psychology

psychology

second canadian edition

Saundra K. Ciccarelli
Gulf Coast Community College

•

J. Noland White
Georgia College and State University

•

V. Heather Fritzley
Sheridan College Institute of Technology and Advanced Learning

•

Tom Harrigan
Red River Community College

PEARSON

Toronto

Vice-President, Editorial Director: Gary Bennett
Editor-in-Chief: Michelle Sartor
Acquisitions Editor: Matthew Christian
Sponsoring Editor: Kathleen McGill
Marketing Manager: Lisa Gillis
Developmental Editor: Paul Donnelly
Project Managers: Sarah Lukaweski, Rachel Thompson
Manufacturing Coordinator: Susan Johnson
Production Editor: PreMediaGlobal

Copy Editor: Deborah Cooper-Bullock
Proofreader: PreMediaGlobal
Compositor: PreMediaGlobal
Photo & Permissions Researcher: Christina Beamish
Art Director: Julia Hall
Cover and Interior Designer: Miriam Blier
Cover Image: (single butterfly in top half) Shutterstock, (group of butterflies below) Jeffrey Coolidge/Getty Images

Credits and acknowledgments for material borrowed from other sources and reproduced, with permission, in this textbook appear on the appropriate page within the text [or on page C-1].

Original edition published by Pearson Education, Inc., Upper Saddle River, New Jersey, USA. Copyright © 2012 Pearson Education, Inc. This edition is authorized for sale only in Canada.

If you purchased this book outside the United States or Canada, you should be aware that it has been imported without the approval of the publisher or the author.

10 9 8 7 6 5 4 3 2 [CKV]

Library and Archives Canada Cataloguing in Publication

Psychology / Saundra K. Ciccarelli ... [et al.]. -- 2nd Canadian ed.
  Includes index.
   ISBN 978-0-13-259440-0
  1. Psychology—Textbooks. I. Ciccarelli, Saundra K.
  BF121.C52 2012
   150   C2011-904896-5

ISBN 978-0-13-259440-0

Brief Contents

Brief Contents

Contents

1
The Science of Psychology   2

2
The Biological Perspective   42

3

Sensation and Perception 88

4

Consciousness: Sleep, Dreams, Hypnosis, and Drugs 134

 8

Development Across the Lifespan   302

9

Motivation and Emotion   350

10

Stress and Health   396

11
Personality   438

12
Social Psychology   476

13
Psychological Disorders   520

14
Psychological Therapies 564

Preface

Dear Reader,

Instructors and students alike experience frustration during lectures when students are unprepared for class. Our goal is to focus on the students and motivate them to learn. We set out to write in a style that draws readers into an ongoing dialogue about psychology. Our aim is to help introduce readers to psychology, its history, its breadth, its mysteries, and its applications. Response from students and instructors using the first edition has been very gratifying—particularly the feedback from students who are reading our book and are excited by this introduction to the fascinating field of psychology. In this second Canadian edition, you'll find some new opening stories highlighting chapter topics and the inclusion of new research (such as the update on stem cell research in Chapter 2 and new information on animal language in Chapter 7). We've reordered some of the chapters so that learning, memory, and cognition now appear together. We've also streamlined the text from 15 to 14 chapters by integrating key content on gender and sexuality into other chapters. New art enhances each chapter as well.

We also want to see students inspired to use the study materials that accompany their text. Students want to do well; they are motivated when goals are clearly laid out and when they know content will "be on the test." By creating an integrated learning and assessment package, we hope to encourage students to focus on the learning objectives and assist instructors in continually assessing students' progress in mastering these objectives. Instructors using the first edition have indicated that these features are working—students are better able to understand the content, and instructors using our resources are better able to track the progress and address the needs of their classes. You'll find that the learning objectives for each chapter have been reorganized into a more streamlined format. Some exciting new study aids have also been added. "Brainstorming" questions at the end of some practice quizzes challenge students to think beyond the material presented. There are also new icons within each chapter leading to Web-based expansions on topics, allowing instructors and students access to extra information, videos, podcasts, and simulations.

We are deeply indebted to the many reviewers who have taken the time to give insightful feedback and suggestions on improving the first edition, as well as the numerous students who have helped us determine the most important changes while staying true to our original intentions and message of the book. We thank you for your time and effort.

Sincerely,
Sandy Ciccarelli
J. Noland White
V. Heather Fritzley
Tom Harrigan

LEARNER-CENTERED APPROACH
Curiosity and Dialogue

In recent years there has been an increased focus on a more learner-centered approach in higher education. A learner-centered approach encourages dialogue and recognizes the importance of actively engaging students. The first edition of this textbook came about because we recognized the importance of motivating students to read. When we say "read," we mean really read the text, not just skim it looking for answers to some study guide questions or trying to cram it all in the night before the exam. We set out to write in a style that draws the reader into an ongoing dialogue about psychology. We also want to see students inspired to use the study materials integrated with the text. Our goal is to awaken students' curiosity and energize their desire to learn more, and we are delighted with the feedback from students and instructors who have used our text and who tell us this approach is working.

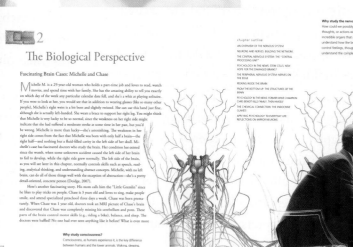

Chapter Opening Prologues are designed to capture student interest immediately. Taken from a case study or recent event in the news, these openers engage students in the material from the very start of the chapter. The design truly captures the imagination of students and adds to the appeal of the chapter content.

ScanLife™ Barcode

To access more tests and your own personalized study plan that will help you focus on the areas you need to master before your next class test, be sure to go to **www.MyPsychLab.com**, Pearson Education Canada's online psychology website, available with the access code packaged with your book.

Scanlife™ barcodes at the beginning of each chapter allow students to download **Study on the Go** content.

Student Voice Questions encourage students to stop, to clarify, and to think critically.

Written by students for students, these questions create a dialogue between the text and the reader and encourage students to ask similar questions in the classroom or online. Cited by students and instructors alike as a truly unique and key feature of the first edition, for the second edition we highlight photographs of students who used the text in their introductory class and who provided questions, comments, and invaluable feedback on the book.

ing a really unethical and lengthy experiment) to find out if smoking behaviour and life expectancy are related to each other is to use the medical records of people who have already died. (For privacy's sake, personal information such as names and social insurance numbers would be removed, with only facts such as age, gender, and weight available to researchers.) Researchers would look for two facts from each record: the number of cigarettes the person smoked per day and the age of the person at death.

Now the researcher has two sets of numbers for each person in the study. Those numbers go into a mathematical formula and produce a number called the *correlation coefficient*. The correlation coefficient represents two things: the strength of the linear relationship and its direction.

Direction: How can a mathematical relationship have a direction? Whenever researchers talk about two variables being related or correlated to each other, what they really mean is that when they graph the variables together on a scatterplot (see Figure 1.3), they can see a linear pattern. If they see a linear pattern, then knowing the value of one variable allows them to estimate the value of the other variable. For example, if researchers found that smoking and life expectancy are indeed related in a linear fashion, they should be able to predict how long someone might live if they know how many cigarettes a person smokes in a day. But which way does that prediction work? If a person smokes a lot of cigarettes, does that mean that he or she will live a longer life or a shorter one? Does life expectancy go up or down as smoking increases? That is what is meant by the *direction* of the relationship.

◄ Direction? How can a mathematical relationship have a direction?

But I've heard about people who, under hypnosis, ▶ remember being abused as children. Aren't those memories sometimes real?

So can we trust any of our memories at all?

why asking people whether they saw a particular person at a crime scene (causing them to imagine the image of that person) might affect the memories those people have of the crime when questioned some time later—the person they were asked to think about may be falsely remembered as having been present.

Clearly, memories obtained through hypnosis should not be considered as accurate without solid evidence from other sources.

But I've heard about people who, under hypnosis, remember being abused as children. Aren't those memories sometimes real? Some researchers argue that false memory syndrome is not as prevalent as many believe it to be. For example, Wendy Hovdestad and Connie Kristiansen (1996) of Carleton University argued that of the individuals with recovered memories, only 3.9 to 13.6 percent satisfied the criteria for false memory syndrome. The fact that some people recover false memories under certain conditions does not mean that child molestation does not really happen; nor does it mean that a person who was molested might not push that unwanted memory away from conscious thought. Molestation is a sad fact: According to the Canadian National Advisory Council of Women, one in three females and one in six males experience some form of sexual abuse before the age of 18.

So can we trust any of our memories at all? On a more positive and promising note (and in contrast to research supporting false memory syndrome relating to trauma), recent research by Steven Porter and Kristine Peace (2007) of Dalhousie University suggests that victims may actually be able to recall the details of trau-

CHAPTER 5   LEARNING   179

IT MAKES YOUR MOUTH WATER: CLASSICAL CONDITIONING

In the early 1900s, when Freud was just becoming famous in Europe and the structuralists and functionalists were arguing over consciousness in the ivy-covered halls of universities, research scientists were unhappy with psychology's focus on mental activity. ⓛⓘⓝⓚ *to Chapter One: The Science of Psychology, pp. 6–10.* Many were looking for a way to bring some kind of objectivity and scientific research to the field.

It was not a psychologist who accomplished that goal. It was a Russian *physiologist* (a person who studies the workings of the body) named Ivan Pavlov (1849–1936) who accidentally stumbled across the basic principles of a particular kind of learning (Pavlov, 1926).

One thing that is often difficult for students to do is make connections from topics in one chapter to topics in other chapters. Throughout each chapter, when one topic has a relationship to another topic, a ⓛⓘⓝⓚ symbol is shown that includes specific chapter and page numbers. The links refer to content covered within the same chapter or in earlier chapters as well as in subsequent chapters—giving students a real sense of the connections in all of the material.

semantic network model
model of memory organization that
assumes information is stored in the
brain in a connected fashion, with
concepts that are related stored
physically closer to each other than
concepts that are not highly related.

network, with nodes (focal points) of related information linked to each other in a kind of hierarchy.* To verify the statement "a canary is a bird" requires moving to only one node, but "a canary is an animal" requires moving through two nodes and should take longer. This was exactly the result of the 1969 study, leading the researchers to develop the **semantic network model**, which assumes that information is stored in the brain in a connected fashion, with concepts that are related stored physically closer to each other than concepts that are not highly related (Collins & Quillian, 1969).

_____
*Hierarchy: an ordered list or series

With the diversity of today's classroom, many ESL students' lack of vocabulary is a big stumbling block. If a word is defined at the end of the same page on which it occurs, students stand a far better chance of understanding what they are reading. In this text, these **Vocabulary Terms** are defined at the bottom of the page on which they first appear. Feedback on these terms from ESL students has been very positive; they say it helps them better understand the chapter content as a whole.

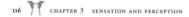

116   CHAPTER 3   SENSATION AND PERCEPTION

shape constancy
the tendency to interpret the shape of an object as being constant, even when its shape changes on the retina.

brightness constancy
the tendency to perceive the apparent brightness of an object as the same even when the light conditions change.

Another perceptual constancy is the tendency to interpret the shape of an object as constant, even when it changes on the retina. This is called **shape constancy** and is why a person still perceives a coin as a circle even if it is held at an angle that makes it appear to be an oval on the retina. Dinner plates on a table are also seen as round, even though from the angle of viewing they are oval (see Figure 3.14).

The third form of perceptual constancy is called **brightness constancy**, the tendency to perceive the apparent brightness of an object as the same even when the light conditions change. If a person is wearing black pants and a white shirt, for example, in broad daylight the shirt will appear to be much brighter than the pants. But if the sun is covered by thick clouds, even though the pants and shirt have less light to reflect than previously, the shirt will still appear to be just as much brighter than the pants as before—because the different amount of light reflected from each piece of clothing is still the same difference as before (Zeki, 2001).

In the **Running Glossary**, psychological terms are set in bold in the text and defined in the margins.

New Simulate/Explore/Watch Icons integrated in the text lead to Web-based expansions on topics, allowing instructors and students access to extra information, videos, podcasts, and simulations. The icons are not exhaustive; many more resources are available than those highlighted in the book, but the icons do draw attention to some of the most high-interest materials available at **www.pearsonmylab.com**.

NEW

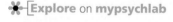
Simulate on **mypsychlab**

Simulate

Provides interactive simulations and experiments to help students better understand key topic areas, such as the scientific method, dependent and independent variables, the anatomy of the brain, and many more.

NEW

✳️ Explore on **mypsychlab**

Explore

Expands on chapter content, providing students with engaging activities and readings on compelling topics, such as Gardner's Multiple Intelligences, Theories of Motivation, Internal & External Attributions, Bystander Intervention, Genetic Counseling, and much more.

THE INFORMATION-PROCESSING MODEL: THREE STAGES OF MEMORY

6.2   *What is the information-processing model of memory?*

Exactly how does memory work? When the storage process occurs, where does that information go and why? Memory experts have proposed several different ways of looking at memory. The model that many researchers feel is the most comprehensive, and perhaps the most influential over the past several decades, is the **information-processing model**, an approach that focuses on the way information is processed, or handled, through three different stages of memory. The processes of encoding, storage, and retrieval are seen as part of this model.

The link between cognitive psychology and information-processing theory was

Simulate on **mypsychlab**
The Information Processing Model

plish, and our lives are full of them. It's easy to think of fears people might have that are conditioned or learned: a child's fear of the dentist's chair, a puppy's fear of a rolled-up newspaper, or the fear of dogs that is often shown by a person who has been attacked by a dog in the past. But other emotions can be conditioned, too.

The next time you watch television, watch the commercials closely. Advertisers often use certain objects or certain types of people in their ads to generate a certain emotional response in viewers, hoping that the emotional response will become associated with their product. Sexy models, cute babies, and adorable puppies are some of the examples of stimuli the advertising world uses to tug at our heartstrings, so to speak.

Other television messages are meant to elicit a fear response, such as messages about what drugs will do to your brain. In a classic public service message from the 1980s, a woman holds up an egg and says, "This is your brain." She then drops the

✳️ Explore on **mypsychlab**
Classical Conditioning of Little Albert

NEW

👁 **Watch** on **mypsychlab**

Watch fascinating video clips that highlight classic content on John Watson, Albert Bandura, and Jean Piaget, as well as contemporary clips on post-traumatic stress disorder, anatomy of a human brain, social influence, and more.

---

they are being compared to can lead to bias in such testing.

Intelligence tests are useful measuring devices but should not necessarily be assumed to be measures of all types of intelligent behaviour, or even good measures for all groups of people, as the next section discusses.

👁 Watch on mypsychlab
Robert Guthrie: Demographics and Intelligence Testing

IQ TESTS AND CULTURAL BIAS The problem with trying to measure intelligence with a test that is based on an understanding of the world and its resources is that not everyone comes from the same "world." People raised in a different culture, or even a different economic situation, from the one in which the designer of an IQ test is raised are not likely to perform well on such a test.

It is very difficult to design an intelligence test that is completely free of *cultural bias*, a term referring to the tendency of IQ tests to reflect, in language, dialect, and content, the culture of the person or persons who designed the test. A person who comes from the same culture (or even socioeconomic background) as the test designer may have an unfair advantage over a person who is from a different cultural or socioeconomic background (Helms, 1992). If people raised in an Asian culture are given a test designed within a traditional Western culture, such as Canada, many

---

Practice Quizzes are included in each chapter at the end of every major section. This embedded assessment encourages students to stop, review, and reinforce their learning before moving on.

PRACTICE QUIZ: HOW MUCH DO YOU REMEMBER?

Pick the best answer.

1. Which of the following is NOT one of the common ethical rules?
   a. Participants have to give informed consent.
   b. Deception cannot be used in any studies with human beings.
   c. The rights and well-being of the participants must come first.
   d. Data must remain confidential.

2. We use animals in research because
   a. animals have simple behaviour that makes it easy to see changes.
   b. animals don't live as long as humans and are easier to control.
   c. we can do things to animals that we can't do to people.
   d. all of the above are true.

3. A famous newscaster advertises a new magnetic mattress for controlling pain. If Nathaniel decides to order the mattress because he believes that such a well-known personality should know

whether or not it works, he has made an error in which of the following?
   a. Few "truths" do not need to be tested.
   b. All evidence is not equal in quality.
   c. Authority or expertise does not make the claims of the authority or expert true.
   d. Critical thinking requires an open mind.

4. Critical thinking means making judgments based on
   a. emotional issues.   c. reason and logical evaluation.
   b. keeping a closed mind.   d. authority and expertise.

5. Which pseudo-psychology claims to understand personality through a study of the bumps on one's skull?
   a. phrenology   c. graphology
   b. palmistry   d. astrology

Answers: 1-b, 2-d, 3-c, 4-c, 5-a.

Test Yourself Sample exams are found at the end of every chapter. Both the quizzes and the end-of-chapter tests are in multiple-choice format to replicate the experience most students have with graded assessments.

TEST YOURSELF

Pick the best answer.

1. Which of the following is the definition of personality?
   a. the characteristics with which each person is born
   b. the moral and ethical behaviour of a person
   c. the unique way an individual thinks, feels, and acts
   d. changes in behaviour according to experiences

2. Which of Freud's parts of the personality is the most like short-term memory?
   a. conscious   c. unconscious
   b. preconscious   d. subconscious

3. Stephen wants a new MP3 player that he saw in the local electronics store, but he doesn't have enough money to pay for it. Which structure of Stephen's personality would urge him to take the player while no one in the store was looking?
   a. id   c. superego
   b. ego   d. libido

4. Which structure of the personality, according to Freud, works on the reality principle?
   a. id   c. superego
   b. ego   d. libido

5. The _____ develops in the _____ stage as a result of identification.
   a. ego; oral   c. superego; phallic
   b. id; oral   d. superego; latency

6. Three-year-old Brandon has watched his father, a chef, when he prepares meals for the family. This year, Brandon has asked for a play kitchen for his birthday. Freud would say that Brandon is beginning the process of _____ as a way of resolving his Oedipal conflict.
   a. compensation   c. sublimation
   b. identification   d. denial

7. According to Adler, middle children tend to be
   a. overachieving.
   b. competitive.
   c. resentful of the freedom of the older child.
   d. filled with feelings of superiority.

8. Research has begun to show some support for which of Freud's concepts?
   a. the existence of an id, ego, and superego
   b. the order of the psychosexual stages
   c. the concept of an unconscious mind
   d. the existence of the Oedipus complex

9. To explain a person's personality, behaviourists would look to
   a. early childhood emotional traumas.
   b. the unconditional positive regard given to the person by his or her parents.
   c. the early experiences of rewards and punishments for certain behaviour.
   d. the constellation of personality traits possessed by the person.

10. For Bandura, one of the most important person variables in determining personality is
   a. self-efficacy.   c. self-determination.
   b. self-concept.   d. self-motivation.

11. Unlike psychoanalysis, the social cognitive view of personality
   a. tries to explain how people become the people they are.
   b. stresses the importance of early childhood in personality development.
   c. is fully able to explain all the complexities of human behaviour.
   d. has been scientifically tested.

12. The striving for fulfillment of one's potential is called
   a. self-concept.   c. self-actualization.
   b. self-efficacy.   d. the ideal self.

13. According to Rogers, anxiety and neurotic behaviour result from
   a. unconscious conflicts and desires.
   b. a mismatch between the real and ideal self.
   c. receiving too much unconditional positive regard from significant others.
   d. learned habits of behaviour.

14. Which of the following viewpoints has different goals from the other three?
   a. psychoanalytic   c. humanism
   b. behaviourism   d. trait theory

15. How many source traits did Cattell use in developing his personality inventory?
   a. 5   c. 16
   b. 10   d. 23

16. The five-factor model of personality traits includes all but which of the following?
   a. openness to experience   c. extraversion
   b. self-sufficiency   d. neuroticism

A detailed **Chapter Summary** highlights all the important parts of the chapter.

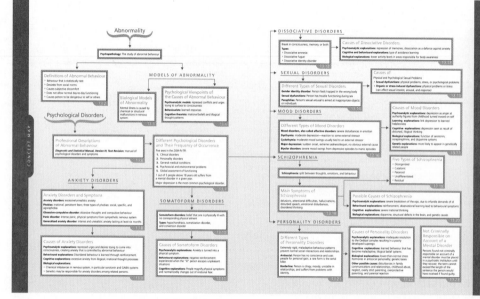

A **Concept Map** at the end of each chapter provides students with a graphic summary of content, emphasizing the key objectives of each chapter. By pulling the content together in this highly visual manner, students can better understand the connections and grasp how the chapter material fits together.

Other features of each chapter are special sections covering interesting topics related to the chapter material, especially topics of diversity and cultural interest. These are not set off from the text in boxes, and the author refers to these features in the chapter content, making it more likely that students will read the enriching material. The test bank, practice quizzes, and the tests at the end of each chapter include questions on this material, further encouraging students to read it.

Each section ends with **Questions for Further Study** that encourage students to think critically about the content they have just read.

TEACHING AND LEARNING PACKAGE
Integration and Feedback

It is increasingly true today that as valuable as a good textbook is, it is still only one element of a comprehensive learning package. The teaching and homework package that accompanies the second Canadian edition of *Psychology* is the most comprehensive and integrated on the market. We have made every effort to provide high-quality instructor supplements that will save you preparation time and will enhance the time you spend in the classroom. We are grateful to the participants of numerous focus groups who helped guide the revisions for different elements of the integrated package, as well as those instructors and students who reviewed the first edition supplements and provided wonderful feedback.

b. playing video games
c. number of hours spent playing video games
d. the type of video game played

20. In that same experiment, the experimental group would
a. not play the video games.
b. take the memory test while the control group would not.
c. not take the memory test while the control group would.
d. play the video games.

d. the rights of the animals must be weighed against the study value to science.

Answers: 1.-a, 2.-b, 3.-c, 4.-b, 5.-a, 6.-b, 7.-d, 8.-a, 9.-c, 10.-d, 11.-a, 12.-d, 13.-a, 14.-d, 15.-c, 16.-b, 17.-a, 18.-b, 19.-a, 20.-d, 21.-d, 22.-b, 23.-c, 24.-b, 25.-c.

ScanLife™ Barcode

To access more tests and your own personalized study plan that will help you focus on the areas you need to master before your next class test, be sure to go to **www.MyPsychLab.com**, Pearson Education Canada's online psychology website, available with the access code packaged with your book.

Study on the Go

Featured at the end of each chapter, you will find a unique barcode providing access to Study on the Go, an unprecedented mobile integration between text and online content. Students link to Pearson's unique Study on the Go content directly from their smartphones, allowing them to study whenever and wherever they wish! Go to one of the sites below to see how you can download an app to your smartphone for free. Once the app is installed, your phone will scan the code and link to a website containing Pearson's Study on the Go content,

The **Test Item File** has been thoroughly revised to meet the needs of this new edition. Containing almost 3,000 questions in a variety of formats (multiple choice, true/false, short answer, essay), it has been edited to ensure clarity and accuracy.

including the popular study tools Glossary Flashcards, Audio Summaries, and Quizzes, which can be accessed anytime.

ScanLife
http://getscanlife.com/

NeoReader
http://get.neoreader.com/

QuickMark
http://www.quickmark.com.tw/

19. The key to the partial report method of Sperling's study of sensory memory was to _____.
    a) have the participants report the entire matrix of letters they saw as fast as they could
    b) have the participants report the entire matrix of letters but mask the letters after presentation with a very bright light

    Incorrect. Masking was used by a later study.

    c) cue the participants, using a tone, as to which line of the matrix they were to report

    Correct. A cue was used by Sperling to allow the participants to retrieve the marked set of letters and let Sperling measure the duration of sensory memory.

    d) test the use of chunking

    ANS: c, p. 233, C, LO=6.3, (3)

An additional feature for the test bank is the inclusion of **rationales for the correct answer and the key distracter** in the multiple-choice questions. The rationales help instructors reviewing the content to further evaluate the questions they are choosing for their tests and give instructors the option to use the rationales as an answer key for their students. Feedback from current customers indicates this unique feature is very useful for ensuring quality and quick response to student queries.

The new edition test bank comes with **NEW** Pearson MyTest, a powerful assessment generation program that helps instructors easily create and print quizzes and exams. Questions and tests can be authored online, allowing instructors ultimate flexibility and the ability to efficiently manage assessments anytime, anywhere! Instructors can easily access existing questions and edit, create, and store using simple drag-and-drop and Word-like controls. Data on each question provides information on difficulty level and page number. In addition, each question maps to the text's major section and learning objective. For more information go to **www.PearsonMyTest.com**.

The completely revised **Instructor's Resource Manual** offers an exhaustive collection of resources. For each chapter, you'll find activities, exercises, assignments, handouts, and demos for in-class use, as well as guidelines on integrating the many Pearson media resources into your classroom and syllabus. This resource saves prep work and helps you maximize your classroom time.

6.2 What are some of the different models of how memory works?

Models of Memory
1. Information processing models are
   a. Computer is a metaphor for memory
   b. Input, output; access, storage, retrieval
   c. Atkinson-Shiffrin model of memory (figure 6.3)
2. PDP –Parallel Distributed Processing (Figure 6.4)
   a. Brain is a metaphor for memory
   b. Connectionist model
   c. Concepts are interconnected in a network
   d. Concepts are activated which activate other concepts, in parallel with each other

The Three-Box Model of Memory
Sensory Register: Fleeting Impressions
1. Includes separate memory subsystems for each of the senses
2. Acts as a holding bin until we select items for attention
3. Pattern recognition compares a stimulus to information long-term me short-term m

538

CLASSROOM ACTIVITIES, DEMONSTRATIONS, AND EXERCISES

Activity 1: Misconceptions About Psychology

One of the most popular and venerable activities for the introductory course is the administration and subsequent discussion of misconceptions about psychology. Although a new 65-item multiple-choice test was developed by McCutcheon (1991), the most popular test is the Test of Common Beliefs developed by Vaughan (1977). Vaughan's test, however, has been criticized for the ambiguity of some of the items (Brown, 1984; Gardner & Dalsing, 1986; Ruble, 1986), the fact that all items have "false" as the correct response, which may lead to a response set tendency (Vaughan, 1977), and the finding that many of the items are not really misconceptions since they are often correctly answered (Gardner & Dalsing, 1986; Lamal, 1979). Griggs and Ransdell (1987) compared responses to Vaughan's Test of Common Beliefs from students that had taken an introductory psychology course in high school to those of several other studies (Lamal, 1979; Gardner & Dalsing, 1986; Vaughan, 1977). Using a criterion of at least a 50% error rate for an item (that is, they were answered as "true"), they identified 15 questions that met the criterion in at least two studies and had not been subject to earlier criticisms of ambiguity. These items are reproduced in Handout Master 1.1 and are ordered from highest to lowest with respect to their average error rate. You can

LECTURE LAUNCHERS AND DISCUSSION TOPICS

Lecture/Discussion 1: How Do We Know What We Know?

How do you know that
John A. Macdonald was the first prime minister of Canada?
you really have a stomach?

Dependence on observation is one of the hallmarks of science, but it is not the only way humans acquire knowledge. There are, in fact, many questions that cannot be answered by scientific methods and for which other means of acquiring knowledge are more appropriate. Begin by asking the following questions.

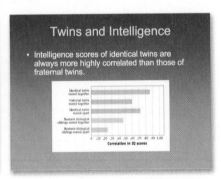

PowerPoint Presentations bring the powerful Ciccarelli design right into the classroom, drawing students into the lecture and providing wonderful interactive activities, visuals, and videos.

Also included are **Personal Response System** questions that help generate discussion and provide instant feedback on how your students are responding to the lecture content.

All of the following are sysptoms of ADHD EXCEPT:

1. Feelings of restlessness
2. Not paying attention when spoken to by others
3. Impatient and impulsive
4. Inability to pay attention to details
5. Prolonged atention but to inappropriate aspects of the social situation.

Instructor's Resource CD-ROM

This resource CD brings all of the text instructor resources together in one convenient place, including the test bank, Instructor's Resource Manual, Personal Response System questions, and PowerPoint Presentations. Most of these instructor supplements are also available for download from a password-protected section of Pearson Education Canada's online catalogue (**vig.pearsoned.ca**). Navigate to your book's catalogue page to view a list of those supplements that are available. See your local sales representative for details and access.

CourseSmart goes beyond traditional expectations–providing instant, online access to the textbooks and course materials you need at a lower cost for students. And even as students save money, you can save time and hassle with a digital eTextbook that allows you to search for the most relevant content at the very moment you need it. Whether it's evaluating textbooks or creating lecture notes to help students with difficult concepts, CourseSmart can make life a little easier. For more information, visit **www.coursesmart.com**.

Technology Specialists. Pearson's Technology Specialists work with faculty and campus course designers to ensure that Pearson technology products, assessment tools, and online course materials are tailored to meet your specific needs. This highly qualified team is dedicated to helping schools take full advantage of a wide range of educational resources, by assisting in the integration of a variety of instructional materials and media formats. Your local Pearson Education sales representative can provide you with more details on this service program.

Pearson Custom Library

For enrollments of at least 25 students, you can create your own textbook by choosing the chapters that best suit your own course needs. *To begin building your custom text, visit www.pearsoncustomlibrary.com*. You may also work with a dedicated Pearson Custom editor to create your ideal text—publishing your own original content or mixing and matching Pearson content. *Contact your local Pearson Representative to get started*.

ONLINE OPTIONS

for *Psychology,* Second Canadian Edition

MyPsychLab

The moment you know.

Educators know it. Students know it. It's that inspired moment when something that was difficult to understand suddenly makes perfect sense. Our MyLab products have been designed and refined with a single purpose in mind—to help educators create that moment of understanding with their students.

MyPsychLab delivers **proven results** in helping individual students succeed. It provides **engaging experiences** that personalize, stimulate, and measure learning for each student. And, it comes from a **trusted partner** with educational expertise and an eye on the future.

MyPsychLab can be used by itself or linked to any learning management system. To learn more about how MyPsychLab combines proven learning applications with powerful assessment, visit www.MyPsychLab.com.

MyPsychLab—the moment you know

peerScholar

Firmly grounded in published research, peerScholar is a powerful online pedagogical tool that helps develop your students' critical and creative thinking skills. peerScholar facilitates this through the process of creation, evaluation and reflection. Working in stages, students begin by submitting a written assignment. peerScholar then circulates their work for others to review, a process that can be anonymous or not depending on your preference. Students receive peer feedback and evaluations immediately, reinforcing their learning and driving the development of higher-order thinking skills. Students can then re-submit revised work, again depending on your preference. Contact your Pearson Representative to learn more about peerScholar and the research behind it.

DEVELOPMENT STORY

Insight and Collaboration

The creation of this text and package for both the first and second Canadian editions is the result of the most extensive development investment in a text that this discipline has ever experienced. Over 1,000 instructors and students have contributed. Over 250 manuscript reviewers provided invaluable feedback. Expert reviewers in critical topic areas provided feedback on the currency and accuracy of the research. A full-time development editor analyzed feedback from our customers and reviewers and worked with the authors, editing the prose line by line for clarity. More than 100 focus-group participants contributed to decisions regarding text organization and content coverage as well as pedagogical innovation. Student reviewers have been involved in evaluating the clarity of the writing style and the value of the in-text learning tools and assessment features—you will see many of these student reviewers in the photos included with the student voice questions in the margins of the text. We are grateful to all who provided feedback on changes for the second edition text as well as changes to the design—which we hope you find as inviting as we do!

Acknowledgments

We, the authors, would very much like to express our sincere appreciation to the many colleagues and friends who through either their knowledge, patience, interest, or advice helped us put the words down in a coherent fashion and more importantly guided us with their inspiration through the tough times.

We are especially indebted to the following reviewers who gave us both positive and critical feedback during the development of the second Canadian edition:

Trudi Chalmers, Red Deer College
Mary Close, Canadore College
Laura Dane, Douglas College
Deborah Gural , Red River College
Rick Healey, Memorial University of Newfoundland
Alan Ho, Ambrose University College
Arlene Johnsrude , SIAST
Anjanie McCarthy, Fanshawe College
Heather Poole, University of Ottawa
Barry Smith, Red River College
Connie Winder, George Brown College
Sue Walling, Memorial University of Newfoundland

We cannot forget the overwhelming support of the publisher, Pearson Canada, and their many exceptional personnel that kept us on track—specifically, Ky Pruesse for inviting us to take part at the outset, and Matthew Christian for his ongoing support; Paul Donnelly for being such an understanding and supportive developmental editor; and our production team, including Sarah Lukaweski, Melena Fenn, and Deborah Cooper-Bullock. Finally, we acknowledge all the Canadian psychological researchers we cited or not, whose tireless efforts made this book possible.

First and foremost, I would like to thank my family for their unwavering support and understanding throughout this process and throughout my life. Thanks also to my close friends and colleagues (whom I also consider friends) who have been there for me every step of the way. I would also like to thank my co-author Tom Harrigan for his calming words and reassurances—Tom, at deadline time, you kept me sane when I thought I was going to lose my mind.

V. Heather Fritzley
Sheridan College

First, I would again like to acknowledge all the reviewers - your insights were invaluable. Second, I would like to give a few kudos to the many students in my classes who offered suggestions for this second edition. Unfortunately, we could not find a way to download all of the material directly to your brain in 30 seconds - maybe next edition? And last, but certainly NOT least, I'm indebted to the following individuals who made this possible:

Evelyn Harrigan, Mom of Tom

V. Heather Fritzley, Sheridan College

Saundra K. Ciccarelli, Golf Coast Community College

J. Noland White, Georgia College & State University

Duncan Mackinnon, Pearson Education

Tom Harrigan
Red River College

About the Authors

Saundra K. Ciccarelli is a Professor of Psychology at Gulf Coast Community College in Panama City, Florida. She received her Ph.D. in Developmental Psychology from George Peabody College of Vanderbilt University, Nashville, Tennessee. She is a member of the American Psychological Association and the Association for Psychological Science. Originally interested in a career as a researcher in the development of language and intelligence in developmentally delayed children and adolescents, Dr. Ciccarelli had publications in the American Journal of Mental Deficiency while still at Peabody. However, she discovered a love of teaching early on in her career. This led her to the position at Gulf Coast Community College, where she has been teaching Introductory Psychology and Human Development for over 27 years. Her students love her enthusiasm for the field of psychology and the many anecdotes and examples she uses to bring psychology to life for them. Before writing this text, Dr. Ciccarelli authored numerous ancillary materials for several introductory psychology and human development texts.

J. Noland White is an Assistant Professor of Psychology and currently the interim Director of Retention and Advising at Georgia College & State University (GCSU) in Milledgeville, Georgia. He received both his B.S. and M.S. in Psychology from GCSU and joined the faculty there in 2001 after receiving his Ph.D. in Counseling Psychology from the University of Tennessee. As a licensed psychologist, Dr. White has worked as a consultant in a variety of settings, including adult mental health, developmental disabilities, and juvenile justice. Back on campus, he has an active lab and with his students is currently investigating the psychophysiological characteristics and neuropsychological performance of adults with and without ADHD. Outside of the lab, Dr. White is engaged in collaborative research examining the effectiveness of incorporating iPods and podcasting in and out of the college classroom to facilitate student learning. In April 2008, he was a recipient of the GCSU Excellence in Teaching Award.

Tom Harrigan has taught thousands of undergraduate students at Red River College, the University of Manitoba, the University of Winnipeg, and Lakehead University over the last 15 years. Tom received his undergraduate degree in Science with honours from Laurentian University, then completed his master's degree in Experimental Psychology at Lakehead University, and continued his move west completing a Ph.D. in Behavioural Neuroscience at the University of Manitoba. Tom's research interest in helping students learn more effectively has, with the support of Pearson Education Canada, led to the development of HandsOnPsych, a CD-ROM based set of interactive psychology modules. Tom currently holds a position in the nursing department at Red River College where he teaches Introduction to Psychology, Statistics, and a variety of psychology related courses, and is researching student perceptions associated with the use of cheat sheets. He is also excited to see the return of the NHL to Winnipeg!

Dr. V. Heather Fritzley received her Ph.D. in Psychology from Queen's University in Kingston, Ontario. She is currently a full-time psychology professor at Sheridan Institute of Technology and Advanced

Learning in Ontario. Dr. Fritzley specializes in social psychology and she has conducted research on the effect of various questioning techniques on young children's responses and children's eyewitness abilities. She is the co-author of *Mastering Social Psychology, 1st Canadian Edition*, a textbook for students in social psychology courses. Dr. Fritzley teaches a variety of psychology courses including Introductory Psychology, Social Psychology, The Psychology of Good and Evil, Research Methods, Personality Psychology, Cognitive Psychology, The Psychology of Cults, and The Psychology of Prejudice. She is very passionate about the quest for knowledge and believes that the best teachers are the ones who are always learning. When Dr. Fritzley is not teaching, she enjoys cheering on the Toronto Maple Leafs, reading thrillers, taking photographs, and playing soccer.

1 The Science of Psychology

What Can Psychology Do for Me?

Have you ever wondered …

… why some people are outgoing and others are shy?

… how you could develop a better memory?

… why it's so easy for little children to learn another language when it's so difficult for adults?

… if ESP really exists?

… why you find some people attractive but not others?

… if taking the pill makes women choose poor mates?

… why some people become serial killers?

… if NHL hockey players have some unique personality characteristics?

… what scores on an IQ test really mean?

… how to juggle school, work, and parents, while still maintaining an active personal life?

… how different men and women really are?

… why you sleep and why you dream?

… if hypnosis is real?

… why buying lottery tickets can be so addictive?

… why people tend to get sick right before final exam week?

… why identical twins aren't so identical when it comes to their personalities?

… if you can teach your parents to be more environmentally conscious?

… what happens to your brain when you use an illegal drug?

If you've ever been curious about any of these questions, this book is for you. Psychologists study all of these things and more. If you've puzzled about it, thought about doing it, or actually done it, chances are psychology has an explanation for it.

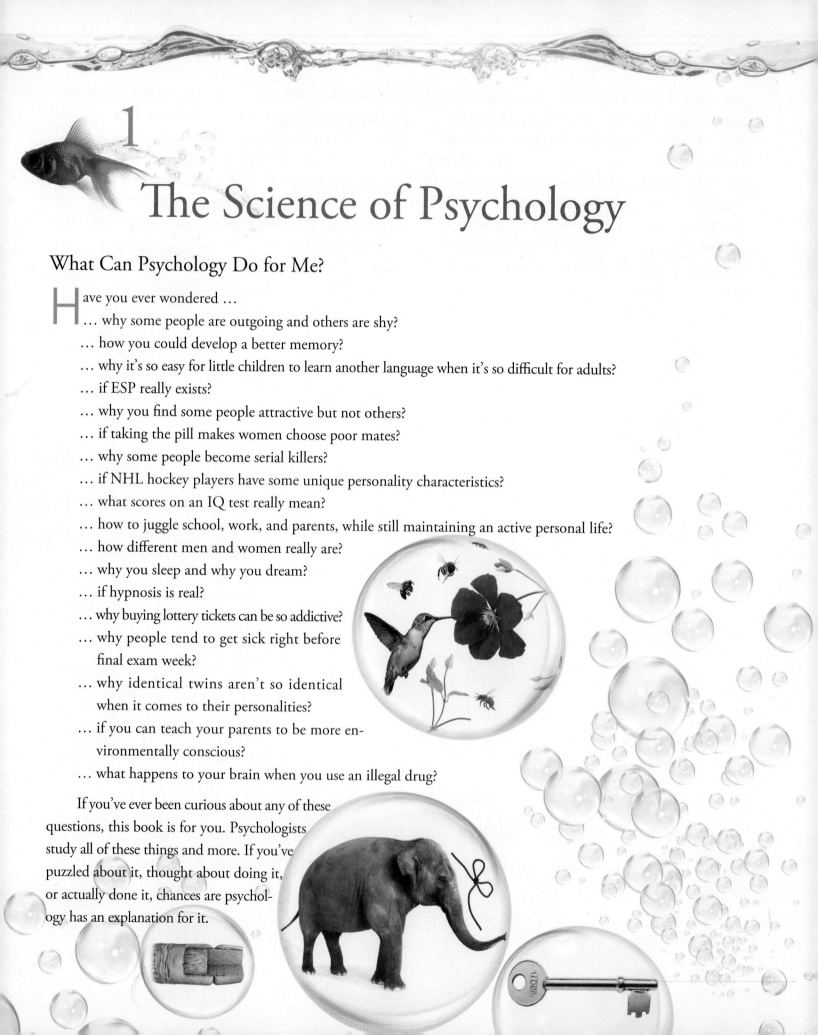

Why study psychology?

Psychology not only helps us understand why other people do the things they do, it also helps us better understand ourselves and our reactions to other people. Psychology can help you understand how your brain and body are connected, how to improve your learning abilities and memory, and how to deal with the stresses of life, both ordinary and extraordinary. In studying psychology, an understanding of the methods psychologists use is important because research can be flawed, and knowing how research should be done can bring those flaws to light. Finally, the critical thinking that psychology and its methods of research promote can be used to evaluate not just research but also claims of all kinds, including those of advertisers and politicians.

1

Study Help Note: For each section of every chapter in this text, there are numbered learning objectives. These learning objectives represent the key questions that you should be able to understand and answer after reading the chapter. They appear at the beginning of each chapter, at the beginning of each relevant section in the chapter, and in the chapter summary.

1.1 What is the definition and what are four primary goals of psychology?

1.2 What were the basic ideas of structuralism and functionalism, and who were the important people in those early fields?

1.3 What were the basic ideas and who were the important people behind the early approaches known as *Gestalt*, *psychoanalysis*, and *behaviourism*?

1.4 What are the basic concepts of the modern perspectives known as *psychodynamics, behaviourism, humanism, biopsychology, cognitive psychology, the sociocultural perspective*, and *the evolutionary perspective*?

1.5 What were the contributions of Skinner, Maslow, Rogers, and Hebb?

1.6 What's the difference between a psychiatrist and a psychologist, and what other types of professionals work in the various areas of psychology?

1.7 Why is psychology a science, and what are the steps in using the scientific method?

1.8 How do psychologists use naturalistic and laboratory settings to describe behaviour, and what are the advantages and disadvantages associated with these settings?

1.9 How do psychologists use case studies and surveys to describe behaviour, and what are some drawbacks to each of these methods?

1.10 What is the correlational technique, and what does it tell researchers about relationships?

1.11 How do researchers use operational definitions, independent and dependent variables, experimental and control groups, and random assignment in designing an experiment?

1.12 What are the placebo and the experimenter effects, and how do single-blind and double-blind studies control for those effects?

1.13 What are the ethical concerns when conducting research with people and animals?

1.14 What are the basic principles of critical thinking, and how can using critical thinking help people in their everyday lives?

1.15 How might critical thinking be applied to a real-world example?

WHAT IS PSYCHOLOGY?

THE FIELD OF PSYCHOLOGY

Some people believe that psychology is just the study of people and what makes them tick. Psychologists do study people, but they study animals, too. What makes people and animals "tick" is what goes on inside their bodies and brains as well as what they do.

1.1 *What is the definition and what are four primary goals of psychology?*

Psychology is the scientific study of behaviour and mental processes. *Behaviour* includes all of our outward or overt actions and reactions, such as talking, facial expressions, and movement. *Mental processes* refer to all the internal, covert activity of our minds, such as thinking, feeling, and remembering. Why "scientific"? To study behaviour and mental processes in both animals and humans, researchers have to observe them. Whenever a human being is observing anyone or anything, there's always a possibility that the observer will see only what he or she expects to see. Psychologists don't want to let these possible biases* cause them to make faulty observations. They want to be as precise and measure as carefully as they can, so they use the scientific method to study psychology.

PSYCHOLOGY'S GOALS

Every science has goals. In physics, the goals concern learning how the physical world works. In astronomy, the goals are to chart the universe and understand both how it

psychology
the scientific study of behaviour and mental processes.

*Biases: personal judgments based on beliefs rather than facts

4

came to be and what it is becoming. In psychology, there are four goals that aim at uncovering the mysteries of human and animal behaviour: description, explanation, prediction, and control.

DESCRIPTION: WHAT IS HAPPENING?   The first step in understanding anything is to give it a name. *Description* involves observing a behaviour and noting everything about it: what is happening, where it happens, to whom it happens, and under what circumstances it seems to happen.

For example, a teacher might notice that a young girl in his grade 2 classroom is behaving oddly. She's not turning in her homework, her grades are slipping badly, and she seems to have a very negative attitude toward school.

That's *what* she is doing. The description of what she is doing gives a starting place for the next goal: *Why* is she doing it?

EXPLANATION: WHY IS IT HAPPENING?   To find out why the girl is doing all these things, the teacher would most likely ask the school counsellor to administer some tests. Her parents might be asked to take her to a pediatrician to make sure that there is no physical illness, such as an allergy. They might also take her to a psychologist to be assessed. In other words, they are looking for an *explanation* for her behaviour. Finding explanations for behaviour is a very important step in the process of forming theories of behaviour. A *theory* is a general explanation of a set of observations or facts. The goal of description provides the observations, and the goal of explanation helps to build the theory.

If all the tests seem to indicate that the young girl has a learning problem, such as dyslexia (an inability to read at expected levels for a particular age and degree of intelligence), the next step would be trying to predict what is likely to happen if the situation stays the same.

PREDICTION: WHEN WILL IT HAPPEN AGAIN?   Determining what will happen in the future is a *prediction.* In the example, the psychologist or counsellor would predict (based on previous research into similar situations) that this little girl will probably continue to do poorly in her school work and may never be able to reach her full learning potential. Clearly, something needs to be done to change this prediction, and that is the point of the last of the four goals of psychology: changing or modifying behaviour.

CONTROL: HOW CAN IT BE CHANGED?   *Control,* or the modification of some behaviour, has been somewhat controversial in the past. Some people hear the word *control* and think *brainwashing,* but that is not the focus of this goal. The goal is to change a behaviour from an undesirable one (such as failing in school) to a desirable one (such as academic success).

In the example of the young girl, certain learning strategies can be used to help a child (or an adult) who has dyslexia improve reading skills (Aylward et al., 2003; Shaywitz, 1996). The psychologist and educators would work together to find a training strategy that will work best for this particular girl.

Not all psychological investigations will try to meet all four of these goals. In some cases, the main focus might be on description and prediction, as it would be for a personality theorist who wants to know what people are like (description) and what they might do in certain situations (prediction). Some psychologists are interested in both description and explanation, as is the case with experimental psychologists who design research to find explanations for observed (described) behaviour. Therapists,

The researcher in the foreground is watching the children through a one-way mirror to get a description of their behaviour. Observations such as this are just one of many ways that psychologists have of investigating behaviour. Why is it important for the researcher to be behind a one-way mirror?

of course, would be more interested in control, although the other three goals would be important in getting to that goal.

These goals have not really changed in the years since psychology's beginnings, but the methods of achieving them certainly have changed. In the next section, we'll take a look at the early pioneers in psychology.

PRACTICE QUIZ: HOW MUCH DO YOU REMEMBER?

Study Help Note: These practice quizzes are spaced throughout each chapter to give you an opportunity to check your understanding of the material in each section and provide practice for exams. The answers to each quiz can be found upside down at the end of each quiz.

Pick the best answer.

1. In the definition of psychology, *behaviour* means
   a. internal, covert processes.
   b. mental processes.
   c. outward or overt actions and reactions.
   d. only human behaviour.

2. A psychologist is interested in what a particular person might do in a stressful situation. This psychologist is most interested in the goal of
   a. description.
   b. explanation.
   c. prediction.
   d. control.

3. Dr. Watson designs a special behaviour program for helping children who are bullies learn how to be less aggressive and more successful in social relationships. Dr. Watson is most interested in the goal of
   a. description.
   b. explanation.
   c. prediction.
   d. control.

4. The first step in studying animal behaviour is to observe animals and record everything they do, when they do it, and what is going on around them when they do it. This meets the goal of
   a. description.
   b. explanation.
   c. prediction.
   d. control.

5. Experimental psychologists, who design experiments to determine the causes of behaviour, would be most interested in the goal of
   a. description.
   b. explanation.
   c. prediction.
   d. control.

Answers: 1.-c, 2.-c, 3.-d, 4.-a, 5.-b.

PSYCHOLOGY THEN: THE HISTORY OF PSYCHOLOGY
IN THE BEGINNING: WUNDT, INTROSPECTION, AND THE LABORATORY

How long has psychology been around—and where did it begin? ▶

How long has psychology been around—and where did it begin? Psychology is a relatively new field in the realm of the sciences, only about 125 years old. It's not that no one thought about what makes people tick before then; on the contrary, there were philosophers*, medical doctors, and physiologists** who thought about little else. Famous philosophers such as Plato, Aristotle, and Descartes wrote of the relationship between the soul (or mind) and the body (Durrant, 1993; Everson, 1995; Jackson, 2001; Kenny, 1968, 1994).

Philosophers tried to understand or explain the human mind and its connection to the physical body, while medical doctors and physiologists wondered about the physical connection between the body and the brain. For example, physician and physicist Gustav Fechner (1860) is often credited with performing some of the first scientific experiments that would form a basis for experimentation in psychology with his studies of perception, and physician Hermann von Helmholtz (1852, 1863) performed groundbreaking experiments in visual and auditory perception. Ⓛ Ⓘ Ⓝ Ⓚ *to Chapter Three: Sensation and Perception, p. 88.*

MyPsychLab

Research on **www.MyPsychLab.com**
Psychology Timeline

---

*Philosophers: people who seek wisdom and knowledge through thinking and discussion

**Physiologists: scientists who study the physical workings of the body and its systems

1.2 *What were the basic ideas of structuralism and functionalism, and who were the important people in those early fields?*

It really all started to come together in a laboratory in Leipzig, Germany, in 1879. It was here that Wilhelm Wundt (VILL-helm Voont, 1832–1920), a physiologist, attempted to apply scientific principles to the study of the human mind. In his laboratory, students from around the world were taught to study the structure of the human mind. Wundt believed that the mind was made up of thoughts, experiences, emotions, and other basic elements. To inspect these nonphysical elements, students had to learn to think objectively about their own thoughts—after all, they could hardly read someone else's mind. Wundt called this process **objective introspection**, the process of objectively examining and measuring one's own thoughts and mental activities (Rieber & Robinson, 2001). For example, Wundt might have placed an object, such as a rock, into a student's hand and had that student tell him everything that he was feeling as a result of having the rock in his hand—all the sensations stimulated by the rock.

German physiologist Wilhelm Wundt participates in an experiment in his laboratory as students look on.

This was really the first attempt by anyone to bring objectivity and measurement to the concept of psychology. This attention to objectivity, together with the establishment of the first true experimental laboratory in psychology, is why Wundt is known as the "father of psychology."

TITCHENER AND BALDWIN AND STRUCTURALISM IN NORTH AMERICA

Two of Wundt's students, Edward Titchener (1867–1927) and James Mark Baldwin (1861–1934), helped bring Wundt's ideas to North America. Titchener, at Cornell University in Ithaca, New York, expanded on Wundt's original ideas, calling his new viewpoint **structuralism**, because the focus of study was the structure of the mind. He believed that every experience could be broken down into its individual emotions and sensations (Brennan, 2002). Although Titchener agreed with Wundt that consciousness, the state of being aware of external events, could be broken down into its basic elements, Titchener also believed that the introspection method could be used on thoughts just as it was on physical sensations. For example, Titchener might have asked his students to introspect about things that are blue rather than actually giving them a blue object and asking for reactions to it. Such an exercise might have led to something like the following: "What is blue? There are blue things, such as the sky or a bird's feathers. Blue is cool and restful. Blue is calm …" and so on.

Structuralists would be interested in all of the memories and sensations this woman is experiencing as she smells the flowers.

In 1889, James Mark Baldwin was hired by the University of Toronto to establish the first experimental psychological laboratory in Canada. Baldwin's appointment as professor of logic, metaphysics, and ethics was very controversial at the time. Faculty and students were resistant to the idea of an "outsider" teaching in Toronto and petitioned against and denounced Baldwin's elemental view of mental life. Despite the initial controversy, Baldwin's lab flourished, and he became a popular professor on campus. Baldwin was fascinated with the mental development of his two daughters and became the first psychologist to experiment with children, which later would inspire prominent psychologists such as Piaget and Kohlberg (Hoff, 1992; Wright & Myers, 1982). Ⓛ Ⓘ Ⓝ Ⓚ *to Chapter Eight: Development Across the Lifespan, p. 302.*

Baldwin also became a very influential presence in the psychological community. He was a founding member of the American Psychological Association (APA) in 1892 and, after relocating to Princeton in 1893, he became the APA's president in 1897.

Structuralism was a dominant force in the early days of psychology, but it eventually died out in the early 1900s, as the structuralists were busily fighting among

objective introspection
the process of examining and measuring one's own thoughts and mental activities.

structuralism
early perspective in psychology associated with Wilhelm Wundt and Edward Titchener, in which the focus of study is the structure or basic elements of the mind.

James Mark Baldwin, a founding father of Canadian psychology.

So what happened ▶ next? Where did psychology go from here?

functionalism
early perspective in psychology associated with William James, in which the focus of study is how the mind allows people to adapt, live, work, and play.

themselves over just which key elements of experience were the most important. A competing view arose not long after Wundt's laboratory was established, shortly before structuralism came to America.

WILLIAM JAMES AND FUNCTIONALISM

Harvard University was the first school in the United States to offer classes in psychology in the late 1870s. These classes were taught by one of Harvard's most illustrious instructors, William James (1842–1910). James began teaching anatomy and physiology but, as his interest in psychology developed, he began teaching psychology almost exclusively (Brennan, 2002). His comprehensive textbook on the subject, *Principles of Psychology*, is so brilliantly written that copies are still in print (James, 1890, 2002).

Unlike Wundt and Titchener, James believed that trying to study consciousness was like trying to study the wind. Conscious ideas are constantly flowing in an ever-changing stream, and once you start thinking about what you were just thinking about, what you were thinking about is no longer what you *were* thinking about, it's what you *are* thinking about, and … excuse me, I'm a little dizzy. I think you get the picture, anyway.

Instead, James focused on how the mind allows people to *function* in the real world—how people work, play, and adapt to their surroundings—a viewpoint he called **functionalism**. (He was heavily influenced by Charles Darwin's ideas about *natural selection*, in which physical traits that help an animal adapt to its environment and survive are passed on to its offspring, becoming part of the animal's traits.) If physical traits could aid in survival, why couldn't behavioural traits do the same? Animals and people whose behaviour helped them to survive would pass on those traits to their offspring, perhaps by teaching or even by some mechanism of heredity. For example, a behavioural trait or preference for foods rich in fats and sugar may have greatly increased the survival of our primitive ancestors, but those same preferences in today's society may lead to obesity.

So what happened next? Where did psychology go from here? In the new field of psychology, functionalism offered an alternative viewpoint to the structuralists. But like so many of psychology's early ideas, it is no longer a major perspective. Instead, one can find elements of functionalism in the modern fields of *educational psychology* (studying the application of psychological concepts to education) and *industrial/organizational psychology* (studying the application of psychological concepts to businesses, organizations, and industry), as well as other areas in psychology. Functionalism also played a part in the development of one of the more modern perspectives, evolutionary psychology, discussed later in this chapter.

GESTALT PSYCHOLOGY: THE WHOLE IS GREATER THAN THE SUM OF ITS PARTS

Meanwhile, back in Germany, other psychologists were attacking the concepts of psychology in yet another way. Max Wertheimer (VERT-hi-mer), like James, objected to the structuralist point of view but for different reasons. Wertheimer felt that psychological events such as perceiving and sensing could not be broken down into smaller elements and still be properly understood. You can take an MP3 player apart, for example, but then you no longer have an MP3 player—you have a pile of unconnected bits and pieces. As a melody is made up of individual notes and can be recognized only if the notes are in their correct relationship to one another, so perception can be understood only as a whole, entire event. Hence the familiar slogan, "The whole is greater than the sum of its parts." The Gestalt psychologists believed that people naturally seek out patterns ("wholes") in the sensory information available to them. See Figure 1.1 for an example of Gestalt perceptual patterns.

1.3   *What were the basic ideas and who were the important people behind the early approaches known as Gestalt, psychoanalysis, and behaviourism?*

Wertheimer and others devoted their efforts to studying sensation and perception in this new perspective, **Gestalt psychology**. *Gestalt* (Gesh-TALT) is a German word meaning "good form" or "good figure," which fit well with the focus on studying whole patterns rather than small pieces of them. Today, Gestalt ideas are part of the study of *cognitive psychology*, a field that focuses not only on perception but also on learning, memory, thought processes, and problem solving; the basic Gestalt principles of perception are still taught within this newer field (Ash, 1998; Kohler, 1992; Wertheimer, 1982). The Gestalt approach has also been influential in psychological therapy, becoming the basis for a major therapeutic technique called *Gestalt therapy.* ⓛⓘⓝⓚ *to Chapter Fourteen: Psychological Therapies, p. 564.*

SIGMUND FREUD'S PSYCHOANALYSIS

It should be clear by now that psychology didn't start in one place and at one particular time. People of several different viewpoints were trying to promote their own perspectives on the study of the human mind and behaviour in different places all over the world. Up to now, this chapter has focused on the physiologists who became interested in psychology, and their focus was on understanding consciousness but little else. The medical profession took a whole different approach to psychology.

What about Freud? Everybody talks about him when they talk about psychology. How does he figure into the beginnings of psychology? Sigmund Freud had become a noted physician in Austria while the structuralists argued, the functionalists specialized, and the Gestaltists were looking at the big picture. He was a medical doctor—a neurologist, someone who specializes in disorders of the nervous system—and he and his colleagues had long sought a way to understand the patients who were coming to them for help.

Freud's patients suffered from nervous disorders for which he and other doctors could find no physical cause. Therefore, it was thought, the cause must be in the mind, and that is where Freud began to explore. He proposed that there is an *unconscious* (unaware) mind into which we push, or *repress*, all of our threatening urges and desires. He believed that these repressed urges, in trying to surface, created the nervous disorders in his patients (Freud et al., 1990). ⓛⓘⓝⓚ *to Chapter Eleven: Theories of Personality, p. 438.*

Freud stressed the importance of early childhood experiences, believing that personality was formed in the first six years of life, and that if there were significant problems, those problems must have begun in those early years.

Some of his more well-known followers were Alfred Adler, Carl Jung, and his own daughter, Anna Freud. Anna Freud began what became known as the *ego movement* in psychology, a movement that produced one of the most famous psychologists in the study of personality development, Erik Erikson. ⓛⓘⓝⓚ *to Chapter Eight: Development Across the Lifespan, p. 302.*

Freudian **psychoanalysis**, the theory and therapy based on his ideas, has been the basis of much modern psychotherapy (a process in which a trained psychological professional helps a person gain insights into and change his or her behaviour), but his ideas often lacked scientific rigour. Thus, another major and more scientifically based viewpoint has actually become more influential in the field of psychology as a whole.

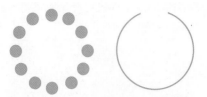

FIGURE 1.1 **A Gestalt Perception**
The eye tends to "fill in" the blanks here and see both of these figures as circles rather than as a series of dots or a broken line.

Psychoanalyst Sigmund Freud walks with his daughter Anna, also a psychoanalyst.

◄   What about Freud? Everybody talks about him when they talk about psychology. How does he figure into the beginnings of psychology?

Gestalt psychology
early perspective in psychology that focuses on perception and sensation, particularly the perception of patterns and whole figures.

psychoanalysis
the theory and therapy based on the work of Sigmund Freud.

Physiologist Ivan Pavlov uses a dog to demonstrate the conditioned reflex to students at the Russian Military Medical Academy.

👁 Watch on **mypsychlab**
Archival Footage of Little Albert

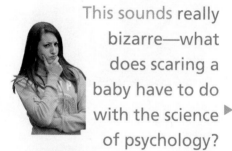

This sounds really bizarre—what does scaring a baby have to do with the science of psychology? ▶

American psychologist John Watson is known as the "father of behaviourism." Behaviourism focuses only on observable behaviour.

behaviourism
the science of behaviour that focuses on observable behaviour only.

PAVLOV, WATSON, AND BEHAVIOURISM

Ivan Pavlov, like Freud, was not a psychologist. He was a Russian physiologist who, working with dogs, had shown that an involuntary reflex such as salivation, which is normally produced by having food in one's mouth, could be elicited by a totally new and formally unrelated stimulus,* such as the ring of a bell. Pavlov would ring the bell, give the dogs food, and the dogs would salivate because of the food in their mouths. After doing this several times, the dogs would salivate to the ring of bell before the food was presented—a learned (or conditioned) reflexive response (Klein & Mowrer, 1989). This process was called *conditioning*. ⓛ ⓘ ⓝ ⓚ *to Chapter Five: Learning, p. 176.*

In the early 1900s, John B. Watson had tired of the arguing among the structuralists; he challenged the functionalist viewpoint, as well as psychoanalysis, with his own "science of behaviour," or **behaviourism** (Watson, 1924). Watson wanted to bring psychology back to a focus on scientific inquiry, and he felt that the only way to do that was to ignore the whole "consciousness" issue and focus only on *observable behaviour*—something that could be directly seen and measured. He based a lot of his ideas on the work of Russian physiologist Ivan Pavlov.

OF BABIES AND RATS Watson was certainly aware of Freud's work and his views on unconscious repression. Freud believed that all behaviour stems from some unconscious motivation, whereas Watson believed that all behaviour is learned. Freud had stated that a *phobia*, an irrational fear, is really a symptom of an underlying, repressed conflict and cannot be "cured" without years of psychoanalysis to uncover and understand the repressed material.

Watson believed that phobias are learned through the process of conditioning and set out to prove it. He took a baby, known as *Little Albert*, and taught him to fear a white rat by making a loud, scary noise every time the infant saw the rat, until finally seeing the rat caused the infant to cry and become fearful (Watson & Rayner, 1920). Even though Little Albert was not afraid of the rat at the start, the experiment worked very well—in fact, Little Albert became afraid of anything white and fuzzy, including white beards and furry rabbit skins. (This experiment occurred before there were such things as ethics committees. Today, this study would not be permitted because of the potential psychological harm to the child.)

This sounds really bizarre—what does scaring a baby have to do with the science of psychology? Watson wanted to prove that all behaviour was a result of a stimulus–response relationship such as that described by Pavlov. Because Freud and his ideas about unconscious motivation were becoming a dominant force, Watson felt the need to show the world that a much simpler explanation could be found. Although scaring a baby sounds a little cruel, he felt that the advancement of the science of behaviour was worth the relatively brief discomfort of the baby.

Behaviourism, like psychoanalysis, is still a major perspective in psychology today. It has also influenced the development of other perspectives, such as *cognitive psychology*.

---

*Stimulus: anything that causes an organism to have a reaction or response

PSYCHOLOGY NOW: MODERN PERSPECTIVES

1.4   *What are the basic concepts of the modern perspectives known as psychodynamics, behaviourism, humanism, biopsychology, cognitive psychology, the sociocultural perspective, and the evolutionary perspective?*

Even today, there isn't one single perspective that is used to explain all human behaviour and mental processes. There are actually seven modern perspectives, with two of those being holdovers from the early days of the field.

PSYCHODYNAMIC PERSPECTIVE

Freud's theory is still with us today in use by many professionals in therapy situations. It is far less common than it was a few decades ago, however, and even those who use his techniques modify them for modern use. In the more modern **psychodynamic perspective**, the focus is still on the unconscious mind and its influence over conscious behaviour and on early childhood experiences, but with less emphasis on sex and sexual motivations and more emphasis on the development of a sense of self and the discovery of other motivations behind a person's behaviour.

Freud had a number of followers who took his original ideas and modified them to their own perspectives. Their students modified those theories, until today there is a kind of neo-Freudianism (Freud et al., 1918/1990; Meadow & Clevans, 1978). Therapists often speak of Freudian complexes and use much of his terminology in their work with clients. Part of the reason that Freudian concepts are so enduring is the lack of any way to scientifically test them and, therefore, show them to be either useful or useless. ⓁⒾⓃⓀ *to Chapter Eleven: Theories of Personality, p. 438.*

BEHAVIOURAL PERSPECTIVE

Like psychoanalysis, behaviourism is still very influential. When its primary supporter, Watson, moved on to greener pastures in the world of advertising, B. F. Skinner became the new leader of the field.

1.5   *What were the contributions of Skinner, Maslow, Rogers, and Hebb?*

Skinner not only continued research in classical conditioning but also developed a theory of how voluntary behaviour is learned, called *operant conditioning* (Skinner,

psychodynamic perspective
modern version of psychoanalysis that is more focused on the development of a sense of self and the discovery of other motivations behind a person's behaviour than sexual motivations.

Behaviourist B. F. Skinner puts a rat through its paces. What problems might arise from applying information gained from studies with animals to human behaviour?

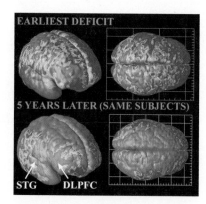

These brain scans show the increasing malfunction of the brains of schizophrenics over a five-year period, highlighting the focus of the biological perspective.

biopsychological perspective
perspective that attributes human and animal behaviour to biological events occurring in the body, such as genetic influences, hormones, and the activity of the nervous system.

1938). In this theory, behavioural responses that are followed by pleasurable consequences are strengthened, or *reinforced*. For example, a child who cries and is rewarded by getting his mother's attention will cry again in the future. Skinner's work is discussed in much greater depth in Chapter Five. Ⓛ Ⓘ Ⓝ Ⓚ *to Chapter Five: Learning, p. 218.* In addition to the psychodynamic and behavioural perspectives, five newer perspectives have developed within the past 50 years.

HUMANISTIC PERSPECTIVE

One of the newer perspectives, often called the *third force* in psychology, was really a reaction to both psychodynamic theory and behaviourism. In the early to mid 1900s, if you were a psychologist you were either a psychoanalyst or a behaviourist—there weren't any other major viewpoints to rival those two. Behaviourism was seen as a very "mechanical" theory—stimulus goes in, response comes out, and what happens in the middle is of no interest. The environment determines behaviour and the individual has little input into his or her development. Psychoanalysis wasn't mechanistic, but in this theory the workings of the physical body (in the form of sexual and aggressive instincts) determine behaviour, and the individual, once again, has little to do with his or her own destiny.

Some professionals began to develop a perspective that would allow them to focus on people's ability to direct their own lives. These theorists wanted to shift the focus to the aspects of human nature that make us uniquely human—our appreciation for beauty, for example. In a very real sense, then, this approach owes far more to the early roots of psychology in the field of philosophy than the more scientific fields of medicine and physiology. Humanists held the view that people have *free will*, the freedom to choose their own destiny. Two of the earliest and most famous founders of this view were Abraham Maslow (1908–1970) and Carl Rogers (1902–1987).

Both Maslow and Rogers emphasized the human potential, the ability of each person to become the best person he or she could be (Maslow, 1968; Rogers, 1961). They believed that studying animals in laboratories (as the behaviourists did) or people with nervous disorders (as the psychoanalysts did) could not lead to a better understanding of this human potential for *self-actualization*, as Maslow termed it—achieving one's full potential or actual self. Today, humanism is still very influential in psychotherapy. Ⓛ Ⓘ Ⓝ Ⓚ *to Chapter Fourteen: Psychological Therapies, p. 564.*

BIOPSYCHOLOGICAL PERSPECTIVE

In the **biopsychological perspective**, human and animal behaviour is seen as a direct result of events in the body. Hormones, brain chemicals, tumours, and diseases are some of the biological causes of behaviour and mental events. Ⓛ Ⓘ Ⓝ Ⓚ *to Chapter Two: The Biological Perspective, p. 42.*

For example, evidence is mounting for a biological cause (perhaps even genetic) for *schizophrenia*, a mental disorder involving delusions (false beliefs), hallucinations (false sensory impressions), and extremely distorted thinking (Brzustowicz et al., 2004; Maziade et al., 1997). Ⓛ Ⓘ Ⓝ Ⓚ *to Chapter Thirteen: Psychological Disorders, p. 520.*

Biopsychology, or the study of the biological bases of behaviour and mental processes, isn't really as new a perspective as one might think. In fact, Wundt was greatly influenced by advances in the field of physiology—a branch of biology that studies the functions of living things—as evidenced by the title of his first textbook of psychology, *Principles of Physiological Psychology*. Despite these early beginnings, the influence of behaviourism in the early and mid 1900s pushed the biopsychological perspective to the side because it was difficult to study and observe the inner workings of the brain. However, one prominent Canadian psychologist, Donald Hebb (1904–1985), argued against the prevailing behaviouristic view, stating that brain activity could be directly related to behavioural and mental acts.

PSYCHOLOGY IN THE NEWS

Was Prominent Canadian Psychologist Donald Hebb a CIA Operative?

Donald Olding Hebb was born in Chester, Nova Scotia. He graduated from Dalhousie University with a bachelor of arts degree in 1925 and hoped to become a novelist. Following graduation, Hebb taught in Nova Scotia and Quebec, and in 1928 he became a part-time psychology graduate student at McGill University. At McGill, Hebb was greatly influenced by the physiological approach to psychology taught to him by Boris Babin, who had worked directly with Ivan Pavlov. In 1934, Hebb left Montreal to work on his PhD at the University of Chicago, but within a year he followed his advisor to Harvard University. In 1937, Hebb went back to Montreal and worked with Wilder Penfield researching the effects of brain injury and surgery on behaviour (Ferguson, 1982).

In 1939, Hebb accepted a teaching position at Queen's University, where he showed that detrimental early-life experiences could influence the problem-solving ability of adult rats. This groundbreaking research is today one of the basic tenets of developmental psychology and was instrumental in the creation of the Head Start programs that promote school readiness by enhancing the cognitive and social skills of disadvantaged preschoolers.

Hebb went back to the United States in 1942 to again work with his PhD advisor, but he returned to McGill in 1947. It was here that Hebb studied an array of topics including sensory deprivation, which some believe formed the basis of the Central Intelligence Agency's (CIA) sensory isolation torture and which became a standard interrogation technique. This connection has led to speculation that Hebb may have willingly or unwillingly worked with the CIA. In 1947, Hebb published his most influential work, a book titled *The Organization of Behavior: A Neuropsychological Theory*. In this book, Hebb proposed a theory that linked physical experience with changes in brain structure and function. The gist of his theory, which became known as *Hebbian learning* or *Hebb's Law*, states that when one brain cell (A) repeatedly excites another brain cell (B), some growth process occurs that enables brain cell A to more easily excite brain cell B in the future (Hebb, 1949). In other words, brain cells that fire together wire together. This seemingly simple theory opened the door to a vast array of research that inspired many of the studies that you will read about in this textbook (Klien, 1999).

Donald Olding Hebb, arguably Canada's most famous psychologist. His groundbreaking ideas continue to influence psychologists around the world.

COGNITIVE PERSPECTIVE

Cognitive psychology focuses on how people think, remember, store, and use information. It became a major force in the field in the 1960s. It wasn't a new idea, as the Gestalt psychologists had themselves supported the study of mental processes of learning. The development of computers (which just happened to make great models of human thinking), the work of Piaget with children, Chomsky's analysis of Skinner's views of language, and discoveries in biological psychology stimulated an interest in studying the processes of thought. The **cognitive perspective**, with its focus on memory, intelligence, perception, thought processes, problem solving, language, and learning, has become a major force in psychology. ⓁⒾⓃⓀ *to Chapter Seven: Cognition, p. 260.*

cognitive perspective
perspective that focuses on memory, intelligence, perception, problem solving, and learning.

SOCIOCULTURAL PERSPECTIVE

Another modern perspective in psychology is the **sociocultural perspective**, which actually combines two areas of study: *social psychology*, which is the study of groups, social roles, rules of social actions, and relationships; and *cultural psychology*, which is the study of cultural norms,* values, and expectations. These two areas are related in that they are both about the effect that people have on one another, either individually or in a larger group, such as a culture (Peplau & Taylor, 1997). (L)(I)(N)(K) *to Chapter Twelve: Social Psychology, p. 476.*

The sociocultural perspective is important because it reminds people that how they and others behave (or even think) is influenced not only by whether they are alone, with friends, in a crowd, or part of a group but also by the particular culture in which they live. For example, consider a tobacco company trying to sell cigarettes by using the image of a smoking cowboy riding his horse into the sunset. In Canada and the United States, an advertising campaign using this theme was hugely successful because our individualistic culture embraces rugged masculinity. In China, which has more of a collectivist culture in which strong cohesive groups are emphasized, this same campaign had Chinese people wondering what the cowboy had done wrong!

EVOLUTIONARY PERSPECTIVE

The **evolutionary perspective** focuses on the biological bases for universal mental characteristics that all humans share. It seeks to explain general mental strategies and traits, such as why we lie, how attractiveness influences mate selection, why fear of snakes is so universal, and why people like music and dancing, among many others.

In this perspective, human behaviour results from the interaction of two equally important components. First, the mind is seen as a set of information-processing modules, often referred to as *adaptations*, designed by the same process of natural selection that Darwin (1859) first theorized. Second, input from the environment is necessary to develop new adaptations or activate existing ones. Our current or existing adaptations developed over thousands and thousands of generations in response to challenges in the environment. In other words, these adaptations allowed human beings to solve the problems we faced in the early days of human evolution—the problems of the early hunters and gatherers. For example, *evolutionary psychologists* (psychologists who study the evolutionary origins of human behaviour) would view the human behaviour of not eating substances that have a bitter taste (such as poisonous plants) as an adaptive** behaviour that evolved as early humans came into contact with such bitter plants. Those who ate the bitter plants would die, while those who spit them out survived to pass on their "I don't like this taste" genes to their offspring, who would pass on the genes to their offspring, and so on, until after a long period of time there is an entire population of humans that naturally avoid bitter-tasting substances.

That explains why people don't like bitter stuff, like the white part of an orange peel, but that's really a physical thing. How would this work for something psychological, such as relationships? Relationships between men and women are one of the many areas in which evolutionary psychologists conduct research. For example, in one study, researchers surveyed young adults about their relationships

Psychologists with an evolutionary perspective would be interested in the adaptive physical and emotional characteristics that brought this couple together.

That explains why people don't like bitter stuff, like the white part of an orange peel, but that's really a physical thing. How would this work for something psychological, such as relationships? ▶

sociocultural perspective
perspective that focuses on the relationship between social behaviour and culture.

evolutionary perspective
perspective that focuses on the biological bases of universal mental characteristics that all humans share.

---

*Norms: standards or expected behaviour
**Adaptive: having the quality of adjusting to the circumstances or need; in the sense used here, a behaviour that aids in survival

with the opposite sex, asking the participants how likely they would be to forgive either a sexual infidelity or an emotional one (Shackelford et al., 2002). Evolutionary theory would predict that men, on the one hand, would find it more difficult to forgive a woman who had sex with someone else than a woman who was only emotionally involved with someone, because the man cannot be sure that the children the woman bears are his (Geary, 2000). Why put all that effort into providing for what could be another man's offspring? Women, on the other hand, should find it more difficult to forgive an emotional infidelity, as they are always sure that their children are their own, but (in evolutionary terms, mind you) they need the emotional loyalty of the men to provide for those children (Buss et al., 1992; Daly et al., 1982). The results of the study bore out the prediction: men found it more difficult to forgive a partner's sexual straying and were more likely to break up with the woman than if the infidelity were purely emotional; for women, the opposite results were found.

PRACTICE QUIZ: HOW MUCH DO YOU REMEMBER?

Pick the best answer.

1. Which of the following pairs represents the two psychology perspectives that were also part of the historical beginnings of psychology?
   a. humanism and behaviourism
   b. behaviourism and psychodynamics
   c. psychodynamics and humanism
   d. cognitive psychology and psychodynamics

2. Which perspective is known as the *third force* in psychology?
   a. psychoanalysis
   b. behaviourism
   c. cognitive psychology
   d. humanism

3. Elsie suffered a stroke and had to be hospitalized. While in the hospital, she talked in strange, garbled words and seemed to think that she was being held against her will. Which of the following perspectives BEST explains Elsie's odd behaviour?
   a. psychodynamics
   b. cognitive psychology
   c. behaviourism
   d. biopsychology

4. Which perspective would a researcher be taking if she were studying the way children store and retrieve information?
   a. psychoanalysis
   b. behaviourism
   c. cognitive psychology
   d. evolutionary perspective

5. Which of the following historical perspectives gave rise, at least in part, to the evolutionary perspective?
   a. behaviourism
   b. psychoanalysis
   c. structuralism
   d. functionalism

6. Which of the following best summarizes Hebb's Law?
   a. brain cells that flock together stray apart
   b. brain cells that fire together wire together
   c. brain cells that play together stay together
   d. brain cells that are opposites attract one another

Answers: 1.-b, 2.-d, 3.-d, 4.-c, 5.-d, 6.-b.

TYPES OF PSYCHOLOGICAL PROFESSIONALS

There are a number of professionals who work in the field of psychology. These professionals have different training, different focuses, and may have different goals from the typical psychologist.

1.6 *What's the difference between a psychiatrist and a psychologist, and what other types of professionals work in the various areas of psychology?*

A **psychiatrist** has a medical doctorate (MD) degree and is a medical doctor who has specialized in the diagnosis and treatment of psychological disorders. Psychiatrists can prescribe medicine in addition to providing therapy and counselling, and they typically work in private practice or hospital settings.

A **psychoanalyst** is usually either a psychiatrist (MD) or a psychologist (PhD, PsyD, or EdD) who has special training in the theories of Sigmund Freud and his

psychiatrist
a medical doctor who has specialized in the diagnosis and treatment of psychological disorders.

psychoanalyst
either a psychiatrist or a psychologist who has special training in the theories of Sigmund Freud and his method of psychoanalysis.

Psychiatric social workers use many tools to help children deal with problems such as divorce or abuse. How might using hand puppets help this young girl talk about the problems in her life?

psychiatric social worker
a social worker with some training in therapy methods who focuses on the environmental conditions that can have an impact on mental disorders, such as poverty, overcrowding, stress, and drug abuse.

psychologist
a professional with an academic degree and specialized training in one or more areas of psychology.

method of psychoanalysis. Psychoanalysts, like psychiatrists, usually work in private practice or hospital settings.

A **psychiatric social worker** is trained in the area of social work and usually possesses a master of social work (MSW) degree or a licensed clinical social work (LCSW) degree. These professionals focus more on the environmental conditions that can have an impact on mental disorders, such as poverty, overcrowding, stress, and drug abuse. They work out of clinics, hospitals, and social service organizations.

In Canada, a **psychologist** typically has no medical training but does have a doctorate degree and is licensed or registered in the province where he or she conducts business. Some provinces (e.g., Nova Scotia) will register an individual who holds a master's degree in psychology as a psychologist. Most registered psychologists in Canada are further classified as either clinical or counselling psychologists. Clinical psychologists often treat people with psychological illnesses and study the diagnosis, causes, and treatment of mental disorders. Counselling psychologists are more likely to treat people suffering with personal problems that do not necessarily involve a full-blown psychological illness. Psychologists can also work as professors and researchers in colleges and universities. Your instructor and the authors of this text fall into this category. Some psychologists may work for the government, helping to develop policy, and some may work in industry, designing better equipment or workplaces.

As you can see, psychologists must undergo intense academic training, learning about many different areas of psychology before choosing an area in which to specialize (see Figure 1.2).

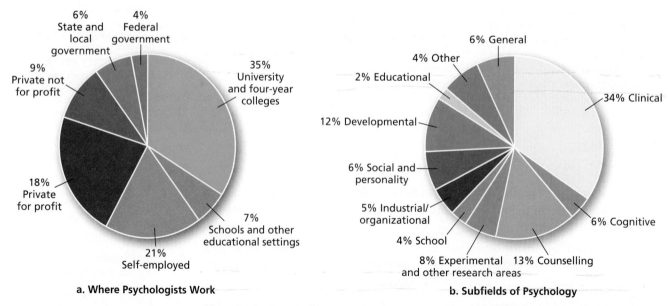

a. Where Psychologists Work

b. Subfields of Psychology

FIGURE 1.2 **Work Settings and Subfields of Psychology** (a) There are many different work settings for psychologists. Although not obvious from the chart, many psychologists work in more than one setting. For example, a clinical psychologist may work in a hospital setting as well as teach at a university or college (J. Tsapogas et al., 2006). (b) This pie chart shows the specialty areas of psychologists who recently received their doctorates (T. B. Hoffer et al., 2007).

Note: Because of rounding, percentages may not total to 100 percent.

PRACTICE QUIZ: HOW MUCH DO YOU REMEMBER?

Pick the best answer.

1. Which of the following professionals in psychology focuses more on the environmental conditions that affect mental disorders?
   a. psychiatrist
   b. psychoanalyst
   c. psychiatric social worker
   d. psychologist

2. Which of the following specialties in psychology deals with diagnosis and treatment of disorders?
   a. clinical
   b. development
   c. personality
   d. experimental

3. Max is interested in becoming a psychologist. He is most interested in how people in groups behave differently from people who act alone. He would most likely specialize in _____ psychology.
   a. comparative
   b. educational
   c. school
   d. social

4. Dr. Roaden works in a school system, dealing directly with children who have emotional, academic, and behavioural problems. Dr. Roaden is most likely which type of psychologist?
   a. personality
   b. developmental
   c. school
   d. comparative

Answers: 1.–c, 2.–a, 3.–d, 4.–c.

PSYCHOLOGY: THE SCIENCE
WHY PSYCHOLOGISTS USE THE SCIENTIFIC METHOD

Have you ever played the "airport game"? You sit at the airport (bus terminal, doctor's office, or any other place where people come and go and you have a long wait) and try to guess what people do for a living based only on their appearance. Although it's a fun game, the guesses are rarely correct. People's guesses also sometimes reveal the biases that they may have about certain physical appearances: men with long hair are musicians, people wearing suits are executives, and so on. On the other hand, psychology is about trying to determine facts and reduce uncertainty.

1.7   *Why is psychology a science, and what are the steps in using the scientific method?*

In psychology, researchers want to see only what is really there, not what their biases might want them to see. The way to do that is by using the **scientific method**, a system for reducing bias and error in the measurement of data.

The first step in any investigation is to have a question to investigate, right? So the first step in the scientific method is the following:

1. **Perceiving the Question:** You notice something interesting happening in your surroundings for which you would like to have an explanation. An example might be that you've noticed that your children seem to get a little more aggressive with each other after watching a particularly violent children's cartoon program on Saturday morning. You wonder if the violence in the cartoon could be creating the aggressive behaviour in your children. This step is derived from the goal of description: What is happening here?

   Once you have a question, you want an answer. The next logical step is to form a tentative answer or explanation for the behaviour you have seen. This tentative explanation is known as a **hypothesis**.

2. **Forming a Hypothesis:** Based on your initial observations about what's going on in your surroundings, you form an educated guess about the explanation for your observations, putting it into the form of a statement that can be tested in some way. This is not as easy as it sounds. An educated guess means you will have to

The scientific method can be used to determine whether children who watch violence on television are more likely to be aggressive than those who do not.

scientific method
system of gathering data so that bias and error in measurement are reduced.

hypothesis
tentative explanation of a phenomenon based on observations.

review the scientific literature on the topic, which can take quite a long time. This literature review will guide you logically to a testable research hypothesis. Going back to the previous example, you might say, based on the available scientific literature, "Children who watch violent cartoons will become more aggressive."

The next step is testing the hypothesis. People have a tendency to notice only things that agree with their view of the world, a kind of selective perception called *confirmation bias*. (L)(I)(N)(K) *to Chapter Seven: Cognition, p. 260.* For example, if a person is convinced that all men with long hair smoke cigarettes, that person will tend to notice only those long-haired men who are smoking and ignore all the long-haired men who don't smoke. The scientific method is designed to overcome this tendency to look at only the information that confirms people's biases by forcing them to actively seek out information that might contradict their biases (or hypotheses). So when you test your hypothesis, you are trying to determine whether the factor you suspect has an effect and the results were not due to luck or chance. That's why psychologists keep doing research over and over—to get more evidence that hypotheses are "supported."

3. **Testing the Hypothesis:** The method you use to test your hypothesis will depend on exactly what kind of answer you think you might get. You might make more detailed observations or do a survey in which you ask questions of a large number of people, or you might design an experiment in which you would deliberately change one thing to see if it causes changes in the behaviour you are observing. In the example, the best method would probably be an experiment in which you select a group of children, randomly show half of them a cartoon with violence and the other half of them a cartoon with no violence, and then measure aggressive behaviour in some defined way in each group.

Once you have the measures from your experiment, in this case the aggressive scores, you will organize and analyze them with some kind of statistical procedure. The statistical results will form the basis of the next step.

4. **Drawing Conclusions:** Once you know the results, you will find that either your hypothesis was supported, which means that your experiment worked—your measurements supported your initial observations outlined in your hypothesis—or it wasn't supported, which means that you need to go back to square one and think of another possible explanation for what you have observed. (Could it be that Saturday mornings make children a little more aggressive? Or Saturday breakfasts?). Once you have your conclusions it is time to tell other researchers what you have found. (L)(I)(N)(K) *to Appendix A: Statistics* (online in your eText).

Why tell anyone what happened if it failed? Just because one experiment or other study did not find support for the hypothesis does not necessarily mean that the hypothesis is incorrect. Your study might have been poorly designed, or there might have been factors not under your control that interfered with the study. But other researchers are asking the same kinds of questions that you might have asked. They need to know what has already been found out about the answers to those questions so that they can continue investigating, adding more knowledge about the answers to those questions. Even if your own investigation didn't go as planned, that tells other researchers what *not* to do in the future. So the final step in any scientific investigation is reporting the results.

5. **Report Your Results:** At this point, you would want to write up exactly what you did, why you did it, how you did it, and what you found, so that others can learn from what you have already accomplished—or failed to accomplish. Another reason for reporting your results is that even if your research gave you the answer you

◁ Why tell anyone what happened if it failed?

expected, your investigation might have been done incorrectly, or the results might have been a fluke or due to chance alone. So if others can **replicate** your research (do exactly the same study over again and get the same results), it gives much more support to your findings. This allows others to predict behaviour based on your findings and to use the results of those findings to modify or control behaviour, the last two goals in psychology.

This might be a good place to make a distinction between questions that can be scientifically or empirically studied and those that cannot. For example, "What is the meaning of life?" is not a question that can be studied using the scientific or empirical method. Empirical questions are those that can be tested through direct observation or experience. For example, "Has life ever existed on Mars?" is a question that scientists are trying to answer through measurements, experimentation, soil samples, and other methods. Eventually they will be able to say with some degree of confidence that life could have existed or could not have existed. That is an empirical question because it can be supported or disproved by gathering real evidence. The meaning of life, however, is a question of belief for each person. One does not need proof to *believe*, but scientists need proof (in the form of objectively gathered evidence) to *know*.

In psychology, researchers try to find the answers to empirical questions. Questions that involve beliefs and values are best left to philosophy and religion.

DESCRIPTIVE METHODS

1.8   *How do psychologists use naturalistic and laboratory settings to describe behaviour, and what are the advantages and disadvantages associated with these settings?*

There are a number of different ways to investigate the answers to research questions, and which one researchers use depends on the kind of question they want to answer. If they want to simply gather information about what has happened or what is happening, they would want a method that gives them a detailed description.

NATURALISTIC OBSERVATION   Sometimes all that researchers need to know is what is happening to a group of animals or people. The best way to look at the behaviour of animals or people is to watch them behave in their normal environment. That's why animal researchers such as Jane Goodall went to the areas where chimpanzees lived and watched them eat, play, mate, and sleep in their own natural surroundings. With people, researchers might want to observe them in their workplaces, homes, or on playgrounds. For example, if someone wanted to know how the parents of Canadian minor hockey league players acted, the researcher might become a coach and record the behaviour of parents at the local rink. Dr. Paul Valliant, a Laurentian University professor, did just that. He, like many Canadian parents, became the coach to his son's hockey team and began taking notes on how parents interacted with their own sons and daughters, other players and parents, referees, and fans. Dr. Valliant observed both good and bad parental behaviour and published his observations in a book titled *Minor Hockey to NHL: Parents Survival Guide*.

What is the advantage of naturalistic observation? It allows researchers to get a realistic picture of how behaviour occurs because they are actually watching that behaviour. In a more artificial setting, such as a laboratory, they might get

replicate
in research, repeating a study or experiment to see if the same results will be obtained, in an effort to demonstrate reliability of results.

Researcher Jane Goodall watches chimpanzees behave in their natural environment. How might her presence have affected the behaviour of the chimpanzees?

behaviour that is contrived or artificial rather than genuine. Of course, there are precautions that must be taken. In many cases, animals or people who know they are being watched will not behave normally anyway. This is called the **observer effect**, so often the observer needs to remain hidden from view. When researching humans, this is often a difficult thing to do. In a mall setting with teenagers, a researcher might find that pretending to read a book is a good disguise, especially if he or she wears glasses to hide the movement of the eyes. Then the researcher would be able to look up at what goes on between the teens without them knowing that they were being watched. In other cases, researchers might use one-way mirrors, or they might actually become participants in a group, a technique called **participant observation**.

Are there disadvantages? Unfortunately, yes. One of the disadvantages of naturalistic observation is the possibility of **observer bias**. That happens when the person doing the observing has a particular opinion about what he or she is going to see or expects to see. If that is the case, sometimes that person sees only those actions that support that expectation and ignores actions that don't fit. A way around that is to have *blind observers*: people who do not know what the research question is and, therefore, have no preconceived notions about what they "should" see. It's also a good idea to have more than one observer, so that the various observations can be compared.

Another disadvantage is that each naturalistic setting is unique and unlike any other. Observations that are made at one time in one setting may not hold true for another time, even if the setting is similar, because the conditions are not going to be exactly the same time after time—researchers don't have that kind of control over the natural world. For example, famed gorilla researcher Dian Fossey had to battle poachers who set traps for the animals in the area of her observations (Mowat, 1988). The presence and activities of the poachers affected the normal behaviour of the gorillas she was trying to observe.

LABORATORY OBSERVATION   Sometimes observing behaviour in animals or people is just not practical in a natural setting. For example, a researcher might want to observe the reactions of animals to a mirror image of themselves and record the reactions with a camera mounted behind the one-way mirror. That kind of equipment might be difficult to set up in a natural setting. In a laboratory observation, the researcher would bring the animal to the equipment, controlling the type of animal, the number of animals, and everything else that goes on in the laboratory.

Laboratory settings have the disadvantage of being an artificial situation that might result in artificial behaviour—animals and people often react differently in the laboratory than they would in the real world. The main advantage of this method is the degree of control that it gives to the observer.

Both naturalistic and laboratory observations can lead to the formation of hypotheses that can later be tested.

1.9   *How do psychologists use case studies and surveys to describe behaviour, and what are some drawbacks to each of these methods?*

CASE STUDIES   Another descriptive technique is called the **case study**, in which one individual is studied in great detail. In a case study, researchers try to learn everything they can about that individual. For example, Sigmund Freud based his entire

observer effect
tendency of people or animals to behave differently from normal when they know they are being observed.

participant observation
a naturalistic observation in which the observer becomes a participant in the group being observed.

observer bias
tendency of observers to see what they expect to see.

case study
study of one individual in great detail.

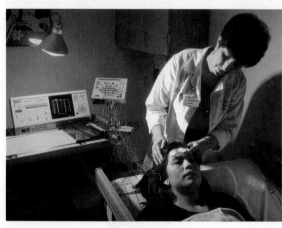

Psychologists use many kinds of tools to observe behaviour. In this scene, a researcher is attaching electrodes to a woman to gather information about her sleep habits.

theory of psychoanalysis on his numerous case studies of his patients in which he gathered information about their childhoods and relationships with others from the very beginning of their lives to the present. L I N K to *Chapter Eleven: Theories of Personality, p. 438.*

The advantage of the case study is the tremendous amount of detail it provides. It may also be the only way to get certain kinds of information. For example, one famous case study is the story of Phineas Gage, who had a railroad spike driven through his head and suffered a major personality change as a result (Damasio et al., 1994). Researchers couldn't study that case with naturalistic observation, and an experiment was out of the question. Imagine anyone responding to an ad in the newspaper that read:

Wanted: 50 people willing to suffer non-fatal brain damage for scientific study of the brain. Will pay all medical expenses.

It's pretty certain that anyone who actually answered that ad might already be suffering from some pretty extensive brain damage.

The disadvantage of the case study is that researchers can't really apply the results to other similar people. In other words, they can't assume that if another person had the same kind of experiences growing up, he or she would turn out just like the person in the case study. People are unique and have too many complicating factors in their lives to be that predictable. So what researchers find in one case won't necessarily apply or generalize to others.

SURVEYS   Sometimes what psychologists want to know about is pretty personal— such as what people do in their sexual relationships, for example. The only way to find out about very private (covert) behaviour is to ask questions.

In the survey method, researchers will ask a series of questions about the topic they are studying. Surveys can be conducted in person in the form of interviews or on the telephone, on the internet, or with a questionnaire. The questions in interviews or on the telephone can vary, but usually all the questions in a survey are the same for everyone answering the survey. In this way, researchers can ask lots of questions and survey hundreds of people.

That is the big advantage of surveys, aside from their ability to get at private information. Researchers can get a tremendous amount of data on a very large group of people. Of course, there are disadvantages. One disadvantage is that researchers have to be very careful about the group of people they survey. If they want to find out what first-year college students think about politics, for example, they can't really ask every single first-year college student in Canada. But they can select a **representative sample** from that group. For example, they could randomly* select a certain number of first-year students from several different colleges across Canada. Why randomly? Because the sample has to be *representative* of the **population**, which is the entire group in which the researcher is interested. If researchers selected only first-year students from large urban schools, for example, they would certainly get different opinions than they might get from students at small community colleges. But if they take a lot of colleges and select their *participants* (people who are part of the study) randomly, they will be more certain of getting answers that a broad selection of college students would typically give.

*Randomly: in this sense, chosen so that each member of the group has an equal chance of being chosen

Explore on **mypsychlab**
Phineas Gage

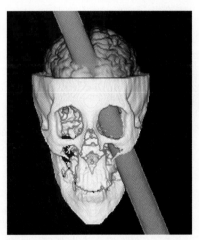

This is a computer-generated reconstruction of the damaged skull of Phineas Gage. The red area shows the path taken by the steel rod driven through his skull by an explosion in 1848.

representative sample
randomly selected sample of subjects or participants from a larger population of subjects or participants.

population
the entire group of people or animals in which the researcher is interested.

"Next question: I believe that life is a constant striving for balance, requiring frequent tradeoffs between morality and necessity, within a cyclic pattern of joy and sadness, forging a trail of bittersweet memories until one slips, inevitably, into the jaws of death. Agree or disagree?"

That point brings up the other major disadvantage of the survey technique: People aren't always going to give researchers accurate answers. The fact is, people tend to misremember things, distort the truth, and may lie outright—even if the survey is an anonymous questionnaire. Remembering is not a very accurate process sometimes, especially when people think that they might not come off sounding very desirable or socially appropriate. Some people deliberately give the answer they think is more socially correct rather than their true opinion, so that no one gets offended, in a process called *courtesy* or *social desirability bias*.

Both the wording of survey questions and the order in which they appear on the survey can affect the outcome. It is difficult to find a wording that will be understood in exactly the same way by all those who read the question, for example. Questions can be worded in such a way that the desired answer becomes obvious (often resulting in socially desirable biased–type answers), or a question that appears at the end of a survey might be answered quite differently than if it had appeared at the beginning. These limitations force researchers to take survey results with a grain of salt**—results may not be as accurate as they would like them to be. An intriguing finding on a survey will often lead a researcher to do more research, but this time using a more controlled research method, such as a correlation or an experiment. These advanced research methods are reviewed next.

PRACTICE QUIZ: HOW MUCH DO YOU REMEMBER?

Pick the best answer.

1. In the scientific method, the first step is
   a. reporting your results.
   b. perceiving a question.
   c. drawing conclusions.
   d. testing the hypothesis.

2. In a naturalistic observation, the phenomenon in which the behaviour of the participants being observed changes because they are being watched is called
   a. observer bias.
   b. participant observation.
   c. observer effect.
   d. representative sampling.

3. The use of _____ helps to control for the effect of observer bias.
   a. blind observers
   b. a single trained observer
   c. randomly selected observers
   d. none of the above

4. The main disadvantage of a case study is that it is not
   a. easily done, because of the large number of participants.
   b. generalizable to other similar conditions.
   c. detailed enough for most research questions.
   d. biased.

5. Which of the following is the BEST example of a representative sample?
   a. You ask your fellow students to be participants in a study of adult memory.
   b. You choose people shopping in an expensive store in the mall to respond to your survey.
   c. You ask people from your church to participate in a study of family values.
   d. You choose people randomly from the telephone book to respond to your survey.

Answers: 1-b, 2-c, 3-a, 4-c, 5-d.

FINDING RELATIONSHIPS

The methods discussed so far only provide descriptions of behaviour. Only two methods allow researchers to know more than just a description of what has happened: correlations and experiments. Correlation is a statistical technique, a particular way of organizing numerical information so that it is easier to look for patterns in the information. In fact, the data from the descriptive methods just discussed are often analyzed using the correlational technique.

**Grain of salt: a phrase meaning to be skeptical; to doubt the truth or accuracy of something

1.10 *What is the correlational technique, and what does it tell researchers about relationships?*

CORRELATIONS A **correlation** is a measure of the relationship between two or more variables. A *variable* is anything that can change or vary—scores on a test, temperature in a room, gender, and so on. For example, researchers might be curious to know whether cigarette smoking is connected to life expectancy (the number of years a person can be expected to live). Obviously, the scientists can't hang around people who smoke and wait to see when those people die. The only way (short of performing a really unethical and lengthy experiment) to find out if smoking behaviour and life expectancy are related to each other is to use the medical records of people who have already died. (For privacy's sake, personal information such as names and social insurance numbers would be removed, with only facts such as age, gender, and weight available to researchers.) Researchers would look for two facts from each record: the number of cigarettes the person smoked per day and the age of the person at death.

Now the researcher has two sets of numbers for each person in the study. Those numbers go into a mathematical formula and produce a number called the *correlation coefficient.* The correlation coefficient represents two things: the strength of the linear relationship and its direction.

Direction? How can a mathematical relationship have a direction? Whenever researchers talk about two variables being related or correlated to each other, what they really mean is that when they graph the variables together on a scatterplot (see Figure 1.3), they can see a linear pattern. If they see a linear pattern, then knowing the value of one variable allows them to estimate the value of the other variable. For example, if researchers found that smoking and life expectancy are indeed related in a linear fashion, they should be able to predict how long someone might live if they know how many cigarettes a person smokes in a day. But which way does that prediction work? If a person smokes a lot of cigarettes, does that mean that he or she will live a longer life or a shorter one? Does life expectancy go up or down as smoking increases? That is what is meant by the *direction* of the relationship.

In terms of the correlation coefficient (represented by the small letter *r*), the number researchers get from the formula will either be a positive number or a negative number. If positive, the two variables increase in the same direction—as one goes up, the other goes up; or as one decreases, the other also decreases. If the correlation coefficient is negative, the two variables have an inverse relationship—as one increases, the other decreases. If researchers find that the more cigarettes a person smoked, the younger that person was when he or she died, that would mean that the correlation between the two variables is negative. (As smoking goes up, life expectancy goes down—an inverse relationship.)

The strength of the relationship between the variables will be determined by the actual number itself. That number will always range between +1.00 and –1.00. If the relationship is a strong one, the number will be closer to +1.00 or to –1.00. A correlation of +0.89 for example, would be a very strong positive correlation. That might represent the relationship between scores on the GPA and an IQ test, for example. A correlation of –0.89 would be equally strong but negative. That would be more like the correlation researchers would probably find between smoking cigarettes and the age at which a person dies (see Figure 1.3 for some examples).

Notice that the closer the number is to zero, the weaker the relationship becomes. Researchers would probably find that the correlation coefficient for the relationship between people's weight and the number of freckles they have is pretty close to zero, for example.

correlation
a measure of the relationship between two variables.

✳ Explore on **mypsychlab**
Correlations Do Not Show Causation

◀ Direction? How can a mathematical relationship have a direction?

© The New Yorker Collection 1994 Leo Cullum from cartoonbank.com. All Rights Reserved.

FIGURE 1.3 **Scatterplot Examples**
Five scatterplots showing direction and strength of correlation. It should be noted that perfect correlations, whether positive or negative, rarely occur in the real world.

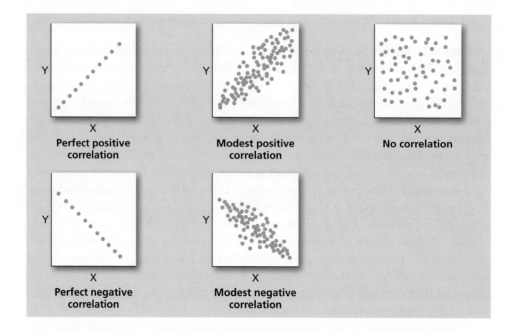

Perfect positive correlation

Modest positive correlation

No correlation

Perfect negative correlation

Modest negative correlation

Go back to the cigarette thing—if we found that the correlation between ▶ cigarette smoking and life expectancy was high, does that mean that smoking causes your life expectancy to be shortened?

experiment
a deliberate manipulation of a variable to see if corresponding changes in behaviour result, allowing the determination of cause-and-effect relationships.

Go back to the cigarette thing—if we found that the correlation between cigarette smoking and life expectancy was high, does that mean that smoking causes your life expectancy to be shortened? Not exactly. The biggest error that people make concerning correlation is to assume that it means one variable is the cause of the other. Remember that *correlation does not prove causation.* That means that just because two variables are related to each other, researchers cannot assume that one of them causes the other one to occur. They could both be related to some other variable that is the cause of both. For example, population is the cause of increasing numbers of many kinds of services in a particular area, including churches and bars. The number of churches in any given area can be used to predict the number of bars because the two are correlated through their common link to population, not because churches cause bars to be built or vice versa.

To sum up, a correlation will tell researchers whether or not there is a linear relationship between the variables, how strong the relationship is, and in what direction the relationship goes. Also, even though correlation does not prove causation, it can provide a starting point for examining causal relationships with another type of study, the experiment.

THE EXPERIMENT The only research method that will allow researchers to determine the cause of a behaviour is the **experiment**. In an experiment, researchers deliberately manipulate (change in some purposeful way) the variable they think is causing some behaviour while holding all the other variables that might interfere with the experiment's results constant and unchanging. That way, if they get changes in behaviour (an effect, in other words), they know that those changes must be due to the manipulated variable. For example, remember the discussion of the steps in the scientific method. It talked about how to study the effects of watching violent cartoons on children's aggressive behaviour. The most logical way to study that particular relationship is by an experiment.

First, researchers might start by selecting the children they want to use in the experiment. The best method to do that is the same method they would use for selecting a sample of people to participate in the experiment—random selection. Ideally, researchers would decide on the age they wanted to study. Let's say that they want to know the effects of the experiment on children who are 3 to 4 years old. Then researchers could go to daycare centres to randomly select a certain number of children of that age. Of course, that wouldn't include the children who don't go to a daycare centre. Another way to get a sample in the age range might be to ask several pediatricians to send letters to parents of children of that age and then randomly select the sample from those children whose parents responded positively.

1.11 *How do researchers use operational definitions, independent and dependent variables, experimental and control groups, and random assignment in designing an experiment?*

The Variables   Another important step is to decide on the variable the researchers want to manipulate (which would be the one they think causes changes in behaviour) and the variable they want to measure to see if there are any changes (this would be the effect on behaviour of the manipulation). Often, deciding on the variables in the experiment comes before selection of the participants or subjects.

In the example of aggression and children's cartoons, the variable that researchers think causes changes in aggressive behaviour is the violence in the cartoons. Researchers would want to manipulate that in some way, and to do that they have to define the term *violent cartoon*. They would have to find a cartoon that contains violence or make one. Then they would show that cartoon to the participants and try to measure their aggressive behaviour afterward. In measuring the aggressive behaviour, they would have to specify exactly what they mean by "aggressive behaviour" so that it can be measured. This is called an **operational definition** because it specifically names the operations (steps or procedures) that the experimenter must use to control or measure the variables in the experiment. An operational definition of aggressive behaviour might be a checklist of very specific actions, such as hitting and pushing, that an observer can mark off as the children complete the items on the list. If the observers were just told to look for "aggressive behaviour," the researchers would probably get half a dozen or more different interpretations of what aggressive behaviour is.

The name for the variable that is manipulated in any experiment is the **independent variable** because it is *independent* of anything the participants do. The participants in the study do not get to choose or vary the independent variable, and their behaviour does not affect this variable at all. Since the independent variable is manipulated it must have at least two levels. One level is considered a control or baseline level and the other level is considered the experimental level. In the preceding example, the levels of the independent variable would be the presence (experimental) or absence (control) of violence in the cartoons.

The response of the participants to the manipulation of the independent variable *is* a dependent relationship, so the response of the participants that is measured is known as the **dependent variable**. Their behaviour, if the hypothesis is correct, should *depend* on which level of the independent variable they were exposed to. In the example, the dependent variable would be the measure

◄━●━ **Simulate** on **mypsychlab**
Distinguishing Independent and Dependent Variables

operational definition
a researcher's definition of a variable of interest that precisely describes the variable and how it is to be measured.

independent variable
variable in an experiment that is manipulated by the experimenter.

dependent variable
variable in an experiment that represents the measurable response or behaviour of the participants in the experiment.

The act of hitting each other with toy swords could be part of an operational definition of aggressive behaviour.

of aggressive behaviour in the children. The dependent variable is always the thing (response of participants or result of some action) that is measured to see just how the independent variable may have affected it.

The Groups If researchers do all of this and find that the children's behaviour is aggressive, can they say that the aggressive behaviour was caused by the violence in the cartoon? No, what has been described so far is not enough. The researchers may find that the children who watch the violent cartoon are aggressive, but how would they know if the children's aggressive behaviour was caused by the cartoon or was just the natural aggressive level of those particular children or the result of the particular time of day they were observed? Those sorts of *confounding variables* (variables that interfere with each other and their possible effects on some other variable of interest) are the kind researchers have to control for in some way. For example, if participants in an experiment were supposed to take only a potassium supplement but also took an iron supplement, any effects the potassium might have had on what the experimenter was measuring would be confused (confounded) with the effects that the iron supplement might have also had. The best way to control for confounding variables is to have a group of participants for each level of the independent variable—in our case, a group that watches the violent cartoon and a group that watches a non-violent cartoon for the same length of time. Then the researchers would measure the aggressive behaviour in both groups. If the aggressive behaviour is significantly greater in the group that watched the violent cartoon (and the researchers would use statistics to determine this), then the researchers can say that in this experiment, violent cartoon watching caused greater aggressive behaviour.

Recall from above that any independent variable must have at least two levels since it is manipulated by the experimenter. The name given to the group that gets exposed to the level of the independent variable that involves the manipulation (the violent cartoon in this example) is the **experimental group** because it is the group that receives the experimental manipulation. The other group, the one that would get exposed to the level of the independent variable that involves either no treatment or some kind of treatment that should have no effect (like the group that watches the non-violent cartoon in the example), is called the **control group** because it is used to *control* for the possibility that other factors might be causing the effect that is being examined. If researchers were to find that both the group that watched the violent cartoon (experimental group) and the group that watched the non-violent cartoon (control group) were equally aggressive, they would have to assume that the violent content did not influence aggressive behaviour at all.

> If researchers do all of this and find that the children's behaviour is aggressive, can they say that the aggressive behaviour was caused by the violence in the cartoon?

CONTROL GROUP   OUT OF CONTROL GROUP.

experimental group
participants in an experiment who are exposed to the level of the independent variable that should influence the dependent variable.

control group
participants in an experiment who are exposed to the level of the independent variable that should *not* influence the dependent variable. They may receive a placebo treatment.

PSYCHOLOGY IN THE NEWS

Free Cocaine Offered for Psychological Study at McGill

Five years ago, Marco Leyton, a psychology professor at McGill University, began to study the effects of cocaine on the human brain in hopes of finding a way to stop the strong cravings experienced by addicts. His study was recently judged the best among 50 applicants for funding in the medical category of research related to brain and behaviour. For that success he received an additional $600 000 in funding from the Canadian Institutes of Health Research to continue his study for another five years. Each year, Dr. Leyton recruits about 10 male and female participants to take part in his study. Each participant is paid roughly $8 per hour to snort one, two, three, four, or even five lines of coke. The participants are then instructed to lie down on a bed, and as the drug begins to take effect, three-dimensional photographs of their brains are taken.

Would you like to participate in this study? Would you want to be in the experimental group or the control group? Unfortunately, if you were a participant in this study, you would not get to pick which group you are in. Participants in any experiment are assigned randomly to either the control group or the experimental group. This means that if you were a participant, you would have an equal chance of being in either the control group or the experimental group. Randomization helps to ensure that any confounding or extraneous variables that we did not account for are equally distributed across the control and experimental groups.

Do you think the study is safe? For example, what would happen if a participant became addicted to cocaine after participating in the study? To put your mind at ease, any psychology study is governed by a strict ethical code, which you will become familiar with at the end of this chapter. For example, the participants in Dr. Leyton's study had to be fully informed about the study and give their consent; they also had to be previous users of cocaine; and after the drug was consumed the participants were required to stay overnight so they could be continuously monitored by doctors and nurses. Nonetheless, the issues raised by this one study—the research questions, the ethical issues they raise, the practical considerations required, and the connections to "real life"—are both a microcosm and the tip of the iceberg in the types of experimental studies that a psychologist can perform.

Questions for Further Discussion

1. Can you think of any other factors that might affect the results of Dr. Leyton's study?

2. Do you think the potential benefits of helping or even curing cocaine addiction outweigh the potential costs involved in Dr. Leyton's study?

3. How might the results of this study be applied to help people with drug addictions?

The Importance of Randomization It's been mentioned that the best way to select the participants for any study is randomly, but once researchers have their participants they must be assigned to either the experimental group or the control group. **Random assignment** of each participant to one or the other condition is also the best way to assure control over those other interfering, or *extraneous*, variables. Random assignment means that each participant has an equal chance of being assigned to each condition. If researchers simply put all the children from one daycare centre or one pediatrician's recommendations into the experimental group and the same for the control group, they would run the risk of biasing their research. Some daycare centres may have more naturally aggressive children, for example, or some pediatricians may have a particular client base in which the children are very passive. So researchers want to take the entire participant group and assign each person randomly to one or the other of the groups in the study. Sometimes this is as simple as picking names out of a hat.

random assignment
process of assigning subjects or participants to the experimental or control groups randomly, so that each subject or participant has an equal chance of being in either group.

This elderly woman has Alzheimer's disease, which eventually causes a severe loss of memory. If she was given a drug to improve her memory, the researcher could not be certain that any improvement shown was caused by the drug or by the elderly woman's belief that the drug would work. The expectations of any person in an experimental study can affect the outcome of the study, a phenomenon known as the *placebo effect.*

1.12 *What are the placebo and the experimenter effects, and how do single-blind and double-blind studies control for those effects?*

EXPERIMENTAL HAZARDS: THE PLACEBO EFFECT AND THE EXPERIMENTER EFFECT There are a few other problems that might arise in any experiment, even with the use of control groups and random assignment. For example, say a new drug is supposed to improve memory in people who are in the early stages of *Alzheimer's disease* (a form of mental deterioration that occurs in some people as they grow old). ⓛⓘⓝⓚ *to Chapter Six: Memory, p. 218.* Researchers would want to test the drug to see if it really is effective in helping to improve memory, so they would get a sample of people who are in the early stages of the disease, divide them into two groups, give one group the drug, and then test for improvement. They would probably have to do a test of memory both before and after the administration of the drug to be able to measure improvement.

Let me see if I've got this straight. The group that gets the drug would be the experimental group, and the one that doesn't is the control group, right? Right, and getting or not getting the drug are the levels of the independent variable, whereas the measure of memory improvement is the dependent variable. But there's still a problem with doing the experiment this way. What if the researchers do find that the drug group had greater memory improvement than the group that received nothing? Can they really say that the drug itself caused the improvement? Or is it possible that the participants who received the drug *knew* that they were supposed to improve in memory and, therefore, made a major effort to do so? The improvement may have had more to do with participants' *belief* in the drug than the drug itself, a phenomenon known as the **placebo effect**: the expectations of the participants in a study can influence their behaviour. In medical research, the control group is often given a harmless substitute for the real drug, such as a sugar pill or an injection of salt water, and this substitute (which has no medical effect) is called the *placebo.* If there is a placebo effect, the control group will show changes in the dependent variable even though the participants in that group received only a placebo.

There is another way that someone's expectations about the outcome of the experiment can influence the results, even when the participants are animals rather

◉ **Watch** on **mypsychlab**

Konrad Lorenz: Controlling an Experiment

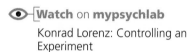

Let me see if I've got this straight. The group that gets the drug ▶ would be the experimental group, and the one that doesn't is the control group, right?

placebo effect
the phenomenon in which the expectations of the participants in a study can influence their behaviour.

than people. It's called the **experimenter effect**, and it has to do with the experimenter's expectations, not the participants' expectations. As discussed earlier in the section about naturalistic observations, sometimes observers are biased—they see what they expect to see. This can also happen in an experiment. If the researcher is doing the measuring of the dependent variable, it's possible that he or she could give the participants clues about how they are supposed to respond—with body language, tone of voice, or even eye contact. It wouldn't be deliberate, but it does happen. It could go something like this in the example: You, the Alzheimer's patient, are in the experimenter's office to take your second memory test after trying the drug. The experimenter seems to pay a lot of attention to you and to every answer that you give in the test, so you get the feeling that you are supposed to have improved a lot. So you try harder, and any improvement you do have may be caused only by your own increased effort, not by the drug. That's the experimenter effect: The behaviour of the experimenter caused the participant to change his or her response pattern.

Single-Blind and Double-Blind Studies Fortunately, there are ways to control for these effects. The classic way to control for the placebo effect is to give the control group an actual placebo—some kind of treatment that doesn't affect behaviour at all. In the drug experiment, the placebo would have to be some kind of sugar pill or saline (salt) solution that looks like and is administered just like the actual drug. The participants in both the experimental and the control groups would not know which group they are actually in and whether or not they got the real drug or the placebo. That way, if their expectations have any effect at all on the outcome of the experiment, the experimenter will be able to tell by looking at the results for the control group and comparing them to the experimental group. Even if the control group improves a little, the drug group should improve significantly more if the drug is working. This is called a **single-blind study**, because the participants are "blind" to the treatment they receive.

For a long time, this type of experiment was the only kind researchers did in psychology. But researchers Robert Rosenthal and Lenore Jacobson reported in their 1968 book, *Pygmalion in the Classroom*, that when teachers were told that some students had a high potential for success and others a low potential, the students showed significant gains or decreases in their performance on standardized tests depending on which "potential" they were supposed to have (Rosenthal & Jacobson, 1968). Actually, the students had been selected randomly and randomly assigned to one of the two groups, "high" or "low." Their performances on the tests were affected by the attitudes of the teachers concerning their potential. This study and similar studies after it highlighted the need to have the experimenter be "blind" as well as the participants in research. So in a **double-blind study**, neither the participants nor the person or persons measuring the dependent variable know who got what. That's why everything in a double-blind experiment gets coded in some way, so that only after all the measurements have been taken can anyone determine who was in the experimental group and who was in the control group.

Perhaps the most serious weakness of experiments is **external validity**. Lack of external validity refers to the fact that the participants or the control conditions necessary for an experiment may not realistically duplicate what is seen in the real world. For example, consider you are interested in studying the impact that layoffs have on workers who remain on the job. You devise an experiment in which you randomly assign groups of students to perform a proofreading task for course credit. Then you "let go," or lay off, some of the students (who actually are still working with you, so you never really lay them off) and record the reactions of the remaining students (Brockner et al., 1986). Can you be sure the reactions of the students are the same as the reactions of workers who remain on the job after losing a 20-year co-worker and

experimenter effect
tendency of the experimenter's expectations for a study to unintentionally influence the results of the study.

single-blind study
study in which the participants do not know if they are in the experimental or the control group.

double-blind study
study in which neither the participants nor the experimenter knows if the participants are in the experimental or control group.

external validity
the ability to generalize the results of an experiment to real-world situations.

personal friend to a layoff? Probably not! Lack of external validity can limit our ability to generalize the results of a study to the real world.

Other Experimental Designs In the field of developmental psychology, researchers are always looking for the ways in which a person's age influences his or her behaviour. The problem is that age is a variable that cannot be randomly controlled. In a regular experiment, for example, participants can be randomly assigned to the various conditions: drug or placebo, special instructions or no special instructions, and so on. But participants cannot be randomly assigned to different age groups. It would be like saying, "Okay, these people are now going to be 20, and these others will be 30."

To get around this problem, researchers use alternative designs (called *quasi-experimental designs*) that are not considered true experiments because of the inability to randomly assign participants to the experimental and control groups (Gribbons & Herman, 1997). These designs are discussed more fully in Chapter Eight. ⓛⓘⓝⓚ *to Chapter Eight: Development Across the Lifespan, p. 302.*

PRACTICE QUIZ: HOW MUCH DO YOU REMEMBER?

Pick the best answer.

1. It's pretty common knowledge that the more you study, the higher your grade will be. What kind of correlation is this relationship?
   a. positive
   b. negative
   c. zero
   d. causal

2. Which of the following would indicate the strongest relationship between two variables:
   a. +1.04
   b. −0.89
   c. +0.75
   d. +0.54

3. In an experiment to test the effects of alcohol on memory, the experimenter gives vodka mixed in orange juice to one group of participants and orange juice with no vodka to the other group. She then measures the memory skills of both groups by means of a memory test. In this study, the independent variable would be

   a. scores on the memory test.
   b. the presence or absence of vodka in the orange juice.
   c. intelligence.
   d. a placebo.

4. In that same experiment, the control group is the one that gets
   a. only one drink of orange juice with vodka.
   b. a fake test of memory.
   c. only something to eat.
   d. the orange juice without vodka.

5. In a _____ study, neither the experimenter nor the participants knows who is in the control group and who is in the experimental group.
   a. placebo
   b. single-blind
   c. double-blind
   d. triple-blind

Answers: 1-a, 2-b, 3-b, 4-d, 5-c.

ETHICS OF PSYCHOLOGICAL RESEARCH

> The study that Dr. Watson did with "Little Albert" and the white rat seems pretty cruel, when you think about it. Do researchers today do that kind of study?

The study that Dr. Watson did with "Little Albert" and the white rat seems pretty cruel, when you think about it. Do researchers today do that kind of study? Actually, as psychology began to grow and more research with people was being done, psychologists began to realize that some protections had to be put in place. No one wanted to be thought of as a "mad scientist," and if studies were permitted that could actually harm people, the field of psychology might die out pretty quickly. Scientists in other areas of research were also realizing that ethical treatment of the participants in studies had to be ensured in some way. Ethical treatment, of course, means that people who volunteer for a study will be able to expect that no physical or psychological harm should come to them.

1.13 *What are the ethical concerns when conducting research with people and animals?*

In Canada all universities and colleges (where most psychological research is carried out) are required to have *ethics committees* or *research ethic boards (REBs)*. REBs are

TABLE 1.1 RESEARCH METHODS USED IN PSYCHOLOGY

RESEARCH METHOD	DESCRIPTION	STRENGTHS	WEAKNESSES
Naturalistic and Laboratory Observation	Systematic observation of behaviour in natural or more controlled settings	Gives a realistic picture of how behaviour occurs, which can help generate theories and hypotheses.	Prone to the observer effect and observer biases. Cannot establish cause-and-effect relationships.
Case Study	The detailed study of one or a few individuals	Very detailed and often unique kinds of information can be gathered.	The results cannot be applied or generalized to other people. Sometimes the researcher may lose objectivity.
Surveys	Large numbers of persons are asked a series of questions about some topic.	A lot of data is generated quickly.	The results may not be accurate and therefore not generalizable unless the researchers ensure a representative sample. People taking the survey may not provide accurate responses because of poor memory, distortions of the truth, or courtesy bias.
Correlations	Two or more variables are measured to see whether they are related in some fashion.	A lot of data can be gathered quickly in both controlled and non-controlled settings. If a relationship exists, the strength of the relationship can be determined.	It is very difficult to establish cause-and-effect relationships.
The Experiment	The deliberate manipulation of a variable to see if a corresponding change in some other variable exists	Cause-and-effect relationships can be determined. Confounding variables can be greatly controlled.	It can sometimes lack external validity.

comprised of groups of psychologists or other professionals who look over each proposed research study and judge it according to its safety and consideration for the participants in the study. These REBs look at all aspects of the proposed research, from the written materials that explain the research to the potential participants to the equipment that may be used in the study itself.

THE GUIDELINES FOR DOING RESEARCH WITH PEOPLE

There are quite a few ethical concerns when dealing with human participants in an experiment or other type of study. The ethical code of conduct that all psychologists must follow is set and overseen in Canada by the Canadian Psychological Association (CPA) and the three main federal granting agencies: the Social Sciences and Humanities Research Council of Canada (SSHRC), the Canadian Institutes for Health Research (CIHR), and the Natural Sciences and Engineering

"He says he wants a lawyer."
© The New Yorker Collection 1999 Tom Chalkley from cartoonbank.com. All Rights Reserved.

Simulate on mypsychlab

Ethics of Psychological Research

Research Council (NSERC). Below is a list of the most common ethical guidelines that must be addressed in every psychological study:

1. *Rights and well-being of participants must be weighed against the study's value to science.* In other words, people must come first, research second.

2. *Participants must be allowed to make an informed decision about their voluntary participation in any study.* This means that researchers have to explain the study to the people they want to include before they do anything to them or with them—even children—and the explanation must be in terms that the participants can understand. If researchers are using infants, their parents have to be informed and give their consent. This is known as *informed consent.*

3. *Deception must be justified.* In some cases, it is necessary to deceive the participants. If that happens, the deception has to be because the study wouldn't work any other way, and the participants must be told after the study exactly why the deception was important. This is called *debriefing.* Debriefing participants helps them understand why they were deceived and the importance of their responses to that deception.

4. *Participants may withdraw from the study at any time.* The participants must be allowed to drop out for any reason. Sometimes people get bored with the study, decide they don't have the time, or don't like what they have to do, for example. Children are particularly likely to decide not to play. Researchers have to let them go, even if it means getting more participants.

5. *Participants must be protected from risks or told explicitly of risks.* For example, if researchers are using any kind of electrical equipment, care must be taken to ensure that no participant will experience a physical shock from faulty electrical equipment.

6. *Investigator must debrief participants, telling the true nature of the study and expectations of results.* This is important in all types of studies but particularly in those involving a deception.

7. *Data must remain confidential.* Freud recognized the importance of confidentiality, referring to his patients in his books and articles with false names. This is also why psychologists and other researchers today tend to report only group results rather than results for a single individual, so that no one could possibly be recognized (American Psychological Association, 1992).

In Canada, the issue of confidentiality with respect to the communications between client and therapist is likely very different from what you are accustomed to seeing on American television shows. Canadian laws do not protect the communications between client and therapist. Thus, Canadian courts can make psychologists testify to the content of their discussions with clients. In addition, laws in Canada require that psychologists report certain types of information, for example, murder or child abuse, revealed by their clients. To avoid these possible conflicts, Canadian psychologists often spend a good amount of time ensuring that the client or research participant fully understands these confidentiality limits.

Psychologists also study animals to find out about behaviour, often drawing comparisons between what the animals do and what people might do under similar conditions.

But why not just study the people in the first place? Some research questions are extremely important but difficult or impossible to answer by using human participants. Animals live shorter lives, so looking at long-term effects becomes much easier. Animals are also easier to control—the scientist can control diet, living arrangements, and even genetic relatedness. The white laboratory rat has become a

But why **not just study the people** in the first place?

recognized species different from ordinary rats, bred with its own kind for many decades until each white rat is essentially a little genetic "twin" of all the others. Animals also engage in much simpler behaviour than humans do, making it easier to see the effects of manipulations. But the biggest reason that researchers use animals in some research is that animals can be used in ways that researchers could never use people. For example, it took a long time for scientists to prove that nicotine causes cancer because they had to do correlational studies with people and experiments only with animals. There's the catch—researchers can do many things to animals that they can't do to people. That might seem cruel at first, but when you think that without animal research there would be no vaccines for deadly diseases, no insulin treatments for diabetics, no transplants, then the value of the research and its benefits to humankind far outweigh the hazards to which the research animals are exposed.

There are also ethical considerations when dealing with animals in research, just as there are with humans. In Canada, these ethical standards are set by the Canadian Council on Animal Care (CCAC). The core principle held by the CCAC focuses on how to avoid exposing all research or teaching animals to any *unnecessary* pain or suffering. So if surgery is part of the study, it is done under anaesthesia. If the research animal must die in order for the effects of some drug or other treatment to be examined in an autopsy, the death must be accomplished humanely. Avoiding unnecessary pain and suffering extends to animals not only during the actual research study but also during the entire time the animal is in the care of the researcher. For example, social animals such as rats and primates must be housed in a social or communal environment to ensure they receive proper social stimulation, which promotes more normal development. (L)(I)(N)(K) *to Chapter Eight: Development Across the Lifespan, p. 302.*

If Canadian researchers fail to meet any of the guidelines set forth by the CCAC, they may be subject to criminal prosecution under the *Cruelty to Animals Act*, or at the very least have their research privileges taken away. Animals are used in only about 7 percent of all psychological studies (Committee on Animal Research and Ethics, 2004).

These rabbits are part of a drug-testing study. Their bodies are enclosed in the metal cases to prevent movement during the test. What steps might the researchers using these animals take to treat the animals ethically?

CRITICAL THINKING

What good is all this focus on science and research going to do for me? I live in the real world, not a laboratory. The real world is full of opportunities for scientific thinking. Think about all of those commercials on television for miracle weight loss, hair restoration, or herbal remedies for arthritis, depression, and a whole host of physical and mental problems. Wouldn't it be nice to know how many of these claims people should believe? Wouldn't you like to know how to evaluate claims like these and possibly save yourself some time, effort, and money? That's exactly the kind of "real-world" problem that critical thinking can help sort out.

1.14 *What are the basic principles of critical thinking, and how can using critical thinking help people in their everyday lives?*

THE CRITERIA FOR CRITICAL THINKING

According to Beyer (1995), **critical thinking** means making reasoned judgments. The word *reasoned* means that the judgment should be logical and well thought out. There are four basic criteria for critical thinking that people should try to remember when faced with statements about the world around them (Gill, 1991; Shore, 1990):

1. *There are very few "truths" that do not need to be subjected to testing.* Although people may accept religious beliefs and personal values on "faith," everything else in

What good is all this focus on science and research going to do for me? I live in the real world, not a laboratory.

⊙─[**Watch** on **mypsychlab**
Debate Over Abstinence Only Education

critical thinking
making reasoned judgments about claims.

Linus Pauling is a two-time winner of the Nobel Prize. He proposed the use of vitamin C supplements to prevent the common cold, but scientific evidence has repeatedly failed to find support for his belief.

I guess I understand the importance of critical thinking—there seems to be a lot of people out there who will ▶ fall for anything.

pseudo-psychologies
systems of explaining human behaviour that are not based on or consistent with scientific evidence.

life needs to have supporting evidence. Questions that can be investigated empirically should be examined using established scientific methods. One shouldn't accept anything at face value but should always ask, "How do you know that? What is the evidence?"

2. *All evidence is not equal in quality.* This is one of the most important steps in critical thinking and one that is often overlooked. People need to look at how evidence is gathered before deciding that it provides good support for an idea. For example, there are poorly done experiments, incorrect assumptions based on correlations rather than experiments, and studies in which there was either no control group or no attempt made to control for placebo effects or experimenter effects.

3. *Just because someone is considered to be an authority or to have a lot of expertise does not make everything that person claims automatically true.* One should always ask to see the evidence rather than just take an expert's word for anything. How good is the evidence? Are there other alternative explanations? For example, Linus Pauling, a famous and respected scientist, made claims about the benefits of vitamin C for curing the common cold. Although research is beginning to support the idea that vitamin C may help fight cancer, the research has also found that large doses of this vitamin don't do anything for curing the common cold (Padayatty & Levine, 2001).

4. *Critical thinking requires an open mind.* Although it is good to be skeptical, people don't need to be so skeptical that they actually close their minds to things that are possible. At the same time, it's good to have an open mind, but not so open as to be gullible or apt to "swallow anything." Critical thinking requires a delicate balance between skepticism and willingness to consider possibilities. For example, scientists have yet to see any convincing evidence that there was once life on Mars. That doesn't mean that scientists totally dismiss the idea of life on Mars, just that there is no convincing evidence *yet*.

PSEUDO-PSYCHOLOGIES: WHY DO PEOPLE FALL FOR FAKERY?

I guess I understand the importance of critical thinking—there seems to be a lot of people out there who will fall for anything. Actually, the kind of people who fall for the dumbest-sounding scams is rather surprising. Many very intelligent people fall prey to the same kinds of faulty reasoning that less "sophisticated" persons do. Con artists and scammers know the flaws in human nature pretty well, and that's how they survive.

Some of the easiest things to fall for are the **pseudo-psychologies**, systems of explaining human behaviour that are not based on scientific evidence and that have no real value other than being entertaining (Bunge, 1984). Because people like to try to understand themselves, they often participate in these activities.

People, including some reputable scientists of the Victorian era, used to believe that bumps on the skull were indicators of various personality traits, resulting in the "science" of *phrenology*. Franz Gall, a German anatomy teacher, popularized phrenology in the 1800s. His research was flawed and often quite biased. He also thought that skull size was related to intelligence, and he set out to demonstrate that people of different races had smaller skulls than Caucasians and were therefore less intelligent. He deliberately chose skulls of a size to "prove" his assumption.

Another false system is *palmistry*, or the reading of palms. There is overwhelming evidence that the lines of the palm have absolutely no relationship to personality and cannot predict the future (Ben-Shakhar et al., 1986; Dean et al., 1992), yet many people still believe that palm readers are for real. What about handwriting?

Surely one's personality would be revealed in handwriting. The pseudo-psychology called *graphology*, or the analysis of personality through handwriting, even has respectable companies using handwriting analysis to select prospective employees, yet graphologists score close to zero on tests of accuracy in personality measurement (Ben-Shakhar et al., 1986).

PRACTICE QUIZ: HOW MUCH DO YOU REMEMBER?

Pick the best answer.

1. Which of the following is NOT one of the common ethical rules?
   a. Participants have to give informed consent.
   b. Deception cannot be used in any studies with human beings.
   c. The rights and well-being of the participants must come first.
   d. Data must remain confidential.

2. We use animals in research because
   a. animals have simple behaviour that makes it easy to see changes.
   b. animals don't live as long as humans and are easier to control.
   c. we can do things to animals that we can't do to people.
   d. all of the above are true.

3. A famous newscaster advertises a new magnetic mattress for controlling pain. If Nathaniel decides to order the mattress because he believes that such a well-known personality should know whether or not it works, he has made an error in which of the following?
   a. Few "truths" do not need to be tested.
   b. All evidence is not equal in quality.
   c. Authority or expertise does not make the claims of the authority or expert true.
   d. Critical thinking requires an open mind.

4. Critical thinking means making judgments based on
   a. emotional issues.   c. reason and logical evaluation.
   b. keeping a closed mind.   d. authority and expertise.

5. Which pseudo-psychology claims to understand personality through a study of the bumps on one's skull?
   a. phrenology   c. graphology
   b. palmistry   d. astrology

APPLYING PSYCHOLOGY TO EVERYDAY LIFE: USING CRITICAL THINKING—DOES ASTROLOGY WORK?

1.15 *How might critical thinking be applied to a real-world example?*

Astrology is a pseudo-psychology that attempts to predict the future and explain personality by using the positions of the stars and planets at the moment of birth. Many people see astrology as a form of entertainment, but others take it quite seriously, planning their daily activities and making important life choices based on their horoscopes. But is there any validity to believing that the positions of the objects in the rest of the universe have any effect at all on one's personality or daily successes or failures? Here's an example of critical thinking applied to astrology:

This is a map of sixteenth-century astrologer Tycho Brahe's Earth-centred universe. He rejected Copernicus's notion that the planets, including Earth, revolved around the sun, preferring his own theory that Earth was the centre of the universe.

1. *Are astrologer's charts up to date?* The basic astrological charts were designed more than 3000 years ago. The stars, planets, and constellations are no longer in the same positions in the sky because of changes in the rotation of Earth's axis over long periods of time—more than 24 degrees in just the past 2000 years (Dean & Kelly, 2000; Kelly, 1980). So a Gemini is really a Cancer and will be a Leo in another 2000 years.

2. *What exactly is so important about the moment of birth?* Why not the moment of conception? What happens if a baby is born by Caesarean section and not at the time it would have been born naturally? Is that person's whole life messed up?

3. *Why would the stars and planets have any effect on a person? Is it gravity?* The body mass of the doctor who delivers the baby has a far greater gravitational pull on the infant's body than the moon. (Maybe people should use skinny obstetricians?)

→◉─Simulate on mypsychlab

The Pseudoscience of Astrology

Research shows no connection between astrological signs and personality, careers, skills, marriage rates, divorce rates, or even physical characteristics (Dean & Kelly, 2000; Kelly, 1980). Studies of thousands of predictions by astrologers showed that only a very small percentage of those predictions actually came true (Dean & Kelly, 2000), and the ones that did come true were very vague or easily guessed from current events. ("I predict that a famous star will have plastic surgery this year.")

Questions for Further Discussion

1. Why might reasonably educated people believe in astrology?
2. Is there any harm in using astrology to make decisions in one's life?

CHAPTER SUMMARY

What Is Psychology?

1.1 *What is the definition and what are four primary goals of psychology?*

- Psychology is the scientific study of behaviour and mental processes.
- The four goals of psychology are description, explanation, prediction, and control.

Psychology Then: The History of Psychology

1.2 *What were the basic ideas of structuralism and functionalism, and who were the important people in those early fields?*

- In 1879 psychology began as a science of its own in Germany, with the establishment of Wundt's psychology laboratory. He developed the technique of objective introspection.
- Titchener, a student of Wundt, brought psychology in the form of structuralism to North America. Structuralism died out in the early twentieth century.
- James proposed a counter point of view called *functionalism*, which stresses the way the mind allows us to adapt.
- Functionalism influenced the modern fields of educational psychology, evolutionary psychology, and industrial/organizational psychology.

1.3 *What were the basic ideas and who were the important people behind the early approaches known as Gestalt, psychoanalysis, and behaviourism?*

- Wertheimer and others studied sensation and perception, calling the new perspective Gestalt ("good form") psychology.
- Freud proposed, in his theory of psychoanalysis, that the unconscious mind controls much of our conscious behaviour.
- Watson proposed a science of behaviour called *behaviourism*, which focused only on the study of observable stimuli and responses.
- Watson and Rayner demonstrated that a phobia could be learned, by conditioning a baby to be afraid of a white rat.

Psychology Now: Modern Perspectives

1.4 *What are the basic concepts of the modern perspectives known as psychodynamics, behaviourism, humanism, biopsychology, cognitive psychology, the sociocultural perspective, and the evolutionary perspective?*

- Modern Freudians such as Anna Freud, Jung, and Adler changed the emphasis in Freud's original theory into a kind of neo-Freudianism.

1.5 *What were the contributions of Skinner, Maslow, Rogers, and Hebb?*

- Skinner's operant conditioning of voluntary behaviour became a major force in the twentieth century. He introduced the concept of reinforcement to behaviourism.
- Humanism, which focuses on free will and the human potential for growth, was developed by Maslow and Rogers, among others, as a reaction to the deterministic nature of behaviourism and psychoanalysis. The humanistic perspective emphasized the potential of all humans to become the best people they could possibly be.
- Biopsychology emerged as the study of the biological basis of behaviour.

Psychology in the News: Was Prominent Canadian Psychologist Donald Hebb a CIA Operative?

- Hebb was a Canadian psychologist who championed the biopsychological perspective. Hebb was the first psychologist to link physical experience with changes in brain structure and function. Essentially, his theory suggests brain cells that fire together wire together. His theory opened the door to a vast array of research that inspired many future psychologists.
- Cognitive psychology is the study of learning, memory, language, and problem solving.
- The sociocultural perspective focuses on the relationship between social behaviour and culture.
- The principles of evolution and the knowledge we currently have about evolution are used in the evolutionary perspective to look at the way the mind works and why it works as it does. Behaviour is seen as having an adaptive or survival value.

Types of Psychological Professionals

1.6 *What's the difference between a psychiatrist and a psychologist, and what other types of professionals work in the various areas of psychology?*

- Psychiatrists are medical doctors who provide diagnosis and therapy for persons with mental disorders, whereas psychoanalysts are psychiatrists or psychologists with special training in the theory of psychoanalysis.
- Psychiatric social workers are social workers with special training in the influences of the environment on mental illness.

- Psychologists have academic degrees; can counsel, teach, and research; and may specialize in any one of a large number of areas within psychology.
- There are many different areas of specialization in psychology, including clinical, counselling, developmental, social, and personality as areas of work or study.

Psychology: The Science

1.7   *Why is psychology a science, and what are the steps in using the scientific method?*

- Psychologists use the scientific method to determine facts and control the possibilities of error and bias when observing behaviour. The five steps of the scientific method are perceiving the question, forming a hypothesis, testing the hypothesis, drawing conclusions, and reporting the results.

1.8   *How do psychologists use naturalistic and laboratory settings to describe behaviour, and what are the advantages and disadvantages associated with these settings?*

- Naturalistic observations involve watching animals or people in their natural environments but have the disadvantage of lack of control.
- Laboratory observations involve watching animals or people in an artificial but controlled situation, such as a laboratory.

1.9   *How do psychologists use case studies and surveys to describe behaviour, and what are some drawbacks to each of these methods?*

- Case studies are detailed investigations of one subject or participant, whereas surveys involve asking standardized questions of large groups of people who represent a sample of the population of interest.
- Information gained from case studies cannot be applied to other cases. People responding to surveys may not always tell the truth or remember information correctly.

1.10   *What is the correlational technique, and what does it tell researchers about relationships?*

- Correlation is a statistical technique that allows researchers to discover and predict relationships between variables of interest.
- A positive correlation means an increase in one variable is matched by an increase in the other variable, whereas a negative correlation means an increase in one variable is matched by a decrease in the other variable.
- Correlations cannot be used to prove cause-and-effect relationships.

Psychology in the News: Free Cocaine Offered for Psychological Study at McGill

1.11   *How do researchers use operational definitions, independent and dependent variables, experimental and control groups, and random assignment in designing an experiment?*

- Experiments are tightly controlled manipulations of variables that allow researchers to determine cause-and-effect relationships.
- The independent variable in an experiment is the variable that is deliberately manipulated by the experimenter to see if related changes occur in the behaviour or responses of the participants; it is given to the experimental group.
- The dependent variable in an experiment is the measured behaviour or responses of the participants.
- The control group receives nothing or a placebo treatment.
- Random assignment of participants to groups within an experiment helps control for individual differences both within and between the groups that might otherwise interfere with the experiment's outcome. In Dr. Leyton's cocaine experiment at McGill, participants were randomly assigned to either the experimental or control groups, the independent variable was the dose of cocaine, and the dependent variable was changes in brain activity as observed with the brain scanner.

1.12   *What are the placebo and the experimenter effects, and how do single-blind and double-blind studies control for those effects?*

- The placebo effect occurs in an experiment when the expectations of the control group influences their behaviour. The experimenter effect occurs when the expectations of the experimenter unintentionally influence the results of an experiment.
- Fortunately, these expectation effects can be controlled for. Single-blind studies are experiments in which the participants do not know whether they are in the experimental or control group, so expectations in both groups are similar. Double-blind studies are experiments in which neither the experimenters nor the participants know which is the control or experimental group until after the study is complete, making it impossible for the experimenter to unintentionally influence the results.

Ethics of Psychological Research

1.13   *What are the ethical concerns when conducting research with people and animals?*

- In Canada all universities and colleges are required to have ethics committees or *research ethic boards (REBs)*. REBs are comprised of groups of psychologists or other professionals who look over each proposed research study and judge it according to its safety and consideration for the participants in the study.
- When human beings are to be used in a research study, the REBs review the study to ensure that the study complies with the following ethical guidelines: the protection of rights and well-being of participants, informed consent, justification when deception is used, the right of participants to withdraw at any time, protection of participants from physical or psychological harm, confidentiality, and debriefing of participants at the end of the study.
- Animals in psychological research make useful models because they are easier to control than humans, they have simpler behaviour, and they can be used in ways that are not permissible with humans. When animals are used in a study, REBs ensure that all animals will not be exposed to any unnecessary pain or suffering.

Critical Thinking

1.14   *What are the basic principles of critical thinking, and how can using critical thinking help people in their everyday lives?*

- Critical thinking is the ability to make reasoned judgments. The four basic criteria of critical thinking are that there are few concepts that do not need to be tested, evidence can vary in quality, experts and authorities do not automatically make something true, and keeping an open mind is important.
- Faulty reasoning and a failure to use critical thinking can lead to belief in false systems such as palmistry and graphology.

Applying Psychology to Everyday Life: Using Critical Thinking—Does Astrology Work?

1.15   *How might critical thinking be applied to a real-world example?*

- When critical thinking principles are applied to the pseudo-psychology of astrology, the conclusion is that astrology does not work. Empirical research findings support this conclusion.

1 KEY TERMS

behaviourism 10
biopsychological perspective 12
case study 20
cognitive perspective 13
control group 26
correlation 23
critical thinking 33
dependent variable 25
double-blind study 29
evolutionary perspective 14
experiment 24
experimental group 26
experimenter effect 29
external validity 29

functionalism 8
Gestalt psychology 9
hypothesis 17
independent variable 25
objective introspection 7
observer bias 20
observer effect 20
operational definition 25
participant observation 20
placebo effect 28
population 21
pseudo-psychologies 34
psychiatric social worker 16
psychiatrist 15

psychoanalysis 9
psychoanalyst 15
psychodynamic perspective 11
psychologist 16
psychology 4
random assignment 27
replicate 19
representative sample 21
scientific method 17
single-blind study 29
sociocultural perspective 14
structuralism 7

TEST YOURSELF

Study Help Note: These longer quizzes appear at the end of every chapter and cover all the major learning objectives that you should know after reading the chapter. These quizzes also provide practice for exams. The answers can be found printed upside down at the end of the test.

Pick the best answer.

1. In the definition of psychology, mental processes means
   a. internal, covert processes.
   b. outward behaviour.
   c. overt actions and reactions.
   d. only animal behaviour.
2. A psychologist is interested in finding out why identical twins have different personalities. This psychologist is most interested in the goal of
   a. description.   c. prediction.
   b. explanation.   d. control.
3. Psychologists who give potential employees tests that determine what kind of job those employees might best fit are interested in the goal of
   a. description.   c. prediction.
   b. explanation.   d. control.
4. Which early theorist developed his perspective on psychology by basing it on Darwin's "survival of the fittest" doctrine?
   a. Wilhelm Wundt   c. John Watson
   b. William James   d. Sigmund Freud
5. Who is most associated with the technique of introspection?
   a. Wilhelm Wundt   c. John Watson
   b. William James   d. Max Wertheimer
6. *Operant conditioning* and *reinforcement* are terms most associated with which perspective?
   a. psychodynamic   c. humanistic
   b. behavioural   d. cognitive
7. Who championed the biopsychological perspective by claiming that brain cells that fire together wire together?
   a. Charles Darwin   c. Sigmund Freud
   b. Carl Rogers   d. Donald Hebb

8. Jenna suffers from a nervous tic of washing her hands repeatedly and being unable to resist washing them again and again. Which perspective would explain Jenna's handwashing behaviour as a result of repressed conflicts?
   a. psychodynamics   c. behaviourism
   b. cognitive psychology d. biopsychology
9. Which perspective looks at perception, learning, and memory?
   a. psychoanalysis   c. cognitive psychology
   b. behaviourism   d. evolutionary perspective
10. Which perspective assumes that human behaviour may have developed in certain directions because it served a useful function in preserving the species?
   a. psychoanalysis   c. cognitive psychology
   b. behaviourism   d. evolutionary perspective
11. A person who has suffered a major stroke and is now experiencing severe personality problems because of the damage would best be advised to see a
   a. psychiatrist.   c. psychiatric social worker.
   b. psychoanalyst.   d. psychologist.
12. In the scientific method, forming an educated guess is called
   a. reporting your results.   c. drawing conclusions.
   b. perceiving a question.   d. forming a hypothesis.
13. The main advantage of the laboratory observation method is
   a. the degree of control it allows the observer.
   b. the degree of participation it allows the observer.
   c. the observer effect.
   d. the opportunity for representative sampling.

14. Harlan wanted to write realistically about street gangs, so he pretended to be a teenager and joined a real gang. This is most similar to the method of
    a. laboratory observation.
    c. the case study.
    b. the observer effect.
    d. participant observation.

15. The main advantage of a case study is
    a. the ease of generalizing the results to others.
    b. being able to determine cause and effect.
    c. the amount of detail it provides about an individual.
    d. the large number of people that can be studied at one time.

16. The entire group that a researcher is interested in is called a
    a. sample
    c. subject pool
    b. population
    d. survey

17. Professor Jones surveyed her six classes and found that students who slept less than five hours the night before the exam received lower exam scores than those students who slept seven hours or more. What kind of correlation is this relationship between hours of sleep and scores?
    a. positive
    c. zero
    b. negative
    d. causal

18. Drinking orange juice is negatively correlated with lowered risk of cancer. Based on this information, which of the following statements is true?
    a. The more orange juice you drink, the higher your risk of cancer.
    b. The more orange juice you drink, the lower your risk of cancer.
    c. The less orange juice you drink, the lower your risk of cancer.
    d. Drinking orange juice causes people to be cancer-free.

19. A researcher designs an experiment to test the effects of playing video games on memory. What would be the dependent variable?
    a. scores on a memory test
    b. playing video games
    c. number of hours spent playing video games
    d. the type of video game played

20. In that same experiment, the experimental group would
    a. not play the video games.
    b. take the memory test while the control group would not.
    c. not take the memory test while the control group would.
    d. play the video games.

21. In Dr. Leyton's experiments on the effects of cocaine on the brain, what is the independent variable?
    a. the informed consent each participant gave
    b. the three-dimensional images of the brain
    c. the amount of cash each participant received
    d. the different doses of cocaine

22. In a _____ study, only the experimenter knows who is in the control group and who is in the experimental group.
    a. placebo
    c. double-blind
    b. single-blind
    d. triple-blind

23. Dr. Silverberg is conducting a study in which she tests infants for memory ability. Before she can begin her study, she must obtain
    a. permission from the infants.
    b. permission from the parents.
    c. informed consent from the parents.
    d. confidential information from the parents.

24. Several years ago two scientists announced that they had achieved "cold fusion" in the laboratory, but further studies failed to replicate their findings and later it was found that the original scientists had used sloppy methods. This highlights which of the following critical thinking principles?
    a. Few "truths" do not need to be tested.
    b. All evidence is not equal in quality.
    c. Authority or expertise does not make the claims of the authority or expert true.
    d. Critical thinking requires an open mind.

25. The core principle of the Canadian Council on Animal Care is
    a. all data on the animals must remain confidential.
    b. all animals must be treated humanely.
    c. no animal shall be exposed to unnecessary pain or suffering.
    d. the rights of the animals must be weighed against the study's value to science.

ScanLife™ Barcode

To access more tests and your own personalized study plan that will help you focus on the areas you need to master before your next class test, be sure to go to **www.MyPsychLab.com**, Pearson Education Canada's online psychology website, available with the access code packaged with your book.

1.1

Psychology
(is the scientific study of behaviour and mental processes)

- has methods for studying phenomena
- has four primary goals
  - describe
  - explain
  - predict
  - control

1.2–3   p. 6

Psychology Then: The History of Psychology
(has roots in several disciplines, including philosophy, medicine, and physiology, and has developed through several perspectives)

- A relatively new science that formally began in 1879 when Wilhelm Wundt ("father of psychology") established the first psychological laboratory in Leipzig, Germany

  was a student of Wundt's

- **Structuralism**
  founded by Edward Titchener

- **Functionalism**
  founded by William James

- **Gestalt psychology**
  founded by Max Wertheimer

- **Psychoanalysis**
  ideas put forth
  by Sigmund Freud

- **Behaviourism**
  associated with work
  of John B. Watson,
  who was greatly influenced by
  Ivan Pavlov's work
  in conditioning/learning

1.4   p. 11

- **Psychodynamic**
  based on Freud's theory

- **Behavioural**
  based on early work
  of Watson
  and later B.F. Skinner

- **Humanistic**
  two pioneers are
  Carl Rogers
  and Abraham Maslow

- **Cognitive**
  has roots in
  Gestalt psychology

Psychology Now:
Modern Perspectives
(No one single perspective is used to explain all human behaviour and processes)

- **Sociocultural**

- **Biopsychological**

- **Evolutionary**

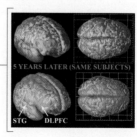

1.5   p. 15

Types of Psychological Professionals
(people working in the field of psychology have a variety of training experiences and different focuses)

- **psychiatrist**
- **psychoanalyst**
- **psychiatric social worker**
- **psychologist**

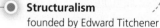

Psychology—The Science

(psychology uses the scientific method to try to determine facts and reduce uncertainty)

- **scientific method**
  - perceiving the question
  - forming a hypothesis
  - testing the hypothesis
  - drawing conclusions
  - reporting your results
- **descriptive data collection methods**
  - naturalistic observation
  - laboratory observation
  - case studies
  - surveys

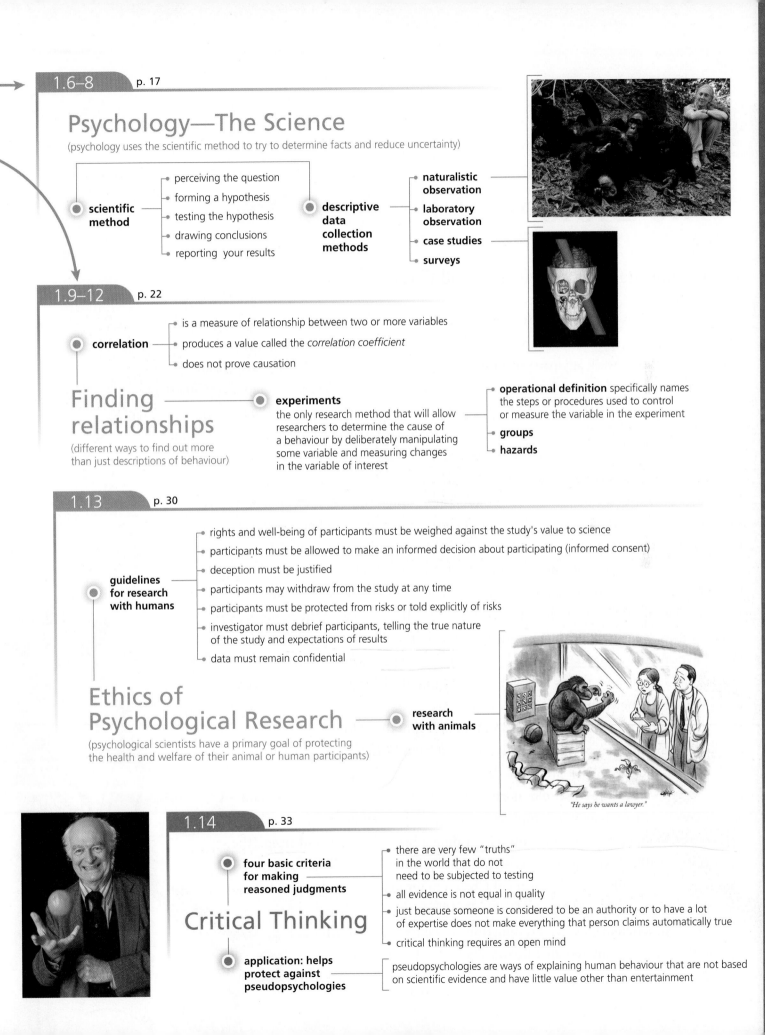

- **correlation**
  - is a measure of relationship between two or more variables
  - produces a value called the *correlation coefficient*
  - does not prove causation

Finding relationships

(different ways to find out more than just descriptions of behaviour)

- **experiments**
  the only research method that will allow researchers to determine the cause of a behaviour by deliberately manipulating some variable and measuring changes in the variable of interest
  - **operational definition** specifically names the steps or procedures used to control or measure the variable in the experiment
  - **groups**
  - **hazards**

- **guidelines for research with humans**
  - rights and well-being of participants must be weighed against the study's value to science
  - participants must be allowed to make an informed decision about participating (informed consent)
  - deception must be justified
  - participants may withdraw from the study at any time
  - participants must be protected from risks or told explicitly of risks
  - investigator must debrief participants, telling the true nature of the study and expectations of results
  - data must remain confidential

Ethics of Psychological Research

(psychological scientists have a primary goal of protecting the health and welfare of their animal or human participants)

- **research with animals**

"He says he wants a lawyer."

- **four basic criteria for making reasoned judgments**
  - there are very few "truths" in the world that do not need to be subjected to testing
  - all evidence is not equal in quality
  - just because someone is considered to be an authority or to have a lot of expertise does not make everything that person claims automatically true
  - critical thinking requires an open mind

Critical Thinking

- **application: helps protect against pseudopsychologies**
  - pseudopsychologies are ways of explaining human behaviour that are not based on scientific evidence and have little value other than entertainment

2

The Biological Perspective

Fascinating Brain Cases: Michelle and Chase

Michelle M. is a 29-year-old woman who holds a part-time job and loves to read, watch movies, and spend time with her family. She has the amazing ability to tell you exactly on which day of the week any particular calendar date fell, and she's a whiz at playing solitaire. If you were to look at her, you would see that in addition to wearing glasses (like so many other people), Michelle's right wrist is a bit bent and slightly twisted. She can use this hand just fine, although she is actually left-handed. She wears a brace to support her right leg. You might think that Michelle is very lucky to be so normal, since the weakness on her right side might indicate that she had suffered a moderate stroke at some time in her past, but you'd be wrong. Michelle is more than lucky—she's astonishing. The weakness in her right side comes from the fact that Michelle was born with only half a brain—the right half—and nothing but a fluid-filled cavity in the left side of her skull. Michelle's case has fascinated doctors who study the brain. Her condition has existed since the womb, when some unknown accident caused the left side of her brain to fail to develop, while the right side grew normally. The left side of the brain, as you will see later in this chapter, normally controls skills such as speech, reading, analytical thinking, and understanding abstract concepts. Michelle, with no left brain, can do all of those things well with the exception of abstraction—she's a pretty detail-oriented, concrete person (Doidge, 2007).

Here's another fascinating story. His mom calls him the "Little Gremlin" since he likes to play tricks on people. Chase is 3 years old and loves to sing, make people smile, and attend specialized preschool three days a week. Chase was born prematurely. When Chase was 1 year old, doctors took an MRI picture of Chase's brain and discovered that Chase was completely missing his cerebellum and pons. These parts of the brain control motor skills (e.g., riding a bike), balance, and sleep. The doctors were baffled! No one had ever seen anything like it before! What is even more amazing is that the ultrasound pictures of Chase's brain *in utero* clearly show a cerebellum. Where did it go? No one knows. But Chase can ride a bike!

How can Michelle and Chase function so well with such different brains? That's just one mystery that we will explore in the pages to come.

Why study the nervous system and the glands?

How could we possibly understand any of our behaviour, thoughts, or actions without knowing something about the incredible organs that allow us to act, think, and react? If we can understand how the brain, the nerves, and the glands interact to control feelings, thoughts, and behaviour, we can begin to truly understand the complex organism called a human being.

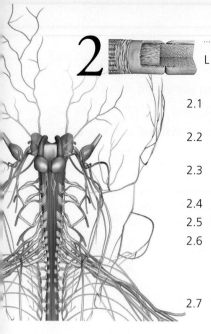

2.1 How do all the parts of the nervous system relate to one another?

2.2 What are neurons and nerves, and how do they work?

2.3 How do neurons communicate with each other and with the body?

2.4 What are the different neurotransmitters?

2.5 How do the brain and spinal cord interact?

2.6 How do the somatic and autonomic nervous systems allow people to interact with their surroundings and control the body's automatic functions?

2.7 How does the autonomic nervous system control the body's automatic functions and its reaction to stress?

2.8 How do psychologists study the brain and how it works?

2.9 What are the different structures of the bottom part of the brain, and what do they do?

2.10 Which structures of the brain control emotion, learning, memory, and motivation?

2.11 Which parts of the cortex control the different senses and the movement of the body?

2.12 Which parts of the cortex are responsible for higher forms of thought, such as language?

2.13 How does the left side of the brain differ from the right side?

2.14 How do the hormones released by glands interact with the nervous system and affect behaviour?

AN OVERVIEW OF THE NERVOUS SYSTEM

2.1 *How do all the parts of the nervous system relate to one another?*

This chapter will discuss a very complex system of cells, organs, and chemicals that work together to produce behaviour, thoughts, and actions. The first part of this complex arrangement is the **nervous system**, a network of cells that carries information to and from all parts of the body. Before beginning the discussion on the cells that make up the nervous system, take a look at Figure 2.1. This figure shows the organization of the various parts of the nervous system and will help you understand how all the different parts work together in controlling the way people and animals think, act, and feel.

nervous system
an extensive network of specialized cells that carries information to and from all parts of the body.

FIGURE 2.1 **An Overview of the Nervous System**

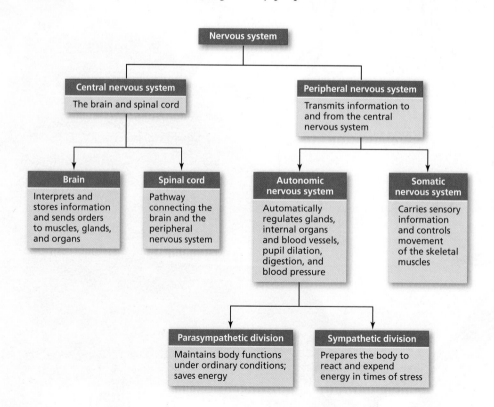

NEURONS AND NERVES: BUILDING THE NETWORK

The field of **neuroscience** is a branch of the life sciences that deals with the structure and functioning of the brain and the neurons, nerves, and nervous tissue that form the nervous system, especially focusing on their relationship to behaviour and learning. It was Santiago Ramón y Cajal, a doctor studying slides of brain tissue, who first theorized that the nervous system was made up of individual cells (Ramón y Cajal, 1995).

2.2   *What are neurons and nerves, and how do they work?*

STRUCTURE OF THE NEURON—THE NERVOUS SYSTEM'S BUILDING BLOCK

Although the entire body is composed of cells, each type of cell has a special purpose and function and, therefore, a special structure. Skin cells are flat, but muscle cells are long and stretchy. Most cells do have three things in common: a nucleus, a cell body, and a cell membrane holding it all together. The **neuron** is the specialized cell in the nervous system that receives and sends messages within that system. Neurons are one of the messengers of the body, and that means that they have a very special structure.

The parts of the neuron that receive messages from other cells are called the **dendrites**. The name *dendrite* means "branch," and this structure does indeed look like the branches of a tree. The dendrites are attached to the cell body, or **soma**, which is the part of the cell that contains the nucleus and keeps the entire cell alive and functioning. The **axon** is a fibre attached to the soma, and its job is to carry messages out to other cells (see Figure 2.2).

neuroscience
a branch of the life sciences that deals with the structure and function of neurons, nerves, and nervous tissue, especially focusing on their relationship to behaviour and learning.

neuron
the basic cell that makes up the nervous system and that receives and sends messages within that system.

dendrites
branchlike structures that receive messages from other neurons.

soma
the cell body of the neuron responsible for maintaining the life of the cell.

axon
tubelike structure that carries the neural message to other cells.

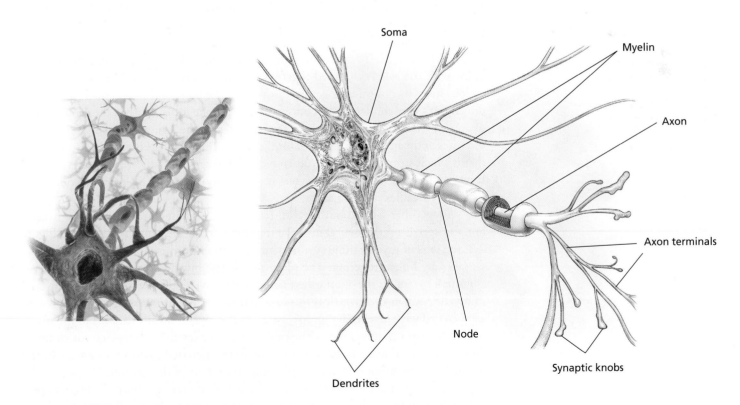

FIGURE 2.2 **The Structure of the Neuron**
The electron micrograph on the left shows neurons with axons and dendrites extending from them.

glial cells
grey fatty cells that provide support for the neurons to grow on and around, deliver nutrients to neurons, produce myelin to coat axons, and clean up waste products and dead neurons.

myelin
fatty substances produced by certain glial cells that coat the axons of neurons to insulate, protect, and speed up the neural impulse.

nerves
bundles of axons coated in myelin that travel together through the body.

Most people think that the brain is made up entirely of neurons. They may also have heard the old saying that people use only 10 percent of their brains. Neither statement is true, however. People use every cell in the brain for *something*. The fact is that neurons make up only 10 percent of the cells in the brain. The other 90 percent of the brain is composed of **glial cells** that serve as a sort of structure on which the neurons develop and work and which hold the neurons in place. *Glial* (Greek for "glue") cells are often considered the glue that holds the brain together. There are several different types of glial cells that perform various functions, such as getting nutrients to the neurons, cleaning up the remains of neurons that have died, communicating with neurons and other glial cells, and providing insulation for neurons. New research has discovered that some glial cells affect both the functioning and structure of neurons and may also "give birth" to new neurons during prenatal development (Breedlove et al., 2007; Bullock et al., 2005).

Why are the glial cells needed for structural support? Well, the neuron's message that travels through the cell is electrical. That means that if one neuron touches another one in the wrong area, they'll short each other out. The glial cells support the neurons to prevent them from touching one another, and some act like the plastic casing on a wire, insulating the electrical messages.

Neurons aren't found only in the brain. If they are spread throughout the human body, how are they kept separated? The answer is simple. Two special types of glial cells, called *oligodendrocytes* and *Schwann cells*, generate a layer of fatty substances called **myelin**. Oligodendrocytes produce myelin in the brain and spinal cord, while Schwann cells produce myelin in the neurons of the body. Myelin wraps around the shaft of the axons, forming a protective and insulating sheath, again, like the plastic casing on a wire. Interestingly, only Schwann cells can guide axonal regrowth after injury. That means that damaged axons can be repaired in the body, but not in the brain or spinal cord. It's really the axons that do the bulk of the travelling through the body, with the somas clumped together near the spinal cord. So the axons of those various neurons can travel together throughout the body and never touch each other directly. It's very similar to the concept of a telephone cable. Within the cable are lots of copper wires coated in plastic. The plastic serves the same insulating purpose for the wires as the myelin sheath does for the axons. Bundled together, they form a cable that is much stronger and less vulnerable to breakage than any wire alone would be. It works the same way in the nervous system. Bundles of myelin-coated axons travel together in "cables" called **nerves**.

A few other facts about myelin: It not only insulates and protects the neuron but also speeds up the neural message travelling down the axon. As shown in Figure 2.2, sections of myelin bump up next to each other on the axon, similar to the way sausages are linked together. The places where the myelin seems to bump are actually small spaces on the axon called *nodes of Ranvier* (nodes), which are not covered in myelin. When the electrical impulse that is the neural message travels down an axon coated with myelin, it "jumps" between the myelin sheath sections to the places where the axon is accessible at the nodes. That makes the message go much faster down the coated axon than it would down an uncoated axon of a neuron in the brain. Thus, the myelin sheath is a very important part of the neuron. Damage to the myelin sheath is a serious problem since the arrival of messages from the brain to particular areas of the body becomes disrupted. If damage to the myelin occurs in brain areas associated with vision, persons may experience double vision; if myelin damage occurs in the brain stem, persons may lose their muscular strength and their ability to control their skeletal muscles, resulting in problems with balance, and they may even become paralyzed.

The disease called *multiple sclerosis* (MS) damages the myelin sheaths (Allen, 1991). In MS, the person's own immune system begins to attack the myelin sheaths and thus disrupts the timing and accuracy of brain messages. This damage leads to the common symptoms of MS: blurred or double vision, muscle weakness, tremors, poor speech, paralysis, and eventual death. While the cause of MS is still unknown, Stevens (1988) and Noseworthy (1999) suggest that exposure to a virus may trigger an attack. Researchers at the University of Calgary have found support for such a theory (Beck, Metz, Svenson, & Patten, 2005). These Calgary researchers looked at the regional differences in rates of MS across Canada and found some surprising results. People who lived in the Prairie and Atlantic provinces had higher rates of MS than those living in British Columbia, Ontario, and Quebec. These regional differences suggest that MS may be caused, in part, by some environmental factor(s), such as exposure to a virus.

Another environmental factor could be a buildup of iron in the brain. Dr. Paolo Zamboni contends that poor blood drainage from the brain results in the formation of iron deposits within the brain that may lead to the development of MS. To test his idea, Zamboni performed surgery (angioplasty) on 65 persons with MS to improve blood drainage from the brain. He reported that two years later 73 percent of persons who received the surgery had improved (Zamboni et al., 2009). Not surprisingly, the publication of this paper had many MS patients around the world, including Canada, seeking the treatment, dubbed the *Liberation Procedure*. Since the procedure was not approved in Canada, many Canadians went abroad for it. Some have shared their experiences with your authors and even documented their experiences on YouTube. The results are promising, but there have also been some serious complications. Recall from Chapter One that replication and control are key components of scientific research. Although encouraging, Zamboni's results will need to be researched further to confirm that the Liberation Procedure works better than placebo and other established MS treatments. Science moves cautiously forward.

Exactly how does this "electrical message" work inside the cell?

GENERATING THE MESSAGE WITHIN THE NEURON—THE NEURAL IMPULSE

A neuron that's at rest—not currently firing a neural impulse or message—is actually electrically charged. The inside of the cell is really a semi-liquid solution in which there are charged particles, or *ions*. A semi-liquid solution surrounds the outside of the cell as well, which also contains ions. The catch is that the ions inside the cell are mostly negatively charged, and the ions outside the cell are mostly positively charged. The cell membrane itself is *semipermeable*, meaning that some substances that are outside the cell can enter through tiny openings, or *gates*, in the membrane, while other substances in the cell can also get outside. Some of the ions inside the cell are positively charged potassium ions which move freely in and out of the cell when the cell is at rest. Most ions inside the cell, however, carry a negative charge and are so big that they can't ever get out. So the inside of the cell is primarily negative when at rest. Outside the cell are positively charged sodium ions, but they are unable to enter the cell membrane when the cell is at rest—the ion gates that would allow them in are closed. But because the outside sodium ions are positive and the majority of inside ions are negative, and because opposite electrical charges attract each other, the sodium ions cluster around the membrane. This difference in charges is an electrical potential. In other words, your neurons act like tiny batteries in which the inside is the negative terminal and the outside the positive terminal. When the neuron is at rest, this difference in charge is called the **resting membrane potential**.

◀ Exactly how does this "electrical message" work inside the cell?

✳ **Explore** on **mypsychlab**
Neuronal Transmission

resting membrane potential
the state of the neuron when not firing a neural impulse.

action potential
the release of the neural impulse consisting of a reversal of the electrical charge within the axon.

Think of the ions inside the cell as a hockey game inside an arena (the cell walls). The sodium ions outside the cell are all the fans wanting to get inside to see the game. When the cell is at rest, the fans are stuck outside because the arena is closed. The sodium ions cannot enter when the cell is at rest, because even though the cell membrane has all these gates, the *particular* gates for the sodium ions are not yet open. But when the cell receives a strong enough stimulation from another cell (meaning that the dendrites are activated), the sodium gates open and sodium rushes in. In our analogy, the gates to the arena are now open and the fans rush in. The only difference is that typically all the gates to an arena would open simultaneously, whereas, in the axon, gate opening is much more of an ordered process. Sodium gates first open where the axon meets the soma (called the *axon hillock*). When the positively charged sodium ions rush in, the charge inside the axon hillock reverses from negative to positive and the charge outside of the hillock reverses from positive to negative.

This electrical charge reversal will now proceed down the axon in a kind of chain reaction. (Picture a long hallway with many doors in which the first door opens, then the second, and so on all the way down the hall.) This electrical charge reversal is known as the **action potential** because the electrical potential is now in action rather than at rest. Each action potential sequence takes about 2 to 3 milliseconds (thousandths of a second), so the neural message travels very fast—from 1 metre per second in the slowest, shortest neurons to 120 metres per second in other neurons (see Figure 2.3).

Now the action potential is travelling down the axon. When it gets to the end of the axon, something else happens that will be discussed momentarily. Meanwhile, what is happening to the parts of the cell that the action potential has already left behind? How does the cell get the "fans" back outside? Remember, the action potential means that the cell is now positive inside and negative outside at the point where the sodium gates opened. Unfortunately, sodium gates close immediately after the action potential has passed, allowing no more "fans" (sodium ions) to enter or leave the cell via this route. So how does the axon get back to its resting state? A couple of things happen. First, the cell membrane literally "pumps" the positive sodium ions back outside the cell, kicking the "fans" out. Second, since this pumping process is a little slow, another type of ion gets into the act. The small, positively charged potassium ions from inside the neuron now move rapidly out of the cell after the action potential passes, helping to more quickly restore the inside of the neuron to a negative charge. This combination of positive potassium ions leaving the inside of the neuron and the sodium pump kicking out the sodium ions returns the neuron to its resting state. The neuron is now ready to "fire off" another message.

Let's sum all that up. When the neuron is stimulated, the sodium gates at the axon hillock open and the electrical charge *at that gate* is reversed. Then the next gate opens and *that* charge is reversed. In the meantime, the *first* gate has been closed and the charge is returning to what it was when it was at rest because positively charged potassium ions leave the inside of the cell and the sodium is pumped out. The action potential is the *sequence* of sodium gates opening down the entire length of the cell.

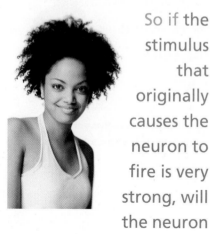

So if the stimulus that originally causes the neuron to fire is very strong, will the neuron fire more strongly than it would if the stimulus were weak? Neurons actually have a threshold for firing, and all it takes is a stimulus that is just strong enough to get past that threshold to make the neuron fire. Here's a simple version of

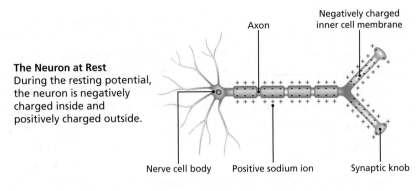

The Neuron at Rest
During the resting potential, the neuron is negatively charged inside and positively charged outside.

Axon

Negatively charged inner cell membrane

Nerve cell body   Positive sodium ion   Synaptic knob

FIGURE 2.3 **The Neural Impulse Action Potential**
In the graph below, voltage readings are shown at a given place on the neuron over a period of 2 or 3 milliseconds (thousandths of a second). At first the cell is resting; it then reaches threshold and an action potential is triggered. After a brief refractory period, the cell returns to its resting potential.

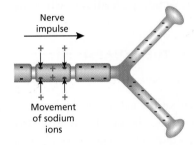

Nerve impulse

Movement of sodium ions

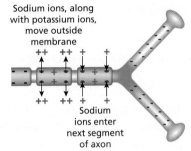

Sodium ions, along with potassium ions, move outside membrane

Sodium ions enter next segment of axon

The Neural Impulse
The action potential occurs when positive sodium ions enter into the cell, causing a reversal of the electrical charge from negative to positive.

The Neural Impulse Continues
As the action potential moves down the axon toward the axon terminals, the cell areas behind the action potential return to their resting state of a negative charge as the positive sodium ions are pumped to the outside of the cell, and the positive potassium ions rapidly leave.

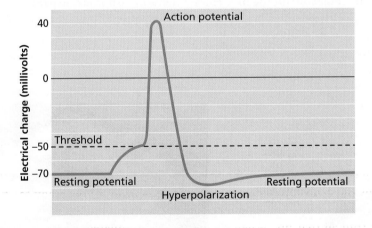

how this works: Each neuron is receiving many signals from other neurons. Some of these signals are meant to cause the neuron to fire, whereas others are meant to prevent the neuron from firing. The neuron constantly adds together the effects of the "fire" messages and subtracts the "don't fire" messages, and if the "fire" messages are great enough, the threshold is crossed and the neuron fires. When a neuron does fire, it fires in an **all-or-none** fashion. Neurons are either firing at full strength or not at all—there's no such thing as "partial" firing of a neuron. It is like a light switch—it's either on or off. When the switch is turned to the on position, the light will come on. When it's turned to the off position, the light will go off.

all-or-none
referring to the fact that a neuron either fires completely or does not fire at all.

So what's the difference between strong stimulation and weak stimulation? A strong message will cause the neuron to fire more quickly (as if someone flicked the light switch on and off as quickly as possible), and it will also cause more neurons to fire (as if there were a lot of lights going on and off instead of just one). The latter point can be demonstrated quite easily. Just touch lightly on the palm of your hand. You feel a very light pressure sensation. Now push hard in the same spot. You will feel a much stronger pressure sensation, and you can see with your own eyes that more of the skin on the palm of your hand is pushed in by your touch—more skin involved means more neurons firing.

Now that we know how the message travels within the axon of the cell, what is that "something else" that happens when the action potential reaches the end of the axon?

SENDING THE MESSAGE TO OTHER CELLS: THE SYNAPSE

2.3 *How do neurons communicate with each other and with the body?*

Look once again at Figure 2.2 on p. 45. The end of the axon actually branches out into several "limbs," which are called **axon terminals**. The tip of each axon terminal has a little knob on it. Figure 2.4 shows this knob blown up to giant size. Notice that the knob (called the **synaptic knob** or sometimes the *terminal button*) is not empty. It has a number of little saclike structures in it called **synaptic vesicles**. The word *vesicle* is Latin and means "little blister" or "fluid-filled sac."

Inside the synaptic vesicles are chemicals suspended in fluid, which are molecules of substances called **neurotransmitters**. What lies next to the synaptic knob? Right next to it is the dendrite of another neuron. Between them is a fluid-filled space called the **synapse** or the synaptic gap. Instead of an electrical charge, the vesicles at the end of the axon contain the molecules of neurotransmitters, whereas the surface

Now that we know how the message travels within the axon of the cell, what is that "something else" that happens when the action potential reaches the end of the axon?

✿ Explore on **mypsychlab**
The Synapse

FIGURE 2.4 **The Synapse**
The nerve impulse reaches the synaptic knobs, triggering the release of neurotransmitters from the synaptic vesicles. The molecules of neurotransmitter cross the synaptic gap to fit into the receptor sites that fit the shape of the molecule.

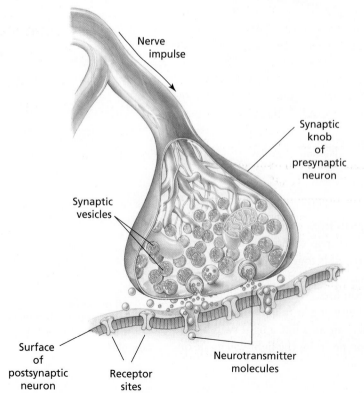

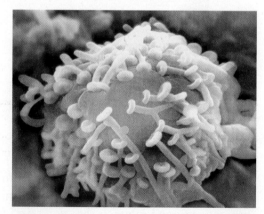

A micrograph of synaptic knobs (small mushroom-like fibres) clustering around another neuron's cell body.

of the dendrite right next to the axon contains special little locks called **receptor sites**. These locks have a special shape that allows only a particular molecule of neurotransmitter to fit into it, just as only a particular key will fit into a keyhole. (The end of the axon containing the neurotransmitters is called the *presynaptic membrane* and the surface of the receiving neuron is called the *postsynaptic membrane*.)

How do the neurotransmitters get across the gap? Recall the action potential making its way down the axon. When that electrical charge reaches the synaptic vesicles, they release their neurotransmitters into the synaptic gap. The molecules then float or diffuse* across the synapse and many of them fit themselves into the receptor sites, either activating or deactivating the next cell. It is this activation of receptors that either stimulates or prevents the action potential in that next cell. Please be aware that the "next cell" can be a neuron as we have indicated, but the "next cell" can also be a muscle or a gland. Muscles and glands have special receptor sites on them, too, just like the dendrite of a neuron.

You may be assuming that activation of receptors via neurotransmitters always causes the next cell to fire its action potential (or, in the case of a muscle or gland, to contract or start secreting its chemicals). But the neurons must also have a way to be turned off. Otherwise, when a person burns a finger, the pain signals from those neurons would not stop until the burn was completely healed. The neurotransmitters found at various synapses around the nervous system (there are at least 50 known neurotransmitters and theoretically several times that number exist) can either turn cells on (called an *excitatory effect*) or turn cells off (called an *inhibitory effect*). Although some people refer to neurotransmitters that turn cells on as **excitatory neurotransmitters** and the ones that turn cells off as **inhibitory neurotransmitters**, it's really more correct to refer to excitatory synapses and inhibitory synapses. In other words, it's not the neurotransmitter itself that is excitatory or inhibitory, but rather it is the effect of that neurotransmitter (either excitatory or inhibitory) at the receptor sites of a particular synapse.

I think I understand the synapse now, but will knowing about neurotransmitters and synapses help me in the real world? Most people have taken medication of some sort at some point in their lives. Knowing how and why drugs affect us can help us understand why a doctor might prescribe a particular drug or why certain drugs are dangerous and should be avoided. Consider a molecule of a drug that is similar in shape to a neurotransmitter and finds its way into a synapse and attaches to a receptor site just like the neurotransmitter would. What would happen? As you likely predicted, the receptor sites of the synapse would either be activated or inhibited. **Agonists** are chemical substances that mimic or enhance the effects of neurotransmitters on the receptor sites of the next cell, which can result in an increase or decrease in the activity of the receiving cell, depending on the effect of the original neurotransmitter (excitatory or inhibitory). So if the original neurotransmitter was excitatory, the effect of the agonist will be to increase that excitation. If it was inhibitory, the effect of the agonist will be to increase that inhibition. For example, there are drugs that bind to receptors in the heart muscle (called *beta* receptors) that act as agonists by increasing the action of the neurotransmitter that stimulates the contractions of certain heart valves. Digoxin, which comes from the foxglove plant, is one example of this kind of agonist drug.

Other drugs act as **antagonists**, chemical substances that block or reduce a cell's response to the action of other chemicals or neurotransmitters. Although an antagonist might sound like it has only an inhibitory effect, it is important to remember

---

*Diffuse: to move from high concentration to low concentration

axon terminals
branches at the end of the axon.

synaptic knob
rounded areas on the end of the axon terminals.

synaptic vesicles
saclike structures found inside the synaptic knob containing chemicals.

neurotransmitter
chemical found in the synaptic vesicles that, when released, has an effect on the next cell.

synapse (synaptic gap)
microscopic fluid-filled space between the synaptic knob of one cell and the dendrites or surface of the next cell.

receptor sites
holes in the surface of the dendrites or certain cells of the muscles and glands, which are shaped to fit only certain neurotransmitters.

excitatory synapse
the effect of the neurotransmitter in the synapse causes the receiving cell to fire.

inhibitory synapse
the effect of the neurotransmitter in the synapse causes the receiving cell to stop firing.

◀ I think I understand the synapse now, but will knowing about neurotransmitters and synapses help me in the real world?

agonists
chemical substances that mimic or enhance the effects of neurotransmitters on the receptor sites of the next cell, increasing or decreasing the activity of that cell.

antagonists
chemical substances that block or reduce a cell's response to the action of other chemicals or neurotransmitters.

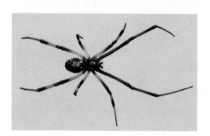

The venom of the black widow spider causes a flood of acetylcholine to be released into the body's muscle system, causing convulsions.

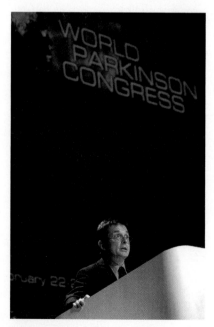

Michael J. Fox speaks at the World Parkinson Congress. Mr. Fox has been diagnosed with Parkinson's disease, which results from too little dopamine released in certain areas of the brain associated with motor control.

that if the neurotransmitter that the antagonist affects is inhibitory itself, the result will actually be an *increase* in the activity of the cell that would normally have been inhibited; the antagonist *blocks* the inhibitory effect. *Beta blockers* are drugs that are used to control high blood pressure and (as the name suggests) serve as antagonists by blocking the effects of the neurotransmitters that stimulate the heart's contractions. This results in slower heart contractions and lowered blood pressure. Two examples of commonly prescribed beta blockers are propranolol (trade name Inderal) and metaprolol (trade name Lopressor). The following discussion of specific types of neurotransmitters provides more examples of agonists and antagonists and explains how they affect the nervous system.

NEUROTRANSMITTERS, MESSENGERS OF THE NETWORK

2.4 *What are the different neurotransmitters?*

The first neurotransmitter to be identified was named *acetylcholine.* It is found at the synapses between neurons and muscle cells. Acetylcholine serves to stimulate the skeletal muscle to contract, but actually slows contractions of heart muscle. If acetylcholine receptor sites on the muscle cells are blocked in some way, then the acetylcholine can't get to the site and the muscle will be incapable of contracting—paralyzed, in other words. This is exactly what happens when *curare*, a drug used by Native South Americans on their blow darts, gets into the nervous system. Curare's molecules are just similar enough to fit into the receptor site without actually stimulating the cell, making curare an antagonist for acetylcholine.

What would happen if the neurons released too much acetylcholine? The bite of a black widow spider does just that. Its venom stimulates the release of excessive amounts of acetylcholine and causes convulsions and possible death. Black widow spider venom is an agonist for acetylcholine. Acetylcholine is also found in the hippocampus, an area of the brain that is responsible for forming new memories, and low levels of acetylcholine have been associated with Alzheimer's disease. LINK *to Chapter Six: Memory, p. 218.*

Although acetylcholine was the first neurotransmitter found to have an excitatory effect at the synapse, the nervous system's major excitatory neurotransmitter is *glutamate*. Like acetylcholine, glutamate plays an important role in learning and memory, and may also be involved in the development of the nervous system.

Another neurotransmitter is *GABA* (or *gamma-aminobutyric acid*). Whereas glutamate is the major excitatory neurotransmitter, GABA is the most common inhibitory neurotransmitter in the brain. GABA can help calm anxiety, for example, it binds to the same receptor sites that are affected by tranquilizing drugs and alcohol. In fact, drinking alcohol enhances the effect of GABA, which causes the general inhibition of the nervous system associated with getting drunk. This makes alcohol an agonist for GABA. LINK *to Chapter Four: Consciousness, p. 134.*

Serotonin is a neurotransmitter found in the lower part of the brain that can have either an excitatory or inhibitory effect, depending on the particular synapse being affected. It is associated with sleep, mood, and appetite. Low levels of serotonin activity have been linked to depression, for example. LINK *to Chapter Thirteen: Psychological Disorders, p. 520.*

Dopamine is found in the brain and, like serotonin, can have different effects depending on the location of its activity. If too little dopamine is released in a certain area of the brain, the result is a disease called *Parkinson's*—the disease currently being battled by former boxing champ Muhammad Ali and Canadian actor Michael J. Fox (Ahlskog, 2003). If too much dopamine is released in another area, the result is a serious mental disorder called *schizophrenia* (Akil et al., 2003). Ⓛ Ⓘ Ⓝ Ⓚ *to Chapter Thirteen: Psychological Disorders, p. 520* (See Table 2.1 for a list of some neurotransmitters and their functions.)

Some neurotransmitters directly control the release of other neurotransmitters. These special neurotransmitters are called *neural regulators* or *neural peptides* (Agnati et al., 1992), one example is *endorphins*. Endorphins are pain-controlling chemicals in the body. When a person is hurt, a neurotransmitter that signals pain is released. When the brain gets this message, it triggers the release of endorphins. The endorphins bind to receptors that open the gates on the axon. This causes the cell to be unable to fire its pain signal, and the pain sensations eventually decrease. For example, sports players may injure themselves during an event and yet not feel the pain until after the event when the endorphin levels go down.

The name *endorphin* comes from the term *endogenous morphine*. (*Endogenous* means "native to the area"—in this case, native to the body.) Scientists studying the nervous system found receptor sites that fit morphine molecules perfectly and decided that a natural substance in the body must have the same effect as morphine. Endorphins are the reason that heroin and the other drugs derived from opium are so addictive—when people take morphine or heroin, their bodies neglect to produce endorphins. When the drug wears off, they are left with no protection against pain at all, and *everything* hurts. Known as withdrawal, this pain is why most people want more heroin, creating an addictive cycle of abuse. Ⓛ Ⓘ Ⓝ Ⓚ *to Chapter Four: Consciousness, p. 134.*

If the neurotransmitters are out there in the synaptic gap and in the receptor sites, what happens to them when they aren't needed anymore?

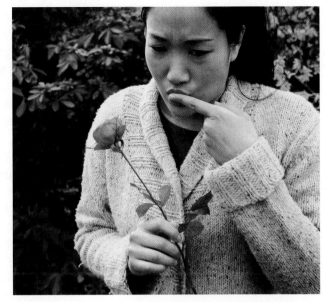

The look on this young woman's face clearly indicates that she has experienced pain in her finger. Pain is a warning signal that something is wrong. In this case it indicates that touching the thorns on the stem of the rose was a bad idea. What might be some of the problems encountered by a person who could feel no pain at all?

◄ If the neurotransmitters are out there in the synaptic gap and in the receptor sites, what happens to them when they aren't needed anymore?

TABLE 2.1 NEUROTRANSMITTERS AND THEIR FUNCTIONS	
NEUROTRANSMITTERS	**FUNCTIONS**
Acetylcholine	Excitatory or inhibitory; involved in memory and controls muscle contractions
Serotonin	Excitatory or inhibitory; involved in mood, sleep, and appetite
GABA (gamma-aminobutyric acid)	Major inhibitory neurotransmitter; involved in sleep and inhibits movement
Glutamate	Major excitatory neurotransmitter; involved in learning, memory formation, and nervous system development
Norepinephrine	Mainly excitatory; involved in arousal and mood
Dopamine	Excitatory or inhibitory; involved in control of movement and sensations of pleasure
Endorphins	Inhibitory neural regulators; involved in pain relief

reuptake
process by which neurotransmitters are taken back into the synaptic vesicles.

CLEANING UP THE SYNAPSE: REUPTAKE AND ENZYMES

The neurotransmitters have to get out of the receptor sites before the next stimulation can occur. Most neurotransmitters will end up back in the synaptic vesicles in a process called **reuptake**. (Think of a little suction tube, sucking the chemicals back into the vesicles.) That way, the synapse is cleared for the next release of neurotransmitters. Some drugs, such as cocaine, can affect the nervous system by blocking the reuptake process (see Figure 2.5 for a visual representation of how cocaine affects dopamine synapses).

One neurotransmitter is not taken back into the vesicles, however. Because acetylcholine is responsible for muscle activity, and muscle activity needs to happen rapidly and continually, it's not possible to wait around for the "sucking up" process to occur. Instead, an enzyme specifically designed to break apart acetylcholine clears the synaptic gap very quickly. There are enzymes that break down the other neurotransmitters as well.

The neurotransmitter serotonin helps regulate and adjust people's moods, but in some people the reuptake process occurs too quickly. This takes the serotonin out of the synapse before it can fully activate the receptors on the next neuron, leaving the person in a state of depression. Most of the drugs used to treat this condition are called *SSRIs* (selective serotonin reuptake inhibitors). SSRIs block the reuptake of serotonin, leaving more serotonin available in the synapse to bond with the receptor sites. Eventually, this elevates mood and lifts the depression. Although doctors used to have a patient taper off the use of antidepressants after the person's depression had lifted, new research has found that keeping a person on a maintenance dose of the drug helps prevent future episodes of depression (Geddes et al., 2003; Taylor et al., 2004).

This section covered the neuron and how neurons communicate. The next section looks at the bigger picture—the nervous system itself. Before reading on, try answering the following questions to test your memory.

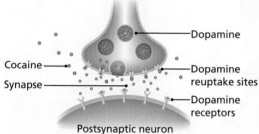

Presynaptic neuron

Dopamine

Cocaine

Synapse

Dopamine reuptake sites

Dopamine receptors

Postsynaptic neuron

FIGURE 2.5 **Reuptake of Dopamine**
Dopamine is removed from the synapse by reuptake sites. Cocaine acts by blocking dopamine reuptake sites, allowing dopamine to remain active in the synapse longer.

PRACTICE QUIZ: HOW MUCH DO YOU REMEMBER?

Pick the best answer.

1. Which cell type is considered to be the "glue" that holds the brain together?
a. neuron
b. brain cell
c. glial
d. cell body

2. Which part of the neuron receives messages from other cells?
a. axon
b. dendrite
c. soma
d. myelin

3. Which one of the following is NOT a function of the myelin sheath?
a. insulation from other axons
b. speeds up the neural message
c. protects the nerve fibre from damage
d. aids in reuptake

4. Which of the following provinces likely has the highest rate of multiple sclerosis?
a. Manitoba
b. British Columbia
c. Ontario
d. Quebec

5. When the neuron's action potential is released, _____ ions are rushing into the axon through openings on the membrane.
a. sodium
b. potassium
c. chloride
d. oxygen

6. When the action potential reaches the end of the axon terminals, it causes the release of
a. an electrical spark that sets off the next neuron.
b. positively charged ions that excite the next cell.
c. negatively charged ions that inhibit the next cell.
d. neurotransmitters that excite or inhibit the next cell.

7. Receiving neurons have special _____ that fit the shape of certain molecules.
a. synaptic vesicles
b. gaps
c. receptor sites
d. branches

8. Which of the following is associated with sleep, mood, and appetite?
a. acetylcholine
b. GABA
c. serotonin
d. endorphin

9. Which neural peptide is responsible for the dulling of the pain response?
a. serotonin
b. dopamine
c. glutamate
d. endorphin

10. Drugs classified as SSRI do what?
a. They activate enzymes in the synapse that break down acetylcholine.
b. They block the reuptake of serotonin.
c. They block the reuptake of GABA.
d. They inactivate enzymes in the synapse that break down endorphins.

THE CENTRAL NERVOUS SYSTEM: THE "CENTRAL PROCESSING UNIT"

The **central nervous system (CNS)** is composed of the brain and the spinal cord. Both the brain and the spinal cord are composed of neurons and glial cells that control the life-sustaining functions of the body as well as all thought, emotion, and behaviour.

2.5 *How do the brain and spinal cord interact?*

THE BRAIN

As the true core of the nervous system, the brain makes sense of the information received from the senses, makes decisions, and sends commands to the muscles and the rest of the body. Later parts of this chapter will cover the brain in more detail. Without the spinal cord, however, the brain would be useless.

THE SPINAL CORD

The **spinal cord** is a long bundle of neurons that serves two vital functions for the nervous system. Look at the cross-sectional view of the spinal cord in Figure 2.6. Note that it seems to be divided into two areas, one around the outside and one inside the cord. If it were a real spinal cord, the outer section would appear to be white and the inner section would seem grey. That's because the outer section is composed mainly of axons and nerves, which appear white, whereas the inner section is mainly composed of cell bodies of neurons, which appear grey. The purpose of the outer section is to carry messages from the body up to the brain and from the brain down to the body. It is simply a message "pipeline."

THE REFLEX ARC: THREE TYPES OF NEURONS The spinal cord's inside section, which is made up of cell bodies separated by glial cells, is actually a primitive sort of "brain." This part of the spinal cord is responsible for certain reflexes—very fast, life-saving reflexes. To understand how the spinal cord reflexes work, it is important to know there are three basic types of neurons: **sensory neurons** (called *afferent neurons*) that carry messages from the senses to the spinal cord, **motor neurons** (called *efferent neurons*) that carry messages from the spinal cord to the muscles and glands, and **interneurons** that connect the sensory neurons to the motor neurons (and make up the inside of the spinal cord and the brain itself; see Figure 2.6). Touch a hot flame, for example, and a sensory, or afferent, neuron will send the pain message to the spinal column where it will enter into the central area of the cord. The interneuron in that central area will then receive the message and send a response along a motor, or efferent, neuron, causing you to pull away. This all happens very quickly. If the pain message had to go all the way up to the brain, the response time would be greatly increased and more damage would be done to the area touching the flame. So having this kind of **reflex arc** controlled by the spinal cord alone allows for very fast response times. (A good way to avoid mixing up the terms *afferent* and *efferent* is to remember "afferent neurons access the spinal cord; efferent neurons exit." The pain message does eventually get to the brain, where other motor responses may be triggered, such as saying "Ouch!" or, if you burned your finger, putting it in your mouth.

If the spinal cord is such an important link between the body and the brain, what happens if it is damaged? Damage to the CNS was once thought to be permanent. Neurons in the brain and spinal cord were not seen as capable of repairing themselves. When people recovered from a stroke, for example, it was assumed

central nervous system (CNS)
part of the nervous system consisting of the brain and spinal cord.

spinal cord
a long bundle of neurons that carries messages to and from the body and to and from the brain. Is responsible for a variety of life-saving reflexes.

sensory neuron
a neuron that carries information from the senses to the central nervous system. Also called an *afferent neuron*.

motor neuron
a neuron that carries messages from the central nervous system to the muscles and the glands of the body. Also called an *efferent neuron*.

interneuron
a neuron found in the centre of the spinal cord that receives information from the sensory neurons and sends commands to the muscles through the motor neurons. Interneurons also make up the bulk of the neurons in the brain.

reflex arc
the connection of the sensory neurons to the interneurons to the motor neurons, resulting in a reflex action.

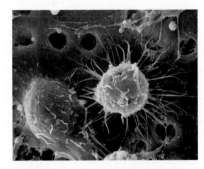

Microphotograph of a bone marrow stem cell.

✱ Explore on **mypsychlab**
The Virtual Brain

If the spinal cord is such an important link between the body and the brain, what happens if it is damaged?

FIGURE 2.6 **The Spinal Cord Reflex**
The pain from the burning heat of the candle flame stimulates the afferent nerve fibres, which carry the message up to the interneurons in the middle of the spinal cord. The interneurons then send a message out by means of the efferent nerve fibres, causing the hand to jerk away from the flame.

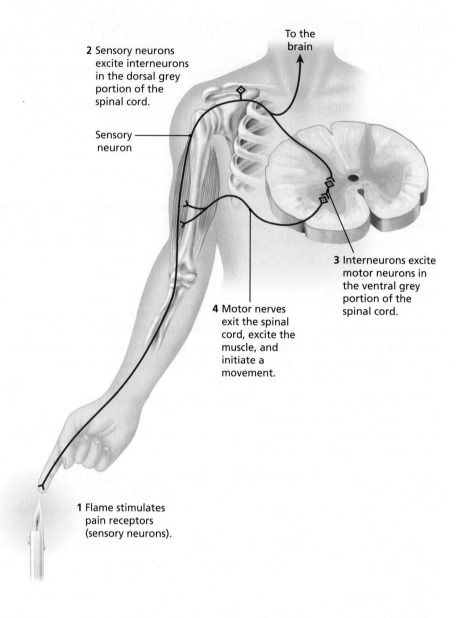

2 Sensory neurons excite interneurons in the dorsal grey portion of the spinal cord.

Sensory neuron

To the brain

3 Interneurons excite motor neurons in the ventral grey portion of the spinal cord.

4 Motor nerves exit the spinal cord, excite the muscle, and initiate a movement.

1 Flame stimulates pain receptors (sensory neurons).

✽ Explore on mypsychlab
The Nerve Impulse and Afferent and Efferent Neurons

that healthy brain cells took over the function of the damaged ones. Scientists have known for a while now that some forms of CNS damage can be repaired by the body's systems, and in recent years great strides have been made in repairing spinal cord damage.

The brain actually exhibits a great deal of *plasticity*, the ability to constantly change both the structure and function of many cells in the brain in response to experience and even trauma (Neville & Bavelier, 2000). Scientists have been able to *implant* nerve fibres from outside the spinal cord onto a damaged area and then "coax" the damaged spinal nerves to grow through these "tunnels" of implanted fibres (Cheng et al., 1996). The first human trials have already begun (Bunge & Pearse, 2003). It is also now known that the brain can change itself quite a bit—by adapting neurons to serve new functions when old neurons die or are damaged. For example, Bryan Kolb, Jan Cioe, and Ian Whishaw (2000) have shown that when parts of the brain involved in the control of complex motor skills are destroyed early in development, other parts of the brain can begin to take over the function of the destroyed areas. Plasticity is also evident as dendrites grow and new synapses are formed in at least some areas of the brain, as people learn new things throughout life (Abraham & Williams, 2003). For instance, Lixia Yang and colleagues at Ryerson University have been working with elderly participants and have found evidence of continued plasticity in even the oldest participants who were more than 80 years of age (Yang, Krampe, & Baltes, 2006). University of Calgary researchers Jaideep Bains and Stephane Oliet (2007) would argue that these 80-plus year olds are learning because their glial cells are helping their neurons form new connections. In a cleverly titled paper, "Glia: They Make Your Memories Stick!" Bains and Oliet (2007) were able to show that the formation of new synapses associated with learning and memory are dependent on glial cells.

Researchers are constantly looking for new ways to repair the brain. For a look at a new and promising treatment for people with diseases such as Parkinson's and Alzheimer's, and for damage from strokes, read the following Psychology in the News section.

stem cells
special cells found in all the tissues of the body that are capable of manufacturing other cell types when those cells need to be replaced because of damage or wear and tear.

peripheral nervous system (PNS)
all nerves and neurons that are not contained in the brain and spinal cord but that run through the body itself.

somatic nervous system
division of the PNS consisting of nerves that carry information from the senses to the CNS and from the CNS to the voluntary muscles of the body.

autonomic nervous system (ANS)
division of the PNS consisting of nerves that control all the involuntary muscles, organs, and glands.

PSYCHOLOGY IN THE NEWS

Stem Cells: New Hope for the Damaged Brains?

Scientists have been researching the possibility of transplanting **stem cells** to repair damaged or diseased brain tissue (see Figure 2.7). Stem cells can create other cells, such as blood cells, nerve cells, and brain cells (National Institutes of Health, 2000). For example, researchers at McMaster University in Hamilton, Ontario, implanted stem cells into mice that showed symptoms consistent with Parkinson's disease. Amazingly, the stem cells became functional and the mice showed significant improvement (Meissner, Kirkham, & Doering, 2005). An ongoing controversy concerns the source of such stem cells, which can be obtained from human embryos, either from terminated pregnancies or fertilization clinics. Many people are opposed to the idea of putting embryos to this use, even if stem cell research promises cures for diseases such as Parkinson's and Alzheimer's or the repair of damaged spinal cords or brain tissue.

A recent study, reported by author and neurologist Alexander Storch of the University of Ulm in Germany, may hold hope for the future of stem cell treatments without the controversial need to use human embryonic tissue (Storch, 2004). In a paper presented at the American Academy of Neurology in San Francisco, Dr. Storch talked about the possibility of obtaining stem cells from adult bone marrow for use in repairing damaged neural tissue. These cells would not only remove the controversy surrounding embryonic stem cells but would also eliminate any immune system problems in transplanting tissues, because the cells would be taken from the adult's own bone marrow. Storch said that a small amount of bone marrow stem cells can be made to grow and produce a large amount of cells that can be converted into the type of cell needed.

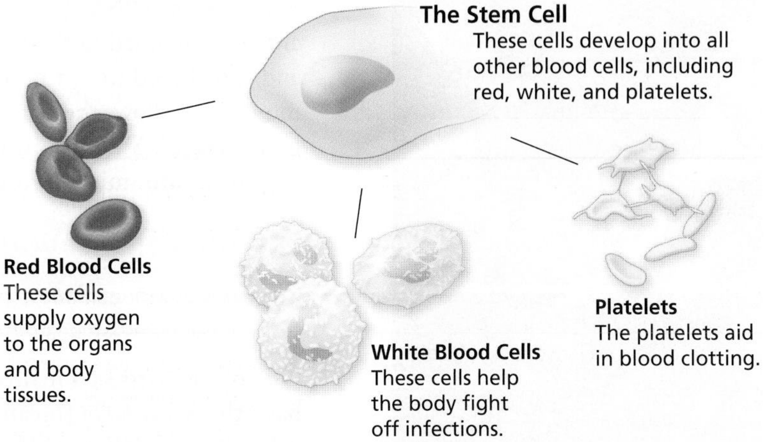

The Stem Cell
These cells develop into all other blood cells, including red, white, and platelets.

Red Blood Cells
These cells supply oxygen to the organs and body tissues.

White Blood Cells
These cells help the body fight off infections.

Platelets
The platelets aid in blood clotting.

FIGURE 2.7 **The Stem Cell**
Stem cells are basic cells that differentiate into specific types of cells, such as these blood cells. Stem cells can also become other types of cells, such as brain cells and nerve cells.

Canadian researchers have also contributed to adult mammalian stem cell research. Recently, researchers at the Hospital for Sick Children in Toronto have found evidence that stem cells taken from the skin of both humans and rodents could be coaxed to become cells that myelinate axons (McKenzie, Biernaskie, Toma, Midha, & Miller, 2006). At the University of Toronto, researchers have found stem cells in the adult rodent eye. These stem cells were successfully turned into other eye cells (Tropepe et al., 2000). In a fascinating finding, Mick Bhatia and his team at McMaster's Stem Cell and Cancer Research Institute were able to produce adult bloods cells from adult skin cells (Szabo et al., 2010). This was the first time adult human cells were coaxed into other adult human cells without first producing a stem cell! Not only is this finding significant from a medical point of view (e.g., for what it could do to increase the blood supply) but it also brings us a step closer to believing that perhaps any cell can be transformed into any other cell.

Although the majority of the studies at present are being conducted only on animals, the future may hold promise for people as well.

Questions for Further Discussion

1. If stem cells could be used to create tissues other than nerves and neurons, what other kinds of disorders might become treatable?

2. What problems might arise from doing the first studies with human subjects in this area?

3. How might understanding stem cell reproduction affect cancer research?

Okay, that takes care of the CNS, except for the detail on the brain. How does the CNS communicate with the rest of the body? ▶

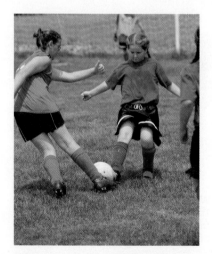

These young soccer players are using their senses and voluntary muscles controlled by the somatic division of the peripheral nervous system. What part of the autonomic nervous system are these girls also using at this time?

THE PERIPHERAL NERVOUS SYSTEM: NERVES ON THE EDGE

Okay, that takes care of the CNS, except for the detail on the brain. How does the CNS communicate with the rest of the body? The term *peripheral* refers to things that are not in the centre or that are on the edges of the centre. The **peripheral nervous system (PNS)** (see Figure 2.8) is made up of all the nerves and neurons that are not contained in the brain and spinal cord. It is this system that allows the brain and spinal cord to communicate with the sensory systems of the eyes, ears, skin, and mouth and allows the brain and spinal cord to control the muscles and glands of the body. The PNS can be divided into two major systems, the **somatic nervous system** and the **autonomic nervous system (ANS)**.

THE SOMATIC NERVOUS SYSTEM

2.6 *How do the somatic and autonomic nervous systems allow people to interact with their surroundings and control the body's automatic functions?*

One of the parts of a neuron is the soma, or cell body. In psychology, a lot of terms have the word *soma* (meaning "body") in them, which indicates that each of these terms has something to do with the body. The somatic nervous system is made up of all the nerves carrying messages from the senses to the CNS (those containing afferent nerves) and all the nerves carrying messages from the CNS to the muscles of the body—specifically, the skeletal muscles that allow people to voluntarily move their bodies (those nerves composed of efferent neurons). When people are walking, raising their hands in class, smelling a flower, or seeing a pretty picture, they are using the somatic nervous system. (As seen in the discussion of spinal cord reflexes, although these muscles are called the *voluntary muscles*, they can move involuntarily when a reflex response occurs. They are called *voluntary* because they *can* be moved at will but are not limited to only that kind of movement.)

Involuntary muscles, such as the heart, stomach, and intestines, together with glands, such as the adrenal glands and the pancreas, are all controlled by clumps of neurons located on or near the spinal column. (The words *on* or *near* are used quite deliberately here. The neurons *inside* the spinal column are part of the CNS, not the PNS.) These large groups of neurons on or near the spinal column make up the *autonomic nervous system*.

THE AUTONOMIC NERVOUS SYSTEM

2.7   *How does the autonomic nervous system control the body's automatic functions and its reaction to stress?*

The word *autonomic* suggests that the functions of this system are more or less automatic, which is basically correct. Whereas the somatic division of the PNS controls the senses and voluntary muscles, the autonomic division controls everything else in the body—organs, glands, and involuntary muscles. The ANS itself is divided into two systems, the *sympathetic division* and the *parasympathetic division*. (For a visual representation of how all the various sections of the nervous system are organized, look back at Figure 2.1 on p. 44.)

THE SYMPATHETIC DIVISION   The **sympathetic division** of the ANS is primarily located on the middle of the spinal column—running from near the top of the rib cage to the waist area. It may help to think of the name in these terms: The sympathetic division is in sympathy with one's emotions. In fact, the sympathetic division is usually called the **fight-or-flight system**, because it allows people and animals to deal with all kinds of stressful events. ⓁⒾⓃⓀ *to Chapter Ten: Stress and Health, p. 396.* Emotions during these events might be anger (hence, the term *fight*) or fear (that's the flight part, obviously) or even extreme joy or excitement. Yes, even joy can be stressful. The sympathetic division's job is to get the body ready to deal with the stress.

What are the specific ways in which this division readies the body to react? (See Figure 2.9.) The pupils seem to get bigger, perhaps to let in more light and, therefore, more information. The heart starts pumping faster and harder, drawing blood away from non-essential organs such as the skin (so at first the person may turn pale) and sometimes even the brain itself (so the person might actually faint). Blood needs lots of oxygen before it goes to the muscles, so the lungs work overtime, too (the person may begin to breathe faster). One set of glands in particular receives special instructions. The adrenal glands will be stimulated to release certain stress-related chemicals (members of a class of chemicals called *hormones*) into the bloodstream. These stress hormones will travel to all parts of the body, but they will affect only certain target organs. Just as a neurotransmitter fits into a receptor site on a cell, the molecules of the stress hormones fit into receptor sites at the

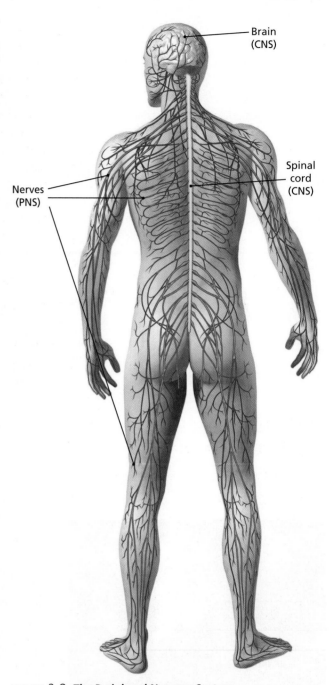

FIGURE 2.8 **The Peripheral Nervous System**

✴ Explore on **mypsychlab**
The Autonomic Nervous System

sympathetic division (fight-or-flight system)
part of the ANS that is responsible for reacting to stressful events and bodily arousal.

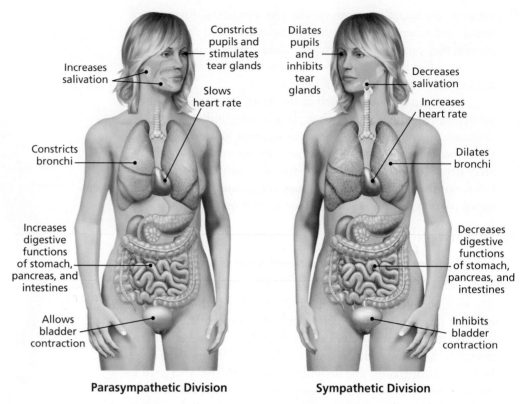

Parasympathetic Division

- Increases salivation
- Constricts pupils and stimulates tear glands
- Slows heart rate
- Constricts bronchi
- Increases digestive functions of stomach, pancreas, and intestines
- Allows bladder contraction

Sympathetic Division

- Dilates pupils and inhibits tear glands
- Decreases salivation
- Increases heart rate
- Dilates bronchi
- Decreases digestive functions of stomach, pancreas, and intestines
- Inhibits bladder contraction

FIGURE 2.9 **Functions of the Parasympathetic and Sympathetic Divisions of the Nervous System**

various target organs—notably, the heart, muscles, and lungs. This further stimulates these organs to work harder. (There are other hormones for other functions that have nothing to do with stress. For more about hormones and glands, see the last section in this chapter, The Chemical Connection: The Endocrine Glands.)

But not every organ or system will be stimulated by the activation of the sympathetic division. Digestion of food and excretion of waste are not necessary functions when dealing with stressful situations, so these systems tend to be "shut down" or inhibited. Saliva, which is part of digestion, dries right up (ever try whistling when you're scared?). Food that was in the stomach sits there like a lump. Usually, the urge to go to the bathroom will be suppressed, but if the person is really scared the bladder or bowels may actually empty (this is why people who die under extreme stress, such as hanging or electrocution, will release their urine and waste). The sympathetic division is also going to demand that the body burn a tremendous amount of fuel, or blood sugar.

Now, all this is going on during a stressful situation. If the stress ends, the activity of the sympathetic division will be replaced by the activation of the parasympathetic division. If the stress goes on so long that all available energy is used up, the person might actually collapse (as a deer might do when being chased by another animal). This collapse occurs because the parasympathetic division over-responds in its inhibition of sympathetic activity. The heart slows down, blood vessels open up, blood pressure in the brain drops, and fainting can be the result.

THE PARASYMPATHETIC DIVISION   If the sympathetic division can be called the fight-or-flight system, the **parasympathetic division** might be called the eat-drink-and-rest system. The neurons of this division are located at the top and bottom of the spinal column, on either side of the sympathetic division neurons (*para* means "beyond" or "next to" and in this sense refers to the neurons located on either side of the sympathetic division neurons).

In looking at Figure 2.9, it might seem as if the parasympathetic division does pretty much the opposite of the sympathetic division, but it's a little more complex than that. The parasympathetic division's job is to restore the body to normal functioning after a stressful situation ends. It slows the heart and breathing, constricts the pupils, and reactivates digestion and excretion. Signals to the adrenal glands stop, because the parasympathetic division isn't connected to the adrenal glands. In a sense, the parasympathetic division allows the body to put back all the energy it burned, which is why people often feel hungry after the stress is over.

The parasympathetic division does more than just react to the activity of the sympathetic division. It is the parasympathetic division that is responsible for most of the ordinary, day-to-day bodily functioning. It keeps the heart beating regularly, breathing normal, and digestion going. People spend the greater part of their 24-hour day eating, sleeping, digesting, and excreting. So it is the parasympathetic division that is normally active. At any given moment, then, one or the other of these divisions, sympathetic or parasympathetic, will determine whether people are aroused or relaxed.

parasympathetic division
part of the ANS that restores the body to normal functioning after arousal and is responsible for the day-to-day functioning of the organs and glands.

This marathon runner collapsed where she stood after finishing the race. Her parasympathetic nervous system is already slowing her breathing and heart rate as her bodily functions begin to return to normal.

PRACTICE QUIZ: HOW MUCH DO YOU REMEMBER?

Pick the best answer.

1. If you burn your finger, your immediate reaction will probably involve all BUT which of the following?
   a. the brain
   b. the spinal cord
   c. sensory neurons
   d. motor neurons

2. Plasticity refers to
   a. the brain's ability to remain stable.
   b. the brain's ability to change its shape and function as a consequence of experience.
   c. the removal of dead brain tissue by glial cells.
   d. the controlled response of a reflex arc.

3. If you are typing on the computer keyboard, the motions of your fingers on the keys are probably being controlled by
   a. the autonomic nervous system.
   b. afferent neurons.
   c. efferent neurons.
   d. autonomic neurons.

4. The neurons of the somatic nervous system control
   a. stress reactions.
   b. organs and glands.
   c. involuntary muscles.
   d. voluntary muscles.

5. What type of cell is responsible for the reproduction of other cells of the body?
   a. blood cells
   b. stem cells
   c. neurons
   d. basal cells

6. Which of the following is NOT a function of the sympathetic division?
   a. increasing digestive activity to supply fuel for the body
   b. dilating the pupils of the eyes
   c. increasing the heart rate
   d. increasing the activity of the lungs

7. Which of the following would be active if you are sleeping?
   a. sympathetic division
   b. parasympathetic division
   c. somatic division
   d. motor division

Answers: 1.-a, 2.-b, 3.-c, 4.-d, 5.-b, 6.-a, 7.-b.

PEEKING INSIDE THE BRAIN

2.8 *How do psychologists study the brain and how it works?*

In ancient times, many early "scientists" would dissect the brains of those who had died—both animals and people—to try to see how the brain worked. The problem, of course, is that it is impossible tell what a structure in the brain is supposed to do if it's dead. A scientist can't even be sure what the brain tissue really looks like when it's inside the skull of a living person instead of sitting on a dissecting table. How can scientists find out what the various parts of the brain do?

CLINICAL STUDIES

One way to get some idea of what the various areas of the brain control is to study animals or people with damage to those areas. In animals, that may mean damaging a part of the brain deliberately. Then researchers test the animal to see what has happened to its abilities. Or they may electrically stimulate some particular area of the animal's brain and watch the result. Both the destruction and stimulation of brain tissue are accomplished by the same basic process. A thin wire insulated everywhere but the very tip is surgically inserted into the brain of the test animal. If brain tissue is to be destroyed, an electrical current strong enough to kill the neurons at the tip of the wire is sent through it. This is called **deep lesioning**. (When cells are destroyed on the surface of the brain or just below it, this is sometimes referred to as *shallow lesioning*.)

If researchers want to only stimulate that area of the brain, the electrical current will be much milder, causing the neurons to react as if they had received a message. This is called *electrical stimulation of the brain (ESB)*. Of course, animals aren't people, even though some people treat them that way, and researchers can't be sure that a human brain is going to function exactly like the brain of a lower animal.

It should be obvious that researchers can't ask human beings to let them destroy areas of their brains. So how do researchers study human brain function? One way is to find people who already have some kind of brain damage or brain disorder and test them to see what they can or cannot do. It isn't an ideal way to study the brain, however, as no two case studies of human brain damage are likely to be in exactly the same area of the brain and involve exactly the same amount of damage. The first of these studies were performed by Dr. Wilder Penfield at the Montreal Neurological Institute. Penfield was particularly intrigued by epilepsy. Penfield saw epilepsy as a short-circuit in the brain, and if he could identify the area of the short-circuit and remove it, he could cure the patient. Penfield also knew that many persons with epilepsy have an "aura" or "sensation" just before a seizure. For example, one of his patients reported that she could always smell burnt toast just before a seizure. Armed with this knowledge, Penfield and his colleagues began to perfect a surgical technique that would later become known as the *Montreal Procedure*. In this procedure, Penfield would apply a local anaesthetic to the person's scalp and then proceed to remove the person's skull to expose the brain. The person had to be fully conscious so that when Penfield gently stimulated different brain areas with his electrical probe the person could report what he or she was feeling. Penfield reasoned that if he could find the area that produced the "aura" and remove it, the epilepsy would also disappear. The procedure worked! Penfield treated more than 1000 patients with this procedure.

THE EEG

A fairly harmless way to study the activity of the living brain is to record the electrical activity of the neurons just below the skull. This has been done for years, using a device called an **electroencephalograph (EEG)** machine. Small metal disks called

electroencephalograph (EEG) machine designed to record the brain wave patterns produced by electrical activity of the surface of the brain.

deep lesioning insertion of a thin, insulated wire into the brain through which an electrical current is sent that destroys the brain cells at the tip of the wire.

microelectrodes are placed directly on the skin covering the skull, using a jellylike substance to help conduct the electrical messages from the neurons just below. These microelectrodes are attached to wires and the wires are attached to pens that rest on a moving graph paper. The microelectrodes can detect electrical activity, which causes the pens to move up and down on the paper, creating squiggly lines or waves that indicate many things, such as stages of sleep, seizures, and even the presence of tumours. The EEG can also be used to determine which areas of the brain are active during tasks such as reading, writing, and speaking (see Figure 2.10).

As can be seen in Figure 2.10a, very fast, irregular waves called *beta waves* indicate waking activity (third and sixth lines in Figure 2.10a). Slightly more regular and slower waves called *alpha waves* are a sign of relaxation, whereas much slower, larger waves called *delta waves* indicate a deep stage of sleep (first and fifth lines in Figure 2.10a). Ⓛ Ⓘ Ⓝ Ⓚ *to Chapter Four: Consciousness, p. 134.*

Scientists have recently developed a new technique involving the way EEG recordings are interpreted (Makeig et al., 2004). The process allows identification of individual signals coming from the different areas of the brain and is called *independent component analysis (ICA)*. ICA allows a more detailed and precise interpretation of the signals coming from different areas of the brain's surface. Another technique using the EEG is called *event-related potential (ERP)*. In ERP, the results of multiple presentations of a stimulus are measured on an EEG and then averaged to remove the variations in random brain activity that occur in the background of any single EEG recording. The result is a measurement of the electrical potential of the brain related to the stimulus event itself or an event-related potential. ERP is being investigated for several different uses. For example, one study has looked at the possibility of using ERP to follow the progression of Alzheimer's disease (Katada et al., 2003), whereas another area of research involves using ERP as a method of lie detection (Allen & Iacona, 1997).

CT SCANS

The EEG allows researchers to look only at the activity of the surface of the brain. Scientists now have several ways to look inside a human brain without harming the person. One way is to take a series of X-rays of the brain, aided by a computer. This is called a CT scan (*CT* stands for **computed tomography**, or "mapping" the brain by computer). CT scans can show stroke damage, tumours, injuries, and abnormal brain structure (see Figure 2.10b).

computed tomography (CT) scan
brain-imaging method using computer-controlled X-rays of the brain.

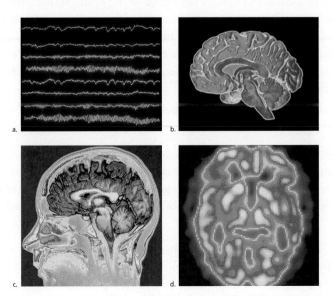

FIGURE 2.10 **Studying the Brain**
These are four methods researchers use to study the brain: EEGs, CT scans, MRIs, and PET scans. (a) An example of an EEG readout. (b) A CT scan (coloured by a computer) showing the detail of a centre cross-section of the brain. (c) An MRI (coloured by a computer) showing enhanced detail of the same view of the brain as in the CT scan. (d) A PET scan showing activity of the brain, using colours to indicate different levels of activity; areas that are very active are white, whereas areas that are inactive are dark blue.

magnetic resonance imaging (MRI) brain-imaging method using radio waves and magnetic fields of the body to produce detailed images of the brain.

positron emission tomography (PET) brain-imaging method in which a radioactive sugar is injected into the subject and a computer compiles a colour-coded image of the activity of the brain, with lighter colours indicating more activity.

medulla the first large swelling at the top of the spinal cord, forming the lowest part of the brain, which is responsible for life-sustaining functions such as breathing, swallowing, and heart rate.

MRI SCANS

As good as a CT scan can be, it still doesn't show very small details within the brain. A newer technique called **magnetic resonance imaging (MRI)** provides much more detail, even allowing doctors to see the effects of very small strokes (see Figure 2.10c). The person getting an MRI scan will be placed inside a machine that generates a powerful magnetic field. The magnetic field allows the computer to create a three-dimensional image of the brain and display "slices" of that image on a screen.

PET SCANS

While CT and MRI scans show the structure of the brain, **PET (positron emission tomography)** scans show the brain in action (see Figure 2.10d). In this method, the person is injected with a radioactive glucose (a kind of sugar). The computer detects the activity of the brain cells by looking at which cells are using up the radioactive glucose and projecting the image of that activity onto a monitor. The computer uses colours to indicate different levels of activity. Areas that are very active usually show up as white or very light, whereas areas that are inactive are dark blue. With this method, researchers can actually have the person perform different tasks while the computer shows what his or her brain is doing during the task.

FUNCTIONAL MRI (FMRI)

Although traditional MRI scans show only structure, there is a technique called *functional MRI (fMRI)* in which the computer tracks changes in the oxygen levels of the blood). By placing this picture of where the oxygen goes in the brain on top of the picture of the brain's structure, researchers can tell what areas of the brain are active. By combining such images taken over a period of time, a sort of "movie" of the brain's functioning can be made (Lin et al., 2007). Functional MRIs can give more detail, tend to be clearer than PET scans, and are fast becoming an incredibly useful tool for research into the workings of the brain.

Okay, now I ▶ understand a little more about how we look inside the brain. What exactly *is* inside the brain?

Okay, now I understand a little more about how we look inside the brain. What exactly *is* inside the brain?

FROM THE BOTTOM UP: THE STRUCTURES OF THE BRAIN

Now it's time to look at the various structures of the brain, starting from the bottom and working up to the top. (A word of caution: This text won't be discussing every single part of the brain, only the parts interesting to psychologists as explorers of human behaviour. Many parts of the brain also overlap in their functions, but a full understanding of the brain is not truly possible within one chapter of an introductory psychology text.)

2.9 *What are the different structures of the bottom part of the brain, and what do they do?*

THE HINDBRAIN

The hindbrain is one of the oldest parts of the brain and, as such, its various components are responsible for controlling our basic life-sustaining reflexes (e.g., breathing, swallowing, heart rate, sleeping). Let's look at some specific hindbrain parts in more detail.

MEDULLA The **medulla** (which, oddly enough, means "marrow" or "inner substance") is located at the top of the spinal column. In Figure 2.11, it is the first "swelling" at the top of the spinal cord, at the very bottom of the brain. This is the part of the brain that a person would least want to have damaged, as it controls life-sustaining functions such as heart rate, breathing, and swallowing. The upper part of the spinal cord and the lower part of the brain are highly interconnected. It is in the medulla that the sensory nerves coming from the left and right sides of the body cross over, so that the sensory information from the left side of the body goes to the right side of the brain and vice versa.

PONS   The **pons** is the larger "swelling" just above the medulla. This term means "bridge," and the pons is indeed the bridge between the lower parts of the brain and the upper sections. As in the medulla, there is a crossover of nerves, but in this case it is the motor nerves carrying messages from the brain to the body. This allows the pons to coordinate the movements of the left and right sides of the body. The pons also influences sleep and dreaming, coordination of movements on the right and left sides of the body, and arousal. The role that the pons plays in sleep and dreams will be discussed in more detail in Chapter Four. (L)(I)(N)(K) to *Chapter Four: Consciousness, p. 134.*

THE RETICULAR FORMATION   The **reticular formation (RF)** is an area of neurons running through the middle of the medulla and the pons and slightly beyond. These neurons are responsible for people's ability to selectively attend to certain kinds of information in their surroundings. Basically, the RF allows people to ignore constant, unchanging information (such as the noise of an air conditioner) and become alert to changes in information (e.g., if the air conditioner stopped, most people would notice immediately).

The RF is also the part of the brain that helps keep people alert and aroused. One part of the RF is called the *reticular activating system (RAS)*, and it stimulates

pons
the larger swelling above the medulla that connects the top of the brain to the bottom and plays a part in sleep, dreaming, left–right body coordination, and arousal.

reticular formation (RF)
an area of neurons running through the middle of the medulla and the pons, and slightly beyond, that is responsible for selective attention.

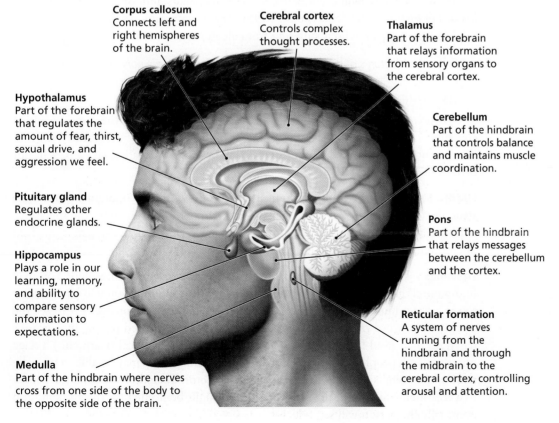

FIGURE 2.11 **The Major Structures of the Human Brain**

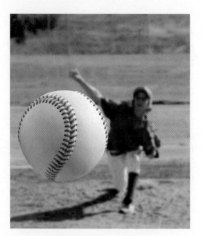

This pitcher must count on his cerebellum to help him balance and coordinate the many fine muscle commands that allow him to pitch the baseball accurately and swiftly. What other kinds of professions depend heavily on the activity of the cerebellum?

So if your cerebellum ▶ is damaged, you might be very uncoordinated?

❋ Explore on **mypsychlab**
The Limbic System

cerebellum
part of the lower brain located behind the pons that controls and coordinates involuntary, rapid, fine motor movement.

limbic system
a group of several brain structures located under the cortex and involved in learning, emotion, memory, and motivation.

the upper part of the brain, keeping people awake and alert. When a person is driving along and someone suddenly pulls out in front of the vehicle, it is the RAS that brings that driver to full attention. It is also the system that lets a mother hear her baby cry in the night, even though she might sleep through other noises. The RAS has also been suggested by brain-scanning studies as a possible area involved in attention deficit hyperactivity disorder, in which children or adults have difficulty maintaining attention to a single task (Durston, 2003).

Studies have shown that when the RF of rats is electrically stimulated while they are sleeping, they immediately awaken. If the RF is destroyed (e.g., by deep lesioning), they fall into a sleeplike coma from which they never awaken (Moruzzi & Magoun, 1949; Steriade & McCarley, 1990). The RF is also implicated in comas in humans (Plum & Posner, 1985).

CEREBELLUM At the base of the skull, behind the pons and below the main part of the brain, is a structure that looks like a small brain (see Figure 2.11). This is the **cerebellum** (meaning "little brain"). The cerebellum is the part of the lower brain that controls all involuntary, rapid, fine motor movement. People can sit upright because the cerebellum controls all the little muscles needed to keep them from falling out of their chair. It also coordinates voluntary movements that have to happen in rapid succession, such as walking, diving, skating, gymnastics, dancing, typing (once it has been learned well), playing a musical instrument, and even the movements of speech. Learned reflexes, skills, and habits are also stored here—which allows them to become more or less automatic. Because of the cerebellum, people don't have to consciously think about their posture, muscle tone, and balance.

So if your cerebellum is damaged, you might be very uncoordinated? Yes. In fact, in a disease called *spinocerebellar degeneration*, the first symptoms are tremors, an unsteady walk, slurred speech, dizziness, and muscle weakness. The person suffering from this disease will eventually be unable to walk, stand, or even get a spoon to his or her own mouth (Schöls et al., 1998). These symptoms are similar to what one might see in a person who is suffering from alcohol intoxication.

2.10 *Which structures of the brain control emotion, learning, memory, and motivation?*

STRUCTURES UNDER THE CORTEX
The cortex, which is discussed in detail later in this chapter, is the outer wrinkled covering of the brain. But there are a number of important structures located just under the cortex and above the brain stem. Each of these structures plays a part in our behaviour (see Figure 2.12).

LIMBIC SYSTEM The **limbic system** (the word *limbic* means "marginal," and these structures are found in the inner margin of the upper brain) includes the thalamus, hypothalamus, hippocampus, and amygdala. In general, the limbic system is involved in emotions, motivation, and learning.

Thalamus Have you ever had to go to the emergency room of a hospital? You may find yourself getting past the receptionist, but most of the time you will have to wait to see a *triage* nurse before you ever get to see the doctor—if you ever get to see the doctor. (The word *triage* refers to a process for sorting injured people into groups based on their need for or likely benefit from immediate medical treatment.) Triage nurses will ask people questions about their complaints. They may be able to partially treat minor complaints before the person sees a doctor. Then they will send the person to a treatment room with the equipment that might be needed for the ailment, and eventually the person will see a doctor.

FIGURE 2.12 **The Limbic System**

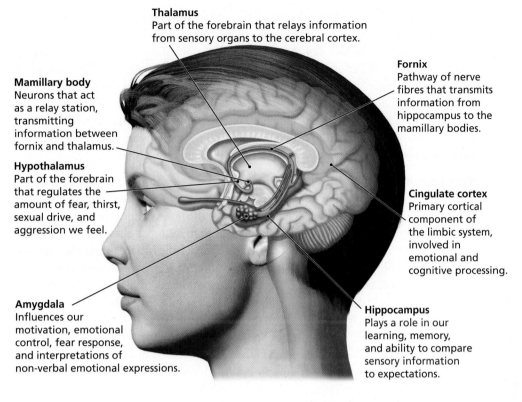

Thalamus
Part of the forebrain that relays information from sensory organs to the cerebral cortex.

Mamillary body
Neurons that act as a relay station, transmitting information between fornix and thalamus.

Hypothalamus
Part of the forebrain that regulates the amount of fear, thirst, sexual drive, and aggression we feel.

Amygdala
Influences our motivation, emotional control, fear response, and interpretations of non-verbal emotional expressions.

Fornix
Pathway of nerve fibres that transmits information from hippocampus to the mamillary bodies.

Cingulate cortex
Primary cortical component of the limbic system, involved in emotional and cognitive processing.

Hippocampus
Plays a role in our learning, memory, and ability to compare sensory information to expectations.

The **thalamus** ("inner chamber") is in some ways similar to a triage nurse. This somewhat round structure in the centre of the brain acts as a kind of relay station for incoming sensory information. Like a nurse, the thalamus might perform some processing of that sensory information before sending it on to the part of the cortex that deals with that kind of sensation—hearing, sight, touch, or taste. Damage to the thalamus might result in the loss or partial loss of any or all of those sensations.

The sense of smell is unique in that signals from the neurons in the sinus cavity go directly into special parts of the brain called *olfactory bulbs*, just under the front part of the brain. Smell is the only sense that cannot be affected by damage to the thalamus.

Hypothalamus   A very small but extremely powerful part of the brain is located just below and in front of the thalamus (see Figure 2.12). The **hypothalamus** ("below the inner chamber") regulates body temperature, thirst, hunger, sleeping and waking, sexual activity, and emotions. It sits right above the *pituitary gland*, which is called the *master gland* because it controls the functions of all the other endocrine glands that will be discussed later in this chapter. The hypothalamus controls the pituitary, so the ultimate regulation of hormones lies with the hypothalamus.

Recently an interesting finding occurred at Toronto Western Hospital. Neurosurgeon Dr. Andres Lozano began treating a 50-year-old man with morbid obesity by electrically stimulating parts of his hypothalamus. He was looking for areas in the hypothalamus that would help suppress the man's appetite. Suddenly the patient experienced a strong sense of déjà vu. He reported remembering being in a park with friends some 30 years previous, when he was about 20 years old. As Dr. Lozano increased the electrical current the memory became more vivid. This was a most unexpected finding as the hypothalamus is not traditionally thought of as a memory centre. Further tests showed that stimulation

thalamus
part of the limbic system located in the centre of the brain, this structure relays sensory information from the lower part of the brain to the proper areas of the cortex and processes some sensory information before sending it to its proper area.

hypothalamus
small structure in the brain located below the thalamus and directly above the pituitary gland, responsible for motivational behaviour such as sleep, hunger, thirst, and sex.

hippocampus
curved structure located within each temporal lobe, responsible for the formation of long-term memories and the storage of memory for location of objects.

amygdala
brain structure located near the hippocampus, responsible for fear responses and memory of fear.

to this part of the hypothalamus increased the activity in the hippocampus (see next section) and temporal lobe, two areas known to be important in memory. What was even more surprising was the fact that the man, who had normal memory before the surgery, started to score far higher on tests of memory and learning as long as the electrodes, which remained in his brain, were stimulated by the pacemaker implanted in his shoulder. This serendipitous finding has led Toronto researchers to implant electrodes into the same hypothalamic area of six Alzheimer's patients to try to improve their memory. The findings are still preliminary, but Dr. Lozano reports that all the patients are doing fine and there has been some indication of improved memory (Hamani et al., 2008).

Hippocampus   **Hippocampus** is the Greek word for "seahorse," and this structure of the brain was given this name because the first scientists who dissected the brain thought it looked like a seahorse. Research has shown that the hippocampus is instrumental in forming long-term (permanent) memories that are then stored elsewhere in the brain (Bigler et al., 1996). Many researchers consider the hippocampus the "gateway to memory." Much of what we know about this gateway function has come from studies done by Dr. Brenda Milner and her colleagues at the Montreal Neurological Institute on one patient named H. M., who had parts of his hippocampus removed on both sides of his brain (Corkin, 1984). You will learn more about H. M. in Chapter Six. ⓛⓘⓝⓚ *to Chapter Six: Memory, p. 218.*

Acetylcholine, the neurotransmitter involved in muscle control, is also involved in the memory function of the hippocampus. People who have Alzheimer's, for example, have much lower levels of acetylcholine in that structure than is normal. The hippocampus is located within the temporal lobes on each side of the brain, and electrical stimulation of the temporal lobe may produce memory-like or dream-like experiences.

The hippocampus may be very close to the area of the brain where the memories for locations of objects are stored as well. Researchers have found that the right parahippocampal gyrus, located alongside the right hippocampus, is more active when a person is planning a travel route (Maguire et al., 1998), which might explain why elderly people who develop memory problems associated with deterioration of the hippocampus also tend to forget where they live, where they parked the car, and similar location problems. Deterioration in the hippocampal area may spread to or affect other nearby areas.

This young man's thirst is regulated by his hypothalamus.

Amygdala   The **amygdala** ("almond") is an area of the brain located near the hippocampus. These two structures seem to be responsible for fear responses and memory of fear. The amygdala, along with the hypothalamus, also activates circuits in the brain stem that control aggressive behaviour (Siegel et al., 1999). Information from the senses goes to the amygdala before the upper part of the brain is even involved, so that people can respond to danger very quickly, sometimes before they are consciously aware of what is happening. In 1939, researchers found that monkeys with large parts of their temporal lobes removed—including the amygdala—were completely unafraid of snakes and humans, both normally fear-provoking stimuli (Klüver & Bucy, 1939). This effect came to be known as the *Klüver–Bucy syndrome.* Rats that have damaged amygdala structures will also show no fear when placed next to a cat (Maren & Fanselow, 1996). Humans with damage to the amygdala also show decreased fear (Adophs et al., 2005).

What about Michelle M. from the story at the beginning? Was she missing any of these structures? ▶

What about Michelle M. from the story at the beginning? Was she missing any of these structures? Michelle M. did have some abnormalities in a few of these structures, but her greatest "missing piece" was one-half of a very important brain structure, the cortex. The next section explores the cortex and its functions.

PRACTICE QUIZ: HOW MUCH DO YOU REMEMBER?

Pick the best answer.

1. Which of the following techniques for peeking inside the brain is associated with the work of Wilder Penfield?
   a. electroencephalogram
   b. electrical stimulation of the brain
   c. magnetic resonance imaging
   d. computed tomography

2. Which of the following techniques uses a radioactive sugar to look at the functioning of the brain?
   a. EEG   c. MRI
   b. CT   d. PET

3. Which brain structure is most responsible for our balance, posture, and muscle tone?
   a. medulla   c. reticular formation
   b. cerebellum   d. pons

4. Damage to which brain structure would most likely result in death?
   a. medulla   c. reticular formation
   b. cerebellum   d. pons

5. If you were to develop a rare condition in which signals from your eyes were sent to the area of the brain that processes sound, and signals from the ears were sent to the area of the brain that processes vision, which part of the brain would most likely be damaged?
   a. hippocampus   c. thalamus
   b. hypothalamus   d. amygdala

6. Which part of the brain did Dr. Andres Lozano stimulate in order to help someone lose weight?
   a. the hippocampus   c. the hindbrain
   b. the hypothalamus   d. the amygdala

7. If you have problems storing new memories, the damage is most likely in the _____ area of the brain.
   a. hippocampus   c. cerebellum
   b. hypothalamus   d. amygdala

8. What are the initials of Canada's most famous amnesiac, whose condition led to the discovery that the hippocampus is the "gateway to memory"?
   a. T. H.   c. H. M.
   b. H. F.   d. Can't remember!

Answers: 1.-b, 2.-d, 3.-b, 4.-a, 5.-c, 6.-b, 7.-a, 8.-c.

THE CORTEX

As stated earlier, the **cortex** ("rind" or outer covering) is the outermost part of the brain, which is the part of the brain most people picture when they think of what the brain looks like. It is made up of tightly packed neurons and actually is only about 2 to 3 millimetres thick on average (Fischl et al., 2001; MacDonald et al., 2000; Zilles, 1990). The tissue appears greyish pink because the tightly packed neural bodies are grey and the small blood vessels appear pink. The cortex is very recognizable because it is full of wrinkles.

Why is the cortex so wrinkled? The wrinkling of the cortex allows a much larger area of cortical cells to exist in the small space inside the skull. If the cortex were to be taken out, ironed flat, and measured, it would be about 1400 square centimetres. As the brain develops before birth, it forms a smooth outer covering on all the other brain structures. This will be the cortex, which will get more and more wrinkled as the brain increases in size and complexity. This increase in wrinkling is called *corticalization* and is the real measure of human intelligence.

2.11 *Which parts of the cortex control the different senses and the movement of the body?*

THE LOBES AND THEIR SPECIALTIES   The cortex is divided into two sections called the **cerebral hemispheres**, which are connected by a thick, tough band of neural bodies called the **corpus callosum** (literally meaning "hard bodies," as calluses on the feet are hard). (Refer back to Figure 2.11 on p. 65.) Each hemisphere can be roughly divided into four sections by looking at the deeper wrinkles, or fissures, in its surface (see Figure 2.13). (Remember, Michelle M.'s left hemisphere never developed—she had only the right hemisphere, and so only the right-side lobes.)

Occipital Lobes   At the base of the cortex, toward the back of the brain, is an area called the **occipital lobe** (the term *occipital* refers to the rear of the head). This area processes visual information from the eyes in the *primary visual cortex*. The *visual association*

◀ Why is the cortex so wrinkled?

◉ **Watch** on **mypsychlab**
The Human Cerebrum

cortex
outermost covering of the brain consisting of densely packed neurons, responsible for higher thought processes and interpretation of sensory input.

cerebral hemispheres
the two sections of the cortex on the left and right sides of the brain.

corpus callosum
thick band of neurons that connects the right and left cerebral hemispheres.

occipital lobe
section of the brain located at the rear and bottom of each cerebral hemisphere containing the visual centres of the brain.

parietal lobes
sections of the brain located at the top and back of each cerebral hemisphere containing the centres for touch, taste, and temperature sensations.

somatosensory cortex
area of neurons running down the front of the parietal lobes responsible for processing information from the skin and internal body receptors for touch, temperature, body position, and possibly taste.

temporal lobes
areas of the cortex located just behind the temples containing the neurons responsible for the sense of hearing and meaningful speech.

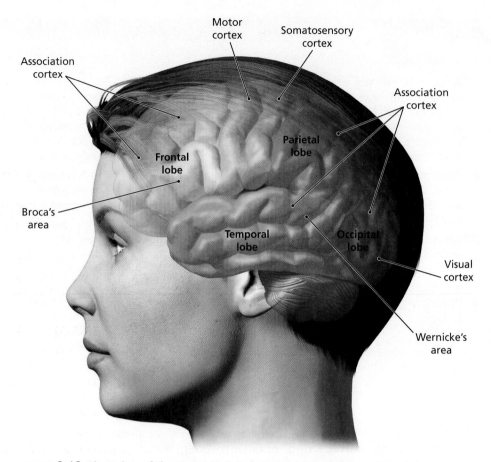

FIGURE 2.13 **The Lobes of the Brain: Occipital, Parietal, Temporal, and Frontal**

This boxer must rely on his parietal lobes to sense where his body is in relation to the floor of the ring and the other boxer, his occipital lobes to see his target, and his frontal lobes to guide his hand and arm into the punch.

These young women are processing the music in their temporal lobes.

cortex, also in this lobe, is the part of the brain that helps identify and make sense of the visual information from the eyes. The famed neurologist Oliver Sacks once had a patient who had a tumour in his right occipital lobe area. He could still see objects perfectly well and even describe them in physical terms, but he could not identify them by sight alone. For example, Sacks once gave him a rose to look at. The man turned it around and around and began to describe it as a "red inflorescence" of some type with a green tubular projection. Only when he held it under his nose (stimulating the sense of smell) did he recognize it as a rose (Sacks, 1990). Each area of the cortex has these association areas that help people make sense of sensory information.

Have you ever wondered why people sometimes "see stars" after being hit in the rear of the head? Because the area of the brain at the back of the head processes vision, any stimulation to that area will be interpreted as vision—hence, the "stars."

Parietal Lobes The **parietal lobes** (*parietal* means "wall") are at the top and back of the brain, just under the parietal bone in the skull. This area contains the **somatosensory cortex**, an area of neurons (see Figure 2.13) running down the front of the parietal lobes on either side of the brain. This area processes information from the skin and internal body receptors for touch, temperature, and body position. The somatosensory cortex is laid out in a rather interesting way—the cells at the top of the brain receive information from the bottom of the body, and as one moves down the area, the signals come from higher and higher in the body. It's almost as if a little upside-down person were laid out along this area of cells.

Temporal Lobes The **temporal lobes** (*temporal* means "of or near the temples") are found just behind the temples of the head. These lobes contain the *primary auditory* *cortex* and the *auditory association area.* If a person receives a blow to the side of the head, that person will probably "hear" a ringing sound. Also found in the left temporal lobe is an area that in most people is particularly involved with language. Oddly, the sense of taste also seems to be processed in the temporal lobe, deep inside a cortical fold, rather than in the parietal lobe (Fresquet et al., 2004).

Frontal Lobes   These lobes are at the front of the brain, hence, the name **frontal lobes**. (It doesn't often get this easy in psychology; feel free to take a moment to appreciate it.) Here are found all the higher mental functions of the brain—planning, personality, memory storage, complex decision making, and (again in the left hemisphere in most people) areas devoted to language. The frontal lobe also helps in controlling emotions by means of its connection to the limbic system. Phineas Gage lacked this emotional control because he had suffered damage to his frontal lobe, which damaged this connection with the limbic system, particularly the amygdala. ⓛⓘⓝⓚ *to Chapter One: The Science of Psychology, p. 21.* People with damage to this area of the brain may also experience problems with performing mental tasks, getting stuck on one step or one wrong answer and repeating it over and over again (Goel & Grafman, 1995).

The frontal lobes also contain the **motor cortex**, a band of neurons located at the back of each lobe (see Figure 2.14). These cells control the movements of the

frontal lobes
areas of the cortex located in the front and top of the brain, responsible for higher mental processes and decision making as well as the production of fluent speech.

motor cortex
section of the frontal lobe located at the back, responsible for sending motor commands to the muscles of the somatic nervous system.

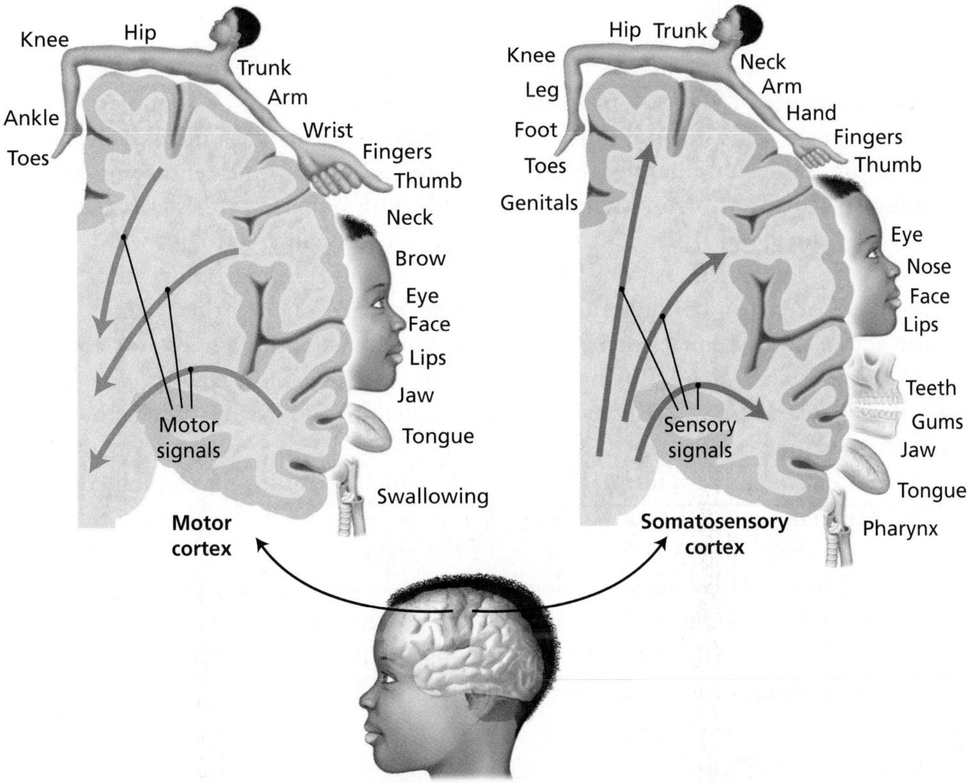

FIGURE 2.14 **The Motor and Somatosensory Cortex** The motor cortex in the frontal lobe controls the voluntary muscles of the body. Cells at the top of the motor cortex control muscles at the bottom of the body, whereas cells at the bottom of the motor cortex control muscles at the top of the body. Body parts are drawn larger or smaller according to the number of cortical cells devoted to that body part. For example, the hand has many small muscles and requires a larger area of cortical cells to control it. The somatosensory cortex, located in the parietal lobe just behind the motor cortex, is organized in much the same manner and receives information about the sense of touch and body position.

You've mentioned association cortex a few times. Do the other lobes of the brain contain association ▶ cortex as well?

body's voluntary muscles by sending commands out to the somatic division of the peripheral nervous system. The motor cortex is laid out just like the somatosensory cortex right next door in the parietal lobes. This mirror-image layout allows for fast response times between the processing of sensory information and the production of motor responses. For example, if a person's hand touches something squishy, the information about that touch sensation is received in the somatosensory cortex area right next to the motor cortex area that will let the person pull his or her hand back quickly.

You've mentioned association cortex a few times. Do the other lobes of the brain contain association cortex as well?

THE ASSOCIATION AREAS OF THE CORTEX

2.12 *Which parts of the cortex are responsible for higher forms of thought, such as language?*

Association areas are made up of neurons in the cortex that are devoted to making connections between the sensory information coming into the brain and stored memories, images, and knowledge. In other words, association areas help people make sense of the incoming sensory input. Although the association areas in the occipital and temporal lobes have already been mentioned, the bulk of the brain's association cortex is in the frontal lobes. Some special association areas are worth talking about in more detail.

BROCA'S AREA   In the left frontal lobe of most people is an area of the brain devoted to the production of speech. (In a small portion of the population, this area is in the right frontal lobe.) More specifically, this area allows a person to speak smoothly and fluently. It is called *Broca's area* after nineteenth-century neurologist Paul Broca, who first studied people with damage to this area (Leonard, 1997). Damage to Broca's area causes a person to be unable to get words out in a smooth, connected fashion. People with this condition may know exactly what they want to say and understand what they hear others say, but they cannot control the actual production of their own words. Speech is halting and words are often mispronounced, such as saying *cot* instead of *clock* or *non* instead of *nine*. This is called **Broca's aphasia**. *Aphasia* refers to an inability to use or understand either written or spoken language (Goodglass et al., 2001). Persons who suffer many head injuries or concussions in their lifetime are at higher risk for developing cognitive impairments such as Broca's aphasia. For a more in-depth discussion of concussions and their effect on the brain, read the tragic story of Chris Benoit, former WWE Champion, in the Psychology in the News section that follows. (Stuttering is a somewhat different problem in that a person has trouble getting words *started*, rather than mispronouncing them or leaving them out, but it may also be related to Broca's area.)

association areas
areas within each lobe of the cortex responsible for the coordination and interpretation of information, as well as higher mental processing.

Broca's aphasia
condition resulting from damage to Broca's area, causing the affected person to be unable to speak fluently, to mispronounce words, and to speak haltingly.

PSYCHOLOGY IN THE NEWS

Former WWE Champion Chris Benoit Kills Family, Then Himself: Was It "Roid Rage" or Brain Injury?

Chris Benoit was born in Montreal and grew up in Edmonton. Chris grew up idolizing wrestling legend Tommy Billington (a.k.a. The Dynamite Kid) and trained with Canada's first family of wrestling, the Harts, in the infamous "Hart Family Dungeon" (Pilson, 2000). In 1986, Chris made his debut in Stampede Wrestling. After successful stints in Japan, where he wrestled as the Pegasus Kid, Chris returned to North America. In 2004, he had reached the pinnacle of the wrestling world. He defeated Shawn Michaels and Triple H in a spectacular triple-threat match at Madison Square Garden in New York City, and was now the WWE's World Champion (Cohen, 2007; Milner, 2007). In recognition of this feat, the City of Edmonton declared April 15, 2004, Chris Benoit Day (CTV.ca News Staff, 2007).

Despite all the fame and fortune, tragedy would strike the Benoit home. In June 2007, police in Atlanta discovered the bodies of Chris, Chris's wife, Nancy, and their son, Daniel, in their suburban home. It was ruled a murder–suicide. Chris had killed his wife, then his son, and finally took his own life. Officers at the scene found anabolic steroids, and it was later confirmed that Chris had elevated levels of testosterone in his blood. Early speculation pointed to "roid rage" to explain Chris's behaviour. Roid rage is a condition that sometimes occurs in long-time and heavy users of anabolic steroids. Symptoms often include increased levels of anti-social behaviour, criminality, mania, and depression. In addition, anabolic steroids are linked to violent outbursts of anger, increased aggression, and hostile behaviour. It is this cluster of impulsive symptoms that is often described as "roid rage." However, as details surrounding the murder–suicide began to surface, many of Chris's actions did not appear impulsive. He sedated his son prior to murdering him and placed bibles beside the bodies of his wife and son (Dornin & Reiss, 2007). Might there be another explanation of Chris's bizarre behaviour?

Upon autopsy of Chris's brain by experts Bennet Omalu and Julian Bailes of the Sports Legacy Institute in West Virginia, it was concluded that Chris's brain was so severely damaged that it resembled the brain of an 85-year-old Alzheimer's patient. The official term used to describe the damage to Chris's brain is *chronic traumatic encephalopathy (CTE)*. CTE's most common symptoms include depression, cognitive impairment, dementia, Parkinsonism, and erratic behaviour, often leading to personal and business problems. CTE has long been known to exist in boxers and soccer players. Former National Football League stars Andre Waters and Terry Long, who both committed suicide recently, suffered from the condition, which can be diagnosed only at autopsy. CTE is thought to develop from a history of head trauma and concussions (Sports Legacy Institute, 2007). This is also likely to be the case for Chris Benoit, who in the ring was often struck in the head by objects such as chairs and ladders. Chris once reported, "I've had more concussions than I can count!" The damage to Chris's brain was extensive (see the photo). Areas of damage included all four cortical lobes, the limbic system, basal ganglia, and brain stem. The experts believe that this brain damage, likely caused by years of impacts to Chris's head during his prolific wrestling career, is the leading factor when attempting to explain Chris's actions. The experts further stated that chronic steroid use does not cause this type of brain damage.

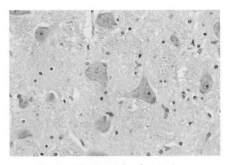

This is a photograph of a section of the cerebral cortex in a non-damaged, healthy brain. Compare this photograph to the one below, showcasing Chris Benoit's cerebral cortex.

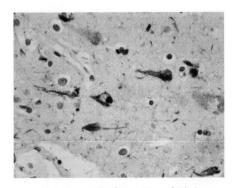

A photograph of a section of Chris Benoit's cerebral cortex. What kinds of damage do you see when you compare Chris's brain with that of the healthy cerebral cortex above? The damage here is thought to have been caused by repeated head injuries experienced during his wrestling career. Similar types of cortical damage are found in other athletes involved in contact sports. Persons with this type of damage to their cerebral cortex often show signs of depression, cognitive impairment (i.e., difficulty with language, memory, or problem solving), dementia, Parkinson's disease, and erratic behaviour.

© 2008 Sports Legacy Institute

Explore on mypsychlab
Brain Damage and Neuroplasticity

Questions for Further Discussion

1. Do you think "roid rage" or CTE is the more likely cause of Chris Benoit's actions?

2. Should helmets be mandatory equipment for skateboarders and snowboarders?

3. Should athletes who are known to have suffered from numerous concussions be forced to retire?

4. Should sports such as boxing and wrestling be banned?

WERNICKE'S AREA   In the left temporal lobe (again, in most people) is an area called *Wernicke's area*, named after the physiologist and Broca's contemporary, Carl Wernicke, who first studied problems arising from damage in this location. This area of the brain appears to be involved in understanding the meaning of words (Goodglass et al., 2001). A person with **Wernicke's aphasia** would be able to speak fluently and pronounce words correctly, but the words would be the wrong ones entirely. For example, Elsie suffered a stroke to the temporal lobe, damaging this area of the brain. In the emergency room, the nurse tried to take her blood pressure, and when the cuff inflated, Elsie said, "Oh, that's so Saturday hard." Now, what does "Saturday hard" mean? Neither the nurse nor Elsie's daughter could figure that one out, but Elsie *thought* she was making sense. She also had trouble understanding what the people around her were saying to her. In another instance, Ernest suffered a stroke at the age of 80 and developed complete aphasia. As he recovered, he showed some telltale signs of Wernicke's aphasia. In one instance, he asked his wife to get him some milk out of the air conditioner. When she told him that he surely meant to say "refrigerator," he got angry and told her he knew what he was saying: "Now get me some milk out of the air conditioner, woman!"

SPATIAL NEGLECT   Remember that not all association areas are in the frontal or temporal lobes. Damage to association areas of the right occipital and parietal cortical lobes can produce an odd condition called **spatial neglect**. For example, a person with damage to the right occipital association cortex may fail to recognize the left side of the visual field and may not shave or apply makeup to the left side of the face. Although spatial neglect can affect the left hemisphere, this condition occurs less frequently and in a much milder form than right-hemisphere neglect (Heilman et al., 1993; Springer & Deutsch, 1998).

THE CEREBRAL HEMISPHERES: ARE YOU IN YOUR RIGHT MIND?

I've heard that some people are right-brained and some are left-brained. Are the two sides of the brain really that different? Most people tend to think of the two cerebral hemispheres as identical twins. Both sides have the same four lobes and are arranged in pretty much the same way. But language seems to be confined to only the left hemisphere in about 90 percent of the population (Toga & Thompson, 2003). What other special tasks do the two halves of the **cerebrum** (the upper part of the brain consisting of the two hemispheres and the structures that connect them) engage in, and how do researchers know about such functions?

2.13 *How does the left side of the brain differ from the right side?*

SPLIT-BRAIN RESEARCH   Roger Sperry was a pioneer in the field of hemisphere specialization. He won a Nobel Prize for his work in demonstrating that the left and right hemispheres of the brain specialize in different activities and functions (Sperry, 1968). In looking for a way to cure epilepsy (severe muscle spasms or seizures result-

---

Wernicke's aphasia
condition resulting from damage to Wernicke's area, causing the affected person to be unable to understand or produce meaningful language.

spatial neglect
condition produced by damage to the association areas of the right hemisphere resulting in an inability to recognize objects or body parts in the left visual field.

cerebrum
the upper part of the brain consisting of the two hemispheres and the structures that connect them.

I've heard that some people are right-brained and some are ▶ left-brained. Are the two sides of the brain really that different?

◀●─ **Simulate** on **mypsychlab**

Split-Brain Experiments

TABLE 2.2 SPECIALIZATION OF THE TWO HEMISPHERES

LEFT HEMISPHERE	RIGHT HEMISPHERE
Controls the right hand	Controls the left hand
Spoken language	Non-verbal
Written language	Visuospatial perception
Mathematical calculations	Music and artistic processing
Logical thought processes	Emotional thought and recognition
Analysis of detail	Processes the whole
Reading	Pattern recognition
	Facial recognition

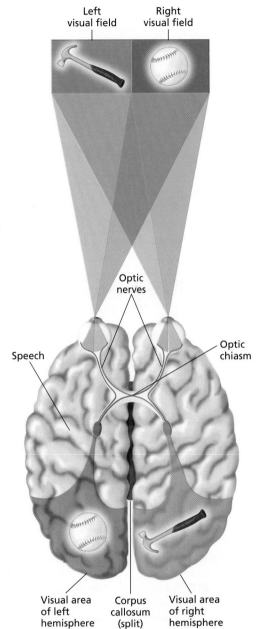

FIGURE 2.15 **The Split-Brain Experiment** Roger Sperry created this experiment to demonstrate the specialization of the left and right hemispheres of the brain.

ing from brain damage), Sperry cut through the corpus callosum, the thick band of neurons that joins the two hemispheres. In early research with animals, this technique worked and seemed to have no side effects. The first people to have this procedure done also experienced relief from their severe epileptic symptoms, but testing found that (in a sense) they now had two brains in one body.

The special testing involves sending messages to only one side of the brain, which is now possible because the connecting tissue, the corpus callosum, has been cut. Figure 2.15 shows a picture of a typical split-brain patient seated in front of a screen.

If a picture of a ball is flashed to the right side of the screen, the image of the ball will be sent to the left occipital lobe. The person will be able to say that he or she sees a ball. If a picture of a hammer is flashed to the left side of the screen, the person will not be able to verbally identify the object or be able to state with any certainty that something was seen. But if the left hand (controlled by the right hemisphere) is used, the person can point to the hammer he or she "didn't see." The right occipital lobe clearly saw the hammer, but the person could not verbalize that fact (Sperry, 1968). By doing studies such as these, researchers have found that the left hemisphere specializes in language, speech, handwriting, calculation (math), sense of time and rhythm (which is mathematical in nature), and basically any kind of thought requiring analysis. The right hemisphere appears to specialize in more global (widespread) processing involving perception; visualization; spatial perception; recognition of patterns, faces, emotions, and melodies; and expression of emotions. It also comprehends simple language but does not produce speech.

Springer and Deutsch (1998) found that, in general, the left hemisphere processes information in a sequence and is good at breaking things down into smaller parts, or performing analysis. The right hemisphere, by contrast, processes information all at once and simultaneously, a more global or holistic* style of processing. Remember the discussion in Chapter One of the early days of psychology, the structuralists and the Gestalt psychologists? One could almost say that the left hemisphere of the brain is a structuralist, who wants to break everything down into its smallest parts, and the right side of the brain is a Gestaltist, who wants to study only the whole (see Table 2.2).

So there really are left-brained and right-brained people? And how could Michelle M. talk and read without a left hemisphere? Actually, unless one is a split-brain patient, the two sides of the brain are always working together as an integrated whole. For example, the right side might recognize someone's face, while

---

*Holistic: relating to or concerned with complete systems or wholes

So there really are left-brained and right-brained people? And how could Michelle M. talk and read without a left hemisphere?

the left side struggles to recall the person's name. People aren't really left- or right-brained, they are whole-brained. (Well, most of them, anyway.) And in the case of Michelle M., neuroscientists think that her right hemisphere was able to "learn" what would normally be left hemisphere tasks through Michelle's own actions and her parents' constant encouragement—neuroplasticity in action!

The separate functions of the left and right sides of the brain are often confused with handedness, or the tendency to use one hand for most fine motor skills. While most right-handed people also have their left hemisphere in control of their other fine motor skills, such as speech, a few right-handers actually have their language functions in the right hemisphere, in spite of the dominance of the left hemisphere for controlling the right hand. Among left-handed people, there are also many who, although right-brain dominant, still have their language functions on the left side of the brain. Why? How much time do you have? There are far too many theories of why we use one hand over the other to cover in this text.

PRACTICE QUIZ: HOW MUCH DO YOU REMEMBER?

Pick the best answer.

1. In which of the following lobes of the cortex would you find the primary auditory area?
   a. frontal
   b. temporal
   c. occipital
   d. parietal

2. Which of the following is the name for the thick band of neurons that connects the left and right sides of the cortex?
   a. fornix
   b. corpus callosum
   c. Wernicke's area
   d. thalamus

3. The higher mental functions, such as thinking and problem solving, are found in the _____ lobe.
   a. frontal
   b. parietal
   c. temporal
   d. occipital

4. When researchers looked at Chris Benoit's 40-year-old brain, what did they find?
   a. It looked like that of an 85-year-old man with Alzheimer's disease.
   b. It looked like any other normal 40-year-old brain.
   c. It was enlarged due to steroid use.
   d. It looked like a 20-year-old brain because of Benoit's superior conditioning.

5. In an old *Twilight Zone* episode, a man wakes up one morning to find that people around him are using words that make no sense to him, and they also don't seem to understand him. His wife tells him that their son forgot his dinosaur today, and when he looks puzzled, she holds up the son's lunchbox and repeats, "You know, his dinosaur." This man's predicament is most like which of the following disorders?
   a. Wernicke's aphasia
   b. Broca's aphasia
   c. apraxia
   d. spatial neglect

6. If you are a split-brain patient, which of the following would be true?
   a. Objects in your left visual field would be easily named.
   b. Objects in your left visual field are invisible.
   c. Objects in your right visual field would be easily named.
   d. Objects in your right visual field are invisible.

Answers: 1.-b, 2.-b, 3.-a, 4.-a, 5.-a, 6.-c.

THE CHEMICAL CONNECTION: THE ENDOCRINE GLANDS

How do the glands fit into all of this? Aren't there more glands than just the adrenal glands? How do they affect our behaviour? Glands are organs in the body that secrete chemicals. Some glands, such as salivary glands and sweat glands, secrete their chemicals directly onto the body's tissues through tiny tubes, or ducts. This kind of gland affects the functioning of the body but doesn't really affect behaviour. (It might affect the behaviour of people around a person who is drooling or stinky, though.) Other glands, called **endocrine glands**, have no ducts and secrete their chemicals directly into the bloodstream (see Figure 2.16). The chemicals secreted by this type of gland are called **hormones**. As mentioned earlier in the chapter when talking about

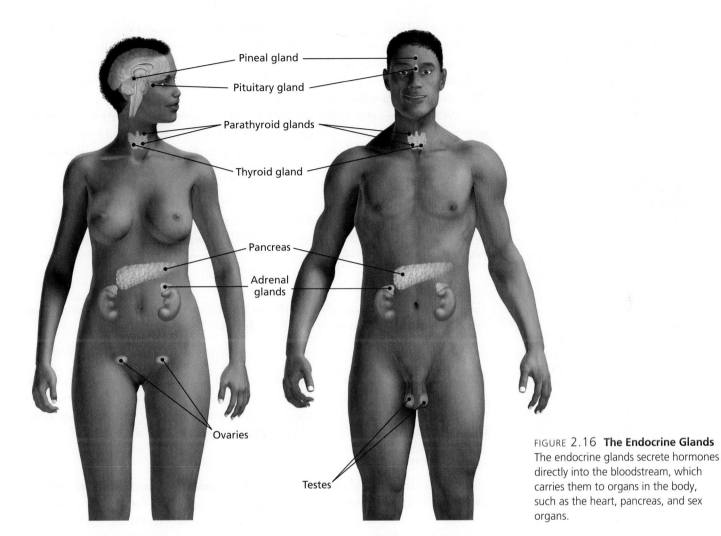

- Pineal gland
- Pituitary gland
- Parathyroid glands
- Thyroid gland
- Pancreas
- Adrenal glands
- Ovaries
- Testes

FIGURE 2.16 **The Endocrine Glands**
The endocrine glands secrete hormones directly into the bloodstream, which carries them to organs in the body, such as the heart, pancreas, and sex organs.

the sympathetic division of the autonomic nervous system, these hormones flow into the bloodstream, which carries them to their target organs. The molecules of these hormones then fit into receptor sites on those organs to fulfill their function, affecting behaviour as they do so.

2.14 *How do the hormones released by glands interact with the nervous system and affect behaviour?*

The hormones affect behaviour and emotions by controlling muscles and organs such as the heart, pancreas, and sex organs. Some theories of emotion state that the surge in certain hormones actually triggers the emotional reaction (Izard, 1988; Zajonc, 1980, 1984). ⓛⓘⓝⓚ *to Chapter Nine: Motivation and Emotion, p. 350.* Some of the hormones produced by endocrine glands also influence the activity of the brain, producing excitatory or inhibitory effects (Mai et al., 1987).

THE PITUITARY, MASTER OF THE HORMONAL UNIVERSE

The **pituitary gland** is located in the brain itself, just below the hypothalamus. The hypothalamus controls the glandular system by influencing the pituitary. That is because the pituitary gland is the *master gland*, the one that controls or influences all the other endocrine glands. One part of the pituitary controls things associated with

✳️⬛ **Explore** on **mypsychlab**
Virtual Brain: Hormones and Sex

hormones
chemicals released into the bloodstream by endocrine glands.

endocrine glands
glands that secrete chemicals called *hormones* directly into the bloodstream.

pituitary gland
gland located in the brain that secretes human growth hormone and influences all other hormone-secreting glands (also known as the *master gland*).

pineal gland
endocrine gland located near the base of the cerebrum that secretes melatonin.

thyroid gland
endocrine gland found in the neck that regulates metabolism.

pancreas
endocrine gland that controls the levels of sugar in the blood.

gonads
the sex glands that secrete hormones that regulate sexual development and behaviour as well as reproduction.

ovaries
the female gonads.

testes
the male gonads.

adrenal glands
endocrine glands located on top of each kidney that secrete more than 30 different hormones to deal with stress, regulate salt intake, and provide a secondary source of sex hormones affecting the sexual changes that occur during adolescence.

pregnancy, such as production of milk for nursing infants and the onset of labour, as well as the levels of salt and water in the body. Another part of the pituitary secretes several hormones that influence the activity of the other glands. Most notable of these hormones is a *growth hormone* that controls and regulates increases in size as children grow from infancy to adulthood.

As the master gland, the pituitary forms a very important part of a feedback system, one that includes the hypothalamus and the organs targeted by the various hormones. The balance of hormones in the entire endocrine system is maintained by feedback from each of these "players" to the others.

THE PINEAL GLAND

The **pineal gland** is also located in the brain, nearer to the back. It secretes a hormone called *melatonin*, which regulates the sleep–wake cycle. (LINK) to *Chapter Four: Consciousness, p. 134.*

THE THYROID GLAND

The **thyroid gland** is located inside the neck and secretes a hormone called *thyroxin* that regulates metabolism (how fast the body burns its available energy).

PANCREAS

The **pancreas** controls the level of blood sugar in the body by secreting *insulin* and *glucagons*. If the pancreas secretes too little insulin, it results in *diabetes*. If it secretes too much insulin, it results in *hypoglycemia*, or low blood sugar, which causes a person to feel hungry all the time and often become overweight as a result.

THE GONADS

The **gonads** are the sex glands, including the **ovaries** in the female and the **testes** in the male. They secrete hormones that regulate sexual behaviour and reproduction. They do not control all sexual behaviour, though. In a very real sense, the brain itself is the master of the sexual system—human sexual behaviour is not controlled totally by instincts and the actions of the glands as in the animal world but also by psychological factors such as attractiveness.

THE ADRENAL GLANDS

Everyone has two **adrenal glands**, one on top of each kidney. The origin of the name is simple enough; *renal* comes from a Latin word meaning "kidney" and *ad* is Latin for "to," so *adrenal* means "to or on the kidney." Each adrenal gland is actually divided into two sections, the *adrenal medulla* and the *adrenal cortex*. It is the adrenal medulla that releases epinephrine and norepinephrine when people are under stress and that aids in sympathetic arousal.

The adrenal cortex produces more than 30 different hormones called *corticoids* (also called *steroids*) that regulate salt intake and help initiate and control stress reactions, and also provides a source of sex hormones in addition to those provided by the gonads. One of the most important of these adrenal hormones is *cortisol*, which is released when the body experiences stress, both physical stress (such as illness, surgery, or extreme heat or cold) and psychological stress (such as an emotional upset). (LINK) *to Chapter Ten: Stress and Health, p. 396.* Cortisol is important in the release of glucose into the bloodstream during stress, providing energy for the brain itself, and the release of fatty acids from the fat cells that provide the muscles with energy.

Pick the best answer.

1. The endocrine glands secrete chemicals called
   a. pheromones into the bloodstream.
   b. hormones into the bloodstream.
   c. pheromones onto bodily tissues.
   d. hormones onto bodily tissues.

2. Andrew never grew to be very tall. The doctor told his parents that Andrew's _____ gland did not secrete enough growth hormone, causing his small stature.
   a. pituitary   **c.** thyroid
   b. adrenal   **d.** pancreas

3. If the pancreas secretes too little insulin, it causes
   a. diabetes.
   b. hypoglycemia.
   c. hypothyroidism.
   d. virilism.

Answers: 1.-b, 2.-a, 3.-a.

APPLYING PSYCHOLOGY TO EVERYDAY LIFE: REFLECTIONS ON MIRROR NEURONS

You have probably heard the old phrase "monkey see, monkey do." Neuroscientists have now discovered that the phrase "monkey see, monkey *cortex* do" is more appropriate. Psychologist Giacomo Rizzolatti and his colleagues at the University of Parma, Italy, while using implanted electrodes to examine neural activity in macaque monkeys, made an interesting discovery (Rizzolatti et al., 1996). The researchers wanted to determine which neurons were specifically involved in controlling the movement of the hands. They discovered that the same neurons that fired when the monkeys clutched a piece of food would also fire when the monkeys merely *watched the researchers* handle food. These neurons, which fire when an animal performs an action but also when an animal observes that same action being performed by another, are called **mirror neurons**. Brain-imaging techniques in human studies indicate that we, too, have mirror neurons (Buccino et al., 2001; Buccino et al., 2004; Iacoboni et al., 1999).

Psychologists are very excited about what the existence of mirror neurons means for social interaction and its influence on the brain and perception. Have you ever winced and ducked when watching someone in a hockey game get hit? Blame those mirror neurons. Do you see someone looking happy and feel you just have to smile also? Mirror neurons again—monkey see, monkey *feel*. Researchers have known for decades that in the first few weeks of life human infants will imitate the facial expressions of adults (Meltzoff, 1990, 2007; Meltzoff & Moore, 1989). Now mirror neurons seem to provide the neurological explanation for why infants can do this. We are apparently social creatures from the very beginning, reacting to the mere sight of what we see others doing.

Does the knowledge researchers are gathering about mirror neurons have any practical applications? Some studies find that when a stroke patient needs to relearn a motor skill, watching another person perform that skill can be effective in regaining it (Binkofski & Buccino, 2006; Ertelt et al., 2007).

Experts in the field of *autism*, a disorder that is primarily social, are now becoming convinced that autism may be due at least in part to a faulty mirror system in the brain (Dapretto et al., 2006; Oberman et al., 2005; Oberman & Ramachandran, 2007). Autistic people may not like to touch or be touched, do not communicate well if at all, and tend not to make eye contact. In one study (Dapretto et al., 2006), autistic children and non-autistic children were asked to imitate the facial expressions

mirror neurons
neurons that fire when an animal or person performs an action and also when an animal or person observes that same action being performed by another.

As this boy imitates the motions his father goes through while shaving, certain areas of his brain are more active than others, areas that control the motions of shaving. But even if the boy were only *watching* his father, those same neural areas would be active—the neurons in the boy's brain would *mirror* the actions of the father he is observing.

they saw in a series of pictures, and researchers measured neural activity in the mirror neuron system. Although both groups of children were able to imitate the expressions in the pictures, the autistic children showed no neural activity in the mirror system while doing so. The control group of non-autistic children *did* show such mirror system activity. The researchers believe that this lack of a normally functioning mirror system in the autistic children may help explain why autistic people have difficulty with empathy (the ability to understand the emotions of others) as well as with language skills. Their mirror neuron systems respond only to what they themselves do and not to what they see other people doing—autistic people are "locked out" of that system of social reflection.

The implications for therapy with psychological disorders have not yet been fully explored. Could having depressed patients watch others enjoying themselves and laughing lift the depression? If a child with an intense fear of dogs watched someone calmly pet and play with a dog, would that help the child become less afraid? Is it possible that effective exercises could be developed to train or correct the defective mirror neuron systems of autistic children and adults, thereby enabling them to communicate and interact with others more socially? The future is ours to see—through the looking glass of social interactions.

Questions for Further Discussion

1. What are some other psychological disorders that might be treated by having the affected person observe someone else's behaviour or facial expression?

2. In what ways might mirror neurons be involved in how children learn to speak and form words?

2 | CHAPTER SUMMARY

An Overview of the Nervous System

2.1. How do all the parts of the nervous system relate to one another?

- The nervous system is a complex network of cells that carries information to and from all parts of the body.

Neurons and Nerves: Building the Network

2.2. What are neurons and nerves, and how do they work?

- The brain is made up of two types of cells, neurons and glial cells.
- Neurons have dendrites, which receive input, a soma or cell body, and axons that carry the neural message to other cells.
- Glial cells separate, support, and insulate the neurons from each other and make up 90 percent of the brain.
- Myelin insulates and protects the axons of neurons that travel in the body. These axons bundle together in "cables" called *nerves*. Myelin also speeds up the neural message.

2.3. How do neurons communicate with each other and with the body?

- A neuron contains charged particles called ions. When at rest, the neuron is negatively charged on the inside and positively charged on the outside. When stimulated, this reverses the charge by allowing positive sodium ions to enter the cell. This is the action potential.

- Neurons fire in an all-or-nothing manner. It is the speed and number of neurons firing that tell researchers the strength of the stimulus.
- Synaptic vesicles in the end of the axon terminal release neurotransmitter chemicals into the synapse, or gap, between one cell and the next. The neurotransmitter molecules fit into receptor sites on the next cell, stimulating or inhibiting that cell's firing. There are excitatory and inhibitory synapses.

2.4. What are the different neurotransmitters?

- The first known neurotransmitter was acetylcholine. It stimulates muscles and helps in memory formation. Curare is a poison that blocks its effect.
- GABA is the major inhibitory neurotransmitter; high amounts of GABA are released when a person drinks alcohol.
- Serotonin is associated with sleep, mood, and appetite.
- Dopamine is associated with Parkinson's and schizophrenia.
- Endorphins are neural regulators that control our pain response.
- Most neurotransmitters are taken back into the synaptic vesicles in a process called *reuptake*.
- Acetylcholine is cleared out of the synapse by enzymes that break up the molecules.

The Central Nervous System—The "Central Processing Unit"

2.5. *How do the brain and spinal cord interact?*

- The central nervous system consists of the brain and the spinal cord.
- The brain is the true core of the nervous system. It takes information from the senses, processes it, makes decisions, and sends commands to the rest of the body.
- The spinal cord serves two functions. The outer part of the cord transmits messages to and from the brain, whereas the inner part controls life-saving reflexes such as the pain response.
- Spinal cord reflexes involve sensory neurons, interneurons, and motor neurons, forming a simple reflex arc.
- Great strides are being made in spinal cord repair and the growth of new neurons in the central nervous system.

Psychology in the News: Stem Cells: New Hope for the Damaged Brains?

- Research suggests that stem cells can be obtained from adult bone marrow, making the repair and replacement of damaged neurons more feasible.

The Peripheral Nervous System—Nerves on the Edge

- The peripheral nervous system is all the neurons and nerves that are not part of the brain and spinal cord and that extend throughout the body.
- There are two systems within the peripheral nervous system, the somatic nervous system and the autonomic nervous system.

2.6. *How do the somatic and autonomic nervous systems allow people to interact with their surroundings and control the body's automatic functions?*

- The somatic nervous system contains afferent neurons that carry sensory messages to the central nervous system, and it also contains efferent neurons that carry messages from the central nervous system to the voluntary muscles.
- The autonomic nervous system consists of the parasympathetic division and the sympathetic division. The sympathetic division is our fight-or-flight system, reacting to stress, whereas the parasympathetic division restores and maintains normal day-to-day functioning of the organs.

2.7. *How does the autonomic nervous system control the body's automatic functions and its reaction to stress?*

- The autonomic nervous system controls the organs, glands, and involuntary muscles. It is composed of two systems, the sympathetic and parasympathetic division. The sympathetic division is in sympathy with our emotions and thus is responsible for our reaction to stress. When activated, the sympathetic division—sometimes called our *fight-or-flight system*—dilates our pupils, makes our heart pump faster and harder, and draws blood away from non-essential organs such as the skin. Lungs work overtime to oxygenate the blood and the adrenal glands release stress-related chemicals into the bloodstream. The parasympathetic division does virtually the opposite of the sympathetic division. Its job is to restore the body to normal functioning after a stressful situation ends. It constricts the pupils, slows the heart and breathing, and reactivates digestion and excretion.

Peeking Inside the Brain

2.8. *How do psychologists study the brain and how it works?*

- We can study the brain by using deep lesioning to destroy certain areas of the brain in laboratory animals or by electrically stimulating those areas (ESB).
- We can use case studies of human brain damage to learn about the brain's functions but cannot easily generalize from one case to another. Wilder Penfield established the Montreal Neurological Institute where he treated patients with severe epilepsy by directly stimulating their brains. This procedure became known as the Montreal Procedure and allowed Penfield to create highly detailed brain maps that are still used by neurosurgeons today.
- The EEG machine allows researchers to look at the activity of the surface of the brain through the use of microelectrodes placed on the scalp and connected to graph paper.
- CT scans are computer-aided X-rays of the brain and show a great deal of brain structure.
- MRI scans use a magnetic field and a computer to give researchers an even more detailed look at the structure of the brain. A related technique, fMRI, allows researchers to look at the activity of the brain over a time period.
- PET scans use a radioactive sugar injected into the bloodstream to track the activity of brain cells, which is enhanced and colour-coded by a computer.

From the Bottom Up: The Structures of the Brain

2.9. *What are the different structures of the bottom part of the brain, and what do they do?*

- The medulla is at the very bottom of the brain and top of the spinal column. It controls life-sustaining functions such as breathing and swallowing. The nerves from each side of the body cross over to opposite sides in this structure.
- The pons is above the medulla and acts as a bridge between the lower part of the brain and the upper part. It influences sleep, dreaming, arousal, and coordination of movement on the left and right sides of the body.
- The reticular formation runs through the medulla and the pons and controls our selective attention and arousal.
- The cerebellum is found at the base and back of the brain and coordinates fine, rapid motor movement, learned reflexes, posture, and muscle tone.

2.10. *Which structures of the brain control emotion, learning, memory, and motivation?*

- The thalamus is the switching station that sends sensory information to the proper areas of the cortex.
- The hypothalamus controls hunger, thirst, sleep, sexual behaviour, sleeping and waking, and emotions. It also controls the pituitary gland.
- The limbic system consists of the thalamus, hypothalamus, hippocampus, and amygdala.
- The hippocampus is the part of the brain responsible for storing memories and remembering locations of objects.
- The amygdala controls our fear responses and memory of fearful stimuli.

2.11. *Which parts of the cortex control the different senses and the movement of the body?*

- The cortex is the outer covering of the cerebrum and consists of a tightly packed layer of neurons about 2 millimetres in thickness. Its wrinkles, or corticalization, allow for greater cortical area and are associated with greater intelligence.

- The cortex is divided into two cerebral hemispheres connected by a thick band of neurons called the *corpus callosum*.
- The occipital lobes at the back and base of each hemisphere process vision and contain the primary visual cortex.
- The parietal lobes at the top and back of the cortex contain the somatosensory area, which processes our sense of touch, temperature, and body position. Taste is also processed in this lobe.
- The temporal lobes contain the primary auditory area and are also involved in understanding language.
- The frontal lobes contain the motor cortex, which controls the voluntary muscles, and are also where all the higher mental functions occur, such as planning, language, and complex decision making.

2.12. *Which parts of the cortex are responsible for higher forms of thought, such as language?*

- Association areas of the cortex are found in all the lobes but particularly in the frontal lobes. These areas help people make sense of the information they receive from the lower areas of the brain.
- An area called Broca's area in the left frontal lobe is responsible for producing fluent, understandable speech. If damaged, the person has Broca's aphasia, in which words will be halting and pronounced incorrectly.
- An area called Wernicke's area in the left temporal lobe is responsible for the understanding of language. If damaged, the person has Wernicke's aphasia, in which speech is fluent but nonsensical. The wrong words are used.
- Spatial neglect comes from damage to the association areas on one side of the cortex, usually the right side. A person with this condition will ignore information from the opposite side of the body or the opposite visual field.

Psychology in the News: **Former WWE Champion Chris Benoit Kills Family, Then Himself: Was it "Roid Rage" or Brain Injury?**

- Following a murder–suicide, an autopsy revealed that former WWE champion Chris Benoit's brain resembled that of an 85-year-old man suffering from Alzheimer's disease. The researchers speculated that this brain damage likely resulted from repeated head trauma and that brain damage, and not steroid abuse, was the causal factor of Benoit's tragic behaviour.

2.13. *How does the left side of the brain differ from the right side?*

- Studies with split-brain patients, in which the corpus callosum has been severed to correct epilepsy, reveal that the left side of the

brain seems to control language, writing, logical thought, analysis, and mathematical abilities. The left side processes information sequentially.

- The right side of the brain processes information globally and controls emotional expression, spatial perception, and recognition of faces, patterns, melodies, and emotions. The left hemisphere can speak but the right cannot.

The Chemical Connection: The Endocrine Glands

2.14. *How do the hormones released by glands interact with the nervous system and affect behaviour?*

- Endocrine glands secrete chemicals called hormones directly into the bloodstream, influencing the activity of the muscles and organs.
- The pituitary gland is found in the brain just below the hypothalamus. It has two parts, the anterior and the posterior. It controls the levels of salt and water in the system and, in women, the onset of labour and lactation, as well as secreting growth hormone and influencing the activity of the other glands.
- The pineal gland is also located in the brain. It secretes melatonin, a hormone that regulates the sleep–wake cycle in response to changes in light.
- The thyroid gland is located inside the neck. It controls metabolism (the burning of energy) by secreting thyroxin.
- The pancreas controls the level of sugar in the blood by secreting insulin and glucagons. Too much insulin produces hypoglycemia, whereas too little causes diabetes.
- The gonads are the ovaries in women and testes in men. They secrete hormones to regulate sexual growth, activity, and reproduction.
- The adrenal glands, one on top of each kidney, control the stress reaction through the adrenal medulla's secretion of epinephrine and norepinephrine. The adrenal cortex secretes more than 30 different corticoids (hormones) controlling salt intake, stress, and sexual development.

Applying Psychology to Everyday Life: Reflections on Mirror Neurons

- Italian scientist Rizzolatti and colleagues discovered the existence of mirror neurons, neurons that not only fire when performing an action but also fire when the organism merely watches an action being performed by another.
- Mirror neurons may explain much of human social interaction, and may be useful in understanding disorders such as autism. There may also be practical applications in the treatment of stroke patients who need to regain lost skills and in therapy for psychological disorders such as depression.

2 KEY TERMS

deep lesioning   62
dendrites   45
electroencephalograph (EEG)   62
endocrine glands   77
excitatory synapse   51
frontal lobes   71
glial cells   46
gonads   78
hippocampus   68
hormones   77
hypothalamus   67
inhibitory synapse   51
interneuron   55
limbic system   66
magnetic resonance imaging (MRI)   64
medulla   64
mirror neuron   79
motor cortex   71
motor neuron   55

myelin   46
nerves   46
nervous system   44
neuron   45
neuroscience   45
neurotransmitter   50
occipital lobe   69
ovaries   78
pancreas   78
parasympathetic division   61
parietal lobes   70
peripheral nervous system (PNS)   58
pineal gland   78
pituitary gland   77
pons   65
positron emission tomography (PET)   64
receptor sites   51
reflex arc   55
resting membrane potential   47

reticular formation (RF)   65
reuptake   54
sensory neuron   55
soma   45
somatic nervous system   58
somatosensory cortex   70
spatial neglect   74
spinal cord   55
stem cells   57
sympathetic division
   (fight-or-flight system)   59
synapse (synaptic gap)   50
synaptic knob   50
synaptic vesicles   50
temporal lobes   70
testes   78
thalamus   67
thyroid gland   78
Wernicke's aphasia   74

TEST YOURSELF

Pick the best answer.

1. In the structure of the neuron, the _____ sends information to other cells.
   a. axon   **c.** soma
   b. dendrite   **d.** myelin

2. Which type of cell makes up 10 percent of the brain?
   a. glial cells   **c.** stem cells
   b. neurons   **d.** afferent cells

3. Damaged nerve fibres in the body can repair themselves because they are coated with _____, which forms a protective tunnel around the nerve fibres.
   a. glial   **c.** myelin
   b. soma   **d.** neurilemma

4. When a neuron is in the resting potential state, where are the sodium ions?
   a. inside the cell   **c.** inside the soma
   b. outside the cell   **d.** in the synapse

5. How does one neuron communicate with another neuron?
   a. An electrical spark jumps over the gap between cells.
   b. Charged particles leap from one cell to the next.
   c. Chemicals in the end of one neuron float across the gap to fit into holes on the next neuron.
   d. The end of one neuron extends to touch the other neuron.

6. Which neurotransmitter is associated with the control of the pain response?
   a. acetylcholine   **c.** serotonin
   b. GABA   **d.** endorphin

7. Which of the following is the correct path of a reflex arc?
   a. motor neuron to interneuron to sensory neuron
   b. motor neuron to sensory neuron to interneuron
   c. sensory neuron to interneuron to motor neuron
   d. sensory neuron to motor neuron to the brain

8. The synaptic plasticity associated with learning new things and creating new memories is dependent on
   a. neurons only.   **c.** neither a nor b.
   b. glial cells only.   **d.** both a and b.

9. Voluntary muscles are controlled by the _____ nervous system.
   a. somatic   **c.** sympathetic
   b. autonomic   **d.** parasympathetic

10. Your heart races. You begin to breathe faster. Your pupils enlarge and your appetite is gone. Your _____ division has just been activated.
   a. sympathetic   **c.** autonomic
   b. parasympathetic   **d.** somatic

11. Stem cells are
   a. immature neurons.
   b. immature glial cells.
   c. found only in embryos and the eye of adult mammals.
   d. basic cells that can differentiate into any specific type of cell.

12. Which of the following techniques for imaging the brain would NOT be advisable for a person with a metal plate in his or her head?
   a. EEG   **c.** MRI
   b. CT   **d.** PET

13. Imagine the motor cortex of an elephant. Which structure would likely be especially prominent?
   a. the ears   **c.** the trunk
   b. the mouth   **d.** the legs

14. Maria suffered a stroke that damaged a part of her brain. She fell into a sleeplike coma and cannot be awakened. If we know that the area of damage is somewhere in the brain stem, which structure is most likely damaged?
   a. medulla   **c.** reticular formation
   b. pons   **d.** cerebellum

15. Alex, who is 2 months old, is having his picture taken. The photographer tries to sit him up, but Alex keeps sinking down. Alex cannot sit upright yet because the _____ in his brain stem is not yet fully developed.
    a. medulla
    c. reticular formation
    b. pons
    d. cerebellum
16. Which sense is NOT sent to the cortex by the thalamus?
    a. hearing
    c. taste
    b. smell
    d. vision
17. Which part of the brain is the link between the brain and the glandular system?
    a. hippocampus
    b. thalamus
    c. hypothalamus
    d. amygdala
18. What serendipitous finding did Dr. Lozano find?
    a. Stimulation of hippocampus, which was hypothesized to reduce weight, actually caused significantly weight gain.
    b. Stimulation of the hypothalamus, which was hypothesized to curb appetite, actually increased memory.
    c. Stimulation of the hypothalamus, which was hypothesized to curb appetite, actually increased musical ability.
    d. Stimulation of the hippocampus, which was hypothesized to increase memory, actually curbed appetite.
19. Jeff is undergoing brain surgery to remove a tumour. The surgeon applies electrical simulation to various areas around the tumour, causing Jeff to report tingling sensations in various areas of his skin. The tumour is most likely in which lobe of Jeff's brain?
    a. frontal
    c. occipital
    b. temporal
    d. parietal
20. Experts believe that Chris Benoit suffered from chronic traumatic encephalopathy (CTE). What is the most likely cause of this?
    a. genetics
    b. poor nutrition in early childhood
    c. repeated concussions
    d. excessive steroid use, especially of testosterone and human growth hormone

21. Linda is recovering from damage to her brain. Her main symptom is a speech problem; instead of saying, "I am going to P. T. (physical therapy) at nine o'clock," she says, "I go … P. T … non o'cot." Linda's problem is
    a. spatial neglect.
    c. Broca's aphasia.
    b. visual agnosia.
    d. Wernicke's aphasia.
22. Recognizing the face of someone you run into at the mall is a function of the _____ hemisphere; being able to retrieve that person's name from memory is a function of the _____ hemisphere.
    a. left; right
    c. right; right
    b. right; left
    d. left; left
23. Heather is beautifully proportioned, but at 18 years of age she is still no taller than the average 10-year-old. Heather most likely had a problem in her _____ gland(s) while she was growing up.
    a. pituitary
    c. thyroid
    b. adrenal
    d. pineal
24. Melatonin is secreted by the _____ gland(s).
    a. pituitary
    c. thyroid
    b. adrenal
    d. pineal
25. Which childhood disorder is thought to be due, at least in part, to a faulty mirror neuron system?
    a. ADHD (attention deficit hyperactivity disorder)
    b. conduct disorder
    c. autism
    d. measles

Answers: 1.-a, 2.-b, 3.-d, 4.-b, 5.-c, 6.-d, 7.-c, 8.-d, 9.-a, 10.-a, 11.-d, 12.-c, 13.-c, 14.-c, 15.-d, 16.-b, 17.-c, 18.-b, 19.-d, 20.-c, 21.-c, 22.-b, 23.-a, 24.-d, 25.-c.

ScanLife™ Barcode

To access more tests and your own personalized study plan that will help you focus on the areas you need to master before your next class test, be sure to go to **www.MyPsychLab.com**, Pearson Education Canada's online psychology website, available with the access code packaged with your book.

2.1–3

Neurons and Nerves

(the brain is composed of glial cells and neurons)

- **glial cells**
  separate, support, and insulate the neurons from each other

- **neurons**
  specialized cells in nervous system

- have specialized components

- have an electrical charge at rest— the resting potential
- are affected by neurotransmitters
- fire in an all-or-nothing manner
- are separated by a gap called the synapse

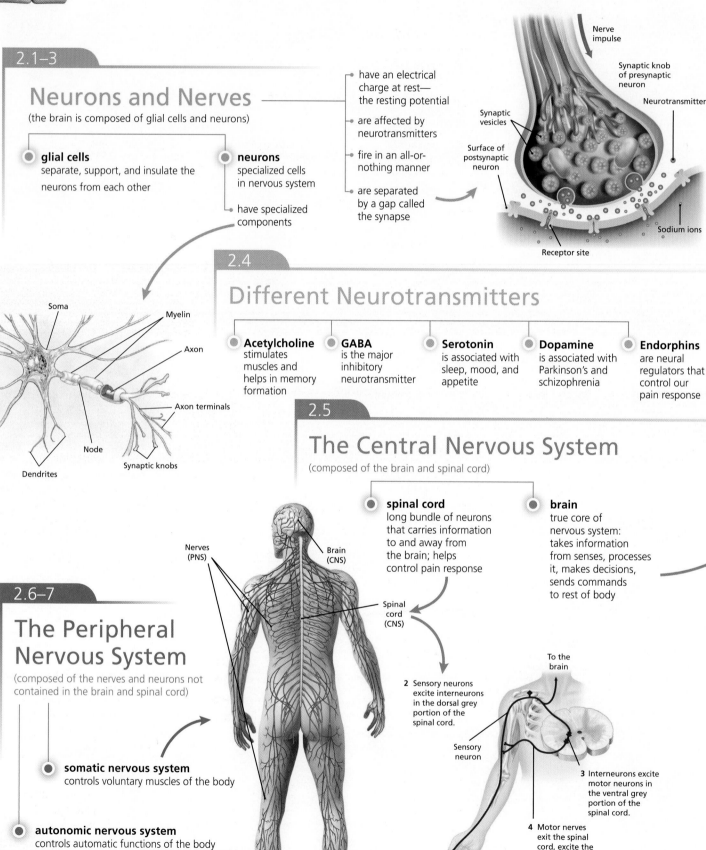

Nerve impulse

Synaptic knob of presynaptic neuron

Neurotransmitter

Synaptic vesicles

Surface of postsynaptic neuron

Sodium ions

Receptor site

Soma
Myelin
Axon
Axon terminals
Node
Synaptic knobs
Dendrites

2.4

Different Neurotransmitters

- **Acetylcholine**
  stimulates muscles and helps in memory formation

- **GABA**
  is the major inhibitory neurotransmitter

- **Serotonin**
  is associated with sleep, mood, and appetite

- **Dopamine**
  is associated with Parkinson's and schizophrenia

- **Endorphins**
  are neural regulators that control our pain response

2.5

The Central Nervous System

(composed of the brain and spinal cord)

- **spinal cord**
  long bundle of neurons that carries information to and away from the brain; helps control pain response

- **brain**
  true core of nervous system: takes information from senses, processes it, makes decisions, sends commands to rest of body

Nerves (PNS)

Brain (CNS)

Spinal cord (CNS)

2.6–7

The Peripheral Nervous System

(composed of the nerves and neurons not contained in the brain and spinal cord)

- **somatic nervous system**
  controls voluntary muscles of the body

- **autonomic nervous system**
  controls automatic functions of the body and its reaction to stress (via the sympathetic and parasympathetic divisions)

To the brain

2 Sensory neurons excite interneurons in the dorsal grey portion of the spinal cord.

Sensory neuron

3 Interneurons excite motor neurons in the ventral grey portion of the spinal cord.

4 Motor nerves exit the spinal cord, excite the muscle, and initiate a movement.

1 Flame stimulates pain receptors (sensory neurons).

Peeking Inside the Brain

(methods for studying the structures and/or activity of the living brain)

- clinical studies
- electroencephalogram (EEG)
- computed tomography (CT)
- magnetic resonance imaging (MRI)
- positron emission tomography (PET)

From the Bottom Up: The Structures of the Brain

- **structures under the cortex**
  - **thalamus**
  - **hypothalamus**
  - **hippocampus**
  - **amygdala**

- **the hindbrain**
  - **medulla**
  - **pons**
  - **reticular formation**
  - **cerebellum**

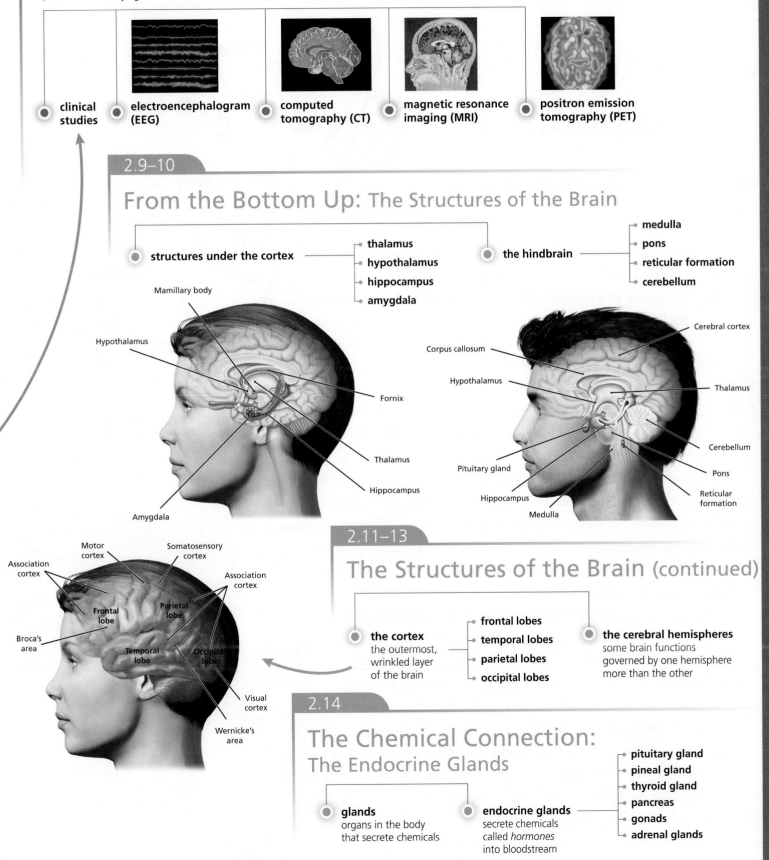

Mamillary body
Hypothalamus
Fornix
Thalamus
Hippocampus
Amygdala

Corpus callosum
Hypothalamus
Pituitary gland
Hippocampus
Medulla
Cerebral cortex
Thalamus
Cerebellum
Pons
Reticular formation

Motor cortex
Somatosensory cortex
Association cortex
Association cortex
Frontal lobe
Parietal lobe
Broca's area
Temporal lobe
Occipital lobe
Visual cortex
Wernicke's area

The Structures of the Brain (continued)

- **the cortex**
  the outermost, wrinkled layer of the brain
  - **frontal lobes**
  - **temporal lobes**
  - **parietal lobes**
  - **occipital lobes**

- **the cerebral hemispheres**
  some brain functions governed by one hemisphere more than the other

The Chemical Connection: The Endocrine Glands

- **glands**
  organs in the body that secrete chemicals

- **endocrine glands**
  secrete chemicals called *hormones* into bloodstream
  - **pituitary gland**
  - **pineal gland**
  - **thyroid gland**
  - **pancreas**
  - **gonads**
  - **adrenal glands**

3

Sensation and Perception

Is Your Cellphone or BlackBerry a Fifth Limb?

Have you ever heard your cellphone ringing and there's nobody there? Or reached for your vibrating BlackBerry only to find that you were not wearing it? If you have, then you are not alone. In fact, this phenomenon has become so prevalent it has jokingly been termed *ringxiety* or *faux-cellarm* in the cyber community. Countless people are reporting that they feel like their cellphones are part of them or that without their cellphones they do not feel whole, because their phones, like their other senses, connect them to the world. Although experimental research on the topic is scant, some psychologists have likened the phenomenon to phantom limb pain, a condition in which limb amputees continue to feel the presence of their lost limb and may even try to reach out for things with their missing limb.

Prominent Canadian pain guru Ronald Melzack believes that phantom limb pain occurs because of the organization of the parietal lobe's somatosensory cortex. After a limb is lost, neurons in the somatosensory cortex continue to function and, because of the lack of normal stimulation, begin to reorganize. For instance, neurons that originally controlled the lost limb may make connections to neurons that sense your nose; thus, touching your nose activates not only the nose neurons but also the lost limb's neurons. As a result, you feel the presence of your original limb even though it is not there. Similar plasticity may be occurring with your ringing cellphone or vibrating BlackBerry. The repeated ringing or vibrating of these devices from a common bodily area continually activates the same neurons within your somatosensory cortex, and these neurons then begin to reorganize the somatosensory cortex—perhaps creating the representation of a fifth limb within your cortex. So if you forget your cellphone or BlackBerry for whatever reason, the neurons within the somatosensory cortex fire indiscriminately; as a result, you reach for your new fifth limb even though it is not there. Maybe machines are really becoming part of us (Simon, 2007)!

Why study sensation and perception?

Without sensations to tell us what is outside our own mental world, we would live entirely in our own minds, separate from one another and unable to find food or any other basics that sustain life. Sensations are the mind's window to the world that exists around us. Without perception we would be unable to understand what all those sensations mean—perception is the process of interpreting the sensations we experience so that we can act upon them.

3

THE ABCs OF SENSATION

How do we get ▶ information from the outside world into our brains?

How do we get information from the outside world into our brains? There is so much information in the world outside the body and brain. That information has to have a way to get into the brain, where it can be used to determine actions and responses. The way into the brain is through the sensory organs and the process of sensation.

WHAT IS SENSATION?

3.1. *What are each of the following: sensation, transduction, the just noticeable difference, subliminal perception, and synesthesia?*

Sensation occurs when special receptors in the sense organs are activated, allowing various forms of outside stimuli to become neural signals in the brain. (This process of converting outside stimuli, such as light, into neural activity is called **transduction**.) Let's take a closer look at these special receptors.

SENSORY RECEPTORS The *sensory receptors* are specialized forms of neurons, the cells that make up the nervous system. Instead of receiving neurotransmitters from other cells, these receptor cells are stimulated by different kinds of energy—for example, the receptors in the eyes are triggered by light, whereas vibrations trigger the receptors in the ears.

SENSORY THRESHOLDS

The various sense organs—eyes, ears, nose, skin, and taste buds—are actually quite sensitive to stimulation. The following questions capture two of the most interesting aspects of sensory abilities: What is the smallest amount of energy needed for a person to consciously detect a stimulus? What is the smallest difference between two stimuli that a person can detect? Gustav Fechner (1801–1887) studied something he called the **absolute threshold** (Fechner, 1860). The absolute threshold is the smallest amount of energy needed for a person to consciously detect a stimulus 50 percent of the time it is present. For example, how much salt must be added to a glass of water before the change in taste can be detected in at least half of the taste tests? Table 3.1 provides some examples of absolute thresholds for various senses. Ernst Weber (1795–1878)

sensation
the activation of receptors in the various sense organs.

transduction
the process of converting outside stimuli, such as light, into neural activity.

absolute threshold
the smallest amount of energy needed for a person to consciously detect a stimulus 50 percent of the time it is present.

TABLE 3.1 **EXAMPLES OF ABSOLUTE THRESHOLDS**

SENSE	THRESHOLD
Sight	A candle flame at 50 kilometres on a clear, dark night
Hearing	The tick of a watch 7 metres away in a quiet room
Smell	One drop of perfume diffused throughout a three-room apartment
Taste	1 teaspoon of sugar in 7.5 litres of water
Touch	A bee's wing falling on the cheek from 1 centimetre above

did studies to try to determine the smallest difference between two weights that could be detected. His research led to the formulation known as Weber's law of **just noticeable differences (jnd,** or the **difference threshold**). A jnd is the smallest difference between two stimuli that is detectable 50 percent of the time, and Weber's law simply means that whatever the difference between stimuli might be, it is always a constant. In other words, if the amount of sugar a person would need to add to a cup of coffee that is already sweetened with 5 teaspoons is 1 teaspoon, then the percentage of change needed to detect a just noticeable difference is ⅕, or 20 percent. So if the coffee has 10 teaspoons of sugar in it, the person would have to add another 20 percent, or 2 teaspoons, to be able to taste the difference half of the time.

I've heard about people being influenced by stuff in movies and on television, things that are just below the level of conscious awareness. Is that true?

SUBLIMINAL PERCEPTION   Stimuli that are below the level of conscious awareness are called *subliminal stimuli*. (The word *limin* means "threshold," so *sublimin* means "below the threshold.") These stimuli are just strong enough to activate the sensory receptors but not strong enough for people to be consciously aware of them. Many people believe that these stimuli act upon the unconscious mind, influencing behaviour in a process called *subliminal perception.*

Although the following story is now widely recognized as false, it has taken on the status of an urban legend.* The story highlights the fears that many people had concerning subliminal perception when psychologists first introduced the concept. The story goes like this: In 1957, a market researcher named James Vicary claimed that over a six-week period, 45 699 patrons at a movie theatre in Fort Lee, New Jersey, were shown two advertising messages, *Eat Popcorn* and *Drink Coca-Cola*, while they watched the film *Picnic*. According to Vicary, these messages were flashed for 0.003 second once every 5 seconds. Vicary claimed that over the six-week period the sales of popcorn rose 57.7 percent and the sales of Coca-Cola rose 18.1 percent.

For years, Vicary's claims were often accepted as established facts. The real truth? Vicary never described his study in print. Legitimate researchers were unable to duplicate his findings. Finally, in an interview with *Advertising Age* in 1962, Vicary admitted what many researchers had long suspected: The original study was a complete deception—Vicary never did it (Merikle, 2000; Pratkanis, 1992). Researchers have gathered scientific evidence that subliminal perception does not work in advertising

*Urban legend: a story that is so often repeated that people have come to believe that it is true

just noticeable difference (jnd, or the difference threshold)
the smallest difference between two stimuli that is detectable 50 percent of the time.

✱⊣Explore on **mypsychlab**
Weber's Law

◀ I've heard about people being influenced by stuff in movies and on television, things that are just below the level of conscious awareness. Is that true?

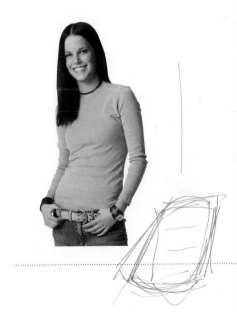

(Bargh et al., 1996; Moore, 1988; Pratkanis & Greenwald, 1988; Trappey, 1996; Vokey & Read, 1985).

Despite the lack of influence of subliminal perception in advertising, the University of Waterloo's Dr. Philip Merikle has shown that under the right conditions, subliminal stimuli may influence us. Using a procedure known as *visual priming*, he presented participants with visual images so quickly that they could not consciously state what the images were. Although the participants were unable to identify the visual images, Dr. Merikle and his colleagues did show that these visual primes could influence how participants responded to subsequent stimuli (Merikle & Daneman, 1998). For example, suppose participants were subconsciously primed with negative images of snakes, fires, and accidents, and then shown photographs of people going about their daily business. What do you think might happen if the participants were asked to rate the attitudes and beliefs of the persons in the photographs? Participants who were exposed to the subconscious negative primes were more likely to ascribe negative attitudes and beliefs toward the persons in subsequent photos (Krosnick, Betz, Jussim, & Lynn, 1992).

So are advertisers trying to control what we do and how we act through subliminal perception? Well, the answer is, of course, no! While some studies have found that subliminal stimuli may influence our affective attributes, there is no evidence to suggest they can control or cause us to act in any fashion. Although some advertisers may have tried this, the world is full of complex motives, and people are not as easily influenced as one might think (Pratkanis, 1992). Even the so-called hidden pictures that some artists airbrush into the art in advertisements aren't truly subliminal—if someone points it out, it can be seen easily enough. Hey, if subliminal study perception really really worked, don't you think that hard authors of textbooks send in psychology me would be some money of the first people to use it? No one sent the authors any money when this appeared in the first edition.

Is my friend lying to me? She swears that every time she looks at the number five she sees the colour yellow. Your friend may have a rare—about 1 in 25 000—and interesting condition called **synesthesia**. A person with synesthesia is referred to as a *synesthete*. In synesthesia, some of the signals from the various sensory organs are processed in the wrong cortical areas, resulting in the sense information being interpreted as more than one sensation. For example, researchers at the University of Saskatchewan scanned the brain of a colour–digit synesthete. They were able to show that some brain areas associated with vision were activated while the synesthete was listening to arithmetic (Elias, Saucier, Hardie, & Sarty, 2003). Interestingly, there are reports of synesthesia for most possible sensory combinations, with a fusion of sight and sound being most common (Baron-Cohen et al., 1996; Cytowic, 1989). For example, some synesthetes may say that the sight of green grass smells like coffee, or that the sound of a note of music is grey.

HABITUATION AND SENSORY ADAPTATION

3.2. *How can some sensations be ignored?*

In Chapter Two, it was stated that the lower centres of the brain sort through sensory stimulation and "ignore" or prevent conscious attention to stimuli that do not change. The brain is interested only in changes in information. That's why people don't really "hear" the noise of the air conditioner unless it suddenly cuts off or the noise made in some classrooms unless it gets very quiet. Although they actually are *hearing* it, they aren't paying attention to it. This is called **habituation**, and it is the way the brain deals with unchanging information. (L I N K) *to Chapter Two: The Biological Perspective, p. 42.*

So are advertisers ▶ trying to control what we do and how we act through subliminal perception?

Is my friend lying to ▶ me? She swears that every time she looks at the number five she sees the colour yellow.

synesthesia
a rare condition in which some of the signals from the various sensory organs are processed in the wrong cortical areas, resulting in the sense information being interpreted as more than one sensation.

habituation
tendency of the brain to stop attending to constant, unchanging information.

Is that why sometimes I can smell the odour of the garbage can in the kitchen when I first come home, but after a while the smell seems to go away? The process by which constant and unchanging information from the senses of taste, touch, smell, and vision is ignored is a different process from habituation. The difference is that for taste, touch, smell, and vision, any sensory stimulus that does not change is ignored by the actual sensory receptors, not by the lower part of the brain (as in habituation). In **sensory adaptation**, the sensory receptor cells become less responsive to an unchanging stimulus. Without sensory adaptation, clothes would probably drive people crazy because they would be constantly aware of every piece of clothing or jewellery they have on. They would feel the seat of the chair they are sitting on constantly instead of just when they move. Bad odours such as the garbage-can smell would never go away.

For example, many Canadians bring in a new year with a polar bear swim. At first, the water feels as though it is freezing (and it is); but, after a minute or two, the water may feel a bit more refreshing. Even if you have never had the pleasure of a polar bear swim, you have undoubtedly entered a cool lake on a hot summer's day and thought the water was freezing. After a few minutes though, you scream to your friends, "Come in—the water is perfect!"

So, if I stare at something long enough, it will disappear? No; the eyes are a little different. Even though the sensory receptors in the back of the eyes would adapt to and become less responsive to a constant visual stimulus, under ordinary circumstances the eyes are never that still. There's a constant movement of the eyes, tiny little vibrations called *saccades* that people don't notice consciously. These movements keep the eyes from adapting to what they see. That's a good thing, because otherwise many students would no doubt go blind from staring off into space. But what if we lost those saccadic movements for a while, would the objects we stare at disappear? The answer is yes. The eyes also show sensory adaptation. We know this because of specially designed contact lenses created at McGill University in Montreal (Pritchard, 1961). These lenses enabled researchers to focus and hold steady, even if the eye moved, an image at the back of the eye. The result was fascinating: People reported seeing the image and then it would magically disappear, and reappear, and disappear, and so on.

◀ Is that why sometimes I can smell the odour of the garbage can in the kitchen when I first come home, but after a while the smell seems to go away?

◀ So, if I stare at something long enough, it will disappear?

sensory adaptation
tendency of sensory receptor cells to become less responsive to a stimulus that is unchanging.

The Annual Polar Bear Swim in Maple Bay. Let's hope these adventurous Canadians experience sensory adaptation quickly—brrrrr!

PRACTICE QUIZ: HOW MUCH DO YOU REMEMBER?

Pick the best answer.

1. The smallest difference between two stimuli that can be detected 50 percent of the time it is present is called
   a. absolute threshold.
   c. sensation.
   b. just noticeable difference.
   d. sensory adaptation.

2. When receptor cells for the senses are activated, the process called has begun.
   a. perception
   c. adaptation
   b. sublimation
   d. sensation

3. Using visual priming, researchers have been able to show that subliminal stimuli
   a. can influence only how we act.
   b. can influence only our complex emotions
   c. can influence only our attitudes and beliefs
   d. cannot influence us in any way.

4. Which two sensory modalities are most commonly fused in synesthesia?
   a. vision–smell
   c. vision–hearing
   b. touch–taste
   d. touch–vision

5. You are holding a piece of candy in your mouth. After a while, the candy doesn't taste as strong as it did when you first tasted it. What has happened?
   a. sensory adaptation
   c. threshold adaptation
   b. subliminal perception
   d. perceptual defence

6. Vicary's study of subliminal advertising was remarkable in that
   a. it demonstrated the use fulness of subliminal perception.
   b. people actually bought more colas and popcorn after seeing the movie.
   c. the subliminal stimuli had no effect on buying behaviour.
   d. it never happened.

7. Which of your senses does not adapt to a constant stimulus at the level of the receptor cells?
   a. vision
   c. hearing
   b. touch
   d. smell

Answers: 1.b.,2.d.,3.c.,4.c.,5.a.,6.d.,7.c.

THE SCIENCE OF SEEING

► I've heard that light is waves, but I've also heard that light is made of particles— which is it?

I've heard that light is waves, but I've also heard that light is made of particles— which is it? Light is a complicated phenomenon. Although scientists have long argued over the nature of light, they agree that light has the properties of both waves and particles. The following section gives a brief history of how scientists have tried to "shed light" on the mystery of light.

PSYCHOLOGICAL PROPERTIES OF LIGHT: CATCHING THE WAVES

3.3. *What is light?*

Although Isaac Newton believed light to consist of particles, in 1802 Thomas Young demonstrated that light behaves like waves. Research at the turn of the twentieth century provided evidence for both views—sometimes light behaves like particles and sometimes like waves. It was Albert Einstein who first demonstrated that light is actually both: He proposed tiny "packets" of waves called *photons*. These photons actually have wavelengths associated with them—hence, the wavelike properties (van der Merwe & Garuccio, 1994).

When people experience light, they are not really aware of its dual nature. There are three psychological aspects to the experience of light: brightness, colour, and saturation.

Brightness is determined by the amplitude of the wave—how high or how low the wave actually is. The bigger the wave, the brighter the light will be. Smaller amplitude waves are dimmer. *Colour*, or hue, is determined by the wavelength—the distance from one crest to another. Long wavelengths are found at the red end of the *visible spectrum* (the portion of the whole spectrum of light that is visible to the human eye; see Figure 3.1), whereas shorter wavelengths are found at the blue end.

FIGURE 3.1 **The Visible Spectrum**
The wavelengths that people can see are only a small part of the whole electromagnetic spectrum.

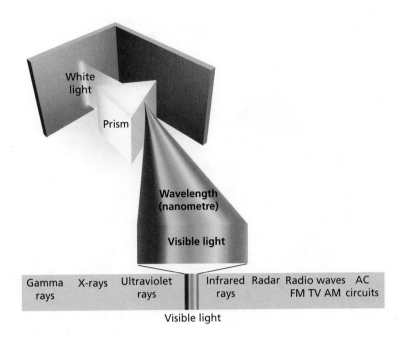

Saturation refers to the purity of the colour people see: A highly saturated red, for example, would contain only red wavelengths, whereas a less saturated red might contain a mixture of wavelengths. For example, when a child is using the red paint from a set of poster paints, the paint on the paper will look like a pure red, but if the child mixes in some white paint, the paint will look pink. The hue is still red but it will be a less saturated red because of the presence of other wavelengths. Mixing in any other colour would also lessen the saturation.

THE STRUCTURE OF THE EYE

How does the eye know how to interpret all of that information? The best way to explain how the eye processes light is to talk about what happens to an image as the light from that image travels through the eye. Refer to Figure 3.2 to follow the path of the image.

3.4. *How do the parts of the eye work together?*

FROM FRONT TO BACK: THE PARTS OF THE EYE   The surface of the eye is covered in a clear membrane called the *cornea*. The cornea not only protects the eye but also focuses most of the light coming into the eye (the vision-improving technique called *LASIK* actually uses this fact by making small incisions in the cornea with a laser to change the focus in the eye).

The next visual layer is a clear, watery fluid called the *aqueous humour*. This fluid is continually replenished and supplies nourishment to the eye. The light from the visual image then enters the interior of the eye through a hole, called the *pupil*, in a round muscle called the *iris* (the coloured part of the eye). The iris can change the size of the pupil, letting in more or less light. That also helps focus the image; people try to do the same thing by squinting.

Behind the iris, suspended by muscles, is another clear structure called the *lens*. The flexible lens finishes the focusing process begun by the cornea, and it can change its shape from thick to thin in a process called **visual accommodation**, which allows

◀ How does the eye know how to interpret all of that information?

visual accommodation
the change in the thickness of the lens as the eye focuses on objects that are far away or close.

FIGURE 3.2 **The Structure of the Eye**
Light enters the eye through the cornea
and pupil. The iris controls the size of
the pupil. From the pupil, light passes
through the lens to the retina, where it
is transformed into nerve impulses. The
nerve impulses travel to the brain along
the optic nerve.

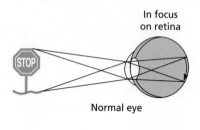

Normal eye

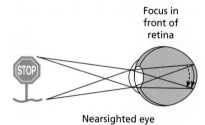

Nearsighted eye

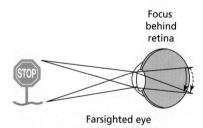

Farsighted eye

FIGURE 3.3 **Common Visual
Problems: Nearsightedness
and Farsightedness** This figure
shows the problem of focusing on
distant objects when the eyeball
is too long (nearsightedness) and
the problem of focusing on near
objects when the eyeball is too short
(farsightedness).

cones
visual sensory receptors found at the
back of the retina, responsible for
colour vision and sharpness of vision.

rods
visual sensory receptors found at the
back of the retina, responsible for non-
colour sensitivity to low levels of light.

blind spot
area in the retina where the axons of
the three layers of retinal cells exit the
eye to form the optic nerve, insensitive
to light.

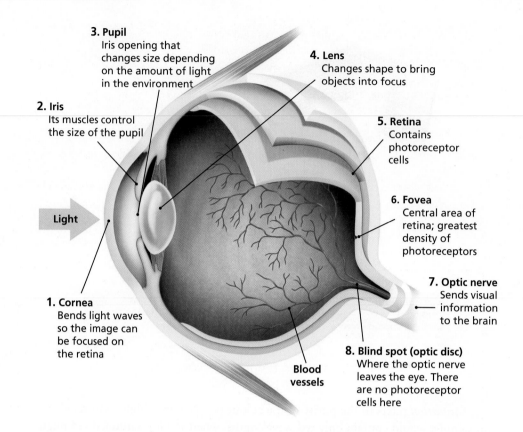

3. Pupil
Iris opening that
changes size depending
on the amount of light
in the environment

4. Lens
Changes shape to bring
objects into focus

2. Iris
Its muscles control
the size of the pupil

5. Retina
Contains
photoreceptor
cells

6. Fovea
Central area of
retina; greatest
density of
photoreceptors

Light

7. Optic nerve
Sends visual
information
to the brain

1. Cornea
Bends light waves
so the image can
be focused on
the retina

8. Blind spot (optic disc)
Where the optic nerve
leaves the eye. There
are no photoreceptor
cells here

Blood
vessels

people to focus on objects that are close or far away, as shown in Figure 3.3. People
lose this ability as the lens hardens through aging (a process called *presbyopia*), causing the need for bifocals, because holding objects at arm's length can no longer be
used to compensate.

Once through the lens, light passes through a large, open space filled with a
clear, jellylike fluid called the *vitreous humour*. This fluid, like the aqueous humour,
also nourishes the eye and gives it shape.

RETINA, RODS, AND CONES   The final stop for light within the eye is the *retina*,
a light-sensitive area at the back of the eye containing three layers: ganglion* cells,
bipolar cells, and the special cells (*photoreceptors*), called **rods** and **cones**, which respond to the various light waves (see Figure 3.4a). The rods and the cones are the
business end of the retina—the part that actually receives the photons of light and
transduces it into neural signals, sending it first to the bipolar cells (called *bipolar*, or
"two-ended," because they connect the rods and cones to the cells in the optic nerve)
and then to the ganglion cells that form the optic nerve with their axons entering the
brain (see Figure 3.5).

THE BLIND SPOT   The eyes don't adapt to constant stimuli under normal circumstances because of saccadic movements. But if people stare with one eye at one spot
long enough, they may see a blank space form because there is a "hole" in the retina—
the place where all the axons of those ganglion cells leave the retina to become the optic
nerve. There are no rods or cones here, so this is referred to as the **blind spot**. You can
demonstrate the blind spot for yourself by following the directions in Figure 3.4b.
We tend not to perceive our blind spots because our brains use information from
receptors around the blind spot to "fill in" the gaps in our retinal images—yes, your
brain will actually make up what it thinks should be there.

*Ganglion: a mass of nerve tissue and cells in the peripheral nervous system

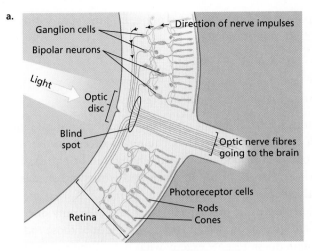

a.

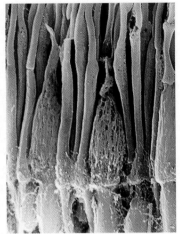

FIGURE 3.4 **The Parts of the Retina**
(a) Light passes through ganglion and bipolar cells until it reaches and stimulates the rods and cones. Nerve impulses from the rods and cones travel along a nerve pathway to the brain. On the right of the figure is a photomicrograph of the long, thin rods and the shorter, thicker cones; the rods outnumber the cones by a ratio of about 20 to 1. (b) The blind spot demonstration. Hold the book in front of you. Close your right eye and stare at the picture of the dog with your left eye. Slowly bring the book closer to your face. The picture of the cat will disappear at some point, because the light from the picture of the cat is falling on your blind spot.

b.

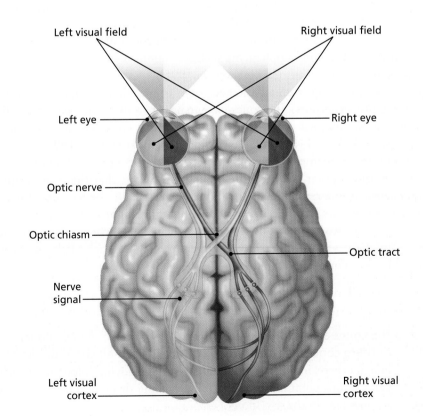

FIGURE 3.5 **Crossing of the Optic Nerve**   Light rays enter the eyes to fall on the retina. Light falling on the left side of each eye's retina (from the right visual field, shown in yellow) will stimulate a neural message that will travel along the optic nerve to the left visual cortex in the occipital lobe of the left hemisphere. Notice that the message from the left eye goes directly to the left occipital lobe, while the message from the right eye crosses over to the left hemisphere (the optic chiasm is the point of crossover). The optic nerve tissue from both eyes joins together to form the left optic tract before going on to the left occipital lobe. For the left visual field (shown in blue), the messages from both right sides of the retinas will travel along the right optic track to the right visual cortex in the same manner.

✳ Explore on mypsychlab
The Visual Cortex

Sometimes when I ▶ "space out" and stare at a page, a blank spot forms in what I'm staring at. What is that, adaptation?

dark adaptation
the recovery of the eye's sensitivity to visual stimuli in darkness after exposure to bright lights.

light adaptation
the recovery of the eye's sensitivity to visual stimuli in light after exposure to darkness.

While this deer may see quite well when using its rods at night, the bright headlights of a car will activate the cones. The cones will take a few minutes to fully adapt to the brightness, leaving the deer blinded by the light until then.

You said the cones are used in colour vision. There are so many colours in the world— are there cones that detect each colour? Or ▶ do all cones detect all colours?

Sometimes when I "space out" and stare at a page, a blank spot forms in what I'm staring at. What is that, adaptation?

HOW THE EYE WORKS

3.5. *How do the eyes see, and how do the eyes see different colours?*

Rods and cones are each responsible for different aspects of vision. The rods (about 120 million of them in each eye) are found all over the retina except in the very centre, which contains only cones. Rods are sensitive to changes in brightness but not to changes in wavelength, so they see only in black and white and shades of grey. They can be very sensitive because they are all on a "party line." That means that many rods are hooked up to only one bipolar cell, so that if even only one rod is stimulated by a photon of light, the brain perceives the whole area of those rods as stimulated. But because the brain doesn't know exactly what part of the area is actually "calling in" the message, the visual acuity (sharpness) is pretty low. That's why things seen in low levels of light, such as twilight or a dimly lit room, are fuzzy and greyish. Because rods are located on the periphery of the retina, they are responsible for peripheral vision.

Because rods work well in low levels of light, they are also the cells that allow the eyes to adapt to low light. **Dark adaptation** occurs as the eye recovers its ability to see when going from a brightly lit state to a dark state. The brighter the light was, the longer it takes the rods to adapt to the new lower levels of light (Bartlett, 1965). This is why the bright headlights of an oncoming car can leave a person less able to see for a while after the car has passed. Fortunately, this is usually a temporary condition and the rods readapt to the dark night relatively quickly. Complete dark adaptation takes about 30 minutes and takes longer as people get older, causing many older persons to be less able to see at night and in darkened rooms (Klaver et al., 1998). This age-related change can cause *night blindness*, in which a person has difficulty seeing well enough to drive at night or get around in a darkened room or house. Some research indicates that taking supplements such as vitamin A can reverse or relieve this symptom in some cases (Jacobsen et al., 1995).

When going from a darkened room to one that is brightly lit, the opposite process occurs. The cones have to adapt to the increased level of light, and they accomplish this **light adaptation** much more quickly than the rods adapt to darkness—it takes a few seconds at most (Hood, 1998). There are 6 million cones in each eye; of these, 50 000 have a private line to the optic nerve (one bipolar cell for each cone). This means that the cones found in the very centre of the retina, in an area called the *fovea*, are the receptors for visual acuity. It also means that the cones need a lot more light to function than the rods do, so cones work best in bright light, which is also when people see things most clearly. Cones are also sensitive to different wavelengths of light, so they are responsible for colour vision.

COLOUR VISION

You said the cones are used in colour vision. There are so many colours in the world—are there cones that detect each colour? Or do all cones detect all colours? Although experts in the visual system have been studying colour and its nature for many years, at this point in time there is an ongoing theoretical discussion about the role the cones play in the sensation of colour.

THEORIES OF COLOUR VISION   Two theories about how people see colours were originally proposed in the 1800s. The first is called the **trichromatic** ("three colours") **theory**. First proposed by Thomas Young in 1802 and later modified by Hermann von Helmholtz in 1852, this theory proposed three types of cones: red cones, blue cones, and green cones, one for each of the three primary colours of light.

Wait a minute—I thought the primary colours were red, yellow, and blue. Red, yellow, and blue are the primary colours when talking about *painting or pigment mixing*, not when talking about light itself. Paints *reflect* light, and the way reflected light mixes is different from the way direct light mixes. For example, if an artist were to blend red, yellow, and blue paints together, the result would be a mess—a black mess. But if the artist were to blend a red, green, and blue light together by focusing lights of those three colours on one common spot, the result would be white, not black.

In the trichromatic theory, different shades of colours correspond to different amounts of light received by each of these three types of cones. These cones then fire their message to the brain's vision centres. It is the combination of cones and the rate at which they are firing that determine the colour that will be seen. For example, if the red and green cones are firing in response to a stimulus at fast enough rates, the colour the person sees is yellow. If the red and blue cones are firing fast enough, the result is magenta. If the blue and green cones are firing fast enough, a cyan colour (blue-green) appears. Look again at Figure 3.1 on p. 95, the visible spectrum. Adding the long red wavelengths to the much shorter green ones will produce something in the middle—yellow.

In 1964, Brown and Wald identified three types of cones in the retina, each sensitive to one of the primary colour wavelengths. The actual colours and wavelengths turn out to be just a little different from Young and Helmholtz's original three: Blue-violet or "blue cones" (420 nanometres), green-yellow or "green cones" (530 nanometres), and yellow-green or "red cones" (560 nanometres) are the most sensitive wavelengths. Interestingly, people vary considerably in the number of "red" and "green" cones they have, but these differences do not appear to affect colour vision. Blue cones represent only about 8 percent of all cones.

THE AFTERIMAGE   The trichromatic theory would, at first glance, seem to be more than adequate to explain how people perceive colour. But there's an interesting phenomenon that this theory cannot explain. If a person stares at a picture of the Canadian flag for a little while—say, for 30 seconds—and then looks away to a blank white wall or sheet of white paper, that person will see an **afterimage** of the flag. Afterimages occur when a visual sensation persists for a brief time after the original stimulus is removed. The person would also notice rather quickly that the colours of the "flag" in the afterimage are all wrong—green for red, and black for white. If you follow the directions for Figure 3.6, in which the "flag" is green and black, you should see a flag coloured with the usual red and white.

Hey, now the afterimage of the flag has normal colours! Why does this happen? The phenomenon of the colour afterimage is explained by the second theory of colour perception, called the **opponent-process theory** (De Valois & Jacobs, 1968; Hurvich, 1969). In this theory, there are actually four primary colours: red, green, blue, and yellow. The cones are arranged in pairs, red with green and blue with yellow. If one member of a pair is stimulated, the other member cannot be working—so there are no reddish-greens or bluish-yellows.

So how does this cause the colour afterimage? If a person tires out one of the members of the pairs (by looking at a red image for about a minute, for example), it weakens that member's ability to inhibit the other cell. When the person then looks away from the red image, there will be a green afterimage as the other member of the pair fires away.

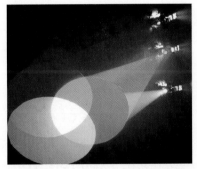

◄ Wait a minute—I thought the primary colours were red, yellow, and blue.

In trichromatic theory, the three types of cones combine to form different colours, much as these three coloured lights combine.

◄ Hey, now the afterimage of the flag has normal colours! Why does this happen?

trichromatic theory
theory of colour vision that proposes three types of cones: red, blue, and green.

afterimage
image that occurs when a visual sensation persists for a brief time after the original stimulus is removed.

opponent-process theory
theory of colour vision that proposes four primary colours with cones arranged in pairs: red and green, and blue and yellow.

FIGURE 3.6 **Colour Afterimage**
Stare at the white dot in the centre of this oddly coloured flag for about 30 seconds. Now look at a white piece of paper or a white wall. Notice that the colours are now the normal, expected colours of the Canadian flag. They are also the primary colours that are opposites of the colours in the picture, and evidence for the opponent-process theory of colour vision.

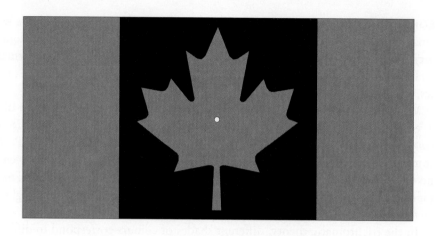

So which theory accounts for colour blindness? I've heard that there are two kinds of colour blindness, people who can't tell red from green and people who can't tell blue from yellow. ▶

So which theory is the right one? Both theories play a part in colour vision. Recently scientists have found that opponent-processing occurs at various levels along the visual pathway. For instance, some ganglion cells in the retina will increase their firing rate to yellow and decrease their firing rate to blue, and others will do the opposite. Similar observations have been found inside the thalamus in an area called the *lateral geniculate nucleus (LGN)*. The LGN is part of the pathway that visual information takes to the occipital lobe. Together, the ganglion cells and the cells in the LGN appear to be responsible for opponent processing of colour vision and the afterimage effect.

So which theory accounts for colour blindness? I've heard that there are two kinds of colour blindness, people who can't tell red from green and people who can't tell blue from yellow.

COLOUR BLINDNESS From the mention of red-green and yellow-blue colour blindness, one might think that the opponent-process theory explains this problem. But in reality colour blindness is caused by defective cones in the retina of the eye.

Persons who have normal colour vision are referred to as *trichromats*. They can detect red-green, yellow-blue, and black-white. Most persons who are colour blind are

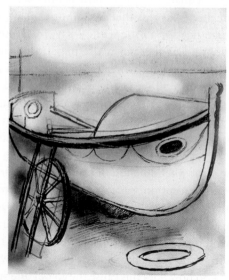

The painting on the left was done by a person with normal (trichromatic) colour vision. The painting in the centre was done by a person with dichromatic red-green colour blindness. (*Source:* From Oliver Sacks's story "The Case of the Colorblind Person" in his book *An Anthropologist on Mars* [1995].) The painting on the right was done by a *monochromat*, a person who sees no colour at all. Although some monochromats have no functioning cones and see very poorly, others are like this person and have some functioning cones, allowing them to have visual acuity.

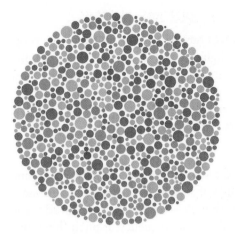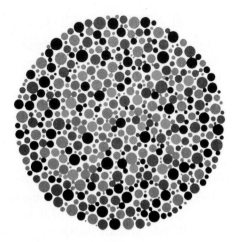

FIGURE 3.7 **The Ishihara Colour Test**
In the circle on the left, the number 8 is visible only to those with normal colour vision. In the circle on the right, people with normal vision will see the number 96, while those with red-green colour blindness will see nothing but a circle of dots.

dichromats. They cannot detect either red-green or yellow-blue. The most common type of dichromat has a deficiency in the red-green system (*red-green colour blindness*). These dichromats have normal visual acuity but see the world in blues, yellows, and shades of grey. Much less common are yellow-blue dichromats. Their blue cones do not work, and their visual world consists of reds, greens, and shades of grey. A very rare type of colour blindness is the *monochromat*, who is sensitive only to the black-white system and thus is totally colour blind. To monochromats, everything appears in shades of grey. To get an idea of what a test for colour blindness is like, look at Figure 3.7.

I've heard that most colour-blind people are men. Is that true? Yes, because the defective genes involved in red-green colour blindness are located on the X chromosome. Men inherit only one X chromosome (their sex chromosomes are XY), while women inherit two (their sex chromosomes are XX). So women would need to inherit two defective X chromosomes to develop red-green colour blindness, while men need only to inherit one. Since the probability of inheriting two defective X chromosomes is reduced, red-green colour blindness occurs in only about 1 percent of females but in 7 to 8 percent of males. This pattern of inheritance is known as *sex-linked inheritance*. Blue-yellow colour blindness appears equally in men and women and thus involves a faulty gene that is not located on the X chromosome. It is rare, affecting fewer than 1 in 10 000 people.

◀ I've heard that most colour-blind people are men. Is that true?

PRACTICE QUIZ: HOW MUCH DO YOU REMEMBER?

Pick the best answer.

1. Which of the following terms refers to the psychological effect of the amplitude of light waves?
   a. colour
   b. brightness
   c. saturation
   d. hue

2. Which of the following represents the correct path of light through the eye?
   a. iris, cornea, lens, retina
   b. cornea, vitreous humour, iris, lens, aqueous humour, retina
   c. cornea, pupil, lens, vitreous humour, retina
   d. cornea, lens, pupil, iris, retina

3. If you wanted to see a star better at night, what should you do?
   a. Look directly at it, because the cones will focus better at night.
   b. Look off to the side, using the cones in the periphery of the retina.
   c. Look directly at it, because the rods can see sharply at night.
   d. Look off to the side, using the rods in the periphery of the retina.

4. Which theory of colour vision accounts better for the afterimage?
   a. trichromatic theory
   b. opponent-process theory
   c. both a and b
   d. neither a nor b

5. Which statement about colour blindness is true?
   a. There are more men who are colour-blind than women.
   b. can influence only our complex emotions.
   c. Some colour-blind people see only in blue.
   d. Some colour-blind people see only in blue and red.

Answers: 1.b, 2.c, 3.d, 4.b, 5.a.

THE HEARING SENSE: CAN YOU HEAR ME NOW?

If light works like ▶
waves, then do sound
waves have similar
properties?

If light works like waves, then do sound waves have similar properties? The properties of sound are indeed similar to those of light, as both senses rely on waves. But the similarity ends there, as the physical properties of sound are different from those of light.

PERCEPTION OF SOUND: GOOD VIBRATIONS

3.6. *What is sound?*

Sound waves do not come in little packets the way light comes in photons. Sound waves are simply the vibrations of the molecules of air that surround us. Sound waves do have the same properties of light waves, though—wavelength, amplitude, and *purity*. Wavelengths are interpreted by the brain as the frequency or pitch (high, medium, or low). Amplitude is interpreted as volume, how soft or loud a sound is (see Figure 3.8). Finally, what would correspond to saturation or purity in light is called *timbre* in sound, a richness in the tone of the sound. And just as people rarely see pure colours in the world around us, they also seldom hear pure sounds. The everyday noises that surround people do not allow them to hear many pure tones.

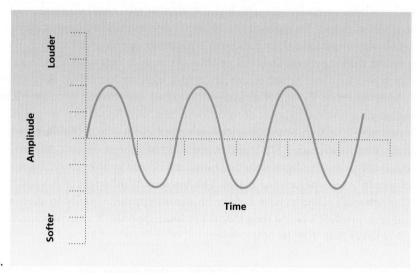

a.

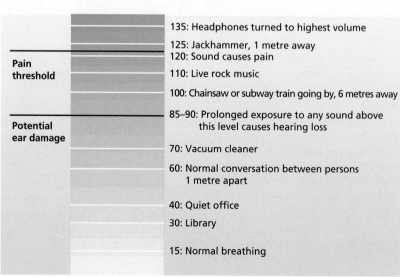

b.

FIGURE 3.8 **Sound Waves and Decibels** (a) A typical sound wave. The bigger the wave, the louder the sound; the smaller the wave, the softer the sound. If the waves are close together in time (high frequency), the sound will be perceived as a high pitch. Waves that are farther apart (low frequency) will be perceived as having a lower pitch. (b) Decibels of various stimuli. A *decibel* is a unit of measurement for loudness. Psychologists study the effects that noise has on stress, learning, performance, aggression, and psychological and physical well-being. Research on the hazards of loud noises led the National Basketball Association to put an 85-decibel limit on the sound system played at basketball arenas (Heisler, 1995).

Just as a person's vision is limited by the visible spectrum of light, a person is also limited in the range of frequencies he or she can hear. Frequency is measured in cycles (waves) per second, or **hertz (Hz)**. Human limits are between 20 and 20 000 Hz, with the most accurate hearing occurring at around 1000 Hz. (In comparison, dogs can hear between 50 and 60 000 Hz, whereas dolphins can hear up to 200 000 Hz.) To hear the higher and lower frequencies of a piece of music on a CD, for example, a person would need to increase the amplitude—which explains why some people like to "crank it up."

Is there a pathway through the ear, like the layers of the eye?

Is there a pathway through the ear, like the layers of the eye?

THE STRUCTURE OF THE EAR: FOLLOW THE VIBES

3.7. *How do the parts of the ear work together to hear sounds?*

The ear is a series of structures, each of which plays a part in the sense of hearing, as shown in Figure 3.9.

THE OUTER EAR The *pinna* is the visible, external part of the ear that serves as a kind of concentrator, funnelling the sound waves from the outside into the structure of the ear. People try to mimic this function when they curl their hand around their ear to hear better —they're trying to make the pinna larger. The antlers of a male moose may act in a similar fashion. Canadian scientists at the University of Guelph have determined that the antlers of male moose reflect sounds—including the sweet sounds of potential mates— toward the ear (Bubenik & Bubenik, 2008).

The pinna is the entrance to the **auditory canal** (or ear canal), the short tunnel that runs down to the *tympanic membrane*, or eardrum. The eardrum is a thin section of skin that tightly covers the opening into the middle part of the ear, just like a drum skin covers the opening in a drum. And just like that drum skin, when sound waves hit the eardrum, it vibrates and causes three tiny bones in the middle ear to vibrate.

THE MIDDLE EAR: HAMMER, ANVIL, AND STIRRUP The three tiny bones in the middle ear are known collectively as the auditory ossicles and individually as the hammer, anvil, and stirrup. The names come from the shape of each of the bones. When the eardrum vibrates, the hammer resting against the eardrum also vibrates, causing a chain reaction in the anvil and the stirrup. As the vibrations travel down the bones, they are amplified somewhat. The stirrup, the last bone in the chain, rests against another membrane of tissue called the *oval window*, which in turn covers the entrance to the inner ear.

THE INNER EAR The oval window vibrates when the stirrup vibrates, setting up another chain reaction within the inner ear.

Cochlea The inner ear is a snail-shaped structure called the **cochlea**, which is filled with fluid. When the oval window vibrates, it causes the fluid in the cochlea to vibrate. This fluid surrounds a membrane running through the middle of the cochlea called the *basilar membrane*.

"And only you can hear this whistle?"

Natural hearing aids

Peter Bubenik, a math professor at Cleveland State University, helped confirm a family theory that a bull moose's antlers help the animal to hear better.

How it works
1. Sound waves bounce off the broad palms of the bony antlers.

2. The moose moves its ears toward the antlers to "tune in" to the amplified sound.

SOURCES: Peter Bubenik; European Journal of Wildlife Research

KEN MARSHALL | THE PLAIN DEALER

hertz (Hz)
cycles or waves per second, a measurement of frequency.
auditory canal
short tunnel that runs from the pinna to the eardrum.
cochlea
snail-shaped structure of the inner ear that is filled with fluid.

FIGURE 3.9 **The Structure of the Ear** (a) This figure shows the entire ear, beginning with the outer ear (pinna, ear canal, and eardrum). The vestibular organ includes the semicircular canals and the otolith organs (inside the round structures just above the cochlea). (b) The middle ear. Sound waves entering through the ear canal cause the eardrum to vibrate, which causes each of the three bones of the middle ear to vibrate, amplifying the sound. The stirrup rests on the oval window, which transmits its vibration to the fluid in the inner ear. (c) The inner ear. Large spaces are filled with fluid (shown in purple) that vibrates as the oval window vibrates. A thin membrane suspended in this fluid is called the *basilar membrane*, which contains the organ of Corti, the structure composed of the hairlike cells that transduce sound waves to neural impulses. The neural impulses make their way to the auditory cortex of the brain via the auditory nerve. (d) A close-up view of the basilar membrane (in brown) with the hair cells of the organ of Corti (in dark purple). Notice the axons (small black lines) leaving the hair cells to form the auditory nerve.

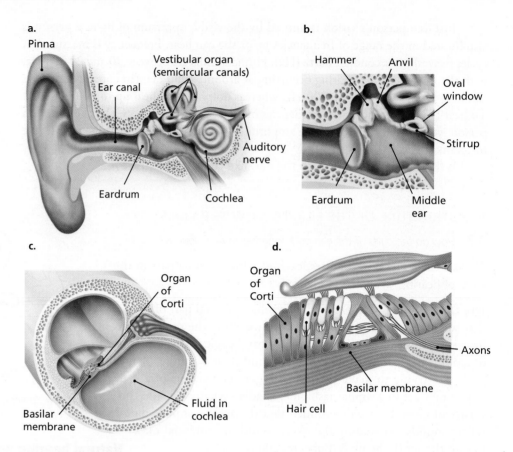

> I think I have it straight— but all of that just explains how soft and loud sounds get to the brain from the outside. How do we hear different kinds of sounds, such as high pitches and low pitches? ▶

✱ Explore on **mypsychlab**
Major Structures of the Ear

auditory nerve
bundle of axons from the hair cells in the inner ear.

pitch
psychological experience of sound that corresponds to the frequency of the sound waves; higher frequencies are perceived as higher pitches.

Basilar Membrane and the Organ of Corti The basilar membrane is the resting place of the *organ of Corti*, which contains the receptor cells for the sense of hearing. When the basilar membrane vibrates, it vibrates the organ of Corti, causing it to brush against a membrane above it. On the organ of Corti are special cells called *hair cells*, which are the receptors for sound and transduce sound waves to neural messages. When these auditory receptors or hair cells are bent up against the other membrane, it causes them to send a neural message through the **auditory nerve** (which contains the axons of all the receptor neurons) and into the brain, where the auditory cortex will interpret the sounds.

Thus, the sound waves go in through the pinna and vibrate the eardrum, which then vibrates the hammer, anvil, and stirrup, which in turn vibrate the oval window. This causes the fluid in the cochlea to vibrate, which vibrates the basilar membrane, which then causes the organ of Corti to move up and bend its hair cells, which send signals about hearing to the brain. Of course, the louder the sound in the outside world, the stronger the vibrations that stimulate more of those hair cells, which the brain interprets as loudness.

I think I have it straight—but all of that just explains how soft and loud sounds get to the brain from the outside. How do we hear different kinds of sounds, such as high pitches and low pitches?

THEORIES OF PITCH

Pitch refers to how high or low a sound is. There are two theories about how the brain receives information about pitch.

PLACE THEORY: HEARING IN HIGH PLACES The older **place theory** was proposed in 1863 by Hermann von Helmholtz of the Young–Helmholtz theory of colour vision fame. In this theory, the pitch a person hears depends on where the hair cells that are stimulated are located on the organ of Corti. For example, if the person is hearing a high-pitched sound, all the hair cells near the oval window will be stimulated, but if the sound is low-pitched, all the hair cells that are farther away on the organ of Corti will be stimulated.

FREQUENCY THEORY: THE LOW-DOWN ON PITCH   The **frequency theory**, developed by Ernest Rutherford in 1886, states that pitch is related to how fast the basilar membrane vibrates. The faster the membrane vibrates, the higher the pitch; the slower it vibrates, the lower the pitch. (In this theory, all the auditory neurons would be firing at the same time.)

So which theory is right? It turns out that both theories are right up to a certain point. In the case of place theory, research has found that for this theory to be right, the basilar membrane has to vibrate unevenly—which it does when the frequency of the sound is *above* 1000 Hz. For the frequency theory to be correct, the neurons associated with the hair cells would have to fire as fast as the basilar membrane vibrates. This only works up to 100 Hz, because neurons simply can't fire any faster than 100 times per second.

The place theory works for pitches above 1000 Hz, and the frequency theory works for pitches up to 100 Hz. What happens in between? The likeliest explanation of what happens between 100 and 1000 Hz is called the **volley principle**. In this explanation, when frequencies are above 100 Hz, the auditory neurons do not all fire at once. Instead, they take turns firing in a process called *volleying* or *the volley principle*. If a person hears a tone of about 300 Hz, it means that three groups of neurons have taken turns sending the message to the brain—the first group for the first 100 Hz, the second group for the next 100 Hz, and so on.

TYPES OF HEARING IMPAIRMENTS

3.8. *What is a hearing impairment?*

Hearing impairment is the term used to refer to difficulties in hearing. A person can be partially hearing impaired or totally hearing impaired.

3.9. *What can be done to help people with a hearing impairment?*

The treatment for hearing loss will vary according to the reason for the impairment.

CONDUCTION HEARING IMPAIRMENT   *Conduction hearing impairment* can result from either a damaged eardrum (which would prevent sound waves from being carried into the middle ear properly) or damage to the bones of the middle ear. In the latter case, sounds cannot be conducted from the eardrum to the cochlea. Middle ear damage is often from ear infections that are not treated quickly enough or from chronic ear infections. In this case, hearing aids may be of some use in restoring hearing.

NERVE HEARING IMPAIRMENT   In *nerve hearing impairment*, the problem lies either in the inner ear or in the auditory pathways and cortical areas of the brain. Normal aging causes loss of hair cells in the cochlea, and exposure to loud noises can damage hair cells. *Tinnitus* is a fancy word for an extremely annoying ringing in one's ears, and it can also be caused by infections or loud noises—including loud music in headphones, so you might want to turn down that music player! On a positive note, University of Toronto researchers have found that older musicians do *not* experience age-associated changes in their auditory cortex that typically contribute to declines in auditory perception (Zendel & Alain, 2009). So the old adage "use it or lose it" may apply to hearing. So, no matter how old you are, get out there and learn to play a new instrument.

Because the damage is to the nerves or the brain, nerve hearing impairment cannot be helped with ordinary hearing aids, which are basically sound amplifiers. A new technique

place theory
theory of pitch that states that different pitches are experienced by the stimulation of hair cells in different locations on the organ of Corti.

frequency theory
theory of pitch that states that pitch is related to the speed of vibrations in the basilar membrane.

volley principle
theory of pitch that states that frequencies above 100 Hz cause the hair cells (auditory neurons) to fire in a volley pattern, or take turns in firing.

FIGURE 3.10 **Cochlear Implant**
(a) In a cochlear implant, a microphone implanted just behind the ear picks up sound from the surrounding environment. A speech processor, attached to the implant and worn outside the body, selects and arranges the sound picked up by the microphone. The implant itself is a transmitter and receiver, converting the signals from the speech processor into electrical impulses that are collected by the electrode array in the cochlea and then sent to the brain. (b) This child is able to hear with the help of a cochlear implant. Hearing spoken language during the early years of a child's life helps in the development of the child's own speech.

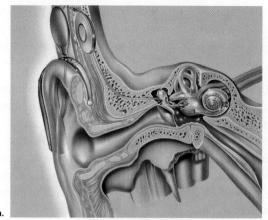
a.

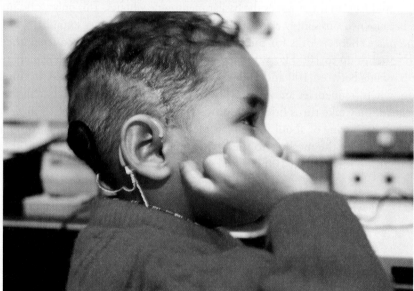
b.

for restoring hearing to those with nerve hearing impairment makes use of an electronic device called a *cochlear implant*. This device bypasses the outer and middle ears by sending signals from a microphone worn behind the ear to a sound processor worn on the belt or in a pocket, which then translates those signals into electrical stimuli that are sent to a series of electrodes implanted directly into the brain (see Figure 3.10). The brain then processes the electrode information as sound. With an implant, people can hear some speech and their own speech to a degree that allows more communication with others.

PRACTICE QUIZ: HOW MUCH DO YOU REMEMBER?

Pick the best answer.

1. Which of the following properties of sound would be the most similar to the colour or hue of light?
   a. pitch
   b. loudness
   c. purity
   d. timbre

2. The eardrum is also called the
   a. pinna
   b. oval window
   c. tympanic membrane
   d. cochlea

3. The _____ theory explains how we hear sounds above 1000 Hz.
   a. place
   b. frequency
   c. volley
   d. adaptive

4. If the bones of the middle ear begin to deteriorate, you will develop _____ hearing impairment.
   a. nerve
   b. stimulation
   c. brain pathway
   d. conduction

5. Why might you want to decrease the amount of loud music being pumped directly into the ear canal?
   a. to avoid tinnitus later in life
   b. to avoid growing antlers
   c. to avoid conductive hearing loss
   d. no need to avoid—I'll just get a cochlear implant!

CHEMICAL SENSES: IT TASTES GOOD, BUT IT SMELLS TERRIBLE

3.10. *How do the senses of taste and smell work?*

The sense of taste (taste in food, not taste in clothing or friends) and the sense of smell are very closely related. Have you ever noticed that when your nose is stopped up, your sense of taste is affected, too? That's because the sense of taste is really a combination of taste and smell. Without the input from the nose, there are actually only four, and possibly five, kinds of taste sensors in the mouth.

GUSTATION: HOW WE TASTE THE WORLD

TASTE BUDS   *Taste buds* are the common name for the taste receptor cells, special kinds of neurons found in the mouth that are responsible for the sense of taste, or **gustation**. Most taste buds are located on the tongue, but there are a few on the roof of the mouth, the cheeks, and under the tongue as well. How sensitive people are to various tastes depends on how many taste buds they have; some people have only around 500, whereas others have 20 times that number. The latter are called *supertasters* and need far less seasoning in their food than those with fewer taste buds (Bartoshuk, 1993).

So taste buds are those little bumps I can see when I look closely at my tongue? No, those "bumps" are called papillae, and the taste buds line the walls of these papillae (see Figure 3.11).

Explore on **mypsychlab**
The Four Basic Tastes

gustation
the sensation of taste.

So taste buds are those little bumps I can see when I look closely at my tongue?

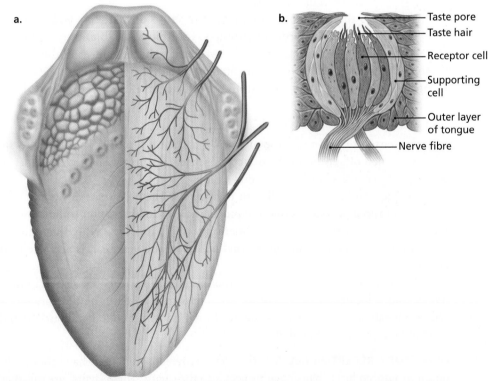

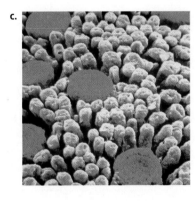

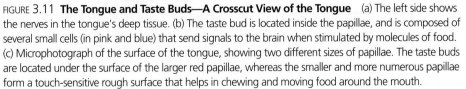

FIGURE 3.11 **The Tongue and Taste Buds—A Crosscut View of the Tongue**   (a) The left side shows the nerves in the tongue's deep tissue. (b) The taste bud is located inside the papillae, and is composed of several small cells (in pink and blue) that send signals to the brain when stimulated by molecules of food. (c) Microphotograph of the surface of the tongue, showing two different sizes of papillae. The taste buds are located under the surface of the larger red papillae, whereas the smaller and more numerous papillae form a touch-sensitive rough surface that helps in chewing and moving food around the mouth.

olfaction (olfactory sense)
the sensation of smell.

Each taste bud has about 20 receptors that are very similar to the receptor sites on receiving neurons at the synapse. Ⓛ Ⓘ Ⓝ Ⓚ *to Chapter Two: The Biological Perspective, p. 42.* In fact, the receptors on taste buds work exactly like receptor sites on neurons—they receive molecules of various substances that fit into the receptor like a key into a lock. Taste is often considered a chemical sense because it works with molecules of foods in the same way that neural receptors work with neurotransmitters. When the molecules (dissolved in saliva) fit into the receptors, a signal is fired to the brain, which then interprets the taste sensation.

What happens to the taste buds when I burn my tongue? Do they repair themselves? I know when I have burned my tongue, I can't taste much for a while, but the taste comes back. Actually, in general, the taste receptors get such a workout that they have to be replaced every 10 to 14 days (McLaughlin & Margolskee, 1994). And when the tongue is burned, the damaged cells no longer work. As time goes on, those cells get replaced and the taste sense comes back. Ever wonder why some people make a point of cleaning their tongue? The coating that people get on their tongue is no doubt partly composed of dead taste cells.

THE FIVE BASIC TASTES In 1916, a German psychologist named Hans Henning proposed that there are four primary tastes: sweet, sour, salty, and bitter. In 1996, Lindemann proposed that there is a fifth kind of taste receptor that detects a pleasant "brothy" taste associated with foods such as chicken soup, tuna, kelp, cheese, and soy products, among others. Lindemann also proposed that this fifth taste be called *umami*, a Japanese word that describes the taste. The five taste sensations work together, along with the sense of smell and the texture, temperature, and "heat" of foods, to produce thousands of taste sensations.

How does the sense of smell affect the sense of taste? As you said, when I have a cold I can taste hardly anything—everything is so bland. Everything becomes bland because you can taste only sweet, salty, bitter, sour, and umami—and because your nose is stuffed up when you have a cold, you don't get all the enhanced variations of those tastes that come from the sense of smell.

THE SENSE OF SCENTS: OLFACTION

Like the sense of taste, the sense of smell is a chemical sense. The ability to smell odours is called **olfaction**, or the **olfactory sense**. (It's pretty easy to remember that, because "old factories" really smell, don't they?)

People don't actually smell with their noses. The outer part of the nose serves the same purpose for odours that the pinna and ear canal serve for sounds: Both are merely ways to get the sensory information to the part of the body that will translate it into neural signals. So the external nose, like the outer ear, is just a collection device.

The part of the olfactory system that turns odours into signals the brain can understand is located at the top of the nasal passages. This area of olfactory receptor cells is only about 2.5 centimetres square in each cavity yet contains about 10 million olfactory receptors (see Figure 3.12).

OLFACTORY RECEPTOR CELLS The *olfactory receptor cells* each have about a half-dozen to a dozen little "hairs" that project into the cavity. These "hairs" are called *cilia*. Like taste buds, there are receptor sites on these hair cells that send signals to the brain when stimulated by the molecules of substances that are in the air moving past them.

Wait a minute—you mean that when I'm smelling something like a skunk, there are little particles of skunk odour in my nose? Yes. When a person is sniffing something, the sniffing serves to move molecules of whatever the person is trying

---

Sidebar callouts:

▶ What happens to the taste buds when I burn my tongue? Do they repair themselves? I know when I have burned my tongue, I can't taste much for a while, but the taste comes back.

▶ How does the sense of smell affect the sense of taste? As you said, when I have a cold I can taste hardly anything—everything is so bland.

👁 Watch on **mypsychlab**
Alzheimer's Smell Test

Wait a minute—you mean that when I'm smelling something like a skunk, there are little particles of skunk odour *in* my nose? ▶

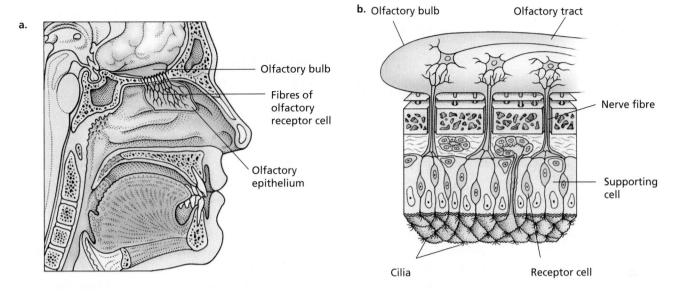

FIGURE 3.12 **The Olfactory Receptors** (a) A cross-section of the nose and mouth. This drawing shows the nerve fibres inside the nasal cavity that carry information about smell directly to the olfactory bulb just under the frontal lobe of the brain (shown in green). (b) A diagram of the cells in the nose that process smell. The olfactory bulb is on top, shown in green. Notice the tiny hairlike cells that project into the nasal cavity. These are the receptors for the sense of smell.

to smell into the nose and into the nasal cavities. That's okay when it's the smell of baking bread, apple pie, flowers, and the like, but when it's skunk, rotten eggs, dead animals—well, try not to think about it too much.

Olfactory receptors are like taste buds in another way, too. Olfactory receptors also have to be replaced as they naturally die off, about every five to eight weeks. Unlike the taste buds, there are more than five types of olfactory receptors. In fact, there are at least 1000 of them.

Don't I remember from Chapter Two that the sense of smell is different in some way from the other senses? Yes, the signals from the olfactory receptors in the nasal cavity do not follow the same path as the signals from all the other senses. Vision, hearing, taste, and touch all go through the medulla (where the signals from one side of the body cross over to the opposite side) and up through the brain stem, the thalamus, and finally to the area of the cortex that processes that particular sensory information. But the sense of smell has its own special place in the brain—the olfactory bulbs.

THE OLFACTORY BULBS The **olfactory bulbs** are located right on top of the sinus cavity on each side of the brain directly beneath the frontal lobes. (Refer back to Figure 3.12.) The olfactory receptors send their neural signals directly up to these bulbs, bypassing the entire lower brain and its selective attention filter, the reticular formation.

If the olfactory signals bypass the part of the brain that lets us ignore constant and unchanging information, does that mean that we can't "ignore" smells? Fortunately, people can ignore a smell that is constant and unchanging; but, it doesn't involve the reticular formation.

Remember when sensory adaptation was covered earlier in the chapter? The text stated that certain sensory receptors become less sensitive to a constant stimulus as time goes by, so that eventually a person no longer perceives the stimulus. This adaptation is why people don't continue to smell the odour of the kitchen garbage can after being home for a while.

olfactory bulbs
areas of the brain located just above the sinus cavity and just below the frontal lobes that receive information from the olfactory receptor cells.

◀ Don't I remember from Chapter Two that the sense of smell is different in some way from the other senses?

If the olfactory signals bypass the part of
◀ the brain that lets us ignore constant and unchanging information, does that mean that we can't "ignore" smells?

PSYCHOLOGY IN THE NEWS

Can Humans Smell Danger and Great Potential Mates?

Smelling Danger

A team of researchers led by Dr. Johan Lundstrom at the Montreal Neurological Institute has shown that humans are very good at smelling the difference between someone we know and someone we don't know. Researchers asked 15 participants to smell four different body odours: their own, that of a stranger, a friend's, and an artificial body odour. When the researcher asked each participant to identify each smell, they were correct 90 percent of the time. Then each participant was again asked to smell and identify each odour, but this time their brain activity was being recorded with a PET (positron emission tomography) scanner. The researchers found a number of interesting results. First, the brain appears to process real body odours in different brain areas than artificial odours. Second, only the body odour of a stranger activated parts of the brain known to be important in the processing of fear and danger, the amygdala and insular cortex. And third, although the accuracy of identifying each smell dropped when near the PET scanner (the researchers believe that being near the PET scanner made the participants nervous), the brain could not be fooled. Even if a participant reported that the smell of a stranger was that of a friend, the amygdala turned on (Lundstrom, Boyle, Zatorre, & Jones-Gotman, 2008). When asked about the results of his study, Dr. Lundstrom, who now works at the Monell Chemical Senses Center in Philadelphia, said, "Our study demonstrates that the olfactory system has preferential processing for behaviourally important stimuli. This means that stimuli that are perceived as very important to us, either for survival, finding food, or mate selection, are processed faster and more accurately" (Derfel, 2007).

Smelling Great Mates

Ladies, imagine this. Men are given clean T-shirts and asked to wear them overnight. The T-shirts are then bagged, and blood samples are taken from the men. Women are then asked to sniff each T-shirt and rate the smell for attractiveness. They, too, provide blood samples. Researchers then determine the type of genes that make up each participant's major histocompatibility complex (MHC). MHC genes are involved in your immune response. The results from studies such as this are intriguing. In general, women tend not to like the smell of most men. When women are ovulating, however, they prefer the scents of men who have the most *dissimilar* MHC complexes. This finding suggests that mixing up the immune response genes may create healthier and fitter offspring. Even more interesting is the finding that women taking birth control pills preferred the scents of men with similar MHC complexes (Wedekind, Seebeck, Bettens, & Paepke, 1995; Roberts, Gosling, Carter, & Petrie, 2008)! Does the pill make women select bad mates? Garver-Apgar et al. (2006) have found that women who share fewer MHC genes with their partners are more satisfied in their relationships and more likely to be faithful than women who have partners with similar MHC complexes. So maybe the nose really does know!

Questions for Further Discussion

1. How might Dr. Lundstrom have gotten his odour samples?

2. Why do some retailers infuse their shops with specific odours?

3. Why might the pill make women select bad mates?

SOMESTHETIC SENSES: WHAT THE BODY KNOWS

So far, this chapter has covered vision, hearing, taste, and smell. That leaves touch. What is thought of as the sense of touch is really several sensations, originating in several different places in—and on—the body. It's really more accurate to refer to these as the *body senses*, or **somesthetic senses**. The first part of that word, *soma*, means "body," as mentioned in Chapter Two. The second part, *esthetic*, means "feeling," hence the name. There are three somesthetic sense systems, the **skin senses** (having to do with touch, pressure, temperature, and pain), the **kinesthetic sense** (having to do with the location of body parts in relation to the ground and to each other), and the **vestibular senses** (having to do with movement, balance, and body position).

TOUCH, PRESSURE, AND TEMPERATURE

3.11. *How does the sense of touch work, and what happens when people experience pain?*

Here's a good trivia question: What organ of the body is about 2 square metres in size? The answer is the skin. Skin is an organ. Its purposes include more than simply keeping bodily fluids in and germs out; skin also receives and transmits information from the outside world to the central nervous system (specifically, to the somatosensory cortex Ⓛ Ⓘ Ⓝ Ⓚ *to Chapter Two: The Biological Perspective, pp. 70–71*). Information about light touch, deeper pressure, heat, cold, and even pain is collected by special receptors in the skin's layers.

TYPES OF SENSORY RECEPTORS IN THE SKIN   There are about half a dozen different receptors in the layers of the skin (see Figure 3.13). Some of them will respond to only one kind of sensation. For example, the *Pacinian corpuscles* are just beneath the skin and respond only to pressure. There are nerve endings that wrap around the ends of the hair follicles, a fact people may be well aware of when they tweeze their eyebrows. These nerve endings are sensitive to both pain and touch. There are *free nerve endings* just beneath the uppermost layer of the skin that respond to changes in temperature and to pressure—and pain.

How exactly does pain work? Why is it that sometimes I feel pain deep inside?   There are pain nerve fibres in the internal organs as well as receptors for pressure. How else would people have a stomach ache or intestinal pain? Or get that full feeling of pressure when they've eaten too much or their bladder is full?

Margin glossary

somesthetic senses
the body senses, consisting of the skin senses, the kinesthetic sense, and the vestibular senses.

skin senses
the sensations of touch, pressure, temperature, and pain.

kinesthetic sense
sense of the location of body parts in relation to the ground and each other.

vestibular senses
the sensations of movement, balance, and body position.

Her sense of touch is allowing this blind girl to "read" a Braille book with her fingers. The fingertips are extremely sensitive to fine differences in texture, allowing her to distinguish between small dots representing the different letters of the alphabet.

◀ How exactly does pain work? Why is it that sometimes I feel pain deep inside?

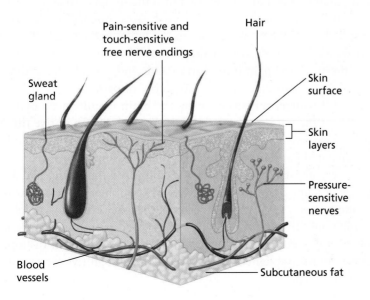

FIGURE 3.13 **Cross-Section of the Skin and Its Receptors**   The skin is composed of several types of cells that process pain, pressure, and temperature. Some of these cells are wrapped around the ends of the hairs on the skin and are sensitive to touch on the hair itself, while others are located near the surface and still others just under the top layer of tissue.

Figure labels: Pain-sensitive and touch-sensitive free nerve endings; Hair; Sweat gland; Skin surface; Skin layers; Pressure-sensitive nerves; Blood vessels; Subcutaneous fat

There are actually different types of pain. Some receptors detect pain (and pressure) in the organs, a type of pain called *visceral pain*. But pain sensations in the skin, muscles, tendons, and joints are carried on large nerve fibres and are called *somatic pain*. Somatic pain is the body's warning system that something is being, or is about to be, damaged and tends to be sharp and fast. Another type of somatic pain is carried on small nerve fibres and is slower and more of a general ache. This somatic pain acts as a kind of reminder system, keeping people from further injury by reminding them that the body has already been damaged. For example, if you hit your thumb with a hammer, the immediate pain sensation is of the first kind—sharp, fast, and bright. But later the bruised tissue simply aches, letting you know to take it easy on that thumb.

People may not like pain, but the function it serves as a warning system is vitally important. There are people who are born without the ability to feel pain, rare conditions called *congenital analgesia* and *congenital insensitivity to pain with anhidrosis (CIPA)*. Children with these disorders cannot feel pain when they cut or scrape themselves, leading to an increased risk of infection when the cut goes untreated (Mogil, 1999). They fear nothing—which can be a horrifying trial for the parents and teachers of such a child. These disorders affect the neural pathways that carry pain, heat, and cold sensations. (Those with CIPA have an additional disruption in the body's heat/cold sensing perspiration system [anhidrosis], so that the person is unable to cool off the body by sweating.)

PAIN: GATE-CONTROL THEORY

The best current explanation for how the sensation of pain works is called *gate-control theory*, first proposed by Canadian psychologist Ronald Melzack and British physiologist Patrick Wall (1965) and later refined and expanded by them (Melzack & Wall, 1996) at McGill University. In this theory, the pain signals must pass through a "gate" located in the spinal cord. The activity of the gate can be closed by non-pain signals coming into the spinal cord from the body and by signals coming from the brain. This helps to explain why rubbing a sore spot can help to reduce the feeling of pain. The gate is not a physical structure but instead represents the relative balance in neural activity of cells in the spinal cord that receive information from the body and then send information to the brain.

Stimulation of the pain receptor cells releases a chemical called *substance P* (for pain, naturally). Substance P released into the spinal cord activates other neurons that send their messages through spinal gates (opened by the pain signal). From the spinal cord, the message goes to the brain, activating cells in the thalamus, somatosensory cortex, areas of the frontal lobes, and the limbic system. The brain then interprets the pain information and sends signals that either open the spinal gates farther, causing a greater experience of pain, or close them, dampening the pain. Of course, this decision by the brain is influenced by the psychological aspects of the pain-causing stimulus. Anxiety, fear, negative thinking, and helplessness can intensify pain. For example, researchers at Dalhousie University in Halifax separated participants into two groups: Group 1 consisted of those who viewed pain very negatively, and Group 2 comprised those who had a much less negative view of pain. Both groups were asked to submerge their arms in icy cold water for one minute, and every 20 seconds they reported how much pain they were experiencing. Those in Group 1, who viewed pain much more negatively than Group 2, reported much higher pain experiences (Sullivan, Bishop, & Pivik, 1995). These results highlight the negative role that cognitive factors can have on the perception of pain.

Anhidrosis is a rare genetic disorder that makes 5-year-old Ashlyn unable to feel pain. She must be examined carefully for scrapes and cuts after recess at school because she cannot feel when she hurts herself, putting her at risk for infection. What are some of the problems that Ashlyn and her parents may face as she grows older?

But cognitive factors can also be a positive influence on our perception of pain. Laughter, distraction, and a sense of control (e.g., Zen meditation) can diminish it. This is likely why Toronto Maple Leaf great Bobby Baun was able to score the winning overtime goal against Detroit in Game Six of the 1964 Stanley Cup final despite having broken his leg. Baun also refused an X-ray after the game because he thought the doctors would find something to keep him out of the lineup for Game Seven. He played Game Seven, the Leafs won the Cup, and then he learned of his broken leg. Those same psychological aspects can also influence the release of the *endorphins*, the body's natural version of morphine. Ⓛ Ⓘ Ⓝ Ⓚ *to Chapter Two: The Biological Perspective, p. 42.* Endorphins can inhibit the transmission of pain signals in the brain, and in the spinal cord they can inhibit the release of substance P. As discussed in the section on neurotransmitters in Chapter Two, the release of endorphins is perhaps one explanation for "runner's high" (the pleasurable feeling a runner may experience after running a long distance) and the effectiveness of acupuncture.

I've always heard that women are able to stand more pain than men. Is that true? The statement that women are better able to tolerate higher levels of pain than are men is a generalization that has no basis in fact. Some people also have heard that men are very childish about pain and do not cope well with pain, but that is also a myth. The fact is that research has shown that women apparently feel pain more intensely than do men, and they also report pain more often than men do (Chesterton et al., 2003; Faucett et al., 1994; Norrbrink et al., 2003). Men have been shown to cope better with many kinds of pain, possibly because men are often found to have a stronger belief than women that they can control their pain by their own efforts (Jackson et al., 2002). We may all be able to lower our sensitivity to pain though. Researchers at the Université de Montréal have shown, using MRI results, that persons who practise Zen meditation have thicker brain regions that regulate emotions and pain (i.e., the anterior cingulate gyrus). This increased cortical thickness may account for the reduced sensitivity to pain seen in persons who meditate (Grant et al., 2010).

THE KINESTHETIC SENSE

3.12. *What sense allows the body to know how it is moving and when it is balanced?*

The *proprioceptive receptors (proprioceptors)*, located in the skin, joints, muscles, and tendons, are part of the body's sense of position in space—the location of the arms, legs, and so forth in relation to one another and in relation to the ground. This sense is called *kinesthesia*, from the Greek words *kinein* (to move) and *aesthesis* (sensation). When you close your eyes and raise your hand above your head, you know where your hand is because the proprioceptors tell you about the changes in pressure within the muscles.

What about motion sickness? I get queasy every time I have to ride in the back seat of a car or travel on a boat—what kinds of receptors are responsible for that? Actually, it's not the proprioceptors in the body that make people get sick. The culprits are special structures in the ear that make up the *vestibular sense*—the sense of balance.

THE VESTIBULAR SENSE

The name of this particular sense comes from a Latin word that means "entrance" or "chamber." The latter definition is probably the one that fits better here, as the structures for this sense are located in the innermost chamber of the ear. There are two kinds of vestibular organs, the otolith organs and the semicircular canals.

The *otolith organs* are tiny sacs found just above the cochlea. These sacs contain a gelatin-like fluid within which tiny crystals are suspended (much like pieces of fruit

◀ I've always heard that women are able to stand more pain than men. Is that true?

What about motion sickness? I get queasy every time I have to ride in the back seat of a car or travel on a boat—what kinds of receptors are responsible for that?

These Cirque du Soleil performers are balancing themselves and each other in an amazing feat of coordination and muscular control. They must use not only their vestibular organs to help maintain their balance but also their kinesthetic sense to be aware of exactly where each body part is in relation to the others.

in a bowl of Jell-O). The head moves and the crystals cause the fluid to vibrate, setting off some tiny hairlike receptors on the inner surface of the sac, telling the person that he or she is moving forward, back, sideways, or up and down. (It's pretty much the way the cochlea works but with movement as the stimulus instead of sound vibrations.)

The *semicircular canals* are three somewhat circular tubes that are also filled with fluid and will stimulate hairlike receptors when rotated. There are three tubes, one in each of the three planes of motion. Remember learning in geometry class about the *x*-, *y*-, and *z*-axes? Those are the three planes through which the body can rotate, and when it does, it sets off the receptors in these canals. Ever spin around and around like a top when you were a kid? When you stopped, the fluid in the horizontal canal was still rotating and making you feel dizzy because your body was telling you that you were still moving, but your eyes were telling you that you had stopped.

MOTION SICKNESS This disagreement between what the eyes say and what the body says is pretty much what causes *motion sickness*, the tendency to get nauseated when in a moving vehicle, especially one with an irregular movement. Normally, the vestibular sense coordinates with the other senses. But for some people, the information from the eyes may conflict a little too much with the vestibular organs, and dizziness, nausea, and disorientation are the result. This explanation of motion sickness is known as **sensory conflict theory** (Oman, 1990). Actually, people can probably blame the dizziness for the nausea; in human evolutionary history, many poisons make a person dizzy, and the most adaptive thing to do is to expel the poison. So although there isn't any poison in a case of motion sickness, the person may "expel" something anyway.

One way some people overcome motion sickness is to focus on a distant point or object. That point won't seem to move like the objects closer to the car window, for example, and so this causes less conflict. This is also how ballerinas and ice skaters manage not to get sick when turning rapidly and repeatedly—they focus their eyes at least once on some fixed object every so many turns.

sensory conflict theory
an explanation of motion sickness in which the information from the eyes conflicts with the information from the vestibular senses, resulting in dizziness, nausea, and other physical discomforts.

Pick the best answer.

1. The receptors on our taste buds work most like
   a. receptors in the ears.
   b. receptors in the eyes.
   c. receptor sites on neurons.
   d. receptors in the skin.

2. Which of the following statements about olfactory receptors is FALSE?
   a. Olfactory receptors are replaced every few years.
   b. There are at least 1000 types of olfactory receptors.
   c. Signals from the receptors go directly to the olfactory bulbs in the brain.
   d. Olfactory receptors have hairlike projections called cilia.

3. After some time has passed, you can no longer smell the odour of the paper mill that you noticed when you first walked into your classroom. Which is the most likely reason for this?
   a. The smell has gone away.
   b. You've adapted to the smell, even though it's still there.
   c. Your nose fell asleep.
   d. You fell asleep.

4. Pain sensations in the skin, muscles, tendons, and joints that are carried on large nerve fibres are called
   a. visceral pain.
   b. somatic pain.
   c. referred pain.
   d. indigenous pain.

5. In gate-control theory, substance P
   a. opens the spinal gates for pain.
   b. closes the spinal gates for pain.
   c. is unrelated to pain.
   d. is similar in function to endorphins.

6. Which of the following is most likely to open the pain gate?
   a. negative thinking about pain
   b. excitement over an upcoming big game
   c. rubbing a sore spot
   d. both a and b

7. A bowl of gelatin with fruit in it will wiggle more than if it contained no fruit. This is most similar to the way the _____ work.
   a. semicircular canals
   b. proprioceptors
   c. otolith organs
   d. none of the above

Answers: 1-c, 2-a, 3-b, 4-b, 5-a, 6-a, 7-c.

THE ABCs OF PERCEPTION

3.13. *What are perception and perceptual constancies?*

Perception is the method by which people take all the sensations they experience at any given moment and interpret them in some meaningful fashion. Perception has some individuality to it—no two people will perceive the world in exactly the same way. Two people might be looking at a cloud, for example, and while one thinks it's shaped like a horse, the other thinks it's more like a cow. They both *see* the same cloud, but they *perceive* a different interpretation. As individual as perception might be, there are some rules for how people perceive the world around them. The following section discusses some of these basic principles.

THE CONSTANCIES: SIZE, SHAPE, AND BRIGHTNESS

There's an old cartoon that shows a very large man speaking to a very small man. He's saying, "Excuse me for shouting—I thought you were much farther away." This cartoon makes use of the concept of a perceptual constancy for size. **Size constancy** is the tendency to interpret an object as always being the same size, regardless of its distance from the viewer (or the size of the image it casts on the retina). So if an object that is normally perceived to be about 2 metres tall appears very small on the retina, it will be interpreted as being very far away. Evidence for size constancy has been found in 6-month-old infants (McKenzie et al., 1980), 4-month-olds (Day & McKenzie, 1981), and newborns (Slater et al., 1990). Yet size constancy cannot be fully present at birth, or it must require some kind of environmental stimulation to be maintained, because in cases of people who have been blind since birth and who then have sight restored, size constancy is absent or severely limited (Gregory, 1990; Sacks, 1995).

perception
the method by which the sensations experienced at any given moment are interpreted and organized in some meaningful fashion.

size constancy
the tendency to interpret an object as always being the same actual size, regardless of its distance from the viewer.

shape constancy
the tendency to interpret the shape of an object as being constant, even when its shape changes on the retina.

brightness constancy
the tendency to perceive the apparent brightness of an object as the same even when the light conditions change.

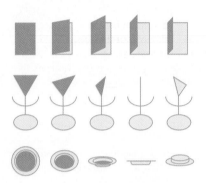

FIGURE 3.14 **Shape Constancy** Three examples of shape constancy are shown here. The opening door is actually many different shapes, yet we still see it as basically a rectangular door. We do the same thing with a triangle and a circle—although when we look at them from different angles they cast quite differently shaped images on our retina, we experience them as a triangle and a circle because of shape constancy.

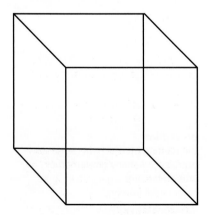

FIGURE 3.15 **The Necker Cube** This drawing is an example of a reversible figure. It can also be described as an ambiguous figure, since it is not clear which pattern should predominate.

Another perceptual constancy is the tendency to interpret the shape of an object as constant, even when it changes on the retina. This is called **shape constancy** and is why a person still perceives a coin as a circle even if it is held at an angle that makes it appear to be an oval on the retina. Dinner plates on a table are also seen as round, even though from the angle of viewing they are oval (see Figure 3.14).

The third form of perceptual constancy is called **brightness constancy**, the tendency to perceive the apparent brightness of an object as the same even when the light conditions change. If a person is wearing black pants and a white shirt, for example, in broad daylight the shirt will appear to be much brighter than the pants. But if the sun is covered by thick clouds, even though the pants and shirt have less light to reflect than previously, the shirt will still appear to be just as much brighter than the pants as before—because the different amount of light reflected from each piece of clothing is still the same difference as before (Zeki, 2001).

THE GESTALT PRINCIPLES

Remember the discussion of the Gestalt theorists in Chapter One? Those scientists were studying the very same concepts, the rules of human perception. Although Gestalt psychology has become a kind of therapy orientation today, the original focus on perception still remains in the basic principles of perception first laid out by those early pioneers in the field. These principles are based on the idea that people have a natural tendency to force patterns onto whatever they see. Following are some of the basic principles of this tendency to group objects and perceive whole shapes.

3.14. *What are the Gestalt principles of perception?*

FIGURE–GROUND RELATIONSHIPS   Take a look at the drawing of the cube in Figure 3.15. Which face of the cube is at the front? Look again. Do the planes and corners of the cube seem to shift as you look at it?

This image is called the *Necker cube*. It has been around officially since 1832, when a Swiss scientist who was studying the structure of crystals first drew it in his published papers. The problem with this cube is that there are no cues for depth, so the viewer is never really sure which plane or edge is at the back and which is at the front.

A similar illusion can be seen in Figure 3.16. In this picture, the viewer can switch perception back and forth from two faces looking at each other to the outline of a goblet in the middle. Which figure is the foreground and which is the background?

Figure–ground relationships refer to the tendency to perceive objects, or figures, as existing on some background. People seem to have a preference for picking out figures from backgrounds even as early as birth, and this is the first visual ability to reappear after a cataract patient regains sight. The illusions in Figures 3.15 and 3.16 are **reversible figures**, in which the figure and the ground can be switched back and forth.

PROXIMITY   Another very simple rule of perception is the tendency to perceive objects that are close to one another as part of the same grouping, a principle called **proximity**, or nearness (see Figure 3.17).

SIMILARITY   **Similarity** refers to the tendency to perceive things that look similar as being part of the same group (see Figure 3.17). This is one reason why sports teams wear uniforms that are all the same colour—it allows people viewing the game to perceive team members as one group even when they are scattered around the rink, field, or court.

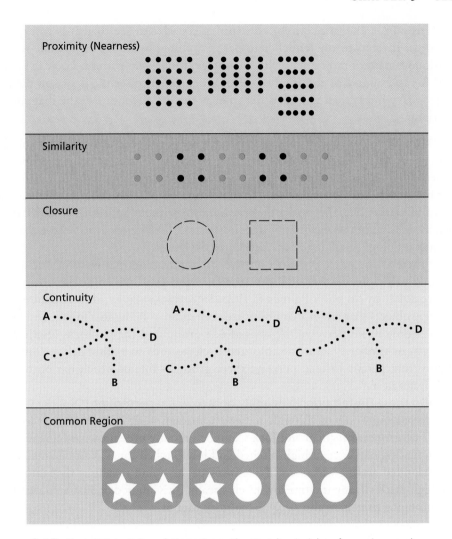

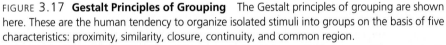

FIGURE 3.16 **Figure–Ground Illusion** What do you see when you look at this picture? Is it a wine goblet? Or two faces looking at each other? This drawing is an example in which the figure and the ground seem to "switch" each time you look at the picture.

✳—Explore on **mypsychlab**
Ambiguous Figures

FIGURE 3.17 **Gestalt Principles of Grouping** The Gestalt principles of grouping are shown here. These are the human tendency to organize isolated stimuli into groups on the basis of five characteristics: proximity, similarity, closure, continuity, and common region.

Proximity: The dots on the left can be seen as horizontal or vertical rows—neither organization dominates. But just by changing the proximity of certain dots, as in the other two examples, we experience the dots as vertical columns (middle) or horizontal rows (right).

Similarity: The similarity of colour here makes you perceive these dots as forming black squares and colour squares rather than two rows of black and coloured dots.

Closure: Even though the lines are broken, we still see these figures as a circle and a square—an example of how we tend to "close" or "fill in" missing parts from what we know of the whole.

Continuity: Because of continuity, we are much more likely to see the figure on the left as being made up of two lines, A to B and C to D, than we are to see it as a figure made up of lines A to D and C to B or A to C and B to D.

Common Region: Similarity would suggest that people see two groups, stars and circles. But the coloured backgrounds define a visible common region, and the tendency is to perceive three different groups.

CLOSURE   **Closure** is the tendency to complete figures that are incomplete (see Figure 3.17). In class, one instructor usually draws a series of curved lines, spaced a few centimetres apart, in a circular pattern on the board. When students are asked what they see, they invariably say "a circle." But it isn't a circle at all—just curved lines laid out in a circular formation. The brain fills in the spaces between the arcs to perceive a circle. In the same way, a talented artist can give the impression of an entire face with just a few cleverly placed strokes of the pen or brush—the viewers fill in the details.

figure–ground
the tendency to perceive objects, or figures, as existing on a background.

reversible figures
visual illusions in which the figure and ground can be reversed.

proximity
the tendency to perceive objects that are close to each other as part of the same grouping.

similarity
the tendency to perceive things that look similar to each other as being part of the same group.

closure
the tendency to complete figures that are incomplete.

continuity
the tendency to perceive things as simply as possible with a continuous pattern rather than with a complex, broken-up pattern.

contiguity
the tendency to perceive two things that happen close together in time as being related.

depth perception
the ability to perceive the world in three dimensions.

Do these Gestalt ▶ principles apply only to visual perception?

CONTINUITY   The principle of **continuity** is easier to see than it is to explain in words. It refers to the tendency to perceive things as simply as possible with a continuous pattern rather than with a complex, broken-up pattern. Look at Figure 3.17 for an example of continuity. Isn't it much easier to see the figure on the left as two wavy lines crossing each other than as the little sections in the diagram to the right?

CONTIGUITY   **Contiguity** isn't shown in Figure 3.17, because it involves not just nearness in space but also nearness in time. Basically, contiguity is the tendency to perceive two things that happen close together in time as being related. Usually the first occurring event is seen as causing the second event. Ventriloquists make great use of this principle. They make the vocalizations without appearing to move their own mouths but move the dummy's mouth instead. The tendency to believe that the dummy is doing the talking is due largely to contiguity.

There is one other principle of perceptual grouping that was not one of the original principles. It was added to the list (and can be seen at the bottom of Figure 3.17) by Stephen Palmer (1992). In *common region*, the tendency is to perceive objects that are in a common area or region as being in a group. In Figure 3.17, people could perceive the stars as one group and the circles as another on the basis of similarity. But the coloured backgrounds so visibly define common regions that people instead perceive three groups—one of which has both stars and circles in it.

Do these Gestalt principles apply only to visual perception? No, the Gestalt laws do not apply only to vision. In a classic Canadian study done in 1971 at McGill University, Albert Bregman and Jock Campbell rapidly presented participants with an alternating sequence of high-pitched and low-pitched tones. Participants amazingly reported hearing what seemed like two separate sound streams at the same time, one high-pitch stream and one low-pitch stream. This study demonstrated that Gestalt grouping principles also apply to auditory stimuli.

DEPTH PERCEPTION

The ability to see the world in three dimensions is called **depth perception**. It's a handy ability, because without it people would have a hard time judging how far away objects are. How early is depth perception developed? People who have had sight restored have almost no ability to perceive depth if they were blind from birth. Yet, like the constancies, depth perception seems to be present in infants at a very young age. The following Classic Studies in Psychology section presents one of the most famous studies in the field of depth perception.

Of course, the youngest babies in Gibson and Walk's classic study were 6 months old, and that might be old enough to have learned depth cues. In later studies, researchers (Campos et al., 1970) were able to demonstrate depth perception in infants as young as 2 months. These researchers placed very young infants on either the deep side or the shallow side and measured their heart rate. A decreasing heart rate in infants is associated with interest, whereas an increasing rate is associated with fear. The heart rate of the infants did not alter when they were placed on the shallow side but decreased when placed on the deep side. They were interested but not afraid. The older infants in the Gibson and Walk study were old enough to have experience with falling and tumbling down, and

CLASSIC STUDIES IN PSYCHOLOGY

The Visual Cliff

3.15. *How do people perceive the world in three dimensions?*

In the late 1950s, psychologist Eleanor Gibson was on a picnic at a local park. She was watching toddlers playing near the edge of a drop-off and began to wonder how the children knew not to step off the drop. (Most people would probably be yelling at the toddlers to get away from the cliff, but most people aren't psychologists.) This simple observation led to one of the most famous experiments in the field of developmental psychology.

Eleanor Gibson and her fellow researcher, Michael Walk, wondered if infants could perceive the world in three dimensions and devised a way to test babies for depth perception (Gibson & Walk, 1960). They built a special table (see Figure 3.18) that had a big drop on one side. The surface of the table on both the top part and the lower part on the floor were covered in a patterned tablecloth, so that the different size of the patterns would be a cue for depth (remember, in size constancy, if it looks smaller, people assume it is farther away from them). The whole table was then covered by a clear glass top, so that a baby could safely be placed on or crawl across the "deep" side.

The infants tested in this study ranged from 6 months to 14 months old. They were placed on the middle of the table and then encouraged (usually by their mothers) to crawl over either the shallow side or the deep side. Most babies—81 percent—refused to crawl over the deep side, even though they could touch it with their hands and feel that it was solid. They were upset and seemed fearful when encouraged to crawl across. Gibson and Walk interpreted this as a very early sign of the concept of depth perception.

Questions for Further Discussion

1. Does the fact that 19 percent of the infants did crawl over the deep side of the visual cliff necessarily mean that those infants could not perceive the depth?

2. What other factors might explain the willingness of the 19 percent to crawl over the deep side?

3. Are there any ethical concerns in this experiment?

4. Ducks aren't bothered by the visual cliff at all—why would that be?

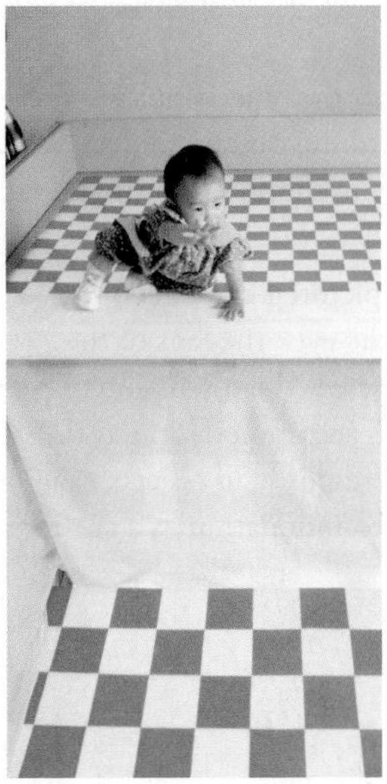

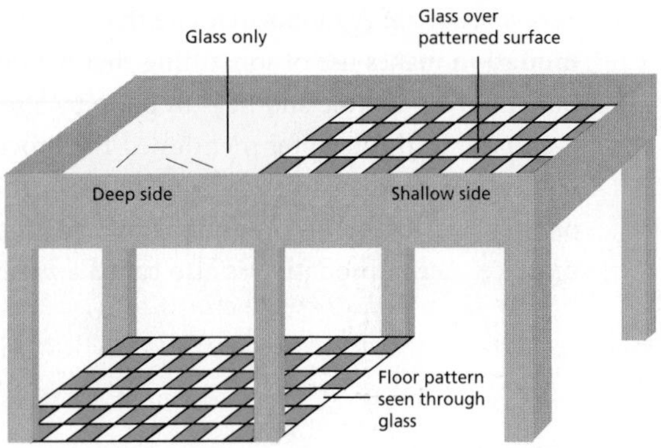

Watch on **mypsychlab**

Eleanor Gibson, Richard Walk, and the Visual Cliff

Glass only

Glass over patterned surface

Deep side

Shallow side

Floor pattern seen through glass

FIGURE 3.18 **The Visual Cliff Experiment**   In the visual cliff experiment, the table has both a "shallow" and a "deep" side, with glass covering the entire table. When an infant looks down at the deep side, the squares in the design on the floor look smaller than the ones on the shallow side, forming a visual cue for depth. Notice that this little girl seems to be very reluctant to cross over the deep side of the table, gesturing to be picked up instead.

it is probably this experience that caused them to fear the depth. Based on the reactions of the infants in the Campos study, it is very likely that the ability to perceive the world in three dimensions is more or less inborn. It is fear of depth that requires learning and experience.

There are various cues for perceiving depth in the world. Some require the use of only one eye (**monocular cues**) and some are a result of the slightly different visual patterns that exist when the visual fields* of both eyes are used (**binocular cues**).

MONOCULAR CUES   Monocular cues are often referred to as pictorial depth cues, because artists can use these cues to give the illusion of depth to paintings and drawings. Examples of these cues can be seen in Figure 3.19.

1. *Linear perspective*: When looking down a long highway, the two sides of the highway appear to merge together in the distance. This tendency for parallel lines to appear to converge on each other is called **linear perspective**. It works in pictures because people assume that in the picture, as in real life, the converging lines meet a great distance away from where they are.

2. *Relative size*: The principle of size constancy is at work in **relative size**, when objects that people expect to be of a certain size appear to be small, they are, therefore, assumed to be much farther away. Movie makers use this principle to make their small models seem gigantic and in the distance.

3. *Overlap*: If one object seems to be blocking another object, people assume that the blocked object is behind the first one and therefore farther away. This cue is also known as **interposition**.

4. *Aerial perspective*: The farther away an object is, the hazier the object will appear to be, a process called **aerial perspective**. This is why distant mountains often look fuzzy, and buildings far in the distance are blurrier than those that are close. At greater distances more tiny particles of dust, dirt, and other pollutants in the air can come between the object and a person's eyes, causing blurred vision.

5. *Texture gradient*: If there are any large expanses of pebbles, rocks, or patterned roads (such as a cobblestone street) nearby, go take a look at them one day. The pebbles or bricks that are close to you are very distinctly textured, but as you look farther off into the distance, their texture becomes smaller and finer. **Texture gradient** is another trick used by artists to give the illusion of depth in a painting.

6. *Motion parallax*: The next time you're in a car, notice how the objects outside the car window seem to zip by very fast when they are close to the car, and objects in the distance seem to move more slowly. This discrepancy in motion of near and far objects is called **motion parallax**.

7. *Accommodation*: A monocular cue that is not one of the pictorial cues, **accommodation** makes use of something that happens inside the eye. The lens of the human eye is flexible and held in place by a series of muscles. The discussion of the eye earlier in this chapter mentioned the process of visual accommodation as the tendency of the lens to change its shape, or thickness, in response to objects near or far away. The brain can use this information about accommodation as a cue for distance. Accommodation is also called a *muscular cue*.

monocular cues (pictorial depth cues)
cues for perceiving depth based on one eye only.

binocular cues
cues for perceiving depth based on both eyes.

linear perspective
the tendency for parallel lines to appear to converge on each other.

relative size
perception that occurs when objects that a person expects to be of a certain size appear to be small and are therefore assumed to be much farther away.

interposition (overlap)
the assumption that an object that appears to be blocking part of another object is in front of the second object and closer to the viewer.

aerial perspective
the haziness that surrounds objects that are farther away from the viewer, causing the distance to be perceived as greater.

texture gradient
the tendency for textured surfaces to appear to become smaller and finer as distance from the viewer increases.

motion parallax
the perception of motion of objects in which close objects appear to move more quickly than objects that are farther away.

accommodation
as a monocular clue, the brain's use of information about the changing thickness of the lens of the eye in response to looking at objects that are close or far away.

*Visual field: the entire area of space visible at a given instant without moving the eyes

FIGURE 3.19 **Examples of Pictorial Depth Cues**   (a) Both the lines of the trees and the sides of the road appear to come together in the distance. This is an example of linear perspective. (b) Notice how the larger pebbles in the foreground seem to give way to smaller and smaller pebbles near the middle of the picture. Texture gradient causes the viewer to assume that as the texture of the pebbles gets finer, the pebbles are getting farther away. (c) In aerial perspective, the farther away something is the hazier it appears because of fine particles in the air between the viewer and the object. (d) The depth clue of relative size appears in this photograph. Notice that the flowers in the distance appear much smaller than those in the foreground. Relative size causes smaller objects to be perceived as farther away from the viewer.
Source: Shepard, T. H. (2001).

BINOCULAR CUES   As the name suggests, these cues require the use of two eyes.

1. *Convergence*: Another muscular cue, **convergence** refers to the rotation of the two eyes in their sockets to focus on a single object. If the object is close, the convergence is pretty great (almost as great as crossing the eyes). If the object is far away, the convergence is much less. Hold your finger up in front of your nose, and then move it away and back again. That feeling you get in the muscles of your eyes is convergence (see Figure 3.20a).

2. *Binocular disparity*: **Binocular disparity** is a scientific way of saying that because the eyes are a few centimetres apart, they don't see exactly the same image. The brain interprets the images on the retina to determine distance from the eyes. If

convergence
the rotation of the two eyes in their sockets to focus on a single object, resulting in greater convergence for closer objects and lesser convergence if objects are distant.

binocular disparity
the difference in images between the two eyes, which is greater for objects that are close and smaller for distant objects.

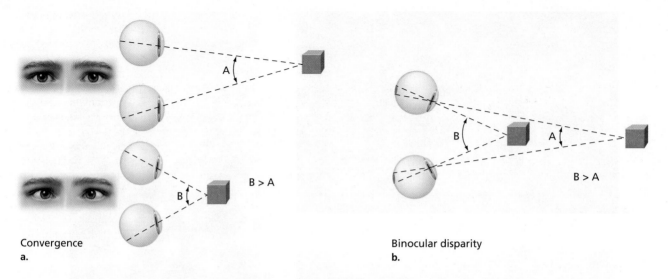

Convergence
a.

Binocular disparity
b.

FIGURE 3.20 **Binocular Cues to Depth Perception** (a) Convergence is a depth cue that involves the muscles of the eyes. When objects are far away, the eye muscles are more relaxed; when objects are close, the eye muscles move together, or converge. (b) Binocular disparity. Because your eyes are separated by several centimetres, each eye sees a slightly different image of the object in front of you. In A, the object is far enough away that the difference is small. In B, while the object is closer, there is a greater difference between what each eye sees. The brain interprets this difference as the distance of the object.

You've mentioned the word illusion several times. Exactly what are illusions, and why is it so easy to be fooled by them?

Müller-Lyer illusion
illusion of line length that is distorted by inward-turning or outward-turning corners on the ends of the lines, causing lines of equal length to appear to be different.

the two images are very different, the object must be pretty close. If they are almost identical, the object is far enough away to make the retinal disparity very small. You can demonstrate this cue for yourself by holding an object in front of your nose. Close one eye, note where the object is, and then open that eye and close the other. There should be quite a difference in views. But if you do the same thing with an object that is across the room, the image doesn't seem to "jump" or move nearly as much, if at all (see Figure 3.20b).

In spite of all the cues for perception that exist, even the most sophisticated perceiver can still fail to perceive the world as it actually is, as the next section demonstrates.

PERCEPTUAL ILLUSIONS

You've mentioned the word *illusion* several times. Exactly what are illusions, and why is it so easy to be fooled by them? An *illusion* is a perception that does not correspond to reality. People *think* they see something when the reality is quite different. Another way of thinking of illusions is as visual stimuli that "fool" the eye. (Illusions are different from hallucinations in that a hallucination's origin is in the brain itself—a person is seeing or hearing something that is actually not there at all. An illusion is a distorted perception of something that *is* there.)

3.16. *How do visual illusions work?*

MÜLLER-LYER ILLUSION One of the most famous visual illusions, the **Müller-Lyer illusion**, is shown in Figure 3.21. The distortion happens when the viewer tries to determine whether the two lines are exactly the same length. They are identical, but one line—the line with the angles on the end facing outward—looks longer than the other. Why is this illusion so powerful? The explanation is that most people live in a world with lots of buildings. Buildings have corners. When a person is outside a building, the corner of the building is close to that person, while the walls seem to

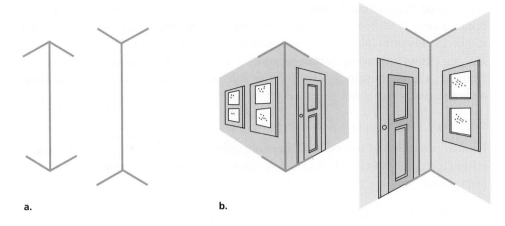

a.   b.

FIGURE 3.21 **The Müller-Lyer Illusion**   (a) Which line is longer? In industrialized Western countries, people generally see the lines in part (a) in situations such as in part (b). According to one theory, they have become accustomed to seeing right angles in their environment and assume that the short, slanted lines are forming a right angle to the vertical line. They make that assumption because they are accustomed to seeing corners, such as the ones shown in the figure on the right. Consequently, in the figure on the left, they tend to perceive the line on the right as slightly longer than the line on the left.

be moving away. When the person is inside a building, the corner of the room seems to move away from the viewer while the walls are coming closer. In the illusion, the line with the angles facing inward is like the outside of the building, and the one with the angles facing outward is like the inside of the room. In their minds, people "pull" the inward-facing angles toward them like the outside corners of a building, and they make the outward-facing angles "stretch" away from them like the inside corners of the room (Enns & Coren, 1995; Gregory, 1990).

Segall and colleagues (1966) found that people in Western cultures, having carpentered buildings with lots of straight lines and corners (Segall and colleagues refer to this as a "carpentered world") are far more susceptible to this illusion than people from non-Western cultures (having round huts with few corners—an "uncarpentered world"). Gregory (1990) found that Zulus, for example, rarely see this illusion. They live in round huts arranged in circles, use curved tools and toys, and experience few straight lines and corners in their world.

THE MOON ILLUSION   Another common illusion is the *moon illusion*, in which the moon on the horizon appears to be much larger than the moon in the sky (Plug & Ross, 1994). One explanation for this is that the moon high in the sky is all alone, with no cues for depth surrounding it. But on the horizon, the moon appears behind trees and houses, cues for depth that make the horizon seem very far away. The moon is seen as being behind these objects and, therefore, farther away from the viewer. Because people know that objects that are farther away from them and still seem large are very large indeed, they "magnify" the moon in their minds—a misapplication of the principle of size constancy. This explanation of the moon illusion is called the *apparent distance hypothesis*.

The moon illusion. When this moon is high in the night sky it will still be the same size to the eye as it is now. Nevertheless, it is perceived to be much larger when on the horizon. In the sky, there are no objects for comparison, but on the horizon, objects such as this tree are seen as being in front of a very large moon.

ILLUSIONS OF MOTION   Sometimes people perceive an object as moving when it is really still. One example of this is mentioned in Chapter Twelve, in the context of a famous experiment in conformity: the *autokinetic effect*. (L)(I)(N)(K) *to Chapter Twelve: Social Psychology, p. 479*. In this effect, a small, stationary light in a darkened room will appear to move or drift because there are no surrounding cues to indicate that the light is *not* moving. Another is the *stroboscopic motion* seen in motion pictures, in which a rapid series of still pictures will seem to be in motion. Many a student has discovered that drawing little figures on the edges of a notebook and then flipping the pages quickly will also produce this same illusion of movement.

Another movement illusion related to stroboscopic motion is the *phi phenomenon*, in which lights turned on in sequence appear to move. For example, if a light

perceptual set (perceptual expectancy)
the tendency to perceive things a certain way because previous experiences or expectations influence those perceptions.

top-down processing
the use of pre-existing knowledge to organize individual features into a unified whole.

bottom-up processing
the analysis of the smaller features to build up to a complete perception.

✳ Explore on mypsychlab
Top-Down Processing

✳ Explore on mypsychlab
Five Well-Known Illusions

FIGURE 3.22 **Perceptual Set**
Look at the drawing in the middle. What do you see? Now look at the drawings on each end. Would you have interpreted the middle drawing differently if you had looked at the drawing of the man or the kneeling woman first?

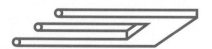

FIGURE 3.23 **The Devil's Trident**
At first glance, this seems to be an ordinary three-pronged figure. But a closer look reveals that the three prongs cannot be real as drawn. Follow the lines of the top prong to see what goes wrong.

is turned on in a darkened room and then turned off, and then another light a short distance away is flashed on and off, it will appear to be one light moving across that distance. This principle is used to suggest motion in many theatre marquee signs, flashing arrows indicating direction that have a series of lights going on and off in a sequence, and even in strings of decorative lighting, such as the "chasing" lights seen on houses at holiday times.

FACTORS THAT INFLUENCE PERCEPTION

Human perception of the world is obviously influenced by things such as culture and misinterpretations of cues. Following are other factors that cause people to alter their perceptions.

3.17. *What factors can influence perception?*

PERCEPTUAL SETS AND EXPECTANCIES   People often misunderstand what is said to them because they were expecting to hear something else. People's tendency to perceive things a certain way because their previous experiences or expectations influence them is called **perceptual set** or perceptual expectancy. Although expectancies can be useful in interpreting certain stimuli, they can also lead people down the wrong path. For example, look at Figure 3.22. The drawing in the middle is a little difficult to identify. People who start looking at these five drawings by looking at the drawing on the far left (which is clearly a man's face) tend to see the middle drawing as a man's face. But people who start looking from the far right (where the drawing is a kneeling woman with one arm over her chest and one touching her knee) see the middle picture as a woman. What you see depends on what you expect to see.

The way in which people interpret what they perceive can also influence that perception. For example, people can try to understand what they perceive by using information they already have (as is the case in a perceptual expectancy). But if there is no existing information that relates to the new information, they can look at each feature of what they perceive and try to put it all together into one whole.

Anyone who has ever worked on a jigsaw puzzle knows that it's a lot easier to put it together if there is a picture of the finished puzzle to act as a guide. It also helps to have worked the puzzle before—people who have done that already know what it's going to look like when it's finished. In the field of perception, this is known as **top-down processing**—the use of pre-existing knowledge to organize individual features into a unified whole. This is also a form of perceptual expectancy.

If the puzzle is one the person has never worked before or if that person has lost the top of the box with the picture on it, he or she would have to start with a small section, put it together, and keep building up the sections until the recognizable picture appears. This analysis of smaller features and building up to a complete perception is called **bottom-up processing** (Cave & Kim, 1999). In this case, there is no expectancy to help organize the perception, making bottom-up processing more difficult in some respects. Fortunately, the two types of processing are used together in perceiving the surrounding world.

Would people of different cultures perceive objects differently because of different expectancies? Some research suggests that this is true. For example, take a look at Figure 3.23.

This figure is often called *the devil's trident*. Europeans and North Americans insist on making this figure three dimensional, so they have trouble looking at it—the figure is impossible if it is perceived in three dimensions. But people in more "primitive" native cultures have little difficulty with seeing or even reproducing this figure, because they see it as a two-dimensional drawing, quite literally a collection of lines and circles rather than a solid object (Deregowski, 1969).

PRACTICE QUIZ: HOW MUCH DO YOU REMEMBER?

Pick the best answer.

1. The tendency to perceive a quarter as being round even when it is viewed at an angle is called
   a. size constancy.
   b. shape constancy.
   c. brightness constancy.
   d. colour constancy.

2. A reversible figure, such as the Necker cube, makes use of which principle of perception?
   a. shape constancy
   b. expectancy
   c. figure–ground relationships
   d. depth perception

3. Which of the following is NOT a monocular cue for depth?
   a. convergence
   b. linear perspective
   c. overlap
   d. texture gradient

4. An illusion
   a. is the same thing as a hallucination.
   b. exists only in the brain cells of the viewer.
   c. is a distorted perception of an actual stimulus.
   d. corresponds directly to reality.

5. Ned found a decaying carcass lying on the beach one day. Looking at the size of the body (which had decomposed quite a bit), Ned decided that it was the body of a sea monster, something like the Loch Ness monster in Scotland. If we know that Ned loves to read about weird, mythical animals, we might expect that he has made an error of perception because of
   a. perceptual set.
   b. perceptual defence.
   c. bottom-up processing.
   d. none of the above

6. The first time Joe had to put together a child's bicycle, it took a long time. But several bicycles later, he's a whiz at constructing them. His improved speed and skill can be attributed to
   a. bottom-up processing.
   b. top-down processing.
   c. perceptual set.
   d. perceptual expectancy.

Answers: 1-b, 2-c, 3-a, 4-c, 5-a, 6-b.

APPLYING PSYCHOLOGY TO EVERYDAY LIFE: THINKING CRITICALLY ABOUT ESP

Extrasensory perception (ESP) is usually defined as a claim of perception that occurs without the use of normal sensory channels such as sight, hearing, touch, taste, or smell. People who claim to have one or more of these abilities are commonly called psychics. It was J. B. Rhine, a professor at Duke University, who first coined the term ESP in 1927 and, in fact, invented the field of **parapsychology**, the scientific study of ESP, ghosts, and all things that do not normally fall into the realm of ordinary psychology (Rhine, 1935). Dr. Rhine invented the Zener cards (see Figure 3.24) to test for one of the ESP abilities, telepathy.

There are supposedly several different kinds of extrasensory perception. Here's a list of the more common "abilities" that psychics are supposed to have:

1. *Telepathy:* The word literally means "distant feeling" and is commonly used to refer to the claimed ability to read another person's thoughts, or mind reading.

2. *Clairvoyance:* Literally "clear sight," this term refers to the supposed ability to "see" things that are not actually present. This ability is also claimed by many so-called psychic detectives, who believe that they can find lost objects, people, or even the bodies of murder victims by touching objects associated with the people in question.

3. *Precognition:* Precognition is the supposed ability to know something in advance of its occurrence or to predict a future event. Note that precognition is often confused with clairvoyance. The difference is that in clairvoyance, what is "seen" is something that exists at the present time, whereas precognition is supposed to involve "seeing" the future.

parapsychology
the study of ESP, ghosts, and other subjects that do not normally fall into the realm of ordinary psychology.

FIGURE 3.24 **Zener Cards**
These five shapes, star, circle, cross, wavy lines, and square, are used in a test for telepathy, a form of extrasensory perception. One person (the sender) looks at each card after pulling it from a randomly shuffled deck of these five cards and thinks about the image on the card. The person being tested for telepathy, who cannot see the card, is supposed to guess what the shape is. An accuracy rate greater than chance is taken as an indication of telepathic ability.

Research has been conducted since the time of Rhine's early experiments with mixed results. Many of the earlier methodologies used in researching psychic phenomena were flawed, making their results useless (Randi, 1980, 1982). Critics and skeptics point to the lack of consistent scientific evidence or ability to replicate experiments, which seem to support viewing ESP and other psychic abilities as fakery, fraud, and misdirection. Believers claim that ESP is a talent that does not work "on command" and is detrimentally affected by the presence of skepticism during tests.

Is there a case for ESP, or "psi" as it is sometimes called? Here's a quotation from the online *Skeptic's Dictionary*:

> Most ESP claims do not get tested, but parapsychologists have attempted to verify the existence of ESP under controlled conditions. Some, like Charles Tart and Raymond Moody, claim success; others, such as Susan J. Blackmore, claim that years of trying to find experimental proof of ESP have failed to turn up any proof of indisputable, repeatable psychic powers. Defenders of psi claim that the gansfeld [sic] experiments, the CIA's remote viewing experiments and attempts to influence randomizers at Princeton Engineering Anomalies Research have produced evidence of ESP. Psychologists who have thoroughly investigated parapsychological studies, like Ray Hyman and Blackmore, have concluded that where positive results have been found, the work was fraught with fraud, error, incompetence, and statistical legerdemain. (Carroll, 2002)

One of the most promising research techniques is the ganzfeld experiment, in which a person who is the "receiver" is placed in a room and wears special goggles (table-tennis balls cut in half and secured over the eyes) and earphones that produce white noise. This creates a kind of sensory deprivation. A "sender" in another room tries to mentally send images or video clips to the receiver. In one set of studies published in *Psychological Bulletin* (Bem & Honorton, 1994), these experiments seemed to produce a "hit rate" greater than that predicted by chance and were taken as evidence that some kind of mental telepathy had taken place. But later studies that examined all the ganzfeld studies that had been completed demonstrated that there were no consistent findings across studies, no replication, and no support for any kind of telepathy (Milton & Wiseman, 2001).

Dr. Michael Persinger and his colleagues at Laurentian University in Sudbury, Ontario, have provided what amounts to a rational, testable, and very controversial explanation for the apparent perception of various psychic abilities. In a series of experiments over the past 20 years, Persinger used a modified snowmobile helmet (see photo below) to demonstrate that weak electromagnetic stimulation of the right temporal lobe can produce religious or paranormal experiences in some participants (Hill & Persinger, 2003). One skeptical ESP authority mentioned above, Dr. Susan Blackmore, agreed to wear Dr. Persinger's helmet. The following is an excerpt of her experience:

For the first ten minutes or so nothing seemed to happen. To tell the truth I felt rather daft. Instructed to describe aloud anything that happened I did not know what to say and felt under pressure to say something—anything. Then suddenly all my doubts were gone. "I'm swaying. It's like being on a hammock." Then it felt for all the world as though two hands had grabbed my shoulders and were bodily yanking me upright. I knew I was still lying in the reclining chair, but someone, or something, was pulling me up.

Something seemed to get hold of my leg and pull it, distort it, and drag it up the wall. I felt as though I had been stretched half way up to the ceiling.

Then came the emotions. Totally out of the blue, but intensely and vividly, I felt suddenly angry—not just mildly cross but that sort of determinedly clear-minded anger out of which you act—only there was nothing and no one to act on. After perhaps ten seconds it was gone but later was replaced by an equally sudden fit of fear. I was just suddenly terrified—of nothing in particular. Never in my life have I had such powerful sensations coupled with the total lack of anything to blame them on. I was almost looking around the little room to find who was doing it.

Of course, I knew that it was all caused by the magnetic field changes but what, I wondered, would I feel if such things happened spontaneously. What if I woke in the middle of the night with all those feelings? I knew I would want, above all, to find an explanation, to find out who had been doing it to me. To have such powerful feelings and no reason for them is horrible. You feel as if you are going mad. If someone told me an alien was responsible and invited me to join an abductees' support group, I might well prefer to believe the idea; rather than accept I was going mad. (Blackmore, 1994)

Dr. Blackmore's experience is typical of the experiences described by others who have worn the helmet, but she knew what she was getting into and her expectations may have contributed to her experience, an example of the placebo effect. Dr. Pehr Granqvist and his colleagues (2005) recently tried to replicate Persinger's findings without success. The enterprise that is science will continue to move forward in this fascinating area of research.

Questions for Further Discussion

1. Cellphones emit magnetic fields similar to the ones used by Dr. Persinger. Do you think these devices may be altering neural functioning and affecting our sleep or cognitive functioning?

2. Do you think belief in the paranormal is a fundamental human characteristic that promotes survival?

A participant sports the modified snowmobile helmet while she relaxes in an experimental chamber at Laurentian University. Soon weak magnetic fields will be applied to her brain's temporal lobes and she may experience sensations similar to those of Dr. Blackmore's (see text for details).

CHAPTER SUMMARY

The ABCs of Sensation

3.1. *What are each of the following: sensation, the just noticeable difference, subliminal perception, and synesthesia?*

• Sensation is the activation of receptors located in the eyes, ears, skin, nasal cavities, and tongue.

• Sensory receptors are specialized forms of neurons that are activated by different stimuli such as light and sound.

• A just noticeable difference is the point at which a stimulus is detectable half the time it is present.

• Weber's law of just noticeable differences states that the just noticeable difference between two stimuli is always a constant.

- Absolute thresholds are the smallest amount of energy needed for conscious detection of a stimulus at least half the time it is present.
- Subliminal stimuli are just below the level of conscious awareness but have not been shown to affect behaviour in day-to-day life.
- Synesthesia is a rare condition in which some of the signals from the various sensory organs are processed in the wrong cortical areas, resulting in the sense information being interpreted as more than one sensation. The most common type of synesthesia is a fusion of sight and sound.

3.2. *How can some sensations be ignored?*

- Habituation occurs when the brain ignores a constant stimulus.
- Sensory adaptation occurs when the sensory receptors stop responding to a constant stimulus.

The Science of Seeing

3.3. *What is light?*

- Light is the part of the electromagnetic spectrum that people see and has properties of both waves and particles. Light perception consists of brightness, colour, and saturation. Brightness corresponds to the amplitude of light waves, whereas colour corresponds to the length of the light waves. Saturation is the psychological interpretation of wavelengths that are all the same (highly saturated) or varying (less saturated).

3.4. *How do the parts of the eye work together?*

- Light enters the eye and is focused through the cornea, passes through the aqueous humour, and then through the hole in the iris muscle called the *pupil*.
- The lens also focuses the light on the retina, where it passes through ganglion and bipolar cells to stimulate the rods and cones.

3.5. *How do the eyes see, and how do the eyes see different colours?*

- Rods detect changes in brightness but do not see colour, and they function best in low levels of light. They do not respond to different colours and are found everywhere in the retina except the centre, or fovea.
- Cones are sensitive to colours and work best in bright light. They are responsible for the sharpness of visual information and are found in the fovea.
- Trichromatic theory of colour perception assumes three types of cones: red, green, and blue. All colours would be perceived as combinations of these three.
- Opponent-process theory of colour perception assumes four primary colours: red, green, blue, and yellow. Cones are arranged in pairs, and when one member of a pair is activated, the other is not.
- Colour blindness is either a total lack of colour perception or colour perception that is limited to yellows and blues or reds and greens only.

The Hearing Sense: Can You Hear Me Now?

3.6. *What is sound?*

- Sound has three aspects: pitch (frequency), loudness, and timbre (purity).

3.7. *How do the parts of the ear work together to hear sounds?*

- Sound enters the ear through the visible outer structure, or pinna, and travels to the eardrum and then to the small bones of the middle ear.
- The bone called the *stirrup* rests on the oval window, causing the cochlea and basilar membrane to vibrate with sound.

- The organ of Corti on the basilar membrane contains the auditory receptors, which send signals to the brain about sound qualities as they vibrate.
- Place theory states that the location of the hair cells on the organ of Corti correspond to different pitches of sound. This explains pitch above 1000 Hz.
- Frequency theory states that the speed with which the basilar membrane vibrates corresponds to different pitches of sound. This explains pitch below 100 Hz.
- The volley principle states that neurons take turns firing for sounds above 100 Hz and below 1000 Hz.

3.8. *What is a hearing impairment?*

- Conduction hearing impairment is caused by damage to the outer or middle ear structures, whereas nerve hearing impairment is caused by damage to the inner ear or auditory pathways in the brain.

3.9. *What can be done to help people with a hearing impairment?*

- In some cases, cochlear implants can restore hearing to those with damage to the hearing nerves.

Chemical Senses: It Tastes Good, But It Smells Terrible

3.10. *How do the senses of taste and smell work?*

- Gustation is the sense of taste. Taste buds in the tongue receive molecules of substances, which fit into receptor sites.
- The five basic types of taste are sweet, sour, salty, bitter, and umami (brothy).
- Olfaction is the sense of smell. The olfactory receptors in the upper part of the nasal passages receive molecules of substances and create neural signals that then go to the olfactory bulbs under the frontal lobes.

Psychology in the News: **Can Humans Smell Danger and Great Potential Mates?**

- The human brain appears to process real body odours in different brain areas than artificial odours. For example, the body odour of a stranger and not that of a friend activated parts of the brain known to be important in the processing of fear and danger, the amygdala and insular cortex.

Somesthetic Senses: What the Body Knows

- The somesthetic senses include the skin senses and the vestibular senses.

3.11. *How does the sense of touch work, and what happens when people experience pain?*

- Pacinian corpuscles respond to pressure, certain nerve endings around hair follicles respond to pain and pressure, and free nerve endings respond to pain, pressure, and temperature.
- The gate-control theory of pain states that when receptors sensitive to pain are stimulated, a neurotransmitter called substance P is released into the spinal cord, activating other pain receptors by opening "gates" in the spinal column and sending the message to the brain.

3.12. *What sense allows the body to know how it is moving and when it is balanced?*

- The kinesthetic senses allow the brain to know its position in space through the activity of special receptors called *proprioceptors* that are responsive to pressure inside the body.

- The vestibular sense also contributes to the body's sense of spatial orientation through the activity of the otolith organs (up and down movement) and the semicircular canals (movement through arcs).
- Motion sickness is explained by sensory conflict theory, in which information from the eyes conflicts with information from the vestibular sense, causing nausea.

The ABCs of Perception

3.13. What are perception and perceptual constancies?
- Perception is the interpretation and organization of sensations.
- Size constancy is the tendency to perceive objects as always being the same size, no matter how close or far away they are.
- Shape constancy is the tendency to perceive objects as remaining the same shape even when the shape of the object changes on the retina of the eye.
- Brightness constancy is the tendency to perceive objects as a certain level of brightness, even when the light changes.

3.14. What are the Gestalt principles of perception?
- The Gestalt psychologists developed several principles of perception that involve interpreting patterns in visual stimuli. The principles are figure–ground relationships, proximity, similarity, closure, continuity, contiguity, and common region.

Classic Studies in Psychology: The Visual Cliff

3.15. How do people perceive the world in three dimensions?
- Depth perception is the ability to see in three dimensions. Infants as young as 2 months can detect depth.
- Monocular cues for depth perception include linear perspective, relative size, overlap, aerial perspective, texture gradient, motion parallax, and accommodation.

- Binocular cues for depth perception include convergence and binocular disparity.

3.16. How do visual illusions work?
- Illusions are perceptions that do not correspond to reality or are distortions of visual stimuli.
- The Müller-Lyer illusion involves the misperception of two lines of equal length as being different in length because of angles placed on the ends of each line.
- The moon illusion occurs when the moon appears to be larger on the horizon than high in the sky. It is explained by the apparent distance hypothesis, which involves a misinterpretation of size constancy.

3.17. What factors can influence perception?
- Perceptual set or expectancy refers to the tendency to perceive objects and situations in a particular way because of prior experiences.
- Top-down processing involves the use of pre-existing knowledge to organize individual features into a unified whole.
- Bottom-up processing involves the analysis of smaller features, building up to a complete perception.

Applying Psychology to Everyday Life: Thinking Critically About ESP
- Extrasensory perception (ESP) is a claim of perception that occurs without the use of normal sensory channels such as sight, hearing, touch, taste, or smell.
- Claimed ESP abilities include telepathy, clairvoyance, and precognition.
- Research has produced some support for ESP, but critics claim these studies were flawed. Other research has failed to find any support for the claims of ESP.

3 KEY TERMS

TEST YOURSELF

Pick the best answer.

1. You find that you have to add 1 teaspoon of sugar to a cup of coffee that already has 5 teaspoons of sugar in it to notice the difference in sweetness. If you have a cup of coffee with 10 teaspoons of sugar in it, how many teaspoons would you have to add to notice the difference in sweetness at least half the time?
   a. 1
   b. 2
   c. 4
   d. 5

2. Which of your senses habituates rather than adapts to constant stimuli?
   a. vision
   b. touch
   c. hearing
   d. smell

3. When Heather hears the number 2 she always sees green. Heather may have a rare condition known as
   a. synesthesia.
   b. habituation.
   c. monochrome colour blindness.
   d. Ishihara.

4. Which of the following is responsible for controlling how much light enters the eye?
   a. cornea
   b. lens
   c. retina
   d. iris

5. Which type of retinal cell forms the optic nerve?
   a. rods
   b. cones
   c. ganglion cells
   d. bipolar cells

6. Which type of retinal cell is responsible for peripheral vision?
   a. rods
   b. cones
   c. ganglion cells
   d. bipolar cells

7. Which set of colours are the primary colours when mixing light?
   a. red, yellow, and blue
   b. red, blue, and green
   c. blue, green, and yellow
   d. red, green, and yellow

8. Which of the following properties of sound would be the most similar to the brightness of light?
   a. pitch
   b. loudness
   c. purity
   d. timbre

9. The thin membrane stretched over the opening to the inner ear is the
   a. pinna.
   b. oval window.
   c. tympanic membrane.
   d. cochlea.

10. The _____ theory explains how we hear sounds between 100 and 1000 Hz.
    a. place
    b. frequency
    c. volley
    d. adaptive

11. If a severe ear infection damages the bones of the middle ear, you may develop _____ hearing impairment.
    a. nerve
    b. stimulation
    c. brain pathway
    d. conduction

12. The sense of taste is closely related to the sense of
    a. sight.
    b. hearing.
    c. smell.
    d. touch.

13. The "bumps" on the tongue that are visible to the eye are the
    a. taste buds.
    b. papillae.
    c. taste receptors.
    d. olfactory receptors.

14. The olfactory receptor cells are located in the
    a. tops of the nasal passages.
    b. auditory passages.
    c. roof of the mouth.
    d. lining of the outer nose.

15. Which of the following statements about olfactory receptors is TRUE?
    a. Olfactory receptors are replaced every five to eight weeks.
    b. There are fewer than 50 types of olfactory receptors.
    c. Signals from the receptors go through the brain stem and then to the cortex.
    d. Olfactory receptors respond to pressure.

16. In the spinal cord, _____ inhibit(s) the release of substance P.
    a. hormones
    b. serotonin
    c. norepinephrine
    d. endorphins

17. We know when we are moving up and down in an elevator because of the movement of tiny crystals in the
    a. outer ear.
    b. inner ear.
    c. otolith organs.
    d. middle ear.

18. Ellis turns around and around in a circle. When he stops, he feels like his head is still spinning. What is responsible for this sensation?
    a. semicircular canals
    b. proprioceptors
    c. otolith organs
    d. otolith crystals

19. An old comedy routine on television had a character who would line up the heads of people who were very far away from him between his fingers. Then he would pinch his fingers together and say gleefully, "I'm crushing your head, I'm crushing your head." The comedian was playing around with which perceptual constancy?
    a. size constancy
    b. shape constancy
    c. brightness constancy
    d. colour constancy

20. When Bregman presented two alternating streams of sounds to his participants, one high-pitched and the other low-pitched, participants reported hearing what seemed like two separate sound streams at the same time. Which Gestalt grouping principle is likely at work here?
    a. common region
    b. closure
    c. similarity
    d. continuity

21. Researchers have been able to demonstrate depth perception in babies as young as
    a. 1 month.
    b. 2 months.
    c. 3 months.
    d. 4 months.

22. Which of the following occurs when one object seems to block another object?
    a. convergence
    b. linear perspective
    c. overlap
    d. texture gradient

23. The Müller-Lyer illusion exists in cultures in which there are
    a. more men than women.
    b. more women than men.
    c. lots of trees.
    d. buildings with lots of corners.

24. Allison opened her new jigsaw puzzle but soon realized that the puzzle pieces inside had nothing to do with the picture on the box. With no picture to go by, she realized she would have to use
a. bottom-up processing.
b. top-down processing.
c. perceptual expectancy.
d. perceptual set.

25. Which supposed ESP ability involves being able to "see" something that is not physically present by touching another object?
a. precognition
b. telepathy
c. clairvoyance
d. telekinesis`

Answers: 1-b, 2-c, 3-a, 4-d, 5-c, 6-a, 7-b, 8-b, 9-b, 10-c, 11-d, 12-c, 13-b, 14-a, 15-a, 16-d, 17-c, 18-a, 19-a, 20-c, 21-b, 22-c, 23-d, 24-a, 25-c.

ScanLife™ Barcode

To access more tests and your own personalized study plan that will help you focus on the areas you need to master before your next class test, be sure to go to **www.MyPsychLab.com**, Pearson Education Canada's online psychology website, available with the access code packaged with your book.

The ABCs of Sensation

Sensation and the Central Nervous System

Sensation: activation of sense organ receptors

Sensory receptors: specialized neurons activated by stimuli

Thresholds:

▸ **Just noticeable difference:** smallest detectable stimulus change

▸ **Absolute thresholds:** smallest amount of energy for stimulus detection

▸ **Subliminal stimuli:** Not been shown to affect day-to-day behaviour

Synesthesia: rare condition in which some sensory signals are processed in the wrong areas, so sense information is interpreted as more than one sensation

3.1

Ignoring Sensations

Habituation: ignoring a constant stimulus

Sensory adaptation: sensory neurons stop responding to constant stimuli

3.2

Colour Vision

Trichromatic and opponent-process theories: two processes that work together

Trichromatic theory of colour perception: three types of cones for long, medium, and short wavelengths

Opponent processes: at the ganglion cell level combine long versus medium cones to produce red and green. Medium and long cones combine together versus the short-wavelength cone to produce yellow and blue.

Colour blindness: total lack of colour perception or colour perception that is limited to yellows and blues or reds and greens only

The Science of Seeing

Light

Light: form of electromagnetic radiation described by wavelength and amplitude

Colour or hue: in part determined by wavelength

▸ Long wavelengths—red end of the visible spectrum

▸ Shorter wavelengths—blue end of the visible spectrum

Brightness: corresponds to the amplitude of light waves

Saturation: refers to the purity of the colour people see

3.3

Parts of the Eye

Pathway of Light:
Cornea →
Pupil →
Lens →
Retina →
(Hits the rods and cones)

3.4

How the Eyes See and How the Eyes See Different Colours

3.5

Pupil
Iris
Lens
Retina
Cornea
Blind spot (Optic disc)
Light
Optic nerve
Blood vessels

Rods, Cones

Rods: low light levels, no role in colour vision, poor acuity, located peripherally

Cones: work at bright light levels, see colour, provide central and sharp vision

The Hearing Sense

Sound

Sound consists of pressure waves in the air.

Sound has three aspects:

▸ pitch (frequency)
▸ loudness
▸ timbre (purity)

3.6

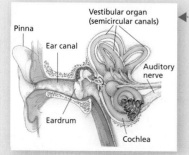

Vestibular organ (semicircular canals)
Pinna
Ear canal
Auditory nerve
Eardrum
Cochlea

Parts of the Ear

Sound: → pinna, → eardrum → bones of middle ear (hammer, anvil, stirrup)
Stirrup causes the cochlea and basilar membrane to vibrate with sound.
The organ of Corti on the basilar membrane contains the auditory receptors.

3.7

Hearing Impairment

Conduction hearing impairment: damage to the outer or middle ear structures

Nerve hearing impairment: damage to the inner ear or auditory pathways

Cochlear implant: an electronic device in the inner ear to restore hearing

3.8–9

Perception of Pitch

Place theory: organ of Corti hair cells corresponding to pitches above 1000 hertz

Frequency theory: basilar membrane vibrates corresponding to pitches below 100 hertz

Volley theory: neurons take turns firing for sounds above 100 hertz and below 1000 hertz

Chemical Senses

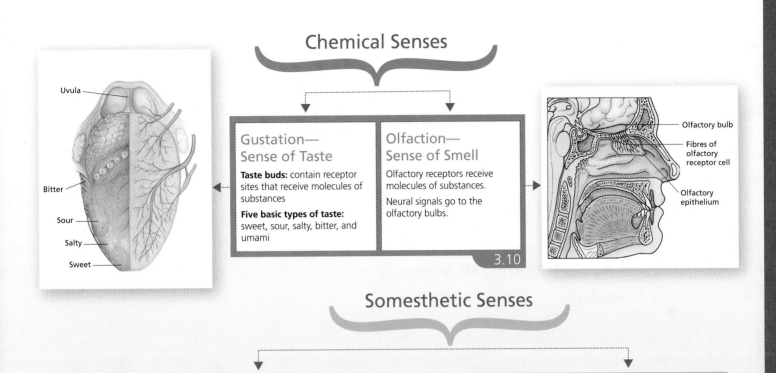

Gustation— Sense of Taste

Taste buds: contain receptor sites that receive molecules of substances

Five basic types of taste: sweet, sour, salty, bitter, and umami

Olfaction— Sense of Smell

Olfactory receptors receive molecules of substances.

Neural signals go to the olfactory bulbs.

3.10

Labels on tongue diagram: Uvula, Bitter, Sour, Salty, Sweet

Labels on olfaction diagram: Olfactory bulb, Fibres of olfactory receptor cell, Olfactory epithelium

Somesthetic Senses

Sense of Touch and Pain

Touch:
- Pacinian corpuscles
- Nerve endings around hair
- Free nerve endings

Gate-control theory of pain:
- Stimulation of pain receptors cause transmitter release into the spinal cord.
- Activates other pain receptors by opening "gates" in the spinal column

3.11

Kinesthetic Sense: Movement and Balance

Kinesthetic sense: relays position in space and based on proprioceptors

Vestibular sense: body's sense of spatial orientation

Based on: otolith organs and **semicircular canals**

3.12

The ABCs of Perception

Perception and Perceptual Constancies

Size constancy: Objects seem the same size, no matter their distance.

Shape constancy: Objects seem same shape despite retinal image changes.

Brightness constancy: Changes in lighting do not affect brightness perception.

3.13

Gestalt Principles of Perception

Figure–ground relationships
- Proximity
- Similarity
- Closure
- Continuity
- Contiguity
- Common region

3.14

How People Perceive the World in Three Dimensions

Depth perception is the ability to see in three dimensions.

Monocular cues (pictorial depth cues):
Depth cues based on one eye only
- Linear perspective
- Interposition (overlap)
- Texture gradient
- Accommodation
- Relative size
- Aerial perspective
- Motion parallax

Binocular cues: Cues for perceiving depth based on both eyes
- Convergence
- Binocular disparity

3.15

Visual Illusions

Müller-Lyer illusion: involves the misperception of two lines of equal length

Moon illusion: Moon appears to be larger on the horizon.

3.16

Factors That Influence Perception

Perceptual set or expectancy: tendency to perceive according to prior experiences

Top-down processing: Knowledge organizes individual features into a unified whole.

Bottom-up processing: Analysis of smaller feature builds up to a complete perception.

3.17

4

Consciousness: Sleep, Dreams, Hypnosis, and Drugs

Canadian Soldiers Battle 3-Metre-Tall Marijuana Plants and the Munchies

Imagine: You are a Canadian soldier in Afghanistan tracking Taliban militants, and midway through your shift as a Leopard tank gunner, you come across what seems like an impenetrable forest of 3-metre-tall marijuana plants. You are surprised to learn that the plants are very efficient at absorbing energy, making them extremely difficult to penetrate with your thermal devices and thus ideal cover for Taliban militants. So to take away this strategic advantage, you try to burn the plants with phosphorous or diesel. It doesn't work very well. Some of the plants on the periphery burn, but the majority in the centre are so full of water that they simply will not burn. Some members of your platoon decide to cut down a few of the giant plants to camouflage their armoured vehicles. A few hours later, as your shift comes to an end, you notice that you and some of your platoon members who were downwind of the burning plants are feeling unusually happy and relaxed and have a strong craving for snack foods. So you instruct the tank operator to pull the tank up to the drive-through window at the Kandahar base Tim Hortons and proceed to order a dozen doughnuts. Another soldier yells out, "I think we've all got the marijuana munchies."

Later that evening, while debriefing Canada's top military commander General Rick Hillier, you are quoted as saying, "Sir, three years ago before I joined the army, I never thought I'd say, 'That damn marijuana!'" (Reuters, 2006).

Why study consciousness?

Consciousness, as humans experience it, is the key difference between humans and the lower animals. Waking, sleeping, dreaming, daydreaming, and other forms of conscious awareness make up the better part of the human experience. Drug use is on the rise, not only as recreation but also for many health and psychological conditions, including the treatment of children. It seems obvious that we need to understand how drugs affect our thinking and behaviour in everyday life. In a very real sense, to understand consciousness is to understand what it means to be who we are.

4.1. What does it mean to be conscious, and are there different levels of consciousness?

4.2. Why do people sleep, and how does sleep work?

4.3. What is seasonal affective disorder, and are Canadians at greater risk?

4.4. What is the purpose of sleep?

4.5. What are the different stages of sleep?

4.6. Can sleepwalking and sexsomnia be a defence for committing a crime?

4.7. What is dreaming, and what happens if people don't dream?

4.8. What changes might occur in sleep as a result of learning a new motor task?

4.9. What kinds of problems can happen during sleep?

4.10. Why do people dream, and what do they dream about?

4.11. What is hypnosis, and how does it work?

4.12. What is the difference between a physical dependence and a psychological dependence on a drug?

4.13. What are some examples of stimulants and the dangers associated with taking them?

4.14. What are some different types of depressants, and how can they be harmful?

4.15. What kind of drug is alcohol, and what are the dangers of drinking too much?

4.16. How do narcotics work, and why are they so addictive?

4.17. How do hallucinogens work?

4.18. What is marijuana, and what are the risks of using it?

4.19. What are some medicinal uses for marijuana?

4.20. How serious is the problem of sleep deprivation?

WHAT IS CONSCIOUSNESS?

What exactly is meant by the term *consciousness*? I've heard it a lot, but I'm not sure that I know everything it means. *Consciousness* is one of those terms that most people think they understand until someone asks them to define it. But if you are sitting there trying to define it now, don't worry if you have trouble coming up with a definition that satisfies you. Various scientists, psychologists, neuroscientists, philosophers, and even computer scientists (who have been trying to develop an artificial intelligence for some time now) have tried to define consciousness, and so there are several definitions—one for nearly every field in which consciousness is studied. The early psychologist and functionalist William James devoted quite a bit of space in his textbook to the concept of a "stream of consciousness" in which ideas, sensations, and thoughts flow from one into another (James, 1894). Philosopher Daniel Dennett, in his 1991 book *Consciousness Explained*, asserts that there is no single stream of consciousness but rather multiple "channels," each of which is handling its own tasks (Dennett, 1991). All of these channels operate in parallel, a kind of chaos of consciousness. People must somehow organize all this conscious experience, and that organization is influenced by their particular social groups and culture.

Do animals experience consciousness in the same way as people? That is a question too complex to answer fully here, but many researchers of animal behaviour, language, and cognition have some reason to propose that there is a kind of consciousness in at least some animals, although its organization would naturally not be the same as human consciousness (Block, 2005; Browne, 2004; Hurley & Nudds, 2006).

DEFINITION OF CONSCIOUSNESS

4.1 *What does it mean to be conscious, and are there different levels of consciousness?*

For our purposes, a more useful definition of consciousness might be the following: **Consciousness** is your awareness of everything that is going on around you and inside your own head at any given moment (Farthing, 1992). That includes thoughts, sensations, and feelings. Much of people's time awake is spent in a state called **waking consciousness**, in which their thoughts, feelings, and sensations are clear and

---

What exactly is ▶ **meant by the term *consciousness*? I've heard it a lot, but I'm not sure that I know everything it means.**

consciousness
a person's awareness of everything that is going on around him or her at any given moment.

waking consciousness
state in which thoughts, feelings, and sensations are clear and organized, and the person feels alert.

organized, and they feel alert. But there are many times in daily activities and in life when people experience states of consciousness that differ from this organized waking state. These variations in consciousness are called *altered states of consciousness*.

ALTERED STATES OF CONSCIOUSNESS

An **altered state of consciousness** occurs when there is a shift in the quality or pattern of a person's mental activity (Tart, 1986). Thoughts may become fuzzy and disorganized and people may feel less alert, or their thoughts may take bizarre turns as they so often do in dreams. You may also divide your conscious awareness, as when you drive to work or school and then wonder how you got there—one level of conscious awareness was driving, while the other was thinking about the day ahead, perhaps. This altered state of divided consciousness can be a dangerous thing, as many people who try to drive and talk on a cellphone at the same time have discovered. Driving and carrying on a conversation on a phone are both processes that should demand focused attention, and it is simply not possible to do both at once in a safe and efficient manner. Studies have shown that driving while talking on a cellphone, even a hands-free phone, puts a person at the same degree of risk as driving under the influence of alcohol (Alm & Nilsson, 1995; Briem & Hedman, 1995; Strayer & Drews, 2007; Strayer & Johnston, 2001; Strayer et al., 2006).

There are many pathways to altered states of consciousness: using drugs, daydreaming, being hypnotized, or achieving a meditative state. Ⓛ Ⓘ Ⓝ Ⓚ *to Chapter Ten: Stress and Health, p. 396.* But the most common altered state people experience is the one they spend about one-third of their lives in on a nightly basis—sleep.

ALTERED STATES: SLEEP

Have you ever wondered why people have to sleep? They could get so much more work done if they didn't have to sleep, and they would have more time to play and do creative things.

THE NECESSITY OF SLEEP

4.2 *Why do people sleep, and how does sleep work?*

Sleep was once referred to as "the gentle tyrant" (Webb, 1992). People can try to stay awake, and sometimes they may go for a while without sleep, but eventually they *must* sleep. One reason for this is that sleep is one of the human body's *biological rhythms*, natural cycles of activity that the body must go through. Some biological rhythms are monthly, such as the cycle of a woman's menstruation, whereas others are far shorter, such as the beat of the heart. But many biological rhythms take place on a daily basis, such as the rise and fall of blood pressure and body temperature, or the production of certain body chemicals (Moore-Ede et al., 1982). The most obvious of these is the sleep–wake cycle (Baehr et al., 2000).

THE RHYTHMS OF LIFE: CIRCADIAN RHYTHMS   The sleep–wake cycle is a **circadian rhythm**. The term actually comes from two Latin words, *circa* (about) and *diem* (day). So a circadian rhythm is a cycle that takes "about a day" to complete.

For most people, this means that they will experience several hours of sleep at least once during every 24-hour period. The sleep–wake cycle is ultimately controlled by the brain, specifically by an area within the *hypothalamus*, the tiny section of the brain that influences the glandular system. Ⓛ Ⓘ Ⓝ Ⓚ *to Chapter Two: The Biological Perspective, p. 42.*

---

altered state of consciousness
state in which there is a shift in the quality or pattern of mental activity as compared to waking consciousness.

circadian rhythm
a cycle of bodily rhythm that occurs over a 24-hour period.

Sleep, according to Webb (1992), is the "gentle tyrant." As this picture shows, when the urge to sleep comes upon a person, it can be very difficult to resist—no matter where that person is at the time. Can you think of a time or place at which you fell asleep without meaning to do so? What do you think were the factors in your "sleep attack"?

> There was a big fuss ▶ over something called melatonin a few years ago—isn't melatonin supposed to make people sleep?

THE ROLE OF THE HYPOTHALAMUS: THE MIGHTY MITE There was a big fuss over something called *melatonin* a few years ago—isn't melatonin supposed to make people sleep? Melatonin is only one part of the sleep story. Deep within the hypothalamus is an area called the *suprachiasmatic* (SOO-prah-ki-AS-ma-tik) *nucleus*, the internal clock that tells people when to wake up and when to fall asleep (Quintero et al., 2003; Yamaguchi et al., 2003; Zisapel, 2001). The suprachiasmatic nucleus (SCN) is sensitive to changes in light. As daylight fades, the SCN tells the *pineal gland* (located in the base of the brain) to secrete the hormone melatonin (Bondarenko, 2004; Delagrange & Guardiola-Lemaitre, 1997). As melatonin accumulates, a person will feel sleepy. As the light coming into the eyes increases (as it does in the morning), the SCN tells the pineal gland to stop secreting melatonin, allowing the body to awaken. Some psychologists playfully refer to melatonin as the *Dracula hormone* because it comes out only at night. Melatonin supplements are often used to treat sleep disturbances caused by changes in our circadian rhythms, such as jet lag or shift work (Folkard, 2006).

Melatonin is not the entire story. There is also ongoing research into the role of the neurotransmitter serotonin in the regulation of sleep (Veasey, 2003). As the day goes by, serotonin levels in the nervous system increase and seem to produce sleepiness. This would explain why, at the end of the day, it is very difficult for people to stay awake past their usual bedtime. The serotonin level is high enough at that time to produce an intense feeling of sleepiness.

Body temperature plays a part in inducing sleep, too. The SCN, as part of the hypothalamus, controls body temperature. The higher the body temperature, the more alert people are; the lower the temperature, the sleepier they are. When people are asleep at night, their body temperature is at its lowest level.

In studies in which volunteers spent several days without access to information about day or night, their sleep–wake cycles lengthened (Czeisler, 1995; Czeisler et al., 1980). The daily activities of their bodies, such as sleeping, waking, waste production, blood pressure rise and fall, and so on, took place over a period of 25 hours rather than 24. Based on this research, it appears that the SCN may be responsible for resetting the body's biological "clock" to a 24-hour cycle every day.

In the same studies, body temperature dropped consistently even in the absence of light (Czeisler et al., 1980). As body temperature dropped, sleep began, giving further support to the importance of body temperature in the regulation of sleep.

CLASSIC STUDIES IN PSYCHOLOGY

Seasonal Affective Disorder (SAD): Are Canadians at Greater Risk?

4.3 *What is seasonal affective disorder, and are Canadians at greater risk?*

In 1984, Dr. Rosenthal and his colleagues described a variant of major depression that they termed **seasonal affective disorder (SAD)**. The symptoms of this condition had many similarities to that of normal depression, such as feelings of fatigue, worthlessness, and helplessness, and loss of interest and pleasure in normal activities. LINK to Chapter Thirteen: Psychological Disorders, p. 520.

However, what was unique about these symptoms was that they appeared only during the autumn or winter months, and then they disappeared in the spring and summer months. In addition, people had other symptoms not typically seen in depressed persons. For instance,

seasonal affective disorder (SAD) a mood disorder caused by the body's reaction to low levels of sunlight in the winter months.

people with SAD seemed to sleep much more than traditionally depressed persons and had an increased appetite for foods high in carbohydrates. The increased sleep and increased caloric intake resulted in significant winter weight gain.

Canadian researcher Raymond Lam, at the University of British Columbia, has spent many years studying SAD. He has shown that SAD is twice as common in females and that as one moves farther and farther away from the equator, the likelihood of suffering from SAD increases (Lam & Levitt, 1999). Lam reasons that the short days and long nights of winter may alter the body's sleep–wake cycle, which, in turn, may affect our ability to regulate mood. Recall that our internal clock, the suprachiasmatic nucleus, is very sensitive to light. In the presence of light, it instructs the pineal gland to stop producing melatonin; in the absence of light, melatonin levels increase and people become sleepy. We also know that melatonin is made from serotonin. Thus, as melatonin levels increase, serotonin levels decrease. In Chapter Two, we learned that serotonin is an important neurotransmitter in the regulation of sleep, mood, and appetite, and that low levels of serotonin have been linked to depression. LINK to Chapter Two: The Biological Perspective, p. 42.

This woman is experiencing full-spectrum light therapy, one of the main treatments recommended for people suffering from seasonal affective disorder (SAD).

Perhaps, during the long Canadian winter nights, the increased production of melatonin makes some people sleepy so they sleep a lot, and the resulting decrease in serotonin makes them crave carbohydrates and become more prone to depression. Because SAD often improves in the spring and summer, one form of treatment involves daily exposure to bright lamps that simulate real daylight. Lam has shown that this type of photo treatment is more effective than placebo, and the side effects (e.g., headache, eye strain, feeling "wired," and nausea) are generally mild. But photo treatment does not help everyone with SAD. Fortunately, traditional drug treatments for depression, such as fluoxetine (trade name Prozac), are also effective for treating SAD (Lam, Levitt, Levitan, Enns, Morehouse, & Michalak et al., 2006).

Questions for Further Discussion

1. Are blind persons more likely to experience depression or SAD?

2. Would going to Mexico, Cuba, Florida, or the Bahamas for spring break decrease the risk of developing SAD?

3. What are some possible reasons to explain the finding that Canadian women are more likely than Canadian men to experience SAD?

THE PRICE OF NOT SLEEPING

4.4   *What is the purpose of sleep?*

Although people can do without sleep for a while, they cannot do without it altogether. In one experiment, rats were placed on moving treadmills over water. They couldn't sleep normally because they would then fall into the water and be awakened, but they did drift repeatedly into **microsleeps**, or brief sidesteps into sleep lasting only seconds (Goleman, 1982; Konowal et al., 1999). People can have microsleeps, too, and if this happens while they are driving, it's obviously bad news (Dinges, 1995; Lyznicki et al., 1998; Thomas et al., 1998). Microsleep periods are no doubt responsible for a lot of car accidents that occur when drivers have had very little sleep.

What will missing out on one night's sleep do to a person? For most people, a missed night of sleep will result in concentration problems and the inability to do simple tasks that normally would take no thought at all, such as loading a CD into a player. More complex tasks, such as math problems, suffer less than these simple tasks. When sleep loss is complicated by an emotional trauma (such as the death of a loved one), the concentration problems and disorientation may be more severe.

Microsleeps are a common cause of accidents while driving. If this woman continues to drive while she is this sleepy, she may fall asleep at the wheel for only a few moments. Those few moments can mean disaster—for her and for others on the road with her.

microsleeps
brief sidesteps into sleep lasting only a few seconds.

Contrary to popular belief, sleep deprivation often affects younger people more than older people, who need less sleep. Does this young man look well rested and able to successfully complete the task of brushing his teeth?

Okay, so we obviously ▶ need to sleep. But what does it do for us? Why do we have to sleep at all?

sleep deprivation
any significant loss of sleep, resulting in problems in concentration and irritability.

adaptive theory
theory of sleep proposing that animals and humans evolved sleep patterns to avoid predators by sleeping when predators are most active.

restorative theory
theory of sleep proposing that sleep is necessary to the physical health of the body and serves to replenish chemicals and repair cellular damage.

Even so, **sleep deprivation**, or loss of sleep, is a serious problem, which many people have without realizing it. People stay up too late at night during the week, get up before they've really rested to go to work or school, and then try to pay off the "sleep debt" on the weekend. All of that disrupts the normal sleep–wake cycle and isn't good for anyone's health. Students, for example, may stay up all night to study for an important test the next day. In doing so, they will lose more information than they gain, as a good night's sleep is important for memory and the ability to think well. Some typical symptoms of sleep deprivation include trembling hands, inattention, staring off into space, droopy eyelids, and general discomfort (Naitoh, Kelly, & Englund, 1989), as well as emotional symptoms such as irritability and even depression.

Just how serious is missing a few nights' sleep? Sleep researchers conducted a study in which healthy adults between the ages of 21 and 38 were randomly placed in one of four restricted sleep conditions (Van Dongen et al., 2003). Participants began the experiment with at least three days of regular sleep and then were either allowed to get only four hours, six hours, or eight hours (this was the control group) of sleep each day for 14 days. A fourth group of participants was totally deprived of sleep (by being kept awake by the researchers) for three days in a row. Measurements of the participants' cognitive abilities and physical alertness were taken every two hours during the scheduled "awake" times. The results showed that even in the six-hour sleep condition, participants' abilities to function mentally and physically were as negatively affected as if they had been entirely deprived of sleep for two nights. All participants in the sleep-deprived and no-sleep conditions were seriously impaired in their functioning and were relatively unaware of the seriousness of the impairment. That the participants did not seem to be aware of their problems in functioning may account for the impression many people have that a few nights of poor sleep is not that serious. The results of this study seem to indicate that even moderate sleep loss is a serious problem.

The Adaptive Theory of Sleep   Okay, so we obviously need to sleep. But what does it do for us? Why do we have to sleep at all? According to the **adaptive theory** of why organisms sleep, sleep is a product of evolution (Webb, 1992). Animals and humans evolved different sleep patterns to avoid predators during the predators' normal hunting times, which are generally at night. If a prey animal (one the predator will eat) is out and about at night, it is likely to be eaten. If, instead, it is in a safe place sleeping and conserving energy, it remains safe. If this is true, then one would expect prey animals to sleep mostly at night and for shorter periods of time than predator animals, whereas the predator animals can sleep in the daytime and as much as they want. In fact, animals such as lions, which have very few natural predators, sleep nearly 15 hours a day, while animals such as gazelles, which are prey, sleep a total of only 4 hours a day, usually in short naps.

The Restorative Theory of Sleep   The other major theory of why organisms sleep is called **restorative theory**, which states that sleep is necessary to the physical health of the body. During sleep, chemicals that were used up during the day's activities are replenished and cellular damage is repaired (Adam, 1980; Moldofsky, 1995). There is evidence that most bodily growth and repair occur during the deepest stages of sleep, when enzymes responsible for these functions are secreted in higher amounts. This may account for the fact that children in periods of rapid growth need to sleep more and also helps to explain why children who are experiencing disrupted sleep (as is the case in situations of domestic violence) suffer delays in growth (Gilmore & Skuse, 1999; Swanson, 1994).

Which of these theories is correct? The answer is that both are probably needed to understand why sleep occurs the way it does. Adaptive theory explains why people sleep *when* they do, and restorative theory explains why people *need* to sleep.

How Much Sleep Do People Need?   How much sleep is enough sleep? The answer varies from person to person because of each person's age and possibly inherited sleep needs (Feroah et al., 2004). Most people need about 7 to 8 hours of sleep each 24-hour period to function well. Some people are short sleepers, needing only 4 to 5 hours, whereas others are long sleepers and need 9 to 10 hours of sleep (McCann & Stewin, 1988).

THE STAGES OF SLEEP

So are there different kinds of sleep? Do you go from being awake to being asleep and dreaming—is it instant? There are actually two kinds of sleep: **REM (rapid eye movement)** and **non-REM (NREM) sleep**. REM sleep is a relatively active type of sleep when most of a person's dreaming takes place, whereas NREM sleep is a much deeper, more restful kind of sleep. There are also several different stages of sleep that people go through each night in which REM sleep and NREM sleep occur. A machine called an *electroencephalograph (EEG)* allows scientists to see the brain wave activity as a person passes through the various stages of sleep and to determine what type of sleep the person has entered (Aserinsky & Kleitman, 1953). See Figure 4.1 for a look at what happens in each stage of sleep.

A person who is wide awake and mentally active will show a brain wave pattern on the EEG called *beta waves*. Beta waves are very small and very fast. As the person relaxes and gets drowsy, slightly larger and slower **alpha waves** appear. The alpha waves are eventually replaced by even slower and larger **theta waves**.

In March 2011, an air traffic controller, who was working his fourth consecutive midnight shift, fell asleep at Reagan National Airport in Washington DC, forcing two planes to land with no help from the tower. Researchers have found that air traffic controllers such as the one pictured here were significantly more impaired in performance after working an eight-hour midnight shift as compared to a day or evening shift of equal length (Heslegrave & Rhodes, 1997).

◀ So are there different kinds of sleep? Do you go from being awake to being asleep and dreaming—is it instant?

This tree-dwelling loris, like most nocturnal animals, has very large eyes. The adaptive theory of sleep assumes that animals in danger from predators tend to sleep at night. With its nightly activities confined safely to the trees, the loris has no need to fear predators at night and instead sleeps during the day.

This lioness is a predator and has no need to sleep at night to protect herself. She sleeps and hunts on and off during the day in perfect safety, while the animals that the lioness preys upon sleep at night in the safety of dens or other shelter.

PRACTICE QUIZ: HOW MUCH DO YOU REMEMBER?

Pick the best answer.

1. When our mental activity undergoes a change in quality or pattern, this is called a(n)
   a. waking consciousness.
   b. altered state of consciousness.
   c. transient state of consciousness.
   d. hallucination.

2. The sleep–wake cycle is a(n) _____ rhythm, normally occurring every 24 hours.
   a. annual
   b. monthly
   c. circadian
   d. nocturnal

3. The suprachiasmatic nucleus instructs the _____ gland to release _____.
   a. pineal; melatonin
   b. pineal; serotonin
   c. pituitary; melatonin
   d. pituitary; serotonin

4. What is the relationship between long winter nights, melatonin, and serotonin?
   a. Long winter nights decrease the production of melatonin and serotonin.
   b. Long winter nights increase serotonin and decrease melatonin.
   c. Long winter nights increase melatonin and decrease serotonin.
   d. Long winter nights increase the production of melatonin and serotonin.

5. Which of the following does NOT have a role in determining when we sleep?
   a. light and dark information
   b. body temperature
   c. digestion
   d. serotonin

6. Which theory of why we sleep explains why we sleep *when* we do?
   a. restorative theory
   b. adaptive theory
   c. reactive theory
   d. REM theory

Answers: 1-b, 2-c, 3-a, 4-c, 5-c, 6-b.

4.5 *What are the different stages of sleep?*

NON-REM STAGE ONE: LIGHT SLEEP   As theta wave activity increases and alpha wave activity fades away, people are said to be entering Stage One sleep, or light sleep. Several rather interesting things can happen in this NREM stage of sleep. If people are awakened at this point, they will probably not believe that they were actually asleep. They may also experience vivid visual events called *hypnagogic images* (Mavromatis, 1987; Mavromatis & Richardson, 1984). (The Greek word *hypnos* means "sleep.") These images are bits and pieces of what may eventually become dreams but are most often seen as flashes of light. Some people have very vivid images that seem realistic. Many researchers now believe that people's experiences of ghostly visits, alien abductions, and near-death experiences may be most easily explained by these images (Moody & Perry, 1993). (They can also occur just as people are about to wake up and are then called *hypnopompic images*.)

A much more common occurrence is called the *hypnic jerk* (Mahowald & Schenck, 1996; Oswald, 1959). Have you ever been drifting off to sleep when your knees, legs, or sometimes your whole body gives a big "jerk"? Although experts have no solid proof of why this occurs, many believe that it has something to do with the possibility that our ancestors slept in trees: The relaxation of the muscles as one drifts into sleep causes a "falling" sensation, at which point the body jerks awake to prevent the "fall" from the hypothetical tree (Coolidge, 2006; Sagan, 1977).

NON-REM STAGE TWO: SLEEP SPINDLES   As people drift further into sleep, the body temperature continues to drop. Heart rate slows, breathing becomes more shallow and irregular, and the EEG will show the first signs of *sleep spindles*, brief bursts of activity lasting only a second or two. Theta waves still predominate in this stage, but if people are awakened during this stage, they will be aware of having been asleep.

NON-REM STAGES THREE AND FOUR: DELTA WAVES ROLL IN   In the third stage of sleep, the slowest and largest waves make their appearance. These waves are called **delta waves**. In Stage Three, delta waves make up only about 20 to 50 percent of the brain wave pattern.

Simulate on **mypsychlab**
Stages of Sleep

non-REM (NREM) sleep
any of the stages of sleep that do not include REM.

rapid eye movement (REM)
stage of sleep in which the eyes move rapidly under the eyelids and the person is typically experiencing a dream.

alpha waves
brain waves that indicate a state of relaxation or light sleep.

theta waves
brain waves indicating the early stages of sleep.

delta waves
long, slow waves that indicate the deepest stage of sleep.

a.

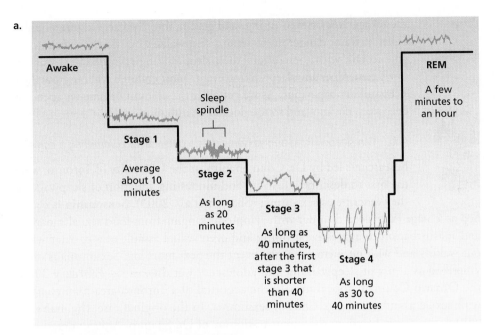

Awake

Stage 1

Average about 10 minutes

Sleep spindle

Stage 2

As long as 20 minutes

Stage 3

As long as 40 minutes, after the first stage 3 that is shorter than 40 minutes

Stage 4

As long as 30 to 40 minutes

REM

A few minutes to an hour

FIGURE 4.1 **Eight-Hour Sleep Cycle** (a) The four stages of sleep and REM sleep comprise the sleep cycle, repeated four or five times during a single night's sleep. A normal sleep cycle takes an average of an hour and a half, with Stage Four being longer in the beginning of the night and REM sleep being longer in the last part of the sleep period, just before awakening. (b) The EEG shows brain activity (bottom line) during REM sleep. The larger graphs in the middle (third and fourth from the top) show muscle activity, which is much slower during REM sleep and accounts for the larger, slower waves on these graphs.

b.

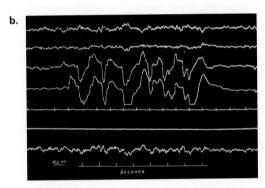

Once delta waves account for more than 50 percent of total brain activity, the person is said to have entered Stage Four sleep, the deepest stage of sleep. It is during this stage that growth hormones (often abbreviated as *GH*) are released from the pituitary gland and reach their peak. The body is at its lowest level of functioning. Eventually, the delta waves make up 100 percent of the brain activity for this stage of sleep.

People in deep sleep are very difficult to awaken. If something does wake them, they may be very confused and disoriented at first. It is not unusual for people to wake up in this kind of disoriented state only to hear the crack of thunder and realize that a storm has begun. Children, who need deep sleep so that their bodies will grow, are even more difficult to wake up when in this state than are adults.

The fact that children do sleep so deeply may explain why certain sleep disorders are more common in childhood. In fact, many sleep disorders are more common in boys than in girls because boys sleep more deeply than do girls because of high levels of the male hormone testosterone (Miyatake et al., 1980; Thiedke, 2001).

Stage Four Sleep Disorders **Sleepwalking**, or **somnambulism**, occurs in about 20 percent of the population and is at least partially due to heredity (Abe et al., 1984; Kales et al., 1980). It is much more common in childhood and also occurs more frequently in boys than in girls. Although the old movies portray sleepwalkers as zombielike, with arms outstretched, in reality a sleepwalker may do nothing more than sit up in bed. But other sleepwalking episodes may involve walking around the house, looking in

Sleepwalking is more common among children than adults. Although this young girl may appear to be awake, she is still deeply asleep. When she awakens in the morning, she will have no memory of this sleepwalking episode.

sleepwalking (somnambulism) occurring during deep sleep, an episode of moving around or walking around in one's sleep.

"Wait Don't! It can be dangerous to wake them."
©The New Yorker Collection J. Dator from
cartoonbank.com. All Rights Reserved.

sexsomnia
a rare Stage Four sleep disorder in which persons may groan loudly, masturbate, or even sexually assault a partner without waking and with no memory of their behaviour.

night terrors
relatively rare disorder in which the person experiences extreme fear and screams or runs around during deep sleep without waking fully.

nightmares
bad dreams occurring during REM sleep.

> But that sounds like ▸
> the description of a
> nightmare—what's the
> difference?

the refrigerator or even eating, and getting into the car. Despite popular belief, it is not dangerous to wake a sleepwalker, but do not expect to be able to talk with them about their sleepwalking episode. Sleepwalkers rarely remember any sleepwalking event. Most children will outgrow their sleepwalking behaviour. As we get older the amount of time we spend in deep sleep declines and so too does somnambulism.

4.6 *Can sleepwalking and sexsomnia be a defence for committing a crime?*

Researchers led by Dr. Colin Shapiro, at the University of Toronto, were the first to describe a distinct and interesting variation of sleepwalking they describe as sexsomnia (Shapiro et al., 2003). **Sexsomnia** is classified as a Stage Four sleep disorder with symptoms ranging from loud sexual moaning and masturbation to aggressive groping and even sexual assault of a partner without waking and with no memory of the event the next morning. Sexsomnia is often described as a mix of sleepwalking and adolescent wet dreams. In February 2008, the Ontario Court of Appeal upheld the acquittal of a Toronto area man charged with sexual assault on the grounds of sexsomnia. In the original case, the man's acquittal was largely based on the expert testimony of Dr. Shapiro. After undergoing a sleep study, Dr. Shapiro showed that the man displayed every conceivable symptom of sexsomnia and that the diagnosis was a "slam dunk." Specifically the man's brain wave pattern showed a tendency to abruptly elevate him out of periods of deep sleep, which is considered the hallmark of the disorder. The man also had several other features of sexsomnia, notably a history of sleepwalking and previous sexsomnia as described by an ex-girlfriend. In addition, the man had been sleep deprived, drinking alcohol, and under considerable emotional stress, which are common triggers for a sexsomnic episode. In the end, the judge ruled that the man had been so deep in sleep that he could not have formed the intention to commit a sexual assault.

Night Terrors **Night terrors** are a rare disorder, although they are more likely in children and are likely to disappear as the child grows older (Garland & Smith, 1991). A night terror is essentially a state of panic experienced while sound asleep. People may sit up, scream, run around the room, or flail at some unseen attacker. It is not uncommon for people to feel unable to breathe as well. Considering that people suffering a night terror episode are in a deep stage of sleep and breathing shallowly, one can understand why breathing would seem difficult when they are suddenly active. Most people do not remember what happened during a night terror episode, although a few people can remember vividly the images and terror they experienced.

But that sounds like the description of a nightmare—what's the difference? There are some very real differences between night terrors and **nightmares**. Nightmares are usually vividly remembered immediately upon waking. A person who has had a nightmare, unlike a person experiencing a night terror, will actually be able to come awake and immediately talk about the bad dream. Perhaps the most telling difference is that nightmares occur during REM sleep rather than deep NREM sleep, which means that people don't move around in a nightmare as they do in a night terror experience.

REM SLEEP

4.7 *What is dreaming, and what happens if people don't dream?*

Think back to the description of the four stages of sleep. After spending some time in Stage Four, the sleeping person will go back up through Stage Three, Stage Two, and then into a stage in which the eyes move rapidly under the eyelids, the body is almost as aroused as in a waking state, and brain waves resemble beta waves—the kind of brain activity that usually signals wakefulness. (This high level of brain activity has led some to call this stage *paradoxical sleep.*) The person is still asleep but is in REM sleep.

When a person in REM sleep is awakened, he or she almost always reports being in a dream state (Shafton, 1995). REM sleep is, therefore, associated with dreaming, and 90 percent of dreams actually take place in REM sleep. People do have dreams in the other NREM stages, but REM dreams tend to be more vivid, more detailed, longer, and more bizarre than the dreams of NREM sleep. NREM dreams tend to be more like thoughts about daily occurrences and far shorter than REM dreams (Foulkes & Schmidt, 1983; Takeuchi et al., 2003).

The Need for REM Sleep Why two kinds of sleep? And why would REM sleep ever be considered restful when the body is almost awake and the brain is so active? REM sleep seems to serve a different purpose than does NREM, or deep sleep. After a very physically demanding day, people tend to spend more time in NREM deep sleep than is usual. But an emotionally stressful day leads to increased time in REM sleep (Horne & Staff, 1983).

4.8 *What changes might occur in sleep as a result of learning a new motor task?*

Carlyle Smith of Trent University in Peterborough, Ontario, has been studying the effect of sleep on long-term memory in both humans and animals (Smith, 2001, 2003). He and his colleagues have demonstrated that both REM sleep (Smith, Nixon, & Nader, 2004) and Stage Two NREM sleep (Fogel & Smith, 2006) are important for memory associated with learning a new motor task. More specifically, Smith has shown that when a person is learning a new motor task, different sleep patterns emerge that are dependent on the initial skill level of the individual. If the person was already fairly good at performing the new motor task, he or she shows significant increases in Stage Two NREM sleep. Individuals who initially have a hard time learning the new motor task show increases in REM activity (Peters, Smith, & Smith, 2007). Perhaps the dreams people have in REM sleep are a way of dealing with the stresses, tensions, and any new learning the day may bring, whereas deeper learning of a motor task and physical activity would demand more time for the building of new synapses and recovery of the body in NREM sleep. Also, if deprived of REM sleep (as would occur with the use of sleeping pills or other depressant drugs such as alcohol), a person will experience greatly increased amounts of REM sleep the next night, a phenomenon called **REM rebound** (Vogel, 1975, 1993).

Interestingly, REM sleep in early infancy differs from adult REM sleep. First, babies spend nearly half of their sleep in REM as compared to 20 percent in adulthood. Second, the brain wave patterns on EEG recordings are not exactly the same in infant REM when compared to adult REM recordings, and infants can and do move around quite a bit during REM sleep (Carskadon & Dement, 2005; Davis et al., 2004; Sheldon, 2002; Tucker et al., 2006). These two differences can be explained: When infants are engaged in REM sleep, they are not dreaming but rather forming new connections between neurons (Carskadon & Dement, 2005; Davis et al., 2004; Sheldon, 2002). The infant brain is highly plastic, and much of brain growth and development takes place during REM sleep.

Nightmares and REM Behaviour Disorder What would happen if we *could* act out our dreams? Would it be like sleepwalking? Being able to act out one's dreams, especially nightmares, is a far more dangerous proposition than sleepwalking. Nightmares are bad dreams, and some nightmares can be utterly terrifying. Children tend to have more nightmares than adults do because they spend more of their sleep in the REM state, as discussed earlier. As they age, they have fewer nightmares because they have less opportunity to have them. But some people still suffer from nightmares as adults.

REM rebound
increased amounts of REM sleep after being deprived of REM sleep on earlier nights.

What would happen if we *could* act out our dreams? Would it be like sleepwalking?

REM behaviour disorder
a rare disorder in which the mechanism that blocks the movement of the voluntary muscles fails, allowing the person to thrash around and even get up and act out nightmares.

Some people have a rare disorder in which the brain mechanisms that normally inhibit the voluntary muscles fail, allowing the person to thrash around and even get up and act out nightmares. This disorder is called **REM behaviour disorder**, which is a fairly serious condition (Shafton, 1995). Usually seen in men older than age 60, it can happen in younger men and in women. For more about this disorder, see the Psychology in the News section that follows.

SLEEP DISORDERS

There are a number of other problems that can occur during sleep in addition to sleepwalking, sexsomnia, nightmares, and REM behaviour disorder.

4.9 *What kinds of problems can happen during sleep?*

INSOMNIA Most people think that **insomnia** is the inability to sleep. Although that is the literal meaning of the term, in reality insomnia is the inability to get to sleep, stay asleep, or get a good quality of sleep (Kryger, Lavie, & Rosen, 1999).

PSYCHOLOGY IN THE NEWS

Murderous Dreams

According to a compilation of information by Dr. Lawrence Martin at Case Western Reserve University in Cleveland, Ohio, a specialist in pulmonary* and sleep medicine, at least 20 cases of "murder while sleepwalking" have been recorded. The term *sleepwalking* as used in these cases probably refers to the very real condition called *REM behaviour disorder*. Use of this disorder as a defence in a murder trial has sometimes been successful. Here is a short description of a well-known Canadian case and its outcome.

Kenneth Parks, a 23-year-old man from Toronto, had been suffering from severe insomnia stemming from the loss of his job and from financial problems. On May 23, 1987, he got up early in the morning, got in his car, and drove 23 kilometres to the home of his wife's parents. He stabbed his mother-in-law to death, attacked his father-in-law, and then drove to the police. Once there, he told them that he thought he had killed some people. At that point, he looked down at his hands and seemed to realize for the first time that they were severely cut—several of the tendons in both hands had to be surgically repaired.

Parks had loved his mother-in-law, and there was no history of bad feelings or hostility prior to the attack. He did have a history of sleepwalking, and his defence team, which included sleep experts and psychiatrists, concluded that he was indeed unaware of his actions at the time of the crime. He was acquitted (Denno, 2002; Martin, 2004). In 2006, Mr. Parks ran for a school trustee position on the Durham District School Board. He was unsuccessful.

Kenneth Parks was found not guilty of murder after it was concluded that he was "asleep" when he committed the crime and therefore was not conscious of his actions.

Questions for Further Discussion

1. Should sleepwalking be a valid defence for a crime as serious as murder? What about other kinds of crimes?

2. What kind of evidence should be required to convince a jury that a crime was committed while sleepwalking?

*Pulmonary: having to do with the lungs

There are many causes of insomnia, both psychological and physiological. Some of the psychological causes are worrying, trying too hard to sleep, or anxiety. Some of the physiological causes are too much caffeine, indigestion, or aches and pain.

There are several steps people can take to help them sleep. Obvious ones are consuming no caffeinated drinks or foods that cause indigestion before bedtime, taking medication for pain, and dealing with anxieties in the daytime rather than facing them at night. That last bit of advice is easy to say but not always easy to do. Here are some other helpful hints (Kupfer & Reynolds, 1997):

1. Go to bed only when you are sleepy. If you lie in bed for 20 minutes and are still awake, get up and do something such as reading or watching television until you feel sleepy, and then go back to bed.

2. Don't do anything in your bed but sleep. Your bed should be a cue for sleeping, not studying or watching television. Because sleeping is a reflex response, using the bed as a cue for sleeping is a kind of learning called *classical conditioning*, or the pairing of cues and reflex responses. Ⓛ Ⓘ Ⓝ Ⓚ *to Chapter Five: Learning, p. 176.*

3. Don't try too hard to get to sleep, and especially do not look at the clock and calculate how much sleep you aren't getting. That just increases the tension and makes it more difficult to sleep.

4. Don't take sleeping pills or drink alcohol or other types of drugs that slow down the nervous system (see the section about depressants later in this chapter). These drugs force you into deep sleep and do not allow you to get any REM sleep or the lighter stages. When you try to sleep without these drugs the next night, you will experience REM rebound, which will cause you to feel tired and sleepy the next day. REM rebound is one way to experience the form of insomnia in which a person sleeps but sleeps poorly.

If none of these things seem to be working, there are sleep clinics and sleep experts who can help people with insomnia. The Canadian Sleep Society's website at **www.css.to** has information about sleep medicine clinics in Canada.

SLEEP APNEA   Gerald was a snorer. Actually, that's an understatement. Gerald could give a jet engine some serious competition. Snoring is fairly common, occurring when the breathing passages (nose and throat) get blocked. Most people snore only when they have a cold or some other occasional problem, but some people snore every night and quite loudly, like Gerald. It is this type of snoring that is often associated with a condition called **sleep apnea**, in which the person stops breathing for nearly half a minute or more. When breathing stops, there will be a sudden silence, followed shortly by a gasping sound as the person struggles to get air into the lungs. Many people do not wake up while this is happening, but they do not get a good, restful night's sleep because of the apnea.

Apnea is a serious problem. Not only does it disturb nightly sleep, making the person excessively sleepy in the daytime, but it can also cause heart problems (Flemons, 2002). If a person suspects the presence of apnea, a visit to a physician is the first step in identifying the disorder and deciding on a treatment. With mild apnea, treatment may be a device worn on the nose at night to open the nostrils and prevent blockage. Obesity is a primary cause of apnea, especially in men, so another solution might be to lose excess weight. There are also sprays that are supposed to shrink the tissues lining the throat (much as a nasal decongestant spray shrinks the tissues of the

This woman has insomnia. In insomnia, a person has trouble getting to sleep, staying asleep, or getting enough sleep. How will this woman feel when she wakes up in the morning?

⊙─Watch on **mypsychlab**
SIDS

✳─Explore on **mypsychlab**
Sleeping and Dreaming

insomnia
the inability to get to sleep, stay asleep, or get a good quality of sleep.

sleep apnea
disorder in which the person stops breathing for nearly half a minute or more.

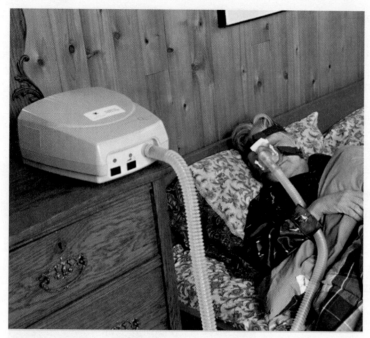

This man is wearing a CPAP, or continuous positive air pressure device. The CPAP gently forces air through his nasal passages, keeping his airways open and preventing sleep apnea. Why might wearing a CPAP become a problem for some apnea sufferers?

"On your application it says you have narcolepsy. What is that?"

www.CartoonStock.com.

⊙▬ Watch on mypsychlab

Living with Narcolepsy

narcolepsy
sleep disorder in which a person falls immediately into REM sleep during the day without warning.

nasal passages). Some people sleep with a device that delivers a continuous stream of air under mild pressure, called a *continuous positive airway pressure (CPAP)* device. Others undergo a simple surgery in which the *uvula* (the little flap that hangs down at the back of the throat) and some of the soft tissues surrounding it are removed.

Some very young infants also experience a kind of apnea due to immaturity of the brain stem. These infants are typically placed on monitors that sound an alarm when breathing stops, allowing caregivers to help the infant begin breathing again. Although sleep apnea in infants is often associated with sudden infant death syndrome (SIDS), it is not necessarily a cause: Many infants who die of SIDS were never diagnosed with sleep apnea (Blackmon et al., 2003).

NARCOLEPSY   A genetic disorder affecting 1 in every 2000 persons, **narcolepsy** is a kind of "sleep seizure." In narcolepsy, the person may slip suddenly into REM sleep during the day (especially when the person experiences strong emotions). Another symptom is excessive daytime sleepiness that results in the person falling asleep throughout the day at inappropriate times and in inappropriate places (Overeem et al., 2001). These sleep attacks may occur many times and without warning, making the operation of a car or other machinery very dangerous for the *narcoleptic* (person who suffers from narcolepsy). The sudden REM attacks are especially dangerous because of the symptom of *cataplexy*, or a sudden loss of muscle tone. This REM paralysis may cause injuries if the person is standing when the attack occurs.

Research suggests that narcolepsy is due to a loss of hypocretin-secreting neurons located in the hypothalamus (Nishino et al., 2000). The same hypnogogic images that may accompany Stage One sleep may also occur in the narcoleptic person. Table 4.1 has a more detailed list of known sleep disorders.

TABLE 4.1 COMMON SLEEP DISORDERS	
NAME OF DISORDER	**PRIMARY SYMPTOMS**
Somnambulism	Sitting, walking, or performing complex behaviour while asleep
Sexsomnia	Sexual behaviour while asleep
Night terrors	Extreme fear, agitation, screaming while asleep
Restless leg syndrome	Uncomfortable sensations in legs causing movement and loss of sleep
Nocturnal leg cramps	Painful cramps in calf or foot muscles
Hypersomnia	Excessive daytime sleepiness
Circadian rhythm disorders	Disturbances of the sleep–wake cycle such as jet lag and shift work
Enuresis	Urinating while asleep in bed

PRACTICE QUIZ: HOW MUCH DO YOU REMEMBER?

Pick the best answer.

1. In which stage of sleep is a person who is very difficult to awaken?
   a. Stage One
   b. Stage Two
   c. Stage Three
   d. Stage Four

2. Which of the following is NOT a characteristic of REM sleep?
   a. paralysis of voluntary muscles
   b. increased heart rate
   c. slower, deeper breathing
   d. increased body temperature

3. What is the main identifying feature of sexsomnia?
   a. increased REM
   b. a history of sleepwalking behaviour
   c. sleep deprivation and alcohol consumption
   d. an abrupt elevation from deep sleep

4. Three-year-old Sara watches her dad and his buddies throw a miniature football around as they get set to watch the Grey Cup. Once the game starts, Sara picks up the football and starts tossing it around the house. What might we expect to find with respect to Sara's sleep pattern that night?
   a. more NREM sleep
   b. less NREM sleep
   c. less REM sleep
   d. more REM sleep

5. Acting out your nightmares is a rare condition called
   a. sleep apnea.
   b. night terrors.
   c. narcolepsy.
   d. REM behaviour disorder.

6. In which disorder does breathing stop for nearly half a minute or more?
   a. sleep apnea
   b. night terrors
   c. sleepwalking
   d. narcolepsy

7. Which of the following is bad advice for someone suffering from insomnia?
   a. Do not watch television or read in bed.
   b. Avoid coffee, tea, and other caffeine-containing products before bed.
   c. Do not study or work in bed.
   d. Lie in bed until you fall asleep, even if it takes several hours.

8. Nightmares occur in _____ sleep, whereas night terrors occur in _____ sleep.
   a. Stage One; Stage Two
   b. REM; NREM
   c. Stage Four; Stage One
   d. NREM; REM

Answers: 1-d, 2-c, 3-d, 4-d, 5-d, 6-a, 7-d, 8-b.

DREAMS

4.10   *Why do people dream, and what do they dream about?*

Dreams have long been a source of curiosity. People of ancient times tried to find meaning in dreams. Some saw dreams as prophecy, some as messages from the spirits. But the real inquiry into the process of dreaming began with the publication of Freud's *The Interpretation of Dreams* (1900).

FREUD'S INTERPRETATION: DREAMS AS WISH FULFILLMENT

Sigmund Freud (1856–1939) believed that the problems of his patients stemmed from conflicts and events that had been buried in their unconscious minds since childhood. These early traumas were seen as the cause of *neurotic behaviour* in adulthood, in which his patients suffered from symptoms such as a type of paralysis that had no physical basis, or repetitive, ritualistic handwashing. One of the ways Freud devised to get at these early memories was to examine the dreams of his patients, believing that conflicts, events, and desires of the past would be represented in symbolic form in the dreams.

MANIFEST CONTENT   The *manifest content* of a dream is the actual dream itself. For example, if Chad has a dream in which he is trying to climb out of a bathtub, the manifest content of the dream is exactly that—he's trying to climb out of a bathtub.

Seems like quite a stretch. Wouldn't there be lots of ▶ other possible interpretations?

Dreams are often filled with unrealistic and imaginative events and images. A common dream is that of flying. What do you think flying might represent in a dream?

My dreams can be really weird, but sometimes they seem pretty ordinary or even ▶ seem to mean something. Can dreams be more meaningful?

LATENT CONTENT   But, of course, Freud would no doubt find more meaning in Chad's dream than is at first evident. He believed that the true meaning of a dream lay hidden, or *latent*, and was expressed only in symbols. In the dream, the water in the tub might symbolize the waters of birth, and the tub itself Chad's mother's womb. In Freudian terms Chad may be dreaming about being born.

Seems like quite a stretch. Wouldn't there be lots of other possible interpretations? Yes, and today many professionals are no longer as fond of Freud's dream analysis as they once were. But there are still some people who insist that dreams have symbolic meaning. For example, dreaming about being naked in a public place is very common, and most dream analyzers interpret that as feeling open and exposed, an expression of childhood innocence, or even a desire for sex. Exactly how the dream is interpreted depends on the other features of the dream and what is happening in the person's waking life.

The development of techniques for looking at the structure and activity of the brain (see Chapter Two, p. 62) has led to an explanation of why people dream that is more concrete than that of Freud.

THE ACTIVATION-SYNTHESIS HYPOTHESIS

Using brain-imaging techniques such as a PET scan (see Chapter Two), researchers have found evidence that dreams are products of activity in the lower brain stem (Hobson, 1988; Hobson & McCarley, 1977; Hobson et al., 2000). This lower area inhibits the neurotransmitters that would allow movement of the voluntary muscles while sending random signals to the areas of the cortex that interpret vision, hearing, and so on.

When signals from the lower brain bombard the cortex during waking consciousness, the association areas of the cortex interpret those signals as seeing, hearing, and so on. Because those signals come from the real world, this process results in an experience of reality. But when people are asleep, the signals from the brain stem are random and not necessarily attached to actual external stimuli, yet the brain must somehow interpret these random signals. It *synthesizes* (puts together) an explanation of the cortex's activation from memories and other stored information.

In this theory, called the **activation-synthesis hypothesis**, a dream is merely another kind of thinking that occurs when people sleep. It is less realistic because it comes not from the outside world of reality but from within people's memories and experiences of the past. The frontal lobes, which people normally use in daytime thinking, are more or less shut down during dreaming, which may also account for the unrealistic and often bizarre nature of dreams (Macquet & Franck, 1996).

My dreams can be really weird, but sometimes they seem pretty ordinary or even seem to mean something. Can dreams be more meaningful? Some dream experts suggest that dreams may have more meaning than Hobson and McCarley originally theorized. A survey questioning subjects about their dream content, for example, concluded that much of the content of dreams is meaningful, consistent over time, and fits in with past or present emotional concerns rather than being bizarre, meaningless, and random (Domhoff, 1996).

Hobson and colleagues have reworked the activation-synthesis hypothesis to reflect concerns about dream meaning, calling it the **activation-information-mode model (AIM;** Hobson et al., 2000). In this newer version, information that is accessed during waking hours can have an influence on the synthesis of dreams. In other words, when the brain is "making up" a dream to explain its own activation, it uses bits and pieces of the person's experiences from the previous day or the past few days.

This tendency to use information from a person's daily life may also include information that is being suppressed. Suppression is a conscious, deliberate effort to refuse to think about or remember certain events or information. Some theorists see Freud's emphasis on repression (the unconscious forgetting of such information) as suppression. Whether it is called *repression* or *suppression*, there is some evidence from cognitive studies that Freud may not have been entirely wrong about the appearance in dreams of information a person would rather forget. For example, in one study of nearly 300 smokers who quit smoking for from one to four weeks, a significant number of participants reported having dreams about smoking and feeling strong negative emotions such as guilt and panic during the dream (Hajek & Belcher, 1991).

WHAT DO PEOPLE DREAM ABOUT?

Do people dream in black and white or colour? And do women have different kinds of dreams than men do? What about gamers? Calvin Hall collected more than 10 000 dreams and concluded that most dreams reflect the events that occur in everyday life (Hall, 1966). Although most people dream in colour, people who grew up in the era of black and white television sometimes have dreams in black and white. There are gender differences, although whether those differences are caused by hormonal/genetic influences, sociocultural influences, or a combination of influences remains to be seen. In his book *Finding Meaning in Dreams*, Dr. William Domhoff (1996) concluded that across many cultures, men more often dream of other males whereas women tend to dream about males and females equally. Men across various cultures also tend to have more physical aggression in their dreams than do women, with women more often being the victims of such aggression in their dreams. Domhoff also concluded that where there are differences in the content of dreams across cultures, the differences make sense in light of the culture's "personality." For example, American culture is considered fairly aggressive when compared to the culture of the Netherlands, and the aggressive content of the dreams in both cultures reflects this difference: There were lower levels of aggression in the dreams of those from the Netherlands when compared to the American dream content.

Girls and women tend to dream about people they know, personal appearance concerns, and their dreams emphasize family and home. Boys and men tend to have more male characters in their dreams, which are also typically in outdoor or unfamiliar settings and may involve weapons, tools, cars, and roads. Men also report more sexual dreams, usually with unknown and attractive partners (Domhoff, 1996; Foulkes, 1982; Van de Castle, 1994).

In dreams people run, jump, talk, and do all the actions that they do in normal daily life. In fact, nearly 50 percent of the dreams recorded by Hall (1966) had sexual content, although later research has found lower percentages (Van de Castle, 1994). Then there are dreams of flying, falling, trying to do something and failing, all of which are very common dreams, even in other cultures (Domhoff, 1996). So is a dream of being naked in public.

Jayne Gackenbach at Grant MacEwan University in Edmonton has been studying the dream content of heavy video game users, or "gamers." She and her colleagues have found that high-end gamers had more dead and imagination characters in their dreams and more dream bizarreness than low-end gamers, which is consistent with previous findings that events of the day make up the majority of dream content (Gackenbach et al. 2009; Gackenbach, Kuruvilla, & Dopko, 2009).

activation-synthesis hypothesis
theory that the higher cortical centres of the brain create dreams in response to the random activation of brain stem cells that occurs during REM sleep periods.

activation-information-mode model (AIM)
revised version of the activation-synthesis explanation of dreams in which information that is accessed during waking hours can have an influence on the synthesis of dreams.

◀ Do people dream in black and white or colour? And do women have different kinds of dreams than men do? What about gamers?

PRACTICE QUIZ: HOW MUCH DO YOU REMEMBER?

Pick the best answer.

1. In Freud's theory, the symbolic content of dreams is called
   a. manifest content.
   b. latent content.
   c. symbolic content.
   d. hidden content.

2. Which dream theory states that dreams are simply the brain's way of explaining random neural activity while sleeping?
   a. Freudian dream theory
   b. dreams for survival theory
   c. activation-synthesis hypothesis
   d. Hall's dreams as reflections of everyday life

3. According to Hobson and McCarley, the _____ area of the brain sends signals to the _____, creating what we interpret as dreams.
   a. cerebellum; forebrain
   b. forebrain; cerebellum
   c. cortex; pons
   d. pons; cortex

4. The _____ lobes "shut down" during dreaming, explaining the often bizarre nature of dreams.
   a. frontal
   b. temporal
   c. occipital
   d. parietal

5. Shelia once had a dream in which she was trying to reach something important but couldn't. The harder she tried, the less she could move—it was like moving in molasses. This is most likely explained by
   a. anxiety.
   b. REM paralysis.
   c. Stage Four paralysis.
   d. a night terror.

Answers: 1-b, 2-c, 3-d, 4-a, 5-b.

hypnosis
state of consciousness in which the person is especially susceptible to suggestion.

👁 **Watch** on **mypsychlab**

Hypnosis: Mary

Is it true that people can be hypnotized into doing things that they would never ▶ do under normal conditions?

ALTERED STATES: HYPNOSIS

Hypnosis is a state of consciousness in which a person is especially susceptible to suggestion. Although a lot of misunderstandings exist about hypnosis, it can be a useful tool when properly managed.

STEPS IN HYPNOTIC INDUCTION

4.11 *What is hypnosis, and how does it work?*

There are several key steps in inducing hypnosis. According to Druckman and Bjork (1994), although every hypnotist may have a different style or use different words, these four elements are always present:

1. The hypnotist tells the person to focus on what is being said.
2. The person is told to relax and feel tired.
3. The hypnotist tells the person to "let go" and accept suggestions easily.
4. The person is told to use vivid imagination.

The real key to hypnosis seems to be a heightened state of suggestibility. People can be hypnotized when active and alert, but only if they are willing to be hypnotized. Only 80 percent of all people can be hypnotized, and only 40 percent are good hypnotic subjects. People who fantasize a lot, who daydream and have vivid imaginations, as well as people who get "really into" whatever task they are doing are more susceptible to hypnosis than others (Silva & Kirsch, 1992).

A test of *hypnotic susceptibility*, or the degree to which a person is a good hypnotic subject, often makes use of a series of suggestions. The more suggestions the person responds to, the more susceptible that person is. (See Table 4.2 for a list of some common suggestions developed at Stanford University.)

FACT OR MYTH: WHAT CAN HYPNOSIS REALLY DO?

Is it true that people can be hypnotized into doing things that they would never do under normal conditions? Books, movies, and television programs have often misrepresented the effects of hypnosis. Although the popular view is that the hypnotized person is acting involuntarily, the fact is that the hypnotized person is really the one in control. In fact, the hypnotist may only be a guide into a more

TABLE 4.2 SAMPLE ITEMS FROM THE STANFORD HYPNOTIC SUSCEPTIBILITY SCALE: FORM A (SHSS:A)		
1. Postural sway	5. Finger lock	9. Hallucination (fly)
2. Eye closure	6. Arm rigidity (left arm)	10. Eye catalepsy
3. Hand lowering (left)	7. Hands moving together	11. Posthypnotic (changes chairs)
4. Immobilization (right arm)	8. Verbal inhibition (name)	12. Amnesia

Source: Adapted from Hypnotic Susceptibility by E. Hilgard (1965). New York: Harcourt, Brace and World.

relaxed state, while the subject actually hypnotizes himself or herself (Kirsch & Lynn, 1995). So relax, you won't be committing any immoral acts or doing anything really objectionable under hypnosis because you are really the one in control. People cannot be hypnotized against their will. The tendency to act as though their behaviour is automatic and out of their control is called the *basic suggestion effect* (Kihlstrom, 1985); it gives people an excuse to do things they might not otherwise do because the burden of responsibility for their actions falls on the hypnotist.

Some people say that a hypnotized person can be super strong or endure pain without feeling it. Is any of that true? Dr. Nicholas Spanos (1942–1994), of Carleton University, in Ottawa, was a leader in determining whether hypnosis could really change what we see or feel. Spanos and his colleagues used some very creative experimental designs to hone in on the sensory effects of hypnosis. In one study, 45 hypnotized participants were told that they were being shown a blank page; however, the page actually contained the number 8. Participants were then unhypnotized and asked to report what they saw on the page. Only 15 participants said they saw the blank page. In an attempt to increase accuracy, the 15 participants who said they saw a blank page were then told that only "fakers" said that. After a few minutes, the participants were given a chance to redeem themselves and handed a piece of paper and asked to draw what they saw. Fourteen of 15 correctly drew the number 8. Thus, 44 of 45 hypnotized participants correctly identified the 8 on the page, when they were told that nothing was there. These findings suggest that hypnosis does not alter the ability of our physical senses, but rather alters what we report (Spanos, Flynn, & Gabora, 1989).

So the answer to the question of whether a hypnotized person can be super strong or endure pain without feeling it is no and yes. Persons may report changes in their sensory experience, but the sensory system is likely performing normally. For a look at what hypnosis can and cannot do, see Table 4.3.

In general, hypnosis is a handy way to help people relax and control pain. These are subjective experiences and very much under people's mental influence. Actual

◀ Some people say that a hypnotized person can be super strong or endure pain without feeling it. Is any of that true?

✴ Explore on **mypsychlab**
Hypnosis

TABLE 4.3 FACTS ABOUT HYPNOSIS	
HYPNOSIS CAN	**HYPNOSIS CANNOT**
Create amnesia for whatever happens during the hypnotic session, at least for a brief time (Bowers & Woody, 1996)	Give people superhuman strength (People may use their full strength under hypnosis, but it is no more than they had before hypnosis.)
Relieve pain by allowing a person to remove conscious attention from the pain (Holroyd, 1996)	Reliably enhance memory (There's an increased risk of false memory retrieval because of the suggestible state hypnosis creates.)
Alter sensory perceptions (Smell, hearing, vision, time sense, and the ability to see visual illusions can all be affected by hypnosis.)	Regress people back to childhood (Although people may *act* like children, they do and say things children would not.)

physical behaviour is more difficult to change, and that is why hypnosis is not as effective at changing eating habits or helping people to stop smoking (Druckman & Bjork, 1994). Hypnosis is sometimes used in psychological therapy to help people cope with anxiety or deal with cravings for food or drugs.

THEORIES OF HYPNOSIS

There are two views of why hypnosis works. One emphasizes the role of *dissociation*, or a splitting of conscious awareness, whereas the other involves a kind of social role-playing.

HYPNOSIS AS DISSOCIATION: THE HIDDEN OBSERVER Ernest Hilgard (1991; Hilgard & Hilgard, 1994) believed that hypnosis worked only on the immediate conscious mind of a person, while a part of that person's mind (a "hidden observer") remained aware of all that was going on. It's the same kind of dissociation that takes place when people drive somewhere familiar and then wonder how they got there. One part of the mind, the conscious part, is thinking about dinner or a date or something else, while the other part is doing the actual driving. When people arrive at their destination, they don't really remember the actual trip. In the same way, Hilgard believes that there is a hidden part of the mind that is very much aware of the hypnotic subject's activities and sensations, even though the "hypnotized" part of the mind is blissfully unaware of these same things.

In one study (Miller & Bowers, 1993), subjects were hypnotized and told to put their arms in ice water, although they were instructed to feel no pain. There had to be pain—most people can't even get an ice cube out of the freezer without *some* pain—but subjects reported no pain at all. The subjects who were successful at denying the pain also reported that they imagined being at the beach or in some other place that allowed them to dissociate from the pain.

HYPNOSIS AS SOCIAL ROLE-PLAYING: THE SOCIAL-COGNITIVE EXPLANATION The other theory of why hypnosis works began with an experiment in which people who were *not* hypnotized were instructed to behave as if they were (Sarbin & Coe, 1972). These people had no trouble copying many actions previously thought to require a hypnotic state, such as being rigidly suspended between two chairs. Researchers (Sarbin & Coe, 1972) also found that people who were not familiar with hypnosis, and had no idea what the "role" of a hypnotic subject was supposed to be, could not be hypnotized. Similarly, Canadian university students in Ottawa were hypnotized and asked to go back in time and remember their births, their time in the womb, and even a previous life. Interestingly, about one-third of the students recalled a previous life. However, the students were poor at answering simple questions about their previous life. Questions such as was your country at war, who was your leader, or what kind of money did you use were rarely answered correctly. The researchers concluded that the students' memories were

Stage hypnotists often make use of people's willingness to believe that something ordinary is extraordinary. This woman was hypnotized and suspended between two chairs after the person supporting her middle stepped away. The hypnotist led the audience to believe that she could not do this unless hypnotized, but in reality anyone can do this while fully conscious.

based on the places and events of their current lives, cues provided by the hypnotist, and the desire to fulfill their role as a hypnotized participant (Spanos & Menary et al., 1991)

Add to those findings the later findings of Kirsch (2000) that expectancies of the hypnotized person play a big part in how the person responds and what the person does under hypnosis. The **social-cognitive theory of hypnosis** assumes that people who are hypnotized are not in an altered state but are merely playing the role expected of them in the situation. They might believe that they are hypnotized, but in fact it is all a very good performance, so good that even the "subjects" are unaware that they are role-playing. Social roles are very powerful influences on behaviour, as anyone who has ever worn a uniform can understand—the uniform stands for a particular role that becomes very easy to play (Zimbardo, 1970; Zimbardo et al., 2000). (L I N K) *to Chapter Twelve: Social Psychology, p. 476.*

PRACTICE QUIZ: HOW MUCH DO YOU REMEMBER?

Pick the best answer.

1. Which of the following is NOT one of the steps in inducing hypnosis?
  a. putting the person to sleep
  b. telling the person to relax
  c. telling the person to use vivid imagination
  d. telling the person to "let go"

2. The tendency to act as though your behaviour is out of your control and involuntary is called (the)
  a. hypnosis effect.   **c.** basic suggestion effect.
  b. basic involuntary effect.   **d.** none of the above

3. Hypnosis has been successfully used to
  a. give a person superhuman strength.
  b. recall memories accurately and completely.

  c. reduce sensations of pain.
  d. regress a person back to infancy.

4. In the _____ theory of hypnosis, the person has a part of the mind that is not hypnotized and that is fully aware of the proceedings.
  a. social-cognitive   **c.** role-playing
  b. dissociative   **d.** expectancy

5. About one-third of hypnotized Canadian students could recall a previous life, but few could answer simple questions regarding this previous life. This finding supports the _____ theory of hypnosis.
  a. expectancy   **c.** social-cognitive
  b. role-playing   **d.** dissociative

Answers: 1-a, 2-c, 3-c, 4-b, 5-c.

ALTERED STATES: PSYCHOACTIVE DRUGS

While some people seek altered states of consciousness in sleep, daydreaming, meditation, or even hypnosis, others take a shortcut. They use drugs, called **psychoactive drugs**, that alter thinking, perception, memory, or some combination of those abilities. Although some of these drugs can be useful under certain circumstances, they all pose risks as well. One of the dangers of such drugs is their potential to create either a physical or psychological dependence, both of which can lead to a lifelong pattern of abuse as well as the risk of taking increasingly larger doses, leading to one of the clearest dangers of dependence: a drug overdose. Drug overdoses do not have to happen only with illegal drugs; even certain additives in so-called natural supplements can have a deadly effect. For example, in January 2003, Steve Bechler, a prospective pitcher for the Baltimore Orioles, died after taking three ephedra pills on an empty stomach (Shekelle et al., 2003). Ephedra is a substance derived from a shrub found in desert areas and has been used in supplements that claim to promote weight loss.

✳ ⌐**Explore** on **mypsychlab**
  What Altered States Have You Experienced?

social-cognitive theory of hypnosis
theory that people who are hypnotized are not in an altered state but are merely playing the role expected of them in the situation.

psychoactive drugs
drugs that alter thinking, perception, and memory.

withdrawal
physical symptoms that can include nausea, pain, tremors, crankiness, and high blood pressure, resulting from a lack of an addictive drug in the body systems.

psychological dependence
the feeling that a drug is needed to continue a feeling of emotional or psychological well-being.

But not all drugs produce physical dependence, right? For example, some people say that you can't get ▶ physically dependent on marijuana. If that's true, why is it so hard for some people to quit smoking pot?

One of the dangers of psychoactive drugs is that they may lead to physical or psychological dependence. Cocaine is a powerful and addictive stimulant and can be sniffed in through the nose or injected, as the man in this photograph is doing.

PHYSICAL DEPENDENCE

4.12   *What is the difference between a physical dependence and a psychological dependence on a drug?*

Drugs that people can become physically dependent on cause the user's body to crave the drug (Abadinsky, 1989; Fleming & Barry, 1992; Pratt, 1991). After using the drug for some period of time, the body becomes unable to function normally without the drug and the person is said to be dependent or addicted.

DRUG TOLERANCE   One sign of physical dependence is the development of a *drug tolerance* (Pratt, 1991). As the person continues to use the drug, larger and larger doses of the drug are needed to achieve the same initial effects of the drug.

WITHDRAWAL   Another sign of a physical dependence is that the user experiences symptoms of **withdrawal** when deprived of the drug. Depending on the drug, these symptoms can range from headaches, nausea, and irritability to severe pain, cramping, shaking, and dangerously elevated blood pressure. These physical sensations occur because the body is trying to adjust to the absence of the drug. Many users will take more of the drug to alleviate the symptoms of withdrawal, which makes the entire situation worse. In Chapter Five, we will discuss the concept of *negative reinforcement*, the tendency to continue a behaviour that leads to the removal of or escape from unpleasant circumstances or sensations. Negative reinforcement is a very powerful motivating factor, and scores of drug-dependent users exist as living proof of that power.

But not all drugs produce physical dependence, right? For example, some people say that you can't get physically dependent on marijuana. If that's true, why is it so hard for some people to quit smoking pot?

PSYCHOLOGICAL DEPENDENCE

Not all drugs cause physical dependence; some cause **psychological dependence**, or the feeling that the drug is needed to continue a feeling of emotional or psychological well-being, which is a very powerful factor in continued drug use. The body may not need or crave the drug, and people may not experience the symptoms of physical withdrawal or tolerance, but they will continue to use the drug because they *think* they need it. In this case, it is the rewarding properties of using the drug that cause a dependency to develop. In Chapter Five, this is called *positive reinforcement*, or the tendency of a behaviour to strengthen when followed by pleasurable consequences. Negative reinforcement is also at work here, as taking the drug will lower levels of anxiety.

Although not all drugs produce physical dependence, *any* drug can become a focus of psychological dependence. Indeed, because there is no withdrawal to go through and from which to recover, psychological dependencies can last forever. Some people who gave up smoking pot decades ago still say that the craving returns every now and then (Roffman et al., 1988).

The effect of a particular drug depends on the category to which it belongs and the particular neurotransmitter the drug affects. LINK *to Chapter Two: The Biological Perspective, pp. 51–53.* This chapter will describe several of the major drug categories: **stimulants** (drugs that increase the functioning of the nervous system), **depressants** (drugs that decrease the functioning of the nervous system), **narcotics** (drugs that are derived from the opium poppy), and **psychogenic drugs** (those that cause hallucinations, as well as marijuana and hashish).

STIMULANTS: UP, UP, AND AWAY

Stimulants are a class of drugs that cause the nervous system and many of the organs connected to it to increase their activity, at least temporarily. In simple terms, stimulants "speed up" the nervous system. Many of these drugs are called *uppers* for this reason.

4.13   *What are some examples of stimulants and the dangers associated with taking them?*

AMPHETAMINES   **Amphetamines** are stimulants that are synthesized (made) in laboratories rather than being found in nature. Among the amphetamines are drugs such as Benzedrine, Methedrine, and Dexedrine. Truck drivers use amphetamines to stay awake while driving long hours, and many doctors used to prescribe these drugs as diet pills for overweight people.

Like other stimulants, amphetamines cause the sympathetic nervous system to go into overdrive. ⓛ ⓘ ⓝ ⓚ *to Chapter Two: The Biological Perspective, pp. 59–60.* Stimulants won't give people any extra energy, but they will cause people to burn up whatever energy reserves they do have. They also depress the appetite, which is another function of the sympathetic division. When the energy reserves are exhausted, or the drug wears off, a "crash" is inevitable.

This is why people who take amphetamines often develop a physical dependency on the drug and quickly develop a tolerance. When the "crash" or depression comes, the tendency is to take more pills to get back "up." The person taking these pills finds that it takes more and more pills to get the same stimulant effect. Doses can easily become toxic and deadly. Nausea, vomiting, high blood pressure, and strokes are possible, as is a condition called *amphetamine psychosis.* This condition causes addicts to become delusional (losing contact with what is real) and paranoid. They think people are out to "get" them. Violence is a likely outcome, both against the self and others (Kratofil, Baberg, & Dimsdale, 1996).

Of course, amphetamines are also used to treat narcolepsy, the sleep disorder discussed earlier in this chapter. They are still used as diet pills, but only on a short-term basis and under strict medical supervision. The diet aids that people buy over the counter usually contain another relatively mild stimulant, caffeine.

COCAINE   Unlike amphetamines, **cocaine** is a natural drug found in coca plant leaves. It produces feelings of euphoria (a feeling of great happiness), energy, power, and pleasure. It also deadens pain and suppresses the appetite. It was used rather liberally by both doctors and dentists (who used it in numbing the mouth prior to extracting a tooth, for example) near the end of the nineteenth century and the beginning of the twentieth century, until the deadly effects of its addictive qualities became known. Many patent medicines contained traces of cocaine, including the famous Coca-Cola. The good news is that even in 1902, there wasn't enough cocaine in a bottle of cola to affect even a fly, and by 1929, all traces of cocaine were removed (Allen, 1994).

Cocaine is a highly dangerous drug, not just for its addictive properties. Some people have convulsions and may even die when using cocaine for the first time (Lacayo, 1995). It has devastating effects on the children born to mothers who use cocaine, causing learning disabilities, hyperactivity, delayed language development, and tremors, among other symptoms (Blatt et al., 2000; Frank et al., 2001). Laboratory animals have been known to press a lever to give themselves cocaine rather than eating or drinking, even to the point of starvation and death (Iwamoto & Martin, 1988; Ward et al., 1996).

stimulants
drugs that increase the functioning of the nervous system.

depressants
drugs that decrease the functioning of the nervous system.

narcotics
a class of opium-related drugs that suppress the sensation of pain by binding to and stimulating the nervous system's natural receptor sites for endorphins.

psychogenic drugs
drugs, including hallucinogens and marijuana, that produce hallucinations or increased feelings of relaxation and intoxication.

amphetamines
stimulants that are synthesized (made) in laboratories rather than being found in nature.

cocaine
a natural drug derived from the leaves of the coca plant.

✱⃞ **Explore** on **mypsychlab**
Drug Addiction and Brain Reward Circuits

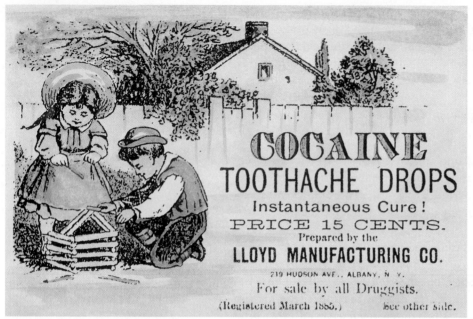

Far from being illegal, cocaine was once used in many health drinks and medications, such as this toothache medicine used in the late 1800s.

Hasn't nicotine just been the victim of a lot of bad press? After all, it's legal, unlike cocaine and heroin. ▶

Nicotine is highly addictive, and many smokers will go to great lengths to be able to smoke—including smoking right next to a "No Smoking" sign.

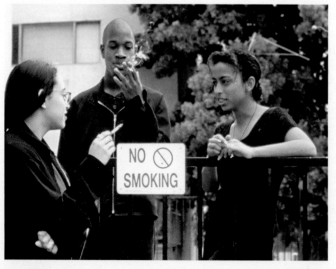

What are the signs of physical dependency? Although cocaine users do not go through the same kind of physical withdrawal symptoms that users of heroin, alcohol, and other physically addictive drugs go through, users will experience a severe mood swing into depression (the "crash"), followed by extreme tiredness, nervousness, an inability to feel pleasure, and paranoia. The brain is the part of the body that develops the craving for cocaine because of chemical changes caused by the drug (Hurley, 1989). There are three basic signs of physical dependency:

- *Compulsive use:* If cocaine is available, the person has to use it. He or she can't say no to it.

- *Loss of control:* Once people start using it, they can't stop until it is all gone or they have exhausted themselves to the point at which they can no longer function.

- *Disregard for the consequences of use:* Cocaine addicts will lie, cheat, steal, lose their jobs, damage or break up relationships, and use rent money to buy cocaine—nothing else matters to them but the drug.

As addictive as cocaine is, there is one other stimulant that comes in a very close second. The Surgeon General's Report (Centers for Disease Control and Prevention [CDC], 1992) reports that although crack cocaine (a less pure, cheaper version found on the streets) produces addiction in every person who uses it, nicotine produces addiction in 99 percent of the people who use it.

NICOTINE   Hasn't nicotine just been the victim of a lot of bad press? After all, it's legal, unlike cocaine and heroin. Every year, nearly 45 000 people in Canada die from illnesses related to smoking. And don't forget the non-smokers. It is estimated that in Canada another 1000 persons die from second-hand smoke. That's more people than those who die from motor-vehicle accidents, alcohol, cocaine, heroin and other drug abuse, AIDS, suicide, or homicide *combined* (Health Canada, 2005). Remember, cocaine, heroin, morphine, and many other currently controlled substances or illegal drugs once used to be legal. One has to wonder what would have been the fate of these drugs if as many people had been making money off of them at that time as do those who farm, manufacture, and distribute tobacco products today.

Nicotine is a relatively mild but nevertheless toxic stimulant, producing a slight "rush" or sense of arousal as it raises blood pressure and accelerates the heart, as well as providing a rush of sugar into the bloodstream by stimulating the release of adrenalin (Rezvani & Levin, 2001). As is the case with many stimulants, it also has a relaxing effect on most people (remember the effect of Ritalin on hyperactivity) and seems to reduce stress (Pormerleau & Pormerleau, 1994).

Although fewer Canadians are smoking (down to about 20 percent from about 50 percent in the mid 1960s), Canadian teens

(15–19 years) and young adults (20–24 years) continue to smoke at fairly high rates, at 18 percent and 26 percent respectively (Health Canada, 2005). This is alarming news when one considers the toxic nature of nicotine: In the 1920s and 1930s, it was used as an insecticide and is considered to be highly toxic and fast-acting (Gosselin et al., 1984). Although the amount of nicotine in a cigarette is low, first-time smokers often experience nausea as a result of the toxic effects after just a few puffs.

Quitting is a good idea but difficult to accomplish for many people. Although there are a lucky few who can quit "cold turkey" without ever smoking again, the majority of people who quit will start smoking again, even after having quit for years.

Why is it so difficult to quit? Aside from the powerfully addictive nature of nicotine, the physical withdrawal symptoms can be as bad as those resulting from alcohol, cocaine, or heroin abuse (Epping-Jordan et al., 1998). People don't think about nicotine as being as bad as cocaine or heroin because nicotine is legal and easily obtainable; but, in terms of its addictive power, nicotine is *more powerful* than heroin or alcohol (Henningfield et al., 1990).

There are many ways to quit, but the most effective methods involve delayed smoking (Cincirpini et al., 1995). In delayed smoking, the smoker begins by delaying that first cigarette of the morning, increasing the delay by a little bit every morning. Next, the total number of cigarettes smoked each day is reduced. There are also medications that can help smokers deal with the cravings for nicotine while they try to quit, as well as nicotine-containing gums and patches (worn on the skin to deliver a measured dose of nicotine in decreasing doses). The gum and patch methods deliver nicotine in a much safer, less addictive way, allowing the smoker to control the cravings until quitting completely (Benowitz, 1996; Henningfield, 1995; Stitzer & De Wit, 1998).

CAFFEINE   Although many people will never use amphetamines or take cocaine, and others will never smoke or will quit successfully, there is one stimulant that almost everyone uses, with many using it every day. Of course, this is **caffeine**, the stimulant found in coffee, tea, most sodas, chocolate, and even many over-the-counter drugs.

Caffeine is another natural substance, like cocaine and nicotine, and is found in coffee beans, tea leaves, cocoa nuts, and at least 60 other types of plants (Braun, 1996).

It is a mild stimulant, helps maintain alertness, and can increase the effectiveness of some pain relievers such as Aspirin. Caffeine is often added to pain relievers for that reason and is the key ingredient in medications meant to keep people awake.

Using coffee to help induce sobriety is a common caffeine myth. All one would get is a wide-awake drunk. Coffee is fairly acidic, too, and acids are not what the stomach of a person with a hangover needs. (And since the subject has come up, drinking more alcohol or "hair of the dog that bit you" just increases the problem later on—the best cure for a hangover is lots of water, to put back all the fluids that alcohol takes out of the body, and sleep.)

Recently, a Kentucky man who allegedly strangled his wife with an extension cord, used "caffeine intoxication" as his defence. First claiming that his steady intake of diet pills and energy drinks rendered him temporarily insane as he carried out the murder and later claiming that his caffeine intoxication led him to falsely confess to the alleged murder.

For a comparison of the amounts of caffeine in some common foods, see Table 4.4.

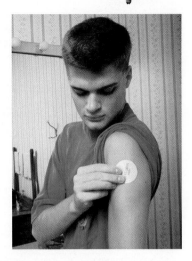

The harmful effects of nicotine are now well known, but many people continue to smoke or chew tobacco in spite of warnings such as the one shown here cautioning pregnant women not to smoke. The nicotine patch this man is placing on his upper arm will deliver a controlled dose of nicotine throughout the time he is wearing it to prevent the physical craving for the drug. As he continues to move to smaller doses, his addiction will lessen and eventually disappear.

Sleep deprivation causes this man to struggle to wake up. Caffeine can help with alertness but may worsen his sleep deprivation when he tries to get a decent night's sleep tonight.

nicotine
the active ingredient in tobacco.

caffeine
a mild stimulant found in coffee, tea, and several other plant-based substances.

TABLE 4.4 AVERAGE CAFFEINE CONTENT OF SOME BEVERAGES	
PRODUCT (250 MILLILITRES EXCEPT AS NOTED)	CAFFEINE (MILLIGRAMS)
Brewed coffee	60–120
Decaffeinated coffee	2–4
Espresso/cappuccino (30 millilitres)	30–50
Tea brewed 1 minute	9–33
Tea brewed 3 minutes	20–46
Tea brewed 5 minutes	20–50
Iced tea (250 millilitres/355 millilitres)	15–24/22–36
Hot cocoa	3–32
Milk chocolate (30 millilitres)	1–15
Dark chocolate (30 millilitres)	5–35
Jolt soda (250 millilitres/355 millilitres)	47/71
Mountain Dew (250 millilitres/355 millilitres)	36/54
Coca-Cola (250 millilitres/355 millilitres)	31/46
Pepsi (250 millilitres/355 millilitres)	24/36

Source: Barone and Roberts (1996).

"Nowadays, Hal is ninety-nine per cent caffeine-free."

©The New Yorker Collection, 1989 George Price from cartoonbank.com. All Rights Reserved.

barbiturates
depressant drugs that have a sedative effect.

benzodiazepines
drugs that lower anxiety and reduce stress.

alcohol
the chemical resulting from fermentation or distillation of various kinds of vegetable matter.

DOWN IN THE VALLEY: DEPRESSANTS

Another class of psychoactive drugs is *depressants*, drugs that slow the central nervous system.

4.14 *What are some different types of depressants, and how can they be harmful?*

BARBITURATES OR MAJOR TRANQUILIZERS Commonly known as the *major tranquilizers* (drugs that have a strong depressant effect) or sleeping pills, **barbiturates** are drugs that have a sedative (sleep-inducing) effect. The effects, depending on dosage levels, range from mild sedation or sleepiness to unconsciousness or coma. Overdoses can lead to death as breathing and heart action are stopped. Barbiturates are highly addictive and users can quickly develop a tolerance. Withdrawal can be as serious as convulsions, which are life-threatening (Olin, 1993).

Another danger of barbiturate use is the combination of one of these drugs with alcohol, another kind of depressant drug. A person who takes a dose of barbiturates that is not deadly in and of itself may die from the interaction of that dose with alcohol. This is called a *drug interaction* and is a major contributor to many unfortunate deaths.

BENZODIAZEPINES OR MINOR TRANQUILIZERS The *minor tranquilizers* (drugs having a relatively mild depressant effect) are called **benzodiazepines**. These drugs are used to lower anxiety and reduce stress. They are considered safer than barbiturates and are now the drugs of choice to treat sleep problems, nervousness, and anxiety. Some of the most common are Valium, Xanax, Halcion, Ativan, and Librium.

Even these minor tranquilizers can be addictive, and large doses can be dangerous, as can an interaction with alcohol or other drugs. Rohypnol is a newer tranquilizer that has become famous as the "date rape" drug. Unsuspecting victims drink something that has been doctored with this drug, which renders them unconscious. Rape or some other form of sexual assault can then be carried out without fear that the victim will remember it or be able to report it (Armstrong, 1997).

ALCOHOL

4.15 *What kind of drug is alcohol, and what are the dangers of drinking too much?*

The most commonly used and abused depressant is **alcohol,** the chemical resulting from fermentation or distillation of various kinds of vegetable matter. It is estimated that anywhere from 600 000 to 700 000 Canadians aged 15 years or older suffer from alcoholism (Statistics Canada, 2002). Aside from the obvious health risks to the liver, brain, and heart, alcohol is associated with loss of work time, loss of a job, and loss of economic stability. Alcohol-related car accidents are a leading cause of death among 15- to 25-year-olds in Canada.

SIGNS OF ALCOHOL ABUSE Many people are alcoholics but deny the fact, a common psychological defence. ⓁⒾⓃⓀ *to Chapter Ten: Stress and Health, p. 396.* They believe that getting drunk, especially in university, is a ritual of adulthood.

But drunkenness is a major sign of alcoholism. Some other danger signs are feeling guilty about drinking, drinking in the morning, drinking to recover from drinking, drinking alone, being sensitive about how much one drinks when others mention it, drinking so much that one does and says things one later regrets, drinking enough to have blackouts or memory loss, drinking too fast, lying about drinking, and drinking enough to pass out.

If you are concerned about your own drinking or are worried about a friend or loved one, please talk with a medical professional or visit an easy to use and free online assessment site such as the following: **http://notes.camh.net/efeed.nsf/ feedback**.

I have friends who insist that alcohol is a stimulant because they feel more uninhibited when they drink, so why is it considered a depressant? Alcohol is often confused with stimulants. Many people think this because alcohol makes a person feel "up" and euphoric (happy). Actually, alcohol is a depressant that gives the illusion of stimulation, because the very first thing alcohol depresses is a person's natural inhibitions, or the "don'ts" of behaviour. Inhibitions are all the social rules people have learned that allow them to get along with others and function in society. Inhibitions also keep people from taking off all their clothes and dancing on the table at a crowded bar—inhibitions are a good thing.

Alcohol, as stated in Chapter Two, indirectly stimulates the release of a neurotransmitter called *GABA*, the brain's major depressant (Brick, 2003). GABA slows down or stops neural activity. As more GABA is released, the brain's functioning actually becomes more and more inhibited, depressed, or slowed down. The areas of the brain that are first affected by alcohol are unfortunately the areas that control social inhibitions, so alcohol (because of its simulation of GABA) has the effect of depressing the inhibitions. As the effects continue, motor skills, reaction time, and speech are all affected.

You might be surprised to learn that only one drink can have a fairly strong effect on some people. People who are not usually drinkers will feel the effects of alcohol much more quickly than those who have built up a tolerance. Women also feel the effects sooner, as their bodies process alcohol differently than men's bodies do. (Women are typically smaller, too, so alcohol has a quicker impact on women.) See Table 4.5 for a look at what constitutes a "drink" and the effects of various numbers of drinks on the system and behaviour of the drinker.

Why do humans like to drink alcohol? Maybe it's because we have an evolutionary hangover! Primates have

Watch on **mypsychlab**
Drugs and Alcohol in Eastern Europe

Watch on **mypsychlab**
Teen Drinking Test

I have friends who insist that alcohol is a stimulant because they feel more uninhibited when they drink, so why is it considered a depressant?

Although many young adults see drinking as a rite of passage into adulthood, few may understand the dangers of "binge" drinking, or drinking four to five drinks within a limited amount of time. Inhibitions are lowered and poor decisions may be made, such as driving while intoxicated. Binge drinking, a popular activity on some campuses, can also lead to alcoholism.

TABLE 4.5 BLOOD ALCOHOL LEVEL AND BEHAVIOUR ASSOCIATED WITH AMOUNTS OF ALCOHOL

A drink is a drink. Each contains 15 millilitres (0.5 ounces) of alcohol.

So a drink is …

- 1 can of beer (355 millilitres, 4–5% alcohol)
- 1 glass of wine (120 millitres, 12% alcohol)
- 1 shot of most liquors (30 millitres, 40–50% alcohol)

At times "a drink" is really the equivalent of more than just one drink, like when you order a drink with more than one shot of alcohol in it, or you do a shot followed by a beer.

AVERAGE NUMBER OF DRINKS	BLOOD ALCOHOL LEVEL	BEHAVIOUR
1–2 drinks	0.05%	Feeling of well-being
		Release of inhibitions
		Judgment impaired
		Coordination and level of alertness lowered
		Increased risk of collision while driving
3–5 drinks	0.10%	Reaction time significantly slowed
		Muscle control and speech impaired
		Limited night and side vision
		Loss of self-control
		Crash risk greatly increased
6–7 drinks	0.15%	Consistent and major increases in reaction time
8–10 drinks	0.20%	Loss of equilibrium and technical skills
		Sensory and motor capabilities depressed
		Double vision and legal blindness (20/200)
		Unfit to drive for up to 10 hours
10–14 drinks	0.20% and 0.25%	Staggering and severe motor disturbances
10–14 drinks	0.30%	Not aware of surroundings
10–14 drinks	0.35%	Surgical anaesthesia
		Lethal dosage for a small percentage of people
14–20 drinks	0.40%	Lethal dosage for about 50% of people
		Severe circulatory/respiratory depression
		Alcohol poisoning/overdose

Source: Adapted from the *Moderate Drinking Skills Study Guide* (2004). Eau-Claire, WI: University of Wisconsin.

opium
substance derived from the opium poppy, from which all narcotic drugs are derived.

morphine
narcotic drug derived from opium, used to treat severe pain.

heroin
narcotic drug derived from opium that is extremely addictive.

been eating fruit for millions of years, and the ripest fruit, which we desire most, contains alcohol. So according to the *frugivory by-product hypothesis*, the reason so many of us like alcohol is because it artificially activates, at an unconscious level, an adaptive mechanism for consuming the ripest fruit (Dudley, 2002).

NARCOTICS: I FEEL YOUR PAIN

4.16 *How do narcotics work, and why are they so addictive?*

Narcotics are a class of drugs that suppress the sensation of pain by binding to and stimulating the nervous system's natural receptor sites for endorphins, the neurotransmitters that naturally deaden pain sensations (Olin, 1993). Because they also slow down the action of the nervous system, drug interactions with alcohol and other depressants are possible—and deadly. All narcotics are a derivative of a particular plant-based substance, opium.

OPIUM Opium, made from the opium poppy, has pain-relieving and euphoria-inducing properties that have been known for at least 2000 years. It was commonly used by ladies of the Victorian era in a form called *laudanum* and was still prescribed as *paregoric* for teething infants in the middle of the twentieth century. It was in 1803 that opium was developed for use as a medication by a German physician. The new form—morphine—was hailed as "God's own medicine" (Hodgson, 2001).

MORPHINE Morphine was created by dissolving opium in an acid and then neutralizing the acid with ammonia. Morphine was thought to be a wonder drug, although its addictive qualities soon became a major concern to physicians and their patients. Morphine is still used today but in carefully controlled doses and for short periods of time.

HEROIN Ironically, **heroin** was first hailed as the new wonder drug—a derivative of morphine that did not have many of the disagreeable side effects of morphine. The theory was that heroin was a purer form of the drug, and that the impurities in

PRACTICE QUIZ: HOW MUCH DO YOU REMEMBER?

Pick the best answer.

1. What are two signs of physical dependency?
a. drug tolerance and psychological cravings
b. psychological cravings and withdrawal
c. drug tolerance and withdrawal
d. psychological cravings and nausea

2. Larger and larger doses of amphetamines can lead to a severe mental disturbance and paranoia called
a. amphetamine neurosis.
b. amphetamine psychosis.
c. amphetaminism.
d. amphetamine toxicity.

3. Which of the following is NOT one of the three signs of cocaine abuse?
a. withdrawal
b. compulsive use
c. loss of control
d. disregard for consequences

4. Caffeine replaced _____ in patent medicines and over-the-counter preparations in the early 1900s.
a. cocaine
b. morphine
c. opium
d. nicotine

5. The "date rape" drug, Rohypnol, is one of the _____.
a. major tranquilizers
b. barbiturates
c. minor tranquilizers
d. opiates

6. Several of Marnie's friends suspect that she is using some sort of drug. She is very thin, stays awake for long periods of time, and is often jittery, nervous, and somewhat paranoid. If Marnie is using a drug, it is likely to be
a. alcohol.
b. an amphetamine.
c. sleeping pills.
d. benzodiazapine.

Answers: 1.-c, 2.-b, 3.-a, 4.-a, 5.-c, 6.-b.

morphine were the substances creating the harmful side effects. It did not take long, however, for doctors and others to realize that heroin was even more powerfully addictive than morphine or opium. Its use as a medicine ceased, but it is still used by many people.

Why are morphine and heroin so addictive? Think back to Chapter Two. That chapter discussed the roles of endorphins in relieving pain. Opium and its derivatives, morphine and heroin, duplicate the action of endorphins so well that the nervous system slows or stops its production of the neurotransmitter. When the drug wears off, there is no protection against any kind of pain, causing the severe symptoms of withdrawal associated with these drugs. The addict who tries to quit using the drug feels such pain that the urge to use again becomes unbearable.

Methadone is also a derivative of opium but does not produce the euphoric "high" of morphine or heroin. It is used to control heroin dependency and can be taken only once a day to control the withdrawal symptoms that would otherwise follow when stopping heroin use (Kahan & Sutton, 1998). Two other drugs, buprenorphine and naltrexone, are also used to treat opiate addictions (Ward et al., 1999).

There are also non-drug treatments that make use of behavioural therapies, such as *contingency management therapy* in which patients earn vouchers for negative drug tests (Tusel et al., 1994). The vouchers can be exchanged for healthier, more desirable items such as food. These behavioural therapies can include residential and outpatient approaches. ⓁⒾⓃⓀ *to Chapter Five: Learning, p. 176. Cognitive-behavioural interventions* work to change the way people think about the stresses in their lives and react to those stressors, working toward more effective coping without resorting to heroin.

HALLUCINOGENS: HIGHER AND HIGHER

4.17 *How do hallucinogens work?*

Hallucinogens fall under the category of psychogenic drugs. Hallucinogens actually stimulate the brain into altering its interpretation of sensations (Olin, 1993) and can produce sensory distortions very similar to the disorder *synesthesia,* ⓁⒾⓃⓀ *to Chapter Three: Sensation and Perception, p. 88*, in which sensations cross over each other—colours have sound, sounds have smells, and so on. False sensory perceptions, called *hallucinations*, are often experienced, especially with the more powerful

Why are **morphine and heroin so addictive?**

hallucinogens
drugs that cause false sensory messages, altering the perception of reality.

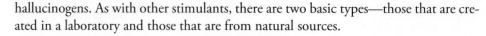

LSD (lysergic acid diethylamide)
powerful synthetic hallucinogen.

PCP
synthesized drug now used as an animal tranquilizer that can cause stimulant, depressant, narcotic, or hallucinogenic effects.

MDMA (Ecstasy or X)
designer drug that can have both stimulant and hallucinatory effects.

stimulatory hallucinogenics
drugs that produce a mixture of psychomotor stimulant and hallucinogenic effects.

hallucinogens. As with other stimulants, there are two basic types—those that are created in a laboratory and those that are from natural sources.

MANUFACTURED HIGHS There are several drugs that were developed in the laboratory instead of being found in nature. Perhaps because these drugs are manufactured, they are often more potent than drugs found in the natural world.

LSD **LSD**, or **lysergic acid diethylamide**, is synthesized from a grain fungus called *ergot*. Ergot fungus commonly grows on rye grain but can be found on other grains as well. First manufactured in 1938, LSD is one of the most potent, or powerful, hallucinogens (Lee & Shlain, 1986). It takes only a very tiny drop of LSD to achieve a "high."

People who take LSD usually do so to get that high feeling. Some people feel that LSD helps them to expand their consciousness or awareness of the world around them. Colours seem more intense, sounds more beautiful, and so on. But the fact is that LSD takes people out of the real world and dumps them into a world of the brain's creation. This is not always a pleasant experience, just as dreams are not always filled with positive emotions. "Bad trips" or very disturbing experiences are quite common, and there is no way to control what kind of "trip" the brain is going to decide to take.

One of the greater dangers in using LSD is the effect it has on a person's ability to perceive reality. Real dangers and hazards in the world may go unnoticed by a person "lost" in an LSD fantasy, and people under the influence of this drug may make poor decisions, such as trying to drive while high.

PCP Another synthesized drug was found to be so dangerous that it became useful only in veterinary medicine as a tranquilizer. The drug is **PCP** (which stands for

Many of these young people enjoying themselves at a rave may be using MDMA, or Ecstasy. The dehydrating effect of the drug, together with the intense dancing and physical activity at raves, can have a deadly effect on the user.

phenyl cyclohexyl piperidine, a name which is often contracted as *phencyclidine*), which can have many different effects. Depending on the dosage, it can be a hallucinogen, stimulant, depressant, or an analgesic (pain-killing) drug. As with LSD, PCP users can experience hallucinations, distorted sensations, and very unpleasant effects. PCP can also lead to acts of violence against others or suicide (Brecher et al., 1988; Cami et al., 2000). Users may even physically injure themselves unintentionally because PCP causes them to feel no warning signal of pain.

MDMA (Ecstasy) This last synthetic drug is technically an amphetamine but is capable of producing hallucinations as well. In fact, both **MDMA** (a "designer drug" known on the streets as **Ecstasy** or simply **X**) and PCP are now classified as **stimulatory hallucinogenics**, drugs that produce a mixture of psychomotor stimulant and hallucinogenic effects (Shuglin, 1986). Although many users of MDMA believe that it is relatively harmless, it can be deadly. MDMA is a common drug at "raves" or all-night dance parties. One of the properties of this drug is to dehydrate the body and raise body temperature, so it is very important that someone taking this drug drink enough water. But excessive drinking of water can also lead to coma and death, as excess fluid can disrupt the salt content of body tissue, making it impossible for all body parts to function properly. Nightclubs that sponsor raves usually pass out or sell bottled water to offset the dehydration, but in the midst of having fun it is easy for a person to forget to drink enough—or to drink far too much. Adding to the risk is the possibility that Ecstasy users are also consuming alcohol, and that interaction increases the dehydration and rise in body temperature (Leccese et al., 2000).

NON-MANUFACTURED HIGHS A number of substances found in nature can produce hallucinogenic effects. Although some people might refer to these substances as "natural" highs, they are still drugs and still potentially dangerous.

Mescaline Mescaline comes from the buttons found on the peyote cactus and has long been a part of many Native American religious and spiritual rituals. The duration of its hallucinogenic effects can last longer than those of LSD (Aghajanian & Marek, 1999). Native Americans have used mescaline in combination with sitting in a hut or other enclosed space while water is poured over very hot rocks. This sauna effect, together with the drug, may produce sensations of being out of one's own body or talking with spirits, which is the purpose of these rituals (Lyvers, 2003).

Psilocybin Psilocybin (sill-luh-SIGH-bun) is another naturally occurring hallucinogen, contained in a certain kind of mushroom, often referred to as "magic mushrooms." Like mescaline, it has also been used in similar rituals by several native cultures (Aghajanian & Marek, 1999).

Is using mescaline or psilocybin addictive? Neither mescaline nor psilocybin has been shown to create physical dependency, but as with any psychoactive drug, psychological dependency is possible (Lyvers, 2003).

MARIJUANA

4.18 *What is marijuana, and what are the risks of using it?*

One of the best known and most commonly abused of the psychogenic drugs, **marijuana** (also called *pot* or *weed*) comes from the leaves and flowers of the hemp plant called *Cannabis sativa*. (*Hashish* is the substance scraped from these leaves, and both marijuana and hashish are called *cannabinoids*.) The active ingredient in marijuana is *tetrahydrocannabinol (THC)*. Marijuana is best known for its ability to produce a feeling of well-being, mild intoxication, and mild sensory distortions or hallucinations (Olin, 1993; Tart, 1970).

The effects of marijuana are relatively mild compared to the other hallucinogens. In fact, an inexperienced user who doesn't know what to expect upon smoking that first marijuana cigarette or *joint* may feel nothing at all. Most people do report a feeling of mild euphoria and relaxation, along with an altered time sense and mild visual distortions. Higher doses can lead to hallucinations, delusions, and the all-too-common paranoia. Most studies of marijuana's effects have concluded that while marijuana can create a powerful psychological dependency, it does not produce physical dependency or physical withdrawal symptoms. Newer studies, however, suggest that long-term marijuana use can produce signs of withdrawal such as irritability, sleep difficulties, and increased aggression (Budney et al., 2001; Kouri et al., 1999).

Even at mild doses, it is not safe to operate heavy machinery or drive a car while under the influence of marijuana. The effect on a person's reaction time and perception of surroundings is too damaging to the ability to make the split-second decisions that are required in driving.

mescaline
natural hallucinogen derived from peyote cactus buttons.

psilocybin
natural hallucinogen found in certain mushrooms.

marijuana (pot or weed)
mild hallucinogen derived from the leaves and flowers of a particular type of hemp plant.

◀ Is using mescaline or psilocybin addictive?

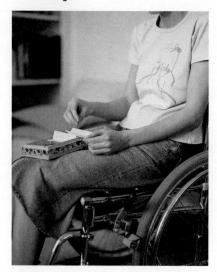

This woman is preparing a cannabis (marijuana) cigarette. Cannabis is reported to relieve pain in cases of multiple sclerosis and chronic pain from nerve damage. In Canada, cannabis was approved for use in certain medical conditions in 2001.

Marijuana is most commonly smoked like tobacco, but some people have been known to eat it baked into brownies or other foods. This is a kind of double duty for the doctored food, as marijuana stimulates the appetite.

Although no one has ever been known to die from an overdose of marijuana, it is not exactly a healthy habit. Marijuana smokers get considerably more *carcinogens* (cancer-causing substances), carbon dioxide, and tar exposure than do the smokers of ordinary cigarettes. This is partly caused by the higher content of these substances in marijuana and partly by the pot smoker's tendency to inhale more deeply and hold in the smoke longer than tobacco smokers do (Wu et al., 1988). A recent review of the literature suggests that some adolescent users of high potency marijuana may be putting themselves at increased risk for the development of schizophrenia, a brain disorder that involves delusions and hallucinations (Moore et al., 2007). LINK to *Chapter Thirteen: Psychological Disorders, p. 520.* It appears that young developing brains are much more susceptible to THC than more mature brains. This is particularly alarming since it is estimated that in Canada 22 percent of males and 10 percent of females between the ages of 15 and 24 regularly use marijuana.

4.19 *What are some medicinal uses for marijuana?*

Marijuana also has some medical benefits. In Canada, it has been successfully used to treat a variety of medical conditions, including the nausea and vomiting that occur following cancer chemotherapy; eye swelling in glaucoma; and the seizures and muscle spasms associated with epilepsy, multiple sclerosis, or spinal cord injury (Zimmer & Morgan, 1997). Given these medical benefits, the Canadian government revised the Narcotic Control Regulations in 2001 and enacted the Marijuana Medical Access Regulations. These new regulations made it no longer a crime for persons suffering from a severe illness such as cancer or multiple sclerosis to benefit from marijuana. It is estimated that 200 000 Canadians are currently using marijuana for its beneficial medical effects.

Table 4.6 summarizes the various types of drugs, their common names, and their effects on human behaviour.

TABLE 4.6 HOW DRUGS AFFECT CONSCIOUSNESS

DRUG CLASSIFICATION	COMMON NAME	MAIN EFFECT
Depressants		
Alcohol	Beer, wine, spirits	Relaxation
Barbiturates (tranquilizers)	Nembutal, Seconal	
Stimulants		
Amphetamines	Methamphetamine, speed, Ritalin, Dexedrine	Stimulation, excitement
Cocaine	Cocaine, crack	
Nicotine	Tobacco	
Caffeine	Coffee, tea	
Narcotics		
Opiates	Morphine, heroin	Euphoria
Psychedelics and Hallucinogens		
	Marijuana, hashish, LSD, Ecstasy	Distorts consciousness, alters perception

PRACTICE QUIZ: HOW MUCH DO YOU REMEMBER?

Pick the best answer.

1. All narcotics are derived from
   a. cannabis.
   b. opium.
   c. mescaline.
   d. morphine.

2. This drug was at first hailed as the new wonder drug, because the impurities that supposedly caused many of the addictive and unpleasant side effects of the previous version had been removed. In fact, _____ was even more addictive and deadly.
   a. laudanum
   b. heroin
   c. morphine
   d. ergot

3. Which of the following hallucinogens is NOT a synthetically created drug?
   a. psilocybin
   b. LSD
   c. PCP
   d. MDMA

4. Of the following, which comes from the peyote cactus?
   a. mescaline
   b. psilocybin
   c. marijuana
   d. ergot

5. Which of the following is a long-term effect of marijuana use?
   a. lung cancer
   b. asthma
   c. immune system damage
   d. all of the above

6. Which of the following statements about marijuana is TRUE?
   a. Marijuana is not physically addictive.
   b. It is safe to drive under the influence of pot.
   c. Marijuana is more healthful than tobacco.
   d. Short-term memory is enhanced by smoking marijuana.

7. Which of following has NOT been associated with a medical use of marijuana?
   a. reduced swelling of the eye in glaucoma
   b. decreased nausea and vomiting in cancer patients undergoing chemotherapy
   c. decreased spasms in persons with multiple sclerosis
   d. increased memory retention in Alzheimer's disease

Answers: 1.-b, 2.-b, 3.-a, 4.-a, 5.-d, 6.-a, 7.-d.

APPLYING PSYCHOLOGY TO EVERYDAY LIFE: ARE COLLEGE STUDENTS SLEEP DEPRIVED?

4.20   *How serious is the problem of sleep deprivation?*

Sleep deprivation has long been considered a fact of life for many people, especially college and university students. Dr. William Dement (1997), one of the most renowned sleep experts in the field, believes that people are ignorant of the detrimental effects of sleep deprivation. Here are some of the facts he points out concerning the widespread nature of sleep deprivation:

- 55 percent of drowsy driving fatalities occur under the age of 25.

- 56 percent of the adult population reports that daytime drowsiness is a problem.

- In a study of 1000 people who reported no daytime drowsiness, 34 percent were actually found to be dangerously sleepy.

- In samples of undergraduates, nurses, and medical students, 80 percent were dangerously sleep deprived.

Dr. Dement cautions that drowsiness should be considered a red alert. Contrary to many people's belief that drowsiness indicates the first step in falling asleep, he states that drowsiness is the last step—if you are drowsy, you are seconds away from sleep.

The National Commission on Sleep Disorders (1997) estimates that "sleep deprivation costs $150 billion a year in higher stress and reduced workplace productivity." Sleep deprivation was one of the factors indicated in such disasters as the explosion of the *Challenger*, the *Exxon Valdez* oil spill, and the Chernobyl disaster.

Here are more disturbing facts (Williamson & Feyer, 2000; National Sleep Foundation, 2008):

- 30 to 40 percent of all heavy truck accidents can be attributed to driver fatigue.

- Drivers who are awake for 17 to 19 hours were more dangerous than drivers with a blood alcohol level of 0.05.

- 16 to 60 percent of road accidents involve sleep deprivation (the wide variation is due to the inability to confirm the cause of accidents, as the drivers are often killed).

- Sleep deprivation is linked to higher levels of stress, anxiety, depression, and unnecessary risk-taking.

- Sleep deprivation signals people to eat more, and the foods they crave are generally sugar, salt, and carbohydrates. So if you are overweight, you may be sleep-starved!

- There is a link between sleep deprivation and cardiovascular disease.

Clearly, sleep deprivation is a serious and all-too-common problem. In today's 24-hour-a-day society, stores are always open, services such as banking and transportation are always available, and many professionals (such as nurses, doctors, and firefighters) must work varying shifts around the clock (Knauth, 1993). As stated earlier, shift work can seriously disrupt the normal sleep–wake cycle, often causing insomnia.

CAUSES OF SLEEP DEPRIVATION

Many of the sleep disorders that were discussed in this chapter are themselves causes of sleep deprivation. Sleep apnea, narcolepsy, sleepwalking, night terrors, and a condition called *restless leg syndrome,* in which a person constantly moves his or her legs because they are tingly or have crawling sensations, are all causes. Yet these problems are not the sole, or most common, cause of sleep deprivation.

The most obvious cause is the refusal of many people to go to sleep at a reasonable time, so that they can get the eight hours of sleep that most adults need to function well (Bonnet & Arand, 1995). People want to watch that last bit of news or get a little more work done or party into the wee hours. Another reason for sleep loss is worry. People live in stressful times, and many people worry about a variety of concerns: debts, the stock market, relationships, war, rising crime, and so on. Finally, some medications that people take, both prescription and over-the-counter drugs, interfere with the sleep–wake cycle. For example, decongestants that some people take to relieve sinus congestion may cause a racing heartbeat, preventing them from relaxing enough to sleep.

The student in the background is unable to stay awake during his class, indicating that he is seriously sleep-deprived. Has this happened to you?

HOW CAN YOU TELL IF YOU ARE SLEEP-DEPRIVED?

According to Fahey (1993), you may be sleep-deprived if you

- actually need your alarm clock to wake up
- find getting out of bed in the morning is a struggle
- feel tired, irritable, or stressed out for much of the day
- have trouble concentrating or remembering
- fall asleep watching television, in meetings, lectures, or warm rooms
- fall asleep after heavy meals or after a low dose of alcohol
- fall asleep within five minutes of getting into bed. (A well-rested person actually takes 15 to 20 minutes to fall asleep.)

If you are interested in learning more about sleep deprivation and sleep disorders that can cause it, try searching the internet. There are some excellent sites about sleep and sleep disorders, including many with online tests that can help people decide whether they have a sleep disorder. Here are a few good sites:

- Sleepnet.com at **www.sleepnet.com** has a test for many kinds of sleep disorders and provides detailed information about sleep disorders.
- The National Sleep Foundation at **www.sleepfoundation.org** has many links to sites with information about sleep, sleep disorders, and sleep tips.

Questions for Further Discussion

1. What are some possible behavioural changes that might help to reverse the disturbing sleep deprivation trend?

2. There is a relationship between weight gain and sleep deprivation. Do you think you can sleep yourself thin?

4 CHAPTER SUMMARY

What Is Consciousness?

4.1 *What does it mean to be conscious, and are there different levels of consciousness?*

- Consciousness is a person's awareness of everything that is going on at any given moment. Most waking hours are spent in waking consciousness.
- Altered states of consciousness are shifts in the quality or pattern of mental activity.

Altered States: Sleep

4.2 *Why do people sleep, and how does sleep work?*

- Sleep is a circadian rhythm, lasting 24 hours, and is a product of the activity suprachiasmatic nucleus (SCN), which is located in the hypothalamus; the hormone melatonin; the neurotransmitter serotonin; and body temperature.

Classic Studies in Psychology: Seasonal Affective Disorder (SAD): Are Canadians at Greater Risk?

4.3 *What is seasonal affective disorder, and are Canadians at greater risk?*

- Seasonal affective disorder (SAD) is a variant of depression linked to low levels of sunlight experienced during the long Canadian winters.
- Persons with SAD often have symptoms consistent with depression, such as being tired and feeling helpless and hopeless, but also have symptoms inconsistent with depression such as having an increased appetite for carbohydrates and sleeping too much, which often leads to significant weight gain during the winter months.
- Because lack of sunlight is thought to be a contributing factor to SAD, a unique treatment involves sitting in front of bright full-spectrum lights.

4.4 *What is the purpose of sleep?*

- Adaptive theory states that sleep evolved as a way to conserve energy and keep animals safe from predators that hunt at night.
- Restorative theory states that sleep provides the body with an opportunity to restore chemicals that have been depleted during the day as well as the growth and repair of cell tissue.
- The average amount of sleep needed by most people is about 7 to 8 hours within each 24-hour period.

4.5 *What are the different stages of sleep?*

- Stage One sleep is light sleep.
- Stage Two sleep is indicated by the presence of sleep spindles, bursts of activity on the EEG.
- Stage Three is highlighted by the first appearance of delta waves, the slowest and largest waves, whereas Stage Four is predominantly delta waves, and the body is at its lowest level of functioning.

- Sleepwalking and sleeptalking occur in Stage Four sleep.
- Night terrors are attacks of extreme fear that the victim has while sound asleep.

4.6 *Can sleepwalking and sexsomnia be a defence for committing a crime?*

- The Ontario Court of Appeal recently upheld the acquittal of a man charged with sexual assault. His successful defence was based on his sexsomnia condition.

4.7 *What is dreaming, and what happens if people don't dream?*

- REM sleep occurs four or five times a night, replacing Stage One sleep in the sleep–wake cycle, and is accompanied by paralysis of the voluntary muscles.
- Nightmares are bad or unpleasant dreams that occur during REM sleep.
- REM behaviour disorder is a rare condition in which REM paralysis fails and the person moves violently while dreaming, often acting out the elements of the dream.

4.8 *What changes might occur in sleep as a result of learning a new motor task?*

- When learning a new motor task, different sleep patterns emerge dependent on the initial skill level of the individual. If an individual is initially fairly good at performing the new motor task, they show significant increases in Stage Two NREM sleep. Individuals who initially have a hard time learning the new motor task show increases in REM activity.

Psychology in the News: Murderous Dreams

- Sleepwalking has been used as a defence in numerous cases of murder. In many of these cases, the defendant has been acquitted because of the sleepwalking defence.

4.9 *What kinds of problems can happen during sleep?*

- Insomnia is an inability to get to sleep, stay asleep, or get enough sleep.
- Sleep apnea occurs when a person stops breathing for nearly half a minute or more, followed by gasping for breath.
- Narcolepsy is a genetic disorder in which the person suddenly and without warning collapses into REM sleep.

Dreams

4.10 *Why do people dream, and what do they dream about?*

- Manifest content of a dream is the actual dream and its events. Latent content of a dream is the symbolic content, according to Freud.
- Without outside sensory information to explain the activation of the brain cells in the cortex by the pons area, the association areas of the cortex synthesize a story, or dream, to explain that activation in the activation-synthesis hypothesis.

- A revision of activation-synthesis theory, the activation-information-mode model (AIM) states that information experienced during waking hours can influence the synthesis of dreams.

Altered States: Hypnosis

4.11 *What is hypnosis, and how does it work?*

- The hypnotist will tell the person to relax and feel tired, to focus on what is being said, to let go of inhibitions and accept suggestions, and to use vivid imagination.
- Hypnosis cannot give increased strength, reliably enhance memory, or regress people to an earlier age or an earlier life, but it can produce amnesia, reduce pain, and alter sensory impressions.
- Hilgard believed that a person under hypnosis is in a state of dissociation, in which one part of consciousness is hypnotized and susceptible to suggestion, while another part is aware of everything that occurs.
- Other theorists believe that the hypnotized subject is merely playing a social role, that of the hypnotized person. This is called the *social-cognitive theory of hypnosis.*

Altered States: Psychoactive Drugs

4.12 *What is the difference between a physical dependence and a psychological dependence on a drug?*

- Drugs that are physically addictive cause the user's body to crave the drug. When deprived of the drug, the user will go through physical withdrawal.
- Drug tolerance occurs as the user's body becomes conditioned to the level of the drug. After a time, the user must take more and more of the drug to get the same effect.
- In psychological dependence, the user believes that he or she needs the drug to function well and maintain a sense of well-being. Any drug can produce psychological dependence.

4.13 *What are some examples of stimulants and the dangers associated with taking them?*

- Stimulants are drugs that increase the functioning of the nervous system.
- Amphetamines are synthetic drugs such as Benzedrine or Dexedrine. They help people stay awake and reduce appetite but are highly physically addictive.
- Cocaine is highly addictive and can cause convulsions and death in some first-time users.
- Nicotine is a mild stimulant and is very physically addictive.
- Caffeine is the most commonly used stimulant, found in coffee, tea, chocolate, and many sodas.

4.14 *What are some different types of depressants, and how can they be harmful?*

- Barbiturates, benzodiazepines, and alcohol are types of depressants.
- Barbiturates, also known as major tranquilizers, have a sedative effect and are used as sleeping pills.
- The minor tranquilizers are benzodiazepines such as Valium or Xanax.
- When barbiturates or benzodiazepines are combined with alcohol, a drug interaction occurs, which can lead to unconsciousness and death.

4.15 *What kind of drug is alcohol, and what are the dangers of drinking too much?*

- Alcohol is the most commonly used and abused depressant.
- As noted above, alcohol can interact with other depressants, leading to serious consequences.
- Heavy drinking can lead to impaired reaction times, poor muscle control, memory impairments, alcoholism, and death.

4.16 *How do narcotics work, and why are they so addictive?*

- Narcotics are pain-relieving drugs of the depressant class that are derived from the opium poppy.
- Opium is the earliest form of this drug.
- Morphine is a more refined version of opium but is highly addictive.
- Heroin was believed to be a purer form of morphine and therefore less addictive, but in fact is even more powerfully addictive.
- Methadone has the ability to control the symptoms of heroin or morphine withdrawal without the euphoria, or "high," of heroin or morphine.
- Narcotics are addictive because they duplicate the actions of our bodies own endorphin neurotransmitters. They duplicate the actions so well that our bodies actually begin to produce fewer endorphin neurotransmitters. As a consequence, when the drug wears off, there is very little natural protection against pain and people experience severe withdrawal symptoms and a powerful urge to reuse.

4.17 *How do hallucinogens work?*

- Hallucinogens are stimulants that alter the brain's interpretation of sensations, creating hallucinations. Three synthetically created hallucinogens are LSD, PCP, and MDMA.
- Three naturally occurring hallucinogens are mescaline, psilocybin, and marijuana.

4.18 *What is marijuana, and what are the risks of using it?*

- Marijuana is a mild hallucinogen, producing a mild euphoria and feelings of relaxation in its users.
- Larger doses of marijuana can lead to hallucinations and paranoia. It is carcinogenic and impairs learning and memory.

4.19 *What are some medicinal uses for marijuana?*

- Marijuana has been successfully used to treat a variety of medical conditions, including the nausea and vomiting that occurs following cancer chemotherapy; eye swelling in glaucoma; and the seizures and muscle spasms associated with epilepsy, multiple sclerosis, or spinal cord injury.

Applying Psychology to Everyday Life: Are College Students Sleep Deprived?

4.20 *How serious is the problem of sleep deprivation?*

- Sleep deprivation is a serious disorder responsible for a large portion of traffic accidents and fatalities as well as increased stress, depression, anxiety, reduced productivity, weight gain, cardiovascular disease, and risk-taking behaviour.
- Causes of sleep deprivation include sleep disorders such as apnea and narcolepsy, failure of people to go to sleep or stay asleep for an adequate amount of time, worrying, and the influence of some drugs.

4 KEY TERMS

activation-information-mode model (AIM)   151

activation-synthesis hypothesis   150

adaptive theory   140

alcohol   162

alpha waves   142

altered state of consciousness   137

amphetamines   157

barbiturates   162

benzodiazepines   162

caffeine   159

circadian rhythm   137

cocaine   157

consciousness   136

delta waves   136

depressants   143

hallucinogens   165

heroin   164

hypnosis   152

insomnia   147

LSD (lysergic acid diethylamide)   165

marijuana (pot or weed)   167

MDMA (Ecstasy or X)   166

mescaline   166

microsleeps   139

morphine   164

narcolepsy   148

narcotics   157

nicotine   159

night terrors   145

nightmares   145

non-REM (NREM) sleep   142

opium   164

PCP   165

psilocybin   166

psychoactive drugs   156

psychogenic drugs   157

psychological dependence   156

rapid eye movement (REM)   142

REM behaviour disorder   146

REM rebound   146

restorative theory   140

seasonal affective disorder (SAD)   138

sexsomnia   144

sleep apnea   148

sleep deprivation   140

sleepwalking (somnambulism)   144

social-cognitive theory of hypnosis   155

stimulants   157

stimulatory hallucinogenics   166

theta waves   142

waking consciousness   136

withdrawal   156

TEST YOURSELF

Pick the best answer.

1. Which of the following situations is NOT an altered state of consciousness?
   a. You are daydreaming.
   b. You have been drinking beer.
   c. You are concentrating on a math test.
   d. You are asleep.

2. Which of the following is NOT an example of a circadian rhythm?
   a. menstrual cycle
   b. sleep–wake cycle
   c. blood pressure changes
   d. body temperature changes

3. When light begins to fade at the end of the day, the suprachiasmatic nucleus in the _____ signals the pineal gland to release _____.
   a. hippocampus; melatonin
   b. hippocampus; serotonin
   c. hypothalamus; melatonin
   d. hypothalamus; serotonin

4. As you move closer to the equator, the incident of SAD _____.
   a. doubles
   b. triples
   c. increases
   d. decreases

5. Which of the following was NOT listed as one of the factors involved in the ability to go to sleep?
   a. body mass
   b. body temperature
   c. serotonin levels
   d. melatonin levels

6. The symptoms of sleep deprivation include all but which of the following?
   a. trembling hands
   b. inability to concentrate
   c. feeling of general discomfort
   d. hypnic jerk

7. You hear about an accident that took place at 3:00 a.m. The car was travelling along and then seemed to drift into the opposing lane of traffic, hitting an oncoming car head on. Given the early morning time, you suspect that the driver of the car that drifted over the centre line most likely experienced a
   a. lapse in judgment.
   b. microsleep episode.
   c. hypnogogic episode.
   d. hypnopompic episode.

8. It might be best to say that adaptive theory explains _____, while restorative theory explains _____.
   a. why we *need* to sleep; *when* we sleep
   b. *where* we sleep; why we *need* to sleep
   c. why we *need* to sleep; *where* we sleep
   d. *when* we sleep; why we *need* to sleep

9. In which stage of sleep do night terrors occur?
   a. Stage One
   b. Stage Two
   c. Stage Three
   d. Stage Four

10. Sleepwalking
   a. is partly hereditary.
   b. occurs more frequently in girls than in boys.
   c. occurs in about 50 percent of the population.
   d. lasts well into late adulthood in most people.

11. In those prone to sexsomnia, which of the following is NOT considered a trigger to bringing on an episode?
   a. sleep deprivation
   b. excessive activity
   c. heavy drinking of alcohol
   d. emotional stress

12. Night terrors
    a. are the same thing as nightmares.
    b. are always vividly remembered afterward.
    c. are more common in children.
    d. take place in one of the lighter stages of sleep.

13. Which of the following statements about REM sleep is false?
    a. The eyes move rapidly back and forth under the eyelids.
    b. Most people report that they were dreaming if awakened.
    c. The body is aroused and brain waves resemble waking beta waves.
    d. Lack of REM sleep produces psychological disorders.

14. If you are in REM sleep but are able to move around and act out your dreams, you may have a rare condition called
    a. REM behaviour disorder.
    b. somnambulism.
    c. nightmare disorder.
    d. narcolepsy.

15. If you suddenly and without warning slip into REM sleep during the day, often falling down as you do so, you may have the condition called
    a. sleep apnea.
    b. insomnia.
    c. narcolepsy.
    d. epilepsy.

16. A sleep disorder that may require the use of a machine to force air gently into the nasal passages is called
    a. sleep apnea.
    b. insomnia.
    c. narcolepsy.
    d. cataplexy.

17. Hypnosis has been shown to do all of the following BUT
    a. induce amnesia for what happens during the hypnotic state.
    b. provide pain relief without medication.
    c. alter sensory perceptions.
    d. regress people back to their early childhood experiences.

18. Jackie used Ecstasy while she was in college, but now that she has a government job she has avoided using any recreational drugs. Although she had no problem quitting, she still finds that every now and then she gets a strong craving to use Ecstasy again. Her craving is most likely the result of
    a. psychological dependence.
    b. physical dependency.
    c. withdrawal.
    d. none of the above

19. Which of the following is NOT a naturally occurring substance?
    a. nicotine
    b. amphetamine
    c. caffeine
    d. cocaine

20. Roughly how many Canadians die each year as the result of smoking related illness and second-hand smoke?
    a. 20 000–30 000
    b. 30 000–40 000
    c. 40 000–50 000
    d. 50 000–60 000

21. Which of the following is NOT a depressant?
    a. alcohol
    b. valium
    c. PCP
    d. barbiturate

22. Alcohol actually _____ the release of GABA, a neurotransmitter that inhibits many brain functions.
    a. depresses
    b. decreases
    c. stimulates
    d. prevents

23. "Magic mushrooms" are the source of
    a. marijuana.
    b. psilocybin.
    c. mescaline.
    d. Ecstasy.

24. High doses of marijuana can lead to
    a. death.
    b. hallucinations and delusions.
    c. extreme arousal.
    d. none of the above.

25. Which of the following statements concerning sleep deprivation is FALSE?
    a. Driving after 17 to 19 hours without sleep is less dangerous than having a blood alcohol level of 0.05.
    b. Sleep deprivation accounts for 30–40 percent of all accidents involving heavy trucks.
    c. Sleep deprivation accounts for 16–60 percent of all road accidents.
    d. Sleep deprivation can cause stress, anxiety, and depression and increase risky behaviour.

Answers: 1.-c, 2.-a, 3.-c, 4.-d, 5.-a, 6.-d, 7.-b, 8.-d, 9.-d, 10.-a, 11.-b, 12.-c, 13.-d, 14.-a, 15.-c, 16.-a, 17.-d, 18.-a, 19.-b, 20.-c, 21.-c, 22.-c, 23.-b, 24.-b, 25.-a.

ScanLife™ Barcode

To access more tests and your own personalized study plan that will help you focus on the areas you need to master before your next class test, be sure to go to **www.MyPsychLab.com**, Pearson Education Canada's online psychology website, available with the access code packaged with your book.

4.1

What Is Consiousness?

a person's awareness of everything that is going on at any given moment

- most waking hours are spent in waking consciousness
- altered states of consciousness are shifts in the quality or pattern of mental activity

4.2–4

hypothalamus contains the suprachiasmatic nucleus (SCN)

- SCN is sensitive to light—influences pineal gland's secretion of melatonin (↑ melatonin = ↑ sleepiness)
- light through eyes relayed to SCN; SCN signals pineal gland to stop producing melatonin (↓ melatonin = ↑ alertness / ↓ sleepiness)
- SCN also influences body temperature (↓ temperature = ↑ sleepiness)

seasonal affective disorder is a variant of depression linked to low levels of sunlight

- long Canadian winters can make Canadians more susceptible

Sleep: The Necessity of Sleep

(sleep is one of the body's daily (circadian) biological rhythms; sleep–wake cycle controlled by the brain including the hypothalamus and the neurotransmitter serotonin)

people can live without sleep for a while, can't live without it altogether

- **sleep deprivation**
- **amount of sleep needed**
- **adaptive theory of sleep**
- **restorative theory of sleep**

Presleep

Awake, alert
Beta waves

Awake, relaxed
Alpha waves

Non-REM

Sleep stage 1
Theta waves

Sleep stage 2
Sleep Spindle
Spindle (burst of activity)

Sleep stage 3

Sleep stage 4
Delta waves

REM

REM stage

4.5–9

Sleep: Stages and Disorders

consist of both REM (rapid eye movement) and non-REM stages

- **non-REM Stage 1**
- **non-REM Stage 2**
- **non-REM Stages 3 & 4**
- **REM sleep**

sleepwalking and sexsomnia can be a defence for committing a crime

learning a new motor task affects the sleep patterns of individuals

- an individual who initially has a hard time shows increases in REM activity
- an individual who is initially fairly good at performing the new motor task shows significant increases in Stage Two NREM sleep

people can live without sleep for a while, can't live without it altogether

- **insomnia** → **coffee**
- **sleep apnea** → **loud snoring**
- **narcolepsy** → **hypocretin**

Table 4.1 Common Sleep Disorders	
NAME OF DISORDER	**PRIMARY SYMPTOMS**
Somnambulism	Sitting, walking, or performing complex behaviour while asleep
Night terrors	Extreme fear, agitation, screaming while asleep
Restless leg syndrome	Uncomfortable sensations in legs causing movement and loss of sleep
Nocturnal leg cramps	Painful cramps in calf or foot muscles
Hypersomnia	Excessive daytime sleepiness
Circadian rhythm disorders	Disturbances of the sleep–wake cycle such as lag and shift work
Enuresis	Urinating while asleep in bed

Dreams

Why do we dream?
- **Freud's interpretation:** wish fulfillment—conflicts, events, and desires represented in symbolic form in dreams
- **activation–synthesis hypothesis**

What do people dream about? typically about events that occur in everyday life; most in colour; content influenced by gender and culture

CAST OF DREAM
THE MONSTER ...... YOUR FATHER
KIND WOMAN ...... YOUR MOTHER
POLICEMAN .... YOUR ANALYST
FIRST STRANGER .... YOUR BROTHER
SECOND STRANGER .. YOUR SISTER
LITTLE BOY ..... YOU

Hypnosis
(state of consciousness during which person is more susceptible to suggestion)

- can be assessed by scale of hypnotic susceptibility
- induction typically involves relaxed focus and "permission to let go"; person being hypnotized is in control and cannot be hypnotized against his or her will
- can be used in therapy—help people deal with pain, anxiety, or cravings (e.g., food, drug)
- **theories**
  - **dissociation:** one part of mind is aware of actions/activities taking place, while the "hypnotized" part is not
  - **social-cognitive theory** suggests that people assume roles based on expectations for a given situation

"Nowadays, Hal is ninety-nine per cent caffeine-free."

Why do some people continue to use or become addicted to psychoactive drugs?
- **physical dependence:** user's body needs a drug to function; drug tolerance and withdrawal are warning signs/symptoms
- **psychological dependence:** user believes drug is needed to function

Psychoactive Drugs
(drugs that alter thinking, perception, or memory)

types

stimulants
increase functioning of nervous system
- **amphetamines**
- **cocaine**
- **nicotine**
- **caffeine**

depressants
have sedative effect
- **barbiturates**
  major tranquilizers
- **benzodiazepines**
  minor tranquilizers—Valium, Xanax, Halcion, Activan, Librium, Rohypnol
- **alcohol**

narcotics
euphoria-producing and pain relieving drugs derived from opium
- **morphine**
- **heroin**
- **methadone**
  does not produce euphoria; used to treat heroin addiction

hallucinogens
alter brain's interpretation of sensations
- **manufactured**
  - **LSD**
  - **PCP**
  - **MDMA (Ectasy)**
- **nonmanufactured**
  - **mescaline**
  - **psilocybin**
  - **marijuana**
    can treat symptoms related to chemotherapy, glaucoma, epilepsy, multiple sclerosis, or spinal cord injury

Table 4.3 Facts About Hypnosis

HYPNOSIS CAN:	HYPNOSIS CANNOT:
Create amnesia for whatever happens during the hypnotic session, at least for a brief time (Bowers & Woody, 1996).	Give people superhuman strength. (People may use their full strength under hypnosis, but it is no more than they had before hypnosis.
Relieve pain by allowing a person to remove conscious attention from the pain (Holroyd, 1996).	Reliably enhance memory. (There's an increased risk of false memory retrieval because of the suggestible state hypnosis creates.)
Alter sensory perceptions. (Smell, hearing, vision, time sense, and the ability to see visual illusions can all be affected by hypnosis.)	Regress people back to childhood. (Although people may act like children, they do and say things children would not.)
Help people relax in situations that normally would cause them stress, such as flying on an airplane (Muhlberger et al., 2001).	Regress people to some "past life." There is no scientific evidence for past life regression (Lilienfeld et al., 2004)

5 Learning

Diet Foods for Kids May Lead to Obesity

Have you ever ingested a particular food and vomited shortly thereafter? What was your reaction the next time you came in close proximity to that food or drink? Like most people, you probably avoided it. This avoidance reaction stems from a special type of learning called *conditioned-taste aversion*.

University of Alberta professor David Pierce contends that animals and people not only learn to avoid foods that have made them sick but also learn to connect the taste of a particular food with its caloric value. To prove this, Dr. Pierce employed a unique experimental design (Pierce et al., 2007). Initially he trained young rats to associate a sweet taste with either the presence or absence of calories. In other words, half the rats were on a diet and half were not. Those young rats not on the diet received calories when they ate a sweet food; those on the diet did not get calories when they ate sweet food. Dr. Pierce then exposed all the rats to a calorie-rich, sweet-tasting pre-meal. Finally, he monitored how much the young rats ate over the next three hours after helping themselves to the sweet pre-meal. What he found was remarkable. The rats on the diet, those that had learned to associate the sweet taste with no calories, ate significantly more over the next three hours than the non-diet rats. This finding suggests that substituting diet versions of foods may contribute to overeating.

Dr. Pierce believes that a similar process may be occurring in humans. The use of diet foods from an early age to adulthood may be teaching people the wrong caloric value of foods through this taste-conditioning process. And, like the rats, people may begin to overeat and gradually gain weight. This learning of taste and caloric value may also help to explain recent findings that link consumption of diet pop to the development of obesity. Maybe diet pop drinkers are overeating and gaining weight because they have learned to associate sweet tastes with few calories?

Why study learning?

If we had not been able to learn, we would have died out as a species long ago. Learning is the process that allows us to adapt to the changing conditions of the world around us. We can alter our actions until we find the behaviour that leads us to survival and rewards, and we can eliminate actions that have been unsuccessful in the past. Without learning, there would be no buildings, no agriculture, no life-saving medicines, and no human civilization.

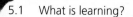

DEFINITION OF LEARNING

5.1 *What is learning?*

The term *learning* is one of those concepts whose meaning is crystal clear until one has to put it in words. "Learning is when you learn something." "Learning is learning how to do something." A more useful definition is as follows: Learning is any relatively permanent change in behaviour brought about by experience or practice.

What does "relatively permanent" mean? And how does experience change what we do? The "relatively permanent" part of the definition refers to the fact that when people learn anything, some part of their brain is physically changed to record what they've learned. This is actually a process of memory, for without the ability to remember what happens, people cannot learn anything. Although there is no conclusive proof as yet, research suggests strongly that once people learn something, it is always present somewhere in memory (Barsalou, 1992). They may be unable to "get" to it, but it's there. ⓁⒾⓃⓀ *to Chapter Six: Memory, p. 218.*

As for the part about experience or practice, think about the last time you did something that caused you a lot of pain. Are you going to do it again? Of course not. You don't want to experience that pain again, so you change your behaviour to avoid the painful consequence. This is how children learn not to touch hot stoves. Of course, if a person does something that results in a very pleasurable consequence, that person is more likely to do that same thing again. This is another change in behaviour.

So, is any kind of change learning? Not all change is accomplished through learning. Any kind of change in the way an organism *behaves* is learning. Changes such as an increase in height or the size of the brain are another kind of change controlled by a genetic blueprint. This kind of change is called *maturation*, and it is not the same as learning. For example, children learn to walk *when* they do because their nervous systems, muscle strength, and sense of balance have reached the point where walking is possible for them—all factors controlled by maturation, not by how much practice those children have had in trying to walk. No amount of experience or practice will help that child walk before maturation makes it possible—in spite of what some eager parents might wish.

▶ What does "relatively permanent" mean? And how does experience change what we do?

the neighborhood. Jerry Van Amerongen

An instantaneous learning experience.

© Reprinted with special permission of King Features Syndicate.

IT MAKES YOUR MOUTH WATER: CLASSICAL CONDITIONING

In the early 1900s, when Freud was just becoming famous in Europe and the structuralists and functionalists were arguing over consciousness in the ivy-covered halls of universities, research scientists were unhappy with psychology's focus on mental activity. **LINK** *to Chapter One: The Science of Psychology, pp. 6–10.* Many were looking for a way to bring some kind of objectivity and scientific research to the field.

It was not a psychologist who accomplished that goal. It was a Russian *physiologist* (a person who studies the workings of the body) named Ivan Pavlov (1849–1936) who accidentally stumbled across the basic principles of a particular kind of learning (Pavlov, 1926).

5.2 *What is classical conditioning, and who first studied it?*

Studying the digestive system in his dogs, Pavlov had built a device that would accurately measure the amount of saliva produced by the dogs when they were fed a measured amount of food. Normally, when food is placed in the mouth of any animal, the salivary glands automatically start releasing saliva to help with chewing and digestion. This is a normal *reflex* (involuntary response) in both animals and humans. The food causes a particular reaction, the salivation. A *stimulus* can be defined as any object, event, or experience that causes a *response*, the reaction of an organism. In the case of Pavlov's dogs, the food is the stimulus and salivation is the response.

PAVLOV AND THE SALIVATING DOGS

What first annoyed and then intrigued Pavlov was that his dogs began salivating when they weren't supposed to be salivating. Some dogs would start salivating when they saw the lab assistant bringing their food, others when they heard the clatter of the food bowl in the kitchen, and still others when it was the time of day they were usually fed. Pavlov spent the rest of his career studying what eventually he termed **classical conditioning**, learning to make a reflex response to a stimulus other than the original, natural stimulus that normally produces it.

ELEMENTS OF CLASSICAL CONDITIONING

Pavlov eventually identified several key elements that must be present and experienced in a particular way for conditioning to take place.

5.3 *What are the important concepts in classical conditioning?*

UNCONDITIONED STIMULUS The original, naturally occurring stimulus mentioned in the preceding paragraph is called the **unconditioned stimulus (UCS)**. The term *unconditioned* means "unlearned" or "naturally occurring." This is the stimulus that ordinarily leads to the reflex, involuntary response. In the case of Pavlov's dogs, the food served is the unconditioned stimulus.

UNCONDITIONED RESPONSE The reflex response to the unconditioned stimulus is called the **unconditioned response (UCR)** for much the same reason. It is unlearned and occurs because of genetic "wiring" in the nervous system. For example, in Pavlov's experiment, the food given to the dogs is the UCS, and the salivation to that food is the UCR.

CONDITIONED STIMULUS Pavlov determined that almost any kind of stimulus could become associated with the unconditioned stimulus (UCS) if it is paired

Dr. Ivan Pavlov and students working in his laboratory. Pavlov, a Russian physiologist, was the first to study and write about the basic principles of classical conditioning.

Watch on **mypsychlab**
Classic Footage of Pavlov

classical conditioning
learning to make a reflex response to a stimulus other than the original, natural stimulus that normally produces the reflex.

unconditioned stimulus (UCS)
a naturally occurring stimulus that leads to an involuntary response.

unconditioned response (UCR)
an involuntary response to a naturally occurring or unconditioned stimulus.

with the UCS often enough. In his original study, for example, the sight of the food dish itself became a stimulus for salivation *before* the food was given to the dogs. Every time the dogs received food (to which they naturally salivated), they saw the dish. At this point, the dish was called a **neutral stimulus (NS)** because it had no effect on salivation. After being paired with the food so many times, the dish came to produce the same salivation response, although a somewhat weaker one, as did the food itself. When a previously neutral stimulus, through repeated pairing with the unconditioned stimulus, begins to cause the same kind of reflexive response, learning has occurred. The neutral stimulus can now be called a **conditioned stimulus (CS)**. (*Unconditioned* means "unlearned," and *conditioned* means "learned.")

CONDITIONED RESPONSE   The response that is given to the CS is not usually quite as strong as the original unconditioned response (UCR), but it is essentially the same response. However, because it comes as a response to the conditioned stimulus, it is called the **conditioned response (CR)** or sometimes the *conditioned reflex*.

PUTTING IT ALL TOGETHER: PAVLOV'S CANINE CLASSIC, OR DING, DONG, BELL

5.4   What was Pavlov's classic experiment in conditioning?

Classical conditioning is not as complex as it sounds. What gets tough is keeping all the letters straight: UCS, UCR, CS, and CR. Pavlov did a classic experiment in which he paired the ringing of a bell with the presentation of food to see if the dogs would eventually salivate to the sound of the bell. Since the bell did not normally produce salivation, it was the neutral stimulus (NS) before any conditioning took place. The repeated pairing of the NS and the UCS is usually called *acquisition*, because the organism is in the process of acquiring learning. Figure 5.1 is a chart of how each element of the conditioning relationship worked in Pavlov's experiment.

Notice that the responses, CR and UCR, are the same: salivation. They simply differ in what they are the response *to*. An unconditioned stimulus (UCS) is always followed by an unconditioned response (UCR), and a conditioned stimulus (CS) is always followed by a conditioned response (CR).

Is this rocket science? No, not really. Classical conditioning is actually one of the simplest forms of learning. It's so simple that it happens to people all the time without their even being aware of it. Does your mouth water when you merely *see* an advertisement for your favourite food on television? Does your stomach get upset every time you hear the high-pitched whine of the dentist's drill? These are both examples of classical conditioning.

After all the dog stories, your salivation response to the television ad probably needs no explanation, but what about the dentist's drill? Over the course of many visits, the body comes to associate that sound (CS) with the anxiety or fear (UCR) the person has felt while receiving a painful dental treatment (UCS), and so the sound produces a feeling of anxiety (CR), whether that person is in the chair or just in the outer waiting area.

Although classical conditioning happens quite easily, researchers have discovered a few basic principles:

1. The CS must come *before* the UCS. If Pavlov rang the bell just after he gave the dogs the food, they did not become conditioned (Rescorla, 1988).

2. The CS and UCS must come very close together in time—ideally, only several seconds apart. When Pavlov tried to stretch the time between the potential CS and

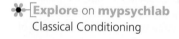
Explore on **mypsychlab**
Classical Conditioning

neutral stimulus (NS)
stimulus that has no effect on the desired response.

conditioned stimulus (CS)
stimulus that becomes able to produce a learned reflex response by being paired with the original unconditioned stimulus.

conditioned response (CR)
learned reflex response to a conditioned stimulus.

Classical conditioning in the real world. These children are no doubt salivating to the sound of the ice cream truck's bell, much as Pavlov's dogs were conditioned to respond. What other kinds of stimuli might make a person salivate?

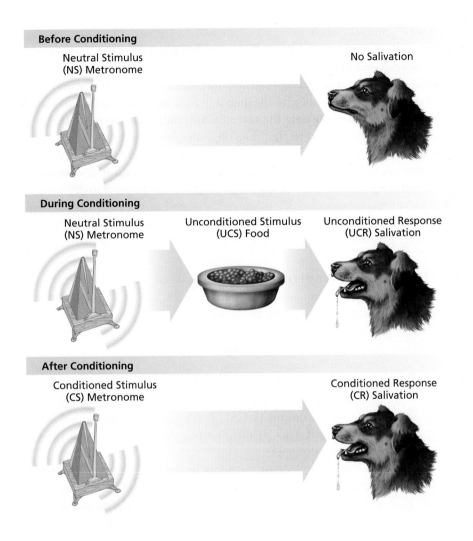

Before Conditioning

Neutral Stimulus
(NS) Metronome → No Salivation

During Conditioning

Neutral Stimulus
(NS) Metronome → Unconditioned Stimulus
(UCS) Food → Unconditioned Response
(UCR) Salivation

After Conditioning

Conditioned Stimulus
(CS) Metronome → Conditioned Response
(CR) Salivation

FIGURE 5.1 **Classical Conditioning** Before conditioning takes place, the sound of the bell does not cause salivation and is a neutral stimulus, or NS. During conditioning, the sound of the bell occurs just before the presentation of the food, the UCS. The food causes salivation, the UCR. When conditioning has occurred after several pairings of the bell with the food, the bell will begin to elicit a salivation response from the dog without any food. This is learning, and the sound of the bell is now a CS and the salivation to the bell is the CR.

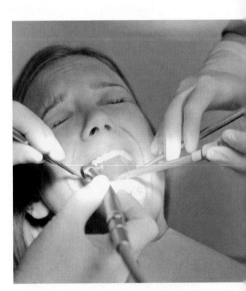

Could this be you? The anxiety that many people feel while in the dentist's office is a conditioned response, with the dentist's chair and the smells of the office acting as conditioned stimuli.

◀ That seems simple enough. But I have to know—did Pavlov's dogs salivate to the doorbell, too?

the UCS to several minutes, no association was made. Too much could happen in the longer interval of time to interfere with conditioning (Pavlov, 1926; Wasserman & Miller, 1997).

3. The neutral stimulus must be paired with the UCS several times, often many times, before conditioning can take place (Pavlov, 1926).

4. The CS is usually some stimulus that is distinctive or stands out from other competing stimuli. The bell was a sound that was not normally present in the laboratory and, therefore, was distinct (Pavlov, 1926; Rescorla, 1988).

That seems simple enough. But I have to know—did Pavlov's dogs salivate to the doorbell, too? They certainly could have, if the doorbell were similar in sound to the CS bell, and if the dogs were near enough to hear the doorbell, and assuming Pavlov even had a doorbell.

STIMULUS GENERALIZATION AND DISCRIMINATION Pavlov did find that similar-sounding bells would produce the same conditioned response from his dogs. He and other researchers found that the strength of the response to the similar bells was not as strong as to the original one, but the more similar the other bell tone was to the original bell tone, the more similar the strength of the response was as well (Siegel,

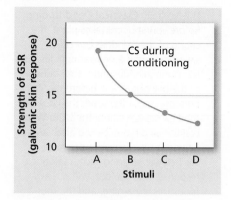

FIGURE 5.2 **Strength of the Generalized Response (GSR)** An example of generalization. The subjects had been conditioned originally to a CS (A) of a given frequency. When tested with the original tone, and with tones B, C, and D of differing frequencies, a clear generalization effect appeared. The closer the frequency of the test tone to the frequency of tone A, the greater was the magnitude of the response to the tone. (Howland, 1937)

stimulus generalization
the tendency to respond to a stimulus that is similar only to the original conditioned stimulus with the conditioned response.

stimulus discrimination
the tendency to stop making a generalized response to a stimulus that is similar to the original conditioned stimulus because the similar stimulus is never paired with the unconditioned stimulus.

extinction
the disappearance or weakening of a learned response following the removal or absence of the unconditioned stimulus (in classical conditioning) or the removal of a reinforcer (in operant conditioning).

reinforcer
any event or object that, when following a response, increases the likelihood of that response occurring again.

spontaneous recovery
the reappearance of a learned response after extinction has occurred.

1969). (See Figure 5.2.) The tendency to respond to a stimulus that is similar only to the original conditioned stimulus is called **stimulus generalization**. For example, a person who reacts with anxiety to the sound of a dentist's drill might react with some slight anxiety to a similar-sounding machine, such as an electric coffee grinder.

Of course, Pavlov did not give the dogs any food after the similar bell sounded. They received food following only the correct CS. It didn't take long for the dogs to stop responding (generalizing) to the "fake" bell sounds altogether. Because only the real CS was followed with food, they learned to tell the difference, or *discriminate*, between the "fake" bells and the real one, a process called **stimulus discrimination**. Stimulus discrimination occurs when an organism learns to respond to different stimuli in different ways. For example, although the sound of the coffee grinder might produce a little anxiety in the dental-drill-hating person, after a few uses that sound will no longer produce anxiety because it isn't associated with dental pain.

EXTINCTION AND SPONTANEOUS RECOVERY What would have happened if Pavlov had stopped giving the dogs food after the real CS? Pavlov did just that, and the dogs gradually stopped salivating to the sound of the bell. When the bell (CS) was repeatedly presented in the absence of the UCS (food, in this case), the salivation (CR) "died out" in a process called **extinction**.

Why does the removal of an unconditioned stimulus lead to extinction of the conditioned response? Look back at Figure 5.1. Once conditioning is acquired, the conditioned stimulus (CS) and conditioned response (CR) will always come *before* the original unconditioned stimulus (UCS). The UCS now serves as a **reinforcer** (strengthener) of the CS–CR association. Remove the reinforcer, and the CR it strengthens will weaken and disappear.

The term *extinction* is a little unfortunate in that it seems to mean that the original conditioned response is totally gone, dead, never coming back, just like the dinosaurs. Remember the definition of learning is any relatively *permanent* change in behaviour. The fact is that once people learn something, it's almost impossible to "unlearn" it. People can learn new things that replace it, or lose their way to it in memory, but it's still there. In the case of classical conditioning, this is easily demonstrated.

After extinguishing the conditioned salivation response in his dogs, Pavlov waited a few weeks, putting the bell away. There were no more training sessions and the dogs were not exposed to the bell's ringing in that time at all. But when Pavlov took the bell back out and rang it, the dogs all began to salivate, although it was a fairly weak response and didn't last very long. This brief recovery of the conditioned response proves that the CR is still in there somewhere. It isn't dead and gone, it's just suppressed or inhibited by the lack of an association with the unconditioned stimulus of food (which is no longer reinforcing the CR). As time passes, this inhibition weakens, especially if the original conditioned stimulus has not been present for a while. In **spontaneous recovery,** the conditioned response can briefly reappear when the original CS returns, although the response is usually weak and short-lived. See Figure 5.3 for a graph showing both extinction and spontaneous recovery.

If Pavlov had followed the dogs' spontaneous salivation to the bell with food, their conditioning would have resurfaced in no time at all. This would be an example of retraining. Retraining is made simpler by the fact that the extinguished response isn't really gone, it is just suppressed.

People experience classical conditioning in many ways. A person whose car has been hit from behind in a car accident, for example, will spend the next few weeks cringing every time another vehicle gets too close to the rear of the car. That cringing

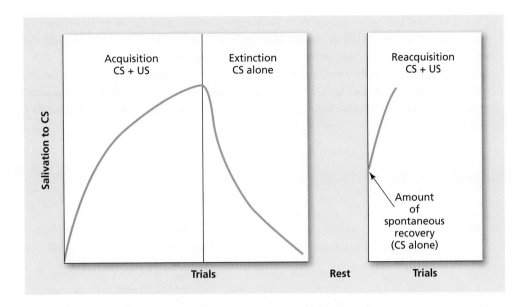

FIGURE 5.3 **Extinction and Spontaneous Recovery**   This graph shows the acquisition, extinction, spontaneous recovery, and reacquisition of a conditioned salivary response. Typically, the measure of conditioning is the number of drops of saliva elicited by the CS on each trial. Note that on the day following extinction, the first presentation of the CS elicits quite a large response.

reaction is a conditioned response. The crash itself was the UCS and the closeness of the other cars becomes a CS. People who are allergic to cats sometimes sneeze when they see a *picture* of a cat. Remember the discussion of how to treat insomnia in Chapter Four (p. 147)? One of the recommendations was to avoid reading, working, watching television, or eating in bed. The bed should be used only for sleeping (a reflex) and will eventually become a conditioned stimulus for sleeping.

higher-order conditioning
occurs when a strong conditioned stimulus is paired with a neutral stimulus, causing the neutral stimulus to become a second conditioned stimulus.

HIGHER-ORDER CONDITIONING   Another concept in classical conditioning is **higher-order conditioning** (see Figure 5.4). This occurs when a strong conditioned stimulus is paired with a neutral stimulus. The strong CS can actually play the part of a UCS, and the previously neutral stimulus becomes a *second* conditioned stimulus.

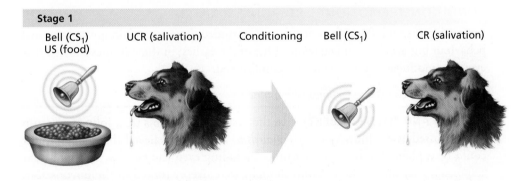

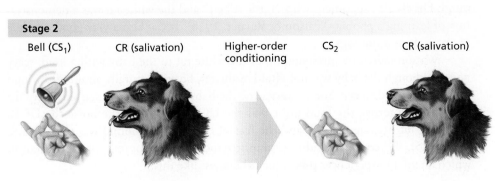

FIGURE 5.4 **Higher-Order Conditioning**   In Stage 1, a strong salivation response is conditioned to occur to the sound of the bell (CS1). In Stage 2, finger snapping (CS2) is repeatedly paired with the ringing of the bell (CS1) until the dog begins to salivate to the finger snapping alone. This is called higher-order conditioning, because one CS is used to create another, "higher" CS.

For example, let's assume that Pavlov has conditioned his dogs to salivate at the sound of the bell. What would happen if just before Pavlov rang the bell, he snapped his fingers? The sequence would now be snap-bell-salivation, or NS-CS-CR. If this happens enough times, the finger snap will eventually also produce a salivation response. The finger snap becomes associated with the bell through the same process that the bell became associated with the food originally and it is now another conditioned stimulus.

PRACTICE QUIZ: HOW MUCH DO YOU REMEMBER?

Pick the best answer.

1. Which of the following statements about learning is NOT true?
   a. Learning is another word for maturation.
   b. Learning is relatively permanent.
   c. Learning involves changes in behaviour.
   d. Learning involves experiences.

2. Ed noticed that whenever he used his electric can opener, his cat would come into the kitchen and act hungry—drooling and mewing pitiably. He reasoned that because he used the can opener to open the cat's food, the sound of the can opener had become a(n)
   a. unconditioned stimulus.   c. unconditioned response.
   b. conditioned stimulus.   d. conditioned response.

3. Which of the following statements about conditioning is FALSE, according to Pavlov?
   a. The CS and UCS must come close together in time.
   b. The CS must come immediately after the UCS.
   c. The neutral stimulus and UCS must be paired several times before conditioning takes place.
   d. All of the above are true.

4. The chapter-opening story describes how Dr. Pierce taught rats to associate sweet-tasting foods with no calories. He then exposed these rats to a sweet-tasting, calorie-rich pre-meal and found that over the next three hours these rats ate significantly more than control rats. Which of the following explains these results best?
   a. extinction   c. stimulus discrimination
   b. spontaneous recovery   d. stimulus generalization

5. When a conditioned response briefly reappears after it has been extinguished, this is called
   a. spontaneous recovery.   c. extinction.
   b. higher-order conditioning.   d. stimulus generalization.

6. The use of a strong CS to create a second CS is called
   a. spontaneous recovery.   c. extinction.
   b. higher-order conditioning.   d. stimulus generalization.

Answers: 1-a, 2-b, 3-b, 4-d, 5-a, 6-b.

CONDITIONED EMOTIONAL RESPONSES: RATS!

Later scientists took Pavlov's concepts and expanded them to explain not only animal behaviour but also human behaviour. One of the earliest of these studies showed that even an emotional response could be conditioned.

5.5   *What is a conditioned emotional response?*

WATSON AND "LITTLE ALBERT"   In the first chapter of this text, John B. Watson was discussed as the founder of *behaviourism*. He firmly believed that all behaviour could be explained in terms of learning, including even the *phobias* (irrational fear responses) that the Freudian camp thought were deeply rooted in the unconscious mind. His classic experiment with "Little Albert" and the white rat was a demonstration of learning a phobia (Watson & Rayner, 1920). It was also a very good example of classical conditioning.

Watson paired the presentation of the white rat to the baby with a loud, scary noise. Although the baby was not afraid of the rat, he was naturally afraid of the loud noise and started to cry. Soon, every time the baby saw the rat, he started to cry. In conditioning terms, the loud noise was the UCS, the fear of the noise the UCR, the white rat became the CS, and the fear of the rat (the phobia) was the CR (see Figure 5.5). (Of course, no ethics committee today would approve an experiment in which an infant experiences psychological distress like this.)

FIGURE 5.5 **Conditioning of "Little Albert"** After Little Albert had been conditioned to fear a white rat, he became afraid of anything white and fuzzy, including John Watson himself with a white fuzzy mask on his face. Can you think of any emotional reactions you experience that might be classically conditioned emotional responses?

The learning of phobias is a very good example of a certain type of classical conditioning, the **conditioned emotional response (CER)**. Conditioned emotional responses are some of the most common forms of classical conditioning to accomplish, and our lives are full of them. It's easy to think of fears people might have that are conditioned or learned: a child's fear of the dentist's chair, a puppy's fear of a rolled-up newspaper, or the fear of dogs that is often shown by a person who has been attacked by a dog in the past. But other emotions can be conditioned, too.

The next time you watch television, watch the commercials closely. Advertisers often use certain objects or certain types of people in their ads to generate a certain emotional response in viewers, hoping that the emotional response will become associated with their product. Sexy models, cute babies, and adorable puppies are some of the examples of stimuli the advertising world uses to tug at our heartstrings, so to speak.

Other television messages are meant to elicit a fear response, such as messages about what drugs will do to your brain. In a classic public service message from the 1980s, a woman holds up an egg and says, "This is your brain." She then drops the egg into a grease-filled, smoking hot skillet and says, "This is your brain on drugs. Any questions?" This spot was supposed to cause disgust by showing the egg being cracked into a filthy-looking skillet and getting immediately fried to a crisp.

It is even possible to become classically conditioned by simply watching someone else respond to a stimulus, in a process called **vicarious conditioning** (Bandura & Rosenthal, 1966). Many years ago, children received vaccination shots in school. The nurse lined the children up, and one by one they had to go forward to get a needle in the arm. When some children received their shots, they cried quite a bit. By the time the nurse got near the end of the line of children, they were all crying—many of them before she ever touched needle to skin. They had learned their fear reflex from watching the reactions of the other children. Researchers at McMaster University suggest that animals can also learn vicariously (Galef & Whiskin, 1995). They conditioned rats to become sick upon tasting a particular flavour. Not only did these rats refuse to consume the flavour that made them sick, but so too did their cage mates who were never previously exposed to the flavour (Whiskin & Bielavska, 1997). From these observations it is likely that vicarious learning plays a significant role in all mammals as they learn about all kinds of things from watching their parents.

✳ **Explore** on **mypsychlab**
Classical Conditioning of Little Albert

conditioned emotional response (CER)
emotional response that has become classically conditioned to occur to learned stimuli, such as a fear of dogs or the emotional reaction that occurs when seeing an attractive person.

vicarious conditioning
classical conditioning of a reflex response or emotion by watching the reaction of another person.

OTHER CONDITIONED RESPONSES IN HUMANS

Many experiments, such as the one described above, have shown that laboratory rats will develop a **conditioned taste aversion** for any liquid or food they swallow up to six hours before becoming nauseated. Researchers found that rats that were given a sweetened liquid and then injected with a drug or exposed to radiation that caused nausea would not touch the liquid again (Garcia et al., 1989; Garcia & Koelling, 1966). In a similar manner, alcoholics who are given a drug to make them violently nauseated when they drink alcohol may learn to avoid drinking any alcoholic beverage. The chemotherapy drugs that cancer patients receive also can create severe nausea, which causes those people to develop a taste aversion for any food they have eaten before going in for the chemotherapy treatment (Berteretche et al., 2004).

But I thought that it took several pairings of these stimuli to bring about conditioning. How can classical conditioning happen so fast?

BIOLOGICAL PREPAREDNESS Conditioned taste aversions are an example of something called **biological preparedness**. Most mammals, who find their food by smell and taste, will learn to avoid any food that smells or tastes like something they ate just before becoming ill. It's a survival mechanism; if they continued eating a "bad" food, they might die. The mammalian body seems to be prepared to associate smell and taste with getting sick (Garcia & Koelling, 1966; Seligman, 1970). Although most conditioning requires repeated pairings of CS with UCS, when the response is nausea, one pairing seems to be all that is necessary. Taste aversion conditioning is so effective that it has even been used by renowned psychologist Dr. John Garcia and colleagues as a tool to stop coyotes from killing ranchers' sheep and also to stop the ranchers from wiping out the coyote population entirely (Gustavson et al., 1976). Garcia and his fellow researchers laced sheep meat with lithium chloride and left it for the coyotes to find. The coyotes ate the drugged meat, got extremely sick, and avoided eating sheep for quite some time afterward. The coyotes got to live, and the ranchers got to keep their sheep.

It's interesting to note that birds, which find their food by sight, will avoid any object or insect that simply *looks* like the one that made them sick. A certain species of moth has colouring that mimics the monarch butterfly. The butterfly is poisonous to birds, but the moth isn't. The moths' mimicry causes birds to avoid eating them, even though they are quite edible. Whereas mammals are biologically prepared to associate taste with illness, birds are biologically prepared to associate visual characteristics with illness (Shapiro et al., 1980).

5.6 *How is classical conditioning related to advertising?*

Advertisers often use classical conditioning principles to persuade you to buy something. University of British Columbia professor Gerald Gorn divided two McGill University management classes into four groups and told them that an advertising agency wanted their help in choosing music for a pen commercial. Half of the students in one management class were shown slides of a blue pen as music they liked, from the *Grease* soundtrack, played in the background. The other half of the students in this class were shown slides of a beige pen as music from India, which most

---

But I thought that it took several pairings of these stimuli to bring about conditioning. How can ▶ classical conditioning happen so fast?

Conditioned taste aversions in nature: This moth is not poisonous to birds, but the monarch butterfly whose colouring the moth imitates is quite poisonous. Birds find their food by vision and will not eat anything that resembles the monarch.

conditioned taste aversion
development of a nausea or aversive response to a particular taste because that taste was followed by a nausea reaction, occurring after only one association.

biological preparedness
the tendency of animals to learn certain associations, such as taste and nausea, with only one or a few pairings because of the survival value of the learning.

students disliked, played in the background. In the other management class, half the students were shown the beige pen with the liked music from *Grease*, and the rest saw the blue pen and heard the Indian music. Later each participant was given a choice of either a blue pen or a beige pen.

What do you think happened? As Professor Gorn predicted, 79 percent of participants picked the colour of the pen associated with the music they liked, and 70 percent of those who heard music they disliked chose the colour of the pen they had never seen (Gorn, 1982). In this study, the music was the UCS that elicited the UCR of either good feelings (liked music) or bad feelings (disliked music). The pen served as the CS and, when presented alone, produced the CR of either good or bad feelings, depending on the type of music it was associated with. Interestingly, most students commented that the music had no influence on their pen choice, but the results suggest that the music had a significant effect. From this study it is easy to see why advertisers often associate well-liked music and famous people with their products.

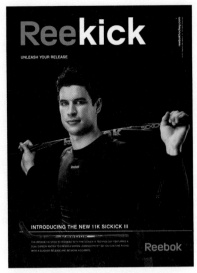

Sidney Crosby uses his considerable star power to endorse Reebok. Try to determine the UCS, UCR, CS, and CR.

WHY DOES CLASSICAL CONDITIONING WORK?

5.7 *Why does classical conditioning work?*

There are two ways to explain how one stimulus comes to "stand in" for another. One is the original explanation given by Pavlov, whereas the other is based on a cognitive explanation.

Pavlov believed that the CS, through its association close in time with the UCS, came to activate the same place in the animal's brain that was originally activated by the UCS. He called this process **stimulus substitution**. But if a mere association in time is all that is needed, why would conditioning *fail to happen* when the CS is presented immediately *after* the UCS?

Robert Rescorla (1988) found that the CS has to provide some kind of information about the coming of the UCS in order to achieve conditioning. In other words, the CS must predict that the UCS is coming. In one study, Rescorla exposed one group of rats to a tone, and just after the tone's onset and while the tone was still able to be heard, an electric shock was administered for some of the tone presentations. Soon the rats became agitated and reacted in fear by shivering and squealing at the onset of the tone, a kind of conditioned emotional response. But with a second group of rats, Rescorla again sounded a tone, but administered the electric shock only *after* the tone *stopped*, not while the tone was being heard. That group of rats responded with fear to the *stopping* of the tone (Rescorla, 1968).

The tone for the second group of rats provided a different kind of information than the tone in the first instance. For the first group, the tone means the shock is coming, whereas for the second group, the tone means there is no shock while the tone is on. It was the particular *expectancy* created by pairing the tone or absence of tone with the shock that determined the particular response of the rats. Because this explanation involves the mental activity of consciously expecting something to occur, it is an example of an explanation for classical conditioning called the **cognitive perspective**.

stimulus substitution
original theory in which Pavlov stated that classical conditioning occurred because the conditioned stimulus became a substitute for the unconditioned stimulus by being paired closely together.

cognitive perspective
modern theory in which classical conditioning is seen to occur because the conditioned stimulus provides information or an expectancy about the coming of the unconditioned stimulus.

PRACTICE QUIZ: HOW MUCH DO YOU REMEMBER?

Pick the best answer.

1. In Watson's experiment with "Little Albert," the UCS was
   a. the white rat.
   c. the fear of the rat.
   b. the loud noise.
   d. the fear of the noise.

2. Often people with certain types of cancer must take chemotherapy treatments. The drugs used in these treatments are powerful and usually cause strong nausea reactions. If Cindy had scrambled eggs for breakfast and then took a chemotherapy treatment later that same morning, what might we predict based on conditioned taste aversion research?
   a. Cindy will probably develop a strong liking for scrambled eggs.
   b. Cindy will probably be able to eat scrambled eggs with no nausea at all.
   c. Cindy will probably get nauseated the next time she tries to eat scrambled eggs.
   d. None of the above is likely.

3. Your pet parakeet eats some cooked spaghetti noodles. Later the poor bird gets very ill. What would the research on biological preparedness predict?
   a. The parakeet will probably not eat shell macaroni because it smells similar to spaghetti.
   b. The parakeet will probably not eat shell macaroni because it tastes similar to spaghetti.
   c. The parakeet will probably not eat linguini noodles because they are long and thin and look similar to spaghetti.
   d. The parakeet will eat spaghetti again.

4. The fact that the CS must come immediately before the UCS, and not after, is a problem for the _____ theory of why classical conditioning works.
   a. stimulus substitution
   c. cognitive substitution
   b. cognitive perspective
   d. stimulus perspective

5. Rescorla found that the CS must _____ the UCS for conditioning to take place.
   a. replace
   c. come at the same time as
   b. come after
   d. predict

6. Rat A receives a dose of radiation after drinking mint-flavoured water. In his home cage, which he shares with Rat B, he becomes ill. What will happen when Rat B is offered mint-flavoured treats?
   a. Rat B will slowly begin to nibble at the treats and will eventually eat them.
   b. Rat B will not eat the treats.
   c. Rat B will immediately consume the treats.
   d. Rat B will eat the treats and then become ill.

7. In an advertisement, Wayne Gretzky is posing, giving a thumbs-up, by a Ford truck. In this ad, what is the UCS?
   a. the Ford truck
   b. the good feeling associated with seeing Wayne Gretzky
   c. Wayne Gretzky
   d. The UCS cannot be determined in this example.

8. For the past three months, every time Steve has been out at the local bar he takes Ecstasy. One evening he attends a house party, ingests Ecstasy, and becomes so sick that he needs to go to the hospital. In this case, the local bar acted as a(n) _____, preparing his body for the drug.
   a. unconditioned stimulus
   c. unconditioned response
   b. conditioned stimulus
   d. conditioned response

Answers: 1-b, 2-c, 3-c, 4-a, 5-d, 6-b, 7-c, 8-b.

So far, all learning seems to involve reflex behaviour. What about how we learn voluntary ▶ behaviour such as brushing and flossing?

If Pavlov is the person to associate with classical conditioning, who first studied operant conditioning? ▶

WHAT'S IN IT FOR ME? OPERANT CONDITIONING

So far, all learning seems to involve reflex behaviour. What about how we learn voluntary behaviour such as brushing and flossing? There are two kinds of behaviour that all organisms are capable of doing: involuntary (reflexive) and voluntary. If Inez blinks her eyes because a gnat flies close to them, that's a reflex and totally involuntary. But if she then swats at the gnat to frighten it, that's a voluntary choice. She *had* to blink, but she *chose* to swat.

5.8 *What is operant conditioning and Thorndike's Law of Effect?*

Classical conditioning is the kind of learning that occurs with reflexive, involuntary behaviour. The kind of learning that applies to voluntary behaviour is called **operant conditioning**, and it is both different from and similar to classical conditioning. If Pavlov is the person to associate with classical conditioning, who first studied operant conditioning?

FRUSTRATING CATS: THORNDIKE'S PUZZLE BOX AND THE LAW OF EFFECT

Edward L. Thorndike (1874–1949) was one of the first researchers to explore and attempt to outline the laws of learning voluntary responses, although the field was not yet called *operant conditioning*. Thorndike placed a hungry cat inside a "puzzle box" from which the only escape was to press a lever located on the floor of the box (see Figure 5.6). Cats definitely do *not* like being confined, as anyone who has ever tried to stuff one into a travel box will know (and probably has the scars to prove it), and there's a dish of food *outside* the box, so the cat is highly motivated to get out. Thorndike observed that the cat would move around the box, pushing and rubbing up against the walls in an effort to escape. Eventually, the cat would accidentally push the lever, opening the door. Upon escaping, the cat was fed from a dish placed just outside the box. The lever is the stimulus, the pushing of the lever is the response, and the consequence is both escape (good) and food (even better).

The cat did not learn the connection between the lever and the escape right away. After a number of trials in a box like this one, the cat took less and less time to push the lever to deliberately open the door—it had made an association between pushing the lever and opening the door (see Figure 5.7). Each time the cat rubbed and pushed at the part of the box that had led to freedom and food more quickly.

Based on this research, Thorndike developed the **Law of Effect**: If a response is followed by a pleasurable consequence, it will tend to be repeated. If a response is followed by an unpleasant consequence, it will tend not to be repeated (Thorndike, 1911). This basic principle is behind learning voluntary behaviour. In the case of the cat in the box, pushing the lever was followed by a pleasurable consequence (getting out and getting fed), so pushing the lever became a repeated response.

Who first called it operant conditioning? Thorndike's work began the study of voluntary learning, but the person who has had the greatest influence on the field

operant conditioning
the learning of voluntary behaviour through the effects of pleasant and unpleasant consequences to responses.

Law of Effect
law stating that if a response is followed by a pleasurable consequence, it will tend to be repeated, and if followed by an unpleasant consequence, it will tend not to be repeated.

◄●┤Simulate on **mypsychlab**
Operant Conditioning

◄ Who first called it operant conditioning?

FIGURE 5.6 **Thorndike Puzzle Box**
A typical Thorndike puzzle box. The cat is placed inside the box and can get out by pushing on the little platform to one side of the door—at first, accidentally. Each time the cat managed to escape, it would be put back into the box until, through trial and error, it knew to push on the platform to open the door.

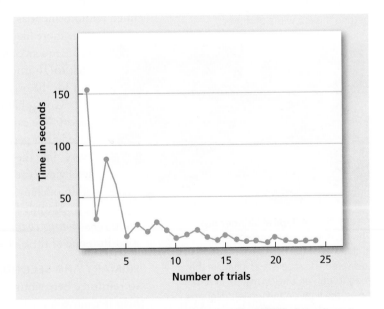

FIGURE 5.7 **Graph of the Time to Learn in Thorndike's Experiment**
This is one of the earliest "learning curves" in the history of the experimental study of conditioning. The time required by one of Thorndike's cats to escape from the puzzle box gradually decreased with additional trials but with obvious reversals.

operant
any behaviour that is voluntary.

reinforcement
any event or stimulus that, when following a response, increases the probability that the response will occur again.

and who gave it the name *operant conditioning* was B. F. Skinner. He is also known as behaviourism's biggest supporter.

B. F. SKINNER: THE BEHAVIOURIST'S BEHAVIOURIST

5.9 *What was Skinner's contribution to operant conditioning?*

B. F. Skinner (1904–1990) was the behaviourist who assumed leadership of the field after John Watson. He was even more determined than Watson that psychologists should study only measurable, observable behaviour. In addition to his knowledge of Pavlovian classical conditioning, Skinner found in the work of Thorndike a way to explain all behaviour as the product of learning. He even gave the learning of voluntary behaviour a special name: *operant conditioning* (Skinner, 1938). Voluntary behaviour is that which people and animals do to *operate* in the world. When people perform a voluntary action, it is to get something they want or avoid something they don't want, right? So voluntary behaviour, for Skinner, is **operant** behaviour, and the learning of such behaviour is operant conditioning.

The heart of operant conditioning is the effect of consequences on behaviour. Thinking back to the section on classical conditioning, learning a reflex really depends on what comes *before* the response—the unconditioned stimulus and what will become the conditioned stimulus. These two stimuli are the *antecedent* stimuli (*antecedent* means something that comes before another thing). But in operant conditioning, learning depends on what happens *after* the response—the consequence. In a way, operant conditioning could be summed up as "If I do this, what's in it for me?"

THE CONCEPT OF REINFORCEMENT

5.10 *What are the important concepts in operant conditioning?*

"What's in it for me" represents the concept of **reinforcement**, one of Skinner's major contributions to behaviourism. The word itself means to strengthen, and Skinner defined reinforcement as anything that, when following a response, causes that response to be more likely to happen again. Typically, this means that reinforcement is a consequence that is in some way pleasurable to the organism, which relates back to Thorndike's Law of Effect. The "pleasurable consequence" is what's in it for the organism—the reward, so to speak.

Going back to Thorndike's puzzle box research, what was "in it" for the cat? We can see that the escape from the box and the food that the cat received after getting out are both *reinforcement* of the lever-pushing response. Every time the cat got out of the box, it got reinforced for doing so. In Skinner's view, this reinforcement is the reason that the cat learned anything at all. In operant conditioning, reinforcement is the key to learning.

Skinner had his own version of a puzzle box called a *Skinner box* or *operant conditioning chamber* (see Figure 5.8). His early research often involved placing a rat into one of these chambers and training it to push down on a bar to get food.

PRIMARY AND SECONDARY REINFORCERS The events or items that can be used to reinforce behaviour are not all alike. Let's say that a friend of yours asks you to help her move some books from the trunk of her car to her apartment on the second floor. She offers you a choice of $25 or a candy bar. Unless you're really hungry, you'll most likely choose the money, right? With $25, you could buy more than one candy bar. (At today's prices, you might even be able to afford three.)

"Once it became clear to me that, by responding correctly to certain stimuli, I could get all the bananas I wanted, getting this job was a pushover."

FIGURE 5.8 **A Typical Skinner Box**
This rat is learning to press the bar in the wall of the cage to get food (delivered a few pellets at a time in the food trough on the lower left). In some cases, the light on the top left might be turned on to indicate that pressing the bar will lead to food or to warn of an impending shock delivered by the grate on the floor of the cage.

Now pretend that your friend offers the same deal to a 3-year-old child who lives downstairs for carrying up some of the paperback books: $25 or a candy bar. Which reward will the child more likely choose? Most children at that age have no clear idea of the value of money, so the child will probably choose the candy bar. The money and the candy bar represent two basic kinds of *reinforcers*, items or events that when following a response will strengthen it. The reinforcing properties of money must be learned, but candy gives immediate reward in the form of taste and satisfying hunger.

A reinforcer such as a candy bar that satisfies a basic need such as hunger is called a **primary reinforcer**. Examples would be any kind of food (hunger drive), liquid (thirst drive), or touch (pleasure drive). Infants, toddlers, preschool-age children, and animals can be easily reinforced by using primary reinforcers. (It's not a good idea, however, to start thinking of reinforcers as rewards—freedom from pain is also a basic need, so pain itself can be a primary reinforcer when it is *removed*. Removal of a painful stimulus fills a basic need just as eating food when hungry fills the hunger need.)

A **secondary reinforcer** such as money, however, gets its reinforcing properties from being associated with primary reinforcers in the past. A child who is given money to spend soon realizes that the boring paper can be traded for candy and treats—primary reinforcers—and so money becomes reinforcing in and of itself. If a person praises a puppy while petting him (touch, a primary reinforcer), the praise alone will eventually make the puppy squirm with delight.

That sounds very familiar. Isn't this related to classical conditioning? Secondary reinforcers do indeed get their reinforcing power from the process of classical conditioning. After all, the pleasure people feel when they eat, drink, or get a back rub is a reflex response, and any reflex can be classically conditioned to occur to a new stimulus. In the case of money, the candy is a UCS for pleasure (the UCR) and the money is present just before the candy is obtained. The money becomes a CS for pleasure, and people certainly do feel pleasure when they have a lot of money, don't they?

In the case of the puppy, the petting is the UCS, and the pleasure at being touched and petted is the UCR. The praise, or more specifically the tone of voice, becomes the CS for pleasure. Although classical and operant conditioning often "work together," as in the creation of secondary reinforcers, they are two different processes. Table 5.1 presents a brief look at how the two types of conditioning differ from each other.

◄ That sounds **very** familiar. Isn't this related to classical conditioning?

TABLE 5.1 COMPARING TWO KINDS OF CONDITIONING	
OPERANT CONDITIONING	**CLASSICAL CONDITIONING**
Goal is to increase the rate of an already occurring response.	Responses are voluntary.
Consequences are important in forming an association.	Reinforcement must be immediate.
An expectancy develops for reinforcement to follow a correct response.	Goal is to create a new response to a stimulus that doesn't normally produce that response.
Responses are involuntary and reflexive.	Antecedent stimuli are important in forming an association.
CS must occur immediately before the UCS.	An expectancy develops for UCS to follow CS.

primary reinforcer
any reinforcer that is naturally reinforcing by meeting a basic biological need, such as hunger, thirst, or touch.

secondary reinforcer
any reinforcer that becomes reinforcing after being paired with a primary reinforcer, such as praise, tokens, or gold stars.

Javier Bardem receives an Academy Award for his role in *No Country for Old Men*. The award, the applause of the audience, and the attention of the photographers are all positive reinforcement.

5.11 *What is the difference between negative reinforcement and punishment?*

POSITIVE AND NEGATIVE REINFORCEMENT Reinforcers can also differ in the way they are used. Most people have no trouble at all understanding that following a response with some kind of pleasurable consequence (like a reward) will lead to an increase in the likelihood of that response being repeated. But many people have trouble understanding that the opposite is also true: Following a response with *the removal or escape* from something *unpleasant* will also increase the likelihood of that response being repeated. Remember the idea that pain can be a reinforcer if it is removed? If a person's behaviour gets pain to stop, the person is much more likely to do that same thing again—which is part of the reason people can get addicted to painkilling medication.

There are really only two kinds of things people ever experience as consequences in the world: things they like (food, money, candy, sex, praise, and so on) and things they don't like (spankings, being yelled at, and experiencing any kind of pain, to name a few). There are also only two possibilities for experiencing these two kinds of consequences: Either people experience them directly (such as getting money for working or getting yelled at for misbehaving) or they don't experience them, (such as losing an allowance for misbehaving or avoiding a scolding by lying about misbehaviour). These four consequences are named and described in Table 5.2.

First, take a look at the left column of Table 5.2, the one labelled "Reinforcement." Getting money for working is another example of **positive reinforcement**, the reinforcement of a response by the *addition* or experience of a pleasurable consequence, such as a reward or a pat on the back. That one everyone understands. But avoiding a penalty by turning one's income tax return in on time is an example of negative reinforcement. **Negative reinforcement** is the reinforcement of a response by the removal, escape from, or avoidance of an unpleasant stimulus. Because the behaviour (turning in the tax return before the deadline) results in *avoiding* an unpleasant stimulus (a penalty), the likelihood that the person will behave that way again (turn it in on time in the future) is *increased*—just as positive reinforcement will increase a behaviour's likelihood. Examples are the best way to understand the difference between these two types of reinforcement, so try to figure out which of the following examples would be positive reinforcement and which would be negative reinforcement:

1. Arnie's father nags him to wash his car. Arnie hates being nagged, so he washes the car so his father will stop nagging.

2. Trey learns that talking in a funny voice gets him lots of attention from his classmates, so now he talks that way often.

3. Allen is a server at a restaurant and always tries to smile and be pleasant because that seems to lead to bigger tips.

positive reinforcement
the reinforcement of a response by the addition or experiencing of a pleasurable stimulus.

negative reinforcement
the reinforcement of a response by the removal, escape from, or avoidance of an unpleasant stimulus.

TABLE 5.2 FOUR WAYS TO MODIFY BEHAVIOUR

	REINFORCEMENT	PUNISHMENT
Positive (Adding)	Something valued or desirable	Something unpleasant
	Positive Reinforcement	*Punishment by Application*
	Example: getting a gold star for good behaviour in school	Example: getting a spanking for disobeying
Negative (Removing/ Avoiding)	Something unpleasant	Something valued or desirable
	Negative Reinforcement	*Punishment by Removal*
	Example: avoiding a ticket by stopping at a red light	Example: losing a privilege such as going out with friends

4. An Li turns in her report to her teacher on the day it is due because papers get marked down a letter grade for every day they are late.

Here are the answers:

1. Arnie is being negatively reinforced for washing his car because the nagging (unpleasant stimulus) stops when he does so.

2. Trey is getting positive reinforcement in the form of his classmates' attention.

3. Allen's smiling and pleasantness are positively reinforced by the customers' tips.

4. An Li is avoiding an unpleasant stimulus (the marked-down grade) by turning in her paper on time, which is an example of negative reinforcement.

I'm confused—I thought taking something away was a kind of punishment?

TWO KINDS OF PUNISHMENT People get confused because "negative" sounds like it ought to be something bad, like a kind of punishment. **Punishment** is actually the opposite of reinforcement. It is any event or stimulus that, when following a response, causes that response to be less likely to happen again. Punishment *weakens* responses, whereas reinforcement (whether it is *positive or negative) strengthens* responses. There are two ways in which punishment can happen, just as there are two ways in which reinforcement can happen.

Now take a look at the right column of Table 5.2, labelled "Punishment." **Punishment by application** occurs when something unpleasant (such as a spanking, scolding, or other unpleasant stimulus) is added to the situation or *applied*. This is the kind of punishment that most people think of when they hear the word *punishment*. In 2004, the Supreme Court of Canada upheld Section 43 of the Criminal Code, which allows parents, teachers, and caregivers to use reasonable force when disciplining children between the ages of 2 and 12. This is also the kind of punishment that many child development specialists strongly recommend parents avoid using with their children because it can easily escalate into abuse (Dubowitz & Bennett, 2007; Saunders & Goddard, 1998; Straus, 2000; Straus & Stewart, 1999; Straus & Yodanis, 1994; Trocmé et al., 2001). A spanking might be *physically* harmless if it is only two or three swats with a hand, but if done in anger or with a belt or other instrument, it becomes abuse, both physical and emotional.

Punishment by removal, on the other hand, is the kind of punishment most often confused with negative reinforcement. In this type of punishment, behaviour is punished by the removal of something pleasurable or desired after the behaviour occurs. "Grounding" a teenager is removing the freedom to do what the teenager wants to do and is an example of this kind of punishment. Other examples would be placing a child in a time out (removing the attention of the others in the room), fining someone for disobeying the law (removing money), and punishing aggressive behaviour by taking away television privileges. This type of punishment is far more acceptable to child development specialists because it involves no physical aggression and avoids many of the problems caused by more aggressive punishments.

The confusion over the difference between negative reinforcement and punishment by removal makes it worth examining the difference just a bit more. Negative reinforcement occurs when a response is followed by the *removal* of an *unpleasant* stimulus. If something unpleasant has just gone away as a consequence of that response, wouldn't that response tend to happen again and again? If the response increases, the consequence has to be a kind of *reinforcement*. The problem is that the name sounds like it should be

I'm confused—I ◄ thought taking something away was a kind of punishment?

punishment
any event or object that, when following a response, makes that response less likely to happen again.

punishment by application
the punishment of a response by the addition or experiencing of an unpleasant stimulus.

punishment by removal
the punishment of a response by the removal of a pleasurable stimulus.

This young man's father is applying punishment by removal as he takes the car keys away from his son.

TABLE 5.3 NEGATIVE REINFORCEMENT VERSUS PUNISHMENT BY REMOVAL	
EXAMPLE OF NEGATIVE REINFORCEMENT	**EXAMPLE OF PUNISHMENT BY REMOVAL**
Stopping at a red light to avoid getting in an accident.	Losing the privilege of driving because you caused too many accidents.
Mailing an income tax return by the due date to avoid paying a penalty.	Having to lose some of your money to pay the penalty for late tax filing.
Obeying a parent before the parent reaches the count of "three" to avoid getting a scolding.	Being "grounded" (losing your freedom) because of disobedience.

some kind of punishment because of the word *negative*, and that's exactly the problem that many people experience when they are trying to understand negative reinforcement. They get negative reinforcement mixed up with punishment by removal, in which a *pleasant* thing is removed (such as having your driver's license taken away because you caused a bad accident). Because something is removed (taken away) in both cases, people think that they will both have the effect of punishment, or weakening a response. The difference between them lies in *what* is taken away. In the case of negative reinforcement, it is an *unpleasant* thing; in the case of this particular form of punishment, it is a *pleasant* or desirable thing. For a head-to-head comparison of negative reinforcement and this particular type of punishment by removal, see Table 5.3.

You said earlier ▶
that there are some
problems with
punishment, and that
many psychologists
don't recommend
using it. What are the
problems?

You said earlier that there are some problems with punishment, and that many psychologists don't recommend using it. What are the problems?

PROBLEMS WITH PUNISHMENT   Although punishment can be effective in reducing or weakening a behaviour, it has several drawbacks. The job of punishment is much more difficult than that of reinforcement. In using reinforcement, all one has to do is strengthen a response that is already there. But punishment is used to weaken a response, and getting rid of a response that is already well established is not that easy. (Ask any parent or pet owner.) Many times punishment serves only to temporarily suppress or inhibit a behaviour until enough time has passed. For example, punishing a child's bad behaviour doesn't always eliminate the behaviour completely. As time goes on, the punishment is forgotten, and the "bad" behaviour may occur again in a kind of spontaneous recovery of the old (and probably pleasurable for the child) behaviour.

Look back at Table 5.2 under the "Punishment" column. Punishment by application can be quite severe, and severe punishment does do one thing well: It stops the behaviour immediately (Bucher & Lovaas, 1967; Carr & Lovass, 1983). It may not stop it permanently, but it does stop it. In a situation in which a child might be doing something dangerous or self-injurious, this kind of punishment is sometimes more acceptable (Duker & Seys, 1995). For example, if a child starts to run into a busy street, the parent might scream at the child to stop and then administer several rather severe swats to the child's rear. If this is not usual behaviour on the part of the parent, the child will most likely never run into the street again.

Other than in situations in which a dangerous behaviour needs to be stopped immediately, severe punishment has too many drawbacks to be really useful. It should also be discouraged because of its potential for leading to abuse (Dubowitz & Bennett, 2007; Gershoff, 2000; Millan et al., 1999; Trocmé et al., 2001):

• Severe punishment may cause the child (or animal) to avoid the punisher instead of the behaviour being punished, so the child (or animal) learns the wrong response.

- Severe punishment may encourage lying to avoid the punishment (a kind of negative reinforcement)—again, not the response that is desired.

- Severe punishment creates fear and anxiety, emotional responses that do not promote learning (Baumrind, 1997; Gershoff, 2000; Gershoff, 2002). If the point is to teach something, this kind of consequence isn't going to help.

- Hitting provides a successful model for aggression (Gershoff, 2000; Milner, 1992).

That last point is worth a bit more discussion. In using an aggressive type of punishment, such as spanking, the adult is actually modelling (presenting a behaviour to be imitated by the child). After all, the adult is using aggression to get what the adult wants from the child. Children sometimes become more likely to use aggression to get what they want when they receive this kind of punishment (Bryan & Freed, 1982; Larzelere, 1986), and the adult has lost an opportunity to model a more appropriate way to deal with parent–child disagreements. Since aggressive punishment does tend to stop the undesirable behaviour, at least for a while, the parent who is punishing actually experiences a kind of negative reinforcement: "When I spank, the unpleasant behaviour goes away." This reinforcement may increase the tendency to use aggressive punishment over other forms of discipline and could even lead to child abuse (Dubowitz & Bennett, 2007). Finally, some children are so desperate for attention from their parents that they will actually misbehave on purpose. The punishment is a form of attention, and these children will take whatever attention they can get, even negative attention.

Punishment by removal is less objectionable to many parents and educators and is the only kind of punishment that is permitted in many public schools. But this kind of punishment also has its drawbacks—it teaches the child what *not* to do but not what the child should do. Both punishment by removal and punishment by application are usually only temporary in their effect on behaviour. After some time has passed, the behaviour will most likely return as the memory of the punishment gets weaker, allowing spontaneous recovery.

If punishment doesn't work very well, what can a parent do to keep a child from behaving badly?

HOW TO MAKE PUNISHMENT MORE EFFECTIVE   The way to make punishment more effective involves remembering a few simple rules:

1. *Punishment should immediately follow the behaviour it is meant to punish.* If the punishment comes long after the behaviour, it will not be associated with that behaviour. (This rule is also true of reinforcement.)

2. *Punishment should be consistent.* This actually means two things. First, if the parent says that a certain punishment will follow a certain behaviour, then the parent must make sure to follow through and do what he or she promised to do. Second, punishment for a particular behaviour should stay at the same intensity or increase slightly but never decrease. For example, if a child is scolded for jumping on the bed the first time, the second time this behaviour happens the child should also be punished by scolding or by a stronger penalty, such as removal of a favourite toy. But if the first misbehaviour is punished by spanking and the second by only a scolding, the child learns to "gamble" with the possible punishment.

3. *Punishment of the wrong behaviour should be paired, whenever possible, with reinforcement of the right behaviour.* Instead of yelling at a 2-year-old for eating with her fingers, the parent should pull her hand gently out of her plate while saying something such as "No, we do not eat with our fingers. We eat with our fork,"

✳ Explore on **mypsychlab**
The Controversy Surrounding Spanking

If punishment **doesn't** work very well, what can a parent do to keep a child from behaving badly?

If the parents in this store give in to their whining child, they will be positively reinforcing his whining. But they will receive negative reinforcement for giving in when the child's obnoxious whining stops.

and then placing the fork in the child's hand and praising her for using it. "See, you are doing such a good job with your fork. I'm so proud of you." Pairing punishment (the mild correction of pulling her hand away while saying "No, we do not eat with our fingers") with reinforcement allows parents (and others) to use a much milder punishment and still be effective. It also teaches the desired behaviour rather than just suppressing the undesired one.

PRACTICE QUIZ: HOW MUCH DO YOU REMEMBER?

Pick the best answer.

1. In Thorndike's puzzle box experiments, the cats were rewarded by
   a. getting out of the box.
   b. getting food.
   c. being petted and praised.
   d. both a and b.

2. _____ is an example of a primary reinforcer, whereas _____ is an example of a secondary reinforcer.
   a. A candy bar; a gold star
   b. A gold star; money
   c. Food; a drink
   d. A gold star; candy

3. _____ occurs when a response is followed by experiencing something pleasurable.
   a. Positive reinforcement
   b. Negative reinforcement
   c. Punishment
   d. Generalization

4. Cindy hates to clean up after dinner. One night she volunteers to bathe the baby before cleaning up. When she finishes with the baby and returns to the kitchen, her husband has cleaned up everything. Which of the following statements is most *likely* true?
   a. Cindy will start cleaning up.
   b. Cindy's husband has positively reinforced her for bathing the baby.
   c. Cindy's husband has negatively reinforced her for bathing the baby.
   d. Cindy will never bathe the baby again.

5. Bennie is afraid of snakes. He won't even look at pictures of them in a book, turning the page or closing the book instead. When he sees a picture of a snake, his anxiety goes up, but when he avoids looking at the picture, his anxiety goes down. It is most correct to say that Bennie's avoidance behaviour is being
   a. punished because he feels anxious after doing so.
   b. punished because he will never get better.
   c. positively reinforced because he is rewarded by his anxiety going down.
   d. negatively reinforced because he is rewarded by his anxiety going down.

Answers: 1-d, 2-a, 3-a, 4-c, 5-d.

Yes, it was really hard. How do circus trainers get their animals to do ▸ all those complicated tricks?

✱ Explore on mypsychlab
Shaping

shaping
the reinforcement of simple steps in behaviour that lead to a desired, more complex behaviour.

successive approximations
small steps in behaviour, one after the other, that lead to a particular goal behaviour.

MORE CONCEPTS IN OPERANT CONDITIONING

Operant conditioning is more than just the reinforcement of simple responses. For example, have you ever tried to teach a pet to do a trick?

Yes, it was really hard. How do circus trainers get their animals to do all those complicated tricks?

SHAPING When you see an animal perform tricks in a circus or in a show at the zoo, you are seeing the result of applying the rules of conditioning—both classical and operant—to animals. But the more complex tricks are a form of operant conditioning called **shaping**, in which small steps toward some ultimate goal are reinforced until the goal itself is reached (Skinner, 1974).

For example, if Jody wanted to train his dog to jump through a hoop, he would have to start with some behaviour that the dog is already capable of doing on its own. Then he would gradually "mould" that starting behaviour into the jump—something the dog is capable of doing but not likely to do on its own. Jody would have to start with the hoop on the ground in front of Rover's face, and then call the dog through the hoop, using a treat as bait. After Rover steps through the hoop (as the shortest way to the treat), Jody should give Rover the treat (positive reinforcement). Then he could raise the hoop just a little, reward him for walking through it again, raise the hoop, reward him … until Rover is jumping through the hoop to get the treat. The goal is achieved by reinforcing each **successive approximation** (small steps one after the other that get closer and closer to the goal).

EXTINCTION, GENERALIZATION, AND SPONTANEOUS RECOVERY IN OPERANT CONDITIONING *Extinction* in classical conditioning involves the removal of the UCS, the unconditioned stimulus that eventually acts as a reinforcer of the CS–CR bond. It should come as no surprise, then, that extinction in operant conditioning involves the removal of the reinforcement. Have you ever seen a child throw a temper tantrum in the checkout line because the little one wanted some candy or a toy? Many exasperated parents will cave in and give the child the treat, positively reinforcing the tantrum. The parent is also being negatively reinforced for giving in, because the obnoxious behaviour stops. The only way to get the tantrum behaviour to stop is to remove the reinforcement, which means no candy, no treat, and if possible, no attention from the parent.

Ignoring a child's tantrum in public is a lot more difficult than ignoring it at home, but it can be done. In fact, most of the other people in the store who witness the tantrum will most likely silently applaud a parent who does not give in and groan inwardly when they see the child's tantrum rewarded.

Just as in classical conditioning, operantly conditioned responses also can be generalized to stimuli that are similar to only the original stimulus. For example, what parent has not experienced that wonderful moment when Baby, who is just learning to label objects and people, refers to every man she sees as "Dada." The name "Dada" is a response to the presence of her own father and is reinforced by his delight and attention to her. But in the beginning, she will generalize her "Dada" response to any man. As other men fail to reinforce her for this response, she'll learn to discriminate between them and her father and call only her father "Dada." In this way, the man who is actually her father becomes a **discriminative stimulus**. A discriminative stimulus is any stimulus, such as a stop sign or a doorknob, that provides the organism with a cue for making a certain response in order to obtain reinforcement.

Spontaneous recovery (the recurrence of a conditioned response after extinction) will also happen with operant responses. Remember the hoop-jumping dog? Anyone who has ever trained animals to do several different tricks will say that when first learning a new trick, most animals will try to get reinforcers by performing their *old* tricks. Rover might very well have tried to roll over, speak, and shake paws to get that treat before finally walking through the hoop.

This dog has been trained to help its physically challenged owner. Operant conditioning principles can be used to train animals to do many useful tasks, including opening the refrigerator.

One way to deal with this child's temper tantrum is to ignore it. The lack of reinforcement for the tantrum behaviour will eventually result in extinction.

discriminative stimulus
any stimulus, such as a stop sign or a doorknob, that provides the organism with a cue for making a certain response in order to obtain reinforcement.

PRACTICE QUIZ: HOW MUCH DO YOU REMEMBER?

Pick the best answer.

1. Elizabeth's parents want her to put her clothes in the hamper. At first, they praise her for putting the clothes together in one pile. Then they praise her for getting the clothes on the same side of the room as the hamper. When she gets the clothes on top of the hamper, she gets praise. Finally, her parents praise her when she puts her clothes in the hamper. This is an example of
   a. negative reinforcement.
   b. punishment.
   c. extinction.
   d. shaping.

2. Marcella starts whining in the grocery store because she wants some candy. Her father refuses to give her candy and ignores her whining. What will happen?
   a. generalization
   b. extinction
   c. spontaneous recovery
   d. discrimination

3. The first time Giorgio sees a duck, his mother tells him, "That's a duck. Can you say duck?" He repeats the word gleefully. The next day he is watching a cartoon and sees a chicken on the television. He points at the chicken and says, "Duck!" This is an example of
   a. generalization.
   b. extinction.
   c. spontaneous recovery.
   d. discrimination.

4. Ella is teaching her parrot a new word. Every time the parrot says a sound that is close to the new word, she gives it a treat. But the parrot keeps repeating other words it has learned in the past, trying to get a treat that way. The parrot is exhibiting
   a. generalization
   b. extinction.
   c. spontaneous recovery.
   d. discrimination.

SCHEDULES OF REINFORCEMENT: WHY THE ONE-ARMED BANDIT IS SO SEDUCTIVE

The timing of reinforcement can make a tremendous difference to the speed at which learning occurs and the strength of the learned response. Skinner (1956) found that reinforcing each and every response was not necessarily the best schedule of reinforcement for long-lasting learning.

5.12 *What are the schedules of reinforcement?*

THE PARTIAL REINFORCEMENT EFFECT   Alicia's mother gives her a quarter every night she remembers to put her dirty clothes in the clothes hamper. Bianca's mother gives her a dollar at the end of the week, but only if Bianca has put her clothes in the hamper every night. After a time, the mothers stop giving the girls the money. Which child will stop putting her clothes in the hamper more quickly?

The answer might be surprising. It will more likely be Alicia, who has expected to get a reinforcer (the quarter) after *every single response.* As soon as the reinforcers stop, the behaviour extinguishes. Bianca has expected to get a reinforcer only after *seven correct responses.* When the reinforcers stop, Bianca might continue to put the clothes in the hamper for several more days or even another whole week, hoping that the reinforcer will eventually come anyway.

Bianca's behaviour illustrates the **partial reinforcement effect** (Skinner, 1956): A response that is reinforced after some, but not all, correct responses will be more resistant to extinction than a response that receives **continuous reinforcement** (a reinforcer for each and every correct response). Imagine being paid for every hamburger you make or every report you turn in. In the real world, people tend to receive partial reinforcement rather than continuous reinforcement for their work.

Partial reinforcement can be accomplished according to different patterns or schedules. On the one hand, it may be the number of responses that is important, as it would be if one had to sell a certain number of raffle tickets in order to get a prize. On the other hand, it might be a certain interval of time that's important, such as an office safe that can be opened only at a certain time of day. It wouldn't matter how many times one tried to open the safe if the effort didn't come at the right *time.* When it is the number of responses that is important, the schedule is called a *ratio schedule* because a certain number of responses is required for each reinforcer (e.g., 50 raffle tickets for each prize). When the timing of the response is more important, it is called an *interval schedule.*

The other way in which schedules of reinforcement can differ is in whether the number of responses or interval of time is *fixed* (the same in each case) or *variable* (a different number or interval is required in each case). So it is possible to have a fixed ratio schedule, a variable ratio schedule, a fixed interval schedule, and a variable interval schedule (Skinner, 1961).

FIXED RATIO SCHEDULE OF REINFORCEMENT   In a **fixed ratio schedule of reinforcement**, the number of responses required to receive each reinforcer will always be the same number. If Professor Conner were teaching a rat to press a lever to get food pellets, she might require 20 lever pushes for each food pellet, or a fixed ratio of 20:1. If she were to graph the rat's progress, she would end up with something like the second graph of Figure 5.9.

"Remember, every time he gives you a pellet, reinforce that behaviour by pulling the lever."

partial reinforcement effect
the tendency for a response that is reinforced after some, but not all, correct responses to be very resistant to extinction.

continuous reinforcement
the reinforcement of each and every correct response.

fixed ratio schedule of reinforcement
schedule of reinforcement in which the number of responses required for reinforcement is always the same.

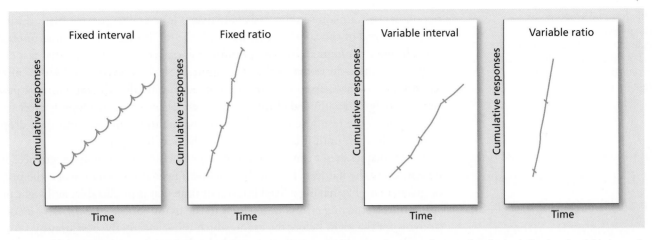

FIGURE 5.9 **Schedules of Reinforcement**   These four graphs show the typical pattern of responding for both fixed and variable interval and ratio schedules of reinforcement. The responses are cumulative, which means new responses are added to those that come before, and all graphs begin after the learned pattern is well established. Slash marks mean that a reinforcement has been given. In both the fixed interval and fixed ratio graphs, there is a pause after each reinforcement as the learner briefly "rests." The "scalloped" shape of the fixed interval curve is a typical indicator of this pause, as is the stair-step shape of the fixed ratio curve. In the variable interval and ratio schedules, no such pause occurs, because the reinforcements are unpredictable. Notice that both fixed and variable interval schedules are slower (less steep) than the two ratio schedules because of the need to respond as quickly as possible in the ratio schedules.

Notice two things about this graph: The rate of responding is very fast and there are little "breaks" in the response pattern immediately after a reinforcer is given. The rapid response rate occurs because the rat wants to get to the next reinforcer as fast as possible, and the number of lever pushes counts. The pauses or breaks come right after a reinforcer, because the rat knows "about how many" lever pushes will be needed to get to the next reinforcer because it's always the same. Fixed schedules are predictable, and that allows rest breaks.

In human terms, anyone who does piecework, in which a certain number of items have to be completed before payment is given, is reinforced on a fixed ratio schedule. Some sandwich shops give out punch cards that get punched one time for each sandwich purchased. When the card has 10 punches, for example, the person might get a free sandwich.

VARIABLE RATIO SCHEDULE OF REINFORCEMENT   In Figure 5.9 the last graph is also very fast, but it's so much smoother. Why? A **variable ratio schedule of reinforcement** is one in which the number of responses changes from one trial to the next. In the rat example, the rat might be expected to push the bar an *average* of 20 times to get reinforcement. That means that sometimes the rat would push the lever only 10 times before a reinforcer comes, but at other times it might take 30 lever pushes or more.

The graph at the lower right of Figure 5.9 shows a curve that is just as rapid a response rate as the fixed ratio schedule because the number of responses still matters. But the graph is much smoother because the rat is taking no rest breaks. It can't afford to do so because it *doesn't know* how many times it may have to push that lever to get the next food pellet. It pushes as fast as it can and eats while pushing. It is the *unpredictability* of the variable schedule that makes the responses more or less continuous.

FIXED INTERVAL SCHEDULE OF REINFORCEMENT   The kind of reinforcement schedule most people are more familiar with is called a **fixed interval schedule of reinforcement**, in which a reinforcer is received after a certain, fixed interval of time has passed. If people receive a paycheque once every two weeks (provided that they show up to work in those two weeks), they are being reinforced on this kind of schedule.

As shown in the first graph of Figure 5.9, this schedule of reinforcement does not produce as fast a rate of response as does the fixed ratio schedule. The number of

◀ In Figure 5.9 the graph on the lower left is also very fast, but it's so much smoother. Why?

variable ratio schedule of reinforcement
schedule of reinforcement in which the number of responses required for reinforcement is different for each trial or event

fixed interval schedule of reinforcement
schedule of reinforcement in which the interval of time that must pass before reinforcement becomes possible is always the same.

variable interval schedule of reinforcement
schedule of reinforcement in which the interval of time that must pass before reinforcement becomes possible is different for each trial or event.

So if a scheduled test is a fixed interval, then would a pop quiz be a variable interval schedule? ▶

responses doesn't matter in this case, only that at least one response is made during the specific interval of time. In the example with the rat, it might be required to press the lever during a five-minute interval of time. It doesn't have to press the bar fast or even very many times—just once in the five minutes. It is the first correct response after the interval of time has passed that gets reinforced. Eventually, the rat will start pushing the lever only as the interval of time nears its end, causing the scalloping effect you see in the graph. The response rate goes up just before the reinforcer and then drops off immediately after, until it is almost time for the next food pellet.

Paycheques aren't the only kind of fixed schedule that people experience. When do you study the hardest? Isn't it right before a test? If you know when the test is to be given, that's like having a fixed interval of time that is predictable, and you can save your greatest studying efforts until closer to the exam. (Some students save *all* of their studying for the night before the exam, which is not exactly the best strategy.) Another example of a fixed interval schedule would be the way that most people floss and brush their teeth most rigorously the few days before their next dental exam. In this case, they are probably hoping for negative reinforcement. The cleaner they get their teeth before the appointment, the less time they might have to spend in that chair.

So if a scheduled test is a fixed interval, then would a pop quiz be a variable interval schedule?

VARIABLE INTERVAL SCHEDULE OF REINFORCEMENT Pop quizzes are unpredictable. Students don't know which day they might be given a pop quiz, so the best strategy is to study a little every night just in case there is a quiz the next day. Pop quizzes are good examples of a **variable interval schedule of reinforcement**, in which the interval of time after which the organism must respond in order to receive a reinforcer changes from one time to the next. For example, the rat might receive a food pellet every five minutes *on average*. Sometimes it might be two minutes, sometimes ten, but the rat must push the lever at least once after that interval to get the pellet. Because the rat can't predict how long the interval is going to be, it pushes the bar more or less continuously, producing the smooth third graph of Figure 5.9. Once again, the number of responses is not important, so the rate of responding is not as fast as a variable ratio schedule.

Another example of a variable interval schedule might be the kind of fishing in which people put their fishing line in the water and wait—and wait, and wait, until a fish takes the bait—if they are lucky. They have to put the line in the water only once, but they might refrain from taking it out for fear that just when they do, the biggest fish in the world would swim by. Dialing a busy phone number also uses this kind of schedule, as people don't know *when* the call will go through, so they keep dialing and dialing.

Regardless of the schedule of reinforcement one uses, there are some things that can be done to make using reinforcement of a behaviour as effective as possible. One thing also concerns timing: A reinforcer should be given as immediately as possible after the desired behaviour. Delaying reinforcement tends not to work well, especially when dealing with animals and small children. (Older children and adults can think about future reinforcements, such as saving up one's money to buy a highly desired item, so delayed reinforcement can work with them.) Care should also be taken to reinforce *only* the desired behaviour—for example, many parents make the mistake of giving a child who has not done some chore the promised treat anyway, which completely undermines the child's learning of that chore or task.

5.13 *Why are video lottery terminals and other games of chance so addictive?*

In human terms, one-armed bandits, slot machines, or video lottery terminals (VLTs) reinforce on a variable ratio schedule of reinforcement. People put their coins in (response), but they don't know how many times they will have to do this before

Slot machines provide reinforcement in the form of money on a variable ratio schedule, making the use of these machines very addictive for many people. People don't want to stop for fear the next pull of the lever will be that "magic" one that produces a jackpot.

reinforcement (the jackpot) comes. People who do this tend to sit there until they either win or run out of money. They don't dare stop because the "next one" might hit that jackpot. Brian Cox and his colleagues at the University of Manitoba estimate that 2 percent of the Canadian population is at risk for developing a gambling problem, and the risk is even higher if the person has easy access to the most addictive form of gambling, VLTs (Beaudoin & Cox, 1999; Cox, Yu, Afini, & Ladouceur, 2005). VLTs also use classical conditioning techniques to keep people playing. When you win (UCS), you feel good (UCR). And winning is paired with lights and sounds emanating from the VLT. Over many pairings the lights and sounds produce good feelings in you, even if they are not coming from *your* VLT. And soon, through higher-order conditioning, the sight of a VLT or even the place where you play will become associated with good feelings.

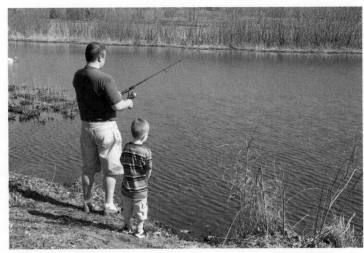

When people go fishing, they never know how long they may have to dangle the bait in the water before snagging a fish. This is an example of a variable interval schedule of reinforcement and explains why some people, such as this father and son, are reluctant to pack up and go home.

Buying lottery tickets is much the same thing, as is any kind of gambling. People don't know how many tickets they will have to buy, and they're afraid that if they don't buy the next one, that will be the ticket that would have won, so they keep buying and buying.

STIMULUS CONTROL: SLOW DOWN, IT'S THE COPS

5.14 How do operant stimuli control behaviour?

The beginning of the discussion of operant conditioning states that there are stimuli associated with learning voluntary behaviour, even though it is the consequences of that behaviour that create the learning process. These stimuli act as cues in the environment.

DISCRIMINATIVE STIMULI   As stated earlier, a *discriminative stimulus* is any stimulus that provides an organism with a cue for making a certain response in order to obtain reinforcement. For example, a stop sign is a cue for stopping, which is usually followed by negative reinforcement—people don't get a ticket or don't get hit by another vehicle. A doorknob is a cue for where to grab the door to successfully open it. In fact, if a door has a knob, people always turn it, but if it has a handle, people usually push it, right? The two kinds of opening devices each bring forth a different response from people, and their reward is opening the door.

Other examples of discriminative stimuli are all around. What do you do when you are out driving and you see a vehicle with flashing lights in the rearview mirror? You slow down and hope the officer is after someone else. The point is that you *slow down*, and you do that any time you see a vehicle that *might* be a patrol car. People are so well conditioned to respond to the sight of a police vehicle by slowing down that even empty police vehicles slow down traffic.

APPLYING OPERANT CONDITIONING: BEHAVIOUR MODIFICATION

5.15 What is behaviour modification?

Operant conditioning principles such as reinforcement and shaping have been used for many years to change undesirable behaviour and create desirable responses in animals and humans—particularly in school children. The term **behaviour modification** refers to the application of operant conditioning to bring about such changes. People might recall their grade school teacher offering gold stars or some other incentive as a reward for reading a certain number of books or giving a reward such as a wooden stick that could be traded in for a treat.

✳ Explore on **mypsychlab**
Schedules of Reinforcement

behaviour modification
the use of operant conditioning techniques to bring about desired changes in behaviour.

For example, if a teacher wants to use behaviour modification to help a child learn to be more attentive during the teacher's lectures, the teacher may do the following:

1. Select a target behaviour, such as making eye contact with the teacher.
2. Choose a reinforcer. This may be a gold star applied to the child's chart on the wall, for example.
3. Put the plan in action. Every time the child makes eye contact, the teacher gives the child a gold star. Inappropriate behaviour (such as looking out of the window) is not reinforced with gold stars.
4. At the end of the day, the teacher gives the child a special treat or reward for having a certain number of gold stars. This special reward is decided on ahead of time and discussed with the child.

Both gold stars and wooden sticks can be considered *tokens*, secondary reinforcers that can be traded in for other kinds of reinforcers. The use of tokens to modify behaviour is called a token economy. LINK *to Chapter Fourteen: Psychological Therapies, p. 564.* In the example, the child is collecting gold stars to "buy" the special treat at the end of the day. When one thinks about it, the system of money is very much a token economy. People are rewarded for working for money, which they then trade in for food, shelter, and so on.

Another tool that behaviourists can use to modify behaviour is the process of *time out*. Time out is a form of mild punishment by removal in which a misbehaving animal, child, or adult is placed in a special area away from the attention of others. Essentially, the organism is being "removed" from any possibility of positive reinforcement in the form of attention. When used with children, time out should be limited to one minute for each year of age, with a maximum time out of 10 minutes (longer than that and the child can forget why the time out occurred).

Applied behaviour analysis (ABA) is the modern term for a form of behaviour modification that uses shaping techniques to mould a desired behaviour or response. It can be said to have begun with the work of Lovaas (1964) and his associates, although the basic techniques are those first outlined by Skinner. Lovaas used small pieces of candy as reinforcers to teach social skills and language to children with *autism*. (Autism is a disorder in which the person has great difficulty in communicating with others, often refusing to look at another person. People who are autistic may also fail to learn to speak at all, and they normally do not like to be touched. The character played by Dustin Hoffman in the movie *Rain Man* was autistic.)

In ABA, skills are broken down to their simplest steps and then taught to the autistic child through a system of reinforcement. Prompts (such as moving a child's face back to looking at the teacher or the task) are given as needed when the child is learning a skill or refuses to cooperate. As the child begins to master a skill and receives reinforcement in the form of treats or praise, the prompts are gradually withdrawn until the child can do the skill independently. ABA is the most successful treatment for children with autism (Frea & Vittimberga, 2000). As a result, in Canada, most provinces now fund ABA programs. ABA is a growing field, with many Canadian universities offering excellent programs at both the undergraduate and graduate levels. A person graduating from one of these programs may act as a consultant to schools or other institutions or may set up a private practice. Typical uses for ABA are helping children with disorders, training animals, and developing effective teaching methods for children and adults of all levels of mental abilities (Baer et al., 1968).

A relatively newer technique called **neurofeedback** has been used to treat a child's attention problems in the classroom. Although this technique uses the latest in technology, the basic principles behind it are much older. Neurofeedback involves

applied behaviour analysis (ABA)
modern term for a form of behaviour modification that uses shaping techniques to mould a desired behaviour or response.

neurofeedback
form of biofeedback using brain-scanning devices to provide feedback about brain activity in an effort to modify behaviour.

trying to change brain-wave activity. In neurofeedback, the person is connected to an *electroencephalograph*, a machine that records the brain's electrical activity. Neurofeedback devices can be integrated into video-game–style programs. In one case, a young boy with attention problems was able to make a car on a screen go faster or slower in response to his own changing brain activity, which reflected his mental state of relaxation or excitement (Gevensleben, 2009; Radford, 2004).

Neurofeedback has been used to treat a number of disorders and conditions in the last few years, including epilepsy (Sterman, 2000; Sterman & Lantz, 2001), anxiety disorders (Egner et al., 2002; Norris et al., 2001), depression and anger (Hammond, 2001a; Putnam, 2001), drug addiction (Trudeau, 2000), chronic fatigue syndrome (Hammond, 2001b; Mueller et al., 2001), obsessive-compulsive disorder (Hammond, 2003), autism (Jarusiewicz, 2002), and attention-deficit hyperactivity disorder (Linden et al., 1996; Monastra et al., 2002; Rossiter & La Vaque, 1995). Playing a video game to help solve problems such as anxiety and attention problems? It sounds like a child's dream world.

◄●─ **Simulate** on **mypsychlab**
Neurofeedback for ASD

PRACTICE QUIZ: HOW MUCH DO YOU REMEMBER?

Pick the best answer.

1. Jessica's mother was upset to find that Jessica had used her crayons to draw flowers on her bedroom wall. Her mother took the crayons away from her and made Jessica wash the drawings off the wall. Which of the following statements is true for Jessica?
   a. Having her crayons taken away was a form of punishment by removal.
   b. Being made to wash off the drawings was a form of punishment by application.
   c. Having her crayons taken away was a form of negative reinforcement.
   d. Both a and b.

2. Which schedule of reinforcement best illustrates the responses of a person playing a VLT?
   a. fixed ratio
   b. variable ratio
   c. fixed interval
   d. variable interval

3. Which of the following is NOT a problem with punishment?
   a. The effect of punishment is often temporary.
   b. Severe punishment creates fear and anxiety.
   c. Mild punishment can be paired with reinforcement of the correct behaviour.
   d. Aggressive punishment can model aggressive behaviour for the child.

4. Professor Elliot told his students that if his door was open, it meant that he was available to them and would gladly answer any ques-

tions they might have. But if his door was pushed almost completely shut, it meant that he was busy and would prefer not to answer questions at that time. Professor Elliot's door being open was a _____ for _____.
   a. discriminative stimulus; asking questions
   b. discriminative stimulus; not asking questions
   c. discriminative response; asking questions
   d. discriminative response; not asking questions

5. What is the most likely explanation for why fear caused by severe punishment tends to make the punishment ineffective?
   a. Fear causes the child to remember the behaviour that was punished.
   b. Fear creates resentment that makes the child rebellious and disobedient.
   c. Fear interferes with the child's ability to learn from the punishment.
   d. None of the above are true.

6. Applied behaviour analysis
   a. involves the process of shaping.
   b. is useful only for teaching autistic children.
   c. is different from behaviour modification.
   d. cannot be used with animals.

Answers: 1-d, 2-b, 3-c, 4-a, 5-c, 6-a.

COGNITIVE LEARNING THEORY

5.16 *What is cognitive learning theory?*

In the early days of behaviourism, the original focus of Watson, Skinner, and many of their followers was on observable behaviour. Anything that might be occurring inside a person or animal's head during learning was considered to be of no interest to

latent learning
learning that remains hidden until its application becomes useful.

cognitive map
a mental representation of the environment.

"Bathroom? Sure, it's just down that hall to the left, jog right, left, another left, straight past two more lefts, then right, and it's at the end of the third corridor on your right."
©The New Yorker Collection 2000 Pat Byrnes from cartoonbank.com. All Rights Reserved.

the behaviourist because it could not be seen or directly measured. But in the 1950s, and more intensely in the 1960s, many psychologists were becoming aware that *cognition*, the mental events that take place inside a person's mind while behaving, could no longer be ignored (Kendler, 1985). One of these early cognitive learning scientists was Edward Tolman (1886–1959).

TOLMAN'S MAZE-RUNNING RATS: LATENT LEARNING

5.17 *What was Tolman's classic study on latent learning?*

One of psychologist Edward Tolman's best-known experiments in learning involved teaching three groups of rats the same maze, one at a time (Tolman & Honzik, 1930). In the first group, each rat was placed in the maze and rewarded with food for making its way out the other side. The rat was then placed back in the maze, rewarded, and so on until the rat could successfully solve the maze with no errors—the typical maze-learning experience (see Figure 5.10).

The second group of rats was treated exactly like the first, except that they never received any reinforcement upon exiting the maze. They were simply put back in again and again, until the tenth day of the experiment. On that day, the rats in the second group began to receive reinforcement for getting out of the maze.

The third group of rats, serving as a control group, was also not reinforced and was not given reinforcement for the entire duration of the experiment.

A strict Skinnerian behaviourist would predict that only the first group of rats would learn the maze successfully because learning depends on reinforcing consequences. At first, this seemed to be the case. The first group of rats did indeed solve the maze after a certain number of trials, whereas the second and third groups seemed to wander aimlessly around the maze until accidentally finding their way out.

On the tenth day, however, something happened that would be difficult to explain using only Skinner's basic principles. The second group of rats, upon receiving the reinforcement for the first time, *should* have then taken as long as the first group to solve the maze. Instead, they began to solve the maze almost immediately (see Figure 5.11).

Tolman concluded that the rats in the second group, while wandering around in the first nine days of the experiment, had indeed learned where all the blind alleys, wrong turns, and correct paths were. They had simply not *demonstrated* this learning because there was no reason to do so. The learning had remained hidden, or latent, until the rats had a reason to demonstrate their learning by getting to the food. Tolman called this **latent learning** and suggested that the rats may have formed a mental representation or a **cognitive map** of the maze.

Marcia Spetch and her colleagues at the University of Alberta have been studying the cognitive maps of animals and people because the ability to locate, remember, and recognize important places and objects is a fundamental aspect of survival. In her studies, Dr. Spetch uses colour monitors equipped with touch-sensitive frames. Scenes are presented on the monitors as test participants try to find a goal object by touching the monitor. Once participants can reliably find the

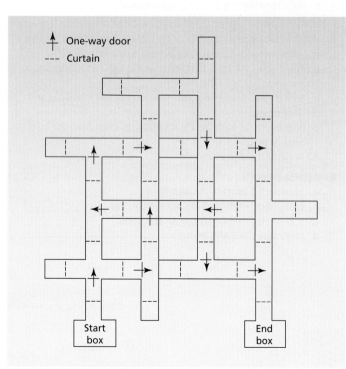

FIGURE 5.10 **A Typical Maze** This maze example is like the one used in Tolman's experiments in latent learning. A rat is placed in the Start box. The trial is over when the rat gets to the End box.

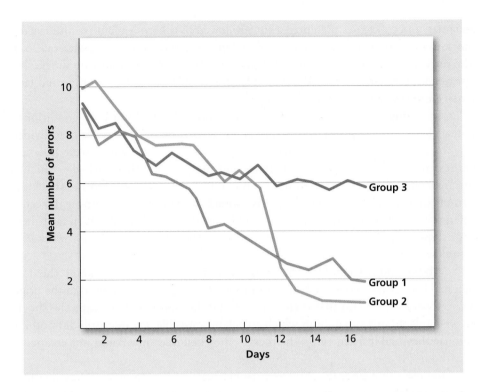

FIGURE 5.11 **Learning Curves for Three Groups of Rats**   In the results of the classic study of latent learning, Group 1 was rewarded on each day while Group 2 was rewarded for the first time on Day 11. Group 3 was never rewarded. Note the immediate change in the behaviour of Group 2 on Day 12 (Tolman & Honzik, 1930).

goal object, Dr. Spetch can manipulate the scene to determine which cues (e.g., physical landmarks and/or geometry) were most important for remembering the location of a goal object. Not surprisingly, Dr. Spetch has been able to show that pigeons, marmoset monkeys, and humans all use visual cues as beacons or landmarks when searching for a goal (MacDonald, Spetch, Kelly, & Cheng, 2004; Spetch, Cheng, & MacDonald, 1996). However, when the positions of the landmarks within a scene are changed in the images, adult humans are much better at adapting their previously learned strategy to locate the goal than pigeons, marmoset monkeys, or human children. These results suggest that most species that rely on locomotion to gain access to food and mates likely possess cognitive maps, but that the cognitive map of the adult human appears to be uniquely suited for change and adaptation.

Latent learning and cognitive maps together demonstrate that conditioned learning involves much more than simply making associations between two stimuli, or a response and a reward. It also involves gaining knowledge about important aspects of the entire behavioural context, such as how the world is organized and the consequences of making a response. This knowledge can then be used in the future to help solve problems and reach new goals, or sometimes, as in the next section, it may even impede problem solving.

SELIGMAN'S DEPRESSED DOGS: LEARNED HELPLESSNESS

5.18 *What is learned helplessness?*

Martin Seligman is now famous for founding the field of *positive psychology*, a new way of looking at the entire concept of mental health and therapy. But in the mid to late 1960s, Seligman and his colleagues accidentally discovered an unexpected phenomenon while doing experiments on dogs using classical conditioning (Seligman, 1975). Their original intention was to study escape and avoidance learning.

Simulate on mypsychlab
Latent Learning

Simulate on mypsychlab
Learned Helplessness

learned helplessness
the tendency to fail to act to escape from a situation because of a history of repeated failures in the past.

Why would the conditioned dogs refuse to move when shocked? ▶

I know some people who seem to act just ▶ like those dogs—they live in a h0orrible situation but won't leave. Is this the same thing?

Seligman and colleagues presented a tone followed by a harmless but painful electric shock to one group of dogs (Overmier & Seligman, 1967; Seligman & Maier, 1967). The dogs in this group were harnessed so that they could not escape the shock. The researchers assumed that the dogs would learn to fear the sound of the tone and later try to escape from the tone before being shocked.

These dogs, along with another group of dogs that had not been conditioned to fear the tone, were placed into a special box consisting of a low fence that divided the box into two compartments (see Figure 5.12). The dogs, which were now un-harnessed, could easily see over the fence and jump over if they wished—which is precisely what the dogs that had not been conditioned did as soon as the shock occurred. Imagine the researchers' surprise when, instead of jumping over the fence when the tone sounded, the previously conditioned dogs just sat there. In fact, these dogs showed distress but didn't try to jump over the fence *even when the shock itself began.*

Why would the conditioned dogs refuse to move when shocked? The dogs that had been harnessed while being conditioned had apparently learned in the original tone/shock situation that there was nothing they could do to escape the shock. So when placed in a situation in which escape was possible, the dogs still did nothing because they had learned to be "helpless." They believed they could not escape, so they did not try.

I know some people who seem to act just like those dogs—they live in a horrible situation but won't leave. Is this the same thing? Seligman extended this theory of **learned helplessness**, the tendency to fail to act to escape from a situation because of a history of repeated failures in the past, to explain *depression.* Depressed people seem to lack normal emotions and become somewhat apathetic, often staying in unpleasant work environments or bad marriages or relationships rather than trying to escape or better their situation. Seligman proposed that this depressive behaviour is a form of learned helplessness. Depressed people may have learned in the past that they seem to have no control over what happens to them (Alloy & Clements, 1998).

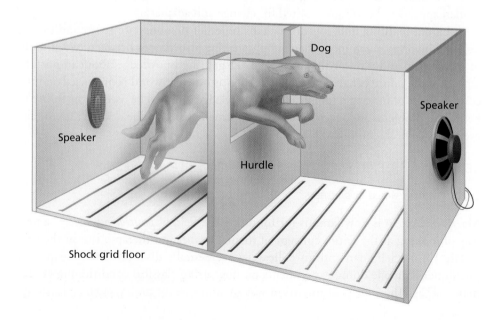

FIGURE 5.12 **Seligman's Apparatus** In Seligman's studies of learned helplessness, dogs were placed in a two-sided box. Dogs that had no prior experience with being unable to escape a shock would quickly jump over the hurdle in the centre of the box to land on the "safe" side. Dogs that had previously learned that escape was impossible would stay on the side of the box in which the shock occurred, not even trying to go over the hurdle.

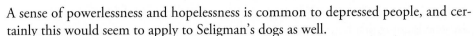

A sense of powerlessness and hopelessness is common to depressed people, and certainly this would seem to apply to Seligman's dogs as well.

Think about how this might apply to other situations. Many students feel that they are bad at math because they have had problems with it in the past. Is it possible that this belief could make them not try as hard or study as much as they should? Isn't this kind of thinking also an example of learned helplessness?

KOHLER'S SMART CHIMP: INSIGHT LEARNING

5.19 *What is insight?*

Another exploration of the cognitive elements of learning came about almost by accident. Wolfgang Köhler (1887–1967) was a Gestalt psychologist who became marooned on an island in the Canaries (a group of islands off the coast of North Africa) when World War I broke out. Stuck at the primate research lab that had first drawn him to the island, he turned to studies of animal learning.

In one of his more famous studies (Köhler, 1925), he set up a problem for one of the chimpanzees. Sultan the chimp was faced with the problem of how to get to a banana that was placed just out of his reach outside his cage. Sultan solved this problem relatively easily, first trying to reach through the bars with his arm, and then using a stick that was lying in the cage to rake the banana into the cage. As chimpanzees are natural tool users, this behaviour is not surprising and is still nothing more than simple trial-and-error learning.

But then the problem was made more difficult. The banana was placed just out of reach of Sultan's extended arm with the stick in his hand. At this point there were two sticks lying around in the cage, which could be fitted together to make a single pole that would be long enough to reach the banana. Sultan first tried one stick, and then the other (simple trial and error). After about an hour of trying, Sultan seemed to have a sudden flash of inspiration. He pushed one stick out of the cage as far as it would go toward the banana and then pushed the other stick behind the first one. Of course, when he tried to draw the sticks back, only the one in his hand came. He jumped up and down and was very excited, and when Köhler gave him the second stick, he sat on the floor of the cage and looked at them carefully. He then fitted one stick into the other and retrieved his banana. Köhler called Sultan's rapid "perception of relationships" **insight** and determined that insight could not be gained through trial-and-error learning alone (Köhler, 1925). Although Thorndike and other early learning theorists believed that animals could not demonstrate insight, Köhler's work seems to demonstrate that insight requires a sudden "coming together" of all the elements of a problem in a kind of "aha" moment that is not predicted by traditional animal learning studies. More recent research has also found support for the concept of animal insight (Heinrich, 2000; Heyes, 1998; Zentall, 2000), but there is still controversy over how to interpret the results of those studies (Wynne, 1999).

Another of Köhler's chimpanzees, Grande, has just solved the problem of how to get to the banana by stacking boxes. Does this meet the criteria for insight, or was it simple trial-and-error learning?

OBSERVATIONAL LEARNING

5.20 *What is observational learning?*

Another type of learning theory that departs from the traditional theories of Pavlov and Skinner and depends at least partly on cognition is that of **observational learning**,

insight
the sudden perception of relationships among various parts of a problem, allowing the solution to the problem to come quickly.

observational learning
learning new behaviour by watching a model perform that behaviour.

Explore on **mypsychlab**
Bandura's Study on Observational Learning

Ah, but would that child have imitated the model if the model had been punished? Wouldn't the *consequences* of the model's behaviour make a difference? ▶

the learning of new behaviour through the observation of a model (watching someone else who is doing that behaviour).

BANDURA AND THE BOBO DOLL

5.21 *What was Bandura's classic Bobo doll study?*

Bandura's classic study in observational learning involved having a preschool child in a room in which the experimenter and a model interacted with toys in the room in front of the child (Bandura et al., 1961). In one condition, the model interacted with the toys in a non-aggressive manner, completely ignoring the presence of a "Bobo" doll (a punch-bag doll in the shape of a clown). In another condition, the model became very aggressive with the doll, kicking it and yelling at it, throwing it in the air and hitting it with a hammer.

When each child was left alone in the room and had the opportunity to play with the toys, a camera filming through a one-way mirror caught the children who were exposed to the aggressive model beating up on the Bobo doll in exact imitation of the model. The children who saw the model ignore the doll did not act aggressively toward the toy. Obviously, the aggressive children had learned their aggressive actions from merely watching the model—with no reinforcement necessary.

Ah, but would that child have imitated the model if the model had been punished? Wouldn't the *consequences* of the model's behaviour make a difference? In later studies, Bandura showed a film of a model beating up the Bobo doll. In one condition, the children saw the model rewarded afterward. In another, the model was punished. When placed in the room with toys, the children in the first group beat up the doll, but the children in the second group did not. But when Bandura told the children in the second group that he would give them a reward if they could show him what the model in the film did, each child duplicated the model's actions. Both groups had learned from watching the model, but only the children watching the successful (rewarded) model imitated the aggression with no prompting (Bandura, 1965). Apparently, consequences do matter in motivating a child (or an adult) to imitate a particular model. The tendency for some movies and television programs to make "heroes" out of violent, aggressive "bad guys" is particularly disturbing in light of these findings. In fact, Bandura began this research to investigate possible links between children's exposure to violence on television and aggressive behaviour toward others.

The fact that learning can take place without actual performance (a kind of latent learning) is called the **learning/performance distinction**.

THE FOUR ELEMENTS OF OBSERVATIONAL LEARNING

Are there other ▶
elements of observed
behaviour that make it
more or less likely to be
learned?

Are there other elements of observed behaviour that make it more or less likely to be learned? Bandura (1986) concluded, from these studies and others, that observational learning required the presence of four elements.

5.22 *What are the four elements of observational learning?*

ATTENTION   To learn anything through observation, the learner must first pay attention to the model. For example, a person at a fancy dinner party who wants to know which utensil to use has to watch the person who seems to know what is correct. Certain characteristics of models can make attention more likely. For example, people pay more attention to those people they perceive as similar to them and to people whom they perceive as attractive.

MEMORY   The learner must also be able to retain the memory of what was done, such as remembering the steps in preparing a dish that was first seen on a cooking show.

IMITATION   The learner must be capable of reproducing, or imitating, the actions of the model. A 2-year-old might be able to watch someone tie shoelaces and might even remember most of the steps, but the 2-year-old's chubby little fingers will not have the dexterity necessary for actually tying the laces. A person with extremely weak ankles might be able to watch and remember how some ballet move was accomplished but will not be able to reproduce it.

MOTIVATION   Finally, the learner must have the desire to perform the action. That person at the fancy dinner, for example, might not care which fork or which knife is the "proper" one to use. Also, if a person expects a reward because he or she has been given one in the past or has been promised a future reward (such as the children in the second group of Bandura's study), or has witnessed a model getting a reward (such as the children in the first group), that person will be much more likely to imitate the observed behaviour. Successful models are powerful figures for imitation but rarely would we be motivated to imitate someone who fails or is punished.

(An easy way to remember the four elements of modelling is to remember *AMIM*, which stands for the first letters of each of the four elements. This is a good example of using a strategy to improve memory.)

Albert Bandura's famous Bobo doll experiment. This doll was used to demonstrate the impact of observing an adult model performing aggressive behaviour on the later aggressive behaviour of children. The children in these photos are imitating the adult model's behaviour even though they believe they are alone and are not being watched.

PRACTICE QUIZ: HOW MUCH DO YOU REMEMBER?

Pick the best answer.

1. Cognition refers to
   a. behaviour that is observable and external.
   b. behaviour that is directly measurable.
   c. the mental events that take place while a person is behaving.
   d. memories.

2. In Tolman's maze study, the fact that the group of rats receiving reinforcement only after the tenth day of the study solved the maze far more quickly than did the rats who had been reinforced from the first day can be interpreted to mean that these particular rats
   a. were much smarter than the other rats.
   b. had already learned the maze in the first nine days.
   c. had the opportunity to cheat by watching the other rats.
   d. were very hungry and therefore learned much more quickly.

3. Cognitive maps are
   a. mental representations of our environment.
   b. similar in pigeons and humans.
   c. similar in marmoset monkeys and humans.
   d. both a and c are correct

4. Seligman found many similarities between his "helpless" dogs and people suffering from
   a. aggressive behaviour syndrome.
   b. mental illness.
   c. schizophrenia.
   d. depression.

5. Köhler determined that Sultan's two-stick solution to the banana problem was an example of insight because it was
   a. the result of trial-and-error learning.
   b. sudden and rapid.
   c. arrived at after a long time period.
   d. intelligent.

6. In Bandura's study with the Bobo doll, the children in the group that saw the model punished did not imitate the model at first. They would imitate the model only if given a reward for doing so. The fact that these children had obviously learned the behaviour without actually performing it is an example of
   a. latent learning.   c. classical conditioning.
   b. operant conditioning.   d. insight learning.

7. Miranda wanted to make a casserole she saw on a food show on television. She bought the ingredients, put them together, baked it, and served it at dinner that night. To her horror, it tasted awful. She realized that she had left out a key ingredient and vowed next time to write everything down as she watched the show. Miranda's dinner disaster was an example of failing at which of Bandura's four elements of observational learning?
   a. attention   c. imitation
   b. memory   d. motivation

APPLYING PSYCHOLOGY TO EVERYDAY LIFE: CAN YOU REALLY TOILET TRAIN YOUR CAT?

5.23 *What is a real-world example of the use of conditioning?*

(This article has been excerpted with permission of the author and cat-trainer extraordinaire Karawynn Long. Karawynn Long is a published writer and web designer who lives in Seattle with her family. Sadly, since this article was written, her cat Misha passed away. Long can be reached at her website **www.karawynn.net/mishacat/ toilet.html**. The italicized words in square brackets are the text authors' comments.)

There have been more books and articles about toilet-training cats than you'd think. In the summer of 1989, when Misha was a small kitten with big ears and enough meow for five cats, I searched out and read a half-dozen of them. And then tried it myself, and discovered there were a couple of things they all failed to mention ... here's what worked for me and Misha.

The central idea is that the transition from litter box to toilet should be accomplished in a series of stages. [*This is shaping.*] You make a small change and then give your cat time to adjust before you make another small change. If at any time Felix gives the whole thing up and goes on the rug instead, you're pushing him too far too fast; back up a stage or two and try again, more slowly.

READY? FIRST START BY TRAINING YOURSELF ...

The very most important thing to remember is: Lid Up, Seat Down. Post a note on the back of the door or the lid of the toilet if you think you (or your housemates or guests) might forget. And if you are accustomed to closing the bathroom door when it's empty, you'll have to break that habit too. [*In operant conditioning, this is part of "preparing the training arena."*]

Begin by moving the cat's current litter box from wherever it is to one side of the toilet. Make sure he knows where it is and uses it. Rest (this means doing nothing for a period of between a day and a week, depending on how flappable your cat is). Next put something—a stack of newspapers, a phone book, a cardboard box—under the litter box to raise it, say, about an inch. (Magazines are too slick; you don't want the litter box sliding around and making your cat feel insecure. Tape the litter box down if you need to.) Rest. Get another box or phone book and raise it a little higher. Rest. Continue this process until the bottom of the litter box is level with the top of the toilet seat. (For Misha I raised it about two inches per day.) [*Notice that this is the step-by-step process typically used in shaping.*]

At the beginning of this process, your cat could just step into the litter box; later he began jumping up into it, until at some point he probably started jumping up onto the toilet seat first and stepping into the box from there. Lift the seat on your toilet and measure the inside diameter of the top of the bowl at its widest point. Venture forth and buy a metal mixing bowl of that diameter. Do not (I discovered this the hard way) substitute a plastic bowl. A plastic bowl will not support the cat's weight and will bend, dropping into the toilet bowl and spilling litter everywhere, not to mention startling the cat.

Now you move the litter box over so that it's sitting directly over the toilet seat. (If your cat has shown reluctance over previous changes, you might want to split this into two stages, moving it halfway onto the seat and then fully over.) Take away the stack of phone books or whatever you used. Rest. [*Again, notice that everything has to be done in small steps. This is the heart of the shaping process—requiring too large a step will stop the process.*]

Here's the cool part. Take away the litter box entirely. (Ta da!) Nestle the metal mixing bowl inside the toilet bowl and lower the seat. Fill the bowl with about two

Misha's first attempt without the box. He scored two out of a possible four.

inches of litter (all of this is much easier if you have the tiny granules of litter that can be scooped out and flushed).

Naturally, any humans using the toilet at this point will want to remove the metal bowl prior to their own use and replace it afterward. The next week or two the whole process is likely to be something of an annoyance; if you begin to think it's not worth it, just remember that you will never have to clean a litter box again.

Watch your cat using the bathroom in the metal bowl. Count the number of feet he gets up on the toilet seat (as opposed to down in the bowl of litter). The higher the number, the luckier you are and the easier your job is going to be …

… because next you have to teach him proper squatting posture. Catch him beginning to use the toilet as much of the time as possible and show him where his feet are supposed to go. Just lift them right out of the bowl and place them on the seat (front legs in the middle, hind legs on the outside). If he starts out with three or, heaven forbid, all four feet in the bowl, just get the front two feet out first. Praise him all over the place every time he completes the activity in this position. [*The praise is the positive reinforcement, and should be done with each successful step.*]

Misha demonstrates proper squatting posture. Note the look of firm concentration.

(Misha is very doglike in that he craves approval and praise. If your cat is indifferent to this sort of thing, you can also reward him with small food treats and wean him from them later when the toilet behaviour has "set." Just keep the treats as small and infrequent as possible—half a Pounce or similar treat per occasion should be plenty.) [*If treats are too frequent, it will make it difficult to phase out the reinforcer after the behaviour is well learned.*]

When he is regularly using the toilet with his front feet out (and some cats naturally start from this position), begin lifting a hind foot out and placing it on the seat outside the front paws. Your cat will probably find this awkward at first and try to replace the foot in the litter. Be persistent. Move that foot four times in a row if you have to, until it stays there. Praise and/or treat.

Repeat with the other hind foot, until your cat learns to balance in that squat. Once he's getting all four feet regularly on the seat, it's all easy from here.

Which is fortunate, because the last bit is also the most unpleasant. I suggest that you postpone this stage until you have at least a weekend, and preferably several days, when you (or another responsible party) will be at home most of the time. I skipped through this part in about two days; I only hope that your cat allows you to move along that fast.

Begin reducing the litter in the bowl. Go as fast as he'll feel comfortable with, because as the litter decreases, the odor increases. You'll want to be home at this point so that you can praise him and dump out the contents of the bowl immediately after he's finished, to minimize both the smell and the possibility that your cat, in a confused attempt to minimize the smell on his own, tries to cover it up with litter that no longer exists and ends up tracking unpleasantness into the rest of the house.

By the time you're down to a token teaspoonful of litter in the bottom of the bowl, your next-door neighbors will probably be aware of the precise instant your cat has used the toilet. This is as bad as it gets. The next time you rinse out the metal bowl, put a little bit of water in the bottom. Increase the water level each time, just as you decreased the litter level. Remember—if at any point Felix looks nervous enough about the change to give the whole thing up and take his business to the corner behind the door, back up a step or two and try the thing again more slowly. [*Shaping takes a lot of patience, depending on the behaviour being shaped and the learning ability of the animal—or person.*]

Once the water in the mixing bowl is a couple of inches deep and your cat is comfortable with the whole thing, you get to perform the last bit of magic. Take the mixing bowl away, leaving the bare toilet. (Lid Up, Seat Down.)

Voila! Your cat is now toilet trained.

Some useful books on using operant conditioning to toilet train cats:

Brotman, E. (2001). *How to Toilet Train Your Cat: The Education of Mango*. Sherman Oaks: CA, Bird Brain Press.

Kunkel, P., & Mead K. P. (1991). *How to Toilet Train Your Cat: 21 Days to a Litter-Free Home*. New York: Workman Publishing Company.

Questions for Further Discussion

1. Why would this technique probably not work with a dog?

2. Are there any safety concerns with teaching a cat in this way?

3. Are there any other difficulties that might arise when doing this training?

CHAPTER SUMMARY

Definition of Learning

5.1 *What is learning?*

- Learning is any relatively permanent change in behaviour brought about by experience or practice and is different from maturation, which is genetically controlled.

It Makes Your Mouth Water: Classical Conditioning

5.2 *What is classical conditioning, and who first studied it?*

- Pavlov accidentally discovered the phenomenon in which one stimulus can, through pairing with another stimulus, come to produce a similar response. He called this *classical conditioning*.

5.3 *What are the important concepts in classical conditioning?*

- The unconditioned stimulus (UCS) is the stimulus that is naturally occurring and produces the reflex, or involuntary unconditioned response (UCR). Both are called *unconditioned* because they are not learned.
- The conditioned stimulus (CS) begins as a neutral stimulus, but when paired with the unconditioned stimulus eventually begins to elicit the reflex on its own. The reflex response to the conditioned stimulus is called the conditioned response (CR), and both stimulus and response are learned.

5.4 *What was Pavlov's classic experiment in conditioning?*

- Pavlov paired a sound with the presentation of food to dogs and discovered several principles for classical conditioning: The neutral stimulus (NS) and UCS must be paired several times and the CS must precede the UCS by only a few seconds.
- Other important aspects of classical conditioning include stimulus generalization, stimulus discrimination, extinction, spontaneous recovery, and higher-order conditioning.

5.5 *What is a conditioned emotional response?*

- Watson was able to demonstrate that an emotional disorder called a *phobia* could be learned through classical conditioning. He did this by exposing a baby to a white rat and a loud noise, producing conditioned fear of the rat in the baby.
- Vicarious conditioning is classical conditioning of a reflex response or emotion by watching the reaction of another person.

- Conditioned taste aversions occur when an organism becomes nauseated some time after eating a certain food, which then becomes aversive to the organism.
- Some kinds of conditioned responses are more easily learned than others because of biological preparedness.

5.6 *How is classical conditioning related to advertising?*

- Advertisers often use classical conditioning principles to persuade you to buy something. When advertisers associate well-liked music or famous people with their products they are using the principles of classical conditioning.

5.7 *Why does classical conditioning work?*

- Pavlov believed that the NS became a substitute for the UCS through association in time.
- The cognitive perspective asserts that the CS has to provide some kind of information or expectancy about the coming of the UCS for conditioning to occur.

What's in It for Me? Operant Conditioning

5.8 *What is operant conditioning and Thorndike's Law of Effect?*

- Operant conditioning is learning to make voluntary responses through the effects of positive and negative consequences.
- Thorndike developed the Law of Effect: A response followed by a pleasurable consequence will be repeated, but a response followed by an unpleasant consequence will not be repeated.

5.9 *What was Skinner's contribution to operant conditioning?*

- B. F. Skinner named the learning of voluntary responses *operant conditioning* because voluntary responses are what we use to operate in the world around us.

5.10 *What are the important concepts in operant conditioning?*

- Skinner developed the concept of reinforcement, the process of strengthening a response by following it with a pleasurable, rewarding consequence.
- A primary reinforcer is something such as food or water that satisfies a basic, natural drive, whereas a secondary reinforcer is something that becomes reinforcing only after being paired with a primary reinforcer.

- In positive reinforcement, a response is followed by the presentation of a pleasurable stimulus, whereas in negative reinforcement, a response is followed by the removal or avoidance of an unpleasant stimulus.

- Shaping is the reinforcement of successive approximations to some final goal, allowing behaviour to be moulded from simple behaviour already present in the organism.

- Extinction, generalization, discrimination, and spontaneous recovery also occur in operant conditioning.

5.11 *What is the difference between negative reinforcement and punishment?*

- Negative reinforcement increases the likelihood of some response by removing, escaping from, or avoiding an unpleasant stimulus.

- Punishment is any event or object that decreases the likelihood of some response. Punishment can occur by application (addition or experience of something unpleasant, such as a scolding) or by removal (some pleasurable stimulus is removed, such as your computer time is taken away).

5.12 *What are the schedules of reinforcement?*

- Continuous reinforcement occurs when each and every correct response is followed by a reinforcer.

- Partial reinforcement, in which only some correct responses are followed by reinforcement, is much more resistant to extinction. This is called the *partial reinforcement effect*.

- In a fixed ratio schedule of reinforcement, a certain number of responses is required before reinforcement is given.

- In a variable ratio schedule of reinforcement, a varying number of responses is required to obtain reinforcement.

- In a fixed interval schedule of reinforcement, at least one correct response must be made within a set interval of time to obtain reinforcement.

- In a variable interval schedule of reinforcement, reinforcement follows the first correct response made after an interval of time that changes for each reinforcement opportunity.

5.13 *Why are video lottery terminals and other games of chance so addictive?*

- VLTs are highly addictive to some individuals because they are programmed to pay out using a variable ratio schedule, which produces very fast responding that is difficult to extinguish because you never know which "play" will be a winner.

- VLTs also use flashing lights and ringing bells on winning "plays" that quickly become associated with the good feeling of winning. Soon the lights and sounds of the VLTs that may come from other machines may make you feel good, even if you don't win.

- For some people, VLTs may offer an escape from the pressures and anxieties of everyday life, which can become very reinforcing.

5.14 *How do operant stimuli control behaviour?*

- Discriminative stimuli are cues, such as a flashing light on a police car or a sign on a door that says "Open," that provide information about what response to make to obtain reinforcement.

5.15 *What is behaviour modification?*

- Operant conditioning can be used in many settings, on both animals and people, to change or modify behaviour. This use is termed *behaviour modification* and includes the use of reinforcement and shaping to alter behaviour.

- Token economies are a type of behaviour modification in which secondary reinforcers, or tokens, are used.

- Applied behaviour analysis (ABA) is the modern version of behaviour modification and makes use of shaping by breaking desired behaviour down into discrete steps.

Cognitive Learning Theory

5.16 *What is cognitive learning theory?*

- Cognitive learning theory states that learning requires cognition, or the influence of an organism's thought processes.

5.17 *What was Tolman's classic study on latent learning?*

- Tolman found that rats that were allowed to wander in a maze but were not reinforced still showed evidence of having learned the maze once reinforcement becomes possible. He termed this hidden learning *latent learning*, a form of cognitive learning.

5.18 *What is learned helplessness?*

- Seligman found that dogs that had been placed in an inescapable situation failed to try to escape when it became possible to do so, remaining in the painful situation as if helpless to leave. Seligman called this phenomenon *learned helplessness* and found parallels between learned helplessness and depression.

5.19 *What is insight?*

- Köhler found evidence of insight, the sudden perception of the relationships among elements of a problem, in chimpanzees.

Observational Learning

5.20 *What is observational learning?*

- Observational learning is learning through watching others perform, or model, certain actions.

5.21 *What was Bandura's classic Bobo doll study?*

- Bandura's famous Bobo doll experiment demonstrated that young children will imitate the aggressive actions of a model even when there is no reinforcement for doing so.

5.22 *What are the four elements of observational learning?*

- Bandura determined that four elements need to be present for observational learning to occur: attention, memory, imitation, and motivation.

Applying Psychology to Everyday Life: Can You Really Toilet Train Your Cat?

5.23 *What is a real-world example of the use of conditioning?*

- Writer Karawynn Long used shaping, reinforcement, and classical conditioning to train her cat to use the toilet in her bathroom instead of a litter box.

5 KEY TERMS

applied behaviour analysis (ABA)   202
behaviour modification   201
biological preparedness   186
classical conditioning   179
cognitive map   205
cognitive perspective   187
conditioned emotional response
  (CER)   185
conditioned response (CR)   180
conditioned stimulus (CS)   180
conditioned taste aversion   186
continuous reinforcement   198
discriminative stimulus   197
extinction   182
fixed interval schedule of reinforcement   199
fixed ratio schedule of reinforcement   198
higher-order conditioning   183

insight   207
latent learning   205
Law of Effect   189
learned helplessness   207
learning/performance distinction   208
negative reinforcement   192
neurofeedback   202
neutral stimulus (NS)   180
observational learning   208
operant   190
operant conditioning   189
partial reinforcement effect   198
positive reinforcement   192
primary reinforcer   191
punishment   193
punishment by application   193
punishment by removal   193

reinforcement   190
reinforcer   182
secondary reinforcer   191
shaping   196
spontaneous recovery   182
stimulus discrimination   182
stimulus generalization   182
stimulus substitution   187
successive approximation   196
unconditioned response (UCR)   179
unconditioned stimulus (UCS)   179
variable interval schedule of
  reinforcement   200
variable ratio schedule of reinforcement   199
vicarious conditioning   185

TEST YOURSELF

Pick the best answer.

1. Learning is
   a. any temporary change in behaviour.
   b. a change in behaviour due to maturation.
   c. any permanent change in behaviour brought about by experience.
   d. any permanent change in behaviour due to maturation.

2. In your school dorm, any time you take a shower, someone always flushes the toilet and causes the water in your shower to turn icy cold, making you cringe. After several episodes like this, you find that you tend to cringe whenever you hear a toilet flush, no matter where you are. In this example, what is the conditioned stimulus?
   a. the cold water
   b. the sound of the flushing
   c. the cringing reaction
   d. the sight of a toilet

3. You move out of your dorm into an apartment shared with three other people. Unlike the shower in the dorm, this shower does not turn cold when the toilet is flushed, and you eventually stop cringing every time you hear the flushing sound. What has occurred?
   a. stimulus generalization
   b. stimulus discrimination
   c. spontaneous recovery
   d. extinction

4. When one conditioned stimulus is used to create another, this is called
   a. spontaneous recovery.
   b. extinction.
   c. higher-order conditioning.
   d. shaping.

5. Tenia ate out with some friends and had fried oysters. The next morning she was nauseated and sick for much of the day. The next time she saw someone eating fried oysters, she felt queasy and quickly looked away. Her queasiness at the sight of the fried oysters was probably due to
   a. higher-order conditioning.
   b. a conditioned taste aversion.
   c. stimulus substitution.
   d. stimulus generalization.

6. Research suggests that classical conditioning plays an important role in drug addiction. The UCS is the drug, the UCR is the body's response to the drug, and the CS is the environment where the repeated drug exposure takes place. If this is the case, what might you expect to find if you interview heroin addicts who survived an overdose?
   a. The majority overdosed because they tried to administer a higher dose.
   b. The majority overdosed because they received a bad supply of heroin.
   c. The majority overdosed because they were using in an unfamiliar place or under unfamiliar circumstances.
   d. The majority overdosed because they wanted to die.

7. To prevent an outbreak of meningitis, children are lined up to receive a vaccination. Some of the children cry after receiving their shot and soon thereafter all the children in the line are crying even before getting the vaccination. This is an example of
   a. emotional conditioning.
   b. vicarious conditioning.
   c. biological preparedness.
   d. stimulus substitution.

8. The fact that some kinds of stimuli (such as a taste) are more easily and quickly connected to a response (such as nausea) is explained by the concept of
   a. biological preparedness.
   b. psychological preparedness.
   c. instinctive drift.
   d. stimulus substitution.

9. In classical conditioning, the _____ are important in learning, but in operant conditioning, it is the _____ that determine whether learning will occur.
   a. antecedents; consequences
   b. consequences; antecedents
   c. rewards; punishments
   d. punishments; rewards

10. Who added the concept of reinforcement to learning theory?
    a. John Watson
    b. Edward Thorndike
    c. B. F. Skinner
    d. Ivan Pavlov

11. Which of the following is an example of a secondary reinforcer?
    a. receiving a candy bar
    b. receiving a glass of water
    c. petting a dog
    d. praising a child

12. Joaquin's parents have given his 2-year-old daughter, Marie, a very noisy jack-in-the-box toy for her birthday. Marie loves to turn the crank and make the puppet pop up, over and over and over. Desperate to have some peace and quiet, Joaquin gives Marie a popsicle, which distracts her and produces the quiet he was craving. But when the popsicle is finished, Marie goes back to the toy, cranking and cranking. Joaquin tries another popsicle. What kind of reinforcement process is taking place in this situation?
    a. Marie is being positively reinforced for playing with the toy by receiving the treat.
    b. Joaquin is being positively reinforced for giving her the treat by the quiet that follows.
    c. Joaquin is being negatively reinforced for giving her the treat by the absence of the noise.
    d. Both a and c are correct.

13. Sherry wants her dog to heel on command. At first she gives the dog a treat for coming to her when she speaks the command, "Heel!" Then she rewards the dog only when it stands at her side when she gives the command and, finally, rewards the dog only when it is at her side and facing front. Sherry is using
    a. higher-order conditioning.
    c. shaping.
    b. biological readiness.
    d. generalization.

14. One-year-old Ben learned to say the word *duck* when his mother showed him a duck in their backyard. That evening he sees a cartoon with a rooster in it and says "duck," pointing to the rooster. Ben is exhibiting
    a. generalization.
    c. spontaneous recovery.
    b. discrimination.
    d. shaping.

15. Dennis buys a lottery ticket every Saturday, using the same set of numbers. Although he has won $25 on only one occasion, he keeps buying the tickets. In fact, he's a little afraid that if he doesn't buy a ticket, that would be the one that would win really big. The fact that Dennis seems addicted to buying lottery tickets is a common characteristic of which schedule of reinforcement?
    a. fixed ratio
    c. variable ratio
    b. fixed interval
    d. variable interval

16. Which type of gambling is considered to be the most addictive?
    a. poker
    c. lottery ticket buying
    b. horse-racing
    d. video lottery terminals

17. Which of the following individuals is most likely to spend the most money on lottery tickets?
    a. Ted, who runs an automotive dealership
    b. Sara, who is a nurse
    c. Bill, who is retired and lives on a government pension
    d. Tina, who is on maternity leave from her high school

18. Liz failed her math test, so her parents told her that she could not play video games until her grade improved. Her parents are using

    a. positive reinforcement.
    c. punishment by removal.
    b. negative reinforcement.
    d. punishment by application.

19. To make punishment more effective, it should be
    a. very intense.
    b. applied every other time the bad behaviour occurs.
    c. an aggressive type, such as spanking.
    d. paired with reinforcement of the correct behaviour.

20. In applied behaviour analysis,
    a. skills are broken down into their smallest steps and then reinforced.
    b. punishment by application is often used to control behaviour.
    c. researchers develop new theories of learning rather than actually solving problems.
    d. the basic form of learning used is classical conditioning.

21. The first day on campus was very frustrating for Tyler. He couldn't seem to find any of his classes. Just a week later he easily finds one of the campus computer labs that he has never been to before. This change in performance is likely the result of
    a. the development of a cognitive map of the campus.
    b. stimulus generalization.
    c. insight.
    d. learning/performance distinction.

22. Jody has had repeated failures at asking guys out on dates. Finally, she gives up. One day at the office a really nice guy seems interested in her, but she refuses to even approach him. What concept might explain her reluctance?
    a. latent learning
    c. insight learning
    b. learned helplessness
    d. observational learning

23. Jared's father is ill and cannot prepare his famous chili recipe, which Jared has watched his father make many times. When his father tells Jared that he must cook the chili, he panics at first. But then Jared finds that he knows how to put the recipe together anyway. His ability to prepare the recipe is an example of
    a. latent learning.
    c. insight learning.
    b. learned helplessness.
    d. discovery learning.

24. Archimedes was told by the king to find a way to prove that a gold crown was really gold. While in his bath, he noticed the water that his body displaced out of the tub and shouted, "Eureka!" which means "I have found it!" If the crown was really gold, it should displace the same amount of water as an equal amount of real gold. This is a famous example of
    a. latent learning.
    c. insight.
    b. learned helplessness.
    d. observational learning.

25. Jared realized that he had learned how to prepare his father's famous chili recipe by watching his father in the kitchen for many years. This kind of learning is called
    a. discovery learning.
    c. insight learning.
    b. helplessness learning.
    d. observational learning.

Answers: 1-c, 2-b, 3-d, 4-c, 5-b, 6-c, 7-b, 8-a, 9-a, 10-c, 11-d, 12-d, 13-c, 14-a, 15-c, 16-d, 17-c, 18-c, 19-d, 20-a, 21-a, 22-b, 23-a, 24-c, 25-d.

ScanLife™ Barcode

To access more tests and your own personalized study plan that will help you focus on the areas you need to master before your next class test, be sure to go to **www.MyPsychLab.com**, Pearson Education Canada's online psychology website, available with the access code packaged with your book.

5.1

Learning

any relatively permanent change in behaviour brought about by experience or practice; is different from maturation, which is genetically controlled

5.2–4

- **discovered by Ivan Pavlov** — focused on observable, measurable behaviour
  worked with salivating dogs

  - **several key elements must be present and experienced**
    - **unconditioned stimulus (UCS)**
    - **unconditioned response (UCR)**
    - **conditioned stimulus (CS)**
    - **conditioned response (CR)**

Classical Conditioning (part 1)

(learning to make an involuntary response to a stimulus other than the original, natural stimulus that normally produces it)

- **basic principles for classical conditioning to occur**
  - CS must come before the UCS
  - CS and UCS must come very close together in time (< 5 sec)
  - CS must be paired with the UCS many times
  - CS must be distinct from other competing stimuli

- **key features**
  - **stimulus generalization**
  - **stimulus discrimination**
  - **extinction**
  - **spontaneous recovery**
  - **higher-order conditioning**

Before Conditioning

Neutral Stimulus (NS) Bell — No Salivation

During Conditioning

Neutral Stimulus (NS) Bell — Unconditioned Stimulus (UCS) Food — Unconditioned Response (UCR) Salivation

After Conditioning

Conditioned Stimulus (CS) Bell — Conditioned Response (CR) Salivation

5.5–7

Classical Conditioning (part 2)

(learning to make a involuntary response to a stimulus other than the original, natural stimulus that normally produces it)

- **other features**
  - **conditioned emotional responses**
  - **conditioned taste aversion**
- **Why does it work?**
  - Pavlov
  - cognitive perspective
  - **vicarious conditioning**
- **used in advertising to persuade**

"Bathroom? Sure, it's just down the hall to the left, jog right, left, another left, straight past two more lefts, then right, and it's at the end of the third corridor on your right."

P. BYRNES.

5.16–19

Cognitive Learning Theory

(focuses on role of cognition, or thought processes, on learning)

- **Tolman**
  worked with rats in a maze, finding evidence of latent learning

- **Seligman**
  originally studying escape and avoidance learning in dogs, finding evidence of learned helplessness

- **Köhler**
  worked with chimpanzees— set up a problem situation, finding evidence of insight

One-way door
Curtain

Start box
End box

Thorndike
was among the first to study learning of voluntary responses

— developed Law of Effect

Skinner
led field of behaviourism after Watson

— coined term *operant conditioning*

Operant Conditioning (part 1)

(learning to make voluntary responses through the effects of positive or negative consequences)

- primary reinforcers
- secondary reinforcers
- positive reinforcement
- negative reinforcement

reinforcement — any event or stimulus, that when following a response increases the probability that the response will occur again

"Remember, every time he gives you a pellet, reinforce that behavior by pulling the lever."

punishment
is any event or stimulus, that when following a response, decreases the probability that the response will occur again

- punishment by application
- punishment by removal

Fixed interval
Fixed ratio
Variable interval
Variable ratio
(Cumulative responses / Time)

schedules of reinforcement

- timing of reinforcement
- continuous reinforcement
- partial reinforcement

Operant Conditioning (part 2)

(learning to make voluntary responses through the effects of positive or negative consequences)

— **behaviour modification**

Table 5.2 Four Ways to Modify Behaviour

	REINFORCEMENT	PUNISHMENT
Positive (Adding)	Something valued or desirable	Something unpleasant
	Positive Reinforcement	*Punishment by Application*
	Example: getting a gold star for good behaviour in school	Example: getting a spanking for disobeying
Negative (Removing/ Avoiding)	Something unpleasant	Something valued or desirable
	Negative Reinforcement	*Punishment by Removal*
	Example: avoiding a ticket by stopping at a red light	Example: losing a privilege such as going out with friends

Observational Learning

(the learning of a new behaviour through the observation of a model; typically associated with classic work of Bandura and Bobo doll study)

children observing
an adult model's aggressive or nonaggressive behaviours tended to later act in the same manner they saw modelled; no reinforcement was necessary

— later research suggested that potential consequences can influence motivation to imitate a particular model

key elements for learner

- pay attention to the model
- able to remember what was done
- capable of reproducing, or imitating, the actions of the model
- have the desire or motivation to perform the action

6
Memory

Two-Time Guinness World Record Holder for Greatest Memory: Dave Farrow

Canadian Dave Farrow, from Kitchener, ON, is the only person in North America to hold a Guinness record for memorizing playing cards. In 1996, he was able to memorize 52 decks of cards (a total of 2704 cards) after seeing them only once. As a result, he was placed in the Guinness World Records for having the greatest memory. In 2007, he managed to break the record again by memorizing and accurately recalling 59 decks of cards (a total of 3068 cards).

In high school, Dave Farrow was diagnosed with attention deficit hyperactivity disorder (ADHD) and dyslexia and was constantly told he was not "college material." So how did he go from being all but written off by the educational system to being a memory champion? After being told that he would not succeed, instead of giving up, he became motivated to learn everything he could about human memory and how his own mind worked. He researched memory techniques, both ancient and contemporary, and started to create his own techniques as well. In two years' time, he had improved his grades significantly and started teaching his techniques to his peers.

Today, Farrow is an expert in the field of memorization, known for his memory enhancement techniques (called the *Farrow Memory System*) as well as his techniques for overcoming obstacles related to learning disabilities. He has started three successful companies and has made appearances on *Live! with Regis & Kelly*, *The Today Show*, CTV, CBC, CNN, Fox News, and the Discovery Channel. In addition, as the name of this opening vignette suggests, you can also find him in the Guinness World Records (ProSpeakers Bureau, 2011). If you'd like to know more about Farrow, you can check out his website at **www.davefarrow.com**.

Why study memory?

Without memory, how would we be able to learn anything? The ability to learn is the key to our very survival, and we cannot learn unless we can remember what happened the last time a particular situation arose. Why study forgetting? If we can learn about the ways in which we forget information, we can apply that learning so that forgetting occurs less frequently.

6

LEARNING OBJECTIVES

6.1   What is memory, and what are the three processes of memory?

6.2   What is the information-processing model of memory?

6.3   What is sensory memory?

6.4   What is short-term memory, and how does it differ from working memory?

6.5   What is long-term memory?

6.6   Can culture influence what gets encoded into long-term memory?

6.7   What are the different types of long-term memory, and how is information stored in long-term memory organized?

6.8   What are some other models of memory?

6.9   What kinds of cues help people remember?

6.10   How do the retrieval processes of recall and recognition differ, and how reliable are our memories of events?

6.11   How are long-term memories formed, and what kinds of problems do people experience as a result?

6.12   What is false memory syndrome?

6.13   Why do we forget?

6.14   How and where are memories formed in the brain?

6.15   What is amnesia?

6.16   What is Alzheimer's disease?

6.17   How can the implementation of false memories be used beneficially?

---

memory
as an active system that receives information from the senses, organizes and alters the information as it stores it away, and then retrieves the information from storage.

encoding
the set of mental operations that people perform on sensory information to convert that information into a form that is usable in the brain's storage systems.

storage
holding on to information for some period of time.

So it sounds like ▶ encoding works just like the senses, which we read about in Chapter Three.

MEMORY

6.1   *What is memory, and what are the three processes of memory?*

Is memory a place or a process? The answer to that question is not simple. In reading through this chapter, it becomes clear that memory is a process but that it also has a "place" in the brain. Perhaps the best definition of **memory** is that it is an active system that receives information from the senses, organizes and alters the information as it stores it away, and then retrieves the information from storage (Baddeley, 1996, 2003).

Although there are several different models of how memory works, all of them involve the same three processes: getting the information into the memory system, storing it there, and getting it back out.

PUTTING IT IN: ENCODING

The first step in the memory system is to get sensory information (sight, sound, etc.) into a form that the brain can use, a process called **encoding**. Encoding is the set of mental operations that people perform on sensory information to convert that information into a form that is usable in the brain's storage systems. For example, when people hear a sound, their ears turn the vibrations in the air into neural messages from the auditory nerve, which makes it possible for the brain to interpret that sound. **LINK** to *Chapter Three: Sensation and Perception, p. 88.*

So it sounds like encoding works just like the senses, which we read about in Chapter Three. Encoding is not limited to turning sensory information into signals for the brain; instead, it can take a different form in each of the three different storage systems, or stages of memory. In one stage of memory storage, encoding can take the form of rehearsing information over and over to keep it in memory, whereas in another stage encoding involves elaborating on the meaning of the information—but let's elaborate on that later.

KEEPING IT IN: STORAGE

The next step in memory is to hold on to the information for some period of time, a process called **storage**. This period of time will actually be of different lengths, depending on the stage of memory being used. For example, in one stage of memory

Scrabble™ player Marlon Hill (right) poses with Eric Chalkin, director of the documentary *Word Wars*, a film about top-rated players of this classic word game. A game such as this requires retrieval of not only the words but also the word spellings from previously stored memories.

people hold on to information just long enough to work with it, about 20 seconds or so. In another stage of memory, people hold on to information more or less permanently.

GETTING IT OUT: RETRIEVAL

The biggest problem many people have is **retrieval**, getting the information they know they have out of storage. Have you ever handed in a test and *then* remembered several other things you could have added? Retrieval problems are quite common.

THE INFORMATION-PROCESSING MODEL: THREE STAGES OF MEMORY

6.2   *What is the information-processing model of memory?*

Exactly how does memory work? When the storage process occurs, where does that information go and why? Memory experts have proposed several different ways of looking at memory. The model that many researchers feel is the most comprehensive, and perhaps the most influential over the past several decades, is the **information-processing model**, an approach that focuses on the way information is processed, or handled, through three different stages of memory. The processes of encoding, storage, and retrieval are seen as part of this model.

The link between cognitive psychology and information-processing theory was discussed briefly in Chapter One. Information-processing theory, which looks at how thought processes such as memory work, uses as its model for human thought the way that a computer functions (Massaro & Cowan, 1993). Data are encoded in a way that the computer can understand and use. The computer stores that information on a disk, hard drive, or—these days—a memory stick, and then the data are retrieved out of storage as needed. It was also information-processing theorists who first proposed that there are three stages or types of memory systems (see Figure 6.1): sensory memory, short-term memory, and long-term memory (Atkinson & Shiffrin, 1968).

Simulate on **mypsychlab**

The Information Processing Model

retrieval
getting information that is in storage into a form that can be used.

information-processing model
model of memory that assumes the processing of information for memory storage is similar to the way a computer processes memory in a series of three stages.

FIGURE 6.1 **Three-Stage Process of Memory** Information enters through the sensory system, briefly registering in sensory memory. Selective attention moves the information into short-term memory, where it is held while attention (rehearsal) continues. If the information receives enough rehearsal, it will enter and be stored in long-term memory.

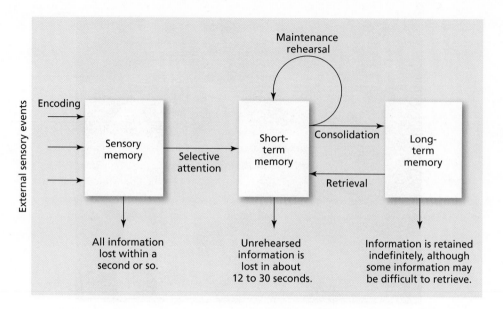

SENSORY MEMORY: WHY DO PEOPLE DO DOUBLE TAKES?

6.3 *What is sensory memory?*

Sensory memory is the first stage of memory, the point at which information enters the nervous system through the sensory systems—eyes, ears, and so on. Think of it as a door to the world that is open for a brief time. Looking through the door, one can see many people and objects, but only some of them will actually make it through the door itself.

Information is encoded into sensory memory as neural messages in the nervous system. As long as those neural messages are travelling through the system, it can be said that people have a "memory" for that information that can be accessed if needed. For example, say Elaina is driving down the street, looking at the people and cars on either side of her vehicle. All of a sudden she thinks, "What? Was that my exboyfriend?" and she looks back to check. How did she know to look back? Her eyes had already moved past the man, but some part of her brain must have just processed what she saw (most likely the reticular formation, which notices new and important information). This action is called a double take and can be explained only by the presence, however brief, of a memory for what she saw.

Two kinds of sensory memory have been studied extensively: the iconic (visual) and echoic (hearing). In the sections that follow, these and other types of memories, as well as several of the experiments that have added a great deal of information to the understanding of memory, will be discussed.

ICONIC SENSORY MEMORY The incident where Elaina thought she saw her ex is an example of how visual sensory memory, or **iconic memory**, works. *Icon* is the Greek word for "image." Iconic memory was studied in several classic experiments by George Sperling (1960).

Capacity of Iconic Memory Sperling had found in his early studies that if he presented a row of letters using a machine that allowed very fast presentation (50 milliseconds), his participants could remember only about four or five of the letters, no matter how many had been presented.

Sperling became convinced that this method was an inaccurate measure of the capacity of iconic memory because the human tendency to read from top to bottom

sensory memory
the first stage of memory, the point at which information enters the nervous system through the sensory systems.

iconic memory
visual sensory memory, lasting only a fraction of a second.

took long enough that the letters on the bottom of the grid may have faded from memory by the time the person had "read" the letters at the top. He developed a method called the *partial report method*, in which he showed a grid of letters similar to those in Figure 6.2 but immediately sounded a high, medium, or low tone just after the grid was shown. Participants were told to read off the top row of letters if they heard the high tone, the middle row for the medium tone, or the lowest row for the low tone. As they didn't hear the tone until after the grid went away, they couldn't look at just one row in advance (see Figure 6.2).

Using this method, Sperling found that participants could accurately report any of the three rows. This finding meant that the entire grid was in iconic memory and available to the participants. The capacity of iconic memory is everything that can be seen at one time.

Duration of Iconic Memory Sperling also found that if he delayed the tone for a brief period of time, after about half a second, participants could no longer recall any of the letters from the grid. The icon had completely faded out of sensory memory in that brief time.

In real life, information that has just entered iconic memory will be pushed out very quickly by new information, a process called *masking* (Cowan, 1988). Research suggests that after only a quarter of a second, old information is replaced by new information.

Although it is rare, some people do have what is properly called **eidetic imagery**, or the ability to access a visual memory for 30 seconds or more. Although the popular term *photographic memory* is often used to refer to this rare ability, some people claiming to have "photographic memories" actually mean that they have very good memories. Having a very good memory and having eidetic imagery ability are two very different things. People with eidetic imagery ability might be able to look quickly at a page in a book, and then, by focusing on a blank wall or piece of paper, "read" the words from the image that still lingers in their sensory memory. Although it might sound like a great ability to have as a student, it actually provides little advantage when taking tests because it's just like having an open-book test. If a student can't *understand* what's written on the pages, having the book open is useless. It is unknown why some people have this ability. It is more common in children and tends to diminish by adolescence or young adulthood (Haber, 1979; Leask et al., 1969; Stromeyer & Psotka, 1971).

If iconic memory last such a brief time, what use is it to us?

Function of Iconic Memory Iconic memory actually serves a very important function in the visual system. Chapter Three discussed the way the eyes make tiny little movements called *saccades* that keep vision from adapting to a constant visual stimulus, so that what is stared at steadily doesn't slowly disappear. Iconic memory helps the visual system view surroundings as continuous and stable in spite of these saccadic movements. It also allows enough time for the brain stem to decide whether the information is important enough to be brought into consciousness.

ECHOIC SENSORY MEMORY Another type of sensory memory is **echoic memory**, or the brief memory of something a person has just heard. A good example of echoic memory is the "What?" phenomenon. You might be reading or concentrating on the television, and your roommate walks up and asks you how your classes are going. You may say "What?" at first and then, after a second or two, answer, "I guess they're going okay," or whatever comment is appropriate. You didn't really process the question from the other person as he or she said it. You heard it, but your brain didn't interpret it immediately. Instead, it took several seconds for

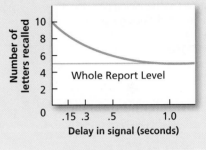

Rows of Letters	Tone Signalling Which Row to Report
LHTY	High tone
EPNR	Medium tone
SBAX	Low tone

FIGURE 6.2 **Iconic Memory Test** Sample grid of letters for Sperling's test of iconic memory. To determine if the entire grid existed in iconic memory, Sperling sounded a tone associated with each row after the grid's presentation. Participants were able to recall the letters in the row for which they heard the tone. The graph shows the decrease in the number of letters recalled as the delay in presenting the tone increased.

◀ If iconic memory lasts such a brief time, what use is it to us?

eidetic imagery
the ability to access a visual memory for 30 seconds or more.

echoic memory
the brief memory of something a person has just heard.

Once these piano strings have been attached to the tuning pins, the piano can be tuned. Tuning a piano requires the use of echoic sensory memory. What other occupations might find a good echoic memory to be an asset?

If the lower centres of ▶ the brain do decide that the information is important enough, what happens to the information at that point?

you to realize that (1) something was said, (2) it may have been important, and (3) you'd better try to remember what it was. If you realize all this within a few seconds (the average duration of echoic memory), you will more than likely be able to "hear" an echo of the statement in your head, a kind of instant replay.

Echoic memory's capacity is limited to what can be heard at any one moment and is smaller than the capacity of iconic memory, although it lasts longer—about two to four seconds (Murray & Hitchcock, 1969; Schweickert, 1993).

Echoic memory is very useful when a person wants to have meaningful conversations with others. It allows the person to remember what someone said just long enough to recognize the meaning of a phrase. As with iconic memory, it also allows people to hold on to incoming auditory information long enough for the lower brain centres to decide whether the information is important enough to become conscious. It is echoic memory that allows a musician to tune a musical instrument, for example. The memory of the tuning fork's tone lingers in echoic memory long enough for the person doing the tuning to match that tone on the instrument.

If the lower centres of the brain do decide that the information is important enough, what happens to the information at that point?

SHORT-TERM (WORKING) MEMORY

6.4 *What is short-term memory, and how does it differ from working memory?*

Information moves from sensory memory to the next stage of memory, called *short-term memory*, through the process of **selective attention**, or the ability to focus on only one stimulus from among all sensory input (Broadbent, 1958). This process is different from *divided attention*, which is the process of focusing on more than one stimulus at a time. When a person is thinking actively about some information, that information is said to be conscious (see Chapter Four). It can also be said to be in **short-term memory (STM)**, the memory system in which information is held for brief periods of time while being used.

Imagine that you are driving to a friend's house for a party when you realize you forgot to bring the potato chips. You don't want to turn around and go back home, so you call her to get directions to the nearest store. As you are talking to her, the radio is playing in the background. You need to be able to "selectively attend" to her voice while ignoring the radio so that you don't get lost. By paying attention to your friend, you are moving the directions she is giving you into your STM. According to researchers Katharine Arbuthnott of the University of Regina and Jamie Campbell of the University of Saskatchewan (2000), selective attention involves two processes: excluding irrelevant information (e.g., the song on the radio) and eliminating no-longer-relevant information (e.g., your friend asking whether you are bringing potato chips). They also concluded that some people are better than others at these two processes (Arbuthnott & Campbell, 2000).

Selective attention is responsible for the "cocktail party effect" that has been long established in studies of perception and attention (Cherry, 1953; Handel, 1989). If you've ever been at a party where there's a lot of noise and many conversations going on in the background, but you are able to notice when someone says your name, you have experienced this effect. The areas of the brain that are involved in selective attention were working even though you were not consciously aware of it, and when that important bit of information (your name) appeared, those areas brought the information to your conscious awareness (Hopfinger et al., 2000; Stuss et al., 2002). The only time this attention filter is not working at its peak is during deep Stage Four sleep, and it is still

selective attention
the ability to focus on only one stimulus from among all sensory input.

short-term memory (STM)
the memory system in which information is held for brief periods of time while being used.

Each person at this gathering is involved in a conversation with others, with dozens of such conversations going on at the same time all around. Yet if a person in another conversation says the name of one of the people in the crowd, that person in the crowd will be able to selectively attend to his or her name. This occurrence is known as the *cocktail party effect*.

functioning even then (LaBerge, 1980). For example, a mother might be able to sleep through the noise of a train that passes nearby every night but immediately awakens when hearing the soft sound of her baby crying. The train sound may be louder but is not important, whereas the baby's cry is most certainly important.

STM tends to be encoded in auditory (sound) form. That simply means that people tend to "talk" inside their own heads. Although some images are certainly stored in STM in a kind of visual "sketchpad" (referred to as the *visuospatial sketchpad* by Baddeley, 1986), auditory storage accounts for much of short-term encoding. Even a dancer planning out moves in her head will not only visualize the moves but also be very likely to verbally describe the moves in her head as she plans. An artist planning a painting certainly has visual information in STM but may also keep up an internal dialogue that is primarily auditory. Research in which participants were asked to recall numbers and letters showed that errors were nearly always made with numbers or letters that *sounded like* the target but not with those that *looked like* the target word or number (Conrad & Hull, 1964).

Some memory theorists use the term *working memory* as another way of referring to STM. This is not entirely correct: STM has traditionally been thought of as a thing or a place into which information is put. **Working memory** is more correctly thought of as an active system that processes the information present in STM. Working memory is thought to consist of three interrelated systems: a central executive (a kind of "CEO" or "big boss") that controls and coordinates the other two systems, the visuospatial sketchpad, and a kind of auditory "recorder" (Baddeley, 1986; Baddeley & Hitch, 1974; Engle & Kane, 2004). The central executive acts as interpreter for both the visual and auditory information, and the visual and auditory information is itself contained in STM. For example, when a person is reading a book, the sketchpad will contain images of the people and events of the particular passage being read, while the recorder "plays" the dialogue in the person's head. The central executive helps interpret the information from both systems and pulls it all together. In a sense, then, STM can be seen as being a part of the working memory system (Bayliss et al., 2005; Colom et al., 2006; Kail & Hall, 2001).

◉─ Watch on mypsychlab
Memory

working memory
an active system that processes the information present in short-term memory.

6 8 2 5

5 7 2 1 4

3 5 9 7 2 1

9 2 5 4 6 3 8

2 8 3 7 1 5 6 9

7 3 2 4 9 6 8 5 1

6 5 4 7 8 9 3 2 1 7

FIGURE 6.3 **Digit-Span Test**
Instructions for the digit-span test:
Listen carefully as the instructor reads
each string of numbers out loud.
As soon as each string is ended (the
instructor may say "go"), write down
the numbers in the exact order in
which they were given.

This woman must hold the phone
number she is reading in short-term
memory long enough to dial it into her
cellphone.

What do you mean
by *rehearsal*? How
long can short-term
memories last when
rehearsal is a factor? ▶

As an example, let's say you run into someone familiar at the mall. You pull that person's name from your more permanent memory and visualize that name along with the memory of the last time you saw the person, almost as if you were viewing it on a screen. At the same time, you will hear the name in your head. The central executive pulls these different types of information together, and you are able to successfully greet your old friend. *Where* you see and hear this is in STM; the *process* that allows this to happen and coordinates it is working memory.

Another way to think about STM is as if it were a kind of desk where you do your work. You might pull some files out of storage (permanent memory) or someone might hand you some files (sensory input). While the files are on your desk, you can see them, read them, and work with them. The "files" are now conscious material and will stay that way as long as they are on the desk. If they are not that important or only necessary for a little while, they get "thrown out" (forgotten as you fail to pay attention to them). If they are important, they might get stored away in the filing system (permanent memory), where they are not conscious until they are once again retrieved—brought out onto the desk.

CAPACITY: THE MAGICAL NUMBER SEVEN George Miller (1956) wanted to know how much information humans can hold in STM at any one time (or how many "files" will fit on the "desk"). He used a memory test called the *digit-span test*, in which a series of numbers is read to participants in the experiment, who are then asked to recall the numbers in order. Each series gets longer and longer, until the participants cannot recall any of the numbers in order (see Figure 6.3).

What you will discover is that everyone you test will get past the first two sequences of numbers, but some people will make errors on the six-digit span, about half of the people you test will slip up on the seven-digit span, and very few will be able to get past the nine-digit span without errors. This finding led Miller to conclude that the capacity of STM is about seven items or pieces of information, plus or minus two items, or from five to nine bits of information. Miller called this the "magical number seven, plus or minus two." So the "desk" isn't really very big and can hold only so many "files."

Chunking There is a way to "fool" STM into holding more information than is usual. Think of it as "stacking" related files on the desk. If the bits of information are combined into meaningful units, or chunks, more information can be held in STM. If someone were to recode the last sequence of numbers as "654-789-3217," for example, instead of 10 bits of information, there would be only three "chunks" that read like a phone number. This process of recoding, or reorganizing, the information is called *chunking*. Chances are that anyone who can easily remember more than eight or nine digits in the digit-span test is probably recoding the numbers into chunks.

People do not just use chunking for individual digits or letters. This strategy can also be used to remember larger categories, such as television networks (e.g., CBC, CTV, TSN) or items on a grocery list.

WHY DO YOU THINK THEY CALL IT SHORT TERM? How long is the "short" of short-term memory? Research has shown that STM lasts from about 12 to 30 seconds without rehearsal (Atkinson & Shiffrin, 1968; Brown, 1958; Peterson & Peterson, 1959). After that, the memory seems to rapidly "decay" or disappear.

What do you mean by rehearsal? How long can short-term memories last if rehearsal is a factor? Most people learn that saying something they want to remember over and over again in their heads, such as repeating a phone number they need just long enough to dial it, can help them remember longer. This process is known as

maintenance rehearsal, which is one of the two types of rehearsal discussed by University of Toronto's Craik and Lockhart (1972). The other type of rehearsal, which will be discussed in detail later, is known as *elaborative rehearsal*. With maintenance rehearsal, a person is simply continuing to pay attention to the information to be held in memory, and since attention is how that information got into STM in the first place, it works quite well (Atkinson & Shiffrin, 1968; Rundus, 1971). With this type of rehearsal, information will stay in STM until rehearsal stops. When rehearsal stops, the memory rapidly decays and is forgotten. If anything interferes with maintenance rehearsal, memories are also likely to be lost. For example, if someone is trying to count a stack of five-dollar bills by reciting each number out loud while counting, and someone else asks that person the time and interferes with the counting process, the person who is counting will probably forget what the last number was and have to start all over again. STM helps people keep track of things such as counting.

Interference in STM can also happen if the amount of information to be held in STM exceeds its capacity (about five to nine "bits" of information, remember). Information already in STM may be "pushed out" to make room for newer information. This is why it might be possible to remember the first few names of people you meet at a party; but, as more names are added, they displace the older names. A better way to remember a person's name is to associate the name with something about the person's appearance, a process that helps move the name from STM into more permanent storage. This more permanent storage is long-term memory, which is the topic of the next section.

It is very important for this pharmacist to count out the number of pills in the prescription accurately. Short-term memory allows her to remember the last number she counted; but if she is interrupted, she will have to start all over again. Short-term memory is very susceptible to interference.

◀⦿ Simulate on **mypsychlab**
Digit Span

PRACTICE QUIZ: HOW MUCH DO YOU REMEMBER?

Pick the best answer.

1. Eldon has just finished his test and handed it in. As he walks out of the classroom, he realizes that there were a few more things he should have included in the long-answer portion of the test. Eldon's problem is in the memory process of
a. encoding.   **c.** retrieval.
b. storage.   **d.** retention.

2. Long ago (in the dark ages of television), when a television set was turned off, it took a while for the last image that was on the screen to fade away. This is most like
a. iconic memory.   **c.** short-term memory.
b. echoic memory.   **d.** long-term memory.

3. Which type of memory allows us to have meaningful conversations?
a. iconic memory
b. echoic memory
c. short-term memory
d. long-term memory

4. Fethia learned her multiplication facts by repeating them over and over until she had them memorized. Fethia was using what kind of rehearsal?
a. repetitive   **c.** elaborative
b. imagery   **d.** maintenance

Answers: 1-c, 2-a, 3-b, 4-d.

LONG-TERM MEMORY

6.5 *What is long-term memory?*

The third stage of memory is **long-term memory (LTM)**, the system into which all the information is placed to be kept more or less permanently. In terms of capacity, LTM is unlimited (Bahrick, 1984; Barnyard & Grayson, 1996). Think about it: Would there ever really come a time when you could not fit one more piece of information into your head? When you could learn nothing more? Perhaps if humans lived much longer lives, there might be a way to "fill up" the brain's memory stores. But in practical terms, there is always room for more information (in spite of what some students may believe).

maintenance rehearsal practice of saying some information to be remembered over and over in one's head to maintain it in short-term memory.

long-term memory (LTM) the system of memory into which all the information is placed to be kept more or less permanently.

> I once memorized a poem by repeating it over and over and over—which is maintenance rehearsal, right? I still remember most of the poem, so it must be in LTM. So can maintenance rehearsal get information into LTM?

As for duration, the name *long-term* says it all. There is a physical change in the brain itself when a LTM is formed. This physical change is relatively permanent. That means that many of the memories people have stored away for a long, long time—even since childhood—are probably always there. That does not mean that people can always retrieve those memories. The memories may be *available* but not *accessible*, meaning that they are still there, but for various reasons people cannot get to them.

I once memorized a poem by repeating it over and over and over—which is maintenance rehearsal, right? I still remember most of the poem, so it must be in LTM. So can maintenance rehearsal get information into LTM? Information that is rehearsed long enough may actually find its way into LTM. After all, it's how most people learn their social insurance or credit card numbers and the letters of the alphabet (although people cheated a little on the latter by putting the alphabet to music, which makes it easier to retrieve). Most people tend to learn poems and the multiplication tables by maintenance rehearsal, otherwise known as rote learning. *Rote* is like "rotating" the information in one's head, saying it over and over again. But maintenance rehearsal is not the most efficient way of putting information into long-term storage, because to get the information back out, one has to remember it almost exactly as it went in. Try this: What is the fifteenth letter of the alphabet? Did you have to recite or sing through the song to get to that letter?

Although many long-term memories are encoded as images (think of the *Mona Lisa*), sounds, smells, and tastes (Cowan, 1988), in general LTM is encoded in meaningful form, a kind of mental storehouse of the meanings of words, concepts, and all the events that people want to keep in mind. Even the images, sounds, smells, and tastes involved in these events have some sort of meaning attached to them that gives them enough importance to be stored long-term. If STM can be thought of as a working "surface" or "desk," then LTM can be thought of as a huge series of filing cabinets behind the desk, in which files are stored in an organized fashion, according to meaning.

These actors are memorizing their lines in a play. They will use rehearsal (repeating and practising their lines over and over) until they can recite their parts perfectly. Their lines will be stored in long-term memory. Is there any way that the actors could use elaborative rehearsal to help them remember their lines?

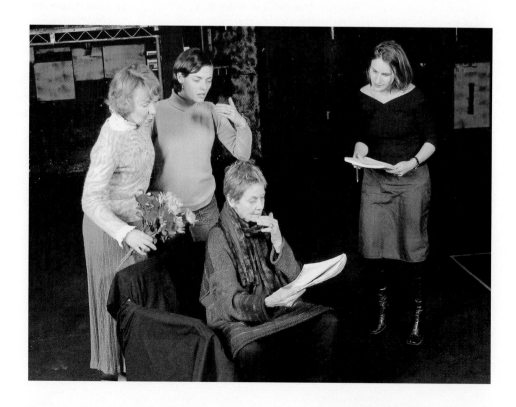

Files have to be placed into the cabinets in a certain organized fashion to be useful. How else could anyone ever remember any kind of information quickly if the files were not in some order? The best way to encode information into LTM in an organized fashion is to make it meaningful through *elaborative rehearsal* (Craik & Lockhart, 1972).

ELABORATIVE REHEARSAL   **Elaborative rehearsal** is a way of transferring information from STM into LTM by making that information meaningful in some way (Postman, 1975). The easiest way to do this is to connect new information with something that is already well known (Craik & Lockhart, 1972; Postman, 1975). For example, the French word *maison* means "house." A person could try to memorize that (using maintenance rehearsal) by saying over and over, "*Maison* means house, *maison* means house." But it would be much easier and more efficient if that person simply thought, "*Maison* sounds like masons, and masons build houses." That makes the meaning of the word tie in with something the person already knows (masons, who lay stone or bricks to build houses) and helps in remembering the French term.

Craik and Lockhart (1972) theorized that information that is more "deeply processed," or processed according to its meaning rather than just the sound or physical characteristics of the word or words, will be remembered more efficiently and for a longer period of time. Elaborative rehearsal is a deeper kind of processing than maintenance rehearsal and so leads to better long-term storage (Craik & Tulving, 1975).

We can also organize material in our LTM in a way that will make it more likely for us to remember it. Memory strategies known as *mnemonics* can aid people in remembering great amounts of information. An example of a mnemonic can be found in elementary school music classes; for example, the phrase "Every Good Boy Deserves Fudge" is often taught to music students as a way of remembering the treble clef line notes (the first letter in each word of the phrase corresponds to each note that falls on a line in the clef). In an analysis of students' ability to remember radio advertisements, Smith and Phillips (2001) from the University of Manitoba found that advertisements that used rhyming mnemonics were more likely to be remembered, even after a week had passed.

CULTURE AND LONG-TERM MEMORY

6.6   *Can culture influence what gets encoded into long-term memory?*

Many researchers are starting to focus on the impact of culture on memory. Studies have shown that culture affects the encoding, storage, and retrieval of information in long-term memory (e.g., Grön, Schul, Bretschneider, Wunderlich, & Riepe, 2003; Lang, 2001; MacDonald, Uesiliana, & Hayne, 2000; Wagar & Cohen, 2003). Brandon Wagar of the University of Waterloo is interested in the effect of culture on the encoding of information into LTM (and also *what* information is encoded). Wagar and Cohen (2003) found that European Canadians were faster to recognize individual traits but slower to recognize collective traits than Asian Canadians, suggesting that culture does indeed play a role in the encoding of information into LTM. Contemporary research has also used brain-imaging techniques to determine the effects culture may have on memory. Using such brain scans, Grön and colleagues (2003) found that even though North American and Chinese participants' behavioural performance was similar, the two groups exhibited different patterns of brain activation on memory recall tasks.

I can remember a lot of stuff from my childhood. Some of it is stuff I learned in school and still remember, and some of it is more personal, like the first day of school. Are there different kinds of long-term memories?

elaborative rehearsal
a method of transferring information from STM into LTM by making that information meaningful in some way.

I can remember a lot of stuff from my childhood. Some of it is stuff I learned in school and still remember, and some of it is more personal, like the first day of school. Are there different kinds of long-term memories?

procedural (non-declarative) memory
type of long-term memory that includes memory for skills, emotional responses, habits, and simple conditioned reflexes. These memories are not conscious but are implied to exist because they affect conscious behaviour.

anterograde amnesia
loss of memory from the point of injury or trauma forward, or the inability to form new long-term memories.

implicit memory
memory that is not easily retrieved into conscious awareness, such as procedural memory.

TYPES OF LONG-TERM INFORMATION

6.7 *What are the different types of long-term memory, and how is information stored in long-term memory organized?*

Long-term memories include general facts and knowledge, personal facts, and even skills that can be performed. From his observations of amnesiacs, Paul Kolers, while at the University of Toronto, concluded that LTM falls into at least two categories: Memory for skills is called *procedural (non-declarative) memory* because it usually involves a series of steps or procedures; memory for facts is called *declarative memory* because facts are things that are known and can be declared (stated outright; Kolers, 1975). These two types of LTM are quite different.

Procedural (Non-declarative) LTM Memories for skills that people know how to do, such as tying shoelaces and riding a bicycle, are a kind of LTM called **procedural (non-declarative) memory**. Procedural memories also include emotional associations, habits, and simple conditioned reflexes that may or may not be in conscious awareness. ⓛⓘⓝⓚ *to Chapter Five: Learning, p. 176*. Referring back to Chapter Two, the amygdala is the most probable location for emotional associations, such as fear, and the cerebellum in the hindbrain is responsible for storage of memories of conditioned responses, skills, and habits (Squire et al., 1993).

Evidence that separate areas of the brain control procedural memory comes from studies of people with damage to the hippocampus area of the brain. This damage causes them to have **anterograde amnesia**, in which new long-term memories cannot be formed. In one study (Cohen et al., 1985), patients with this disorder were taught how to solve a particular puzzle called the Tower of Hanoi (see Figure 6.4). One of the more famous anterograde amnesia patients, H. M., is discussed in detail later in this chapter on p. 250.

Although the patients were able to learn the sequence of moves necessary to solve the puzzle, when brought back into the testing room at a later time they could not remember ever having seen the puzzle before—or, for that matter, the examiner. Each trial was like the first one ever for these patients, as they were unable to store the LTM of having been in the room or having met the examiner previously. Yet they were able to solve the puzzle even while claiming that they had never seen it before. Their procedural memories for how to solve the puzzle were evidently formed and stored in a part of the brain separate from the part controlling the memories they could no longer form.

The patients in this study had the kind of memory problems that people with Alzheimer's disease have. Yet even people with Alzheimer's disease do not forget how to walk, talk, fasten clothing, or even tie shoelaces (although they do lose motor ability because the brain eventually fails to send the proper signals). These are all procedural, non-declarative memories. They may not be able to tell someone who asks that they know how to do these things, but they can still do them. Alzheimer's disease affects the hippocampus and the frontal cortex (involved in decision making and planning) and eventually affects other areas of the brain after it has progressed nearly to the end (Kanne et al., 1998). In fact, it would be rare to find someone who has lost procedural memory. Literally, these are the kind of memories people "never forget."

Procedural memory is often called **implicit memory** because memories for these skills, habits, and learned reflexes are not easily retrieved into conscious awareness. The fact that people have the knowledge of how to tie their shoelaces, for example, is *implied* by the fact that they can actually tie them. But have you ever tried to tell someone how to tie laces without using your hands to show them? The participants in the Tower of Hanoi study provide a good example of implicit memory, as they could solve the puzzle but had no conscious knowledge of how to do so. Such

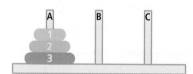

FIGURE 6.4 **Tower of Hanoi** The Tower of Hanoi is a puzzle that is solved in a series of steps by moving one disc at a time. The goal is to move all of the discs from the first peg to another peg; the rule is that a larger disc can never be moved on top of a smaller one. Amnesia patients were able to learn the procedure for solving the puzzle but could not remember that they knew how to solve it.

knowledge is in people's memories because they use this information, but they are often not consciously aware of this knowledge (Roediger, 1990). Although procedural memories are implicit, not all implicit memories are necessarily procedural. A memory from one's early childhood of being frightened by a dog, for example, may not be a conscious memory in later childhood but may still be the cause of that older child's fear of dogs. Conscious memories for events in childhood, on the contrary, are usually considered to be a different kind of LTM called *declarative memory.*

Declarative LTM   Procedural memory is about the things that people can *do*, but **declarative memory** is about all the things that people can *know*—the facts and information that make up knowledge. People know things such as the names of the planets in the solar system, that adding two and two makes four, and that a noun is the name of a person, place, or thing. These are general facts, but people also know about the things that have happened to them personally. For example, I know what I ate for breakfast this morning and what I saw on the way to work, but I don't know what you had for breakfast or what you might have seen. As the well-known Canadian researcher Endel Tulving and his colleagues have pointed out, there are two types of declarative long-term memories: *semantic* and *episodic* (Nyberg & Tulving, 1996; Tulving, 1972).

One type of declarative memory is general knowledge that anyone has the ability to know. Most of this information is what is learned in school or by reading. This kind of LTM is called **semantic memory**. The word *semantic* refers to meaning, so this kind of knowledge is the awareness of the meanings of words, concepts, and terms, as well as names of objects, math skills, and so on. This knowledge is also the type that is used on game shows such as *Jeopardy*. Semantic memories, like procedural memories, are relatively permanent. But it is possible to "lose the way to" this kind of memory, as discussed in the section on forgetting.

The other kind of factual memory is the personal knowledge that each person has of his or her daily life and personal history, a kind of autobiographical memory. Memories of what has happened to people each day, certain birthdays, anniversaries that were particularly special, childhood events, and so on are called **episodic memory**, because they represent episodes from their lives.

Endel Tulving, with the help of many colleagues, has conducted much research on an amnesiac from Mississauga, ON, named Kent Cochrane (known as *K. C.*). K. C. was involved in a motorcycle accident when he was 30 years old and sustained damage to his episodic memory. K. C.'s collection of semantic facts and the procedural skills he acquired in the first 30 years of his life (e.g., riding a bike) have not been affected, but he is unable to recollect any specific event that he was a part of or witnessed. The case of K. C. provides support for the distinction between semantic and episodic memory.

Unlike procedural and semantic long-term memories, episodic memories tend to be updated and revised more or less constantly. You can probably remember what you had for breakfast today, but what you had for breakfast two years ago on this date is most likely a mystery. Episodic memories that are especially *meaningful*, such as the memory of the first day of school or your first date, are more likely to be kept in LTM (although they may not be as exact as people sometimes assume they are). The updating process is a kind of survival mechanism, because although semantic and procedural memories are useful and necessary on an ongoing basis, no one really needs to remember every little detail of every day. As becomes obvious later, the ability to forget some kinds of information is very necessary.

Episodic and semantic memories are forms of **explicit memory**, memories that are easily made conscious and brought from long-term storage into STM. The knowledge of

Procedural knowledge, such as tying one's shoelaces, often must be learned by doing, as it is difficult to put into words. Once this child learns how to tie laces, the knowledge will always be there to retrieve.

declarative memory
type of long-term memory containing information that is conscious and known.

semantic memory
type of declarative memory containing general knowledge, such as knowledge of language and information learned in formal education.

episodic memory
type of declarative memory containing personal information not readily available to others, such as daily activities and events.

explicit memory
memory that is easily made conscious and brought from long-term storage into short-term memory, such as declarative memory.

FIGURE 6.5 **Types of Long-Term Memories** Long-term memory can be divided into declarative memories, which are factual and typically conscious (explicit) memories, and nondeclarative memories, which are skills, habits, and conditioned responses that are typically unconscious (implicit). Declarative memories are further divided into episodic memories (personal experiences) and semantic memories (general knowledge).

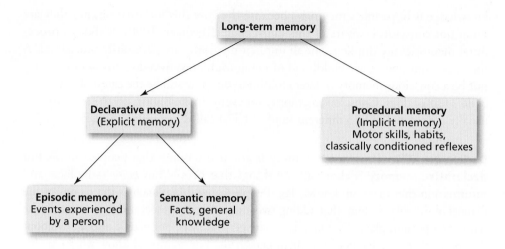

semantic memories such as important dates in history, science concepts, and so on can be brought out of the "filing cabinet" and placed on the "desk" where that knowledge becomes *explicit*, or obvious. The same is often true of personal, episodic memories.

> But sometimes I can't remember all the provinces and territories of Canada or what I had for breakfast yesterday. Doesn't that make these memories implicit instead of explicit?

The difference between implicit memories, such as balancing on a bicycle, and explicit memories, such as naming all the provinces and territories, is that it is impossible or extremely difficult to bring implicit memories into consciousness. Explicit memories can be forgotten but always have the potential to be made conscious. When someone reminds you of what you had for breakfast the day before, for example, you will remember that you had that knowledge all along—it was just temporarily "mislaid." For a look at the connections among all these types of LTM, see Figure 6.5.

LONG-TERM MEMORY ORGANIZATION As stated before, LTM has to be fairly well organized for retrieval to be so quick. Can you remember the name of your grade 1 teacher? If you can, how long did it take you to pull that name out of LTM and "put it on the desk" of STM? It probably took hardly any time at all. Think of it this way: If a person who puts documents in a filing cabinet just stuffs them in any drawer with no system of organization, when a particular document is needed it requires searching through every drawer. But if documents are filed away alphabetically, and perhaps even according to type of document (assignments in one folder, tests in another, etc.), it becomes very easy to retrieve a particular document.

Research suggests that LTM is organized in terms of related meanings and concepts (Collins & Loftus, 1975; Collins & Quillian, 1969). In their original study, Collins and Quillian (1969) had participants respond "true" or "false" as quickly as possible to sentences such as "a canary is a bird" and "a canary is an animal." Looking at Figure 6.6, it is apparent that information exists in a kind of network, with nodes (focal points) of related information linked to each other in a kind of hierarchy.* To verify the statement "a canary is a bird" requires moving to only one node, but "a canary is an animal" requires moving through two nodes and should take longer. This was exactly the result of the 1969 study, leading the researchers to develop the **semantic network model**, which assumes that information is stored in the brain in a connected fashion, with concepts that are related stored physically closer to each other than concepts that are not highly related (Collins & Quillian, 1969).

But sometimes I ▶ can't remember all the provinces and territories of Canada or what I had for breakfast yesterday. Doesn't that make these memories implicit instead of explicit?

semantic network model model of memory organization that assumes information is stored in the brain in a connected fashion, with concepts that are related stored physically closer to each other than concepts that are not highly related.

---

*Hierarchy: an ordered list or series

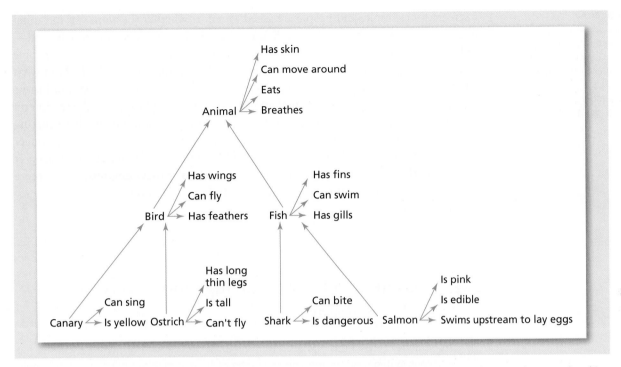

FIGURE 6.6 **An Example of a Semantic Network**   In the semantic network model of memory, concepts that are related in meaning are thought to be stored physically near each other in the brain. In this example, canary and ostrich are stored near the concept node for "bird," whereas shark and salmon are stored near "fish." But the fact that a canary is yellow is stored directly with that concept.

The parallel distributed processing model (Rumelhart et al., 1986), which will be discussed in the next section, can be used to explain how rapidly the different points on the networks can be accessed. Although the access of nodes within a particular category (e.g., *birds*) may take place in a serial fashion, explaining the different response times in the Collins and Quillian (1969) study, access across the entire network may take place in a parallel fashion, allowing several different concepts to be targeted at the same time (e.g., one might be able to think about *birds*, *cats*, and *trees* simultaneously). The activation of one memory triggers the activation of related memories, which is known as *spreading activation*.

Perhaps the best way to think of how information is organized in LTM is to think about the internet. A person might go to one website and from that site link to many other related sites. Each related site has its own specific information but is also linked to many other related sites, and a person can have more than one site open at the same time. This grouping is very similar to the way in which the mind organizes the information stored in LTM.

✖ Explore on **mypsychlab**
Encoding, Storage, and Retrieval in Memory

OTHER MODELS OF MEMORY

6.8   *What are some other models of memory?*

LEVELS-OF-PROCESSING MODEL

The information-processing model assumes that how long a memory will be remembered depends on the stage of memory in which it is stored. Other researchers have proposed that how long a memory will be remembered depends on the depth (i.e., the effort made to understand the meaning) to which the information is processed (Cermak & Craik, 1979; Craik & Lockhart, 1972). If the word *BALL* is flashed on

levels-of-processing model
model of memory that assumes information that is more "deeply processed," or processed according to its meaning rather than just the sound or physical characteristics of the word or words, will be remembered more efficiently and for a longer period of time.

a screen, for example, and people are asked to report whether the word was in capital or lowercase letters, the word itself does not have to be processed very much at all—only its visual characteristics need enter into conscious attention. But if those people were to be asked to use that word in a sentence, they would have to think about what a ball is and how it can be used. They would have to process its meaning, not just its "looks," which requires more mental effort. As was discussed earlier in the section on elaborative rehearsal, researchers have found in numerous experiments that thinking about the meaning of something is a deeper level of processing and results in longer retention of the word (Cermak & Craik, 1979; Craik & Tulving, 1975; Watson et al., 1999). This model of memory is called the **levels-of-processing model**. For more about this model of memory, see the Classic Studies in Psychology box.

CLASSIC STUDIES IN PSYCHOLOGY
Craik, Lockhart, Tulving, and Levels of Processing

Dr. Endel Tulving has had a profound impact on the field of memory. Tulving has contributed more to the understanding of human memory than almost any other scientist. His theories not only laid the groundwork for subsequent memory research but also helped researchers achieve a greater understanding of disorders such as Alzheimer's disease. Tulving has received international recognition for the work that he has done, including being elected to six national academies of science worldwide. He has also been recognized in Canada, being named an Officer of the Order of Canada in 2006 and inducted into the Canadian Medical Hall of Fame in 2007.

The contributions of Dr. Fergus Craik, like Tulving's, are numerous and have shed much light on the workings of human memory. Craik's work with colleague Robert Lockhart served as a foundation for one of the best-known models of memory in the field of psychology. In 1972, Craik and Lockhart decided to go against the status quo by focusing on the processes involved in memory instead of on memory stores or structures. As a result, Craik and Lockhart's levels-of-processing model was created. This model was then tested by Craik and Tulving in a famous study.

In 1975, while at the University of Toronto, Craik and Tulving decided to collaborate on a study that has now become a classic in the field of memory research. They tested the levels-of-processing model by investigating whether recall is affected by the depth of processing. Participants were presented with a series of 60 words and then were required to answer one of three questions pertaining to them. One of the three questions required semantic processing (i.e., processing according to meaning), the second required phonemic processing (i.e., processing according to sound), and the third required structural processing (i.e., processing according to physical aspects).

According to Craik and Tulving (1975), processing on a semantic level (e.g., Does the word *nurse* make sense in a story involving a car accident?) is deeper than processing on a phonemic level (e.g., Does the word *car* rhyme with the word *star*?), which, in turn, is deeper than processing on a structural level (e.g., is the word *PHONE* in capital letters?).

Participants were then required to pick out the original words they had heard from a list of 180 words, in which the original words were mixed with a series of new words. Craik and Tulving found that participants were better at recalling the semantically processed words than the acoustically and visually processed words, demonstrating that deeper processing results in enhanced memory performance.

Drs. Craik (left), Lockhart (middle) and Tulving (right) have contributed a great deal to the understanding of memory.

Craik, Lockhart, and Tulving are now all retired from the University of Toronto, but they still remain as professors emeriti. Craik and Tulving also continue to work together at the Rotman Research Institute in Toronto, where they collaborate on research projects, articles, and books.

Questions for Further Discussion

1. How might students use the work of Craik, Lockhart, and Tulving to help them do better in school?

2. Does the development of a new model or theory in psychology always mean that previous models or theories become "outdated" or incorrect?

3. What would psychology (and other sciences) be like if researchers such as Craik, Lockhart, and Tulving never challenged the status quo?

PARALLEL DISTRIBUTED PROCESSING MODEL

In the **parallel distributed processing (PDP) model**, memory is seen as a simultaneous process, with the creation and storage of memories taking place across a series of mental networks "stretched" across the brain (McClelland & Rumelhart, 1988; Rumelhart et al., 1986).

Supporters of this model base their viewpoint on the way neural processing actually takes place in the brain: Neural connections appear to be organized in a parallel manner and in sequential pathways in the brain (Hinton et al., 1986; Sartori & Umilta, 2000). Instead of information for a memory being processed only in a series of steps, the brain runs several different processes at the same time, or in parallel, to one another, while at the same time spreading that information across the entire network of neural connections. This process enables people to retrieve many different aspects of a memory all at once, allowing much faster reactions and decisions.

So which model is right? "Which model is right?" is not the correct question. The correct question is "Which model explains the findings of researchers about how memory works?" The answer to that question is that all of these models can be used to explain some, if not all, research findings. So although the information-processing model of memory may take centre stage, it is important to remember the concepts of the levels at which information is processed and the way in which those processes may take place while reading the rest of this chapter.

◄◎⊢Simulate on **mypsychlab**

Depth of Processing

parallel distributed processing (PDP) model
a model of memory in which memory processes are proposed to take place at the same time over a large network of neural connections.

◄ So which model is right?

PRACTICE QUIZ: HOW MUCH DO YOU REMEMBER?

Pick the best answer.

1. Of the following, which is the most similar to the concept of long-term memory?
  a. a revolving door
  b. a filing cabinet
  c. a desktop
  d. a computer keyboard

2. Long-term memories are encoded in terms of
  a. sounds.
  b. visual images.
  c. meanings of words and concepts.
  d. all of the above

3. Which type of LTM is seldom, if ever, lost by people with Alzheimer's disease?
  a. procedural
  b. semantic
  c. episodic
  d. both (b) and (c)

4. In the game show *Who Wants to Be a Millionaire?* contestants are asked a series of questions of general information, although of increasing difficulty. The type of memory needed to access the answers to these kinds of questions is
  a. procedural.
  b. semantic.
  c. episodic.
  d. working.

5. The internet, with its series of links from one site to many others, is a good analogy for the organization of
  a. short-term memory.
  b. episodic memory.
  c. long-term memory.
  d. procedural memory.

6. When Edie studies her psychology terms, she tries to tie each concept to something she already knows. She thinks about the meaning of the concept rather than just saying the words over and over. Which model of memory would best explain Edie's approach to encoding memories?
  a. levels of processing
  b. parallel distributed processing
  c. information processing
  d. three-stage

Answers: 1-b, 2-d, 3-a, 4-b, 5-c, 6-a.

GETTING IT OUT: RETRIEVAL OF LONG-TERM MEMORIES

My problem isn't so much getting information into my head, as finding it later. Oddly enough, most people's problems with getting information stored in LTM back out again has to do with *how* they put that information *into* LTM.

RETRIEVAL CUES

6.9 *What kinds of cues help people remember?*

Remember the previous discussion about maintenance rehearsal versus elaborative rehearsal? One of the main reasons that maintenance rehearsal is not a very good way to get information into LTM is that saying something over and over gives only one kind of **retrieval cue** (a stimulus for remembering), the sound of the word or phrase. When people try to remember a piece of information by thinking of what it means and how it fits in with what they already know, they are giving themselves cues for meaning in addition to sound. The more cues stored with a piece of information, the easier the recall of that information will be (Roediger, 2000; Roediger & Guynn, 1996).

ENCODING SPECIFICITY AND STATE-DEPENDENT LEARNING: CONTEXT AND MOOD EFFECTS ON MEMORY RETRIEVAL Although most people would assume that cues for retrieval would have to be directly related to the concepts being studied, almost anything in one's surroundings is capable of becoming a cue. If you usually eat peanuts while watching a Toronto Blue Jays game, for example, the next time you eat peanuts you might find yourself thinking of the Toronto Blue Jays. This connection between surroundings and remembered information is called *encoding specificity* (Tulving & Thomson, 1973).

Have you ever had to take a test in a different classroom than the one in which you learned the material being tested? Do you think that your performance on that test was hurt by being in a different physical context? Researchers have found strong evidence for the concept of **encoding specificity**, the tendency for memory of any kind of information to be improved if the physical surroundings available when the memory is first formed are also available when the memory is being retrieved (Reder et al., 1974;

**My problem isn't ►
so much getting
information *into* my
head, as finding
it later.**

retrieval cue
a stimulus for remembering.

encoding specificity
the tendency for memory of any kind of information to be improved if the physical surroundings available when the memory is first formed are also available when the memory is being retrieved.

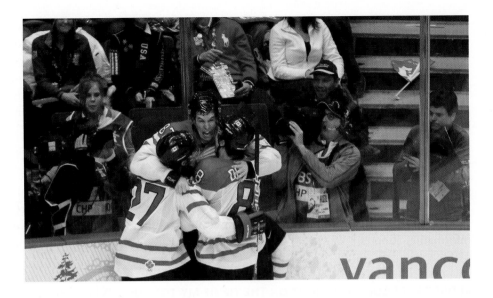

Sidney Crosby celebrates after scoring the game-winning (and gold medal earning) goal in the 2010 Winter Olympics. From that point on, Crosby's memories related to scoring this goal will be easier to access whenever he is happy because he was happy after scoring the goal. State-dependent learning makes it easier for people to recall information stored while in a particular emotional state (such as the happiness of Sid the Kid) if the recall occurs in a similar emotional state.

Tulving & Thomson, 1973). For example, encoding specificity would predict that the best place to take one's psychology test is in the same room in which you learned the material. Also, it's very common to walk into a room and know that there was something you wanted but, in order to remember it, you have to go back to the room you started in to use your surroundings as a cue for remembering.

David Smith and his colleagues at Bishop's University in Lennoxville, QC, examined whether odour can act as a contextual retrieval cue for remembering a list of words. They had 47 university students learn a list of 12 pleasant and 12 unpleasant words while exposed to one of two odours (jasmine or perfume). The participants then had to relearn the list with either the same or an alternate odour present. The results showed that relearning in an environment with the same odour (e.g., if they first learned the list while smelling jasmine and then had to relearn the list while again smelling jasmine) was superior to performance in a mismatched odour condition (Smith, Standing, & de Man, 1992).

Physical surroundings at the time of encoding a memory are not the only kinds of cues that can help in retrieval. In *state-dependent learning*, memories formed during a particular physiological or psychological state will be easier to recall while in a similar state. State-dependent learning has also been a subject of research. Eric Eich, from the University of British Columbia, and Janet Metcalfe, from the University of California, San Diego, conducted a study in which they had participants try to recall words that they had either read or thought up while listening to music that was either happy or sad. When later tested for memory of the words, the words that were read or created while participants were in a happy mood were recalled better if the mood at recall was also happy but far less well if the mood at recall was sad. The reverse was also true (Eich & Metcalfe, 1989).

Reprinted with special permission of King Features Syndicate.

6.10 *How do the retrieval processes of recall and recognition differ, and how reliable are our memories of events?*

Why do multiple-choice tests seem so much easier than essay tests for most students? There are two kinds of memory retrieval: recall and recognition. It is the

Why do multiple-choice tests seem so much easier than essay tests for most students?

recall
type of memory retrieval in which the information to be retrieved must be "pulled" from memory with very few external cues.

recognition
the ability to match a piece of information or a stimulus to a stored image or fact.

serial position effect
tendency of information at the beginning and the end of a body of information to be remembered more easily and accurately than information in the middle of the body of information.

primacy effect
tendency to remember information at the beginning of a body of information better than the information that follows.

difference between these two retrieval methods that makes some kinds of exams seem more difficult than others. In **recall**, on the one hand, memories are retrieved with few or no external cues, such as filling in the blanks in an application form. **Recognition**, on the other hand, involves looking at or hearing information and matching it to what is already in memory. A word-search puzzle, in which the words are already written down in the grid and simply need to be circled, is an example of recognition. The following section takes a closer look at these two important processes.

RECALL: HMM . . . LET ME THINK

When playing a game of Trivial Pursuit with friends, the question acts as the cue for retrieval of the answer. This is an example of recall, as are essay-question, short-answer, and fill-in-the-blank tests that are used to measure a person's memory for information (Borges et al., 1977; Gillund & Shiffrin, 1984; Raaijmakers & Shiffrin, 1992).

RETRIEVAL FAILURE: IT'S RIGHT ON THE TIP OF MY TONGUE   Whenever people find themselves struggling for an answer, recall has failed (at least temporarily). Sometimes the answer seems so very close to the surface of conscious thought that it feels like it's "on the tip of the tongue." This feeling is sometimes called the *tip of the tongue (TOT)* phenomenon (Brown & McNeill, 1966; Burke et al., 1991). Although people may be able to say how long the word is or name letters that start or even end the word, they cannot retrieve the sound or actual spelling of the word to allow it to be pulled into the auditory "recorder" of STM so that it can be fully retrieved.

How can a person overcome TOT? The best solution is the one "everyone" seems to know: Forget about it. When you "forget about it," the brain apparently continues to work on retrieval. Some time later (perhaps when you run across a similar sounding word in your surroundings), the word or name will just "pop out." This tendency can make for interesting conversations, because when that particular word does "pop out," it usually has little to do with the current conversation.

THE SERIAL POSITION EFFECT   Another interesting feature of recall is that information at the beginning and the end of a body of information, such as a poem or song, tends to be remembered more easily and accurately than information in the middle of the body of information. This characteristic is called the **serial position effect** (Murdock, 1962).

A good demonstration of this phenomenon involves instructing people to listen to and try to remember words that are read to them that are spaced about four or five seconds apart. People typically use maintenance rehearsal by repeating each word in their heads. They are then asked to write as many of the words down as they can remember. If the frequency of recall for each word in the list is graphed, it will nearly always look like the graph in Figure 6.7.

Words at the very beginning of the list tend to be remembered better than those that follow. This effect is called the **primacy effect** and is due to the fact that the first few words, when the listener has nothing already in STM to interfere with their rehearsal, will receive far more rehearsal time than the words in the middle, which are constantly being replaced by the next word on the list (Craik, 1970; Murdock, 1962). In fact, the first words may actually move into LTM if they are rehearsed long enough, because rote memorization, although not the best way to remember something, can lead to long-term storage.

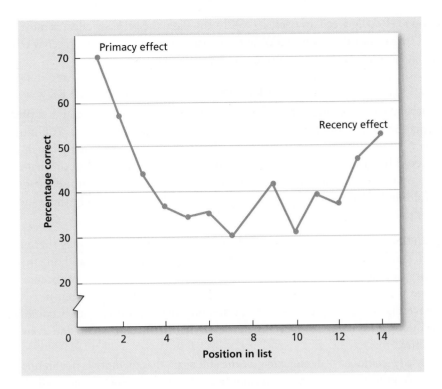

FIGURE 6.7 **Serial Position Effect**
In the serial position effect, information at the beginning of a list will be recalled at a higher rate than information in the middle of the list (primacy effect), because the beginning information receives more rehearsal and may enter LTM. Information at the end of a list is also retrieved at a higher rate (recency effect), because the end of the list is still in STM, with no information coming after it to interfere with retrieval.

At the end of the graph there is another increase in recall. This is the **recency effect** and is usually attributed to the fact that the last word or two was *just heard* and is still in STM for easy retrieval, with no new words entering to "push" the most recent word or words out of memory (Bjork & Whitten, 1974; Murdock, 1962). The serial position effect works with many different kinds of information. In fact, business schools often teach their students that they should try not to be "in the middle" for job interviews. Going first or last in the interview process is much more likely to make a person's interview more memorable.

In an interesting demonstration of the serial position effect, Cornell and Heth of the University of Alberta found that if children get lost when asked to retrace a route (e.g., on the way home from school), they tend to get lost in the middle of the route, not at the beginning or the end. According to Cornell and Heth (2006), as children walk a route, they create representations of landmarks. Cornell and Heth made children give verbal recall of their route and also complete tasks where they had to put pictures of their route in order. It was found that children performed better when asked about the beginning and end of the route than when asked about the middle of the route. As a result of the work done by Cornell and colleagues, parents and police officers now know where to start looking when a child gets lost on the way to or from school.

The serial position effect is often used to demonstrate that there are indeed two memory systems, STM and LTM. Memory researchers point to the primacy effect as a result of LTM storage and the recency effect as a result of STM. But the serial position effect can also apply to LTM exclusively (Baddeley & Hitch, 1974; Roediger & Crowder, 1976). Think about the prime ministers of Canada. How many of them can you remember? Everyone remembers Sir John A. Macdonald because he was *first*. After Macdonald, though, it becomes a struggle to remember who came next. Even if a person can get the first several, the middle prime ministers are almost impossible to remember. But everyone remembers who is prime minister right now and who was prime minister before him, and so on, up until about the time of

recency effect
tendency to remember information at the end of a body of information better than the information ahead of it.

These people are waiting to audition for a play. The person who auditions first and the one who auditions last have the greatest chance of being remembered when the time comes for the director to choose. The serial position effect will cause the impression made by the people in the "middle" to be less memorable.

false positive
error of recognition in which people think that they recognize some stimulus that is not actually in memory.

childhood (Roediger & Crowder, 1976). In this case, the primacy effect is most likely caused by Macdonald's importance in Canadian history, whereas the recency effect is more likely an effect of the importance of recent events.

RECOGNITION: HEY, DON'T I KNOW YOU FROM SOMEWHERE?

The other form of memory retrieval is *recognition*, the ability to match a piece of information or a stimulus to a stored image or fact (Borges et al., 1977; Gillund & Shiffrin, 1984; Raaijmakers & Shiffrin, 1992). Recognition is usually much easier than recall because the cue is the actual object, word, sound, and so on that one is simply trying to detect as familiar and known. Examples of tests that use recognition are multiple-choice, matching, and true–false tests. The answer is right there and simply has to be matched to the information already in memory.

FALSE POSITIVES   Recognition isn't foolproof, however. Sometimes there is just enough similarity between a stimulus that is not already in memory and one that is in memory so that a **false positive** occurs (Muter, 1978). A false positive occurs when a person thinks that he or she has recognized something or someone but in fact does not have that something or someone in memory. False positives can become disastrous in certain situations, especially those relating to the courtroom and eyewitness testimony.

Many studies have demonstrated time and again that memory is not an unchanging, stable process but rather is a constantly changing one. People continually update and revise their memories of events without being aware that they are doing so, and they incorporate information gained after the actual event, whether correct or incorrect.

PSYCHOLOGY IN THE NEWS
Wrongfully Convicted

In 1959, Steven Truscott, just 14 years old at the time, was sentenced to be hanged for murdering his schoolmate and friend, 12-year-old Lynne Harper. On June 9 that same year, Truscott gave Harper a ride on his bicycle and was the last known person to see her alive. Two days later, her body was found in a wooded area about 180 kilometres west of Toronto. It was determined that Harper had been raped and strangled.

Within two days of discovering her body, police charged Truscott with her murder. At the trial, the Crown's case was based on four main pieces of evidence, one of them being eyewitness evidence as to when and where Truscott was seen on the night that Harper disappeared. The Crown used this evidence, even though there were many conflicting eyewitness reports, to establish the "fact" that Truscott took Harper into the wooded area where she was later found dead (Robins, 2008).

After only 15 days of trial, Truscott was found guilty and was handed the death penalty. He spent three and a half months on death row, believing that the construction outside his prison was actually the construction of scaffolding for his hanging. His sentence was later commuted to life imprisonment and he ended up spending the next 10 years of his life behind bars before he was finally paroled.

In 2006, the Ontario Court of Appeal started hearings in the case. One of the witnesses, Karen Jutsi, who was only 9 years old at the time of the murder, stated that her original eyewitness report was incorrect. She claimed to be shocked when she read her statement years later.

Steven Truscott spent 10 years behind bars for a murder that he did not commit. It is believed that the controversy surrounding Truscott's case is what led to Canada's abolition of the death penalty in 1976.

On August 28, 2007, Steven Truscott was finally acquitted, with the court calling his conviction a "miscarriage of justice." He was later awarded $6.5 million in compensation, nearly 50 years after he was charged and found guilty of Harper's murder.

It is believed that the controversy surrounding Truscott's case is what led to Canada's abolition of the death penalty in 1976 (CBC News, 2008; CityNews.ca Staff, 2008).

This case is just one of many wrongful convictions that have happened throughout Canadian history. Other well-known cases include those of Guy Paul Morin, David Milgaard, and Thomas Sophonow. According to the Innocence Project at Osgoode Hall Law School at York University, an estimated 25 percent of wrongful convictions involve faulty eyewitness testimony, as distinguished from identification error.

Questions for Further Discussion

1. What factors may be involved in faulty eyewitness testimony? Does faulty eyewitness testimony relate solely to memory, or could there be other influences as well?

2. What are some things the Canadian legal system can do to reduce the number of wrongful convictions resulting from faulty eyewitness testimony?

AUTOMATIC ENCODING: FLASHBULB MEMORIES

Although some long-term memories need extensive maintenance rehearsal or effortful encoding in the form of elaborative rehearsal to enter from STM into LTM, many other kinds of long-term memories seem to enter permanent storage with little or no effort at all, in a kind of **automatic encoding** (Mandler, 1967; Schneider et al., 1984).

A special kind of automatic encoding takes place when an unexpected event or episode in a person's life has strong emotional associations, such as fear, horror, or joy. Memories of highly emotional events can often seem vivid and detailed, as if the person's mind took a "flash picture" of the moment in time. These kinds of memories are called **flashbulb memories** (Neisser, 1982; Neisser & Harsch, 1992; Winningham et al., 2000).

It has been established that flashbulb memories can exist on a grand scale. But personal flashbulb memories also exist. These memories tend to be major emotional events, such as the first date, an embarrassing event, or a particularly memorable birthday party.

Why do flashbulb memories seem so vivid and exact? The answer lies in the emotions felt at the time of the event. Emotional reactions stimulate the release of hormones that have been shown to enhance the formation of long-term memories (McEwen, 2000). But is this kind of memory really all that accurate? Although some researchers have found evidence for a high degree of accuracy in flashbulb memories of *major events*, such as 9/11, others have found that while flashbulb memories are often convincingly real, they are just as subject to decay and alterations over time as other kinds of memories (Neisser & Harsch, 1992). Researchers at the University of Toronto asked participants about their recollections concerning both the events of 9/11 and their activities at the time of the tragedy. It was found that although students who reported greater emotional involvement in the events were better at recalling details of the event, they were worse at remembering the details surrounding their activities when the event occurred (Smith, Bibi, & Sheard, 2003). Apparently, no memories are completely accurate after the passage of time. The next section will discuss some of the reasons for faulty memories.

automatic encoding
tendency of certain kinds of information to enter long-term memory with little or no effortful encoding.

flashbulb memories
type of automatic encoding that occurs because an unexpected event has strong emotional associations for the person remembering it.

Events such as the horror of 9/11 are so emotional that the memories for the event are stored automatically. Such "flashbulb" memories seem to be very accurate, as if the person's mind took a flash picture of that moment in time, but are actually no more accurate than any other memory.

PRACTICE QUIZ: HOW MUCH DO YOU REMEMBER?

Pick the best answer.

1. The best place to take your math exam to ensure good retrieval of math concepts is in
   a. the math classroom.
   b. an auditorium, to prevent cheating.
   c. the English classroom.
   d. the special testing room used for all exams.

2. Sarah can remember names of the first two people she was introduced to at Ted's party, and she can remember the name of the last person she met, but the names of the dozen or so people in between are gone. This is an example of the
   a. encoding specificity effect.
   b. serial position effect.
   c. tip-of-the-tongue effect.
   d. reintegrative effect.

3. This quiz question, as well as the other quiz questions, makes use of which form of retrieval of memories?
   a. rehearsal
   b. relearning
   c. recall
   d. recognition

4. Which of the following statements about flashbulb memories is FALSE?
   a. They may be formed by the hormones released at emotional moments.
   b. They are vivid and detailed.
   c. They are unusually accurate.
   d. They can be personal or concern world events.

Answers: 1-a, 2-b, 3-d, 4-c

THE RECONSTRUCTIVE NATURE OF LONG-TERM MEMORY RETRIEVAL: HOW RELIABLE ARE MEMORIES?

> I think my memory is pretty good, but my brother and I often have arguments about things that happened when we were kids. Why don't we have the same exact memories? We were both there!

I think my memory is pretty good, but my brother and I often have arguments about things that happened when we were kids. Why don't we have the same exact memories? We were both there! People tend to assume that their memories are accurate when, in fact, memories are revised, edited, and altered on an almost continuous basis. The reason for the changes that occur in memory has to do with the way in which memories are formed as well as how they are retrieved.

CONSTRUCTIVE PROCESSING OF MEMORIES

6.11 *How are long-term memories formed, and what kinds of problems do people experience as a result?*

Many people have the idea that when they recall a memory, they are recalling it as if it were an "instant replay." One of the first to propose this idea was a Canadian, Wilder Penfield. Penfield (1957) believed that "The brain records the past like a continuous strip of movie film, complete with sound track" (p. 265). In reality, memories (including flashbulb memories) are never quite accurate, and the more time that passes, the more inaccuracies creep in. As new memories are created in LTM, old memories can get "lost," but they are more likely to be changed or altered in some way (Baddeley, 1988).

Think about the example of the filing system used to talk about LTM. What if different parts of each file (the sound, the image, the meaning, etc.) are stored in different areas of the filing system? When a person wants to retrieve that piece of information, files have to be pulled out of several places and put back together into the original item. Isn't it very likely that some pieces of the original item will not be retrieved? In fact, isn't it likely that some may never have been properly stored in the first place, and that some information gets added in that was not originally part of the file?

For more than 30 years, Dr. Elizabeth Loftus has been one of the world's leading researchers in the area of memory. Her focus has been on the accuracy of recall of memories—or rather, the inaccuracies of memory retrieval. Loftus and many others have demonstrated time and again that memory is not an unchanging, stable process but rather is a constantly changing one. People continually update and revise their memories of events without being aware that they are doing so, and they incorporate information gained after the actual event, whether correct or incorrect.

Loftus, along with other researchers (Bruck, Ceci, Francoeur, & Barr, 1995; Hyman & Loftus, 1998, 2002), has provided ample evidence for the **constructive processing** view of memory retrieval. In this view, memories are literally "built" from the pieces stored away at encoding. Each time a memory is retrieved, it may be altered or revised in some way to include new information, or details that were there at encoding may be left out of the new retrieval.

MEMORY RETRIEVAL PROBLEMS

Some people may say that they have "total recall." What they usually mean is that they feel that their memories are more accurate than those of other people. As should be obvious by now, true total recall is not a very likely ability for anyone to have. Here are some reasons why people have trouble recalling information accurately.

THE MISINFORMATION EFFECT   Elizabeth Loftus, in addition to her studies concerning eyewitness testimony, has also done several similar studies that demonstrate the **misinformation effect**. In this effect, misleading information that is presented *after* an event has taken place can affect the accuracy of the memory for that event (Loftus et al., 1978). In one study, participants viewed a slide presentation of a traffic accident. The actual slide presentation contained a stop sign; but, in a written summary of the presentation, the sign was referred to as a yield sign. Participants who were given this misleading information after viewing the slides were far less accurate in their memories for the kind of sign present than were participants given no such information. One of the interesting points to be made by this study is that information that comes not only after the original event but also in an entirely different format (i.e., written instead of visual) can cause memories of the event to be incorrectly reconstructed.

While a great deal of Loftus's work focuses on adults, other researchers have focused on the suggestibility of children. When Maggie Bruck was at McGill University, she collaborated on a research project investigating whether children's reports regarding a visit to their pediatrician could be influenced by misleading information (Bruck et al., 1995). The children visited their pediatrician to get an inoculation, an event that is usually stressful for a child. Results showed that, after one year had passed, children who had been given misleading information about the actions of the pediatrician included more false memories in their reports than those who were not given any misleading information.

constructive processing
referring to the retrieval of memories in which those memories are altered, revised, or influenced by newer information.

misinformation effect
the tendency of misleading information presented after an event to alter the memories of the event itself.

Elizabeth Loftus and colleagues (1978) have shown that participants who are given misleading information after viewing slides such as these were far less accurate in their memories for the kind of sign present than were participants who were not given misleading information.

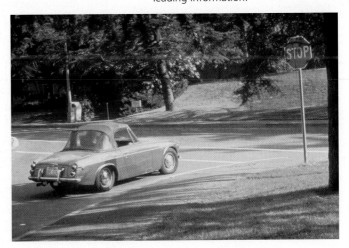

RELIABILITY OF MEMORY RETRIEVAL

6.12 *What is false memory syndrome?*

If memory is edited and changed when people are in a state of waking consciousness, alert and making an effort to retrieve information, how much more might memory be changed when people are in an altered state of conscious, such as hypnosis? *False memory syndrome* refers to the creation of inaccurate or false memories through the suggestion of others, often while the person is under hypnosis (Hochman, 1994).

For example, research has shown that although hypnosis may make it easier to recall some real memories, it also makes it easier to recall false memories. Hypnosis also has been found to increase the confidence people have in their memories, regardless of whether those memories are real or false. False memories have been accidentally created by therapist suggestions during hypnotic therapy sessions (especially those that involve age regression in which therapists lead their hypnotized patients to believe that they are at a younger age in order to relive certain experiences; Bowman, 1996).

The debate as to whether hypnosis leads to false memories is still going strong today, with contradictory findings being put forth by numerous researchers. Currently, the Canadian Psychological Association maintains that current research supports the existence of repressed memories and also that memories can be altered in response to suggestions. (L I N K) *to Chapter Four: Consciousness, p. 134.* For more information on false memory syndrome, visit the False Memory Syndrome Foundation website at **www.fmsonline.org**.

Some recent evidence suggests false memories are created in the brain in much the same way as real memories are formed, especially when visual images are involved (Gonsalves et al., 2004). Researchers, using MRI scans, looked at the brain activity of people who were looking at real visual images and then were asked to imagine looking at visual images. They found that these same people were often unable to later distinguish between the images they had really seen and the imagined images when asked to remember which images were real or imagined. This result might explain why asking people whether they saw a particular person at a crime scene (causing them to imagine the image of that person) might affect the memories those people have of the crime when questioned some time later—the person they were asked to think about may be falsely remembered as having been present.

Clearly, memories obtained through hypnosis should not be considered as accurate without solid evidence from other sources.

But I've heard about people who, under hypnosis, ▶ remember being abused as children. Aren't those memories sometimes real?

But I've heard about people who, under hypnosis, remember being abused as children. Aren't those memories sometimes real? Some researchers argue that false memory syndrome is not as prevalent as many believe it to be. For example, Wendy Hovdestad and Connie Kristiansen (1996) of Carleton University argued that of the individuals with recovered memories, only 3.9 to 13.6 percent satisfied the criteria for false memory syndrome. The fact that some people recover false memories under certain conditions does not mean that child molestation does not really happen; nor does it mean that a person who was molested might not push that unwanted memory away from conscious thought. Molestation is a sad fact: According to the Canadian National Advisory Council of Women, one in three females and one in six males experience some form of sexual abuse before the age of 18.

So can we trust any of ▶ our memories at all?

So can we trust any of our memories at all? On a more positive and promising note (and in contrast to research supporting false memory syndrome relating to trauma), recent research by Steven Porter and Kristine Peace (2007) of Dalhousie University suggests that victims may actually be able to recall the details of traumatic events such as physical or sexual assault later with as much clarity as on the day they happened. Porter and Peace recorded participants' memories surrounding both a traumatic event and a positive event. The participants were re-interviewed three months and five years later. It was found that participants' memory for the positive event changed dramatically while their memory for the central details of the traumatic criminal event was remarkably reliable.

There is also evidence to suggest that false memories cannot be created for just any kind of memory. The *memories* must at least be plausible, according to the research of cognitive psychologist and memory expert Kathy Pezdek, who, with her colleagues, has done several studies demonstrating the resistance of children to the creation of implausible false memories (Hyman et al., 1998; Pezdek et al., 1997; Pezdek & Hodge, 1999).

The idea that only plausible events can become false memories runs contrary to the earlier work of Loftus and colleagues and to research concerning some very implausible false memories that have been successfully implanted, such as a memory for satanic rituals and alien abductions (Mack, 1994). Loftus and colleagues (Mazzoni et al., 2001) conducted several experiments in which they found that implausible events could be made more plausible by having the experimenters provide false feedback to the participants, who read articles telling of the implausible events as if they had actually happened to other people. The false feedback involved telling the participants that their responses to a questionnaire about fears were typical of people who had been through one of the false events (much as a well-meaning therapist might suggest to a client that certain anxieties and feelings are typical of someone who has been abused). These manipulations were so successful that participants not only developed false memories for the events but also even contradicted their own earlier statements in which they denied having these experiences in childhood. The researchers concluded that two steps must occur before people will be likely to interpret their thoughts and fantasies about false events as true memories:

1. The event must be made to seem as plausible as possible.

2. Individuals are given information that helps them believe that the event could have happened to them personally.

◄●─Simulate on mypsychlab

Creating False Memories

PRACTICE QUIZ: HOW MUCH DO YOU REMEMBER?

Pick the best answer.

1. The _____ of memory retrieval states that each time a memory is retrieved, it may be altered or revised in some way to include new information, or details that were there at encoding may be left out.
   a. instant replay view
   b. constructive processing view
   c. levels-of-processing view
   d. misinformation effect

2. In their 1978 study, Loftus and colleagues had participants view a slide presentation of an accident. Later, some of the participants were asked a question about a yield sign when the actual slides contained pictures of a stop sign. When these same participants were later asked about what kind of sign was at the accident, they were very likely to be confused in this situation. This is an example of the
   a. instant replay effect.
   b. constructive processing effect.
   c. levels-of-processing effect.
   d. misinformation effect.

3. Which of the following statements about memory retrieval while under hypnosis is true?
   a. These memories are more accurate than other kinds of memories.
   b. People recalling memories under hypnosis are more confident in their memories, regardless of accuracy.
   c. Hypnosis makes it *more difficult* to recall memories in general.
   d. Age regression through hypnosis can increase the accuracy of recall of early childhood memories.

4. Pezdek and colleagues found that for a person to interpret thoughts and fantasies about false events as true memories
   a. the event must seem as plausible as possible.
   b. the person must believe in repression.
   c. there is very little information provided about the event.
   d. they need to hear about the event *only* once.

► Why do we forget things? And why do we forget some things but not others?

WELL, FOR CRYING OUT LOUD! AL TOWBRIDGE! WHAT IS IT, NINE YEARS, SEVEN MONTHS, AND TWELVE DAYS SINCE I LAST RAN INTO YOU? TEN-THIRTY-TWO A.M., A SATURDAY, FELCHER'S HARDWARE STORE. YOU WERE BUYING SEALER FOR YOUR BLACKTOP DRIVEWAY. TELL ME, AL, HOW DID THAT SEALER WORK? DID IT HOLD UP?

MR. TOTAL RECALL

curve of forgetting
a graph showing a distinct pattern in which forgetting is very fast within the first hour after learning a list and then tapers off gradually.

WHAT WERE WE TALKING ABOUT? FORGETTING

Why do we forget things? And why do we forget some things but not others?

6.13 Why do we forget?

Think for a minute: What would it be like if people didn't forget anything? At first, the answer seems to be that such a phenomenal memory would be great, right? Anything people learned would always be there. But what if people *couldn't* forget? That is exactly the problem experienced in the case of A. R. Luria's (1968) famous *mnemonist*, Mr. S. (A mnemonist is a memory expert or someone with exceptional memory ability.) Mr. S. was a performing mnemonist, astonishing his audiences with lists of numbers that he memorized in minutes. But Mr. S. found that he *was unable to forget* the lists. He also could not easily separate important memories from trivial ones, and each time he looked at an object or read a word, images stimulated by that object or word would flood his mind. He eventually invented a way to "forget" things—by writing them on a piece of paper and then burning the paper (Luria, 1968).

The ability to forget seems necessary to one's sanity, if the experience of Mr. S. is any indicator. But how fast do people forget things? Are there some things that are harder or easier to forget?

EBBINGHAUS AND THE FORGETTING CURVE

Hermann Ebbinghaus (1913) was one of the first researchers to study forgetting. Because he did not want any verbal associations to aid him in remembering, he created several lists of "nonsense syllables," pronounceable but meaningless (such as *GEX* and *WOL*). He memorized a list, waited a specific amount of time, and then tried to retrieve the list, graphing his results each time. The result has become a familiar graph: the **curve of forgetting**. This graph clearly shows that forgetting happens quickly within the first hour after learning the lists and then tapers off gradually (see Figure 6.8). In other words, forgetting is greatest just after learning. This curve can be applied to other types of information as well. Although meaningful material is forgotten much more slowly and much less completely, the pattern obtained when testing for forgetting is similar (Conway et al., 1992).

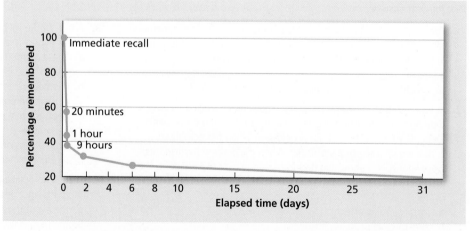

FIGURE 6.8 **Curve of Forgetting** Ebbinghaus found that his recall of words from his memorized word lists was greatest immediately after learning the list but rapidly decreased within the first hour. After the first hour, forgetting levelled off.

ENCODING FAILURE

People forget things for several reasons. One of the simplest is that some things never get encoded in the first place. Your friend, for example, may have said something to you as he walked out the door, and you may have heard him; but, if you weren't paying attention to what he said, it would not get past sensory memory. This isn't forgetting so much as it is **encoding failure**, the failure to process information into memory. Researchers developed a test of encoding failure using images of pennies (Nickerson & Adams, 1979). Look at Figure 6.9. Which view of a penny is the correct one? People see pennies nearly every day, but how many people actually look at what's on the penny and try to remember it?

FIGURE 6.9 **Which Penny Is Real?** Most people do not really look at the face of a penny. Which of these pennies represents an actual penny? The answer can be found on the next page.

→●─Simulate on mypsychlab

Forgetting

encoding failure
the failure to process information into memory.

memory trace
physical change in the brain that occurs when a memory is formed.

decay
loss of memory because of the passage of time, during which the memory trace is not used.

disuse
another name for *decay*, assuming that memories that are not used will eventually decay and disappear.

MEMORY TRACE DECAY THEORY

One of the older theories of forgetting involves the concept of a **memory trace**. A memory trace is some physical change in the brain, perhaps in a neuron or in the activity between neurons, that occurs when a memory is formed (Brown, 1958; Peterson & Peterson, 1959). Over time, if these traces are not used, they may **decay**, fading into nothing. It would be similar to what happens when a number of people walk across a particular patch of grass, causing a path to appear in which the grass is trampled down and perhaps turns brown. But if people stop using the path, the grass grows back and the path disappears.

Forgetting in sensory memory and STM seems easy to explain as decay: Information that is not brought to attention in sensory memory or continuously rehearsed in STM will fade away. But is decay a good explanation for forgetting from LTM? When referring to LTM, decay theory is usually called **disuse**, and the phrase "use it or lose it" takes on great meaning (Bjork & Bjork, 1992). Although the fading of information from LTM through disuse sounds logical, there are many times when people can recall memories they had assumed were long forgotten. In addition, students are often tested more than once on the same material and perform better on the later tests than they did on the initial test. There must be other factors aside from decay involved in the forgetting of long-term memories.

The fact that this woman can remember the things shown in the pictures even after many years makes it unlikely that the memory trace decay theory can explain all forgetting in long-term memory.

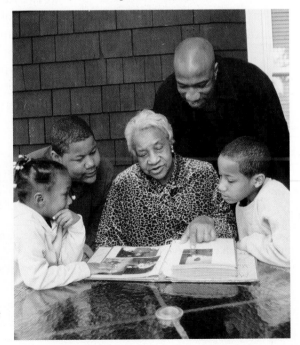

INTERFERENCE THEORY

A possible explanation of LTM forgetting is that although most long-term memories may be stored more or less permanently in the brain, those memories may not always be accessible to attempted retrieval because other information interferes (Anderson & Neely, 1995). And even memories that are accessible are subject to constructive processing, which can lead to inaccurate recall. A great deal of research indicates that interference is the key process in forgetting (e.g., Bower, Thompson, & Tulving, 1994). An analogy might be this: The can of paint that Phillip wants may very well be on some shelf in his storeroom, but there's so much other junk in its way that he can't see it and can't get to it. In the case of LTM, interference can come from two different "directions."

Proactive Interference

French, learned **beforehand**, interferes proactively

Study French	Study Spanish	Spanish Test

Retroactive Interference

Spanish, learned **afterward**, interferes retroactively

Study French	Study Spanish	French Test

FIGURE 6.10 **Proactive and Retroactive Interference**
If a student were to study for a French exam and then a Spanish exam, interference could occur in two directions. When taking the Spanish exam, the French information studied first may proactively interfere with retrieval of the Spanish information. But when taking the French exam, the more recently studied Spanish information may retroactively interfere with the retrieval of the French information.

The answer to Figure 6.9 on p. 31 is D.

proactive interference
memory retrieval problem that occurs when older information prevents or interferes with the retrieval of newer information.

retroactive interference
memory retrieval problem that occurs when newer information prevents or interferes with the retrieval of older information.

People who are used to driving on the right side of the road experience quite a bit of proactive interference when trying to learn to drive in England, where cars are driven on the left. When this man returns home from vacation, he may experience retroactive interference in trying to remember to drive on the right side of the road again.

PROACTIVE INTERFERENCE Have you ever switched your phone number? You may have found yourself remembering your old phone number or some of its digits instead of the new number when you gave the new number to friends. The reason why this causes problems is because of **proactive interference**: the tendency for older or previously learned material to interfere with the retrieval of newer, more recently learned material (see Figure 6.10).

RETROACTIVE INTERFERENCE When newer information interferes with the retrieval of older information, this is called **retroactive interference** (see Figure 6.10). What happens when you have to update your personal information for school records or a store you hold an account with? You will likely have to remember your previous phone number to do so. Chances are your new number will interfere with the recollection of your old number.

The different ways that forgetting occurs are summarized in Table 6.1.

TABLE 6.1 TYPES OF FORGETTING	
TYPE OF FORGETTING	**DESCRIPTION**
Encoding Failure	The information is not attended to and fails to be encoded.
Decay or Disuse	Information that is not accessed decays from the storage system over time.
Proactive Interference	Older information already in memory interferes with the retrieval of newer information.
Retroactive Interference	Newer information interferes with the retrieval of older information.

PRACTICE QUIZ: HOW MUCH DO YOU REMEMBER?

Pick the best answer.

1. Salvatore was introduced to a number of new people on his first day at his new job. According to Ebbinghaus, when should Salvatore expect to have forgotten the greatest number of the names he has just learned?
   a. within the first hour after learning the names
   b. within the first day after learning the names
   c. near the end of the first week on the job
   d. near the middle of the first week on the job

2. When a person "forgets" what someone has just said because he or she wasn't paying attention to the speaker at all, it is an example of the _____ explanation of forgetting.
   a. interference
   b. memory trace
   c. encoding failure
   d. repression

3. Decay theory works well to explain forgetting in
   a. sensory memory only.
   b. short-term memory only.
   c. long-term memory only.
   d. sensory memory and short-term memory.

4. Edna took sociology in the fall semester and is now taking psychology. Some of the concepts are similar, and Edna finds that she sometimes has trouble recalling some of the major sociology theorists. She keeps getting them confused with psychology theorists. Edna's problem is most likely due to
   a. encoding failure.
   b. proactive interference.
   c. retroactive interference.
   d. none of the above

5. Brian went from Canada, where he grew up, to England. The first week he was there, he had a terrible time remembering to drive on the left side of the road. His problem is most likely due to
   a. encoding failure.
   b. retroactive interference.
   c. proactive interference.
   d. none of the above

Answers: 1-a, 2-c, 3-d, 4-b, 5-c.

MEMORY AND THE BRAIN: THE PHYSICAL ASPECTS OF MEMORY

6.14   *How and where are memories formed in the brain?*

The physical change that takes place in the brain when a memory is formed is called the *engram*. Researchers have evidence that specific areas of the brain may be the places in which engrams are formed and that these areas are different for different types of memory. For example, procedural memories seem to be stored in the cerebellum (Boyd & Winstein, 2004; Daum & Schugens, 1996). Research involving PET scanning techniques strongly suggests that short-term memories are stored in the prefrontal cortex (the very front of the frontal lobe) and the temporal lobe (Cabeza & Nyberg, 2000; Goldman-Rakic, 1998; Rao et al., 1997). Ⓛ Ⓘ Ⓝ Ⓚ *to Chapter Two: The Biological Perspective, p. 42.*

As for semantic and episodic long-term memories, evidence suggests that these memories are also stored in the frontal and temporal lobes but not in exactly the same places, nor in the same location as short-term memories (Cabeza & Nyberg, 2000; Weis et al., 2004). In fact, after reviewing 275 PET and fMRI studies, Roberto Cabeza, of the University of Alberta, and Lars Nyberg, of Umea University in Sweden, found that different areas were activated in episodic memory tasks involving encoding from areas that were activated in episodic memory tasks involving retrieval (Cabeza & Nyberg, 2000). As discussed in Chapter Two, memories relating to fear are stored in the amygdala.

All that explains is the "where" of memory. Did scientists ever find out the "what," or the exact physical change that happens in the brain when memories are stored?

NEURAL ACTIVITY AND STRUCTURE IN MEMORY FORMATION

Several studies have offered evidence that the engram is not simply one physical change but many: changes in the number of receptor sites, changes in the sensitivity of the synapse through repeated stimulation (called *long-term potentiation*), and

◄─●─ **Simulate** on **mypsychlab**
Virtual Brain: Learning and Memory

All that explains is the "where" of memory. Did scientists ever find ◄ out the "what," or the exact physical change that happens in the brain when memories are stored?

consolidation
the changes that take place in the structure and functioning of neurons when an engram is formed.

retrograde amnesia
loss of memory from the point of some injury or trauma backward, or loss of memory for the past.

changes in the dendrites and the proteins within the neurons (Alkon, 1989; Kandel & Schwartz, 1982; Squire & Kandel, 1999). All these changes serve to increase the neural connections and make connections that already exist more sensitive to stimulation. These changes that take place as an engram is forming are called **consolidation**. Although people may learn quickly, the memory of what has been learned takes some time to form completely.

As discussed in Chapter One, Canadian Donald Hebb presented one of the most influential physiological theories of memory. Hebb put forth the idea that when two neurons are active at the same time, the synapses between them are strengthened. So when specific groups of neurons are firing more than others, patterns of firing are created. According to Hebb, these patterns must be established in order for memories to be transferred from STM to LTM. When it comes to remembering information, certain neurons are repeatedly activated by various events, making those events better remembered and more easily retrieved (Hebb, 1949). Hebb's work led to the idea of long-term potentiation, which is mentioned above. ⓛⓘⓝⓚ *to Chapter One: The Science of Psychology, p. 13.*

THE HIPPOCAMPUS AND MEMORY

In the discussion of the hippocampus (a part of the limbic system) in Chapter Two (p. 68), the hippocampus was identified as the part of the brain responsible for the formation of new long-term memories. One of the clearest pieces of evidence of this function comes from the study of a man known as H. M. (Milner et al., 1968), the American amnesiac mentioned at the beginning of this chapter.

H. M. was about 17 when he began to suffer from severe epileptic seizures. A few years later, H. M.'s hippocampi were completely removed in an attempt to remove what the surgeon incorrectly believed was the source of the seizures. The last thing H. M. could remember was being rolled on the gurney to the operating room, and that was the last memory he was ever able to form. The hippocampus was not the source of his problem. It was, however, apparently the source of his ability to store any new information he encountered, because without either hippocampus, he was completely unable to remember anything new. Consolidation had become impossible. He had a magazine that he carried around, reading and rereading the stories, because each time he did so the stories were completely new to him. As with most amnesiacs of this type (although H. M.'s case was quite severe), his procedural memory was still intact. It was only new declarative memory—both semantic and episodic—that was lost.

WHEN MEMORY FAILS: ORGANIC AMNESIA

6.15 *What is amnesia?*

There are two forms of severe loss of memory disorders caused by problems in the functioning of the memory areas of the brain.

RETROGRADE AMNESIA   If the hippocampus is that important to the formation of memories, what would happen if it was temporarily "disconnected"? People who are in accidents in which they receive a head injury often are unable to recall the accident itself. Sometimes they cannot remember the last several hours or even days before the accident. This type of amnesia (literally, "without memory") is called **retrograde amnesia**, which is loss of memory from the point of injury backward (Hodges, 1994). What apparently happens in this kind of memory loss is that the consolidation process, which was busy making the physical changes to allow new memories to be stored, gets disrupted and loses everything that was not already nearly "finished."

Think about this: You are working on your computer, trying to finish a history paper that is due tomorrow. Your computer saves the document every 10 minutes, but you are working so furiously that you've written a lot in the past 10 minutes. Then the power goes out—horrors! When the power comes back on, you find that while all the files you had already saved are still intact, your history paper is missing that last 10 minutes' worth of work. This is similar to what happens when someone's consolidation process is disrupted. All memories that were in the process of being stored but are not yet permanent are lost.

ANTEROGRADE AMNESIA   The kind of amnesia that H. M. experienced is called anterograde amnesia, the loss of memories from the point of injury or illness forward (Squire & Slater, 1978). Movies such as *Memento* and *50 First Dates* have centred on characters with anterograde amnesia. People with this kind of amnesia, like H. M., have difficulty remembering anything new. This amnesia is also the kind most often seen in people with *senile dementia*, a mental disorder in which severe forgetfulness, mental confusion, and mood swings are the primary symptoms. (Dementia patients also may suffer from retrograde amnesia in addition to anterograde amnesia.) If retrograde amnesia is like losing a document in the computer because of a power loss, anterograde amnesia is like discovering that your hard drive has become defective—you can read data that are already on the hard drive, but you can't store any new information. As long as you are looking at the data in your open computer window (i.e., attending to it), you can access it, but as soon as you close that window (stop thinking about it), the information is lost because it was never transferred to the hard drive (LTM).

INFANTILE AMNESIA   What is the earliest memory you have? Chances are you cannot remember much that happened to you before age 3. When a person does claim to "remember" some event from infancy, a little investigation usually reveals that the "memory" is really based on what family members have told the person about that event and it is not a genuine memory at all. This type of "manufactured" memory often has the quality of watching yourself in the memory as if it were a movie and you were an actor. In a genuine memory, you would remember the event through your own eyes—as if you were the camera.

Why can't people remember events from the first two or three years of life? One explanation of **infantile amnesia** involves the type of memory that exists in the first few years of life, when a child is still considered an infant. Early memories tend to be implicit and, as stated earlier in this chapter, implicit memories are difficult to bring to consciousness. Explicit memory, which is the more verbal and conscious form of memory, does not really develop until after about age 2, when the hippocampus is more fully developed and language skills blossom (Carver & Bauer, 2001).

Katherine Nelson (1993) also gives credit to the social relationships that small children have with others. As children are able to talk about shared memories with adults, they begin to develop their **autobiographical memory**, or the memory for events and facts related to one's personal life story.

In a recent paper on culture and autobiographical memory, Michael Ross of the University of Waterloo and Qi Wang of Peking University in China point out that there is overwhelming evidence of cultural differences in terms of autobiographical memory (Ross & Wang, 2010). One example is that there appear to be cultural disparities when it comes to the dates of earliest memories, with North American children generally having earlier memories than children from Asian cultures. According to Ross and Wang (2010), adults of European descent recall events that they date at about 3.5 years of age, while adults of Asian descent tend to recall events that are anywhere from 6 to 17 months later than their counterparts of European descent.

Canadian hockey player Steve Moore makes his first public appearance after suffering major injuries in a hockey game in 2004. In addition to a broken neck, Moore suffered a concussion and developed a form of retrograde amnesia.

 **Explore** on mypsychlab
Amnesia

infantile amnesia
the inability to retrieve memories from much before age 3.

autobiographical memory
the memory for events and facts related to one's personal life story.

One Canadian study that supports this notion was conducted by Carole Peterson of Memorial University in Newfoundland and her colleagues. Peterson, Wang, and Hou (2009) examined the earliest childhood memories of 8-, 11-, and 14-year-old European Canadian and Chinese children and found that the European Canadian children reported earlier first memories than did Chinese children, regardless of their age.

In addition, Wang and Ross (2007) found cultural differences in the *content* of autobiographical memories: participants of European heritage tended to remember personal experiences and feelings, while those of Asian heritage tended to recollect memories based on group actions and interpersonal relationships.

Ross and Wang (2010) argue that these cultural differences, along with others in autobiographical memory, are due to differences in physical environments, self-views, the motivation to self-enhance, behavioural and emotional regulation, socialization, and language.

WHEN MEMORY FAILS: ALZHEIMER'S DISEASE

6.16 *What is Alzheimer's disease?*

People with Alzheimer's disease need constant reminders of where they are, what day it is, and what time it is. As the disease progresses, they may forget how to read, rendering these signs useless.

In 2008, approximately 480 600 Canadians (1.5 percent of Canada's population) were suffering from Alzheimer's disease or related dementias (Alzheimer Society of Canada, 2009). In addition, it is predicted that this number will skyrocket to 1 125 200 (2.8 percent of Canada's population) by the year 2038. The Alzheimer Society of Canada claims that the economic burden of Alzheimer's disease and related dementias doubles every decade, increasing from $15 billion in 2008 to $153 billion in 2038 (2009).

Symptoms of Alzheimer's disease usually begin with changes in memory, which may be rather mild at first but become more severe over time, causing the person to become more and more forgetful about everyday tasks, such as remembering to turn off the stove. Eventually more dangerous forgetting occurs, such as taking extra doses of medication or leaving something cooking on the stove unattended. The person with this disorder repeats things in conversation, thoughts become disorganized, and messages get garbled. As Alzheimer's progresses, the ability to do simple calculations such as balancing a chequebook is lost, along with remembering how to do simple tasks such as bathing or getting dressed. It is a costly disease to care for, and caretakers often face severe emotional and financial burdens in caring for a loved one who is slowly becoming a stranger.

What can be done? There is at present no cure, but in recent years several new medications have been developed that seem to slow the progress of the disease, and new research into the cause gives hope that a cure may one day be a reality. Examples of such medication used in mild-to-moderate Alzheimer's include cholinesterase inhibitors, such as Aricept, which prevent the breakdown of the neurotransmitter acetylcholine, which is important in memory function. Ⓛ Ⓘ Ⓝ Ⓚ *to Chapter Two: The Biological Perspective, p. 52.* An example of a medication used in moderate-to-severe Alzheimer's is memantine, which helps relieve the symptoms of more advanced Alzheimer's disease. Recently, ongoing research is showing that the best treatment protocol is the combination of cholinesterase inhibitors with memantine (Alzheimer Society Toronto, 2007). In addition, according to a media release from the University of British Columbia, doctors may now be able to detect and treat Alzheimer's disease before it progresses to severe degrees of cognitive impairment (UBC Public Affairs, 2007). Dr. Howard Feldman, head of the Division of Neurology at the University of British Columbia's Faculty of Medicine, co-led the development of new guidelines for diagnosing Alzheimer's disease with an international group of researchers.

The new guidelines will change diagnostic criteria so that advanced techniques, such as brain imaging and examining spinal fluid, will be used to detect the early stages of the disease. This early detection will make possible the testing of new preventative vaccines or even treatments that can be used on fully affected patients. In addition, other treatments that can be administered in the early stages of the disease to reduce symptoms can also be tested.

Recently, Dr. Andres Lozano at the University of Toronto has discovered that deep-brain stimulation (LINK) to *Chapter Fourteen: Psychological Therapies, p. 595* may help slow the progression of early Alzheimer's disease through the implantation of electrodes into the hippocampus (LINK) to *Chapter Two: The Biological Perspective, p. 68*, which plays a major role in memory. This treatment is still in its very early stages, and empirical results regarding its effectiveness won't be known for at least a few years (CBC News, 2010).

Watch on **mypsychlab**
Alzheimer's and Dementia

PRACTICE QUIZ: HOW MUCH DO YOU REMEMBER?

Pick the best answer.

1. The physical trace of memory in the brain is called the
   a. memogram.
   c. sonogram.
   b. engram.
   d. pachygram.

2. Katherine is trying to hold the names of the students she just met in her psychology class in short-term memory. According to studies, these short-term memories will be stored in which part of the brain?
   a. cerebellum
   c. amygdala
   b. hippocampus
   d. prefrontal lobes

3. Research suggests that memory formation is a function of
   a. changes in the number of receptor sites.
   b. changes in the sensitivity of the synapse.
   c. changes in the dendrites and proteins within neurons.
   d. all of the above

4. The role of the _____ in the formation of new long-term memories was first made apparent in the case of H. M., a famous amnesiac.
   a. hippocampus
   c. frontal lobes
   b. amygdala
   d. cerebellum

5. T. J. was in a car accident and suffered a concussion. After he recovered, he found that he could not remember the accident itself or the events of the morning leading up to the accident. T. J. had which kind of amnesia?
   a. retrograde
   c. Alzheimer's disease
   b. anterograde
   d. infantile amnesia

Answers: 1-b, 2-d, 3-d, 4-a, 5-a

APPLYING PSYCHOLOGY TO EVERYDAY LIFE: USING FALSE MEMORIES TO PREVENT ALCOHOL ABUSE

6.17   *How can the implementation of false memories be used beneficially?*

Recent research by Dr. Daniel Bernstein from Kwantlen Polytechnic University in British Columbia and his colleagues has focused on the possible health benefits that false memory can provide, such as getting people to eat their vegetables and preventing overeating and alcohol abuse (Bernstein, Laney, Morris, & Loftus, 2005; Bernstein & Loftus, 2009; Laney, Morris, Bernstein, Wakefield, & Loftus, 2008). Bernstein and his colleagues gave participants false feedback about certain foods (e.g., dill pickles, eggs, asparagus). When the false feedback was negative (e.g., the participants were led to believe that as children they had become ill after eating a dill pickle), the participants were less interested in eating that food than were the participants who did not receive false feedback. When the false feedback about a particular food was positive (e.g., as children they had loved eating asparagus), the participants reported liking that food more and were willing to pay more for that food than the other participants who hadn't received false feedback.

The use of false memories can also be used to prevent alcohol abuse. At the 2006 International Conference on Memory in Sydney, Australia, Bernstein presented unpublished research demonstrating that people's liking of rum can be lessened by implanting the false belief that they had been sick as a result of drinking rum in the past. This research is still in its infancy, and much more work needs to be done before any conclusive statements regarding the health benefits of false memories can be made, but it looks promising at the moment.

Questions for Further Discussion

1. How could the procedure Bernstein used in his study be used in a smoking cessation program?

2. What ethical issues need to be taken into consideration before this research can be applied to the health field?

CHAPTER SUMMARY

Memory

6.1 *What is memory, and what are the three processes of memory?*

- Memory can be defined as an active system that receives information from the senses, organizes and alters the information as it stores it away, and then retrieves the information from storage.
- The three processes are encoding, storage, and retrieval.

The Information-Processing Model: Three Stages of Memory

6.2 *What is the information-processing model of memory?*

- The information-processing model assumes that the processing of information for memory storage is similar to the way a computer processes memory in a series of three stages.
- Information-processing theorists propose that there are three stages or types of memory systems: sensory memory, short-term memory, and long-term memory.

6.3 *What is sensory memory?*

- Iconic memory is the visual sensory memory, in which an afterimage or icon will be held in neural form for about one-fourth to one-half second.
- Echoic memory is the auditory form of sensory memory and takes the form of an echo that lasts for up to four seconds.

6.4 *What is short-term memory, and how does it differ from working memory?*

- Short-term memory is where information is held while it is conscious and being used. It holds about seven, plus or minus two, chunks of information and lasts about 30 seconds without rehearsal.
- STM can be lost through failure to rehearse, decay, interference by similar information, and the intrusion of new information into the STM system, which pushes older information out.
- Some memory theorists use the term *working memory* as another way of referring to short-term memory. This is not entirely correct: short-term memory has traditionally been thought of as a thing or a place into which information is put. Working memory is more correctly thought of as an active system that processes the information present in short-term memory.

6.5 *What is long-term memory?*

- Long-term memory is the system in which memories that are to be kept more or less permanently are stored. It is unlimited in capacity and relatively permanent in duration.
- Information that is more deeply processed, or processed according to meaning, will be retained and retrieved more efficiently.

6.6 *Can culture influence what gets encoded into long-term memory?*

- Studies have shown that culture affects the encoding, storage, and retrieval of information in long-term memory.
- Contemporary research has used brain-imaging techniques to determine the effects culture may have on memory.

6.7 *What are the different types of long-term memory, and how is information stored in long-term memory organized?*

- Procedural memories are memories for skills, habits, and conditioned responses. Declarative memories are memories for general facts and personal experiences and include both semantic memories and episodic memories.
- Implicit memories are difficult to bring into conscious awareness, whereas explicit memories are those that a person is aware of possessing.
- Long-term memory is organized in the form of semantic networks, or nodes of related information spreading out from a central piece of knowledge.

Other Models of Memory

6.8 *What are some other models of memory?*

- In the levels-of-processing model of memory, information that gets more deeply processed is more likely to be remembered.
- In the parallel distributed processing model of memory, information is simultaneously stored across an interconnected neural network that stretches across the brain.

Classic Studies in Psychology: Craik, Lockhart, Tulving, and Levels of Processing

- In 1972, Craik and Lockhart decided to go against the status quo by focusing on the processes involved in memory instead of on memory stores or structures. As a result, Craik and Lockhart's levels-of-processing model was created.

- This model was then tested by Craik and Tulving in a famous study. Craik and Tulving (1975) showed that participants were better at recalling semantically processed words than acoustically and visually processed words, demonstrating that deeper processing leads to increased memory performance.

Getting It Out: Retrieval of Long-Term Memories

6.9   *What kinds of cues help people remember?*

- Retrieval cues are words, meanings, sounds, and other stimuli that are encoded at the same time as a new memory.
- Encoding specificity occurs when physical surroundings become encoded as retrieval cues for specific memories.
- State-dependent learning occurs when physiological or psychological states become encoded as retrieval cues for memories formed while in those states.

6.10   *How do the retrieval processes of recall and recognition differ, and how reliable are our memories of events?*

- Recall is a type of memory retrieval in which the information to be retrieved must be "pulled" out of memory with few or no cues, whereas recognition involves matching information with stored images or facts.
- The serial position effect, or primacy or recency effect, occurs when the first items and the last items in a list of information are recalled more efficiently than items in the middle of the list.

Psychology in the News: Wrongfully Convicted

- Loftus and others have found that people constantly update and revise their memories of events, adding information to a memory that occurred later even when that information is in error.
- Automatic encoding of some kinds of information requires very little effort to place information into long-term memory.
- Memory for particularly emotional or traumatic events can lead to the formation of flashbulb memories, memories that seem as vivid and detailed as if the person were looking at a snapshot of the event but that are no more accurate than any other memories.

The Reconstructive Nature of Long-Term Memory Retrieval: How Reliable Are Memories?

6.11   *How are long-term memories formed, and what kinds of problems do people experience as a result?*

- Memories are reconstructed from the various bits and pieces of information that have been stored away in different places at the time of encoding in a process called *constructive processing*.
- The misinformation effect refers to the tendency of people who are asked misleading questions or given misleading information to incorporate that information into their memories for a particular event.

6.12   *What is false memory syndrome?*

- Rather than improving memory retrieval, hypnosis makes the creation of false memories more likely.
- False memory syndrome is the creation of false or inaccurate memories through suggestion, especially while hypnotized.
- Pezdek and colleagues assert that false memories are more likely to be formed for plausible false events than for implausible ones.

What Were We Talking About? Forgetting

6.13   *Why do we forget?*

- Ebbinghaus found that information is mostly lost within one hour after learning and then gradually fades away. This is known as the curve of forgetting.

- A failure to encode information will not produce a memory.
- Memory trace decay theory assumes the presence of a physical memory trace that decays with disuse over time.
- Forgetting in LTM is most likely due to proactive or retroactive interference.

Memory and the Brain: The Physical Aspects of Memory

6.14   *How and where are memories formed in the brain?*

- Different memories are stored in different parts of the brain.
- Procedural memories appear to be stored in the cerebellum.
- Both short-term memories and long-term memories are stored in the frontal and temporal lobes but not in exactly the same places nor in the same location.
- Memories relating to fear are stored in the amygdala.
- Consolidation consists of the physical changes in neurons that take place during the formation of a memory.
- The hippocampus appears to be responsible for the storage of new long-term memories. If it is removed, the ability to store anything new is completely lost.

6.15   *What is amnesia?*

- In retrograde amnesia, memory for the past (prior to the injury) is lost, which can be a loss of only minutes or a loss of several years.
- In anterograde amnesia, memory for anything new becomes impossible, although old memories may still be retrievable.
- Most people cannot remember events that occurred before age 2 or 3. This is called infantile amnesia and is most likely because of the implicit nature of infant memory.
- As children are able to talk about shared memories with adults, they begin to develop their autobiographical memory, which is the memory for events and facts related to one's personal life story.
- Recent research indicates that autobiographical memory is deeply affected by culture.

6.16   *What is Alzheimer's disease?*

- Symptoms of Alzheimer's disease usually begin with changes in memory, which may be rather mild at first but become more severe over time, causing the person to become more and more forgetful about everyday tasks. Eventually, more dangerous forgetting occurs.
- The primary memory difficulty in Alzheimer's is anterograde amnesia, although retrograde amnesia can also occur as the disease progresses.
- There are various drugs in use or in development for use in slowing or stopping the progression of Alzheimer's disease.
- New guidelines will change the criteria so that advanced brain-imaging techniques and different processes, such as examining spinal fluid, will be used to detect the early stages of the disease.
- Early detection will make possible the testing of new preventative vaccines or even treatments that can be used on fully affected patients. In addition, other pharmacological treatments that can be administered in the early stages of the disease to reduce symptoms can also be tested.

Applying Psychology to Everyday Life: Using False Memories to Prevent Alcohol Abuse

6.17   *How can the implementation of false memories be used beneficially?*

- There exist possible health benefits that false memory can provide, such as getting people to eat their vegetables and preventing overeating and alcohol abuse.

6 KEY TERMS

anterograde amnesia   230
autobiographical memory   251
automatic encoding   241
consolidation   250
constructive processing   243
curve of forgetting   246
decay   247
declarative memory   231
disuse   247
echoic memory   223
eidetic imagery   223
elaborative rehearsal   229
encoding   220
encoding failure   247
encoding specificity   236
episodic memory   231

explicit memory   231
false positive   240
flashbulb memories   241
iconic memory   222
implicit memory   230
infantile amnesia   251
information-processing model   221
levels-of-processing model   234
long-term memory (LTM)   227
maintenance rehearsal   227
memory   220
memory trace   247
misinformation effect   243
parallel distributed processing (PDP)
   model   235
primacy effect   238

proactive interference   248
procedural (non-declarative) memory   230
recall   238
recency effect   239
recognition   238
retrieval   221
retrieval cue   236
retroactive interference   248
retrograde amnesia   250
selective attention   224
semantic memory   231
semantic network model   232
sensory memory   222
serial position effect   238
short-term memory (STM)   224
storage   220
working memory   225

TEST YOURSELF

Pick the best answer.

1. Memory can best be described as
   a. a series of storage bins or boxes.
   b. a process of storage.
   c. an active system that encodes, stores, and retrieves information.
   d. a series of passive data files.
2. In the _____ model of memory, memories are simultaneously created and stored across a mental network.
   a. levels-of-processing
   b. parallel distributed processing
   c. transfer-appropriate processing
   d. information-processing
3. Roberta looked up from her book, realizing that Joaquin had just said something to her. What was it? Oh, yes, he had just asked her whether she wanted to go out to dinner. Roberta's ability to retrieve what Joaquin said is due to her
   a. iconic sensory memory.
   b. echoic sensory memory.
   c. short-term memory.
   d. tactile sensory memory.
4. Although Sperling found evidence that iconic memory lasts about half a second, in reality, information gets pushed out rather quickly by newer information. Evidence suggests that iconic memory really lasts about _____ of a second.
   a. three-quarters
   b. half
   c. one-quarter
   d. one-tenth
5. The duration of echoic memory is _____ than iconic memory, but its capacity is probably _____.
   a. shorter; larger
   b. longer; smaller
   c. longer; about the same
   d. shorter; about the same

6. When Greg tried to remember the name of his employer's wife, he had trouble getting the right name. At first he thought it might be Sandy or Candy, but he finally realized that it was Mandy. Greg's confusion is evidence that short-term memories are primarily encoded in _____ form.
   a. acoustic   c. ltactile
   b. visua   d. optical
7. Although the capacity of short-term memory is limited, more items can be held in this kind of storage through the process of
   a. chunking.   c. rote rehearsal.
   b. decoding.   d. data compression.
8. The best method for encoding long-term memories is probably to use
   a. maintenance rehearsal.   c. elaborative rehearsal.
   b. rote rehearsal.   d. sleep learning.
9. The levels-of-processing concept of Craik and Tulving would suggest that which of the following questions would lead to better memory of the word *frog*?
   a. Does it rhyme with *blog*?
   b. Is it in capital letters?
   c. Is it written in cursive?
   d. Would it be found in a pond?
10. Which type of long-term memory is revised and updated more or less constantly?
   a. procedural
   b. declarative
   c. semantic
   d. episodic
11. Knowledge that we gain from school is called _____ memory.
   a. procedural
   b. declarative
   c. semantic
   d. episodic

12. The semantic network model of memory would suggest that which of the following questions would take longest to answer?
    a. Is a collie a dog?
    b. Is a collie a mammal?
    c. Is a collie an animal?
    d. There would be no difference in answering times.

13. The research of Eich and Metcalfe would suggest that if you were really angry when you were learning Spanish, you should be _____ when taking the final exam for best retrieval.
    a. really calm
    b. unemotional
    c. angry
    d. depressed

14. Which of the following is NOT an example of a test using recall?
    a. short answer
    b. essay
    c. fill in the blanks
    d. true–false

15. The serial position effect predicts that the information that will be remembered best from a list will come at the _____ of the list.
    a. beginning
    b. end
    c. middle
    d. beginning and the end

16. Melanie was having a difficult time describing the man who took her purse in the mall parking lot. The officer showed her some pictures of people who had been involved in similar crimes, and she was quickly able to point out the right man. Melanie's situation is a reminder that in comparing recognition to recall, recognition tends to be
    a. easier.
    b. slower.
    c. more difficult.
    d. less accurate.

17. Is eyewitness testimony usually accurate?
    a. Yes, because seeing is believing.
    b. No, because eyewitnesses are not usually honest.
    c. Yes, because eyewitnesses are very confident about their testimony.
    d. No, because there is a great possibility of a "false positive" identification.

18. The passage of time and frequency of events are examples of knowledge that is often subject to
    a. encoding specificity.
    b. automatic encoding.
    c. flashbulb memories.
    d. eidetic imagery.

19. When retrieving a long-term memory, bits and pieces of information are gathered from various areas and put back together in a process called
    a. consolidation.
    b. reintegration.
    c. constructive processing.
    d. automatic processing.

20. Ebbinghaus found that information is forgotten
    a. more rapidly as time goes by.
    b. gradually at first, and then increasing in speed of forgetting.
    c. quickly at first, and then tapering off gradually.
    d. most quickly one day after learning.

21. A problem with using memory trace decay theory to explain forgetting from long-term memory is that
    a. older people can still remember things from their early years.
    b. there is no physical change in the brain when forming long-term memories.
    c. older memories always get lost, while newer memories always remain.
    d. older people cannot remember events in their childhood.

22. You started out by using WordPerfect and then moved to Microsoft Word because your company demanded that all documents be in Word. If you have trouble with Word, it is most likely due to
    a. proactive interference.
    b. retroactive interference.
    c. anterograde interference.
    d. consolidation problems.

23. The main type of memory problem that people with dementia, including Alzheimer's, typically have is called
    a. psychogenic amnesia.
    b. retrograde amnesia.
    c. retroactive amnesia.
    d. anterograde amnesia.

24. One theory that explains infantile amnesia states that these memories are
    a. never fully stored and therefore not available.
    b. explicit and not retrievable consciously.
    c. implicit and not retrievable consciously.
    d. repressed.

25. Which of the following is an example of an advanced technique that may be used to diagnose Alzheimer's disease?
    a. brain imaging
    b. examination of the spinal fluid
    c. both a and b
    d. none of the above

Answers: 1-c, 2-b, 3-b, 4-c, 5-b, 6-a, 7-a, 8-c, 9-d, 10-d, 11-c, 12-c, 13-c, 14-d, 15-d, 16-a, 17-d, 18-b, 19-b, 20-c, 21-a, 22-a, 23-d, 24-c, 25-c.

ScanLife™ Barcode

To access more tests and your own personalized study plan that will help you focus on the areas you need to master before your next class test, be sure to go to **www.MyPsychLab.com**, Pearson Education Canada's online psychology website, available with the access code packaged with your book.

Memory: Three Processes

Memory: system that actively stores and retrieves information

Three processes are
▸ Encoding ▸ Storage ▸ Retrieval

6.1

Information-Processing Model

▸ Processing of information in memory is similar to the way a computer processes memory.
▸ Three stages or types of memory systems: sensory memory, short-term memory, and long-term memory

6.2

Information-Processing Theory: Three Stages of Memory

Long-Term Memory

▸ Memories are more or less permanent.
▸ Unlimited in capacity
▸ Deeply processed information is retained and retrieved more efficiently.
▸ Culture affects the encoding, storage, and retrieval of information in long-term memory.

6.5–6.6

Sensory Memory

Iconic memory:
▸ Visual representation in neural form
▸ Lasts 1/4 second

Echoic memory:
▸ Auditory form
▸ Lasts for up to four seconds

6.3

Short-Term or Working Memory

▸ Holds information before storage into LTM or information that is currently in use
▸ Capacity of 7 ± 2 chunks of information
▸ Duration of 12 to 30 seconds without rehearsal

Loss of STM contents:
▸ Failure to rehearse
▸ Decay
▸ Interference by similar information
▸ Intrusion of new information into STM

6.4

Types of Long-Term Memory

Procedural memories: skills, habits, and conditioned responses

Declarative memories: general facts and personal experiences. Includes

  Semantic memories: general knowledge, such as knowledge of language and information learned in formal education

  Episodic memories: personal information such as daily activities and events

Implicit memories: difficult to bring into conscious awareness

Explicit memories: Person is aware of possessing.

Long-Term Memory Organization

Semantic networks: nodes of related information spreading out from a central piece of knowledge

6.7

THREE-STAGE MODEL OF MEMORY

Maintenance rehearsal

Sensory memory → Selective attention → Short-term memory → Encoding → Long-term memory

Retrieval

All information is lost within a second or so.

Unrehearsed information is lost in about 12 to 30 seconds.

Some information is retained indefinitely; some is lost with the passage of time.

Other Models of Memory

▸ **Levels-of-processing model:** Information that is processed at a deeper level is more likely to be remembered.
▸ **Parallel distributed processing model:** Information is simultaneously stored across an interconnected neural network that stretches across the brain.

6.8

Psychology in the News: Wrongfully Convicted

Eyewitness Testimony Reliability

Loftus and others have found
▸ People update and revise their memories of events.
▸ Add information to a memory that occurred later
▸ Revisions occur even if information is in error.

6.10

Flashbulb Memory

▸ Vivid and detailed memories caused by emotional or traumatic events
▸ No more accurate than any other memories

6.10

Use of Cues for Remembering

Retrieval cue: a stimulus for remembering. Retrieval cues are encoded at same time as new memory.

Encoding specificity: Physical surroundings become encoded as retrieval cues.

State-dependent learning: physiological/psychological states used as retrieval cues

6.9

Differences Between Recall and Recognition

Recall: Information must be "pulled" out of memory.

Recognition: involves matching information with stored images or facts

Serial position effect: First items and last items in a list are recalled better than middle items.

6.10

Long-Term Memory Formation

Constructive processing: Memories are reconstructed from information that is stored during encoding.

Memory Retrieval Problems

Misinformation effect: Misleading questions or information may be incorporated into memory.

False memory syndrome: creation of false or inaccurate memories through suggestion, hypnosis

6.11–12

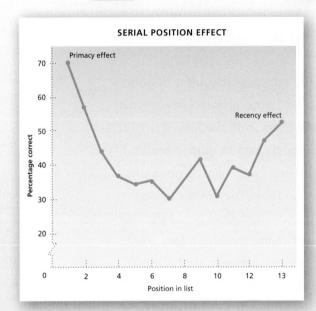

SERIAL POSITION EFFECT

Primacy effect

Recency effect

Percentage correct

Position in list

Reasons We Forget

TYPES OF FORGETTING	DESCRIPTION
Encoding Failure	The information is not attended to and fails to be encoded.
Decay or Disuse	Information that is not accessed decays from the storage system over time.
Proactive Interference	Older information already in memory interferes with the retrieval of newer information.
Retroactive Interference	Newer information interferes with the retrieval of older information.

6.13

Memory and Brain

Procedural memories: cerebellum

Short-term memories: cortical prefrontal and temporal lobes

Semantic and episodic memories: frontal and temporal lobes

Memory for fear: amygdala

Memory Formation in the Brain

Consolidation: neuronal changes during formation of a memory

Hippocampus: responsible for new long-term memory storage, removal destroys ability to store anything new

6.14

Amnesia

Retrograde amnesia: past memories lost; can be for minutes or several years

Anterograde amnesia: new memory formation blocked; old memories retrievable

Infantile amnesia: lack of memories before the ages 2–3; because of implicit nature of infant memory

6.15

Alzheimer's Disease

▸ Alzheimer's disease usually begins with mild forgetfulness and eventually progresses to more severe forgetting.

▸ The primary memory difficulty in Alzheimer's is anterograde amnesia.

▸ Various drugs are in use or in development that will slow or stop the progression of Alzheimer's disease.

6.16

Benefits of False Memories

▸ May provide possible health benefits, such as preventing overeating and alcohol abuse.

6.17

7

Cognition: Thinking, Intelligence, and Language

First Human–Machine Poker Championship Held in Vancouver

The field of artificial intelligence has come a long way since the term was first used by John McCarthy at a conference devoted to the subject in 1959. In lay terms, *artificial intelligence* is the development of machines that can think like humans. Researchers from the University of Alberta's GAMES (Game-playing, Analytical methods, Minimax search, and Empirical Studies) group have spent a great deal of time developing some of the world's best game-playing programs. Their programs include *Chinook*, the official world checkers champion; *Poki*, the world's strongest poker program; and *Polaris*, a poker-playing program that took on two top-level poker professionals (Phil Laak and Ali Eslami) in the first human–machine poker championship in July 2007.

The $50 000 match took place in Vancouver and was held in conjunction with the annual conference of the Association for the Advancement of Artificial Intelligence. According to all involved, the competition was very exciting. In the first session, Eslami won $390 from *Polaris* while Laak lost $465 to the computer. Because the difference was not statistically significant, it was counted as a tie. In the second match, Laak ended up being ahead by $1570 while Eslami lost $2495, which meant that *Polaris* achieved the first win in the match. In session three, Laak won $1455 while Eslami lost only $625, leading to a victory for humans. In the fourth and deciding session, both Eslami and Laak ended up winning a small amount from *Polaris*, rendering humanity as the official winner of the first human–machine poker championship.

Although some may view the 1–1–2 record of the program as a failure, the GAMES group researchers considered *Polaris*'s performance a great success. It was able to compete with some of the best poker-playing professionals in the world. In fact, when it comes down to money, the program lost only a measly $395.

For more information on the University of Alberta's GAMES group, visit **www. cs.ualberta.ca/~games**.

Why study the nature of thought?

To fully understand how we do any of the things we do (such as learning, remembering, and behaving), we need to understand how we think. How do we organize our thoughts? How do we communicate those thoughts to others? What do we mean by intelligence? Why are some people able to learn so much faster than others?

HOW PEOPLE THINK

What does it mean to think? People are thinking all the time and talking about thinking as well: "What do you think?" "Let me think about that." "I don't think so." What does it mean to think? **Thinking,** or **cognition** (from a Latin word meaning "to know"), can be defined as mental activity that goes on in the brain when a person is processing information—organizing it, understanding it, and communicating it to others. Thinking includes memory, but it is much more. When people think, they are not only aware of the information in the brain but also make decisions about it, compare it to other information, and use it to solve problems.

Thinking also includes more than just a kind of verbal "stream of consciousness." When people think, they often have images as well as words in their minds.

7.1 *How are mental images and concepts involved in the process of thinking?*

MENTAL IMAGERY

As stated in Chapter Six, short-term memories are encoded in the form of sounds and also as visual images, forming a mental picture of the world. Thus, **mental images** (representations that stand in for objects or events and have a picturelike quality) are one of several tools used in the thought process.

Here's an interesting demonstration of the use of mental images. Get several people together and ask them to tell you *as fast as they can* how many windows are in the place where they live. Usually you'll find that the first people to shout out an answer have fewer windows in their houses than the ones who take longer to respond. You'll also notice that most of them look up, as if looking at some image that only they can see. If asked, they'll say that to determine the number of windows, they pictured where they live and simply counted windows as they "walked through" the image.

So more windows means more time to count them in your head? I guess mentally "walking" through a bigger house in your head would take longer than "walking" through a smaller one. That's what researchers think, too. They have found that it does take longer to view a mental image that is larger or covers more distance than a smaller, more compact one (Kosslyn et al., 2001; Ochsner & Kosslyn, 1994).

Mental imagery is something people use every day. It helps them remember where they parked the car, find furniture that fits the space they have for it, and relax by

thinking (cognition)
mental activity that goes on in the brain when a person is organizing and attempting to understand information and communicating information to others.

mental images
mental representations that stand for objects or events and have a picture-like quality.

> So more windows means more time to count them in your head? I guess mentally "walking" through a bigger house in your head would take longer than "walking" through a smaller one. ▶

Mentally "walking" through this very large house in your head would take longer than "walking" through the smaller house; researchers have found that it takes people longer to view a mental image that is larger or covers more distance than a smaller, more compact one.

creating daydreams. It allows them to find their way home and to other places by using their learned "mental maps" of how to get to familiar locations. (L I N K) *to Chapter Five: Learning, p. 176.* Mental imagery is also a very useful tool for remembering things (Paivio, 1971, 1986; Thomas, 2001).

People are even able to mentally rotate, or turn, images (Shepherd & Metzler, 1971). (See Figure 7.1.) In a creative study done by York University's Irwin Silverman and colleagues (2000), undergraduate students were led into a densely wooded area on campus and asked to find their way back. The researchers found that there was a strong connection between skill at finding the way back and the ability to mentally rotate objects (or route, as the case may be; Silverman et al., 2000).

Researchers have found that there exist gender differences when it comes to mental rotation abilities (Lippa, Collaer, & Peters, 2010; Silverman, Choi, & Peters, 2007). Richard Lippa of California State University, Marcia Collaer of Middlebury College, and Michael Peters of the University of Guelph investigated mental rotation in more than 90 000 women and 111 000 men from 53 different countries. They found that in every single country, men's mean performance was better than that of women's. Similarly, when Irwin Silverman of York University, Jean Choi of the University of Lethbridge, and Michael Peters of the University of Guelph investigated ability to perform three-dimensional mental rotations in men and women of seven different ethnicities and from 40 different countries, they found that men scored significantly higher than women in all 7 ethnic groups and in all 40 countries.

In the brain, creating a mental image is almost the opposite of seeing an actual image. With an actual image, the information goes from the eyes to the visual cortex of the occipital lobe and is processed, or interpreted, by other areas of the cortex that compare the new information to information already in memory. (L I N K) *to Chapter Two: The Biological Perspective, p. 42.* In creating a mental image, other areas of the cortex associated with stored knowledge send information to the visual cortex, where

Now look at this object:

Two of these four drawings show the same object. Can you find the two? Put a big X across them.

FIGURE 7.1 **Example of a Mental Rotation Task** This is an example of a mental rotation task. Look at the object on the left and find the two "identical" images (under varying degrees of rotation) on the right.

✳ Explore on **mypsychlab**
Mental Rotation

Images are not the only way we think, are they?

concepts
ideas that represent a class or category of objects, events, or activities.

formal concepts
concepts that are defined by specific rules or features.

natural concepts
concepts people form as a result of their experiences in the world.

prototype
an example of a concept that closely matches the defining characteristics of a concept.

But what about things ▶ that don't easily fit the rules or features? What if a thing has some, but not all, features of a concept?

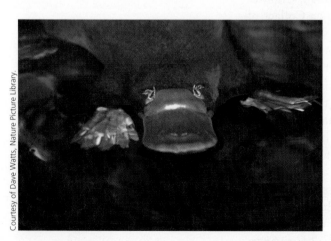

A duck-billed platypus is classified as a mammal yet shares features with birds, such as webbed feet and a bill, and also lays eggs. The platypus is an example of a "fuzzy" natural concept.

the image is perceived in the "mind's eye" (Kosslyn et al., 1993; Sparing et al., 2002). PET scans show areas of the visual cortex being activated during the process of forming an image, providing evidence for the role of the visual cortex in mental imagery (Kosslyn et al., 1993, 1999, 2001).

CONCEPTS

Images are not the only way in which we think, are they? Mental images are only one form of mental representation. Another aspect of thought processes is the use of concepts. **Concepts** are ideas that represent a class or category of objects, events, or activities. People use concepts to think about objects or events without having to think about all the specific examples of the category. For example, a person can think about "fruit" without thinking about every kind of fruit there is in the world, which would take far more effort and time.

Concepts not only contain the important features of the objects or events people want to think about but also allow the identification of new objects and events that may fit the concept. For example, dogs come in all shapes, sizes, colours, and lengths of fur. Yet most people have no trouble recognizing dogs as dogs, even though they may never before have seen that particular breed of dog.

Concepts can have very strict definitions, such as the concept of a square as a shape with four equal sides. Concepts defined by specific rules or features are called **formal concepts** and are pretty rigid. To be a square, for example, an object must be a two-dimensional figure with four equal sides and four angles adding up to 360 degrees. If an object has those features, it is not only a square but also cannot be anything BUT a square.

But what about things that don't easily fit the rules or features? What if a thing has some, but not all, features of a concept? In everyday life, people are surrounded by objects, events, and activities that are not as clearly defined as the definition of a square. What is a vehicle? Cars and trucks leap immediately to mind, but what about a bobsled? How about a raft? Those last two objects aren't quite as easy to classify as vehicles immediately, but they fit some of the rules for "vehicle." These are examples of **natural concepts**, concepts people form not as a result of the application of a strict set of rules but rather as the result of their experiences with these concepts in the world (Ahn, 1998; Barton & Komatsu, 1989; Gelman, 1988; Rosch, 1973). Whereas formal concepts are well-defined, natural concepts are "fuzzy" (Hampton, 1998). Is a whale a fish or a mammal? Is a platypus a mammal or a bird? People may know that whales are technically mammals, but whales also share a lot of fish-defining characteristics. Mammals have fur; birds lay eggs and have beaks. The duck-billed platypus has and does all three (has fur, lays eggs, and has a beak), yet it is classified as a mammal, not a bird.

Natural concepts are important in helping people understand their surroundings in a less structured manner than the formal concepts that are taught in school, and they form the basis for interpreting those surroundings and the events that may occur in everyday life.

Everyone's experiences aren't going to be the same, right? So how do people develop those basic concepts if they are all having different experiences?

PROTOTYPES When someone says "fruit," what's the first image that comes to mind? More than likely, it's a specific kind of fruit such as an apple, pear, or orange. It's less likely that someone's first impulse will be to say "guava" or "papaya," or even "banana," unless that person comes from a tropical area. In Canada, apples are a good example of a **prototype**, a concept that closely matches the defining characteristics of the concept (Mervis & Rosch, 1981; Rosch, 1977). Fruit is sweet, grows on trees, has seeds, and is usually round—all very applelike qualities. Coconuts are sweet and they also grow on trees, but many people in the Northern hemisphere have never actually seen a coconut tree. They have more likely seen apple trees. So people who have very different experiences with fruit, for instance, will have different prototypes, which are the most basic examples of concepts.

What about someone who lives in a tropical area? Would his or her prototype for fruit be different? And would people's prototypes be different in different cultures? More than likely, prototypes develop according to the exposure a person has to objects in that category. So someone who grew up in an area where there are many coconut trees might think of coconuts as more prototypical than apples, whereas someone growing up in North America would more likely see apples as a prototypical fruit (Aitchison, 1992). Research suggests that what a person knows about a particular type of object does affect the person's prototype for the category (Lynch et al., 2000; Shafto & Coley, 2003). For example, people who are not that knowledgeable about trees tend to pick a tree that is found where they live as the prototypical tree (such as a maple tree), whereas experts in tree identification tend to select trees that have more ideal characteristics (tall, for example) rather than one specific type of tree. For non-experts, familiarity was important in selecting a prototype; but, for experts, central characteristics more representative of trees in general were the standard (Lynch et al., 2000).

Culture also matters in the formation of prototypes. Research on concept prototypes across various cultures found greater differences and variations in prototypes between cultures that were dissimilar than between cultures that are more similar (Lin & Schwanenflugel, 1995; Lin, Schwanenflugel, & Wisenbaker, 1990; Schwanenflugel & Rey, 1986). So there would be greater differences in prototypes between Taiwan and Canada than between English Canadians and French Canadians living in Montreal.

How do prototypes affect thinking? People tend to look at potential examples of a concept and compare them to the prototype to see how well they match—which is why it takes most people much longer to think about olives and tomatoes as fruit because they aren't sweet, one of the major characteristics of the prototype of fruit (Rosch & Mervis, 1975).

No matter what type, concepts are one of the ways people deal with all the information that bombards their senses every day and allow them to organize their perceptions of the world around them. Not only do concepts help people think, they are also an important tool in *problem solving*, a type of thinking that people engage in every day and in many different situations.

PROBLEM SOLVING AND DECISION MAKING

Problem solving is certainly a big part of any college or university student's life. Is there any one "best" way to go about solving a problem? Put a coin in a bottle and then cork the opening. How can you get the coin out of the bottle without pulling out the cork or breaking the bottle? (For the solution, see p. 267.)

As stated earlier, images and concepts are mental tools that can be used to solve problems. For the preceding problem, you are probably trying to create an image of the bottle with a coin in it. **Problem solving** occurs when a goal must be reached by thinking and behaving in certain ways. Problems range from figuring out how to cut a recipe in half to understanding complex mathematical proofs to deciding what to major in at college or university. There are several different ways in which people can think in order to solve problems.

problem solving
process of cognition that occurs when a goal must be reached by thinking and behaving in certain ways.

What about someone who lives in a tropical area? Would his or her prototype for fruit be different? And would people's prototypes be different in different cultures?

Both of these animals are dogs. They both have fur, four legs, a tail—but the similarities end there. With so many variations in the animals we call "dogs," what is the prototype for "dog"?

Problem solving is certainly a big part of any college or university student's life. Is there any one "best" way to go about solving a problem?

Cartoon Stock www.cartoonstock.com
Nicola Jones nikj@cartoonstock.com

This child is trying one piece after another until finding the piece that fits. This is an example of trial-and-error learning.

trial and error (mechanical solution) problem-solving method in which one possible solution after another is tried until a successful one is found.

algorithms very specific, step-by-step procedures for solving certain types of problems that guarantee a solution to a problem providing they are used correctly.

heuristic an educated guess based on prior experiences that helps narrow down the possible solutions for a problem. Also known as a *rule of thumb*.

7.2 What methods do people use to solve problems and make decisions?

TRIAL AND ERROR (MECHANICAL SOLUTIONS) One method is to use **trial and error**, also known as a **mechanical solution**. Trial and error refers to trying one solution after another until finding one that works. For example, if Shelana has forgotten the PIN for her online banking website, she can try one combination after another until she finds the one that works, if she has only a few such PINs that she normally uses. Mechanical solutions can also involve solving by *rote*, or a learned set of rules. This is how word problems were solved in grade school, for example. One type of rote solution is to use an algorithm.

ALGORITHMS **Algorithms** are specific, step-by-step procedures for solving certain types of problems. When applied properly, algorithms will always result in a correct solution, if there is a correct solution to be found and you have enough time to find it. Mathematical formulas are algorithms. Many puzzles, such as a Rubik's Cube, have a set of steps that, if followed exactly, will always result a solution. But algorithms aren't always practical to use. For example, if Shelana didn't have a clue what those four numbers might be, she *might* be able to figure out her forgotten PIN by trying *all possible combinations* of four digits, 0 through 9. She would eventually find the right four-digit combination—provided she hasn't starved to death or died of old age. Computers, however, can run searches like this one very quickly, so the systematic search algorithm is a useful part of some computer programs.

HEURISTICS Unfortunately, humans aren't as fast as computers and need some other way to narrow down the possible solutions to only a few. One way to do this is to use a heuristic. A **heuristic**, or "rule of thumb," is a simple rule that is intended to apply to many situations. Whereas an algorithm is very specific and will always lead to a solution, a heuristic is an educated guess based on prior experiences that helps narrow down the possible solutions for a problem. For example, if a student is typing a paper in a word-processing program and wants to know how to format the page, he or she could try to read an entire manual on the word-processing program. That would take a while. Instead, the student could type "format" into the help feature's search program or click on the word "Format" on the toolbar. Doing either action greatly reduces the amount of information the student will have to look at to get an answer. Using the help feature or clicking on the appropriate toolbar word will also work for similar problems.

Will using a rule of thumb always work, like an algorithm? Using a heuristic is faster than using an algorithm in many cases, but unlike algorithms, heuristics will *not* always lead to the correct solution. What you gain in speed is sometimes lost in accuracy. For example, one kind of heuristic (called a *representative heuristic*) for categorizing objects simply assumes that any object (or person) that shares characteristics with the members of a particular category is also a member of that category. This tool is handy when it comes to classifying plants but doesn't work as well when applied to people. Are all people with dark skin from Africa? Does everyone with red hair also have a bad temper? Are all blue-eyed blonds from Sweden? See the point? The representative heuristic can be used—or misused—to create and sustain stereotypes (Tversky & Kahneman, 1974).

A useful heuristic that works much of the time is to work backward from the goal. For example, if you want to know the shortest way to get to the new bookstore in town, you already know the goal, which is finding the bookstore. There are probably several ways to get there from your house, and some shorter than others.

Assuming you have the address of the store, the best way to determine the shortest route is to look up the location of the store on a map of the city and then trace a route back to where you live.

What if my problem is writing a term paper? Starting at the end isn't going to help me much! Sometimes it's better to break a goal down into subgoals, so that as each subgoal is achieved, the final solution is that much closer. Writing a term paper, for example, can seem overwhelming until it is broken down into steps: choose a topic, research the topic, organize what has been gathered, write one section at a time, and so on. Other examples of heuristics include making diagrams to help organize the information concerning the problem or testing possible solutions to the problem one by one and eliminating those that do not work.

Another kind of heuristic is **means–end analysis**, in which a person determines the difference between the current situation and the goal and then tries to reduce that difference by various means (methods). For example, Katrina has to prepare a 15-minute speech for her political science class. The current situation is that she has nothing prepared and the goal is a 15-minute speech. Katrina needs to reduce this large discrepancy between her current situation and her goal. To do so, she can break her daunting task into smaller subgoals, such as (a) choosing a topic; (b) doing research on the topic; (c) organizing all the information she has collected; (d) writing her first draft, and so on. By completing each of these subgoals (steps), Katrina is reducing the distance between her current state and her ultimate goal of having a 15-minute speech. What might have seemed an impossible task to Katrina at first became doable once it was broken down into smaller subgoals.

INSIGHT Sometimes I have to find answers to problems one step at a time, but in other cases the answer seems to just "pop" into my head all of a sudden. Why do some answers come so easily to mind? When the solution to a problem seems to come suddenly to mind, it is called *insight*. Chapter Five (p. 207) discussed Köhler's (1925) work with Sultan the chimpanzee, which demonstrated that even some animals can solve problems by means of a sudden insight. In humans, insight often takes the form of an "aha" moment—the solution seems to come in a flash. A person may realize that this problem is similar to another one that he or she already knew how to solve or might see that an object can be used for a different purpose than its original one, such as using a dime as a screwdriver.

Remember the problem of the bottleneck discussed earlier in this chapter? The task was to get the coin out of the bottle without removing the cork or breaking the bottle. The answer is simple: Push the cork into the bottle and shake out the coin. Aha!

Insight is not really a magical process, although it can seem like magic. What usually happens is that the mind simply reorganizes a problem, sometimes while the person is thinking about something else (Durso et al., 1994).

Here's a problem that can be solved with insight: Marsha and Marjorie were born on the same day of the same month of the same year to the same mother and the same father yet they are not twins. How is that possible? Think about it and then look for the answer at the end of this section.

In summary, thinking is a complex process involving the use of mental imagery and various types of concepts to organize the events of daily life. Problem solving is a special type of thinking that involves the use of many tools, such as trial-and-error thinking, algorithms, and heuristics, to solve different types of problems.

◀ What if my problem is writing a term paper? Starting at the end isn't going to help me much!

◀ Sometimes I have to find answers to problems one step at a time, but in other cases the answer seems to just "pop" into my head all of a sudden. Why do some answers come so easily to mind?

means–end analysis
heuristic in which the difference between the starting situation and the goal is determined and then steps are taken to reduce that difference.

PRACTICE QUIZ: HOW MUCH DO YOU REMEMBER?

Pick the best answer.

1. Mental images
   a. represent abstract ideas.
   b. have a picturelike quality.
   c. consist entirely of unconscious information..
   d. are always prototypes.

2. Knowing that the definition of psychology is the scientific study of behaviour and mental processes is an example of a
   a. prototypical concept.   **c.** formal concept.
   b. natural concept.   **d.** mental image.

3. A "rule of thumb" is another name for a
   a. heuristic.   **c.** trial-and-error solution.
   b. algorithm.   **d.** means–end analysis.

4. What type of problem-solving strategy would be best to use when solving a problem in algebra class?
   a. heuristic   **c.** trial-and-error solution
   b. algorithm   **d.** means–end analysis

5. Miguel was struggling with the answer to one of the questions on his psychology midterm. Seeing that the answer was not going to come easily, he went on to answer some of the other easier questions. Then, suddenly, the answer to the problematic question just seemed to "pop" into his head. Miguel's experience is an example of
   a. means–end analysis.   **c.** an algorithm.
   b. a heuristic.   **d.** insight.

Answers: 1-b, 2-c, 3-a, 4-b, 5-d.

Explore on mypsychlab
Obstacles to Problem Solving

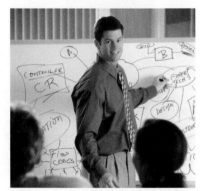

One rule of thumb, or heuristic, involves breaking down a goal into subgoals. The man standing in front of the whiteboard has diagrammed the steps needed to reach the company's goal.

functional fixedness
a block to problem solving that comes from thinking about objects in terms of only their typical functions.

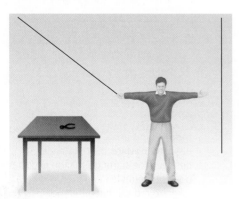

The string problem: How do you tie the two strings together if you cannot reach them both at the same time?

FIGURE 7.2 **The String Problem**

Answer to Insight Problem on page 267: Marsha and Marjorie are two of a set of triplets. Gotcha!

PROBLEMS WITH PROBLEM SOLVING

7.3   *Why does problem solving sometimes fail, and what is meant by creative thinking?*

Methods of problem solving such as using insight are not foolproof. Sometimes a solution to a problem remains just "out of reach" because the elements of the problem are not arranged properly or because people get stuck in certain ways of thinking that act as barriers to solving problems. Such ways of thinking occur more or less automatically, influencing attempts to solve problems without any conscious awareness of that influence. Here's a classic example:

Two strings are hanging from a ceiling but are too far apart to allow a person to hold one and walk to the other. Nearby is a table with a pair of pliers on it (see Figure 7.2). The goal is to tie the two pieces of string together. How? For the solution to this problem, see p. 271. FIGURE 7.2 **The String Problem**

People can become aware of automatic tendencies to try to solve problems in ways that are not going to lead to solutions and in becoming aware can abandon the "old" ways for more appropriate problem-solving methods. Three of the most common barriers to successful problem solving are functional fixedness, mental sets, and confirmation bias.

FUNCTIONAL FIXEDNESS   One problem-solving difficulty involves thinking about objects only in terms of their typical uses, which is a phenomenon called **functional fixedness** (literally, "fixed on the function"). Have you ever searched high and low for a screwdriver to fix something around the house? All the while there are several objects close at hand that could be used to tighten a screw: a butter knife, a key, or even a dime in your pocket. Because the tendency is to think of those objects in terms of cooking, unlocking, and spending, we sometimes ignore the less obvious possible uses. The string problem is an example of functional fixedness. The pair of pliers is often seen as useless until the person realizes it can be used as a weight (see p. 271).

One of the authors of this textbook used to use a boot tray as a toboggan to joyride down the local hill during winters. It is obvious from this example that this particular author is not a victim of functional fixedness.

MENTAL SETS Functional fixedness is actually a kind of **mental set**, which is defined as the tendency for people to persist in using problem-solving patterns that have worked for them in the past. Solutions that have worked in the past tend to be the ones people try first, and people are often hesitant or even unable to think of other possibilities. Look at the accompanying figure.

Can you draw four straight lines so that they pass through all nine dots *without lifting your pencil from the page and without touching any dot more than once*?

People are taught from the earliest grades to stay within the lines, right? That tried-and-true method will not help in solving the dot problem. The solution involves drawing the lines beyond the actual dots, as seen in Figure 7.3.

CONFIRMATION BIAS Another barrier to logical thinking, called **confirmation bias**, is the tendency to search for evidence that fits one's beliefs while ignoring any evidence to the contrary. This is similar to a mental set, except that what is "set" is a belief rather than a method of solving problems. For example, believers in ESP tend to remember the few studies that seem to support their beliefs and psychic predictions that worked out while at the same time "forgetting" the cases in which studies found no proof or psychics made predictions that failed to come true. They remember only that which confirms their bias toward a belief in the existence of ESP.

CREATIVITY

So far, we've talked about only logic and pretty straightforward thinking. How do people come up with totally new ideas, things no one has thought of before? Not every problem can be answered by using information already at hand and the rules of logic in applying that information. Sometimes a problem requires coming up with entirely new ways of looking at the problem or unusual, inventive solutions. This kind of thinking is called **creativity**: solving problems by combining ideas or behaviour in new ways (Csikszentmihalyi, 1996).

DIVERGENT AND CONVERGENT THINKING The logical method for problem solving that has been discussed so far is based on a type of thinking called **convergent thinking**. In convergent thinking, a problem is seen as having only one answer and all lines of thinking will eventually lead to (converge on) that single answer if the problem solver uses previous knowledge and logic (Ciardiello, 1998). For example, the question "In what ways are a pencil and a pen alike?" can be answered by listing the features that the two items have in common—both can be used to write, both have similar shapes, and so on—in a simple comparison process. Convergent thinking

mental set
the tendency for people to persist in using problem-solving patterns that have worked for them in the past.

confirmation bias
the tendency to search for evidence that fits one's beliefs while ignoring any evidence that does not fit those beliefs.

creativity
the process of solving problems by combining ideas or behaviour in new ways.

convergent thinking
type of thinking in which a problem is seen as having only one answer, and all lines of thinking will eventually lead to that single answer if the problem solver uses previous knowledge and logic.

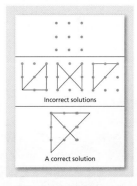

FIGURE 7.3 **The Solution to the Dot Problem** When people try to solve this problem, a mental set causes them to think of the dots as representing a box, and they try to draw the line while staying in the box. The only way to connect all nine dots without lifting the pencil from the paper is to draw the lines so they extend out of the box of dots—literally "thinking outside the box."

So far, we've talked about only logic and pretty straightforward thinking. How do people come up with totally new ideas, things no one has thought of before?

works well for routine problem solving but may be of little use when a more creative solution is needed.

Divergent thinking is the reverse of convergent thinking. Here a person starts at one point and comes up with many different, or divergent, ideas or possibilities based on that point (Finke, 1995). For example, if someone were to ask the question, "What is a pencil used for?" the convergent answer would be "to write." But if the question is put this way: "How many different uses can you think of for a pencil?" the answers multiply: "Writing, poking holes, a weight for the tail of a kite, a weapon."

What are the characteristics of a creative, divergent thinker? Theorists in the field of creative thinking have found through examining the habits of highly creative people that the most productive periods of divergent thinking for those people tend to occur when they are doing some task or activity that is more or less automatic, such as walking or swimming (Csikszentmihalyi, 1996; Gardner, 1993a; Goleman, 1995). These automatic tasks take up some attentional processes, leaving the remainder to devote to creative thinking. The fact that all of one's attention is not focused on the problem is actually a benefit because divergent thinkers often make links and connections at a level of consciousness just below alert awareness so that ideas can flow freely without being censored by the higher mental processes (Goleman, 1995). In other words, having part of one's attention devoted to walking, for example, allows the rest of the mind to "sneak up on" more creative solutions and ideas.

Divergent thinkers will obviously be less prone to some of the barriers to problem solving, such as functional fixedness. For example, what would most people do if it suddenly started to rain while they are stuck in their office with no umbrella? How many people would think of using a see-through vinyl tote bag as a makeshift umbrella?

Creative, divergent thinking is often a neglected topic in the education of young people. Although some people are naturally more creative, it is possible to develop one's creative ability. The ability to be creative is important—coming up with topics for a research paper, for example, is something that many students have trouble doing. Cross-cultural research (Basadur et al., 2002; Colligan, 1983) has found that divergent thinking and problem-solving skills can be easily taught in cultures such as that of the Japanese and the Omaha Native Americans. In these cultures, creativity in many areas is not normally prized and the preference is to hold to well-established traditions, such as that of traditional dances that have not varied for centuries.

divergent thinking
type of thinking in which a person starts from one point and comes up with many different ideas or possibilities based on that point.

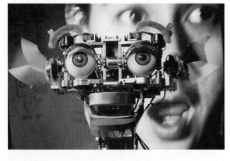

Cynthia Breazeal is a researcher at the Artificial Intelligence Lab at MIT. Here she is pictured with the robot she designed called Kismet. Designed to help with the study of infant emotional expressions, Kismet can display several "moods" on its face as emotional expressions. This is divergent thinking at its best—a "baby" that won't cry, wet, or demand to be fed.

Ripley's Believe It or Not! building in Niagara Falls, Ontario, is considered to be a creative piece of architecture. The architects who designed the building did not follow the typical architectural methods used to design buildings.

Many people have the idea that creative people are also a little different from other people. There are artists and musicians, for example, who actually encourage others to see them as eccentric. But the fact is that creative people are actually pretty normal. According to Csikszentmihalyi (1997),

1. Creative people usually have a broad range of knowledge about a lot of subjects and are good at using mental imagery.

2. Creative people aren't afraid to be different—they are more open to new experiences than many people, and they tend to have more vivid dreams and daydreams than others do.

3. Creative people value their independence.

4. Creative people are often unconventional in their work but not in other aspects of their lives.

You might be asking yourself how one would go about measuring creativity. Because there are so many differing viewpoints on what creativity actually is, it is difficult to determine whether a person is creative and if so, just how creative the person is. Despite this difficulty, many measures of creativity have been devised. One of the best-known and most widely used forms of creativity assessment is the Torrance Tests of Creative Thinking (TTCT) created by E. Paul Torrance (1962). The Torrance Tests involve three components. The first component, Thinking Creatively with Pictures, presents the participants with three exercises involving pictures to assess five mental characteristics: fluency, originality, elaboration, abstractness of titles, and resistance to closure. In the second component, the Figural TTCT, participants are asked to state what abstract images might be. Finally, in the third component, the Verbal TTCT presents participants with a situation and gives them the opportunity to ask questions and to "just suppose" (e.g., "Just suppose people were able to fly. How would the world be different?") For examples of TTCT, go to http://php.indiana.edu/~cjbonk/bobweb/DemonstratorTTCT.doc.

Cartoon Stock www.cartoonstock.com
Nicola Jones nikj@cartoonstock.com

Explore on **mypsychlab**
Intuition and Discovery in Problem Solving

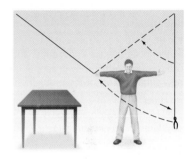

The solution to the string problem is to use the pliers as a pendulum to swing the second string closer to you.

Solution to the string problem

PRACTICE QUIZ: HOW MUCH DO YOU REMEMBER?

Pick the best answer.

1. Al goes out one frosty morning to find that his car is covered with a thick layer of frost. He needs to get to work and looks for his ice scraper. Unable to find it, he thinks a moment, reaches into his pocket and takes out a credit card from his wallet. In using the credit card as a makeshift ice scraper, Al has overcome
   a. functional fixedness.
   b. confirmation bias.
   c. creativity bias.
   d. confirmation fixedness.

2. Randall believes that aliens crashed in Western Canada in the 1950s. When looking for information about this on the internet, he ignores any sites that are skeptical of his belief and visits only sites that support his belief. This is an example of
   a. functional fixedness.
   b. confirmation bias.
   c. creativity bias.
   d. confirmation fixedness.

3. When a problem is seen as having only one answer, with all lines of thinking leading to that answer, this is known as _____ thinking.
   a. divergent
   b. creative
   c. convergent
   d. mental set

4. Which of the following statements about creative people is TRUE?
   a. They are not very good at mental imagery.
   b. They are not afraid to be different.
   c. They value their dependence on others.
   d. They are often very conventional in their work.

5. Which is NOT one of the three components of the Torrance Tests of Creative Thinking?
   a. Verbal TTCT
   b. Fluency TTCT
   c. Thinking Creatively with Pictures
   d. Figural TTCT

Answers: 1-a, 2-b, 3-c, 4-b, 5-b.

I know I've heard and ▶
even used the term a
lot, but exactly what is
intelligence?

👁 Watch on **mypsychlab**
Intelligence: Robert Sternberg

intelligence
the ability to learn from one's
experiences, acquire knowledge, and
use resources effectively in adapting to
new situations or solving problems.

g factor
the ability to reason and solve
problems, or general intelligence.

s factor
the ability to excel in certain areas, or
specific intelligence.

This child is displaying only one of the many forms that intelligence can take, according to Gardner's multiple intelligences theory.

INTELLIGENCE

I know I've heard and even used the term a lot, but exactly what is intelligence?
The word *intelligence* is thrown around quite frequently in many different settings. For example, you may see a member of a dating website filling out "intelligence" as one of his or her requirements for potential partners. Doctors treating patients with an intellectual disability will use their assumptions about intelligence to predict how well their patients will function. These differences are important as not everyone is in agreement on just what intelligence truly is.

DEFINITION

7.4 *How do psychologists define intelligence, and how do various theories of intelligence differ?*

Is intelligence merely a score on some test, or is it practical knowledge of how to get along in the world? Is it making good grades or being a financial success or a social success? Ask a dozen people and you will probably get a dozen different answers. Psychologists have come up with a workable definition that combines many of the ideas just listed: They define **intelligence** as the ability to learn from one's experiences, acquire knowledge, and use resources effectively in adapting to new situations or solving problems (Sternberg & Kaufman, 1998; Wechsler, 1975). These are the characteristics that people need to be able to survive in their culture.

THEORIES OF INTELLIGENCE

Although we have defined intelligence in a general way, there are differing opinions of the specific knowledge and abilities that make up the concept of intelligence. It is these differing opinions as to the nature and number of intelligence-related abilities that are discussed in the following different views of intelligence.

SPEARMAN'S G FACTOR Spearman (1904) saw intelligence as two different abilities, both measurable by intelligence tests. The ability to reason and solve problems was labelled **g factor** for *general intelligence*, whereas a person's ability to excel in certain areas such as music, business, or art was labelled **s factor** for *specific intelligence*.
A traditional intelligence quotient (IQ) test would most likely measure g factor, but Spearman believed that superiority in one type of intelligence predicts superiority overall. Although his early research found some support for specific intelligences, other researchers (Guilford, 1967; Thurstone, 1938) felt that Spearman had oversimplified the concept of intelligence. Intelligence began to be viewed as composed of numerous factors. In fact, Guilford (1967) proposed that there were 120 types of intelligence.

GARDNER'S MULTIPLE INTELLIGENCES One of the later theorists to propose the existence of several kinds of intelligence was Gardner (1993b, 1999a). Although many people use the terms *reason*, *logic*, and *knowledge* as if they are the same ability, Gardner believes that they are different aspects of intelligence, along with several other abilities. He originally listed seven different kinds of intelligence but then added an eighth type (Gardner, 1998) and then a ninth type (Gardner, 1999b). The nine types of intelligence are described in Table 7.1.
The idea of multiple intelligences has great appeal, especially for educators, as it takes into account the cultural context

TABLE 7.1 GARDNER'S NINE INTELLIGENCES		
TYPE OF INTELLIGENCE	DESCRIPTION	SAMPLE OCCUPATION
Verbal/linguistic	Ability to use language	Writers, speakers
Musical	Ability to compose and/or perform music	Musicians, even those who do not read musical notes but can perform and compose
Logical/mathematical	Ability to think logically and to solve mathematical problems	Scientists, engineers
Visual/spatial	Ability to understand how objects are oriented in space	Pilots, astronauts, artists, navigators
Movement	Ability to control one's body motions	Dancers, athletes
Interpersonal	Sensitivity to others and understanding motivation of others	Psychologists, managers
Intrapersonal	Understanding of one's emotions and how they guide actions	Various people-oriented careers
Naturalist	Ability to recognize the patterns found in nature	Farmers, landscapers, biologists, botanists
Existentialist	Ability to see the "big picture" of the human world by asking questions about life, death, and the ultimate reality of human existence	Various careers, philosophical thinkers

of intelligence and the complexity of and differences in human competencies. Despite this appeal, Gardner's theory has not been readily accepted in the academic world. According to Smith (2002), Gardner's work will always represent a problem for people who believe that intelligence is what is measured by an intelligence test. Critics of the theory claim that there is little scientific evidence that such intelligences are anything more than different abilities and that those abilities are not necessarily the same thing as what is typically meant by *intelligence* (Hunt, 2001). Because Gardner never created a properly designed set of tests to identify and measure each of the different intelligences, these critics argue that his theory is problematic because it is based solely on his intuitions and not on empirical research. Gardner originally planned to create a test for each of the different intelligences, but he decided against it after he realized that such testing could lead to labelling, which in turn could lead to prejudice and discrimination (Gardner, 1999a).

Despite the criticisms it has faced, Gardner's theory has been warmly received by educators and policymakers all over North America, who have implemented Gardner's ideas in the development of school curricula and in the area of hiring (Morris, 2010; Smith, 2002). Human Resources and Skills Development Canada regards Gardner's model as fundamental because it believes that more than just a traditional IQ test is necessary to measure intelligence (Morris, 2010).

STERNBERG'S TRIARCHIC THEORY Sternberg (1988, 1997) has theorized that there are three kinds of intelligence. Called the **triarchic theory of intelligence** (*triarchic* means "three"), this theory is similar to one proposed more than 2000 years ago by Aristotle; he proposed a theory that intelligence is composed of theoretical, productive, and practical aspects.

In Sternberg's theory, the three aspects are *analytical, creative,* and *practical intelligence.* **Analytical intelligence** refers to the ability to break down problems into component parts, or analysis, for problem solving. In Western countries, such as Canada, it is the type of intelligence that is measured on tests and valued in schools.

Sternberg's practical intelligence is a form of "street smarts" that includes the ability to adapt to one's environment and solve practical problems. These girls are giving their younger brother a drink of water by using a folded leaf as an impromptu cup.

triarchic theory of intelligence
Sternberg's theory that there are three kinds of intelligences: analytical, creative, and practical.

analytical intelligence
the ability to break down problems into component parts, or analysis, for problem solving.

Analytical intelligence is commonly referred to as "book smarts." Although analytical intelligence is valued more in Western cultures than in Eastern cultures (Tweed & Lehman, 2002), it is applicable to people of all cultures. **Creative intelligence** is the ability to deal with new and different concepts and to come up with new ways of solving problems (divergent thinking, in other words). **Practical intelligence** is best described as "street smarts," or the ability to use information to get along in life. People with a high degree of practical intelligence know how to be tactful, how to manipulate situations to their advantage, and how to use inside information to increase their odds of success.

How might these three types of intelligence be illustrated? All three might come into play when planning and completing an experiment. For example:

- *Analytical:* Being able to run a statistical analysis on data from the experiment.
- *Creative:* Being able to design the experiment in the first place.
- *Practical:* Being able to get funding for the experiment.

Practical intelligence has become a topic of much interest and research. Sternberg (1996, 1997) has found that practical intelligence predicts success in life but has a surprisingly low relationship to academic (analytical) intelligence. In fact, the higher one's degree of practical intelligence, the less likely that person is to succeed in a university or other academic setting.

Research has found that teaching students to use all three types of intelligence has resulted in improved achievement in school (Grigorenko, Jarvin, & Sternberg, 2002). Sternberg strongly believes that changes need to be made in the assessment of intelligence, as it currently mostly measures analytic abilities. According to Sternberg (2006), a more well-rounded instruction and testing system that includes creative and practical aspects of intelligence could lead to a better educational experience for all students.

MEASURING INTELLIGENCE

7.5   *How is intelligence measured, and how are intelligence tests constructed?*

The history of intelligence testing spans the twentieth century and has at times been marked by controversies and misuse. A full history of how intelligence testing developed would take at least an entire chapter, so this section will discuss only some of the better-known forms of testing and how they came to be.

It doesn't sound like that would be easy to measure on a test—how do IQ tests work, anyway? The measurement of intelligence by some kind of test is a concept that is less than a century old. It began when educators in France realized that some students needed more help with learning than others did. If a way could be found to identify these students, they could be given a different kind of education than the more capable students.

BINET'S MENTAL ABILITY TEST   In those early days, a French psychologist named Alfred Binet was asked by the French Ministry of Education to design a formal test of intelligence that would help identify children who were unable to learn as quickly or as well as others, so that they could be given remedial education. Eventually, he and colleague Théodore Simon came up with a test that distinguished not only between fast and slow learners but also between children of different age groups as well (Binet & Simon, 1916). They noticed that the fast learners seemed to give answers to questions that older children might give, whereas the slow learners gave answers that were more typical of a younger child. Binet decided that the key element to be tested was

👁 Watch on **mypsychlab**
Gender and Spatial Ability

It doesn't **sound like**
that would be easy to
measure on a test—
how do IQ tests work,
anyway? ▶

👁 Watch on **mypsychlab**
Classic Footage—Assessment of Memory With the Stanford-Binet Intelligence Scale

creative intelligence
the ability to deal with new and different concepts and to come up with new ways of solving problems.

practical intelligence
the ability to use information to get along in life and become successful.

a child's *mental age*, or the average age at which children could successfully answer a particular level of questions.

STANFORD-BINET AND IQ Terman (1916), a researcher at Stanford University, adopted German psychologist William Stern's method for comparing mental age and *chronological age* (number of years since birth) for use with the translated and revised Binet test. Stern's (1912) formula was to divide the mental age (MA) by the chronological age (CA) and multiply the result by 100 to get rid of any decimal points. The resulting score is called an **intelligence quotient (IQ)**. (A quotient is a number that results from dividing one number by another.)

$$IQ = MA/CA \times 100$$

For example, if a child who is 10 years old takes the test and scores a mental age of 15 (is able to answer the level of questions typical of a 15-year-old), the IQ would look like this:

$$IQ = 15/10 \times 100 = 150$$

The quotient has the advantage of allowing testers to compare the intelligence levels of people of different age groups. Today, the *Stanford-Binet Intelligence Scales,* Fifth Edition (SB5; Roid, 2003) is used by many educators across North America to make decisions about the placement of students into different educational programs. See Table 7.2 for descriptions of some items similar to those from the SB5.

THE WECHSLER TESTS Although the original Stanford-Binet Test is now in its fifth edition and includes different questions for people of different age groups, it is not the only IQ test that is popular today. David Wechsler (1981, 1990, 1991) was the first to devise a series of tests designed for specific age groups (also given to an individual, not just groups, as is the Stanford-Binet test). Originally dissatisfied with the fact that the Stanford-Binet was designed for children but being administered to adults, he developed an IQ test specifically for adults. He later designed tests specifically for older school-age children and preschool children as well as those in the early grades. The Wechsler Adult Intelligence Scale (WAIS-IV), the Wechsler Intelligence Scale for Children (WISC-IV), and the Wechsler Preschool and Primary Scale of Intelligence (WPPSI-III) are the three versions of this test, and in Canada these tests

intelligence quotient (IQ) a number representing a measure of intelligence, resulting from the division of mental age by chronological age and then multiplying that quotient by 100.

TABLE 7.2 PARAPHRASED ITEMS FROM THE STANFORD-BINET INTELLIGENCE TEST		
AGE*	**TYPE OF ITEM**	**DESCRIPTION OF ITEM**
2	Board with three differently shaped holes	Child can place correct shape into matching hole on board.
4	Building block bridge	Child can build a simple bridge out of blocks after being shown a model.
7	Similarities	Child can answer such question as "In what way are a ship and a car alike?"
9	Digit reversal	Child can repeat four digits backward.
Average adult	Vocabulary	Child can define 20 words from a list.

* Age at which item typically is successfully completed.

Source: Roid, G. H. (2003).

TABLE 7.3	PARAPHRASED SAMPLE ITEMS FROM THE WECHSLER ADULT INTELLIGENCE SCALE (WAIS-IV)

VERBAL SCALE

Information	What is steam made of? What is pepper? Who wrote *Tom Sawyer*?
Comprehension	Why is copper often used in electrical wire? What is the advantage of keeping money in a bank?
Arithmetic	Three women divided 18 golf balls equally among themselves. How many golf balls did each person receive?
	If two buttons cost $0.15, what will be the cost of a dozen buttons?
Similarities	In what way are a circle and a triangle alike? In what way are a saw and a hammer alike?
Vocabulary	What is a hippopotamus? What does *resemble* mean?

PERFORMANCE SCALE

Picture Arrangement	A story is told in three or more cartoon panels placed in the incorrect order; put them together to tell the story.
Picture Completion	Point out what's missing from each picture.
Block Design	After looking at a pattern or a design, try to arrange small cubes in the same pattern.
Object Assembly	Given pieces with part of a picture on each, put them together to form such objects as a hand or a profile.
Digit Symbol	Learn a different symbol for each number and then fill in the blank under the number with the correct symbol. (This test is timed.)

Simulated items similar to those in the *Wechsler Adult Intelligence Scale,* Third Edition (2005).

are now used more frequently than the Stanford-Binet. These tests differ from the Stanford-Binet in that they each have a verbal and a performance (non-verbal) scale, as well as providing an overall score of intelligence. The verbal component scale tests vocabulary, comprehension, and general knowledge, whereas the performance component scale tests such skills as arranging blocks to match a pattern, identifying missing parts in pictures, and putting pictures representing a story in order. Table 7.3 has some sample verbal and performance items from the WAIS-IV.

TEST CONSTRUCTION: GOOD TEST, BAD TEST? All tests are not equally good tests. Some tests might be easy to use, but if they don't actually measure what they are supposed to measure, they are useless. They are thought of as "invalid" (untrue) tests. **Validity** is the degree to which a test actually measures what it's supposed to measure. Other tests may fail to give the same results on different occasions for the same person when that person has not changed—also useless. These would be considered unreliable tests. **Reliability** of a test refers to the test producing consistent results each time it is given to the same individual or group of people. For example, if Nicholas takes a personality test today and then again in a month or so, the results should be very similar if the personality test is reliable. And what does a test score mean? To what, or whom, is it compared?

Take the hypothetical example of Professor Stumpwater, who for reasons best known only to him believes that intelligence is related to the speed of a person's text messaging. Let's say that he develops an adult intelligence test based on how fast people can send text messages. What do we need to look at to determine whether his test is a good one?

Standardization of Tests First of all, we would want to look at how he tried to standardize his test. *Standardization* refers to the process of giving the test to a large group

Watch on mypsychlab

Are Intelligence Tests Valid?

validity
the degree to which a test actually measures what it's supposed to measure.

reliability
the tendency of a test to produce the same scores again and again each time it is given to the same person.

of people that represents the kind of people for whom the test is designed. Standardization groups are chosen randomly from the population for whom the test is intended and, like all samples, must be representative of that population. If a test is designed for children, for example, then a large sample of randomly selected children would be given the test. All test subjects would take the test under the same conditions. In the professor's case, this would mean that he would have to allow his sample members to send the same number of text messages on the same phone under the same conditions, and so on.

Norms The scores from the standardization group would be called the *norms*, the standards against which all others who take the test would be compared. Most tests of intelligence follow a *normal curve*, or a distribution in which the scores are the greatest around the *mean*, or average, and become less and less the farther from the mean they occur (see Figure 7.4). (L I N K) to *Appendix A: Statistics* (online in your eText).

In Figure 7.4, percentages represent the percentage of scores falling under a section of the curve for each *standard deviation (SD)* from the mean on the Wechsler IQ test. The standard deviation is the average variation of scores from the mean.

In the case of the professor's text messaging test, he might find that a certain speed is the average, which he would interpret as average intelligence. People who scored extremely well on the text messaging test would be compared to the average, as well as people with unusually poor scores.

The normal curve allows IQ scores to be more accurately estimated. The old IQ scoring method using the simple formula devised by Stern produces raw IQ scores that start to become meaningless as the person's chronological age passes 16 years. (Once a person becomes an adult, the idea of questions that are geared for a particular age group loses its power. For example, what kind of differences would there be between questions designed for a 30 year old versus a 40 year old?) Test designers replaced the old ratio IQ of the earlier versions of IQ tests with **deviation IQ scores**, which are based on the normal curve distribution (Eysenck, 1994): IQ is assumed to be normally distributed with a mean IQ of 100 and a typical standard deviation of about 15 (the standard deviation can vary according to the particular test).

With respect to validity and reliability, the professor's test fares poorly. If the results of the professor's test were compared with other established intelligence tests, there would probably be no relationship at all. Speed of text messaging has nothing to do with intelligence, so the test is not a valid, or true, measure of intelligence.

On the other hand, his test might work well for some people and poorly for others on the question of reliability. Some people who are fast and regular text messagers tend to score about the same for each test that they complete, so for them, the text messaging IQ would be fairly reliable. But others, especially those who do not send text messages or text infrequently, would have widely varying scores from time to time. For those people, the test would be very unreliable, and if a test is unreliable for some, it's not a good test.

A test can fail in validity but still be reliable. If for some reason Professor Stumpwater chose to use height as a measure of intelligence, an adult's score on Stumpwater's "test" would always be the same, as height does not change very much after the late teens. But the opposite is not true. If a test is unreliable, how can it accurately measure what it is supposed to measure? For example, adult intelligence remains fairly constant. If a test meant

◄●┤Simulate on **mypsychlab**
Normal Curve

deviation IQ scores
a type of intelligence measure that assumes that IQ is normally distributed around a mean of 100 with a standard deviation of about 15.

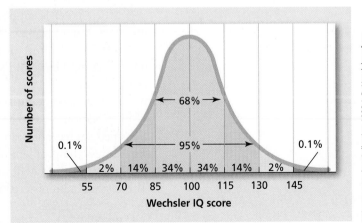

FIGURE 7.4 **The Normal Curve** On the Wechsler IQ test, the percentages under each section of the normal curve represent the percentage of scores falling within that section for each *standard deviation (SD)* from the mean.

to measure that intelligence gives different scores at different times, it's obviously not a valid measure of intelligence.

Just because an IQ test gives the same score every time a person takes it doesn't mean that the score is actually measuring real intelligence, right? That's right—think about the definition of intelligence for a moment: the ability to learn from one's experiences, acquire knowledge, and use resources effectively in adapting to new situations or solving problems. How can anyone define what effective use of resources might be? Does everyone have access to the same resources? Is everyone's "world" necessarily perceived as being the same?

Likewise, real intelligence would not be measured if people taking the test were asked outdated questions. To keep the norms in IQ tests current, and thus ensure the reliability and validity of the tests, most IQ tests are revised approximately every 10 to 15 years (Dulcan, 2010). Updating norms is extremely important in intelligence testing because cohort differences between the people being tested and the norms they are being compared to can lead to bias in such testing.

Intelligence tests are useful measuring devices but should not necessarily be assumed to be measures of all types of intelligent behaviour, or even good measures for all groups of people, as the next section discusses.

IQ TESTS AND CULTURAL BIAS The problem with trying to measure intelligence with a test that is based on an understanding of the world and its resources is that not everyone comes from the same "world." People raised in a different culture, or even a different economic situation, from the one in which the designer of an IQ test is raised are not likely to perform well on such a test.

It is very difficult to design an intelligence test that is completely free of *cultural bias*, a term referring to the tendency of IQ tests to reflect, in language, dialect, and content, the culture of the person or persons who designed the test. A person who comes from the same culture (or even socioeconomic background) as the test designer may have an unfair advantage over a person who is from a different cultural or socioeconomic background (Helms, 1992). If people raised in an Asian culture are given a test designed within a traditional Western culture, such as Canada, many items on the test might make no sense to them. For example, one kind of question might be the following: Which one of the five is least like the other four?

DOG–CAR–CAT–BIRD–FISH

The answer is supposed to be "car," which is the only one of the five that is not alive. But a Japanese child, living in a culture that relies on the sea for so much of its food and culture, might choose "fish," because none of the others are found in the ocean. That child's test score would be lower but not because the child is unintelligent.

A Canadian example of the problem of cultural bias can be found in the testing of First Nations youth. Many people have argued that the intelligence of First Nations peoples has not been accurately measured because of biased testing procedures. To address the problem of cultural bias in the intelligence testing of the Eastern James Bay Cree, Mawhinney (1983) developed the Cree Picture Vocabulary Test. This test was administered in the Cree language and was designed in accordance with the Cree experience.

Attempts have been made to create intelligence tests that are as free of cultural influences as is humanly possible. Many test designers have come to the conclusion that it may be impossible to create a test that is completely free of cultural bias (Carpenter et al., 1990). Instead, they are striving to create tests that are at least *culturally fair*. These tests use questions that do not create a disadvantage for people whose

Watch on **mypsychlab**
Robert Guthrie: Demographics and Intelligence Testing

These high school students are taking a standardized test. How fair is it to expect all of these young people, many who may be from different cultural backgrounds, to interpret every question on the test in the exact manner that the test designer intended?

culture differs from that of the majority. Many items on a "culturally fair" test require the use of non-verbal abilities such as rotating objects rather than items about verbal knowledge that might be culturally specific.

If intelligence tests are so flawed, why do people still use them? The one thing that IQ tests do well is predict academic success for those who score at the higher and lower ends of the normal curve. (For those who score in the average range of IQ, the predictive value is less clear.) The kinds of tests students are given in school are often similar to intelligence tests, and so people who do well on IQ tests typically do well on other kinds of academically oriented tests as well, such as the newly developed Pan-Canadian Assessment Program, the Scholastic Aptitude Test (SAT), the Graduate Record Exam (GRE), and actual college and university examinations. These achievement tests are very similar to IQ tests but are administered to groups of people rather than to individuals.

◀ If intelligence **tests** are so flawed, why do people still use them?

PRACTICE QUIZ: HOW MUCH DO YOU REMEMBER?

Pick the best answer.

1. According to Spearman, a traditional IQ test would most likely measure
  a. practical intelligence.
  b. specific intelligence.
  c. general intelligence.
  d. emotional intelligence.

2. In Gardner's view, astronauts, navigators, and artists would be high in _____ intelligence.
  a. verbal/linguistic
  b. visual/spatial
  c. interpersonal
  d. intrapersonal

3. Sternberg has found that _____ intelligence is a good predictor of success in life but has a low relationship to _____ intelligence.
  a. practical; academic
  b. practical; creative
  c. academic; practical
  d. academic; creative

4. Using the Stanford-Binet IQ formula, what IQ would a person have whose mental age is 10 and whose chronological age is 15?
  a. 150
  b. 1.50
  c. 0.67
  d. 67

5. Professor Beckett designed an IQ test. To standardize this test, the professor should be careful to do which of the following?
  a. Use only a small sample to prevent possible cheating on the test.
  b. Select the people in the sample from the population of people for whom the test is designed.
  c. Select only university professors to take the test so that they can critique the questions on the test.
  d. Test each member of the sample under different conditions.

6. _____ would be the problem with a test that provides a consistent score for some people each time it is administered but yields different scores for other people.
  a. Reliability
  b. Validity
  c. Standardization
  d. Normalization

Answers: 1-c, 2-b, 3-a, 4-d, 5-b, 6-a.

INDIVIDUAL DIFFERENCES IN INTELLIGENCE

Another use of IQ tests is to identify people who differ from those of average intelligence by a great degree. Although one such group is composed of those who are sometimes called *geniuses* (who fall at the extreme high end of the normal curve for intelligence), the other group is made up of people who, for various reasons, are considered intellectually delayed and whose IQ scores fall well below the mean on the normal curve.

INTELLECTUAL DISABILITY

7.6   *What is intellectual disability, and what causes it?*

According to the American Association on Intellectual and Developmental Disabilities (AAIDD), **intellectual disability** is "characterized by significant limitations both in intellectual functioning and in adaptive behaviour as expressed in conceptual, social, and practical adaptive skills. This disability originates before age 18" (Schalock, Luckasson, & Shogren, 2007, p. 118). American clinicians are not the only ones who use the definition provided by the AAIDD; Canadian clinicians use it as well. According to the World Health Organization (1985), in industrialized countries such as Canada, intellectual disability occurs in about 3 percent of the population.

The term *intellectual disability* is increasingly being used instead of *mental retardation* (Schalock et al. 2007), a term still commonly used to refer to the condition, which, in fact, is still used in the *Diagnostic and Statistical Manual*, Fourth Edition (*DSM-IV*). The *DSM-IV* is the manual used to classify and diagnose mental disorders; it will be discussed further in Chapter Thirteen. Ⓛ Ⓘ Ⓝ Ⓚ *to Chapter Thirteen: Psychological Disorders, p. 520.* However, in line with recommendations from the AAIDD, the new edition of the *DSM* (*DSM-V*), which is set for publication in 2013, is expected to replace the term *mental retardation* with *intellectual disability* (Shogren, 2011).

So how would a professional go about deciding whether a child has an intellectual disability? Is the IQ test the primary method? Diagnosis of intellectual disability, according to the AAIDD guidelines (AAIDD, 2011), should not depend on IQ tests scores alone (generally an IQ score of around 70 indicates a significant limitation in intellectual functioning). Instead, scores from standardized tests determining limitations in adaptive behaviour should also be used. Adaptive behaviour includes three types of skills: conceptual skills (e.g., language and reading skills and time and number concepts), social skills (e.g., skills relating to dealing with others, self-esteem, gullibility, and the ability to avoid being taken advantage of), and practical skills (e.g., occupational skills, personal care, and proper use of money). In addition, the AAIDD stresses that before a diagnosis of intellectual disability can be made, professionals must take into account factors such as cultural, environmental, and linguistic diversity.

Classifications   Intellectual disability can vary from mild to extremely severe. Even with their flaws, IQ test scores are still used to classify the various levels of disability, as can be seen in Table 7.4.

Causes   So what causes intellectual disability? There are numerous environmental and biological causes of intellectual disability. Examples of environmental factors that can lead to intellectual disability include malnutrition and various environmental toxins such as lead and mercury poisoning.

The three most common biological causes of intellectual disability are Down syndrome (also known as *Trisomy 21*) Ⓛ Ⓘ Ⓝ Ⓚ *to Chapter Eight: Development Across the Lifespan, p. 302*, fetal alcohol syndrome, and fragile X syndrome. *Fetal alcohol syndrome* is a condition that results from exposing a developing embryo to

---

So how would a
professional go about
deciding whether a
child has an intellectual
disability? Is the IQ test
the primary method? ▶

So what **causes**
intellectual disability? ▶

intellectual disability
characterized by significant limitations both in intellectual functioning and in adaptive behaviour as expressed in conceptual, social, and practical adaptive skills.

alcohol (i.e., the mother drinks alcohol while she is pregnant, and thus this condition can be easily prevented by the mother avoiding alcohol while pregnant), and intelligence levels range from below average to an intellectual disability (Olson & Burgess, 1997). In *fragile X syndrome*, a male has a thin, frail-looking area on his X chromosome of the twenty-third pair. As children, people with this syndrome typically have a mild intellectual disability, but the degree of this disability strengthens as they become adults (Dykens et al., 1994).

There are many other causes of intellectual disability (Murphy et al., 1998). Lack of oxygen at birth; damage to the fetus in the womb from diseases, infections, or drug use by the mother; and even diseases and accidents during childhood can lead to intellectual disability.

One thing should always be remembered: Intellectual disability affects the person's intellectual capabilities. People with intellectual disabilities are just as responsive to love and affection as anyone else and need to be loved and to have friends just as all people do. Intelligence is only one characteristic; warmth, friendliness, caring, and compassion also count for a great deal and should not be underrated.

This middle-aged man is named Jack. Jack lives in a small town in Arkansas and serves as a deacon at the local church. He is loved and respected and leads a full and happy life. Jack also has Down syndrome, which is discussed in Chapter Eight.

Mainstreaming in Canadian Schools Approximately 50 years ago, Canadian children with intellectual disabilities were segregated from other children—they were placed into separate, special schools. Today, Canadian public schools are more inclusive. There is now a legal requirement in Canada that all students receive free and appropriate education (Dworet & Bennett, 2002). This includes children who speak different languages, children from different religious or cultural backgrounds, and children with varying intellectual challenges, among others. This practice of including children with intellectual disabilities in regular schools is commonly referred to as **mainstreaming**.

mainstreaming
process of educating students with intellectual disabilities in regular schools, often in classes with students without intellectual disabilities.

TABLE 7.4 CLASSIFICATIONS OF INTELLECTUAL DISABILITY

CLASSIFICATION	RANGE OF IQ SCORES	ADAPTIVE LIMITATIONS	DELAYED POPULATION
Mild	55–70	Can reach grade 6 skill level. Capable with training of living independently and being self-supporting.	90%
Moderate	40–55	Can reach grade 2 skill level. Can work and live in sheltered environments with supervision.	6%
Severe	25–40	Can learn to talk and perform basic self-care but needs constant supervision.	3%
Profound	Below 25	Very limited ability to learn; may be able to learn only very simple tasks; poor language skills and limited self-care.	1%

Source: Table based on classifications in the *DSM-IV* (American Psychiatric Association [APA], 2000a).

The degree of mainstreaming varies across the provinces of Canada. In Quebec, less than 50 percent of all children with an intellectual disability are educated in regular classrooms, almost 25 percent are educated in separate special-education schools, and the remaining students are educated in special-education classes within regular schools. In contrast, in Prince Edward Island, almost 75 percent of children with an intellectual disability are educated in regular classrooms and virtually none are in special-education schools (Canadian Council on Learning, 2007).

There has been much debate over whether mainstreaming is a good idea. Evidence has been found for both sides of the debate; but, overall, it appears that the process of including children with intellectual disabilities in regular classrooms leads to better academic and social skills in children with disabilities (Baker, 1994; Carlberg & Kavale, 1980; Wang & Baker, 1985). Also important, studies have found that not only was the academic progress of students without disabilities not negatively affected by mainstreaming, students without disabilities were also found to experience positive academic, social, and emotional gains from inclusive classrooms (Bear & Proctor, 1990; Helmstetter, Peck, & Giangreco, 1994; Staub & Peck, 1995).

Of course, as with anything else, there are exceptions to every rule. Whether a certain child with an intellectual disability will be successful in a regular school obviously depends on the nature and severity of his or her disability.

GIFTEDNESS

7.7   What is giftedness, and does being intellectually gifted guarantee success in life?

At the other end of the intelligence scale are those who fall on the upper end of the normal curve (see Figure 7.4 on p. 277) above an IQ of 130 (about 2 percent of the population). The term applied to these people is **gifted**, and if the IQ falls above 140 (less than half of 1 percent of the population), the term is often *genius*. Some people use the term *genius* only for people with extremely high IQs or with other qualities that are extreme, such as creativity (Kamphaus, 1993).

I've heard that geniuses are sometimes a little "nutty" and odd. Are geniuses, especially the really high-IQ ones, "not playing with a full deck," as the saying goes? People have long held many false beliefs about people who are very, very intelligent. One common phrase around the turn of the twentieth century was "early ripe, early rot," which meant that people expected young geniuses to lose their genius early in life (Shurkin, 1992). Other beliefs were that gifted people are weird and socially awkward, physically weak, and more likely to suffer from mental illnesses. From these beliefs comes the "mad scientist" of the cinema (think Dr. Evil of *Austin Powers*) and the "evil genius" of literature—Dr. Frankenstein, Dr. Jekyll, and Superman's arch-enemy, Lex Luthor, to name a few.

These beliefs were shattered by a groundbreaking study that was initiated in 1921 by Lewis M. Terman, a psychologist at Stanford University. Terman (1925) selected 1528 children to participate in a longitudinal study. ⓛⓘⓝⓚ *to Chapter Eight: Development Across the Lifespan, p. 302.* These children, 857 boys and 671 girls, had IQs (as measured by the Stanford-Binet) ranging from 130 to 200.

The early findings of this major study (Terman & Oden, 1947) demonstrated that the gifted were socially well adjusted and often skilled leaders. They were also above average in height, weight, and physical attractiveness, putting an end to the myth of the weakling genius. Terman was also able to demonstrate that his gifted children were not only less susceptible to mental illness than the general population but also *more* resistant to mental illnesses. Only those with the highest IQs (180 and above)

I've heard that geniuses are sometimes a little "nutty" and odd. Are geniuses, especially the really high-IQ ones, "not playing with a full ▶ deck," as the saying goes?

United Media/United Feature Syndicate, Inc.

"I'm sorry, but I'm not allowed to sell you that smart phone without first verifying your IQ."

gifted
the 2 percent of the population falling on the upper end of the normal curve and typically possessing an IQ of 130 or above.

were found to have some social and behavioural adjustment problems *as children* (Janos, 1987). For more on Terman's famous study, see the Classic Studies in Psychology section that follows.

There has been a debate as to how exactly a gifted child becomes gifted. As you will see later in the chapter, the nature/nurture controversy is alive and well in the area

CLASSIC STUDIES IN PSYCHOLOGY

Terman's Termites

Terman's "Termites" as they came to be called, were also typically successful as adults. They earned more academic degrees and had higher occupational and financial success than their average peers (at least, the men in the study had occupational success—women at this time did not typically have careers outside the home). Their occupations included doctors, lawyers, business executives, university professors, scientists, and even one famous science-fiction writer and an Oscar-winning director (Edward Dmytryk, director of the 1954 *The Caine Mutiny*), among others.

Terman's (1925) longitudinal study is still going on today, although many of his original subjects have passed away and those who remain are in their 80s. Terman himself died in 1956, but several other researchers (including Robert Sears, one of the original Termites) have kept track of the remaining Termites over the years (Holahan & Sears, 1996).

By 2000, only about 200 Termites were still living. Although the study was marred by several flaws, it still remains one of the most important and rich sources of data on an entire generation. Terman's study was actually the first truly longitudinal study (**LINK** to *Chapter Eight: Development Across the Lifespan, p. 302*) ever to be accomplished, and scientists have collected data about the effects of phenomena such as World War II and the influence of personality traits on how long one lives from the questionnaires filled out by the participants over the years.

Terman and Oden (1959) compared the 100 most successful men in the group to the 100 least successful by defining *successful* as holding jobs that related to or used their intellectual skills. The more successful men earned more money, had careers with more prestige, and were healthier and less likely to be divorced or alcoholics than the less successful men. The IQ scores were relatively equal between the two groups, so the differences in success in life had to be caused by some other factor or factors. Terman and Oden found that the successful adults were different from the others in three ways: They were more goal oriented, more persistent in pursuing those goals, and were more self-confident than the less successful Termites.

What were the flaws in this study? Terman acquired his participants by getting recommendations from teachers and principals, not through random selection, so there was room for bias in the pool of participants from the start. It is quite possible that the teachers and principals were less likely, especially in 1921, to recommend students who were "troublemakers" or different from the majority. Consequently, Terman's original group consisted of almost entirely white, urban, and middle-class children, with the majority (856 out of 1528) being male. There were two African Americans, six Japanese Americans, and one Native American.

Another flaw is the way Terman interfered in the lives of his "children." In any good research study, the investigator should avoid becoming personally involved in the lives of the participants of the studies to reduce the possibility of biasing the results. Terman seemed to find it nearly impossible to remain objective (Leslie, 2000). He became like a surrogate father to many of them, even going so far as to write a letter urging authorities to give Edward Dmytryk every consideration as they tried to determine whether 14-year-old runaway Edward was indeed being abused by his father or just telling a tall tale. Terman's letter did the trick, and Edward went to a good foster home and grew up to become a famous Hollywood director of

Stanford University psychologist Lewis Terman is pictured at his desk in 1942. Terman spent a good portion of his career researching children with high IQ scores and was the first to use the term *gifted* to describe these children.

23 films. This is just one example of how Terman not only observed his participants but also influenced the course of their lives above and beyond their own intelligence levels.

Flawed as it may have been, Terman's groundbreaking study did accomplish his original goal of putting to rest the myths that existed about genius in the early part of the twentieth century. Gifted children and adults are no more prone to mental illnesses or odd behaviour than any other group, and they also have their share of failures as well as successes. Genius is obviously not the only factor that influences success in life—personality and experiences are strong factors as well. For example, the homes of the children in the top 2 percent of Terman's group had an average of 450 books in their libraries, a sign that the parents of these children valued books and learning, and these parents were also more likely to be teachers, professionals, doctors, and lawyers. The experiences of these gifted children growing up would have been vastly different from those in homes with less emphasis on reading and lower occupational levels for the parents.

Questions for Further Discussion

1. Thinking back to the discussion of research ethics in Chapter One (pp. 30–33), what ethical violations may Terman have committed while involved in this study?

2. If gifted children thrive when growing up in more economically sound and educationally focused environments, what should the educational system strive to do to nourish the gifted? Should the government get involved in programs for the gifted?

3. In Terman and Oden's 1959 study of the successful and unsuccessful Termites, what might be the problems associated with the definition of *successful* in the study?

of intelligence. Some researchers argue that intelligence is inborn while others argue that experience and learning are the major determinants of a person's intelligence. Recent research findings concerning the effect of musical training on children's development have supported the latter argument. For information regarding the effects of musical training on children's cognitive abilities, read the following Psychology in the News section.

PSYCHOLOGY IN THE NEWS

Music Lessons Make for Brighter Kids

7.8. *How does musical training affect children's cognitive abilities?*

aurel Trainor of McMaster University in Hamilton and Takako Fujioka of the Rotman Research Institute in Toronto used brain-scanning techniques to compare developmental changes in children between the ages of 4 and 6 over the course of a year. It was found that music lessons can help advance brain development in children as young as 4 years of age, even when it seems as though the children are just making random noise. One finding in particular was that there were changes in the attentional systems of children who took music lessons, affecting their ability to pay attention to the world around them (Canadian Press, 2006).

Trainor and her colleagues believe that as kids are learning music, networks in their brains are being formed and solidified. Trainor also adds that musical training could lead to improvements in mathematical ability, literacy, memory, and IQ, among other things.

According to Trainor, while much research by E. Glenn Schellenberg from the University of Toronto has shown that music lessons improve IQ scores in older children, this study is the first to identify the positive effect of music lessons on the cognitive abilities of preschool children.

Questions for Further Discussion

1. If government spending were up to you, how would you allocate funding to each of the major areas of education (i.e., what would be the percentage of funds allocated to the maths and sciences, the arts, languages, etc.)?

2. How might this study's findings affect parental decisions regarding their children's extra-curricular activities?

3. In what ways are the findings regarding changes in the attentional systems of children taking music lessons relevant to other subject areas in school?

4. Aside from brain-scanning techniques, what are some methods that researchers could use to determine whether music lessons do, in fact, have a beneficial effect on children's cognitive development?

PRACTICE QUIZ: HOW MUCH DO YOU REMEMBER?

Pick the best answer.

1. Jarod is 35 years old, but his mind has never gone beyond the level of a grade 2 child. Jarod would be classified as having a _____ intellectual disability.
   a. mild
   b. moderate
   c. severe
   d. profound

2. A male with a mild intellectual disability that becomes more severe as he ages probably suffers from
   a. Down syndrome.
   b. fetal alcohol syndrome.
   c. hydrocephaly.
   d. fragile X syndrome.

3. Elizabeth was tested while in grade school and was found to have an IQ of 134. Elizabeth's intelligence level can be labelled as
   a. average.
   b. somewhat above normal.
   c. gifted.
   d. genius.

4. Which of the following statements about the successful "Termites" in the Terman and Oden (1959) study is FALSE?
   a. The successful men earned more money.
   b. The successful men were more likely to be divorced.
   c. The unsuccessful men were less healthy.
   d. The unsuccessful men held jobs of lower prestige.

5. According to Laurel Trainor, music training could lead to improvements in
   a. literacy.
   b. memory.
   c. IQ.
   d. all of the above

Answers: 1-b, 2-d, 3-c, 4-b, 5-d.

7.9 *What is emotional intelligence, and how is it measured?*

EMOTIONAL INTELLIGENCE What about people who have a lot of "book smarts" but not much common sense? There are people like that, who never seem to get ahead in life, in spite of having all that so-called intelligence. It is true that not everyone who is intellectually able is going to be a success in life (Mehrabian, 2000). Often the people who are most successful are those who didn't do all that well in the regular academic setting.

One of the early explanations for why people who succeed in life often did poorly in school and those who did well in school did not excel in the "real" world was that success relies on a certain degree of **emotional intelligence**, the awareness of and ability to manage one's own emotions as well as the ability to be self-motivated, to feel what others feel, and to be socially skilled (Persaud, 2001).

The concept of emotional intelligence was first introduced by Salovey and Mayer (1990) and was later expanded on by Goleman (1995). Goleman proposed that emotional intelligence is a more powerful influence on success in life than more traditional views of intelligence. One who is emotionally

Emotional intelligence includes empathy, which is the ability to feel what others are feeling. This doctor is not only able to listen to her patient's problems but also able to show by her facial expression, body language, and gestures that she understands how the patient feels.

emotional intelligence
the awareness of and ability to manage one's own emotions as well as the ability to be self-motivated, able to feel what others feel, and socially skilled.

intelligent possesses self-control of emotions such as anger, impulsiveness, and anxiety. Empathy, the ability to understand what others feel, is also a component, as are an awareness of one's own emotions, sensitivity, persistence even in the face of frustrations, and the ability to motivate oneself (Salovey & Mayer, 1990).

> That all sounds very ▶
> nice, but how can
> anything like this be
> measured? Is there
> research to support this
> idea?

That all sounds very nice, but how can anything like this be measured? Is there research to support this idea? In one study, researchers asked 321 participants to read passages written by non-participants and to guess what the non-participants were feeling while they were writing (Mayer & Geher, 1996). The assumption was that people who were good at connecting thoughts to feelings would also have a high degree of empathy and emotional intelligence. The participants who more correctly judged the writers' emotional experiences (assessed by both how well each participant's emotional judgments agreed with a group consensus and the non-participant's actual report of feelings) also scored higher on the empathy measure and lower on the defensiveness measure. These same participants also had higher SAT scores (self-reported), leading Mayer and colleagues to conclude not only that emotional intelligence is a valid and measurable concept but also that general intelligence and emotional intelligence may be related: Those who are high in emotional intelligence are also smarter in the traditional sense (Mayer et al., 2000).

More recently, James Parker and his colleagues at Trent University in Peterborough, Ontario, have found a relationship between first-year students' level of emotional intelligence and their academic success (Parker, Hogan, Eastabrook, Oke, & Wood, 2006). They point out that post-secondary education is one of the most stressful experiences of a young person's life (Parker et al., 2006). In fact, it is so stressful that many students who enroll in a particular program end up dropping out before graduation (Gerdes & Mallinckrodt, 1994). Examples of stressors that first-year students face include moving away from home, having to be financially independent for the first time (and possibly having to take a job in order to pay tuition), making new friends, and dealing with an increased workload.

According to Parker and colleagues, much of the previous work looking at predictors of academic performance in post-secondary education has focused on grades in high school or standardized measures of cognitive abilities. These so-called predictors have not been found to be reliable indictors of academic success in college or university. Because of this failure to find a relationship that many believed to exist, researchers started turning to other possibilities, such as emotional intelligence. Researchers began finding a link between academic achievement in post-secondary education and emotional intelligence—a link that was not found with other factors.

One of the most academically supported assessments of emotional intelligence is the Mayer-Salovey-Caruso Emotional Intelligence Test (MSCEIT). According to the EI Skills Group (2011), the MSCEIT is based on an ability model of emotional intelligence, where emotional intelligence is conceptualized as having four separate components: Identify (in which one must identify emotion(s) expressed by a face or in designs; Use (in which one must generate an emotion and then solve a problem with that mood); Understand (in which one must understand the cause(s) of the emotion(s); and finally, Manage (in which one must be able to manage their emotions to obtain a positive result; see Figure 7.5).

Identifying Emotions

Indicate how much of each emotion is present in this picture.

Emotion	Not Much				Very
Happiness	1	2	3	4	5
Fear	1	2	3	4	5
Sadness	1	2	3	4	5
Surprise	1	2	3	4	5

Using Emotions

What mood(s) might be helpful to feel when meeting in-laws for the very first time?

Mood	Not Useful				Useful
Tension	1	2	3	4	5
Surprise	1	2	3	4	5
Joy	1	2	3	4	5

Understanding Emotions

Tom felt anxious, and became a bit stressed when he thought about all the work he needed to do. When his supervisor brought him an additional project, he felt ____.
(Select the best choice.)

a) Overwhelmed
b) Depressed
c) Ashamed
d) Self-conscious
e) Jittery

Managing Emotions

Debbie just came back from vacation. She was feeling peaceful and content. How well would each action preserve her mood?

Action 1: She started to make a list of things at home that she needed to do.
    Very Ineffective..1.....2.....3.....4.....5..Very Effective

Action 2: She began thinking about where and when she would go on her next vacation.
    Very Ineffective..1.....2.....3.....4.....5..Very Effective

Action 3: She decided it was best to ignore the feeling since it wouldn't last anyway.
    Very Ineffective..1.....2.....3.....4.....5..Very Effective

FIGURE 7.5 **Example MSCEIT Items**   These sample items are from the Mayer-Salovey-Caruso Emotional Intelligence Test (MSCEIT).

Although his own work and that of his colleagues provide empirical support for the concept of emotional intelligence, Mayer (1999) has criticized the presentation of emotional intelligence in popular magazines and bestselling (but non-scientific) books by stating the following in an online article for the American Psychology Association:

> "The popular literature's implication—that highly emotionally intelligent people possess an unqualified advantage in life—appears overly enthusiastic at present and unsubstantiated by reasonable scientific standards."

THE NATURE/NURTURE CONTROVERSY REGARDING INTELLIGENCE

7.10   *What is the influence of heredity and environment on the development of intelligence?*

Are people born with all the "smarts" they will ever have, or does experience and learning count for something in the development of intellect? The influence of nature (heredity or

Wait a minute—if monozygotic twins have a correlation of 0.86, wouldn't that mean that intelligence is 86 percent inherited? ▶

FIGURE 7.6 **Correlations Between IQ Scores of Persons with Various Relationships**   In the graph on the left, the degree of genetic relatedness seems to determine the agreement (correlation) between IQ scores of the various comparisons. For example, monozygotic twins, who share 100 percent of their genes, are more similar in IQ than dizygotic twins, who share only about 50 percent of their genes, even when raised in the same environment. In the graph on the right, monozygotic twins are still more similar to each other in IQ than are other types of comparisons, but being raised in the same environment increases the similarity considerably.

genes) and nurture (environment) on personality traits has long been debated in the field of human development (ⓛⓘⓝⓚ *to Chapter Eight: Development Across the Lifespan, p. 302*), and intelligence is one of the traits that has been examined closely.

TWIN STUDIES   The problem with trying to separate the role of genes from that of environment is that controlled, perfect experiments are neither practical nor ethical. Instead, researchers find out what they can from *natural experiments*, circumstances existing in nature that can be examined to understand some phenomenon. *Twin studies* are an example of such circumstances.

As you will learn in Chapter Eight, monozygotic twins (commonly referred to as *identical twins*, which is a misnomer because no two people are actually identical) are those who originally came from one fertilized egg and, therefore, share almost the same genetic inheritance. Any differences between them on a certain trait, then, should be caused by environmental factors. Dizygotic twins (commonly referred to as *fraternal twins*) come from two different eggs, each fertilized by a different sperm, and share only the amount of genetic material that any two siblings would share. ⓛⓘⓝⓚ *to Chapter Eight: Development Across the Lifespan, p. 302*. By comparing the IQs of these two types of twins reared together (similar environments) and reared apart (different environments), as well as persons of other degrees of relatedness, researchers can get a general, if not exact, idea of how much influence heredity has over the trait of intelligence (see Figure 7.6).

As can be easily seen from the chart, the greater the degree of genetic relatedness, the stronger the correlation is between the IQ scores of those persons. The fact that genetically monozygotic twins show a correlation of 0.86 means that the environment must play a part in determining some aspects of intelligence as measured by IQ tests. If heredity alone were responsible, the correlation between genetically monozygotic twins should be 1.00. At this time, researchers have determined that the estimated *heritability* (proportion of change in IQ within a population that is caused by hereditary factors) for intelligence is about 0.50 or 50 percent (Plomin & DeFries, 1998).

Wait a minute—if monozygotic twins have a correlation of 0.86, wouldn't that mean that intelligence is 86 percent inherited? Although the correlation between monozygotic twins is higher than the estimated heritability of 0.50, that similarity is not entirely due to the twin's genetic similarity. Twins who are raised in the same household obviously share very similar environments as well. Even twins who are reared apart are usually placed in homes that are similar in socioeconomic and ethnic

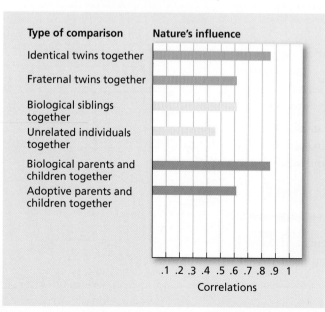

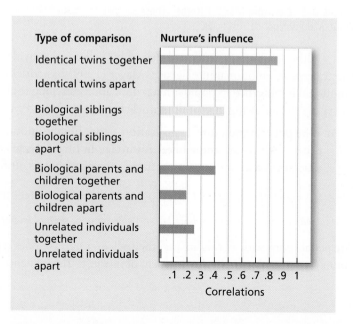

background—more similar than one might think. So when twins who are genetically similar are raised in similar environments, their IQ scores are also going to be similar.

Heritability is worth a little more explanation because findings show that genes have significant influence on human behaviour. A trait such as height is one that is highly heritable; in a group of people who are all nearly equal in nourishment, for example, differences between them in height will be caused almost entirely by differences in their genes. But something such as table manners is very low in heritability; table manners are a result of experience and upbringing, not genetics (Dickens & Flynn, 2001).

One of the things that people need to understand about heritability is that estimates of heritability apply only to changes in IQ within a *group* of people, *not to the individual people themselves.* Each individual is far too different in experiences, education, and other non-genetic factors to predict exactly how a particular set of genes will interact with those factors in that one person. It is only differences among people *in general* that can be investigated for the influence of genes (Dickens & Flynn, 2001). You will learn in Chapter Eight that our genes are designed to take their cues from nurture; our environments dictate how our genes express ourselves throughout our lives (Ridley, 2003). (L)(I)(N)(K) *to Chapter Eight: Development Across the Lifespan, p. 302.* Genes always interact with environmental factors, and in some cases extreme environments can modify even very heritable traits, as would happen in the case of a severely malnourished child's growth pattern.

"I told my parents that if grades were so important they should have paid for a smarter egg donor."

THE BELL CURVE AND MISINTERPRETATION OF STATISTICS In 1994, Herrnstein and Murray published the controversial book *The Bell Curve,* in which they cite large amounts of statistical studies (never published in scientific journals prior to the book) that led them to make the claim that IQ is largely inherited. These authors go further by also implying that people from lower economic levels are poor because they are unintelligent.

In their book, Herrnstein and Murray made several statistical errors and ignored the effects of environment and culture. First, they assumed that IQ tests actually do measure intelligence. As discussed earlier, IQ tests are not free of cultural or socioeconomic bias. So all Herrnstein and Murray really found was a correlation between race and *IQ,* not race and *intelligence.* Second, they assumed that intelligence itself is very heavily influenced by genetics, with a heritability factor of about 0.80. The current estimate of the heritability of intelligence is about 0.50 (Plomin & DeFries, 1998).

Herrnstein and Murray also failed to understand that heritability applies only to differences that can be found *within* a group of people as opposed to those *between* groups of people or individuals (Gould, 1981). Heritability estimates can be made accurately only from a group that was exposed to a similar environment.

One of their findings was that Japanese Americans are at the top of the IQ ladder, a finding that they attribute to racial and genetic characteristics. They seem to ignore the cultural influence of intense focus on education and achievement by Japanese American parents (Neisser et al., 1996).

Another researcher who has created a lot of controversy by claiming to find evidence supporting the existence of racial differences in IQ is Canadian J. Philippe Rushton of the University of Western Ontario. According to Rushton, findings regarding differences in head circumference, brain size, and estimated cranial space support his conclusion that Asians are the most intelligent group of people, followed by whites, and then blacks (Rushton, 1991, 1992).

Scientists (Beardsley, 1995; Kamin, 1995) have concluded that, despite the claims of *The Bell Curve* and Rushton, there is no real scientific evidence for genetic differences in intelligence *between* different racial groups. A series of studies, using blood-group testing for racial grouping (different racial groups have different rates of certain blood groups, allowing a statistical estimation of ancestry), found no significant relationship between ethnicity and IQ (Neisser et al., 1996).

Although *The Bell Curve* stated that Japanese Americans are genetically superior in intelligence, the book's authors overlook the influence of cultural values. Japanese American parents put much time and effort into helping their children with schoolwork.

ARTIFICIAL INTELLIGENCE (AI)

7.11   *What is artificial intelligence?*

Many people might think that interest in **artificial intelligence (AI)**, or the creation of a machine that can think like a human, is a relatively recent phenomenon. But the idea of a mechanical "man" or robot is ancient. In Greek mythology, the god Hephaestus created a bronze man called Talos 1, the guardian of Crete. In a sense, Mary Shelley's *Frankenstein* (1818/1969) was an artificially created being as well. The first use of the term *robot* was in Karel Capek's famous play *R. U. R.* (Rossum's Universal Robots) in 1923 (Capek & Capek, 1923).

Today, artificial intelligence is represented in computer programs such as *Polaris*, which was discussed in the chapter-opening story, and *Deep Blue*, a chess program that allowed a computer to beat the world chess champion, Garry Kasparov, in 1997 (Kasparov had beaten *Deep Blue* in 1996, four games to two). In 2003, Kasparov played *Deep Blue*'s "descendent," *Deep Junior*, and managed only a draw. *Deep Junior*, unlike *Deep Blue*, was programmed to consider only the strongest possible positions in detail (Knight, 2003). Interestingly, *Deep Blue* was programmed to use heuristics, the same kind of decision-making processes that humans use when playing chess. *Deep Junior* used algorithms (the more typical way in which computers are programmed). *Deep Junior* was able to play Kasparov to a draw by using strategies that were less like human thinking than *Deep Blue*'s strategies.

Should scientists be trying to create artificial intelligence that mimics human thought processes? That is one of the arguments among researchers in the field of AI (Hoffmann, 1998; Weizenbaum, 1976). Scientists will no doubt continue to try to refine robotic machines that can be used to go where humans cannot safely go, such as the depths of the oceans and the farthest reaches of our solar system. Will those machines think like machines, think like humans, or use a blend of machine and human cognitive processes? Only the future knows.

Chess genius Garry Kasparov plays against the artificial intelligence program *Deep Junior*. The outcome was a draw.

artificial intelligence (AI)
the creation of a machine that can think like a human.

PRACTICE QUIZ: HOW MUCH DO YOU REMEMBER?

Pick the best answer.

1. Which of the following is NOT part of the definition of emotional intelligence?
   a. ability to manage one's emotions
   b. ability to feel what others feel
   c. being socially skilled
   d. succeeding at practical tasks

2. Emotional intelligence has been found to be _____ to academic success in college or university; grades in high school have been found to be _____ to academic success in college or university.
   a. related; unrelated
   b. related; related
   c. unrelated; unrelated
   d. unrelated; related

3. The four components of the MSCEIT include
   a. Identify, Strategize, Manipulate, and Manage.
   b. Identify, Use, Understand, and Manage.
   c. Use, Think, Manipulate, and Apply.
   d. Apply, Think, Manage, and Manipulate.

4. Researchers have determined that the estimated heritability for intelligence is about
   a. 75 percent.   c. 50 percent.
   b. 25 percent.   d. 100 percent.

5. Which of the following was NOT one of the errors of the authors of *The Bell Curve*?
   a. They assumed that IQ tests are good measures of intelligence.
   b. They found a correlation between race and IQ, not race and intelligence.
   c. They assumed that intelligence was heavily influenced by genetics.
   d. They assumed that heritability applied only to differences within groups of people.

6. The main difference between the AI programs *Deep Blue* and *Deep Junior* is that *Deep Blue* used _____ whereas *Deep Junior* was programmed to use _____.
   a. algorithms; heuristics   c. heuristics; algorithms
   b. heuristics; rules of thumb   d. algorithm; rules of thumb

LANGUAGE

7.12   *How is language defined, and what are its different elements and structure?*

Language is a system for combining symbols (such as words) so that an infinite number of meaningful statements can be made for the purpose of communicating with others. Language allows people not only to communicate with one another but also to represent their own internal mental activity. In other words, language is a very important part of how people think. This section focuses on the characteristics of language. Theories of language development are covered in Chapter Eight.

THE LEVELS OF LANGUAGE ANALYSIS

The structures of languages all over the world share common characteristics. Languages involve word order, word meanings, the rules for making words into other words, the sounds that exist within a language, the rules for practical communication with others, and the meanings of sentences and phrases.

GRAMMAR   Grammar is the system of rules governing the structure and use of a language. According to famed linguist Noam Chomsky (2006; Chomsky et al., 2002), humans have an innate ability to understand and produce language through a device he calls the *language acquisition device (LAD)*. While humans may learn the *specific* language (e.g., English, Spanish, Mandarin) through the processes of imitation, reinforcement, and shaping (Ⓛ Ⓘ Ⓝ Ⓚ *to Chapter Five: Learning, p. 176*), the complexities of the grammar of a language are, according to Chomsky, to some degree "wired in" to the developing brain. The LAD "listens" to the language input of the infant's world and then begins to produce language sounds and eventually words and sentences in a pattern found across cultures. This pattern is discussed in greater detail in Chapter Eight. Ⓛ Ⓘ Ⓝ Ⓚ *to Chapter Eight: Development Across the Lifespan, p. 302.* Grammar includes rules for the order of words known as *syntax, morphology* (the study of the formation of words), *phonemes* (the basic sounds of language), and *pragmatics* (the practical social expectations and uses of language).

SYNTAX   Syntax is a system of rules for combining words and phrases to form grammatically correct sentences. Consider the following sentence: "Where does the Canadian prime minister live?" The adjective *Canadian* comes before the noun *prime minister*, and the verb is a complex one involving both *does* and *live*. In English, this makes perfect sense. In Spanish, the word order of the sentence with the exact same meaning would be "*¿Dónde vive el primer ministro canadiense?*" Literally translated, it says "Where lives the prime minister Canadian?" which is incorrect syntax in English but perfectly correct in Spanish. As one can imagine, syntax is quite important. Just a simple mix-up can cause sentences to be completely misunderstood. For example, "John kidnapped the boy" has a different meaning from "John, the kidnapped boy" although all four words are the same (Lasnik, 1990).

MORPHEMES   Morphemes are the smallest units of meaning within a language. For example, the word *playing* consists of two morphemes, *play* and *ing*.

Morphemes themselves are governed by **semantics**, rules for determining the meaning of words and sentences. Sentences, for example, can have the same semantic meaning while having different syntax: "Johnny hit the ball" and "the ball was hit by Johnny."

PHONEMES   Phonemes are the basic units of sound in a language. The *a* in the word *car* is a very different phoneme from the *a* in the word *day*, even though it is the same letter of the alphabet. The difference is in how we say the sound of the *a* in each

---

👁‑**Watch** on **mypsychlab**
Is Music a Universal Language?

language
a system for combining symbols (such as words) so that an unlimited number of meaningful statements can be made for the purpose of communicating with others.

grammar
the system of rules governing the structure and use of a language.

syntax
the system of rules for combining words and phrases to form grammatically correct sentences.

morphemes
the smallest units of meaning within a language.

semantics
the rules for determining the meaning of words and sentences.

phonemes
the basic units of sound in language.

Pragmatics involves the practical aspects of communicating. This young mother is talking and then pausing for the infant's response. In this way, the infant is learning about taking turns, an important aspect of language development. What kinds of games do adults play with infants that also aid the development of language?

word. Phonemes are more than just the different ways in which we pronounce single letters, too. *Th*, *sh*, and *au* are also phonemes. Phonemes for different languages are also different, and one of the biggest problems for people who are trying to learn another language is the inability to both hear and pronounce the phonemes of that other language. Although infants are born with the ability to recognize all phonemes (Werker & Lalonde, 1988), after about nine months, that ability has deteriorated and the infant recognizes only the phonemes of the language to which the infant is exposed (Boyson-Bardies et al., 1989).

PRAGMATICS   The **pragmatics** of language have to do with the practical aspects of communicating with others, or the social "niceties" of language. Simply put, pragmatics involve knowing things such as how to take turns in a conversation, the use of gestures to emphasize a point or to indicate a need for more information, and the different ways in which one speaks to different people (Yule, 1996). For example, adults speak to small children differently than they do to other adults by using simpler words. Both adults and children use higher pitched voices and many repeated phrases when talking to infants. Part of the pragmatics of language includes knowing just what rhythm and emphasis to use when communicating with others, called *intonation*. When speaking to infants, adults and children are changing the inflection when they use the higher pitch and stress certain words differently than others. Some languages, such as Japanese, are highly sensitive to intonation, meaning that changing the pronunciation of a particular word can change its meaning entirely (Beckman & Pierrehumbert, 1986). For example, the Japanese name *Yoshiko* should be pronounced with the accent or stress on the first syllable: YO-she-koh. This pronunciation of the name means "woman-child." But if the stress is placed on the second syllable (yo-SHE-ko), the name means "woman who urinates."

THE RELATIONSHIP BETWEEN LANGUAGE AND THOUGHT

7.13   *Does language influence the way people think?*

As with the controversy of nature versus nurture, researchers have long debated the relationship between language and thought. Does language actually influence thought, or does thinking influence language?

Two very influential developmental psychologists, Jean Piaget and Lev Vygotsky, often debated the relationship of language and thought (Duncan, 1995). Piaget (1926, 1962) theorized that concepts preceded and aided the development of language. For example, a child would have to have a concept or mental schema for "mother" before being able to learn the word *mama*. In a sense, concepts become the "pegs" upon which words are "hung." Piaget also noticed that preschool children seemed to spend a great deal of time talking to themselves—even when playing with another child. Each child would be talking about something totally unrelated to the speech of the other, in a process Piaget called *collective monologue*. Piaget believed that this kind of non-social speech was very egocentric (i.e., from the child's point of view only, with no regard for the listener) and that as the child became more socially involved and less egocentric, these non-social speech patterns would decrease.

pragmatics
aspects of language involving the practical ways of communicating with others, or the social "niceties" of language.

Vygotsky, however, believed almost the opposite. He theorized that language actually helped develop concepts and that language could also help the child learn to control behaviour—including social behaviour (Vygotsky, 1962, 1978, 1987). For Vygotsky, the word helped form the concept: Once a child had learned the word *mama*, the various elements of "mama-ness"—warm, soft, food, safety, and so on—could come together around that word. Vygotsky also believed that the "egocentric" speech of the preschool child was actually a way for the child to form thoughts and control actions. This "private speech" was a way for children to plan their behaviour and organize actions so that their goals could be obtained. Since socializing with other children would demand much more self-control and behavioural regulation on the part of the preschool child, Vygotsky believed that private speech would actually *increase* as children became more socially active in the preschool years. This was, of course, the opposite of Piaget's assumption, and the evidence seems to bear out Vygotsky's view: Children, especially bright children, do tend to use more private speech when learning how to socialize with other children or when working on a difficult task (Berk, 1992; Berk & Spuhl, 1995; Bivens & Berk, 1990).

LINGUISTIC RELATIVITY HYPOTHESIS   The hypothesis that language shapes and influences thoughts was accepted by many theorists, with a few notable exceptions, such as Piaget. One of the best-known versions of this view is the Sapir–Whorf hypothesis (named for the two theorists who developed it, Edward Sapir and his student, Benjamin Lee Whorf). This hypothesis assumes that the thought processes and concepts within any culture are determined by the words of the culture (Sapir, 1921; Whorf, 1956). It has come to be known as the **linguistic relativity hypothesis**, meaning that thought processes and concepts are controlled by (are relative to) language. That is, the words people use determine much of the way in which they think about the world around them.

One of the most famous examples used by Whorf to support this idea was that of the Inuit, Aboriginals living in the Arctic. Supposedly, the Inuit have many more words for *snow* than do people in other cultures. One estimate was 23 different words, whereas other estimates have ranged in the hundreds. Unfortunately, this anecdotal evidence has turned out to be false, and is more myth than reality (Pullum, 1991). In fact, English speakers also have many different words for *snow* (*sleet*, *slush*, *powder*, and *dusting*, to name a few).

Is there evidence for the linguistic relativity hypothesis? Neither Sapir nor Whorf provided any scientific studies that would support their proposition. There have been numerous studies by other researchers, however. For example, in one study researchers assumed that a language's colour names would influence the ability of the people who grew up with that language to distinguish among and perceive colours. The study found that basic colour terms did directly influence colour recognition memory (Lucy & Shweder, 1979). But an earlier series of studies of the perception of colours (Rosch-Heider, 1972; Rosch-Heider & Olivier, 1972) had already found just the opposite effect: Members of the Dani tribe, who have only two names for colours, were no different in their ability to perceive all colours than were the English speakers in the study. More recent studies (Davies et al., 1998a, 1998b; Laws et al., 1995; Pinker & Bloom, 1990) support Rosch-Heider's findings and the idea of a **cognitive universalism** (concepts are universal and influence the development of language) rather than linguistic relativity.

Other research suggests that although the linguistic relativity hypothesis may not work for fine perceptual discriminations such as those in the Rosch-Heider studies, it may be an appropriate explanation for concepts of a higher level. In one study,

linguistic relativity hypothesis
the theory that thought processes and concepts are controlled by language.

cognitive universalism
theory that concepts are universal and influence the development of language.

researchers showed pictures of two animals to preschool children (Gelman & Markman, 1986). The pictures were of a flamingo and a bat. The children were told that the flamingo feeds its baby mashed-up food but the bat feeds its baby milk. Then they were shown a picture of a blackbird (which looked more like the bat than the flamingo). Half the children were told that the blackbird was a bird, while the other children were not. When asked how the blackbird fed its baby, the children who had been given the bird label were more likely to say that it fed its baby mashed-up food than were the children who were not given the label, indicating that the preschoolers were making inferences about feeding habits based on category membership rather than perceptual similarity—the word *bird* helped the children who were given that label to place the blackbird in its proper higher-level category.

Psychologists cannot deny the influence of language on problem solving, cognition, and memory. Sometimes a problem can simply be worded differently to have the solution become obvious, and memory is certainly stored in terms of the semantics of language. L I N K *to Chapter Six: Memory, p. 218.* Language can definitely influence the perception of others as well—"computer geek" and "software engineer" might be used to describe the same person, but one phrase is obviously less flattering and the image brought to mind is different for the two terms. In the end, trying to determine whether language influences thoughts or thoughts influence language may be like trying to determine which came first, the chicken or the egg.

ANIMAL STUDIES IN LANGUAGE   I've heard that chimpanzees can be taught to use sign language. Is this for real, or are the chimps just performing tricks like the animals you can see in the circus or the zoo? There are really two questions about animals and language. The first is "Can animals communicate?" and the second is "Can animals use language?" The answer to the first question is a definite yes. Animals communicate in many ways. They use sounds, such as the rattle of a rattlesnake or the warning growl of an angry dog. There are also physical behaviours, such as the "dance" of honeybees that tells other bees where a source of pollen is (Gould & Gould, 1994) or where a safe flower can be found (Abbott & Dukas, 2009). But the answer to the second question is more complicated because language is defined as the use of symbols, and symbols are things that stand for something else. Words are symbols, and gestures can be symbols. But the gestures used by animals are instinctual, meaning they are controlled by the animal's genetic makeup. The honeybee doing the "dance" is controlled completely by instinct, as is the growling dog. In human language, symbols are used quite deliberately and voluntarily, not by instinct, and abstract symbols have no meaning until people assign meaning to them.

I've heard that chimpanzees can be taught to use sign language. Is this for real, or are the chimps just performing tricks like the animals you ▶ can see in the circus or the zoo?

7.14 *Are animals capable of learning language?*

Can animals be taught to use abstract symbols? There have been attempts to teach animals how to use sign language (as animals lack the vocal structure to form spoken words), but many of these attempts were simply not "good science." The most successful of these experiments (which also has its critics) has been with Kanzi, a bonobo chimpanzee trained to press abstract symbols on a computer keyboard (Savage-Rumbaugh & Lewin, 1994). Kanzi actually was not the original subject of the study—his mother, Matata, was the chimp being trained. She did not learn many of the symbols, but Kanzi watched his mother use the keyboard and appeared to learn how to use the symbols through that observation. At last count, Kanzi could understand about 150 spoken English words. Trainers who speak to him are not in his view, so he is not responding to physical cues or symbols. He has managed to follow complex instructions correctly up to the level of a 2½ year old (Savage-Rumbaugh et al., 1998).

Kanzi looks at the keyboard used in teaching language to chimpanzees. Kanzi's language abilities were learned through watching the researchers train his mother rather than directly—much as a human infant learns through listening to the speech of adults.

The most recent studies with Kanzi have him making sounds that seem to have consistent meaning across different situations (Tagliatatela et al., 2003). Nearly 100 videotaped hours of Kanzi engaged in day-to-day activities were analyzed for these sounds. The researchers were able to identify four sounds that seemed to represent banana, grapes, juice, and the word *yes*. (However, remember that four sounds do not come close to making an entire language.)

Other studies with dolphins (Herman et al., 1993) and a parrot (Pepperberg, 1998) have also met with some success. Is it real language? The answer seems to be a qualified yes. The qualification is that none of the animals that have achieved success so far can compare to the level of language development of a 3-year-old human child (Pinker, 1995). However, linguists still debate whether these animals are truly learning language if they are not also learning how to use syntax—combining words into grammatically correct sentences as well as being able to understand the differences between sentences such as "The girl kissed the boy" and "The boy kissed the girl." As yet, there is no evidence that any of the animals trained in language have been able to master syntax (Demers, 1988; Johnson, 1995; Pinker, 1995).

PRACTICE QUIZ: HOW MUCH DO YOU REMEMBER?

Pick the best answer.

1. The system of rules for combining words and phrases to make meaningful sentences is called
   a. grammar.
   b. phonics.
   c. syntax.
   d. morphology.

2. Grammar includes all but which of the following aspects of language?
   a. tone
   b. sounds
   c. order
   d. meaning

3. The sounds of the letters *b, z, c,* and *d* are examples of
   a. morphemes.
   b. phonemes.
   c. semantics.
   d. syntax.

4. The Dani have only two words for colour yet can distinguish between many different colours. This finding supports the language theory of
   a. Sapir and Whorf.
   b. Lucy and Shweder.
   c. Pullum.
   d. Rosch-Heider.

5. The quality of language produced by animals cannot yet compare to the level achieved by a _____ human.
   a. 1-year-old
   b. 2-year-old
   c. 3-year-old
   d. 5-year-old

Answers: 1-c, 2-a, 3-b, 4-d, 5-c.

APPLYING PSYCHOLOGY TO EVERYDAY LIFE
THE COGNITIVE BENEFITS OF MULTILINGUALISM

7.15. *Is learning more than one language beneficial?*

Canada is different from many countries in that it has two official languages: English and French. English tends to be the predominant language across Canada, with approximately 59 percent of the population speaking English as their first language. In contrast, approximately 23 percent of Canadians identify French as their first language and the remaining 18 percent identify a language other than English or French as their native tongue (Statistics Canada, 2001).

Over the years, researchers have debated whether learning more than one language has a beneficial effect on cognitive abilities. One researcher who has investigated this topic in great detail is Dr. Ellen Bialystok of York University in Toronto. Bialystok has found that bilingualism leads to many cognitive advantages in children, young adults, and older adults. For example, bilingualism in children leads to more advanced ability in solving problems in which there is misleading perceptual information (Bialystok & Shapero, 2005). Bilingual older adults have been found to maintain higher levels of cognitive control beyond 60 years of age (Bialystok, Craik, & Ryan, 2006).

From the research conducted by Bialystok and colleagues, it is apparent that the Official Languages Act of Canada, which recognizes and promotes the use of Canada's two official languages, has numerous positive effects on the Canadian population.

Questions for Further Discussion

1. Why do you think learning more than one language is beneficial to cognition?

2. Do you think researchers would find cognitive differences between adults who learned a second language in adulthood and those who had learned the second language during their childhood? What differences would you expect to find?

CHAPTER SUMMARY

How People Think

7.1   *How are mental images and concepts involved in the process of thinking?*

- Thinking (cognition) is mental activity that occurs in the brain when information is being organized, stored, communicated, or processed.
- Mental images represent objects or events and have a picturelike quality.
- Concepts are ideas that represent a class or category of events, objects, or activities.
- Prototypes are examples of a concept that more closely match the defining characteristics of that concept.

7.2   *What methods do people use to solve problems and make decisions?*

- Problem solving consists of thinking and behaving in certain ways to reach a goal.
- Mechanical solutions include trial-and-error learning and rote solutions.
- Algorithms are a type of rote solution in which one follows step-by-step procedures for solving certain types of problems.
- A heuristic or "rule of thumb" is a strategy that narrows down the possible solutions for a problem.
- Insight is the sudden perception of a solution to a problem.

7.3   *Why does problem solving sometimes fail, and what is meant by creative thinking?*

- Functional fixedness is the tendency to perceive objects as having only the use for which they were originally intended and, therefore, failing to see them as possible tools for solving other problems.

- Confirmation bias is the tendency to search for evidence that confirms one's beliefs, ignoring any evidence to the contrary.
- Divergent thinking involves coming up with as many different answers as possible. This is a kind of creativity (combining ideas or behaviour in new ways).
- Creative people are usually good at mental imagery and have knowledge of a wide range of topics, are unafraid to be different, value their independence, and are often unconventional in their work but not in other areas.
- One of the best known and most widely used forms of creativity assessment are the Torrance Tests of Creative Thinking (TTCT) created by E. Paul Torrance.
- The Torrance Tests involve three components: Thinking Creatively with Pictures, the Figural TTCT, and the Verbal TTCT.

Intelligence

7.4   *How do psychologists define intelligence, and how do various theories of intelligence differ?*

- Intelligence is the ability to learn from one's experiences, acquire knowledge, and use resources effectively in adapting to new situations or solving problems.
- Spearman proposed general intelligence, or g factor, as the ability to reason and solve problems, whereas specific intelligence, or s factor, is the ability to excel in certain areas such as music or business.
- Gardner proposed nine different types of intelligence, ranging from verbal, linguistic, and mathematical to interpersonal and intrapersonal intelligence.

- Sternberg proposed three types of intelligence: analytical, creative, and practical.

7.5 *How is intelligence measured, and how are intelligence tests constructed?*

- The Stanford-Binet Intelligence Test yields an IQ score that is determined by dividing the mental age of the person by the chronological age and multiplying that quotient by 100.
- The Wechsler Intelligence Tests yield a verbal score and a performance score as well as an overall score of intelligence.
- Standardization, validity, and reliability are all important factors in the construction of an intelligence test.
- Deviation IQs are based on the normal curve, defining different levels of intelligence based on the deviation of scores from a common mean.
- IQ tests are often criticized for being culturally biased.

7.6 *What is intellectual disability, and what causes it?*

- Intellectual disability is a condition in which IQ falls below 70 and adaptive behaviour is severely deficient for a person of a particular chronological age.
- The four levels of delay are mild, 55–70 IQ; moderate, 40–55 IQ; severe, 25–40 IQ; and profound, below 25 IQ.
- Causes of intellectual disability include deprived environments as well as chromosome and genetic disorders and dietary deficiencies.

7.7 *What is giftedness, and does being intellectually gifted guarantee success in life?*

- Gifted persons are defined as those having IQ scores at the upper end of the normal curve (130 or above).

Classic Studies in Psychology: Terman's "Termites"

- Terman conducted a longitudinal study that demonstrated that gifted children grow up to be successful adults for the most part.
- Terman's study has been criticized for a lack of objectivity because Terman became too involved in the lives of his participants, even to the point of interfering on their behalf.

Psychology in the News: Music Lessons Make for Brighter Kids

7.8 *How does musical training affect children's cognitive abilities?*

- Music lessons can help advance brain development in children as young as 4 years of age.
- Specifically, musical training can lead to improvements in mathematical ability, literacy, memory, and IQ, among other things.

7.9 *What is emotional intelligence, and how is it measured?*

- Emotional intelligence is the awareness of and ability to manage one's own emotions as well as the ability to be self-motivated, able to feel what others feel, and socially skilled.
- One of the most academically supported assessments of emotional intelligence is the Mayer-Salovey-Caruso Emotional Intelligence Test

(MSCEIT). The MSCEIT is based on an ability model of emotional intelligence, in which emotional intelligence is conceptualized as having four separate components: Identify, Use, Understand, and Manage.

7.10 *What is the influence of heredity and environment on the development of intelligence?*

- Stronger correlations are found between IQ scores as genetic relatedness increases. Heritability of IQ is estimated at 0.50.
- In 1994, Herrnstein and Murray published *The Bell Curve*, in which they made widely criticized claims about the heritability of intelligence.

Artificial Intelligence (AI)

7.11 *What is artificial intelligence?*

- Artificial intelligence refers to the attempt to create a machine that thinks like a human being.
- Although some computers have been designed that can play chess and perform in similar ways to a human, the true flexibility of human thought processes has yet to be developed in a machine.

Language

7.12 *How is language defined, and what are its different elements and structure?*

- Language is a system for combining symbols so that an infinite number of meaningful statements can be created and communicated to others.
- Grammar is the system of rules by which language is governed and includes the rules for using phonemes, morphemes, and syntax. Pragmatics refers to practical aspects of language.

7.13 *Does language influence the way people think?*

- Sapir and Whorf originally proposed that language controls and helps the development of thought processes and concepts, an idea known as the *linguistic relativity hypothesis*.
- Other researchers have found evidence that concepts are universal and directly influence the development of language, called the *cognitive universalism viewpoint*.

7.14 *Are animals capable of learning language?*

- Studies with chimpanzees, parrots, and dolphins have been somewhat successful in demonstrating that animals can develop a basic kind of language, including some abstract ideas.
- Controversy exists over the lack of evidence that animals can learn syntax, which some feel means that animals are not truly learning and using language.

Applying Psychology to Everyday Life: The Cognitive Benefits of Multilingualism

7.15 *Is learning more than one language beneficial?*

- Canadian researchers have found that bilingualism leads to many cognitive advantages in children, young adults, and older adults.

7 KEY TERMS

algorithms   266

analytical intelligence   273

artificial intelligence (AI)   290

cognitive universalism   293

concepts   264

confirmation bias   269

convergent thinking   269

creative intelligence   274

creativity   269

deviation IQ scores   277

divergent thinking   270

emotional intelligence   285

formal concepts   264

functional fixedness   268

g factor   272

gifted   282

grammar   291

heuristic   266

intellectual disability   280

intelligence   272

intelligence quotient (IQ)   275

language   291

linguistic relativity hypothesis   293

mainstreaming   281

means–end analysis   267

mental images   262

mental set   269

morphemes   291

natural concepts   264

phonemes   291

practical intelligence   274

pragmatics   292

problem solving   265

prototype   264

reliability   276

s factor   272

semantics   291

syntax   291

thinking (cognition)   262

trial and error (mechanical solution)   266

triarchic theory of intelligence   273

validity   276

TEST YOURSELF

Pick the best answer.

1. Mental activity that goes on in the brain when a person is processing information is called
   a. mentation.
   c. thinking.
   b. a concept.
   d. mental imagery.

2. Concepts that are formed as a result of everyday experience, which are not always well defined, are known as _____ concepts.
   a. formal
   c. prototypical
   b. natural
   d. mental

3. On a popular quiz show, contestants are asked to match the audience in naming certain items. One contestant, when asked to "name a type of vehicle" replied "wheelchair!" The audience groaned, because they knew that the contestant was pretty far off the mark. The contestant should have picked a vehicle that was closer to a _____ for vehicles to match the audience's response.
   a. formal concept
   c. fuzzy concept
   b. natural concept
   d. prototype

4. Algorithms are a type of _____
   a. mechanical solution.
   c. rule of thumb.
   b. heuristic.
   d. means–end analysis.

5. The _____ heuristic can be used to create and maintain stereotypes.
   a. availability
   c. insight
   b. representative
   d. means–end analysis

6. Which of the following artificial intelligence programs was able to beat world chess champion Garry Kasparov?
   a. *Deep Blue*
   c. *Deep Junior*
   b. *Deep Purple*
   d. *Deep Senior*

7. When people persist in trying to solve a problem the same way they have always gone about solving problems, they have developed
   a. a mental set.
   c. confirmation bias.
   b. functional fixedness.
   d. transformation bias.

8. Which of the following questions would be more likely to produce divergent thinking?
   a. "What is a stapler?"
   b. "How do you spell *stapler*?"
   c. "How many uses can you think of for a stapler?"
   d. "What does a stapler look like?"

9. Which of the following is NOT part of the definition of intelligence?
   a. ability to adapt
   b. ability to solve problems
   c. ability to be creative
   d. ability to use resources effectively

10. Keneisha is only 11 years old, but she can answer questions that most 15-year-olds can answer. Fifteen is Keneisha's
    a. chronological age.
    c. IQ.
    b. mental age.
    d. standard age.

11. Which of the following makes the Wechsler tests different from the Stanford-Binet?
    a. The Wechsler tests are administered to individuals.
    b. The Wechsler is designed only for children.
    c. The Stanford-Binet is designed only for adults.
    d. The Wechsler provides both a verbal and a performance score.

12. A test that gives similar scores for a person each time the person takes it is considered to be a _____ test.
    a. reliable
    c. standardized
    b. valid
    d. creative

13. When a test allows a person from one particular background to have an unfair advantage over persons from other backgrounds, it is called
    a. culturally free.
    c. culturally biased.
    b. culturally fair.
    d. unreliable.

14. Denny has a flat upper lip, wide-set eyes, and problems with his heart in addition to having a mild intellectual disability. Denny most likely suffers from
    a. Down syndrome.
    b. fetal alcohol syndrome.
    c. fragile X syndrome.
    d. cretinism.

15. In Terman's study of gifted children, social and behavioural problems were found only in those
    a. with IQs of 150 or higher.
    b. with IQs of 180 or higher.
    c. with IQs of 180 or higher (problems occurred in adulthood).
    d. with IQs of 180 or higher (problems occurred in childhood).

16. According to Sternberg, "street smarts" is another way of talking about which kind of intelligence?
    a. analytical
    b. creative
    c. practical
    d. emotional

17. Which type of intelligence, according to Sternberg, would most likely be measured by traditional intelligence tests?
    a. analytical
    b. creative
    c. practical
    d. emotional

18. Goleman has proposed that _____ intelligence is a more powerful influence on success in life than other forms of intelligence.
    a. analytical
    b. creative
    c. practical
    d. emotional

19. Which of the following is NOT one of the four components of the MSCEIT?
    a. identifying emotion
    b. using emotion
    c. applying emotion
    d. understanding emotion

20. Which term refers to the practical aspects of language?
    a. pragmatics
    b. semantics
    c. morphology
    d. grammar

21. The current estimate of heritability of intelligence is
    a. 0.90.
    b. 0.86.
    c. 0.50.
    d. 0.34.

22. The basic units of sound are called
    a. morphemes.
    b. phonemes.
    c. semantics.
    d. syntax.

23. The linguistic relativity hypothesis states that
    a. language shapes thoughts.
    b. thoughts shape language.
    c. language and thought develop independently.
    d. language and thought influence each other.

24. Which of the following is NOT one of the animals that has been taught to use language with some success?
    a. chimpanzee
    b. parrot
    c. dog
    d. dolphin

25. What was one of the specific findings relating to bilingualism in the research conducted by Dr. Ellen Bialystok?
    a. Bilingualism was found to lead to more advanced ability in solving problems in which there is misleading perceptual information in young children.
    b. When it comes to older adults, people who are bilingual have been found to maintain higher levels of cognitive control beyond 60 years of age.
    c. Both a and b are true.
    d. Neither a nor b are true.

Answers: 1-c, 2-b, 3-d, 4-a, 5-b, 6-a, 7-a, 8-c, 9-c, 10-b, 11-d, 12-a, 13-c, 14-b, 15-d, 16-c, 17-a, 18-d, 19-c, 20-a 21-c, 22-b, 23-a, 24-c, 25-c.

ScanLife™ Barcode

To access more tests and your own personalized study plan that will help you focus on the areas you need to master before your next class test, be sure to go to **www.MyPsychLab.com**, Pearson Education Canada's online psychology website, available with the access code packaged with your book.

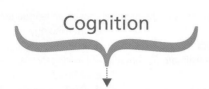

Cognition

Occurs when information is being organized, stored, communicated, or processed

Mental Images

Represent objects or events and have a picturelike quality

Nature of a Concept

Concepts: ideas that represent a class or category of events, objects, or activities

Prototypes: concepts that closely match defining characteristics of a concept

7.1

Problem Solving

Problem Solving and Decision Making

Problem solving consists of thinking and behaving in certain ways to reach a goal.

Mechanical solutions: trial-and-error learning and rote solutions

Algorithms: methods of problem solving that always guarantee a solution

Heuristics: strategies that narrow down possible solutions for a problem but do not guarantee a solution

Insight: sudden perception of a solution to a problem

7.2

Barriers to Problem Solving

Functional fixedness: perceiving objects as having only one use, failing to see other uses

Confirmation bias: searching for evidence that confirms one's beliefs, ignoring contrary evidence

Creative Thinking

Divergent thinking: coming up with as many different answers as possible

7.3

Intelligence Tests and Measuring Intelligence

Stanford-Binet Intelligence Test: yields an IQ score

IQ = MA/CA x 100

Wechsler Intelligence Tests: yield a verbal and a performance score as well as an overall score of intelligence

Intelligence Test Construction

Important factors in test construction: standardization, validity, and reliability

Deviation IQs: based on deviations of the mean of a normal curve

IQ tests: often criticized for being culturally biased

7.5

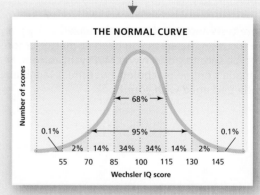

THE NORMAL CURVE

Intellectual Disability and Its Causes

Intellectual or developmental disability:

▸ Condition in which IQ falls below 70

▸ Adaptive behaviour severely deficient at a particular chronological age

Causes include: deprived environments, chromosome and genetic disorders, and dietary deficiencies

7.6

CONCEPT MAP

Intelligence

Ability to learn from one's experiences, acquire knowledge, and use resources effectively in adapting to new situations or solving problems.

Theories of Intelligence

Spearman proposed
- **General intelligence or g factor:** ability to reason and solve problems
- **Specific intelligence or s factor:** ability to excel in certain areas

Gardner: proposed eight different types of intelligence (from verbal/linguistic, musical, logical/mathematical, visual/spatial, movement, interpersonal, intrapersonal, naturalist, and existentialist)

Sternberg proposed three types of intelligence: analytical, creative, and practical

7.4

Giftedness

Gifted persons: having IQ scores at the upper end of the normal curve (130 or above)

Being Intellectually Gifted—Terman's Termite's

Terman demonstrated that gifted children usually grow up to be successful adults.

7.7

Musical Training and Cognition

Music lessons can help advance brain development in children as young as age 4 (improvements in mathematical ability, literacy, memory, and IQ)

7.8

Emotional Intelligence

Ability to manage one's own emotions and to be self-motivated, empathetic, and socially skilled

Mayer-Salovey-Caruso Emotional Intelligence Test:

based on an ability model of emotional intelligence with four separate components: Identify, Use, Understand, and Manage

7.9

Influence of Heredity and Environment on Intelligence

- Stronger correlations are found between IQ scores as genetic relatedness increases
- Heritability of IQ is estimated at 0.50

7.10

Artificial Intelligence

- **Artificial intelligence:** attempt to create a machine that thinks like a human being
- Computers have been designed that play chess and perform in similar ways to humans.
- True flexibility of human thought has yet to be developed in a machine.

7.11

Language

System for combining symbols so that an infinite number of meaningful statements can be created and communicated to others

Elements and Structure of Language

Grammar: system of rules by which language is governed

Parts of language:
- **phonemes**—basic units of sound in language
- **morphemes**—smallest units of meaning within a language
- **syntax**—system of rules for combining words and phrases

Pragmatics: practical aspects of language

7.12

Language and Thinking

Sapir and Whorf linguistic relativity hypothesis: Language controls and helps development of thought processes and concepts.

Cognitive universalism viewpoint: Concepts are universal and directly influence the development of language.

8.13

Animal Language

- Chimpanzees, parrots, and dolphins have demonstrated a basic kind of language, including some abstract ideas.
- Controversy exists over lack of evidence that animals can learn syntax.

8.14

Learning More than One Language

Canadian researchers have found that bilingualism leads to many cognitive advantages in children and adults.

8.15

8

Development Across the Lifespan

"Little Canadian Mozart"

André Mathieu (1929–1968), a pianist and composer, was born in Montreal, Quebec, on February 18, 1929. He composed his first piece (*Trois Études*) at age 4. When he was only 6 years old, he became an overnight sensation after giving a recital of his compositions at the Ritz-Carlton Hotel in Montreal. He went on to stun audiences in Paris at age 7 and in New York City at age 10. He was so talented that famous Russian composer Sergei Rachmaninov claimed that Mathieu was "a genius, more so than I am" (Analekta, 2011; The Canadian Encyclopedia, 2011).

According to the Cambridge Dictionaries Online, the term *child prodigy* is used to refer to a "a young child who has very great ability in something" (Cambridge Dictionaries Online, 2011). Why do some children, such as Mathieu, show amazing abilities at such a young age, while other children do not? Was Mathieu "born that way" or was the encouragement of his father enough to develop Mathieu's musical talent? This nature versus nurture debate is nothing new. Scholars have been debating about issues such as these since the beginning of time. This particular debate will be addressed at the beginning of this chapter in the Nature Versus Nurture section.

Unfortunately, Mathieu's musical career did not live up to Rachmaninov's expectations—his fame peaked when he was about 21 years of age. After having a disastrous affair, suffering from alcoholism, and living in poverty, Mathieu died of unknown causes at age 39 (Analekta, 2011). Recently, in May 2010, Alliance Vivafilm released a critically acclaimed movie titled *L'enfant Prodige* (*The Child Prodigy*), documenting the life story of Mathieu.

Why study human development?

Understanding how we come to be the people we are is a critical step in understanding ourselves as we are today as well as who we may become as we grow older. From the moment of conception, we are each headed down a pathway of change, influenced by our biology, environment, and social interactions, to a destination that is the same for all of us. The twists and turns of the pathway are what make each of us unique individuals. In this chapter, we'll look at the influences that help determine our developmental pathway through life.

8 LEARNING OBJECTIVES

8.1 What are some of the special research methods used to study development?

8.2 What is the relationship between heredity and environmental factors in determining development, and how do researchers study such a relationship?

8.3 How do chromosomes, genes, and DNA determine a person's characteristics or disorders, and what causes multiple births?

8.4 How do conjoined twins adjust to being separated?

8.5 What happens during the germinal, embryonic, and fetal periods of pregnancy, and what are some hazards in prenatal development?

8.6 What kinds of physical changes take place in infancy and childhood?

8.7 What are two ways of looking at cognitive development, and how does language develop?

8.8 How do infants and children develop personalities and form relationships with

others, and what are Erikson's stages of psychosocial development for children?

8.9 How are gender roles developed?

8.10 How much influence do biology and learning have on gender role development?

8.11 What are the theories about how children learn their gender roles?

8.12 What are the physical, cognitive, and personality changes that occur in adolescence, including concepts of morality and Erikson's search for identity?

8.13 What are the physical, cognitive, and personality changes that occur during adulthood and aging, including Erikson's last three psychosocial stages and patterns of parenting?

8.14 How do psychologists explain why aging occurs, and what are the stages of death and dying?

8.15 What are some of the implications of the Human Genome Project?

ISSUES IN STUDYING HUMAN DEVELOPMENT

What is development? In the context of life, **human development** is the changes that occur in people as they age, from conception until death. As such, developmental psychology involves the scientific study of the changes that occur in people over their lifetimes. This chapter will touch on almost all of the topics covered in the other chapters of this text, such as personality, cognition, biological processes, and social interactions. But in this chapter, all of those topics will be studied in the context of changes that occur as a result of the process of human development.

8.1 *What are some of the special research methods used to study development?*

As briefly discussed in Chapter One, research in development is affected by the problem of age. In any experiment, the participants who are exposed to the independent variable (the variable in an experiment that is deliberately manipulated by the experimenter) should be randomly assigned to the different experimental conditions. The problem in developmental research is that the age of the people in the study should always be an independent variable, but people cannot be randomly assigned to different age groups.

There are some special designs that are used in researching age-related changes: the **longitudinal design**, in which one group of people is followed and assessed at different times as the group ages; the **cross-sectional design**, in which several different age groups are studied at one time; and the **cross-sequential design**, which is a combination of the longitudinal and cross-sectional designs (Baltes et al., 1988).

The longitudinal design has the advantage of looking at real age-related changes as those changes occur in the same individuals. Disadvantages of this method are the lengthy amount of time, money, and effort involved in following participants over the years as well as the loss of participants when they move away, lose interest, or die. The cross-sectional design has the advantages of being quick, relatively inexpensive, and easier to accomplish than the longitudinal design. The main disadvantage is that

human development
the changes that occur in people as they age from conception until death.

longitudinal design
research design in which one participant or group of participants is studied over a long period of time.

cross-sectional design
research design in which several different age groups of participants are studied at one particular point in time.

cross-sequential design
research design in which participants are first studied by means of a cross-sectional design but also followed and assessed for a period of no more than six years.

304

one is no longer comparing an individual to that same individual as he or she ages; instead, individuals of different ages are being compared to one another. Differences between age groups are often a problem in developmental research. For example, if comparing the IQ scores of 30 year olds to 80 year olds to see how aging affects intelligence, questions arise concerning the differing experiences those two age groups have had in educational opportunities that might affect IQ scores in addition to any effects of aging. This example illustrates the **cohort effect**, which occurs when participants are born around the same time (e.g., in the same year or even the same decade). Because they were born during the same time period, they are more likely to share various characteristics with one another, such as years spent in school or attitudes toward same-sex marriage. Therefore, it can sometimes be difficult to draw conclusions regarding the effects of aging because any effects found may not be due to aging itself but instead to the fact that the participants of one age group were born during a particular time period and thus share similar characteristics.

In studying human development, developmental psychologists have outlined many theories of how these age-related changes occur. There are some areas of controversy, however, and one of these is the issue of nature versus nurture.

NATURE VERSUS NURTURE

8.2   *What is the relationship between heredity and environmental factors in determining development, and how do researchers study such a relationship?*

Nature refers to heredity, the influence of inherited characteristics on personality, physical growth, intellectual growth, and social interactions. **Nurture** refers to the influence of the environment on all of those same things and includes parenting styles, physical surroundings, economic factors, and anything that can have an influence on development that does not come from within the person.

So, is a person like Hitler born that way, or did something happen to make him the person he was? How much of a person's personality and behaviour are determined by nature and how much are determined by nurture? This is a key question, and the answer is quite complicated. It is also quite important: Are people like Adolf Hitler, Paul Bernardo, and Robert Pickton the result of bad genes? Or was it bad parenting or life-altering experiences in childhood? Or are they the unique combination of both hereditary and environmental influences? After many years of scientific research, most psychologists now agree that the last possibility is the most likely explanation for most of human development: All that people are and all that people become is the product of an interaction between nature and nurture (Ridley, 1999). Matt Ridley, a scientist and science journalist, has authored many acclaimed publications regarding this controversy. In his 2003 book, *Nature via Nurture: Genes, Experience, and What Makes Us Human*, he argues what scientists now almost all agree on: that the nature versus nurture debate is futile and that nature and nurture interact to make us who we are. Ridley (2003) argues that it's now time to focus on the idea that genes are designed to take their cues from nurture. That is, our environments dictate how our genes express ourselves throughout our lives (Mysterud, 2003).

Behavioural genetics is a relatively new field in the investigation of the origins of behaviour in which researchers try to determine how much of behaviour is the result of genetic inheritance and how much is due to a person's experiences. For more information on behavioural genetics and links to other sites, go to **www.ornl.gov/ sci/techresources/Human_Genome/home.shtml**.

How do researchers investigate whether a behaviour is caused by nature or nurture? Twins, which will be discussed in The Zygote and Twinning on p. 309 and in

cohort effect
when participants who are born around the same time are more likely to share various characteristics with one another than with those who were born during a different time period.

nature
the influence of our inherited characteristics on our personality, physical growth, intellectual growth, and social interactions.

nurture
the influence of the environment on personality, physical growth, intellectual growth, and social interactions.

◄ So, is a **person like** Hitler born that way, or did something happen to make him the person he was?

How do **researchers** investigate whether a behaviour is caused by ◄ nature or nurture?

The Human Genome Project was completed in 2003 and identified approximately 20 000 to 25 000 genes in the human genetic material. For more on the Human Genome Project, see Applying Psychology to Everyday Life on p. 342.

Psychology in the News on p. 310, provide developmental psychologists with another way to look at the contribution of nature and nurture to human development. Researchers may seek out identical twins who have been separated at birth, looking at all the ways those twins are alike in spite of being raised in different environments. These studies are commonly referred to as *twin studies*. LINK to Chapter Eleven: *Theories of Personality, p. 438;* LINK to Chapter Seven: Cognition, *p. 260.*

TWIN STUDIES

Monozygotic twins (commonly referred to as *identical twins*, which is a misnomer because no two people are actually identical) share almost 100 percent of their genetic material, having come from one fertilized egg, whereas dizygotic twins (commonly referred to as *fraternal twins*) share only about 50 percent of their genetic material, as any other pair of siblings would. By comparing monozygotic twins to dizygotic twins, especially when twins can be found who were not raised in the same environment, researchers can begin to find evidence of possible genetic influences on various traits, including personality.

A great example of longitudinal twin research can be found in Canadian-born researcher Steven Pinker's Twins Studies at Harvard project, which is being conducted in collaboration with his colleague Jennifer Ganger. Together, they are conducting longitudinal research on the language development of monozygotic and dizygotic twin pairs. Language development will be discussed later in this chapter.

ADOPTION STUDIES

Another tool of behavioural geneticists is to study adopted children and their adoptive and birth families. If studying monozygotic twins raised in different environments can help investigators understand the genetic influences on personality, then studying *unrelated* people who are raised in the *same* environment should help investigators discover the influence of environment. By comparing adopted children to their adoptive parents and siblings and, if possible, to their biological parents who have not raised them, researchers can uncover some of the shared and non-shared environmental and genetic influences on personality.

PRENATAL DEVELOPMENT

Any study of the human lifespan must begin by looking at the complex material contained in the cells of the body that carries the instructions for life itself. After discussing the basic building blocks of life, this text will discuss how the processes of conception and the development of the infant within the womb take place.

CHROMOSOMES, GENES, AND DNA

8.3 *How do chromosomes, genes, and DNA determine a person's characteristics or disorders, and what causes multiple births?*

Genetics is the science of heredity. Understanding how genes transmit human characteristics and traits involves defining a few basic terms.

Imagine a long ladder. Now imagine that the ladder is made of very soft rubber, and it is twisted around itself along its whole length. **DNA (deoxyribonucleic acid)** is a very special kind of molecule (the smallest particle of a substance that still has all the properties of that substance). DNA consists of two strands, each composed of certain sugars and phosphates. The two strands wind around each other in a spiral, much like the two sides of the ladder wind around each other. Linking the two

genetics
the science of inherited traits.

DNA (deoxyribonucleic acid)
special molecule that contains the genetic material of the organism.

strands together are chemical elements called *amines* or *bases* arranged in a particular pattern. The rungs of the rubber ladder would be like these chemical links. See Figure 8.1 for a realistic representation of DNA.

Because of DNA's unique shape, each molecule of DNA is linked end to end with the others, forming a very long strand. Sections of this DNA strand are linked by the amines, which are usually referred to by letters A, T, G, and C (adenine, thymine, guanine, and cytosine, respectively). Amines are organic structures that contain the genetic codes for building the proteins that make up organic life (e.g., hair colouring, muscle, and skin) and that control the life of each cell. Each section of DNA containing a certain sequence (ordering) of these amines is called a **gene**. So a gene is nothing more than a section of the DNA strand that has the same sequence of amines. Genes are located on rod-shaped structures called **chromosomes**, which are found in the nucleus of a cell.

Humans have a total of 46 chromosomes in each cell of their bodies (with the exception of the egg and the sperm). Twenty-three of these chromosomes come from the mother's egg and the other 23 from the father's sperm. Most characteristics are determined by 22 such pairs, called the *autosomes*. The last pair determines the sex of the person. These two chromosomes are called the *sex chromosomes*.

DOMINANT AND RECESSIVE GENES

The 46 chromosomes can actually be arranged in pairs, with one member of each pair coming from the mother and the other member from the father. Think about just one of these pairs for the moment.

In this particular pair of chromosomes, assume that there is a gene for hair colour on each chromosome. The actual colour of the person's hair will be determined by those two genes, one gene from each parent. If both genes are for brown hair, the person will obviously have brown hair, right? And if both are for blond hair, the person's hair will be blond.

But what if one gene is for brown hair and the other is for blond hair? The answer lies in the nature of each gene. Some genes that are more active in influencing the trait are called **dominant**. A dominant gene will always be expressed in the actual trait, in this case the hair colour. A person with a dominant brown hair colour gene will have brown hair, no matter what the other gene is, because brown is the most dominant of all the hair colours.

Some genes are less active in influencing the trait and will be expressed in the actual trait only if they are paired with another less active gene. These genes tend to recede, or fade, into the background when paired with a more dominant gene, so they are called **recessive**. Blond hair colour is the most recessive colour and will show up in a person's actual hair colour only if that person has a blond hair colour gene from each parent. (Figure 8.2 illustrates how dominant and recessive genes work for eye colour.)

What about red hair? And why do some people have mixed hair colour, like a strawberry blond? In reality, the pattern of genetic transmission of traits can be a little complicated. Almost all traits are controlled by more than one pair of genes in a process called *polygenic inheritance*. (*Polygenic* means "many genes.") Sometimes certain kinds of genes tend to group themselves with certain other genes, like the genes for blond hair and blue eyes. Other genes are so equally dominant or equally recessive that they combine their traits in the organism. For example, genes for blond hair and red hair are recessive. When a child inherits one of each from his or her parents, instead of one or the other controlling the child's hair colour, they may blend together to form a strawberry-blond mix.

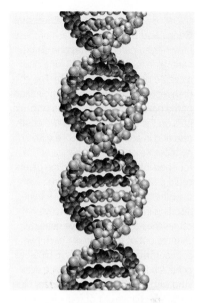

FIGURE **8.1 DNA Molecule**   In this model of a DNA molecule, the two strands making up the sides of the "twisted ladder" are composed of sugars and phosphates. The "rungs" of the ladder that link the two strands are amines. Amines contain the genetic codes for building the proteins that make up organic life.

gene
section of DNA having the same arrangement of chemical elements.

chromosome
tightly wound strand of genetic material or DNA.

dominant
a gene that actively controls the expression of a trait.

recessive
a gene that influences the expression of a trait only when paired with an identical gene.

◀ What about red hair? And how come some people have mixed hair colour, like a strawberry blond?

FIGURE 8.2 **Dominant and Recessive Genes and Eye Colour** Each of these brown-eyed parents carries one dominant gene for brown eyes (B) and one recessive gene for blue eyes (b). The children represent the possible combinations of the parents' genes. Each parent could pass on the dominant brown-eye genes, resulting in a brown-eyed child with no recessive genes (one chance out of four possible combinations). One parent could pass on the dominant gene while the other passes on the recessive gene, resulting in a child with brown eyes who carries the recessive blue-eye gene (two chances out of four). Finally, each parent could pass on the recessive blue-eye gene, leading to a child with blue eyes who carries two recessive genes for blue eyes (one chance out of four). In other words, each child this couple bears has a 25 percent chance of having blue eyes.

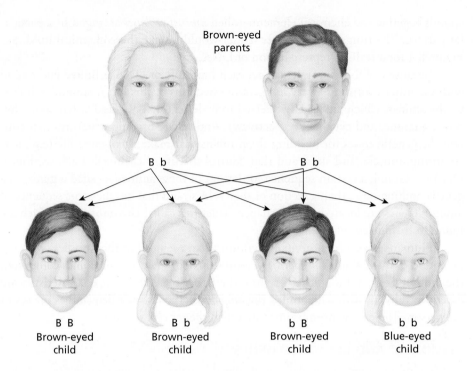

Brown-eyed parents

B b   B b

B B   B b   b B   b b
Brown-eyed   Brown-eyed   Brown-eyed   Blue-eyed
child   child   child   child

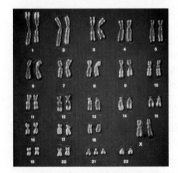

Down syndrome (Trisomy 21) is a form of developmental delay caused by an extra chromosome 21.

GENETIC AND CHROMOSOME DISORDERS

Several genetic disorders are carried by recessive genes. Diseases carried by recessive genes are inherited when a child inherits two recessive genes, one from each parent. Examples of disorders inherited in this manner are cystic fibrosis (a disease of the respiratory and digestive tracts) and sickle-cell anemia (a blood disorder).

Sometimes the chromosome itself is the problem. Although each egg and each sperm are supposed to have only 23 chromosomes, in the creation of these cells a chromosome can end up in the wrong cell, leaving one cell with only 22 and the other with 24. If either of these cells survives to "mate," the missing or extra chromosome can cause mild to severe problems in development (Barnes & Carey, 2002; Gardner & Sutherland, 1996; Public Health Agency of Canada, 2003).

PRACTICE QUIZ: HOW MUCH DO YOU REMEMBER?

Pick the best answer.

1. In a _____ design, several different age groups of participants are studied at one time.
   a. longitudinal
   b. cross-sectional
   c. cross-sequential
   d. cross-longitudinal

2. The design that combines the two other development designs is called
   a. cross-sequential.
   b. cross-sectional.
   c. longitudinal.
   d. cross-longitudinal.

3. If researchers want to investigate whether a personality characteristic is inherited, they can do this by
   a. comparing monozygotic twins to dizygotic twins.
   b. comparing adopted children to their adoptive and birth families.
   c. Neither a nor b can help researchers discover if a personality characteristic is inherited.
   d. Both a or b can help researchers discover if a personality characteristic is inherited.

4. In the analogy of the rubber ladder, the sequence of amines would be represented by the _____ of the ladder.
   a. sides
   b. length
   c. rungs
   d. wood

5. Brandon has blue eyes, even though both his mother and father have brown eyes. What do we know about Brandon's parents?
   a. At least one of his parents has a recessive blue-eye colour gene.
   b. Each of his parents must have one recessive blue-eye colour gene.
   c. Each of his parents must have one dominant blue-eye colour gene.
   d. Neither of his parents has a blue-eye colour gene.

The most common chromosome disorder is *Down syndrome*, also known as Trisomy 21, a disorder in which there is an extra chromosome in what would normally be the twenty-first pair. Down syndrome occurs in an estimated 1 in 700 to 1 in 1000 births, with little variation across the world (Public Health Agency of Canada, 2003). According to the Canadian Down Syndrome Society, about 500 babies are born with Down Syndrome each year in Canada (Canadian Down Syndrome Society, 2011). Characteristics associated with Down syndrome include chubby cheeks, large, round eyes, larger tongue, smaller limbs and smaller body frame, and intellectual disability (Barnes & Carey, 2002; Hernandez & Fisher, 1996). Although life expectancy is shorter in people with Down syndrome, most people with the disease grow up to live happy and productive lives.

FROM CONCEPTION TO BIRTH

Life begins at the moment of **conception**, the moment at which a female becomes pregnant. From conception to the actual birth of the baby is a period of approximately 40 weeks, during which a single cell becomes a complete infant. It is also during this time that many things can have a positive or negative influence on the developing infant.

THE ZYGOTE AND TWINNING   When an egg (also called an **ovum**) and a sperm unite in the process of **fertilization**, the resulting single cell will have a total of 46 chromosomes and is called a **zygote**. Normally, the zygote will begin to divide, first into two cells, then four, then eight, and so on, with each new cell also having 46 chromosomes, because the DNA molecules produce duplicates of themselves before each division. (This division process is called *mitosis*.) Eventually, the mass of cells becomes a baby. Sometimes this division process doesn't work exactly this way, and twins or multiples are the result.

There are actually two kinds of twins. As discussed earlier in the chapter, twins who are commonly referred to as "identical" are **monozygotic twins**, meaning that the two babies come from one (mono) fertilized egg (zygote). Early in the division process, the mass of cells splits completely—no one knows exactly why—into two separate masses, each of which will develop into a separate infant. The infants will be the same sex and have almost identical features because they each possess the same set of 46 chromosomes.

The other type of twin is more an accident of timing and is more common in women who are older and who are from certain ethnic groups, for example, it is more common in Nigerian women than it is in Japanese women (Allen & Parisi, 1990; Bonnelykke, 1990; Imaizumi, 1998). A woman's body may either release more than one egg at a time or release an egg after a woman has already conceived once. If two eggs are fertilized, the woman may give birth to fraternal or **dizygotic twins** (two zygotes), or possibly triplets or some other multiple number of babies (Bryan & Hallett, 2001). This is also more likely to happen to women who are taking fertility drugs to help them get pregnant (see Figure 8.3).

Sometimes in the twinning process, the mass of cells does not completely split apart. When this occurs, *conjoined* twins will result, and they will be joined at the point where the two cell masses remained "stuck." This joining may involve only soft tissues or may involve the sharing of certain body parts and/or organs, as happened in the case of Tinashe and Tinotenda Mufuka, which is discussed in the Psychology in the News section that follows.

It was once commonly believed (and taught) that identical twins were 100 percent alike in terms of their DNA, and that any differences in the twins were the result

conception
the moment at which a female becomes pregnant.

ovum
the female sex cell, or egg.

fertilization
the union of the ovum and sperm.

zygote
cell resulting from the uniting of the ovum and sperm.

monozygotic twins
identical twins formed when one zygote splits into two separate masses of cells, each of which develops into a separate embryo.

dizygotic twins
often called *fraternal twins*, occurring when two eggs each get fertilized by two different sperm, resulting in two zygotes in the uterus at the same time.

FIGURE 8.3 **Monozygotic and Dizygotic Twins** Because twins who are commonly referred to as being 'identical' come from one fertilized egg (zygote), they are called *monozygotic*. Fraternal twins, who come from two different fertilized eggs, are called *dizygotic*.

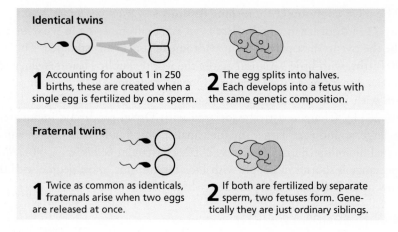

Identical twins

1 Accounting for about 1 in 250 births, these are created when a single egg is fertilized by one sperm.

2 The egg splits into halves. Each develops into a fetus with the same genetic composition.

Fraternal twins

1 Twice as common as identicals, fraternals arise when two eggs are released at once.

2 If both are fertilized by separate sperm, two fetuses form. Genetically they are just ordinary siblings.

of the environment in which they were raised. Recently, however, geneticists such as Dr. Shiva Singh of the University of Western Ontario have found that the environment is not the only contributor to the differences between identical twins—there exist differences at the genetic level as well (S. Singh, personal communication, May 23, 2011). This recent discovery has many implications: one of the biggest being its impact on twin studies. The basic assumption about monozygotic and dizygotic twins involved in such studies (that monozygotic twins share 100 percent of the same DNA and dizygotic twins 50 percent) will now have to be modified before any conclusions can be drawn about any phenomenon under investigation.

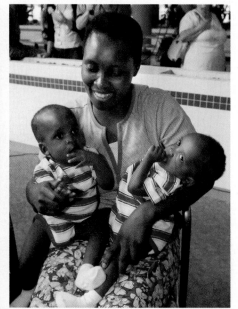

Tinashe and Tinotenda Mufuka, joined at the stomach and sharing one liver, were born in July 2004 in rural Zimbabwe. They were brought to Toronto's Hospital for Sick Children in December 2004 to be separated. The brothers, now separated, are back in Zimbabwe and doing much better than was expected.

PSYCHOLOGY IN THE NEWS

Tinashe and Tinotenda Mufuka, Saved by Chance

8.4 *How do conjoined twins adjust to being separated?*

The story begins in June 2004 when a pregnant woman named Elizabeth Mufuka walked into a Salvation Army hospital in rural Zimbabwe ("Separate Lives," 2005). Dr. Paul Thistle, an obstetrician who had trained at the University of Toronto and had been helping the poverty-stricken people of Zimbabwe for more than 10 years, was the doctor in charge of the small hospital. Thistle made the surprising discovery that she was carrying twin boys who were attached at the torso: a phenomenon that occurs in only about 1 in 60 000 pregnancies. This discovery was disturbing because even in countries with the best health care, most sets of conjoined twins don't survive, and if they do, they normally can't be separated for fear of damaging one (or both) of the children's vital organs.

After the boys were delivered by Caesarean section on July 20, 2004, Thistle decided that the fate of the boys would be more promising if they were taken to a country where they could be cared for properly and where they could also be separated. Thanks to a humanitarian fund at the Hospital for Sick Children, the boys and their mother arrived in Toronto in December 2004. Because of malnutrition and subsequent infections and sicknesses, it took some time for the boys to build up the appropriate strength needed for the operation. In March 2005, the boys were healthy enough to be separated. The delicate operation involved more than 25 people and took about four hours—two hours to separate the boys and another two hours for the skin grafts that cover the wounds.

The operation was a success. Tinashe and Tinotenda were the tenth set of conjoined twins to be separated at the Hospital for Sick Children. In July 2005, just four months after the surgery, the twins and their mother went back home to Zimbabwe (Stancl, 2006). Dr. Thistle is also back at Howard hospital and is the family's *chiremba*, or family doctor. According to him, the boys haven't experienced any major medical problems and although they have a long road ahead of them, their chances are now as good as any other child growing up in rural Zimbabwe.

Questions for Further Discussion

1. Do you think that the attachment bond between the brothers is greater than that between twins who were not born conjoined?

2. What kinds of difficulties (physical, emotional, and/or social) might Tinashe and Tinotenda face as they grow up?

THE GERMINAL PERIOD

8.5 *What happens during the germinal, embryonic, and fetal periods of pregnancy, and what are some hazards in prenatal development?*

Once fertilization has taken place, the zygote begins dividing and moving down to the *uterus*, the muscular organ that will contain and protect the developing infant. This process takes about a week, followed by about week during which the mass of cells, now forming a hollow ball, firmly attaches itself to the wall of the uterus. This two-week period is called the **germinal period** of pregnancy. The *placenta* also begins to form during this period. The placenta is a specialized organ that provides nourishment and filters away waste products from the developing baby. The *umbilical cord* also begins to develop at this time, connecting the organism to the placenta.

germinal period
first two weeks after fertilization, during which the zygote moves down to the uterus and begins to implant in the lining.

👁 **Watch** on **mypsychlab**
Prenatal Ultrasound

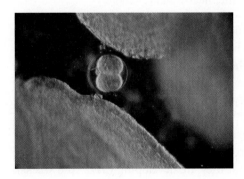

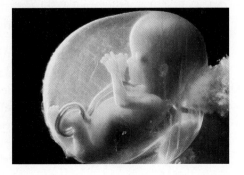

The three periods of pregnancy are the germinal period, lasting about two weeks; the embryonic period, from about two to eight weeks; and the fetal period, which lasts from eight weeks until the end of pregnancy.

How does it get from ▶ the mass of cells to a baby, with eyes, nose, hands, feet, and so on? How do all those different things come from the same original single cell?

embryo
name for the developing organism from two weeks to eight weeks after fertilization.

embryonic period
the period from two to eight weeks after fertilization, during which the major organs and structures of the organism develop.

critical periods
times during which certain environmental influences can have an impact on the development of the infant.

teratogen
any factor that can cause a birth defect.

fetal period
the time from about eight weeks after conception until the birth of the child.

fetus
name for the developing organism from eight weeks after fertilization to the birth of the baby.

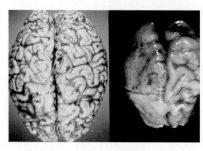

This image shows the brains of two 6-week old infants. The brain on the left is that of a "normal" developing 6-week old. The brain on the right is that of a 6-week old whose mother abused alcohol while she was pregnant. You can notice the differences right away. From this image, it is obvious that alcohol is a very strong teratogen.

How does it get from the mass of cells to a baby, with eyes, nose, hands, feet, and so on? How do all those different things come from the same original single cell? During the germinal period, the cells begin to differentiate, or develop into specialized cells, in preparation for becoming all the various kinds of cells that make up the human body—skin cells, heart cells, and so on. Perhaps the most important of these cells are the *stem cells*, which stay in a somewhat immature state until needed to produce more cells. Researchers are currently looking into ways to use stem cells found in the umbilical cord to grow new organs and tissues for transplant or to repair neurological damage (Chen & Ende, 2000; Holden & Vogel, 2002; Lu & Ende, 1997; Master, McLeod, & Mendez, 2007). ⓛⓘⓝⓚ *to Chapter Two: The Biological Perspective, p. 42.*

Over the past decade, stem cell research has been a much debated topic, with one camp arguing that it is not ethical and the other arguing that is highly necessary. One of the major activists urging that the research continue is Michael J. Fox, a famous Canadian actor who suffers from Parkinson's disease. Janet Rossant, a developmental biologist at Mount Sinai Hospital in Toronto, has pointed out that the debate has been much more controversial in the United States than it has been in Canada. In Canada, there is a general consensus that embryo research, as long as there are strict ethical guidelines in place and specific goals set, is acceptable (Jarmul, 2002).

Embryonic stem cells are not the only type of stem cell; there are also adult stem cells (often referred to as *somatic stem cells*). Somatic stem cells have been used in medical treatment for quite some time. The use of these cells as a treatment is less controversial than the use of embryonic stem cells as they are taken from the bodily tissues of a consenting adult (e.g., bone marrow and fat cells).

THE EMBRYONIC PERIOD Once firmly attached to the uterus, the developing organism is called an **embryo**. The **embryonic period** will last from two weeks after conception to eight weeks, and during this time the cells will continue to specialize and become the various organs and structures of a human infant. By the end of eight weeks after conception, the embryo is about 2 centimetres long and has primitive eyes, nose, lips, teeth, arms and legs, and a beating heart. Although no organ is fully developed or completely functional at this time, nearly all are "there."

Critical Periods As soon as the embryo begins to receive nourishment from the mother through the placenta, it becomes vulnerable to hazards such as diseases of the mother, drugs, and other toxins that can pass from the mother through the placenta to the developing infant. (Since the developing organism in the germinal stage is not yet connected to the mother's system, the organism is not usually vulnerable to outside influences in that stage.) It is during the embryonic period that we most clearly see **critical periods**, times during which some environmental influence can have an impact—often devastating—on the development of the infant. The structural development of the arms and legs, for example, is affected only during the time that they are developing (3 1/2 to 8 weeks), whereas the heart's structure is most affected very early in this period (2 1/2 to 6 1/2 weeks). Other physical and structural problems can occur with the central nervous system (2 to 5 weeks), eyes (3 1/2 to 8 1/2 weeks), and the teeth and roof of the mouth (about 7 to 12 weeks).

Prenatal Hazards: Teratogens Any substance such as a drug, chemical, virus, or other factor that can cause a birth defect is called a **teratogen**. Common teratogens include drugs (e.g., cocaine, nicotine, and caffeine), alcohol, and mercury. These teratogens can have numerous negative effects on the developing embryo. For example, nicotine can lead to miscarriages, low birth weight, and/or learning difficulties, and alcohol can lead to fetal alcohol syndrome (developmental delay, delayed growth) and/or learning difficulties.

THE FETAL PERIOD: GROW, BABY, GROW The **fetal period** is the time from about eight weeks after conception until the birth of the child (now called a **fetus**) and is a period of tremendous growth. The fetus's length increases by about 20 times, and its weight increases from about 30 grams at two months to a little over 3 kilograms. The organs, while accomplishing most of their differentiation in the embryonic period, continue to develop and become functional. Muscles begin to contract in the third month. In the fourth month, the mother will begin to feel this movement as a tiny "flutter" or "quickening" at first, and by the fifth month, the flutter will become a "kick."

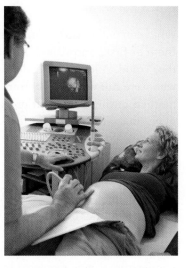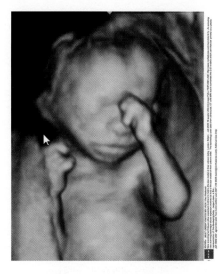

The last few months continue the development of fat and the growth of the body, until about the end of the thirty-eighth week. At that time, the fetus is pushed out of the mother's body in the process of labour and childbirth and becomes a baby. Babies born before 38 weeks are called *preterm* and may need life support to survive. This is especially true if the baby weighs less than about 2.5 kilograms at birth.

The most likely time for a *miscarriage*, or *spontaneous abortion*, is in the first three months, when the organs are forming and first becoming functional (Speroff et al., 1999). Statistics Canada includes miscarriage in the category "fetal loss," along with stillbirths and abortions. In 2004, fetal loss occurred in 8788 cases of 445 899 Canadian pregnancies (Statistics Canada, 2007b). This number is substantially lower than has been reported in the past. When a miscarriage occurs, it is most likely caused by a genetic defect in the way the embryo or fetus is developing that will not allow the infant to survive. In other words, there isn't anything that the mother did wrong or that could have been done to prevent the miscarriage.

This pregnant woman is getting a sonogram. Sonograms allow doctors to see any physical deformities and make accurate measurements of gestational age without risk to the mother or the fetus. Imaging techniques are now even more advanced: Parents can see three-dimensional images of their children before they are even born. Here, a mother is able to see her baby in three dimensions at a special clinic in Surrey, British Columbia. These techniques are controversial because Health Canada recommends that soon-to-be parents avoid unnecessary sonograms of their babies for health reasons. Although clinic operators promise safety, Health Canada insists that sonograms should not be used to get a picture of the baby for non-medical reasons.

PRACTICE QUIZ: HOW MUCH DO YOU REMEMBER?

Pick the best answer.

1. The fertilized egg cell is called a
   a. zygote.
   b. ovum.
   c. sperm.
   d. blastocyst.

2. Which of the following statements about Tinashe and Tinotenda Mufuka is FALSE?
   a. They were successfully separated.
   b. They are surprisingly healthy.
   c. They are expected to not be as well adjusted as other children from rural Zimbabwe.
   d. They were attached at the torso and shared a liver.

3. The first two weeks of pregnancy are called the _____ period.
   a. fetal
   b. embryonic
   c. placental
   d. germinal

4. The period of pregnancy that contains the clearest examples of critical periods is the _____ period.
   a. germinal
   b. embryonic
   c. fetal
   d. gestational

5. Miscarriages are usually the result of
   a. something the mother did during her pregnancy.
   b. some type of trauma to the mother during her pregnancy.
   c. some form of physical defect in the way the embryo or fetus is developing.
   d. some form of genetic defect in the way the embryo or fetus is developing.

What can babies do? ▶ Aren't they pretty much unaware of what's going on around them at first?

I've heard that babies can't see or hear very much at ▶ birth. Is that true?

INFANCY AND CHILDHOOD DEVELOPMENT

What can babies do? Aren't they pretty much unaware of what's going on around them at first? Surprisingly, babies can do a lot more than researchers used to believe they could. A lot of the early research on infants just after birth was done on babies who were still very drowsy from the general anaesthesia that used to be given to their mothers during the labour process. Drowsy babies don't tend to respond well, as one might imagine. In the next few sections, it becomes obvious that infants accomplish a great deal throughout infancy, even in the first few days of life on the outside.

PHYSICAL DEVELOPMENT

8.6. *What kinds of physical changes take place in infancy and childhood?*

Immediately after birth, several things start to happen. The respiratory system begins to function, filling the lungs with air and putting oxygen into the blood. The blood now circulates only within the infant's system because the umbilical cord has been cut. Body temperature is now regulated by the infant's own activity and body fat (which acts as insulation) rather than by the amniotic fluid. The digestive system generally takes the longest to adjust to life outside the womb. This is another reason for the baby's excess body fat. It provides fuel until the infant is able to take in enough nourishment on its own. That is why most babies lose a little weight in the first week after birth.

REFLEXES   Babies come into this world able to interact with it. Infants have a set of *innate* (existing from birth) involuntary behaviour patterns called *reflexes*. Until an infant is capable of learning more complex means of interaction, reflexes help the infant to survive. Figure 8.4 shows five infant reflexes.

Pediatricians use these and other reflexes to determine whether an infant's nervous system is working properly.

BABY, CAN YOU SEE ME? BABY, CAN YOU HEAR ME? SENSORY DEVELOPMENT
I've heard that babies can't see or hear very much at birth. Is that true? Although most infant sensory abilities are fairly well developed at birth, some require a bit more time to reach "full power." The sense of touch is the most well developed, which makes perfect sense when one realizes how much skin-to-womb contact the baby has had in the last months of pregnancy. The sense of smell is also highly developed. Breast-fed babies can actually tell the difference between their own mother's milk scent and another woman's milk scent within a few days after birth.

Taste is also nearly fully developed. At birth, infants show a preference for sweets (and human breast milk is very sweet), and by four months have developed a

FIGURE 8.4 **Five Infant Reflexes**
Shown here are (a) grasping reflex, (b) startle reflect (also known as the *Moro reflex*), (c) rooting reflex (when you touch a baby's cheek it will turn toward your hand, open its mouth, and search for the nipple), (d) stepping reflex, and (e) sucking reflex. These infant reflexes can be used to check on the health of an infant's nervous system. If a reflex is absent or abnormal, it may indicate brain damage or some other neurological problem.

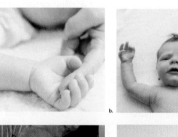

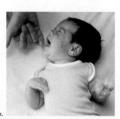

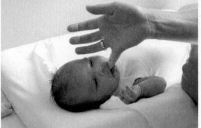

preference for salty tastes (which may come from exposure to the salty taste of their mother's skin). Sour and bitter, two other taste sensations, produce spitting up and the making of horrible faces (Ganchrow et al., 1983).

Hearing is functional before birth but may take a little while to reach its full potential after birth. The fluids of the womb must clear out completely. From birth, newborns seem most responsive to high pitches, as in a woman's voice, and low pitches, as in a male's voice.

The least functional sense at birth is vision. The eye, as stated in Chapter Three, is quite a complex organ. (L I N K) *to Chapter Three: Sensation and Perception, p. 96.* The rods, which see in black and white and have little visual acuity, are fairly well developed at birth, but the cones, which see colour and provide sharpness of vision, will take about another six months to fully develop. So the newborn has relatively poor colour perception when compared to sharply contrasting lights and darks until about 2 months of age (Adams, 1987) and has fairly "fuzzy" vision, much as a near-sighted person would have. The lens of the newborn stays fixed until the muscles that hold it in place mature. Until then the newborn is unable to shift what little focus it has from close to far. Thus, newborns actually have a fixed distance for clear vision of about 18 to 25 centimetres, which is the distance from the baby's face to the mother's face while nursing (Slater, 2000). This focal distance may also be the reason adults almost instinctively hold a baby at about this distance from their own faces.

Newborns also have visual preferences at birth, as discovered by researchers using measures of the time that infants spent looking at certain visual stimuli (Fantz, 1961). They found that infants prefer to look at complex patterns rather than simple ones, three dimensions rather than two, and that the most preferred visual stimulus was a human face. More recently, using a form of the preference method, researchers from McMaster University in Hamilton, Ontario, have found that newborns' preferences were influenced by the stimuli's resemblance to a human face. They concluded that newborns appear to be predisposed to look toward faces (Mondlach et al., 1999). The fact that infants prefer human voices and human faces (DeCasper & Fifer, 1980; DeCasper & Spence, 1986; Fantz, 1964; Maurer & Young, 1983) makes it easier for them to form relationships with their caretakers and to develop language later on.

FROM CRAWLING TO A BLUR OF MOTION: MOTOR DEVELOPMENT   Infants manage a tremendous amount of development in motor skills from birth to about 2 years of age. Figure 8.5 shows some of the major physical milestones of infancy. When looking at the ages listed, remember that these ages are averages based on large samples of infants. An infant may reach these milestones earlier or later than the average and still be considered to be developing normally.

✱ Explore on mypsychlab
Infant's Perceptual and Cognitive Milestones

👁 Watch on mypsychlab
The Growing Child

FIGURE 8.5 **Six Motor Milestones** Shown here are (a) raising head and chest—2 to 4 months, (b) rolling over—2 to 5 months, (c) sitting up with support—4 to 6 months, (d) sitting up without support—6 to 7 months, (e) crawling—7 to 8 months, and (f) walking—8 to 18 months. The motor milestones develop as the infant gains greater voluntary control over the muscles in its body, typically from the top of the body downward. This pattern is seen in the early control of the neck muscles and the much later development of control of the legs and feet.

An infant's normal development is related to many factors, such as nutrition, care, and health. One important way to protect an infant's health is to make sure that immunizations against various illnesses are given at the appropriate times. In the last few decades, parents of young children have begun to resist getting their children immunized against diseases such as measles, mumps, and rubella (MMR). This trend is probably due to a number of factors. First, the parents of these children have grown up in an era in which immunizations during infancy were common, making them unaware of the seriousness of the childhood diseases those immunizations prevent. They have not seen the serious consequences that can result from outbreaks of such diseases: blindness, deafness, developmental delay, and even death (Public Health Agency of Canada, 2006).

Second, many of these parents have become influenced by misinformation that has been placed on the internet and handed out by often well-meaning but uninformed people that highlights the dangers of immunization (Stratton et al., 2001a, 2001b). For example, some people believe that children who get the vaccination will develop the disease itself. Most vaccines are made from dead viruses, and it is impossible to get the disease in this way. Vaccines that use very weak live viruses (such as the chicken pox vaccine) might cause a child to develop a mild version of the disease, but the risk is very small, and the full-blown disease is far more serious and deadly (Public Health Agency of Canada, 2006). Another common concern of people who are anti-immunization is that the MMR vaccine causes autism in children. Autism is a complex neurological disorder in which the more visible symptoms used for diagnosis, such as language delays and difficulties in speaking, do not appear until 2 to 3 years of age. The MMR vaccine is typically given at about 1 year or shortly after and so seems to be followed by the "onset" of autism. But research indicates that the timing of the vaccine and the first easily visible signs of autism is simply a coincidence; studies have consistently failed to show any link between the vaccine and autism (Gilberg & Coleman, 2000; Madsen et al., 2002; Taylor et al., 1999). In addition, early signs of autism can now be observed long before the delivery of the MMR vaccine (Mars et al., 1998; Rutherford, 2008). Using an eye-tracking tool, Mel Rutherford of McMaster University has been able to diagnose infants with autism spectrum disorder as early as 9 months of age (Rutherford, 2008).

COGNITIVE DEVELOPMENT

By the time the average infant is 1 year old, it has tripled its birth weight and added about another 30 centimetres to its height. The brain triples in weight in the first two years, reaching about 75 percent of its adult weight. By age 5, the brain is at 90 percent of its adult weight. This increase makes possible a tremendous amount of major advances in **cognitive development**, including the development of thinking, problem solving, and memory.

8.7   *What are two ways of looking at cognitive development, and how does language develop?*

PIAGET'S THEORY: FOUR STAGES OF COGNITIVE DEVELOPMENT   Early researcher Jean Piaget developed his theory from detailed observations of infants and children, most especially his own three children. Piaget made significant contributions to the understanding of how children think about the world around them, and shifted the view of children's thinking from that of "little adults" to something quite different from adult thinking. Piaget believed that children form mental concepts or **schema** as they experience new situations and events. For example, if Sandy points to a picture of an apple and tells her child, "That's an apple," the child forms

cognitive development
the development of thinking, problem solving, and memory.

schema
a mental concept formed through experiences with objects and events.

TABLE 8.1 PIAGET'S STAGES OF COGNITIVE DEVELOPMENT	
STAGE	**COGNITIVE DEVELOPMENT**
Sensorimotor (0 to 2 years)	• Explore world by using senses and movement. • Develop object permanence and the understanding that concepts and mental images represent objects, people, and events.
Preoperational (2 to 7 years)	• Develop capacity for symbolic thought. • Can't conserve, logically reason, or simultaneously consider many characteristics of an object.
Concrete Operational (7 to 12 years)	• Develop conservation and reversibility of thought. • Can think logically and understand analogies but only about concrete events.
Formal Operational (12 years to adulthood)	• Develop abstract reasoning about hypothetical events or situations. • Think about logical possibilities. • Use abstract analogies. • Systematically examine and test hypotheses. (Not everyone can eventually reason in all these ways.)

sensorimotor stage
Piaget's first stage of cognitive development in which the infant uses its senses and motor abilities to interact with objects in the environment.

object permanence
the knowledge that an object exists even when it is not in sight.

preoperational stage
Piaget's second stage of cognitive development in which the preschool child learns to use language as a means of exploring the world.

a schema for "apple" that looks something like that picture. Piaget also believed that children first try to understand new things in terms of schema they already possess, a process called *assimilation.* The child might see an orange and say "apple" because both objects are round. When corrected, the child might alter the schema for apple to include "round" and "red." The process of altering or adjusting old schemas to fit new information and experiences is *accommodation* (Piaget, 1952, 1962, 1983).

Piaget also proposed that there are four distinct stages of cognitive development that occur from infancy to adolescence, as shown in Table 8.1 (Piaget, 1952, 1962, 1983).

The Sensorimotor Stage   The **sensorimotor stage** is the first of Piaget's stages. It concerns infants from birth to age 2. In this stage, infants use their senses and motor abilities to learn about the world around them. At first, infants have only the involuntary reflexes present at birth to interact with objects and people. As their sensory and motor development progresses, they begin to interact deliberately with objects by grasping, pushing, tasting, and so on. Infants move from simple repetitive actions, such as grabbing their toes, to complex patterns such as trying to put a shape into a sorting box.

Near the end of this period, infants develop a sense of **object permanence**, the knowledge that an object exists even when it is not in sight. For example, the game of peek-a-boo is important in teaching infants that Mommy's smiling face is always going to be behind her hands. This is a critical step in developing language, as words themselves are symbols of things that may not be present. Symbolic thought, which is the ability to represent objects in one's thoughts with symbols such as words, becomes possible by the end of this stage, with children of 2 years capable of thinking in simple symbols and of planning out actions.

Is that why it's so easy for little children to believe in Santa Claus and the Tooth Fairy when they're little?

The Preoperational Stage   The **preoperational stage** (ages 2 to 7) is a time of developing language and concepts. Children, who can now move freely about in their world, no longer have to rely only on senses and motor skills but now can ask questions

Is that why it's so easy for little children to believe in Santa Claus and the Tooth Fairy when they're little?

egocentrism
the inability to see the world through anyone else's eyes.

centration
in Piaget's theory, the tendency of a young child to focus only on one feature of an object while ignoring other relevant features.

conservation
in Piaget's theory, the ability to understand that simply changing the appearance of an object does not change the object's nature.

irreversibility
in Piaget's theory, the inability of the young child to mentally reverse an action.

FIGURE 8.6 **Conservation Experiment** A typical conservation task consists of pouring equal amounts of water into two glasses of the same size and shape. When the water from one of these glasses is poured into a taller, narrower glass, children who cannot yet conserve tend to focus (centrate) on the height of the water in the second glass, assuming that the second glass now has more water than the first one. In the second example, pennies are laid out in two equal lines. When the pennies in the top line are spaced out, the child who cannot yet conserve will centrate on the top line and assume that there are actually more pennies in that line.

and explore their surroundings more fully. Pretending and make-believe play become possible because children at this stage can understand, through symbolic thinking, that a line of wooden blocks can "stand in" for a train. They are limited, however, in several ways. They are not yet capable of logical thought—they can use simple mental concepts but are not able to use those concepts in a more rational, logical sense. They tend to be overwhelmed by what they see, so when children of this age see Santa Claus in a book, on television, or at the mall, Santa Claus becomes real to them. It doesn't occur to them to think about how Santa might get to every child's house in one night or why those toys are the same ones they saw in the store just last week.

Another limitation is **egocentrism**, the inability to see the world through anyone else's eyes except one's own. For the preoperational child, everyone else must see what the child sees, and what is important to the child must be important to everyone else. For example, the 4-year-old niece of one of the authors insisted on buying her mother a Barbie for Christmas because that is what *she* thought was the best present. This desire was egocentric, yet completely unselfish.

Children in this stage may be able to count up to 10 or 20, but they won't understand that in the bottom example in Figure 8.6 both rows have the same number of coins. Instead of counting the coins, they are overwhelmed by the longer *appearance* of the top row of coins. A child who complains that his piece of pie is smaller than his brother's may be quite happy once his original piece is cut into two pieces—now he thinks he has more than his brother. He has focused only on the number of pieces, not the actual amount of the pie. Focusing only on one feature of some object rather than taking all features into consideration is called **centration**. In the coin example in Figure 8.6, children of this stage will focus on the length of the top line of coins only and ignore the number of coins. Centration is one of the reasons that children in this stage often fail to understand that changing the way something looks does not change its substance. The ability to understand that altering the appearance of something does not change its amount (as in the coin example), its volume, or its mass is called **conservation**.

Preoperational children fail at conservation not only because they centrate (such as focusing on the number of pieces of pie) but also because they are unable to "mentally reverse" actions. This feature of preoperational thinking is called **irreversibility**. For example, if a preoperational child sees liquid poured from a short, wide glass into a tall, thin glass, the child will assume that the second glass holds more liquid (see Figure 8.6). This failure to "conserve" (save) the volume of liquid as it takes on a

Type of conservation	Initial presentation	Transformation	Question	Preoperational child's answer
Liquids	Two equal glasses of liquid	Pour one into a taller, narrower glass.	Which glass contains more?	The taller one.
Number	Two equal lines of pennies	Increase spacing of pennies in one line.	Which line has more pennies?	The longer one.

different shape in the tall, thin glass is caused not only by the child's centration on the height of the liquid in the second glass but also by the inability of the child to imagine pouring the liquid back into the first glass and having it be the same amount again.

Concrete Operations   In the **concrete operations stage** (ages 7 to 12), children finally become capable of conservation and reversible thinking. Centration no longer occurs as children become capable of considering all the relevant features of any given object. They begin to think more logically about beliefs such as Santa Claus and ask questions, eventually coming to their own more rational conclusions about the fantasies of early childhood. They are in school, learning all sorts of science and math, and are convinced that they know more than their parents at this point. In fact, they become so logical and focused on "the rules" that they find it difficult to alter rules— their thinking is set in "concrete."

This "concrete" thinking is the major limitation of this stage. Children in this stage are unable to deal effectively with *abstract concepts.* Abstract concepts are those that do not have some physical, touchable reality. For example, "freedom" is an abstract concept. People can define it, they can get a good sense of what it means, but there is no "thing" that they can point to and say, "This is freedom." *Concrete concepts,* which are the kind of concepts understood by children of this age, are about objects, written rules, and real things. Children need to be able to see it, touch it, or at least see it in their heads to be able to understand it.

These concrete operational children, seen in a science class, have begun to think logically and are able to solve many kinds of problems that were not possible for them to solve while in the preoperational stage.

Formal Operations   In the last of Piaget's stages, **formal operations** (age 12 to adulthood), abstract thinking becomes possible. Teenagers not only understand concepts that have no physical reality but also get deeply involved in *hypothetical thinking,* or thinking about possibilities and even impossibilities. "What if everyone just got along?" "If women were in charge of countries, would there be fewer wars?"

Piaget did not believe that everyone would necessarily reach formal operations. Studies show that only about half of all adults in North America reach formal operations (Sutherland, 1992). That does not mean that the adults who do not develop this type of thinking are somehow less intelligent; it simply means that they use a more practical kind of intelligence that suits their particular lifestyle. Successful university or college students, however, need formal operational thinking to succeed in their post-secondary education, as most classes require critical thinking, problem-solving abilities, and abstract thinking based on formal operational skills (Powers, 1984).

Educators have put Piaget's ideas into practice by allowing children to learn at their own pace, by "hands-on" experience with objects, and by teaching concepts to children who are at an appropriate cognitive level (Brooks & Brooks, 1993). But Piaget's theory has also been criticized on several points. Some researchers believe that the idea of distinct stages of cognitive development is not completely correct and that changes in thought are more continuous (Courage & Howe, 2002; Feldman, 2003; Schwitzgebel, 1999; Siegler, 1996). Others point out that Piaget underestimated the abilities of children. For example, preschoolers are not as egocentric as Piaget seemed to believe (Flavell, 1999), and object permanence exists much earlier than Piaget thought (Aguiar & Baillargeon, 2003; Baillargeon, 1986).

VYGOTSKY'S SOCIOCULTURAL THEORY: THE IMPORTANCE OF BEING THERE
Russian psychologist Lev Vygotsky developed a theory of how children think that did not match the prevailing political ideas in Russia. After his death from tuberculosis in 1934, his ideas were suppressed by the government but kept alive by his students and later republished. Vygotsky's pioneering work in developmental psychology has had a profound influence on school education in Russia, and interest in his theories

concrete operations stage
Piaget's third stage of cognitive development in which the school-age child becomes capable of logical thought processes but is not yet capable of abstract thinking.

formal operations
Piaget's last stage of cognitive development in which the adolescent becomes capable of abstract thinking.

scaffolding
process in which a more skilled learner gives help to a less skilled learner, reducing the amount of help as the less skilled learner becomes more capable.

zone of proximal development (ZPD)
Vygotsky's concept of the difference between what a child can do alone and what that child can do with the help of a teacher.

This boy is helping his younger sister learn to read a book. Vygotsky's view of cognitive development states that the help of skilled others aids in making cognitive advances such as this one.

It sounds as though language is pretty important in all this, is ▶ that right?

continues to grow throughout the world (Bodrova & Leong, 1996). Vygotsky wrote about children's cognitive development but differed from Piaget in his emphasis on the role of others in cognitive development (Vygotsky, 1934/1962, 1978, 1987). Whereas Piaget stressed the importance of the child's interaction with objects as a primary factor in cognitive development, Vygotsky stressed the importance of social interactions with other people, typically more highly skilled children and adults. Vygotsky believed that children develop cognitively when someone else helps them by asking leading questions and providing examples of concepts in a process called **scaffolding**. In scaffolding, the more highly skilled person gives the learner more help at the beginning of the learning process and then begins to withdraw help as the learner's skills improve (Rogoff, 1994).

Vygotsky also proposed that each developing child has a **zone of proximal development (ZPD)**, which is the difference between what a child can do alone versus what a child can do with the help of a teacher. For example, if little Jenny can do math problems up to the grade 4 level on her own but with the help of a teacher can successfully work problems at a grade 6 level, her ZPD is two years. Suzi might be the same age as Jenny (and might even score the same on a traditional IQ test), but if Suzi can work math problems only at a grade 5 level with the help of the teacher, Suzi's ZPD is not as great as Jenny's. This might be a better way of thinking about intelligence: It isn't what you know (as measured by traditional tests), it's what you *can do.*

Vygotsky's ideas have been put into practice in education through the use of cooperative learning, in which children work together in groups to achieve a common goal, and in reciprocal teaching, in which teachers lead students through the basic strategies of reading until the students themselves become capable of teaching the strategies to others.

So, Piaget focused on the child's cognitive development as if the other people in the child's world were not all that important to the acquisition of knowledge and the development of skills. This is not necessarily wrong; children are able to grasp many ideas and concepts through their own thought processes and interactions with objects, discovering basic principles and characteristics of objects in individual play. In contrast, Vygotsky theorized that other people, acting as teachers and mentors, were a crucial part of the cognitive development of the child (Duncan, 1995). Another difference between Piaget and Vygotsky (and also a shortcoming of Piaget's work) is that Piaget underestimated the impact that culture has on cognitive development, whereas Vygostky believed that cognitive development could not be studied without consideration of cultural impact.

STAGES OF LANGUAGE DEVELOPMENT   It sounds as though language is pretty important in all this, is that right? The development of language is indeed a very important milestone in the cognitive development of a child because language allows children to think in words rather than just images, to ask questions, to communicate their needs and wants to others, and to form concepts (Bloom, 1974; Bloom, 2000). Early views of language development were based on Skinnerian principles of reinforcement, basically proposing that language develops as a result of the child being reinforced, or rewarded. However, Noam Chomsky argued strongly against this viewpoint. As was discussed in Chapter Seven, Chomsky proposed a language acquisition device (LAD), an innate "program" that contained a schema for human language. ⓁⒾⓃⓀ *to Chapter Seven: Cognition, p. 291.* The children matched the language they heard against this schema and, thus, language developed in a well-researched sequence (Chomsky, 1957, 1964, 1981, 1986).

A great deal of support exists for the idea that language abilities are innate. First, children from different parts of the world go through similar stages of language development, regardless of the language that is native to the area. In addition, deaf infants go through the same stages as hearing infants (Brown, 1973). In their first months of life, deaf infants and hearing infants sound very much alike. Both will cry, coo, and deaf infants will even begin to babble like a hearing infant (Hoff, 2005). However, it is during the babbling stage that differences will begin to appear. Laura Ann Petitto of the University of Toronto is just one of many researchers who has shown that deaf infants will actually begin to babble with their hands (Pettito, 2001). Although differences in the type of babbling (oral versus manual) exist, deaf infants and hearing infants do go through the same stages of language acquisition.

There are several stages of language development that all children experience, no matter what culture they live in or what language they will learn to speak (Brown, 1973):

1. **Cooing:** At around 2 months of age, babies begin to make vowel-like sounds.
2. **Babbling:** At about 6 months, infants add consonant sounds to the vowels to make a babbling sound, which at times can almost sound like real speech. Deaf children actually decrease their babbling after 6 months while increasing their use of primitive hand signs and gestures (Petitto & Marentette, 1991; Petitto et al., 2001).
3. **One-word speech:** Somewhere just before or around age 1, most children begin to say actual words. These words are typically nouns and may seem to represent an entire phrase of meaning. They are called *holophrases* (whole phrases in one word) for that reason. For example, a child might say "Milk!" and mean "I want some milk!" or "I drank my milk!"
4. **Telegraphic speech:** At around 1½ years, toddlers begin to string words together to form short, simple sentences by using nouns, verbs, and adjectives. "Baby eat," "Mommy go," and "Doggie go bye-bye" are examples of telegraphic speech. Only the words that carry the meaning of the sentence are used.
5. **Whole sentences:** As children move through the preschool years, they learn to use grammatical terms and increase the number of words in their sentences, until by age 6 or so they are nearly as fluent as an adult, although the number of words they know is still limited when compared to adult vocabulary.

Other support for the idea that language learning is innate comes from findings that children learn how to speak correctly even when not consistently corrected, and children have been found to invent their own language when they have not been exposed to adult language. As an example, in Managua, Nicaragua, deaf children were left to their own devices when it came to communicating with one another. As a result, Nicaraguan Sign Language (NSL), now recognized by scientists as a true language, was born.

But does the work of Chomsky and the findings that universal stages of language development exist prove that language abilities are due only to nature? Of course not. Recall the previous discussion of the infamous nature–nurture debate. Psychologists usually agree that nature and nurture both contribute to development, and the development of language is no exception. Children's environment and culture obviously have a profound impact on their language learning as well. One piece of evidence that supports this idea comes from the story of Genie, an abused child who was not exposed to language until she was 13 years old. Genie, although eventually able to understand and produce some words, was not able to master language. For many researchers, this case study provided evidence for the idea of critical periods, which

⊙─ ⃞Watch on mypsychlab
Play in Early Childhood

This infant has already learned some of the basics of language, including the use of gestures to indicate meaning and enhance communication.

were discussed in relation to embryonic development earlier in the chapter and are relevant to many different issues relating to development. When it comes to language learning, the critical period is that time (usually the first decade of life) during which children must be exposed to language in order for them to master it. Some researchers believe that other factors may have contributed to Genie's inability to master language (e.g., the severe physical and emotional abuse; lack of cognitive stimulation; and the possibility of a pre-existing neurological problem; Grimshaw, Adelstein, Bryden, & MacKinnon, 1998). However, most researchers argue that because Genie had not been exposed to language during the first 10 years of her life, her ability to use language was significantly impaired.

It is important to note that many researchers disagree with the use of the term *critical period* when it comes to language acquisition and instead choose to use the term *sensitive period*. They argue that although *mastery* of language after childhood is extremely difficult, if not impossible, people can still become proficient at a language (e.g., think of learning a second language) after the first decade of life.

PRACTICE QUIZ: HOW MUCH DO YOU REMEMBER?

Pick the best answer.

1. Which sense is least functional at birth?
   - **a.** touch
   - **b.** taste
   - **c.** smell
   - **d.** vision

2. What is the first voluntary movement that allows an infant to get from one place to another?
   - **a.** sitting without support
   - **b.** rolling over
   - **c.** raising the head when placed face down
   - **d.** standing

3. Which of the following statements concerning vaccinations is FALSE?
   - **a.** The side effects of vaccines are far less harmful than the effects of the diseases they prevent.
   - **b.** Most children today do not need immunizations, as the diseases have been eliminated.
   - **c.** Vaccines are one of the most effective ways to prevent the transmission of the diseases they treat.
   - **d.** Vaccinations are particularly important when travelling to other countries where the diseases still exist.

4. In which of Piaget's stages would a child be who has just developed object permanence?
   - **a.** sensorimotor
   - **b.** preoperational
   - **c.** concrete operational
   - **d.** formal operational

5. Vygotsky defines _____ as the difference between what a child can do alone and what that child can do with help.
   - **a.** scaffolding
   - **b.** habituation
   - **c.** zone of proximal development
   - **d.** metamemory

6. "Daddy go bye-bye" is an example of
   - **a.** telegraphic speech.
   - **b.** babbling.
   - **c.** a holophrase.
   - **d.** cooing.

Answers: 1.-d, 2.-b, 3.-b, 4.-a, 5.-c, 6.-a.

PSYCHOSOCIAL DEVELOPMENT

8.8 *How do infants and children develop personalities and form relationships with others, and what are Erikson's stages of psychosocial development for children?*

The psychological and social development of infants and children involves the development of personality, relationships, and a sense of being male or female. Although these processes begin in infancy, they will continue in many respects well into adulthood.

Why are some children negative and whiny while others are sweet and good-natured?

TEMPERAMENT   One of the first ways in which infants demonstrate that they have different personalities (long-lasting characteristics that make each person different from other persons) is in their **temperament**, the behavioural and emotional characteristics that are fairly well established at birth. Researchers (Chess & Thomas, 1986; Thomas & Chess, 1977) have been able to identify three basic temperament styles of infants:

1. **Easy:** "Easy" babies are regular in their schedules of waking, sleeping, and eating and are adaptable to change. Easy babies are happy babies and when distressed are easily soothed.

2. **Difficult:** "Difficult" babies are almost the opposite of easy ones. Difficult babies tend to be irregular in their schedules and are very negative about change of any kind. They are loud, active, and tend to be crabby rather than happy.

3. **Slow to warm up:** This kind of temperament is associated with infants who are less negative, quieter, and more regular than difficult children but who are slow to adapt to change. If change is introduced gradually, these babies will "warm up" to new people and new situations.

Of course, not all babies will fall neatly into one of these three patterns—some children may be a mix of two or even all three patterns of behaviour, as Chess and Thomas (1986) discovered. Even so, longitudinal research strongly suggests that these temperament styles last well into adulthood (Korn, 1984), although they are somewhat influenced by the environment in which the infant is raised. For example, a "difficult" infant who is raised by parents who are themselves very loud and active may not be perceived as difficult by the parents, whereas a child who is slow to warm up might be perceived as difficult if the parents themselves like lots of change and noise. The first infant is in a situation in which the "goodness of fit" of the infant's temperament to the parents' temperament is very close, but the parents of the second infant are a poor fit in temperament for that less active child (Chess & Thomas, 1986).

I'd sure hate to have a difficult child! How does a baby's temperament affect the way the parents deal with the baby? A baby's temperament is going to be connected to how parents deal with many issues. Babies with easy temperaments allow parents to plan around their schedules, for example. Planning around the varying sleeping and eating behaviours of a difficult infant is much trickier (Bates, 1989; Sheeber & Johnson, 1992). As children grow, their temperament and how well it matches a parent's own temperament becomes an issue in discipline and in the formation of emotional bonds to the parents or other caregivers (Cameron et al., 1989; Goldsmith & Campos, 1982; Skolnick, 1986).

ATTACHMENT   The emotional bond that forms between an infant and a primary caregiver is called **attachment**. Attachment is a very important development in the social and emotional life of the infant, usually forming within the first six months of the infant's life and showing up in a number of ways during the second six months, such as wariness of strangers and fear of being separated from the caregiver. Although attachment to the mother is usually the primary attachment, infants can attach to fathers and to other caretakers as well.

◀ Why are some children negative and whiny while others are sweet and good-natured?

◀ I'd sure hate to have a difficult child! How does a baby's temperament affect the way the parents deal with the baby?

temperament
the behavioural characteristics that are fairly well established at birth, such as easy, difficult, and slow to warm up.

attachment
the emotional bond between an infant and the primary caregiver.

CLASSIC STUDIES IN PSYCHOLOGY
Insworth and the Strange Situation Paradigm

Mary Ainsworth completed her PhD in developmental psychology at the University of Toronto in 1939. After graduating, she stayed at the university to teach for a few years before deciding to enlist in the Canadian Women's Army Corp in 1942 (during World War II). In the 1960s, after working with John Bowlby in England and spending some time studying mother–child interactions in Africa, Ainsworth (1985; Ainsworth et al., 1978) came up with a special experimental design to measure the attachment of an infant to the caretaker, called the *Strange Situation*. This test involved exposing an infant to a series of leave-takings and returns of the mother and a stranger. Through this measurement technique Ainsworth and another colleague identified four attachment styles:

1. **Secure**: Infants labelled as *secure* were willing to detach themselves from their mothers when they first entered the room with their mothers. They explored happily, looking back at their mothers and returning to them every now and then (sort of like "touching base"). When the stranger came in, these infants were wary but calm as long as their mother was nearby. When the mother left, the infants got upset. When the mother returned, the infants approached her, were easily soothed, and were glad to have her back.

2. **Avoidant**: In contrast, avoidant babies, although somewhat willing to explore, did not "touch base." They did not look at the stranger or the mother and reacted very little to her absence or her return, seeming to have no interest or concern.

3. **Ambivalent**: The word *ambivalent* means to have mixed feelings about something. Ambivalent babies in Ainsworth's study were clingy and unwilling to explore, were very upset by the stranger regardless of the mother's presence, protested mightily when the mother left, and were difficult to soothe. When the mother returned, these babies would demand to be picked up but, at the same time, would push the mother away or kick her in a mixed reaction to her return.

4. **Disorganized-disoriented**: In subsequent studies, other researchers (Main & Hesse, 1990; Main & Solomon, 1990) found that some babies seemed unable to decide just how they should react to the mother's return. These disorganized-disoriented infants would approach her but with their eyes turned away from her, as if afraid to make eye contact. In general, these infants seemed fearful and showed a dazed and depressed look on their faces.

It should come as no surprise that the mothers of each of the four types of infants also behaved differently from one another. Mothers of secure infants were loving, warm, sensitive to their infant's needs, and responsive to the infant's attempts at communication. Mothers of avoidant babies were unresponsive, insensitive, and coldly rejecting. Mothers of ambivalent babies tried to be responsive but were inconsistent and insensitive to the baby's actions, often talking to the infant about something totally unrelated to what the infant was doing at the time. Mothers of disorganized-disoriented babies were found to be abusive or neglectful in interactions with the infants.

Attachment is not necessarily the result of the behaviour of the mother alone, however. The temperament of the infant may play an important part in determining the reactions of the mothers (Goldsmith & Campos, 1982; Skolnick, 1986). For example, an infant with a difficult temperament is difficult to soothe. A mother with this kind of infant might come to avoid unnecessary contact with the infant, as did the mothers of the avoidant babies in Ainsworth's studies.

Critics of Ainsworth's Strange Situation research focus on the artificial nature of the design and wonder if infants and mothers would behave differently in the more familiar surroundings of home, even though Ainsworth's experimental observers also observed the

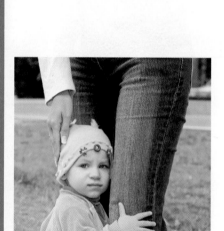

This toddler shows reluctance to explore his environment, instead clinging to his mother's legs. Such clingy behaviour, if common, can be a sign of an ambivalent attachment.

infants and mothers in the home prior to the Strange Situation (Ainsworth, 1985). Other research has found results supporting Ainsworth's findings in home-based assessments of attachment (Blanchard & Main, 1979). Other studies have also found support for the concept of attachment styles and stability of attachment over the first six years of life (Lutkenhaus et al., 1985; Main & Cassidy, 1988; Owen et al., 1984; Wartner et al., 1994). Even adult relationships can be seen as influenced by the attachment style of the adult—those who are avoidant tend to have numerous shallow and brief relationships with different partners, whereas those who are ambivalent tend to have repeated break-ups and make-ups with the same person (Bartholomew, 1990; Hazan & Shaver, 1987).

Questions for Further Discussion

1. Do you think it is possible for adults to change their attachment style once they're grown and in their own adult relationships?

2. Do you think it is possible for an infant who meets the criteria of one of the categories to later change categories? For example, what might happen to a securely attached child if a traumatic event occurred during the first year of the baby's life?

3. There is a lot of focus on mothers in Ainsworth's work. What about infants who are raised by their fathers? Do you think the findings would be similar?

As daycare has become more widely acceptable and common, many parents have been concerned about the effect of daycare on attachment. Psychologist Jay Belsky and colleagues (Belsky, 2005; Belsky & Johnson, 2005; Belsky et al., 2007) have studied the attachment of infants in daycare and concluded that although higher quality of daycare (low child-to-caregiver ratio, low turnover in caregivers, and caregivers educated in child-care techniques and theory) is important, especially for cognitive development, positive development including attachment was more clearly related to the quality of parenting that the infants and toddlers received at home.

Evidence that similar attachment styles are found in other cultures demonstrates the need to consider attachment as an important first step in forming relationships with others, one which may set the stage for all relationships that follow (Hu & Meng, 1996; Juffer & Rosenboom, 1997; Keromoian & Leiderman, 1986). Recently, Lachlan McWilliams and S. Jeffrey Bailey of Acadia University in Nova Scotia discovered just how important attachment styles can be. Their research has shown that any form of insecure attachment can have a negative impact on one's physical health. The findings of their study indicate that insecure attachment is a risk factor for the development of disease and chronic illness, such as chronic pain, stroke, heart attack, high blood pressure, and ulcers (McWilliams & Bailey, 2010).

HARLOW AND CONTACT COMFORT As psychologists began to study the development of attachment, they at first assumed that attachment to the mother occurred because the mother was associated with satisfaction of primary drives such as hunger and thirst. The mother is present when the food (a primary reinforcer) is presented, so the mother becomes a secondary reinforcer capable of producing pleasurable feelings. L I N K *to Chapter Five: Learning, p. 176.*

Psychologist Harry Harlow felt that attachment had to be influenced by more than just the provision of food. He conducted a number of studies of attachment by using infant rhesus monkeys (Harlow, 1958). Noticing that the monkeys in his lab liked to cling to the soft cloth pad used to line their cages, Harlow designed a study to examine the importance of what he termed *contact comfort*, the seeming attachment of the monkeys to something soft to the touch.

The wire surrogate "mother" provides the food for this infant rhesus monkey. But the infant spends all its time with the soft, cloth-covered surrogate. According to Harlow, this demonstrates the importance of contact comfort in attachment.

Watch on mypsychlab

Harlow's Monkeys: Contact Comfort

I've heard that you shouldn't pick up a baby every time it cries—that if you do, it might spoil the baby.

He isolated eight baby rhesus monkeys shortly after their birth, placing each in a cage with two surrogate (substitute) "mothers." The surrogates were actually a block of wood covered in soft padding and terry cloth and a wire form, both heated from within. For half of the monkeys, the wire "mother" held the bottle from which they fed, while for the other half the soft "mother" held the bottle. Harlow then recorded the time each monkey spent with each "mother." If time spent with the surrogate is taken as an indicator of attachment, then learning theory would predict that the monkeys would spend more time with whichever surrogate was being used to feed them.

The results? Regardless of which surrogate was feeding them, the monkeys all spent significantly more time with the soft, cloth-covered surrogate. In fact, all monkeys spent very little time with the wire surrogate, even if this was the one with the bottle. Harlow and his colleagues concluded that "contact comfort was an important basic affectional or love variable" (Harlow, 1958, p. 574).

Harlow's work represents one of the earliest investigations into the importance of touch in the attachment process and remains an important part of human development.

Researchers now know that touch can have numerous benefits for both preterm and full-term infants (Ferber & Makhoul, 2004). For example, skin-to-skin contact between mothers and infants has been shown to have a positive impact on infants' sleeping patterns. This skin-to-skin contact has been labelled *kangaroo care* (because it mimics the kangaroo's pouch) and is now frequently used in neonatal intensive care units in hospitals all over the world. Research indicates that kangaroo care has significantly improved cognitive, physical, and emotional outcomes in preterm infants (Ferber & Makhoul, 2004).

ERIKSON'S THEORY: THE FIRST FOUR STAGES I've heard that you shouldn't pick up a baby every time it cries—that if you do, it might spoil the baby. Unfortunately, a lot of people have not only heard this advice but also acted on it by frequently ignoring an infant's crying, which turns out to be a very bad thing for babies. When a baby under 6 months of age cries, it is an instinctive reaction meant to get the caretaker to tend to the baby's needs—hunger, thirst, pain, and even loneliness. Research has shown that babies whose cries are tended to consistently (that is, the infant is fed when hungry, changed when wet, and so on) in the early months are more securely attached as late as age 1 than those infants whose caretakers frequently allow the infants to cry when there is a need for attention—hunger, pain, or wetness, for example (Brazelton, 1992; Heinicke et al., 2000). Erikson, a psychodynamic theorist who emphasized the importance of social relationships in the development of personality, would certainly disagree with letting a baby "cry it out," although allowing an infant who has been fed, changed, burped, and checked to cry on occasion will not damage attachment.

Erikson, who trained as a Freudian psychoanalyst but became convinced that social interactions were more important in development than sexual development, believed that development occurred in a series of eight stages, with the first four of these stages occurring in infancy and childhood (Erikson, 1950; Erikson & Erikson, 1997). (Freud's stages of psychosexual development are covered in detail in Chapter Eleven. LINK to Chapter Eleven: *Theories of Personality*, p. 438.) Each stage is an emotional *crisis*, or a kind of turning point, in personality, and the crisis in each stage must be successfully met for normal, healthy psychological development.

Erikson focused on the relationship of the infant and the child to significant others in the immediate surroundings—parents and then later teachers and even peers. Table 8.2 summarizes the conflict in each of the eight stages and some of the implications for future development (Erikson, 1950; Erikson & Erikson, 1997). For now, just focus on the first four stages. The remaining four will be discussed later in the chapter.

TABLE 8.2 ERIKSON'S PSYCHOSOCIAL STAGES OF DEVELOPMENT

STAGE	DEVELOPMENTAL CRISIS	SUCCESSFUL DEALING	UNSUCCESSFUL DEALING
1. Infant Birth to 1 year old	**Trust Versus Mistrust** Babies learn to trust or mistrust others based on whether or not their needs—such as food and comfort—are met.	If babies' needs are met, they learn to trust people and expect life to be pleasant.	If babies' needs are not met, they learn not to trust.
2. Toddler 1 to 3 years old	**Autonomy Versus Shame and Doubt** Toddlers realize that they can direct their own behaviour.	If toddlers are successful in directing their own behaviour, they learn to be independent.	If toddlers' attempts at being independent are blocked, they learn self-doubt and shame for being unsuccessful.
3. Preschool Age 3 to 5 years old	**Initiative Versus Guilt** Preschoolers are challenged to control their own behaviour, such as controlling their exuberance when they are in a restaurant.	If preschoolers succeed in taking responsibility, they feel capable and develop initiative.	If preschoolers fail in taking responsibility, they feel irresponsible, anxious, and guilty.
4. Elementary School Age 5 to 12 years old	**Industry Versus Inferiority** When children succeed in learning new skills and obtaining new knowledge, they develop a sense of industry, a feeling of competence arising from their work and effort.	When children succeed at learning new skills, they develop a sense of industry, a feeling of competence and self-esteem arising from their work and effort.	If children fail to develop new abilities, they feel incompetent, inadequate, and inferior.
5. Adolescence 13 to early twenties	**Identity Versus Role Confusion** Adolescents are faced with deciding who or what they want to be in terms of occupation, beliefs, attitudes, and behaviour patterns.	Adolescents who succeed in defining who they are and finding a role for themselves develop a strong sense of identity.	Adolescents who fail to define their identity become confused and withdraw or want to inconspicuously blend in with the crowd.
6. Early Adulthood Twenties and thiarties	**Intimacy Versus Isolation** The task facing those in early adulthood is to be able to share who they are with another person in a close, committed relationship.	People who succeed in this task will have satisfying intimate relationships.	Adults who fail at this task will be isolated from other people and may suffer from loneliness.
7. Middle Adulthood Forties and fifties	**Generativity Versus Stagnation** The challenge is to be creative, productive, and nurturant of the next generation.	Adults who succeed in this challenge will be creative, productive, and nurturant, thereby benefiting themselves, their family, community, country, and future generations.	Adults who fail will be passive, and self-centered, feel that they have done nothing for the next generation, and feel that the world is no better off for their being alive.
8. Late Adulthood Sixties and beyond	**Ego Integrity Versus Despair** The issue is whether a person will reach wisdom, spiritual tranquility, a sense of wholeness, and acceptance of his or her life.	Elderly people who succeed in addressing this issue will enjoy life and not fear death.	Elderly people who fail will feel that their life is empty and will fear death.

PRACTICE QUIZ: HOW MUCH DO YOU REMEMBER?

Pick the best answer.

1. According to Thomas and Chess, a child that is very irregular in sleeping and eating, resists change, and is negative and loud is labelled a(n) _____ child.
   a. easy
   b. difficult
   c. slow-to-warm-up
   d. negative

2. What kind of attachment, according to Ainsworth, is shown by a baby who explores the room and gets upset when the mother leaves, but is easily soothed and is happy to see the mother when she returns?
   a. secure
   b. avoidant
   c. ambivalent
   d. disorganized-disoriented

3. Mothers who were abusive and/or neglectful were associated with the _____ type of attachment.
   a. secure
   b. avoidant
   c. ambivalent
   d. disorganized-disoriented

4. In Erikson's _____ stage of psychosocial development, the child learns self-control and begins to feel more capable.
   a. trust versus mistrust
   b. autonomy versus shame and doubt
   c. initiative versus guilt
   d. industry versus inferiority

When do little kids ▶ learn the difference between girls and boys?

8.9 *How are gender roles developed?*

GENDER ROLE DEVELOPMENT When do little kids learn the difference between girls and boys? Most children begin to realize the difference between girls and boys at about age 2, and most can say which one they are at that age. But knowing one's sex (the physical characteristic of being male or female) is not the same thing as knowing the different behaviour expected of a male or a female (**gender**). The behaviour that goes along with being male or female is heavily influenced by cultural expectations as well as biology, and is referred to as **gender identity**.

GENDER ROLES AND GENDER TYPING

Gender roles are the culture's expectations for behaviour of a person who is perceived as male or female, including attitudes, actions, and personality traits associated with a particular gender within that culture (Tobach, 2001; Unger, 1979). **Gender typing** is the process by which people learn their culture's preferences and expectations for proper "masculine" and "feminine" behaviour. The process of developing a person's gender identity (a sense of being male or female) is influenced by both biological and environmental factors (in the form of parenting and other child-rearing behaviours), although which type of factor has greater influence is still controversial.

Most researchers today would agree that biology has an important role in gender identity, at least in certain aspects of gender identity and behaviour (Diamond & Sigmundson, 1997; Reiner, 1999, 2000). In one study, 25 genetically male children who were born with ambiguous genitalia were surgically altered and raised as girls. Now older children and teenagers, they prefer male play activities. Fourteen of these children have openly declared themselves to be boys (Reiner, 2000).

Gender identity, like physical sex, is also not always as straightforward as males who are masculine and females who are feminine. People's sense of gender identity does not always match their external appearance or even the sex chromosomes that determine whether they are male or female (Califia, 1997; Crawford & Unger, 2004; White, 2000). Biology and environment both have an influence on the concept of a person's gender identity. In a disorder called *gender identity disorder* (L I N K *to Chapter Thirteen: Psychological Disorders, p. 541*), a person feels that he or she is occupying the body of the wrong sex; a man may feel that he was meant to be a woman or a woman may feel that she was meant to be a man (American Psychiatric Association, 2000). Some people with this disorder feel so strongly that they are in the wrong sex that they have surgery to become the sex they feel they were always meant to be. These people are generally termed *transsexuals.* Other people are born with ambiguous gender and may also have issues with gender identity. Although the causes of gender identity disorder are not fully understood, there is some evidence for both prenatal influences and early childhood experiences as causes (Stein, 1984; Ward, 1992; Zhou et al., 1995).

Many First Nations have long recognized the role of the male *winkte* (the Lakota word for "wants to be like a woman") in their societies and traditionally were not only tolerant of such different individuals but also had important places for them in the social structure as caretakers of children, cooks, and menders and creators of clothing, and even had certain rituals for bestowing luck upon a hunt (Medicine, 2002). Although some winkte (now often referred to as people with "two spirits") were homosexuals, many were not and would now be recognized as having an alternate gender identity. Unfortunately, as First Nations have modernized and become more integrated into the larger European-dominated culture of North America, the tolerant attitudes of other Native Americans toward the winkte have begun to be replaced with homophobic attitudes and aggressive behaviour toward those who are different in this way (Medicine, 2002).

gender
the behaviour associated with being male or female.

gender identity
one's perception of being male or female and the behaviour that is associated with that gender.

gender roles
the culture's expectations for masculine or feminine behaviour, including attitudes, actions, and personality traits associated with being male or female in that culture.

gender typing
the process of acquiring gender role characteristics.

8.10   *How much influence do biology and learning have on gender role development?*

BIOLOGICAL INFLUENCES   What are the biological influences on gender? Aside from the obvious external sexual characteristics of the genitals, there are also hormonal differences between men and women. Some researchers believe that exposure to these hormones during fetal development not only causes the formation of the sexual organs but also predisposes the infant to behaviour that is typically associated with one gender or the other. There have been several studies of infant girls who were exposed to androgens before birth (e.g., some drugs that prevent miscarriages are male hormones). These studies found that, during childhood, these girls tended to play with typically "boy" toys, to wrestle and play rough, and to play with boys rather than with other girls (Berenbaum & Snyder, 1995; Money & Mathews, 1982; Money & Norman, 1987). However, when these girls grew up, they became more typically "female" in their desire for marriage and motherhood, which many of these same researchers took as evidence that upbringing won out over the hormonal influences.

Was their early "tomboy" nature due to the influence of the male hormones? This is difficult to prove, as the parents of these girls were told about their infants' exposure to male hormones during the pregnancy and may have formed assumptions about the effects of such hormones on their children. It is entirely possible that these girls were simply allowed, or even encouraged, to be more "masculine" as small children because the parents were expecting them to be masculine. As these same girls grew older, they were exposed to the gender role expectations of teachers, friends, and the media, which may have influenced them to become more like the feminine gender stereotype in contrast to their earlier "masculine" style of behaviour.

A recent study examined the way in which men and women respond to visual sexual stimuli and found that although men and women may report being equally aroused by erotic pictures, what happens in their brains is quite different (Hamann et al., 2004). Using the fMRI brain-scanning technique, the researchers found that the amygdala and hypothalamus (areas involved in emotional and sexual responses) were more strongly active in men than in women who viewed the pictures. ⓁⒾⓃⓀ *to Chapter Two: The Biological Perspective, p. 42.* The researchers concluded that the male brain's enhanced reaction might be a product of natural selection, as early human males who could quickly recognize a sexually receptive female would have had a greater opportunity to mate and pass on their genes to their offspring.

ENVIRONMENTAL INFLUENCES   Even if the girls who were exposed to androgens prenatally were initially influenced by these hormones, it seems fairly clear that their later "reversion" to more feminine ways was at least somewhat influenced by the pressures of society. In most cultures, males and females are expected to play certain roles (gender roles, in other words), and the pressure that can be brought to bear on a person who does not conform to these expectations can be tremendous. In most Western cultures, the pressure to be masculine is even greater for boys than the pressure to be feminine is for girls. The term *tomboy* is not generally viewed as an insult, but there are no terms for a boy who acts in a feminine manner that are not insulting—*sissy*, for example, is not a nice term at all. And although studies of parents' influence on their children's gender typing show that both parents have an impact, they also show that the fathers are almost always more concerned about their sons showing male gender behaviour than their daughters showing female gender behaviour (Lytton & Romney, 1991).

CULTURE AND GENDER   A person's culture is also an environmental influence. Previous cross-cultural research has found relatively little influence of cultural differences on gender roles and ideas of masculine and feminine behaviour (Best & Williams, 2001).

◀ Was their early "tomboy" nature due to the influence of the male hormones?

In studies where infant girls were exposed to androgens (male hormones) while in their mothers' wombs, the girls became "tomboys" as children, preferring to play with typically masculine toys and participate in male-dominated play activities. Yet when these same girls grew into puberty and adulthood, they became more feminine in their behaviour. What do these findings mean for the nature–nurture controversy?

◉ ⟦**Watch** on **mypsychlab**
Boys in Crisis

Studies have found that the most obvious influences of culture on male and female gender roles and behaviour have been in the area of traditional versus non-traditional views. In the traditional view, women are seen as more responsible for domestic duties: child-rearing, home care, cooking, and so on. Men are seen as more responsible for the external activities of working to feed the family and chores that require heavy physical labour, such as farming or construction work. For a long time, the traditional view of the roles of the sexes prevailed in cross-cultural research, which some have seen as caused by the biological differences between men and women: Not only do men have more physical upper body strength, which might be needed for heavy physical labour, but also men are freer than women in some senses, as women are the bearers of children and are responsible for breastfeeding their infants (Best & Williams, 2001).

In the past few decades, however, a change has occurred in cultures that are of different "personalities." Cultures that are more individualistic and have fairly high standards of living are becoming more non-traditional, especially for women in those cultures, whereas the more traditional views seem to be held by collectivistic cultures that have less wealth; although even in the latter, women are more likely to be less traditional than men (Gibbons et al., 1991). Other studies have found that the most non-traditional ideas about gender roles and gender behaviour are found in countries such as the Netherlands, Germany, Italy, and England, whereas the most traditional ideas predominate in African and Asian countries such as Nigeria, Pakistan, and -Japan (Best & Williams, 2001). The United States, often seen as very non-traditional by researchers, actually was somewhere in the middle in these studies, perhaps because of the large variation in subcultures that exists within this multicultural country. Although Canada was not included in this particular set of studies, it is reasonable to assume that it would also fall somewhere in the middle because of its multicultural nature. Environment, even in the form of culture, seems to play at least a partial and perhaps dominant role in gender behaviour.

PRACTICE QUIZ: HOW MUCH DO YOU REMEMBER?

Pick the best answer.

1. Developing a person's sense of being male or female is called
   a. gender role.
   c. gender typing.
   b. gender identity.
   d. gender stereotyping.

2. Which of the following is not a biological influence on gender?
   a. hormones secreted during fetal development
   b. the influence of hormones taken by the pregnant mother
   c. exposure to playmates of a particular gender
   d. sex chromosomes

3. In _____ cultures, gender roles are seen as more traditional, whereas in _____ cultures they may be more non-traditional, especially for women.
   a. individualistic; collectivistic
   b. collectivistic; individualistic
   c. European; Asian
   d. affluent; poor

Answers: 1-b, 2-c, 3-b.

THEORIES OF GENDER ROLE DEVELOPMENT

8.11 *What are the theories about how children learn their gender roles?*

How do children acquire the knowledge of their society or culture's gender role expectations? How does that knowledge lead to the development of a gender identity? Although early psychodynamic theorists such as Freud, (L)(I)(N)(K) *to Chapter Eleven: Theories of Personality, p. 438,* believed that children would learn their gender identities as a natural consequence of resolving the sexual conflicts of early childhood, many modern theorists focus on learning and cognitive processes for the development of gender identity and behaviour.

SOCIAL LEARNING THEORY   Social learning theory, which emphasizes learning through observation and imitation of models, attributes gender role development to those processes. Children observe their same-sex parents behaving in certain ways and imitate that behaviour. When the children imitate the appropriate gender behaviour, they are reinforced with positive attention. Inappropriate gender behaviour is either ignored or actively discouraged (Fagot & Hagan, 1991; Mischel, 1966).

Of course, parents are not the only gender role models available to children. In addition to older brothers and sisters, family friends, teachers, and peers, children are exposed to male and female behaviour on television and in other media. In fact, television, movies, and children's books are often filled with very traditional male and female roles. In these books, doctors are males and nurses are female far more often than the other way around, for example. Although some children's books and television programs make a genuine effort to present males and females in non-typical occupations, there are far more that maintain traditional roles for men and women. All one has to do to find evidence of these traditional gender roles in the media is watch a Disney movie: The heroes are usually good-looking, overly muscled men, while the women are weaker than the men and often need to be rescued.

GENDER SCHEMA THEORY   A theory of gender role development that combines social learning theory with cognitive development is called **gender schema theory** (Bem, 1987, 1993). In this theory, based on the Piagetian concept of schemas, children develop a schema, or mental pattern, for being male or female in much the same way that they develop schemas for other concepts, such as "dog." As their brains mature, they become capable of distinguishing among various concepts. For example, a "dog" might at first be anything with four legs and a tail, but as a child encounters dogs and other kinds of animals and is given instruction, "dog" becomes more specific and the schema for "dog" becomes well defined.

In a similar manner, children develop a concept for "boy" and "girl." Once that schema is in place, children can identify themselves as "boy" or "girl" and will notice other members of that schema. They notice the behaviour of other "boys" or "girls" and imitate that behaviour. Rather than being simple imitation and reinforcement, as in social learning theory, children acquire their gender role behaviour by organizing that behaviour around the schema of "boy" or "girl."

ADOLESCENCE

Adolescence is the period of life from about age 13 to the early 20s, during which a young person is no longer physically a child but is not yet an independent, self-supporting adult. In the past, adolescence was always defined as the "teens," from ages 13 to 19. But adolescence isn't necessarily determined by chronological age. It also concerns how a person deals with life issues such as work, family, and relationships. So although there is a clear age of onset, the end of adolescence may come early or late for different individuals.

PHYSICAL DEVELOPMENT
I thought that adolescence was just the physical changes that happen to your body.

👁 **Watch** on **mypsychlab**
Gender Versus Sex: Florence Denmark

As children develop the concept of gender, they begin to imitate the behaviour of those they see as similar to themselves. This young girl is learning that women wear cosmetics while she plays at helping her mother put on her makeup. As she grows, she will incorporate more of her mother's behaviour and ideas about what it is to be female into her own personality.

I thought that adolescence was just the physical changes that happen to your body.

puberty
the physical changes that occur in the body as sexual development reaches its peak.

PUBERTY

8.12 *What are the physical, cognitive, and personality changes that occur in adolescence, including concepts of morality and Erikson's search for identity?*

The clearest sign of the beginning of adolescence is the onset of **puberty**, the physical changes in both *primary sex characteristics* (growth of the actual sex organs such as the penis or the uterus) and *secondary sex characteristics* (changes in the body such as the development of breasts and body hair) that occur in the body as sexual development reaches its peak.. Puberty occurs as the result of a complex series of glandular activities, stimulated by the "master gland," or the pituitary gland, when the proper genetically determined age is reached. Certain psychosocial and environmental factors such as stress, exercise, and nutrition may also have an impact on the timing of puberty (Ellis et al., 1999; Graber et al., 1995). The thyroid gland increases the rate of growth, the adrenal glands and sex glands stimulate the growth of characteristics such as body hair, muscle tissue in males, and the menstrual cycle in girls, for example (Grumbach & Kaplan, 1990; Grumbach & Styne, 1998). Puberty often begins about two years after the beginning of the *growth spurt*, the rapid period of growth that takes place at around age 10 for girls and around age 12 for boys.

In addition to an increase in height, physical characteristics related to being male or female undergo rapid and dramatic change. In fact, the rate of growth and development in puberty approaches that of development in the womb. For females, breast tissue begins to enlarge, hips begin to widen, the uterus grows, and eventually the menstrual cycle begins. For boys, the penis and testicles increase in size, muscles become more defined, and the voice begins to deepen. For both sexes, oily secretions increase (causing pimples and even acne in many teens), hair grows on the pubic area and under the arms, and body odour becomes more noticeable. After about four years, the changes of puberty are relatively complete.

COGNITIVE DEVELOPMENT

If I'm remembering correctly, teenagers should be in Piaget's formal operations stage. So why don't many teenagers think just like adults? The cognitive development of adolescents is less visible than the physical development but still represents a major change in the way adolescents think about themselves, their peers and relationships, and the world around them.

PIAGET'S FORMAL OPERATIONS REVISITED Adolescents, especially those who receive a formal high-school education, move into Piaget's final stage of formal operations, in which abstract thinking becomes possible. This cognitive advance is primarily due to the final development of the frontal lobes of the brain, the part

If I'm remembering ▶ correctly, teenagers should be in Piaget's formal operations stage. So why don't many teenagers think just like adults?

Reprinted with special permission of King Features Syndicate.

of the brain that is responsible for organizing, understanding, and decision making (Giedd et al., 1999; Sowell et al., 1999). Teenagers begin to think about hypothetical situations, leading to a picture of what an "ideal" world would be like. Many become convinced that such a world is possible to achieve if only everyone else would just listen to the teenager.

As discussed earlier, Piaget's concept of stages has been criticized as too simplistic. The evidence now points to gradual, continuous cognitive development (Feldman, 2003; Siegler, 1996). Even so, Piaget's theory has had a tremendous impact in the education of children and in stimulating research about children's cognitive development (Satterly, 1987). Children from different cultures usually come to understand the world in the way that Piaget described, although the age at which this understanding comes varies from one child to another.

Although headed into an adult style of thinking, adolescents are not yet completely free of egocentric thought. At this time in life, however, their egocentrism shows up in their preoccupation with their own thoughts. They do a lot of introspection (turning inward) and may become convinced that their thoughts are as important to others as they are to themselves. Two ways in which this adolescent egocentrism emerges are the personal fable and the imaginary audience (Elkind, 1985; Lapsley et al., 1986; Vartanian, 2000).

In the **personal fable**, adolescents have spent so much time thinking about their own thoughts and feelings that they become convinced that they are special and that no one else has ever had these thoughts and feelings before them. The personal fable is not without a dangerous side. Because they feel unique, teenagers may feel that they are somehow protected from the dangers of the world and so do not take the precautions that they should. This may result in an unwanted pregnancy, severe injury or death while racing in a car, drinking and driving, and drug use, to name a few possibilities.

The **imaginary audience** shows up as extreme self-consciousness in adolescents. They become convinced that *everyone is looking at them* and that they are always the centre of everyone else's world, just as they are the centre of their own. This explains the intense self-consciousness that many adolescents experience concerning what others think about how the adolescent looks or behaves.

MORAL DEVELOPMENT   Another important aspect in the cognitive advances that occur in adolescence concerns the teenager's understanding of "right" and "wrong." Harvard University professor Lawrence Kohlberg was a developmental psychologist who, influenced by Piaget and others, developed a theory of the development of moral thinking. Through looking at how people of various ages responded to stories about people caught up in moral dilemmas (see Figure 8.7 for a typical story), Kohlberg (1973) outlined three levels of moral development, or the knowledge of right and wrong behaviour. These levels are summarized in Table 8.3, along with an example of each type of thinking.

Although these stages are associated with certain age groups, adolescents and adults can be found at all three levels. For example, a juvenile delinquent tends to be preconventional in moral thinking.

Kohlberg's theory has been criticized as being male oriented, especially since he used only males in his studies (Gilligan, 1982). Carol Gilligan (1982) proposed that men and women have different perspectives on morality: Men tend to judge as moral the actions that lead to a fair or just end, whereas women tend to judge as moral the actions that are non-violent and hurt the fewest people. There still exists much debate as to whether gender differences really exist in moral development. Gilligan

personal fable
type of thought common to adolescents in which young people believe themselves to be unique and protected from harm.

imaginary audience
type of thought common to adolescents in which young people believe that other people are just as concerned about the adolescent's thoughts and characteristics as they themselves are.

FIGURE 8.7 **Example of a Moral Dilemma** *Source*: Kohlberg, 1969, p. 379.

Example of a Moral Dilemma

A woman in Europe was dying from a rare disease. Her only hope was a drug that a local druggist had discovered. The druggist was charging ten times more than it cost him to make it. Heinz, the husband of the dying woman, had desperately tried to borrow money to buy the drug, but he could borrow only half of the amount he needed. He went to the druggist, told him that his wife was dying, and asked to let him pay the druggist later or to sell the drug at a lower cost. The druggist refused, saying that he had discovered the drug and he was going to make money from it. Later, Heinz broke into the druggist's store to steal the drug for his wife. Should Heinz have done that? Why?

and others (e.g., Baumrind, 1986; Finlay & Love, 1998) believe that there are gender differences in moral development, while others have not found consistent support for such differences. For example, Larry Walker (1984, 1986, 1989, 1991), from the University of British Columbia, has done a lot of research on moral development and has found that the moral reasoning of males and females is extremely similar.

PSYCHOSOCIAL DEVELOPMENT

The development of personality and social relationships in adolescence primarily concerns the search for a consistent sense of self or personal identity.

ERIKSON'S IDENTITY VERSUS ROLE CONFUSION The psychosocial crisis that must be faced by the adolescent, according to Erikson, is that of **identity versus role confusion** (see Table 8.2 on p. 327). In this stage, the teenager must choose from among many options for values in life and beliefs concerning things such as political issues, career options, and marriage (Feldman, 2003). From those options, a consistent sense of self must be found. Erikson believed that teens who have successfully resolved the conflicts of the earlier four stages are much better "equipped" to resist peer pressure and find their own identity during the adolescent years. Those

preconventional morality
first level of Kohlberg's stages of moral development in which the child's behaviour is governed by the consequences of the behaviour.

conventional morality
second level of Kohlberg's stages of moral development in which the person's behaviour is governed by conforming to the society's norms of behaviour.

postconventional morality
third level of Kohlberg's stages of moral development in which the person's behaviour is governed by moral principles that have been decided on by the individual and which may be in disagreement with accepted social norms.

identity versus role confusion
fifth stage of personality development in which the adolescent must find a consistent sense of self.

TABLE 8.3 **KOHLBERG'S THREE LEVELS OF MORALITY**		
LEVEL OF MORALITY	**HOW RULES ARE UNDERSTOOD**	**EXAMPLE**
Preconventional* morality (typically very young children)	The consequences determine morality; behaviour that is rewarded is right, that which is punished is wrong.	A child who steals a toy from another child and does not get caught does not see that action as wrong.
Conventional morality (older children, adolescents, and most adults)	Conformity to social norms is right; nonconformity is wrong.	A child criticizes his or her parent for speeding because speeding is against the stated laws.
Postconventional morality (about 20 percent of the population)	Moral principles determined by the person are used to determine right and wrong and may disagree with societal norms.	A reporter who wrote a controversial story goes to jail rather than reveal the source's identity.

*The term *conventional* refers to general standards or norms of behaviour for a particular society, which will differ from one social group or culture to another.

teens who are not as successful come into the adolescent years with a lack of trust in others, feelings of guilt and shame, low self-esteem, and dependency on others. Peer pressure is quite effective on teenagers who desperately want to "fit in" and have an identity of some sort and who feel that others will not want to be with them unless they conform to the expectations and demands of the peer group. They play the part of the model child for the parents, the good student for the teachers, and the "cool" juvenile delinquent to their friends and will be confused about which of the many roles they play are really their own identity.

PARENT–TEEN CONFLICT   Even for the majority of adolescents who end up successfully finding a consistent sense of self, there will be conflicts with parents. Many researchers believe that a certain amount of "rebellion" and conflict is a necessary step in breaking away from childhood dependence on the parents and becoming a self-sufficient adult. Although many people think that these conflicts are intense and concern very serious behaviour, the reality is that most parent–teen conflict is over trivial issues—hair, clothing, taste in music, and so on. On the really big moral issues, most parents and teens would be quite surprised to realize that they are in agreement.

Actresses Lindsay Lohan, Amanda Seyfried, Lacey Chabert, and Rachel McAdams on the set of Mark S. Waters's comedy movie *Mean Girls*. This movie portrays the ins and outs of peer pressure and the desire to fit in that many adolescents face.

Watch on **mypsychlab**
Josh: Adolescence and Making Choices

PRACTICE QUIZ: HOW MUCH DO YOU REMEMBER?

Pick the best answer.

1. Which of the following statements about adolescence is FALSE?
   a. It begins with the onset of puberty.
   b. It is a time during which the young person is no longer a child but is not yet an adult.
   c. It ends when puberty is complete.
   d. It is a time of preoccupation with one's own thoughts.

2. Which term refers to the feeling of being unique and protected?
   a. formal operations
   b. imaginary audience
   c. personal fable
   d. puberty

3. According to Kohlberg, most adolescents are at the _____ level of morality.
   a. preconventional
   b. conventional
   c. postconventional
   d. preliminary

4. According to Erikson, the task of the adolescent is to
   a. find a consistent sense of self.
   b. develop a sense of initiative.
   c. find intimacy with another.
   d. develop a sense of industry.

5. Which of the following issues typically creates a lot of conflict between most teens and their parents?
   a. serious issues of drug and alcohol use
   b. trivial issues of hair, clothing, and music choices
   c. issues of postconventional morality
   d. issues of achieving an identity

Answers: 1-c, 2-c, 3-b, 4-a, 5-b.

ADULTHOOD

When exactly does adulthood begin? Adulthood can be thought of as the period of life from the early 20s onward. Exactly when adulthood begins is not always easy to determine. In some cultures, adulthood is reached soon after puberty (Bledsoe & Cohen, 1993; Ocholla-Ayayo et al., 1993). Some people feel that it begins after graduation from high school, whereas others would say adulthood doesn't begin until after graduation from college or university. Others define it as the point when a person becomes totally self-sufficient with a job and a home separate from his or her parents.

When exactly does adulthood begin?

8.13 *What are the physical, cognitive, and personality changes that occur during adulthood and aging, including Erikson's last three psychosocial stages and patterns of parenting?*

PHYSICAL DEVELOPMENT

Aging is usually portrayed in a negative light, which often leads to stereotypes of the elderly and **ageism**. Before you read the section below, it is important to note that even though most people do slow down with age (compared to when they were in their 20s), many also find that with age comes stability and happiness. Healthy older adults with strong social support networks report higher levels of satisfaction and have fewer complaints compared to younger adults.

Adulthood can also be divided into at least three periods: young adulthood, middle age, and late adulthood. Physical changes in young adulthood are relatively minimal. The 20s are a time of peak physical health, sharp senses, and mature cognitive abilities; but, even in the early 20s, the signs of aging are already beginning. Oil glands in the neck and around the eyes begin to malfunction, contributing to wrinkles in those areas near the end of the 20s and the beginning of the 30s. The 30s may not bring noticeable changes, but vision and hearing are beginning to decline and by around age 40, bifocal lenses may become necessary as the lens of the eye hardens, becoming unable to change its shape to shift focus.

In the 40s, skin begins to show more wrinkles, hair turns grey (or falls out), vision and hearing decline further, and physical strength may begin to decline (Frontera et al., 1991). In the 50s, these changes continue. Throughout middle age, if exercise is not a priority, weight may increase as the rate at which the body functions slows down. Height begins to decrease, with about a centimetre of height lost for every 10 years past age 40, although people with the bone-loss disease osteoporosis may lose up to 20 centimetres or more (Cummings & Melton, 2002). Although sexual functioning usually does not decline in middle age, opportunities for sexual activity may be fewer than in the days of young adulthood (Hodsen & Skeen, 1994; Williams, 1995). Children, mortgages, and career worries can put a damper on middle-age romance.

"I don't eat organic foods. At my age I can use all the preservatives I can get."

Cartoonstock Nicola Jones nikj@cartoonstock.com

ageism
discrimination against individuals because of their age.

MENOPAUSE   For women, the 40s are a time of great physical changes. At this time in life a woman's reproductive organs become unreliable, as levels of the female hormone estrogen decline in preparation for the end of reproduction. The uterus slowly begins to get smaller in size, menstrual cycles become irregular, and some women begin to experience "hot flashes," a sudden sensation of heat and sweating that may keep them up at night. Interestingly, in some cultures, particularly those in which the diet contains high amounts of soy products, hot flashes are almost nonexistent (Cassidy et al., 1994; Lock, 1994). These changes are called the *climacteric*, and the period of 5 to 10 years over which these changes occur is called *perimenopause*. At an average age of 51, most women will cease ovulation altogether, ending their reproductive years. The cessation of ovulation and the menstrual cycle is called **menopause** (Mishell, 2001).

Do men go through anything like menopause? Men also go through a time of sexual changes, but it is much more gradual and less dramatic than menopause. In males, **andropause** (Carruthers, 2001) may begin in the mid 20s with a decline in several hormones, primarily testosterone (the major male hormone). Physical symptoms are also less dramatic but no less troubling: fatigue, irritability, possible problems in sexual functioning, and reduced sperm count. Males, however, rarely lose all reproductive ability.

EFFECTS OF AGING ON HEALTH   It is in middle age that many health problems first occur, although their true cause may have begun in the young adulthood years. Young adults may smoke, drink heavily, stay up late, and fail to protect their skin from sun damage, and the wear and tear that this lifestyle causes on their bodies will not become obvious until their 40s and 50s.

Some of the common health problems that may show up in middle age are high blood pressure, skin cancer, heart problems, arthritis, and obesity. High blood pressure can be caused by lifestyle factors such as obesity and stress but may also be related to hereditary factors (Rudd & Osterberg, 2002). Sleep problems, such as loud snoring and sleep apnea (in which breathing stops for 10 seconds or more), may also take their toll on physical health. There is some evidence that high blood pressure

menopause
the cessation of ovulation and menstrual cycles and the end of a woman's reproductive capability.

andropause
gradual changes in the sexual hormones and reproductive system of males.

◄ Do men go through anything like menopause?

Cartoonstock Nicola Jones nikj@cartoonstock.com

and sleep apnea are linked, although the link may be as simple as the common cause of obesity (Nieto et al., 2000). The most common causes of death in middle age are heart disease, cancer, and stroke—in that order (McGinnis & Foege, 1993).

COGNITIVE DEVELOPMENT

Intellectual abilities do not decline overall, although speed of processing does slow down. Compared to a younger adult, a middle-aged person may take a little longer to solve a problem. However, a middle-aged person also has more life experience and knowledge to bring to bear on a problem, which counters the lack of speed. In one study (Salthouse, 1984), for example, older typists were found to outperform younger typists, even though they typed more slowly than the younger subjects. The older typists, because of years of practice, had developed a skill of looking farther ahead in the document they were typing, so that they could type more continuously without looking back at the document. This allowed them to complete their typing more quickly than the younger typists.

CHANGES IN MEMORY Changes in memory ability are probably the most noticeable changes in middle-age cognition. People find themselves having a hard time remembering a particular word or someone's name. This difficulty in retrieval is probably not evidence of a physical decline (or the beginning of Alzheimer's disease) but is more likely caused by the stresses a middle-aged person experiences and the sheer amount of information that a person of middle years must try to keep straight (Craik, 1994; Launer et al., 1995; Sands & Meredith, 1992).

HOW TO KEEP YOUR BRAIN YOUNG People who exercise their mental abilities have been found to be far less likely to develop memory problems and even senile dementias such as Alzheimer's disease in old age (Ball et al., 2002; Colcombe et al., 2003; Fiatarone, 1996). Working challenging crossword puzzles, for example, can be a major factor in maintaining a healthy level of cognitive functioning. Reading, having an active social life, taking classes, and staying physically active can all have a positive impact on the continued well-being of the brain (Bosworth & Schaie, 1997; Cabeza et al., 2002; Singh-Manoux et al., 2003). Because there has been so much focus on the importance of performing mental exercises, many people don't realize how important physical activity is when it comes to maintaining cognitive functioning. According to Kenneth Rockwood and Laura Middleton of Dalhousie University in Halifax, the risk of cognitive problems such as Alzheimer's disease is lower in people who engage in physical activity than in people who do not exercise (Rockwood & Middleton, 2007).

PSYCHOSOCIAL DEVELOPMENT

In adulthood, concerns involve career, relationships, family, and approaching old age. The late teens and early 20s may be college or university years for many, although other young people go to work directly from high school. The task of choosing and entering a career is very serious and a task that many young adults have difficulty accomplishing. A post-secondary student may change majors more than once during the first few years of college or university, and even after obtaining a bachelor's degree many may either get a job in an unrelated field or go on to a different type of career choice in graduate school. Those who are working may also change careers several times and may experience periods of unemployment while between jobs.

ERIKSON'S INTIMACY VERSUS ISOLATION: FORMING RELATIONSHIPS In young adulthood, Erikson saw the primary task to be finding a mate. True **intimacy** is an

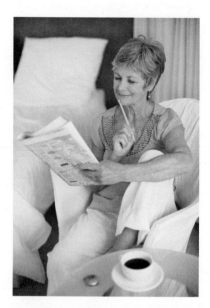

This middle-aged woman works on a crossword puzzle. Mental exercises such as this are one way to keep the brain healthy and fit. What might be some other ways to exercise one's brain?

intimacy
an emotional and psychological closeness that is based on the ability to trust, share, and care, while still maintaining a sense of self.

emotional and psychological closeness that is based on the ability to trust, share, and care, while still maintaining one's sense of self. ⓛⓘⓝⓚ *to Chapter Twelve: Social Psychology, p. 476.* Young adults who have difficulty trusting others and who are unsure of their own identities may find *isolation* instead of intimacy—loneliness, shallow relationships with others, and even a fear of real intimacy.

Erikson saw **intimacy versus isolation** as the sixth stage of personality development. For example, many marriages end in divorce within a few years, with one partner leaving the relationship—and even the responsibilities of parenting—to explore personal concerns and those unfinished issues of identity.

ERIKSON'S GENERATIVITY VERSUS STAGNATION: PARENTING   In middle adulthood, persons who have found intimacy can now focus outward on others (see Table 8.2 on p. 327). Erikson saw this as parenting the next generation and helping them through their crises, a process he called **generativity**. Educators, supervisors, health-care professionals, doctors, and community volunteers might be examples of positions that allow a person to be generative. Those who are unable to focus outward but are still dealing with issues of intimacy or even identity are said to be *stagnated.* People who frequently hand the care of their children over to grandparents or other relatives so that they can go out and "have fun" may be unable to focus on anyone else's needs but their own. Erikson considered **generativity versus stagnation** the seventh stage of personality development.

What kind of parent is the best parent—one who's really strict or one who's pretty easy going?

Parenting Styles   Parenting children is a very important part of most people's middle adulthood. Diana Baumrind (1967) outlined three basic styles of parenting, each of which may be related to certain personality traits in the child raised by that style of parenting.

Authoritarian parenting tends to be overly concerned with rules. This type of parent is stern, rigid, demanding perfection, controlling, uncompromising,* and has a tendency to use physical punishment. The parent who does the punishment often shows little warmth or affection to the child—which may be from a desire to appear stern more than from an actual lack of love. Children raised in this way are often insecure, timid, withdrawn, and resentful. As teenagers, they will very often rebel against parental authority in very negative and self-destructive ways, such as delinquency (criminal acts committed by minor children), drug use, or premarital sex (Baumrind, 1991, 2005).

Permissive parenting occurs when parents put very few demands on their children for behaviour. Parents who have a **permissive neglectful parenting** style simply aren't involved with their children; they ignore them and allow them to do whatever they want, until it interferes with what the parents want. At that point, this relationship may become an abusive one. With **permissive indulgent parenting**, parents seem to be too involved with their children. They allow their "little angels" to behave in any way they wish, refusing to set limits on the child's behaviour or to require any kind of rules for fear of having a negative impact on the child's natural development or for fear that the child will not love them if they set and enforce limits. Children from both kinds of permissive parenting tend to be selfish, immature, dependent, lacking in social skills, and unpopular with peers.

---

*Uncompromising: not making or accepting any viewpoint other than one's own, allowing no other viewpoints.

intimacy versus isolation
sixth stage of personality development in which in which those in early adulthood strive to share who they are with another person in a close, committed relationship.

generativity
providing guidance to one's children or the next generation, or contributing to the well-being of the next generation through career or volunteer work.

generativity versus stagnation
seventh stage of personality development in which those in middle adulthood strive to be creative, productive, and nurturant of the next generation.

authoritarian parenting
style of parenting in which parent is rigid and overly strict, showing little warmth to the child.

◀ What kind of parent is the best parent—one who's really strict or one who's pretty easy going?

◀●⃞ Simulate on **mypsychlab**
Baumrind's Parenting Styles

permissive parenting
style of parenting in which parent makes few, if any, demands on a child's behaviour.

permissive neglectful parenting
style of permissive parenting in which parents are uninvolved with child or child's behaviour.

permissive indulgent parenting
style of permissive parenting in which parents are so involved that children are allowed to behave without set limits.

Authoritative parenting involves combining firm limits on behaviour with love, warmth, affection, respect, and a willingness to listen to the child's point of view. Authoritative parents are more democratic, allowing the child to have some input into the formation of rules but still maintaining the role of final decision maker. Punishment tends to be nonphysical, such as restrictions, time outs, or loss of privileges. Authoritative parents set limits that are clear and understandable, and when a child crosses the limits, they allow an explanation and then agree on the right way to handle the situation.

PRACTICE QUIZ: HOW MUCH DO YOU REMEMBER?

Pick the best answer.

1. The period of 5 to 10 years during which a woman's reproductive system begins to decline is called
   a. climacteric.
   b. perimenopause.
   c. menopause.
   d. all of the above.

2. Which of the following has NOT been shown to help maintain a healthy level of cognitive functioning?
   a. working crossword puzzles
   b. reading
   c. going to plays
   d. relaxing

3. According to Erikson, achieving true intimacy is difficult if one's _____ is not already established.
   a. identity
   b. independence
   c. career
   d. marriage

4. According to Baumrind, _____ parenting may lead to an abusive relationship.
   a. authoritarian
   b. authoritative
   c. permissive neglectful
   d. permissive indulgent

Answers: 1-b, 2-d, 3-a, 4-c.

authoritative parenting
style of parenting in which parents combine warmth and affection with firm limits on a child's behaviour.

integrity versus despair
eighth and final stage of personality development in which those in late adulthood strive to reach wisdom, spiritual tranquility, a sense of wholeness, and acceptance of his or her life.

integrity
sense of wholeness that comes from having lived a full life and the ability to let go of regrets; the final completion of the ego.

Why do people have to age? What makes us grow older, get wrinkles, and so on? ►

ERIKSON'S EGO INTEGRITY VERSUS DESPAIR: DEALING WITH MORTALITY As a person's life enters the stage known as *late adulthood*, the reality of one's eventual death becomes more and more difficult to ignore (see Table 8.2 on p. 327). Erikson (1980) believed that at this time, people enter the **integrity versus despair** stage of personality development. They look back on the life they have lived in a process called a *life review*. In the life review, people must deal with mistakes, regrets, and unfinished business. If people can look back and feel that their lives were relatively full and can come to terms with regrets and losses, then a feeling of **integrity** or wholeness results. Integrity is the final completion of the identity, or ego. If people have many regrets and lots of unfinished business, they feel *despair*, a sense of deep regret over things that will never be accomplished because time has run out.

THEORIES OF AGING

8.14 *How do psychologists explain why aging occurs, and what are the stages of death and dying?*

Why do people have to age? What makes us grow older, get wrinkles, and so on? There are a number of theories of why people physically age. One theory states that the hormonal system gets out of balance, causing the immune system that keeps people healthy to start failing. But this theory fails to state why the hormonal system fails in the first place. Another has to do with the effect of outside influences, whereas two others have to do with biological influences.

CELLULAR CLOCK THEORY   One of the biologically based theories is the *cellular clock theory* (Hayflick, 1977). In this theory, cells are limited in the number of times they can reproduce to repair damage. Evidence for this theory is the existence of *telomeres*, structures on the ends of chromosomes that shorten each time a cell reproduces (Martin & Buckwalter, 2001). When telomeres are too short, cells cannot reproduce and damage accumulates, resulting in the effects of aging.

WEAR-AND-TEAR THEORY   The theory that points to outside influences such as stress, physical exertion, and bodily damage is known as the *wear-and-tear theory of aging.* In this theory, the body's organs and cell tissues simply wear out with repeated use and abuse. Damaged tissues accumulate and produce the effects of aging. *Collagen,* for example, is a natural elastic tissue that allows the skin to be flexible. As people age, the collagen "wears out," becoming less and less "stretchy" and allowing skin to sag and wrinkle (Cua et al., 1990; Kligman & Balin, 1989).

FREE RADICAL THEORY   The *free radical theory* is actually the latest version of the wear-and-tear theory in that it gives a biological explanation for the damage done to cells over time. *Free radicals* are oxygen molecules that have an unstable electron (negative particle). They bounce around the cell, stealing electrons from other molecules and increasing the damage to structures inside the cell. As people get older, more and more free radicals do more and more damage, producing the effects of aging (Hauck & Bartke, 2001; Knight, 1998).

I've heard that most older people just want to be left alone to have some peace and quiet. Is that true?

ACTIVITY THEORY   **Activity theory** (Havighurst et al., 1968) proposes that an elderly person adjusts more positively to aging when remaining active in some way. Even if a career must end, there are other ways to stay active and involved in life. Elderly people who volunteer, who have hobbies, and who also maintain their friendships with others have been shown to be happier and live longer than those who withdraw themselves from activity. Contrary to the view of the elderly as voluntarily withdrawing from activities, the withdrawal of many elderly people is not voluntary at all. Others simply stop inviting elderly people to social activities and including them in their lives.

STAGES OF DEATH AND DYING

There are several ways of looking at the process of dying. One of the more well-known theories is that of Elisabeth Kübler-Ross (1997), who conducted extensive interviews with dying persons and their caretakers.

Figure 8.8 illustrates the five stages of reaction that Kübler-Ross theorized people go through when faced with death (Backer et al., 1994; Kübler-Ross, 1997).

These stages are *denial*, in which people refuse to believe that the diagnosis of death is real; *anger*, which is really anger at death itself and the feelings of helplessness to change things; *bargaining*, in which the dying person tries to make a deal, with doctors or even with God; *depression*, which is sadness from losses already experienced (e.g., loss of a job or one's dignity) and those yet to come (e.g., not being able to see a child grow up); and finally *acceptance*, when the person has accepted the inevitable and quietly awaits death.

✳ Explore on mypsychlab
Ages and Stages of Cognitive and Moral Development

One way to age successfully and maintain psychological health is to remain active and involved in life. This woman is volunteering in a grade school classroom. This not only encourages her to feel useful but also helps her stay mentally alert and socially involved.

◀ I've heard that most older people just want to be left alone to have some peace and quiet. Is that true?

activity theory
theory of adjustment to aging that assumes older people are happier if they remain active in some way, such as volunteering or developing a hobby.

FIGURE 8.8 **Stages of the Grief Cycle** Elisabeth Kübler-Ross believes people go through these five stages of reaction when faced with death.

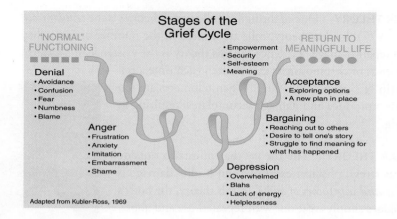

Obviously, some people do not have time to go through all of these stages or even go through them in the listed order (Schneidman, 1983, 1994). Some theorists do not agree with the stage idea, seeing the process of dying as a series of ups and downs, with hope on the rise at times but falling at other times, being replaced by an increase in despair or disbelief (Schneidman, 1983, 1994; Weisman, 1972). Still others question the idea of common reactions among dying people, stating that the particular disease or condition and its treatment, the person's personality before the terminal diagnosis, and other life history factors make the process of dying unique and unpredictable (Kastenbaum & Costa, 1977). The danger in holding too strictly to a stage theory is that people may feel there is a "right" way and a "wrong" way to face death, when in fact each person's dying process is unique.

PRACTICE QUIZ: HOW MUCH DO YOU REMEMBER?

Pick the best answer.

1. In Erikson's last crisis, the life review is
   a. a process of assigning blame.
   b. looking back on the life one has lived.
   c. an analysis of one's parents' lives.
   d. the writing of a biography.

2. A sense of completeness of one's ego, or identity, is called
   a. life review.
   b. intelligence.
   c. integrity.
   d. generativity.

3. According to research, if an older person wants to adjust more positively to aging, he or she should
   a. quietly withdraw from social life.
   b. limit his or her range of activities.
   c. disengage from life.
   d. remain active in some way.

4. In which theory of aging do telomeres become the major means of aging cells?
   a. wear-and-tear theory
   b. cellular clock theory
   c. free radical theory
   d. hormonal imbalance theory

5. In the _____ stage of reaction to death and dying, a person may promise to do everything the doctor says if the doctor will say that the person can live a little longer.
   a. denial
   b. anger
   c. bargaining
   d. depression

Answers: 1.-b, 2.-c, 3.-d, 4.-b, 5.-c.

APPLYING PSYCHOLOGY TO EVERYDAY LIFE: AFFORDABLE PERSONAL GENOMES

8.15 *What are some of the implications of the Human Genome Project?*

Many scientific breakthroughs relating to how exactly the human body is designed have occurred in the past ten years. One of these breakthroughs is the completion of the Human Genome Project. The Human Genome Project began in 1990 and was completed in 2003. In simple terms, a genome is an organism's complete set of DNA. One of the major outcomes of the project was the identification of an estimated 20 000 to 25 000 genes in the human genetic material. More recently, the genomes of single individuals have been sequenced. Drs. J. Craig Venter and James Watson (of the famous scientist pair Watson and Crick) have posted their full genetic codes on the internet for the world to see. Dr. Stephen Scherer and his team at the Centre for Applied Genomics at Toronto's Hospital for Sick Children collaborated on the genetic profiling of Dr. Craig Venter.

It is now estimated that people will be able to buy a profile of their own personal genomes within the next few years for approximately $1000. According to Tim Caulfield of the University of Alberta, this is an incredible achievement that we should be excited about, but we should also beware of the hype and the actual clinical and societal implications. Being able to buy a profile of your own personal genome is good in the sense that if you discover that you're at increased risk for developing heart disease or Alzheimer's disease, you can take preventative measures. However, there are other things to consider. Dr. Scherer cautions that there will not be enough genetic counsellors to meet demand once personal genomes are available to the public. In addition, there are concerns relating to privacy. As argued by David Wiesenthal and Neil Wiener of York University, genetic testing may result in a significant loss of people's privacy rights (Canadian Press, 2007).

Questions for Further Discussion

1. How would you feel if your complete genome was available to the public?

2. What are some of the positive and negative implications of knowing your complete DNA profile?

CHAPTER SUMMARY

Issues in Studying Human Development

8.1 *What are some of the special research methods used to study development?*

- Three special research methods used in developmental research are the longitudinal design, the cross-sectional design, and the cross-sequential design.

8.2 *What is the relationship between heredity and environmental factors in determining development, and how do researchers study such a relationship?*

- The issue of nature (heredity) versus nurture (environmental influences) is the focus of behavioural genetics.

- Researchers can study the relationship between heredity and environmental factors by examining the similarities and differences between monozygotic (identical) and dizygotic (fraternal) twins or by examining the similarities and differences between adopted children and their adoptive and birth families.

Prenatal Development

8.3 *How do chromosomes, genes, and DNA determine a person's characteristics or disorders, and what causes multiple births?*

- A chromosome is a tightly wound strand of genetic material or DNA.

- A gene is a section of DNA having the same arrangement of chemical elements.

- DNA (deoxyribonucleic acid) is a special molecule that contains the genetic material of the organism.

- Dominant genes control the expression of a trait, whereas recessive gene traits are expressed only when paired with another recessive gene for the same trait. Almost all traits are the result of combinations of genes working together in a process called *polygenic inheritance*.

- The most common chromosome disorder is Down syndrome. Examples of genetic disorders include cystic fibrosis and sickle-cell anemia.

- The fertilized egg cell is called a *zygote* and divides into many cells, eventually forming the baby.

- Monozygotic twins are formed when the zygote splits into two separate masses of cells, each of which will develop into a baby almost identical to the other. When the two masses do not fully separate, conjoined twins occur.

- Dizygotic twins are formed when the mother's body releases multiple eggs and at least two are fertilized, or when another ovulation occurs even though the mother has already become pregnant.

- Geneticists have discovered that the environment is not the only contributor to the differences between monozygotic twins—there exist differences at the genetic level as well, which means that "identical" twins are not truly "identical".

Psychology in the News: Tinashe and Tinotenda Mufuka, Saved by Chance

8.4   *How do conjoined twins adjust to being separated?*

- Attached at the torso, conjoined twins Tinashe and Tinotenda were taken to the Hospital for Sick Children in Toronto, where they were separated successfully by doctors.

- Although the twins did experience some physical setbacks, they have experienced no major medical problems.

- The twins are now back home in rural Zimbabwe and have the chance to live life just as any other Zimbabwean brothers would.

8.5   *What happens during the germinal, embryonic, and fetal periods of pregnancy, and what are some hazards in prenatal development?*

- The germinal period is the first two weeks of pregnancy in which the dividing mass of cells (blastocyst) moves down the fallopian tube into the uterus.

- The embryonic period begins at two weeks after conception and ends at eight weeks. The vital organs and structures of the baby form during this period, making it a critical one in which teratogens can affect the development of those organs and structures.

- The fetal period is from the beginning of the ninth week until the birth of the baby. During the fetal period, tremendous growth occurs, length and weight increase, and organs continue to become fully functional.

- Any substance that can cause a birth defect is called a *teratogen*. Common teratogens include drugs, alcohol, and mercury. These teratogens can have numerous negative effects on the developing embryo.

Infancy and Childhood Development

8.6   *What kinds of physical changes take place in infancy and childhood?*

- Four critical areas of adjustment for the newborn are respiration, digestion, circulation, and temperature regulation.

- Infants are born with reflexes that help the infant survive until more complex learning is possible. Some of the reflexes include sucking, rooting, Moro (startle), and grasping.

- The senses, except for vision, are fairly well developed at birth. Vision is blurry and lacking in full colour perception until about 6 months of age. Gross and fine motor skills develop at a fast pace during infancy and early childhood.

- Immunizations are far less dangerous than the diseases they are designed to prevent and are one of the most effective weapons in the fight against infectious diseases.

8.7   *What are two ways of looking at cognitive development, and how does language develop?*

- Piaget's stages include the sensorimotor stage of sensory and physical interaction with the world, preoperational thought in which language becomes a tool of exploration, concrete operations in which logical thought becomes possible, and formal operations in which abstract concepts are understood and hypothetical thinking develops.

- Vygotsky believed that children learn best when being helped by a more highly skilled peer or adult in a process called *scaffolding*. The zone of proximal development is the difference between the mental age of tasks the child performs without help and those the child can perform with help.

- The stages of language development are cooing, babbling, one-word speech (holophrases), and telegraphic speech. Although some language is learned through imitation and reinforcement, infants may possess a language acquisition device (LAD) that governs the learning of language during infancy and early childhood.

8.8   *How do infants and children develop personalities and form relationships with others, and what are Erikson's stages of psychosocial development for children?*

- The three basic infant temperaments are easy (regular, adaptable, and happy), difficult (irregular, non-adaptable, and irritable), and slow to warm up (adjust to change only gradually).

Classic Studies in Psychology: Ainsworth and the Strange Situation Paradigm

- The four types of attachment are secure, avoidant (unattached), ambivalent (insecurely attached), and disorganized-disoriented (insecurely attached and sometimes abused or neglected).

- Harlow's classic research with infant rhesus monkeys demonstrated the importance of contact comfort in the attachment process, contradicting the earlier view that attachment was merely a function of associating the mother with the delivery of food.

- In Erikson's stage of trust versus mistrust, the infant must gain a sense of predictability and trust in caretakers or risk developing a mistrustful nature; in autonomy versus shame and doubt, the toddler needs to become physically independent.

- In initiative versus guilt, the preschool child is developing emotional and psychological independence; in industry versus inferiority, school-age children are gaining competence and developing self-esteem.

8.9   *How are gender roles developed?*

- Gender is the psychological aspects of being male or female.

- Gender roles are the culture's expectations for male and female behaviour and personality.

- Gender typing is the process by which people in a culture learn the appropriate gender role behaviour.

- Gender identity is a one's perception of being male or female and the behaviour that is associated with that gender.

8.10 *How much influence do biology and learning have on gender role development?*

- There are both biological influences, in the form of hormones and chromosomes, and environmental influences, in the form of parenting, surroundings, and culture, on the formation of gender role development.

- Gender stereotyping occurs when people assign characteristics to a person based on the person's male or female status rather than actual characteristics.

8.11 *What are the theories about how children learn their gender roles?*

- Social learning theorists believe that gender identity is formed through reinforcement of appropriate gender behaviour as well as imitation of gender models.
- Gender schema theorists believe that gender identity is a mental schema that develops gradually, influenced by the growth of the brain and organization of observed male or female behaviour around the schema.
- Puberty is a period of about four years during which the sexual organs and systems fully mature and secondary sex characteristics such as body hair, breasts, menstruation, deepening voices, and the growth spurt occur.
- Adolescents engage in two kinds of egocentric thinking called the *imaginary audience* and the *personal fable*.
- Kohlberg proposed three levels of moral development: preconventional morality, conventional morality, and postconventional morality.
- In Erikson's identity versus role confusion crisis the job of the adolescent is to achieve a consistent sense of self from among all the roles, values, and futures open to him or her.

Adolescence

8.12 *What are the physical, cognitive, and personality changes that occur in adolescence, including concepts of morality and Erikson's search for identity?*

- Adolescence is the period of life from about age 13 to the early 20s during which physical development reaches completion.

Adulthood

8.13 *What are the physical, cognitive, and personality changes that occur during adulthood and aging, including Erikson's last three psychosocial stages and patterns of parenting?*

- Adulthood begins in the early 20s and ends with death in old age. It can be divided into young adulthood, middle adulthood, and late adulthood.
- The 20s are the peak of physical health; in the 30s, the signs of aging become more visible. In the 40s, visual problems may occur, weight may increase, strength may decrease, and height begins to decrease.
- Women experience a physical decline in the reproductive system called the *climacteric*, ending at about age 50 with menopause, when a woman's estrogen levels are at zero and her reproductive capabilities are at an end. Men go through andropause, a less dramatic change in testosterone and other male hormones, beginning in the mid 20s.

- Many health problems such as high blood pressure, skin cancers, and arthritis begin in middle age, with the most common causes of death in middle age being heart disease, cancer, and stroke.
- Reaction times slow down, but intelligence and memory remain relatively stable.
- Erikson's crisis of young adulthood is intimacy versus isolation, in which the young person must establish an intimate relationship, usually with a mate.
- Diana Baumrind (1967) outlined three basic styles of parenting, each of which may be related to certain personality traits in the child raised by that style of parenting: Permissive parenting is the style of parenting in which parent makes few, if any demands on a child's behaviour; authoritative parenting is the style of parenting in which parents combine warmth and affection with firm limits on a child's behaviour; and authoritarian parenting is the style of parenting in which the parent is rigid and overly strict, showing little warmth to the child.
- The crisis of middle adulthood is generativity versus stagnation, in which the task of the middle-aged adult is to help the next generation through its crises, either by parenting, mentoring, or working at a career that leaves some legacy to the next generation.
- Erikson's final crisis is integrity versus despair, in which an older adult must come to terms with mortality.

8.14 *How do psychologists explain why aging occurs, and what are the stages of death and dying?*

- Research strongly indicates that remaining active and involved results in the most positive adjustment to aging.
- The cellular clock theory is based on the idea that cells can reproduce only so many times; once that limit is reached, damaged cells begin to accumulate.
- The wear-and-tear theory of physical aging states that as time goes by, repeated use and abuse of the body's tissues cause it to be unable to repair all the damage.
- The free radical theory states that oxygen molecules with an unstable electron move around the cell, damaging cell structures as they go.
- The five stages of reaction to death and dying are denial, anger, bargaining, depression, and acceptance.

Applying Psychology to Everyday Life: Affordable Personal Genomes

8.15 *What are some of the implications of the Human Genome Project?*

- The genome is a person's complete set of DNA.
- One of the major outcomes of the Human Genome Project was the identification of 20 000 to 25 000 genes in human genetic material.
- It is estimated that personal genomes will be available to the public for approximately $1000 in the next five years and, because of this, there will be an increased demand for genetic counsellors.

8 KEY TERMS

activity theory   341
adolescence   331
ageism   336
andropause   337
attachment   323
authoritarian parenting   339
authoritative parenting   340
centration   318
chromosome   307
cognitive development   316
cohort effect   305
conception   309
concrete operations stage   319
conservation   318
conventional morality   334
critical periods   311
cross-sectional design   304
cross-sequential design   304
dizygotic twins   309
DNA (deoxyribonucleic acid)   306
dominant   307
egocentrism   318
embryo   311
embryonic period   311
fertilization   309

fetal period   313
fetus   313
formal operations   319
gender   328
gender identity   328
gender roles   328
gender schema theory   331
gender typing   328
gene   307
generativity   339
generativity versus stagnation   339
genetics   306
germinal period   311
human development   304
identity versus role confusion   334
imaginary audience   333
industry versus inferiority   327
initiative versus guilt   327
integrity   340
integrity versus despair   340
intimacy   338
intimacy versus isolation   339
irreversibility   318
longitudinal design   304

menopause   337
monozygotic twins   309
nature   305
nurture   305
object permanence   317
ovum   309
permissive indulgent parenting   339
permissive neglectful parenting   339
permissive parenting   339
personal fable   333
postconventional morality   334
preconventional morality   334
preoperational stage   317
puberty   332
recessive   307
scaffolding   320
schema   316
sensorimotor stage   317
temperament   323
teratogen   312
zone of proximal development (ZPD)   320
zygote   309

TEST YOURSELF

Pick the best answer.

1. Differences between age groups would cause the most serious problems for which developmental research method?
   a. longitudinal
   b. cross-cultural
   c. cross-sectional
   d. cross-sequential

2. Cystic fibrosis is a _____ disorder if a person has one gene for the disease but does not have cystic fibrosis.
   a. dominant
   b. recessive
   c. sex-linked
   d. polygenic

3. Which of the following represents dizygotic twins?
   a. One egg is fertilized by two different sperm.
   b. One egg splits and is then fertilized by two different sperm.
   c. Two eggs get fertilized by two different sperm.
   d. Two eggs are fertilized by the same sperm.

4. The critical period for pregnancy is the
   a. germinal period.
   b. embryonic period.
   c. fetal period.
   d. last trimester.

5. Which of the following is NOT a risk associated with failing to have a child immunized?
   a. The child may get a deadly disease such as measles or diphtheria.
   b. The child may become immune to the diseases.
   c. Others may be exposed to the diseases that the child can develop.
   d. The child will be more likely to develop a disease with a high fever that can cause brain damage.

6. In the _____ reflex, the baby moves its head toward any light touch to its face.
   a. sucking
   b. startle
   c. rooting
   d. grasping

7. Which of the newborn's senses is the most fully developed at birth?
   a. hearing
   b. vision
   c. smell
   d. touch

8. At what age can the typical infant sit without support?
   a. 3 months
   c. 8 months
   b. 6 months
   d. 12 months
9. By age 5, the brain is at _____ percent of its adult weight.
   a. 25
   c. 90
   b. 50
   d. 100
10. In which of Piaget's stages does the child become capable of understanding conservation?
    a. sensorimotor
    c. formal operational
    b. preoperational
    d. concrete operational
11. According to Vygotsky, giving a child help in the form of asking leading questions and providing examples is called
    a. scaffolding.
    c. private speech.
    b. the zone of proximal development
    d. habituation.
12. Little Kashif held up his empty cup to his mother and said, "Milk!" His use of this word is labelled
    a. a holophrase.
    c. babbling.
    b. telegraphic speech.
    d. cooing.
13. As an infant, Liz never liked change, but if you introduce new things gradually, she will eventually accept them without too much fuss. Liz is most likely
    a. easy.
    c. slow to warm up.
    b. difficult.
    d. securely attached.
14. In the Strange Situation experiment, _____ babies were clingy, were unwilling to explore, were very upset when Mommy left the room, and demanded to be held but pushed her away at the same time when she returned.
    a. secure
    c. ambivalent
    b. avoidant
    d. disorganized-disoriented
15. In Erikson's crisis of _____, children are developing a sense of competence and self-esteem.
    a. trust versus mistrust
    c. initiative versus guilt
    b. autonomy versus shame and doubt
    d. industry versus inferiority
16. In gender schema theory, gender identity
    a. first forms as a mental concept of "boy" or "girl."
    b. is acquired through simple imitation of models.
    c. occurs through observational learning.
    d. is acquired through positive reinforcement of appropriate gender behaviour

17. Samantha refuses to go to school because her chin has a "huge" pimple on it and she is afraid that everyone will laugh at her and point. Samantha is a victim of
    a. the imaginary audience.
    c. abstract egocentrism.
    b. the personal fable.
    d. formal operations.
18. Erikson's fifth stage of psychosocial development is
    a. identity versus role confusion.
    c. generativity versus stagnation.
    b. intimacy versus isolation.
    d. integrity versus despair.
19. Vision and hearing begin to decline in the
    a. 20s.
    c. 40s.
    b. 30s.
    d. 50s.
20. A decline in testosterone in the mid 20s is called
    a. perimenopause.
    c. climacteric.
    b. menopause.
    d. andropause.
21. The crisis of middle adulthood, according to Erikson, is
    a. identity versus role confusion.
    c. generativity versus stagnation.
    b. intimacy versus isolation.
    d. integrity versus despair.
22. Rebellion in the teenage years is the most likely outcome of _____ parenting.
    a. authoritarian
    c. permissive neglectful
    b. authoritative
    d. permissive indulgent
23. Collagen, an elastic tissue that becomes less elastic as we get older, is a good example of the _____ theory of aging.
    a. wear-and-tear
    c. free radical
    b. cellular clock
    d. active
24. According to Kübler-Ross, when bargaining fails, _____ usually results.
    a. denial
    c. depression
    b. anger
    d. acceptance
25. Which of the following is NOT one of the implications of the Human Genome Project?
    a. People will be able to buy their own genome at an affordable price within the next decade.
    b. Researchers will be able to better understand disorders such as schizophrenia.
    c. There will be issues surrounding privacy rights once personal genomes are available.
    d. There will be a decreased need for genetic counsellors once personal genomes are available.

Answers: 1.-c, 2.-b, 3.-c, 4.-b, 5.-b, 6.-c, 7.-d, 8.-b, 9.-c, 10.-d, 11.-a, 12.-a, 13.-c, 14.-c, 15.-d, 16.-a, 17.-a, 18.-a, 19.-b, 20.-d, 21.-c, 22.-a, 23.-a, 24.-c, 25.-c.

ScanLife™ Barcode

To access more tests and your own personalized study plan that will help you focus on the areas you need to master before your next class test, be sure to go to **www.MyPsychLab.com**, Pearson Education Canada's online psychology website, available with the access code packaged with your book.

Developmental Research Methods

Longitudinal design: same participants over a long period

Cross-sectional design: participants of different ages

Cross-sequential design: participants first studied cross-sectionally and then followed for six years

8.1

Heredity and Environmental Factors

▸ Behavioural genetics—nature (hereditary factors) vs. nurture (environmental influences)

▸ Relationship studied by examining the similarities and differences between either monozygotic (identical) and dizygotic (fraternal) twins, or adopted children and their adoptive and birth families

8.2

Prenatal Development

Infancy and Childhood Development

Chromosomes, Genes, DNA, and a Person's Characteristics or Disorders

Chromosome: tightly wound strand of genetic material or DNA

Gene: section of DNA having the same arrangement of chemical elements

DNA (deoxyribonucleic acid): special molecule that contains the genetic material of the organism

Dominant genes: control the expression of a trait

Recessive genes: expressed when paired with another recessive gene

Traits: results of combinations

Most common chromosome disorder: Down syndrome

Genetic disorders: cystic fibrosis, sickle-cell anemia

Zygote: fertilized and dividing egg cell

8.3

Monozygotic and Dizygotic Twins

Monozygotic twins

1 Accounting for about 1 in 250 births, these are created when a single egg is fertilized by one sperm.

2 The egg splits into halves. Each develops into a fetus with almost the same genetic composition.

Dizygotic twins

1 Twice as common as identicals, fraternals arise when two eggs are released at once.

2 If both are fertilized by separate sperm, two fetuses form. Genetically they are just ordinary siblings.

8.4

Germinal, Embryonic, and Fetal Periods— Hazards in Prenatal Development

Germinal period:

▸ First two weeks of pregnancy

▸ Dividing mass of cells (blastocyst) moves down fallopian to uterus

Embryonic period:

▸ Two weeks after conception to eight weeks

▸ Vital organs and structures form during this period.

▸ Teratogens, such as drugs or alcohol, likely to affect the development of organs & structures

Fetal period:

▸ Beginning of ninth week until birth

▸ Tremendous growth occurs, length and weight increase.

▸ Organs continue to become fully functional.

8.5

Physical Changes in Infancy and Childhood

Four critical areas of adjustment for the newborn: respiration, digestion, circulation, and temperature regulation

Infant reflexes aid infant survival: sucking, rooting, Moro (startle), grasping, and stepping

Senses: except for vision, are fairly well developed at birth

Vision: blurry and lacking in full colour perception until infant is 6 months old

Gross and fine motor skills: develop at a fast pace during infancy and early childhood

Facts/Myths Concerning Infant Immunizations

▸ Immunizations far less dangerous than the diseases they prevent.

▸ Most effective weapons in the fight against infectious diseases

8.6

Tow Views of Cognitive Development

Piaget's Stages:

▸ **Sensorimotor stage:** sensory and physical interaction

▸ **Preoperational thought:** language—tool of exploration

▸ **Concrete operations:** logical thought possible

▸ **Formal operations:** abstract concepts and hypothetical thinking

Vygotsky's theory:

▸ **Scaffolding:** Children learn when helped by peer/adult.

▸ **Zone of proximal development:** difference between mental age of tasks child performs without help and with help

Stages of Language Development

cooing, babbling, one-word speech (holophrases), and telegraphic speech

Language Learning

▸ Some learning through reinforcement and imitation

▸ Infants may possess a language acquisition device (LAD) that governs learning of language during infancy and early childhood.

8.7

Development of Personalities and Forming Relationships

Three basic infant temperaments:

▸ **Easy** (regular, adaptable, and happy)

▸ **Difficult** (irregular, non-adaptable, irritable)

▸ **Slow to warm up** adjust to change only gradually

Four types of attachment: secure, avoidant, ambivalent, disorganized-disoriented

8.8

Erikson's First Four Stages of Psychosocial Development

1. **Trust vs. mistrust:** predictability/trust vs. mistrust
2. **Autonomy vs. shame and doubt:** physical independence
3. **Initiative vs. guilt:** emotional/psychological independence
4. **Industry vs. inferiority:** competence and developing self-esteem

Contact comfort and attachment:
- Harlow's classic research demonstrated the importance of contact comfort.
- Contradicted earlier view that attachment was based on mother's food delivery

8.8

HARLOW'S EXPERIMENT

Gender: psychological aspects of being male or female

Gender roles: culture's expectation for male and female behaviour and personality

Gender typing: process by which people in a culture learn appropriate gender role behaviour

Gender identity: person's sense of being male or female

8.9

Gender Role Development

Gender stereotyping occurs when people assign characteristics to a person based on the person's male or female status rather than actual characteristics

8.10

Learning Gender Roles

- **Social learning theorists:** Imitation and reinforcement lead to correct gender behaviour.
- **Gender schema theorists:** gender as a concept that is developed over time

8.11

Adolescence

From age 13 to the early 20s—physical development reaches completion

Puberty

- Period of about four years during which the sexual organs and systems fully mature
- Secondary sex characteristics such as body hair, breasts, menstruation, deepening voice, and growth spurt occur.

8.12

Formal Operations and Moral Thinking

Adolescents engage in two kinds of egocentric thinking: imaginary audience and personal fable.

Kohlberg: Three levels of moral development: preconventional, conventional, and postconventional morality

8.12

Erikson's Adolescent Identity Versus Role Confusion Crisis

Adolescents try to achieve consistent sense of self from among all the roles, values, and futures open to them.

8.12

Adulthood

Adulthood and Aging

Characteristics of aging:
- 20s: peak of physical health
- 30s: Aging becomes more visible.
- 40s: Visual problems occur, weight increases, strength and height decrease.

Gender issues:
- Women: decline in reproductive capacity ending at about age 50 with menopause
- Men: andropause changes in testosterone and other male hormones

Health problems in aging:
- High blood pressure, arthritis, cancer, skin cancers, heart disease, strokes
- Reaction times slow, intelligence/memory remain stable.

8.13

The Human Genome Project

- The genome is a person's complete set of DNA.
- The Human Genome Project identified 20 000–25 000 genes in human genetic material.
- Personal genomes will probably be available to the public for approximately $1000 in the next five years.

8.15

Erikson's Stages in Adulthood

Intimacy vs. isolation: young adulthood—establishing intimate relationships

Generativity vs. stagnation: middle adulthood—help the next generation through its crises

Integrity vs. despair: final crisis—coming to terms with mortality

8.13

Patterns of Parenting

Permissive parenting: style of parenting in which parent makes few, if any demands on a child's behaviour

Authoritative parenting: style of parenting in which parents combine warmth and affection with firm limits on a child's behaviour

Authoritarian parenting: style of parenting in which the parent is rigid and overly strict, showing little warmth to the child

8.13

Theories of Aging

Cellular clock theory: Cells have limited reproduction times.

Wear-and-tear theory: Repeated use and abuse of the body's tissues cause it to be unable to repair all the damage.

Free radical theory: Oxygen molecules with unstable electrons move around the cell, damaging cell structures as they go.

Death and Dying

Five stages of reaction to death and dying: denial, anger, bargaining, depression, and acceptance

8.14

9
Motivation and Emotion

For the Love of the Game

Throughout his professional hockey career, Canadian hockey legend Mario Lemieux experienced many setbacks relating to his health. For example, he had a herniated disk removed in 1990. Because of his back problems, he sat out most of the 1990–1991 season. Despite this injury and his time away from his beloved sport, he returned at the end of the season with unbridled motivation. During the 1991 playoffs, he scored 44 points in 23 games and led his team to the Stanley Cup.

Back problems were not the only health problems Lemieux had to face. In 1992, he was diagnosed with Hodgkin's disease (cancer of the lymphatic system). Despite missing many games because of treatment, Lemieux still managed to win the scoring title that season.

Like Lemieux, many athletes, both professional and amateur, have returned to their sport after bouts with injuries and serious illness because they are highly *motivated* to do so. The stories of such athletes are stores of true motivation.

chapter outline

Why study motivation and emotion?

The study of motivation not only helps us understand why we eat and drink the way we do, but also why some people are more driven to achieve than others. Emotions are a part of everything we do, affecting our relationships with others and our own health, as well as influencing important decisions. In this chapter, we will explore the motives behind our actions and the origins and influences of emotions.

9.1. How do psychologists define motivation, and what are the key elements of the early instinct and drive-reduction approaches to motivation?

9.2. What are the characteristics of the three types of needs?

9.3. What are the key elements of the arousal and incentive approaches to motivation?

9.4. How do Maslow's humanistic approach and self-determination theory explain motivation, and how has evolutionary theory changed how researchers view Maslow's hierarchy?

9.5. What biological and social factors influence hunger?

9.6. What are some problems in eating behaviour?

9.7. What is the difference between intracellular thirst and extracellular thirst?

9.8. How is the sex drive different from the hunger and thirst drives?

9.9. What are the physical differences between females and males, and what does it mean to be "intersex"?

9.10. How did Kinsey study human sexual behaviour, and what were the findings of the Janus Report?

9.11. What are the different sexual orientations, and how do they develop?

9.12. What are the three elements of emotion?

9.13. How does culture affect the expression and interpretation of emotional expressions?

9.14. How do the James–Lange and Cannon–Bard theories of emotion differ?

9.15. What are the key elements in cognitive arousal theory, the facial feedback hypothesis, and the cognitive-mediational theory of emotion?

9.16. How do people get to be high achievers?

APPROACHES TO UNDERSTANDING MOTIVATION

9.1. *How do psychologists define motivation, and what are the key elements of the early instinct and drive-reduction approaches to motivation?*

Motivation is the process by which activities are started, directed, and continued so that physical or psychological needs or wants are met (Petri, 1996). The word itself comes from the Latin word *movere*, which means "to move." Motivation is what "moves" people to do the things they do. For example, when a person is relaxing in front of the television and begins to feel hungry, the physical need for food might cause the person to get up, go into the kitchen, and search for something to eat. If the hunger is great enough, the person might even cook something. The physical need of hunger caused the action (getting up), directed it (going to the kitchen), and sustained the search (finding or preparing something to eat). Hunger is only one example, of course. Loneliness may lead to calling a friend or going to a place where there are people. The desire to get ahead in life motivates many people to go to college or university. Just getting out of bed in the morning is motivated by the need to keep a roof over one's head and food on the table by going to work.

There are different types of motivation. Sometimes people are driven to do something because of an external reward of some sort (or the avoidance of an unpleasant consequence), as when someone goes to work at a job to make money and avoid losing possessions such as a house or a car. (L I N K) *to Chapter Five: Learning, p. 176.* When the motivation is external (coming from outside the self), it is called **extrinsic motivation**. In extrinsic motivation, a person performs an action because it leads to an outcome that is separate from the person (Ryan & Deci, 2000). Examples would be giving a child money for every "A" on a report card, offering a bonus to an employee for increased performance, or tipping a server in a restaurant for good service. The child, employee, and server are motivated to work for the external or extrinsic rewards. In contrast, **intrinsic motivation** is the type of motivation in which a person performs an action because the act itself is rewarding or satisfying in some internal manner.

motivation
the process by which activities are started, directed, and continued so that physical or psychological needs or wants are met.

extrinsic motivation
type of motivation in which a person performs an action because of the potential external rewards that may be obtained as a result.

intrinsic motivation
type of motivation in which a person performs an action because the act itself is rewarding or satisfying in some internal manner.

Previous research has found a negative impact on intrinsic motivation when an external reward is given for the performance (Deci et al., 1999), but a more recent paper by Canadian Judy Cameron and colleagues at the University of Alberta discusses the results of other studies that find negative effects only for tasks that are not interesting in and of themselves (Cameron et al., 2001). When the task itself is interesting to the person, external rewards may increase intrinsic motivation, at least in the short term. Although this recent finding is intriguing, further research is needed to determine whether the long-term effects of extrinsic rewards on intrinsic motivation are consistently negative, as the bulk of the research has shown up to now.

But don't we sometimes do things for both kinds of motives? There are usually elements of both intrinsic and extrinsic motives in many of the things people do. Most teachers, for example, work for money to pay bills (the extrinsic motive) but may also feel that they are helping young children to become better adults in the future, which makes the teachers feel good about themselves (the intrinsic motive).

INSTINCT APPROACHES

One of the earliest approaches to motivation focused on the biologically determined and innate patterns of behaviour that exist in both people and animals called **instincts**. Just as animals are governed by their instincts to do things such as mating and protecting their territory, early researchers proposed that human beings may also be governed by similar instincts (James, 1890; McDougall, 1908). According to these **instinct approach** theorists, in humans the instinct to reproduce is responsible for sexual behaviour, and the instinct for territorial protection may be related to aggressive behaviour.

William McDougall (1908) proposed a total of 18 instincts for humans, including curiosity, flight (running away), pugnacity (aggressiveness), and acquisition (gathering possessions). As the years progressed, psychologists added more and more instincts to the list until there were thousands of proposed instincts. However, none of these early theorists did much more than give names to these instincts. Although there were plenty of descriptions, such as "submissive people possess the instinct of submission," there was no attempt to explain why these instincts exist in humans, if they exist at all (Petri, 1996).

Freud's psychoanalytic theory still includes the concept of instincts that reside in the id (the part of the personality containing all the basic human needs and drives). Link *to Chapter Eleven: Theories of Personality, p. 438.* Even so, instinct approaches have faded away because although they could describe human behaviour, they could not explain it. But these approaches did accomplish one important thing by forcing psychologists to realize that some human behaviour is controlled by hereditary factors. This idea remains central in the study of human behaviour today.

DRIVE-REDUCTION APPROACHES

The next approach to gain support involved the concepts of needs and drives. A **need** is a requirement of some material (such as food or water) that is essential for survival of the organism. When an organism has a need, it leads to a psychological tension as well as a physical arousal that motivates the organism to act in order to fulfill the need and reduce the tension. This tension is called a **drive** (Hull, 1943).

Drive-reduction theory proposes just this connection between internal physiological states and outward behaviour. In this theory, there are two kinds of drives. **Primary drives** are those that involve biological needs of the body such as hunger

But don't we
sometimes do things
for both kinds of
◀ motives?

Call Centre Comics Ozzie info@ callcentercomics.com

instincts
the biologically determined and innate patterns of behaviour that exist in both people and animals.

instinct approach
approach to motivation that assumes people are governed by instincts similar to those of other animals.

need
a requirement of some material (such as food or water) that is essential for survival of the organism.

drive
a psychological tension and physical arousal arising when there is a need that motivates the organism to act in order to fulfill the need and reduce the tension.

drive-reduction theory
approach to motivation that assumes behaviour arises from physiological needs that cause internal drives to push the organism to satisfy the need and reduce tension and arousal.

primary drives
those drives that involve biological needs of the body such as hunger and thirst.

(Top) The human body needs water, especially when a person is working hard or under stress, as this man appears to be. Thirst is a survival need of the body, making it a primary drive, according to drive-reduction theory. What other kinds of needs might be primary drives?

(Bottom) Some people are driven to do strenuous, challenging activities even when there is no physical need to do so. When a drive is acquired through learning, it is called an *acquired*, or *secondary*, *drive*. Fulfilling an acquired drive provides secondary reinforcement. What might this rock climber find reinforcing about scaling this cliff?

acquired (secondary) drives
those drives that are learned through experience or conditioning, such as the need for money or social approval.

homeostasis
the tendency of the body to maintain a steady state.

need for achievement (nAch)
a need that involves a strong desire to succeed in attaining goals, not only realistic ones but also challenging ones.

and thirst, whereas **acquired (secondary) drives** are those that are learned through experience or conditioning, such as the need for money or social approval. If this sounds familiar, it should. The concepts of primary and secondary reinforcers from Chapter Five are related to these drives. Primary reinforcers satisfy primary drives, and secondary reinforcers satisfy acquired, or secondary, drives. Ⓛ Ⓘ Ⓝ Ⓚ *to Chapter Five: Learning, p. 176.*

This theory also includes the concept of **homeostasis**, or the tendency of the body to maintain a steady state. One could think of homeostasis as the body's version of a thermostat—thermostats keep the temperature of a house at a constant level, and homeostasis does the same thing for the body's functions. When there is a primary drive need, the body is in a state of imbalance. This stimulates behaviour that brings the body back into balance, or homeostasis. For example, if Jarrod's body needs food, he feels hunger and the state of tension/arousal associated with that need. He will then seek to restore his homeostasis by eating something, which is the behaviour stimulated to reduce the hunger drive (see Figure 9.1).

Although drive-reduction theory works well to explain the actions people take to reduce tension created by needs, it does not explain all human motivation. Why do people eat when they are not really hungry? People don't always seek to reduce their inner arousal, either—sometimes they seek to increase it. Bungee-jumping, rock climbing, and watching horror movies are all activities that increase the inner state of tension and arousal, and many people love doing these activities. Why would people do such things if they don't reduce some need or restore homeostasis? The answer is complex: There are different types of needs, different effects of arousal, different incentives, and different levels of importance attached to many forms of behaviour. The following theories explore some of these factors in motivation.

DIFFERENT STROKES FOR DIFFERENT FOLKS: NEEDS   Obviously, motivation is about needs. Drive-reduction theory talks about needs, Maslow talks about needs, and many other theories of motivation include the concept of needs or something similar. In many of these theories, most needs are the result of some inner physical drive (such as hunger or thirst) that demands to be satisfied. Even Maslow begins with such physical needs, although later he includes more psychological needs such as self-esteem and companionship. Harvard University psychologist David C. McClelland (1961, 1987) proposed a theory of motivation that highlights the importance of three psychological needs not typically considered by the other theories: achievement, affiliation, and power.

9.2.   *What are the characteristics of the three types of needs?*

Need for Achievement: How to Succeed by Excelling at Everything   The **need for achievement** (abbreviated as **nAch** in McClelland's writings) involves a strong desire to succeed in attaining goals, not only realistic ones but also challenging ones. People who are high in nAch look for careers and hobbies that allow others to evaluate them because these high achievers also need to have feedback about their performance in addition to the achievement of reaching the goal. Although many of these people do become wealthy, famous, and publicly successful, others fulfill their need to achieve in ways that lead only to their own personal success, not material riches—they just want the challenge.

Achievement motivation appears to be strongly related to success in school, occupational success, and the quality and amount of what a person produces (Collins et al., 2004; Gillespie et al., 2002; Spangler, 1992).

Ted Rogers (right), the Canadian billionaire, stands triumphant at the purchase of the Blue Jays baseball team with former Toronto Mayor Mel Lastman (centre) and Paul Godfrey, the Jays' chief executive. Many people who are as wealthy as the Rogers family continue to buy new houses, new businesses, clothing, and cars (among other things) even though they do not need them. This is an example of need for power.

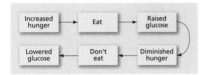

FIGURE 9.1 **Homeostasis** In homeostasis, the body maintains balance in the body's physical states. For example, this diagram shows how increased hunger (a state of imbalance) prompts a person to eat. Eating increases the level of glucose (blood sugar), causing the feelings of hunger to reduce. After a period without eating, the glucose levels become low enough to stimulate the hunger drive once again, and the entire cycle is repeated.

Need for Affiliation: Popularity Rules   Another psychological need is for friendly social interactions and relationships with others. Called the **need for affiliation (nAff)**, people high in this need seek to be liked by others and to be held in high regard by those around them. This makes high affiliation people good team players, whereas a person high in achievement just might run over a few team members on the way to the top.

Need for Power: The One Who Dies with the Most Toys Wins   The final psychological need proposed by McClelland is the **need for power (nPow)**. Power is not about reaching a goal but about having control over other people. People high in this need would want to have influence over others and make an impact on them. They want their ideas to be the ones that are used, regardless of whether their ideas will lead to success. Status and prestige are important, so these people wear expensive clothes, live in expensive houses, drive fancy cars, and dine in the best restaurants. Whereas someone who is a high achiever may not need a lot of money to validate the achievement, someone who is high in the need for power typically sees the money (and cars, houses, jewellery, and other "toys") as the achievement. The subtitle for this section is a saying from a popular bumper sticker but is really a comment on the more negative aspect of the need for power. For the person high in the need for power, it's all about who has the most expensive "toys" in the end.

9.3.   *What are the key elements of the arousal and incentive approaches to motivation?*

AROUSAL APPROACHES

Another explanation for human motivation involves the recognition of yet another type of need, the need for stimulation. A **stimulus motive** is one that appears to be unlearned but causes an increase in stimulation. Examples would be curiosity, playing, and exploration.

In **arousal theory**, people are said to have an optimal (best or ideal) level of tension. Task performances, for example, may suffer if the level of arousal is too high (such as severe test anxiety) or even if the level of arousal is too low (such as boredom). For many kinds of tasks, a moderate level of arousal seems to be best. This relationship between task performance and arousal is called the **Yerkes-Dodson law** (Teigen, 1994; Yerkes & Dodson, 1908). However, this effect is modified by the difficulty level of the task: Easy tasks demand a somewhat "high-moderate" level for optimal

Watch on **mypsychlab**
Carl Rogers on Drive Theory

need for affiliation (nAff)
the need for friendly social interactions and relationships with others.

need for power (nPow)
the need to have control or influence over others.

stimulus motive
a motive that appears to be unlearned but causes an increase in stimulation, such as curiosity.

arousal theory
theory of motivation in which people are said to have an optimal (best or ideal) level of tension that they seek to maintain by increasing or decreasing stimulation.

Yerkes-Dodson law
law stating that performance is related to arousal; moderate levels of arousal lead to better performance than do levels of arousal that are too low or too high. This effect varies with the difficulty of the task: easy tasks require a high-moderate level while more difficult tasks require a low-moderate level.

If people are supposed to be seeking a level of arousal somewhere around the middle, why do some people love to do things like bungee-jumping? ▶

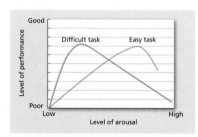

Last Thanksgiving, I had eaten about all I could. Then my aunt brought out her wonderful pumpkin pie and I couldn't resist—I ate a piece, even though I was not at all hungry. What makes us do things even when we don't have the drive or need to do them? ▶

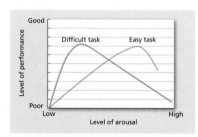

FIGURE 9.2 **Arousal and Performance** The optimal level of arousal for task performance depends on the difficulty of the task. We generally perform easy tasks well if we are highly aroused (green) and accomplish difficult tasks well if we are not very aroused (red).

performance, whereas difficult tasks require a "low-moderate" level. Figure 9.2 shows this relationship in graphic form.

Maintaining an optimal level of arousal, then, may involve reducing tension or creating it (Hebb, 1955). For example, students who experience test anxiety (a high level of arousal) may seek out ways to reduce that anxiety in order to improve test performance. Students who are not anxious at all may not be motivated to study well, lowering their test performance. Many arousal theorists believe that the optimal level of arousal for most people under normal circumstances is somewhere in the middle, neither too high nor too low.

If people are supposed to be seeking a level of arousal somewhere around the middle, why do some people love to do things like bungee-jumping? Even though the average person might require an average level of arousal to feel content, there are some people who need less arousal and some who need more. The person who needs more arousal is called a **sensation seeker** (Zuckerman, 1979, 1994). Sensation seekers seem to need more complex and varied sensory experiences than do other people. The need does not always have to involve danger. For example, students who travel to other countries to study tend to score higher on scales of sensation seeking than do students who stay at home (Schroth & McCormack, 2000). Table 9.1 has some sample items from a typical sensation-seeking scale.

INCENTIVE APPROACHES

Last Thanksgiving, I had eaten about all I could. Then my aunt brought out her wonderful pumpkin pie and I couldn't resist—I ate a piece, even though I was not at all hungry. What makes us do things even when we don't have the drive or need to do them? It's true that sometimes there is no physical need present, yet people still eat, drink, or react as if they did have a need. Even though that piece of pie was not necessary to reduce a hunger drive, it was very rewarding, wasn't it? And on past occasions, that pie was also delicious and rewarding, so there is anticipation of that reward now. The pie becomes an incentive to eat. **Incentives** are things that attract or lure people into action. In fact, the dictionary (Merriam-Webster, 2003) lists *incentive* as meaning the same thing as *motive*.

In **incentive approaches**, behaviour is explained in terms of the external stimulus and its rewarding properties. These rewarding properties exist independently of any need or level of arousal and can cause people to act only upon the incentive. Thus, incentive theory is actually based, at least in part, on the principles of learning that were discussed in Chapter Five. **LINK** *to Chapter Five: Learning, p. 176.*

One of the earliest incentive approaches clearly demonstrates the relationship to learning, particularly the early cognitive learning theories found in the work

TABLE 9.1 SAMPLE ITEMS FROM THE ZUCKERMAN–KUHLMAN PERSONALITY QUESTIONNAIRE	
SCALE ITEM	SENSATION SEEKING
I sometimes do "crazy" things just for fun.	High
I prefer friends who are excitingly unpredictable.	High
I am an impulsive person.	High
Before I begin a complicated job, I make careful plans.	Low
I usually think about what I am going to do before doing it.	Low

Source: Adapted from Zuckerman (2002).

of Edward Tolman (1932). **Expectancy-value theories** are a class of incentive theories based on the work of Tolman and others (Lewin, 1936; Rotter, 1954). In general, these theories assume that the actions of humans cannot be predicted or fully understood without understanding the beliefs, values, and the importance that people attach to those beliefs and values at any given moment in time.

The incentive approach does not explain the motivation behind all behaviour. Many theorists today see motivation as a result of both the "push" of internal needs or drives and the "pull" of a rewarding external stimulus. For example, sometimes a person may actually be hungry (the push) but choose to satisfy that drive by selecting a candy bar instead of a rice cake. The candy bar has more appeal to most people and therefore has more "pull" than the rice cake.

9.4. *How do Maslow's humanistic approach and self-determination theory explain motivation, and how has evolutionary theory changed how researchers view Maslow's hierarchy?*

HUMANISTIC APPROACHES: MASLOW'S HIERARCHY OF NEEDS

Another approach to the study of motivation is based on the work of Abraham Maslow (1987). Maslow was one of the early humanistic psychologists who rejected the dominant theories of psychoanalysis and behaviourism in favour of a more positive view of human behaviour. ⬤L⬤I⬤N⬤K *to Chapter One: The Science of Psychology, p. 2.* Maslow proposed that a person must strive to meet several levels of needs before achieving the highest level of personality fulfillment. According to Maslow, **self-actualization** is the point, which is seldom reached, at which people have satisfied the lower needs and achieved their full human potential.

These needs include both deficiency needs and growth needs. Deficiency needs are needs of the body, such as the need for food or water, whereas growth needs are for desires such as having friends or feeling good about oneself. According to Maslow, for a person to achieve self-actualization, which is the highest level of growth needs, the primary, basic needs must first be fulfilled. Figure 9.3 shows the typical way to

sensation seeker
someone who needs more arousal than the average person.

incentives
things that attract or lure people into action.

incentive approaches
theories of motivation in which behaviour is explained as a response to the external stimulus and its rewarding properties.

expectancy-value theories
incentive theories that assume the actions of humans cannot be predicted or fully understood without understanding the beliefs, values, and the importance that a person attaches to those beliefs and values at any given moment in time.

self-actualization
according to Maslow, the point, which is seldom reached, at which people have sufficiently satisfied the lower needs and achieved their full human potential.

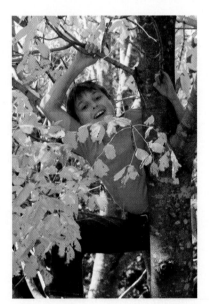

This daring preschool boy has climbed high into this massive tree, and looks as though he might try to climb higher still.

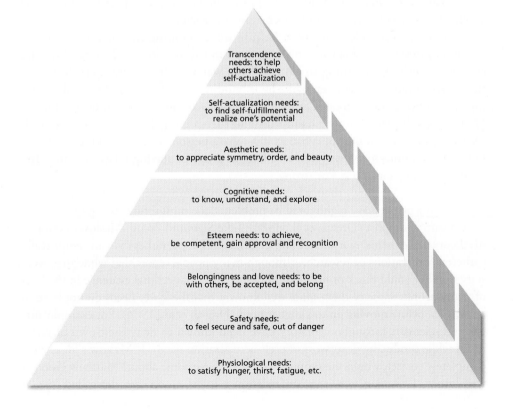

Transcendence needs: to help others achieve self-actualization

Self-actualization needs: to find self-fulfillment and realize one's potential

Aesthetic needs: to appreciate symmetry, order, and beauty

Cognitive needs: to know, understand, and explore

Esteem needs: to achieve, be competent, gain approval and recognition

Belongingness and love needs: to be with others, be accepted, and belong

Safety needs: to feel secure and safe, out of danger

Physiological needs: to satisfy hunger, thirst, fatigue, etc.

FIGURE 9.3 **Maslow's Hierarchy of Needs** Maslow proposed that human beings must fulfill the more basic needs, such as physical and security needs, before being able to fulfill the higher need of self-actualization.

represent Maslow's series of needs as a pyramid, with the most basic needs for survival at the bottom and the highest needs at the top. This type of ranking is called a *hierarchy*.

The lowest level of the pyramid consists of physiological needs such as food, water, and rest. Once those needs are met, safety becomes important and involves feeling secure. Belongingness and love are the needs for friends and companions as well as to be accepted by others, and self-esteem is the need to feel that one has accomplished something good or earned the esteem of others. Although Maslow's original hierarchy included only one more level of self-actualization needs, Maslow later inserted two other needs just below this level (Maslow, 1971; Maslow & Lowery, 1998). Just above the esteem needs on the hierarchy come the cognitive needs, or the need to know and understand the world. This need is typical of an academic person who learns for the sake of gathering knowledge. Above the cognitive needs are the aesthetic needs, which include the need for order and beauty and are typical of artistic people. Once all these needs are met, it is possible to be concerned about self-actualization needs, or needs that help a person reach his or her full potential and capabilities as a human being. Although it does not appear in Figure 9.3, Maslow also added a higher need called *transcendence* above the self-actualization needs (Maslow, 1971). Transcendence involves helping others to achieve their full potential. ⓛⓘⓝⓚ *to Chapter Eight: Development Across the Lifespan, p. 302.*

People move up the pyramid as they go through life, gaining wisdom and the knowledge of how to handle many different situations. But a shift in life's circumstances can result in a shift down to a lower need. For example, someone might be near the top, fulfilling the need for growth in ways that lead to self-actualization (appreciation of beauty, need for truth and justice, and helping others to grow, for example). But if that person loses her job and cannot find another one for quite some time, her money will start running out. She might take a job that is not good for her self-esteem out of love for her family and the need to provide a safe place for them to live and food for them to eat. She would be starting at the level of love and working her way back up. Moving up and down and then back up can occur frequently—even from one hour to the next. Times in a person's life in which self-actualization is achieved, at least temporarily, are called **peak experiences**. For Maslow, the process of growth and self-actualization is the striving to make peak experiences happen again and again.

Here's an example that might help in understanding this hierarchy. In the movie *Castaway*, Tom Hanks's character is stranded on a deserted island. His first concern is to find something to eat and fresh water to drink—without those two things, he cannot survive. Even while he is building a crude shelter, he is still thinking about how to obtain food. Once he has those needs met, however, he gets lonely. He finds a volleyball, paints a handprint and then a crude face on it, and names it "Wilson." He talks to the volleyball as if it were a person, at first as a kind of way to talk out the things he needs to do and later as a way of staying relatively sane. The need for companionship is *that* strong.

Although Maslow's theory has had a powerful influence, it is not without its critics. Some people have highlighted its problems, the most serious being that there is little scientific support (Drenth et al., 1984). Like Sigmund Freud, Maslow developed his theory based on his own personal observations of people rather than any empirically gathered observations or research. Although many people report that while they were starving, they could think of nothing but food, there is anecdotal evidence in the lives of many people, some of them quite well known, that the lower needs do not have to be satisfied before moving on to a higher need (Drenth et al., 1984). For example, artists and scientists throughout history have been known to deny their own physical needs while producing great works (a self-actualization need). If Maslow's ideas were completely correct, would the term *starving artist* have come about? Matthew Good, a well-known Canadian musician, suffers from a severe mood disorder called *bipolar*

In the movie *Castaway*, the character played by actor Tom Hanks feels the need for a companion so badly that he names this volleyball "Wilson." He comes to think of "Wilson" as such a good friend that he almost fails in his attempt to escape the island on which he is stranded to "rescue" the ball when it falls off his makeshift raft.

peak experiences
according to Maslow, times in a person's life during which self-actualization is temporarily achieved.

affective disorder, which causes the sufferer to have severe periods of depression and insecurity. ⓁⒾⓃⓀ *to Chapter Thirteen: Psychological Disorders, p. 520.* This diagnosis should place him on the lowest levels of the hierarchy, yet he was the lead singer of one of Canada's most successful alternative rock bands in the 1990s.

Does this theory apply universally? Maslow's work was based on his studies of Americans. Cross-cultural research suggests that the order of needs on the hierarchy does not always hold true for other cultures, particularly those cultures with a stronger tendency than the culture of the United States to avoid uncertainty, such as Greece and Japan. In those countries, security needs are much stronger than self-actualization needs in determining motivation (Hofstede, 1980; Hofstede et al., 2002). This means that people in those cultures value job security more than they do job satisfaction (holding an interesting or challenging job). In countries such as Sweden and Norway that stress the quality of life as being of greater importance than what a person produces, social needs may be more important than self-actualization needs (Hofstede et al., 2002). ⓁⒾⓃⓀ *to Chapter Eleven: Theories of Personality, p. 438.*

Other theorists have developed and refined Maslow's hierarchy. Clayton Alderfer developed one of the more popular versions of this refinement. In his theory, the hierarchy has only three levels: *existence needs*, which include the physiological needs and basic safety needs that provide for the person's continued existence; *relatedness needs*, which include some safety issues as well as belongingness and self-esteem needs and are related to social relationships; and *growth needs*, which include some self-esteem issues and the self-actualization needs that help people develop their full potential as human beings (Alderfer, 1972).

Alderfer believed that more than one need could be active at a time and that progression up and down the hierarchy is common as one type of need assumes greater importance at a particular time in a person's life than other needs. This makes Alderfer's hierarchy of needs less rigid and more in line with observations about life's "ups and downs."

◀ Does this theory apply universally?

✳ Explore on mypsychlab
Maslow's Hierarchy of Needs

PSYCHOLOGY IN THE NEWS

Turning Maslow's Hierarchy Upside-Down

Almost 70 years after Maslow's classic 1943 paper outlining his hierarchy of needs, University of British Columbia's Mark Schaller and three of his U.S. colleagues have recently created a stir with their new thesis, which turns the hierarchy upside-down. In an evolution-infused argument that is offending some non-parents and singles, Kenrick, Griskevicius, Neuberg, and Schaller (2010) maintain that the need to find and keep a significant other and raise healthy children is more important than the pursuit of self-actualization. In addition, the authors argue that the concept of self-actualization may not be universal—that it seems to be appealing to only those within Western societies. Kenrick and colleagues (2010) have addressed the complaints put forth by childless couples and singles by claiming that the impulse to "parent" can also be seen as a need to "nurture" another being. In other words, people don't need to actually have children, they can act as mentors or nurture others who are not their own children (Todd, 2010).

Schaller and his colleagues don't argue that Maslow's model needs to be discarded. Instead, they suggest that Maslow's conception can be combined with more recent theoretical developments in the fields of evolutionary biology, anthropology, and psychology to make it stronger and more relevant to the findings of today (see Figure 9.4). According to Kenrick and colleagues (2010), the updated model preserves many of Maslow's original ideas, for example, the hierarchical nature of the model and some of the needs (e.g., physiological, safety, and esteem needs). It differs in that self-actualization, instead of being its own distinct need at the

FIGURE 9.4 **An updated hierarchy of human motives** Kenrick and colleagues (2010) have proposed an updated hierarchy of fundamental human motives based on Maslow's (1943) hierarchy of needs (see Figure 9.3 on p. 357).

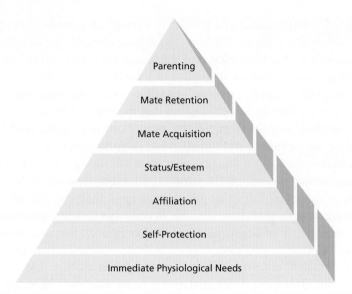

Parenting

Mate Retention

Mate Acquisition

Status/Esteem

Affiliation

Self-Protection

Immediate Physiological Needs

top of the pyramid, is theorized to be incorporated into the status/esteem needs category. In addition, the top of the revised pyramid includes goals relating to reproduction: mate acquisition, mate retention, and parenting. Finally, Kenrick and colleagues (2010) propose that the goals (needs) should be depicted in such a way that they are overlapping (not stacked one on top of another as was originally depicted in Maslow's model) because as we live our lives, we never stop trying to attain any of the goals (needs) included in the hierarchy.

Todd (2010) points out that while some people may see this revised model as overemphasizing humans' need to reproduce and thus pass on their genes, it's at least a start at challenging the idea that self-actualization should take precedence in our lives.

Questions for Further Discussion

1. Do you think that there will be cross-cultural differences in terms of how well this revised model will be received?

2. Evolutionary psychology is becoming increasingly popular. Why do you think this is?

SELF-DETERMINATION THEORY (SDT)

Another theory of motivation that is important today is the **self-determination theory (SDT)** of Richard Ryan and Edward Deci (2000). It has been used to explain motivation in many different areas, for example, athletics and exercise, education, and employment. Formally, the SDT comprises five "mini-theories": cognitive evaluation theory (CET), causality orientations theory (COT), goal contents theory (GCT), basic psychological needs theory (BPNT), and, finally, organismic integration theory (OIT). The latter two mini-theories (BPNT and OIT) will be discussed in detail below. For a brief description of all five mini-theories, see Table 9.2.

BASIC PSYCHOLOGICAL NEEDS THEORY (BPNT) This subcomponent of the SDT states that optimal functioning and psychological health depends on the person's levels of three inborn and universal psychological needs: autonomy, competence, and relatedness. Contexts that support high levels of these three psychological needs promote optimal functioning and psychological well-being, while contexts that do not support high levels of these needs lead to decreased functioning and well-being (University of Rochester, 2008).

The **need for autonomy** is defined as our need to feel as though we make our own choices and are in control. As mentioned previously in the discussion on *learned*

self-determination theory (SDT)
theory of human motivation in which the social context of an action has an effect on the type of motivation existing for the action.

need for autonomy
the psychological need that involves knowing that one's actions are self-determined rather than controlled by others.

TABLE 9.2 THE FIVE "MINI-THEORIES" OF THE SELF-DETERMINATION THEORY

MINI-THEORY	BRIEF DESCRIPTION
Cognitive Evaluation Theory (CET)	• Focuses on intrinsic motivation and the effects that social contexts have on intrinsic motivation (e.g., how rewards impact one's motivation to complete an activity just for its own sake)
Causality Orientations Theory (COT)	• Focuses on whether people desire to be autonomous or controlled in terms of how their behaviour is regulated • Describes three separate orientations relating to how people regulate their actions: *Autonomy orientation:* regulation is based on a person's personal interests and goals *Control orientation:* regulation is based on external rewards and approval from others *Impersonal or amotivated orientation:* people believe that outcomes are beyond their control and therefore feel incompetent, anxious, and helpless
Goal Contents Theory (GCT)	• Focuses on the differences between intrinsic and extrinsic goals and how these goals affect motivation and psychological wellness • Extrinsic goals such as popularity/fame have been associated with lower wellness and lower psychological well-being, while intrinsic goals such as personal growth are associated with better wellness and psychological well-being
Basic Psychological Needs Theory (BPNT)	• Focuses on three inborn and universal psychological needs (autonomy, competence, and relatedness) that help people gain a complete sense of self and whole, healthy relationships with others
Organismic Integration Theory (OIT)	• Focuses on various forms of extrinsic motivation, including external regulation, introjected regulation, identified regulation, and integrated regulation • Uses forms of extrinsic motivation that fall along a continuum of internalization, ranging from completely non-self-determined (amotivation) to completely self-determined (intrinsic regulation), with the four subtypes mentioned above falling in between these two polar opposites in increasing order of self-determination

Source: Adapted from the University of Rochester (2008).

helplessness, LINK *to Chapter Five: Learning, p. 206*, control is very important to people. When we feel as though we are in control and that we are able to make our own choices, our need for autonomy is being met. However, if we feel as though someone else is making decisions for us, our need for autonomy is being frustrated, which can lead to problems in psychological functioning. For example, if you feel that your parents limit your freedom and make crucial decisions about your life that you should be making, you are likely to be bothered by it. Environments differ in terms of how much autonomy can be fostered. If individuals are in an environment that does not often allow them the freedom to make their own decisions (e.g., military, church), they may not develop to their full potential. A more autonomy-supportive environment, such as a school setting in which students get to work at their own pace, can lead to greater intrinsic motivation and greater psychological functioning (S. Tombs, personal communication, November 3, 2009).

The **need for competence** is the need to challenge oneself and be successful in overcoming that challenge. We are satisfied (and thus, happy) when we set goals and achieve those goals. It is important to note that the challenges that people set out

need for competence
the psychological need that humans have to succeed at challenging tasks and to receive positive feedback from others.

need for relatedness
the psychological needs that humans have to form emotional bonds with those around them.

to overcome should match their skill level. If the challenge matches an individual's skill level appropriately, the individual will experience what has been labelled as *flow*, or being completely absorbed in an activity (S. Tombs, personal communication, November 3, 2009). If the skill level is too high for the individual, the result will be anxiety. In contrast, if the skill level is too low, the individual will likely become bored. The optimal mix for flow to occur is if one's skill level and challenge level are moderately high or high (S. Tombs, personal communication, November 3, 2009). Structure is important in the development of competence. Environments must be structured in such a way that people receive appropriate guidance toward desired outcomes (e.g., a teacher may explain to his students what is expected of them on a given assignment). Positive feedback, which can be of various types (e.g., a good grade from a teacher, an improved performance, task completion) will satisfy the need for competence (S. Tombs, personal communication, November 3, 2009).

The **need for relatedness** is the need to develop emotional bonds with others. We need to have relationships with others who we care about and who care about us. These close emotional bonds help us handle stress more effectively and improve our psychological well-being (Tombs, 2010). In this psychological need, the *quality* of our relationships is what is important, not the *quantity* of relationships. We need to know that the other person cares about our well-being, values us, and values us for the person we truly are. If these three conditions are not met, we will experience loneliness and our psychological (and physical) well-being will suffer (S. Tombs, personal communication, November 3, 2009).

Ryan and Deci (2000) argue that these psychological needs are just as important as physiological needs because they motivate us to learn about the world around us, master challenges, and ultimately, further develop as humans. If these psychological needs are met, people will be able to function effectively and experience wellness. If these needs are not met, people will ultimately suffer (University of Rochester, 2008).

ORGANISMIC INTEGRATION THEORY (OIT)   This subtheory of the SDT proposes that there are various forms of extrinsic motivation. According to the OIT, these different types of extrinsic motivation (external regulation, introjected regulation, identified regulation, and integrated regulation) fall along a continuum* of *internalization* (the process of people becoming increasingly in control of regulating their own behaviour so that their actions are more self-determined than externally determined; see Figure 9.5). The continuum ranges from completely non-self-determined (amotivation) to completely self-determined (intrinsic regulation), with the four subtypes of extrinsic motivation falling in between these two polar opposites in increasing order of self-determination (University of Rochester, 2008). This theory

FIGURE 9.5 **Self-determination Continuum as Outlined by the Organismic Integration Theory**
The OIT, which is part of the SDT, describes four forms of extrinsic motivation and places these different types of motivation along a continuum of internalization, ranging from completely non-self-determined (amotivation) to completely self-determined (intrinsic motivation; adapted from Markland, 2011).

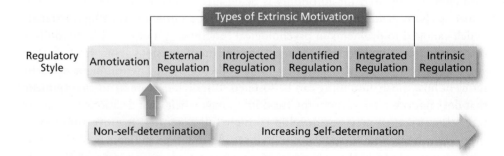

*Continuum: a sequence of values, elements, or behaviour that varies by small degrees

does not see self-determination as "all" or "nothing" (i.e., either you're self-determined or you aren't); instead, it explains *how* self-determined a person is (Markland, 2011). With greater internalization comes greater persistence in tasks, more engagement in activities, and more positive self-evaluations (Ryan & Deci, 2000).

Amotivation can be defined as the state of lacking intention to act and is the result of a person not seeing value in an activity, feelings of incompetence when it comes to the activity, or the belief that the activity will not result in a desirable outcome (Ryan & Deci, 2000). People who never enjoyed playing sports as children, who believe that they are not very good at playing sports, or believe that playing sports wouldn't do much to make their life better, would be amotivated when it comes to sport-playing behaviour.

To the right of amotivation on the continuum is *external regulation*, which is the least self-determined form of extrinsic motivation and the type of extrinsic motivation typically contrasted with intrinsic motivation. Externally regulated behaviours are performed only to obtain an external reward or to satisfy an external demand, with no desire to perform the behaviour for its own sake (Ryan & Ceci, 2000). If a talented, but uninterested, teenager is told by her overly enthusiastic hockey parents that she must play hockey in order to receive a car that she wants and that teenager decides to continue playing hockey, that teenager's behaviour would be labelled as *externally regulated*—she is playing solely to obtain that car.

Beside external regulation on the continuum is *introjected regulation*. Behaviours regulated in this fashion are performed because of feelings of pressure; they are completed to avoid guilt or anxiety, or to gain self-esteem. An example of this type of regulation can be found in the story of a middle-aged man, with a family history of heart disease, who used to be greatly involved in sports and exercise before he had a lot of responsibilities. Because he feels anxiety and guilt when he thinks about the possibility of leaving his children without a father, he decides to take up sports again (Markland, 2011).

Next is *identified regulation*, which occurs when a person consciously accepts the behaviour as important in achieving outcomes that are valuable to them (Markland, 2011). An example of behaviour that is regulated in this way would be a woman in a fast-paced, highly demanding job ensuring that she goes to the gym five times a week because she finds that the exercise decreases her stress levels and makes her think more clearly. Because this woman consciously realizes that the exercise is making her more efficient at her job, she will continue going to the gym (Markland, 2011).

The most self-determined form of extrinsic motivation is *integrated regulation*. This type of regulation occurs when people examine their values and needs and come to realize that a behaviour is important to them and that performing the behaviour is part of their overall view of who they are as people. Integrated regulation is very much like *intrinsic motivation* (which is at the extreme right of the continuum and completely self-determined), but it is still considered to be a form of extrinsic motivation as there is still a presumed instrumental value to the behaviour (i.e., there is still some form of external reward to be gained from performing the behaviour; Ryan & Deci, 2000). If a man quits his nine-to-five office job to work at a fitness club as a personal trainer because he loves to exercise, wants to teach others how to exercise, and believes that exercise and being fit is part of who he is as a person, his behaviour would be regulated in this way. Although he enjoys exercise immensely and believes that it defines part of who he is as a person, he still gains external rewards from performing the behaviour (e.g., he gains a sense of self, improving his self-esteem; Markland, 2011). Finally, people who engage in sports and exercise, even if their competence level is not very high, just for the love of the activity (without any pressure from guilt, self-esteem, or others) are participating in the activity because of intrinsic motivation. The action is completely self-determined.

For more information on the SDT, visit Deci and Ryan's website at the University of Rochester: **www.psych.rochester.edu/SDT/index.php**.

PRACTICE QUIZ: HOW MUCH DO YOU REMEMBER?

Pick the best answer.

1. The process by which activities are started, directed, and sustained to meet a person's wants is called a(n)
   a. drive.
   b. incentive.
   c. motivation.
   d. instinct.

2. People high in the need for _____ want to be liked by others and are good team players.
   a. achievement
   b. affiliation
   c. power
   d. emotion

3. In the _____ approach, people are said to have an optimal level of tension.
   a. drive-reduction
   b. arousal
   c. incentive
   d. humanistic

4. The most basic needs in Maslow's hierarchy are _____ needs.
   a. esteem
   b. love
   c. safety
   d. physiological

5. Jamal gets a new toy for every good grade on his report card in grade 1. Jamal will be
   a. intrinsically motivated.
   b. extrinsically motivated.
   c. motivated by needs.
   d. intrinsically rewarded.

6. The psychological need defined as "the need to feel as though we make our own choices" is
   a. the need for competence.
   b. the need for control.
   c. the need for autonomy.
   d. the need for relatedness.

7. According to the organismic integration theory, when it comes to increasing self-determination, what is the correct order of the four subtypes of extrinsic motivation?
   a. external regulation, introjected regulation, identified regulation, integrated regulation
   b. introjected regulation, integrated regulation, external regulation, identified
   c. external regulation, identified regulation, integrated regulation, introjected regulation
   d. none of the above is the correct order

Answers: 1-c, 2-b, 3-b, 4-d, 5-b, 6-c, 7-a.

WHAT, HUNGRY AGAIN? WHY PEOPLE EAT

9.5. What biological and social factors influence hunger?

The eating habits of people today have become a major concern and a frequent topic of news programs, talk shows, and scientific research. There are countless pills, supplements, and treatments to help people eat less and others to help people eat more. For many, eating is not only a basic survival behaviour but also a form of entertainment.

PHYSIOLOGICAL COMPONENTS OF HUNGER

▶ **Why do we eat? I mean, what causes us to feel hungry in the first place?**

Why do we eat? I mean, what causes us to feel hungry in the first place? There are actually several factors involved in the hunger drive. Cannon (Cannon & Washburn, 1912) believed that stomach contractions, or "hunger pangs," caused hunger and that the presence of food in the stomach would stop the contractions and appease the hunger drive. Oddly enough, having an empty stomach is not the deciding factor in many cases. Although the stomach does have sensory receptors that respond to the pressure of the stretching stomach muscles as food is piled in and that send signals to the brain indicating that the stomach is full (Geliebter, 1988), people who have had their stomachs removed (e.g., as in the case of someone with severe stomach cancer) still get hungry (Janowitz, 1967).

THE ROLE OF HORMONES One factor in hunger seems to be the insulin response that occurs after we begin to eat. **Insulin** and **glucagons** are hormones that are secreted by the pancreas to control the levels of fats, proteins, and carbohydrates in the whole body, including glucose (blood sugar). Insulin reduces the level of glucose in the bloodstream, whereas glucagons increase the level. Insulin, normally released in greater amounts after eating has begun, causes a feeling of more hunger because of the drop in blood-sugar levels. Carbohydrates, especially those that are highly refined (such as table sugar), cause the insulin level to spike even more than other foods do because there is such a large amount of glucose released by these foods at one time. High blood sugar leads to more insulin released, which leads to a low blood-sugar level, increased appetite, and the tendency to overeat. That is the basic principle behind many of the newest diets that promote low-carbohydrate intake. The proponents of these new diets argue that if people control their carbohydrate intake, they can control the insulin reaction and prevent hunger cravings later on, which will lead to weight loss. In contrast, opponents to these diets are not as optimistic about the effectiveness and long-term benefits of the low-carb approach. Much more research needs to be done before any conclusions regarding the safety and effectiveness of low-carbohydrate diets can be drawn.

THE ROLE OF THE HYPOTHALAMUS The stomach and the pancreas are only two of the factors in hunger. In Chapter Two, the role of the hypothalamus in controlling many kinds of motivational stimuli, including hunger, was seen as a result of its influence on the pituitary. But the hypothalamus itself has two separate areas, controlled by the levels of glucose and insulin in the body, which appear to control eating behaviour.

The *ventromedial hypothalamus (VMH)* may be involved in stopping the eating response when glucose levels go up (Neary et al., 2004). In one study, rats whose VMH areas (located to the front and centre of the hypothalamus) were damaged would no longer stop eating—they ate and ate until they were quite overweight (Hetherington & Ranson, 1940). (See Figure 9.6 for a picture of a rat with this kind of damage.) However, they did not eat everything in sight. They actually got rather picky, only overeating food that appealed to them (Ferguson & Keesey, 1975; Parkinson & Weingarten, 1990). In fact, if all the food available to them was unappealing, they did not become obese and in some cases even lost weight.

The other part of the hypothalamus, located on the side, is called the *lateral hypothalamus (LH)*. It seems to influence the onset of eating when insulin levels go up (Neary et al., 2004). Damage to this area caused rats to stop eating to the point of starvation. They would eat only if force-fed and still lost weight under those conditions (Anand & Brobeck, 1951; Hoebel & Teitelbaum, 1966).

WEIGHT SET POINT AND BASAL METABOLIC RATE Obviously, the role of the hypothalamus in eating behaviour is complex. Some researchers believe that the hypothalamus affects the particular level of weight that the body tries to maintain, called the **weight set point** (Leibel et al., 1995; Nisbett, 1972). Injury to the hypothalamus does raise or lower the weight set point rather dramatically, causing either drastic weight loss or weight gain.

Metabolism, the speed at which the body burns available energy, and exercise also play a part in the weight set point. Some people are no doubt genetically wired to have faster metabolisms, and those people can eat large amounts of food without gaining weight. Others have slower metabolisms and may eat a normal or even less than normal amount of food and still gain weight or have difficulty losing it (Bouchard et al., 1990). The rate at which the body burns energy when a person is

FIGURE 9.6 **Obese Laboratory Rat**
This rat has reached a high level of obesity because its ventromedial hypothalamus has been deliberately damaged in the laboratory. The result is a rat that no longer receives signals of being satiated, and so the rat continues to eat and eat and eat.

✳—[**Explore** on **mypsychlab**
The Effects of the Hypothalamus on Eating

insulin
a hormone secreted by the pancreas to control the levels of fats, proteins, and carbohydrates in the body by reducing the level of glucose in the bloodstream.

glucagons
hormones that are secreted by the pancreas to control the levels of fats, proteins, and carbohydrates in the body by increasing the level of glucose in the bloodstream.

weight set point
the particular level of weight that the body tries to maintain.

basal metabolic rate (BMR)
the rate at which the body burns
energy when the organism is resting.

leptin
a hormone that, when released into the
bloodstream, signals the hypothalamus
that the body has had enough food
and reduces the appetite while
increasing the feeling of being full.

resting is called the **basal metabolic rate (BMR)** and is directly tied to the set point. As a person's BMR decreases (as it does in adulthood), that person's weight set point increases. Adolescents have a very high BMR and, therefore, a lower weight set point, meaning they can eat far more than an adult of the same size and not gain weight. But when that adolescent becomes an adult, the BMR begins to decline. If the eating habits of the teenage years are maintained, excessive weight gain is not far behind.

THE BIOLOGY OF OBESITY   Why are some people so naturally slender, whereas others seem likely to become overweight? Scientists now believe that a hormone called **leptin** plays a key role in appetite control. Leptin is a protein that is secreted as a hormone (a chemical that travels by way of the blood to all parts of the body) by the fatty tissues of the body. When released into the bloodstream, leptin signals the hypothalamus that the body has had enough food, reducing appetite and increasing the feeling of being full (Friedman & Halaas, 1998).

Leptin enters the bloodstream from the fat cells, travelling to the hypothalamus in the brain, where it binds to receptors and causes the hypothalamus to signal the body either to stop eating or to eat more. High levels of leptin, which are produced when enough food is consumed, cause appetite to decrease, whereas low levels of leptin signal a condition of starvation and lead to increased appetite and the urge to eat (Brunner et al., 1997). This is the normal feedback loop for appetite control in the brain.

Having found this link, scientists experimented on obese mice by giving them a high dosage of leptin, which should lead to a decrease in appetite and to weight loss. Although at first the results seemed promising, more recent studies have found that certain strains of obese mice do not lose weight when leptin levels are increased, suggesting a resistance to leptin—their bodies can respond only to certain levels of leptin, and when the levels are too high, the body stops responding, allowing appetite to remain out of control (Friedman, 2003).

To make matters worse, the genes that once helped people survive famine and times of want may be the very genes that are now responsible for the rise in obesity (Friedman, 2003). Essentially, humans once lived in two major groupings: the hunter-gatherers, who had to take food as they could get it and often faced very lean times, and the herder-farmers, who lived in areas where cultivating food and raising domesticated animals was possible. The hunter-gatherer population would benefit most from genes that allowed their bodies to store energy very efficiently against the lean times.

What aided the hunter-gatherer population in ancient times, then, may be what is causing people descended from that population to store excess amounts of energy—obese people are storing up for a famine that does not come: "Obesity is not a personal failing. In trying to lose weight, the obese are fighting a difficult battle—a battle against biology, a battle that only the intrepid take on and one in which only a few prevail" (Friedman, 2003, p. 856).

Dr. Gregory Steinberg, a Canadian researcher who is currently doing work at the University of Melbourne in Australia, has been studying the biological factors involved in eating behaviour for many years. Steinberg has shown that when it comes to the ability to stimulate fat metabolism, hormones such as leptin are inhibited by certain proteins. This finding may explain why some of the mice in the above experiment were leptin-resistant (Canadian Institutes of Health Research, 2006)

SOCIAL COMPONENTS OF HUNGER

People often eat when they are not really hungry. There are all sorts of social cues that tell people to eat, such as the convention of eating breakfast, lunch, and dinner at certain times. A large part of that convention is actually the result of classical conditioning. ⓛⓘⓝⓚ *to Chapter Five: Learning, p. 176.* The body becomes conditioned to respond with the hunger reflex at certain times of the day; through association with the act of eating, those times of the day have become conditioned stimuli for hunger. Sometimes a person who has just eaten a late breakfast will still "feel" hungry at noon, simply because the clock says it's time to eat. People also respond to the appeal of food. How many times has someone finished a huge meal only to be tempted by that luscious-looking dessert on the dessert cart?

Food can also be used in times of stress as a comforting routine, an immediate escape from whatever is unpleasant (Dallman et al., 2003). Rodin (1981, 1985) found that the insulin levels that create hunger may actually increase *before* food is eaten (similar to the way Pavlov's dogs began salivating before they received their food). Like getting hungry at a certain time of day, this physiological phenomenon may also be due to classical conditioning: In the past, eating foods with certain visual and sensory characteristics led to an insulin spike, and this pairing occurred so frequently that now just looking at or smelling the food produces the spike before the food is consumed (Stockhorst, 1999).

Social factors such as the presence of other people will also influence how much a person eats. C. Peter Herman and Janet Polivy of the University of Toronto and Deborah Roth of the University of Pennsylvania have concluded that the presence of others strongly influences the amount of food a person will eat. In their review on the effect of other people on an individual's food intake, Herman and colleagues (2003) make two broad conclusions. First, social influences have more impact than any other influence in eating. The presence of other people can override the effects of feeling full and even the effects of extreme hunger. Also, observers can stop people from eating food that they really enjoy. Second, the presence of other people may make people eat more or it may make people eat less, depending on the circumstances. If a person is around other people who continue to eat, they will be more likely to keep eating. In contrast, if a person is around other people who have stopped eating, they will be less likely to keep eating (Herman, Roth, & Polivy, 2003).

MALADAPTIVE EATING PROBLEMS

9.6. *What are some problems in eating behaviour?*

It would be nice if people all over the world ate just the amount of food that they needed and were able to maintain a healthy, normal weight. Unfortunately, that is not the case for many people. Some people weigh far more than they should, whereas others weigh far less.

OBESITY   There are several factors that create *obesity*, a condition in which the body weight of a person is 20 percent or more over the ideal body weight for that person's height. Actual definitions of obesity vary. Some definitions consider 20 to 29 percent to be overweight and limit obesity to 30 percent. Others may use different criteria for men and women. For example, Health Canada (2002) states that men are obese at 20 percent over the ideal weight and women at 30 percent. However it is defined, a significant factor in obesity is heredity. There appear to be several sets of genes, some on different chromosomes, that influence a person's likelihood of becoming obese (Barsh et al., 2000). If there is a history of obesity in a particular family, each family member has a risk of becoming obese that is double or triple the risk of people who do not have a family history of obesity (Bouchard, 1997). In recent years, a hormone called *leptin* (which was discussed previously) has been identified as one of the factors that controls appetite and it may also play an important role in obesity.

(Top) Cultural factors play an important part in why people eat. Women in Japan have been found to be motivated to eat by hunger and social demands, as this woman and her family are doing.

(Bottom) Women in Canada may eat because they are depressed or for other emotional reasons, rather than just to appease hunger or in a social situation. Obviously, this woman does not need the social trappings of a bowl, dining table, and the company of others to motivate her eating habits—unless you count the cat.

⊙ Watch on mypsychlab
Urban Sprawl and Obesity

Portia de Rossi (who has since changed her name to Portia Degeneres after marrying her partner Ellen Degeneres) is an actress who has made it big in Hollywood. She bravely went public with her battle with anorexia and has since written a memoir titled *Unbearable Lightness: A Story of Loss and Gain.* During the worst stages of her battle with anorexia, she weighed only 37.2 kilograms (82 pounds). Hollywood is a major contributor to the concept of very thin women as beautiful and desirable. This is a far cry from the days of sex symbol Marilyn Monroe, who was rumoured to be a size 12.

anorexia nervosa
a condition in which a person reduces eating to the point that a weight loss of 15 percent below the ideal body weight or more occurs.

Another factor is certainly overeating. Around the world, as developing countries get stronger economies and their food supplies become stable, the rates of obesity increase dramatically and quickly (Barsh et al., 2000). Foods become more varied and enticing as well, and an increase in variety is associated with an increase in eating beyond the physiological need to eat (Raynor & Epstein, 2001). In industrialized societies, when workers spend more hours in the workplace, there is less time available for preparing meals at home and more incentive to dine out (Chou et al., 2004). When the "dining out" choices include fast food and soft drinks, as is so often the case, obesity rates increase.

Frighteningly, according to Mark Tremblay of the University of Saskatchewan and J. Douglas Willms of the University of New Brunswick, obesity rates in children have increased substantially in the past couple of decades. For example, between 1981 and 1996, the prevalence of obesity tripled from 5 to 15 percent among Canadian children between the ages of 7 and 13 (Tremblay & Willms, 2003). Tremblay and Willms (2003) believe that this threefold increase supports the idea that environmental factors (e.g., access to fast food, inactive pastimes such as playing video games), and not genetic factors, explain the increase in childhood obesity. In sum, as cultures become more industrialized and follow Western cultural lifestyles, negative aspects of those lifestyles such as obesity also increase.

ANOREXIA NERVOSA   Jennifer is an attractive 20-year-old overachiever who rigidly maintains her weight with diet, exercise, and self-discipline. Although she is thin, she is still dissatisfied with her appearance and weight and strives to lose more. Jennifer is 1.7 metres (5 feet, 6 inches) tall and weighs only 38.5 kilograms (85 pounds; Rideout, 2005). Why does Jennifer think she needs to lose more weight?

Anorexia nervosa is a condition in which a person (typically young and female) reduces eating to the point that a weight loss of 15 percent below expected body weight or more is the result. At a weight loss of 40 percent below expected body weight, hospitalization is necessary. Hormone secretion becomes abnormal, especially in the thyroid and adrenal glands. The heart muscles become weak and heart rhythms may alter. Other physical effects of anorexia include diarrhea, loss of muscle tissue, loss of sleep, and low blood pressure.

Some anorexics will eat in front of others but then force themselves to throw up or take large doses of laxatives. They are often obsessed with exercising and with food—cooking elaborate meals for others while eating nothing themselves. They have extremely distorted body images, seeing fat where others see only skin and bones.

What causes anorexia is not yet fully understood. Some theories involve biological explanations, such as a serotonin imbalance. Others point to psychological factors such as a rejection of sexual maturity (anorexia usually begins in the early teens and often causes menstruation to cease), sexual abuse, perfectionism with a desire to control as many aspects of one's life as possible, and family dysfunction (Abraham & Llewellyn-Jones, 2001; Mitchell, 1985). Still others focus on sociocultural factors, such as exposure to Hollywood types.

After reviewing the research investigating the various factors believed to be involved in the development of eating disorders, Janet Polivy and C. Peter Herman of the University of Toronto have concluded that no one factor on its own seems to cause anorexia, but some factors seem to contribute more than others. Some of these factors include low self-esteem, negative emotion (e.g., depression or anxiety), need for control, and obsessive thoughts (Polivy & Herman, 2002).

What can be done to treat anorexia? If the anorexic weight loss is severe (40 percent or more below expected normal weight), dehydration, severe chemical imbalances, and possibly organ damage may result. Hospitalization should occur before this dangerous point is reached. In the hospital, the anorexic's physical needs will be treated, even to the point of force-feeding in extreme cases. Anorexia nervosa is

classified as a clinical (mental) disorder in the *Diagnostic and Statistical Manual of Mental Disorders, Version IV-Text Revision* or *DSM-IV-TR* (APA, 2000a), which is a listing of disorders and their symptoms used by psychological professionals to make diagnoses. **LINK** *to Chapter Thirteen: Psychological Disorders, p. 520.* As a result, psychological counselling will also be part of the hospital treatment, which may last from two to four months. Those anorexics who are not so severely malnourished as to be in immediate danger can be treated outside of the hospital setting, typically receiving supportive psychotherapy, behavioural therapy, and perhaps group therapy. Family therapy is nearly always indicated in cases in which the family of the anorexic is contributing in some way to the behaviour. **LINK** *to Chapter Fourteen: Psychological Therapies, p. 564.* The prognosis for full recovery is not as hopeful as it should be because only 40 to 60 percent of all anorexics who receive treatment will recover. For some anorexics who do gain weight, the damage to the heart and other body systems may still be so great that an early death is a possibility (Neumarker, 1997).

BULIMIA In her late 20s, Carrie is the expected weight for her height but obsesses about food. She alternates between starving herself and then bingeing on large amounts of food. After bingeing, she makes herself throw up to rid her body of the food she has just eaten. Typically, she binges on fattening, sugary foods such as cookies, ice cream, and breads (Rideout, 2005). Why does Carrie eat like this?

Bulimia is a condition in which a person develops a cycle of "bingeing," or overeating enormous amounts of food at one sitting, and "purging" after eating (Hay & Bacaltchuk, 2002). "Purging" can occur in various forms, such as deliberate vomiting, laxative use, diuretic use, excessive exercise, and/or fasting. Bulimia has some similarities with anorexia: The victims are usually female, obsess about their appearance, diet excessively, and believe themselves to be fat even when they are quite obviously not fat. But bulimics are typically a little older than anorexics at the onset of the disorder—early 20s rather than early puberty. Like Carrie, bulimics often maintain a normal weight, making bulimia difficult to detect. The most obvious difference is that the bulimic will eat, and eat to excess, bingeing on huge amounts of food (as much as 50 000 calories in one sitting). A typical binge may include four litres of ice cream, a pack of cookies, and four litres of milk—all consumed as quickly as possible.

But wait a minute—if they're so concerned about gaining weight, why do they binge at all? Bulimics have very distorted views of how much food is too much food, and eating one cookie while trying to control weight can lead to a binge—after all, since the diet is completely blown, why not go all out?

One might think that bulimia is not as damaging to the health as anorexia. After all, the bulimic is in no danger of starving to death. But bulimia comes with many serious health consequences: severe tooth decay and erosion of the lining of the esophagus from the acidity of the vomiting; enlarged salivary glands; potassium, calcium, and sodium imbalances that can be very dangerous; damage to the intestinal tract from overuse of laxatives; heart problems; fatigue; and seizures (Berg, 1999). All forms of eating disorders wreak havoc on the human body.

As with anorexia, many causes have been proposed. Several research studies indicate a genetic component for both bulimia and anorexia (Fumeron et al., 2001; Strober et al., 2000; Vink et al., 2001). Psychological issues of control have also been cited, but biological evidence suggests that brain chemistry and, in particular, the neurotransmitter *serotonin* is involved in both bulimia and anorexia (Fumeron et al., 2001; Jimerson et al., 1997). Other studies investigating the role of biological factors point to leptin, the hormone that was discussed previously (Ferron et al., 1997).

Treatment of bulimia, which like anorexia is listed as a clinical (mental) disorder in the *DSM-IV-TR* (APA, 2000a), can involve many of the same measures taken to treat anorexia: hospitalization, drugs that affect serotonin levels, and psychotherapy.

◀ But wait a minute—if they're so concerned about gaining weight, why do they binge at all?

bulimia
a condition in which a person develops a cycle of "bingeing," or overeating enormous amounts of food at one sitting, and "purging" or using inappropriate compensatory behaviour in an attempt to get rid of the food after eating.

The prognosis for the bulimic's recovery is somewhat more hopeful than that of anorexia. Cognitive therapy, which involves helping clients to understand how illogical and irrational their thought patterns have become, has been successful in treating bulimia (DeAngelis, 2002). A cognitive therapist is very direct, forcing clients to see how their beliefs do not stand up when considered in "the light of day" and helping them form new and more constructive ways of thinking about themselves and their behaviour. ⓛⓘⓝⓚ *to Chapter Fourteen: Psychological Therapies, p. 564.*

The following websites provide access to information, help, and professional referrals for people with eating disorders:

- **www.nedic.ca** (National Eating Disorder Information Centre)
- **www.sheenasplace.org** (Sheena's Place)

CULTURE AND EATING DISORDERS Although many researchers have believed eating disorders, especially anorexia, to be culture-bound syndromes that show up only in cultures obsessed with being thin (as many Western cultures are), eating disorders are also found in other cultures (Miller & Pumariega, 1999). What differs between Western and non-Western cultures is the rates at which such disorders appear. For example, both Chinese women who reside in China and Chinese women who live in Western cultures are far less likely to suffer from eating disorders than are non-Hispanic white women (Pan, 2000). Why wouldn't the Chinese women who live in Western cultures be more likely to have eating disorders after being exposed to the Western cultural obsession with thinness? Pan (2000) assumes that whatever Chinese cultural factors "protect" Chinese women from developing eating disorders may also still have a powerful influence on these women who live in the Western world.

One problem with looking at anorexia and bulimia in other cultures is that the behaviour of starving oneself may be seen in other cultures as having an entirely different purpose than in Western cultures. One key component of anorexia, for example, is a fear of being fat, a fear that is missing in many other cultures. Yet women in those cultures have starved themselves for other socially recognized reasons such as religious fasting or specific ideas about nutrition (Castillo, 1997).

Anorexia and bulimia have also been thought to occur only rarely in black women, but that characterization seems to be changing. Researchers are seeing an increase in anorexia and bulimia among young black women of all socioeconomic levels (Crago et al., 1996; Mintz & Betz, 1998; Pumariega & Gustavson, 1994). If clinicians and doctors are not aware that these disorders can affect more than the typical white, young, middle- to upper-middle-class woman, important signs and symptoms of eating disorders in non-white or non-Western people may allow these disorders to go untreated until it is too late.

OTHER DRIVES

THIRST

Like hunger, thirst is also a basic biological drive. Because our bodies are made up mostly of water (roughly 75 percent), our need for water is constant. In fact, without water, a human can survive for only about three to five days. In contrast, that same person could live for approximately three weeks without food.

9.7. What is the difference between intracellular thirst and extracellular thirst?

There are two types of thirst: intracellular thirst and extracellular thirst. When you eat a lot of pretzels or salty popcorn at the movies, you will notice that you start to feel thirsty. This is due to your cells releasing some of their own water to fix the resulting disturbance in the water–sodium balance outside of your cells. This type of thirst is known as **intracellular thirst**. When you sweat a lot because you're at the gym or you're on a beach in sunny Cancun, you will also feel thirsty. This thirst is the result

intracellular thirst
thirst triggered by a loss of fluid within bodily cells.

of losing fluid from your bodily tissues and is known as **extracellular thirst**. In addition to sweating, extracellular thirst can also result from having the stomach flu (i.e., from vomiting and diarrhea) or from a night of heavy drinking.

extracellular thirst
thirst triggered by a loss of fluid between bodily cells.

SEX

9.8. *How is the sex drive different from the hunger and thirst drives?*

Sexual motivation is different from hunger and thirst motivation because while the hunger and thirst drives are very much related to bodily need states, the sex drive is not. There is no clear relationship between the amount of time the drive was last satisfied and the need for it (although some people may argue otherwise).

Many people do not include sex as a primary motive with hunger and thirst because it is not necessary for a person to have sex to survive. For example, priests and nuns take oaths of chastity and still manage to survive. However, it must be noted that sex *is* necessary for the survival of the species.

PRACTICE QUIZ: HOW MUCH DO YOU REMEMBER?

Pick the best answer.

1. Which of the following is not one of the physiological factors in hunger?
   a. stomach
   b. pancreas
   c. hypothalamus
   d. corpus callosum

2. As the basal metabolic rate decreases, the weight set point
   a. decreases.
   b. increases.
   c. stays the same.
   d. varies up and down.

3. Scientists believe that some people become obese because their ancestors were _____ and more likely to store up fat for future times of famine.
   a. herder-farmers
   b. agriculturalists
   c. hunter-gatherers
   d. big overeaters

4. One of the main differences between anorexia and bulimia is that the anorexic
   a. is obsessed about body weight.
   b. tends to be female.
   c. never binges on food.
   d. can suffer from heart problems.

5. Bulimia, unlike anorexia,
   a. produces an obsession with food.
   b. is difficult to detect because the person's weight is often normal.
   c. is not physically harmful.
   d. involves starvation.

6. An example of a situation that could cause intracellular thirst is
   a. eating poutine, a wonderful Canadian treat.
   b. having the stomach flu.
   c. exercising on a hot day.
   d. drinking a bottle of vodka.

Answers: 1.- d, 2.- b, 3.- c, 4.- c, 5.- b, 6.- a.

HUMAN SEXUALITY

Human sexual behaviour is not only responsible for the reproduction of the human race but also is one of the most important motivators of human behaviour. In this section, we discuss the physical side of human sexuality and human sexual behaviour.

THE PHYSICAL SIDE OF HUMAN SEXUALITY To understand human sexual behaviour, it may help to understand the physical structures of the human sexual system and the function of those structures. These structures differ for females and males and develop at different times in an individual's life. As you read this next section, keep in mind that physical sex characteristics are not the same as the experience of gender, the psychological aspects of identifying oneself as male or female. The psychological side of human sexuality (e.g., gender, gender roles, and gender role development) was discussed in Chapter Eight. **LINK** *to Chapter Eight: Development Across the Lifespan, p. 302.*

9.9 *What are the physical differences between females and males, and what does it mean to be "intersex"?*

PRIMARY SEX CHARACTERISTICS The sexual organs include structures that are present at birth and those that develop during *puberty*, the period of physiological changes

FIGURE 9.7 **Male and Female Sexual Organs** These figures show the sexual organs of men and women. With the exception of breast tissue development in the female, which occurs during puberty, all of these structures develop during the prenatal period.

Puberty changes come about two years earlier for girls than for boys, including the growth spurt. This dancing couple are both 13 years old, but the physical difference in height is quite obvious.

primary sex characteristics
sexual organs present at birth and directly involved in human reproduction.

vagina
the tube that leads from the outside of a female's body to the opening of the womb.

uterus
the womb in which a fetus grows during pregnancy.

ovaries
the female sexual glands.

penis
male reproductive organ that contains the urethra, which releases both urine and sperm.

testes (testicles)
the male sex glands.

scrotum
external sack that holds the testes.

prostate gland
gland that secretes most of the fluid that carries the male sex cells, or sperm.

secondary sex characteristics
sexual organs and traits that develop at puberty and are indirectly involved in human reproduction.

menstrual cycle
monthly shedding of the blood and tissue that line the uterus (in preparation for pregnancy) when conception does not occur.

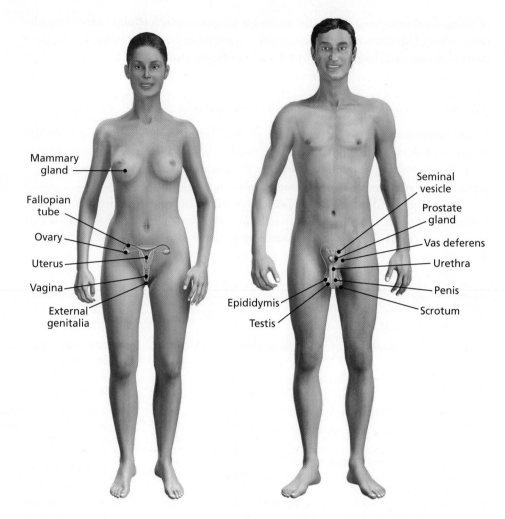

Mammary gland
Fallopian tube
Ovary
Uterus
Vagina
External genitalia

Seminal vesicle
Prostate gland
Vas deferens
Urethra
Penis
Scrotum
Epididymis
Testis

that takes place in the sexual organs and reproductive system during late middle childhood and adolescence. LINK *to Chapter Eight: Development Across the Lifespan, p. 302.*

Female Primary Sex Characteristics   **Primary sex characteristics** are those physical characteristics that are present in the infant at birth. In the female, these characteristics include the **vagina** (the tube leading from the outside of the body to the opening of the womb), **uterus** (the womb), and **ovaries** (the female sex glands). (See Figure 9.7.) Primary sex characteristics are directly involved in human reproduction.

Male Primary Sex Characteristics   In males, the primary sex characteristics include the **penis**, the **testes** or **testicles** (the male sex glands), the **scrotum** (an external pouch that holds the testes), and the **prostate gland** (a gland that secretes most of the fluid that carries the male sex cells, or sperm; see Figure 9.7).

SECONDARY SEX CHARACTERISTICS   **Secondary sex characteristics** develop during puberty and are only indirectly involved in human reproduction. These characteristics serve to distinguish the male from the female and may act as attractants to members of the opposite sex, ensuring that sexual activity and reproduction will occur. They are also, in many cases, a physical necessity for reproduction.

Female Secondary Sex Characteristics   In females, secondary sex characteristics include a growth spurt that usually begins between the ages of 10 and 12 and lasts until about one year after the start of the first **menstrual cycle**. The menstrual cycle is the principle sign of sexual maturity in females, and involves the monthly lining of blood and tissue along the uterus in preparation for pregnancy. When conception does not occur, the uterus lining is shed and the process begins again. Other female secondary sex characteristics include the enlargement of the breasts, which continues for about two years after the growth spurt; wider hips to allow for the passage of a fetus through the pelvic bones; pubic hair; and the deposit of fat on the buttocks and thighs. Some secondary sex characteristics also involve the growth and development of the primary sexual organs. In females, this occurs when the **mammary glands** in the breasts become capable of producing milk for an infant and when the menstrual cycle begins, usually at about age 12 or 13 (Kreipe, 1992; Lee, 1995).

Male Secondary Sex Characteristics   The secondary sex characteristics of males include a deepening voice, facial and chest hair, pubic hair, and the development of coarser skin texture, as well as a large increase in height that continues beyond the growth spurt of the female. The male growth spurt occurs about two years later than the female growth spurt, but males continue to gain height until the late teens. Although the larynx (voice box) increases in size in both sexes, it increases so much in males that part of the tissue forming it becomes visible under the skin of the neck in a structure known as the *Adam's apple*. Primary sex characteristics also undergo changes during puberty, including the production of sperm and the growth of the penis and the testes, which will eventually allow the male to function sexually and reproduce (Kreipe, 1992; Lee, 1995).

How does the person's body know which sexual characteristics to develop? Aren't some babies born with sex organs belonging to both sexes? The primary sex characteristics develop as the fetus is growing in the womb. During the early part of pregnancy, two organs called the *gonads* form in the embryo. At this point, the gonads are undifferentiated: neither male nor fully female. These gonads will eventually develop into either the female sex glands or the male sex glands. If the chromosomes of the twenty-third pair contain two female, or X, chromosomes, the gonads will develop into the ovaries. If the twenty-third pair contains a Y chromosome, the undifferentiated gonads will become the testes. If the gonads become ovaries, these glands will then release female hormones (**estrogens**) and the infant develops female sex organs. If the gonads become testes, male hormones or **androgens** will be released, causing the development of the male sexual organs.

INTERSEX INDIVIDUALS   On rare occasions, an infant is born with sexual organs that are ambiguous—not clearly male or female. This condition used to be commonly referred to as *hermaphroditism*, which was defined as the condition of possessing both male and female sex organs. (The term comes from the name of a Greek god, Hermaphroditus, who was said to have both male and female characteristics.) This term is misleading as it is very rare to find a person who truly has both ovary and testicle material in one body. More commonly, the development of the external genitals is affected by either chromosome defects or the presence of the wrong hormones at a critical time in the development of the fetus in the womb (Hutcheson & Snyder, 2004). In this case, a female clitoris might look more like a penis, or a penis might be so small as to resemble a clitoris. The Intersex Initiative website states, "There is no single 'intersex body'; it encompasses a wide variety of conditions that do not have anything in common except that they are deemed 'abnormal' by the society. What makes intersex people similar is their experiences of medicalization, not biology" (Intersex Initiative, 2008, para. 1). According to the Intersex Initiative (2008), the use of the term *intersexual* should not be used as a noun. Instead, **intersex people** or **people with intersex conditions/experiences** is preferred.

Approximately 1 out of 1500 children is born with this condition (Dreger, 1998, 1999). In the mid to late 1900s, the medical profession's answer to the intersex person was to recommend surgery to make the child more clearly one sex or the other—often in direct contradiction with the child's actual chromosomal

mammary glands
glands within the breast tissue that produce milk when a woman gives birth to an infant.

estrogens
female sex hormones.

androgens
male sex hormones.

intersex people/people with intersex conditions/experiences
people who possess ambiguous sexual organs, making it difficult to determine actual sex from a visual inspection at birth.

How does the person's body know which sexual characteristics to develop? Aren't some babies born with sex organs belonging to both sexes?

Cheryl Chase is an intersex individual, a person who has mixed or ambiguous male and female sex organs. She, along with many other intersex people, is working to stop the practice of surgically altering intersexual infants who are unable to give their own consent for what Chase and colleagues consider to be unnecessary surgery.

intersex
congenital anomaly of the reproductive and sexual system that makes it difficult to determine an infant's sex at birth. Intersex people are born with external genitalia, an endocrine system, and/or internal reproductive organs that are different from those of most other people.

sex. A male with an abnormally small penis might have his testicles removed, his penis reduced, and a vagina constructed to make him appear female. His parents would be told to dress and think of their child as a girl, when in fact he would be a castrated boy. It was easier in those days to construct "females," as a functioning penis was not yet possible with surgery, but a "functioning" vagina was. Being intersex was regarded, and still is by many medical professionals, as an abnormality that must be "fixed."

The **intersex** controversy consists of a large number of intersex individuals who, having developed ways of communicating with one another through the internet and within organizations, are no longer happy with being designated as "abnormal" and forced into surgical alterations while still infants. Parents who resist such surgical treatments are sometimes subjected to intense pressure by the doctors involved. Sexual reassignment is still very common in early infancy and often leads to adolescents or young adults who reject the reassignment and face depression and anxiety (Diamond & Sigmundson, 1997; Dreger, 1999). This rejection of the attempt to "retrain" gender identity indicates that nature, not nurture, may be far more important in determining a person's identity as male or female.

Some adults who were born intersex and experienced the surgery and sexual reassignment as infants are now angry about having their rights violated and being subjected to such a radical procedure without consent (Kessler, 1998). The Intersex Society of North America (ISNA) was formed in 1994 to give support to intersex people and strongly recommends that doctors not seek to perform surgical procedures on intersex children. The goal is to remove the veil of secrecy, so that a child who is intersex can be informed at a relatively early age (far earlier than adolescence) of this condition and that a decision might need to be made in the future about surgery. This allows intersex persons to make the decision for themselves.

HUMAN SEXUAL BEHAVIOUR

9.10   *How did Kinsey study human sexual behaviour, and what were the findings of the Janus Report?*

The study of sexual behaviour is not the study of the sex act, but rather when, with whom, and under what circumstances sexual acts take place. Although there were other attempts to study human sexual behaviour before the mid-twentieth-century studies of Alfred Kinsey (Kinsey et al., 1948; Kinsey et al., 1953), his original work remains an important source of information concerning the different ways in which people engage in the sex act. A movie based on Kinsey's life and work was released in 2004. Even more than half a century later, Kinsey's work is still so controversial that many movie theatres in the United States refused to show the film.

THE KINSEY STUDY   In 1948, zoologist Alfred Kinsey published a controversial report on the results of a massive survey of male sexual behaviour collected from 1938 onwards (Kinsey et al., 1948). His findings concerning the frequency of behaviour such as masturbation, anal sex, and premarital sex rocked many people, who were apparently not ready to believe that so many people had tried "alternative" sexual behaviours. Kinsey believed that sexual orientation was not an either/or situation in which one is either completely heterosexual or completely homosexual but instead that sexual orientation is on a continuum, with some people falling at either extreme and some falling closer to the middle. The idea that there were many people who fit into that middle range of sexual orientation was shocking and, for many, unbelievable (see Table 9.3).

Kinsey used highly trained interviewers who conducted face-to-face interviews with the male participants. A later survey was published in 1953 that dealt exclusively

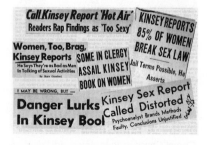

These are actual headlines from various newspapers, all featuring the media's response to Kinsey's controversial survey of human sexual behaviour, the Kinsey Reports, the first of which was published in 1948. How might Kinsey's research be treated today?

TABLE 9.3   KINSEY AND COLLEAGUES' RATING SCALE FOR SEXUAL ORIENTATION

0	1	2	3	4	5	6
Exclusive heterosexual	Predominantly heterosexual; only incidentally homosexual	Predominantly heterosexual; more than incidentally homosexual	Equally heterosexual and homosexual	Predominantly homosexual; more than incidentally heterosexual	Predominantly homosexual; only incidentally heterosexual	Exclusively homosexual

Source: Reprinted by permission of the Kinsey Institute for Research in Sex, Gender, and Reproduction, Inc.

with females (Kinsey et al., 1953). The participants were volunteers supposedly from both rural and urban areas and from different socioeconomic, religious, and educational backgrounds. In reality, a large portion of the participants were well-educated, urban, young Protestants. Table 9.4 lists some of the more interesting findings of the Kinsey study.

Although Kinsey's data are still quoted in many discussions of sexual behaviour, his original surveys were far from perfect. As stated earlier, the participants were almost exclusively white, middle class, and college educated. Older people, those who lived in rural regions, and less educated people were not well represented. Some critics claimed that Kinsey gave far more attention to sexual behaviour that was considered unusual or abnormal than he did to "normal" sexual behaviour (Geddes, 1954). Also, Kinsey's surveys were no less susceptible to the exaggerations, falsifications, and errors of any method using self-report techniques. Finally, a face-to-face interview might cause some people being interviewed to be inhibited about admitting to certain kinds of sexual behaviour, or others might exaggerate wildly, increasing the likelihood of inaccurate data.

THE JANUS REPORT   In 1993, Dr. Samuel S. Janus and Dr. Cynthia L. Janus published the results of the first large-scale study of human sexual behaviour since those of Kinsey (1948) and Masters and Johnson (1966). This national survey, begun in 1983, sampled 3000 people from all 48 mainland states in the United States. Professors in the fields of sociology, psychology, psychiatry, history, biology, and political science received special training in the survey method and supervised experienced graduate student researchers who also collected survey data. Data were collected

TABLE 9.4   KEY FINDINGS FROM KINSEY'S SEXUAL BEHAVIOUR SURVEYS

Males reporting anal sex with spouse: 11 percent.

Nearly 46 percent of males had bisexual experiences.

Between 6 and 14 percent of females had bisexual experiences.

Whereas nearly 21 percent of the males had experienced intercourse by age 16, only 6 percent of females had done so.

Males reporting premarital sex: 67 to 98 percent (varied by economic level).

Females reporting premarital sex: 50 percent.

Nearly 50 percent of all married males had some extramarital experiences, whereas 26 percent of married females had extramarital experiences.

About 10 percent of males were predominantly homosexual.

Between 2 and 6 percent of females were predominantly homosexual.

Males who reported masturbating: 92 percent.

Females who reported masturbating: 62 percent.

Source: Gebhard, P. H., & Johnson, A. B. (1979/1998).

sexual deviance
sexual behaviour that is unacceptable according to societal norms and expectations.

sexual orientation
a person's sexual attraction preference for members of a particular sex.

heterosexual
person attracted to the opposite sex.

homosexual
person attracted to the same sex.

bisexual
person attracted to both men and women.

 Watch on **mypsychlab**
Adolescent Sexual Behaviour

If people have had a homosexual experience as well as heterosexual ones, does that make them bisexuals?

through interviews and mass questionnaires. Survey respondents ranged in age from 18 to more than 65 years, from all levels of marital status, educational backgrounds, and geographical regions in the United States.

One finding of this massive survey was that nearly 80 percent of men and 70 percent of women had masturbated (although about one-fourth to one-third stated that this occurred rarely). Other responses indicated that 19 percent of men and nearly 8 percent of women were involved in full sexual intercourse by age 14. Premarital sex was more commonly reported in men than in women (67 percent for males, 46 percent for females), and men were nearly twice as likely as women to report having at least one extramarital affair. While more than one-fifth of the male respondents and only slightly fewer female respondents reported having at least one homosexual experience, only 9 percent of males and 5 percent of females identified themselves as predominantly homosexual.

In addition to these findings, *The Janus Report on Sexual Behaviour* also looked at **sexual deviance** (sexual behaviour that is unacceptable according to social norms), single people's sexual behaviour, marriage, divorce, the decision to have children, and how religion, political orientation, education, wealth, and geographical region affect sexual behaviour.

SEXUAL ORIENTATION The term **sexual orientation** refers to a person's sexual attraction for members of a particular sex. One of the more important questions that researchers are trying to answer is whether sexual orientation is the product of learning and experience or is biological in origin, or if it is due to an interaction between the environment and biology.

9.11 *What are the different sexual orientations, and how do they develop?*

Heterosexual The most common sexual orientation is **heterosexual**, in which people are sexually attracted to members of the opposite physical sex, as in a man being attracted to a woman or vice versa. (The Greek word *hetero* means "other," so *heterosexual* means "other sexual" or attraction for the other sex.) Heterosexuality is a socially acceptable form of sexual behaviour in all cultures.

Homosexual It is difficult to get an accurate percentage for **homosexual** orientation or sexual attraction to members of one's own sex. (The Greek word *homo* means "same.") The problem concerns the discrimination, prejudice, and mistreatment that homosexual people face in most cultures, making it more likely that a homosexual person will lie about his or her sexual orientation to avoid such negative treatment. The most recent surveys estimate that about 9 percent of men and 5 percent of women are homosexuals, meaning that their sexual orientation is exclusively or predominantly homosexual (Janus & Janus, 1993). However, the same surveys indicate that 22 percent of men and 17 percent of women have had at least one homosexual experience. Apparently, it is not unusual for people to experiment with sexual behaviour while deciding their true sexual identity (see Table 9.5). In 2003, a survey of 135 000 Canadians was conducted and found that 1 percent of the respondents identified themselves as homosexual, with 1.3 percent of men and 0.7 percent of women considering themselves homosexual (Statistics Canada, 2003).

If people have had a homosexual experience as well as heterosexual ones, does that make them bisexuals?

Bisexual A person who is **bisexual** may be either male or female and is attracted to both sexes. Although, as stated in the survey results, a portion of the population has had experiences with both sexes, this does not make these people bisexual, except in the most literal sense, and only for that period of experimentation. In other words, people can have bisexual experiences but are not bisexuals unless this becomes their preferred, stable, sexual identity.

AGE	FEMALE	MALE
Grade school	11%	17%
Junior high	6%	20%
High school	46%	50%
College	37%	13%

TABLE 9.5 WHEN GAY OR BISEXUAL COLLEGE STUDENTS SAY THEY BECAME AWARE OF THEIR SEXUAL ORIENTATION

Source: Elliott, L., & Brantley, C. (1997).

Bisexual people do not necessarily have relationships with both men and women at the same time and may vary in the degree of attraction to one sex or the other over time. Many bisexuals may not act on their desires but instead have a long-term monogamous relationship with only one partner.

For the same reasons that it is difficult to get an accurate percentage for homosexual orientation, obtaining accurate percentages for bisexual orientation or sexual attraction to both members of the opposite sex and also to one's own sex is a challenge. The survey of 135 000 Canadians discussed above found that 0.7 percent of all respondents identified themselves as bisexual, with 0.6 percent of men and 0.9 percent of women considering themselves bisexual (Statistics Canada, 2003).

Development of Sexual Orientation Is sexual orientation a product of the environment, biology, or both? This issue is very controversial, regardless of one's sexual orientation (Diamond, 1995). If sexual orientation is a product of upbringing and environmental experiences, homosexuality and bisexuality can be assumed to be behaviour that can be changed, placing a burden of choice to be "normal" or "abnormal" squarely on the shoulders of homosexual and bisexual people. If it is biological, either through genetic influences or hormonal influences during pregnancy, then it can be seen as a behaviour that is no more a choice than whether the infant is born a male or a female. The implications of sexual orientation as biological leads to some volatile issues: If it is not a choice or a learned behaviour pattern, then society will no longer be able to expect or demand that homosexuals and bisexuals change their sexual behaviour or orientation. Homosexuality and bisexuality become an issue of diversity rather than deviance.

In the past several decades, a large body of research in the areas of biological differences in the brains of heterosexual and homosexual males, genetic influences on sexual orientation, and even prenatal influences on sexual orientation has been amassed by various scientists. One of the earliest studies, for example, found that severe stress experienced by pregnant women during the second trimester of pregnancy (the time during which the sexual differences in genitalia are formed) results in a significantly higher chance of any male children becoming homosexual in orientation (Ellis et al., 1988).

A controversial study by Simon LeVay (1991) found an area of the hypothalamus (which, as discussed in Chapter Two, controls the pituitary gland and, through that gland, the sex glands and adrenal glands that influence sexual behaviour and development) that is three times larger in men than in women. LeVay examined the brain structures of 19 homosexual males, 16 heterosexual males, and 6 deceased women whose sexual orientation was unknown. He found that the same area of the hypothalamus that is larger in men than in women was also two to three times larger in heterosexual men than in homosexual men. Of course, LeVay's findings are based on a quasi-experimental design so causal inferences cannot be made. LINK *to Chapter One: The Science of Psychology, p. 2.* It is possible that the differences in the size of the hypothalamus might be due to increased or decreased sexual activity, for example.

These women are celebrating their wedding day. Canada has allowed same-sex marriages since 2005. Whether or not sexual orientation is determined by biology or by environmental influences is an important question, and the answer to this question will have far-reaching consequences.

There may have been other differences in lifestyle that account for the size difference, or the fact that LeVay was examining dead tissue, which may undergo changes after death that vary over time. Just because there is a relationship between sexual orientation and size of the hypothalamus does not mean that the size of the hypothalamus causes sexual orientation. More research may shed light on this question.

In a recent study that may be interpreted as support of LeVay's findings, researchers discovered that male sheep, or rams, with an exclusively homosexual preference for other rams rather than female sheep (ewes) also have a significantly smaller than normal area in the hypothalamus of their brains when compared to rams that are exclusively heterosexual (Roselli et al., 2004). As in the LeVay (1991) study, the brain structure of the homosexual rams in this study was physically more similar to the brain structure of ewes. However, it is important to remember that these findings represent a correlation only, just as LeVay's do. Neither the findings of LeVay nor the Roselli studies can be interpreted as showing that the cause of homosexuality is definitely biological, much less that it is a specific area of the hypothalamus that causes sexual orientation to be determined.

The evidence for genetic influences on sexual orientation is increasingly convincing. In studies of male and female homosexuals who have identical twins, fraternal twins, or adopted siblings, researchers found that 52 percent of the identical twin siblings were also gay, compared to 22 percent of the fraternal twins and only 11 percent of the adopted brothers and sisters (Bailey & Pillard, 1991). In a similar study with lesbian women only, 48 percent of identical twins were also gay compared to 16 percent of the fraternal twins and 6 percent of the adopted siblings (Bailey et al., 1993). Other research along similar lines has supported these findings (Bailey et al., 2000; Dawood et al., 2000). However, these findings should be interpreted cautiously as well. Twin studies are difficult to conduct without the influence of environment on behaviour. Even twins who are raised apart tend to be reared in similar environments, so that the influence of learning and experience on sexual orientation cannot be entirely ruled out.

There is some evidence that homosexuality may be transmitted by genes carried on the X chromosome, which is passed from mother to son but not from father to son. In 33 out of 40 homosexual brothers, Hamer and colleagues (1993) found an area on the X chromosome (in a location called *Xq28*) that contains several hundred genes that the homosexual brothers had in common in every case, even though other genes on that chromosome were different. This was taken as evidence that the brothers had both inherited a set of genes, donated on the mother's X chromosome, that might be responsible for their sexual orientation. These findings have since been supported in other research (Hu et al., 1995; Turner, 1995).

One of the most common behavioural findings about male homosexuals is that they are consistently feminine as children, according to developmental psychologist J. Michael Bailey (Bailey & Zucker, 1995). Bailey has determined that about three-fourths of feminine boys are homosexual as adults, a far greater rate than in the general population of males. Bailey and Canadian colleague Ken Zucker, who heads the Child and Adolescent Gender Identity Clinic at the University of Toronto's Clarke Institute, interpret these findings as support for the biological foundations of sexual orientation (Bailey & Zucker, 1995). To further support this interpretation, Zucker and his colleagues studied 25 females diagnosed in childhood with gender identity disorder. As young adults, 24 percent of these females were classified as either bisexual or homosexual, which is much higher than the incidence found in the general population (Drummond, Bradley, Peterson-Badali, & Zucker, 2008). Of course, those differences in childhood behaviour could also have been the result of attention and other forms of reinforcement from the social environment. It is simply a very difficult task to separate the environmental influences on any aspect of behaviour from the biological ones.

One thing is certain: The issue of what causes sexual orientation will continue to generate research and controversy for a long time to come.

The first section of this chapter has looked at the motives that drive human behaviour. But people do more than just behave; there are feelings that accompany every human action. The second section of the chapter explores the world of human emotions and how those emotions are connected to both thinking and actions.

PRACTICE QUIZ: HOW MUCH DO YOU REMEMBER?

Pick the best answer.

1. The first scientifically based survey of human sexual behaviour was designed and carried out by
  a. personality psychologists.
  b. a physiological psychologist.
  c. a zoologist.
  d. a psychiatrist.

2. In Kinsey's original data, more _____ than _____ reported having bisexual experiences.
  a. homosexuals; heterosexuals
  b. heterosexuals; homosexuals
  c. women; men
  d. men; women

3. Which group was NOT one of the groups poorly represented in the Kinsey study?
  a. older people
  b. white, middle class
  c. people with little education
  d. people living in rural areas

4. Compared to the Kinsey data, the data from the Janus Report revealed the age of the first sexual experience for about 20 percent of the men and 8 percent of the women to be
  a. 14.
  b. 16.
  c. 17.
  d. 12.

5. LeVay found evidence that homosexual males have a difference from heterosexual males in what area of the brain?
  a. thalamus
  b. cortex
  c. hypothalamus
  d. corpus callosum

6. What percentage of females diagnosed with gender identity in childhood are likely to become bisexual or homosexual in adulthood?
  a. 1.5 percent
  b. 12 percent
  c. 24 percent
  d. 43 percent

Answers: 1.-c, 2.-d, 3.-b, 4.-a, 5.-c, 6.-c.

EMOTION

What part does the way we feel about things play in all of our daily activities— what exactly causes feelings? Although strict behaviourists in the tradition of Watson and Skinner would prefer not to think about it, human beings are full of feelings, or emotions. Although emotions may be internal processes, there are outward physical signs of what people are feeling as well.

THE THREE ELEMENTS OF EMOTION

9.12 *What are the three elements of emotion?*

The Latin word meaning "to move" is the source of both words used in this chapter over and over again—*motive* and *emotion*. **Emotion** can be defined as the "feeling" aspect of consciousness, characterized by a certain physical arousal, a certain behaviour that reveals the feeling to the outside world, and an inner awareness of feelings.

THE PHYSIOLOGY OF EMOTION Physically, when a person experiences an emotion, the sympathetic nervous system creates an arousal. **LINK** *to Chapter Two: The Biological Perspective, p. 42.* The heart rate increases, breathing becomes more rapid, the pupils dilate, and the mouth may become dry. Think about the last time you were angry and then about the last time you were frightened. Weren't the physical symptoms pretty similar? Although facial expressions do differ between various emotional responses (Ekman, 1980; Ekman et al., 1969; Ekman & Friesen, 1978), emotions are difficult to distinguish from one another on the basis of outward bodily reactions alone. In fact, it is quite easy to mistake a person who is actually afraid or angry as being aroused if the person's face is not clearly visible, which can lead to much miscommunication and misunderstanding.

What part does the way we feel about things play in all of our daily activities—what exactly causes feelings?

Watch on **mypsychlab**
Skinner on Emotion

emotion
the "feeling" aspect of consciousness, characterized by a certain physical arousal, a certain behaviour that reveals the emotion to the outside world, and an inner awareness of feelings.

However, in the laboratory, using devices to measure the heart rate, blood pressure, and skin temperature, researchers have found that different emotions are associated with different physiological reactions. For example, fear is associated with a decrease in skin temperature, whereas anger is associated with an increase in skin temperature and a greater increase in blood pressure (Levenson, 1992; Levenson et al., 1992).

Just what parts of the brain are involved in various aspects of emotion? As discussed in Chapter Two, the *amygdala*, a small area located within the limbic system on each side of the brain, is associated with fear in both humans and animals (Davis & Whalen, 2001; Fanselow & Gale, 2003) and is also involved in the processing of facial expressions of human emotions (Morris et al., 1998). When the amygdala is damaged in rats, they cannot be classically conditioned to fear new objects—they apparently cannot remember to be afraid (Davidson et al., 2000; Fanselow & Gale, 2003). In humans, damage to the amygdala has been associated with similar effects (LaBar et al., 1995) and with impairing the ability to determine emotions from looking at the facial expressions of others (Adolphs & Tranel, 2003).

Emotions even work differently depending on which side of the brain is involved. Researchers have found that negative feelings such as sadness, anxiety, and depression seem to be a function of primarily the left hemisphere of the brain (Ahern & Schwartz, 1985; Davidson et al., 1990; Papousek & Schulter, 2002). In a recent study (Papousek & Schulter, 2002), the electrical activity of the brain was tracked using an electroencephalograph (EEG). ⓁⒾⓃⓀ *to Chapter Two: The Biological Perspective, p. 42.* When anxiety and depression were high, so was the activity on the left side of the brain. But when anxiety and depression were reduced, activity levels dropped in the left hemisphere and increased in the right hemisphere.

The ability to interpret the facial expressions of others as a particular emotion also seems to be a function of one side of the brain more than the other. Researchers have found that when people are asked to identify the emotion on another person's face, the right hemisphere is more active than the left, particularly in women (Voyer & Rodgers, 2002). This difference begins weakly in childhood but increases in adulthood, with children being less able to identify negative emotions as well as positive emotions when compared to adults (Barth & Boles, 1999; Lane et al., 1995). This finding is consistent with early research that assigns the recognition of faces to the right hemisphere (Berent, 1977; Ellis, 1983).

THE BEHAVIOUR OF EMOTION: EMOTIONAL EXPRESSION   How do people behave when in the grip of an emotion? Facial expressions, body movements, and actions indicate to others how a person feels. Frowns, smiles, and sad expressions combine with hand gestures, the turning of one's body, and spoken words to produce an understanding of emotion. People fight, run, kiss, and yell, along with countless other actions stemming from the emotions they feel.

Facial expressions can vary across different cultures, although some aspects of facial expression seem to be universal. (See Figure 9.8 for some examples of universal facial expressions.) Charles Darwin (1898) was one of the first to theorize that emotions were a product of evolution and, therefore, universal—all human beings, no matter what their culture, would show the same facial expression because the facial muscles evolved to communicate specific information to onlookers. For example, an angry face would signal to onlookers that they should act submissively or expect a fight. Although Darwin's ideas were not in line with the behaviourist movement of the early and middle twentieth century, which promoted environment rather than heredity as the cause of behaviour, other researchers have since found evidence that at least seven basic emotions have a universal nature (Ekman, 1973; Ekman & Friesen, 1969, 1971). Even children who are blind from birth can produce the appropriate facial

FIGURE 9.8 **Facial Expressions of Emotion** Facial expressions appear to be universal. For example, these faces are interpreted as showing (a) anger, (b) fear, (c) disgust, (d) happiness, (e) surprise, and (f) sadness by people of cultures all over the world. Although the situations that cause these emotions may differ from culture to culture, the expression of particular emotions remains strikingly the same.

expressions for any given situation without ever having witnessed those expressions on others, which strongly supports the idea that emotional expressions have their basis in biology rather than in learning (Charlesworth & Kreutzer, 1973; Fulcher, 1942).

9.13 *How does culture affect the expression and interpretation of emotional expressions?*

To show that emotional expressions are universal, Ekman and Friesen (1969, 1971) showed participants from different cultures photographs of faces to determine whether the same expression would be judged as the same emotion, regardless of the participant's culture. Ekman and Friesen found that people of many different cultures (Japanese, Europeans, Americans, and even the Fore tribe of New Guinea) can consistently recognize at least seven facial expressions: anger, fear, disgust, happiness, surprise, sadness, and contempt (Ekman & Friesen, 1969, 1971). The reason Ekman and Friesen included the Fore tribe of New Guinea (along with another preliterate* culture—the Sadong of Borneo) is because the other participants had most likely been exposed to mass-media portrayals of facial expressions, which represents a threat to the experiments' validity. The participants from the preliterate cultures were shown three photographs, told a story about a particular emotion, and were then asked to pick the picture which went with the story. Although the effect wasn't as strong, the results for the participants from the preliterate cultures replicated those for the participants from the other cultures. Ekman and Friesen's findings regarding the universality of emotional expression have been supported not only by their own subsequent research, but by others who were working independently with their own set of photographs and participants as well (e.g., Izard, 1968, 1969).

Although the emotions and the related facial expressions appear to be universal, exactly when, where, and how an emotion is expressed may be determined by the culture. There are **display rules** that can vary from culture to culture (Ekman, 1973; Ekman & Friesen, 1969). Display rules are learned ways of controlling displays of emotion in social settings. For example, Japanese people have strict social rules about showing emotion in public situations—they simply do not show emotion, remaining cool, calm, and collected, at least on the *outside*. But in a more private situation, as in a parent scolding a child within the home, the adult's facial expression easily would

display rules
learned ways of controlling displays of emotion in social settings.

---
*Preliterate: pertaining to a culture that does not have a written language

be recognized as "angry" by people of any culture. The emotion is universal and the way it is expressed on the face is universal, but whether it is expressed or displayed depends on the learned cultural rules for displaying emotion.

Gilles Kirouac of Laval University and Ursula Hess of the University of Quebec at Montreal have investigated the cultural norms regarding the appropriateness of displaying various emotions in certain contexts (e.g., public versus private). They have argued that these norms affect not only the expression of these emotions (as discussed above) but also the interpretation of these emotions by other people. Specifically, they argue that how emotions are interpreted and explained will differ when someone is aware of someone's social group membership (i.e., culture) and is also aware of the stereotypes regarding the norms for displays of emotion in this group (Kirouac & Hess, 1999). Interpretation of emotions will be discussed further in the next section.

Display rules seem to vary by the type of culture in which they occur. For example, display rules are different between cultures that are individualistic (placing the importance of the individual above the social group) and those that are collectivistic (placing the importance of the social group above that of the individual). While the culture of Canada is individualistic, for example, the culture of Japan is collectivistic. At least part of the difference between the two types of display rules may be due to these cultural differences (Edelmann & Iwawaki, 1987; Hofstede, 1980; Hofstede et al., 2002). ⓛⓘⓝⓚ *to Chapter Eleven: Theories of Personality, p. 438.*

ⓛⓘⓝⓚ *to Chapter Eleven: Theories of Personality, p. 438.*

SUBJECTIVE EXPERIENCE: LABELLING EMOTION   The third component of emotion is interpreting the subjective feeling by giving it a label: anger, fear, disgust, happiness, sadness, shame, interest, and so on. Another way of labelling this component is to call it the *cognitive component*, because the labelling process is a matter of retrieving memories of previous similar experiences, perceiving the context of the emotion, and coming up with a solution—a label.

The label a person applies to a subjective feeling is at least in part a learned response influenced by that person's language and culture. Such labels may differ in people of different cultural backgrounds. For example, a recent study (Tsai et al., 2004) found that Chinese Americans who were still firmly rooted in their original Chinese culture were far more likely to use labels to describe their emotions that referred to bodily sensations (such as "dizzy") or social relationships (such as "friendship") than were more "Westernized" Chinese Americans and European Americans.

In another study, a team of researchers led by Takahiko Masuda of the University of Alberta investigated cultural differences in judging people's emotions from their facial expressions (Masuda et al., 2008). Specifically, the researchers tested the hypothesis that Japanese, more than Westerners, incorporate information from the social context when they judge people's emotions from facial expressions. Participants were asked to look at cartoon images of five people, with the person in the middle being the "central" person (represented as much larger than the other four people). The emotional expressions of the four "background" people matched that of the "central" person in one condition and did not match that of the "central" person in another. Masuda and colleagues (2008) also used eye-tracking techniques to record where exactly the participants were looking.

As was found in Masuda's earlier work (e.g., Masuda & Nisbett, 2001, 2006; Nisbett & Masuda, 2003), the findings of Masuda and colleagues (2008) suggest that Japanese are more likely than their Western counterparts to pay attention to and consider contextual information. Japanese participants were more likely to pay attention and consider the emotional expressions of the four "background" people than were Western participants when they were asked to evaluate the central person's

◀●─ Simulate on **mypsychlab**
Recognizing Facial Expressions of Emotions

Stimulus	First response	Second response

Common sense theory

"I'm shaking because I'm afraid."

Snarling dog → **FEAR** → ANS arousal

Conscious fear

FIGURE 9.9 **Common Sense Theory of Emotion** In the common sense theory of emotion, a stimulus (snarling dog) leads to an emotion of fear, which then leads to bodily arousal (in this case, indicated by shaking) through the autonomic nervous system (ANS).

facial expressions: "Previous findings on East–West differences in contextual sensitivity generalize to social contexts, suggesting that Westerners see emotions as individual feelings, whereas Japanese see them as inseparable from the feelings of the group" (Masuda et al., 2008, p. 365).

In yet another interesting investigation into cross-cultural differences in emotion recognition, Martin G. Beaupre and Ursula Hess of the University of Quebec at Montreal looked at accuracy differences in emotion recognition among sub-Saharan African, Chinese, and French Canadian individuals living in Canada. It was found that French Canadians were more accurate in the recognition of shame and sadness than the other groups, and fear expressions were best recognized by sub-Saharan African Canadians (Beaupre & Hess, 2005).

So which of the three elements is the most important? In the early days of psychology, it was assumed that feeling a particular emotion led first to a physical reaction and then to a behavioural one. Seeing a snarling dog in one's path causes the feeling of fear, which stimulates the body to arousal, followed by the behavioural act of running. People are aroused because they are afraid (see Figure 9.9).

9.14 *How do the James–Lange and Cannon–Bard theories of emotion differ?*

JAMES–LANGE William James (1884, 1890, 1894), who was also the founder of the functionalist perspective in the early history of psychology LINK *to Chapter One: The Science of Psychology, p. 2*, disagreed with this early viewpoint. He believed that the order of the components of emotions was quite different. At nearly the same time, a physiologist and psychologist in Denmark, Carl Lange (1885), came up with an explanation of emotion so similar to that of James that the two names are used together to refer to the theory—**James–Lange theory of emotion** (see Figure 9.10).

In this theory, a stimulus of some sort (e.g., a large snarling dog) produces a physiological reaction. This reaction, which is the arousal of the "fight-or-flight" sympathetic nervous system (wanting to run), produces bodily sensations such as increased heart rate, dry mouth, and rapid breathing. James and Lange believed that the physical arousal led to the labelling of the emotion (*fear*). Simply put, "I am afraid because I am aroused," "I am embarrassed because my face is red," "I am nervous because my stomach is fluttering," and "I am in love because my heart rate increases when I look at her or him."

A problem with the James-Lange theory becomes apparent when you consider people who have spinal cord injuries that prevent the sympathetic nervous system from functioning. Although James and Lange would predict that these people should show decreased emotion because the arousal that causes emotion is no longer there, this does not in fact happen. Several studies of people with spinal cord injuries report that these people are capable of experiencing the same emotions after their injury as before, sometimes even more intensely (Bermond et al., 1991; Chwalisz et al., 1988).

CANNON–BARD Physiologists Walter Cannon (1927) and Philip Bard (1934) theorized that the emotion and the physiological arousal occur more or less at the

So which of the three elements is the most important?

James–Lange theory of emotion theory in which a physiological reaction leads to the labelling of an emotion.

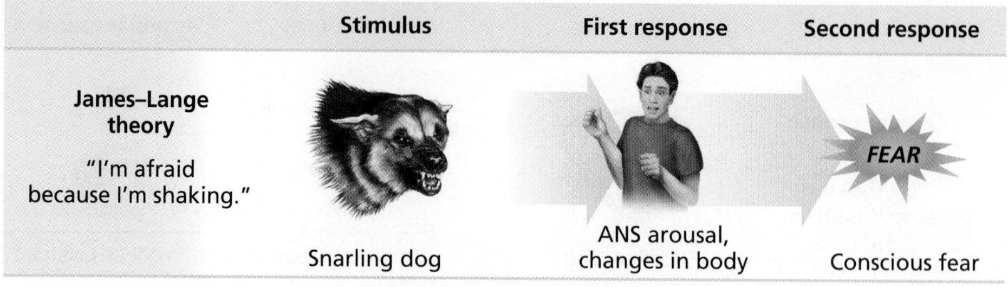

FIGURE 9.10 **James–Lange Theory of Emotion** In the James–Lange theory of emotion, a stimulus leads to bodily arousal first, which is then interpreted as an emotion.

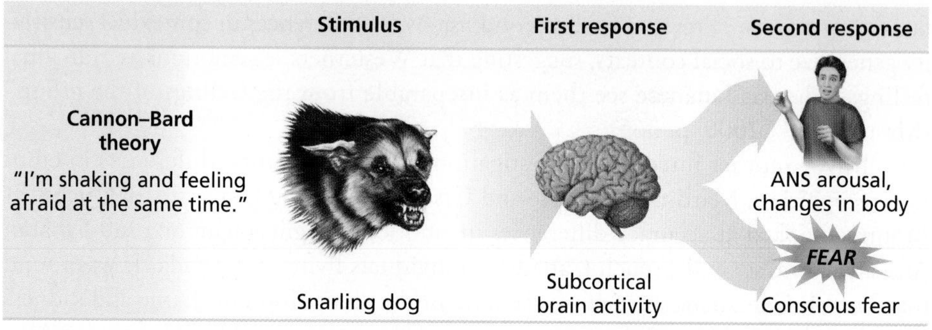

	Stimulus	First response	Second response
James–Lange theory "I'm afraid because I'm shaking."	Snarling dog	ANS arousal, changes in body	**FEAR** Conscious fear

FIGURE 9.11 **Cannon–Bard Theory of Emotion** In the Cannon–Bard theory of emotion, a stimulus leads to activity in the brain, which then sends signals to arouse the body and interpret the emotion at the same time.

	Stimulus	First response	Second response
Cannon–Bard theory "I'm shaking and feeling afraid at the same time."	Snarling dog	Subcortical brain activity	ANS arousal, changes in body **FEAR** Conscious fear

same time. Cannon, an expert in sympathetic arousal mechanisms, did not feel that the physical changes caused by different emotions were distinct enough to allow them to be perceived as different emotions. Bard expanded on this idea by stating that the sensory information that comes into the brain is sent simultaneously (by the thalamus) to both the cortex and the organs of the sympathetic nervous system. According to the **Cannon–Bard theory of emotion**, the fear and the bodily reactions are, therefore, experienced at the same time—not one after the other. "I'm afraid and running and aroused!" (See Figure 9.11.)

This theory also had its critics. Lashley (1938) stated that the thalamus would have to be very sophisticated to make sense of all the possible human emotions and relay them to the proper areas of the cortex and body. This criticism suggests that other areas of the brain must be involved in processing emotional reactions. Studies of people with spinal cord injuries, which seem to suggest that emotions can be experienced without feedback from the sympathetic organs to the cortex and which were cited as a criticism of the James–Lange theory, seem at first to support the Cannon–Bard version of emotions: People do not need feedback from those organs to experience emotion. However, there is an alternate pathway that provides feedback from these organs to the cortex: the *vagus nerve*, one of the cranial nerves (LeDoux, 1994). The existence of this feedback pathway makes the case for the Cannon–Bard theory less convincing. In addition, a major flaw with this particular theory is that Cannon and Bard stated that the three components (appraisal, emotion, and bodily reaction) arise independently of one another, which is not the case (S. Tombs, personal communication, November 3, 2009).

9.15 *What are the key elements in cognitive arousal theory, the facial feedback hypothesis, and the cognitive-mediational theory of emotion?*

SCHACHTER–SINGER AND COGNITIVE AROUSAL THEORY The early theories talked about the emotion and the physical reaction, but what about the mental interpretation of those components? In their **cognitive arousal theory**, Schachter and Singer (1962) proposed that two things have to happen before emotion occurs: the physical arousal and a labelling of the arousal based on cues from the surrounding environment. These two things happen at the same time, resulting in the labelling of the emotion (see Figure 9.12).

Cannon-Bard theory of emotion theory in which the physiological reaction and the emotion are assumed to occur at the same time.

cognitive arousal theory theory of emotion in which both the physical arousal and the labelling of that arousal based on cues from the environment must occur before the emotion is experienced.

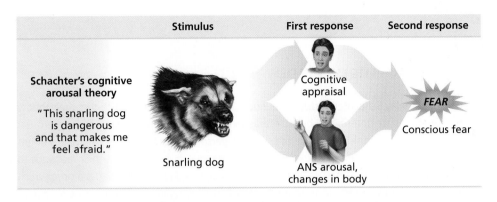

Stimulus	First response	Second response

Schachter's cognitive arousal theory

"This snarling dog is dangerous and that makes me feel afraid."

Snarling dog

Cognitive appraisal

ANS arousal, changes in body

FEAR

Conscious fear

FIGURE 9.12 **Schachter's Cognitive Arousal Theory of Emotion** Schachter's cognitive arousal theory is similar to the James–Lange theory but adds the element of cognitive labelling of the arousal. In this theory, a stimulus leads to both bodily arousal and the labelling of that arousal (based on the surrounding context), which leads to the experience and labelling of the emotional reaction.

Stimulus	First response	Second response

Facial feedback theory

ANS arousal in face

Facial expression

Cognitive interpretation of face motions

FEAR

FIGURE 9.13 **Facial Feedback Theory of Emotion** In the facial feedback theory of emotion, a stimulus such as this snarling dog causes arousal and a facial expression. The facial expression then provides feedback to the brain about the emotion. The brain then interprets the emotion and may also intensify it.

For example, if a person comes across a snarling dog while taking a walk, the physical arousal (heart racing, eyes opening wide) is accompanied by the thought (cognition) that this must be fear. Then and only then will the person experience the fear emotion. In other words, "I am aroused in the presence of a scary dog; therefore, I must be afraid." Evidence for this theory was found in what is now a classic experiment, described in the Classic Studies in Psychology section on p. 386.

THE FACIAL FEEDBACK HYPOTHESIS: SMILE, YOU'LL FEEL BETTER   In his book *The Expression of the Emotions in Man and Animals*, Charles Darwin (1898) stated that facial expressions evolved as a way of communicating intentions, such as threat or fear, and that these expressions are universal within a species rather than specific to a culture. He also believed (as in the James–Lange theory) that when such emotions are expressed freely on the face, the emotion itself intensifies—meaning that the more one smiles, the happier one feels.

Modern psychologists have proposed a theory of emotion that is consistent with much of Darwin's original thinking. Called the **facial feedback hypothesis**, this explanation assumes that facial expressions provide feedback to the brain concerning the emotion being expressed, which in turn not only intensifies the emotion but also actually *causes* the emotion (Buck, 1980; Ekman, 1980; Ekman & Friesen, 1978; Keillor et al., 2002). (See Figure 9.13.)

Does that mean that I don't smile because I'm happy—I'm happy because I smile? As the old song goes, "put on a happy face" and yes, you'll feel happier, according to the facial feedback hypothesis. One fairly recent study does cast some doubt on the validity of this hypothesis, however. If the facial feedback hypothesis is correct, then people who have facial paralysis on both sides of the face should be unable to experience emotions in a normal way. But a case study conducted on just such a person revealed that although she was unable to express emotions on her paralyzed face, she could respond emotionally to slides meant to stimulate emotional reactions, just as anyone else would (Keillor et al., 2002). In addition, it is important to note that this facial feedback effect has been found to differ considerably from person to person and while the effect has been found in many different studies, the overall effects appear to be small in magnitude (S. Tombs, personal communication, November 3, 2009). Clearly, the question of how much the actual facial expression determines the emotional experience has yet to be fully answered.

Does that mean that I don't smile because I'm happy—I'm happy because I smile?

facial feedback hypothesis theory of emotion that assumes that facial expressions provide feedback to the brain concerning the emotion being expressed, which in turn causes and intensifies the emotion.

CLASSIC STUDIES IN PSYCHOLOGY

The Angry/Happy Man

In 1962, Stanley Schachter and Jerome Singer designed an experiment to test their theory that emotions are determined by an interaction between the physiological state of arousal and the label, or cognitive interpretation, that a person places on the arousal. Male student volunteers were told that they were going to answer a questionnaire about their reactions to a new vitamin called *Suproxin*. In reality, they were all injected with epinephrine, a drug which causes physical arousal in the form of increased heart rate, rapid breathing, and a reddened face—all responses that happen during a strong emotional reaction.

Each student then participated in one of two conditions. In one condition, a confederate* posing as one of the participants started complaining about the experimenter, tearing up his questionnaire and storming out. In the other condition, there was one man who acted more like he was very happy, almost giddy and playing with some of the objects in the room. The "angry" man and the "happy" man in both conditions deliberately behaved in the two different ways as part of the experiment.

The facial feedback hypothesis assumes that changing your own facial expression can change the way you feel. Smiling makes people feel happy, and frowning makes people feel sad. This effect seems to have an impact on the people around us as well. If this is true, this smiling woman may make the airline steward handing her the food feel good, too. Is it hard for you to stay in a bad mood when the people around you are smiling and laughing?

After both conditions had played out, participants in each of the two conditions were asked to describe their own emotions. The participants who had been exposed to the "angry" man interpreted their arousal symptoms as anger, whereas those exposed to the "happy" man interpreted their arousal as happiness. In all cases, the actual cause of arousal was the epinephrine and the physical symptoms of arousal were identical. The only difference between the two groups of participants was their exposure to the two different contexts. Schachter and Singer's theory would have predicted exactly these results: Physiological arousal has to be interpreted cognitively before it is experienced as a specific emotion.

Although this classic experiment stimulated a lot of research, much of that research has failed to find much support for the cognitive arousal theory of emotion (Reisenzein, 1983, 1994). But this theory did draw attention to the important role that cognition plays in determining emotions. The role of cognition in emotion has been revisited in some more modern theories of emotion, such as the facial feedback hypothesis and Lazarus's cognitive-mediational theory of emotion.

Questions for Further Discussion

1. How might observing the emotions of others under more normal circumstances (i.e., not in a drugged state) affect a person's own emotional state?

2. According to Schachter and Singer's theory, for your first date with a person, should you choose a happy movie or a sad one?

3. In this experiment, what was the independent variable manipulated by the experimenters? What was the dependent variable?

4. This experiment used deception, as the participants were not told the true nature of the injection they received. What kind of ethical problems might have arisen from this deception? What problems would the experimenters have had in getting this study approved by an ethics committee today?

---

*Confederate: someone who is cooperating with another person on some task

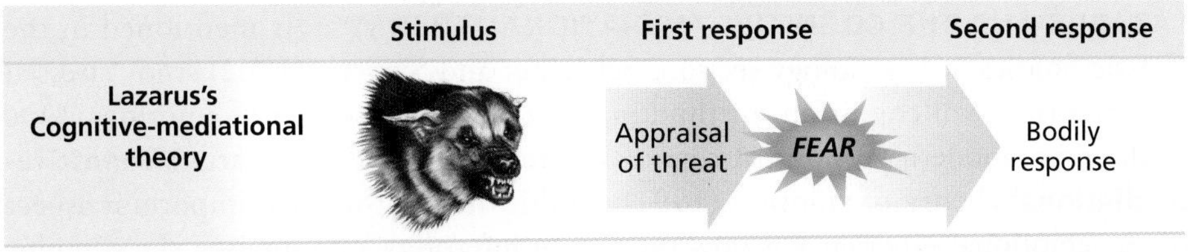

	Stimulus	First response		Second response
Lazarus's Cognitive-mediational theory		Appraisal of threat	**FEAR**	Bodily response

	Stimulus	First response	Second response
Common sense theory "I'm shaking because I'm afraid."	Snarling dog	**FEAR** Conscious fear	ANS arousal
James-Lange theory "I'm afraid because I'm shaking."	Snarling dog	ANS arousal, changes in body	**FEAR** Conscious fear
Cannon-Bard theory "I'm shaking and feeling afraid at the same time."	Snarling dog	Subcortical brain activity	ANS arousal, changes in body **FEAR** Conscious fear
Schachter's cognitive arousal theory "This snarling dog is dangerous and that makes me feel afraid."	Snarling dog	Cognitive appraisal ANS arousal, changes in body	**FEAR** Conscious fear
Facial feedback theory		ANS arousal in face → Facial expression → Cognitive interpretation of face motions	**FEAR**
Lazarus's cognitive-mediational theory		Appraisal of threat **FEAR**	Bodily response

FIGURE 9.14 **Lazarus's Cognitive-Mediational Theory of Emotion** In Lazarus's cognitive-mediational theory of emotion, a stimulus causes an immediate appraisal (e.g., "The dog is snarling and not behind a fence, so this is dangerous"). The cognitive appraisal results in an emotional response, which is then followed by the appropriate bodily response.

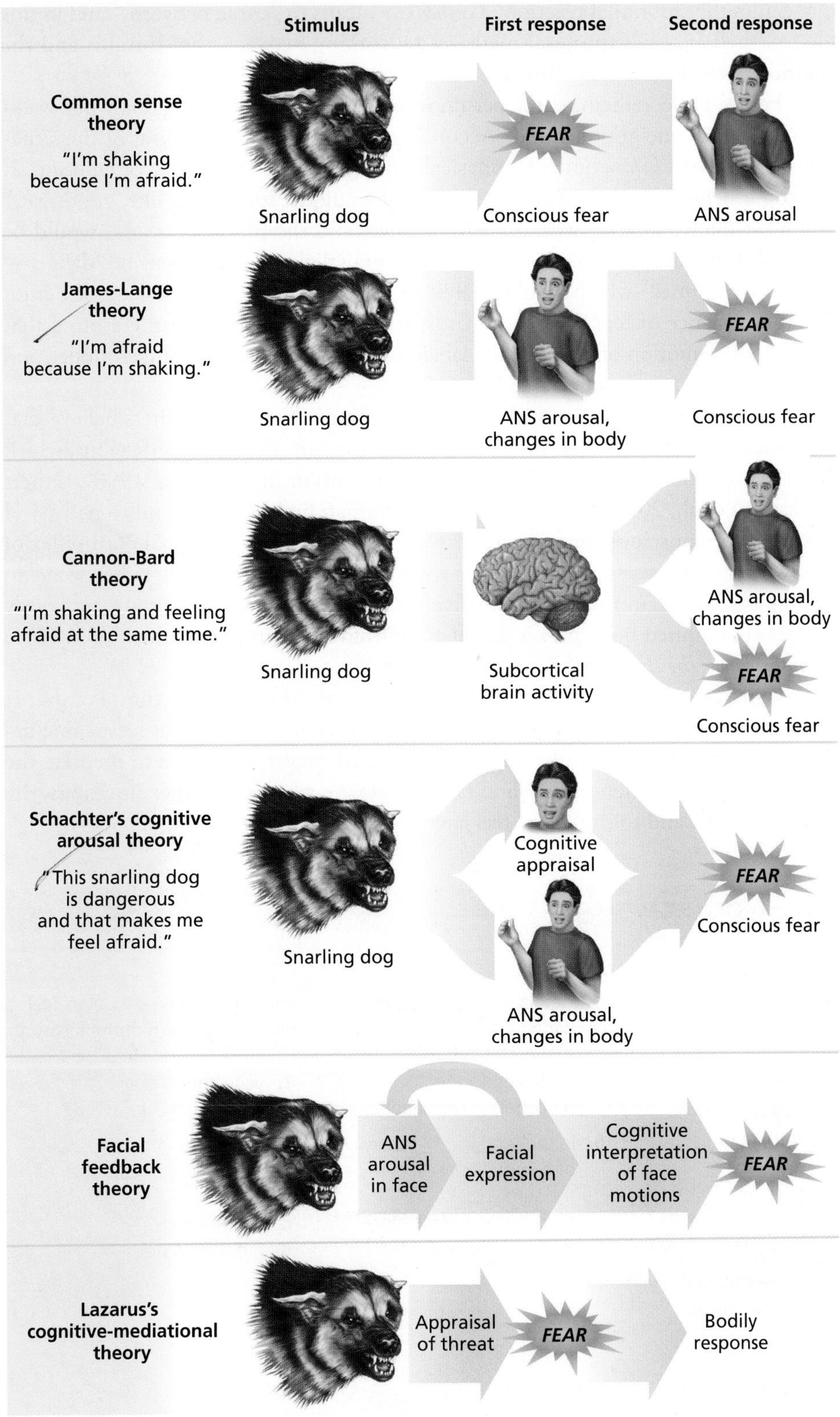

FIGURE 9.15 **Comparison of Theories of Emotion** These figures represent the six different theories of emotion as discussed in the text.

LAZARUS AND THE COGNITIVE-MEDIATIONAL THEORY   As mentioned in the Classic Studies in Psychology section, Schachter and Singer's (1962) study stressed the importance of cognition, or thinking, in the determination of emotions. One of the more modern versions of cognitive emotion theories is Lazarus's **cognitive-mediational theory** of emotion (1991). In this theory, the most important aspect of any emotional experience is how the person interprets, or appraises, the stimulus that causes the emotional reaction. To *mediate* means to "come between," and in this theory, the cognitive appraisal mediates by coming between the stimulus and the emotional response to that stimulus.

For example, remember the person who encountered a snarling dog while walking through the neighbourhood? According to Lazarus, the appraisal of the situation would come *before* both the physical arousal and the experience of emotion. If the dog is behind a sturdy fence, the appraisal would be something like "no threat." The most likely emotion would be annoyance, and the physical arousal would be minimal. But if the dog is not confined, the appraisal would more likely be "danger—threatening animal!" which would be followed by an increase in arousal and the emotional experience of fear. In other words, it's the *interpretation* of the arousal that results in the emotion of fear, not the labelling as in the Schachter–Singer model, and the interpretation comes first (see Figure 9.14).

Not everyone agrees with this theory, of course. Some researchers believe that emotional reactions to situations are so fast that they are almost instantaneous, which would leave little time for a cognitive appraisal to occur first (Zajonc, 1998). Others (Kilhstrom et al., 2000) have found that the human brain can respond to a physical threat before conscious thought enters the picture. The simple spinal cord reflex of pain withdrawal discussed in Chapter Two is an example of this—the reflex occurs so quickly that the brain itself is not involved, and the experience of pain is consciously felt *after* the injured body part is jerked away from the painful stimulus. (L)(I)(N)(K) *to Chapter Two: The Biological Perspective, p. 42.* *Chapter Two: The Biological Perspective, p. 42.*

Which theory is right? Human emotions are so incredibly complex that it might not be out of place to say that all the theories are correct to at least some degree. In certain situations, the cognitive appraisal might have time to mediate the emotion that is experienced (such as falling in love), whereas in other situations, the need to act first and to think and feel later is more important (see Figure 9.15).

cognitive-mediational theory
theory of emotion in which a stimulus must be interpreted (appraised) by a person in order to result in a physical response and an emotional reaction.

Which theory is right? ▶

✳ Explore on **mypsychlab**
Theories of Emotion

PRACTICE QUIZ: HOW MUCH DO YOU REMEMBER?

Pick the best answer.

1. Which of the following is NOT one of the three elements of emotion?
   a. subjective experience
   b. behaviour
   c. attention
   d. physical reaction

2. The theory of emotion that states that the thalamus sends sensory information to the cortex and the sympathetic organs at the same time is the _____ theory.
   a. James–Lange
   b. Cannon–Bard
   c. Schachter–Singer
   d. facial feedback

3. In Schachter and Singer's classic study, participants who were exposed to the "angry" man interpreted their physiological arousal as _____, whereas those who were exposed to the "happy" man interpreted their arousal as _____.
   a. angry; happy
   b. happy; angry
   c. happy; happy
   d. angry; angry

4. Gerald smiles a lot at the office, which makes his co-workers feel happier, too. This effect is best explained by which of the following theories of emotion?
   a. James–Lange
   b. cognitive-mediational
   c. Schachter–Singer
   d. facial feedback

5. In the _____ theory of emotion, the most important aspect of an emotional experience is the interpretation, or appraisal, of the stimulus.
   a. cognitive-mediational
   b. Cannon–Bard
   c. James–Lange
   d. facial feedback

APPLYING PSYCHOLOGY TO EVERYDAY LIFE: CAROL DWECK'S SELF-THEORY OF MOTIVATION

9.16 How do people get to be high achievers?

According to motivation and personality psychologist Carol Dweck (1999), the need for achievement is closely linked to personality factors, including a person's view of how *self* can affect the understanding of how much a person's actions can influence his or her success. (Dweck defines *self* as the beliefs one holds about one's abilities and relationships to others.) This concept is related to the much older notion of *locus of control*, in which people who assume that they have control over what happens in their lives are considered to be *internal* in locus of control, and those who feel that their lives are controlled by powerful others, luck, or fate are considered to be *external* in locus of control (MacDonald, 1970; Rotter, 1966).

Dweck has amassed a large body of empirical research, particularly in the field of education, to support the idea that people's "theories" about their own selves can affect their level of achievement motivation and their willingness to keep trying to achieve success in the face of failure (Dweck, 1986; Dweck & Elliott, 1983; Dweck & Leggett, 1988; Elliott & Dweck, 1988). According to this research, people can form one of two belief systems about intelligence, which in turn affects their motivation to achieve. Those who believe intelligence is fixed and unchangeable often demonstrate an external locus of control, leading them to give up easily or avoid situations in which they might fail—often ensuring their own failure in the process. They are prone to developing learned helplessness, the tendency to stop trying to achieve a goal because past failure has led them to believe that they cannot succeed. L I N K *to Chapter Five: Learning, p. 176.* Their goals involve trying to "look smart" and outperform others ("See, at least I did better than she did"). For example, a student faced with a big exam may avoid coming to class that day, even though that might mean getting an even lower score on a makeup exam.

This does not mean that students with this view of intelligence are always unsuccessful. In fact, Dweck's research (1999) suggests that students who have had a long history of successes may be most at risk for developing a learned helplessness after a big failure precisely because their previous successes have led them to believe in their own fixed intelligence. For example, a child who had never earned anything less than an "A" in school who then receives his first "C" might become depressed and refuse to do any more homework, ensuring future failure.

The other type of person believes that intelligence is changeable and can be shaped by experiences and effort in small increases, or increments. These people tend to show an internal locus of control, believing that their own actions and efforts will improve their intelligence. They work at developing new strategies and get involved in new tasks, with the goal of increasing their "smarts." They are motivated to master tasks and don't allow failure to destroy their confidence in themselves or prevent them from trying again and again, using new strategies each time.

Based on this and other research, Dweck recommends that parents and teachers encourage children to value the learning process more than "looking smart" by always having the right answer (and responding only when sure of that answer, for example). Errors should not be viewed as failures but as a way to improve future

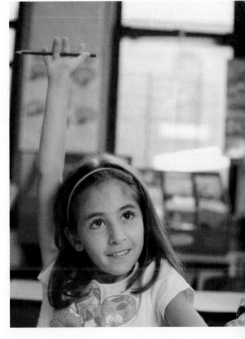

Many people are driven by a need to attain both realistic and challenging goals. This young girl seems eager to provide an answer to the teacher's question, and the teacher's positive feedback will help foster the girl's need for achievement.

performance on the road to mastering whatever the goal in question is. Essentially, this means praising efforts and the methods that children use to make those efforts, not just successes or ability. Instead of saying, "You're right, how smart you are," the parent or teacher should say something such as "You are really thinking hard," or "That was a very clever way to think about this problem." In the past, teachers and parents have been told that praise is good and criticism is bad—it might damage a child's self-esteem. Dweck believes that constructive criticism, when linked with praise of effort and the use of strategies, will be a better influence on the child's self-esteem than endless praise that can become meaningless when given indiscriminately.

Questions for Further Discussion

1. How can this information be used by educators to better educate children? How can it be used by parents to better raise their children?

2. Has reading this section affected your beliefs regarding parenting? If you are already a parent, are you going to parent your child/children differently as a result of reading this section? If you aren't already a parent, but plan on becoming one, will you use this information to help you parent?

9  CHAPTER SUMMARY

Approaches to Understanding Motivation

9.1 *How do psychologists define motivation, and what are the key elements of the early instinct and drive-reduction approaches to motivation?*

- Motivation is the process by which activities are started, directed, and sustained to fulfill physical or psychological needs.

- Intrinsic motivation occurs when people act because the act itself is satisfying or rewarding, whereas extrinsic motivation occurs when people receive an external reward (such as money) for the act.

- Instinct approaches proposed that some human actions may be motivated by instincts, which are innate patterns of behaviour found in both people and animals.

- Drive-reduction approaches state that when an organism has a need (such as hunger), the need leads to psychological tension that motivates the organism to act, fulfilling the need and reducing the tension.

- Primary drives involve needs of the body, whereas acquired (secondary) drives are those learned through experience. Homeostasis is the tendency of the body to maintain a steady state.

9.2 *What are the characteristics of the three types of needs?*

- The need for achievement is a strong desire to succeed in getting to one's goals, both realistic and challenging.

- The need for affiliation is the desire to have friendly social interactions and relationships with others and a desire to be held in high regard by others.

- The need for power concerns having control over others, influencing them, and having an impact on them. Status and prestige are important to people high in this need.

9.3 *What are the key elements of the arousal and incentive approaches to motivation?*

- In arousal theory, a person has an optimal level of arousal to maintain. People who need more arousal than others are called *sensation seekers*.

- In the incentive approach, an external stimulus may be so rewarding that it motivates a person to act toward that stimulus rather than another stimulus or to satisfy a drive.

9.4 *How do Maslow's humanistic approach and self-determination theory explain motivation, and how has evolutionary theory changed how researchers view Maslow's hierarchy?*

- Maslow proposed a hierarchy of needs, beginning with basic physiological needs and ending with self-actualization needs. The more basic needs must be met before the higher needs can be fulfilled.

Psychology in the News: Turning Maslow's Hierarchy Upside-Down

- Kenrick, Griskevicius, Neuberg, and Schaller (2010) maintain that the need to find and keep a significant other and raise healthy children is more important than the pursuit of self-actualization. In addition, the authors argue that the concept of self-actualization may not be universal—that it seems to be appealing to only those within Western societies

- Schaller and his colleagues don't argue that Maslow's model needs to be discarded, instead they suggest that Maslow's conception can be combined with more recent theoretical developments in the field of evolutionary biology, anthropology, and psychology to make it stronger and more relevant to the findings of today.

- Self-determination theory (SDT) is a model of motivation in which three basic needs are seen as necessary to an individual's successful development: autonomy, competence, and relatedness.

- The need for autonomy is the psychological need that involves knowing that one's actions are self-determined rather than controlled by others; the need for competence is the psychological need that humans have to succeed at challenging tasks and to receive positive feedback from others; and the need for relatedness is the psychological needs that humans have to form emotional bonds with those around them

- The SDT comprises five "mini-theories": cognitive evaluation theory (CET), causality orientations theory (COT), goal contents theory (GCT), basic psychological needs theory (BPNT), and, finally, organismic integration theory (OIT).

What, Hungry Again? Why People Eat

9.5   *What biological and social factors influence hunger?*

- The physiological components of hunger include signals from the stomach and the hypothalamus and the increased secretion of insulin.
- When the basal metabolic rate slows down, the weight set point increases and makes weight gain more likely.
- Scientists have researched the role of leptin, a hormone that controls the feeling of being full, in obesity.
- Genetics and insensitivity to leptin may play a part in anorexia and bulimia.
- The social components of hunger include social cues for when meals are to be eaten, cultural customs and food preferences, and the use of food as a comfort device or escape from unpleasantness.

9.6   *What are some problems in eating behaviour?*

- Maladaptive eating problems include obesity, anorexia, and bulimia.

Other Drives

9.7   *What is the difference between intracellular thirst and extracellular thirst?*

- Like hunger, thirst is also a basic biological drive.
- There are two types of thirst: intracellular thirst and extracellular thirst.
- Intracellular thirst is the loss of water from inside the cells of the body and often results from the intake of salty foods.
- Extracellular thirst is the loss of water from bodily tissues and often results from sweating, vomiting, having diarrhea, bleeding, and drinking alcohol.

9.8   *How is the sex drive different from the hunger and thirst drives?*

- Sexual motivation is different from hunger and thirst motivation because while the hunger and thirst drives are very much related to bodily need states, the sex drive is not.
- Although sex is not necessary for survival of an individual, sex *is* necessary for the survival of the species.

Human Sexuality

9.9   *What are the physical differences between females and males, and what does it mean to be "intersex"?*

- The female sexual organs present at birth are the primary sex characteristics of the vagina, uterus, and ovaries.
- The female sexual organs that develop during puberty are secondary sex characteristics consisting of the growth spurt, onset of the menstrual cycle, breast development, widening hips, pubic hair, fat deposits, and further growth and development of the uterus, vagina, and ovaries.
- The primary male sex characteristics are the penis, scrotum, testicles, and prostate gland.
- The secondary male sex characteristics are an enlarged larynx (Adam's apple), deepening voice, facial and chest hair, pubic hair, coarser skin texture, and a large increase in height.

- The term *intersex* refers to a congenital anomaly of the reproductive and sexual system which makes it difficult to determine an infant's sex at birth. Intersex people are born with external genitalia, an endocrine system, and internal reproductive organs that are different from those of most other people.
- This condition used to be commonly referred to as *hermaphroditism*, which was defined as the condition of possessing both male and female sex organs. This term is inaccurate as it is very rare to find a person who truly has both ovary and testicle material in one body.
- Sexual reassignment is still very common in early infancy and often leads to adolescents or young adults who reject the reassignment and face depression and anxiety.

9.10   *How did Kinsey study human sexual behaviour, and what were the findings of the Janus Report?*

- Alfred Kinsey conducted a series of sexual behaviour surveys in the late 1940s and early 1950s, revealing some highly controversial findings about the kinds of sexual behaviour common among people in the United States, including homosexuality, premarital sex, and extramarital sex.
- Janus and Janus, in the mid 1990s, published the results of a large-scale survey of sexual behaviour in the United States. Their survey results did not differ widely from those of Kinsey but looked at many more types of sexual behaviour and factors related to sexual behaviour than did Kinsey's surveys.

9.11   *What are the different sexual orientations, and how do they develop?*

- Heterosexuals are attracted to people of the opposite sex and represent the largest sexual orientation.
- Homosexuals are primarily attracted to people of the same sex and make up about 9 percent of men and 5 percent of women.
- Bisexuals are people who are attracted to both males and females.
- The evidence for biological influences on sexual orientation is increasingly convincing.
- The issue of what causes sexual orientation will continue to generate research and controversy for a long time to come.

Emotion

9.12   *What are the three elements of emotion?*

- Emotion is the "feeling" aspect of consciousness and includes physical, behavioural, and subjective components.

9.13   *How does culture affect the expression and interpretation of emotional expressions?*

- Although the emotions and the related facial expressions appear to be universal, exactly when, where, and how an emotion is expressed may be determined by the culture.
- How emotions are interpreted and explained will differ when someone is aware of the person's culture and the stereotypes surrounding the displaying of emotions in that culture.
- Non-Westerners tend to incorporate information from the social context when they judge people's emotions from facial expressions, while Westerners do not.

9.14   *How do the James–Lange and Cannon–Bard theories of emotion differ?*

- The James–Lange theory states that a stimulus creates a physiological response that then leads to the labelling of the emotion.
- The Cannon–Bard theory asserts that the physiological reaction and the emotion are simultaneous, as the thalamus sends sensory information to both the cortex of the brain and the organs of the sympathetic nervous system.

9.15 *What are the key elements in cognitive arousal theory, the facial feed-back hypothesis, and the cognitive-mediational theory of emotion?*

• In Schachter and Singer's cognitive arousal theory, both the physiological arousal and the actual interpretation of that arousal must occur before the emotion itself is experienced. This interpretation is based on cues from the environment.

• In the facial feedback hypothesis, facial expressions provide feedback to the brain about the emotion being expressed on the face, intensifying the emotion.

Classic Studies in Psychology: The Angry/Happy Man

• In the cognitive-mediational theory of emotion, the cognitive component of emotion (the interpretation) precedes both the physiological reaction and the emotion itself.

• Those participants who were exposed to the "angry" man interpreted their physical arousal as anger, whereas those who were exposed to the "happy" man interpreted their physical arousal as happiness.

Applying Psychology to Everyday Life: Carol Dweck's Self-theory of Motivation

9.16 *How do people get to be high achievers?*

• The self-theory of emotion links the need for achievement to the concept of locus of control. A belief in control over one's life leads to more attempts to achieve, even in the face of failure. Those who believe that they have little control over what happens to them are more likely to develop learned helplessness.

9 KEY TERMS

acquired (secondary) drives   354
androgens   373
anorexia nervosa   368
arousal theory   355
basal metabolic rate (BMR)   366
bisexual   376
bulimia   369
Cannon–Bard theory of emotion   384
cognitive arousal theory   384
cognitive-mediational theory   387
display rules   381
drive   353
drive-reduction theory   353
emotion   379
estrogens   373
expectancy-value theories   357
extracellular thirst   371
extrinsic motivation   352
facial feedback hypothesis   385
glucagons   365
heterosexual   376
homeostasis   354

homosexual   376
incentive approaches   356
incentives   356
instinct approach   353
instincts   353
insulin   365
intersex   374
intersex people/people with intersex conditions/experiences   373
intracellular thirst   371
intrinsic motivation   352
James–Lange theory of emotion   383
leptin   366
mammary glands   373
menstrual cycle   372
motivation   352
need   353
need for achievement (nAch)   354
need for affiliation (nAff)   355
need for autonomy   360
need for competence   361

need for power (nPow)   355
need for relatedness   362
ovaries   372
peak experiences   358
penis   372
primary drives   353
primary sex characteristics   372
prostate gland   372
scrotum   372
secondary sex characteristics   372
self-actualization   357
self-determination theory (SDT)   360
sensation seeker   356
sexual deviance   376
sexual orientation   376
stimulus motive   355
testes (testicles)   372
uterus   372
vagina   372
weight set point   365
Yerkes-Dodson law   355

TEST YOURSELF

Pick the best answer.

1. The approach to motivation that forced psychologists to consider the hereditary factors in motivation was the _____ approach.
   a. arousal
   b. drive-reduction
   c. instinct
   d. incentive

2. The need for money is an example of a(n) _____ drive.
   a. primary
   b. acquired
   c. innate
   d. instinctive

3. Jocelyn needs to be the one whose ideas are always used and craves prestige among others. She drives an expensive car and wears nothing but the most expensive clothes. Jocelyn is high in the need for
   a. achievement.
   b. affiliation.
   c. power.
   d. attention.

4. People who are always looking for a challenge may be high in the need for
   a. achievement.
   b. affiliation.
   c. power.
   d. attention.

5. Gene is trying to choose a snack. There is a bowl of fruit on the table, but there's also a candy bar that he bought yesterday. The fact that Gene feels drawn to choose the candy bar instead of the fruit is an example of the power of
   a. needs.
   b. drives.
   c. incentives.
   d. arousal.

6. According to Maslow, a person who wants to become self-actualized must first satisfy
   a. higher needs before other more basic needs.
   b. more basic needs such as food and safety.
   c. needs for creativity, justice, and the appreciation of beauty.
   d. needs for achievement, affiliation, and power.

7. Shontia works at a daycare centre. The pay is low and the hours are long, but she loves being around children and has no desire to look for a higher-paying job. Shontia's motivation appears to be
   a. intrinsic.   c. selfish.
   b. extrinsic.   d. external.

8. When we eat, the pancreas releases _____, which lowers blood sugar and can increase the feeling of hunger.
   a. glucose   c. thyroxin
   b. insulin   d. adrenaline

9. According to the organismic integration theory, which form of regulation is the most self-determined?
   a. external regulation   c. identified regulation
   b. introjected regulation   d. integrated regulation

10. The structure in the brain that, when damaged, causes rats to stop eating is called the
    a. ventromedial pituitary.   c. ventromedial hypothalamus.
    b. lateral hippocampus.   d. lateral hypothalamus.

11. The rate at which your body burns energy when at rest is called the
    a. basal metabolic rate.   c. basal set point.
    b. weight set point.   d. weight metabolic rate.

12. If there is a history of obesity in a family, each family member has _____ of becoming obese compared to people without such a family history.
    a. the same risk   c. five times the risk
    b. double or triple the risk   d. less risk

13. Unlike anorexics, bulimics
    a. often purge themselves to stay thin.
    b. are obsessed with being too fat.
    c. can do damage to their health.
    d. may appear to be normal in weight.

14. The role of _____, a neurotransmitter that is also implicated in obesity, may provide clues to both bulimia and anorexia.
    a. serotonin   c. dopamine
    b. insulin   d. norepinephrine

15. You caught the stomach flu and have been vomiting for a few hours. As a result, you are very thirsty. What type of thirst would this be classified as?
    a. intracellular thirst   c. extracellular thirst
    b. sedentary thirst   d. non-cellular thirst

16. Which statement about primary sex characteristics is true?
    a. They are directly involved in human reproduction.
    b. They develop during puberty.

c. They are the same for males and females.
d. They include the formation of breasts and growth of the beard.

17. An intersex person is
    a. a person who has sex with both men and women.
    b. another name for a homosexual.
    c. a person born with ambiguous sexual organs.
    d. another name for a heterosexual.

18. Which of the following studies of sexual behaviour was not a survey?
    a. the Kinsey Report   c. Masters and Johnson's study
    b. the Janus Report   d. All of the above were surveys.

19. The most recent surveys indicate that about _____ percent of men and _____ percent of women are predominantly homosexual.
    a. 22; 17   c. 5; 9
    b. 15; 10   d. 9; 5

20. Bisexual people
    a. have multiple relationships with men and women at the same time.
    b. are equally attracted to both sexes.
    c. can be either male or female.
    d. rarely have long-term, monogamous relationships.

21. Your heart is racing, your breathing is rapid, and your mouth is dry. What emotion are you experiencing?
    a. anger
    b. fear
    c. happiness
    d. It is not always possible to distinguish one emotion from another by physiological reactions only.

22. The _____ theory of emotion would predict that people with spinal cord injuries that prevent them from experiencing sympathetic arousal would show decreased emotion.
    a. James–Lange   c. Schachter–Singer
    b. Cannon–Bard   d. facial feedback

23. In Schachter and Singer's classic study, participants were physically aroused by
    a. exposure to a "happy" man.   c. receiving epinephrine.
    b. exposure to an "angry" man. d. watching an exciting film.

24. The theory of emotion that owes a lot to Darwin's work is the _____ theory.
    a. James–Lange   c. Schachter–Singer
    b. Cannon–Bard   d. facial feedback

25. Researchers have found that the human brain
    a. must be consciously aware of a threat before responding.
    b. can respond to a threat before it becomes conscious of the threat.
    c. is not involved in emotions at all.
    d. is important in the spinal cord pain withdrawal reflex.

Answers: 1.-c, 2.-b, 3.-c, 4.-a, 5.-c, 6.-b, 7.-a, 8.-b, 9.-d, 10.-d, 11.-a, 12.-b, 13.-d, 14.-a, 15.-c, 16.-a, 17.-c, 18.-c, 19.-d, 20.-c, 21.-d, 22.-a, 23.-c, 24.-d, 25.-b.

ScanLife™ Barcode

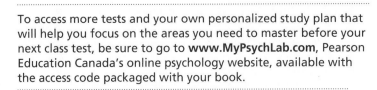

To access more tests and your own personalized study plan that will help you focus on the areas you need to master before your next class test, be sure to go to **www.MyPsychLab.com**, Pearson Education Canada's online psychology website, available with the access code packaged with your book.

Approaches to Motivation

Motivation: process by which activities are started, directed, and sustained to fulfill physical or psychological needs

9.1

Instinct Approaches to Motivation

Human and animal actions may be motivated by innate behaviour patterns.

9.1

Drive-Reduction Approaches to Motivation

Drive-reduction approaches: Needs (such as hunger) motivate the organism to act, fulfilling the need and reducing psychological tension.

Homeostasis: tendency of the body to maintain a steady state

Primary drives: involve survival needs of the body

Secondary drives: those learned through experience

9.1

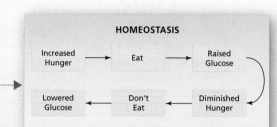

HOMEOSTASIS

Increased Hunger → Eat → Raised Glucose

Lowered Glucose ← Don't Eat ← Diminished Hunger

Arousal Approaches to Motivation

People have an optimal level of arousal to maintain.

Sensation seekers: need more arousal than others

Incentive Approaches to Motivation

External stimuli may be so rewarding that they motivate a person to act toward those stimuli rather than another set of stimuli or to satisfy a drive.

9.3

Three Types of Needs

Need for achievement: desire to succeed in getting to one's goals, both realistic and challenging

Need for affiliation: desire to have friendly social interactions and be held in high regard by others

Need for power: desire to have control over others, influence them, and have an impact on them

9.2

Maslow's Hierarchy of Needs

Begins with basic physiological needs and ends with self-actualization needs. Basic needs must be met before the higher needs can be fulfilled.

From lowest to highest:

Physiological needs, safety needs, belongingness and love needs, esteem needs, cognitive needs, aesthetic needs, self-actualization needs

▶ Researchers have updated Maslow's model by suggesting that Maslow's conception can be combined with more recent theoretical developments in the field of evolutionary biology, anthropology, and psychology to make it stronger and more relevant to the findings of today.

▶ These researchers maintain that finding and keeping a significant other and raising children is more important than self-actualization and that self-actualization may not be universal.

9.4

Eating Behaviours

Self-Determination Theory of Motivation

Self-determination theory (SDT): model of motivation with three basic needs: autonomy, competence, and relatedness

Satisfying these needs increases intrinsic motivation.

The SDT comprises five "mini-theories": cognitive evaluation theory (CET), causality orientations theory (COT), goal contents theory (GCT), basic psychological needs theory (BPNT), and, finally, organismic integration theory (OIT).

9.4

Biological Causes of Hunger

Physiological components: signals from the stomach, increased secretion of insulin, and actions of hypothalamus

Weight gain: When the basal metabolic rate slows down, the weight set point increases and makes weight gain more likely.

Social Causes of Hunger

▶ Social cues for when meals are to be eaten
▶ Cultural customs and food preferences
▶ Use of food as a comfort device or escape

Biological Factors in Obesity

Leptin: hormone that controls the feeling of being full

Genetics: may play a part in anorexia and bulimia, insensitivity to leptin

9.5

Problems in Eating Behaviour

Obesity

Anorexia: weight loss of 15 percent below the ideal body weight

Bulimia: cycle of "binging" and "purging"

9.6

Other Drives

Thirst

- Thirst is a basic biological drive.
- **Intracellular thirst:** loss of water from inside the cells of the body
- **Extracellular thirst:** loss of water from bodily tissues

Sex

- While the hunger and thirst drives are related to bodily need states, the sex drive is not.
- Although sex is not necessary for survival of an individual, sex is necessary for the survival of the species.

9.7–9.8

Male and Female Physical Differences

Female sex characteristics:

Primary: vagina, uterus, ovaries

Secondary: growth spurt, menstrual cycle, breast development, widening hips, pubic hair, fat deposits

Male sex characteristics:

Primary: penis, scrotum, testicles, prostate gland

Secondary: enlarged larynx (Adam's apple), deepening voice, facial and chest hair, pubic hair, coarser skin texture, and a large increase in height

Intersex

a congenital anomaly of the reproductive and sexual system which makes it difficult to determine an infant's sex at birth. Intersex people are born with external genitalia, an endocrine system, and internal reproductive organs, and/or endocrine system that are different from those of most other people

9.9

Kinsey's Study of Human Sexual Behaviour

- Sexual behaviour surveys in the late 1940s and early 1950s
- Highly controversial findings of sexual behaviour, including homo-sexuality, premarital sex, and extramarital sex

Janus Report Findings (mid 1990s)

- Results did not differ widely from those of Kinsey
- Looked at more types of sexual behaviour and factors than Kinsey

9.10

Sexual Orientations

Heterosexuals: attracted to people of the opposite sex

Homosexuals: primarily attracted to people of the same sex

Bisexuals: attracted to both males and females

9.11

Three Elements of Emotion

Emotion is the "feeling" aspect of consciousness and includes physical, behavioural, and subjective components.

9.12

Emotion

Cognitive-Mediational Theory

Cognitive component of emotion (the interpretation) precedes both the physiological reaction and the emotion itself.

9.17

Culture and Emotions

- Some emotions and the related facial expressions are universal, but when, where, and how an emotion is expressed may be determined by the culture.
- Interpretation of emotions differ depending on cultural awareness.

9.13

Theories of Emotion

James–Lange: Stimuli create physiological responses that then lead to the labelling of the emotion.

Cannon–Bard: Physiological reactions and emotions are simultaneous, as the thalamus sends sensory information to both the cortex and sympathetic nervous system.

9.14

Theories of Emotion

Schacter–Singer Cognitive Arousal: Both physiological arousal and actual interpretation of arousal must occur before the emotion itself is experienced; interpretation based on environmental cues.

Facial Feedback Hypothesis: Facial expressions provide feedback to brain about emotions being expressed on the face, intensifying the emotion.

Cognitive–Mediational: the cognitive component of emotion (the interpretation) precedes both the physiological reaction and the emotion itself.

9.15

Classic Studies in Psychology: The Angry/Happy Man

Schachter and Singer's Classic Study of Emotion

Participants exposed to the "angry" man interpreted their physical arousal as anger, while those exposed to the "happy" man interpreted their physical arousal as happiness.

9.15

Carol's Dweck's Self-theory of Motivation

- Links the need for achievement to the locus of control
- A belief in control over one's life leads to more attempts to achieve, even in the face of failure
- A belief that one has little control over one's life is more likely to result in learned helplessness.

9.16

10

Stress and Health

Is Stress Breaking Canadian Soldiers?

On March 15, 2001, Christian McEachern, a highly trained combat soldier, got into his truck and rammed it through the front doors of the Edmonton Garrison headquarters (CTV.ca News, 2003). Christian remembers very little of the incident—he doesn't even remember asking the sergeant to shoot him to put him out of his misery. Years earlier, Christian performed peacekeeping duties in Croatia and Africa where he helplessly witnessed unspeakable atrocities and saw his comrades killed and maimed by landmines.

Upon his return to Canada, he was diagnosed with post-traumatic stress disorder (PTSD). PTSD is not a new disorder. Descriptions of its symptoms date back to ancient Greece. In the American Civil War, the disorder was called *soldier's heart* and in World War I it was referred to as *shell shock*. As its name suggests, PTSD is caused by an individual experiencing or witnessing a traumatic, life-threatening event. War and peacekeeping are not the only triggers of PTSD. Individuals who suffer violent personal attacks, such as rape or a school shooting, or are in serious accidents, or encounter a natural disaster such as a tornado or flood are also at risk for developing PTSD. The main symptom of PTSD is reliving the traumatic event over and over again. Reliving the trauma can happen in the form of flashbacks or nightmares that are so real the persons believe they are truly reliving the traumatic experience and may begin to sweat, have heart palpations, and become very anxious and disoriented. These experiences often force the individuals to withdraw from family and friends and to avoid any situation that may remind them of the traumatic event.

In 2002, Statistics Canada surveyed the Canadian Forces and determined that almost 3 percent of the soldiers had symptoms consistent with PTSD. The more missions the soldiers participated in, the more likely they were to have PTSD symptoms. In February 2008, Veteran Affairs Canada released statistics showing that the number of cases of PTSD has more than tripled since Canada first deployed troops to Afghanistan (Veteran Affairs Canada, 2008). With Canada's involvement in Afghanistan to continue to 2014, we can expect those numbers to grow.

What factors might be responsible in determining who may and may not develop PTSD? Can therapy return those afflicted with PTSD back to health? Is PTSD the only stress-related disorder experienced by those exposed to a life-threatening event? These and many other stress–health questions must be explored to ensure that victims of severe stress are identified and helped, so they can return to a normal, healthy life.

Why study health and stress?

How are they related? Stress is not a rare experience but something that all people experience in varying degrees every day. This chapter will explore the sources of stress in daily life, the factors that can make the experience of stress easier or more difficult, and how stress influences our physical and mental health, as well as ways to cope with the stresses of everyday life and extraordinary experiences.

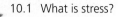

10

STRESS

Life is really about change. Every day, each person faces some kind of challenge, big or small. Just deciding what to wear to work or school can be a challenge for some people, while others find the drive to the workplace or school the most challenging part of the day. There are decisions to be made and changes that will require adapting plans already made. Sometimes there are actual threats to well-being—an accident, a landmine, a fight with the boss, a failed exam, or losing a job, to name a few. All of these challenges, threats, and changes require people to respond in some way.

DEFINITION OF STRESS

10.1   *What is stress?*

Stress is the term used to describe the physical, emotional, cognitive, and behavioural responses to events that are appraised as threatening or challenging.

Stress can show itself in many ways. Physical problems can include unusual fatigue, sleeping problems, frequent colds, and even chest pains and nausea. People under stress may behave differently, too: pacing, eating too much, crying a lot, smoking and drinking more than usual, or physically striking out at others by hitting or throwing things. Emotionally, people under stress experience anxiety, depression, fear, and irritability, as well as anger and frustration. Mental symptoms of stress include problems in concentration, memory, and decision making, and people under stress often lose their sense of humour.

I feel like that most of the time! Most people experience some degree of stress on a daily basis, and post-secondary students are even more likely to face situations and events that require them to make changes and adapt their behaviour: Assigned readings, papers, studying for tests, maintaining physical appearance, juggling jobs, car problems, relationships, and dealing with deadlines are all examples of things that can cause a person to experience stress. Some people feel the effects of stress more than others because what is appraised as a threat by one person might be appraised as an opportunity by another. (For example, think how you and your friends might respond differently to the opportunity to write a 10-page paper for extra credit in the last three weeks of the semester.) Stress-causing events are called **stressors**; they can come from within a person or from an external source and range from relatively mild to severe.

I feel like that most of the time! ▶

stress
the physical, emotional, cognitive, and behavioural responses to events that are appraised as threatening or challenging.

stressors
events that cause a stress reaction.

398

WHAT ARE STRESSORS?

Events that can become stressors range from being stuck behind a person in the 10-items-or-less lane of the grocery store who has twice that amount to dealing with the rubble left after a tornado or a hurricane destroys one's home. Stressors can range from the deadly serious (hurricanes, fires, crashes, combat) to the merely irritating and annoying (delays, rude people, losing one's car keys). Stressors can even be imaginary, as when a couple puts off doing their income tax return, imagining that they will have to pay a huge tax bill, or when a parent imagines the worst happening to a teenage child who isn't yet home from an evening out.

Actually, there are two kinds of stressors: those that cause **distress**, which occurs when people experience unpleasant stressors, and those that cause **eustress**, which results from positive events that still make demands on a person to adapt or change. Marriage, a job promotion, having a baby, and immigrating to Canada may all be positive events for most people, but they all require a great deal of change in people's habits, duties, and even lifestyle, thereby creating stress. Canadian endocrinologist Hans Selye (1936) originally coined the term *eustress* to describe the stress experienced when positive events require the body to adapt.

In an update of Selye's original definition, researchers now define eustress as the optimal amount of stress that people need to promote health and well-being. The arousal theory of Chapter Nine is based on the idea that a certain level of stress, or arousal, is actually necessary for people to feel content (Zuckerman, 1994). **LINK** *to Chapter Nine: Motivation and Emotion, p. 350.* That arousal can be viewed in terms of eustress. Many students are aware that experiencing a little anxiety or stress is helpful to them because it motivates them to study, for example. Without the eustress created by the impending exam, many students might not study very much or at all.

What about the student who is so stressed out that everything he's studied just flies right out of his head? Obviously, a high level of anxiety concerning an impending exam that actually interferes with the ability to study or to retrieve the information at exam time is not eustress but is, in fact, distress. The difference is not only in the degree of anxiety but also in how the person interprets the exam situation. Interpretation, or appraisal, is the topic of the next section.

ENVIRONMENTAL STRESSORS: LIFE'S UPS AND DOWNS

10.2   *What kinds of external events can cause stress?*

CATASTROPHES   Losing one's home in a tornado is an example of a stressor called a **catastrophe**, an unpredictable event that happens on a large scale and creates tremendous amounts of stress and feelings of threat. Wars, hurricanes, floods, fires, airplane crashes, and other disasters are catastrophes. The terrorist-driven destruction of the World Trade Center in New York City on September 11, 2001 or the devastating Japanese earthquake and tsunami on March 11, 2011, are prime examples of catastrophes. In the September 11 example, estimates suggest that nearly 8 percent of the people living in the area near the attacks developed a severe stress disorder, and nearly 10 percent reported symptoms of depression a full two months after the attack (Galea et al., 2002). Even about 4 percent of people who lived nowhere near New York City were affected by the horrifying events of that day and the days that followed. Also, 10 percent of people who spent 12 hours a day or more watching the events unfold on television developed stress-related symptoms (Schlenger et al., 2002). Christopher

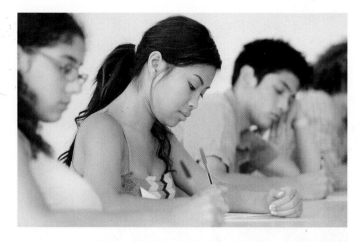

Taking a test is just one of many possible stressors in a student's life. What aspects of post-secondary life have you found to be stressful? Do other students experience the same degree of stress in response to the same stressors?

What about the student who is so stressed out that everything he's studied just flies right out of his head?

distress
the effect of unpleasant and undesirable stressors.

eustress
the effect of positive events, or the optimal amount of stress that people need to promote health and well-being.

catastrophe
an unpredictable, large-scale event that creates a tremendous need to adapt and adjust as well as overwhelming feelings of threat.

This photograph shows people fleeing from the December 2004 tsunami (a giant tidal wave) in Phuket, Thailand. A catastrophe such as this tsunami is a large-scale and unpredictable event that creates intense and often prolonged feelings of stress and threat.

Davis and Stephanie MacDonald (2004) of Carleton University interviewed 80 adults 6 to 12 weeks after the September 11 tragedy, and 11 months later they did a follow-up interview with half the sample. Although these Canadians were not direct victims of the events of September 11, they, like the Americans not living in New York City, did experience significant distress from the television images that they saw. On the positive side, the study also found that the greater the experience of personal distress or threat, the greater the likelihood that persons would engage in helping behaviour and initiate positive changes in their lives—becoming closer to family members and refocusing life's priorities. Their findings suggest that the perception of personal growth may be related to the experience of emotional pain.

ACUTE STRESS DISORDER (ASD) AND POST-TRAUMATIC STRESS DISORDER (PTSD) The severe stress suffered by people after 9/11 is a type of anxiety disorder called **acute stress disorder (ASD)**. Symptoms of ASD include anxiety, recurring nightmares, sleep disturbances, problems in concentration, and moments in which people seem to relive the event in dreams and flashbacks for as long as one month following the event. One recently published study gathered survey information from hurricane evacuees at a major emergency shelter and found that 62 percent of those sampled met the criteria for having acute stress disorder (Mills et al., 2007). When the symptoms associated with ASD last for more than one month, the disorder is then called **post-traumatic stress disorder (PTSD)**. In that same study (Mills et al., 2007), researchers concluded that it was likely that anywhere from 38 to 49 percent of all the evacuees sampled were at risk of developing PTSD.

Peacekeeping is a stressful occupation and Canadians are world famous for their peacekeeping. In fact, in 1992 the Canadian Forces were awarded the Nobel Peace Prize. Cheryl Lamerson and Kevin Kelloway (1996) at the University of Guelph have outlined some of the sources of stress experienced by peacekeepers. Their findings include the following. First, there are the normal stresses that most military combat personnel experience: the possibility of injury or death because of attack, the death of comrades, the handling of dead bodies, and the distance from home and family. Second, there are the unique stresses of the peacekeeping job: Peacekeepers must perform tasks quickly, some of which they may not be adequately trained for. Third, the peacekeeping role is often counterintuitive: Peacekeepers defend and protect the same people who often want to hurt them. And sometimes, because of what they see, peacekeepers take sides in a conflict, which is in direct opposition to the policy of neutrality that they are sworn to uphold. Given these sources of stress, it is easy to see why peacekeepers are at higher risk of developing PTSD.

Women seem to be more vulnerable to PTSD than men. Researchers have found that women have almost twice the risk of developing PTSD than men, and that the likelihood increases if the traumatic experience took place before the woman was 15 years old (Breslau et al., 1997, 1999). Children may also suffer different effects from stress than do adults. Severe PTSD has been linked to a decrease in the size of the hippocampus in children with the disorder (Carrion et al., 2007). The hippocampus is important in the formation of new long-term memories, (L I N K) *to Chapter Six: Memory, p. 218*, and this may have a detrimental effect on learning and the effectiveness of treatments for these children.

acute stress disorder (ASD)
a disorder resulting from exposure to a major stressor, with symptoms of anxiety, recurring nightmares, sleep disturbances, problems in concentration, and moments in which people seem to relive the event in dreams and flashbacks for as long as one month following the event.

post-traumatic stress disorder (PTSD)
a disorder resulting from exposure to a major stressor, with symptoms of anxiety, nightmares, poor sleep, reliving the event, and concentration problems, lasting for more than one month.

Treatment of PTSD may involve the use of medications to control anxiety and other behavioural and cognitive techniques. (L)(I)(N)(K) *to Chapter Fourteen: Psychological Therapies, p. 564.* Dr. Alain Brunet of McGill University in Montreal believes the brain's amazing plasticity may hold the key to effective treatment. To test his hypothesis, people suffering from PTSD were asked to write about their traumatic experience as vividly as possible. Immediately afterward, they received propranolol, a drug that makes memory less emotionally stressful. Once a week over the next six weeks, patients returned to read their script and were again given propranolol. Results suggest that 70 percent of the patients had some remission of PTSD symptoms (Brunet et al., 2007). Brunet believes that propranolol reduces the neural connection between the traumatic memory and the emotional response. So the patients no longer have to "relive" the trauma of the event every time they recall it. The traumatic event becomes "just" a terrible memory. Recall that in Chapter One we learned that "neurons that fire together wire together." This study builds on that: "Neurons that fire apart wire apart," or "neurons that are out of sync fail to link." (L)(I)(N)(K) *to Chapter One: The Science of Psychology, p. 2.*

MAJOR LIFE CHANGES   Thankfully, most people do not have to face the extreme stress of a catastrophe. But stress is present even in relatively ordinary life experiences. Sometimes there are big events, such as marriage, job loss, or going to college or university, that require a person to make adjustments and changes—and adjustments and changes are really the core of stress, according to early researchers in the field (Holmes & Rahe, 1967).

The Social Readjustment Rating Scale (SRRS)   Holmes and Rahe (1967) believed that any life event that required people to change, adapt, or adjust their lifestyles would result in stress. Like Selye, they assume that both negative events (such as getting fired) and positive events (such as getting a promotion) demand that a person adjust in some way, and so both kinds of events are associated with stress. Holmes and Rahe devised a way to measure the amount of stress in a person's life by having that person add up the total "life change units" associated with each major event in their **Social Readjustment Rating Scale (SRRS**; see Table 10.1A). The "life change units" came from sampling 394 people, who were told that marriage represented 50 life change units on a scale from 0 (no changes required) to 100 (extreme changes required). By adding up the points associated with life events that have happened to a person within the past 12 months, a good estimate of the degree of stress being experienced by that person can be obtained.

The researchers found that scores on the SRRS could be associated with increased risk of illness or accidents. Warning: Table 10.1A is *not* a complete listing of the original 43 events and associated life change units and should not be used to calculate a stress "score"! If you would like to calculate your SRRS score, try the free test at this site: **www.stresstips.com/lifeevents.htm**.) Scores of 150 or below were not associated with any significant problems, but scores between 150 and 199 were considered a "mild life crisis" and associated with a 33 percent increase in chance of illness or accident. Scores between 200 and 299 were labelled "moderate life crisis" and associated with a 50 percent increase in risk, whereas scores over 300 were considered a "major life crisis" and represented an 80 percent increase in risk (Holmes & Masuda, 1973). Simply put, if a person's score is 300 or above, that person has a very high chance of becoming ill or having an accident in the near future. Illness includes not only physical conditions such as high blood pressure, ulcers, or migraine headaches but mental illness as well. In one study, researchers found that stressful life events of the kind listed in the SRRS were excellent predictors of the onset of episodes of major depression (Kendler & Prescott, 1999).

◉ Watch on mypsychlab
Bonnie: Living with Post-Traumatic Stress Disorder

Social Readjustment Rating Scale (SRRS) assessment that measures the amount of stress in a person's life over a one-year period resulting from major life events.

TABLE 10.1 TWO STRESS SCALES

A. Sample Items From The Social Readjustment Rating Scale (SRRS)

MAJOR LIFE EVENT	LIFE CHANGE UNIT
Death of spouse	100
Divorce	75
Marital separation	65
Jail term	63
Death of close family member	63
Personal Injury or illness	53
Marriage	50
Dismissal from work	47
Marital reconciliation	45
Pregnancy	40
Death of close friend	37
Change to new kind of work	36
Change in spousal arguments	36
Major mortgage	31
Foreclosure of mortgage or loan	30
Begin or end school	26
Change in living conditions	25
Change in work hours or conditions	20
Change in residence/school/play	19
Change in social activities	18
Small loan or mortgage	17
Vacation	13
Christmas	12
Minor violations of the law	11

Source: Adapted and abridged from Holmes and Rahe (1967).

B. College Undergraduate Stress Scale (CUSS)

STUDENT EVENT	RATING
Being raped	100
Finding out you are HIV-positive	100
Death of a close friend	97
Contracting a sexually transmitted disease (other than AIDS)	94
Concerns about being pregnant	91
Finals week	90
Oversleeping for an exam	89
Flunking a class	89
Having your partner cheat on you	85
Financial difficulties	84
Writing a major term paper; being caught cheating	83
Two exams in one day	80
Getting married	76
Difficulties with parents	73
Talking in front of a class	72
Difficulties with a roommate	66
Job changes (applying, hassles)	65
A class you hate	62
Confrontation with professors	60
Maintaining a steady relationship	55
Commuting to campus or work	54
Experiencing peer pressure; being away from home for the first time	53
Getting straight "A"s	51
Falling asleep in class	40

Source: Adapted and abridged from Renner & Mackin, (1998).

The SRRS was later revised (Miller & Rahe, 1997) to reflect changes in the ratings of the events in the 30 intervening years. Miller and Rahe found that overall stress associated with many of the items on the original list had increased by about 45 percent from the original 1967 ratings. And women in the 1990s reported having more stress in their lives than men.

How can stress cause a person to have an accident? Many studies conducted on the relationship between stress and accidents in the workplace have shown that people under a lot of stress tend to be more distracted and less cautious and, therefore, place themselves at a greater risk for having an accident (Hansen, 1988; Sherry, 1991; Sherry et al., 2003).

The SRRS as it was originally designed seems more appropriate for adults who are already established in their careers than younger people. Some versions of the SRRS use life events more likely to be experienced by college and university students. One of these more recent versions is the **College Undergraduate Stress Scale (CUSS)**, which is represented in its entirety in Table 10.1B (Renner & Mackin, 1998). This scale looks quite different from Holmes and Rahe's original scale because

How can stress cause ▶
a person to have an
accident?

College Undergraduate Stress Scale (CUSS) assessment that measures the amount of stress in a college or university student's life over a one-year period resulting from major life events.

the stressful events listed and rated include those that would be more common or more likely to happen to a college or university student. (Try it. Add up the life change units from the events that you personally have experienced within the past year and then determine your level of risk according to Holmes and Rahe's original scoring system described earlier.)

I notice that Table 10.1B has "falling asleep in class" as its last item. How can falling asleep in class be stressful? It's what happens when the professor catches you that's stressful, isn't it? Ah, but if you fall asleep in class, even if the professor doesn't catch on, you'll miss the lecture notes. You might then have to get the notes from a friend, find enough money to pay for the copy machine, try to read your friend's handwriting, and so on—all stressful situations. Actually, all the events listed on both the SRRS and the CUSS are stressful not just because some of them are emotionally intense but also because there are so many little details, changes, adjustments, adaptations, frustrations, and delays that are caused by the events themselves. The death of a spouse, for example, rates 100 life change units because it requires the greatest amount of adjustment in a person's life. A lot of those adjustments are going to be the little details: planning the funeral, deciding what to do with the spouse's clothes and belongings, getting the notice in the obituaries, answering each condolence card with a thank-you card, dealing with insurance and changing names on policies, and on and on and on. In other words, major life events create a whole host of hassles.

HASSLES   Although it's easy to think about big disasters and major changes in life as sources of stress, the bulk of the stress we experience daily actually comes from little frustrations, delays, irritations, minor disagreements, and similar annoyances. These daily annoyances are called **hassles** (Lazarus, 1993; Lazarus & Folkman, 1984). Experiencing major changes in one's life is like throwing a rock into a pond: There will be a big splash, but the rock itself is gone. What is left behind are all the ripples in the water that came from the impact of the rock. Those ripples are the hassles that arise from the big event.

Lazarus and Folkman (1984) developed a "hassles" scale that has items such as "misplacing or losing things" and "troublesome neighbours." A person taking the test for hassles would rate each item in the scale in terms of how much of a hassle that particular item was for the person. The ratings range between 0 (no hassle or didn't occur) to 3 (extremely severe hassle). Whereas the major life events of Holmes and Rahe's scale (1967) may have a long-term effect on a person's chronic physical and mental health, the day-to-day minor annoyances, delays, and irritations that affect immediate health and well-being are far better predictors of short-term illnesses such as headaches, colds, backaches, and similar symptoms (Burks & Martin, 1985; DeLongis et al., 1988). In one study, researchers found that among 261 participants who experienced headaches, scores on a scale measuring the number and severity of daily hassles were significantly better predictors of headaches than were scores on a life events scale (Fernandez & Sheffield, 1996). The researchers also found that it was not so much the number of daily hassles that predicted headaches but rather the perceived severity of the hassles.

At the University of Calgary, Deborah Dewey and her colleague Shauna Bottos (2004) found that students with chronic headaches reported significantly more daily hassles and had higher levels of perfectionism than students reporting fewer headaches. In addition, the students reporting the greatest number of hassles experienced more intense and longer-lasting headaches. Some of the most commonly reported daily hassles of students include changes in sleeping and eating habits, social activities and relationships, increased class workload, lower-than-expected grades, and computer problems (Ross, Niebling, & Heckert, 1999). Students are not the only group

◀ I notice that Table 10.1B has "falling asleep in class" as its last item. How can falling asleep in class be stressful? It's what happens when the professor catches you that's stressful, isn't it?

hassles
the daily annoyances of everyday life.

Children in the preschool age range find teasing by their peers to be the biggest daily hassle they experience. This boy is obviously upset by the teasing of the other children, who are making fun of his glasses. What other hassles might a child in this age range experience?

◄◉═Simulate on **mypsychlab**
How Stressed Are You?

of Canadians affected by daily hassles. Researchers at the University of Ottawa were able to show that daily hassles increased police officers' reporting of physical symptoms of stress (Otis & Pelletier, 2005). York University researchers have observed an interesting link between major life stressors and daily hassles. Participants who suffered from a major life stressor were much more likely to seek emotional and practical support from others if they were also faced with numerous daily hassles (Flett, Blankstein, Hicken, & Watson, 1995). This finding suggests that one of the possible reasons that daily hassles can have such devastating effect on us is because we rarely ask for help when our normal, everyday stressors start piling up.

A recent study has indicated that hassles may also come from quite different sources depending on a person's developmental stage (Ellis et al., 2001). In this study, researchers surveyed 270 randomly selected people between the ages of 3 and 75. The participants were asked to check off a list of daily hassles and pleasures associated with having "bad days" and "good days," respectively, as well as ranking the hassles in terms of frequency and severity of impact. For children ages 3 to 5, getting teased was the biggest daily hassle. For children in the age 6 to 10 age group, the biggest hassle was getting bad grades. Children from 11 to 15 years old reported feeling pressured to use drugs, whereas older adolescents (ages 16 to 22) cited trouble at school or work. Adults found fighting among family members the greatest source of stress, whereas the elderly people in the study cited a lack of money.

In that same study, the researchers were somewhat surprised to find that elderly people were much more strongly affected by such hassles as going shopping, doctor's appointments, and bad weather than the children and younger adults. It may be that while a young person may view going shopping as an opportunity to socialize, older adults find it threatening: Physically, they are less able to get to a place to shop and may have to rely on others to drive them and help them get around and, thus,

PRACTICE QUIZ: HOW MUCH DO YOU REMEMBER?

Pick the best answer.

1. The optimal amount of stress that people need to promote their health and sense of well-being is called
   a. intensity.
   b. distress.
   c. eustress.
   d. acute stress.

2. Neurons that fire apart
   a. wire together.
   b. fire together.
   c. are in sync.
   d. wire apart.

3. Canadians who experienced great distress after September 11 were more likely to
   a. get closer to their families.
   b. give others a helping hand.
   c. suffer from panic anxiety.
   d. both a and b

4. Anxiety, recurring nightmares, sleep disturbances, and concentration problems that occur for more than one month after a major stressor are symptoms of
   a. acute stress disorder.
   b. post-traumatic stress disorder.
   c. pre-traumatic stress disorder.
   d. general stress disorder.

5. Research has shown that _____ have a long-term effect on physical and mental health, but _____ have a greater impact on short-term health.
   a. hassles; major life events
   b. major life events; hassles
   c. major life events; catastrophes
   d. hassles; catastrophes

6. The College Undergraduate Stress Scale rates being raped as equally stressful when compared with which of the following?
   a. death of a close family member
   b. concerns about being pregnant
   c. being accused of rape
   d. finding out that one is HIV-positive

may take much more time for shopping and doing errands than a younger person would. Mentally, shopping could be seen as threatening because of a lack of financial resources to pay for needed items. Even the need to make decisions might be seen as unpleasant to an older person.

PSYCHOLOGICAL STRESSORS: WHAT, ME WORRY?

Although several specific sources of stress (e.g., marriage, car problems) have already been mentioned, the reasons why people find these events stressful fall into several categories.

10.3   *What are some sources of stress in everyday life?*

PRESSURE   When there are urgent demands or expectations for a person's behaviour coming from an outside source, that person is experiencing **pressure**. Pressure occurs when people feel that they must work harder, faster, or do more, as in meeting a deadline or studying for final exams.

Time pressure is one of the most common forms of pressure. Although some people claim to "work well under pressure," the truth is that pressure can have a negative impact on a person's ability to be creative. Psychologist Teresa Amabile has gathered research within actual work settings strongly indicating that when time pressure is applied to workers who are trying to come up with creative, innovative ideas, creativity levels decrease dramatically—even though the workers may think they have been quite productive because of the effort they have made (Amabile et al., 2002). Researchers in Ontario recently polled 6000 Canadians aged 30 to 59 about their stress. The biggest source of stress was time-crunch pressure, specifically the total number of hours spent on the job. The researchers also report that both men and women find paid work more stressful than household responsibilities. The good news from the study is that stress declines as we age; the bad news is that stress is likely to get worse before it gets better for most Canadians (Beaujot & Andersen, 2007).

UNCONTROLLABILITY   Another factor that increases a person's experience of stress is the degree of control that the person has over a particular event or situation. The less control a person has, the greater the degree of stress. Researchers, in both clinical interviews and experimental studies, have found that lack of control in a situation actually increases PTSD symptoms (Breier et al., 1987).

In two studies carried out in a nursing home with the elderly residents as the participants, researchers Rodin and Langer (Langer & Rodin, 1976; Rodin & Langer, 1977) gave each resident a houseplant. Decisions about watering and how much sun each plant should have were up to each resident. These residents, who were the experimental group, were also given choices such as whether they wanted to see a weekly movie, on which of the two evenings that the movie was shown they wanted to attend, and in what area or room they would like to see their visitors. Participants in the control group, although also given plants, were told that the nurses would take care of the plants and were not encouraged to make decisions for themselves. The follow-up study took place a year and a half later. Using participation in activities, measures of happiness, and other assessments, the researchers found that those who had more control over their lives and who had been given more responsibility were more vigorous, active, and sociable than those in the control group.

First-year college and university students often find the transition from high school to post-secondary school stressful—this is likely not a surprise to you. Researchers at the University of Manitoba have found that competitive learning environments, new social networks, career choices, and more frequent failures are just some of the stresses first-year students face (Perry, 2003). These new demands often

"I suppose this puts my new bike on the back burner?"
©The New Yorker Collection 2005 Bob Zahn from cartoonbank.com. All Rights Reserved.

pressure
the psychological experience produced by urgent demands or expectations for a person's behaviour that come from an outside source.

frustration
the psychological experience produced by the blocking of a desired goal or the fulfillment of a perceived need.

cause many intelligent and motivated students to do poorly academically, especially if they report low amounts of perceived academic control (Perry, Hladkyj, Pekrun, & Pelletier, 2001). There is some good news, too. Students who are motivated and shown how to regain some academic control can significantly boost their academic performance (Hall, Perry, Chipperfield, Clifton, & Haynes, 2006).

The stress-increasing effects of lack of control explain the relationship between unpredictability and stress as well. When potentially stressful situations are unpredictable, as in police work, the degree of stress experienced is increased. An unpredictable situation is one that is not controllable, which may at least partially explain the increase in stress. In one study, rats were either given an electric shock after a warning tone or given a shock with no warning. The rats receiving the unpredictable shocks developed severe stomach ulcers (Weiss, 1972).

FRUSTRATION **Frustration** occurs when people are blocked or prevented from achieving a desired goal or fulfilling a perceived need. As a stressor, frustration can be *external*, such as when a car breaks down, a desired job offer doesn't come through after all, or experiencing a theft of one's belongings. Losses, rejections, failures, and delays are all sources of external frustration.

Obviously, some frustrations are minor and others are more serious. The seriousness of a frustration is affected by how important the goal or need actually is. A person who is delayed in traffic while driving to the mall to do some shopping just for fun will be less frustrated than a person who is trying to get to the mall before it closes to get that last-minute forgotten and important anniversary gift.

Internal frustrations, also known as *personal frustrations*, occur when the goal or need cannot be attained because of internal or personal characteristics. For example,

These parents are fighting in front of their obviously distressed daughter. In some instances, a child who experiences this kind of frustration might act out aggressively toward a sibling or a pet in a form of displaced aggression.

someone who wants to be an astronaut might find that severe motion sickness prevents him or her from such a goal. If a man wants to be a professional basketball player but is only 1.5 metres tall and weighs only 60 kilograms, he may find that he cannot achieve that goal because of his physical characteristics. A person wanting to be an engineer but who has no math skills would find it difficult to attain that goal.

People respond in several typical ways when frustrated. The first is *persistence*, or the continuation of efforts to get around whatever is causing the frustration. Persistence may involve making more intense efforts or changing the style of response. For example, anyone who has ever put coins into a drink machine only to find that the drink does not come out has probably (1) pushed the button again, more forcefully, and (2) pushed several other buttons in an effort to get some kind of response from the machine. If neither of these strategies works, many people may hit or kick the machine itself in an act of aggression.

Aggression, or actions meant to harm or destroy, is unfortunately another typical reaction to frustration. Early psychologists in the field of behaviourism proposed a connection between frustration and aggression, calling it the *frustration–aggression hypothesis* (Dollard et al., 1939; Miller et al., 1941). Ⓛ Ⓘ Ⓝ Ⓚ *to Chapter Twelve: Social Psychology, p. 476.* They believed that although some form of frustration nearly always precedes aggression that does not mean that frustration *always* leads to aggression. In fact, aggression is a frequent and persistent response to frustration, but it is seldom the first response. In a reformulation of the frustration–aggression hypothesis, Berkowitz (1993) stated that frustration creates an internal "readiness to aggress" but that aggression will not follow unless certain external cues are also present. For

aggression
actions meant to harm or destroy.

example, if the human source of a person's frustration is far larger and stronger in appearance than the frustrated person, aggression is an unlikely outcome!

Okay, so if the person who ticked you off is bigger than you—if aggression isn't possible—what can you do? One could try to reason with the person who is the source of frustration. Reasoning with someone is a form of persistence. Trying to "get around" the problem is another way people can deal with frustration. Another possibility is to take out one's frustrations on less threatening, more available targets in a process called **displaced aggression**. Displaced aggression is a form of **displacement**, one of the psychological defence mechanisms discussed later on in this chapter. Anyone who has ever been frustrated by things that occurred at work or school and then later yelled at another person (such as a spouse, parent, or child) has experienced displaced aggression. The person one really wants to strike out at is one's boss, the teacher, or whoever or whatever caused the frustration in the first place. That could be dangerous, so the aggression is reserved for another, less threatening or weaker target. For example, unemployment and financial difficulties are extremely frustrating, as they block a person's ability to maintain a certain standard of living and acquire possessions. In one study, male unemployment and single parenthood were the two factors most highly correlated to rates of child abuse (Gillham et al., 1998). Unemployment is also one of the factors correlated most highly with the murder of abused women, creating four times the risk of murder for women in abusive relationships (Campbell & Wolf, 2003). Both studies are examples of displaced aggression toward the weaker targets of children and women. Such targets often become *scapegoats*, or habitual targets of displaced aggression. Scapegoats are often pets, children, spouses, and even minority groups (who are seen as having less power).

Another possible reaction to frustration is **escape or withdrawal**. Escape or withdrawal can take the form of leaving, dropping out of school, quitting a job, or ending a relationship. Some people manage a psychological escape or withdrawal into apathy (ceasing to care about or act upon the situation), fantasy (which is only a temporary escape), or the use of drugs. Obviously the latter can lead to even more problems.

> Okay, so if the person who ticked you off is bigger than you—if aggression isn't possible—what can you do?

displaced aggression
taking out one's frustrations on some less threatening or more available target; a form of displacement.

displacement
psychological defence mechanism in which emotional reactions and behavioural responses are shifted to targets that are more available or less threatening than the original target.

escape or withdrawal
leaving the presence of a stressor, either literally or by a psychological withdrawal into fantasy, drug abuse, or apathy.

PSYCHOLOGY IN THE NEWS

Suicide in Canada

10.4. *Why do people commit suicide?*

Here are some facts:

- In 2007, nearly 4000 Canadians killed themselves.
- More than 10 percent of Canadians have thought about committing suicide at one point in their lives. Two percent of men and 6 percent of women have attempted suicide.
- Suicide is one of the leading causes of death in both men and women from adolescence to middle age.
- Suicide rates among older Canadian teenagers (15 to 19 years) have more than doubled in the past 40 years. The suicide rate among Canadian First Nations teens is three to four times higher than for teens in the Canadian general population.
- More people die from suicide than homicide.
- The most common method of committing suicide is with a firearm.

Suicide prevention hotline centres are designed to provide help and support to people who are on the verge of committing suicide. Volunteers, such as the one pictured here, act as concerned listeners for the depressed people who call in to the hotline centres.

• Women are 1.5 times more likely to attempt suicide than men, but men are four times more likely to be successful in taking their own lives. More men succeed in committing suicide because they typically use quicker acting and more lethal means such as hanging and guns. Women are more likely to overdose on pills.

• One of the most common reasons for attempting suicide is that suicide appears to be the only answer to an otherwise insoluble problem or a way out of some terrible dilemma.

These facts are based on a report released by Health Canada (2002) on mental illness.

What are the signs of impending suicide? This is a tough question. Some psychologists believe that 90 percent of people who commit suicide leave clear clues; but, at the same time, psychologists find it extremely difficult to predict who will commit suicide. Research suggests that the following may be signs that someone may be contemplating suicide (Shneidman, 1994; Satcher, 2001):

• A profound sense of hopelessness

• Explicit statements about wanting to commit suicide. Please take suicide talk seriously. It is a myth that persons who talk about suicide won't commit suicide. Suicide talk is like a "dress rehearsal" for the real act.

• Asking about God or wondering about the afterlife

• Disposing of their possessions, getting their affairs in order, making a will, or buying a cemetery plot

• Purchasing a gun

• A sudden calm in the previously troubled individual. The person feels relieved that they have finally come to a solution to life's problems.

What can you do if a friend is showing signs of thinking about suicide? Here are some guidelines:

• Ask them if they are feeling suicidal.

• Listen with a sincere attitude of concern and be sympathetic. *Don't* say something like "You're just being silly. You don't really mean it."

• Avoid giving unasked-for advice. You are not a professional, so don't try to be one.

• Ask them if they have experienced feeling like this before and how they managed to cope with it then

• Share a time when you felt the same way and assure them that things can and will change.

• Ask them how they intend to commit suicide. If they have a detailed method they are at greater risk.

• Stay with them; do something together.

• If you have immediate concern, call the police for emergency intervention.

• Give them the number for the suicide prevention hotline in your area and make sure they call.

Above all, a person who tries to prevent a suicide and fails should *not* feel responsible. In the end, if a person committed to the act of suicide succeeds, there was nothing that any bystander could do to prevent it.

Questions for Further Thought

1. How might a parent's or teenager's suicide affect the children or parents left behind?

2. Speculate on possible reasons why the teenage suicide rate is so much higher for Canada's First Nations peoples.

3. Identify specific demographic variables that may increase the likelihood of suicide.

A far more drastic and permanent form of escape is suicide, the taking of one's own life. People who hear about someone's suicide are nearly always mystified by that choice. How can things be so bad that death seems the only option? For current facts about suicide, its causes, and what can be done to prevent it, see the Psychology in the News section above.

CONFLICT   **Conflict** occurs when a person feels pulled toward or drawn to two or more desires or goals but can achieve or experience only one. Lewin (1935) defined three types of conflicts, and his definitions are still used by today's researchers in the area of conflict and conflict resolution.

10.5   *What are the different types of conflict people must face?*

APPROACH–APPROACH CONFLICT   In an **approach–approach conflict**, a person experiences attraction to two desires or goals, each of which is attractive. Typically, this type of conflict, often called a *win-win situation*, is relatively easy to resolve and does not involve a great deal of stress. Because both goals are desirable, the only stress involved is having to choose between them, acquiring one and losing the other. An example of this might be the need to choose between the chocolate cake or key lime pie for dessert or from among several good choices for a date to the prom. "Six on one hand, half a dozen on the other" is a phrase that sums up this conflict nicely.

Avoidance–Avoidance Conflict   **Avoidance–avoidance conflicts** are much more stressful. In this conflict, the choice is between two or more goals or events that are unpleasant. This type of conflict is so common that there are numerous phrases to symbolize it: "Caught between a rock and a hard place," "Between the devil and the deep blue sea," "Out of the frying pan into the fire," and "lose-lose situation" are some of these phrases. Because neither alternative is pleasant, many people avoid making a choice by delaying decisions (Tversky & Shafir, 1992). For example, given the choice of risky back surgery or living with the pain, some people would wait, hoping that the pain would go away on its own and relieve them of the need to make a choice. People who are fearful of dental procedures might face the conflict of suffering the pain of a toothache or going to the dentist.

Approach–Avoidance Conflict   **Approach–avoidance conflicts** are a little different in that they involve only one goal or event. That goal or event may have both positive and negative aspects that make the goal appealing and unappealing at the same time. For example, marriage is a big decision to make for anyone and usually has both attractive features, such as togetherness, sharing good times, and companionship, and also negative aspects, such as disagreements, money issues, and mortgages. This is perhaps the most stressful of all the types of conflict, causing many people to be unable to make up their minds, going back and forth between deciding for or against the goal or event. The original author of this textbook experienced a very stressful approach–avoidance conflict when deciding to write it: On the one hand, there would be money, prestige, and the challenge of doing something new. On the other hand, a tremendous amount of effort and time would be required to write the text, which would take time and energy away from other areas of life. Another example is the offer of a promotion that would require a person to move to a city he or she doesn't like—more money and higher status but all the hassles of moving and living in a less-than-perfect place.

approach–avoidance conflict
conflict occurring when a person must choose or not choose a goal that has both positive and negative aspects.

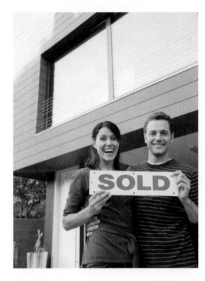

This couple has just purchased their first house, a rite of passage for many young couples. The decision to become a home owner, with the "pulls" of privacy and earning equity and the "pushes" of mortgage payments and upkeep, is often an approach–avoidance conflict.

conflict
psychological experience of being pulled toward or drawn to two or more desires or goals, only one of which may be attained.

approach–approach conflict
conflict occurring when a person must choose between two desirable goals.

avoidance–avoidance conflict
conflict occurring when a person must choose between two undesirable goals.

approach-avoidance conflict
conflict in which there is only one goal or event that is both appealing and unappealing at the same time.

PRACTICE QUIZ: HOW MUCH DO YOU REMEMBER?

Pick the best answer.

1. When people have to work harder, do more work, or work faster, they are experiencing
   a. frustration.
   b. uncontrollability.
   c. pressure.
   d. conflict.

2. The stress-increasing effects of uncontrollability are related to the effects of _____ on stress.
   a. frustration
   b. unpredictability
   c. pressure
   d. conflict

3. Eduardo is on his way to an important job interview when his car breaks down on the highway. Eduardo is likely to experience what kind of frustration?
   a. external
   b. internal
   c. personal
   d. uncontrollable

4. The first response that people typically make to frustration is
   a. persistence.
   b. increasing efforts.
   c. varying efforts
   d. aggression.

5. People who talk about suicide rarely follow through with it. This statement is
   a. true; only 1 percent of people who talk about suicide actually commit suicide.
   b. false; this statement is a myth. Many people use talking about suicide as a dress rehearsal for the real thing.
   c. partially true; 10 percent of people who talk about suicide actually commit suicide.
   d. both true and false; it depends on which country you reside in.

6. Jasmine has just been offered an opportunity to teach at a small college in a rural area of Manitoba. On the one hand, she really needs a job and the money it would bring would allow her to pay off some debts. But the college is in a very small town far away from any major cities and has very little to offer in the way of amusements. She would also be far away from her family and friends. Jasmine is facing what type of conflict in deciding whether to accept the job?
   a. approach–approach
   b. avoidance–avoidance
   c. approach–avoidance
   d. double approach–avoidance

Answers: 1-c, 2-b, 3-a, 4-a, 5-b, 6-c.

PHYSIOLOGICAL FACTORS: STRESS AND HEALTH

▶ When I get all stressed out, I feel pretty terrible. What's the effect of stress on my body?

When I get all stressed out, I feel pretty terrible. What's the effect of stress on my body? Chapter Two discussed in detail the function of the *autonomic nervous system* (ANS), the part of the human nervous system that is responsible for all automatic, involuntary, and life-sustaining activities. ⓁⒾⓃⓀ *to Chapter Two: The Biological Perspective, p. 42.* The ANS consists of two divisions: the *parasympathetic* and the *sympathetic*. It is the sympathetic nervous system (the fight-or-flight system) that reacts when the human body is subjected to stress: heart rate increases, digestion slows or shuts down, and energy is sent to the muscles to help deal with whatever action the stressful situation requires. The parasympathetic system returns the body to normal, day-to-day functioning after the stress has ended. If the stress is great enough and lasts long enough, the parasympathetic system may shut the body down, causing a collapse into what some people might call "nervous exhaustion." Both systems figure prominently in a classic theory of the body's physiological reactions to stress, the general adaptation syndrome.

THE GENERAL ADAPTATION SYNDROME

10.6 *What is happening in the body when a person experiences stress?*

Canadian researcher Hans Selye was the founder of the field of research concerning stress and its effects on the human body. He published more than 1700 papers and 40 books on stress and related problems. In 1968, he received the Order of Canada. Selye studied the sequence of physiological reactions that the body goes through when adapting to a stressor. This sequence (see Figure 10.1) is called the **general adaptation syndrome (GAS)** and consists of three stages (Selye, 1956):

general adaptation syndrome (GAS)
the three stages of the body's physiological reaction to stress, including alarm, resistance, and exhaustion.

- *Alarm:* When the body first reacts to a stressor, the sympathetic nervous system is activated. The adrenal glands release hormones that increase heart rate, blood pressure, and the supply of blood sugar, resulting in a burst of energy. Reactions such as fever, nausea, and headache are common.

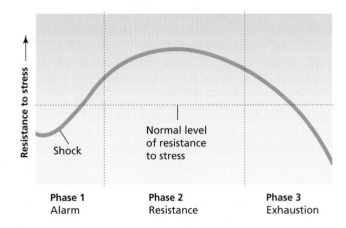

Alarm Stage

Forehead, neck, shoulder, arm, and leg muscles contract

Pupils enlarge

Sugar is released into the bloodstream for energy

Resistance Stage

Breathing is frequent and shallow

Blood pressure remains high

Accelerated heart rate increases blood flow to muscles; blood pressure increases

Hormones from adrenal glands are released into bloodstream

Exhaustion Stage

Sympathetic nervous system is activated by adrenal glands

Liver runs out of sugar

Prolonged muscle tension causes fatigue

FIGURE 10.1 **General Adaptation Syndrome** The diagram at the top shows some of the physical reactions to stress in each of the three stages of the general adaptation syndrome. The diagram at the bottom shows the relationship of each of the three stages to the individual's ability to resist a stressor. In the alarm phase, resistance rapidly increases as the body mobilizes its defence systems. In the resistance stage, the body is working at a much increased level of resistance, using resources until the stress ends or the resources run out. In the exhaustion stage, the body is no longer able to resist as resources have been depleted, and at this point disease and even death are possible.

Resistance to stress →

Shock

Normal level of resistance to stress

Phase 1
Alarm

Phase 2
Resistance

Phase 3
Exhaustion

- *Resistance:* As the stress continues, the body settles into sympathetic division activity, continuing to release the stress hormones that help the body fight off, or resist, the stressor. The early symptoms of alarm lessen and the person or animal may actually feel better. This stage will continue until the stressor ends or the organism has used up all its resources.

- *Exhaustion:* When the body's resources are gone, resistance ends, the parasympathetic division activates, and exhaustion occurs. Exhaustion can lead to the formation of stress-related diseases (i.e., high blood pressure or a weakened immune system) or the death of the organism if outside help is unavailable (Stein-Behrens et al., 1994).

Alarm and resistance are stages that people experience many times throughout life, allowing people to adapt to life's demands (Selye, 1976). It is the prolonged secretion of the stress hormones during the stage of resistance that can lead to the most harmful effects of stress. It was this aspect of Selye's work that convinced other researchers of the connection between stress and certain "diseases of adaptation," as Selye termed them. The most common of these diseases are ulcers and high blood pressure.

Health psychologist Shelly Taylor and her colleagues recently hypothesized that the classic fight-or-flight stress response may be a particularly male response to stress.

Explore on **mypsychlab**
Stress and GAS

immune system
the system of cells, organs, and chemicals in the body that responds to attacks from diseases, infections, and injuries.

psychoneuroimmunology
the study of the effects of psychological factors such as stress, emotions, thoughts, and behaviour on the immune system.

Taylor believes that women are more likely to respond to stress with a pattern of behaviour she calls "tend-and-befriend." Whereas fight-or-flight was likely a more common male response to a stressor in our evolutionary past, Taylor believes that women in times of stress were more likely to care for or tend to their offspring and befriend others to reduce the risk of danger (Taylor et al., 2000). The tend-and-befriend hypothesis has generated much discussion, and empirical evidence does appear to be growing (David & Lyons, 2005; Turton & Campbell, 2005). Tend-and-befriend may explain why in times of stress women are more likely to call another female for support, whereas men like to be left alone.

IMMUNE SYSTEM AND STRESS

10.7 *What is the relationship between stress and the immune system?*

As Selye first discovered, the **immune system** (the system of cells, organs, and chemicals in the body that responds to attacks on the body from diseases and injuries) is affected by stress. The field of **psychoneuroimmunology** concerns the study of the effects of psychological factors such as stress, emotions, thoughts, and behaviour on the immune system (Cohen & Herbert, 1996; Kiecolt-Glaser et al., 1995, 1996, 2002). Researchers in this field have found that stress triggers the same response in the immune system that infection triggers (Maier & Watkins, 1998). Certain enzymes and other chemicals (including antibodies) are created by immune cells when the immune cells, or white blood cells, encounter an infection in the body. The white blood cells surround the bacteria or other infectious material and release their enzymes and chemicals into the bloodstream. From there, these substances activate receptor sites on the *vagus nerve*, the longest nerve that connects the body to the brain. It is the activation of these receptor sites that signals the brain that the body is sick, causing the brain to respond by further activation of the immune system. Mark Schaller, at the University of British Columbia, has shown that a similar kind of immune response can be elicited in people just by having them look at photos of sick people. Schaller had participants watch a 10-minute slide show that contained unpleasant photographs of people who were clearly sick; for example, they had rashes, chicken pox, or mucous running out of their noses. Those participants who saw photos of sickly people had a significant increase in immune response (Schaller et al., 2010). Evolutionarily speaking, this response makes good sense. Seeing a lot of sick people is a good indicator of an increased risk of viral or bacterial assault, and those who were able to mount a quick and vigorous response would have had a survival advantage.

Stress activates this same system but starts in the brain rather than in the bloodstream. The same chemical changes that occur in the brain when it has been alerted by the vagus nerve to infection in the body occurred in laboratory animals when they were kept isolated from other animals or given electric shocks (Maier & Watkins, 1998). This has the effect of "priming" the immune system, allowing it to more successfully resist the effects of the stress, as in Selye's resistance stage of the GAS.

So stress actually increases the activity of the immune system? But then how does stress end up causing those diseases, like high blood pressure? The positive effects of stress on the immune system seem to work only when the stress is not a continual, chronic condition. As stress continues, the body's resources begin to fail in the exhaustion phase of the general adaptation to stress (Kiecolt-Glaser et al., 1987, 1995, 1996; Prigerson et al., 1997). In one study, college students who were undergoing a stressful series of exams were compared to a group of similar students relaxing during a time of no classes and no exams (Deinzer et al., 2000). The exam group tested significantly lower for immune system chemicals that help fight off disease than did the relaxing control group, even as long as 14 days after the exams were over. The

So stress actually increases the activity of the immune system? But then how does stress end up causing those diseases, like high blood pressure? ▶

✳️ Explore on **mypsychlab**
Stress and the Immune System

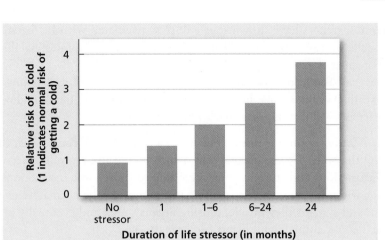

FIGURE 10.2 **Stress Duration and Illness** In this graph, the risk of getting a cold virus increases greatly as the months of exposure to a stressor increase. Although a stress reaction can be useful in its early phase, prolonged stress has a negative impact on the immune system, leaving the body vulnerable to illnesses such as a cold. *Source*: Cohen et al. (1998).

suppression of immune system functioning by stress apparently can continue even after the stress itself is over.

One reason that the early stress reaction is helpful but prolonged stress is not might be that the stress reaction, in evolutionary terms, is really meant only for a short-term response, such as running from a predator (Sapolsky, 2004). That level of intense bodily and hormonal activity isn't really meant to go on and on, as it does for human beings in the modern, stress-filled life we now know. Humans experience the stress reaction over prolonged periods of times and in situations that are not necessarily life-threatening, leading to a breakdown in the immune system (see Figure 10.2).

HEART DISEASE Of course, anything that can weaken the immune system can have a negative effect on other bodily systems. The sympathetic system (active during stress) cannot work at the same time as the parasympathetic system, and vice versa. It is the parasympathetic system, remember, that is responsible for normal, day-to-day functioning of the body, including repairs and "system maintenance," so to speak. For example, stress has been shown to put people at a higher risk for heart attacks and strokes at least in part because the liver, which is activated during parasympathetic functioning, does not have a chance to clear the fat and cholesterol from the bloodstream, leading to clogged arteries and eventually the possibility of heart attacks. In one recent study, middle-aged men were questioned about stress, diet, and lifestyle factors and were examined for biological risk factors for heart disease: obesity, high blood sugar, high triglycerides (a type of fatty acid found in the blood), and low levels of HDL or "good" cholesterol (see Figure 10.3). Stress and the production of stress hormones were found to be strongly linked to all four factors: The more stress the workers were exposed to in their work environment and home life, the more likely they were to exhibit these risk factors (Brunner et al., 2002). Not surprisingly,

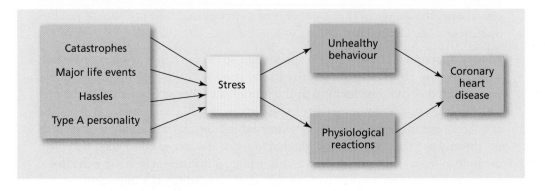

FIGURE 10.3 **Stress and Coronary Heart Disease** The box on the left represents various sources of stress (*Type A personality* refers to someone who is ambitious, always working, and usually hostile). In addition to the physical reactions that accompany the stress reaction, an individual under stress may be more likely to engage in unhealthy behaviour such as overeating, drinking alcohol or taking other kinds of drugs; avoiding exercise; and acting out in anger or frustration. This kind of behaviour also contributes to an increased risk of coronary heart disease.

Canadian researchers have shown that PTSD is associated with increased rates of cardiovascular disease, respiratory disorders, chronic pain, gastrointestinal illness, and cancer (Sareen et al., 2007).

Stress can also lead to certain unhealthy behaviours, such as drinking alcohol; smoking; eating all the wrong, high-fat, high-calorie "comfort" foods; and the avoidance of exercise—all factors associated with poor health.

CANCER   Cancer is not one disease but rather a collection of diseases that can affect any part of the body. Unlike normal cells, which divide and reproduce according to genetic instructions and stop dividing according to those same instructions, cancer cells divide without stopping. The resulting tumours affect the normal functioning of the organs and systems they invade, causing organs to fail and eventually killing the organism. People, animals, and plants can have cancer.

Although stress cannot give a person cancer, stress can have a suppressing effect on the immune system, making the unchecked growth of cancer more likely. In particular, an immune system cell called a **natural killer cell** has as its main functions the suppression of viruses and the destruction of tumour cells (Herberman & Ortaldo, 1981). Stress has been shown to depress the release of natural killer cells, making it more difficult for the body's systems to fight cancerous growths (Zorilla et al., 2001). The hormone adrenaline is released under stress and has been found to interfere with a protein that normally would suppress the growth of cancer cells (Sastry et al., 2007). In other research, stress has been linked to the accumulation of genetic errors that can lead to the formation of cancer cells and tumours: Stress causes the release of hormones that, over time, can cause mistakes in the instructions given by the genes to the cells of the body. As these mistakes "pile up" over the years, cells can begin to grow out of control, causing the growth of tumours and possibly cancer (Kiecolt-Glaser et al., 2002).

Heart disease and cancer are the two biggest killers of Canadians (Statistics Canada, 2005). As we have just seen, the physical effects of prolonged stress on the body and the immune system are profound, but that is only part of the picture of the influence of stress in daily life. The next section looks at how cognitive factors such as how one interprets a stressful event and psychological factors such as one's personality type can affect the impact of stress.

THE INFLUENCE OF COGNITION AND PERSONALITY ON STRESS

10.8   *What are the cognitive factors in stress?*

COGNITIVE FACTORS IN STRESS: LAZARUS'S COGNITIVE APPRAISAL APPROACH   Cognitive psychologist Richard Lazarus developed a cognitive view of stress called the *cognitive–mediational theory* of emotions, in which the way people think about and appraise a stressor is a major factor in how stressful that particular stressor becomes (Lazarus, 1991, 1999; Lazarus & Folkman, 1984). ⓛⓘⓝⓚ *to Chapter Nine: Motivation and Emotion, p. 350.* According to Lazarus, a two-step process assesses the degree of threat or harm of a stressor and how one should react to that stressor (see Figure 10.4).

Primary Appraisal   The first step in appraising a stressor is called **primary appraisal**, which involves estimating the severity of the stressor and classifying it as a threat (something that could be harmful in the future), a challenge (something to be met and defeated), or a harm or loss that has already occurred. If the stressor is appraised as a threat, negative emotions may arise that inhibit the person's ability to cope with the threat. For example, a student who has not read the text or taken good notes will certainly appraise an upcoming exam as threatening. If the stressor is seen as a challenge, however, it is possible to plan to meet that challenge, which is a more positive and

Explore on **mypsychlab**
The Effect of Cognitive Appraisal on Responses to Stressors

natural killer cell
immune system cell responsible for suppressing viruses and destroying tumour cells.

primary appraisal
the first step in assessing stress, which involves estimating the severity of the stressor and classifying it as either a threat or a challenge.

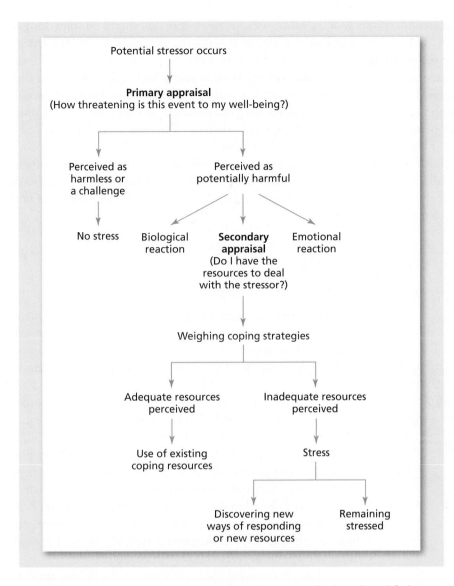

FIGURE 10.4 **Lazarus's Cognitive Appraisal Approach**   According to this approach, there are two steps in cognitively determining the degree of stress created by a potential stressor. Primary appraisal involves determining whether the potential stressor is a threat. If it is perceived as a threat, secondary appraisal occurs in addition to the bodily and emotional reactions. Secondary appraisal involves determining the resources one has to deal with the stress, such as time, money, physical ability, and so on. Inadequate resources lead to increased feelings of stress and the possibility of developing new resources to deal with the stress.

less-stressful approach. For example, the student who has studied, read, and feels prepared is much more likely to appraise the upcoming exam as an opportunity to do well.

Perceiving a stressor as a challenge instead of a threat makes coping with the stressor or the harm it may already have caused more likely to be successful, whereas perceiving it as an embarrassment or imagining failure or rejection is more likely to lead to increased stress reactions, negative emotions, and an inability to cope well (Folkman, 1997; Lazarus, 1993). Think positively!

Secondary Appraisal   In **secondary appraisal**, people who have identified a threat or harmful effect must estimate the resources that they have available for coping with the stressor. Resources might include social support, money, time, energy, ability, or any number of potential resources, depending on the threat. If resources are perceived as adequate or abundant, the degree of stress will be considerably less than if resources are missing or lacking. Using the example of the student and the upcoming exam, a student who feels that she has the time to study and the ability to understand the material in that time will feel much less distress than the student who has little time to study and doesn't feel that she understood much of the lectures covered on the exam.

As another example, let's say that a person's position at a firm has just been downsized. That's a fairly big stressor in most situations, but the degree of stress experienced and the coping abilities of that person will depend on both primary appraisal

secondary appraisal
the second step in assessing a threat, which involves estimating the resources available to the person for coping with the stressor.

and secondary appraisal. In most cases, primary appraisal might go something like this: "I've lost my job! I need a job, so this is bad, very bad!" ("This is a threat!") The secondary appraisal might result in the following: "I don't have much money in savings, and the job market for my skills is pretty bad right now. I don't have anyone I can borrow money from or live with while I'm looking for more work. I'm going to lose everything!" ("I don't have the resources to deal with this!") Contrast that person's situation with this person's situation: "I've been let go, but that's not so bad. I wanted to look for a new job anyhow." ("This is a challenge.") The secondary appraisal might be: "I have some money in savings, and I can live with my brother for a while if nothing turns up quickly. I should be fine." ("I have the resources to deal with this.") Which person is going to experience more stress and have more health problems as a consequence?

THE PSYCHOLOGY OF STRESS: HOW PERSONALITY AND STRESS ARE RELATED

10.9 *What is the relationship between stress and personality?*

"He always times 60 Minutes."
©The New Yorker Collection 1983 Mischa Richter from cartoonbank.com. All Rights Reserved.

Of course, how one cognitively assesses a stressor has a lot to do with one's personality. People with certain kinds of personality traits—such as aggressiveness or a naturally high level of anxiety, for example—seem to create more stress for themselves than may exist in the actual stressor. Even as long ago as the early 1930s, psychologists had evidence that personality characteristics are a major factor in predicting health. A longitudinal study begun in 1932 (Lehr & Thomae, 1987) found that personality was almost as important to longevity (how long people live) as genetic, physical, and lifestyle factors. Other researchers have found that people who live to be very old—into their 90s and even older than 100 years—tend to be relaxed, easygoing, cheerful, and active. People who have opposite personality traits, such as aggressiveness, stubbornness, inflexibility, and tenseness, typically do not live as long as the average life expectancy (Levy et al., 2002).

Those personality traits are some of the factors associated with two personality types that have been related to how people deal with stress and the influence of certain personality characteristics on coronary heart disease.

TYPE A AND TYPE B In 1974, medical doctors Meyer Freidman and Ray Rosenman published a book titled *Type A Behavior and Your Heart.* The book was the result of studies spanning three decades of research into the influence of certain personality characteristics on coronary heart disease (Friedman & Kasanin, 1943; Friedman & Rosenman, 1959; Rosenman et al., 1975). Since then, numerous researchers have explored the link between what Friedman called *Type A* and *Type B personalities.*

Type A people are workaholics. They are very competitive and ambitious, hate to waste time, and are easily annoyed. There is a constant sense of pressure and a strong tendency to try to do several things at once. Often successful but frequently unsatisfied, they always seem to want to go faster and do more, and they get easily upset over small things. A typical Type A finds it difficult to relax and do nothing—Type A people take work with them on vacation, a laptop to the beach, and do business over the phone in the car.

In 1961, the *Western Collaborative Group Study* (Rosenman et al., 1975) assessed 3500 men and followed them for eight years. Participants were asked to agree or disagree with statements such as "I can relax without guilt," in which strong agreement

Type A personality
person who is ambitious, time conscious, extremely hard-working, and tends to have high levels of hostility and anger as well as being easily annoyed.

indicates a Type B personality. The results were that Type A men were three times more likely to develop heart disease than Type B men. **Type B** people are not that competitive or driven, tend to be easygoing and slow to anger, and seem relaxed and at peace. Type B people are more likely to take a book to the beach to cover up their face than to actually read the book (see Figure 10.5).

The *Framingham Heart Study* found that the risk of coronary heart disease for women who work and are also Type A is four times that of Type B working women (Eaker & Castelli, 1988). Other research has narrowed the key factors in Type A personality and heart disease to one characteristic: hostility (Frederickson et al., 1999; Matthews et al., 2004; Williams, 1999; Williams et al., 1980). Williams and his colleagues used the *Minnesota Multiphasic Personality Inventory*, a personality test that looks for certain characteristics that include the level of hostility. ⓁⒾⓃⓀ *to Chapter Eleven: Theories of Personality, p. 438.* In this study, 424 patients who had undergone exploratory surgery for coronary heart disease were examined, and the presence of heart disease was related both to being Type A and to being hostile, with hostility being the more significant factor in the hardening of the arteries to the heart (Williams et al., 1980).

Numerous studies support the link between hostility and increased risk of coronary heart disease. A study of hostility levels and risk factors for heart disease in more than 4000 young adults found that increases in hostility over a five-year follow-up study were associated with a rise in high blood pressure, one of the major risk factors of heart disease (Markovitz et al., 1997). Another study of anger in young men and their risk for premature heart disease found that over a period of slightly more than three decades, the young men who had exhibited high levels of hostility in their youth were far more likely to develop premature cardiovascular disease, particularly heart attacks, than were those men who had lower levels of anger and hostility (Chang et al., 2002). Similar studies found that hostility in college- and university-aged males and females was significantly related to increased risk of heart disease, particularly if levels of hostility rose in middle age (Brondolo et al., 2003; Siegler et al., 2003).

Even children may not escape the hostility–heart disease link. A recent study has found that children and adolescents who scored high on assessments of hostility were more likely to show physical changes such as obesity, resistance to insulin, high blood pressure, and elevated levels of triglycerides three years after the initial measurements of hostility had been made (Raikkonen et al., 2003).

What about people who don't blow their top but try to keep everything in instead? Wouldn't that be bad for a person's health?

TYPE C   A third personality type was identified by researchers Temoshok and Dreher (1992) as being associated with a higher incidence of cancer. **Type C** people tend to be very pleasant and try to keep the peace but find it difficult to express emotions, especially negative ones. They tend to internalize their anger and often experience a sense of despair over the loss of a loved one or a loss of hope. They are often lonely. These personality characteristics are strongly associated with cancer, and people who have cancer and this personality type often have thicker cancerous tumours as well (Eysenck, 1994; Temoshok & Dreher, 1992). Just as the stress of hostility puts the cardiovascular systems of Type A people at greater risk, the internalized negative emotions of the Type C personality may increase the levels of harmful stress hormones, weaken the immune system, and slow recovery.

THE HARDY PERSONALITY   Not all Type A people are prone to heart disease. There are some people who actually seem to thrive on stress instead of letting stress

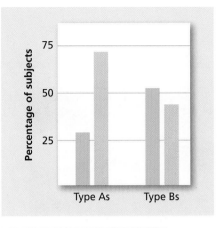

FIGURE 10.5 **Personality and Coronary Heart Disease**   The two bars on the left represent men with Type A personalities. Notice that within the Type A men, there are more than twice as many who suffer from coronary heart disease as those who are healthy. The two bars on the right represent men with Type B personalities. Far more Type B personalities are healthy than Type A personalities, and there are far fewer Type B personalities with coronary heart disease when compared to Type A personalities.
Source: Miller et al. (1991, 1996).

◄ What about people who don't blow their top but try to keep everything in instead? Wouldn't that be bad for a person's health?

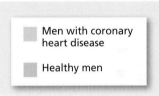

Type B personality
person who is relaxed and laid-back, less driven and competitive than Type A, and slow to anger.

Although Type A men and women may be successful in the world of business, their anger and hostility put them at high risk of coronary heart disease. How would anger and hostility be able to affect the heart?

TYPE Z BEHAVIOR

Type Z behavior
©The New Yorker Collection 1987 Donald Reilly from cartoonbank.com. All Rights Reserved.

Type C personality
pleasant but repressed person, who tends to internalize his or her anger and anxiety and who finds expressing emotions difficult.

hardy personality
a person who seems to thrive on stress but lacks the anger and hostility of the Type A personality.

optimists
people who expect positive outcomes.

pessimists
people who expect negative outcomes.

wear them down. These people have what is called the **hardy personality**, a term first coined by psychologist Suzanne Kobasa (1979). Hardy people (call them "Type H") differ from ordinary, hostile Type A people and others who suffer more ill effects because of stress in three ways:

- Hardy people have a deep sense of *commitment* to their values, beliefs, sense of identity, work, and family life.
- Hardy people also feel that they are in *control* of their lives and what happens to them.
- Hardy people tend to interpret events in primary appraisal differently than people who are not hardy. When things go wrong, they do not see a frightening problem to be avoided but instead a *challenge* to be met and answered.

Why would those three characteristics (often known as *the three C's of hardiness*) lessen the negative impact of stress? Commitment makes a person more willing to make sacrifices and deal with hardships than if commitment were lacking. Think about it: Have you ever had a job that you hated? Every little frustration was very stressful, right? Now think about doing something you love to do. The frustrations that inevitably come with any endeavour just don't seem quite as bad when you are doing something you really want to do, do they?

As for control, uncontrollability is one of the major factors cited as increasing stress, as was discussed earlier in this chapter. Seeing events as challenges rather than problems also changes the level of stress experienced, a difference similar to that felt when riding a roller coaster: If riding the coaster is your own idea, it's fun; if someone makes you ride it, it's not fun.

The four personality types discussed so far could be summed up this way: If life gives them lemons,

- Type A people get enraged and throw the lemons back, having a minor heart attack while doing so.
- Type C people don't say anything but fume inside where no one can see.
- Type B people gather all the lemons and make lemonade.
- Hardy people gather the lemons, make lemonade, sell it, turn it into a franchise business, and make millions.

EXPLANATORY STYLE: OPTIMISTS AND PESSIMISTS   In addition to personality type, other personal factors have an influence on people's reactions to stressors. One of these factors is the attitude that people have toward the things that happen to them in life.

Optimists are people who always tend to look for positive outcomes. For an optimist, a glass is half full, whereas for a pessimist, the glass is half empty. **Pessimists** seem to expect the worst to happen. Researchers have found that optimism is associated with longer life and increased immune system functioning. Mayo Clinic researchers conducted a longitudinal study of optimists and pessimists (as assessed by a scale) over a period of 30 years (Maruta et al., 2002). The results for pessimists were not good: They had a much higher death rate than did the optimists, and those that were still living in 1994 had more problems with physical and emotional health, more pain, less ability to take part in social activities, and less energy than optimists. The optimists had a 50 percent lower risk of premature death and were more calm, peaceful, and happy than the pessimists (Maruta et al., 2002). An earlier study linked being optimistic to higher levels of helper T cells (immune system cells that direct and increase the functioning of the immune system) and higher levels of natural killer cells, the body's antivirus, anticancer cells (Segerstrom et al., 1998).

Martin Seligman is a social learning psychologist who developed the concept of *learned helplessness,* Ⓛ Ⓘ Ⓝ Ⓚ *to Chapter Five: Learning, p. 206,* and began the positive psychology movement. Seligman (2002) has outlined four ways in which optimism may affect how long a person lives:

1. Optimists are less likely to develop learned helplessness, the tendency to stop trying to achieve a goal that has been blocked in the past.

2. Optimists are more likely than pessimists to take care of their health by preventive measures (such as going to the doctor regularly and eating right) because they believe that their actions make a difference in what happens to them. (Remember, this is a characteristic of hardy people as well.)

3. Optimists are far less likely than pessimists to become depressed, and depression is associated with mortality because of the effect of depression on the immune system.

4. Optimists have more effectively functioning immune systems than pessimists, perhaps because they experience less psychological stress.

Regular exercise increases the functioning of the immune system and helps give people a sense of control over their health. Having a sense of control decreases feelings of stress, which also helps the immune system to function well.

Seligman (1998) has also found that optimists are more successful in their life endeavours than pessimists. Optimistic politicians win more elections, optimistic students get better grades, and optimistic athletes win more contests.

Whoa—optimistic students get better grades? How do I become an optimist? Sign me up! Optimism is mostly a matter of controlling mood or emotional reactions to situations. Psychiatrist Dr. Susan Vaughan (2000) has some good advice for optimistic people who want to keep a positive outlook:

- *Alternative thinking:* Optimists tend to take bad things that happen less personally, coming up with alternative explanations for why the bad thing happened. For example, optimists tend to attribute poor exam grades to the difficulty of that particular material or to not having enough time to study. They appraise it as a challenge and assume that they will perform more successfully in the future.

- *Downward social comparison:* Many people make themselves feel better by comparing their performance to that of less competent others, making them feel better and protecting self-esteem. Optimists use *downward social comparison* frequently.

- *Relaxation:* Optimists use relaxation as a way to improve mood, such as exercising, meditating, or reading a good book.

◄ Whoa— optimistic students get better grades? How do I become an optimist? Sign me up!

How to Become an Optimistic Thinker   The way to become an optimist is to monitor one's own thinking. Recognition of negative thoughts is the first step, followed by disputing those same negative thoughts (Seligman, 2002). The problem is that most people don't really think about their thoughts or characterize them as negative or pessimistic, which means that the damaging effects of such thinking are left uncontrolled. Here's a plan to follow to become an optimistic thinker:

1. When a bad mood strikes, stop and think about what just went through your head.

2. When you've recognized the negative statements, treat them as if they came from someone else—someone who is trying to make your life miserable. Think about the damage the statement is doing to you.

3. Argue with those thoughts. Challenge each negative statement and replace it with a more positive statement.

Example:

1. "I'll never get this term paper finished, it's too hard, and there's so much going on that it's impossible!" What words in this statement makes it pessimistic? "Never" is a long time. Why is it too hard? Is it really impossible, or just difficult? Is it just one part of the paper that seems so hard, or is it the whole thing?

2. That statement isn't going to help me at all. It just makes me feel worse and that makes me unmotivated to work on the paper.

3. I can finish the term paper. I'm just going to have to devote more time to working on it. I can make a timetable for finishing the different parts of the paper and stop spending so much time watching television and escaping into other activities that can wait until the paper is finished. I've been in situations like this before and managed, so I can manage now, too.

Note that the third way of thinking is much more positive and hopeful. It includes ways to get around what seemed too hard or impossible in the negative statement. Essentially, the last step in becoming a more optimistic thinker is to learn to argue with yourself and correct distorted or faulty thinking.

How can I recognize distorted thinking when it's my own thoughts in the first place? Recognizing faulty thinking can be difficult at first. The following questions may help people hone in on negative thinking:

1. In thinking about the thoughts you have had in the past few hours, how many of them were negative thoughts? How could you change those thoughts to be more positive?

2. When thinking about people you know who make a lot of negative self-statements or who are always minimizing their efforts or putting themselves down, how does their behaviour make you feel? How do you think their behaviour makes them feel?

How can I recognize ▶ distorted thinking when it's my own thoughts in the first place?

PRACTICE QUIZ: HOW MUCH DO YOU REMEMBER?

Pick the best answer.

1. In the _____ stage of the general adaptation syndrome, the person may actually start to feel better.
   a. alarm
   b. resistance
   c. exhaustion
   d. termination

2. The activation of the immune system response by stress differs from the activation of that system by illness in that
   a. illness activates areas in the brain first.
   b. stress increases the release of natural killer cells.
   c. stress activates a different immune response than does illness.
   d. stress activates areas in the brain first.

3. Adam is very ambitious and driven to succeed. He is easily angered, always wants to be working, and finds it hard to relax. According to research, Adam
   a. is at a high risk for coronary heart disease.
   b. is a hardy personality.
   c. is a Type B personality.
   d. is a Type C personality.

4. Which of the following is NOT one of the three C's of the hardy personality?
   a. commitment
   b. callousness
   c. control
   d. challenge

5. Optimism has been associated with all the following except
   a. taking care of one's health.
   b. increased rates of learned helplessness.
   c. lower rates of depression.
   d. healthy immune systems.

6. According to Lazarus, secondary appraisal involves
   a. estimating the severity of the stressor.
   b. deciding whether the stressor is a problem.
   c. classifying the stressor as a threat or a problem.
   d. estimating the resources a person has available for coping.

Answers: 1-b, 2-d, 3-a, 4-b, 5-b, 6-d.

SOCIAL FACTORS IN STRESS: PEOPLE WHO NEED PEOPLE

10.10   *What is the relationship between stress and social factors?*

Much of the stress in everyday life comes from having to deal with other people and with the rules of social interaction. Overcrowding, for example, is a common source of stress and may be one reason for the increasing rate of *road rage*, or the tendency for drivers to become excessively enraged by ordinary traffic frustrations, sometimes resulting in serious injuries, assaults, and even death (AAA Foundation for Traffic Safety, 1997). Two of the more prominent social factors in creating stressful living conditions are both economically based: poverty and job stress.

POVERTY   Unfortunately, for the roughly 655 000 Canadian families and 788 000 Canadian children living below the poverty line (Statistics Canada, 2007a), life is more stressful for several reasons.

The lack of sufficient money to provide the basic necessities of life can lead to many stressors for both adults and children: overcrowding, poor housing, noisy environments, crime and violence, substance abuse, fewer community services, and increased rates of illness, as poorer persons are less likely to seek medical help when ill or fill their prescriptions (Aligne et al., 2000; Bracey, 1997; Leroy & Symes, 2001; Park et al., 2002; Renchler, 1993; Rouse, 1998; Schmitz et al., 2001; Taylor, Repetti, & Seeman, 1997; Williamson & Fast, 1998). McGill University researchers have also shown that Canadians of lower socioeconomic status are less likely to obtain proper amounts of vitamins and minerals and more likely to buy inexpensive foods that are high in fat, increasing their rate of obesity, which has been associated with poorer health (Johnson-Down, O'Loughlin, Koski, & Gray-Daonald, 1997). While life is stressful at the best of times for most Canadians, for those living below the poverty line stress is only intensified.

JOB STRESS   Canadians are a stressed-out bunch according to a recent poll, with three-quarters of us reporting that we are either sometimes or frequently stressed (CTV.ca News, 2006). The number one reason people gave for their high level of stress was their job, with finances a close second. Even if a person has a job and is making an adequate salary, stresses associated with the workplace add to daily stressors. Some of the typical sources of workplace stress include workload, a lack of variety or meaningfulness in work, lack of control over decisions, long hours, poor physical work conditions, and lack of job security (Murphy, 1995).

👁 **Watch** on **mypsychlab**

Rude Encounters and Bullying in the Workplace

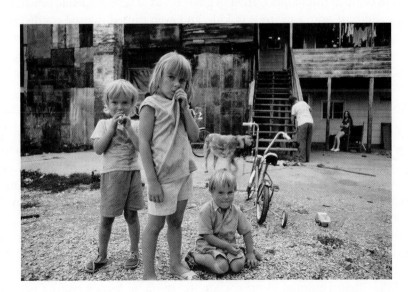

Poverty can lead to many conditions that increase the degree of stress experienced by both adults and children. These children, for example, may face an increased risk of malnutrition, illness, and exposure to violence because of the conditions under which they must live.

There are times when I feel like I've just had it with school and all the work the teachers pile on—is that something like workplace stress? ▶

✳ Explore on **mypsychlab**

This Buddhist group is celebrating Songkran, the New Year, by performing their cultural ritual of pouring water over their elder's palms. Although they are wearing clothing typical of people living in Los Angeles, California, where the ceremony is taking place, they still maintain some of their old cultural traditions.

burnout
negative changes in thoughts, emotions, and behaviour as a result of prolonged stress or frustration.

acculturative stress
stress resulting from the need to change and adapt a person's ways to the majority culture.

Researchers in Ontario and Manitoba reviewed the literature and contend that workplace bullying is a significant contributor to job-related stress. They found that acts of bullying such as yelling, teasing, spreading rumours or lies, or socially excluding a co-worker had affected about 25 percent of all employees at least once in their careers. Interestingly, those who were bullied were more likely to quit their jobs and experience higher anxiety and anger than those who reported being sexually harassed at work (Hershcovis & Barling, 2007). Stress at work can result in the same symptoms as stress from any other source: headaches, high blood pressure, indigestion, and other physical symptoms; anxiety, irritability, anger, depression, and other psychological symptoms; and behavioural symptoms such as overeating, drug use, poor job performance, or changes in family relationships (Anschuetz, 1999).

There are times when I feel like I've just had it with school and all the work the teachers pile on—is that something like workplace stress?

Burnout One of the more serious effects of workplace stress is a condition called *burnout*. **Burnout** can be defined as negative changes in thoughts, emotions, and behaviour as a result of prolonged stress or frustration (Miller & Smith, 1993). Symptoms of burnout are extreme dissatisfaction, pessimism, lowered job satisfaction, and a desire to quit. Although burnout is most commonly associated with job stress, college and university students can also suffer from burnout when the stresses of student life—term papers, exams, assignments and the like—become overwhelming. Amanda Weckwerth and Deborah Flynn (2006) measured burnout in students attending classes at Nipissing University in North Bay, Ontario. Their results suggested that males and females experience burnout differently. Females tended to experience more emotional overextension, leading to feelings of decreased competence and accomplishment. Males tended to feel more depersonalized or emotionally shut down and unable to give psychologically to others. Females were also more likely than males to feel that they could count on others during their stressful time and felt more supported by authority figures, which likely contributed to their continued sense of emotional connection. These results suggest that today's students are experiencing significant stress, and the need for high-quality support services guided by each student's unique stress experience is essential.

Burnout may even be occurring in Canada's youngest students. University of Toronto professors Linda Cameron and Lee Bartel (2008) found that homework assigned to children from kindergarten to grade 6 was of little academic benefit but was often a significant source of stress in kids, and even caused marital conflict in some families, as it interfered with quality family time. Cameron and Bartel (2008) also point out that reading with your child every day is the best way to boost academic success. Fortunately, their research did show that homework was of academic benefit to children in grades 7 through 12. So it will be difficult for you to argue that the homework your professor assigns is of no academic value.

HOW CULTURE AFFECTS STRESS When a person from one culture must live in another culture, that person may experience a great deal of stress. Acculturation is the process of adapting to a new or different culture, often the dominant culture (Sodowsky et al., 1991). The stress resulting from the need to change and adapt to the dominant or majority culture is called **acculturative stress** (Berry & Kim, 1998; Berry & Sam, 1997).

The method that a minority person chooses to enter into the majority culture can also have an impact on the degree of stress that minority person will experience (Berry & Kim, 1988). One method is *integration*: The individual tries to maintain a sense of the original cultural identity while also trying to form a positive relationship with members of the dominant culture. For example, an integrated person will maintain a lot of original cultural traditions within the home and with immediate family members, but will dress like the majority culture and adopt some of those characteristics as well. For people who choose integration, acculturative stress is usually low (Ward & Rana-Deuba, 1999).

In *assimilation*, the minority person gives up the old cultural identity and completely adopts the majority culture's ways. In the early days of the United States, many immigrants were assimilated into the mainstream American culture, even changing their names to sound more "American." Assimilation leads to moderate levels of stress, most likely because of the loss of cultural patterns and rejection by other members of the minority culture who have not chosen assimilation (LaFromboise et al., 1993; Lay & Nguyen, 1998).

Separation is a pattern in which the minority person rejects the majority culture's ways and tries to maintain the original cultural identity. Members of the minority culture refuse to learn the language of the dominant culture, and they live where others from their culture live, socializing only with others from their original culture. Separation results in a fairly high degree of stress, and that stress will be even higher if the separation is forced (by discrimination from the majority group) rather than voluntary (self-imposed withdrawal from the majority culture).

The greatest acculturative stress will most likely be experienced by people who have chosen to be *marginalized*, neither maintaining contact with the original culture nor joining the majority culture. They essentially live on the "margins" of both cultures without feeling or becoming part of either culture. Marginalized individuals do not have the security of the familiar culture of origin or the acceptance of the majority culture and may suffer a loss of identity and feel alienated from others (Roysircai-Sodowsky & Maestas, 2000). Obviously, marginalized people have little in the way of a social support system to help them deal with both everyday stresses and major life changes.

I hear the term *social support system* all the time now. Exactly what is it?

THE POSITIVE BENEFITS OF SOCIAL SUPPORT   A **social support system** is the network of friends, family members, neighbours, co-workers, and others who can offer help to a person in need. That help can take the form of advice, physical or monetary support, information, emotional support, love and affection, or companionship. Research has consistently shown that having a good social support system is of critical importance in a person's ability to cope with stressors: People with good social support systems are less likely to die from illnesses or injuries than those without such support (Kulik & Mahler, 1989, 1993). Marriage, itself a form of social support, is a good predictor of healthy aging and longevity (Gardner & Oswald, 2004; Vaillant, 2002). Social support has been found to have a positive effect on the immune system (Holt-Lunstad et al., 2003) and improves the mental health and physical functioning of people who have lupus, a chronic inflammatory disease that can affect nearly any part of the body (Sutcliffe et al., 1999; Ward et al., 1999), as well as those with cancer and HIV (Carver & Antoni, 2004; Gonzalez et al., 2004). Researchers at York University measured adjustment to university life in 115 first-year undergraduate students in both the first and second semester. They found that increased social support from friends and family improved overall adjustment to university life, but only social support from friends predicted better social adjustment (e.g., "I am very involved with social activities in university") and personal-emotional adjustment (e.g., "Being on my own, taking responsibility for myself, has not been easy"; Friedlander, Reid, Shupak, & Cribbie, 2007).

College or university is often stressful for a young adult who is away from home for the first time. This young woman is being consoled by her fellow students. Social support is one of the most important keys to handling the stresses of any situation. What are some other things the young woman could do to ease her homesickness?

social support system
the network of family, friends, neighbours, co-workers, and others who can offer support, comfort, or aid to a person in need.

I hear the term social support system all the time now. Exactly what is it?

Coping with illness is always made easier when one has social support. Here, a woman recovering in the hospital is visited by a dog. Animals are also a good source of social support, and people who have animals have been shown to recover from illnesses and stressors more quickly (Allen et al., 2002).

Social support can make a stressor seem less threatening because people with such support know that there is help available. Having people to talk to about one's problems reduces the physical symptoms of stress—talking about frightening or frustrating events with others can help people think more realistically about the threat, for example, and talking with people who have had similar experiences can help put the event into perspective. (L I N K) *to Chapter Fourteen: Psychological Therapies, p. 564.* The negative emotions of loneliness and depression, which are less likely to occur with someone who has social support, can adversely affect one's ability to cope (Beehr et al., 2000; Weisse, 1992). Positive emotions, on the contrary, have a decidedly beneficial effect on health, helping people recover from stressful experiences more quickly and effectively (Tugade & Fredrickson, 2004). Positive emotions are more likely to occur in the presence of friends and family.

How people think about a stressor is also a powerful influence on their ability to cope, as the next section will discuss.

PRACTICE QUIZ: HOW MUCH DO YOU REMEMBER?

Pick the best answer.

1. Which of the following is NOT a typical source of stress in the workplace?
   a. heavy workload
   b. lack of variety
   c. lack of shift work
   d. lack of job security

2. Which of the following is NOT a symptom of burnout?
   a. pessimism
   b. dissatisfaction
   c. optimism
   d. desire to quit

3. Larysa moved from Ukraine to the United States. She learned to speak and write English, changed her last name so it would sound more "American," and no longer maintains any of her old culture's styles of dress or customs. Larysa has used which method of entering the majority culture?
   a. integration
   b. assimilation
   c. separation
   d. marginalization

4. Social support
   a. has a positive benefit on health.
   b. can improve the physical functioning of cancer patients.
   c. can improve the physical functioning of people with HIV.
   d. all of the above

Answers: 1-c, 2-c, 3-b, 4-d.

> I have exams and my job and my relationship ▶ to worry about, so I feel pretty stressed out. How do people deal with all the stress they face every day?

COPING WITH STRESS

I have exams and my job and my relationship to worry about, so I feel pretty stressed out. How do people deal with all the stress they face every day? So far, this chapter has talked about what stress is and the factors that can magnify the effects of stress, as well as the effects of stress on a person's physical health. Part of dealing with stress is in knowing those kinds of things so that changes can be made in the factors that are controllable. **Coping strategies** are actions that people can take to master, tolerate, reduce, or minimize the effects of stressors, and they can include both behavioural strategies and psychological strategies.

10.11 *What are two ways that people can deal with stress?*

PROBLEM-FOCUSED COPING

One type of coping strategy is to work on eliminating or changing the stressor itself. When people try to eliminate the source of a stress or reduce its impact through their own actions, it is called **problem-focused coping** (Folkman & Lazarus, 1980; Lazarus, 1993). For example, a student might have a problem understanding a particular professor. The professor is knowledgeable but has trouble explaining the concepts of the course in a way that this student can understand. Problem-focused coping

coping strategies
actions that people can take to master, tolerate, reduce, or minimize the effects of stressors.

problem-focused coping
coping strategies that try to eliminate the source of a stress or reduce its impact through direct actions.

might include talking to the professor after class, asking fellow students to clarify the concepts, getting a tutor, or forming a study group with other students who are also having difficulty and pooling the group's resources.

EMOTION-FOCUSED COPING

Problem-focused coping can work quite well but is not the only method people can use. Most people use both problem-focused coping and **emotion-focused coping** to successfully deal with controllable stressful events (Folkman & Lazarus, 1980; Lazarus, 1993; Stowell et al., 2001). Emotion-focused coping is a strategy that involves changing the way a person feels or emotionally reacts to a stressor. This reduces the emotional impact of the stressor and makes it possible to deal with the problem more effectively. For example, the student who is faced with a professor who isn't easy to understand might share his concerns with a friend, talking it through until calm enough to tackle the problem in a more direct manner. Emotion-focused coping also works for stressors that are uncontrollable and for which problem-focused coping is not possible. Someone using emotion-focused coping may decide to view the stressor as a challenge rather than a threat, decide that the problem is a minor one, write down concerns in a journal, or even ignore the problem altogether.

Ignore it? But won't that just make matters worse? True, ignoring a problem is not a good strategy when there is something a person can actively do about solving the problem. But when it is not possible to change or eliminate the stressor, or when worrying about the stressor can be a problem itself, ignoring the problem is not a bad idea. Researchers working with people who had suffered heart attacks found that those people who worried about a future attack were more likely to suffer from symptoms of post-traumatic stress, such as nightmares and poor sleep (both factors that increase the risk of a future heart attack), than were the people who tried to ignore their worries (Ginzburg et al., 2003).

Using humour can also be a form of emotion-focused coping, as the old saying "laughter is the best medicine" suggests. University of Western Ontario psychologists Rod Martin and Nicholas Kuiper have been studying the relationship between humour, well-being, and stress coping since the early 1980s and are considered authorities on the topic. They have shown that students who have a better sense of humour or can laugh under stressful conditions are less affected by negative life events, have higher self-esteem and better self-concepts, and are more positive in good and bad times (Kuiper & Martin, 1998; Martin, 2007; Martin & Lefcourt, 1983). A study on the effects of laughter found that laughter actually boosted the action of the immune system by increasing the work of natural killer cells (cells that attack viruses in the body). In this study, participants were shown a humorous video for one hour. Blood samples were taken 10 minutes before the viewing, 30 minutes into the viewing, 30 minutes after viewing, and 12 hours after viewing the video. There were significant increases in natural killer cell activity and nearly half a dozen other immune system cells and systems, with some effects lasting the full 12 hours after the video ended (Berk et al., 2001). Martin and Kuiper are cautious, however, with regard to the relationship between humour and the physical aspects of stress (e.g., immune system, blood pressure). After reviewing the literature, they found that this relationship was not as strong as the relationship between humour and the emotional effects of stress (Kuiper, Grimshaw, Leite, & Kirsh, 2004; Martin, 2007). In other words, humour may protect you against anxiety and depression, but it may not be that effective against stress-related physical symptoms such as headaches and high blood pressure.

emotion-focused coping
coping strategies that change the impact of a stressor by changing the emotional reaction to the stressor.

Ignore it? But won't that just make matters ◄ worse?

These life-size models of Marge and Homer Simpson were created for the 350th episode of *The Simpsons* which aired in April 2005. A large part of the success of such comedies can be attributed to the human need to laugh—laughter helps us cope with many of life's stresses.

"I'm sorry, I'm not speaking to anyone tonight. My defense mechanisms seem to be out of order."
©The New Yorker Collection 1985 Joseph Mirachi from cartoonbank.com. All Rights Reserved.

psychological defence mechanisms
unconscious distortions of a person's perception of reality that reduce stress and anxiety.

denial
psychological defence mechanism in which the person refuses to acknowledge or recognize a threatening situation.

repression
psychological defence mechanism in which the person refuses to consciously remember a threatening or unacceptable event, instead "pushing" those events into the unconscious mind.

rationalization
psychological defence mechanism in which a person invents acceptable excuses for unacceptable behaviour.

projection
psychological defence mechanism in which unacceptable or threatening impulses or feelings are seen as originating with someone else, usually the target of the impulses or feelings.

reaction formation
psychological defence mechanism in which a person forms an opposite emotional or behavioural reaction to the way he or she really feels to keep those true feelings hidden from the self and others.

regression
psychological defence mechanism in which a person falls back on childlike patterns of responding in reaction to stressful situations.

identification
defence mechanism in which a person tries to become like someone else to deal with anxiety.

compensation (substitution)
defence mechanism in which a person makes up for inferiorities in one area by becoming superior in another area.

Emotion-focused coping is highly related to several forms of psychological defences first proposed by Sigmund Freud, as the next section discusses.

PSYCHOLOGICAL DEFENCE MECHANISMS

10.12   What are the psychological defence mechanisms?

In Freud's writings on psychoanalysis, he stated that when people experience anxiety (stress) from conflicts between the demands of the body's needs and desires and society's rules for proper behaviour, there are certain unconscious distortions of thought that can protect their sense of self from that anxiety (Freud, 1915), **L I N K** *to Chapter Eleven: Theories of Personality, p. 438.* These unconscious distortions of the perception of reality are called **psychological defence mechanisms** and were further explained by Freud's daughter, Anna Freud (1946). Although Freudian theory has fallen in and out of favour over the past century, the concept of these defence mechanisms has remained quite useful in clinical psychology as a way of describing people's defensive behaviour and irrational thinking. Table 10.2 lists, defines, and gives examples of some of the more common defence mechanisms.

TABLE 10.2 THE PSYCHOLOGICAL DEFENCE MECHANISMS

DEFENCE MECHANISM AND DEFINITION	EXAMPLE
Denial: refusal to recognize or acknowledge a threatening situation.	Ben is an alcoholic who denies being an alcoholic.
Repression: "pushing" threatening or conflicting events or situations out of conscious memory.	Elise, who was sexually abused as a child, cannot remember the abuse at all.
Rationalization: making up acceptable excuses for unacceptable behaviour.	"If I don't have breakfast, I can have that piece of cake later on without hurting my diet."
Projection: placing one's own unacceptable thoughts onto others, as if the thoughts belonged to them and not to oneself.	Keisha is attracted to her sister's husband but denies this and believes the husband is attracted to her.
Reaction formation: forming an emotional reaction or attitude that is the opposite of one's threatening or unacceptable actual thoughts.	Matt is unconsciously attracted to Ben but outwardly voices an extreme hatred of homosexuals.
Displacement: expressing feelings that would be threatening if directed at the real target onto a less threatening substitute target.	Sandra gets reprimanded by her boss and goes home to angrily pick a fight with her husband.
Regression: falling back on childlike patterns as a way of coping with stressful situations.	After his parents bring home a new baby, 4-year-old Jeff starts wetting his bed.
Identification: trying to become like someone else to deal with one's anxiety.	Marie really admires Suzy, the most popular girl in school, and tries to copy her behaviour and dress.
Compensation (substitution): when a person tries to make up for areas in which a lack is perceived by becoming superior in some other area.	Reggie is not good at athletics, so he puts all of his energies into becoming a scholar.
Sublimation: turning socially unacceptable urges into socially acceptable behaviour.	Alain, who is very aggressive, becomes a professional hockey player.

It may have become obvious that nearly all of these techniques are forms of emotion-focused coping strategies, although their misuse can easily lead to more problems, as many of Freud's patients discovered.

Unlike much of the rest of Freud's psychoanalytic theory, research in cognitive psychology has uncovered some scientific support for the concept of unconscious coping mechanisms at work when people experience stress (Cramer, 2000). Although many psychologists in the 1970s and early 1980s rejected the idea of the unconscious mind's influence on conscious behaviour, recent studies in cognitive perception have found support for the influence of experiences for which there is no conscious memory on task performance (Dehaene et al., 2001; Greenwald et al., 1996; Kihlstrom, 1987). These studies deal with the phenomenon of implicit memory. ⓁⓘⓃⓀ *to Chapter Six: Memory, p. 218.* Implicit memory, also called *procedural memory*, is a form of long-term memory in which habits, skills, conditioned responses, emotional associations, and other well-learned procedures are stored. These memories affect conscious behaviour, as in being able to balance on a bicycle, but are not stored in conscious awareness and cannot easily be brought into conscious awareness.

MEDITATION AS A COPING MECHANISM

10.13 *How can meditation help relieve stress?*

Meditation is a mental series of exercises meant to refocus attention and achieve a trancelike state of consciousness. ⓁⓘⓃⓀ *to Chapter Four: Consciousness, p. 134.* Meditation can produce a state of relaxation that can aid in coping with the physiological reactions to a stressful situation.

CONCENTRATIVE MEDITATION Have you ever found yourself staring out into space, or at some little spot on the wall or table, only to realize that your mind has been a complete blank for the past several minutes?

The state just described is really nothing more than **concentrative meditation**, the form of meditation best known to the general public. In concentrative meditation, the goal is to focus the mind on some repetitive or unchanging stimulus (such as a spot or the sound of one's own heart beating) so that the mind can forget daily hassles and problems and the body can relax. In fact, Benson (1975; Benson et al., 1974a, 1974b) found that meditation produces a state of relaxation in which blood pressure is lowered, alpha waves (brain waves associated with relaxation) are increased, and the amounts of melatonin secreted at night (the hormone that helps induce sleep) are increased.

Some people say that if you meditate for only 20 minutes a day, you don't have to sleep at night. That would be nice—think how much more could be accomplished with those extra hours. Unfortunately, although certain meditation groups do make some rather wild claims for meditation, research has shown none of them to be true (Murphy & Donavan, 1997). What research does show is that concentrative meditation is a good way to relax and lower blood pressure in adolescents and adults, men and women, and both white and Black people (Barnes et al., 1997; Schneider et al., 1995; Wenneberg et al., 1997). It isn't the only way, as reading a good book or taking a warm bath also produce relaxation. Even simply resting for the same amount of time as one might meditate can be just as relaxing. The advantage of meditation is that people can do it almost anywhere, even in the classroom just before a big test. (It would be a little difficult to take a warm bath then.)

Other research has suggested that concentrative meditation can reduce the levels of chronic pain (Kabat-Zinn et al., 1986), reduce the symptoms of anxiety,

sublimation
channelling socially unacceptable impulses and urges into socially acceptable behaviour.

This man is practising Zen yoga meditation. Meditation increases relaxation and helps to lower blood pressure and muscle tension.

◄●┤ **Simulate** on mypsychlab
Coping with Stress: Progressive Muscle Relaxation

meditation
mental series of exercises meant to refocus attention and achieve a trancelike state of consciousness.

concentrative meditation
form of meditation in which a person focuses the mind on some repetitive or unchanging stimulus so that the mind can be cleared of disturbing thoughts and the body can experience relaxation.

receptive meditation
form of meditation in which a person attempts to become aware of everything in immediate conscious experience, or an expansion of consciousness.

stress-inoculation training (SIT)
a problem-focused coping method that helps people identify their particular stressors and develop skills that will reduce the negative impact of those stressors.

depression, and hostility (Kabat-Zinn et al., 1985), and reduce stress levels in cancer patients (Speca et al., 2000). Reducing stress levels in cancer patients through meditation will increase the likelihood of recovery and reduce the incidence of recurrence.

RECEPTIVE MEDITATION The other kind of meditation is less well-known and not as easily achieved. It is called **receptive meditation** and involves trying to expand consciousness outward. The best description of what this is like is to think about a time when you were overawed by nature. Perhaps you were standing at the ocean's edge on a starry night and became suddenly aware of how vast the universe really is. Or perhaps you were walking in the woods and listening to all the sounds of the birds and animals surrounding you. Your attention was focused outward rather than inward, and this state is similar to the one that this type of meditation tries to achieve.

THE EFFECTS OF MEDITATION Regardless of which form of meditation people choose to try, the effects are similar (Murphy & Donavan, 1997). Meditation for only 20 minutes can produce lowered blood pressure in people with hypertension (high blood pressure). It can calm anxiety, help people get to sleep, and help people deal with stress.

STRESS-INOCULATION TRAINING AS A COPING MECHANISM

10.14 *What is stress-inoculation training?*

Stress-inoculation training (SIT) is a problem-focused coping method that helps people identify their particular stressors and develop skills that will reduce the negative impact of these stressors. SIT was developed by University of Waterloo professor Donald Meichenbaum (1985, 1993). SIT occurs with a therapist and involves three phases.

In phase one, referred to as the *conceptualization phase*, the person is educated about stress and their personal stress-related behaviour(s) through readings, interviews and testing, and self-monitoring homework assignments. In the homework assignments, clients often keep a stress log, or daily journal of stressful events, and their

These Peruvian villagers are in a cemetery honouring their loved ones who have passed away. The Day of the Dead is not only a celebration of the lives of those who have passed on but also a celebration for the living, who use this holiday to gain a sense of control over one of life's most uncontrollable events—death itself. What rituals or ceremonies do people of other cultures use to cope with death?

associated reactions, thoughts, and emotions. Armed with this information, the client and therapist work together to identify self-defeating thoughts and maladaptive behaviours that the client may be engaging in. For example, suppose an athlete has good results in practice but never performs well in competition. The athlete might say, "I just have to admit to myself that I'm not that good." This self-defeating statement may temporarily reduce stress related to performing poorly in competition as it implies that nothing can be done about the poor performances, but it does nothing to help the athlete perform his or her best. Once these athletes have a good understanding of how they have been talking to themselves and what the statements mean in terms of stress and their performance, then they can move to phase two of SIT.

In phase two, called *skills acquisition and rehearsal*, athletes begin to learn and practise skills that help to change their self-defeating and maladaptive behaviours. Negative statements, such as "I just have to admit to myself that I'm not that good," will be replaced with positive ones, such as "I have trained really hard. This training is going to pay off in the form of some competitive breakthroughs."

In phase three, *application and follow-through*, individuals are given the opportunity to apply their new coping skills to a variety of imagined scenarios (e.g., You have test anxiety and exams are coming up) and evaluate the consequences of their new behaviours. Stress-inoculation training has been used successfully in many settings, for many different types of people, including athletes (Newcomer & Perna, 2003), military personnel (Armfield, 1994), police and teachers (Bishop, 1994), and students (Sheehy & Horan, 2004).

Stress-inoculation training allows the person to take some control over the stressor. The late Norman Endler of York University has shown that when a person establishes some perceived control over the stressor, the chances of coping successfully greatly increase (Endler, Macrodimitris, & Kocovski, 2000).

HOW CULTURE AFFECTS COPING

10.15 *What are the cultural influences on stress?*

Imagine this scene: You are driving out in the country when you come upon an elderly man working on a large wooden box, carefully polishing it. You stop to talk to the man and find out that the box is his own coffin, and he spends his days getting it ready, tending to it with great care. He isn't frightened of dying and doesn't feel strange about polishing his own coffin. How would you react?

If you were from the same rural area of Vietnam as the elderly man, you would probably think nothing strange is going on. For elderly people in the Vietnamese culture, thoughts of death and the things that go along with dying, such as a coffin, are not as stressful as they are to people from Western cultures. In fact, *stress* isn't all that common a term in Vietnamese society compared to Western societies (Phan & Silove, 1999).

In the case of people living in Vietnam and even Vietnamese immigrants in other countries, mental illness is explained by an imbalance between the male and female elements of a person, or by a loss of soul, evil spirits, or a weakening of the nerves. Coping with stress in Vietnamese culture may include rituals, consulting a fortune teller, or eating certain foods (Phan & Silove, 1999).

Obviously, culture is an important factor in the kinds of coping strategies an individual may adopt and even in determining the degree of stress that is experienced. Mental health professionals should make an effort to include an assessment of a person's cultural background as well as immediate circumstances when dealing with adjustment problems because of stress.

Explore on **mypsychlab**
Coping Strategies and Their Effects

HOW RELIGION AFFECTS COPING

10.16 *Can being religious help people cope with stress?*

A belief in a higher power can also be a source of great comfort in times of stress. Religious beliefs can affect the degree of stress people experience and their ability to cope with that stress in several ways (Hill & Butter, 1995; Pargament, 1997).

First, most people who hold strong religious beliefs belong to a religious organization and attend regular religious functions, such as services at a synagogue, mosque, temple, or church. This membership can be a vital part of a person's social support system. People do not feel alone in their struggle, both literally because of the people who surround them in their religious community and spiritually because of the intangible presence of their deity (Koenig et al., 1999).

Another way that religion helps people cope involves the rituals and rites that help people feel better about personal weaknesses, failures, or feelings of inadequacy (Koenig et al., 2001). These include rituals such as confession of sins or prayer services during times of stress. Finally, religious beliefs can give meaning to things that otherwise seem to have no meaning or purpose, such as viewing death as a pathway to a paradise, or the destruction of one's home in a natural disaster as a reminder to place less attachment on material things.

Many religions also encourage healthy behaviour and eating habits through their prohibitions on such activities as overeating, drinking alcohol, smoking, drug use, and sexual activity outside marriage. Some research even suggests that people with religious commitments live longer than those who have no such beliefs, although this is correlational research and should not be interpreted as concluding that religious belief causes longer life expectancies (Hummer et al., 1999; Koenig et al., 1999; Strawbridge et al., 1997; Thoresen & Harris, 2002).

PRACTICE QUIZ: HOW MUCH DO YOU REMEMBER?

Pick the best answer.

1. When a person tries to cope by eliminating or changing the stressor directly, it is known as
   a. a defence mechanism.
   b. problem-focused coping.
   c. self-focused coping.
   d. emotion-focused coping.

2. Darrell is convinced that a woman supervisor in his office is very attracted to him, even though she has given him no outward signs of interest. He watches her frequently and makes excuses to be near her or to talk to her. He interprets everything she says as a veiled reference to her desire for him. If Darrell's supervisor actually has no romantic interest in him, we might conclude that Darrell is
   a. rationalizing.   c. projecting.
   b. repressing.   d. regressing.

3. Rusty drinks beer all day long, often passing out in a stupor after several hours of steady drinking. Yet he refuses to admit that he has a drinking problem, saying that "it's only beer" and continuing to drink. Rusty is most likely using which defence mechanism?
   a. denial   c. displacement
   b. repression   d. reaction formation

4. Kareem is relaxing in a chair with his eyes closed. As he sits quietly, he is focusing on the sound of his own breathing and clearing his mind of other thoughts. Kareem is practising
   a. sensory deprivation.   c. receptive meditation.
   b. concentrative meditation.   d. implosive meditation.

5. Which of the following is NOT one of the ways that religion helps people reduce or cope with stress?
   a. Religion can provide a strong social support system.
   b. Religion includes rituals that can help people feel better about their failings.
   c. Most religions promote healthy lifestyles.
   d. Religion isolates people from those who are different.

Answers: 1-b, 2-c, 3-a, 4-b, 5-d.

APPLYING PSYCHOLOGY TO EVERYDAY LIFE: FOCUS ON WELLNESS

10.17 *What are some ways to promote wellness in one's life?*

Wellness can be defined as the practice of behaviours and lifestyle choices that promote both physical and mental health. Here are some helpful hints on how to promote wellness in one's own life:

- *Exercise.* No one likes to admit it, but exercise is the best way to become healthier. Exercise makes the heart healthier, raises the body's metabolic rate to help maintain a healthy weight, raises good cholesterol and lowers bad cholesterol, strengthens bones, improves sleep quality, reduces tiredness, increases natural killer cell activity to help ward off viruses and cancer, and is a great way to reduce the effects of stress (Fiatarone et al., 1993; Manson et al., 2002).

- *Get involved with others.* The benefits of social support have already been highlighted in this chapter. Make some new friends or join a social organization. Make it a point to do things with other people. Have friends over to dinner or go out shopping with others.

- *Get some sleep.* Most people in the busy, hectic modern world simply do not get enough sleep. As discussed in Chapter Four, sleep serves to restore the body physically and provides a way to manage stress during dreaming. Ⓛ Ⓘ Ⓝ Ⓚ *to Chapter Four: Consciousness, p. 134.* Try to get at least seven to eight hours of sleep each night, including weekends. Try to go to bed and get up at the same time every day to maintain your sleep–wake cycle. Sleep deprivation can lead to a lower production of natural killer cells, which are a necessary and vital part of the immune system (Irwin et al., 1994, 1996).

- *Eat healthful foods.* It's also very easy to eat all the wrong things in today's world. Fortunately, even fast-food restaurants are offering more salads and grilled items to promote healthier eating. Eat breakfast every day, making sure to include a good amount of protein in that meal. Protein in the morning helps improve concentration and alertness, and eating breakfast helps you avoid overeating at lunch or dinner. Eating breakfast has even been shown to decrease the risk of stroke, obesity, and diabetes (Pereira et al., 2003). Be sure to include some healthful snacks at least twice a day.

- *Have some fun.* Playing is important! Schedule some time to just relax, play a game with a friend, read a book, or do something fun. Playing helps prevent burnout.

- *Manage your time.* One of the things that can create a lot of stress is feeling overwhelmed when there are lots of tasks to do. Make a list of the tasks you need to accomplish, putting the most important and urgent ones first. Check each item off the list as you finish it. This gives you a sense of control over your day's activities and rewards you with a sense of accomplishment each time you can check off an item.

- *Take a deep breath.* When feeling stressed, take a moment to cope. Take some deep breaths to help calm yourself and relax tension. If you're so stressed that you feel like crying, find a quiet, private place and cry—crying can relieve stress.

Playing a game, especially one that involves having fun with your friends, is a great way to maintain a sense of wellness and stay physically healthy—especially if the game involves exercise!

Questions for Further Discussion

1. How might studying the evolutionary past of humans lead to living healthier lifestyles?

2. Take a few minutes to write down everything that happened to you yesterday. Start with getting out of bed, what you had for breakfast, how you got stressed while sitting in class or doing homework, how your friends made you feel, and so on, ending when you went to bed. Now look at your day and see if you could apply any of the healthful hints listed above.

10

CHAPTER SUMMARY

Stress

10.1 What is stress?

- Stress is the physical, emotional, cognitive, and behavioural response to events that are appraised as threatening or challenging.
- Stress that has a negative impact is called *distress*. *Eustress* is the optimal amount of stress that people need to function well.

10.2 What kinds of external events can cause stress?

- Catastrophes are events such as floods or crashes that can result in high levels of stress, including acute stress disorder and post-traumatic stress disorder.
- Major life changes create stress by requiring adjustments. Major life changes have an impact on chronic health problems and risk of accidents.
- The daily frustrations and irritations experienced by people, called *hassles*, have an impact on day-to-day health.

10.3 What are some sources of stress in everyday life?

- Four sources of stress are pressure, uncontrollability, frustration, and conflict.
- Frustration, which can be internal or external, may result in persistence, aggression, displaced aggression, or withdrawal.

Psychology in the News: Suicide in Canada

10.4 Why do people commit suicide?

- Suicidal behaviour is highly linked to depression. People who talk about suicide should be taken seriously and need help.

10.5 What are the different types of conflict people must face?

- There are three types of conflicts: approach–approach, avoidance–avoidance, and approach–avoidance.

Physiological Factors: Stress and Health

- The autonomic nervous system consists of the sympathetic system, which responds to stressful events, and the parasympathetic system, which restores the body to normal functioning after the stress has ceased.

10.6 What is happening in the body when a person experiences stress?

- The general adaptation syndrome is the body's reaction to stress and includes three stages of reaction: alarm, resistance, and exhaustion.

10.7 What is the relationship between stress and the immune system?

- Psychoneuroimmunology is the study of the effects of psychological factors such as stress on the immune system.
- Stress causes the immune system to react as though an illness or invading organism has been detected, increasing the functioning of the immune system.
- As the stress continues or increases, the immune system can begin to fail.

10.8 What are the cognitive factors in stress?

- Lazarus's cognitive appraisal approach states that how people think about a stressor determines, at least in part, how stressful that stressor will become.
- The first step in appraising a stressor is called *primary appraisal*, in which the person determines whether an event is threatening, challenging, or of no consequence. Threatening events are more stressful than those seen as challenging.
- The second step is *secondary appraisal*, in which the person assesses the resources available to deal with the stressor, such as time, money, and social support.

10.9 What is the relationship between stress and personality?

- Type A personalities are ambitious, time-conscious, hostile, and angry workaholics who are at increased risk of coronary heart disease, primarily because of their anger and hostility.
- Type B personalities are relaxed and easygoing and have one-third the risk of coronary heart disease as do Type A personalities if male, and one-fourth the risk if female and working outside the home.
- Type C personalities are pleasant but repressed, internalizing their negative emotions.
- Hardy people are hard workers who lack the anger and hostility of the Type A personality, instead seeming to thrive on stress.
- Optimists look for positive outcomes and experience far less stress than pessimists, who take a more negative view.

10.10 What is the relationship between stress and social factors?

- Several social factors can increase the effects of stress: poverty, stresses on the job or in the workplace, and entering a majority culture that is different from one's culture of origin.
- Burnout is a condition that occurs when job stress is so great that the person develops negative thoughts, emotions, and behaviour as well as an extreme dissatisfaction with the job and a desire to quit.
- The four methods of acculturation are integration, assimilation, separation, and marginalization.
- Social support systems are important in helping people cope with stress.

Coping with Stress

10.11 What are two ways that people can deal with stress?

- Problem-focused coping is used when the problem can be eliminated or changed so that it is no longer stressful or so that the impact of the stressor is reduced.
- Emotion-focused coping is often used with problem-focused coping and involves changing one's emotional reactions to a stressor.

10.12 What are the psychological defence mechanisms?

- Psychological defence mechanisms are unconscious distortions of perceived reality and can be a form of emotion-focused coping.

• The different mechanism types are denial, repression, rationalization, projection, reaction formation, displacement, regression, identification, compensation (substitution), and sublimation.

10.13 *How can meditation help relieve stress?*

• Meditation can produce a state of relaxation and reduce the physical reactions common to stressful situations.

• Concentrative meditation involves focusing inward on some repetitive stimulus, such as one's breathing. Receptive meditation involves focusing outward to expand conscious awareness.

10.14 *What is stress-inoculation training?*

• Stress-inoculation training (SIT) is a problem-focused coping method that helps people identify their particular stressors and develop skills that will reduce the negative impact of these stressors.

10.15 *What are the cultural influences on stress?*

• Different cultures perceive stressors differently, and coping strategies will also vary from culture to culture.

10.16 *Can being religious help people cope with stress?*

• People with religious beliefs have been found to cope better with stressful events.

Applying Psychology to Everyday Life: Focus on Wellness

10.17 *What are some ways to promote wellness in one's life?*

• Factors that promote wellness include exercising, taking part in social activities, getting enough sleep, eating healthful foods, having fun, managing one's time, and practising good coping skills.

10 KEY TERMS

acculturative stress 422
acute stress disorder (ASD) 400
aggression 407
approach–approach conflict 409
approach–avoidance conflict 409
avoidance–avoidance conflict 409
burnout 422
catastrophe 399
College Undergraduate Stress Scale (CUSS) 402
compensation (substitution) 426
concentrative meditation 427
conflict 409
coping strategies 424
denial 426
displaced aggression 407
displacement 407
distress 399

emotion-focused coping 425
escape or withdrawal 407
eustress 399
frustration 406
general adaptation syndrome (GAS) 410
hardy personality 418
hassles 403
identification 426
immune system 412
meditation 427
natural killer cell 414
optimists 418
pessimists 418
post-traumatic stress disorder (PTSD) 400
pressure 405
primary appraisal 414
problem-focused coping 424
projection 426

psychological defence mechanisms 426
psychoneuroimmunology 412
rationalization 426
reaction formation 426
receptive meditation 428
regression 426
repression 426
secondary appraisal 415
Social Readjustment Rating Scale (SRRS) 401
social support system 423
stress 398
stress-inoculation training (SIT) 428
stressors 398
sublimation 426
Type A personality 416
Type B personality 417
Type C personality 417

TEST YOURSELF

Pick the best answer.

1. Which of the following is a cognitive symptom of stress?
   a. frequent colds
   b. anxiety
   c. overeating
   d. memory problems

2. How do today's researchers differ from Selye in their view of eustress?
   a. They feel that eustress is more harmful than distress.
   b. They have not found evidence for eustress.
   c. They believe that a certain level of eustress is necessary to promote health.
   d. They believe that distress can be helpful instead of harmful.

3. Appraising a stressor as a challenge results in
   a. more stress.
   b. less stress.
   c. less successful coping.
   d. increased negative emotions.

4. Unpredictable, large-scale events that create a great deal of stress and feelings of threat are called
   a. major life events.
   b. catastrophes.
   c. hassles.
   d. major hassles.

5. After the car accident, Yoshiko suffered from nightmares and other sleeping problems, and she could not concentrate on her work. After about two weeks, these symptoms disappeared and she was able to work and sleep normally again. Yoshiko was suffering from
   a. acute stress disorder.
   b. post-traumatic stress disorder.
   c. mild stress reaction.
   d. shell shock.

6. Lisa's score on the SRRS was 380. According to Holmes and Rahe, Lisa is probably suffering from a
   a. mild life crisis.
   b. moderate life crisis.
   c. major life crisis.
   d. mild stress disorder.

7. Researchers found that the _____ of daily hassles was a far better predictor of headaches than were scores on a life events scale.
   a. number
   b. type
   c. positive quality
   d. perceived severity

8. Differences in the way men and women respond to daily hassles
   a. are greatest during the post-secondary school years.
   b. decrease with age.
   c. were not supported by research.
   d. are present for older adults but not for post-secondary students.

9. Which of the following is NOT a source of stress as discussed in the text?
   a. pressure
   b. uncontrollability
   c. predictability
   d. frustration

10. Who reformulated the frustration–aggression hypothesis?
    a. Dollard
    b. Berkowitz
    c. Miller
    d. Lazarus

11. Rachel's employer gives her a bad review, making Rachel feel lousy. When she arrives at home, she yells at her husband and children. Rachel is displaying
    a. escape.
    b. withdrawal.
    c. displacement.
    d. projection.

12. Trying to decide between two of your favourite desserts is an example of a(n) _____ conflict.
    a. approach–approach
    b. avoidance–avoidance
    c. approach–avoidance
    d. multiple approach–avoidance

13. Phrases such as "caught between a rock and a hard place" and "out of the frying pan, into the fire" refer to _____ conflicts.
    a. approach–approach
    b. avoidance–avoidance
    c. approach–avoidance
    d. multiple approach–avoidance

14. When a person has to make a choice among several goals and each goal has both its good points and its bad points, the person is experiencing a(n) _____ conflict.
    a. approach–approach
    b. avoidance–avoidance
    c. approach–avoidance
    d. multiple approach–avoidance

15. In which of Selye's stages is death a possible outcome?
    a. alarm
    b. resistance
    c. reaction
    d. exhaustion

16. Joe rarely takes any work home, preferring to leave his work worries at the office. He is not ambitious and likes to have a lot of leisure time when it is possible. He is also easygoing and doesn't lose his temper often, preferring to avoid conflict. Which of the following statements about Joe is most likely true?
    a. Joe is a Type A personality.
    b. Joe is a Type B personality.
    c. Joe is a Type C personality.
    d. Joe's risk of coronary heart disease is high.

17. Tad seems to thrive on stress and feels very much in control of his life. He would probably be labelled a _____ personality.
    a. Type A
    b. Type B
    c. Type C
    d. hardy

18. Which of the following is NOT one of the three methods suggested by Vaughan to promote a positive, optimistic mood?
    a. alternative thinking
    b. relaxation
    c. using a scapegoat
    d. downward social comparison

19. Acculturative stress is lowest for people who choose _____ as their method of entering the majority culture.
    a. integration
    b. assimilation
    c. separation
    d. marginalization

20. Shawna is having trouble in algebra She goes to the school's academic help centre for tutoring and spends extra time working algebra problems at home. Shawna's method of coping is
    a. problem focused.
    b. emotion focused.
    c. defensive focused.
    d. internal.

21. Jerome, an 8-year-old boy, constantly teases one of the girls in his grade 3 classroom. He calls her names and chases her on the playground, telling other boys that she has "cooties." If Jerome's real feelings are more like attraction to this girl, we can say that Jerome is exhibiting
    a. displacement.
    b. projection.
    c. reaction formation.
    d. sublimation.

22. Meditation has been shown to accomplish all the following except
    a. relaxation.
    b. reduction in blood pressure.
    c. reduce the need for sleep.
    d. reduce symptoms of anxiety.

23. Who among the following probably has the LEAST ability to cope effectively with stress?
    a. Marian, a very religious person
    b. Mei Ling, who comes from a culture that emphasizes the family
    c. Jackie, who has few friends and whose family lives far away from her
    d. Lenora, who meditates every day

24. Which of the following is NOT one of the guidelines for preventing suicide?
    a. listen with sincerity
    b. ask the person if he or she feels suicidal
    c. share a time when you felt the same way
    d. give the person advice even if he or she doesn't ask for it

25. Which of the following is one of the ways to promote wellness in one's life?
    a. Get enough sleep.
    b. Eat whatever you want, as long as it tastes good.
    c. Don't worry about managing your time.
    d. Avoid getting too involved with other people.

Answers: 1-d, 2-c, 3-b, 4-b, 5-a, 6-c, 7-d, 8-d, 9-c, 10-b, 11-c, 12-a, 13-b, 14-d, 15-d, 16-b, 17-d, 18-c, 19-a, 20-a, 21-c, 22-c, 23-c, 24-d, 25-a.

ScanLife™ Barcode

To access more tests and your own personalized study plan that will help you focus on the areas you need to master before your next class test, be sure to go to **www.MyPsychLab.com**, Pearson Education Canada's online psychology website, available with the access code packaged with your book.

CONCEPT MAP

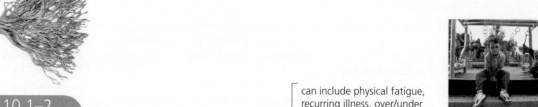

10.1–2

stress is the physical, emotional, cognitive, and behavioural response to events that are appraised as threatening or challenging; first studied systematically by Hans Selye

can include physical fatigue, recurring illness, over/under eating, smoking/drinking more than usual, mood swings, irritability, depression, anger, memory and concentration problems

stress-causing events are called stressors; can come from external or internal sources; range from mild to severe

negative events cause distress; positive events cause eustress, the optimal level of stress required to facilitate healthy adaptation and well-being

external stress-causing events may include catastrophes, major life changes, and daily hassles (differ according to developmental stage)

can be assessed systematically (e.g., Social Readjustment Rating Scale, College Under-graduate Stress Scale)

Stress (part 1)

prolonged or acute stress can cause stress-related disorders that have symptoms including anxiety, recurring nightmares, sleep problems, problems concentrating, and "reliving" the experience through flashbacks or dreams

acute stress disorder (ASD): symptoms present for < 1 month

post-traumatic stress disorder (PTSD): symptoms persist > 1 month

10.3–5

pressure
urgent demands or expectations and uncontrollability

frustration
due to external (losses, rejections, failures, delays) or internal (personal characteristics) factors; can result in several typical responses

- **persistence**
- **aggression**
- **displaced aggression**
- **escape/withdrawal**
  (**suicide** is a drastic form of escape)

Stress (part 2)
(psychological stressors are often related to external events)

conflict

- **approach–approach conflict**
- **avoidance–avoidance conflict**
- **approach–avoidance conflict**

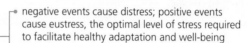

10.6–7

the **autonomic nervous system (ANS)** figures prominently in the body's physiological reactions to stress

Hans Selye identified the **general adaption syndrome (GAS)**, the sequence of physiological reactions the body goes through when adapting to a stressor

- **alarm**
- **resistance**
- **exhaustion**

the field of **psychoneuroimmunology** focuses on the effects of stress on the immune system

Physiological Factors

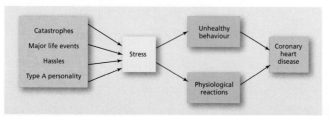

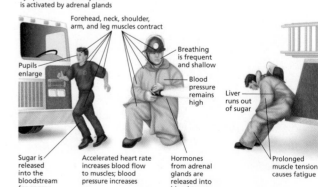

stress-related responses similar to those triggered by infection—increase in white blood cell count, enzymes, and antibodies

body is engineered for short-term, acute stress; prolonged stress/depletion of resources results in reduced functioning of immune system

Lazarus's cognitive–mediational theory of emotions
suggests an individual's appraisal of a stressor is a major factor in determining how stressful that stressor becomes
- primary appraisal
- secondary appraisal

personality differences
affect how one assesses a stressor, the coping strategies used, and possible health outcomes

Cognitive and Personality Factors

- Type A
- Type B
- Type C
- "Type H"

TYPE Z BEHAVIOR

explanatory style
optimists tend to look for positive outcomes, whereas pessimists seem to expect the worst

- Seligman (originally studied concept of learned helplessness) began the positive psychology movement; has suggested that optimism leads to longer life and greater success in life endeavours

- optimism is associated with controlling mood or emotional reactions; can be a learned skill through alternative thinking, downward social comparison, relaxation, and correcting faulty thinking

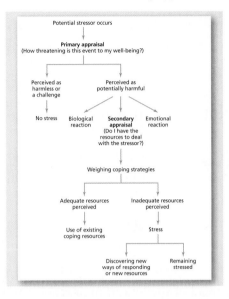

Potential stressor occurs

Primary appraisal
(How threatening is this event to my well-being?)

Perceived as harmless or a challenge → Perceived as potentially harmful

No stress / Biological reaction / **Secondary appraisal** (Do I have the resources to deal with the stressor?) / Emotional reaction

Weighing coping strategies

Adequate resources perceived / Inadequate resources perceived

Use of existing coping resources / Stress

Discovering new ways of responding or new resources / Remaining stressed

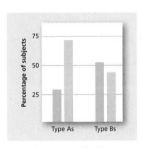

Percentage of subjects — 75, 50, 25 — Type As, Type Bs

- Men with coronary heart disease
- Healthy men

- a great deal of stress can come from dealing with other people and social interactions

- poverty and job stress are prominent, economically based social factors that lead to stressful living conditions
  - poverty results in lack of basic life necessities
  - job stress may be related to workload, lack of control or job security, work schedule, and low job satisfaction

Social Factors

- culturally, stress is affected by status of acculturation (adapting to a new, different, or often dominant culture) and the method chosen to adapt
  - integration
  - assimilation
  - separation
  - marginalization

- in general, having a positive social support system that provides various forms of help (e.g., monetary, physical, emotional support) is a good predictor for healthy aging and longevity

coping strategies
are behavioural and psychological actions taken to master, tolerate, reduce, or minimize the effect of stressors

problem-focused coping
involves working to change or eliminate the stressor itself
- stress-inoculation training (SIT) helps people identify their particular stressors and develop skills that will reduce the negative impact of these stressors

emotion-focused coping
involves changing the way a person feels or emotionally reacts to a stressor
- several unconscious psychological defense mechanisms were proposed by Freud (see Table 10.2); originally psychoanalytical in nature, still useful to describe some thinking and behaviour

Coping with Stress

various methods and behaviours exist to help individuals in dealing with stress
- meditation, in its various forms, helps promote relaxation, calm anxiety, improve sleep, and lower blood pressure
- an individual's culture and/or religious beliefs can affect the appraisal of events as more or less stressful, the coping strategies adopted, and support systems that can offer assistance

11
Personality

Not-So-Identical Twins

Many people have heard the story of the "Jim" twins, James Arthur Springer and James Edward Lewis, identical twins separated at the age of 1 month. At age 39, Springer and Lewis were the first set of twins studied by University of Minnesota psychologist Thomas Bouchard, who examined the differences and similarities between identical and fraternal twins raised apart from each other (Bouchard et al., 1990).

The two "Jims" shared interests in mechanical drawing and carpentry, a love of math and a dread of spelling in high school, and smoked and drank the same amount. It is understandable that many researchers attribute these similarities to the shared genetic material of the "Jim" twins. But Springer and Lewis were both raised in Ohio by parents from relatively similar socioeconomic backgrounds. How much of their similarity to each other might be because of those conditions? And how would genetics explain that they both divorced women named Linda before marrying women named Betty? Are there genes for "divorce Linda, marry Betty"? Obviously not.

Then there's the case of Oskar and Jack. Like the "Jim" twins, they also exhibited a number of similarities in personality and behaviour. No one would accuse Oskar and Jack of being raised in similar environments, however. Born in Trinidad at the time Hitler was rising to power, Jack Yufe was raised by their Jewish father in Trinidad as a Jew, while their mother took Oskar Stohr to occupied Czechoslovakia, where he attended a Nazi-run school and was at one time a Hitler youth. In terms of environment, Oskar and Jack were not-so-identical twins.

If the researchers in the twin study had dug a little deeper, they would also have found countless differences between the twins in the study. To automatically assume that similarities between identical twins are all caused by genetic influences and that differences are caused by environmental influences is bad science. The fact is that any two randomly selected people will find that they have countless things in common, none of which is likely to be caused by hereditary factors.

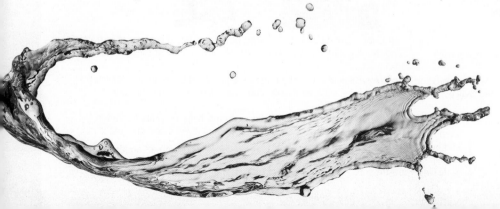

chapter outline

Why study personality?

Personality is the sum total of who you are—your attitudes and reactions, both physical and emotional. It's what makes each person different from every other person in the world. How can any study of human behaviour not include the study of who we are and how we got to be that way?

11

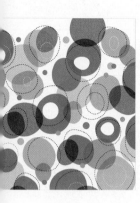

THEORIES OF PERSONALITY

11.1 *What is personality, and how do the various perspectives in psychology view personality?*

As stated in the opening story, **personality** is the unique way in which each individual thinks, acts, and feels throughout life. Personality should not be confused with **character**, which refers to value judgments made about a person's morals or ethical behaviour; nor should it be confused with **temperament**, the enduring characteristics with which each person is born, such as irritability or adaptability. Both character and temperament are vital parts of personality, however.

Personality is an area of the still relatively young field of psychology in which there are several ways that the characteristic behaviour of human beings can be explained. One reason that there is not yet one single explanation of personality that all can agree on is that personality is still difficult to measure precisely and scientifically. At present, there are four main perspectives, or viewpoints, in personality theory:

- The *psychoanalytic perspective* had its beginnings in the work of Sigmund Freud and still exists today. It focuses on the role of the unconscious mind in the development of personality. This perspective is also heavily focused on biological causes of personality differences.

- The *behaviourist perspective* is based on the theories of learning as discussed in Chapter Five. This approach focuses on the effect of the environment on behaviour.

- The *humanistic perspective* first arose as a reaction against the psychoanalytic and behaviourist perspectives and focuses on the role of each person's conscious life experiences and choices in personality development.

- The *trait perspective* differs from the other three in its basic goals: The psychoanalytic, behaviourist, and humanistic perspectives all seek to explain the process that causes personality to form into its unique characteristics, whereas trait theorists are more concerned with the end result—the characteristics themselves. Although some trait theorists assume that traits are biologically determined, others make no such assumption.

personality
the unique and relatively stable ways in which people think, feel, and behave.

character
value judgments of a person's moral and ethical behaviour.

temperament
the enduring characteristics with which each person is born.

440

THE MAN AND THE COUCH: SIGMUND FREUD AND PSYCHOANALYSIS

FREUD'S CULTURAL BACKGROUND

It's difficult to understand how Freud developed his ideas about personality without knowledge of the world in which he and his patients lived. Born in the Austro-Hungarian Empire in 1856, Freud's family moved to Vienna when he was only 4 years old. He lived there until 1938, when the Nazis took over Austria. Dr. Ernest Jones, a former professor of psychiatry at the University of Toronto, was one of the people who helped an ailing Freud, of Jewish background, escape to London. During this time period, Europe was in what is commonly known as the *Victorian Age*, named for Queen Victoria of Great Britain. The Victorian Age was a time of sexual repression. People growing up in this period were told by their church that sex should take place only in the context of marriage and then only to make babies. To enjoy sexual intercourse was considered a sin.

Men were understood to be unable to control their "animal" desires at times, and a good Victorian husband would father several children with his wife and then turn to a mistress for sexual comfort, leaving his virtuous wife untouched. Women, especially those of the upper classes, were not supposed to have sexual urges. It is no wonder that many of Freud's patients were wealthy women with problems stemming from unfulfilled sexual desires or sexual repression. Freud's "obsession" with sexual explanations for abnormal behaviour seems more understandable in light of his cultural background and that of his patients.

Freud came to believe that there were layers of consciousness in the mind. His belief in the influence of the unconscious mind on conscious behaviour, which he published in *The Psychopathology of Everyday Life* (1901), shocked the Victorian world.

11.2 *How did Freud's historical view of the mind and personality form a basis for psychodynamic theory?*

THE IMPORTANCE OF THE UNCONSCIOUS MIND

Freud believed that the mind was divided into three parts: the preconscious, conscious, and unconscious minds (Freud, 1904). This model is referred to as the *topographic model* (see Figure 11.1). According to Freud, the **preconscious mind** is a level of the mind in which all the information, events, concerns, and thoughts that a person is not aware of at the moment are kept. These bits and pieces of the mind can be easily brought into conscious awareness, however, when the need arises. Freud believed that the **conscious mind** is all the things of which a person is aware at any given moment. Whatever is

Sigmund Freud (1856–1939), founder of the psychodynamic movement in psychology.

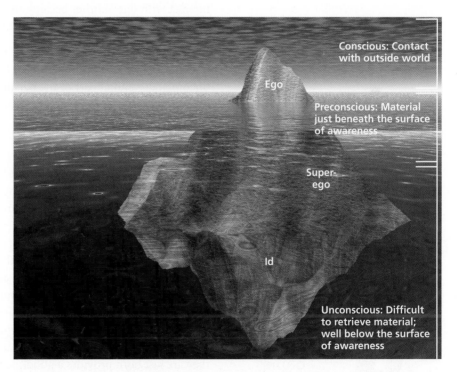

FIGURE 11.1 **Freud's Conception of the Personality** This iceberg represents the three levels of the mind. The part of the iceberg visible above the surface is the conscious mind. Just below the surface is the preconscious mind, everything that is not yet part of the conscious mind. Hidden deep below the surface is the unconscious mind, feelings, memories, thoughts, and urges that cannot be easily brought into consciousness. While two of the three parts of the personality (ego and superego) exist at all three levels of awareness, the id is completely in the unconscious mind.

preconscious mind
level of the mind in which information is available but not currently conscious.

conscious mind
level of the mind that is aware of immediate surroundings and perceptions.

unconscious mind
level of the mind in which thoughts, feelings, memories, and other information are kept that are not easily or voluntarily brought into consciousness.

pleasure principle
principle by which the id functions; the immediate satisfaction of needs without regard for the consequences.

id
part of the personality present at birth and completely unconscious.

libido
the instinctual energy that may come into conflict with the demands of a society's standards for behaviour.

uppermost in one's mind is in the conscious mind. The **unconscious mind** (also called *the unconscious*) was the real departure for the professionals of Freud's day, however. Freud theorized that a part of the mind remains hidden at all times, surfacing only in symbolic form in dreams and in some of the behaviour people engage in without knowing why they have done so. Even when a person makes a determined effort to bring a memory out of the unconscious mind, it will not appear directly, according to Freud. Freud believed that the unconscious mind was the most important determining factor in human behaviour and personality. **LINK** *to Chapter Four: Consciousness, p. 134.*

One of the ways that the unconscious can influence conscious behaviour, for example, is in everyday speech. Have you ever meant to say one thing, only to have it come out as something entirely different? For example, a psychologist preparing an article condemning Freud's theories began her paper by writing, "Fraud's theory... ." In this example, the psychologist obviously meant to write "Freud" but another word came out—a word that Freud would have said revealed the woman's true feelings. This tendency to reveal oneself through errors of speech is called a *Freudian slip*, a slip of the tongue that appears to be accidental but that may provide a clue to the individual's unconscious wishes or urges. Chapter Fourteen discusses other methods used by Freud to uncover the unconscious mind. **LINK** *to Chapter Fourteen: Psychological Therapies, p. 564.*

THE DIVISIONS OF THE PERSONALITY

Freud believed, based on his observations of his patients, that personality itself could be divided into three parts. The way these three parts of the personality develop and interact with one another became the heart of his theory (Freud, 1923, 1933, 1940). This model is referred to as the *structural model*.

ID: IF IT FEELS GOOD, DO IT   The first and most primitive part of the personality, present in the infant, is the **id**. *Id* is a Latin word that means "it." The id is a completely unconscious, amoral part of the personality that exists at birth, containing all the basic biological drives: hunger, thirst, self-preservation, and sex, for example. When these drives are active, the person will feel an increase not only in physical tension but also in psychological tension that Freud called the **libido**, the instinctual energy that may come into conflict with the demands of a society's standards for behaviour. When libidinal energy is high, it's unpleasant for the person, so the goal is to reduce the libido by fulfilling the drive: Eat when hungry, drink when thirsty, and satisfy the sex drive when the need for pleasure is present. Freud emphasized the sexual aspect of libido more than many of his later followers did; he witnessed the struggle to reduce libido yet somehow conform to social rules, such as "sex is wrong outside of marriage."

◀ Wait a minute—Freud thought babies have sex drives? Yes, Freud thought babies have sex drives, which shocked and outraged his colleagues and fellow Victorians. By "sex drive," he really meant "pleasure drive," the need to seek out pleasurable sensations. People do seem to be pleasure-seeking creatures, and even infants seek pleasure from sucking and chewing on anything they can get into their mouths and from the caresses of their mothers and fathers. In fact, thinking about what infants are like when they are just born provides a good picture of the id. Infants are demanding, irrational, illogical, and impulsive. They want their needs satisfied immediately, and they don't care about anyone else's needs or desires. (A word of caution: The fact that infant behaviour seems to fit Freud's concept of the id is not proof that the id exists. It simply means that Freud came up with the concept of the id to fit what he already knew about infants.)

Freud called this need for satisfaction the **pleasure principle**, which can be defined as the desire for immediate gratification of needs with no regard for the consequences. The pleasure principle can be summed up simply as "if it feels good, do it."

EGO: THE EXECUTIVE DIRECTOR   People normally try to satisfy an infant's needs as quickly as possible. Infants are fed when hungry, changed when wet, and tended to

✖ ▢Explore on mypsychlab
Freud's Five Psychosexual Stages of Personality Development

whenever they cry. But as infants begin to grow, adults start denying them their every wish. There will be things they cannot touch or hold, and they must learn to wait for certain things, such as food. Freud would say that reality has reared its ugly head, and the id simply cannot deal with the reality of having to wait or of not getting what it wants. Worse still would be the possibility of punishment as a result of the id's unrestrained actions.

According to Freud, to deal with reality, a second part of the personality develops called the **ego**. The ego, from the Latin word for "I," is mostly conscious and is far more rational, logical, and cunning than the id. The ego works on the **reality principle**, which is the need to satisfy the demands of the id and reduce libido only in ways that will not lead to negative consequences. This means that sometimes the ego decides to deny the id its desires because the consequences would be painful or too unpleasant.

For example, while an infant might reach out and take an object despite a parent's protests, a toddler with the developing ego will avoid taking the object when the parent says, "No!," to avoid punishment but may go back for the object when the parent is not looking. A simpler way of stating the reality principle, then, is "if it feels good, do it, but only if you can get away with it."

SUPEREGO: THE MORAL WATCHDOG   If everyone acted on the pleasure principle, the world would be pretty scary. How does knowing right from wrong come into Freud's theory? Freud called the third and final part of the personality, the moral centre of personality, the **superego**. The superego (also Latin, meaning "over the self") develops as a preschool-aged child learns the rules, customs, and expectations of society. There are actually two parts to the superego: the *ego ideal* and the *conscience*. The **ego ideal** is the sum of all the ideal, or correct and acceptable, behaviour that the child has learned about from parents and others in the society. All behaviour is held up to this standard and judged by the second part of the superego, the **conscience**. The conscience is the part of the personality that makes people feel pride when they do the right thing and guilt, or *moral anxiety*, when they do the wrong thing. It is not until the conscience develops that children have a sense of right and wrong.

THE ANGEL, THE DEVIL, AND ME: HOW THE THREE PARTS OF THE PERSONALITY WORK TOGETHER   Anyone who has ever watched cartoons while growing up has probably seen these three parts of the personality shown in animated form. For example, in one *Simpsons* episode, Marge is going out and tells Bart, Lisa, and Maggie not to steal money from the money jar while she's gone. A devil and an angel appear on the shoulders of all three children when they see the money jar. The devils, telling each child to steal the money, are similar to the id. The angels, telling each child that stealing the money is bad and that they shouldn't do it, are similar to the superego. The children themselves (Bart, Lisa, and Maggie) have to make the ultimate decision as to whether they will steal the money, and thus, they represent the ego.

So, the id makes demands, the superego puts restrictions on how those demands can be met, and the ego has to come up with a plan that will quiet the id but satisfy the superego. Sometimes the id or the superego does not get its way, resulting in a great deal of anxiety for the ego itself. This constant state of conflict is Freud's view of how personality works; it is only when the anxiety created by this conflict gets out of hand that disordered behaviour arises.

The *psychological defence mechanisms* are ways of dealing with stress through unconsciously distorting one's perception of reality. These defence mechanisms were mainly outlined and studied by Freud's daughter, Anna Freud, who was a psychoanalyst (Benjafield, 1996; A. Freud, 1946). For the three parts of the personality to function, the constant conflict among them must be managed, and Freud assumed that the defence mechanisms were one of the most important tools for dealing with the anxiety caused by this conflict. A list of the defence mechanisms, their definitions, and examples of each appears in Table 10.2 in Chapter Ten. LINK *to Chapter Ten: Stress and Health, p. 426.*

---

ego
part of the personality that develops out of a need to deal with reality; mostly conscious, rational, and logical.

reality principle
principle by which the ego functions; the satisfaction of the demands of the id only when negative consequences will not result.

superego
part of the personality that acts as a moral centre.

ego ideal
part of the superego that contains the standards for moral behaviour.

conscience
part of the superego that produces pride or guilt, depending on how well behaviour matches or does not match the ego ideal.

◀ If everyone acted on the pleasure principle, the world would be pretty scary. How does knowing right from wrong come into Freud's theory?

"HOW'LL WE HANDLE THIS?"

PRACTICE QUIZ: HOW MUCH DO YOU REMEMBER?

Pick the best answer.

1. Although Chien's parents have told him that he attended his grandmother's funeral when he was 9 years old, he has no memory of the funeral. According to Freud, Chien's memory of the funeral may be in the _____ mind.
   - **a.** preconscious
   - **b.** conscious
   - **c.** conscience
   - **d.** unconscious

2. Which of Freud's parts of the personality is most like a director?
   - **a.** id
   - **b.** ego
   - **c.** superego
   - **d.** ego ideal

3. According to Freud, which part of the personality makes the person feel pride when doing the right thing?
   - **a.** ego
   - **b.** superego
   - **c.** ego ideal
   - **d.** conscience

4. In Freud's view of the personality, the "devil" would be seen as the
   - **a.** conscience.
   - **b.** id.
   - **c.** ego.
   - **d.** superego.

Answers: 1-d, 2-b, 3-d, 4-b.

> So the **id** exists at birth, but the other two ▶ parts of the personality develop later—how much later? When is personality finished?

Freud believed that mothers should breastfeed their infants to satisfy an infant's need for oral gratification in the oral stage of psychosexual development. The age at which an infant was weaned from the breast was a critical factor in psychoanalytic theory.

fixation
disorder in which the person does not fully resolve the conflict in a particular psychosexual stage, resulting in personality traits and behaviour associated with that earlier stage.

STAGES OF PERSONALITY DEVELOPMENT

So the id exists at birth, but the other two parts of the personality develop later—how much later? When is personality finished? For Freud, the three parts of the personality develop in a series of stages. Because he focused heavily on the sex drive, he believed that the stages were determined by the developing sexuality of the child. At each stage, a different *erogenous zone*, or area of the body that produces pleasurable feelings, becomes important and can become the source of conflicts. Conflicts that are not fully resolved can result in **fixation**, or getting "stuck" to some degree in an earlier stage of development. The child may grow into an adult but will still display infantile and childish habits from that earlier fixated stage.

Because the personality, or *psyche*, develops as a result of sexual development, Freud called these the **psychosexual stages** of personality development.

ORAL STAGE: WEANING AND ORAL FIXATION   The first stage is called the **oral stage** because the erogenous zone is the mouth. This stage occurs from the birth of the infant to about 1 or 1½ years and is dominated by the id. The conflict that can arise here, according to Freud, will be over weaning (taking the mother's breast away from the child, who will now drink from a cup). Weaning that occurs too soon or too late can result in too little or too much satisfaction of the child's oral needs, resulting in the activities and personality traits associated with an orally fixated adult personality: overeating, drinking too much, chain smoking, talking too much, nail biting, gum chewing, and a tendency to be either too dependent and optimistic (when the oral needs are overindulged) or too aggressive and pessimistic (when the oral needs are underindulged).

ANAL STAGE: TOILET TRAINING AND ANAL FIXATION   As the child becomes a toddler (1 or 1½ years to 3 years), Freud believed that the erogenous zone moves from the mouth area to the anus. This stage is called the **anal stage**.

Obviously, Freud thought that the main area of conflict here is toilet training, the demand that the child use the toilet at a particular time and in a particular way. This invasion of reality is part of the process that stimulates the development of the ego during this stage. Freud believed that children in this stage got a great deal of pleasure from both withholding and then releasing their feces at will. These actions allow children to develop self-control as well as please their parents, both desirable goals for children of this age.

Fixation in the anal stage, from toilet training that is too harsh, can take one of two forms. The child who rebels openly against the demands of the parents and other adults will refuse to go in the toilet, instead defecating where and when he or she feels like doing it. According to Freud, this translates in the adult as a person who sees messiness as a statement of personal control and who is somewhat destructive and hostile. These **anal expulsive personalities** (so called because they expelled their feces as children purposefully) are what most people would call *slobs*.

The other anal fixation is the child who is terrified of making a mess and rebels passively—refusing to go at all or retaining the feces. No mess, no punishment. As adults, they are stingy, stubborn, and excessively neat. This type is called the **anal retentive personality**.

PHALLIC STAGE As the child grows older (3 to 6 years), the erogenous zone finally shifts to the genitals. Children have discovered the differences between the sexes by now, and most have also engaged in perfectly normal self-stimulation of the genitals, or masturbation. One can only imagine the horror of the Victorian parent who discovered their child engaged in masturbation. People of that era believed that masturbation led to all manner of evils, including mental illness.

This awakening of sexual curiosity and interest in the genitals is the beginning of what Freud termed the **phallic stage**. The word *phallic* comes from the Greek word *phallos* and means "penis."

Freud believed that boys, upon seeing that girls have no penis, would think that the penis can be lost or cut off, and develop a fear of losing the penis called *castration anxiety*. Girls, he believed, would feel that they were missing something vital and could not be complete without it, leading to feelings of inferiority and *penis envy*. If this seems an odd focus on male anatomy, remember the era—the Western world at that time was very male-oriented and male-dominated.

In an interesting attempt to test Freud's notion of penis envy, Granville Johnson (1966) published a report that discussed the investigation of whether male and female undergraduate students would return their pencils after writing a general psychology exam. It was Johnson's belief that more women would hold on to their pencils, which to him, would confirm Freud's idea of penis envy. Johnson's (1966) findings supported his belief—in comparison to men, women more often failed to return their pencils. From this, Johnson (1966) concluded that (1) the concept of penis envy is valid; (2) women are more dishonest than men; and (3) men are more prone to return pencils. Fortunately, since the time of Freud and Johnson, nearly all psychoanalysts have long since abandoned the concept of penis envy (Horney, 1939, 1973; Slipp, 1993). For example, in 1997, Nicholas Skinner of King's College at the University of Western Ontario conducted a similar experiment to that conducted by Johnson. Skinner observed 395 male and female undergraduate students and found that there were no differences in the rate of pencil-returning between male and female students and also that pencil "stealing" rarely occurred. According to Skinner (1997), Johnson's conclusion that keeping the pencils may be a manifestation of penis envy was not supported.

The conflict in the phallic stage centres on the awakening sexual feelings of the child. Freud essentially believed that boys develop both sexual attraction to their mothers and jealousy of their fathers during this stage, a phenomenon called the **Oedipus complex**. (Oedipus was a king in a Greek tragedy who unknowingly killed his father and married his mother.) One of Freud's followers, Carl Jung, proposed that the term *Oedipus* be reserved only for males and that the complex in females be termed the *Electra complex*, after a female character in another Greek tragedy (Jung, 1933).

psychosexual stages
five stages of personality development proposed by Freud and tied to the sexual development of the child.

oral stage
first stage, occurring in the first year of life, in which the mouth is the erogenous zone and weaning is the primary conflict.

anal stage
second stage, occurring from about 1 or 1½ to 3 years of age, in which the anus is the erogenous zone and toilet training is the source of conflict.

anal expulsive personality
a person fixated in the anal stage who is messy, destructive, and hostile.

anal retentive personality
a person fixated in the anal stage who is neat, fussy, stingy, and stubborn.

phallic stage
third stage, occurring from about 3 to 6 years of age, in which the child discovers sexual feelings.

Oedipus complex
situation, occurring in the phallic stage, in which a child develops a sexual attraction to the opposite-sex parent and jealousy of the same-sex parent.

According to Freud, children in the phallic stage develop a natural curiosity about sexual differences. These girls and boys are at just the right age to have noticed that they have physical differences.

The sexual attraction is not that of an adult male for a female but more of a sexual curiosity that becomes mixed up with the boy's feelings of love and affection for his mother. Of course, his jealousy of his father leads to feelings of anxiety and fears that his father, a powerful authority figure, might get angry and do something terrible—remember that castration anxiety? To deal with this anxiety, two things must occur by the time the phallic stage ends. The boy will *repress* his sexual feelings for his mother and *identify* with his father. *Identification*, as discussed in Chapter Ten, is a defence mechanism used to combat anxiety. The boy tries to be just like his father in every way, taking on the father's behaviour, mannerisms, values, and moral beliefs as his own, so that Daddy won't be able to get angry with the boy. Girls go through a similar process, with their father the target of their affections and their mother as the rival. The result of identification is the development of the superego, the internalized moral values of the same-sex parent.

What happens when things go wrong? If a child does not have a same-sex parent with whom to identify, or if the opposite-sex parent encourages the sexual attraction, fixation can occur. Fixation in the phallic stage usually involves immature sexual attitudes as an adult. People who are fixated in this stage, according to Freud, will often exhibit promiscuous sexual behaviour and be very vain. The vanity is seen as a cover-up for feelings of low self-worth arising from the failure to resolve the complex, and the lack of moral sexual behaviour stems from the failure of identification and the inadequate formation of the superego. Additionally, men with this fixation may be "mama's boys" who never quite grow up, and women may look for much older father figures to marry.

Now the child is about 6 years old and, if passage through the first three stages was successfully accomplished, has all three parts of the personality in place. What next? The personality may be in place, but the place it is in is only 6 years old. Freud named two more periods, one a kind of "holding pattern" and the other the final coming-to-terms with one's own sexuality.

LATENCY STAGE: BOYS HAVE COOTIES AND GIRLS ARE YUCKY   Remember that by the end of the phallic stage, children have pushed their sexual feelings for the opposite sex into the unconscious in another defensive reaction, repression. From age 6 to the onset of puberty, children will remain in this stage of hidden, or *latent*, sexual feelings, so this stage is called **latency**. In this stage, children grow and develop intellectually, physically, and socially but not sexually. This is the age at which boys play with other boys, girls play only with girls, and each thinks the opposite sex is pretty awful.

GENITAL STAGE   When puberty does begin, the sexual feelings that were once repressed can no longer be ignored. Bodies are changing and sexual urges are once more allowed into consciousness, but these urges will no longer have the parents as their targets. When children are 3 years old, their parents are their whole world. When they are 13, their parents often have to walk 20 paces behind them in the mall so none of the 13-year-old's friends will see them. Instead, the focus of sexual curiosity and attraction will become other adolescents or rock stars, movie stars, and other objects of adoration. Since Freud tied personality development into sexual development, the **genital stage** represented the final process in Freud's personality theory as well as the entry into adult social and sexual behaviour. Table 11.1 summarizes the stages of the psychosexual theory of personality development.

THE NEO-FREUDIANS

11.3   *How did Jung, Adler, Horney, and Erikson modify Freud's theory?*

At first Freud's ideas were met with resistance and ridicule by the growing community of doctors and psychologists. Eventually, a number of early psychoanalysts, objecting to Freud's emphasis on biology and particularly on sexuality, broke away from a strict

latency
fourth stage, occurring during the school years, in which the sexual feelings of the child are repressed while the child develops in other ways.

genital stage
fifth and final stage, beginning in puberty and lasting into adulthood, in which the adolescent enters into adult social and sexual behaviour.

TABLE 11.1 FREUD'S PSYCHOSEXUAL STAGES

STAGE	AGE	FOCUS OF PLEASURE	FOCUS OF CONFLICTS	DIFFICULTIES AT THIS STAGE AFFECT LATER . . .
Oral	Birth to 1 years old	Oral activities (such as sucking, feeding, and making noises with the mouth)	Weaning	• Ability to form interpersonal attachments • Basic feelings about the world • Tendency to use oral forms of aggression, such as sarcasm • Optimism or pessimism • Tendency to take charge or be passive
Anal	1 to 3 years old	Bowel and bladder control	Toilet training	• Sense of competence and control • Stubbornness or willingness to go along with others • Neatness or messiness • Punctuality or tardiness
Phallic	3 to 6 years old	Genitals	Sexual awareness	• Development of conscience through identification with same-sex parent • Pride or humility
Latency	6 years old to puberty	Social skills (such as the ability to make friends) and intellectual skills; Dormant period in terms of psychosexual development	School, play, same-sex friendships	• Ability to get along with others
Genital	Puberty to death	Sexual behaviour	Sexual relationship with partner	• Immature love or indiscriminate hate • Uncontrollable working or inability to work

Note: Freud thought that the way a person finds pleasure or is prevented from satisfying urges for pleasure at each stage affects personality. Thus, like Erikson's stage model, described in Chapter Eight, Freud's model argues that the way a person deals with particular psychological challenges or potential areas of conflict has long-term effects on personality.

interpretation of psychoanalytic theory, instead altering the focus of **psychoanalysis** (the term Freud applied to both his explanation of the workings of the unconscious mind and the development of personality and the therapy he based on that theory) to the impact of the social environment. At the same time they retained many of Freud's original concepts, such as the id, ego, superego, and defence mechanisms. These early psychoanalysts became the **neo-Freudians**, or "new" Freudian psychoanalysts. This section briefly covers some of the more famous neo-Freudians.

JUNG   Carl Gustav Jung ("YOONG") disagreed with Freud about the nature of the unconscious mind. Jung believed that the unconscious held much more than personal fears, urges, and memories. He believed that there was not only a **personal unconscious**, as described by Freud, but also a **collective unconscious** as well (Jung, 1933).

According to Jung, the collective unconscious contains a kind of "species" or "racial" memory, memories of ancient fears and themes that seem to occur in many folk tales and cultures. These collective, universal human memories were called **archetypes** by Jung. There are many archetypes, but two of the more well-known are the *anima/animus* (the feminine side of a man/the masculine side of a woman) and the *shadow* (the dark side of personality, called the *devil* in Western cultures). The side of one's personality that is shown to the world is termed the *persona*.

ADLER   Alfred Adler and Freud lived in the same place and at the same time, but Freud's work often overshadowed that of Adler. This is something that has been discussed in detail by Ken Cramer, of the University of Windsor, who made the list of top 10 finalists in TV Ontario's *Big Ideas* Best Lecturers competition for his lecture titled "Alfred Adler: The Most Famous Personality Theorist You Likely Never Heard Of." Cramer mentions that while most people are not familiar with the name *Alfred Adler,*

◉⃞ **Watch on mypsychlab**

Carl Jung: Unconscious

psychoanalysis
Freud's term for both the theory of personality and the therapy based on it.

neo-Freudians
followers of Freud who developed their own competing theories of psychoanalysis.

personal unconscious
Jung's name for the unconscious mind as described by Freud.

collective unconscious
Jung's name for the memories shared by all members of the human species.

archetypes
Jung's collective, universal human memories.

Carl Jung (1875–1961) was a Swiss psychoanalyst who eventually broke away from Freud's emphasis on the sexual content of the unconscious mind. He formed his own theory of analysis known as *analytical psychology*.

they are familiar with many of his ideas. According to Cramer, there are two reasons why most people have not heard of Adler. First, people would take his ideas but not give him the credit he deserved; second, compared to Freud, who was an elegant and prolific writer, Adler did not write very well or very much (University of Windsor, n.d.).

Adler was in disagreement with Freud over the importance of sexuality in personality development. Adler (1927) developed the theory that as young, helpless children, people all develop feelings of inferiority when comparing themselves to the more powerful, superior adults in their world. The driving force behind all human endeavours, emotions, and thoughts for Adler was not the seeking of pleasure but the seeking of superiority. The defence mechanism of *compensation*, in which people try to overcome feelings of inferiority in one area of life by striving to be superior in another area, figured prominently in Adler's theory. (L)(I)(N)(K) *to Chapter Ten: Stress and Health, p. 396.*

Adler (1927) also developed a theory that the birth order of a child affected personality. First-born children with younger siblings feel inferior once those younger siblings get all the attention often overcompensate by becoming overachievers. Middle children have it slightly easier, getting to feel superior over the dethroned older child while dominating younger siblings. They tend to be very competitive. Younger children are supposedly pampered and protected but feel inferior because they are not allowed the freedom and responsibility of the older children. Although some researchers have found evidence to support Adler's birth order theory (Stein, 2001; Sulloway, 1996), and some have even linked birth order to career choices (Leong et al., 2001; Watkins & Savickas, 1990), other researchers point to flawed methodology and the bias of researchers toward the birth order idea (Beer & Horn, 2001; Freese et al., 1999; Ioannidis, 1998).

HORNEY Karen Horney ("HORN-EYE") did not study directly with Freud but studied his work and taught psychoanalysis at the Psychoanalytic Institutes of Berlin and New York. She left the institute because of disagreements with Freud over the differences between males and females and the concept of penis envy, with which she strongly disagreed. She countered with her own concept of "womb envy," stating that men felt the need to compensate for their lack of child-bearing ability by striving for success in other areas (Burger, 1997).

Dr. Alfred Adler (1870–1937) relaxes at his desk in this 1930s photograph. Adler was one of the early psychoanalysts who worked with Sigmund Freud; but, he believed that feelings of inferiority rather than growing sexuality were the keys to personality development.

Dr. Karen Horney (1885–1952) took issue with Freud's emphasis on sexuality, especially the concept of penis envy. She emphasized the importance of feelings of basic anxiety in personality development during early childhood.

Dr. Erik Erikson (1902–1994) was originally an educator. This may have influenced his version of psychoanalytic theory, which emphasized the development of the ego and the importance of social relationships with parents, peers, and other people on personality development.

Rather than focusing on sexuality, Horney focused on the child's sense of **basic anxiety**, the anxiety created in a child born into a world that is so much bigger and more powerful than the child. While people whose parents gave them love, affection, and security would overcome this anxiety, others with less secure upbringings would develop **neurotic personalities** and maladaptive ways of dealing with relationships. Some children, according to Horney, try to deal with their anxiety by moving toward people, becoming dependent and clingy. Others move against people, becoming aggressive, demanding, and cruel. A third way of coping would be to move away from people by withdrawing from personal relationships.

ERIKSON Erik Erikson (1950, 1959, 1982) was an art teacher who became a psychoanalyst by studying with Anna Freud. He also broke away from Freud's emphasis on sex, preferring instead to emphasize the social relationships that are important at every stage of life. Erikson's eight psychosocial stages were discussed in detail in Chapter Eight. (L I N K) *to Chapter Eight: Development Across the Lifespan, p. 327.*

It sounds as if all of these theorists became famous by ditching some of Freud's original ideas. Is Freud even worth studying anymore?

CURRENT THOUGHTS ON FREUD AND THE PSYCHODYNAMIC PERSPECTIVE

11.4 *How does modern psychoanalytic theory differ from that of Freud?*

Although Freud's psychoanalytic theory seems less relevant in today's sexually saturated world, many of his concepts have remained useful and still form a basis for many modern personality theories. As mentioned in Chapter Ten, the idea of the defence mechanisms has research support. The concept of an unconscious mind also has some research support. As strange as the idea of an unconscious mind that guides behaviour must have seemed to Freud's contemporaries, modern researchers have had to admit that influences on human behaviour exist outside of normal conscious awareness. Although much of this research has taken place in the area of hypnosis and subliminal perception (Borgeat & Goulet, 1983; Bryant & McConkey, 1989; Kihlstrom, 1987, 1999, 2001), other researchers have looked at the concept of implicit memory and implicit learning (Frensch & Runger, 2003). (L I N K) *to Chapter Six: Memory, p. 218.*

Recently, Canadian psychiatrist Dr. Norman Doidge wrote an article for *Maclean's* magazine claiming that, with its use of brain scans, neuroscience is supporting Freud's belief that the majority of our thinking, and much of our motivation, is unconscious (Doidge, 2006). In addition, as Donald Carveth of York University pointed out in a 2006 lecture, functional magnetic resonance imaging (fMRI) brain scans have shown that passion, reason, and conscience involve different areas of brain activity, a finding that lends some credibility to Freud's differentiation between the id, ego, and superego (Carveth, 2006).

CRITICISMS OF THE PSYCHODYNAMIC PERSPECTIVE This might be a good time to point out a very important fact about Freud's theory: He did no experiments to arrive at his conclusions about personality. His theory is based on his own observations (case studies) of numerous patients. Basing his suppositions on their detailed memories of their childhoods and life experiences, Freud interpreted their behaviour and reminiscences to develop his theory of psychoanalysis. He felt free to interpret what his patients told him of their childhoods as fantasy or fact, depending on how well those memories fit in with his developing theory. For example, many of Freud's patients told him that they were sexually abused by fathers, brothers, and other close family members. Initially, Freud did believe that his patients' claims of abuse were real

It sounds as if all of these theorists became famous by ◄ ditching some of Freud's original ideas. Is Freud even worth studying anymore?

basic anxiety
anxiety created when a child is born into the bigger and more powerful world of older children and adults.

neurotic personalities
maladaptive ways of dealing with relationships in Horney's theory.

seduction hypothesis
Freud's original belief that sexual abuse was responsible for causing hysteria in his patients.

and that the abuse was responsible for their problems (he called this the **seduction hypothesis**). Freud later rejected this idea, deciding that these memories were in fact fantasies, making them the basis of the Oedipal conflict.

Freud based a great deal of his interpretations of a patient's problems on the interpretations of dreams and the results of the patient's *free association* (talking about anything without fear of negative feedback). These "sources" of information are often criticized as being too ambiguous and without scientific support for the validity of his interpretations. The very ambiguity of these sources of information allowed Freud to fit the patient's words and recollections to his own preferred interpretation, and also increased the possibility that Freud's own suggestions and interpretations might alter the actual memories of the patient, who would no doubt be in a very suggestible state of mind during therapy (Grünbaum, 1984).

Another criticism of Freud's theory concerns the people upon whose dreams, recollections, and comments the theory of psychoanalysis was based. Freud's clients were almost all wealthy Austrian women living in the Victorian era of sexual repression. Critics state that basing his theory on observations made with such a group of clients promoted his emphasis on sexuality as the root of all problems in personality, as women of that social class and era were often sexually frustrated. Freud rarely had clients who did not fit this description, and so his theory is biased in terms of sexual frustrations (Robinson, 1993).

Although most professionals today view Freud's theory with a great deal of skepticism, his influence on the modern world cannot be ignored. Freudian concepts have had an impact on literature, movies, and even children's cartoons. People who have never taken a course in psychology are familiar with some of Freud's most basic concepts, such as the defence mechanisms. He was also one of the first theorists to emphasize the importance of childhood experiences on personality development—in spite of the fact that he never studied children.

It has been only in the past several decades that people have had the necessary tools to examine the concepts of the unconscious mind. One can only wonder how Freud might have changed his theory in light of what is now known about the workings of the human brain and the changes in society that exist today. At present, many people carry on the work (albeit modified work) of Freud, forming various psychoanalysis societies around the world. For example, the Canadian Psychoanalytic Society currently has more than 400 members, coast to coast.

PRACTICE QUIZ: HOW MUCH DO YOU REMEMBER?

Pick the best answer.

1. An area of the body that produces pleasurable sensations is called an _____ zone.
   a. erogenous
   b. fixation
   c. Oedipal
   d. phallic

2. In which psychosexual stage might fixation result in a person who is excessively neat and fussy?
   a. oral
   b. anal
   c. phallic
   d. genital

3. In which psychosexual stage does the defence mechanism of identification figure prominently?
   a. oral
   b. anal
   c. phallic
   d. latency

4. In which psychosexual stage are the sexual feelings repressed?
   a. oral
   b. anal
   c. phallic
   d. latency

5. According to Jung, the part of the mind containing universal human memories is called the _____ unconscious.
   a. personal
   b. cognitive
   c. collective
   d. animistic

6. Which of the neo-Freudians discussed in the text talked about neurotic personalities as moving toward people, moving against people, or moving away from people?
   a. Carl Jung
   b. Alfred Adler
   c. Karen Horney
   d. Erik Erikson

Answers: 1-a, 2-b, 3-c, 4-d, 5-c, 6-c.

THE BEHAVIOURIST AND SOCIAL COGNITIVE VIEW OF PERSONALITY

At the time that Freud's theory was shocking the Western world, another psychological perspective was also making its influence known. Chapter Five discussed the theories of classical and operant conditioning in some detail. *Behaviourists*, researchers who use the principles of conditioning to explain the actions and reactions of both animals and humans, have a very different view of personality.

11.5   *How do behaviourists and social cognitive theorists explain personality?*

For the behaviourist, personality is nothing more than a set of learned responses or **habits** (DeGrandpre, 2000; Dollard & Miller, 1950). In the strictest traditional view of Watson and Skinner, everything a person or animal does is a response to some environmental stimulus that has been reinforced or strengthened by reward in some way.

So how does a pattern of rewarding certain behaviour end up becoming part of some kind of personality pattern? Think about how a traditional behaviourist might explain a shy personality. Beginning in childhood, a person might be exposed to a parent with a rather harsh discipline style (stimulus). Avoiding the attention of that parent would result in less punishment, so that avoidance response is negatively reinforced—the "bad thing" or punishment is avoided by keeping out of sight and quiet. Later, that child might generalize that avoidance response to other authority figures and adults, such as teachers. In this way, a pattern (habit) of shyness would develop. Of course, this is just an example—not all shy people have a parent with such a discipline style.

Of course, many learning theorists today do not use only classical and operant conditioning to explain the development of the behaviour patterns referred to as *personality*. **Social cognitive learning theorists**, who emphasize the importance of both the influences of other people's behaviour and of a person's own expectancies on learning, hold that observational learning, modelling, and other cognitive learning techniques can lead to the formation of patterns of personality. LINK to *Chapter Five: Learning, p. 176.*

One of the more well-researched learning theories that includes the concept of cognitive processes as influences on behaviour is the social cognitive theory of Canadian psychologist Albert Bandura. In the **social cognitive view**, behaviour is governed not just by the influence of external stimuli and response patterns but also by cognitive processes such as anticipating, judging, and memory, as well as learning through the imitation of models.

BANDURA'S RECIPROCAL DETERMINISM AND SELF-EFFICACY

Bandura (1989) believes that three factors influence one another in determining behaviour: the environment, the behaviour itself, and personal or cognitive factors that the person brings into the situation from earlier experiences (see Figure 11.2). These three factors each affect the other two in a reciprocal, or give-and-take, relationship. Bandura calls this relationship **reciprocal determinism**.

The environment includes the actual physical surroundings, the other people who may or may not be present, and the potential for reinforcement in those surroundings. The intensity and frequency of the behaviour will not only be influenced by the environment but will also have an impact on that environment. The person brings into the situation previously reinforced responses (personality, in other words) and mental processes such as thinking and anticipating.

◀ So how does a pattern of rewarding certain behaviour end up becoming part of some kind of personality pattern?

habits
in behaviourism, sets of well-learned responses that have become automatic.

social cognitive learning theorists
theorists who emphasize the importance of both the influences of other people's behaviour and of a person's own expectancies on learning.

social cognitive view
learning theory that includes cognitive processes such as anticipating, judging, memory, and imitation of models.

reciprocal determinism
Bandura's explanation of how the factors of environment, personal characteristics, and behaviour can interact to determine future behaviour.

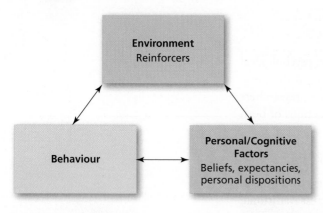

FIGURE 11.2 **Reciprocal Determinism**   In Bandura's model of reciprocal determinism, three factors influence behaviour: the environment, which consists of the physical surroundings and the potential for reinforcement; the person (personal/ cognitive characteristics that have been rewarded in the past); and the behaviour itself, which may or may not be reinforced at this particular time and place.

Here's how this might work: Richard walks into a university classroom filled with other students, but no professor is present at this time. (This is the *environment*.) Part of Richard's *person* characteristics includes the desire to have attention from other people by talking loudly and telling jokes, which has been very rewarding to him in the past (past reinforcements are part of his cognitive processes, or expectancies of future rewards for his behaviour). Also in the past, he has found that he gets more attention when an authority figure is not present. His *behaviour* will most likely be to start talking and telling jokes, which will continue if he gets the reaction he expects from his fellow students. If the professor walks in (the *environment* changes), his behaviour will change. If the other students don't laugh, his behaviour will change. In the future, Richard might be less likely to behave in the same way because his expectations for reward (a cognitive element of his *person* variables) are different.

One of the more important person variables that Bandura talks about is **self-efficacy**, a person's perception of how effective a behaviour will be in any particular circumstance (Bandura, 1998). (Self-efficacy is not the same concept as *self-esteem*, which is the positive values a person places on his or her sense of worth.)

People's sense of self-efficacy can be high or low, depending on what has happened in similar circumstances in the past (success or failure), what other people tell them about their competence, and their own assessment of their abilities. For example, if Fiona has an opportunity to write an extra-credit paper to improve her grade in psychology, she will be more likely to do so if her self-efficacy is high: She has achieved good grades on such papers in the past, her teachers have told her that she writes well, and she knows she can write a good paper. According to Bandura, people high in self-efficacy are more persistent and expect to succeed, whereas people low in self-efficacy expect to fail and tend to avoid challenges (Bandura, 1998).

ROTTER'S SOCIAL LEARNING THEORY: EXPECTANCIES

Julian Rotter (1966, 1978, 1981, 1990) devised a theory based on a basic principle of motivation derived from Thorndike's Law of Effect: People are motivated to seek reinforcement and avoid punishment, as discussed in Chapter 5 on page 189. He viewed personality as a relatively stable set of *potential* responses to various situations. If in the past, a certain way of responding led to a reinforcing or pleasurable consequence, that way of responding would become a pattern of responding, or part of the "personality" as learning theorists see it.

One very important pattern of responding in Rotter's view became his concept of *locus of control*, the tendency for people to assume that they either have control or do not have control over events and consequences in their lives. Ⓛ Ⓘ Ⓝ Ⓚ *to Chapter Nine: Motivation and Emotion, p. 350.* People who assume that their own actions and decisions directly affect the consequences they experience are said to be *internal* in locus of control, whereas people who assume that their lives are more controlled by powerful others, luck, or fate are *external* in locus of control (MacDonald, 1970; Rotter, 1966). Rotter associated people high in internal locus of control with the personality characteristics of high achievement motivation (the will to succeed in any attempted task). Those who give up too quickly or attribute events in their lives to external causes can fall into patterns of learned helplessness and depression (Abramson et al., 1978, 1989; Gong-Guy & Hammen, 1980).

self-efficacy
individual's perception of how effective a behaviour will be in any particular circumstance.

Like Bandura, Rotter (1978, 1981) also believed that an interaction of factors would determine the behavioural patterns that become personality for an individual. For Rotter, two key factors influence a person's decision to act in a certain way given a particular situation: expectancy and reinforcement value. Expectancy is fairly similar to Bandura's concept of self-efficacy in that it refers to the person's subjective feeling that a particular behaviour will lead to a reinforcing consequence. A high expectancy for success is similar to a high sense of self-efficacy and is also based on past experiences with successes and failures.

CURRENT THOUGHTS ON THE BEHAVIOURIST AND SOCIAL COGNITIVE VIEWS

Behaviourism as an explanation of the formation of personality has its limitations. The classic theory does not take mental processes into account when explaining behaviour, nor does it give weight to social influences on learning. The social cognitive view of personality, unlike traditional behaviourism, does include mental processes and their influence on behaviour. Unlike psychoanalysis, the concepts in this theory can and have been tested under scientific conditions (DeGrandpre, 2000; Domjan et al., 2000; Skinner, 1989). Bandura's classic Bobo doll study, described in Chapter Five, for example, made use of experimentation (Bandura, 1965). Ⓛ Ⓘ Ⓝ Ⓚ *to Chapter Five: Learning, p. 208.* Although some critics think that human personality and behaviour are too complex to explain as the result of cognitions and external stimuli interacting, others point out that this viewpoint has enabled the development of therapies based on learning theory that have become effective in changing undesirable behaviour. For example, as you will discover in Chapter Fourteen, systematic desensitization is a therapy that has been very successful in treating people suffering from phobias. Ⓛ Ⓘ Ⓝ Ⓚ *to Chapter Fourteen: Psychological Therapies, p. 564.*

Stanley was deeply disappointed when, high in the Tibetan mountains, he finally found his true self

THE THIRD FORCE: HUMANISM AND PERSONALITY

11.6 *How do humanists such as Carl Rogers explain personality?*

As first discussed in Chapter One, in the middle of the twentieth century the pessimism of Freudian psychoanalysis with its emphasis on conflict and animalistic needs, together with the emphasis of behaviourism on external control of behaviour, gave rise to a "third force" in psychology: the **humanistic perspective**. Humanists such as Carl Rogers and Abraham Maslow wanted psychology to focus on the things that make people uniquely human, such as subjective emotions and the freedom to choose one's own destiny. As Maslow's theory was discussed more fully in Chapter Nine, in this chapter the discussion of the humanistic view of personality will focus on the theory of Carl Rogers. Ⓛ Ⓘ Ⓝ Ⓚ *to Chapter Nine: Motivation and Emotion, p. 350.*

CARL ROGERS AND SELF-CONCEPT

Like Maslow, Rogers (1961) believed that human beings are always striving to fulfill their innate capacities and capabilities and to become everything that their genetic potential will allow them to become. This striving for fulfillment is called the **self-actualizing tendency**. An important tool in human self-actualization is the development of an image of oneself, or the **self-concept**. The self-concept is based on what people are told by others and how the sense of self is reflected in the words

humanistic perspective
the "third force" in psychology that focuses on those aspects of personality that make people uniquely human, such as subjective feelings and freedom of choice.

self-actualizing tendency
the striving to fulfill one's innate capacities and capabilities.

self-concept
the image of oneself that develops from interactions with important, significant people in one's life.

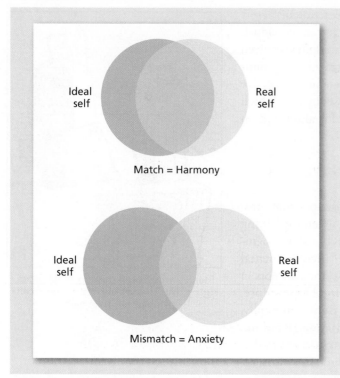

Match = Harmony

Mismatch = Anxiety

FIGURE 11.3 **Real and Ideal Selves**
According to Rogers, the self-concept includes the real self and the ideal self. The real self is a person's actual perception of traits and abilities, whereas the ideal self is the perception of what a person would like to be or thinks he or she should be.

real self
one's perception of actual characteristics, traits, and abilities.

ideal self
one's perception of who one should be or would like to be.

positive regard
warmth, affection, love, and respect that come from the significant others in one's life.

unconditional positive regard
positive regard that is given without conditions or strings attached.

conditional positive regard
positive regard that is given only when the person is doing what the providers of positive regard wish.

fully functioning person
persons who are able to accept reality, live in the present, trust their judgment, acknowledge their freedom and take responsibility for their actions, and finally, make creative contributions to the world.

and actions of important people in one's life, such as parents, siblings, co-workers, friends, and teachers.

REAL AND IDEAL SELF   Two important components of the self-concept are the **real self** (one's actual perception of characteristics, traits, and abilities that form the basis of the striving for self-actualization) and the **ideal self** (the perception of what one should be or would like to be). The ideal self primarily comes from those important, significant others in one's life, most often the parents. Rogers believed that when the real self and the ideal self are very close or similar to each other, people feel competent and capable, but when there is a mismatch between the real and ideal selves, anxiety and neurotic behaviour can be the result (see Figure 11.3).

The two halves of the self are more likely to match if they aren't that far apart at the start. When one has a realistic view of the real self, and the ideal self is something that is actually attainable, there usually isn't a problem of a mismatch. It is when a person's view of self is distorted or the ideal self is impossible to attain that problems arise. Once again, it is primarily how the important people (who can be either good or bad influences) in a person's life react to the person that determines the degree of agreement between real and ideal selves.

CONDITIONAL AND UNCONDITIONAL POSITIVE REGARD   Rogers defined **positive regard** as warmth, affection, love, and respect that come from the significant others (parents, admired adults, friends, and teachers) in people's experience. Positive regard is vital to people's ability to cope with stress and to strive to achieve self-actualization. Rogers believed that **unconditional positive regard**, or love, affection, and respect with no strings attached, is necessary for people to be able to explore fully all that they can achieve and become. Unfortunately, some parents, spouses, and friends give **conditional positive regard**, which is love, affection, respect, and warmth that depend, or seem to depend, on doing what those people want.

Here is an example: In her first year of university, Sasha was thinking about becoming a math teacher, a computer programmer, or an elementary school teacher. Karen, also in her first year, already knew that she was going to be a doctor. While Sasha's parents had told her that what she wanted to become was up to her and that they would love her no matter what, Karen's parents had made it very clear to her as a small child that they expected her to become a doctor. She was under the very strong impression that if she tried to choose any other career, she would lose her parents' love and respect. Sasha's parents were giving her unconditional positive regard, but Karen's parents (whether they intended to do so or not) were giving her conditional positive regard. Karen was obviously not as free as Sasha to explore her potential and abilities.

For Rogers, a person who is in the process of self-actualizing, actively exploring potentials and abilities and experiencing a match between real and ideal selves, is a **fully functioning person**. According to Rogers (1961), individuals are "fully functioning" if they demonstrate the following characteristics: being able to accept reality, live in the present, trust their judgment, acknowledge their freedom and take responsibility for their actions, and finally, make creative contributions to the world. To become fully functioning, a person needs unconditional positive regard. In Rogers's view, Karen would not have been a fully functioning person.

What kinds of people are considered to be fully functioning? Is it the same thing as being self-actualized? Although the two concepts are highly related, there are some subtle differences. Self-actualization is a goal that people are always striving to reach, according to Maslow (1987). (L)(I)(N)(K) *to Chapter Nine: Motivation and Emotion, p. 350.* In Rogers's view, only a person who is fully functioning is capable of reaching the goal of self-actualization. To be fully functioning is a necessary step in the process of self-actualization. Maslow (1987) listed several people that he considered to be self-actualized people: Albert Einstein, Mahatma Gandhi, and Eleanor Roosevelt, for example. Maslow believed that these people had the self-actualized qualities of being creative, autonomous, and unprejudiced. In Rogers's view, these same people would be seen as having trusted their true feelings and innermost needs rather than just going along with the crowd, a description that certainly seems to apply in these three cases.

CURRENT THOUGHTS ON THE HUMANISTIC VIEW OF PERSONALITY

Humanistic views of personality paint a very rosy picture. Some critics believe that the picture is a little too rosy, ignoring the more negative aspects of human nature. For example, would humanistic theory easily explain the development of sociopathic personalities who have no conscience or moral nature? Or could a humanist explain the motivation behind terrorism?

Humanistic theory is also very difficult to test scientifically, as it is obviously difficult to test the notion that people are inherently good. Little research support exists for this viewpoint, which is almost more of a philosophical view of human behaviour than a psychological explanation. Its greatest impact has been in the development of therapies to promote self-growth and help people better understand themselves and others. For example, in Chapter Fourteen, you will read about person-centred therapy, which was developed by Rogers and involves a closer relationship between the therapist and client than in other types of therapy. (L)(I)(N)(K) *to Chapter Fourteen: Psychological Therapies, p. 564.*

◄ What kind of people are considered to be fully functioning? Is it the same thing as being self-actualized?

PRACTICE QUIZ: HOW MUCH DO YOU REMEMBER?

Pick the best answer.

1. According to behaviourists, personality is
   a. driven by unconscious forces.
   b. a set of learned responses.
   c. motivated by a striving for success.
   d. a collection of specific traits.

2. Which of the following is not one of Bandura's three factors in reciprocal determinism?
   a. environment
   b. the person
   c. traits
   d. behaviour

3. Sandy is playing a trivia game with her friends. When it is her turn, she gets the category of geography. She knows very little about geography and has never done well in this category in the past, so her sense of self-efficacy is likely to be
   a. low.
   b. high.
   c. moderate.
   d. the answer cannot be determined from the information provided

4. Eddie knows that he is pretty good at art, but his parents have never encouraged him to develop art as a career because they don't feel that artists have "real" jobs. As a result, Eddie feels that he should concentrate on a more practical career to please his parents. If Eddie is working to be who he *should* be, according to his parents, he is being influenced by his
   a. self-concept.
   b. real self.
   c. superego.
   d. ideal self.

5. Rogers believed that in order for people to become fully functioning, they must receive _____ from the important people in their lives.
   a. unconditional positive regard
   b. conditional positive regard
   c. positive reinforcement
   d. positive modelling

"Can't you give him one of those personalities in a bottle I keep reading about?"

"Can't you give him one of those personalities in a bottle I keep reading about?"
© The New Yorker Collection 1994 Lee Lorenz from cartoonbank.com. All Rights Reserved.

👁 **Watch** on **mypsychlab**
Gordon Allport Discusses Personality Traits

trait theories
theories that endeavour to describe the characteristics that make up human personality in an effort to predict future behaviour.

trait
a consistent, enduring way of thinking, feeling, or behaving.

surface traits
aspects of personality that can easily be seen by other people in the outward actions of a person.

source traits
the more basic traits that underlie the surface traits, forming the core of personality.

introversion
dimension of personality in which people tend to withdraw from excessive stimulation.

✴ **Explore** on **mypsychlab**
The Five-Factor Model

five-factor model (Big Five)
model of personality traits that describes five basic trait dimensions.

TRAIT THEORIES: WHO ARE YOU?

11.7 *What are the history and current views of the trait perspective?*

As discussed in the introduction to this chapter, **trait theories** are less concerned with the explanation for personality development and changing personality than they are with describing personality and predicting behaviour based on that description. A **trait** is a consistent, enduring way of thinking, feeling, or behaving, and trait theories attempt to describe personality in terms of a person's traits.

ALLPORT

One of the earliest attempts to list and describe the traits that make up personality can be found in the work of Gordon Allport (Allport & Odbert, 1936). Allport and his colleague H. S. Odbert literally scanned the dictionary for words that could be traits, finding about 18 000, and then pared that down to 200 traits after eliminating synonyms. Allport believed (with no scientific evidence, however) that these traits were literally wired into the nervous system to guide one's behaviour across many different situations and that each person's "constellation" of traits was unique. (In spite of Allport's lack of evidence, behavioural geneticists have found support for the heritability of personality traits, and these findings are discussed in the next section of this chapter.)

CATTELL AND THE 16PF

Two hundred traits is still a very large number of descriptors. How might an employer be able to judge the personality of a potential employee by looking at a list of 200 traits? A more compact way of describing personality was needed. Raymond Cattell (1990) defined two types of traits as surface traits and source traits. **Surface traits** are like those found by Allport, representing the personality characteristics easily seen by other people. **Source traits** are those more basic traits that underlie the surface traits. For example, shyness, being quiet, and disliking crowds might all be surface traits related to the more basic source trait of **introversion**, a tendency to withdraw from excessive stimulation.

Using a statistical technique that looks for groupings and commonalities in numerical data called *factor analysis*, Cattell discovered 16 source traits (Cattell, 1950, 1966), and although he later determined that there might be another seven source traits to make a total of 23 (Cattell & Kline, 1977), he developed his assessment questionnaire, *The Sixteen Personality Factor Questionnaire* (16PF; Cattell, 1995) based on just 16 source traits (see Figure 11.4). These 16 source traits are seen as trait dimensions, or continuums, in which there are two opposite traits at each end, with many possible degrees of the traits possible along the dimension. For example, someone scoring near the reserved end of the reserved/outgoing dimension would be more introverted than someone scoring in the middle or at the opposite end.

THE BIG FIVE: OCEAN, OR THE FIVE-FACTOR MODEL OF PERSONALITY

Sixteen factors are still quite a lot to discuss when talking about someone's personality. Later researchers attempted to reduce the number of trait dimensions to a more manageable number, with several groups of researchers arriving at more or less the same five trait dimensions (Botwin & Buss, 1989; Jang et al., 1998; McCrae & Costa, 1996). These five dimensions have become known as the **five-factor model**, or the Big Five (see Table 11.2), and represent the core description of human personality—that is, the only dimensions necessary to understand what makes us tick.

As shown in Table 11.2, these five trait dimensions can be remembered by using the acronym *OCEAN*, in which each of the letters is the first letter of one of the five dimensions of personality. Refer to Table 11.2 to see what characteristics describe low scorers and high scorers on each of these five traits.

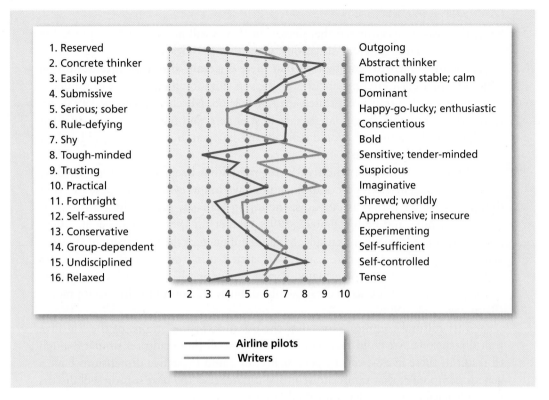

1. Reserved — Outgoing
2. Concrete thinker — Abstract thinker
3. Easily upset — Emotionally stable; calm
4. Submissive — Dominant
5. Serious; sober — Happy-go-lucky; enthusiastic
6. Rule-defying — Conscientious
7. Shy — Bold
8. Tough-minded — Sensitive; tender-minded
9. Trusting — Suspicious
10. Practical — Imaginative
11. Forthright — Shrewd; worldly
12. Self-assured — Apprehensive; insecure
13. Conservative — Experimenting
14. Group-dependent — Self-sufficient
15. Undisciplined — Self-controlled
16. Relaxed — Tense

1 2 3 4 5 6 7 8 9 10

—— Airline pilots
—— Writers

FIGURE 11.4 **Cattell's Self-Report Inventory** This example of personality profiles is based on Cattell's 16PF self-report inventory. The two groups represented are airline pilots and writers. Notice, on the one hand, that airline pilots, when compared to writers, tend to be more controlled, relaxed, self-assured, and far less sensitive. Writers, on the other hand, were more imaginative and better able to think abstractly.
Source: Cattell (1973).

- **Openness to experience** can best be described as a person's willingness to try new things and be open to new experiences.
- **Conscientiousness** refers to how dependable someone is and the care they give to organization and being thoughtful about others.
- **Extraversion** is a term first used by Carl Jung (1933), who believed that all people could be divided into two personality types: extraverts and introverts. **Extraverts** are outgoing and sociable, whereas **introverts** are more solitary and dislike being the centre of attention.
- **Agreeableness** refers to the basic emotional style of a person, whether they show concern for cooperation and harmony with others.
- **Neuroticism** refers to emotional instability or stability.

Costa and McCrae believed that these five traits were independent of one another. In other words, knowing someone's score on extraversion would not give any information about scores on the other four dimensions, allowing for a tremendous amount of variety in personality descriptions.

openness to experience
one of the five factors; willingness to try new things and be open to new experiences.

conscientiousness
one of the five factors; the care a person gives to organization and thoughtfulness of others; dependability.

extraversion
one of the five factors; dimension of personality referring to one's need to be with other people.

extraverts
people who are outgoing and sociable.

introverts
people who prefer solitude and dislike being the centre of attention.

agreeableness
one of the five factors; the emotional style of a person that may range from easygoing, friendly, and likeable to grumpy, crabby, and unpleasant.

neuroticism
one of the five factors; degree of emotional instability or stability.

TABLE 11.2 **THE BIG FIVE**

HIGH SCORER CHARACTERISTICS	FACTOR (OCEAN)	LOW SCORER CHARACTERISTICS
Creative, artistic, curious, imaginative, nonconforming	Openness to experience (O)	Conventional, down-to-earth, uncreative
Organized, reliable, neat, ambitious	Conscientiousness (C)	Unreliable, lazy, careless, negligent, spontaneous
Talkative, optimistic, sociable, affectionate	Extraversion (E)	Reserved, comfortable being alone, stays in the background
Good-natured, trusting, helpful	Agreeableness (A)	Rude, uncooperative, irritable, aggressive, competitive
Worrying, insecure, anxious, temperamental	Neuroticism (N)	Calm, secure, relaxed, stable

Source: Adapted from McRae & Costa (1990).

trait–situation interaction
the assumption that the particular circumstances of any given situation will influence the way in which a trait is expressed.

CURRENT THOUGHTS ON THE TRAIT PERSPECTIVE

Some theorists have cautioned that personality traits will not always be expressed in the same way across different situations. Over four decades ago, Walter Mischel, a social cognitive theorist, emphasized that there is a **trait–situation interaction**, in which the particular circumstances of any given situation are assumed to influence the way in which a trait is expressed (Mischel, 1968; Mischel & Shoda, 1995). An extravert, for example, might laugh, talk to strangers, and tell jokes at a party. That same person, if at a funeral, would still talk and be open, but the jokes and laughter would be less likely to occur.

As mentioned earlier, the five-factor model has been studied and tested by numerous researchers. Cross-cultural studies have found evidence of these five trait dimensions in 11 different cultures, including Canada, Japan, the Philippines, Germany, China, and Peru (Digman, 1990; John et al., 1988; McCrae et al., 2000; Paunonen et al., 1996). For example, Sampo Paunonen of the University of Western Ontario in London, Ontario, tested 575 participants from six different cultures (Canada, Finland, Poland, Germany, Russia, and Hong Kong) and found that the factors found in each country's data resembled the five factors of the five-factor model (Paunonen et al., 1996).

This cultural commonality raises the question of the origins of the Big Five trait dimensions: Are child-rearing practices across all those cultures similar enough to result in these five aspects of personality, or could these five dimensions have a genetic component that transcends cultural differences? The next section will discuss the evidence for a genetic basis for the Big Five.

PSYCHOLOGY IN THE NEWS

Canadians and Americans Aren't That Different

11.8   *Do the personalities of Canadians and Americans differ?*

In 2005, CTV released a story about the work of researchers at the U.S. National Institute on Aging, who have investigated people's beliefs surrounding the traits that make up their country's residents' personalities (Canadian Press, 2005). Terracciano and colleagues (2005) asked thousands of participants in 49 different countries to fill out personality questionnaires. They consistently found that people believed that their personalities reflected the stereotypes of their national character. (McCrae and Terracciano [2006] defined *national character* as "the shared perception of personality characteristics typical of citizens of a particular nation.") For example, Canadians believed they were much more calm than other people because the stereotype of Canadians is that they are very calm. However, when Terracciano and colleagues evaluated the personality inventories, Canadians were not found to be any more calm than American participants. In fact, according to one of the principal investigators, Robert McCrae, Canadians and Americans have almost identical average personality traits. In terms of the five broad trait factors mentioned in the previous section, both Canadians and Americans fell roughly in the middle.

Most Canadians believe that they are significantly different from their neighbours to the south, just as most Americans believe that they are significantly different from their neighbours to the north. Although these beliefs exist, research has found that there are actually very few differences between Canadians and Americans in terms of personality.

According to Canadian researcher Paul Trapnell of the University of Winnipeg, this realization that there is little difference between the two nations in terms of personality may have a negative impact, as national character traits are often used to assert a national identity, which in turn builds self-esteem and allows one to differentiate oneself from people of a different culture. Taking a personality trait such as agreeableness and exaggerating the differences between oneself and a person from a different country in terms of that trait reinforces a person's sense of self-worth.

McCrae and colleagues warn the public about the implications of their work, stating that we should be cautious in making generalizations (i.e., forming stereotypes) about any group of people because these generalizations are often wrong and can lead to prejudice and discrimination.

Questions for Further Discussion

1. What other "national characters" are you aware of? Has reading the above section changed how strongly you ascribe to these beliefs?

2. What are some of the implications (both good and bad) of these generalizations?

3. What are some of the possible problems with the research conducted by Terracciano, McCrae, and colleagues?

PRACTICE QUIZ: HOW MUCH DO YOU REMEMBER?

Pick the best answer.

1. Who believed that traits existed as part of the nervous system?
   a. Costa and McCrae
   b. Allport
   c. Cattell
   d. Rogers

2. According to Cattell, traits that are numerous and can easily be seen by other people are called _____ traits.
   a. central
   b. cardinal
   c. surface
   d. source

3. In the Big Five theory of personality, "C" stands for
   a. conscientiousness.
   b. consciousness.
   c. contrariness.
   d. complexity.

4. Elsie's daughter gave her a microwave oven for her birthday. Elsie has never used a microwave and is scared to use this one. Instead, she lets it sit in her kitchen and uses the stove instead because she has always used the stove. Elsie would probably score very low on
   a. agreeableness.
   b. neuroticism.
   c. introversion.
   d. openness to experience.

5. Recent research has found that the main difference between Canadians and Americans in terms of personality is
   a. Canadians tend to be more agreeable than Americans.
   b. Canadians tend to be more neurotic than Americans.
   c. Canadians tend to be less conscientious than Americans.
   d. No major differences have been found between Canadians and Americans when it comes to personality.

Answers: 1-b, 2-c, 3-a, 4-d, 5-d.

THE BIOLOGY OF PERSONALITY: BEHAVIOURAL GENETICS

What about genetics? How much of our personality is inherited? The field of **behavioural genetics** is devoted to the study of just how much of an individual's personality is due to inherited traits. Animal breeders have known for a long time that selective breeding of certain animals with specific desirable traits can produce changes not only in size, fur colour, and other physical characteristics but also in the temperament of the animals (Isabel, 2003; Trut, 1999). As stated earlier in this chapter, temperament consists of the characteristics with which each person is born and is, therefore, determined by biology to a great degree. If the temperaments of animals can be influenced by manipulating patterns of genetic inheritance, then it is only one small step to assume that at least those personality characteristics related to temperament in human beings may also be influenced by heredity.

How about genetics? How much of our personality is inherited?

behavioural genetics
field of study devoted to discovering the genetic bases for personality characteristics.

Animal breeders have an advantage over those who are studying the influence of genes in human behaviour. Those who breed animals can control the mating of certain animals and the conditions under which those animals are raised. Human research cannot ethically or practically develop that degree of control and so must fall back on the accidental "experiments" of nature and opportunity, studies of twins and adopted persons.

11.9   *What part do biology, heredity, and culture play in personality?*

TWIN STUDIES

The difference between monozygotic (identical) and dizygotic (fraternal) twins was discussed in Chapter Eight. LINK *to Chapter Eight: Development Across the Lifespan, p. 302.* As discussed previously, monozygotic twins share almost 100 percent of their genetic material (remember that no two people are actually identical), having come from one fertilized egg, whereas dizygotic twins share only about 50 percent of their genetic material, as any other pair of siblings would. By comparing monozygotic twins to dizygotic twins, especially when twins can be found who were not raised in the same environment (such as Oskar and Jack or the "Jim" twins in the opening story), researchers can begin to find evidence of possible genetic influences on various traits, including personality (see Figure 11.5).

The results of the Minnesota twin study (of which the "Jim" twins were a part) have revealed that monozygotic twins are more similar than dizygotic twins or unrelated people in intelligence, leadership abilities, the tendency to follow rules, and the tendency to uphold traditional cultural expectations (Bouchard, 1997; Finkel & McGue, 1997); nurturance, empathy, and assertiveness (Neale et al., 1986); and aggressiveness (Miles & Carey, 1997). This similarity holds even if the twins are raised in separate environments.

ADOPTION STUDIES

As was discussed in Chapter Eight, by comparing adopted children to their adoptive parents and siblings and, if possible, to their biological parents who have not raised them, researchers can uncover some of the shared and non-shared environmental and genetic influences on personality. LINK *to Chapter Eight: Development Across the Lifespan, p. 302.*

Adoption studies have confirmed what twin studies have shown: Genetic influences account for a great deal of personality development, regardless of shared or non-shared environments (Hershberger et al., 1995; Loehlin et al., 1985; Loehlin et al., 1998). Through this kind of study, a genetic basis has been suggested for shyness (Plomin et al., 1988) and aggressiveness (Brennan et al., 1997).

CURRENT FINDINGS

Several studies have found that the five personality factors of the five-factor model have nearly a 50 percent rate of heritability across several cultures (Bouchard, 1994; Jang et al., 1996; Loehlin, 1992; Loehlin et al., 1998). Together with the results of the Minnesota twin study and other research (Lubinski, 2000; Lykken & Tellegen, 1996; Plomin, 1994), the studies of genetics and personality seem to indicate that variations in personality traits are about 25 to 50 percent inherited (Jang et al., 1998). This also means that environmental influences apparently account for about half of the variation in personality traits as well. More recently, with researchers from Japan and Germany, Kerry Jang and John Livesley of the University of British Columbia investigated 1209 monozygotic and 701 dizygotic twin pairs from Canada, Japan, and Germany

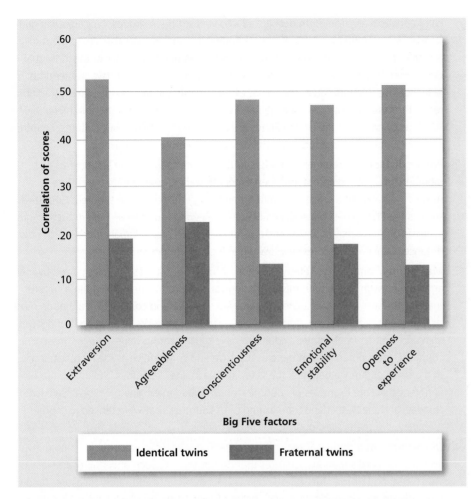

FIGURE 11.5 **Personalities of Monozygotic and Dizygotic Twins** Monozygotic and dizygotic twins differ in the way they express the Big Five personality factors. The scores of monozygotic twins have a correlation of about 50 percent, whereas those of dizygotic twins have a correlation of only about 15 to 20 percent. These findings give support to the idea that some aspects of personality are genetically based. *Source:* Loehlin (1992).

and found direct evidence that the five-factor model reflects underlying genetic structure (Yamagata et al., 2006). According to these researchers, the findings of their 2006 study provide strong support for the claim that the five personality factors have a solid biological basis and that the genetic structure of the five-factor model is universal.

Although the five factors have been found across several cultures, this does not mean that different cultures do not have an impact on personality. For more on this topic, see the Classic Studies in Psychology section that follows.

 CLASSIC STUDIES IN PSYCHOLOGY

Geert Hofstede's Four Dimensions of Cultural Personality

Explore on mypsychlab Theories of Personality (Summary)

In the early 1980s, organizational management specialist Geert Hofstede conducted a massive study into the work-related values of employees of IBM, a multinational corporation (Hofstede, 1980; Hofstede et al., 2002). The study surveyed workers from 64 countries around the world, including Canada. Hofstede analyzed the data collected from this survey and found four basic dimensions of personality along which cultures differed.

1. Individualism/collectivism: Individualistic cultures tend to have loose ties between individuals, with people tending to look after themselves and their immediate families only. Members of such cultures have friends based on shared activities and interests and may belong to many different loosely organized social groups. Autonomy, change, youth, security of the individual, and equality are all highly valued. In a collectivistic

(Top) Canadian Prime Minister Stephen Harper is pictured at the school where he cast his ballot in Calgary, Alberta. Notice that he interacts with the children and does not keep away from the general public, which supports the finding that Canada is lower in power distance than other countries, such as Morocco.

(Bottom) King Mohammed VI of Morocco is pictured on a pilgrimage to Jeddah in Saudi Arabia. Notice that the king and the people of power with him are kept well away from the general public. While this is partly for security reasons, it also indicates a high degree of power distance in this culture.

culture, people are from birth deeply tied into very strong in-groups, typically extended families that include grandparents, aunts and uncles, and cousins. Loyalty to the family is highly stressed, and the care of the family is placed before the care of the individual. Group membership is limited to only a few permanent groups that have tremendous influence over the individual. The values of this kind of culture are duty, order, tradition, respect for the elderly, group security, and respect for the group status and hierarchy. Whereas Canada and the United States are examples of individualistic cultures, countries such as Guatemala, Ecuador, and Panama are much more collectivistic.

2. **Power distance:** This dimension refers to the degree to which the less powerful members of a culture accept and even expect that the power within the culture is held in the hands of a select few rather than being more evenly distributed. Countries such as the Philippines, Malaysia, and Guatemala were found to be high in such expectations, whereas countries such as Austria, Israel, and Denmark were low in power distance. Canada also scores very low when it comes to power distance.

3. **Masculinity/femininity:** Referring to how a culture distributes the roles played by men and women within a culture, this dimension varies more for the men within a culture than for the women. "Masculine" cultures are assertive and competitive, although more so for men than for women, and "feminine" cultures are more modest and caring. Both men and women in "feminine" countries have similar, caring values, but in "masculine" countries, the women are not quite as assertive and competitive as the men, leading to a greater difference between the sexes in "masculine" countries. Japan, Austria, and Venezuela are examples of countries found to be "masculine," whereas Sweden, Norway, and the Netherlands, are examples of countries that were ranked as more "feminine." Canada was found to fall in the middle.

4. **Uncertainty avoidance:** Some cultures are more tolerant of uncertainty, ambiguity, and unstructured situations. Cultures that do not tolerate such uncertainty and lack of structure tend to have strict rules and laws, lots of security and safety measures, and tend toward a philosophical/religious belief of One Truth (and "we have it!"). Cultures that are more accepting of uncertainty are more tolerant of different opinions and have fewer rules. They tend to allow many different religious beliefs to exist side by side and are less anxious and emotional than people in uncertainty-avoiding countries. Examples of uncertainty-avoiding countries include Greece, Portugal, Guatemala, and Uruguay, whereas examples of those that are more tolerant of uncertainty include Singapore, Jamaica, and Denmark. Canada also scores quite low on uncertainty avoidance.

Note that the Big Five personality dimensions of Costa and McCrae (1990) are not necessarily in competition with Hofstede's dimensions. Hofstede's dimensions are *cultural personality traits*, whereas those of the Big Five refer to individuals.

The results of Hofstede's work further illustrate the point made in the Psychology in the News section: Canadians and Americans are not very different when it comes to personality, even when cultural personality traits are being measured. On each of Hofstede's four cultural dimensions, Canada and the United States never fell very far away from one another. Hofstede's findings give us even more evidence that we're not as different as we may think we are.

Questions for Further Discussion

1. Was your own culture listed for any of these dimensions? If so, do you agree with the personality dimension assigned to your culture?

2. If your culture was not listed for a personality dimension, where do you think your culture would fall on that dimension?

3. Do you agree with Hofstede's separation of cultural personality into four factors? Do you think that there may be other dimensions on which various cultures around the world would differ? Provide an example.

ASSESSMENT OF PERSONALITY

11.10   *What are the advantages and disadvantages of using the following measures of personality: interviews, projective tests, behavioural assessment, and personality inventories?*

With all the different theories of personality, how do people find out what kind of personality they have? The methods for measuring or assessing personality vary according to the theory of personality used to develop those methods, as one might expect. However, most psychological professionals doing a personality assessment on a client do not necessarily tie themselves to only one theoretical viewpoint, preferring to take a more *eclectic* view of personality. The eclectic view is a way of choosing the parts of different theories that seem to best fit a particular situation, rather than using only one theory to explain a phenomenon. In fact, looking at behaviour from all four perspectives can often bring insights into a person's behaviour that would not easily come from taking only one perspective. Many professionals will use not only several different perspectives but also several of the assessment techniques that follow. Even so, certain methods are more commonly used by certain kinds of theorists, as can be seen in Table 11.3.

Personality assessments may also differ in the purposes for which they are conducted. For example, sometimes a researcher may administer a personality test of some sort to participants in a research study so that the participants may be classified according to certain personality traits. There are also personality tests available to people who simply want to learn more about their own personalities. Finally, clinical and counselling psychologists, psychiatrists, and other psychological professionals use personality assessment in the diagnosis of disorders of personality. LINK *to Chapter Thirteen: Psychological Disorders, p. 520.*

◀ With all the different theories of personality, how do people find out what kind of personality they have?

TABLE 11.3 WHO USES WHAT METHOD?

TYPE OF ASSESSMENT	MOST LIKELY USED BY ...
Interviews	psychoanalysts, humanistic therapists
Projective Tests: Rorschach Thematic Apperception Test	psychoanalysts
Behavioural Assessments: Direct Observation Rating Scales Frequency Counts	behavioural and social-cognitive therapists
Personality Inventories: Sixteen Personality Factor Questionnaire (16PF) Neuroticism/Extraversion/Openess Personality Inventory (NEO-PI) Myers-Briggs Type Indicator (MBTI) Eysenck Personality Questionnaire (EPQ) Minnesota Multiphasic Personality Inventory-2 (MMPI-2) Minnesota Multiphasic Personality Inventory–2-Restructured Form (MMPI-2-RF)	trait theorists

So an interview is a kind of self-report process?

CartoonStock

interview
method of personality assessment in which the professional asks questions of the client and allows the client to answer, either in a structured or unstructured fashion.

halo effect
tendency of an interviewer to allow positive characteristics of a client to influence the assessments of the client's behaviour and statements.

projection
defence mechanism involving placing, or "projecting," one's own unacceptable thoughts onto others, as if the thoughts actually belonged to those others and not to oneself.

projective tests
personality assessments that present ambiguous visual stimuli to the client and ask the client to respond with whatever comes to mind.

Rorschach inkblot test
projective test that uses 10 inkblots as the ambiguous stimuli.

INTERVIEWS

Some therapists ask questions and note down the answers in a survey process called an **interview**. (L I N K) *to Chapter One: The Science of Psychology, p. 2*. This type of interview, unlike a job interview, is likely to be only *semi-structured* and flow naturally from the beginning comments between the client and the psychologist.

▶ **PROBLEMS WITH INTERVIEWS**   So an interview is a kind of self-report process? Yes, when psychologists interview clients, clients must report on their innermost feelings, urges, and concerns—all things that only they can directly know. The same problems that exist with self-report data (such as surveys) exist with interviews. Clients can lie, distort the truth, misremember, or give what they think is a socially acceptable answer instead of true information. Interviewers themselves can be biased, interpreting what the client says in light of their own belief systems or prejudices. Freud certainly did this when he refused to believe that his patients had actually been sexually molested as children, preferring to interpret that information as a fantasy instead of reality (Russell, 1986).

Another problem with interviews is something called the **halo effect**, which is a tendency to form a favourable or unfavourable impression of someone at the first meeting, so that all of that person's comments and behaviour after that first impression will be interpreted to agree with the impression—positively or negatively. The halo effect can happen in any social situation, including interviews between a psychological professional and a client. First impressions really do count, and people who make a good first impression because of clothing, personal appearance, or some other irrelevant characteristic will seem to have a "halo" hanging over their heads—they can do no wrong after that (Lance et al., 1994; Thorndike, 1920). (Sometimes the negative impression is called the *horn effect*.)

PROJECTIVE TESTS

Psychoanalysts have a goal in dealing with their clients that other personality theorists do not share: The psychoanalyst wishes to uncover the unconscious conflicts, desires, and urges that affect the client's conscious behaviour. No other theorist assigns such importance to the unconscious mind, so psychoanalysts use assessment methods that are meant to "get at" those unconscious, hidden emotions and events.

Think about the definition of the defence mechanism of **projection**: placing, or "projecting," one's own unacceptable thoughts onto others, as if the thoughts actually belonged to those others. What if a person could project unacceptable, unconscious thoughts onto some harmless, ambiguous stimulus, like a picture? For example, have you ever tried to see "shapes" in the clouds? You might see a house where another person might see the same cloud as a horse. The cloud isn't really either of those things but can be *interpreted* as one or the other, depending on the person doing the interpretation. That makes a cloud an ambiguous stimulus—one that is capable of being interpreted in more than one way.

In just this way, psychoanalysts (and a few other psychologists) show their clients ambiguous visual stimuli and ask the clients to tell them what they see. The hope is that the client will project those unconscious concerns and fears onto the visual stimulus, revealing them to the analyst. Tests using this method are called **projective tests**. Although such tests can be used to explore one's personality, they are most commonly used as a diagnostic tool to uncover problems in personality.

THE RORSCHACH INKBLOTS   One of the more well-known projective tests is the **Rorschach inkblot test**, developed in 1921 by Swiss psychiatrist Hermann Rorschach (ROR-shok). There are 10 inkblots, five in black ink on a white background and five in coloured inks on a white background. (See Figure 11.6 for an example of a Rorschach-type inkblot.)

People being tested are asked to look at each inkblot and simply say whatever it might look like to them. Using predetermined categories and responses commonly given by people to each picture (Exner, 1980), psychologists score responses on key factors, such as reference to colour, shape, figures seen in the blot, and response to the whole or to details.

Rorschach tested thousands of inkblots until he narrowed them down to the 10 in use today. They are still frequently used to describe personality, diagnose mental disorders, and predict behaviour (Watkins et al., 1995; Weiner, 1997).

THE TAT First developed in 1935 by psychologist Henry Murray and his colleagues (Morgan & Murray, 1935), the **Thematic Apperception Test (TAT)** consists of 20 pictures, all black and white, that are shown to a client. The client is asked to tell a story about the person or people in the picture, who are all deliberately drawn in ambiguous situations (see Figure 11.7).

Again, the story developed by the client is interpreted by the psychoanalyst, who looks for revealing statements and projection of the client's own problems onto the people in the pictures.

These are only two of the more well-known projective tests. Other types of projective tests include the Sentence Completion test, Draw-a-Person, and House-Tree-Person. In the Sentence Completion test, the client is given a series of sentence beginnings, such as "I wish my mother …" or "Almost every day I feel …" and asked to finish the sentence, whereas in the Draw-a-Person and House-Tree-Person, the client is asked to draw the named items and then the items are analyzed using standardized scoring scales. The therapist/professional will look at things such as presence or absence of items, shading, size, and proportions of body parts. There is some agreement between theorists and researchers when it comes to the analysis of drawings. Oster and Crone (2004) list many different signs that these professionals agree on. Some of these include poor integration of body parts, which is indicative of impulsivity; a lot of shading, which is indicative of anxiety; exaggerated teeth, which is indicative of oral aggression and sarcasm; and the drawing of a profile instead of face-on, which is indicative of someone who is evasive, possibly paranoid and withdrawn (Oster & Crone, 2004).

But how can anyone know if the interpretation is correct? Isn't there a lot of room for error?

PROBLEMS WITH PROJECTIVE TESTS Projective tests are by their nature very **subjective** (valid only within the person's own perception), and interpreting the answers of clients is almost an art. It is certainly not a science and is not known for its accuracy. Problems lie in the areas of reliability and validity. In Chapter Seven, *reliability* was defined as the tendency of a test to give the same score every time it is administered to the same person or group of people, and *validity* was defined as the ability of the test to measure what it is intended to measure. Projective tests, with no standard grading scales, have both low reliability and low validity (Gittelman-Klein, 1978; Lilienfeld, 1999; Wood et al., 1996). A person's answers to the Rorschach, for example, might be quite different from one day to the next, depending on the person's mood and what scary movie might have been on television the previous night.

Projective tests may sound somewhat outdated in today's world of MRIs and PET scans, but many practicing clinical psychologists and psychiatrists still use this

FIGURE 11.6 **Rorschach Inkblot Example** One of the Rorschach inkblots. A person being tested is asked to tell the interviewer what he or she sees in this inkblot. Answers are neither right nor wrong, but may reveal unconscious concerns. What do you see in this inkblot?

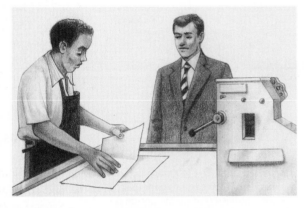

FIGURE 11.7 **Thematic Apperception Test Example** A sample from the Thematic Apperception Test (TAT). When you look at this picture, what story does it suggest to you? Who are the people? What is their relationship?

But how can anyone know if the interpretation is correct? Isn't there a lot of room for error?

Thematic Apperception Test (TAT) projective test that uses 20 pictures of people in ambiguous situations as the visual stimuli.

> Somehow, I can't see a behaviourist using any of these tests; they're too "mental." Do behaviourists even measure personality?

A client may be asked to draw a person during one of their sessions with their therapist. In this drawing, the person is drawn in profile, which, according to Oster and Crone (2004), may indicate that the client is feeling evasive, possibly paranoid, and withdrawn.

subjective
referring to concepts and impressions that are valid only within a particular person's perception and that may be influenced by biases, prejudice, and personal experiences.

direct observation
assessment in which the professional observes the client engaged in ordinary, day-to-day behaviour in either a clinical or natural setting.

type of testing (Butcher & Rouse, 1996; Camara et al., 2000). Some psychologists believe that the latest versions of these tests and others like them still have practical use and some validity (Ganellen, 1996; Weiner, 1997), especially when a client's answers on these tests are used as a starting point for digging deeper into the client's recollections, concerns, and anxieties. However, more reliable and objective methods for assessing personality are available, as the next section discusses.

Somehow, I can't see a behaviourist using any of these tests; they're too "mental." Do behaviourists even measure personality?

BEHAVIOURAL ASSESSMENTS

Behaviourists do not typically want to "look into the mind." Because behaviourists assume that personality is merely habitually learned responses to stimuli in the environment, the preferred method for a behaviourist would be to watch that behaviour unfold in the real world.

In **direct observation**, the psychologist observes the client engaging in ordinary, everyday behaviour, preferably in the natural setting of home, school, or the workplace, for example. A therapist who goes to the classroom and observes that tantrum behaviour happens only when a child is asked to do something involving fine motor abilities (such as drawing or writing) might be able to conclude that the child has difficulty with those skills and throws a tantrum to avoid the task.

Other methods often used by behavioural therapists and other assessors are rating scales and frequency counts. In a **rating scale**, a numerical rating is assigned, either by the assessor or the client, for specific behaviours (Nadeau et al., 2001). In a **frequency count**, the assessor literally counts the frequency of certain behaviours within a specified time limit. Educators make use of both rating scales and frequency counts to diagnose behavioural problems such as attention deficit hyperactivity disorder (ADHD) and aspects of personality such as social skill level through the various grade levels.

PROBLEMS WITH BEHAVIOURAL ASSESSMENTS   Problems with these assessments can include the observer effect (when a person's behaviour is affected by being watched) and observer bias, which can be controlled by having multiple observers and correlating their observations with each other. (L I N K) *to Chapter One: The Science of Psychology, p. 2.* As with any kind of observational method, there is no control over the external environment. A person observing a client for a particular behaviour may not see that behaviour occur within the observation time—much as some car problems never seem to show up when the mechanic is examining the car.

PERSONALITY INVENTORIES

Trait theorists are typically more interested in personality descriptions. They tend to use an assessment known as a **personality inventory**, a questionnaire that has a standard list of questions and requires only certain specific answers, such as "yes," "no," and "can't decide." The standard nature of the questions (everyone gets the same list) and the lack of open-ended answers make these assessments far more objective and reliable than projective tests (Garb et al., 1998), although they are still a form of self-report. One such personality inventory is Cattell's 16PF, described earlier in this chapter. Costa and McCrae (2000) have recently revised their original *Neuroticism/Extraversion/Openness Personality Inventory (NEO-PI)*, which is based on the five-factor model of personality traits. Another inventory in common use is the *Myers-Briggs Type Indicator (MBTI)*. This inventory is based on the ideas of Carl Jung and looks at four personality dimensions. The sensing/intuition (S/I) dimension includes people who prefer to rely on what they can see, hear, and so on through their own physical senses (*sensing*) and, on its opposite end, those who look for patterns and trust their hunches (*intuition*). Sensing people are very detail-oriented, preferring to work only with the known facts, whereas intuitive people are more willing to use metaphors and analogies and look for possibilities. The thinking/feeling (T/F) dimension runs from those who prefer to use logic, analysis, and experiences that can be verified as facts (*thinkers*) to those who tend to make decisions based on their personal values and emotional reactions (*feeling*). Introversion/extraversion (I/E) is the same classic dimension that began with Jung and is represented in nearly every personality theory, including the Big Five. Perceiving/judging (P/J) describes those who are willing to adapt and modify decisions, be spontaneous, are naturally curious, and tend to put off making a final decision so that all possibilities are covered (*perceiving*) as well as those who are the opposite: the action-oriented, decisive, get-the-task-done-and-don't-look-back type (*judging*). These four dimensions can differ for each individual, resulting in 16 (four by four) possible personality types: ISTJ, ISTP, ISFP, ISFJ, and so on (Briggs & Myers, 1998). The Myers-Briggs is often used to assess personality to help people know the kinds of careers for which they may best be suited.

For example, a person who scored high on the extravert, sensing, thinking, and judging dimensions would be an ESTJ. A typical description of this personality type would be a person who needs to analyze information and bring order to the outer world. Such people are organizers, energetic in completing tasks, and practical. They also take their responsibilities seriously and expect others to do so as well. School administrators, for example, are often ESTJs.

To deal with concerns relating to cross-cultural issues such as language, psychologists at the University of Western Ontario and their colleagues in other countries have developed both a verbal self-report measure and a non-verbal measure for use in cross-cultural settings. Douglas Jackson (1984) developed the verbal measure known as the *Personality Research Form (PRF)*, and Sampo Paunonen, Douglas Jackson, and Mirja Keinonen (1990) developed the *Nonverbal Personality Questionnaire (NPQ)*. Using both measures together is beneficial because the use of one test alone can lead to problems. For example, if only verbal measures were used, difficulties may arise with translation from language to language. More recently, Paunonen and colleagues have developed a non-verbal measure of the Big Five personality factors known as the *Five-Factor Nonverbal Personality Questionnaire (FF-NPQ)* to be used in cross-cultural personality research (Paunonen, Ashton, & Jackson, 2001). Paunonen and colleagues (2001) claim that not only are there many benefits to using the FF-NPQ in cross-cultural research, but that it can also be used beneficially with certain populations within various cultures (e.g., people with dyslexia or other linguistic disabilities). However, Paunonen and colleagues also stress the importance of realizing that although the use of this test has many merits, it does not eliminate issues relating to culture bias altogether.

Other common personality tests include the *Eysenck Personality Questionnaire* (Eysenck & Eysenck, 1993) and the *Sixteen Personality Factor Questionnaire* (Cattell, 1994).

THE MMPI-2   By far, the most common personality inventory is the *Minnesota Multiphasic Personality Inventory, Version II (MMPI-2)*, which specifically tests for abnormal behaviour patterns in personality (Butcher & Rouse, 1996; Butcher et al., 2000, 2001). This questionnaire consists of 567 statements such as "I am often very tense" or "I believe I am being plotted against." The person taking the test must answer "true," "false," or "cannot say." The MMPI-2 has 10 clinical scales and 8 validity scales in addition to numerous subscales. Each scale tests for a particular kind of behaviour. The behaviour patterns include relatively mild personality problems such as excessive worrying and shyness as well as more serious disorders such as schizophrenia and depression. The MMPI-2 is used by many different police forces, including the Royal

rating scale
assessment in which a numerical value is assigned to specific behaviour that is listed in the scale.

frequency count
assessment in which the frequency of a particular behaviour is counted.

personality inventory
paper and pencil or computerized test that consists of statements that require a specific, standardized response from the person taking the test.

✴ Explore on **mypsychlab**
Personality Assessment

Canadian Mounted Police, in the personality testing of potential officers. An alternative version (not to be used as a replacement) was published in 2008 (Ben-Porath & Tellegen, 2008) and is referred to as the *Minnesota Multiphasic Personality Inventory, Version II, Restructured Form (MMPI-2-RF)*. It consists of only 338 true/false questions and has two additional clinical scales on top of the 10 used in the MMPI-2.

How can you tell if a person is telling the truth on a personality inventory? *Validity scales*, which are built into any well-designed psychological inventory, are intended to indicate whether or not a person taking the inventory is responding honestly. Responses to certain items on the test will indicate if people are trying to make themselves look better or worse than they are, for example, and certain items are repeated throughout the test in a slightly different form, so that anyone trying to "fake" the test will have difficultly responding to those items consistently (Butcher et al., 2001). For example, if one of the statements is "I am always happy" and a person responds "true" to that statement, the suspicion would be that this person is trying to look better than he or she really is. If several of the validity scale questions are answered in this way, the conclusion is that the person is not being honest.

► How can you tell if a person is telling the truth on a personality inventory?

PROBLEMS WITH PERSONALITY INVENTORIES   The advantage of personality inventories over projective tests and interviews is that inventories are standardized (i.e., everyone gets exactly the same questions, and the answers are scored in exactly the same way). In fact, responses to inventories are often scored on a computer. Observer bias and bias of interpretation are simply not possible because this kind of assessment is objective rather than subjective. The validity and reliability of personality inventories are generally recognized as being greatly superior to that of projective tests (Anastasi & Urbina, 1997).

There are some problems, however. The validity scales, for example, are a good check against cheating, but they are not perfect. Some people are still able to fake their answers and respond in what they feel are the socially appropriate ways (Anastasi & Urbina, 1997; Hicklin & Widiger, 2000). Other problems have to do with human nature itself: Some people may develop a habit of picking a particular answer rather than carefully considering the statement, whereas others may simply grow tired of responding to all those statements and start picking answers at random.

PRACTICE QUIZ: HOW MUCH DO YOU REMEMBER?

Pick the best answer.

1. Which of the following is not one of the traits found to have a genetic component in studies of identical twins?
 a. intelligence
 b. leadership abilities
 c. antagonism
 d. aggressiveness

2. The five-factor model trait dimensions have been shown to have
 a. no relevance in other cultures.
 b. only a 20 percent rate of heritability.
 c. relevance only for Western cultures.
 d. about a 50 percent rate of heritability across cultures.

3. Which of the following countries would be most likely to have an individualistic trait, according to Hofstede?
 a. Japan
 b. Vietnam
 c. Canada
 d. Brazil

4. Which of the following methods is least likely to be used by a behaviourist?
 a. interview
 b. projective test
 c. direct observation
 d. personality inventory

5. Which method of personality assessment offers the most objective measurement?
 a. interview
 b. projective test
 c. direct observation
 d. personality inventory

6. Observer bias would be a problem for any of the following methods except
 a. interview.
 b. projective test.
 c. direct observation.
 d. personality inventory.

APPLYING PSYCHOLOGY TO EVERYDAY LIFE: PROCRASTINATION AND PERSONALITY IN THE TWENTY-FIRST CENTURY

11.11   *How is procrastination related to the Big Five, and how has the creation of the World Wide Web changed how people procrastinate?*

Many psychologists believe that procrastination is linked to personality. One such psychologist is Tim Pychyl, a psychology professor and the director of the Procrastination Research Group (PRG) at Carleton University in Ottawa. The group was created as a result of Pychyl noticing a theme that was present during many of his interviews with research participants. During these interviews, many participants complained that they were having trouble with procrastination and that the procrastination was having a negative impact on their well-being. The group has now become an international research site, involving collaboration between researchers from all over the world (e.g., the United States, Australia, Europe, and the Middle East).

Pychyl and the PRG have focused a great deal on personality traits and situations, specifically looking at the Big Five's relation to procrastination. Pychyl has found that procrastinators tend to be low in conscientiousness and high in impulsivity (which can be related to extraversion or neuroticism). It is believed by many that procrastination is linked to perfectionism, but Piers Steel of the University of Calgary has recently shown that this is not the case. According to Steel, "Procrastinators are actually less likely, not more, to be perfectionists" (2007, p. 81).

Currently, it is estimated that 80 to 95 percent of college and university students procrastinate at one point in time or another (Ellis & Knaus, 1977; O'Brien, 2002) and approximately 75 percent consider themselves procrastinators (Potts, 1987). According to Kachgal, Hansen, and Nutter (2001), these percentages seem to be increasing as we move further into the twenty-first century.

Pychyl and colleagues have looked at the impact of the internet on procrastination. Across the world, internet usage increased from approximately 40 million users in 1996 to 375 million in the year 2000 (Brym & Lenton, 2001). As of 2008, the current estimate of internet users across the world is more than 1.4 billion people! Sixty-six percent of Canadians and 71 percent of Americans are now using the internet on a regular basis (Internet World Stats, 2008). In a 2001 study, Pychyl and his colleagues at the PRG have found that "cyberslacking" is very prevalent among users of the internet: Almost 51 percent of participants procrastinated through internet use on a frequent basis and 47 percent of all time spent online for all participants involved self-reported procrastination (Lavoie & Pychyl, 2001).

Procrastination used to involve such tasks as organizing your closet, alphabetizing your CD collection, or cleaning out your fridge. Now, in this "Internet Age," procrastination has taken on a newer, more technological look—that of Facebook, MSN Messenger, YouTube, or Myspace.

If you are interested in learning about how to combat procrastination or the PRG in general, go to **http://http-server.carleton.ca/~tpychyl/index.html**. (But remember—visiting internet sites can lead to procrastination!)

Questions for Further Discussion

1. Given that procrastination has changed greatly in the past 20 years, do you think that it will change even further in the next 20 years? If so, how will it change?

2. Do you believe that it is possible for a procrastinator to stop procrastinating or is procrastination a characteristic that is inborn and cannot be changed?

3. How might college or university students use the research from the PRG's website to benefit their academic lives?

11

CHAPTER SUMMARY

Theories of Personality

11.1 *What is personality, and how do the various perspectives in psychology view personality?*

- Personality is the unique way individuals think, feel, and act. It is different from character and temperament but includes those aspects.

- The four perspectives in the study of personality are the psychoanalytic, behaviouristic (including social cognitive theory), humanistic, and trait perspectives.

The Man and the Couch: Sigmund Freud and Psychoanalysis

11.2 *How did Freud's historical view of the mind and personality form a basis for psychodynamic theory?*

- According to Freud's topographic model, the three divisions of the mind are the conscious, preconscious, and unconscious.

- Freud's structural model states that there are three parts of personality: the id, ego, and superego.

- The id works on the pleasure principle and the ego works on the reality principle.

- The superego is the moral centre of personality, containing the ego ideal and the conscience, and is the source of moral anxiety.

- The conflicts between the demands of the id and the rules and restrictions of the superego lead to anxiety for the ego, which uses defence mechanisms to deal with that anxiety.

- The personality develops in a series of psychosexual stages: oral (id dominated), anal (ego develops), phallic (superego develops), latency (period of sexual repression), and genital (sexual feelings reawaken with appropriate targets).

- The Oedipus and Electra complexes (sexual "crushes" on the opposite-sex parent) create anxiety in the phallic stage, which is resolved through identification with the same-sex parent.

- Fixation occurs when conflicts are not fully resolved during a stage, resulting in adult personality characteristics reflecting childhood inadequacies.

11.3 *How did Jung, Adler, Horney, and Erikson modify Freud's theory?*

- The neo-Freudians changed the focus of psychoanalysis to fit their own interpretations of the personality.

- Jung developed a theory of a collective unconscious.

- Adler proposed feelings of inferiority as the driving force behind personality and developed birth order theory.

- Horney developed a theory based on basic anxiety and rejected the concept of penis envy.

- Erikson developed a theory based on social rather than sexual relationships, covering the entire lifespan.

11.4 *How does modern psychoanalytic theory differ from that of Freud?*

- Current research has found support for the defence mechanisms and the concept of an unconscious mind that can influence

conscious behaviour, but other concepts cannot be scientifically researched.

The Behaviourist and Social Cognitive View of Personality

11.5 *How do behaviourists and social cognitive theorists explain personality?*

- Behaviourists define personality as a set of learned responses or habits.

- The social cognitive view of personality includes the concept of reciprocal determinism, in which the environment, characteristics of the person, and the behaviour itself all interact.

- Self-efficacy is a characteristic in which a person perceives a behaviour as more or less effective based on previous experiences, the opinions of others, and perceived personal competencies.

- Behaviourist personality theory has scientific support but is criticized as being too simplistic.

The Third Force: Humanism and Personality

11.6 *How do humanists such as Carl Rogers explain personality?*

- Humanism developed as a reaction against the negativity of psychoanalysis and the deterministic nature of behaviourism.

- Carl Rogers proposed that self-actualization depends on proper development of the self-concept.

- The self-concept includes the real self and the ideal self. When these two components do not match or agree, anxiety and disordered behaviour are the results.

- Unconditional positive regard from important others in a person's life helps the formation of the self-concept and the congruity of the real and ideal selves, leading to a fully functioning person.

- Humanistic theory is not scientifically researched but has been effective in therapy situations.

Trait Theories: Who Are You?

11.7 *What are the history and current views of the trait perspective?*

- Trait theorists describe personality traits in order to predict behaviour.

- Allport first developed a list of about 200 traits and believed that these traits were part of the nervous system.

- Cattell reduced the number of traits to between 16 and 23 with a computer method called *factor analysis*.

- Several researchers have arrived at five trait dimensions that have research support across cultures, called the *Big Five* or *five-factor model*. The five factors are openness to experience, conscientiousness, extraversion, agreeableness, and neuroticism (OCEAN).

- Cross-cultural research has found support for the five-factor model of personality traits in a number of different cultures.

- Future research will explore the degree to which child-rearing practices and heredity may influence the five personality factors.

Psychology in the News: Canadians and Americans Aren't That Different

11.8 *Do the personalities of Canadians and Americans differ?*

• Canadians and Americans believe they are significantly different from one another when it comes to personality. Despite these beliefs, research has found that very few differences exist between Canadians and Americans in terms of personality.

The Biology of Personality: Behavioural Genetics

• Behavioural genetics is a field of study of the relationship between heredity and personality.

11.9 *What part do biology, heredity, and culture play in personality?*

• Studies of twins and adopted children have found support for a genetic influence on many personality traits, including intelligence, leadership abilities, traditionalism, nurturance, empathy, assertiveness, neuroticism, and extraversion.

Classic Studies In Psychology: Geert Hofstede's Four Dimensions of Cultural Personality

• Hofstede's cross-cultural management study revealed four basic dimensions of personality along which cultures may vary: individualism/collectivism, power distance, masculinity/femininity, and uncertainty avoidance.

Assessment of Personality

11.10 *What are the advantages and disadvantages of using the following measures of personality: interviews, projective tests, behavioural assessment, and personality inventories?*

• Interviews are used primarily by psychoanalysts and humanists and can include structured or unstructured interviews.

• Disadvantages of interviews can include the halo effect and bias of the interpretation on the part of the interviewer.

• Projective tests are based on the defence mechanism of projection and are used by psychoanalysts. Projective tests include the Rorschach inkblot test and the Thematic Apperception Test.

• Projective tests can be useful in finding starting points to open a dialogue between therapist and client but have been criticized for being low in reliability and validity.

• Behavioural assessments are primarily used by behaviourists and include direct observation of behaviour, rating scales of specific behaviour, and frequency counts of behaviour.

• Behavioural assessments have the disadvantage of the observer effect, which causes an observed person's behaviour to change, and observer bias on the part of the person doing the assessment.

• Personality inventories are typically developed by trait theorists and provide a detailed description of certain personality traits. They are objective tests rather than subjective.

• The NEO-PI is based on the five-factor model, whereas the Myers-Briggs Type Indicator is based on Jung's theory of personality types.

• The MMPI-2 is designed to detect abnormal personality. A newer, alternative version of the MMPI-2 (MMPI-2-RF) has been designed but it is not meant to replace the MMPI-2.

• To conduct cross-cultural research, researchers have developed and used both verbal measures (e.g., the PRF) and non-verbal measures (e.g., FF-NPQ)

• Personality inventories include validity scales to prevent cheating, but such measures are not perfect and cheating is sometimes possible.

Applying Psychology to Everyday Life: Procrastination and Personality in the Twenty-First Century

11.11 *How is procrastination related to the Big Five, and how has the creation of the World Wide Web changed how people procrastinate?*

• Procrastinators tend to be low in conscientiousness and high in impulsivity, which can be linked to extraversion or neuroticism.

• Internet usage has increased from 40 million users in 1996 to more than 1.4 billion users in 2008.

• Research has shown that internet users report spending almost half of their time online procrastinating.

11 KEY TERMS

TEST YOURSELF

Pick the best answer.

1. Which of the following is the definition of personality?
a. the characteristics with which each person is born
b. the moral and ethical behaviour of a person
c. the unique way an individual thinks, feels, and acts
d. changes in behaviour according to experiences

2. Which of Freud's parts of the personality is the most like short-term memory?
a. conscious
b. preconscious
c. unconscious
d. subconscious

3. Stephen wants a new MP3 player that he saw in the local electronics store, but he doesn't have enough money to pay for it. Which structure of Stephen's personality would urge him to take the player while no one in the store was looking?
a. id
b. ego
c. superego
d. libido

4. Which structure of the personality, according to Freud, works on the reality principle?
a. id
b. ego
c. superego
d. libido

5. The _____ develops in the _____ stage as a result of identification.
a. ego; oral
b. id; oral
c. superego; phallic
d. superego; latency

6. Three-year-old Brandon has watched his father, a chef, when he prepares meals for the family. This year, Brandon has asked for a play kitchen for his birthday. Freud would say that Brandon is beginning the process of _____ as a way of resolving his Oedipal conflict.
a. compensation
b. identification
c. sublimation
d. denial

7. According to Adler, middle children tend to be
a. overachieving.
b. competitive.
c. resentful of the freedom of the older child.
d. filled with feelings of superiority.

8. Research has begun to show some support for which of Freud's concepts?
a. the existence of an id, ego, and superego
b. the order of the psychosexual stages
c. the concept of an unconscious mind
d. the existence of the Oedipus complex

9. To explain a person's personality, behaviourists would look to
a. early childhood emotional traumas.
b. the unconditional positive regard given to the person by his or her parents.
c. the early experiences of rewards and punishments for certain behaviour.
d. the constellation of personality traits possessed by the person.

10. For Bandura, one of the most important person variables in determining personality is
a. self-efficacy.
b. self-concept.
c. self-determination.
d. self-motivation.

11. Unlike psychoanalysis, the social cognitive view of personality
a. tries to explain how people become the people they are.
b. stresses the importance of early childhood in personality development.
c. is fully able to explain all the complexities of human behaviour.
d. has been scientifically tested.

12. The striving for fulfillment of one's potential is called
a. self-concept.
b. self-efficacy.
c. self-actualization.
d. the ideal self.

13. According to Rogers, anxiety and neurotic behaviour result from
a. unconscious conflicts and desires.
b. a mismatch between the real and ideal self.
c. receiving too much unconditional positive regard from significant others.
d. learned habits of behaviour.

14. Which of the following viewpoints has different goals from the other three?
a. psychoanalytic
b. behaviourism
c. humanism
d. trait theory

15. How many source traits did Cattell use in developing his personality inventory?
a. 5
b. 10
c. 16
d. 23

16. The five-factor model of personality traits includes all but which of the following?
a. openness to experience
b. self-sufficiency
c. extraversion
d. neuroticism

17. Dr. Phillips is constantly late for his classes and often shows up late for his office hours, leaving students waiting in the hallway outside his door for nearly an hour at times. Using the five-factor model, which dimension would show a very low score for Dr. Phillips?
    a. self-sufficiency
    c. agreeableness
    b. openness to experience
    d. conscientiousness

18. What has research found with respect to beliefs surrounding Canadians' and Americans' personalities?
    a. Canadians and Americans believe that they are very different from one another and, in actuality, are very different from one another.
    b. Canadians and Americans believe that they are very similar to one another but, in actuality, are very different from one another.
    c. Canadians and Americans believe that they are very different from one another but, in actuality, they are not
    d. None of the above.

19. Research by Tim Pychyl and the PRG at Carleton University has found that people who procrastinate are more likely to be high in
    a. impulsivity.
    c. openness to experience.
    b. conscientiousness.
    d. extraversion.

20. The study of the inherited portions of personality is called
    a. twin studies.
    c. behavioural genetics.
    b. adoptive studies.
    d. adoptive genetics.

21. According to Hofstede, cultures that have many strict rules and laws, lots of security and safety measures, and that tend to hold only one philosophical or religious belief are high in
    a. individualism.
    c. masculinity.
    b. power distance.
    d. uncertainty avoidance.

22. If a client is having trouble talking about what is bothering him, a psychoanalyst might turn to a(n) _____ to probe the client's unconscious conflicts.
    a. objective test
    c. personality inventory
    b. projective test
    d. observational study

23. The Rorschach test has people
    a. tell stories about a picture with people in it.
    b. answer hundreds of questions about their feelings and thoughts.
    c. perform tasks while an observer watches through a one-way mirror.
    d. look at ambiguous visual stimuli and tell what they think it is.

24. Which type of assessment would have the least problem with reliability?
    a. subjective test
    c. personality inventory
    b. projective test
    d. observational study

25. Which of the following is not a type of behavioural assessment?
    a. direct observation
    c. rating scale
    b. Thematic Apperception Test
    d. frequency count

Answers: 1.-c, 2.-a, 3.-a, 4.-b, 5.-c, 6.-b, 7.-b, 8.-c, 9.-c, 10.-a, 11.-d, 12.-c, 13.-b, 14.-d, 15.-c, 16.-b, 17.-d, 18.-c, 19.-a, 20.-c, 21.-d, 22.-b, 23.-d, 24.-c, 25.-b.

ScanLife™ Barcode

To access more tests and your own personalized study plan that will help you focus on the areas you need to master before your next class test, be sure to go to **www.MyPsychLab.com**, Pearson Education Canada's online psychology website, available with the access code packaged with your book.

Personality: unique way individuals think, feel, and act	Four perspectives are: 1. Psychoanalytic 2. Behaviourist (including social cognitive theory) 3. Humanist 4. Trait

11.1

Theories of Personality

PSYCHOANALYTIC

BEHAVIOURIST

Jung, Adler, Horney, and Erickson's Modifications of Freud

Jung: theory of a collective unconscious

Adler: feelings of inferiority as the force behind personality

Horney: theory based on basic anxiety, rejected penis envy concept

Erikson: developed a theory based on social relationships

11.3

Freud's View of the Conscious Mind

Three Divisions: conscious, preconscious, and unconscious

11.2

Modern Psychoanalytic Theory

Research supports defence mechanisms, unconscious mind. Other concepts are unable to be scientifically researched.

11.4

Behaviourist Theories of Personality

Personality: set of learned responses or habits

Social cognitive: concept of reciprocal determinism: the environment, person, and behaviour interact

Self-efficacy: person perceives behaviour as more or less effective based on previous experiences, opinions of others, perceived personal competencies.

Behaviourist theory: is criticized as being too simplistic

11.5

Freud's Three Parts of the Personality: Id, Ego, and Superego

▸ **Id:** works on the pleasure principle
▸ **Ego:** works on the reality principle
▸ **Superego:** is the moral centre of personality

Conflict between id and superego leads to anxiety for ego.

11.2

Freudian Stages of Personality Development

Personality develops in a series of psychosexual stages:
▸ Oral (id dominated)   ▸ Anal (ego develops)   ▸ Phallic (superego develops)
▸ Latency (period of sexual repression)   ▸ Genital (sexual feelings)

Oedipus and Electra complexes:
▸ Create anxiety in the phallic stage
▸ Resolved through identification with the same-sex parent

Fixation: occurs when conflicts are not fully resolved during a stage

11.2

Interviews as Measures of Personality

▸ Interviews used primarily by psychoanalysts and humanists
▸ Can include structured or unstructured interviews
▸ Disadvantages: halo effect and biased interpretations

11.10

INK BLOT

THEMATIC APPERCEPTION TEST

Projective Tests

▸ Based on defence mechanism of projection
▸ Include Rorschach inkblots and Thematic Apperception Test
▸ Criticized for being low in reliability and validity

11.10

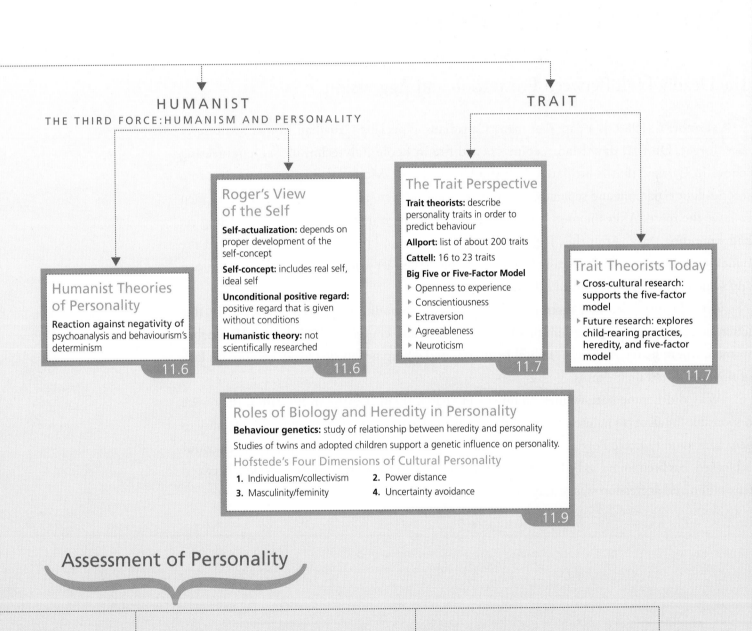

HUMANIST
THE THIRD FORCE: HUMANISM AND PERSONALITY

TRAIT

Roger's View of the Self

Self-actualization: depends on proper development of the self-concept

Self-concept: includes real self, ideal self

Unconditional positive regard: positive regard that is given without conditions

Humanistic theory: not scientifically researched

11.6

Humanist Theories of Personality

Reaction against negativity of psychoanalysis and behaviourism's determinism

11.6

The Trait Perspective

Trait theorists: describe personality traits in order to predict behaviour

Allport: list of about 200 traits

Cattell: 16 to 23 traits

Big Five or Five-Factor Model
▸ Openness to experience
▸ Conscientiousness
▸ Extraversion
▸ Agreeableness
▸ Neuroticism

11.7

Trait Theorists Today

▸ Cross-cultural research: supports the five-factor model
▸ Future research: explores child-rearing practices, heredity, and five-factor model

11.7

Roles of Biology and Heredity in Personality

Behaviour genetics: study of relationship between heredity and personality

Studies of twins and adopted children support a genetic influence on personality.

Hofstede's Four Dimensions of Cultural Personality

1. Individualism/collectivism
2. Power distance
3. Masculinity/feminity
4. Uncertainty avoidance

11.9

Assessment of Personality

Behavioural Assessments Used in Assessing Personality

▸ Include direct observation, rating scales, and frequency counts
▸ Disadvantages: observer effect and observer bias

11.10

Personality Inventories

▸ Developed by trait theorists
▸ Provide detailed description of personality traits
▸ Objective tests rather than subjective
  —NEO-PI: based on the five-factor model
  —Myers-Briggs Type Indicator: based on Jung's theory of personality types
  —MMPI-2: designed to detect abnormal personality

11.10

Procrastination

▸ Procrastinators tend to be low in conscientiousness and high in impulsivity.
▸ Internet users report spending almost half of their time online procrastinating.

11.11

12
Social Psychology

The Deadly Link Between Frustration and Aggression

December 6, 1989, is a date that many Canadians, especially Canadian women, will never forget. On that day, Marc Lepine opened fire in École Polytechnique, an engineering school in Quebec that is affiliated with the Université de Montréal. Lepine went first to a second-floor classroom and separated the women from the men, allowing approximately 50 men to leave the room. After the men left, he opened fire on the nine remaining women, killing six and wounding three. After this, Lepine left the classroom and proceeded to other areas of the building. By the end of his shooting spree, Lepine had killed 14 women, had wounded 9 women and 4 men, and had finally killed himself.

After Lepine's death, a three-page suicide letter was found in his jacket pocket. In this letter, he blamed feminists for ruining his life. The letter also contained a "hit list" of 19 Quebec women, whom he referred to as "radical feminists" and whom he labelled lucky because his lack of time prevented their deaths.

Why did Lepine hate women so much? He hated them because in his mind, they were responsible for all of his failures. In particular, he blamed women and feminism for his inability to gain admission to École Polytechnique. Frustration, which occurs when goal-directed behaviour is blocked, has been found to be linked with aggressive acts. In this particular case, the link between frustration and aggression was deadly.

Why study social psychology?

If people lived in total isolation from other people, there would be no reason to study the effect that other people have on the behaviour of individuals and groups. But human beings are social creatures—we live with others, work with others, and play with others. The people who surround us all of our lives have an impact on our beliefs and values, decisions and assumptions, and the way we think about other people in general. Why are some people prejudiced toward certain other people? Why do we obey some people but not others? What causes us to like, to love, or to hate others? The answers to all these questions and many more can be found in the study of social psychology.

12

LEARNING OBJECTIVES

Chapter One defined psychology as the scientific study of behaviour and mental processes, including how people think and feel. The field of social psychology also looks at behaviour and mental processes but includes as well the social world in which we exist, as we are surrounded by others to whom we are connected and by whom we are influenced in so many ways. It is not the same field as *sociology*, which is the study and classification of human societies. Sociology studies the big picture: how entire groups of people live, work, and play. Although social psychology does look at group behaviour, it is more concerned with the individual person within the group and the influence of the group on the person.

Social psychology is the scientific study of how a person's behaviour, thoughts, and feelings are influenced by the real, imagined, or implied presence of others. Although there are several sections in this chapter, there are really only three main areas under discussion: *social influence*, the ways in which a person's behaviour can be affected by other people; *social cognition*, the ways in which people think about other people; and *social interaction*, the positive and negative aspects of people relating to others.

SOCIAL INFLUENCE: CONFORMITY, COMPLIANCE, AND OBEDIENCE

People live in a world filled with other people. An infant is born into a world with adults who have an impact on the infant's actions, personality, and growth. Adults must interact with others on a daily basis. Such interactions provide ample opportunity for the presence of other people to directly or indirectly influence the behaviour, feelings, and thoughts of each individual in a process called **social influence**. There are many forms of social influence. People can influence others to follow along with their own actions or thoughts, to agree to do things even when the person might prefer to do otherwise, and to be obedient to authorities. The mere presence of others can even influence the way people perform tasks successfully or unsuccessfully.

CONFORMITY

12.1 *What factors influence people to conform to the actions of others?*

Have you ever noticed someone looking up at something? Did the urge to look up to see what that person was looking at become so strong that you actually found yourself looking up? This common practical joke always works, even when people suspect

---

Watch on mypsychlab

Infomercials

---

social psychology
the scientific study of how a person's thoughts, feelings, and behaviour are influenced by the real, imagined, or implied presence of others.

social influence
the process through which the real or implied presence of others can directly or indirectly influence the thoughts, feelings, and behaviour of an individual.

that it's a joke. It clearly demonstrates the power of **conformity**: changing one's own behaviour to more closely match the actions of others.

SHERIF'S EXPERIMENT ON NORM FORMATION   In 1936, social psychologist Muzafer Sherif conducted a study in which participants were shown into a darkened room and exposed to a single point of light. Under those conditions, a point of light will seem to move because of tiny, involuntary movements of the eye known as *saccades*. LINK to *Chapter Three: Sensation and Perception, p. 88*. The participants were not told of this effect (called the *autokinetic effect*) and reported the light moved anywhere from a few inches to several feet. When a confederate (a person chosen by the experimenter to deliberately manipulate the situation) also gave estimates, the original participants began to make estimates of motion that were more and more similar to those of the confederate (Sherif, 1936). This early experiment on conformity has been criticized because the judgments being made were ambiguous (i.e., the light wasn't really moving so any estimate within reason would sound good). Would participants be so easily swayed if the judgments were more specifically measurable and certain?

ASCH'S CLASSIC STUDY ON CONFORMITY   Solomon Asch (1951) conducted his classic study of conformity by having participants gather in a room. They were told that they were participating in an experiment on visual judgment. They were then shown a card with three lines of varying lengths followed by another card with only one line on it. The task was to determine which line on the first card was most similar to the line on the second card (see Figure 12.1).

In reality, only one (usually the next-to-last or the last) person in the group was a real participant. The others were all confederates who were instructed to pick the same *incorrect* line from the comparison lines. Would the real participant, having heard the others pick what seemed to be the wrong answer, change his or her answer to conform to the group's opinion? Surprisingly, the participants conformed a little over one-third of the time. Asch also found that the number of confederates mattered: Conformity increased with each new confederate until there were four confederates; more than that did not increase the participants' tendency to conform (Asch, 1951). In a later experiment, Asch (1956) found that conformity decreased if there was just one confederate who gave the correct answer—apparently, if participants knew that there was at least one other person whose answer was different from that of the group (even if his or her answer was wrong), they felt more comfortable going against the group themselves.

More recent research in North America has found less conformity among participants, perhaps suggesting that the Asch conformity effect was due to the more conforming nature of people in the era and culture of the 1950s (Lalancette & Standing, 1990; Nicholson et al., 1985; Perrin & Spencer, 1980). In other cultures, however, studies have found conformity effects similar to those in Asch's study (Neto, 1995). Still others have found even greater effects of conformity in collectivist cultures such as Hong Kong, Japan, and Zimbabwe (Bond & Smith, 1996; Kim & Markus, 1999). This cultural difference may exist only when face-to-face contact is a part of the task, however. A recent study found that when the Asch

conformity
changing one's own behaviour to match that of other people.

"But Mom, all the girls are doing it."

Conformity

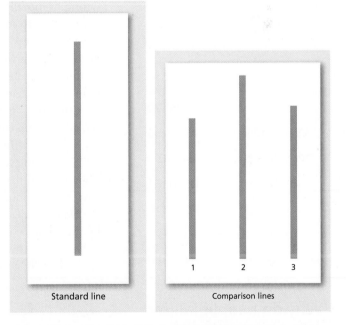

FIGURE 12.1 **Stimuli Used in Asch's Study** Participants in Asch's famous study on conformity were first shown the three comparison lines. They were then shown the standard line and asked to determine to which of the three comparison lines the standard line was most similar. Which line would you pick? What if you were one of several people, and everyone who answered ahead of you chose line 3? How would that affect your answer?

Source: Adapted from Asch (1956).

What about gender— are men or women more conforming? ▶

Many historical events have been at least partly caused by the phenomenon of groupthink. The Walkerton, Ontario, water crisis, in which an E. coli outbreak killed seven people and made hundreds of others sick, is one of those events. According to the local medical officer of health, Dr. Murray McQuigge, the disaster could have been prevented. Apparently, the Walkerton Public Utilities Commission knew there was a problem with the water several days before the public was informed.

I have a friend who watches infomercials on shopping channels and buys items that aren't worth the money or that don't work like they're supposed to work. Why do people fall for pitches like that? ▶

groupthink
kind of thinking that occurs when people place more importance on maintaining group cohesiveness than on assessing the facts of the problem with which the group is concerned.

judgment task is presented in an online format (participants were in communication but not able to see each other), the cultural difference disappears (Cinnirella & Green, 2007).

What about gender—are men or women more conforming? Research shows that gender differences are practically non-existent unless the situation involves behaviour that is not private. If it is possible to give responses in private, conformity is no greater for women than for men, but if a public response is required, women do tend to show more conformity than men (Eagly, 1987; Eagly et al., 2000). This effect may be due to the socialization that women receive in being agreeable and supportive; however, the difference in conformity is quite small.

THE HAZARDS OF GROUPTHINK Before the 1912 sinking of the *Titanic*, the group responsible for the ship's design and construction and the ship's captain and crew assumed the *Titanic* was unsinkable and did not even bother to include enough lifeboats on board for all the passengers. This classic example shows that an error can occur in situations when the pressure to conform to the group norm outweighs any evidence that the group norm is wrong. This kind of thinking, in which people feel it is more important to maintain the group's cohesiveness than to consider the facts more realistically, is called **groupthink** (Hogg & Hains, 1998; Janis, 1972, 1982; Schafer & Crichlow, 1996). Other examples include the *Challenger* disaster of 1986 in which a part on the shuttle was known by a few to be unacceptable (but no one spoke up to delay the launch), the Walkerton water crisis in Canada, and, according to many, the invasion of Iraq by the United States.

Why does groupthink happen? Social psychologist Irving Janis (1972, 1982), who originally gave this phenomenon its name, lists several "symptoms" of groupthink. For example, group members may come to feel that the group can do no wrong, is morally correct, and will always succeed, creating the illusion of invulnerability. Group members also tend to hold stereotyped views of those who disagree with the group's opinions, causing members to think that those who oppose the group have no worthwhile opinions. They exert pressure on individual members to conform to group opinion, prevent those who might disagree from speaking up, and even censor themselves so that the group's mindset will not be disturbed in a "don't rock the boat" mentality. Self-appointed "mind-guards" work to protect the leader of the group from contrary viewpoints.

Several things can be done to minimize the possibility of groupthink (Hart, 1998; McCauley, 1998; Moorhead et al., 1998). For example, leaders should remain impartial and the entire group should seek the opinions of people outside the group. Any voting should be done on secret ballots rather than by a show of hands, and it should be made clear that group members will be held responsible for decisions made by the group.

COMPLIANCE

12.2 *How is compliance defined, and what are four common ways to gain the compliance of another?*

I have a friend who watches infomercials on shopping channels and buys items that aren't worth the money or that don't work like they're supposed to work. Why do people fall for pitches like that? Marketing products is a psychological process. But infomercials are not the only means by which people try to get others to do what they want them to do. **Compliance** occurs when people change their behaviour as a result of another person or group asking or directing them to change. The person or group asking for the change in behaviour typically doesn't have any real authority or power to command a change; when they do have authority, the compliance is called *obedience*, which is the topic of the next major section of this chapter.

A number of techniques that people use to get the compliance of others clearly show the relationship of compliance to the world of marketing, as they refer to techniques that salespeople would commonly use.

FOOT-IN-THE-DOOR TECHNIQUE   Let's say that a neighbour asks you to keep an eye on his house while he is on vacation. You agree, thinking that it's a rather small request. Later that day, or perhaps even in the same conversation, the neighbour asks if you would kindly water his plants while he's gone. This is a little bit more involved and requires more of your time and energy. Will you do it? If you are like most people, you probably will comply with this second larger request.

When compliance with a smaller request is followed by a larger request, people are quite likely to comply because they have already agreed to the smaller one and they want to behave consistently with their previous response (Cialdini et al., 1995; Dillard, 1990, 1991; Freedman & Fraser, 1966). This is called the **foot-in-the-door technique** because the first small request acts as an opener. (Salespeople once literally stuck a foot in the door to prevent the occupant from shutting it so they could continue their sales pitch, hence the name.) Chances are you have already used this technique with your parents or friends. For example, if you have ever asked a parent for a toonie so you can buy a coffee and after receiving it asked for a little bit more money to buy a sandwich as well, you have used this common technique.

DOOR-IN-THE-FACE TECHNIQUE   Closely related to the foot-in-the-door technique is its opposite: the **door-in-the-face technique** (Cialdini et al., 1975). In this method, the larger request comes first, which is usually refused. The first appeal is followed by a second, smaller and more reasonable request that often gets compliance. A good example of this is asking your parents for a brand new car, knowing that your wish will most likely not be granted. Once your request is denied, you can then ask to simply borrow the family car, which you will probably be allowed to do.

This technique relies on the **norm of reciprocity**, which basically assumes that if someone does something for a person, the person should do something in return (Gouldner, 1960). So how does this norm relate to the door-in-the-face technique? According to Cialdini and colleagues (1975), the norm of reciprocity entails that people should make concessions to those who make concessions to them. In the example of asking for a car, because you made a concession in your request by asking for something more reasonable, your parents will feel as though they need to make a concession, too: lending you the family car.

LOWBALL TECHNIQUE   Another compliance technique, also common in the world of sales, is called the **lowball technique** (Burger & Petty, 1981). In this technique, once a commitment is made, the cost of that commitment is increased. (In the sense used here, *cost* does not necessarily mean money; *cost* can also mean time, effort, or other kinds of sacrifices.) A common example will seem familiar to any student who has ever bought a new laptop for school. The commitment to buy the laptop at one low price is quickly followed by the addition of other costs: extended warranties, additional software, taxes and fees, and so on, causing the buyer to spend more money than originally intended.

THAT'S-NOT-ALL TECHNIQUE   Finally, there is the now familiar technique of the infomercial salesperson: the **that's-not-all technique**. In this compliance tactic, the person doing the persuading makes an offer, but before the target of the offer can

compliance
changing one's behaviour as a result of other people directing or asking for the change.

foot-in-the-door technique
asking for a small commitment and, after gaining compliance, asking for a bigger commitment.

door-in-the-face technique
asking for a large commitment and being refused, and then asking for a smaller commitment.

norm of reciprocity
assumption that if someone does something for a person, that person should do something for the other in return.

lowball technique
getting a commitment from a person and then raising the cost of that commitment.

that's-not-all technique
a sales technique in which the persuader makes an offer and then adds something extra to make the offer look better before the target person can make a decision.

👁 **Watch on mypsychlab**
Sales Techniques

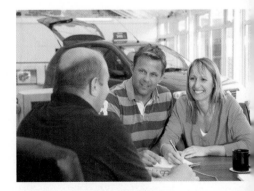

This couple is in the process of buying a new car. Car salespeople often use the lowball technique by quoting what sounds like a reasonable price to potential buyers. Once this couple has committed to buying a particular car, they may find that other costs are tacked on to that original price, such as additional options, extended warranties, and other fees. Can you think of other instances when something like this has happened to you?

make a decision, the persuader throws in something extra to make the deal look even better (Burger, 1986). See if this sounds familiar:

"But wait—that's not all! If you act now, we'll send you this 15-piece set of genuine faux carving knives as a bonus!"

By offering something that the consumer did not ask for in the first place, the persuader has once again activated the norm of reciprocity. Now the consumer feels as though the persuader has "given" something and the consumer should respond by giving in to the persuader's request to buy the product.

Cultural differences exist in people's susceptibility to these techniques. For the foot-in-the door technique in particular, research has shown that people in individualist cultures (such as Canada) are more likely to comply with the second request than are people in collectivist cultures (such as Japan). The research suggests that people in collectivist cultures are not as concerned with being consistent with previous behaviour because they are less focused on their inner motivation than are people in individualist cultures, who are more concerned with their inner motives and consistency (Cialdini et al., 1999; Iyengar & Brockner, in press; Petrova et al., 2003). **LINK** to *Chapter Eleven: Theories of Personality, p. 438.*

OBEDIENCE

12.3 What makes people obey the instructions or orders of others?

There is a difference between the concepts of compliance, which is agreeing to change one's behaviour because someone else asks for the change, and **obedience**, which is changing one's behaviour at the direct order of an authority figure. A salesperson who wants a person to buy a car has no real power to force that person to buy, but an authority figure is a person with social power—such as a police officer, a professor, or a work supervisor—who has the right to demand certain behaviour from the people under the authority figure's command or supervision.

How far will people go in obeying the commands of an authority figure? What factors make obedience more or less likely? Researchers have been investigating these sorts of questions for many years. The answers to these questions became very important not only to researchers but also to people everywhere after the atrocities committed by the soldiers in Nazi Germany—soldiers who were "just following orders."

MILGRAM'S SHOCKING RESEARCH   Social psychologist Stanley Milgram set out to find answers to these questions. He was aware of Asch's studies of conformity and wondered how much impact social influence could have on a behaviour that was more meaningful than judging the length of lines on cards. He designed what has become one of the most famous experiments in the history of psychology.

Through ads placed in the local newspaper, Milgram recruited people who were told that they would be participating in an experiment to test the effects of punishment on learning behaviour (Milgram, 1964a, 1974). Although there were several different forms of this experiment with different participants, the basic premise was the same: The participants believed that they had randomly been assigned to either the "teacher" role or the "learner" role, when in fact the "learner" was an actor already aware of the situation. The "teacher" was given a sample 45-volt shock from the chair in which the "learner" was strapped during the experiment. The task for the learner was a simple memory test for paired words.

The "teacher" was seated in front of a machine through which the shocks would be administered and the level of the shocks changed (see Figure 12.2). For each mistake made by the "learner," the "teacher" was instructed to increase the level of shock

obedience
changing one's behaviour at the command of an authority figure.

by 15 volts. The "learner" (who was not actually shocked) followed a carefully arranged script, showing discomfort, asking for the experiment to end, screaming, and even falling silent as if unconscious—or dead. (See Table 12.1 for samples of the scripted responses of the "learner.") As the "teachers" became reluctant to continue administering the shocks, the experimenter in his authoritative white lab coat said, for example, "The experiment requires you to continue" or "You must continue," and reminded the "teacher" that the experimenter would take full responsibility for the safety of the "learner."

How many of the participants continued to administer what they believed were real shocks? Milgram surveyed psychiatrists, college students, and other adults prior to the experiments for their opinions on how far the participants would go in administering shocks. Everyone predicted that the participants would all refuse to go on at some point, with most believing that the majority of the participants would start refusing as soon as the "learner" protested (i.e., at 150 volts). None of those Milgram surveyed believed that any participant would go all the way to the highest voltage.

So were the predictions right? Far from it—in the first set of experiments, 65 percent of the "teachers" went all the way through the experiment's final 450-volt shock level, although many were obviously uncomfortable and begged to be allowed to stop. Of those "teachers" who did protest and finally stop, not one of them stopped before reaching 300 volts!

So what happened? Were those people sadists? Why would they keep shocking someone like that? No one was more stunned than Milgram himself. He had not believed that his experiments would show such a huge effect of obedience to authority. These results do not appear to be some random "fluke" resulting from a large population of sadistic people residing in the area. These experiments have been repeated at various times, in North America and in other countries, and also with females as participants (only men were included in Milgram's original experiment) and the percentage of participants who went all the way consistently remained between 61 and 66 percent (Blass, 1999).

That's incredible—I just don't believe that I could do something like that to someone else.

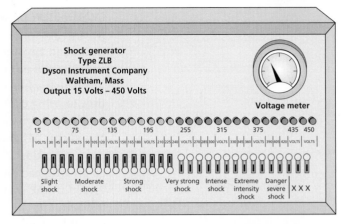

FIGURE 12.2 **Control Panel in Milgram's Experiment** In Stanley Milgram's classic study on obedience, the participants were presented with a control panel like this one. Each participant ("teacher") was instructed to give electric shocks to another person (the "learner," who only pretended to be shocked). Notice the labels under the switches. At what point do you think you would have refused to continue the experiment?

◀ So what happened? Were those people sadists? Why would they keep shocking someone like that?

◀ That's incredible—I just don't believe that I could do something like that to someone else.

TABLE 12.1	SAMPLE SCRIPT ITEMS FROM MILGRAM'S CLASSIC EXPERIMENT
VOLTAGE OF "SHOCK"	**LEARNER'S SCRIPT**
150	"Ugh!! Experimenter! That's all. Get me out of here. I told you I had heart trouble. My heart's starting to bother me now. Get me out of here, please. My heart's starting to bother me. I refuse to go on. Let me out."
210	"Ugh!! Experimenter! Get me out of here. I've had enough. I *won't* be in this experiment any more."
300	(*Agonized scream*) "I absolutely refuse to answer any more. Get me out of here. You can't hold me here. Get me out. Get me out of here."
330	(*Intense and prolonged agonized scream*) "Let me out of here. Let me out of here. My heart's bothering me. Let me out, I tell you. (*Hysterically*) Let me out of here. Let me out of here. You have no right to hold me here. Let me out! Let me out! Let me out of here! Let me out! Let me out!"

Source: Milgram (1964a, 1974).

EVALUATION OF MILGRAM'S RESEARCH   Researchers have looked for particular personality traits that might be associated with high levels of obedience but have not found any one trait or group of traits that consistently predicts who will obey and who will not in experiments similar to Milgram's original studies (Blass, 1991). The people who "went all the way" were not necessarily more dependent or susceptible to being controlled by others; they were simply people like most other people, caught in a situation of "obey or disobey" the authority. Although some have suggested that Milgram's results may have been due to the same kind of foot-in-the-door technique of persuasion as discussed earlier, with participants more likely to go on with each next demanding step of the experiment because they had already agreed to the smaller increments of shock, as yet no research supports this idea (Gilbert, 1981).

Milgram's research also raised a serious ethical question: How far should researchers be willing to go to answer a question of interest? Some have argued that the participants in Milgram's studies may have suffered damaged self-esteem and serious psychological stress from the realization that they were willing to administer shocks great enough to kill another person, just on the say-so of an experimenter (Baumrind, 1964). Milgram (1964b) responded to the criticism by citing his follow-up study of the participants, in which he found that 84 percent of the participants were glad to have been a part of the experiment and only 1.3 percent said that they were sorry they had been in the experiment. A follow-up psychiatric exam one year later also found no signs of harm or trauma in the participants. Even so, most psychologists do agree that under the current ethical rules that exist for such research, this study would never be allowed to happen today. Ⓛⓘⓝⓚ *to Chapter One: The Science of Psychology, p. 2.*

TASK PERFORMANCE: SOCIAL FACILITATION AND SOCIAL LOAFING

12.4   *How does the presence of other people affect a person's performance on a task?*

In addition to the influence that others can have on a person's actions and attitudes, social influence can affect the success or failure of an individual's task performance. The difficulty of the task seems to determine the particular effect of the presence of others as well: If a task is easy, the presence of other people seems to improve performance. If the task is difficult, the presence of others actually has a negative effect on performance. The positive influence of others on performance is called **social facilitation**, whereas the negative influence is sometimes called **social impairment** (Aiello & Douthitt, 2001; Michaels et al., 1982; Zajonc, 1965).

In both social facilitation and social impairment, the presence of other people acts to increase arousal (Zajonc, 1965, 1968; Zajonc et al., 1970). Social facilitation occurs because the presence of others creates just enough increased arousal to improve performance. But the presence of others when the task is difficult produces too high a level of arousal, resulting in impaired performance. Ⓛⓘⓝⓚ *to Chapter Nine: Motivation and Emotion, p. 350.*

All people are not the same, and it would be foolish to expect the rules of social influence to affect different individuals in exactly the same way. For example, people who are lazy tend not to do as well when other people are also working on the same task, but they can do quite well when working on their own. This phenomenon is called **social loafing** (Karau & Williams, 1993, 1997; Latané et al., 1979). The reason for this is that it is easier for a lazy person (a "loafer") to hide laziness when working in a group of people because it is less likely that the individual will be evaluated

---

◉─|Watch **on mypsychlab**

Milgram's Obedience Study

---

social facilitation
the tendency for the presence of other people to have a positive impact on the performance of an easy task.

social impairment
the tendency for the presence of other people to have a negative impact on the performance of a challenging task.

social loafing
the tendency for people to put less effort into a simple task when working with others on that task.

alone—the group will be the focus of the evaluation, and someone in the group will most likely be concerned enough about the evaluation to make sure that the task is completed successfully. The social loafer doesn't feel the need to make any real effort, preferring to let the other members of the group do the work. But when the social loafer is working alone, the focus of evaluation will be on that person only, and as a result, the person feels evaluation apprehension. In that case, the loafer works harder because there is no one else to whom the work can be shifted. Most students experience this social loafing phenomenon at some point during their post-secondary career when they are assigned to work on a group project.

Social loafing depends heavily on the assumption that personal responsibility for a task is severely lessened when working with a group of other people. Studies suggest that although people from Western cultures may readily make that assumption, those from Eastern cultures, who come from a more interdependent cultural viewpoint, tend to assume that each individual within the group is still nearly as responsible for the group's outcome as the group at large (Klehe & Anderson, 2007; Menon et al., 1999). As a result, people from Eastern cultures engage in less social loafing than those from Western cultures (Klehe & Anderson, 2007).

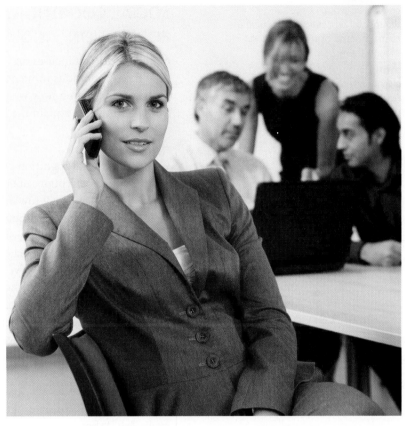

The woman in the foreground is paying more attention to her cellphone than to her colleagues. While they are working hard, she is engaging in some serious social loafing. How do you think her colleagues might feel about her behaviour?

PRACTICE QUIZ: HOW MUCH DO YOU REMEMBER?

Pick the best answer.

1. A person's conformity in a situation like the Asch line study is most likely to be strongest when
   a. the person is in the room with only one other person.
   b. at least one other person agrees with the person.
   c. that person is from Hong Kong.
   d. that person is from Canada.

2. In groupthink, members of the group
   a. have an illusion of invulnerability.
   b. avoid stereotyping those who hold an opposing viewpoint.
   c. like to "rock the boat" every now and then.
   d. sometimes question the moral "rightness" of the group.

3. When members of a cult are trying to enlist a new recruit, they start by asking the recruit to make a small commitment, such as attending a short meeting or helping out at a social function. Then the commitments get more involved, such as staying for a longer period of time and eventually contributing major donations of money and moving in with the cult members. This is most like which of the following techniques?
   a. foot-in-the-door technique   c. lowball technique
   b. door-in-the-face technique   d. that's-not-all technique

4. Which of the following has been shown to be true concerning the "teachers" in Milgram's experiment?
   a. Most of the "teachers" were sorry to have been a part of the experiment.
   b. They were found to be psychologically weak-minded people.
   c. Only a very small percentage said they were sorry they had participated.
   d. They were not ordinary people.

5. Alex, who is in the honours program, failed to do his share of the work on a group project with his four classmates. Alex was most likely engaging in
   a. social facilitation.   c. social loafing.
   b. social impairment.   d. social influencing.

Answers: 1.-c, 2.-a, 3.-a, 4.-c, 5.-c.

social cognition
the mental processes that people use to make sense of the social world around them.

attitude
a tendency to respond positively or negatively toward a certain person, object, idea, or situation.

affect
in psychology, an emotional reaction

SOCIAL COGNITION: ATTITUDES, IMPRESSION FORMATION, AND ATTRIBUTION

Social cognition focuses on the ways in which people think about other people and how those cognitions influence behaviour toward those other people. In this section, we'll concentrate on how we perceive others and form our first impressions of them, as well as how we explain the behaviour of others and ourselves.

ATTITUDES

One area of social cognition concerns the formation and influence of attitudes on the behaviour and perceptions of others. An **attitude** can be defined as a tendency to respond positively or negatively toward a certain idea, person, object, or situation (Triandis, 1971). This tendency, developed through people's experiences as they live and work with others, can affect the way they behave toward those ideas, people, objects, and situations and can include opinions, beliefs, and biases. In fact, attitudes influence the way people view these things *before* they've actually been exposed to them (Petty et al., 2003).

▶ What do you mean—how can an attitude affect something that hasn't happened yet?

What do you mean—how can an attitude affect something that hasn't happened yet? Although new research is showing that some biological and genetic factors may affect attitudes (Olson, Vernon, Harris, & Jang, 2001), for the most part, attitudes are learned through experiences and contact with others and even through direct instruction from parents, teachers, and other important people in a person's life. Because attitudes involve a positive or negative evaluation of things, it's possible to go into a new situation, meet a new person, or be exposed to a new idea with one's "mind already made up" to like or dislike, agree or disagree, and so on (Eagly & Chaiken, 1993; Petty et al., 2003). For example, children are known for making up their minds about certain foods before ever tasting them, simply because the foods are "green." Those children may have tried a green food in the past and disliked it and now will generalize that dislike to any green food, whether they've tasted it or not.

THE ABC MODEL OF ATTITUDES

12.5 *What are the three components of an attitude, how are attitudes formed, and how can attitudes be changed?*

Attitudes are actually made up of three different parts, or components, as shown in Figure 12.3. These components should not come as a surprise to anyone who has been reading the other chapters in this text because, throughout the text, references have been made to personality and traits being composed of the ways people think, feel, and act. By using certain terms to describe these three things, psychologists have come up with a handy way to describe the three components of attitudes (Eagly & Chaiken, 1993, 1998).

Affective Component The *affective component* of an attitude is the way a person feels toward the object, person, or situation. **Affect** is used in psychology to mean "emotions" or "feelings," so the affective component is the emotional component. For example, some people might feel that hockey is fun and entertaining.

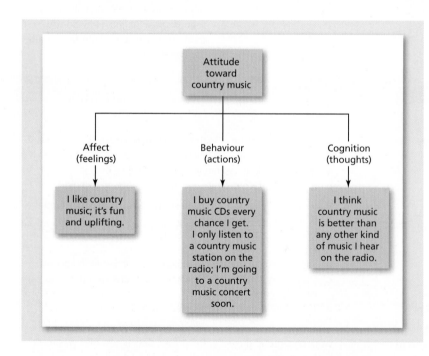

FIGURE 12.3 **Three Components of an Attitude** Attitudes consist of the way a person feels and thinks about something, as well as the way the person chooses to behave. If you like country music, you are also likely to think that country music is good music. You are also more likely to listen to this style of music, buy this type of music, and even go to this type of performance. Each of the three components influences the other two.

Behaviour Component   The *behaviour component* of an attitude is the action that a person takes in regard to the person, object, or situation. For example, people who feel that hockey is fun are likely to tune in to a sports channel on the car radio, play hockey themselves, or go to a hockey game.

Cognitive Component   Finally, the *cognitive component* of an attitude is the way a person thinks about the person, object, or situation. These thoughts, or cognitions, include beliefs and ideas about the focus of the attitude. For example, the hockey lover might believe that hockey is superior to other sports.

THE ATTITUDE–BEHAVIOUR LINK   So if you know what someone thinks or feels about something, you can predict what that person will do, right? Oddly enough, attitudes turn out to be pretty poor predictors of actual behaviour in a number of controlled research studies. One survey of such research conducted in the 1960s found that what people say and what people do are often two very different things (Wicker, 1971). Studies conducted in the decades that followed found that attitudes predict behaviour only under certain conditions. One condition involves situational influences such as *social desirability* (when we act in a way that we believe others want us to act so that we can make a favourable impression). These influences may have an impact on whether someone's actions match their attitudes. For example, someone may hold prejudiced attitudes toward a particular social group, but because prejudiced attitudes are not widely accepted in society today (thankfully), they may not act on those attitudes.

Another factor in matching attitudes and behaviour concerns how specific the attitude itself is. People may hold a general attitude about something without reflecting that attitude in their actual behaviour. For example, doctors generally hold the attitude that people should do everything they can to protect their health and promote wellness, yet many doctors still smoke tobacco, fail to exercise, and often get too little sleep. But a very specific attitude, such as "exercise is important to my immediate health" will more likely be associated with the behaviour of exercising (Ajzen, 2001; Ajzen & Fishbein, 2000).

Some attitudes are stronger than others, and strong attitudes are more likely to predict behaviour than weak ones. A person who quit smoking because of failing health might have a stronger attitude toward second-hand smoking than someone who quit smoking on a dare, for example. The importance or salience* of a particular attitude in a given situation also has an impact on behaviour—the more important the attitude appears, the more likely the behaviour will match the attitude. Someone who is antismoking might be more likely to confront a smoker breaking the rules in a hospital, for example, than a smoker outside the building (Eagly & Chaiken, 1998).

ATTITUDE FORMATION   Attitudes can be formed in many different ways. For many years, it was believed that the only way attitudes are formed is through learning. However, recent Canadian research shows otherwise. The various ways that attitudes can be formed are found below.

Direct Contact   One way in which attitudes are formed is by direct contact with the person, idea, situation, or object that is the focus of the attitude. For example, a student who takes an introductory sociology class and dislikes it will form a negative attitude about sociology in general. Later that negative attitude may be generalized to other courses in the field of sociology.

◀ So if you know what someone thinks or feels about something, you can predict what that person will do, right?

Most non-smokers will not confront a person who is smoking in an appropriate area, as this young woman is doing. But if the young woman were in a hospital waiting room, others would be more likely to confront her. Smoking in an area that is clearly not appropriate would be more important to those with antismoking attitudes.

---

*Salience: importance, or having the quality of being obvious or easily seen

persuasion
the process by which one person tries to change the belief, opinion, position, or course of action of another person through argument, pleading, or explanation.

Direct Instruction   Another way attitudes are formed is through direct instruction, either by parents or some other individual. Parents may tell their children that smoking cigarettes is dangerous and unhealthy, for example. Some children will form a negative attitude about smoking as a result.

Interaction with Others   Sometimes attitudes are formed because the person is around other people with that attitude. If a person's friends, for example, all hold the attitude that smoking is cool, that person is more likely to think that smoking is cool as well (Eddy et al., 2000; Hill, 1990). The attitudes and behaviour of teachers, parents, and siblings matter as well. Researchers found that a non-smoking mother, teacher, or brother had a strong influence on both girls and boys (who are less likely to smoke), although the influence of all three on boys seemed to fade over a seven-year follow-up study (Shean et al., 1994).

Vicarious Conditioning (Observational Learning)   Many attitudes are learned through the observation of other people's actions and reactions to various objects, people, or situations. Just as a child whose mother shows a fear of dogs may develop a similar fear, a child whose mother or father shows a positive attitude toward classical music may grow into an adult with a similarly positive attitude. The emotional components of an attitude can be learned by observing the emotional reactions of others, and the behavioural components can be observed and imitated. This is sometimes how prejudice develops in children; they learn to dislike a particular social group because they've observed the negative emotional reactions of others to members of this group.

Attitudes are influenced not only by other people in a person's immediate world but also by the larger world of the educational system (many attitudes may be learned in school or through reading books) and the mass media of magazines, television, and the movies—the fact of which advertisers and marketing experts are well aware (Gresham & Shimp, 1985; MacKenzie et al., 1986). Also, as James Olson of the University of Western Ontario and Mark Zanna of the University of Waterloo have pointed out, some attitudes are simply formed through what is known as *chance conditioning*, in which learning of the attitude occurs as a result of chance or coincidence (Olson & Zanna, 1993). Advertising companies know how to take advantage of these facts—an estimated $15 billion is spent yearly on television advertising in the United States and Canada alone.

👁 **Watch on mypsychlab**
Learning Attitudes
(Black vs. White)

Sometimes people learn attitudes that aren't necessarily good ones, right? So can attitudes change?

Biological and Genetic Factors   As mentioned previously, for many years, people believed that attitudes are solely the result of learning. James Olson and his colleagues (2001) have shown that although attitudes are more often the result of learning, biological and genetic factors can also influence attitudes. Olson and colleagues found significant differences between the attitudes of identical and fraternal twins: Identical twins' attitudes were more likely to be similar than those of fraternal twins. In addition, the attitudes that were found to be more similar in identical twins than in fraternal twins were more resistant to pressure to conform and more strongly held (Olson et al., 2001). Other research has also supported these findings (e.g., Tesser, 1993). Although more research needs to be done, it seems as though even attitudes may be partly determined by genetics.

▶ **ATTITUDE CHANGE: THE ART OF PERSUASION**   Sometimes people learn attitudes that aren't necessarily good ones, right? So can attitudes change? Because attitudes are mostly learned, they are also subject to change with new learning. The world is full of people, companies, and other organizations that want to change people's attitudes. It's all about the art of **persuasion**, the process by which one person tries to change the belief, opinion, position, or course of action of another person through argument, pleading, or explanation.

Persuasion is not a simple matter. Several factors become important in predicting how successful any persuasive effort at attitude change might be. These factors include the following:

- **Source:** The *communicator* is the person delivering the message. There is a strong tendency to give more weight to people who are perceived as experts, as well as those who seem trustworthy, attractive, and similar to the person receiving the message (Eagly & Chaiken, 1975; Petty & Cacioppo, 1986, 1996; Priester & Petty, 1995). In addition, in Western cultures, communicators who speak more quickly are seen as having more credibility and expertise, which is not the case in Eastern cultures (Peng, Zebrowitz, & Lee, 1993).

- **Message:** The actual message should be clear and well organized (Booth-Butterfield, 1996). It is usually more effective to present both sides of an argument to an audience that has not yet committed to one side or the other (Crowley & Hoyer, 1994; Petty & Cacioppo, 1996; Petty et al., 2003). Messages that are directed at producing fear are more effective if they produce only a moderate amount of fear and also provide information about how to avoid the fear-provoking consequences (Kleinot & Rogers, 1982; Meyrick, 2001; Petty, 1995; Rogers & Mewborn, 1976). In addition, the way the message is communicated (i.e., whether it is written down or videotaped) is important. If the message is complex and difficult to understand, it is better for the message to be in written form. If the message is simple and easy to understand, the message will be more persuasive if it is presented via video rather than written down (Chaiken & Eagly, 1978).

- **Target audience:** The characteristics of the people who are the intended target of the message of persuasion are also important in determining the effectiveness of the message. The age of the audience members can be a factor, for example. Researchers have found that people who are in the young-adult stage of the late teens to the mid 20s are more susceptible to persuasion than are older people (Visser & Krosnick, 1998). In addition, people are often more susceptible to persuasion attempts when they are distracted (Allyn & Festinger, 1961). Where the audience members are from can also have an impact on persuasion. Chanthika Pornpitakpan of the University of Singapore and June Francis of Simon Fraser University in Vancouver studied how Thai and Canadian students responded to persuasive arguments that varied in the perceived expertise of the speaker and in how strong the argument was. It was found that Thai students were more influenced by perceived expertise while Canadian students were more influenced by the strength of the argument (Pornpitakpan & Francis, 2001).

Advertising companies keep these three factors in mind while developing their advertising campaigns.

How easily influenced a person is will also be related to the way people tend to process information. In the **elaboration likelihood model** (ELM) of persuasion (Petty & Cacioppo, 1986), it is assumed that people either elaborate on what they hear (the facts of the message) or they do not elaborate at all, preferring to pay attention to the surface characteristics of the message (e.g., length, who delivers it, how attractive the message deliverer is). Two types of processing are hypothesized in this model (see Figure 12.4): **central-route processing**, sometimes referred to as *systematic*

elaboration likelihood model
model of persuasion stating that people will either elaborate on the persuasive message or fail to elaborate on it, and that the future actions of those who do elaborate are more predictable than those who do not.

central-route processing (systematic processing)
type of information processing that involves attending to the content of the message itself.

How the jurors in this courtroom interpret and process the information they are given will determine the outcome of the trial. Those who listen carefully to what is said by persons involved in the trial are using central-route processing. There may be some jurors, however, who are more affected by the appearance, dress, attractiveness, or tone of voice of the lawyers, defendant, and witnesses. When people are persuaded by factors other than the message itself, it is called *peripheral-route processing*.

processing, in which people attend to the content of the message, and **peripheral-route processing**, sometimes referred to as *heuristic processing*, in which people rely on peripheral cues (cues outside of the message content itself) such as the expertise of the message source, the length of the message, and other factors that have nothing to do with the message content. This style of processing causes people not to pay attention to the message itself but instead to base their decisions on those peripheral factors (Petty & Cacioppo, 1986; Stiff & Mongeau, 2002). For example, one of the authors once participated on a jury panel in which one woman voted "guilty" because the defendant had "shifty eyes" and not because of any of the evidence presented. So which route results in longer-lasting attitude change? Attitudes that are formed through central-route processing tend to be persistent, longer-lasting, and more resistant to attacks.

COGNITIVE DISSONANCE: WHEN ATTITUDES AND BEHAVIOUR CLASH

12.6 *How do people react when attitudes and behaviour are not the same?*

As stated earlier, sometimes what people say and what they do are very different. I once pointed this out to a friend of mine who was behaving this way, and he got really upset over it. Why did he get so upset? When people find themselves doing things or saying things that don't match their idea of themselves as smart, nice, or moral, for example, they experience an emotional discomfort known as **cognitive dissonance** (Aronson, 1997; Festinger, 1957). Most people need to see themselves as smart, moral, and rational. When people are confronted with the knowledge that something they have done or said was a dumb move, immoral, or illogical, they suffer an inconsistency in cognitions. For example, they may have a cognition that says "I'm pretty smart" but also the cognition "That was a dumb thing to do," which causes dissonance. (*Dissonance* is a term referring to an inconsistency or lack of agreement.)

In a classic experiment conducted at Stanford University, psychologist Leo Festinger and colleague James Carlsmith (1959) recruited male volunteers to participate in a study. Each participant was given an hour-long, incredibly boring task: sorting wooden spools into batches of 12 and turning wooden pegs about 90 degrees to the right. The experimenters then asked the participant to help out because a student assistant had failed to show up. Could the participant convince the female participants in the waiting room that the task was fun and interesting? While half of the participants were paid only $1 to try to convince the waiting women, the other participants were paid $20. (In the late 1950s, $20 was a considerable sum of money—the average income was $5000, the average car cost $3000, and gas was only 7 cents a litre.)

At the time of this study, many researchers would have predicted that the more the participant was paid to lie, the more the participant would come to like the task

---

As stated earlier, sometimes what people say and what they do are very different. I once pointed this out to a friend of mine who was behaving this way, and he got really upset over it. Why did he get so upset? ▶

peripheral-route processing (heuristic processing)
type of information processing that involves attending to factors not involved in the message, such as the appearance of the source of the message, the length of the message, and other non-content factors.

cognitive dissonance
sense of discomfort or distress that occurs when a person's behaviour does not correspond to that person's attitudes.

FIGURE 12.4 **The ELM Model: A Cognitive Theory of Persuasion**
According to the elaboration likelihood model (ELM), persuasion can occur in two ways. First, we can be persuaded by carefully and systematically processing the information contained in the persuasive messages (the central route), or second, through less systematic processing based on heuristics or mental shortcuts. Systematic processing occurs when the message is important to us and we have the cognitive resources available to think about it carefully. Heuristic processing is most likely when the message is not important to us or we do not have the cognitive resources (or time) to engage in careful thought.
Source: Based on suggestions by Petty & Cacioppo (1986).

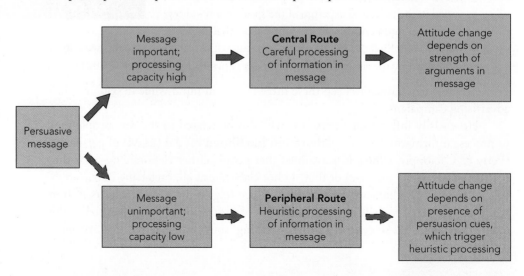

because the participant was getting more reinforcement ($20) for doing so. But what actually happened was that those participants who were paid only $1 for lying actually convinced themselves that the task was interesting and fun. The reason is cognitive dissonance: Participants who were paid only $1 experienced distress at thinking that they would lie to someone for only a dollar. Therefore, they must not be lying—the task really was pretty interesting, after all, and fun, too! Those who were paid more experienced no dissonance because they knew exactly why they were lying—for lots of money—and the money was a sufficient amount to explain their behaviour to their satisfaction. Although most people don't want to be thought of as liars, getting paid enough money to fill the gas tank of one's car three or four times over was incentive enough to tell what probably seemed to be a harmless fib. The fact that those who were paid only $1 had to change their attitude toward the task so that they would not really be lying and could maintain their self-image of honesty is a perfect example of the **insufficient justification effect** (see Figure 12.5).

When people experience cognitive dissonance, the result is unpleasant and the motivation is to change something so that the unpleasant feelings are reduced or eliminated. People can do three basic things to reduce cognitive dissonance:

1. Change the conflicting behaviour to make it match the attitude.

2. Change the current conflicting cognition to justify the behaviour.

3. Form new cognitions to justify the behaviour.

Take the example of Larry, who is a university graduate and a cigarette smoker. On the one hand, Larry is educated enough to know that cigarette smoking is extremely harmful. On the other hand, Larry enjoys his smoking, feeling that it calms him and helps him deal with stress—not to mention the fact that he's thoroughly addicted and finds it difficult to quit. His attitude (smoking is bad for you) doesn't match his behaviour. Larry is experiencing cognitive dissonance and knows he needs to do something to resolve his dilemma.

If Larry chooses the first way of dealing with cognitive dissonance, he'll quit smoking, no matter how difficult it is (Option One). As long as he is working at changing the conflicting behaviour, his dissonance will be reduced. But what if he can't quit? He might decide that smoking isn't as bad as everyone says it is, which changes his original conflicting attitude (Option Two). He might also form a new attitude by deciding that if he smokes "light" cigarettes, he's reducing his risk enough to justify continuing smoking (Option Three).

It's important to point out that the majority of studies on dissonance have been conducted in Western cultures. This focus leads to the important question of whether cognitive dissonance is a universal human experience. Recent studies have found that dissonance does seem to occur in Eastern cultures as well (see Heine & Lehman, 1997; Hoshino-Browne, Zanna, Spencer, Zanna, Kitayama, & Lackenbauer, 2005; Kitayama, Snibbe, Markus, & Suzuki, 2004). However, culture has an influence on the factors that produce dissonance, the magnitude of that dissonance, and how the dissonance is reduced. A study conducted at the University of Waterloo with participants born in Asia and participants born in Canada found that those born in Asia experienced cognitive dissonance when their behaviour didn't match their *social group's* goals and attitudes while those born in Canada experienced dissonance when their behaviour didn't match their *personal* goals and attitudes (Hoshino-Browne et al., 2005). These findings indicate that all individuals, regardless of where they live, experience dissonance when they behave in a way that is inconsistent with their culturally valued self-view (remember that Eastern cultures tend to be more collectivist in nature while Western cultures tend to be more individualistic).

insufficient justification effect when external justification is not sufficient, dissonance is reduced by internally justifying one's behaviour.

Inducement	Attitude
$1	+1.35
$20	−0.50
Control	−0.45

*Based on a −5 to +5 scale, where −5 means "extremely boring" and +5 means "extremely interesting"

FIGURE 12.5 **Cognitive Dissonance: Attitude Toward a Task** After completing a boring task, some participants were paid $1 and some $20 to convince others waiting to do the same task that the task was interesting and fun. Surprisingly, the participants who were paid only $1 seemed to change their own attitude toward the task, rating it as interesting, whereas those who were paid $20 rated the task no differently than a control group did.

Source: Adapted from Festinger and Carlsmith (1959).

PRACTICE QUIZ: HOW MUCH DO YOU REMEMBER?

Pick the best answer.

1. Which of the following represents the cognitive component of an attitude?
   a. "I just love Italian food!"
   b. "Tonight, we're going to that new Italian restaurant."
   c. "Italian food is the best of the European cuisines."
   d. "I'm going to make lasagna tonight."

2. Lilly's mother always listens to the classic rock station on her car radio, so Lilly has grown up hearing that music and noticing how much her mother enjoys it. Now Lilly says that classic rock is her favourite music, too. Lilly's attitude toward classic rock was most likely acquired through
   a. direct contact.
   b. direct instruction.
   c. interaction with others.
   d. vicarious conditioning.

3. Physical attractiveness is most involved in which of the following aspects of persuasion?
   a. the source
   b. the message
   c. the audience
   d. the media

4. Which of the following is not one of the elements of effective persuasion?
   a. the source or communicator
   b. characteristics of the message
   c. presence of supporters
   d. characteristics of the audience

5. "I didn't like the sermon at all today. It was too long, and that preacher wasn't dressed up enough" would be an example of which type of processing?
   a. central-route processing
   b. peripheral-route processing
   c. cognitive-route processing
   d. visual-route processing

6. In the famous Festinger experiment, participants were paid either $1 or $20 to lie to people in the waiting room about how interesting the task was. The participants who convinced themselves that the task really was fun were the ones who were
   a. paid immediately.
   b. paid after one day.
   c. paid only $1.
   d. paid $20.

7. Which of the following statements about cognitive dissonance is accurate?
   a. It occurs only in Western cultures.
   b. It occurs only in Eastern cultures.
   c. It is a universal phenomenon, experienced in the same way across all cultures.
   d. It is a universal phenomenon but is experienced differently across cultures.

Answers: 1.-c, 2.-d, 3.-a, 4.-c, 5.-b, 6.-c, 7.-d.

✳ Explore on **mypsychlab**
Impression Formation and Attributions

IMPRESSION FORMATION

When one person meets another for the first time, it is the first opportunity either person will have to make initial evaluations and judgments about the other. That first opportunity is a very important one in **impression formation**, the forming of the first knowledge a person has about another person. Impression formation includes assigning the other person to a number of categories and drawing conclusions about what that person is likely to do—it's really all about prediction. In a sense, when first meeting another person, the observer goes through a process of concept formation similar to that discussed in Chapter Seven. Impression formation is another kind of social cognition.

At this job fair at Durham College in Ontario, more than 1000 students showed up to network with potential employers. Making a good first impression is important in any networking situation, but when the competition numbers in the thousands, the people who are most likely to find a job are those who are neatly dressed and well groomed.

There is a *primacy effect* in impression formation. ⓁⒾⓃⓀ *to Chapter Six: Memory, p. 218.* The first time people meet someone, they form an impression of that person that persists even though they may later have other contradictory information about that person (DeCoster & Claypool, 2004; Luchins, 1957). So the old saying is pretty much on target: First impressions do count.

Impression formation is one of a number of phenomena that are all part of *social cognition*, the mental processes that people use to make sense out of the social world around them.

12.7   *What are social categorization and implicit personality theories?*

SOCIAL CATEGORIZATION   One of the processes that occur when people meet someone new is the assignment of that person to some kind of category or group. This assignment is usually based on characteristics the new person has in common with other people or groups with whom the perceiver has had prior experience. This **social categorization** is mostly automatic and occurs without conscious awareness of the process (Macrae & Bodenhausen, 2000). Although this is a natural process (human beings are just born categorizers, ⓁⒾⓃⓀ *to Chapter Seven: Cognition, p. 260*), sometimes it can cause problems. When the characteristics used to categorize the person are superficial ones that have become improperly attached to certain ideas, such as "red hair equals a bad temper," social categorization can result in a **stereotype**, a set of characteristics that people believe are shared by all members of a particular social category (Fiske, 1998). Stereotypes are very limiting, causing people to misjudge what others are like and often to treat them differently as a result. Add the process of stereotyping to the primacy effect, and it becomes easy to see how important first impressions really are. That first impression not only has more importance than any other information gathered about a person later on but may include a stereotype that is resistant to change as well (Hilton & von Hipple, 1996; Hugenberg & Bodenhausen, 2003).

It sounds as though we'd be better off if people didn't use social categorization. Social categorization does have an important place in the perception of others. It allows people to access a great deal of information that can be useful about others, as well as helping people to remember and organize information about the characteristics of others (Macrae & Bodenhausen, 2000). Stereotypes will be discussed further in the section on prejudice and discrimination.

IMPLICIT PERSONALITY THEORIES   The categories into which people place others are based on something called an **implicit personality theory**. Implicit personality theories, which form in childhood, are sets of assumptions that people have about how different types of people, personality traits, and actions are all related (Dweck et al., 1995; Erdley & Dweck, 1993). For example, many people have an implicit personality theory that includes the idea that happy people are also friendly people. Although these assumptions or beliefs are not necessarily true, they do serve the function of helping to organize *schemas*, or mental patterns that represent (in this case) what a person believes about certain "types" of people. (The concept of schema here is similar to the complex patterns proposed by Piaget. ⓁⒾⓃⓀ *to Chapter Eight: Development Across the Lifespan, p. 302.*) Of course, the schemas formed in this way can easily become stereotypes when people have limited experience with others who are different from them, especially in superficial ways such as skin colour or other physical characteristics (Levy et al., 1998).

There is some evidence to suggest that implicit personality theories may differ from culture to culture as well as from individual to individual. For example, one study found that Chinese people from Hong Kong and North Americans have different implicit personality theories about how much the personality of an individual is

social categorization
the assignment of a person one has just met to a category based on characteristics the new person has in common with other people with whom one has had experience in the past.

stereotype
a set of characteristics that people believe is shared by all members of a particular social category.

implicit personality theory
sets of assumptions about how different types of people, personality traits, and actions are related to one another.

> It sounds though we'd be better off if people didn't use social categorization.

attribution
the process of explaining one's own behaviour and the behaviour of others.

attribution theory
the theory of how people explain the causes behind behaviour.

situational cause
cause of behaviour attributed to external factors, such as delays, the action of others, or some other aspect of the situation.

dispositional cause
cause of behaviour attributed to internal factors such as personality or character.

fundamental attribution error
the tendency to overestimate the influence of internal factors in determining behaviour while underestimating situational factors.

The people involved in this accident are likely to be late for classes or work. This is a good example of a genuine situational cause for tardiness.

But what else determines which type of cause a person will use? For example, what determines how people explain the behaviour of someone they don't already know or like?

But why do we do that? Why not assume an external cause for everyone?

able to change. Whereas North Americans assume that personality is relatively fixed and unchanging, Chinese people native to Hong Kong assume that personalities are far more changeable (Chiu et al., 1997).

ATTRIBUTION

12.8   *How do people try to explain the actions of others?*

Another aspect of social cognition is the need people seem to have to explain the behaviour of other people. Have you ever watched someone who was doing something you didn't understand? Chances are you were going through a number of possible explanations in your head: "Maybe he sees something I can't see," and so on. It seems to be human nature to want to know why people do the things they do, and if no obvious answer is available, people tend to come up with their own reasons. People also need an explanation for their own behaviour. This need is so great that if an explanation isn't obvious, it can cause cognitive dissonance. The process of explaining both one's own behaviour and the behaviour of other people is called **attribution**.

CAUSES OF BEHAVIOUR   **Attribution theory** was originally developed by social psychologist Fritz Heider (1958) as a way of not only explaining why things happen but also why people choose the particular explanations of behaviour that they do. There are basically two kinds of explanations: those that assume an external cause and those that assume an internal cause.

When the cause of behaviour is assumed to be from external sources, such as the weather, traffic, educational opportunities, and so on, it is said to be a **situational cause**. The observed behaviour is assumed to be caused by whatever situation exists for the person at that time. For example, if John is late for class, his lateness might be explained by heavy traffic or car problems.

On the other hand, if the cause of behaviour is assumed to come from within the individual, it is called a **dispositional cause**. In this case, it is the person's internal personality characteristics that are seen as the cause of the observed behaviour. Someone attributing John's behaviour to a dispositional cause, for example, might assume that John was late for class because he is lazy and unmotivated.

FUNDAMENTAL ATTRIBUTION ERROR   But what else determines which type of cause a person will use? For example, what determines how people explain the behaviour of someone they don't already know or like? The most well-known attributional bias is the **fundamental attribution error**, which is the tendency for people to overestimate the influence of another person's internal characteristics on behaviour and underestimate the influence of the situation. In other words, people tend to explain the actions of others based on what "kind" of person they are rather than looking for outside causes such as social influences or situations (Harman, 1999; Jones & Harris, 1967; Weiner, 1985). (For example, people hearing about Milgram's "shock" study tend to assume that something is wrong with the "teachers" in the study rather than explaining their behaviour within the circumstances of the situation.)

But why do we do that? Why not assume an external cause for everyone? When people observe themselves, they are very aware of the situational influences on their own behaviour. For example, Tardy John was actually the one driving to school, and he knows that heavy traffic and a small accident made him late to school—he was *there*, after all. But someone else looking at John's behaviour doesn't have the opportunity to see all the possible situational influences and has only John himself in focus and, thus, assumes that John's tardiness is caused by some internal personality flaw.

Other research has shown that when students are given an opportunity to make attributions about cheating, they make the fundamental attribution error: If others are cheating, it's because they are not honest people, but if the students themselves were cheating, it would be because of the situation (Bogle, 2000). This happens because of the **self-serving bias**. People tend to choose attributions that make themselves look better as a person, taking credit for when they are successful or do something good for someone (a dispositional attribution) but blaming the situation when they are unsuccessful or do something bad.

Although the fundamental attribution error has been found in North American culture (Jones & Harris, 1967), would the same error occur in a culture that is very different from North American culture, such as Japanese culture? A summary of the research in cross-cultural differences in attribution provides support for the idea that the fundamental attribution error is not a universal one (Peng et al., 2000). The work of Miller (1984) and many other researchers (Cha & Nam, 1985; Choi & Nisbett, 1998; Choi et al., 1999; Lee et al., 1996; Morris & Peng, 1994; Morris et al., 1995; Norenzayan et al., 1999) strongly suggests that in the more interdependent, collectivist cultures found in Hong Kong, Japan, and Korea, people tend to assume that external situational factors are more responsible for the behaviour of other people than are internal dispositional factors—a finding that is exactly the reverse of the fundamental attribution error so common in individualist Western cultures such as Canada.

Part of the reason why cultural differences in the fundamental attribution error have been found may be that there are cultural differences in the tendency to self-serve. Steven Heine and Takeshi Hamamura of the University of British Columbia have found great differences between East Asians and Westerners in terms of self-enhancement. They looked at 91 different studies comparing East Asians and Westerners and found that, overall, Westerners showed a clear self-serving bias while East Asians did not (Heine & Hamamura, 2007).

Even age is a factor in how likely someone is to fall prey to the fundamental attribution error. Several studies (Blanchard-Fields & Horhota, 2005; Follett & Hess, 2002; Leclerc & Hess, 2007) have found that older adults show a stronger bias toward attributing the actions of another to internal causes than do younger people.

Many researchers have pointed out that the word *error* may not be appropriate and instead, refer to this bias in attribution as the *correspondence bias* (Jones, 1979). Yes, there is a tendency for people to explain others' actions as stemming from dispositions, but this may not necessarily result in an *error*—oftentimes, our behaviour does have internal, dispositional causes.

self-serving bias
the tendency to see and represent oneself in the most positive way possible.

PRACTICE QUIZ: HOW MUCH DO YOU REMEMBER?

Pick the best answer.

1. Which of the following statements about stereotypes is FALSE?
   a. Stereotypes are forms of social categories.
   b. Stereotypes are sets of characteristics that people believe are true for all members of a particular social category.
   c. Stereotypes are governed by the recency effect.
   d. Stereotypes are very limiting and can cause discrimination.

2. Mental patterns that represent what a person believes about certain types of people are called
   a. schemas.
   b. stereotypes.
   c. attributions.
   d. attitudes.

3. Elizabeth's room is almost always a mess. Her parents attribute this to Elizabeth's laziness. This is an example of a _____ cause.
   a. situational
   b. dispositional
   c. dispensational
   d. superficial

4. John was late to class, and his friend Eddie assumes that John simply doesn't care about being on time. But when Eddie is late the next day, he blames it on heavy traffic. Eddie has made the
   a. egocentric error.
   b. fundamental attribution error.
   c. assumption error.
   d. false consensus error.

5. In Asian cultures, people tend to explain the behaviour of others as a result of
   a. bad genes.
   b. internal dispositions.
   c. situational factors.
   d. personality traits.

prejudice
an unsupported and often negative attitude about the members of a particular social group.

discrimination
behaving differently toward people based solely or primarily on their membership within a social group.

in-groups
social groups with whom a person identifies; "us."

out-groups
social groups with whom a person does not identify; "them."

✳ Explore on mypsychlab
Unconscious Stereotyping

CartoonStock www.cartoonstock.com

SOCIAL INTERACTION: PREJUDICE, LOVE, AGGRESSION, AND PROSOCIAL BEHAVIOUR

Social influence and social cognition are two of three main areas included in the field of social psychology. The third major area has to do with social interactions with others, or the relationships between people, both casual and intimate. Social interactions include prejudice and discrimination, liking and loving, aggression, and prosocial behaviour.

PREJUDICE AND DISCRIMINATION

12.9 *How are prejudice and discrimination different?*

In talking about attitudes, the idea that some beliefs—stereotypes—can be formed by using only superficial information about a person or group of people was discussed. When a person holds an unsupported and often negative attitude about the members of a particular social group, it is called **prejudice**. When prejudicial attitudes cause members of a particular social group to be treated differently than others in situations that call for equal treatment, it is called **discrimination**. Stereotypes, prejudice, and discrimination relate to the previous discussion of the ABC model of attitudes.

Prejudice is the affective component of the attitude; discrimination represents the behavioural component of the attitude; and stereotyping represents the cognitive component. Although laws can be made to minimize discriminatory behaviour, it is not possible to have laws against holding certain attitudes. In other words, discrimination can be controlled and in some cases eliminated, but the prejudicial attitude that is responsible for the discrimination cannot be so easily controlled or eliminated.

TYPES OF PREJUDICE AND DISCRIMINATION There are many kinds of prejudice. There are also many kinds of discrimination that occur as a result of prejudice. There's ageism, or prejudicial attitudes toward people because of their age; sexism; racism, or prejudice toward those from different ethnic groups; prejudice toward those from different religions, those from different economic levels, those who are overweight, those who are too thin, and so on. Prejudice can also vary in terms of what types of people or groups make the most likely targets. In any society, there will always be **in-groups** and **out-groups**, or "us" versus "them." The in-group is all the people with whom a particular person identifies, and the out-groups are everyone else (Brewer, 2001; Hewstone et al., 2002; Tajfel & Turner, 1986). The formation of in-groups and out-groups begins in childhood (Ruble et al., 2004) and continues as children become adults.

Once an in-group is established, prejudice toward and discriminatory treatment of the out-group or groups soon follow (Brewer, 2001). Members of the out-groups are usually stereotyped according to some superficial characteristic, such as skin colour or hair colour, and getting rid of a stereotype once formed is difficult at best (Cameron et al., 2001; Hamilton & Gifford, 1976). The Classic Studies in Psychology section that follows illustrates how easily in-groups and out-groups can be formed and how quickly prejudice and discrimination follow.

■ ....

 CLASSIC STUDIES IN PSYCHOLOGY
Brown Eyes, Blue Eyes

In a small town in Iowa in 1968, a few days after the assassination of Dr. Martin Luther King, Jr., a grade 2 teacher named Jane Elliot tried to teach her students a lesson about prejudice and discrimination. She divided her students into two groups, those with blue eyes and those with brown eyes.

On the first day of the lesson, the blue-eyed children were given special privileges, such as extra time at recess and getting to leave first for lunch. She also told the blue-eyed children that they were superior to the brown-eyed children, telling the brown-eyed children not to bother taking seconds at lunch because the food would be wasted. She kept the blue-eyed children and the brown-eyed children apart (Peters, 1971).

Although Elliot tried to be critical of the brown-eyed out-group, she soon found that the blue-eyed children were also criticizing, belittling, and were quite vicious in their attacks on the brown-eyed children. By the end of the day, the blue-eyed children felt and acted superior, and the brown-eyed children were miserable. Even the lowered test scores of the brown-eyed children reflected their misery. Two days later, the brown-eyed children became the favoured group and the effects from the first two days appeared again but in reverse this time: The blue-eyed children began to feel inferior and their test scores dropped.

The fact that test scores reflected the treatment received by the out-group is a stunning one, raising questions about the effects of prejudice and discrimination on the education of children who are members of stereotyped out-groups. That the children were so willing to discriminate against their own classmates, some of whom were their close friends before the experiment, is also telling. In his book about this classroom experiment, *A Class Divided*, Peters (1971) reported that the students who were part of the original experiment, when reunited 15 years later to talk about the experience, said that they believed that this early experience with prejudice and discrimination helped them become less prejudiced as young adults.

Questions for Further Discussion

1. Is there anything about this experiment that you find disturbing?

2. How do you think adults might react in a similar experiment?

3. Are there any ethical concerns with what Elliot did in her classroom?

4. What kinds of changes might have occurred in the personalities and performances of the children if the experiment had continued for more than two days with each group?

Scapegoating   Conflicts between groups are usually greater when there are other pressures or stresses going on, such as war, economic difficulties, or other misfortunes. When such pressures exist, the need to find a *scapegoat* becomes stronger. A scapegoat is a person or a group, typically a member or members of an out-group, who serves

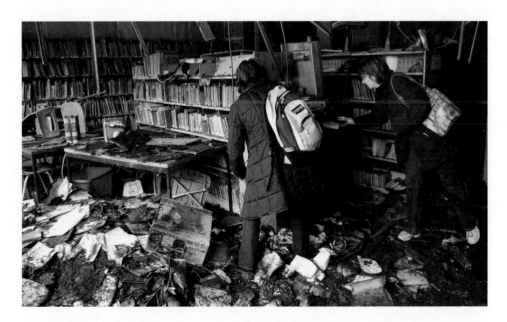

Reporters and school workers inspect the damage at the United Talmud Torah elementary school in Montreal on April 5, 2004. The school's library was firebombed overnight and anti-Semitic literature was left at the scene. Fortunately, because the school was closed for Passover, there were no injuries. For many centuries, Jewish people have often served as scapegoats for many of society's ills.

as the target for the frustrations and negative emotions of members of the in-group. (The term comes from the ancient Jewish tradition of sending a goat out into the wilderness with the symbolic sins of all the people on its head.)

Scapegoats are going to be the group of people with the least power, and the newest immigrants to any area are typically those who have the least power at that time. That is why many social psychologists believe that the rioting that took place in Los Angeles, California, in the spring of 1992 occurred in the areas it did. The infamous Rodney King beating took place at this time. Rodney King was an African American man who was dragged out of his car onto the street and severely beaten by four police officers. The beating was caught on tape by a bystander. At the trial, the officers were found not guilty of assault with a deadly weapon. This decision was followed by a series of violent riots (Knight, 1996).

The puzzling thing about these riots is that the greatest amount of rioting and violence did not take place in the neighbourhoods of the mostly white police officers or in the African American neighbourhoods. The rioting was greatest in the neighbourhoods of the Asian Americans and Asians who were the most recent immigrants to the area. When a group has only recently moved into an area, as the Asians had, that group has the least social power and influence in that new area. So the rioters took out their frustrations *not* on the people seen as directly responsible for those frustrations but on the group of people with the least power to resist.

12.10 *Why are people prejudiced, and how can prejudice be stopped?*

HOW PEOPLE LEARN PREJUDICE   As was seen in the short discussion of the brown eyes–blue eyes experiment, even children have their prejudiced attitudes. Is all prejudice simply a matter of learning, or are there other factors at work? Several theories have been proposed to explain the origins and the persistence of prejudice. In **social cognitive theory**, prejudice is seen as an attitude that is formed as other attitudes are formed, through direct instruction, modelling, and other social influences on learning.

Social Identity Theory   In **social identity theory**, three processes are responsible for the formation of a person's identity within a particular social group and the attitudes, concepts, and behaviour that go along with identification with that group (Tajfel & Turner, 1986). The first process is *social categorization*, as discussed earlier in this chapter. Just as people assign categories to others (such as black, white, student, teacher, and so on) to help organize information about those others, people also assign themselves to social categories to help determine how they should behave. A *reference group* is a group of people to whom people compare themselves, and one's social category determines the reference group that will be used. The second element of social identity theory is *identification*, or the formation of one's **social identity**. A social identity is the part of one's self-concept that includes the view of oneself as a member of a particular social group. This identification process includes the idea of the in-group. The third aspect of social identity theory is **social comparison**, Festinger's (1954) concept in which people compare themselves to others to improve their own self-esteem: "Well, at least I'm better off than that person." Social comparison also allows us to judge how well we are doing at something and how accurate our attitudes and perceptions are. Essentially, we use others as a yardstick to measure our own performance.

With respect to prejudice, social identity theory helps to explain why people categorize or stereotype others, the in-group sense of "us versus them" that people adopt toward out-groups, and people's need to increase their own self-esteem by looking down on others.

social cognitive theory
theory in which cognitive processes are used in relation to understanding the social world.

social identity theory
theory in which the formation of a person's identity within a particular social group is explained by social categorization, social identity, and social comparison.

social identity
the part of the self-concept that includes one's view of self as a member of a particular social category.

social comparison
the comparison of oneself to others to judge how well one is doing at something and how accurate one's attitudes and perceptions are, often in ways that raise one's self-esteem.

Stereotype Vulnerability As discussed previously, stereotypes are the widespread beliefs a person has about members of another group. Not only do stereotypes affect the way people perceive other people, they can also affect the way people see themselves and their performance (Snyder et al., 1977). **Stereotype vulnerability** refers to the effect that a person's knowledge of another's stereotyped opinions can have on that person's behaviour (Steele, 1992, 1997). Research has shown that when people are aware of stereotypes that are normally applied to their own group by others, they feel anxious about behaving in ways that might support that stereotype. This fear results in anxiety and self-consciousness that have negative effects on their performance in a kind of **self-fulfilling prophecy**, or the effect that expectations can have on outcomes.

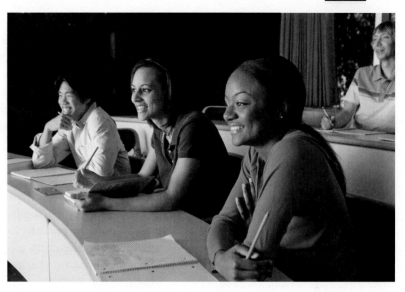

Intergroup contact is one of the best ways to combat prejudice. When people have an opportunity to work together, as the students in this diverse classroom do, they get to know each other on common ground. Can you think of the first time you had direct contact with someone who was different from you? How did that contact change your viewpoint?

Stereotype vulnerability is highly related to *stereotype threat*, in which members of a stereotyped group are made anxious and wary of any situation in which their behaviour might confirm a stereotype (Hyde & Kling, 2001; Steele, 1999). In one study, Margaret Walsh and colleagues at Memorial University of Newfoundland at Corner Brook investigated whether undergraduate women would fall prey to stereotype threat when faced with a standardized test of mathematical problem solving (Walsh, Hickey, & Duffy, 1999). When women were led to believe that the math test had previously revealed gender differences (i.e., when women were led to believe that men performed better than women), they performed worse than men. In contrast, when they were led to believe that the test was merely comparing performance of Canadian students with that of American students, no gender differences were found. According to Walsh and colleagues (1999), the study findings suggest that stereotype threat could be a key factor in explaining gender differences in mathematical problem solving. Similar effects of stereotype threat on performance also have been found with other groups. For example, this phenomenon has been implicated in the poor performance of Black participants relative to white participants on complex verbal tasks (Steele & Aronson, 1995).

OVERCOMING PREJUDICE The best weapon against prejudice is education: learning about people who are different from you can help in many ways. The best way to learn about others is to have direct contact with them and learn to see them as people rather than as "outsiders or strangers." Intergroup contact is very common in college and university settings, for example, where students and faculty from many different backgrounds live, work, and study together. Because they go through many of the same experiences (midterms, finals, and so on), people from these diverse backgrounds find common ground to start building friendships and knowledge of each other's cultural, ethnic, or religious differences.

stereotype vulnerability
the effect that people's awareness of the stereotypes associated with their social group has on their behaviour.

self-fulfilling prophecy
the tendency of one's expectations to affect one's behaviour in such a way as to make the expectation more likely to occur.

contact hypothesis
Gordon Allport's (1954) hypothesis that intergroup contact will reduce prejudice under four conditions: those coming into contact with each other must have equal status, common goals, no competition, and an authority overseeing the contact.

Equal Status Contact In the **contact hypothesis**, Allport (1954) recognized that intergroup contact will lead to reduced prejudice, but only under certain conditions. First, the individuals or groups coming into contact with one another must have equal status (i.e., one must not have power or control over the other); second, they must share common goals; third, there must not be any competition between the individuals or groups; and finally, there must be an authority who is overseeing the contact (Allport, 1954). These conditions, according to Allport (1954), must be met to effectively reduce intergroup prejudice.

realistic conflict theory
theory stating that prejudice and discrimination will be increased between groups that are in conflict (e.g., competing for limited resources).

superordinate goals
shared goals that can be achieved only through cooperation and that can override people's differences from one another.

equal status contact
contact between groups in which the groups have equal status, with neither group having power over the other.

"jigsaw classroom"
educational technique in which each individual is given only part of the information needed to solve a problem, causing the separate individuals to be forced to work together to find the solution.

The creation of superordinate goals, such as having to work together to fix the water supply, was found to reduce prejudice and discrimination in the two conflicting groups of boys in Sherif's experiment.

The idea that contact between social groups can backfire under certain circumstances is illustrated in a famous study (Sherif et al., 1961) called the *Robber's Cave*. In this experiment conducted at a summer camp named Robber's Cave, 22 white, well-adjusted 11- and 12-year-old boys were divided into two groups. The groups each lived in separate cabins and were kept apart from each other for daily activities. During the second week, after in-group relationships had formed, the researchers scheduled highly competitive events pitting one group against the other. Intergroup conflict quickly occurred, with name-calling, fights, and hostility emerging between the two groups. It is obvious that competing for limited resources (e.g., the boys fought for control over the baseball diamond) and, in fact, competition in general, elicited very strong feelings of prejudice from the boys. The idea that competing for resources can lead to prejudice and discrimination is explained by the **realistic conflict theory**. This theory states that the formation of prejudice and the onset of discriminatory treatment are closely tied to the degree of conflict between the in-group and the out-group (Horowitz, 1985; Taylor & Moghaddam, 1994).

The third week involved making the two groups come together for pleasant, non-competitive activities, in the hopes that cooperation would be the result. Instead, the groups used the activities of the third week as opportunities for more hostility. The experimenters deliberately created a series of crises to force the boys to work together. It was only after several weeks of working together on shared goals, called **superordinate goals**, that the boys lost the hostility and formed friendships between the groups. When dealing with the crises, the boys were forced into a situation of **equal status contact**, in which they were all in the same situation with neither group holding power over the other. Equal status contact has been shown to reduce prejudice and discrimination. It appears that personal involvement with people from another group must be cooperative and occur when all groups are equal in terms of power or status to have a positive effect on reducing prejudice (Olson & Zanna, 1993; Pettigrew & Trop, 2000; Robinson & Preston, 1976).

The "Jigsaw Classroom" One way to ensure that contact between people from different backgrounds will occur in a cooperative fashion is to make success at a task depend on the cooperation of each person in a group of people of mixed abilities or statuses. If each member of the group has information that is needed to solve the problem at hand, a situation is created in which people must depend on one another to meet their shared goals (Aronson et al., 1978). Ordinarily, school classrooms are not organized along these lines but are instead more competitive and, therefore, more likely to create conflict between people of different abilities and backgrounds.

In a **"jigsaw classroom,"** students have to work together to reach a specific goal. Each student is given a "piece of the puzzle," or information that is necessary for solving the problem and reaching the goal (Aronson et al., 1978; Clarke, 1994). Students then share their information with other members of the group. Interaction between diverse students is increased, making it more likely that those students will come to see one another as partners and form friendly relationships rather than labelling others as members of an out-group and treating them differently. This technique works at the post-secondary level as well as in the lower school grades (Johnson et al., 1991; Lord, 2001).

PRACTICE QUIZ: HOW MUCH DO YOU REMEMBER?

Pick the best answer.

1. The behavioural component of prejudice is
   a. discrimination.
   b. stereotyping.
   c. implicit personality theorizing.
   d. holding a negative attitude toward a person.

2. The most likely predictor of the development of prejudice and discrimination between two groups is the degree of _____ between the groups.
   a. differences
   b. conflict
   c. distance
   d. emotionality

3. In teacher Jane Elliot's classic study, the most startling finding was that the
   a. blue-eyed children were kinder to their brown-eyed peers.
   b. brown-eyed children were less prejudiced.
   c. both blue-eyed and brown-eyed children performed worse when they were labelled as the inferior group.
   d. children were unwilling to discriminate with respect to the others.

4. Which of the following is not an element of social identity theory?
   a. reference group
   b. social identity
   c. social comparison
   d. superordinate goals

5. Which situation would be LEAST likely to result in a decrease of prejudice?
   a. asking people to work on separate projects but in the same room
   b. asking people to work on a common task
   c. giving each person a piece of information to share with the others to solve a problem
   d. having people of various backgrounds help rescue others from a flood

Answers: 1.–a, 2.–b, 3.–c, 4.–d, 5.–a.

LIKING AND LOVING: INTERPERSONAL ATTRACTION

Prejudice pretty much explains why people don't like each other. What does psychology say about why people like someone else? There are some "rules" for those whom people like and find attractive. Liking or having the desire for a relationship with someone else is called **interpersonal attraction**, and there's a great deal of research on the subject. (Who wouldn't want to know the rules?)

12.11 *What factors govern attraction and love, and what are some different kinds of love?*

THE RULES OF ATTRACTION Several factors are involved in the attraction of one person to another, including both superficial physical characteristics, such as physical beauty and proximity, as well as elements of personality.

Physical Attractiveness When people think about what attracts them to other people, one of the topics that usually arises is the physical attractiveness of the other person. Some research suggests that physical beauty is one of the main factors that influence people's choices for selecting people they want to know better, although other factors may become more important in the later stages of relationships (Eagly et al., 1991; Feingold, 1992; White, 1980).

Proximity—Close to You The closer together people are physically, such as working in the same office building or living in the same dorm, the more likely they are to form a relationship. **Proximity** refers to being physically near someone else. People choose friends and lovers from the pool of people available to them, and availability depends heavily on proximity.

One theory about why proximity is so important involves the idea of repeated exposure to new stimuli. The more people experience something, whether it is a song, a picture, or a person, the more they tend to like it. The phrase "it grew on me"

Proximity and similarity are two of the powerful forces governing interpersonal attraction. Rob Hill and Natasha Swaine, both Leafs fans from Dartmouth, Nova Scotia, were married in a non-traditional way—in Toronto Maple Leaf hockey jerseys.

Simulate on **mypsychlab**
Mere Exposure Effects

interpersonal attraction
liking or having the desire for a relationship with another person.

proximity
physical or geographical nearness.

reciprocity of liking
tendency of people to like other people who like them in return.

romantic love
type of love consisting of intimacy and passion.

companionate love
type of love consisting of intimacy and commitment.

Isn't there a saying that "opposites attract"? Aren't people sometimes attracted to people who are different instead of ▶ similar?

But those aren't all the same kind of relationships. I love my family and I love my friends but in different ▶ ways.

refers to this reaction. When people are in physical proximity to each other, repeated exposure may increase their attraction to each other. This occurrence is referred to as the *mere exposure effect*, which is quite simply defined as "the more we are exposed to something, the more we tend to like it" (Zajonc, 1968).

Birds of a Feather—Similarity   Proximity does not guarantee attraction, just as physical attractiveness does not guarantee a long-term relationship. People tend to like being around others who are *similar* to them in some way. The more people find they have in common with others—such as attitudes, beliefs, and interests—the more they tend to be attracted to those others (Hartfield & Rapson, 1992; Moreland & Zajonc, 1982; Neimeyer & Mitchell, 1998). Similarity as a factor in relationships makes sense when seen in terms of validation of a person's beliefs and attitudes. When other people hold the same attitudes and beliefs and do the same kinds of actions, it makes a person's own concepts seem more correct or valid. Where children are concerned, Canadian researchers Frances Aboud and Morton Mendelson (1998) have found that when it comes to making friends in childhood, similarities in sex, age, race, and preferred activity were more important than values and attitudes.

When Opposites Attract   Isn't there a saying that "opposites attract"? Aren't people sometimes attracted to people who are different instead of similar? There is often a grain of truth in many old sayings, and "opposites attract" is no exception. Some people find that forming a relationship with another person who has *complementary* qualities, or characteristics in the one person that fill a need in the other, can be very rewarding (Carson, 1969; Schmitt, 2002). However, the majority of research shows that similarity tends to draw people together and helps them stay together more so than complementarity (Berscheid & Reis, 1998; McPherson et al., 2001).

Reciprocity of Liking   Finally, people have a very strong tendency to like people who like them, a simple but powerful concept referred to as **reciprocity of liking**. In one experiment, researchers paired college students with other students (Curtis & Miller, 1986). Neither student in any of the pairs knew the other member. One member of each pair was randomly chosen to receive some information from the experimenters about how the *other* student in the pair felt about the first member. In some cases, target students were led to believe that the other students liked them and, in other cases, that the targets disliked them.

When the pairs of students were allowed to meet and talk with each other again, they were friendlier, disclosed more information about themselves, agreed with the other person more, and behaved in a warmer manner *if they had been told* that the other student liked them. The other students came to like these students better as well, so liking produced more liking.

LOVE IS A TRIANGLE—ROBERT STERNBERG'S TRIANGULAR THEORY OF LOVE
Dictionary definitions of love refer to a strong affection for another person because of kinship, personal ties, sexual attraction, admiration, or common interests.

But those aren't all the same kind of relationships. I love my family and I love my friends but in different ways. Psychologists generally agree that there are different kinds of love. One psychologist, Robert Sternberg, outlined a theory of what he determined were the three main components of love and the different types of love that combinations of these three components can produce (Sternberg, 1986, 1988, 1997).

The Three Components of Love   According to Sternberg, love consists of three basic components: intimacy, passion, and commitment.

Intimacy, in Sternberg's view, refers to the feelings of closeness that one has for another person or the sense of having close emotional ties to another. Intimacy in this sense is not physical but psychological. Friends have an intimate relationship because they disclose things to each other that most people might not know, they feel strong emotional ties to each other, and they enjoy the presence of the other person.

Passion is the physical aspect of love. Passion refers to the emotional and sexual arousal a person feels toward the other person. Passion is not simply sex; holding hands, loving looks, and hugging can all be forms of passion.

Commitment involves the decisions one makes about a relationship. A short-term decision might be "I think I'm in love." An example of a more long-term decision is "I want to be with this person for the rest of my life."

The Love Triangles   A love relationship between two people can involve one, two, or all three of these components in various combinations. The combinations can produce seven different forms of love, as can be seen in Figure 12.6.

Two of the more familiar and more heavily researched forms of love from Sternberg's theory are romantic love and companionate love. When intimacy and passion are combined, the result is the more familiar **romantic love**, which is sometimes called *passionate love* by other researchers (Bartels & Zeki, 2000; Diamond, 2003; Hartfield, 1987). Romantic love is often the basis for a more lasting relationship. In many Western cultures, the ideal relationship begins with liking, then becomes romantic love as passion is added to the mix, and finally becomes a more enduring form of love as a commitment is made. Kenneth and Karen Dion, of the University of Toronto, have found that romantic love is more likely to be the basis of Western relationships than of non-Western relationships (Dion & Dion, 1993).

When intimacy and commitment are the main components of a relationship, it is called **companionate love**. In companionate love, people who like each other, feel emotionally close to each other, and understand one another's motives have made a commitment to live together, usually in a marriage relationship. Companionate love is often the binding tie that holds a marriage together through the years of parenting, paying bills, and lessening physical passion (Gottman & Krokoff, 1989; Steinberg & Silverberg, 1987). In many non-Western cultures, companionate love is seen as more sensible. Choices for a mate on the basis of compatibility are often made by parents or matchmakers rather than the couple themselves (Dion & Dion, 1993; Duben & Behar, 1991; Hortaçsu, 1999; Jones, 1997; Thornton & Hui-Sheng, 1994).

Finally, when all three components of love are present, the couple has achieved *consummate love*, the ideal form of love that many people see as the ultimate goal. This kind of love may also evolve into companionate love when the passion lessens during the middle years of a relationship's commitment.

The concept of romantic love, in which two people first feel a passionate attraction for each other and then develop an intimate relationship, is a relatively new one and more typical of Western cultures. In many other cultures, marriages are arranged by the parents of the young couple and based on similarity of personality and commitment, as in this Hindu wedding taking place in Jaipur, India. It is assumed that intimacy and passion will develop over the course of their marriage.

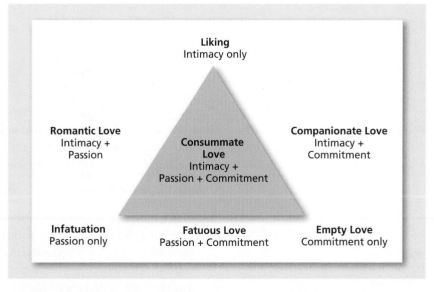

FIGURE 12.6 **Sternberg's Triangular Theory of Love** This diagram represents the seven different kinds of love that can result from combining the three components of love: intimacy, passion, and commitment. Notice that some of these types of love sound less desirable or positive than others. What is the one key element missing from the less positive types *of love*?

Source: Adapted from Sternberg (1986b).

A friend told me that in ▶
an emotionally charged
situation, sometimes
our bodies can "trick"
us into believing we
are in love. What did
she mean?

◉⌐Watch on mypsychlab
Arranged Marriage

A friend told me that in an emotionally charged situation, sometimes our bodies can "trick" us into believing we are in love. What did she mean?

Researchers have shown that physiological arousal intensifies passionate feelings as long as the person believes the arousal is the result of a specific romantic stimulus (e.g., another person who is nearby). Donald Dutton and Arthur Aron of the University of British Columbia have conducted many well-known studies on this phenomenon (e.g., Dutton & Aron, 1974; Dutton & Aron, 1989). In one study, they asked male students to participate in a learning experiment. After being introduced to attractive female partners, one group of the participants were scared to find out that they would be receiving "quite painful" electric shocks (which resulted in physiological arousal). The men were then given a questionnaire that was said to be necessary to determine how they would react to the learning task. On the questionnaire, they were asked how much they would like to date and kiss their female partners. The men in the "scared" (physiologically aroused) condition reported feeling more intense attraction toward their female partners (Dutton & Aron, 1989). Physical arousal may lead people to falsely believe they are attracted to someone.

PRACTICE QUIZ: HOW MUCH DO YOU REMEMBER?

Pick the best answer.

1. Which of the following is not one of the reasons given by the text for interpersonal attraction?
   a. physical attractiveness
   b. similarity
   c. personality
   d. proximity

2. The more you see someone, the more likely you are to _____ that person.
   a. dislike
   b. like
   c. grow tired of
   d. be annoyed by

3. A person who is very low in self-worth is less likely to be affected by the
   a. halo effect.
   b. mere exposure effect.
   c. need complementarity effect.
   d. reciprocity of liking effect.

4. According to Sternberg, the emotional and physical arousal a person feels for another is the _____ component of love.
   a. intimacy
   b. passion
   c. commitment
   d. psychological

5. If you are interested in dating someone and you are scared to ask out him or her for fear of being rejected, when should you approach the person if you finally do get the courage?
   a. after watching a very scary horror movie
   b. after listening to a boring lecture at school
   c. after waking up from a nap
   d. after listening to classical music

Answers: 1.-c, 2.-b, 3.-d, 4.-b, 5.-a.

AGGRESSION

All you have to do is turn on the television or open a newspaper to see the number of violent acts taking place in society today. It seems as though more and more school shootings, armed robberies, and other violent crimes are taking place each day. Researchers have been looking into when and why these aggressive acts occur.

12.12 *What is aggression and what causes it?*

aggression
behaviour intended to hurt or destroy another person.

Unfortunately, violence toward others is another form of social interaction. When one hurts or tries to destroy another, either with words or with physical behaviour, psychologists call it **aggression**. One common cause of aggressive behaviour is frustration, which occurs when a person is prevented from reaching some desired goal. For example, as was mentioned in the chapter-opening story, Marc Lepine believed that women and feminism were preventing him from gaining admission to École Polytechnique, and he became violent as a result. The concept of aggression as a reaction to frustration is known as the *frustration–aggression hypothesis* and was originally proposed by John Dollard and colleagues in 1939. According to the original hypothesis, frustration always leads to some sort of aggression *and* aggression is always the result of frustration. As you have probably already realized, this hypothesis was criticized. Later researchers, namely Len Berkowitz, reformulated the frustration–aggression hypothesis, saying that frustration is just one of the many factors that can cause a negative emotional response (Berkowitz, 1993). Pain, for example, produces negative sensations that are often intense and uncontrollable, leading to frustration and often aggressive acts against the nearest available target (Berkowitz, 1993). Loud noises, excessive heat, the irritation of someone else's cigarette smoke, and even awful smells can lead people to act out in an aggressive manner (Anderson, 1987; Rotton & Frey, 1985; Rotton et al., 1979; Zillmann et al., 1981).

Frustration is not the only source of aggressive behaviour. Many early researchers, including Sigmund Freud (1930), believed that aggression was a basic human instinct. In Freud's view, aggression was part of the death instinct that drove human beings to destroy both others and themselves, and he believed that if aggression were not released it would cause illness. But if aggression is an instinct present in all humans, it should occur in far more similar patterns across cultures than it does. Instinctual behaviour, as often seen in animals, is not modifiable by environmental influences. Modern approaches try to explain aggression as a biological phenomenon or a learned behaviour, or, as in the case of the general aggression model (GAM), both.

AGGRESSION AND BIOLOGY   There is some evidence that human aggression has at least a partial genetic basis. Studies of twins have shown that if one identical twin has a violent temper, the identical sibling will most likely also have a violent temper. This agreement between twins' personalities happens more often with identical twins than with fraternal twins, showing support for the idea that genetics are involved (Miles & Carey, 1997; Rowe et al., 1999). It may be that some gene or combination of genes makes certain people more susceptible to aggressive responses under the right environmental conditions.

As discussed in Chapter Two, certain areas of the brain seem to control aggressive responses. The amygdala and other structures of the limbic system have been shown to trigger aggressive responses when stimulated in both animals and humans (Adams, 1968; Albert & Richmond, 1977; LaBar et al., 1995; Scott et al., 1997). Charles Whitman, the Tower of Texas sniper, who in 1966 killed his mother, his wife, and then shot and killed 12 more people before finally being killed by law enforcement officers, left a note asking for an examination of his brain. An autopsy did reveal a tumour that was pressing into his amygdala (Lavergne, 1997).

There are also chemical influences on aggression. Testosterone, a male sex hormone, has been linked to higher levels of aggression in humans (Archer, 1991). This hormone may help to explain why violent criminals tend to be young, male, and muscular. They typically have high levels of testosterone and low levels of serotonin, another important chemical found in the brain that was discussed in Chapter Two (Alexander et al., 1986; Brown & Linnoila, 1990; Coccaro & Kavoussi, 1996; Dabbs et al., 2001; Robins, 1996).

Don't some people get violent after drinking too much? Does alcohol do something to those brain chemicals? Alcohol does have an impact on aggressive behaviour. Psychologically, alcohol acts to release inhibitions, making people less likely to control their behaviour even if they are not yet intoxicated. Robert Pihl of McGill University and Jordan Peterson of the University of Toronto are just two of many researchers who have found that alcohol also has biological effects on aggression (Pihl & Peterson, 1993). Specifically, alcohol affects the functioning of many neurotransmitters and in particular is associated with a decrease in serotonin. According to Pihl and Peterson, deficiencies in serotonin have been linked to increases in violence. It should also be noted that the effects of alcohol on aggression are also mediated by situational factors, such as the person's frustration level, which was discussed above.

Don't some people get violent after drinking too much? Does alcohol do something to those brain chemicals?

social role
the pattern of behaviour that is
expected of a person who is in a
particular social position.

This photograph shows a "guard"
searching a "prisoner" in Zimbardo's
famous Stanford prison experiment.
The students in the experiment became
so deeply involved in their assigned
roles that Zimbardo had to cancel the
experiment after only six days—less
than half the time originally scheduled
for the study.

What about children
who grow up in
abusive households?
Are they more likely
to become
abusers
because
of their
exposure
to violence?

AGGRESSION AS A LEARNED SOCIAL BEHAVIOUR   Although frustration, genetics, body chemicals, and even the effects of drugs can be blamed for aggressive behaviour to some degree, much of human aggression is also influenced by learning. The social learning theory explanation for aggression states that aggressive behaviour is learned by watching aggressive models get reinforced for their aggressive behaviour (Bandura, 1980; Bandura et al., 1961). (LINK) *to Chapter Five: Learning, p. 176.* Aggressive models can be parents, siblings, friends, or people on television or in video games.

Some evidence suggests that even taking on a particular *social role*, such as that of a soldier, can lead to an increase in aggressive behaviour. A **social role** is the pattern of behaviour that is expected of a person who is in a particular social position. For example, "doctor" is a social role that implies wearing a white coat, asking certain types of questions, and writing prescriptions, among other things. A deeply disturbing experiment was conducted by famed social psychologist Philip Zimbardo at Stanford University in 1971. The experiment was recorded on film from the beginning to a rather abrupt end: About 70 young men, most of whom were college students, volunteered to participate for two weeks. They were told that they would be randomly assigned the social role of either a guard or a prisoner in the experiment. The "guards" were given uniforms and instructions not to use violence but to maintain control of the "prison." The "prisoners" were booked at a real jail, blindfolded, and transported to the campus "prison," actually the basement of one of the campus buildings. On day two, the prisoners staged a revolt (not planned as part of the experiment), which was quickly crushed by the guards. The guards then became increasingly more aggressive, using humiliation to control and punish the prisoners. For example, prisoners were forced to clean out toilet bowls with their bare hands. The staff observing the experiment had to release five of the prisoners who became so upset that they were physically ill. The entire experiment was cancelled on the sixth day, after one of the prisoners reported to Zimbardo that what the experimenters were doing to the young men was terrible (Zimbardo, 1971). For more information on the experiment, go to **www.prisonexp.org**.

The conclusions of Zimbardo and his colleagues highlighted the influence that a social role, such as that of "guard," can have on perfectly ordinary people. Although history is full of examples of people behaving horribly to others while filling a particular role, one need not travel very far into the past to find an example. In 2003, during the war in Iraq, a U.S. army reserve general was suspended from duty while an investigation into reported prisoner abuses was conducted. Between October and December 2003, investigators found numerous cases of cruel, humiliating, and other startling abuses of the Iraqi prisoners by the army military police stationed at the prison of Abu Ghraib (Hersh, 2004). Among the cruelties reported were pouring cold water on naked detainees, beating them with a broom handle or chair, threatening them with rape, and one case of actually carrying out the threat. American soldiers are not the only ones guilty of crimes such as these. A potent Canadian example happened in Somalia in March 1993, when soldiers from the Canadian Airborne Regiment tortured and beat 16-year-old Shidane Arone to death. How could any normal person have done such things? The "guards" in the Stanford prison study were normal people, but the effect of putting on the uniform and taking on the social role of guard changed their behaviour radically. Is it possible that a similar factor was at work at Abu Ghraib and in Somalia? The behaviour of the guards at Abu Ghraib and the Canadian soldiers in Somalia was not part of a formal, controlled study, so further research will be needed to determine to what degree the social roles at work in situations such as this influence the kind of behaviour seen in these real-life examples.

What about children who grow up in abusive households? Are they more likely to become abusers because of their exposure to violence? No one can deny that abused children are exposed to powerful models of aggression. Their abusing parents get reinforced for their aggressive behaviour when they get what they want from the child. No one can deny that there are people who were abused who go on to become abusers. However, contrary to popular belief, most children who suffer abuse do *not* grow up to become abusers themselves—in fact, only one-third of abused children do so (Kaufman & Zigler, 1993; Oliver, 1993). Instead of becoming abusers themselves, some abused children receive help and overcome the damage from their childhood, whereas others withdraw, isolating themselves rather than becoming abusive (Dodge et al., 1990).

VIOLENCE IN THE MEDIA AND AGGRESSION   I've heard that violent television programs can cause children to become more aggressive. How true is that? An early study, by Canadian Albert Bandura, on the effects on small children of an aggressive model viewed over a movie screen was one of the first attempts to investigate the effect of violence in the media on children's aggressive behaviour (Bandura et al., 1961). Ⓛ Ⓘ Ⓝ Ⓚ *to Chapter Five: Learning, p. 176.* Since then, researchers have examined the impact of television and other media violence on the aggressive behaviour of children of various ages. The conclusions have all been similar: Children who are exposed to high levels of violent media are more aggressive than children who are not (Baron & Reiss, 1985; Bushman & Huesmann, 2000; Centerwall, 1989; Geen & Thomas, 1986; Huesmann & Miller, 1994; Huesmann et al., 1997; Huesmann et al., 2003; Villani, 2001). These studies have found that several factors contribute to the normal aggressive tendencies of the child, with more aggressive children preferring to watch more aggressive media, as well as the age at which exposure begins: the younger the child, the greater the impact. Parenting issues also have an impact, as the aggressive impact of television is lessened in homes in which aggressive behaviour is not tolerated and punishment is not physical.

Violent video games have also come under fire as causing violent acting-out in children, especially young adolescents. The tragic shootings at schools in Canada and the United States have, at least in part, been blamed on violent video games that the students seemed to be imitating. A video game called *Super Columbine Massacre*, which recreates the details of the Columbine shooting (where two boys killed 13 of their fellow students), was a favourite of Kimveer Gill, the 25 year old who killed one person and wounded more than a dozen others at Montreal's Dawson College in September 2006.

In a massive meta-analysis of research into the connection between violent media and aggressive behaviour in children, social psychologist Craig Anderson and colleagues (2003) found clear and consistent evidence that even short-term exposure to violent media significantly increases the likelihood that children will engage in both physical and verbal aggression as well as aggressive thoughts and emotions.

The majority of the research now indicates that violent video games do correlate with increased aggression levels of the children who play them, both young children and adolescents (Anderson, 2003; Anderson & Bushman, 2001; Engelhardt, Bartholow, Kerr, & Bushman, in press; Sestir & Bartholow, 2010). However, on a more positive note, recent research also indicates that the opposite may be true: While violent video games are correlated with increased levels of aggression, more relaxing video games have been shown to make players happier and more kind (Bushman & Whitaker, 2011; Sestir & Bartholow, 2010).

THE GENERAL AGGRESSION MODEL   A newer model known as the **general aggression model (GAM)** builds on the social learning perspective to provide an even more complete account of where aggression comes from (Anderson, 1997; Anderson & Bushman, 2002). According to this model, two types of variables will influence an individual's arousal (increasing physiological arousal or excitement), affect (arousing anger), and cognitions (leading the individual to think angry thoughts), which then influence the individual's likelihood of acting in an aggressive manner.

I've heard that violent television programs can cause children to become more aggressive. How true is that?

A U.S. soldier mistreats an Iraqi prisoner at the Abu Ghraib prison in Iraq. Investigators into alleged abuses at this prison found numerous sadistic and brutal acts committed by U.S. military personnel upon the prisoners.

✳ Explore on **mypsychlab**
Bandura's Study on Observation Learning

general aggression model
modern theory of aggression that states that aggression stems from a wide range of variables that influence an individual's arousal, affect, and cognitions.

prosocial behaviour
socially desirable behaviour that benefits others.

altruism
prosocial behaviour that is done with no expectation of reward and may involve the risk of harm to oneself.

These two types of variables are *situational factors* (factors relating to the current situation) and *person factors* (factors relating to the person involved). Examples of situational factors include frustration, insults, or other types of attack; exposure to aggressive models; and anything that causes someone discomfort (e.g., pain). Examples of person factors include personality traits linked to aggression (e.g., high hostility), attitudes and beliefs about aggression (e.g., that it is acceptable), and biological influences (e.g., increased levels of testosterone). According to the GAM, whether an individual will engage in a thoughtful action (e.g., restraining anger and not aggressing) or an impulsive action (e.g., overt aggression) depends on the individual's appraisal of the situation and factors that may restrain the individual, such as the presence of police (see Figure 12.7). This model is still relatively new and is certainly much more complex than previous theories (such as the frustration-aggression hypothesis), but it is gathering a great deal of support.

PROSOCIAL BEHAVIOUR

If you pay attention to the world around you, you will see that as well as committing acts of aggression, people are often inclined to help others. From picking up dropped papers, to holding the door for someone, to more extreme acts such as jumping in front of a car to rescue a child. This far more pleasant form of human social interaction is **prosocial behaviour**, or socially desirable behaviour that benefits others rather than bringing them harm.

12.13 *What is altruism, and how is deciding to help someone related to the presence of others?*

ALTRUISM   One form of prosocial behaviour that almost always makes people feel good about other people is **altruism**, or helping someone in trouble with no expectation of reward and often without fear of one's own safety. Although no one is surprised by the behaviour of a mother who enters a burning house to save her child, some people are often surprised when total strangers step in to help, risking their own lives for people they do not know.

WHY PEOPLE HELP   Sociobiologists, scientists who study the evolutionary and genetic bases of social organizations in both animals and humans, see altruistic behaviour as a way of preserving one's genetic material, even at the cost of one's own life. This is known as the *kin selection theory* and is why the males of certain species of spiders, for example, seem to willingly become "dinner" for the female mates they have just fertilized, ensuring the continuation of their genes through the offspring she will produce (Koh, 1996). It also explains the mother or father who risks life and limb to save a child. But why do people risk their own lives to help total strangers? Sometimes something within us tells us that we ought to help another person, even if he or she is a stranger.

Two social norms have been identified as explanations for this feeling of needing to help someone. The *norm of reciprocity*, which was discussed in relation to compliance techniques earlier in the chapter, is also applicable when it comes to helping. According to sociologist Alvin Gouldner (1960), we should help people who help us. For example, if you are taking part in the

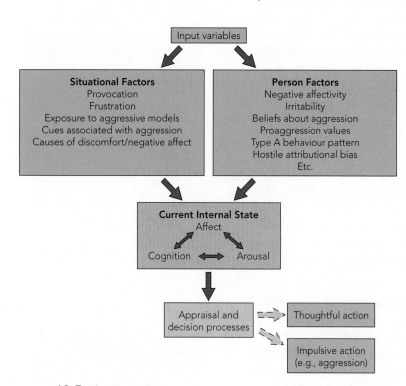

FIGURE 12.7 **The General Aggression Model**

Terry Fox Run and people from school pledge money, the next time they are collecting pledges for a charity, you will feel as though you ought to support them in return. The second norm is the **social-responsibility norm**, which is the belief that we should help people who are in need of help, without consideration of future interactions (Berkowitz, 1972; Schwartz, 1975). For example, when on your way to class you see a person on crutches drop some books, you will most likely feel as though you ought to help. Because the person on crutches is in need of help and cannot easily pick up the books, the norm dictates that we ought to help.

Now that we know why people will help others, even strangers, why do people sometimes refuse to help when their own lives are not at risk, as in the case of Kitty Genovese presented below?

WHY PEOPLE WON'T HELP   At 3:15 a.m. on March 13, 1964, Catherine "Kitty" Genovese had driven into the parking lot of the New York apartment building in which she lived, where a man was waiting in the darkness. Kitty spotted him and ran for the safety of her apartment building, but the man was faster and jumped on her back, stabbing her repeatedly. Kitty was heard to scream, "Oh my God! He stabbed me! Please help me!" But none of the estimated 38 witnesses came to help. At one point, the man was scared off by someone shouting from a window above, but because not one of the witnesses stepped in or called the police, the man returned, raped Kitty, and then stabbed her to death. The entire attack took nearly half an hour.

Kitty Genovese's murder shocked most people when reported in the news in March 1964. People were outraged by the apparent indifference and lack of sympathy for the poor woman's plight. Why did those people simply stand by and watch or listen? Social psychologists would explain that the lack of response to Kitty Genovese's screams for help was not due to indifference or a lack of sympathy but instead to the presence of other people. When other people are present at the scene or are assumed to be present, individuals are affected by two basic principles of social psychology: the bystander effect and diffusion of responsibility.

Bystander Effect   The **bystander effect** refers to the finding that the likelihood of a bystander (someone observing an event and close enough to offer help) helping someone in trouble decreases as the number of bystanders increases. If only one person is standing by, that person is far more likely to help than if there is another person, and the addition of each new bystander decreases the possibility of helping behaviour even more (Darley & Latané, 1968; Eagly & Crowley, 1986; Latané & Darley, 1969). In the case of Kitty Genovese, 38 bystanders were at the windows of the apartment buildings, and none of them helped.

After the Kitty Genovese murder, psychologists became curious about why the bystanders did not call the police right away or try to help in some other way. Two social psychologists, Bibb Latané and John Darley, began a series of research projects to determine the different conditions under which help might or might not be given. In their classic 1968 study, they conducted several experiments, one of which involved pumping smoke into a room where people were filling out questionnaires. Some participants were alone in the room, some were with two other participants, and in a third condition, one participant was in the room with two confederates of the experimenter, who were instructed to visibly notice the smoke but then ignore it. It was found that more participants got up and reported the smoke when they were alone than in the other two conditions (Latané & Darley, 1968). Figure 12.8 illustrates Latané and Darley's findings.

social-responsibility norm
social expectation that people will help those who are dependent on them for help.

bystander effect
the effect that the presence of other people has on the decision to help or not help, with help becoming less likely as the number of bystanders increases.

diffusion of responsibility
occurring when a person fails to take responsibility for actions or for inaction because of the presence of other people who are seen to share the responsibility.

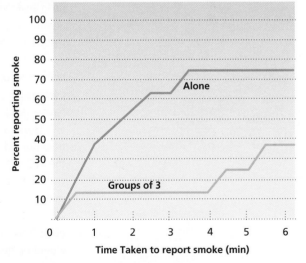

FIGURE 12.8 **Elements Involved in Bystander Response** As you can see in the accompanying graph, the time taken to report smoke and the percentage of people reporting smoke both depended on how many people were in the room at the time the smoke was observed. If a person was alone, he or she was far more likely to report the smoke and report it more quickly than when there were three people (Latané & Darley, 1968).

But why does the ▸
number of bystanders
matter?

✳—Explore on mypsychlab
Bystander Intervention

But why does the number of bystanders matter? **Diffusion of responsibility** is the phenomenon in which a person fails to take responsibility for either action or inaction because of the presence of other people who are seen to share the responsibility (Leary & Forsyth, 1987). Diffusion of responsibility is a form of attribution in which people explain why they acted (or failed to act) as they did because of others. "I was just following orders," "Other people were doing it," and "There were a lot of people there, and I thought one of them would do something" are all examples of statements made in such situations. Kitty Genovese received no help because there were too many potential "helpers," and not one of the people listening to her cries for help took the responsibility to intervene—they thought surely someone else was doing something about it.

This diffusion of responsibility may have been one of the reasons why Toronto subway passengers did nothing while a 79-year-old man was mugged by two attackers. The story of Yusuf Hizel and the failure of his fellow passengers to come to his aid is covered in the Psychology in the News section below.

PSYCHOLOGY IN THE NEWS

Man Robbed on Subway as Bystanders Do Nothing

Around 8:30 p.m. on April 24, 2010, Yusuf Hizel, a 79-year-old man, was travelling eastbound along the Bloor-Danforth line of the Toronto subway system. The man seated beside Hizel asked him for change, and after Hizel refused, a second man approached making the same request. Hizel refused once more and, realizing that he did not feel safe, reached up in an attempt to press the TTC's passenger-assistance alarm (a bright yellow strip that is located around the top of each subway car that makes no sound when pressed but sends an alarm to TTC personnel). He was not able to reach the strip before he was attacked by the two men.

The two men held Hizel down as they stole his wallet. Even though he was crying out for help, none of the other passengers on the train came to Hizel's aid. Not one of the passengers pressed the passenger-assistance alarm or called for help. According to Hizel, "People didn't have a reaction—they just looked at me" (White, 2010).

Hizel, without any help from his fellow passengers, gave chase after his attackers left the train but was unable to catch them. Sadly, Hizel now insists that he will never travel alone on the TTC again; his independence has been taken away (White, 2010).

Many people reacted to this story in disgusted disbelief, some even insisting that Torontonians are heartless and apathetic. (Sounds like people's original opinions of the New Yorkers who witnessed Kitty Genovese's murder, doesn't it?) Others insisted that they also would have been hesitant to act because it would have put their own safety at risk. Latané and Darley would be quick to point out that sometimes things are not what they seem. Perhaps if only one other passenger had been on the subway car that evening, Hizel would have been helped.

Questions for Further Discussion

1. What was your emotional reaction when you read this story?

2. What are some things that we could do as a society to make sure something like this doesn't happen again?

FIVE DECISION POINTS IN HELPING BEHAVIOUR   In all the experiments reported in the preceding section, there were people who did try to help in every condition. What kind of decision-making process might they have gone through before deciding to

TABLE 12.2 HELP OR DON'T HELP: FIVE DECISION POINTS

DECISION POINT	DESCRIPTION	FACTORS INFLUENCING DECISION
Noticing	Realizing that there is a situation that might be an emergency	Hearing a loud crash or a cry for help
Defining an Emergency	Interpreting the cues as signalling an emergency	Loud crash is associated with a car accident; people are obviously hurt.
Taking Responsibility	Personally assuming the responsibility to act	A single bystander is much more likely to act than when others are present (Latané & Darley, 1969).
Planning a Course of Action	Deciding how to help and what skills might be needed	People who feel they have the necessary skills to help are more likely to help.
Taking Action	Actually helping	Costs of helping (e.g., danger to self) must not outweigh the rewards of helping.

help? What are the requirements for deciding when help is needed? Darley and Latané (1968) identified several decision points that a bystander must face before helping someone in trouble. These decision points are outlined in Table 12.2.

Aside from the factors listed in the table, other influences affect the decision to help. For example, the more ambiguous the situation, the less likely it becomes that the situation will be defined as an emergency. If there are other people nearby, especially if the situation is ambiguous, bystanders may rely on the actions of the others to help determine whether or not the situation is an emergency. Since all the bystanders are doing this, it is very likely that the situation will be seen as a non-emergency because no one is moving to help.

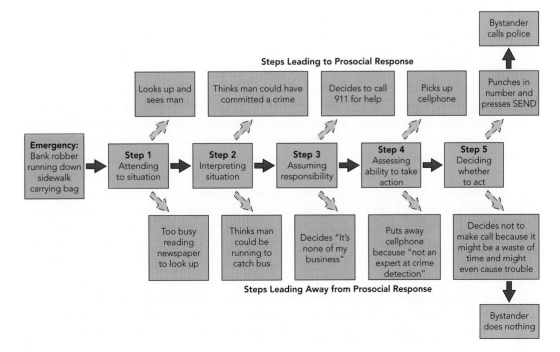

FIGURE 12.9 **Responding to an Emergency: Five Steps to Prosocial Behaviour** A prosocial response to an emergency has been conceptualized as the end point of a series of five steps or choice points. At each step, an individual either becomes less likely or more likely to engage in a prosocial response. (Source: Based on material in Latané & Darley, 1970)

Another factor is the mood of the bystanders. People in a good mood are generally more likely to help than people in a bad mood, but oddly enough, they are not as likely to help if helping would destroy the good mood. Gender of the victim is also a factor, with women more likely to receive help than men if the bystander is male, but not if the bystander is female. Physically attractive people are more likely to be helped. Victims who look like "they deserve what is happening" are less likely to be helped. For example, a man lying on the side of the street who is dressed in shabby clothing and appears to be drunk will be passed by; but, if he is dressed in a business suit, people are more likely to stop and help. Racial and ethnicity differences between victim and bystander also decrease the probability of helping (Richards & Lowe, 2003; Tukuitonga & Bindman, 2002).

PRACTICE QUIZ: HOW MUCH DO YOU REMEMBER?

Pick the best answer.

1. Which of the following has not been studied as a cause of aggressive behaviour?
   a. frustration
   b. pain
   c. alcohol
   d. marijuana

2. The area of the brain that is most involved in aggression is the
   a. amygdala.
   b. pineal gland.
   c. cerebellum.
   d. cortex.

3. Which of the following statements is TRUE?
   a. Abused children always grow up to become abusers.
   b. Abused children rarely grow up to become abusers.
   c. Abused children grow up to become abusers about one-third of the time.
   d. Children who were not abused do not grow up to become abusers.

4. According to the bystander effect, someone in need of help is more likely to get it if there is (are)
   a. no other people standing nearby.
   b. only one other person standing nearby.
   c. several people standing nearby.
   d. a crowd of people standing nearby.

5. In the Latané and Darley experiment, participants were most likely to help when
   a. they were alone in the room.
   b. they were with a friend.
   c. there were three other people in the room.
   d. there was one stranger in the room.

6. Once a situation has been defined as an emergency, the next step in the decision-making process is
   a. noticing.
   b. taking action.
   c. taking responsibility.
   d. planning a course of action.

Answers: 1.-d, 2.-a, 3.-c, 4.-b, 5.-a, 6.-c.

APPLYING PSYCHOLOGY TO EVERYDAY LIFE: ANATOMY OF A CULT

12.14 *Why do people join cults?*

cult
any group of people with a particular religious or philosophical set of beliefs and identity.

The term **cult** literally refers to any group of people with a particular religious or philosophical set of beliefs and identity. In the strictest sense of the word, the Roman Catholic Church and Protestantism are cults within the larger religion of Christianity. But most people associate the term *cult* with a negative connotation: A group of people whose religious or philosophical beliefs and behaviour are so different from that of mainstream organizations that they are viewed with suspicion and seen as existing on the fringes of "normal" behaviour. Although many cults exist without much notice from more mainstream groups, at times members of cults have horrified the public with their actions.

One of the most well-remembered and often cited examples of a cult gone horribly wrong was that of the People's Temple in Jonestown, Guyana, headed by Jim Jones. Originally a Christian offshoot, the People's Temple became a cult under Jones's dictatorial leadership. In 1978, when Jones felt threatened by reporters coming to Guyana, he instructed the entire cult of more than 900 people to commit suicide by either drinking cyanide-laced drinks or shooting each other. A total of 914 people died, including 274 children (WorldIQ.com, 2002).

More recently, 74 followers of the Solar Temple cult died as a result of their involvement with the group. In 1994, 53 members died in Switzerland and Quebec; in 1995, another 16 people died in France; and in 1997, another 5 members died in Quebec. These members believed that one of their leaders, Luc Jouret, was a Knight Templar (a knight endorsed by the Roman Catholic Church during the Middle Ages) who was going to lead them to a planet orbiting Sirius (the dog star). They believed that life was an illusion and that they would be going on to better things once they left Earth.

Why would any person get so caught up in cult beliefs that suicide, and, in some cases, murder becomes a desired behaviour? What kind of person joins a cult in the first place? Although there is no particular personality profile associated with cult membership, cult members do appear to have been in some psychological distress at the time of recruitment by the cult. People who are under a lot of stress, are dissatisfied with their lives, are unassertive, gullible, and dependent, feel a desire to belong to a group, and are unrealistically idealistic are the most likely targets of cult recruitment (Langone, 1996). Young people rebelling against parental authority or trying to become independent of families are prime targets.

In 1978, Reverend Jim Jones, leader of the People's Temple in Jonestown, Guyana, ordered his followers to drink poisoned drinks or shoot each other. Of the cult members, 640 adults died and 274 children were killed either by their own hands or by their parents.

Cult leaders also have certain techniques of persuasion that are common to most cult organizations. The first step is usually something called *love-bombing* by current cult members, who shower the recruit with affection and attention and claim to understand just how the potential cult member feels. Then efforts are made to isolate the recruit from family and friends who might talk them out of joining. This isolation is accomplished in part by keeping the recruits so busy with rigid rituals, ways of dress, meditations, and other activities that they do not allow the recruit time to think about what is happening. All these activities also serve to wear down the resistance of the recruits. Cults also teach their members how to stop questioning thoughts or criticisms, which are typically seen as sins or extremely undesirable behaviour. Access to people and information outside the cult is either kept to a well-guarded minimum or totally shut off (Singer & Lalich, 1995; Zimbardo & Hartley, 1985).

Commitments to the cult are small at first, such as attending a music concert or some other cult function. Eventually, a major step is requested by the cult, such as quitting one's job, turning over money or property to the cult, or similar commitments (remember the foot-in-the-door technique discussed earlier). Leaving a cult is quite difficult, as members of the cult in good standing will often track down a "deserter." Parents, friends, and other family members have been known to hire special "deprogrammers" to help their loved one recover from cult membership, willingly or unwillingly. Sometimes people actually have to "kidnap" their loved one out of the cult environment. Nevertheless, as difficult as it is to leave, 90 percent or more of cult members do eventually get out (Barker, 1983; Galanter, 1983).

Cults have existed all through recorded history and will probably continue to exist in the future. Most cults do not pose a physical threat to their members or others, but the examples of the followers of Jim Jones and Luc Jouret clearly demonstrate that cults, like any group of people, can become deadly.

Questions for Further Discussion

1. In what ways are the methods used by cults on new recruits similar to the methods used by the military when training new soldiers?

2. Is it ethical for the family members of an adult to "kidnap" and deprogram a cult member?

3. Think back to the various compliance techniques discussed earlier in the chapter. Which methods of compliance do cults seem to use to recruit new members?

12 CHAPTER SUMMARY

- Social psychology is the scientific study of how a person's thoughts, feelings, and behaviour are influenced by the real, imagined, or implied presence of other people.

Social Influence: Conformity, Compliance, and Obedience

12.1 *What factors influence people to conform to the actions of others?*

- Asch used a set of comparison lines and a standard line to experiment with conformity, finding that participants conformed to group opinion about one-third of the time, increasing as the number of confederates rose to four, and decreasing if just one confederate gave the correct answer.
- Cross-cultural research has found that collectivistic cultures show more conformity than individualistic cultures. Gender differences do not exist in conformity unless the response is not private, in which case women are more conforming than men.
- Groupthink occurs when a decision-making group feels that it is more important to maintain group unanimity and cohesiveness than to consider the facts realistically.
- Minimizing groupthink involves impartial leadership, seeking outside opinions, using secret ballots, and holding group members responsible for the decisions made by the group.

12.2 *How is compliance defined, and what are four common ways to gain the compliance of another?*

- Compliance occurs when a person changes behaviour as a result of another person asking or directing that person to change.
- Four common ways of getting compliance from others are the foot-in-the-door technique, the door-in-the-face technique, the lowball technique, and the that's-not-all technique.

12.3 *What makes people obey the instructions or orders of others?*

- Milgram conducted experiments in which he found that 65 percent of people obeyed the authority figure of a psychology professor even if it meant hurting, injuring, or possibly killing another person with an electric shock.

12.4 *How does the presence of other people affect a person's performance on a task?*

- When the performance of an individual on a relatively easy task is improved by the presence of others, it is called *social facilitation*. When the performance of an individual on a relatively difficult task is negatively affected by the presence of others, it is called *social impairment*.
- When a person who is lazy is able to work in a group of people, that person often performs less well than if the person were working alone, in a phenomenon called *social loafing*.

Social Cognition: Attitudes, Impression Formation, and Attribution

- Attitudes are tendencies to respond positively or negatively toward ideas, persons, objects, or situations.

12.5 *What are the three components of an attitude, how are attitudes formed, and how can attitudes be changed?*

- The three components of an attitude are the affective (emotional) component, the behavioural component, and the cognitive component.

- Attitudes are often poor predictors of behaviour unless the attitude is very specific or very strong.
- Direct contact with the person, situation, object, or idea can help form attitudes.
- Attitudes can be formed through direct instruction from parents or others.
- Interacting with other people who hold a certain attitude can help an individual form that attitude.
- Attitudes can also be formed through watching the actions and reactions of others to ideas, people, objects, and situations.
- Attitude formation can also be affected by biological and genetic influences.
- Persuasion is the process by which one person tries to change the beliefs, opinions, position, or course of action of another person through argument, pleading, or explanation.
- The key elements in persuasion are the source of the message, the message itself, and the target audience.
- In the elaboration likelihood model, central-route processing involves attending to the content of the message itself, whereas peripheral-route processing involves attending to factors not involved in the message, such as the appearance of the source of the message, the length of the message, and other non-content factors.

12.6 *How do people react when attitudes and behaviour are not the same?*

- Cognitive dissonance is an emotional disturbance that occurs when a person's actions do not match the person's attitudes.
- Cognitive dissonance is lessened by changing the conflicting behaviour, changing the conflicting attitude, or forming a new attitude to justify the behaviour.
- Cognitive dissonance is a universal phenomenon, but it is experienced differently across cultures.
- Impression formation is the forming of the first knowledge a person has about another person.
- The primacy effect in impression formation means that the very first impression one has about a person tends to persist even in the face of evidence to the contrary.
- Impression formation is part of social cognition, or the mental processes that people use to make sense out of the world around them.

12.7 *What are social categorization and implicit personality theories?*

- Social categorization is a process of social cognition in which a person, upon meeting someone new, assigns that person to a category or group on the basis of characteristics the person has in common with other people or groups with whom the perceiver has prior experience.
- One form of a social category is the stereotype, in which the characteristics used to assign a person to a category are superficial and believed to be true of all members of the category.
- An implicit personality theory is a form of social cognition in which a person has sets of assumptions about different types of people, personality traits, and actions that are assumed to be related to each other.
- Schemas are mental patterns that represent what a person believes about certain types of people. Schemas can become stereotypes.

12.8 *How do people try to explain the actions of others?*

- Attribution is the process of explaining the behaviour of others as well as one's own behaviour.

- A situational cause is an explanation of behaviour based on factors in the surrounding environment or situation.
- A dispositional cause is an explanation of behaviour based on the internal personality characteristics of the person being observed.
- The fundamental attribution error is the tendency to overestimate the influence of internal factors on behaviour while underestimating the influence of the situation.
- Some psychologists prefer the term *correspondence bias* to *fundamental attribution error* because dispositional attributions are not always errors.

Social Interaction: Prejudice, Love, Aggression, and Prosocial Behaviour

12.9   *How are prejudice and discrimination different?*

- Prejudice is an unsupported and often negative attitude that a person holds about the members of a particular social group. Discrimination occurs when members of a social group are treated differently because of prejudice toward that group.
- There are many forms of prejudice, including ageism, sexism, racism, and weightism.
- In-groups are the people with whom a person identifies, whereas out-groups are everyone else at whom prejudice tends to be directed.
- Conflict between groups increases prejudice and discrimination according to realistic conflict theory.
- Scapegoating refers to the tendency to direct prejudice and discrimination at out-group members who have little social power or influence. New immigrants are often the scapegoats for frustration and anger of the in-group.

Classic Studies in Psychology: **Brown Eyes, Blue Eyes**

- In 1968, a few days after the assassination of Martin Luther King Jr., a schoolteacher named Jane Elliot divided her class into brown-eyed children and blue-eyed children to teach them a lesson about prejudice.
- The children quickly began to discriminate toward whichever group was the out-group during a certain time period.
- Test scores reflected the treatment received by the out-group, raising questions about the effects of prejudice and discrimination on the education of children who are members of stereotyped out-groups.

12.10   *Why are people prejudiced, and how can prejudice be stopped?*

- Social cognitive theory views prejudice as an attitude acquired through direct instruction, modelling, and other social influences.
- Social identity theory sees a person's formation of a social sense of self within a particular group as being due to three things: social categorization (which may involve the use of reference groups), social identity (the person's sense of belonging to a particular social group), and social comparison (in which people compare themselves to others to improve their own self-esteem or use others as a yardstick by which to judge their own abilities/attitudes/perceptions).
- Stereotype vulnerability refers to the effect that a person's knowledge of the stereotypes that exist against that person's social group can have on that person's behaviour.
- People who are aware of stereotypes may unintentionally come to behave in a way that makes the stereotype real in a self-fulfilling prophecy.
- Intergroup contact is more effective in reducing prejudice if the groups have equal status.

- Prejudice and discrimination are reduced when people must work together to solve a problem because each person has an important key to solving the problem, creating a mutual interdependence. This technique used in education is called the *jigsaw classroom*.
- Prejudice and discrimination can also be reduced when a superordinate goal that is large enough to override all other goals needs to be achieved by all groups.

12.11   *What factors govern attraction and love, and what are some different kinds of love?*

- Many factors govern attraction and love. Some of these include physical attractiveness, physical proximity, similarity, complementarity, and reciprocity of liking.
- Interpersonal attraction refers to liking or having the desire for a relationship with another person.
- Love is a strong affection for another person because of kinship, personal ties, sexual attraction, admiration, or common interests.
- Sternberg states that the three components of love are intimacy, passion, and commitment.
- Romantic love is intimacy with passion, companionate love is intimacy with commitment, and consummate love contains all three components.
- Love is often experienced differently in different cultures.
- Physiological arousal can intensify any emotional reaction, including feelings of being attracted to someone or being in love.

12.12   *What is aggression, and what causes it?*

- Aggression is behaviour intended to hurt or destroy another person, which may be physical or verbal. Frustration is a major source of aggression.
- Frustration often results in aggression, but it is not the sole cause. Instead, it is one of many aversive experiences that may lead to increased aggression.
- Biological influences on aggression may include genetics, the amygdala and limbic system, and testosterone and serotonin levels.
- Social roles are powerful influences on the expression of aggression. Social learning theory states that aggression can be learned through direct reinforcement and through the imitation of successful aggression by a model.
- The general aggression model is a modern theory of aggression that states that aggression stems from a wide range of variables that influence an individual's arousal, affect, and cognitions.
- Studies have concluded that violent television, movies, and video games stimulate aggressive behaviour, both by increasing aggressive tendencies and providing models of aggressive behaviour. Conversely, relaxing video games have been shown to make people happier and nicer.

12.13   *What is altruism, and how is deciding to help someone related to the presence of others?*

- Prosocial behaviour is behaviour that is socially desirable and benefits others.
- Altruism is prosocial behaviour in which a person helps someone else without expectation of reward or recognition, often without fear for his or her own safety.
- The bystander effect means that people are more likely to get help from others if there is only one person nearby or only a few people nearby rather than a larger number. The more people nearby, the less likely it is that help will be offered.

Psychology in the News: Man Robbed on Subway as Bystanders Do Nothing

- Yusuf Hizel, a 79-year-old man, was travelling on the Toronto subway system when he was attacked by two men. Even though he was crying out for help, none of the other passengers on the train came to Hizel's aid. Not one of the passengers pressed the passenger-assistance alarm or called for help.

- Many people reacted to this story in disgusted disbelief, some even insisting that Torontonians are heartless and apathetic.

- Others insisted that they also would have been hesitant to act because it would have put their own safety at risk.

- Perhaps if only one other passenger had been on the subway car that evening, Hizel would have been helped. When others are present at a situation in which help could be offered, there is a diffusion of responsibility among all the bystanders, reducing the likelihood that any one person or persons will feel responsibility for helping.

- The five steps in making a decision to help are noticing, defining an emergency, taking responsibility, planning a course of action, and taking action.

Applying Psychology to Everyday Life: Anatomy of a Cult

12.14 Why do people join cults?

- People who join cults tend to be unhappy, unassertive, gullible, dependent, idealistic, and under stress, and they want to belong. Young people are also likelier to join cults than are older people.

- Cults use love-bombing, isolation, rituals, and activities to keep the new recruits from questions and critical thinking. Cults also use the foot-in-the-door technique.

12 KEY TERMS

aggression 504
altruism 508
attitude 486
attribution 493
attribution theory 493
bystander effect 509
central-route processing (systematic processing) 490
cognitive dissonance 491
companionate love 502
compliance 481
conformity 479
contact hypothesis 499
cult 512
diffusion of responsibility 510
discrimination 496
dispositional cause 493
door-in-the-face technique 481
elaboration likelihood model 489
equal status contact 500
foot-in-the-door technique 481

fundamental attribution error 494
general aggression model 508
groupthink 480
implicit personality theory 493
impression formation 490
in-groups 496
insufficient justification effect 491
interpersonal attraction 501
"jigsaw classroom" 500
lowball technique 481
norm of reciprocity 481
obedience 482
out-groups 496
peripheral-route processing (heuristic processing) 491
persuasion 488
prejudice 496
prosocial behaviour 508
proximity 501
realistic conflict theory 500
reciprocity of liking 502

romantic love 502
self-fulfilling prophecy 499
self-serving bias 495
situational cause 493
social categorization 493
social cognition 486
social cognitive theory 498
social comparison 498
social facilitation 484
social identity 498
social identity theory 498
social impairment 484
social influence 478
social loafing 484
social psychology 478
social role 506
social-responsibility norm 509
stereotype 493
stereotype vulnerability 499
superordinate goals 500
that's-not-all technique 481

TEST YOURSELF

Pick the best answer.

1. Studies have found the degree of conformity to be greater in _____ cultures.
   a. collectivistic
   b. individualistic
   c. Western
   d. European

2. To prevent groupthink, members of a group should do all but which of the following?
   a. Have the leader of the group remain impartial.
   b. Seek outside opinions.
   c. Discourage questions and alternate solutions.
   d. Use secret ballots.

3. Maria's fellow professor asked her to teach an honours class in the spring. Maria agreed only to find out after agreeing that teaching such a course also meant that she would have to attend meetings of the honours professors, go to honours-oriented conventions, and take on special advising duties. Maria had fallen victim to the _____ technique.
   a. foot-in-the-door
   b. door-in-the-face
   c. lowball
   d. that's-not-all

4. Some researchers believe that Milgram's results were a form of the _____ technique of persuasion.
   a. foot-in-the-door
   b. door-in-the-face
   c. lowball
   d. that's-not-all

5. Sandy loves to play pool and has become quite good at the game. Lately, she has noticed that she seems to play better when there

are people watching her than when she is playing alone. This difference in Sandy's playing is most likely the result of
  a. social facilitation.
  c. social loafing.
  b. social impairment.
  d. social laziness.

6. Jerry goes to a lot of dog races because he enjoys them and loves to see the dogs run. For Jerry, going to the dog races a lot represents the _____ component of an attitude.
  a. psychological
  c. cognitive
  b. behavioural
  d. affective

7. Researchers have found that a _____ degree of fear in a message makes it more effective, particularly when it is combined with _____.
  a. maximum; information about how to prevent the fearful consequences
  b. minimum; threats
  c. moderate; threats
  d. moderate; information about how to prevent the fearful consequences

8. Sandy was a juror in the trial for a man accused of stealing guns from a sporting goods store. The defendant was not very well-spoken and came from a very poor background, but Sandy listened carefully to the evidence presented and made her decision based on that. Sandy was using _____ processing.
  a. central-route
  c. cognitive-route
  b. peripheral-route
  d. visual-route

9. Which of the following is not one of the three things people do to reduce cognitive dissonance?
  a. change their behaviour
  c. form a new attitude
  b. change their attitude
  d. ignore the conflict

10. If behaviour is assumed to be caused by internal personality characteristics, this is known as
  a. a situational cause.
  c. a fundamental attribution error.
  b. a dispositional cause.
  d. actor-observer bias.

11. The people with whom a person identifies most strongly are called the
  a. referent group.
  c. out-group.
  b. in-group.
  d. "them" group.

12. Prejudice and discrimination are least likely to develop in which of the following situations?
  a. two different groups of immigrants competing for jobs
  b. two different religious groups, in which each believes that its religion is the right one
  c. two different groups, with one group being blamed for the economic difficulties of the other
  d. two different groups dealing with the aftermath of a hurricane

13. The _____ explanation of prejudice assumes that the same processes that help form other attitudes form prejudiced attitudes.
  a. scapegoat
  c. social cognitive
  b. authoritarian
  d. psychodynamic

14. Patrick is very proud of his Irish heritage and thinks of himself as an Irish Canadian. Patrick has a strong
  a. social identity.
  c. social category.
  b. reference group.
  d. stereotype vulnerability.

15. The self-fulfilling prophecy is a negative outcome of
  a. social identity.
  c. scapegoating.
  b. reference grouping.
  d. stereotype vulnerability.

16. The "Robber's Cave" experiment showed the value of _____ in combating prejudice.
  a. "jigsaw classrooms"
  c. subordinate goals
  b. equal status contact
  d. stereotyping vulnerability

17. Sarah found her soulmate, Jon, when she moved to a small town in Nova Scotia. According to research in interpersonal attraction, the most likely explanation for them "finding" each other is
  a. karma.
  c. fate.
  b. personal attractiveness.
  d. proximity.

18. According to Sternberg, married (committed) people who also have intimacy and passion are in the form of love called _____ love.
  a. companionate
  c. affectionate
  b. romantic
  d. consummate

19. Romantic love is more likely to be the basis of long-term relationships in Canada than in
  a. England.
  c. India.
  b. France.
  d. the United States.

20. The concept of aggression as a basic human instinct driving people to destructive acts was part of early _____ theory.
  a. humanistic
  c. psychoanalytical
  b. behavioural
  d. cognitive

21. The neurotransmitter that seems most involved in aggression is
  a. testosterone.
  c. dopamine.
  b. serotonin.
  d. norepinephrine.

22. Violent video games have been blamed for all but which of the following?
  a. increased levels of aggression in children
  b. increased levels of aggression in adolescents
  c. increased levels of altruism in children
  d. increased incidents of school shootings

23. To which two processes do most social psychologists attribute the failure of Kitty Genovese's neighbours to help her?
  a. bystander effect and altruism
  b. aggression and diffusion of responsibility
  c. altruism and diffusion of responsibility
  d. bystander effect and diffusion of responsibility

24. Cries for help, shouting, and loud noises all help with which step in the decision process for helping?
  a. noticing
  c. taking responsibility
  b. defining an emergency
  d. taking action

25. Cults use all the following except _____ to gain new members.
  a. love-bombing
  c. "foot-in-the-door" technique
  b. isolation
  d. talking with parents of the recruit

Answers: 1.-a, 2.-c, 3.-c, 4.-a, 5.-a, 6.-d, 7.-d, 8.-a, 9.-d, 10.-b, 11.-b, 12.-d, 13.-c, 14.-a, 15.-d, 16.-b, 17.-d, 18.-d, 19.-c, 20.-c, 21.-a, 22.-c, 23.-d, 24.-b, 25.-d.

ScanLife™ Barcode

To access more tests and your own personalized study plan that will help you focus on the areas you need to master before your next class test, be sure to go to **www.MyPsychLab.com**, Pearson Education Canada's online psychology website, available with the access code packaged with your book.

Social Psychology: study of thoughts, feelings, and behaviour influenced by real, imagined, or implied presence of other people

Social Influence

Conforming to the Actions of Others

Asch: Conformity increases with size of group, decreases if at least one other person goes against the majority.

Cross-cultural research: More conformity in collectivistic than individualistic cultures

Gender research: women are more conforming than men in public but not in private, where no differences exist

Groupthink:

Decision makers maintain group unanimity even if incorrect.

Minimizing groupthink involves
▸ Impartial leadership
▸ Seeking outside opinions
▸ Using secret ballots
▸ Holding group members responsible

12.1

Compliance

Occurs when a person changes behaviour as a result of another's influence

Four Common Ways to Gain Compliance
▸ Foot-in-the-door technique
▸ Door-in-the-face technique
▸ Low-ball technique
▸ That's-not-all technique

12.2

Obeying the Instructions of Others

Milgram: 65% of people obeyed a professorial authority figure even if it meant possibly hurting a person.

12.3

Presence of Others Affects Task Performance

Social facilitation: Performance on a task is improved by others' presence.

Social impairment: Performance on an easy task is impaired by others' presence.

Social loafing: People work less in a group than when alone.

12.4

Social Cognition

ATTITUDES ⟷ IMPRESSION FORMATION AND ATTRIBUTION

Attitudes: tendencies to respond positively or negatively toward ideas, persons, objects, or situations

Impression formation: first knowledge a person has about another person; process that people use to make sense of the world

Primacy effect: First impression one has about a person tends to persist.

Three Components of Attitudes, Attitude Formation, and Attitude Change

1. Affective (emotional) component
2. Behavioural component
3. Cognitive component

Factors in Attitude Formation
▸ Attitudes are poor predictors of behaviour.
▸ Direct contact
▸ Direct instruction from parents or others
▸ Interacting with others
▸ Watching actions and reactions of others

Factors in Attitude Change

Persuasion: changing beliefs or actions of another

Key Elements in Persuasion
▸ Source of the message
▸ Message itself
▸ Target audience

Elaboration Likelihood Model
▸ Central-route processing: attending to message content
▸ Peripheral-route processing: attending to factors not involved in message

12.5

Cognitive Dissonance— Attitude Mismatch

Mismatch: Emotional disturbance when a person's actions do not match attitudes

Lessened by changing conflicting behaviours and attitudes, forming new attitudes

12.6

Social Categorization and Implicit Personality Theories

Social categorization: assignment to a category

Stereotype: assignment of characteristics

Implicit personality theory: sets of assumptions about different types of people

Schemas: belief patterns about people

12.7

Explaining Actions

Attribution: process of explaining behaviour

Situational cause: explaining behaviour surrounding environment or situation

Dispositional cause: explaining behaviour based on internal personality characteristics

Fundamental attribution error: overestimating internal factors' influence on behaviour

12.8

Aggression

Behaviour intended to hurt others

Biological factors: genetics, amygdala and limbic system, testosterone/serotonin

Learned factors

▸ **Social learning theory:** reinforcement and imitation of successful aggression (e.g., via social roles)

▸ **Media:** Violent television, movies, and video games can stimulate aggressive behaviour.

▸ **Frustration:** may be linked to aggression

General aggression model: states that aggression stems from a wide range of variables that influence an individual's arousal, affect, and cognitions

12.12

Cults

▸ People who join tend to be young rather than old, and unhappy, gullible, dependent, and under stress, and they want to belong.

▸ Cults use love-bombing, isolation, rituals, and the foot-in-the-door technique

12.14

Altruism

Prosocial behaviour in which a person helps someone else without expectation of reward or recognition, often without fear for one's own safety

Bystander Effect

▸ Presence of others can cause a diffusion of responsibility among all the bystanders.

▸ This diffusion of responsibility leads to a decreased chance of receiving help in an emergency situation.

The Helping Decision—Five Steps

1. Noticing **2.** Defining an emergency **3.** Taking responsibility
4. Planning a course of action **5.** Taking action

12.13

Social Interaction

PREJUDICE AND DISCRIMINATION

LIKING AND LOVING

Prejudice and Discrimination

Prejudice: negative attitudes

Discrimination: differential treatment

In-groups: group person identifies with

Out-groups: treated with prejudice

Realistic conflict theory: Conflict between groups increases prejudice and discrimination

Scapegoating: tendency to direct prejudice and discrimination at out-group members who have little social power or influence

12.9

Causes of and Ways to Stop Prejudice

▸ **Social cognitive theory:** acquired through instruction, modelling, and social influences

▸ **Social identity theory:** sense of self from social categorization, identity, comparison

▸ **Stereotype vulnerability:** Stereotypes may become a self-fulfilling prophecy.

Reducing prejudice

▸ **Equal status-contact:** no group holds power over the others; reduces prejudice

▸ **Jigsaw classroom:** mutual problem solving

▸ **Superordinate goal:** goal that is large enough to override all other goals, which needs to be achieved by all groups

12.10

Factors in Attraction

▸ Physical attractiveness

▸ Proximity

▸ Similarity

▸ Complementary differences

▸ Reciprocity of liking

▸ Physiological arousal can intensify feelings of being in love

Sternberg's Triangular Theory of Love

Liking
Intimacy only

Romantic Love
Intimacy +
Passion

Consummate Love
Intimacy +
Passion + Commitment

Companionate Love
Intimacy +
Commitment

Infatuation
Passion only

Fatuous Love
Passion + Commitment

Empty Love
Commitment only

12.11

13
Psychological Disorders

Tragedy on a Greyhound Bus

On July 30, 2008, Tim McLean, a carnival worker, boarded a Greyhound bus in Edmonton to return home to Winnipeg. Approximately 17 hours later, the bus reached Erikson, Manitoba, where it picked up Vince Li. Li initially sat at the front of the bus, but during a scheduled rest stop he moved to the rear of the bus, taking a seat beside McLean. McLean, with headphones covering his ears and his head against the window, had fallen asleep. According to witnesses, the tragedy that happened next will forever be imprinted on their minds. Li pulled out a large hunting knife and began wildly stabbing McLean's chest and neck regions. The bus pulled over and the other passengers escaped but could only watch in horror as Li displayed McLean's decapitated head. Li continued cutting McLean's body and cannibalized McLean's eyes and parts of his heart. When Portage la Prairie RCMP arrived, Li was still aboard the bus. During an escape attempt, Li was tasered, handcuffed, and taken into custody.

Li was born in China in 1968. He immigrated to Canada and became a Canadian citizen in 2006. Li settled in Winnipeg for a time and worked at a local church and also as a forklift operator. The pastor who hired Li said he appeared happy and never displayed any signs of anger. Rather suddenly, Li left his wife and moved to Edmonton, where he delivered newspapers and worked at a fast-food restaurant and Walmart. Li's newspaper delivery employer described Li as reliable and hard-working, someone who never showed any signs of trouble. Li's wife eventually joined Li in Edmonton.

At trial, Li pleaded not criminally responsible on account of a mental disorder to the charge of second-degree murder. This means that he admitted committing the offence but during the crime could not form the necessary mental intent to be found guilty of the charge. Psychiatrists testified that at the time of the incident Li was suffering from paranoid schizophrenia—a disorder characterized by delusions and hallucinations—and that Li believed God told him that McLean was an evil force that needed to be executed. This voice told Li to "Do it now! If you don't, he's going to kill you." The psychiatrists further stated that Li was responding to treatment, and was beginning to realize what he had done, but still could not accept the fact that he had cannibalized someone. The judge agreed with the psychiatrists, and Li was found not criminally responsible for McLean's murder. Li is currently remanded to a mental health facility in Selkirk, Manitoba. On June 10, 2010, a provincial review board granted Li supervised outdoor walks at the Selkirk facility.

How could a seemingly normal person be capable of such cruel and grotesque behaviour? Is schizophrenia treatable? Is it conceivable that Vincent Li will one day be released into the community?

Why study abnormal behaviour?

Because it is all around us, which raises many questions: How should one react? What should be done to help? What kind of person develops a mental illness? Could this happen to someone close to us? The key to answering these questions is to develop an understanding of just what is meant by abnormal behaviour and the different ways in which behaviour can depart from the "normal" path.

13

WHAT IS ABNORMALITY?

I've heard people call a lot of different things other people do "crazy" or "weird." How do psychologists decide when people are really mentally ill and not just a little odd? Exactly what is meant by the term *abnormal behaviour?* Abnormal compared to what? Who gets to decide what is normal and what is not? Has the term always meant what it means now? These are just a few questions that come to mind when thinking about the study of abnormal behaviour, or **psychopathology** (Wen-Shing & Strelzer, 1997). As can be seen in the following section, definitions of abnormality have depended on cultural ways of explaining behaviour through the ages.

> I've heard people ▶ call a lot of different things other people do "crazy" or "weird." How do psychologists decide when people are really mentally ill and not just a little odd?

A BRIEF HISTORY OF PSYCHOLOGICAL DISORDERS

13.1 *How did people in earlier times explain mental illness?*

Dating from as early as 3000 BCE., archaeologists have found human skulls bearing the evidence of an ancient surgical technique. The skulls have holes cut into them, and the holes were made while the person was still living. In fact, many of the holes show evidence of healing, meaning that the person survived the process. The process of cutting holes into the skull of a living person is called *trepanning* (also spelled *trephining*). Although trepanning is still done today to relieve pressure of fluids on the brain, in ancient times the reason may have had more to do with releasing the "demons" possessing the poor victim (Gross, 1999). Ancient peoples might well have assumed that people who were behaving oddly were possessed by evil spirits. As trepanning had to be rather unpleasant, the disordered person may very well have tried hard to be "normal" after treatment, too.

Hippocrates, a Greek physician during the time in which the rest of the world and even many Greeks believed in the demon possession explanation of mental illness, challenged that belief with his assertion that illnesses of both the body and the

psychopathology
the study of abnormal behaviour.

mind were the result of imbalances in the body's vital fluids, or *humours*. Although Hippocrates was not correct in his assumptions about the humours of the body (phlegm, black bile, blood, and yellow bile), his was the first recorded attempt to explain abnormal behaviour as due to some biological process.

Moving forward in time, people of the Middle Ages believed in spirit possession (through the teachings of the Roman Catholic Church) and the treatment of choice was a religious one: *exorcism*, or the formal casting out of the demon through a religious ritual. During the Renaissance, belief in demon possession (in which the possessed person was at least seen as a victim) gave way to a belief in witchcraft, and mentally ill persons were most likely called witches and put to death.

WHAT IS ABNORMAL?

Defining abnormal behaviour or abnormality is not as simple as it might seem at first. The easy way out is to say that abnormal behaviour is behaviour that is not normal, but what does that mean?

13.2   *What are the different ways in which abnormal behaviour can be defined?*

STATISTICAL DEFINITION   One way to define *normal* and *abnormal* is to use a statistical definition. Frequently occurring behaviour would be considered normal, and behaviour that is rare would be abnormal. That kind of definition works fine with a behaviour such as talking to others, as the two rarer possibilities would be not talking to anyone at all and talking too much to too many people—both of which would be considered abnormal. What about a behaviour such as happiness? Is a medium level of happiness really the "norm" most people strive to reach? A total lack of happiness would be abnormal, but should a person who is very happy really be labelled abnormal? Statistical definitions of abnormality wouldn't work for intelligence either, as only mental retardation (the lower end of a distribution of intelligence in a population) would be considered undesirable and abnormal (Troisi & McGuire, 2002). People possessing a higher degree of intelligence than is "normal" are actually highly respected.

SOCIAL NORM DEVIANCE   Another way of defining abnormality is to see it as something that goes against the norms or standards of the society in which the individual lives. For example, refusing to wear clothing in a society that does not permit nudity would be seen as abnormal. But deviance (variation) from social norms is not always labelled as negative, abnormal behaviour, as in a person who decides to become a monk and live in a monastery in Canada. That would be unusual behaviour and not what the society considers a standard behaviour, but it wouldn't be a sign of abnormality.

Using social nonconformity as a criterion for abnormality also creates a problem when dealing with different cultures. Behaviour that would be labelled *disordered* in one culture may be quite acceptable in another. (See the Psychology in the News section later in this chapter, p. 526.) Even within one culture, the **situational context** (the social or environmental setting of a person's behaviour) can make a difference in how behaviour is labelled. For example, if a man comes to a therapist complaining of people listening in on his phone conversations and spying on all his activities, the therapist's first thought might be that the man is suffering from feelings of persecution. But if the man then explains that he is in a witness protection

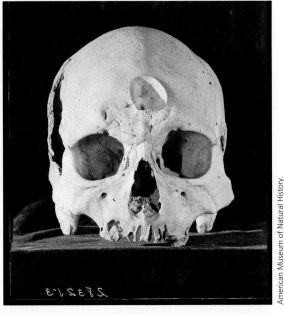

American Museum of Natural History.

This human skull clearly shows the signs of trepanning, a process in which ancient priests or medicine men cut holes into the skulls of a living person, perhaps to release the "demons" making the person's behaviour odd or disturbed. Some who were treated in this way must have survived, as this hole shows some evidence of healing.

Francisco Goya, El Hechizo, 1787–88, Fundacion Lazaro Galdiano.

The illustration shows a priest and his helper performing an exorcism as a demon is dispelled from this tormented woman. This represents what ancient people believed was the cause of mental illness: demonic possession.

situational context
the social or environmental setting of a person's behaviour.

This homeless person has piled on so much clothing that it is impossible to tell if it is a man or a woman. Homeless people are sometimes mentally ill people who have not been able to keep their jobs or find work because of their mental illness, and they often feel that they have nowhere to go for help. Which of the ways to determine if behaviour is abnormal seems to apply to this situation?

So how do psychologists decide what is abnormal?

▶

subjective discomfort
emotional distress or emotional pain.

maladaptive
anything that does not allow a person to function within or adapt to the stresses and everyday demands of life.

psychological disorders
any pattern of behaviour that causes people significant distress, causes them to harm others, or harms their ability to function in daily life.

What causes ▶ psychological disorders?

program, the complaints take on an entirely different and quite understandable tone.

SUBJECTIVE DISCOMFORT   One good sign of abnormality is when the person experiences a great deal of **subjective discomfort**, or emotional distress, while engaging in a particular behaviour. A woman who suffers from a fear of going outside her house, for example, would experience a great deal of anxiety when trying to leave home and distress over being unable to leave. However, all behaviour that might be considered abnormal does not necessarily create subjective discomfort in the person committing the act—a serial killer, for example, does not experience emotional distress after taking someone's life, and some forms of disordered behaviour involve showing no emotions at all.

INABILITY TO FUNCTION NORMALLY   Behaviour that does not allow a person to fit into society or function normally can also be labelled *abnormal*. This kind of behaviour is termed **maladaptive**, meaning that the person finds it difficult to adapt to the demands of day-to-day living. Maladaptive behaviour includes behaviour that may initially help a person cope but has harmful or damaging effects. For example, a woman who cuts herself to relieve anxiety does experience initial relief but is harmed by the action. Maladaptive behaviour is a key element in the definition of abnormality.

THE FINAL DEFINITION OF ABNORMALITY

So how do psychologists decide what is abnormal? Perhaps the shortest definition of abnormality or **psychological disorders** is any pattern of behaviour that causes people significant distress, causes them to harm themselves or others, or harms their ability to function in daily life. To get a clear picture of abnormality, it is often necessary to take all the factors discussed thus far into account. Clinical psychologists and other psychological professionals must consider several different criteria in determining whether or not a behaviour is abnormal (at least two of these criteria must be met to form a diagnosis of abnormality):

1. Is the behaviour unusual, such as experiencing severe panic when faced with a stranger or being severely depressed in the absence of any stressful life situations?
2. Does the behaviour go against social norms?
3. Does the behaviour cause the person significant subjective discomfort?
4. Is the behaviour maladaptive?
5. Does the behaviour cause the person to be dangerous to self or others, as in the case of someone who tries to commit suicide or attacks other people without reason?

MODELS OF ABNORMALITY

What causes psychological disorders? In Chapter Eleven, several different theories of personality were discussed. These theories of personality can be used to describe and explain the formation of not only ordinary behaviour and personality but also disordered behaviour and abnormal personality. How one explains disordered behaviour, then, depends on which theoretical model is used to explain personality in general.

THE BIOLOGICAL MODEL: MEDICAL CAUSES FOR PSYCHOLOGICAL DISORDERS

13.3 *How are psychological disorders related to the brain and body chemistry?*

The **biological model** proposes that psychological disorders have a biological or medical cause (Gamwell & Tomes, 1995). This model explains disorders such as anxiety, depression, and schizophrenia as caused by chemical imbalances, genetic problems, brain damage and dysfunction, or some combination of those causes.

The biological or medical model has had a great deal of influence, especially in the language used to describe disorders: *mental illness*, *symptoms of disorder*, and terms such as *diagnosis*, *mental patient*, *mental hospital*, *therapy*, and *remission* all come from medical terminology. The use of such terms, although still widespread, may tend to bias the assumptions of professionals who are not psychiatrists or medical doctors toward a biological cause for disordered behaviour.

THE PSYCHOLOGICAL MODELS

Although biological explanations of psychological disorders are influential, they are not the only ways or even the first ways in which disorders are explained. Several psychological models attempt to explain disordered behaviour as the result of various forms of emotional, behavioural, or thought-related malfunctioning.

13.4 *How can psychological disorders be explained by the different viewpoints in psychology?*

PSYCHOANALYSIS: HIDING PROBLEMS   The psychoanalytic model, based on the work of Freud and his followers, **LINK** *to Chapter Eleven: Theories of Personality, p. 438,* explains disordered behaviour as the result of repressing, or hiding, one's threatening thoughts, memories, and concerns in the unconscious mind (Carducci, 1998). These repressed thoughts and urges try to resurface, and disordered behaviour develops as a way of keeping the thoughts repressed. For example, a woman who has unacceptable thoughts of sleeping with her brother-in-law might be compelled to wash her hands every time those thoughts threaten to become conscious, ridding herself symbolically of the "dirty" thoughts.

BEHAVIOURISM: LEARNING PROBLEMS   Behaviourists, who define personality as a set of learned responses, have no trouble explaining disordered behaviour as being learned just like normal behaviour (Skinner, 1971; Watson, 1913). For example, when Joanne was a small child, a spider dropped onto her leg, causing Joanne to scream and react with fear. Her mother came running and made a big fuss over her, soothing her and giving her lots of attention. The next time Joanne saw a spider, she screamed again because of the prior fear-provoking incident. She also was rewarded with the attention of everyone in the room. Eventually, Joanne would experience a fear reaction and scream if someone just said the word *spider*. Behaviourists would say that Joanne's fear of the spider was classically conditioned to occur to the mere sight of a spider or even the word, and her screaming reaction was positively reinforced by all the attention and soothing.

COGNITIVE PERSPECTIVE: THINKING PROBLEMS   **Cognitive psychologists**, who study the way people think, remember, and mentally organize information, see abnormal behaviour as resulting from illogical thinking patterns (Mora, 1985). A depressed person, for example, may be taking small problems and blowing them out of proportion: "I flunked my algebra test, so my life is ruined!" A cognitive psychologist might explain Joanne's fear of spiders as distorted thinking: "All spiders are vicious and will bite me, and I will die!" Joanne's particular thinking patterns

Simulate on **mypsychlab**

Closer Look Simulation:
Psychological Disorders

biological model
model of explaining behaviour as caused by biological changes in the chemical, structural, or genetic systems of the body.

cognitive psychologists
psychologists who study the way people think, remember, and mentally organize information.

biopsychosocial model
perspective in which abnormal behaviour is seen as the result of the combined and interacting forces of biology, psychology, culture, and our social environments.

put her at a higher risk of depression and anxiety than those of a person who thinks more logically.

BIOPSYCHOSOCIAL PERSPECTIVE: ALL OF THE ABOVE

In recent years, the biological, psychological, and sociocultural influences on abnormality have no longer been seen as independent causes of abnormal behaviour. Instead, these influences interact with one another to cause the various forms of disorders. For example, a person may have a genetically inherited tendency for a type of disorder, such as anxiety, but may not develop the full-blown disorder unless the family and social environments produce the right stressors at the right time in development. How accepting of such disorders the particular culture is will also play a part in determining the exact degree and form that anxiety disorder might take. This is known as the **biopsychosocial model** of disorder, which has become a very influential way to view the connection between mind and body.

PSYCHOLOGY IN THE NEWS

A Look at Abnormality in Various Cultures

13.5 *How is abnormality viewed in other kinds of cultures?*

As mentioned earlier, what's normal in one culture may be abnormal in another culture. **Cultural relativity** refers to the need to consider the unique characteristics of the culture in which a person with a disorder was nurtured to be able to correctly diagnose and treat the disorder (Castillo, 1997). For example, in most Asian cultures, mental illness is often seen as a shameful thing that brings disgrace to one's family. It may be seen as something inherited and, therefore, something that would hurt the marriage chances of other family members, or it may be seen as stemming from something the family's ancestors did wrong in the past (Ritts, 1999; Ying, 1990). This perception leads many Asian people suffering from disorders that would be labelled as *depression* or even *schizophrenia* to report bodily symptoms rather than emotional or mental ones because bodily ailments are more socially acceptable (Fedoroff & McFarlane, 1998; Lee, 1995; Ritts, 1999).

Some disorders called **culture-bound syndromes** are found only in particular cultures. Here are a few examples, together with the culture in which they are found (Ritts, 1999):

- *Koro:* Found primarily in China and a few other South Asian and East Asian countries, koro involves a fear that one's genitals are shrinking (Pfeiffer, 1982).

- *Taijin-kyofu-sho (TKS):* TKS is found primarily in Japan and also involves excessive fear and anxiety, but in this case it is the fear that one will do something in public that is socially inappropriate or embarrassing such as blushing, staring, or having an offensive body odour (Kirmayer, 1991).

- *Pibloktoq:* Pibloktoq, also known as *arctic hysteria*, is recognized by the Canadian Inuit and is characterized by periods of extreme excitement in which individuals often become irrational (e.g., running in the snow naked) or violent. The unique Inuit diet, which is very high in vitamin A, is thought to play a role in the disorder (Landy, 1985).

- *Susto:* Susto is a kind of magical fright found among the Quechua-speaking people of the Andes. It is seen as a "loss of soul" triggered by some frightening experience, after which the person falls to the ground and experiences appetite and weight loss, weakness, problems sleeping, depression, and apathy (Pfeiffer, 1982).

cultural relativity
the need to consider the unique characteristics of the culture in which behaviour takes place.

culture-bound syndromes
disorders found only in particular cultures.

- *Amok:* The term comes from Southeast Asia, but similar concepts are found in Latin America as well as in certain North American First Nations. Amok results from a perceived insult or slight, which is followed by a period of brooding and then a violent or aggressive outburst, during which the person may attack others and may not remember doing so (Pfeiffer, 1982).

- *Anorexia nervosa:* The eating disorder anorexia, in which individuals starve themselves to become thin, is typically found only in Western cultures such as Canada, the United States, and Great Britain (Bemporad, 1997; Garner & Garfinkel, 1980). There is some evidence that the incidence rates in other non-Western cultures are changing as exposure to Western culture through the media increases (Ritenbaugh et al., 1992) and that in some cultures starvation is not motivated by a desire to be thin but rather by eccentric nutritional ideas or religious fasting (Castillo, 1997; Rieger et al., 2001).

Questions for Further Discussion

1. Think about your own culture. Is there a disorder or behaviour that seems to be unique to your culture?

2. Are there superstitions or magical beliefs in your culture or social group that could become the basis for a disorder?

◉—▭ **Watch** on **mypsychlab**
Current Diagnostic Models

PRACTICE QUIZ: HOW MUCH DO YOU REMEMBER?

Pick the best answer.

1. Who would be most likely to assume that psychological disorders are caused by an imbalance in the fluids of the body?
   a. an ancient Egyptian physician   **c.** an ancient Greek physician
   b. a modern psychiatrist   **d.** a physician of the Middle Ages

2. Lisa has started having feelings of fearfulness about going to school. She has begun to suffer from headaches and stomachaches and has missed several days of school already. Lisa's condition is abnormal from the _____ definition.
   a. statistical   **c.** social deviance
   b. situational context   **d.** subjective discomfort

3. Which model of abnormality explains abnormal behaviour as caused by illogical thinking?
   a. psychoanalytic   **c.** behavioural
   b. cognitive   **d.** biological

4. Elliot is attracted to his beautiful cousin, Ginny, but knows that she is too closely related to him. He believes he has successfully overcome this forbidden attraction but still finds that every time Ginny is near him he is overwhelmed with feelings of anxiety and feels the need to wash his hands. Which model of abnormality would most likely explain Elliot's behaviour?
   a. psychoanalytic   **c.** behavioural
   b. cognitive   **d.** biological

5. What term do the Inuit of Arctic Canada use to describe episodes of extreme irrational or violent excitement?
   a. arctic hysteria   **c.** pibloktoq
   b. koro   **d.** both a and c

6. In Japan, the disorder called _____ centres on a fear of doing something embarrassing or socially inappropriate.
   a. koro   **c.** susto
   b. taijin-kyofu-sho   **d.** amok

Answers: 1-c, 2-d, 3-b, 4-a, 5-d, 6-b.

DIAGNOSTIC AND STATISTICAL MANUAL, VERSION IV, TEXT REVISION (DSM-IV-TR)

13.6 How do psychologists decide what kind of disorder a person has?

In 1952, the first edition of the *Diagnostic and Statistical Manual of Mental Disorders (DSM)* was published to help psychological professionals diagnose psychological disorders. The current version of the *DSM* is called the *Diagnostic and Statistical Manual of Mental Disorders, Version IV, Text Revision* (*DSM-IV-TR*; American Psychiatric

TABLE 13.1 THE AXES OF THE DSM-IV-TR

AXIS	TYPE OF INFORMATION	DESCRIPTION IN BRIEF
Axis I	Clinical Disorders and Other Conditions That May Be a Focus of Clinical Attention	Psychological disorders that impair functioning and are stressful, and factors that are not disorders but that may affect functioning, such as academic or social problems
Axis II	Personality Disorders and Mental Retardation	Rigid, enduring, maladaptive personality patterns and mental retardation
Axis III	General Medical Conditions	Chronic and acute illnesses and medical conditions that may have an impact on mental health
Axis IV	Psychosocial and Environmental Problems	Problems in the physical surroundings of the person that may have an impact on diagnosis, treatment, and outcome
Axis V	Global Assessment of Functioning	Overall judgment of current functioning, including mental, social, and occupational

Source: Adapted from the American Psychiatric Association, *DSM-IV-TR* (2000).

Association, 2000a). The text revision did not change any categories from the previous version of the *DSM-IV*, but it added new text material to the existing categories.

CATEGORIES IN THE *DSM-IV-TR*

13.7   *What are the different types of psychological disorders, and how common are they?*

The *DSM-IV-TR* describes about 250 different psychological disorders. Each disorder is described in terms of its symptoms, the typical path the disorder takes as it progresses, and a checklist of specific criteria that must be met for the diagnosis of that disorder to be made. The manual also divides these disorders and relevant facts about the person being diagnosed along five different categories, or axes (see Table 13.1). A psychologist or psychiatrist assesses the person on each of these five axes.

Axis I, Clinical Disorders, contains the disorders that bring most people to the attention of a psychological professional. With one exception, all the psychological disorders are listed on this axis. The exception is the personality disorders, which are listed on Axis II along with mental retardation. The reason for this is that unlike most psychological disorders that appear at some later point in a person's life, personality disorders seem to exist almost from birth and are relatively stable and enduring. This almost innate quality makes personality disorders more similar to a condition such as mental retardation, which also exists as a part of the individual's biological makeup.

Axis III includes physical disorders that affect a person's psychological *adjustment*, such as juvenile diabetes, chromosome disorders such as Klinefelter's syndrome, and high blood pressure. (In psychology, the term *adjustment* refers to a person's ability to function normally in everyday life.) Axis IV contains information about problems in the person's life that might affect adjustment, such as the death of a loved one, the loss of a job, or poverty. Finally, Axis V is an overall judgment made by the psychological professional of the person's mental health and adjustment, literally a rating on a scale of 0 to 100. For example, scores of 91–100 would be interpreted as

TABLE 13.2 AXIS I DISORDERS OF THE DSM-IV-TR	
DISORDER	**EXAMPLES**
Disorders usually first diagnosed in infancy, childhood, or adolescence	Learning disabilities, ADHD, bedwetting, speech disorder
Delirium, dementia, amnesia, and other cognitive disorders	Alzheimer's, Parkinson's, amnesia caused by physical causes
Psychological disorders caused by a general medical condition	Personality change caused by a brain tumour
Substance-related disorders	Alcoholism, drug addictions
Schizophrenia and other psychotic disorders	Schizophrenia, delusional disorders, hallucinations, paranoid psychosis
Mood disorders	Depression, mania, bipolar disorders
Anxiety disorders	Panic disorder, phobias, stress disorders
Somatoform disorders	Hypochondria, conversion disorder
Factitious disorders	Pathological lying, Munchausen syndrome
Dissociative disorders	Multiple personality, amnesia not caused by physical causes
Sexual and gender identity disorders	Sexual desire disorders, paraphilias
Eating disorders	Anorexia, bulimia
Sleep disorders	Insomnia, sleep terror disorder, sleepwalking, narcolepsy
Impulse-control disorders not elsewhere classified	Kleptomania, pathological gambling, pyromania
Adjustment disorders	Mixed anxiety, conduct disturbances

superior functioning, 71–80 would be considered temporary problems due to stress, and 41–50 would indicate serious symptoms.

For a listing and brief description of the disorders found on Axis I, see Table 13.2.

HOW COMMON ARE PSYCHOLOGICAL DISORDERS?

That table has a pretty long list of disorders, but most people don't get these problems, right? Actually, psychological disorders are more common than most people might think. In any given year, about one in every five Canadian adults will suffer from some form of mental disorder (Public Health Agency of Canada, 2002a).

It is also important to remember that it is quite common for people to suffer from more than one mental disorder at a time, a phenomenon called *comorbidity*. For example, a person with depression may also have a substance abuse disorder, or a person with an anxiety disorder may also suffer from a sleep disorder (NIMH, 2001). Table 13.3 has percentages of selected psychological disorders in Canada.

Before describing the various categories and types of disorders, a word of caution: It's very easy to see oneself in these disorders. Just as medical students often become convinced that they have every one of the symptoms for some rare, exotic disease they have been studying, psychology students studying abnormal behaviour can also become convinced that they have some mental disorder, a problem that can be called *psychology student's syndrome.* The problem is that so many psychological disorders are really ordinary variations in human behaviour taken to an extreme. For example, some people are natural-born worriers. They look for things that can go wrong around every corner. That doesn't make them disordered—it makes them pessimistic

That table has a pretty long list of disorders, but most people don't get these problems, right? ◀

TABLE 13.3 OCCURRENCE OF PSYCHOLOGICAL DISORDERS IN CANADA	
DISORDER CATEGORY	**OCCURRENCE IN CANADIAN ADULTS**
Mood Disorders (all types)	
Major depression	4.4%
Bipolar disorder	1.0%
Anxiety Disorders	
Obsessive-compulsive disorder	1.8%
Panic disorder	0.7%
Social phobia	6.7%
Substance Dependence	3.3%
Eating Disorders	
Anorexia	0.5%
Bulimia	0.8%

Sources: Public Health Agency of Canada (2002a, 2002b); Tiwari & Wang (2006).

Statistically speaking, about one out of every five of the people in this crowd probably suffers from some form of psychological disorder.

But doesn't **everybody** ▶ have anxiety sometimes? What makes it a disorder?

worriers. It doesn't become a disorder until the worrying gets out of hand or takes place when there's nothing to worry about or go wrong. So if you start "seeing" yourself or even your friends and family in any of the following discussions, don't panic—all of you are *probably* okay.

ANXIETY DISORDERS: WHAT, ME WORRY?

13.8 *What are the different types of anxiety disorders and their symptoms?*

The category of **anxiety disorders** includes all disorders in which the most dominant symptom is excessive or unrealistic anxiety. Anxiety can take very specific forms, such as a fear of a specific object, or it can be a very general emotion, such as that experienced by someone who is worried and doesn't know why.

But doesn't everybody have anxiety sometimes? What makes it a disorder?
There's a difference between anxiety that is realistic and has a known source and the kind of anxiety found in disorders. If final exams are coming up and a student hasn't studied enough, that student's anxiety is understandable and realistic. But a student who has studied, has done well on all the class tests, and is very prepared who still worries excessively about passing is showing an unrealistic amount of anxiety. People who are in danger of losing their job might experience quite a bit of anxiety, but its source is obvious and understandable. But people whose life is going well and for whom nothing bad is looming in the future who still feel extremely anxious may be experiencing an anxiety disorder. **Free-floating anxiety** is the term given to anxiety that seems to be unrelated to any realistic, known factor, and it is often a symptom of an anxiety disorder (Freud & Gay, 1977).

Post-traumatic and acute stress disorders are also anxiety disorders but were discussed thoroughly in Chapter Ten and will not be repeated here. Ⓛ Ⓘ Ⓝ Ⓚ *to Chapter Ten: Stress and Health, p. 396.*

PHOBIC DISORDERS: WHEN FEARS GET OUT OF HAND

One of the more specific anxiety disorders is a **phobia**, an irrational, persistent fear of something. The "something" might be an object or a situation or may involve social situations.

anxiety disorders
disorders in which the main symptom is excessive or unrealistic anxiety and fearfulness.

free-floating anxiety
anxiety that is unrelated to any realistic, known source.

phobia
an irrational, persistent fear of an object, situation, or social activity.

When I get up in front of the class to do a presentation, I get really nervous. Is this fear a common phobia?

SOCIAL PHOBIAS (SOCIAL ANXIETY DISORDER)   **Social phobias** (also called *social anxiety disorders*) involve a fear of interacting with others or being in a social situation and are some of the most common phobias people experience (WHO International Consortium in Psychiatric Epidemiology, 2000). University of British Columbia researchers note that persons with a social phobia often worry about their public appearance (e.g., "Do I look okay?" "Do I look foolish?") and are afraid of being evaluated in some negative way by others, so they tend to avoid situations that could lead to something embarrassing or humiliating (Crozier & Alden, 2001). Other Canadian research has shown that persons with social phobia often see themselves as not being as good as others (Antony, Rowa, Liss, Swallow, & Swinson, 2005), and they are very critical of the social skills they have (Taylor & Alden, 2005). A large survey done in Manitoba and Alberta found that among those with social fears, the most common social fears were giving a presentation or speech in front of others (15 percent); walking into a room when everyone in the room was already sitting (13 percent); talking or dealing with a person of authority (10 percent); making eye contact (10 percent); using a public restroom in the presence of others (9 percent); and going out to a party or social event (9 percent; Stein, Torgrud, & Walker, 2000).

SPECIFIC PHOBIAS   A **specific phobia** is an irrational fear of some object or specific situation, such as a fear of dogs, or a fear of being in small, enclosed spaces (**claustrophobia**). Other specific phobias include a fear of injections (*trypanophobia*), fear of dental work (*odontophobia*), fear of blood (*hematophobia*), and fear of heights (**acrophobia**). For a listing of common phobias, see Table 13.4.

AGORAPHOBIA   A third type of phobia is **agoraphobia**, a Greek name that literally means "fear of the marketplace." Although that makes it sound like a social phobia, agoraphobia is a little more complicated. It is actually the fear of being in a place or situation (social or not) from which escape is difficult or impossible if something should go wrong (APA, 2000a). So agoraphobics are often afraid of not only being in crowds but also crossing bridges, travelling in a car or plane, eating in restaurants, and sometimes even of leaving the house. To be in any of these situations or to even think about being in such situations can lead to extreme feelings of anxiety and even panic attacks (see the information about panic attacks on p. 532).

If a person has agoraphobia, it might be difficult to even go to work or the store, right? Exactly. People with specific phobias can usually avoid the object or situation without too much difficulty, and people with social phobias may simply

◀ When I get up in front of the class to do a presentation, I get really nervous. Is this fear a common phobia?

Many people get nervous when they have to speak in front of an audience. Fear of public speaking is a common social phobia. Can you remember a time when you experienced a fear like this?

If a person has agoraphobia, it might be difficult to even go to work or the store, right?

social phobia
fear of interacting with others or being in social situations that might lead to a negative evaluation.

specific phobia
fear of objects or specific situations or events.

claustrophobia
fear of being in a small, enclosed space.

acrophobia
fear of heights.

agoraphobia
fear of being in a place or situation from which escape is difficult or impossible.

TABLE 13.4 **COMMON PHOBIAS AND THEIR SCIENTIFIC NAMES**	
FEAR OF ...	**SCIENTIFIC NAME**
Washing and bathing	Ablutophobia
Spiders	Arachnophobia
Lightning	Ceraunophobia
Dirt, germs	Mysophobia
Snakes	Ophidiophobia
Darkness	Nyctophobia
Fire	Pyrophobia
Foreigners, strangers	Xenophobia
Animals	Zoophobia

Source: Adapted from Culbertson (2003).

Canadian Howie Mandel hosts the popular game show *Deal or No Deal*. He suffers from obsessive-compulsive disorder and a specific phobia, *mysophobia* (fear of germs and contamination). His phobia is so severe that he avoids shaking hands with his enthusiastic contestants, opting instead to exchange fist pounds.

I knew someone who ▶ had just had a baby, and she spent the first few nights home with the baby checking it to see if it was breathing— is that an obsessive-compulsive disorder?

👁 Watch on **mypsychlab**

When Does a Fear Become a Phobia: Sue Minkea

obsessive-compulsive disorder disorder in which intruding, recurring thoughts or obsessions create anxiety that is relieved by performing a repetitive, ritualistic behaviour (compulsion).

panic attack sudden onset of intense panic in which multiple physical symptoms of stress occur, often with feelings that one is dying.

avoid jobs and situations that involve meeting people face to face. But people with agoraphobia cannot avoid their phobia's source because it is simply being outside in the world. A severe case of agoraphobia can make a person's home a prison, leaving the person trapped inside, unable to go to work, shop, or engage in any kind of activity that requires going out of the home.

OBSESSIVE-COMPULSIVE DISORDER

Sometimes people get a thought running through their head that just won't go away, like when a song gets stuck in one's mind. If that particular thought causes a lot of anxiety, it can become the basis for an **obsessive-compulsive disorder** (OCD), a disorder in which intruding thoughts that occur again and again (obsessions, such as a fear that germs are on one's hands) are followed by some repetitive, ritualistic behaviour (compulsion, such as repeated handwashing) meant to lower the anxiety caused by the thought (Clark, 2004; Soomro, 2001). World-renowned OCD expert David Clark at the University of New Brunswick notes that OCD sufferers know their obsessions and compulsions are groundless and excessive but at any given time they may become uncertain of this fact. Children afflicted with OCD, however, may not realize or understand that their obsessive concerns and ritualistic behaviours are groundless and excessive (Clark, 2004). Some other examples of obsessive thoughts and compulsive behaviours include an obsession with having left something undone, resulting in the constant checking and rechecking of one's work, or thinking that one might do something to harm a loved one, leading to counting and recounting the knives in the kitchen.

I knew someone who had just had a baby, and she spent the first few nights home with the baby checking it to see if it was breathing—is that an obsessive-compulsive disorder? No, almost all new parents check their infant's breathing frequently at first. Remember *psychology student's syndrome*? Everyone has a little obsessive thinking from time to time or has some little ritual that just makes them feel better. One woman liked to check on both of her children just before she went to bed, saying a little prayer for their safekeeping each night. She didn't feel *compelled* to do the check and the prayer, however. If she had been an obsessive-compulsive, she would *always have to perform the check and the prayer*, even if it meant getting out of bed or going to wherever the children were sleeping. If she had for some reason been unable to complete the ritual, she would also have experienced extreme anxiety or distress. The distress caused by a failure or inability to successfully complete the compulsive behaviour is a defining feature of OCD. In fact, the woman's children might not have been allowed to sleep anywhere else because of her fear that she could not complete the ritual. It's really a matter of degree.

PANIC DISORDER

Anna, a 14 year old, was sitting in science class watching a film. All of a sudden, she started feeling really strange. Her ears seemed to be stuffed with cotton and her vision was very dim. She was cold, had broken out in a sweat, and felt extremely afraid for no good reason. Her heart was racing and she immediately became convinced that she was dying. A friend sitting behind her saw how pale she had become and tried to ask her what was wrong, but Anna couldn't speak. She was in a state of panic and couldn't move. The friend got the teacher's attention, who motioned to Anna to come over to him. Although she would have sworn she couldn't move, she stood up to go to him and immediately everything returned to normal.

Sound familiar? Anna's symptoms are the classic symptoms of a **panic attack**, a sudden onset of extreme panic with various physical symptoms: racing heart, rapid breathing, a sensation of being "out of one's body," dulled hearing and vision, sweating, and dry mouth (Kumar & Oakley-Browne, 2002). Many people who have a panic attack think that they are having a heart attack and can experience pain as well as panic, but a panic attack is not a diagnosable medical disorder. Psychologically, the person having a panic attack is in a state of terror, thinking that this is it, death is happening, and many people may feel a need to escape. The attack happens without warning and quite suddenly. Although some panic attacks can last as long as half an hour, some last only a few minutes, with most attacks peaking within 10 to 15 minutes.

Having a panic attack is not that unusual. In Canada, it is estimated that 1.6 percent of the population will at some point in their lives suffer from the disorder (Statistics Canada, 2003a). University of Windsor researchers have shown that women are more likely to suffer from panic disorders than men, and that many sufferers often resort to alcohol in an attempt to self-medicate the disorder (Malan, Norton, & Cox, 1993). Researchers have also found evidence that cigarette smoking greatly increases the risk of panic attacks in adolescents and young adults (Johnson, 2000; Zvolensky et al., 2003). Regardless of the age of onset, it is only when panic attacks become so frequent that they affect a person's ability to function in day-to-day life that they become a **panic disorder**. When a fear of having panic attacks in a public place prevents the person from going out into unfamiliar or exposed places, it is called **panic disorder with agoraphobia**.

Many people try to figure out what triggers a panic attack and avoid the situation if possible. If driving a car sets off an attack, they don't drive. If being in a crowd sets off an attack, they don't go where crowds are. It is easy to see how having a panic disorder can often lead to agoraphobia. Psychologists and psychiatrists will classify a person as having either a panic disorder with agoraphobia or a panic disorder without agoraphobia.

GENERALIZED ANXIETY DISORDER

What about people who are just worriers? Can that become a disorder? Remember free-floating anxiety? That's the kind of anxiety that has no real source and may be experienced by people with **generalized anxiety disorder**, in which excessive anxiety and worries (apprehensive expectations) occur more days than not for at least six months. People with this disorder may also experience anxiety about a number of events or activities (such as work or school performance). These feelings of anxiety persist for six months or more and have no real source that can be pinpointed, nor can the person control the feelings even if an effort is made to do so.

People with this disorder are just plain worriers (Ruscio et al., 2001). They worry about money, their children, their lives, their friends, the dog, and anything else that they think might possibly go wrong. They feel tense and edgy, get tired easily, and may have trouble concentrating. They have muscle aches and tension; they experience sleeping problems and are often irritable—all signs of stress. The problem is that the stress comes from their worrying rather than from any real external source. General anxiety disorder is often found occurring with other anxiety disorders and depression. About 1 percent of Canadian adults will experience generalized anxiety disorder in any one-year period (Public Health Agency of Canada, 2002b).

Once again, it is a matter of degree and source: People with generalized anxiety disorder worry more excessively than people who are normal worriers, and they are worried over things that would cause other people no real concern.

"RONALD IS EXTREMELY COMPULSIVE."

www.CartoonStock.com

Actress Sigourney Weaver portrayed an FBI criminal profiler who was attacked by a serial killer in the 1995 movie *Copycat*. Her character developed severe panic disorder with agoraphobia, preventing her from leaving her home. In this still from the film, she is suffering from a panic attack in an elevator during an attempt to escape the killer.

◄ What about **people who are just worriers? Can that become a disorder?**

panic disorder
disorder in which panic attacks occur frequently enough to cause the person difficulty in adjusting to daily life.

panic disorder with agoraphobia
fear of leaving one's familiar surroundings because one might have a panic attack in public.

generalized anxiety disorder
disorder in which a person has feelings of dread and impending doom along with physical symptoms of stress, which lasts six months or more.

Watch on **mypsychlab**
Social Phobia

Anxiety disorders affect children as well as adults.

magnification
the tendency to interpret situations as far more dangerous, harmful, or important than they actually are.

all-or-nothing thinking
the tendency to believe that one's performance must be perfect or the result will be a total failure.

overgeneralization
the tendency to interpret a single negative event as a never-ending pattern of defeat and failure.

minimization
the tendency to give little or no importance to one's successes or positive events and traits.

CAUSES OF ANXIETY DISORDERS

13.9 *How do psychologists explain the causes of anxiety disorders?*

Different perspectives on how personality develops offer different explanations for anxiety disorders. For example, the *psychoanalytic model* sees anxiety as a kind of danger signal that repressed urges or conflicts are threatening to surface (Freud & Gay, 1977). A phobia is seen as a kind of displacement, in which the phobic object is actually only a symbol of whatever the person has buried deep in his or her unconscious mind—the true source of the fear. A fear of knives might mean a fear of one's own aggressive tendencies, or a fear of heights may hide a suicidal desire to jump.

Behaviourists disagree with this interpretation. They believe that anxious behavioural reactions are learned. They see phobias, for example, as nothing more than classically conditioned fear responses, as was the case with "Little Albert" (Rachman, 1990; Watson & Rayner, 1920). ⓛⓘⓝⓚ *to Chapter Five: Learning, p. 176.* Remember Joanne, who was afraid of spiders? She received a lot of attention when she had a phobic reaction. When her friends stopped giving her this attention every time she overreacted to seeing a spider or hearing the word, the reaction was almost completely extinguished. To further support this learning model, Canadian researchers Brian Cox and Steven Taylor (1999) have shown that certain types of phobias (e.g., heights, closed spaces, and blood and injection phobias) often involve early life pairings of the currently phobic object with a fearful experience. These researchers also contend that observational learning, notably modelling, plays an important role in developing a phobia. A child observing a parent acting fearfully to a spider and hearing the parent talk negatively about spiders is more likely to develop arachnophobia.

Cognitive psychologists see anxiety disorders as the result of illogical, irrational thought processes. One way in which people with anxiety disorders show irrational thinking (Beck, 1976, 1984) is through **magnification**, or the tendency to "make mountains out of molehills" by interpreting situations as being far more harmful, dangerous, or embarrassing than they actually are. In panic disorder, for example, a person might interpret a racing heartbeat as a sign of a heart attack instead of just a momentary arousal.

Another distorted thought process is **all-or-nothing thinking**, in which a person believes that his or her performance must be perfect or the result will be a total failure. Canadian researchers have shown that perfectionists often overestimate the consequences of turning in less-than-perfect work, and as a consequence feel compelled to redo the work over and over again, which may contribute to the development of OCD (Antony & Swinson, 1998). **Overgeneralization** (a single negative event interpreted as a never-ending pattern of defeat), jumping to conclusions without facts to support that conclusion, and **minimization** (giving little or no emphasis to one's successes or positive events and traits) are other examples of irrational thinking that can cause excessive anxiety.

Some Canadian psychologists believe that the obsessions seen in OCD may result from trying too hard to control normal obsessions (Clark, 2004). Christine Purdon, now at the University of Windsor, and David Clark assessed the frequency of normal obsession in students at the University of New Brunswick and found that normal obsessions are very common. For example, more than 75 percent of women had obsessed about either leaving the stove on or leaving the house unlocked. Men were more likely to have unwanted sexual thought obsessions. For example, more than 75 percent of men obsessed about seeing strangers naked or having sex in public (Purdon & Clark, 1993). So why do these normal obsessions sometimes become OCD? University of British Columbia researcher Amy Janeck and her colleagues believe that persons who develop OCD are more likely to be preoccupied with their thoughts than persons who do not develop OCD. In other words, persons with OCD do too much thinking about their thinking, which may necessitate compulsive behaviours to reduce the unacceptable or unwanted obsessions (Janeck, Calamari, Riemann, & Heffelfinger, 2003). To make matters worse, Concordia University researchers have discovered that repeated checking may actually worsen your memory for having performed the checking behaviour. For example, repeatedly checking that you unplugged the iron results in more uncertainty later on that you in fact unplugged the iron. This uncertainty may increase obsessive thinking about the iron and contribute to the development of OCD (Radomsky, Gilchrist, & Dussault, 2006).

Evidence exists that *biological* factors contribute to anxiety disorders. Generalized anxiety disorder, for example, has been linked to an imbalance in several neurotransmitters in the nervous system, including serotonin and GABA (Brawman-Mintzer & Lydiard, 1997; Rynn et al., 2000). Recent research has linked panic disorder to a possible defect in the way serotonin binds to its receptors in the nervous system (Neumeister et al., 2004). Some evidence suggests that these chemical imbalances may have a genetic component, meaning that anxiety disorders such as OCD, phobias, and panic disorder can be passed from parent to child through more than just observational learning (Karayiorgou et al., 1997; Lesch et al., 1996; Logue et al., 2003).

Anxiety disorders are found around the world, although the particular form the disorder takes might be different in various cultures. For example, in some Latin American cultures, anxiety can take the form of *ataque de nervios*, or "attack of nerves," in which the person may have fits of crying, shout uncontrollably, experience sensations of heat, and become very aggressive, either verbally or physically. These attacks usually come after a stressful event such as the death of a loved one (APA, 2000a). The Psychology in the News section earlier in this chapter mentioned several syndromes found in certain cultures, such as koro and TKS, that are essentially types of phobias specific to those cultures. Panic disorder is found almost universally at about the same rate all over the world (Weissman et al., 1997).

PRACTICE QUIZ: HOW MUCH DO YOU REMEMBER?

Pick the best answer.

1. Which of the following is not a correct match?
   a. Axis V—Global Assessment of Functioning
   b. Axis I—Personality Disorders
   c. Axis III—General Medical Conditions
   d. Axis IV—Psychosocial and Environmental Problems

2. What percentage of Canadians are likely to suffer from a mental disorder this year?
   a. 10 percent
   b. 15 percent
   c. 20 percent
   d. 25 percent

3. Which of the following is NOT likely to occur in people with social phobia?
   a. feeling that they are not as good as others
   b. feeling that they have enhanced social skills
   c. worrying about their appearance
   d. making eye contact

4. An irrational fear of blood would be a
   a. social phobia.
   b. specific phobia.
   c. type of agoraphobia.
   d. type of acrophobia.

5. Jennifer worries that someone might come into her house at night while she is sleeping and helpless. She checks the locks on the doors and windows several times before she can relax enough to go to bed. Her constant checking of the locks is most similar to
   a. a compulsion.
   b. an obsession.
   c. a panic disorder.
   d. a phobia.

6. Who is least likely to believe that his or her obsessions are groundless and excessive?
   a. Paul, a 30-year-old nurse
   b. Jill, a 28-year-old nurse
   c. Billy, an 8-year-old soccer player
   d. Mary-Anne, a 65-year-old retiree

7. Bud's relatives are concerned that he worries too much. He worries about little things going wrong, he worries about big things going wrong, and sometimes it seems as though he's worrying because there's nothing to worry about. He worries so much that he has a hard time getting things done. Bud most likely has
   a. panic disorder.
   b. obsessive-compulsive disorder.
   c. generalized anxiety disorder.
   d. post-traumatic stress disorder.

8. Sandy has the tendency to make everything seem so much worse than it usually is. Beck would say that Sandy has a tendency to
   a. overgeneralize.
   b. minimize.
   c. do all-or-nothing thinking.
   d. magnify.

Answers: 1. c, 2. b, 3. b, 4. a, 5. b, 6. d.

SOMATOFORM DISORDERS: SICKNESS AS A STATE OF MIND

13.10 *What are the different kinds of somatoform disorders?*

Another category of abnormal behaviour involves the belief that one is physically ill, which is often accompanied by the experience of physical symptoms even though there is no physical illness or problem. Disorders in which people believe they are sick when they are not are called **somatoform disorders**. *Somatoform* means that these disorders take the form of a bodily (somatic) ailment but are not real physical disorders. Although there is no real physical cause, the symptoms are very real to the person experiencing them.

I've heard of something like this—but I thought the name of it was psychosomatic disorder? Somatoform disorders are actually quite different from psychosomatic disorders. In a **psychosomatic disorder** (now called **psychophysiological disorder**), the bodily ailments are real physical ailments caused or worsened by stress. The two disorders are often confused. Unlike psychophysiological disorders, somatoform disorders are *not* real physical ailments, and although the symptoms are real to the person experiencing them, they are quite literally "all in one's head." Concerns about one's health are fairly common in Canada. The Canadian Psychological Association (2000) estimates that 3 to 5 percent of Canadian adults have intense concerns about possible disease and illness, and as many as 20 percent occasionally experience milder concerns regarding their health.

Interestingly, Canadian research has shown that persons suffering from a somatoform disorder are much more likely to bring their "physical problems" to the attention of their physician rather than a mental health professional (Taylor & Asmundson, 2004). This tendency can lead to unnecessary medical treatments that may make matters worse (e.g., side effects of medications) and strain our already overburdened health-care resources.

You have probably heard or used the term *hypochondriac*. This term is often used to describe someone with a somatoform disorder known as *hypochondriasis*. These individuals are constantly worried about having a serious illness and become preoccupied with every body sensation. Another somatoform disorder similar to hypochondriasis is somatization disorder. Persons with somatization disorder complain about specific physical symptoms, such as pain or nausea, but they tend to show much less worry and more "drama" when presenting their symptoms. Persons suffering with hypochondriasis and somatization disorder are not creating their symptoms just to fool others, but they do have a tough time seeing the relationship between their anxiety and their symptoms.

Conversion disorder is one of the most fascinating somatoform disorders. A person experiencing conversion disorder may suddenly experience dramatic and specific symptoms such as blindness, paralysis, deafness, or numbness of certain body parts, none of which have real physical causes. Typically, the problems occur along with some other psychological disorder, such as depression, at a time when there is a stressful situation either already happening or threatening to happen (Hurwitz, 1989).

There are some simple ways to recognize conversion disorders. People with such disorders tend to exhibit a kind of indifference or lack of concern about the symptom, which is understandable if the person has unconscious knowledge that the symptom is not real (Silver, 1996). Another is that the symptom is anatomically impossible, as is the case with blindness for which there is no corresponding damage to the eyes, optic nerve, or parts of the brain responsible for vision (see Figure 13.1). Finally, conversion disorder symptoms disappear when the person is asleep, hypnotized, under anaesthesia, or unconscious (Parobek, 1997; Silver, 1996). Conversion

---

Hypochondriasis

I've heard of ▶ something like this— but I thought the name of it was psychosomatic disorder?

"You know, Burkhart, if you're so damn afraid of the flu maybe you should just stay home."

somatoform disorders
disorders that take the form of bodily illnesses and symptoms but for which there are no real physical disorders.

psychosomatic disorder
disorder in which psychological stress causes a real physical disorder or illness.

psychophysiological disorder
modern term for psychosomatic disorder.

conversion disorder
somatoform disorder in which the person experiences a specific symptom in the somatic nervous system's functioning, such as paralysis, numbness, or blindness, for which there is no physical cause.

TABLE 13.5 SOMATOFORM DISORDERS

DISORDER'S NAME	KEY FEATURES
Conversion Disorder	At least one deficit involving motor or sensory function linked to a significant stressor or conflict.
Hypochondriasis	Preoccupation or fear of having a serious illness. Normal body sensations are misinterpreted as evidence of a serious illness. Those afflicted constantly seek the advice of doctors and burden the health-care system.
Somatization Disorder	Involves recurrent and dramatic complaints of a specific symptom such as nausea, difficulty swallowing, or pain for which no physical cause can be found.
Body Dysmorphic Disorder	Preoccupation and distress with some imagined bodily defect (e.g., my nose is too big) that may lead to social withdrawal and even repeated plastic surgery.

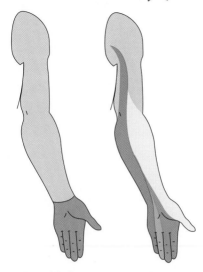

FIGURE 13.1 **Glove Anaesthesia**
Glove anaesthesia is a disorder in which the person experiences numbness from the wrist down (see the drawing on the left). However, real nerve damage would produce numbness down one side of the arm and hand, as shown in the drawing on the right. Thus, because glove anaesthesia is anatomically impossible, it is actually a sign of a conversion disorder.

disorder usually occurs when a stressful situation has also occurred or is threatening to occur, such as a soldier facing the return to combat. See Table 13.5 for a summary of conversion and other somatoform disorders.

CAUSES OF SOMATOFORM DISORDERS

13.11 *What causes somatoform disorders?*

Freud believed that this type of disorder was a way of making anxiety caused by the repression of traumatic events or unacceptable impulses into a physical symptom. The physical symptom was seen as providing some relief from anxiety at first. For example, a woman who was anxious about unwanted sexual thoughts might become "paralyzed" from the waist down, ensuring that she had no way to act on those thoughts. Behaviourists believe that the telling factors in somatoform disorders are that such behaviour results in two kinds of reinforcement: positive reinforcement in the form of attention from doctors, family members, and others; and negative reinforcement from being able to avoid whatever stressful situation is associated with the disorder. A hypochondriac, for example, who believes that his heart is about to give out might resist going back to work or doing strenuous chores around the house; a soldier with conversion paralysis need not face combat again; and a child with a somatization stomachache gets to stay home and avoid the big math test that day. University of British Columbia researchers investigated health anxiety in twins and found that features of hypochondriasis (e.g., believing that one has an undiagnosed disease, and having excessive anxiety about one's health) were caused by both genetic and environmental factors (Taylor, Thordarson, Jang, & Asmundson, 2006). One environmental factor thought to play a prominent role is childhood learning experiences. If children become ill and then learn that they are sickly and frail, they may develop unfounded beliefs (e.g., "I'm always sick and need medical attention"), which may cause them to interpret any minor body ache or pain as a sign of serious disease (Marcus, Gurley, Marchi, & Bauer, 2007; Taylor & Asmundson, 2004).

Cognitive psychologists would again point to the tendency to magnify symptoms and allow false beliefs to dominate one's thinking. In other words, hypochondriacs have a tendency to make "mountains out of molehills" by exaggerating the seriousness of their physical symptoms. This misinterpretation of physical symptoms creates anxiety, and to reduce this anxiety the hypochondriac seeks medical attention.

On Christmas Day 1985, James McDonnell came home to his wife in Larchmont, New York, after 14 years of amnesia. After suffering two separate head injuries in auto accidents, he lost his memory. He went to Philadelphia and found a job in a restaurant. On Christmas Eve, Mr. McDonnell bumped his head and recovered all of his memories. This picture shows the happy reunion with his wife. What kinds of emotional and psychological adjustments do you think Mr. McDonnell and his family might have had to make upon his sudden return?

Turning one's anxiety into physical symptoms is not found in Western culture alone. Somatoform-type disorders are found in many countries, although the specific symptoms may vary from culture to culture (Mezzick et al., 1996). For example, in *dhat* syndrome, young Asian men are excessively afraid that a loss of seminal fluid is depleting their bodies of energy and vitality and often go to doctor after doctor seeking help—exactly what a hypochondriac does (Chadda & Ahuja, 1990).

DISSOCIATIVE DISORDERS: ALTERED CONSCIOUSNESS

13.12 *What are the different types of dissociative disorders?*

Dissociative disorders involve a break, or dissociation, in consciousness, memory, or a person's sense of identity. This "split" is easier to understand when thinking about how people sometimes drive somewhere and then wonder how they got there—they don't remember the trip itself at all. This sort of "automatic pilot" driving happens when the route is familiar and frequently travelled. One part of the conscious mind was thinking about work, school, or whatever was uppermost in the mind while lower centres of consciousness were driving the car, stopping at signs and lights, and turning when needed. This split in conscious attention is very similar to what happens in dissociative disorders. The difference is that in the disorders the dissociation is much more pronounced and involuntary. See Table 13.6 for a summary of the dissociative disorders.

Perhaps the most well-known and controversial dissociative disorder is **dissociative identity disorder**, formerly known as multiple personality disorder.

dissociative disorders
disorders in which there is a break in conscious awareness, memory, the sense of identity, or some combination.

dissociative identity disorder
disorder occurring when a person seems to have two or more distinct personalities within one body.

TABLE 13.6 **DISSOCIATIVE DISORDERS**	
DISORDER'S NAME	**KEY FEATURES**
Dissociative Amnesia	Who am I? Person experiences either complete or partial memory loss for personal information in the absence of an identifiable organic cause. The cause is often a "mental blow" or traumatic event. General knowledge and skills are usually retained. The lost memories often return suddenly after a few days or weeks, but it can take years.
Dissociative Fugue	Who am I and how did I get here? Person suddenly leaves one's current life situation, travels to a new location, assumes a new identity, and has amnesia for past personal material. General knowledge and skills are intact, and person may appear to be leading a normal life. Past identities often return suddenly, and memories of the new life may now vanish from memory.
Depersonalization	Am I dreaming? A temporary loss or change in the usual sense of one's own reality. Persons may feel detached from themselves, their bodies, and/or their surroundings (e.g., feeling robot-like, being on automatic pilot, or observing themselves from outside their bodies).
Dissociative Identity Disorder	How many am I? A person appears to have two or more disorder personalities within one body (see text).

In this disorder, a person seems to experience at least two or more distinct personalities existing in one body. There may be a "core" personality, who usually knows nothing about the other personalities and is the personality that experiences "blackouts" or losses of memory and time. Fugues are common in dissociative identity disorder, with the core personality experiencing unsettling moments of "awakening" in an unfamiliar place or with people who call the person by another name (Kluft, 1984).

First reported in the nineteenth century as a clinical disorder, many believe that cases of so-called "spirit" or "demon possession" were possibly people with this disorder. Freudian psychoanalysts believe that multiple personalities come about as a way of coping with extreme stress, usually in early childhood. Many people who have been diagnosed as "multiples" are women with a history of childhood sexual or physical abuse. It is thought that the dissociation occurs as one aspect of personality emerges to deal with the stress while the rest of the personality remains safely "hidden" in the unconscious mind. Psychoanalysts attempt to "reintegrate" the individual personalities into the core personality, which is a fancy way of saying that the person has to reclaim that part of the personality as part of the whole (Kluft, 1988). (Non-Freudian psychologists, psychiatrists, and therapists use other forms of psychotherapy and/or drugs in the treatment of this disorder.)

With the publication of several famous books, such as *The Three Faces of Eve* (Thigpen & Cleckley, 1992) and *Sybil* (Schreiber, 1973), and movies made from those books, dissociative identity disorder became well known to the public. Throughout the 1980s, the publishing world saw numerous books, some fiction and some a blend of fiction and fact, about this disorder, and psychological professionals began to diagnose this condition at an alarming rate—"multiple personality," as it was then known, had become the "fad" disorder of the late twentieth century, according to some researchers (Aldridge-Morris, 1989; Boor, 1982; Cormier & Thelen, 1998; Showalter, 1997).

In the past decade, the diagnosis of dissociative identity disorder has come under scrutiny, with many professionals now beginning to doubt the validity of previous diagnoses. Even the famous case of "Sybil" has been criticized as a case of the therapist actually "creating" the multiple personalities in her client through suggestion and even direct instruction. Some psychological professionals believe that dissociative identity disorder is actually a misdiagnosis of borderline personality disorder or some other form of anxiety disorder (Lauer et al., 1993).

Is it a real disorder that some people fake, or is there really no such thing as multiple personality? Some skeptics believe that there is no such disorder at all and that clients who demonstrate different "personalities" are simply acting out to get the attention of the therapist or are responding to what the therapist seems to want (Gleaves, 1996). In one Canadian study, ordinary people were given instructions in how to play the role of a multiple personality and were able to exhibit the "symptoms" associated with the disorder quite effectively (Spanos et al., 1985). However, just because someone can act out having the flu does not mean that the flu does not really exist, so being able to reproduce the symptoms of dissociative identity disorder by acting does not automatically mean that such a disorder does not exist. The question is not really "Does dissociative identity disorder exist?" but rather "What causes a person to exhibit the symptoms of dissociative identity disorder?" If the cause is suggestions from the therapist or deliberate deception, then

Watch on **mypsychlab**
Dissociative Identity Disorder:
The Three Faces of Eve

Christine Costner Sizemore is the real face behind *The Three Faces of Eve*, the book that first brought dissociative identity disorder into the public eye. Ms. Sizemore is a successful writer and artist and has been free of symptoms for many years.

◀ Is it a real disorder that some people fake, or is there really no such thing as multiple personality?

there is a problem. If the symptoms of dissociative identity disorder are a sign of a person in deep psychological trouble, then the "reality" of those "personalities" becomes somewhat meaningless—the person is in trouble and needs help (Arrigo & Pezdek, 1998; McHugh, 1993).

CAUSES OF DISSOCIATIVE DISORDERS

13.13 *How do dissociative disorders develop?*

Psychoanalytic theory, of course, sees the repression of threatening or unacceptable thoughts and behaviour at the heart of all disorders, and the dissociative disorders in particular seem to have a large element of repression—motivated forgetting—in them. In the psychoanalytic view, loss of memory or disconnecting one's awareness from a stressful or traumatic event is adaptive in that it reduces the emotional pain (Dorahy, 2001). Dissociation in Freudian theory is a defence mechanism and is associated with emotional or physical trauma (A. Freud, 1946).

Cognitive and behavioural explanations for dissociative disorders are connected: The person may feel guilt, shame, or anxiety when thinking about disturbing experiences or thoughts and start avoiding thoughts about them. This "thought avoidance" is negatively reinforced by the reduction of the anxiety and unpleasant feelings and eventually will become a habit of "not thinking about" these things. This is similar to what many people do when faced with something unpleasant, such as an injection or a painful procedure such as having a root canal. They "think about something else." In doing that, they are deliberately not thinking about what is happening to them at the moment and the experience of pain is decreased. People with dissociative disorders may simply be better at doing this sort of "not thinking" than other people are.

Also, consider the positive reinforcement possibilities for a person with a dissociative disorder: attention from others and help from professionals. Shaping may also play a big role in the development of some cases of dissociative identity disorder. The therapist may unintentionally pay more attention to a client who talks about "feeling like someone else," which may encourage the client to report more such feelings and even elaborate on them. In the wake of the books and movies about multiples, many therapists no doubt were looking very hard for signs of multiple personality in their clients.

There are some possible biological sources for dissociations, as well. Researchers have found that people with **depersonalization disorder** (a mild dissociative disorder in which people feel detached and disconnected from themselves, their bodies, and their surroundings) have lower brain activity in the areas responsible for their sense of body awareness than do people without the disorder (Simeon et al., 2000). Others have found evidence that people with dissociative identity disorders show significant differences in PET scan activity taken when different "personalities" are present (Reinders et al., 2001).

Dissociative disorders can also be found in other cultures. *Amok*, the trance-like state in which a person suddenly becomes highly agitated and violent (found in Southeast Asia and Pacific Island cultures), is usually associated with no memory for the period during which the "trance" lasts (Suryani & Jensen, 1993). But a study that reviewed historical literature throughout the centuries found no mention or tales of what would be labelled as dissociative amnesia in the stories or non-fiction writings of any culture prior to the 1800s (Pope et al., 2007). The authors concluded that dissociative amnesia may be more of a nineteenth-century culture-bound phenomenon than a neuropsychological one.

depersonalization disorder
dissociative disorder in which persons feel detached and disconnected from themselves, their bodies, and their surroundings.

PRACTICE QUIZ: HOW MUCH DO YOU REMEMBER?

Pick the best answer.

1. Which one is not a real physical disorder?
   a. psychosomatic disorder
   b. psychophysiological disorder
   c. somatoform disorder
   d. adaptation disorder

2. According to the Canadian Psychological Association, what percentage of Canadians regularly experience significant concerns about their health?
   a. 1 to 3 percent
   b. 3 to 5 percent
   c. 10 to 20 percent
   d. more than 20 percent

3. Lisa has started having feelings of fearfulness about going to school. She has begun to suffer from headaches and stomachaches and has missed several days of school already. Lisa's illnesses are probably a form of
   a. phobic disorder.
   b. somatization disorder.
   c. generalized anxiety disorder.
   d. dissociative disorder.

4. The misinterpretation of normal physical aches and pains as signs of serious sickness is best described by which of the following?
   a. making mountains out of molehills
   b. fake it until you make it
   c. sticks and stones can break my bones but names will never hurt me
   d. I was born this way

5. Carlo wakes up in a strange motel room. He doesn't know where he is or how he got there, and he's not sure what day it is. This is most likely an episode of dissociative
   a. amnesia.
   b. fugue.
   c. identity disorder.
   d. multiple personality.

6. The fact that the dissociative disorders seem to have a large element of repression in them is related to the _____ explanation of disorders.
   a. behavioural
   b. cognitive
   c. biological
   d. psychoanalytic

Answers: 1-c, 2-b, 3-b, 4-a, 5-b, 6-d.

SEXUAL DISORDERS

13.14   *What are the different types of sexual disorders?*

The *DSM-IV-TR* describes three categories of sexual disorders: gender identity disorder, sexual dysfunctions, and paraphilias.

GENDER IDENTITY DISORDER

The first category of sexual disorder is **gender identity disorder** (GID) in which a person feels psychologically dissatisfied with his or her biological sex. **L I N K** *to Chapter Eight: Development Across the Lifespan, p. 302.* A recent high-profile example of GID is Chaz (formerly Chastity) Bono, who underwent sexual reassignment surgery to become a man.

Are gender identity disorder and homosexuality the same thing? In a word, no! First and foremost, homosexuality is not a psychological disorder. Second, homosexuals do not feel trapped in the wrong body the way persons with GID do. In fact, sexual orientation patterns, **L I N K** *to Chapter Nine: Motivation and Emotion, p. 350,* are of no concern when determining whether a person has GID. For example, before her surgery, Chastity Bono was attracted to females, so she was considered a female homosexual. After sexual reassignment surgery, Chaz is still attracted to females, so he is now a heterosexual man.

SEXUAL FUNCTIONING DISORDERS

13.15   *What causes sexual disorders?*

The second sexual disorders category contains the sexual dysfunctions in which a person has trouble functioning adequately during a sexual encounter. These are common conditions, such as impotence, often helped with drugs such as Viagra. A **sexual dysfunction** is a problem with sexual functioning, or the actual physical workings

Are gender identity disorder and homosexuality the same thing?

◄

gender identity disorder
disorder in which a person feels psychologically dissatisfied with his or her biological sex.

sexual dysfunction
a problem in sexual functioning.

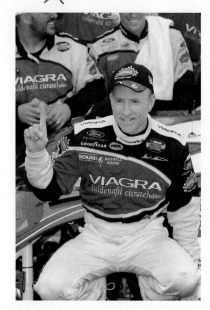

Erectile dysfunction is a major concern to many men who are unable to engage in sexual intercourse with their partners. Medications help some men function once again. Does this ad seem to promise more than just the revival of sexual functioning?

of the sex act. Sexual dysfunctions and problems can be caused by purely organic factors (i.e., illness or side effects from drugs), sociocultural factors (such as negative attitudes toward sexual behaviour), or psychological factors stemming from either personality problems, traumatic events, or relationship problems. More commonly, such problems may stem from a combination of these factors.

Organic factors include physical problems such as illnesses, side effects from medication, the effects of surgeries, physical disabilities, and even the use of illegal and legal drugs, such as cocaine, alcohol, and nicotine. Chronic illnesses such as diabetes, cancer, or strokes also belong in this category of factors.

Sociocultural influences on sexual attitudes and behaviour also exist and may be a source of psychological stress leading to sexual dysfunction. In Canada and some other Western cultures, people may have experienced instruction from their parents (both direct and indirect teaching) that actually helped them to form negative attitudes toward sex and sexual activities, such as masturbation. Some religious upbringing may also foster a sense of guilt about sex and interest in sex. In one study, a relationship between conservative, religious traditionalism and sexual attitudes was found for married members of Jewish, Protestant, and Catholic faiths (Purcell, 1985). The research showed that the more conservative and traditional the married couples were, the less interest and pleasure they took in sexual activity and the more they experienced guilt, shame, and sexual inhibitions. In non-Western cultures, such as that of India, sex may be seen as not only a duty of married couples but also a joy to be celebrated within the context of producing children (Gupta, 1994). In particular, women in India may have an entirely different attitude toward sex because a woman's status in Indian culture depends greatly on her ability to bear children.

Psychological stressors also include individual psychological problems, such as low self-esteem, anxiety over performance of the sex act, depression, self-consciousness about one's body, anxiety disorders, or a history of previous sexual abuse or assault. For example, women who were sexually molested in childhood are two to four times more likely to suffer from pain in the pelvic area on a chronic basis (Reiter & Milburn, 1994).

Another source of psychological stress leading to sexual dysfunctions is the relationship between the two sexual partners. The sexual dysfunction may be only an outward symptom of an underlying problem with the relationship. Examples of such problems might be unresolved arguments, resentment of the partner who feels he or she has less power and influence over the relationship, lack of trust, infidelities, lack of physical attractiveness to the partner, or even lack of sexual skills on the part of one or both partners (Alperstein, 2001).

ORGANIC OR STRESS-INDUCED DYSFUNCTIONS **Organic or stress-induced dysfunctions** are types of sexual problems caused by physical disorders, such as nerve damage, or psychological stress, such as worry and anxiety. (Because body and mind influence each other's functioning, it is difficult to separate these dysfunctions into purely organic and purely stress-induced disorders.) Sexual dysfunctions involve problems in three possible areas of sexual activity: sexual interest, arousal, and response.

How common are problems like these—aren't they pretty rare? Canadian surveys have found that about half of all women (Fisher, Boroditsky, & Morris, 2004) and about 27 percent of men (Auld & Brock, 2002) have experienced some sexual dysfunction in the previous six-month period. These results are similar to a nationwide U.S. survey that found that about 43 percent of women and 31 percent of men report having some sort of sexual dysfunction (Laumann et al., 1999). In the stress-filled world that many people live in today, it isn't all that surprising to find

How common are problems like these— ▶ aren't they pretty rare?

organic or stress-induced dysfunction
sexual problem caused by physical disorder or psychological stress.

TABLE 13.7 ORGANIC OR STRESS-INDUCED DYSFUNCTIONS

Sexual Desire Disorders	Hypoactive Sexual Desire Disorder: Ongoing, abnormally low desire for sexual activity
	Sexual Aversion Disorder: Fear and disgust of sexual contact
Sexual Arousal Disorders	Female Sexual Arousal Disorder: Desire for sexual activity is present, but physical discomfort and a lack of pleasure are experienced during sexual activity.
	Male Erectile Disorder: A male cannot maintain an erection long enough to complete the sexual act.
Orgasmic Disorders	Male Orgasmic Disorder: A male cannot achieve orgasm through vaginal stimulation, even though fully aroused.
	Female Orgasmic Disorder: A female cannot achieve an orgasm even though fully aroused.
	Premature Ejaculation: Some men experience orgasm shortly after penetration, which can cause feelings of sexual inadequacy because the partner does not have time to achieve orgasm.
Sexual Pain Disorders	Vaginismus: Persistent contractions of the vaginal muscles, causing sexual intercourse to be painful or impossible
	Dyspareunia: Pain in the genitals that can occur before, during, or after intercourse; can be experienced by either sex

such a high degree of dysfunction. In fact, the figures may actually be higher than those reported in the survey. As stated in Chapter One, one of the hazards of doing survey research is that people don't always tell the truth. If a person is going to lie about sexual problems, the most likely lie (or distorted truth) would probably be to deny or minimize such problems. Table 13.7 lists some common organic or stress-induced sexual dysfunctions.

For all of the sexual dysfunctions, treatment can include medication, psychotherapy, hormone therapy, stress reduction, and behavioural training. For example, Masters and Johnson (1970) recommended a technique called *sensate focus* for treatment of premature ejaculation, in which each member of a couple engages in a series of exercises meant to focus attention on his or her own sensual experiences during various stages of sexual arousal and activity. Male erectile disorder is now commonly treated with drug therapy.

THE PARAPHILIAS

The third category of sexual disorder is the paraphilias, in which a person's sexual arousal deviates to inappropriate objects or individuals. These problems are behavioural rather than organic in nature. **Paraphilia** (also called *atypical sexual behaviour*) is a disorder in which the person either prefers to, or must, achieve sexual arousal and fulfillment through sexual behaviour that is unusual or not socially acceptable. In some cases, the atypical sexual behaviour is illegal and destructive as well. The term *paraphilia* comes from two Greek words meaning "beyond love," and these disorders are truly "beyond" normal, socially acceptable sexual behaviour. Convicted

paraphilia
a sexual disorder in which the person's preferred method of sexual arousal and fulfillment is through sexual behaviour that is unusual or socially unacceptable

murderer and former Canadian military colonel David Russell Williams may have suffered from sexual sadism, a paraphilia characterized by obtaining sexual arousal from inflicting pain or humiliation on others.

Notice that this a culturally defined term—in some cases, sexual behaviour that is considered abnormal or even illegal in one culture may be quite acceptable in another culture. Whereas some of this alternate sexual behaviour is considered to be a "kinkier" form of sexual expression, in some cases the behaviour indicates a mental illness and may also be a criminal offense. Table 13.8 lists and briefly defines some of the paraphilias.

I've heard about transvestites. Are they gay? And are there women transvestites also? Actually, most transvestites are heterosexual males who may be married and enjoy normal sexual relationships with their wives. The transvestite who cross-dresses for sexual excitement should not be confused with a homosexual male who cross-dresses to attract other males. As for women, there seems to be little evidence that women who wear men's clothing do so for sexual arousal purposes. In fact, it is quite socially acceptable in modern Western society for women to wear clothing that once was considered male. Westerners think nothing of a woman wearing pants, a suit jacket, and even a tie but would look oddly at a man wearing a skirt or a dress, right? In a sense, then, if the culture does not prevent a woman from wearing male-type clothing, there is no "shock" value to doing so—and this may be a big factor in the excitement for men who wear women's clothing. The risk of being "found out" adds to the sexual thrill. Ray Blanchard, who heads the Clinical Sexology Program at the University of Toronto, believes that transvestic fetishism can often lead to GID (Zucker & Blanchard, 1997), as discussed earlier in this chapter. As a result, Blanchard suggests that the lower incidence of GID in women may result because of the low incidence of transvestic fetishism in women (Blanchard, 1989).

Pedophilia is a sexual deviance that is illegal and considered immoral in almost every culture if it is carried out. The *DSM-IV-TR* (American Psychiatric Association, 2000) describes a **pedophile** as a person who has recurring sexual thoughts, fantasies, or behaviour toward prepubescent children (children who have not yet entered puberty). These urges are considered criminal acts if they are acted on. A person must be at least 16 years old and there must be an age difference of at least five years between the person and the object of the sexual fantasies to be considered a pedophile.

Watch on mypsychlab
Video Voyeurism

I've heard about ▶ transvestites. Are they gay? And are there women transvestites also?

pedophilia
deriving sexual arousal and pleasure from touching or having sexual relations with prepubescent (non-sexually mature) children or fantasizing about such contact.

pedophile
a person who has recurring sexual thoughts, fantasies, or engages in sexual actions toward prepubescent (non-sexually mature) children.

TABLE 13.8 PARAPHILIAS	
Festishism	An object or part of the body becomes the focus of sexual interest and arousal, such as shoes, feet, or underwear.
Exhibitionism	The exposure of normally clothed parts of the body to unsuspecting and typically unwilling viewers, such as a "flasher."
Voyeurism	The act of obtaining sexual arousal and gratification through watching other people undress or engage in sexual behaviour, such as a "Peeping Tom."
Frotteurism	The act of becoming sexually aroused or gratified through rubbing up against an unwilling person, usually in a crowded public place.
Necrophilia	Fetishism in which the sexual arousal comes from touching or having intercourse with a corpse.
Transvestism	Fetishism in which sexual arousal and pleasure come from wearing the clothing of the opposite sex.

Contrary to the image most people have of a "dirty old man," the typical pedophile is a young adult male who may be sexually attracted to either females or males of the right age. Many pedophiles are married and have sexual relationships with their wives, yet still engage in their pedophilic fantasies or behaviour. Female pedophiles are rare, but they do exist.

Treatments for the paraphilias can include psychotherapy, conditioning techniques, and even hormone therapy in some cases of pedophilia. **LINK** *to Chapter Fourteen: Psychological Therapies, p. 564.*

There are several possible causes of the different paraphilias. Fetishism is often explained as a kind of classical conditioning in which the object or body part, because of its presence during sexual activity and arousal (the unconditioned stimulus and response), becomes a kind of conditioned stimulus for sexual arousal (the conditioned response). **LINK** *to Chapter Five: Learning, pp. 176.* **Transvestism** can be explained in much the same way. Interestingly, transvestism is more common in cultures in which the male is the major earner of the money, causing some researchers to wonder if cross-dressing may become a way for some men to temporarily assume the female role as a way of relieving the stress of being the breadwinner (Munroe, 1980).

Frotteurism is a condition where sexual gratification is obtained by rubbing one's genitals up against the body of an unwilling person. It is sometimes referred to as "mashing" because it generally occurs in crowded places such as subway trains or buses. The disorder is much more common in men and is thought to develop initially by the random or accidental touching of one's genitals against someone that the person finds sexually exciting. The sexual excitement reinforces and perpetuates the rubbing behaviour. James Horley, at Augustana University College in Camrose, Alberta, studied an individual diagnosed with frotteurism by using a penile plethysmograph—an instrument that measures penile erection. He found that the individual was also sexually aroused by non-consensual sexual activity (i.e., the groping of a woman who was verbally protesting). Horley suggests that frotteurs should be thought of as timid rapists, and that future research may someday reclassify frotteurism as a subtype of rape (Horley, 2001).

Exhibitionism has been explained as a fear of rejection in sexual situations, so that the "flasher" who exposes himself and then runs gets to feel somehow masculine and powerful without the fear of rejection (Miner & Dwyer, 1997). Feelings of inferiority and sexual inadequacy are often given as explanations for paraphilias.

MOOD DISORDERS: THE EFFECT OF AFFECT

13.16   *What are the different types of mood disorders?*

In psychological terms, the word **affect** is used to mean "emotion" or "mood." **Mood disorders** are a disturbance in emotion and are also referred to as *affective disorders.* Although the range of human emotions runs from deep, intense sadness and despair to extreme happiness and elation, under normal circumstances people stay between those extremes—neither too sad nor too happy but content (see Figure 13.2). It is when stress or some other factor pushes a person to one extreme or the other that

transvestism
deriving sexual arousal and pleasure from dressing in the clothing of the opposite sex.

affect
in psychology, an emotional reaction.

mood disorders
a disturbance in emotion; also referred to as *affective disorders.*

FIGURE 13.2 **The Range of Emotions**   Most people experience a range of emotions over the course of a day or several days, such as mild sadness, calm contentment, or mild elation and happiness. A person with a mood disorder experiences emotions that are extreme and, therefore, abnormal.

Extreme Sadness	Mild Sadness	Normal Emotions	Mild Elation	Extreme Elation

But doesn't everybody get a little "down" sometimes? When does being sad become a disorder?

mood disorders can result. Mood disorders can be relatively mild (straying only a short distance from the "average") or they can be extreme (existing at either extreme of the range). The Public Health Agency of Canada (2002c) estimates that roughly 16 percent of Canadian adults have suffered from a mood disorder.

There are two relatively mild mood disorders, although their mildness does not mean that people suffering from these disorders do not need help. **Dysthymia** comes from Greek words meaning "bad spirit" and is a form of mild, chronic depression that lasts for at least two years or more (Klein et al., 2000). **Cyclothymia** means "spirit that moves in circles" and involves a cycle of being sad, then feeling quite happy, and then returning to sad, happy, sad, happy, and so on, with the cycle lasting two years or more. The episodes of elation are called *hypomania*, meaning "low mania." (*Mania* is extremely excessive activity and elation or irritability.) Like dysthymia, it usually begins in childhood or adolescence and includes times of normal feelings that may last less than two months at a time (APA, 2000a).

But doesn't everybody get a little "down" sometimes? When does being sad become a disorder? It is normal to get sad every now and then and even to have a mild "mood swing" on occasion (the "mild" positions on Figure 13.2). But people experiencing normal sadness or moodiness usually return to normal relatively quickly. There's also usually a reason for the sadness—something bad has happened, an opportunity was lost, somebody is sick or has died, and so on. Although both dysthymia and cyclothymia can be triggered by an outside, stressful event, they go on too long to be considered normal reactions that need no treatment or attention.

MAJOR DEPRESSION

When a deeply depressed mood comes on fairly suddenly and either seems to be too severe for the circumstances or exists without any external cause for sadness, it is called **major depression.** Major depression would fall at the far extreme of sadness on Figure 13.2. People suffering from major depression are depressed for most of every day, take little or no pleasure in any activities, feel tired, have trouble sleeping or sleep too much, experience changes in appetite and significant weight changes, experience excessive guilt or feelings of worthlessness, have trouble concentrating, and may have thoughts of death or suicide, including suicide attempts. Some people with this disorder also suffer from delusional thinking and may experience hallucinations. Most of these symptoms occur on a daily basis, lasting for the better part of the day (APA, 2000a).

Major depression is the most common of the diagnosed mood disorders, affecting about 12 percent of adult Canadians living in the community (Patten et al., 2006). And, as shown in Figure 13.3, it is about twice as common in women as it is in men (APA, 2000a; Public Health Agency of Canada, 2002e; Patten, 2006). This is true even across various cultures (Blazer et al., 1994; Weissman et al., 1993). There are many possible explanations for this gender difference, including the different hormonal structure of the female system (e.g., menstruation, hormonal changes during and after pregnancy, menopause) and different social roles played by women in the culture (Blehar & Oren, 1997). Research has found little support for hormonal influences in general, instead finding that the role of hormones and other biological factors in depression is unclear. Instead, studies have found that the degree of differences between male and female rates of depression is decreasing and is non-existent in post-secondary students and single adults, leading some to conclude that social factors such as marital status, career type, and number of children may have more importance in creating the gender difference than biological differences (McGrath et al., 1992; Nolen-Hoeksema, 1990; Weissman & Klerman, 1977).

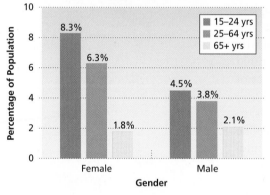

Major Depression by Gender and Age in Canada

FIGURE 13.3 **Prevalence of Major Depression** Women are nearly twice as likely as men to develop major depression before the age of 65.

dysthymia
a moderate depression that lasts for two years or more and is typically a reaction to some external stressor.

cyclothymia
disorder that consists of mood swings from moderate depression to hypomania and lasts two years or more.

major depression
severe depression that comes on suddenly and seems to have no external cause.

Ethnicity is another risk factor for major depression. First Nations, Inuit, and Métis Canadians have higher rates of depression and suicide compared to non-Aboriginal Canadians (Health Canada, 2002). According to a Health Canada (2002) report, the higher rates of depression in Aboriginal Canadians may be linked to a poor sense of self because of conflicting messages about the value of their culture. Cultural instability has also lead to higher rates of family violence and substance abuse, which are known risk factors for depression and suicide. In addition, poverty, childhood separation, and relatively easy access to firearms may also be contributing.

BIPOLAR DISORDERS

Major depression is sometimes referred to as a *unipolar disorder* because the emotional problem exists at only one end, or "pole," of the emotional range. When a person suffers from severe mood swings that go all the way from severe depression to **manic** episodes (excessive excitement, energy, and elation or irritability), that person is said to suffer from a **bipolar disorder**, meaning that emotions cycle between the two poles of possible emotions (APA, 2000a). There is usually no external cause for the extreme ups and downs of the bipolar person. The depressive phases of a bipolar person are indistinguishable from major depression but give way to manic episodes that may last from a few weeks to a few months. In these manic episodes, the person is extremely happy or euphoric without any real cause to be so happy. Restlessness, irritability, an inability to sit still or remain inactive, and seemingly unlimited energy are also common. The person may seem silly to others and can become aggressive when not allowed to carry out the grand (and sometimes delusional) plans that are often the hallmark of the manic phase. Speech may be rapid and jump from one topic to another. Oddly, people in the manic state are often very creative until their lack of organization renders their attempts at being creative useless (Blumer, 2002; McDermott, 2001; Rothenberg, 2001). Bipolar disorder is much rarer than major depression. The reported lifetime prevalence rate is around 2.6 percent (Statistics Canada, 2004) with about 1 percent of Canadian adults currently suffering from the disorder (Public Health Agency of Canada, 2002c).

That sounds almost like a description of an overactive child—can't sit still, can't concentrate—are they related? The answer to that question is actually part of an ongoing controversy. There does seem to be a connection between attention deficit hyperactivity disorder (ADHD) and the onset of bipolar disorder in adolescence (Carlson et al., 1998), but only a small percentage of children with ADHD go on to develop bipolar disorder. The symptoms of bipolar disorder include irrational thinking and other manic symptoms that are not present in ADHD (Geller et al., 1998). Confusion between the two disorders arises because hyperactivity (excessive movement and an inability to concentrate) is a symptom of both disorders.

CAUSES OF MOOD DISORDERS

13.17 *What are the causes of mood disorders?*

Explanations of depression and other mood disorders include psychoanalytic, learning, biological, and genetic theories. Psychoanalytic theories see depression as anger turned inward on the person. This anger, originally aimed at parents or other authority figures who are too threatening to receive the expressions of anger directly, gets repressed by the child and later is displaced to the self in the form of self-blame and self-hate (O'Connor, 1994; O'Connor et al., 1997).

"I've got the bowl, the bone, the big yard. I know I should be happy."

◀ That sounds almost like a description of an overactive child—can't sit still, can't concentrate—are they related?

👁 **Watch** on **mypsychlab**
Living with Bipolar Disorder

manic
having the quality of excessive excitement, energy, and elation or irritability.

bipolar disorder
severe mood swings between major depressive episodes and manic episodes.

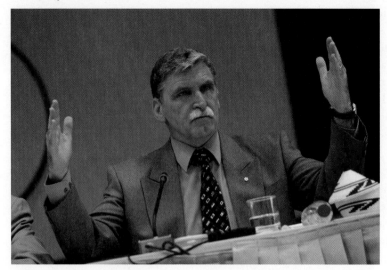

Following his return from Rwanda, Canadian General Romeo Dallaire blamed himself for everything that went wrong there. He sank into depression and became suicidal. With proper medication and counselling he soon began work on his book *Shake Hands with the Devil: The Failure of Humanity in Rwanda* and now feels that those dark days are behind him.

Margaret Trudeau, the former wife of well-known prime minister Pierre Trudeau, gestures while describing her bipolar disorder that affected most of her life. She wants Canadians to know that there is help for mental illness.

Learning theorists link depression to learned helplessness (Seligman, 1975, 1989), whereas social cognitive theorists point to distortions of thinking such as blowing negative events out of proportion and minimizing positive, good events (Beck, 1976, 1984). In the social cognitive view, depressed people continually have negative, self-defeating thoughts about themselves, which depress them further in a downward spiral of despair. Learned helplessness (discussed in Chapter Five) has been linked to an increase in such self-defeating thinking and depression in studies with people who have experienced uncontrollable, painful events (Abramson et al., 1978, 1980). LINK to *Chapter Five: Learning, p. 176.* This link does not necessarily mean that negative thoughts *cause* depression; it may be that depression increases the likelihood of negative thoughts (Gotlib et al., 2001).

Research indicates that major depression often occurs after a stressful event such as the loss of a loved one or divorce (Hammen, 2005). Kate Harkness and her colleagues at Queen's University suggest that stressors may interact with one another over time to influence one's personal risk of depression (Harkness, Bruce, & Lumley, 2006). For example, an abused and neglected child may be more prone to developing depression in response to some future stressful event (e.g., a breakup during adolescence). Researchers in Alberta and Manitoba have shown that individuals who live alone are more prone to depression, suggesting that social support may buffer the effects of stress and reduce the risk of depression (Afifi, Cox, & Enns, 2006).

Biological explanations of mood disorders focus on the effects of brain chemicals such as serotonin, norepinephrine, and dopamine; drugs used to treat depression and mania typically affect the levels of these three neurotransmitters, either alone or in combination (Cohen, 1997; Cummings & Coffey, 1994).

Genes may also play a part in mood disorders. The fact that the more severe mood disorders are not a reaction to some outside source of stress or anxiety but rather seem to come from within the person's own body, together with the tendency of mood disorders to appear in genetically related individuals at a higher rate, suggests rather strongly that inheritance may play a significant part in these disorders (Barondes, 1998; Farmer, 1996). More than 65 percent of people with bipolar disorder have at least one close relative with either bipolar disorder or major depression (NIMH Genetics Workgroup, 1998). Twin studies have shown that if one identical twin has either major depression or bipolar disorder, the chances that the other twin will also develop a mood disorder are about 40 to 70 percent (Muller-Oerlinghausen et al., 2002).

PRACTICE QUIZ: HOW MUCH DO YOU REMEMBER?

Pick the best answer.

1. Which of the following is not a sexual dysfunction primarily stemming from an organic physical disorder?
   a. sexual desire disorder
   b. frotteurism
   c. male erectile disorder
   d. sexual aversion disorder

2. In _____, the person may have the desire for sexual activity but be unable to physically participate.
   a. sexual desire disorder
   b. pedophilia
   c. sexual arousal disorder
   d. orgasmic disorder

3. Which of the following statements about transvestites is FALSE?
  a. Most transvestites are homosexuals.
  b. Transvestites get sexual excitement from wearing the clothing of the opposite sex.
  c. Most transvestites are married.
  d. There is little evidence of women transvestites in Western cultures.

4. In _____, sexual gratification is obtained by rubbing one's genitals up against the body of an unwilling person.
  a. necrophilia
  c. pedophilia
  b. frotteurism
  d. transvestite fetishism

5. Approximately _____ of Canadians will suffer from a mood disorder, _____ from major depression, and _____ from bipolar disorder.
  a. 20 percent; 15 percent; 5 percent
  b. 16 percent; 12 percent; 3 percent
  c. 5 percent; 10 percent; 15 percent
  d. 1 percent; 1 percent; 1 percent

6. Jorge lost his father three years ago. Since then, he has experienced occasional bouts of sadness and depression. Although he usually feels quite happy, sometimes the sadness returns. Jorge's relatively mild mood swings most likely indicate
  a. dysthymia.
  c. major depression.
  b. cyclothymia.
  d. bipolar disorder.

7. Macha woke up one morning in a very sad mood and couldn't think of any reason why she should feel that way. The feeling got worse as the day went on, and although in the days and weeks to follow she occasionally felt normal, she had more sad days than usual. Her feelings were so intense that she couldn't sleep, ate too much, and couldn't take joy in anything. Macha is most likely suffering from
  a. dysthymia.
  c. major depression.
  b. cyclothymia.
  d. bipolar disorder.

8. Which Canadian is most likely to develop depression in life?
  a. Paige, who had a normal childhood and now works as an engineer
  b. Sabrina, who was neglected as a child and is unemployed
  c. Frank, who had a normal childhood and is unemployed
  d. Bill, who was neglected as a child and now works as an engineer

9. Vicki was always coming up with grand plans for making money, none of which lasted very long before she abandoned them. The latest scheme is to buy a huge tract of land and build an expensive dude ranch where people can come to learn how to train their horses, eat at a four-star restaurant, and stay in luxury accommodations—all this in spite of the fact that Vicki and her husband don't have the money to buy the land, the knowledge of how to run a hotel, or a four-star chef handy. Vicki may have
  a. dysthymia.
  c. major depression.
  b. cyclothymia.
  d. bipolar disorder.

Answers: 1-b, 2-c, 3-a, 4-b, 5-b, 6-b, 7-c, 8-b, 9-d.

SCHIZOPHRENIA: ALTERED REALITY

Once known as *dementia praecox*, a Latin-based term meaning "out of one's mind before one's time," **schizophrenia** was renamed by Eugen Bleuler, a Swiss psychiatrist, to better illustrate the division (*schizo*) within the brain (*phren*) among thoughts, feelings, and behaviour that seems to take place in people with this disorder (Bleuler, 1911; Möller & Hell, 2002). Because the term literally means "split mind," it has often been confused with dissociative identity disorder, which was at one time called "split personality." A more modern definition of schizophrenia describes it as a long-lasting **psychotic** disorder (involving a severe break with reality), in which there is an inability to distinguish what is real from what is fantasy, as well as disturbances in thinking, emotions, behaviour, and perception. Schizophrenia afflicts about 300 000 Canadian adults, or about 1 percent of the population (Public Health Agency of Canada, 2002d). It afflicts men and women in equal numbers, but men usually develop the disorder earlier.

SYMPTOMS

13.18 *What are the main symptoms of schizophrenia?*

Schizophrenia includes several different kinds of symptoms. Disorders in thinking are a common symptom and are called **delusions**. Although delusions are not prominent in all forms of schizophrenia, they are the symptom that most people associate with this disorder. Delusions are false beliefs about the world that the person holds and that tend to remain fixed and unshakable even in the face of evidence that disproves the delusions. Common schizophrenic delusions include *delusions of persecution*, in

⊙ Watch on mypsychlab
Living with Schizophrenia

schizophrenia
severe disorder in which the person suffers from disordered thinking, bizarre behaviour, hallucinations, and is unable to distinguish between fantasy and reality.

psychotic
the break away from an ability to perceive what is real and what is fantasy.

delusions
false beliefs held by a person who refuses to accept evidence of their falseness.

Actor Russell Crowe portrayed schizophrenic genius John Forbes Nash in the 2001 film *A Beautiful Mind.*

This photograph shows Keith, Deanna, Joshua, and Luke Laney of New Chapel Hill, Texas, in seemingly happier times. On May 12, 2003, Deanna Laney killed her two young sons by crushing their heads with rocks, believing that God had ordered her to kill her children. On the day of the killings, Deanna suffered a number of visual and auditory hallucinations. Mrs. Laney was found innocent by reason of insanity in 2004 and has been committed to a maximum security state hospital, where she is undergoing treatment for paranoid schizophrenia.

delusional disorder
a psychotic disorder in which the primary symptom is one or more delusions.

hallucinations
false sensory perceptions, such as hearing voices that do not really exist.

flat affect
a lack of emotional responsiveness.

which people believe that others are trying to hurt them in some way; *delusions of reference*, in which people believe that other people, television characters, and even books are specifically talking to them; *delusions of influence*, in which people believe that they are being controlled by external forces, such as the devil, aliens, or cosmic forces; and *delusions of grandeur*, in which people are convinced that they are powerful people who can save the world or have a special mission (APA, 2000a).

Dr. John Nash is a famous mathematician who won the Nobel Prize for mathematics in 1994. His fame, however, is more due to the fact that Nash once suffered from a form of schizophrenia in which he experienced delusions of persecution. He at one time believed that aliens were trying to contact him through the newspaper (delusions of reference). His life story and remarkable recovery from schizophrenia are portrayed in the 2001 movie *A Beautiful Mind,* which starred Russell Crowe as Nash (Kuhn & Nasar, 2001; Nasar, 1998).

Delusional thinking alone is not enough to merit a diagnosis of schizophrenia, as there is a separate category of psychotic disorders called **delusional disorders**, in which the primary symptom is some form of delusion. In schizophrenia, other symptoms must be present (APA, 2000a; Black & Andreason, 1999). Speech disturbances are common: Schizophrenic people will make up words, repeat words or sentences persistently, string words together on the basis of sounds (called *clanging*, such as "come into house, louse, mouse, mouse and cheese, please, sneeze"), and experience sudden interruptions in speech or thought. Thoughts are significantly disturbed as well, with schizophrenic people having a hard time linking their thoughts together in a logical fashion.

People with schizophrenia may also have **hallucinations**, in which they hear voices or see things or people that are not really there. Hearing voices is actually more common and one of the key symptoms in making a diagnosis of schizophrenia. Hallucinations involving touch, smell, and taste are less common but also possible. Although the movie portrayed Nash as having visual hallucinations, he says that he actually heard voices that he eventually learned to ignore (Nasar, 1998).

Emotional disturbances are also a key feature of schizophrenia. **Flat affect** is a condition in which the person shows little or no emotion. Emotions can also be excessive and/or inappropriate—a person might laugh when it would be more appropriate to cry or show sorrow, for example.

The person's behaviour may also become disorganized and extremely odd. For example, some forms of schizophrenia are accompanied by periods of complete immobility, whereas still others may involve weird facial grimaces and odd gesturing. According to the American Psychiatric Association (2000a), at least two or more of the following symptoms must be present frequently for at least one month to diagnose schizophrenia: delusions, hallucinations, disturbed speech, disturbed emotions, and disturbed behaviour.

Attention is also a problem for many schizophrenics. They seem to have trouble "screening out" information and stimulation that they don't really need, causing them to be unable to focus on information that is relevant (Asarnow et al., 1991).

CATEGORIES OF SCHIZOPHRENIA

13.19 *What are the different types of schizophrenia?*

Although all schizophrenics share the symptoms already discussed to a certain degree, the way in which these symptoms show up in behaviour can be used to distinguish among several different types of schizophrenia. There are five basic categories and two major types of schizophrenia (APA, 2000a). The two types differ in the kind of symptoms that predominate.

DISORGANIZED **Disorganized** schizophrenics are very confused in speech, have vivid and frequent hallucinations, and tend to have very inappropriate affect (emotion) or flat affect. They are very socially impaired, unable to engage in the normal social rituals of daily life. Giggling, silliness, nonsensical speech, and neglect of cleanliness are common. They may not bathe or change clothing and may have problems with urinating or defecating in public, either because of incontinence or a deliberate wish to shock those watching.

CATATONIC Although it is becoming rare, **catatonic** schizophrenia involves very disturbed motor behaviour. The person doesn't respond to the outside world and either doesn't move at all, maintaining often odd-looking postures for hours on end (a condition known as *catatonia*) or moves about wildly in great agitation. It's as if there are only two "speeds" for the catatonic, totally off or totally on.

PARANOID The **paranoid** schizophrenic suffers from hallucinations and delusions. Auditory* hallucinations are common, and the delusions are typically persecution, grandeur, or extreme jealousy of another or several other persons. Although their thinking is not as scattered as that of the disorganized schizophrenic, their delusions tend to be bizarre but very systematic.

UNDIFFERENTIATED Sometimes a person with schizophrenic symptoms does not consistently show signs of one of the three previous categories but may instead shift from one pattern to another or show no consistent pattern. This person is usually labelled as having **undifferentiated** schizophrenia.

RESIDUAL Some people have a major episode of schizophrenia that ends, leaving the person in a state between an active episode of schizophrenia and, in some cases, full recovery. If they no longer show the major symptoms of delusions and hallucinations but still have some residual (leftover) symptoms such as negative beliefs, poor language skills, or some unusual ideas and perceptions, they might be given the label of **residual** schizophrenic. They would be considered a little "odd" by others but would be able to function in daily life, unlike a person who is suffering from an active episode of schizophrenia.

Another way of categorizing schizophrenia is to look at the kind of symptoms that predominate. **Positive symptoms** appear to reflect an excess or distortion of normal functions, such as hallucinations and delusions. **Negative symptoms** appear to reflect a decrease of normal functions, such as poor attention or lack of affect (APA, 2000a).

Positive symptoms are associated with overactivity in the dopamine areas of the brain. Dopamine-reducing drugs used to treat schizophrenia are usually effective on these symptoms, and the outlook for recovery is generally good (Davis et al., 1991; Penn, 1998; Rosenzweig et al., 1996).

Negative symptoms include the inability to filter out stimuli to focus attention, flat affect, problems with producing speech, apathy, and withdrawal from others. Negative symptoms, unlike positive symptoms, are associated with *lower* than normal activity in the dopamine systems of the brain and problems in the functioning of the frontal lobe. Studies have found that schizophrenics with negative symptoms have decreased blood flow to the frontal lobe areas (Davis et al., 1991; Perlstein et al., 2001). Unfortunately, this also means that the outlook for recovery from negative-symptom schizophrenia is not good, as these symptoms do not respond well to medications that are effective with positive-symptom schizophrenia.

---

*Auditory: having to do with hearing

disorganized
type of schizophrenia in which behaviour is bizarre and childish and thinking, speech, and motor actions are very disordered.

catatonic
type of schizophrenia in which the person experiences periods of statuelike immobility mixed with occasional bursts of energetic, frantic movement and talking.

paranoid
type of schizophrenia in which the person suffers from delusions of persecution, grandeur, and jealousy, together with hallucinations.

undifferentiated
type of schizophrenia in which the person shows no particular pattern, shifting from one pattern to another, and cannot be neatly classified as disorganized, paranoid, or catatonic.

residual
type of schizophrenia in which there are no delusions and hallucinations, but the person still experiences negative thoughts, poor language skills, and odd behaviour.

positive symptoms
symptoms of schizophrenia that are excesses of behaviour or occur in addition to normal behaviour; hallucinations, delusions, and distorted thinking.

negative symptoms
symptoms of schizophrenia that are less than normal behaviour or an absence of normal behaviour; poor attention, flat affect, and poor speech production.

CAUSES OF SCHIZOPHRENIA

13.20 *What are the possible causes of schizophrenia?*

In psychoanalytic theory, schizophrenia was thought to be the result of a severe breakdown in the ego, which was overwhelmed by the infantile demands of the id. In this theory, the ego retreats into an earlier, more childish stage of development and can no longer distinguish between the fantasies of the id and the realities of the world. It was thought that this regression results from a disturbed relationship between mother and child. Critics of this view point out that schizophrenic people are more than simply childish and infantile in their behaviour, engaging in bizarre behaviour, delusions, and hallucinations that are not common to infants or young children. Psychoanalysts have not been successful in attempts to link early childhood experiences with later development of schizophrenia (Cioffi, 1998).

The woman on the right suffers from schizophrenia, as does 1 percent of the population worldwide. Medication, such as that being given by the nurse on the left, can help some schizophrenic people lead relatively normal lives. Others must remain in institutions.

Behaviourists do not try to account for the onset of schizophrenia but focus on how the particular behavioural symptoms of the different types of schizophrenia might be shaped through the processes of reinforcement and extinction. For example, a person with catatonic schizophrenia might have gained attention from remaining in a statuelike pose, making such poses more likely in the future. Modelling may also play a part in the behavioural explanation of schizophrenia, as patients in a hospital may see the bizarre behaviour of other patients get rewarded with attention and later imitate similar behaviour. This does not explain how people who have never been exposed to other schizophrenics develop their behaviour, however.

Cognitive theorists see the irrational beliefs of the schizophrenic as a more severe form of illogical thinking than is found in anxiety and mood disorders. Cognitive-behavioural treatments of schizophrenia symptoms have had some success in reducing, but not completely erasing, those symptoms (Bradshaw, 1997, 1998). It would seem that cognitive and behavioural theories are more useful in developing treatments to reduce the severity of schizophrenic symptoms than as models for explaining the causes of schizophrenia.

Biological explanations of schizophrenia have generated a significant amount of research pointing to genetic origins, chemical influences (dopamine), and brain structural defects (frontal lobe defects and deterioration of neurons) as the causes of schizophrenia (Gottesman & Shields, 1982; Harrison, 1999; Kety et al., 1994). Dopamine was first suspected when amphetamine users began to show schizophrenialike psychotic symptoms. One of the side effects of amphetamine usage is to increase the release of dopamine in the brain. Drugs used to treat schizophrenia decrease the activity of dopamine, and the prefrontal cortex (an area of the brain involved in planning and organization of information) of people with schizophrenia has been shown to produce lower levels of dopamine than normal (Acar et al., 2003; Harrison, 1999).

Further support for a biological explanation of schizophrenia comes from studies of the incidence of the disorder across different cultures. If schizophrenia were caused mainly by environmental factors, the expectation would be that rates of schizophrenia would vary widely from culture to culture. In fact, the rate of schizophrenia is approximately 1 percent of the population, regardless of the culture (Torrey, 1987).

Family, twin, and adoption studies have provided strong evidence that genes are a major means of transmitting schizophrenia. The highest risk for developing schizophrenia if one has a blood relative with the disorder is faced by monozygotic (identical) twins, who share 100 percent of their genetic material, with a risk factor of about 50 percent

(Gottesman & Shields, 1976, 1982; Gottesman et al., 1987). Dizygotic twins, who share about 50 percent of their genetic material, have about a 17 percent risk, the same as a child with one schizophrenic parent. As genetic relatedness decreases, so does the risk (see Figure 13.4).

Adoption studies also support the genetic basis of schizophrenia. In one study, the biological and adoptive relatives of schizophrenic adoptees were compared to a control group of adoptees without schizophrenia but from similar backgrounds and conditions (Kety et al., 1994). The adoptees with schizophrenia had relatives with schizophrenia but *only among their biological* relatives. When the prevalence of schizophrenia was compared between the biological relatives of the schizophrenic adoptees and the biological relatives of the control group, the rate of the disorder in the relatives of the schizophrenic group was 10 times higher than in the control group (Kety et al., 1994).

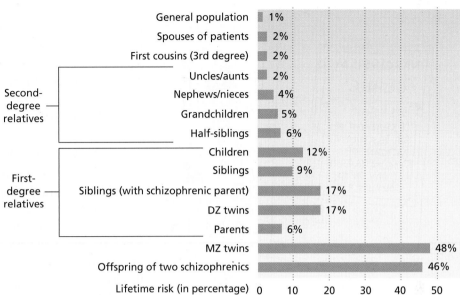

FIGURE 13.4 **Genetics and Schizophrenia**   This graph shows a definite pattern: the greater the degree of genetic relatedness, the higher the risk of schizophrenia in individuals related to each other. The only individual to carry a risk even close to that of identical twins (who share 100 percent of their genes) is a person who is the child of two schizophrenic parents. *Source:* Gottesman**, 1991.**

There's something I don't understand. If one identical twin has the gene and the disorder, shouldn't the other one always have it, too? Why is the rate only 50 percent? If schizophrenia were entirely controlled by genes, identical twins would indeed both have the disorder at a risk of 100 percent, not merely 50 percent. Obviously, there is some influence of environment on the development of schizophrenia. One model that has been proposed is the **stress-vulnerability model**, which assumes that persons with the genetic "markers" for schizophrenia have a physical vulnerability to the disorder but will not develop schizophrenia unless they are exposed to environmental or emotional stress at critical times in development, such as prenatal development (Davis & Bracha, 1996) or puberty (Harrison, 1999; Weinberger, 1987). In fact, Canadian researchers have found that schizophrenia tends to be associated with poor fetal growth, premature birth, and low birth weight (Smith et al. 2001). These factors may help to explain why only one twin out of a pair might develop the disorder when both carry the genetic markers for schizophrenia—the life stresses for the affected twin were different from those of the one who remained healthy.

◄ There's something I don't understand. If one identical twin has the gene and the disorder, shouldn't the other one always have it, too? Why is the rate only 50 percent?

PERSONALITY DISORDERS: I'M OKAY, IT'S EVERYONE ELSE WHO'S WEIRD

13.21   *What are the different kinds of personality disorders?*

Personality disorders are a little different from other psychological disorders in that the disorder does not affect merely one aspect of the person's life, such as a higher than normal level of anxiety or a set of distorted beliefs, but instead affects the entire life adjustment of the person. The disorder is the personality itself, not one aspect of it. In personality disorder, a person has an excessively rigid, maladaptive pattern of behaviour and way of relating to others (APA, 2000a). This rigidity and inability to adapt to social demands and life changes make it very difficult for the individual with

stress-vulnerability model
explanation of disorder that assumes a biological sensitivity, or vulnerability, to a certain disorder will develop under the right conditions of environmental or emotional stress.

personality disorders
disorders in which a person adopts a persistent, rigid, and maladaptive pattern of behaviour that interferes with normal social interactions.

NARCISSISM CLINIC

WORKSHOP: "BREAK OUT OF THE DESTRUCTIVE PATTERN OF GOOGLING YOURSELF ALL DAY ON THE COMPUTER"

SCHWADRON

a personality disorder to fit in with others or have relatively normal social relationships. The *DSM-IV-TR* lists three basic categories of personality disorders (APA, 2000a): those in which the people are seen as odd or eccentric by others, those in which the behaviour of the person is very dramatic or erratic, and those in which the main emotion is anxiety or fearfulness. There are 10 recognized types of personality disorders (see Table 13.9).

ANTISOCIAL PERSONALITY DISORDER

People with **antisocial personality disorder** (APD) are literally "against society." The antisocial person, previously called a *sociopath* or *psychopath*, habitually breaks the law, disobeys rules, tells lies, and uses other people without worrying about their rights or feelings. In Freudian terms, the antisocial personality has no superego or a very weak superego and, therefore, has no real conscience to create guilt feelings when the person does something morally wrong. As a consequence, people with this disorder typically feel no remorse or guilt at lying, cheating, stealing, or even more serious crimes such as murder.

The first thing that usually comes to most people's minds when they hear the term *sociopath* is the *serial killer*, a person who kills others for the excitement and thrill of killing without feeling any guilt. However, most antisocial personalities are not killers. Typically

antisocial personality disorder disorder in which a person has no morals or conscience and often behaves in an impulsive manner without regard for the consequences of that behaviour.

TABLE 13.9 THE PERSONALITY DISORDERS	
PERSONALITY DISORDER	**DESCRIPTION**
Odd or Eccentric Types	
Paranoid	Extreme suspicion of others; mistrustful, often jealous
Schizoid	Loners who are cool, distant, and unwilling and unable to form close relationships with others
Schizotypal	Difficulty in forming social relationships, odd and eccentric behaviour, tendency to hold magical beliefs
Dramatic or Erratic Types	
Antisocial	Lacking in conscience or morals; users and con artists who experience no regret or strong emotions
Borderline	Moody, unstable, lacking in a clear sense of identity, clinging to others
Histrionic	Tendency to overreact and use excessive emotions to draw attention from and manipulate others. Love to be the centre of attention
Narcissistic	Extremely vain and self-involved
Anxious or Fearful Types	
Avoidant	Fearful of social relationships, tend to avoid social contacts unless absolutely necessary
Dependent	Needy, want others to make decisions for them
Obsessive-Compulsive	Controlling, focused on neatness and order to an extreme degree

they borrow money or belongings and don't bother to repay the debt or return the items, they are impulsive, they don't keep their commitments either socially or in their jobs, and they tend to be very selfish, self-centred, manipulative, and unable to feel deep emotions. Despite these obvious character flaws, persons with APD have a superficial charm about them, and most people initially find them charismatic, nice, and fun to be around. University of British Columbia psychologist Robert Hare, a leading authority on APD, believes that this characteristic APD personality begins in childhood or adolescence and continues into adulthood (Hare, 1996). Canadian serial killer Paul Bernardo displayed superficial charm and took lives without feeling guilt or remorse, consistent with APD. Although Canadian data is lacking on the prevalence of APD, an Ontario study pegs the rate of APD at 1.7 percent (Offord et al., 1996).

There is a definite gender difference in antisocial personality disorder, with nearly three to six times as many males diagnosed with this disorder as females (APA, 2000a; Paris, 2004).

BORDERLINE PERSONALITY DISORDER

People with **borderline personality disorder** have relationships with other people that are intense and relatively unstable. They are often moody, manipulative, and untrusting of others. Periods of depression are not unusual, and some may engage in excessive spending, drug abuse, or suicidal behaviour (suicide attempts may be part of the manipulation the borderline personality uses against others in a relationship). Emotions are often inappropriate and excessive, leading to confusion with *histrionic personality disorder*. What makes the borderline different is the confusion over identity issues, in which the person may be unable to focus on consistent life goals, career choices, friendships, and even sexual behaviour (APA, 2000a). As such, many persons who have borderline personality disorder also show many of the behaviours characteristic of other personality disorders. Researchers at the University of Toronto conducted a seven-year follow-up study of persons diagnosed with borderline personality disorder. Those who continued to show elements of borderline personality were also more likely to show elements of avoidant, dependent, and histrionic personality than those who were in remittance of their borderline personality disorder (Links, Heslegrave, & van Reekum, 1998).

The frequency of this disorder in women is nearly two to three times greater than in men (APA, 2000a; Swartz et al., 1990). Numerous causes such as genetic or hormonal influences, childhood experiences with incest or other abuse, and a poor mother–infant relationship during the years in which the identity is forming have all been suggested as a cause of the disorder (Torgersen, 2000; Widiger & Weissman, 1991; Zanarini, 2000).

CAUSES OF PERSONALITY DISORDERS

13.22   *What causes personality disorders?*

Psychoanalytic theorists have blamed an inadequate resolution to the Oedipus complex for the formation of personality disorders. In particular, the antisocial personality can be described as lacking a fully developed superego. More recently, these theories focus on problems in the development of the ego in the anal stage as being responsible for disorders such as narcissism and borderline disorders.

Cognitive-learning theorists do not talk about innate personality traits, normal, disordered, or otherwise. Instead, these theorists talk about how specific behaviour can be learned over time through the processes of reinforcement, shaping, and modelling. More cognitive explanations involve the belief systems formed by the personality disordered persons, such as the paranoia, extreme self-importance, and fear of being unable to cope by oneself of the paranoid, narcissistic, and dependent personalities, for example.

◉ Watch on **mypsychlab**
Living with Borderline Personality Disorder

borderline personality disorder
maladaptive personality pattern in which the person is moody, unstable, lacks a clear sense of identity, and often clings to others.

There is some evidence of genetic factors in personality disorders. Close biological relatives of people with disorders such as antisocial, schizotypal, and borderline are more likely to have these disorders than those who are not related, for example (APA, 2000a; Battaglia et al., 1995; Faraone et al., 1999; Nigg & Goldsmith, 1994). Adoption studies of children whose biological parents had antisocial personality disorder show an increased risk for that disorder in those children, even though raised in a different environment by different people (APA, 2000a).

One interesting finding in genetic studies is that some research shows a greater risk of schizophrenia in relatives of people with schizotypal personality disorder (Kendler & Walsh, 1995; Webb & Levinson, 1993). Only a small proportion of people with schizotypal personality disorder go on to develop full-blown schizophrenia, however (APA, 2000a).

Other causes of personality disorders have been suggested. Antisocial personalities are emotionally unresponsive to stressful or threatening situations when compared to others, which may be one reason that they are not afraid of getting caught (Arnett et al., 1997; Blair et al., 1995; Lykken, 1995). This unresponsiveness seems to be linked to lower than normal levels of stress hormones in antisocial persons (Lykken, 1995).

Disturbances in family relationships and communication have also been linked to personality disorders and, in particular, to antisocial personality disorder (Benjamin, 1996; Livesley, 1995). Childhood abuse, neglect, overly strict parenting, overprotective parenting, and parental rejection have all been put forth as possible causes, making the picture of the development of personality disorders a complicated one. It is safe to say that many of the same factors (genetics, social relationships, and parenting) that help to create ordinary personalities also create disordered personalities.

PRACTICE QUIZ: HOW MUCH DO YOU REMEMBER?

Pick the best answer.

1. Charles believed that a famous song by a popular musical group carried a special, secret message meant only for him. This would be an example of a delusion of
   a. persecution.
   c. influence.
   b. reference.
   d. grandeur.

2. In an old movie, a madman made weird faces and sounds, jumped about wildly in his cell, and laughed and giggled constantly. This bizarre behaviour is typical of the _____ schizophrenic.
   a. disorganized
   c. paranoid
   b. catatonic
   d. residual

3. Which type of schizophrenic is most likely to have delusions of grandeur?
   a. disorganized
   c. paranoid
   b. catatonic
   d. residual

4. Which of the following statements about antisocial personality disorder is TRUE?
   a. Most people with this disorder are vicious killers.
   b. Most people with this disorder are men.
   c. People with this disorder suffer terrible guilt but commit crimes anyway.
   d. People with this disorder feel emotions very deeply and intensely.

5. Which of the following personality disorders is most likely to show elements of other personality disorders?
   a. histrionic personality
   c. narcissistic personality
   b. antisocial personality
   d. borderline personality

Answers: 1-b, 2-a, 3-c, 4-b, 5-d.

APPLYING PSYCHOLOGY TO EVERYDAY LIFE: CANADIAN LAW AND MENTAL ILLNESS

13.23 *What happens to a person who is accused of a crime in Canada and is found not criminally responsible on account of a mental disorder?*

The recent highly publicized murder cases of Vince Li and former colonel David Russell Williams have certainly elevated Canadians' consciousness regarding the law and mental health. Before we actually look at the law, let's review some other Canadian cases. In 1995, well-known Calgary socialite Dorothy Joudrie (1936–2002) shot her estranged husband six times when he returned home to gather some of his belongings. Her husband survived and reported that his wife was unusually calm and detached during the shooting. Police officers, on the contrary, found her quite distraught and very disoriented, with no recollection of what she had just done. Ms. Joudrie was suffering from dissociative amnesia. At trial, it was learned that Dorothy had suffered from years of violent abuse at the hands of her husband, who recently had left her for another women. To cope with her immense guilt, shame, and loneliness, Dorothy turned to alcohol. Dorothy was found not criminally responsible by reason of mental disorder.

In April 2006, the Supreme Court of Canada upheld the acquittal of Rita Graveline, who in a "trancelike and robotic" state killed her abusive and alcoholic husband Michael. Ms. Graveline's defence lawyer told reporters, "All she remembers is going up the stairs—she's dressed—and when she wakes up, she's got a gun in her hands and she's in her husband's bedroom." At her trial, two psychiatrists testified that Ms. Graveline was in a trancelike state known as *automatism* brought on by suppressed rage caused by years of abuse.

It may seem from the examples above that the mental disorder defence is used frequently in Canada. This is not the case. In fact, very few people charged with a crime use this defence (Hart & Roesch, 2007). And don't think for a minute that not criminally responsible on account of a mental disorder means that the person goes free or gets a light sentence. Under provisions in the Canadian Criminal Code of 1985, any person found not guilty by reason of insanity or who is unfit to stand trial because of a mental illness must be indefinitely detained in a psychiatric institution until the disorder improves, at which time they will either be released or found "fit" to stand trial, depending on their circumstances. In many cases, however, the mentally ill person was detained in a mental institution for longer than their sentence would have been had they been found guilty and sent to prison (Harris, Rice, Cormier, 1991). This situation prompted the Supreme Court of Canada to force Parliament to change the Criminal Code, which it did in 1991. One of the major changes was placing limits on how long an accused person could be kept in a psychiatric institution. Changes were also made to the mental disorder defence. The defence of "not guilty by reason of insanity" was change to "not criminally responsible on account of a mental disorder."

Who determines whether a person is not criminally responsive on account of a mental disorder? Ultimately the decision lies with either the judge or the jury. However, judges and juries rely heavily on the testimony provided by mental health professionals who are considered to be expert witnesses. Problems can arise, however, when expert witnesses for the defence and prosecution disagree in their expert opinions. This "battle of the experts" often creates confusion for judges and jurors and highlights the fact that the psychological definition of mental illness, while improving, remains too unreliable, since experts may interpret it differently. We must not forget that at trial an expert witness offers an informed opinion, not the truth, about a mental disorder. It is the judge or jury that must decide whether a mental disorder defence is truly warranted. The conflict between psychology and the law is a particularly interesting area of study called *forensic psychology* that truly demonstrates how psychology can and is being applied to everyday life.

Questions for Further Discussion

1. The defence of "not guilty by reason of insanity" was changed to "not criminally responsible on account of a mental disorder." Explain how are these definitions are similar and different.

2. Under what types of family legal matters (family law) might an expert witness be asked to testify?

3. Thinking back to the chapter-opening story, do you think Vince Li should ever be allowed to re-enter society?

13 CHAPTER SUMMARY

What Is Abnormality?

- Psychopathology is the study of abnormal behaviour.

13.1 *How did people in earlier times explain mental illness?*

- In ancient times, holes were cut in an ill person's head to let out evil spirits in a process called *trepanning*. Hippocrates believed that mental illness came from an imbalance in the body's four humours, whereas in the Middle Ages the mentally ill were labelled as witches.

13.2 *What are the different ways in which abnormal behaviour can be defined?*

- Abnormal behaviour can be defined as behaviour that is statistically rare, is deviant from social norms, causes subjective discomfort, does not allow normal, day-to-day functioning, or causes a person to be dangerous to self or others.

Models of Abnormality

13.3 *How are psychological disorders related to the brain and body chemistry?*

- In biological models of abnormality, the assumption is that mental illnesses are caused by chemical or structural malfunctions in the nervous system.

13.4 *How can psychological disorders be explained by the different viewpoints in psychology?*

- Psychoanalytic theorists assume that abnormal behaviour stems from repressed conflicts and urges that are fighting to become conscious.
- Behaviourists see abnormal behaviour as learned.
- Cognitive theorists see abnormal behaviour as coming from irrational beliefs and illogical patterns of thought.

Psychology in the News: A Look at Abnormality in Various Cultures

13.5 *How is abnormality viewed in other kinds of cultures?*

- Cultural relativity refers to the need to consider the norms and customs of another culture when diagnosing a person from that culture with a disorder.
- Culture-bound syndromes are disorders found only in certain cultures.

Diagnostic and Statistical Manual, Version IV, Text Revision (DSM-IV-TR)

13.6 *How do psychologists decide what kind of disorder a person has?*

- *Diagnostic and Statistical Manual, Version IV, Text Revision (DSM-IV-TR)* is a manual of psychological disorders and their symptoms.

13.7 *What are the different types of psychological disorders and, how common are they?*

- There are five axes in the *DSM-IV-TR*, which include clinical disorders, personality disorders, general medical conditions, psychosocial and environmental problems, and a global assessment of functioning.

- More than one-fifth of all adults older than age 18 suffer from a mental disorder in any given year. Major depression is one of the most common psychological disorders worldwide.

Anxiety Disorders: What, Me Worry?

13.8 *What are the different types of anxiety disorders and their symptoms?*

- Anxiety disorders are all disorders in which the most dominant symptom is excessive and unrealistic anxiety.
- Phobias are irrational, persistent fears. The three types of phobias are social phobias, specific phobias, and agoraphobia.
- Obsessive-compulsive disorder consists of an obsessive, recurring thought that creates anxiety and a compulsive, ritualistic, and repetitive behaviour that reduces that anxiety.
- Panic disorder is the sudden and recurrent onset of intense panic for no reason, with all the physical symptoms that can occur in sympathetic nervous system arousal, and is sometimes accompanied by agoraphobia.
- Generalized anxiety disorder is a condition of intense and unrealistic anxiety that lasts six months or more.

13.9 *How do psychologists explain the causes of anxiety disorders?*

- Psychoanalytic explanations point to repressed urges and desires that are trying to come into conscious, creating anxiety that is controlled by the abnormal behaviour.
- Behaviourists state that disordered behaviour is learned through both positive and negative reinforcement.
- Cognitive psychologists believe that excessive anxiety comes from illogical, irrational thought processes.
- Biological explanations of anxiety disorders include chemical imbalances in the nervous system, in particular serotonin and GABA systems.
- Genetic transmission may be responsible for anxiety disorders among related persons.

Somatoform Disorders: Sickness as a State of Mind

13.10 *What are the different kinds of somatoform disorders?*

- Somatoform disorders are the belief that one is physically ill, although there is no corresponding physical ailment, and include hypochondriasis, somatization disorder, and conversion disorder.

13.11 *What causes somatoform disorders?*

- Psychoanalytic explanations of somatoform disorders assume that anxiety is turned into a physical symptom.
- Behavioural explanations point to the negative reinforcement experienced when the "ill" person escapes unpleasant situations such as combat.
- Cognitive explanations assume that people magnify their physical symptoms and normal bodily changes into ailments out of irrational fear.

Dissociative Disorders: Altered Consciousness

13.12 *What are the different types of dissociative disorders?*

- Dissociative disorders involve a break in consciousness, memory, or both. These disorders include dissociative amnesia, dissociative fugue, and dissociative identity disorder.

13.13 *How do dissociative disorders develop?*

- Psychoanalytic explanations point to repression of memories, seeing dissociation as a defence mechanism against anxiety.
- Cognitive and behavioural explanations see dissociative disorders as a kind of avoidance learning.
- Biological explanations point to lower than normal activity levels in the areas responsible for body awareness in people with dissociative disorders.

Sexual Disorders

13.14 *What are the different types of sexual disorders?*

- There are three different types of sexual disorders: gender identity disorder, in which a person feels trapped in the wrong body; sexual dysfunctions, in which a person has trouble functioning during sex; and the paraphilias, in which a person's sexual arousal is aimed at inappropriate objects or individuals.

13.15 *What causes sexual disorders?*

- Sexual dysfunctions are problems with sexual functioning. They may be caused by physical problems, stress, or psychological problems.
- Organic or stress-induced dysfunctions are caused by a physical problem or by stress and can affect sexual interest, arousal, and response.
- These disorders include hypoactive sexual desire, sexual aversion, female sexual arousal disorder, male erectile disorder, male orgasmic disorder, female orgasmic disorder, premature ejaculation, vaginismus, and dyspareunia.
- The paraphilias are thought to be psychological in origin and involve sexual behaviour that is unusual or not socially acceptable as a preferred way of achieving sexual pleasure.
- The paraphilias include fetishism, exhibitionism, voyeurism, frotteurism, necrophilia, transvestism, and pedophilia.

Mood Disorders: The Effect of Affect

13.16 *What are the different types of mood disorders?*

- Mood disorders, also called affective disorders, are severe disturbances in emotion.
- Dysthymia is a moderate depression that is typically a reaction to some external stressor, whereas cyclothymia consists of moderate mood swings usually tied to an external stressor.
- Major depression has a sudden onset and is extreme sadness and despair, typically with no obvious external cause. It is the most common of the mood disorders and is twice as common in women as in men.
- Bipolar disorders are severe mood swings from major depressive episodes to manic episodes of extreme elation and energy with no obvious external cause.

13.17 *What are the causes of mood disorders?*

- Psychoanalytic theories see depression as anger at authority figures from childhood turned inward on the self.
- Learning theories link depression to learned helplessness.
- Cognitive theories see depression as the result of distorted, illogical thinking.
- Biological explanations of mood disorders look at the function of serotonin, norepinephrine, and dopamine systems in the brain.
- Mood disorders are more likely to appear in genetically related people with higher rates of risk for closer genetic relatives.

Schizophrenia: Altered Reality

- Schizophrenia is a split between thoughts, emotions, and behaviour. It is a long-lasting psychotic disorder in which reality and fantasy become confused.

13.18 *What are the main symptoms of schizophrenia?*

- Symptoms of schizophrenia include delusions (false beliefs about the world), hallucinations, emotional disturbances, attentional difficulties, disturbed speech, and disordered thinking.

13.19 *What are the different types of schizophrenia?*

- The five types of schizophrenic behaviour are disorganized, catatonic, paranoid, undifferentiated, and residual.
- Positive symptoms are excesses of behaviour associated with increased dopamine activity, whereas negative symptoms are deficits in behaviour associated with decreased dopamine activity.

13.20 *What are the possible causes of schizophrenia?*

- Psychoanalytic theories see schizophrenia as resulting from a severe breakdown of the ego, which has become overwhelmed by the demands of the id and results in childish, infantile behaviour.
- Behaviourists focus on how reinforcement, observational learning, and shaping affect the development of the behavioural symptoms of schizophrenia.
- Cognitive theorists see schizophrenia as severely irrational thinking.
- Biological explanations focus on dopamine, structural defects in the brain, and genetic influences in schizophrenia. Rates of risk of developing schizophrenia increase drastically as genetic relatedness increases with the highest risk faced by an identical twin whose twin sibling has schizophrenia.

Personality Disorders: I'm Okay, It's Everyone Else Who's Weird

13.21 *What are the different kinds of personality disorders?*

- Personality disorders are extremely rigid, maladaptive patterns of behaviour that prevent a person from having normal social interactions and relationships.
- In antisocial personality disorder a person has no conscience and uses people for personal gain. A rare form is the serial killer.
- In borderline personality disorder a person is clingy, moody, unstable in relationships, and suffers from problems with identity.

13.22 *What causes personality disorders?*

- Psychoanalysts blame an inadequate resolution to the Oedipal complex for personality disorders, stating that this results in a poorly developed superego.
- Cognitive-learning theorists see personality disorders as a set of learned behaviour that has become maladaptive—bad habits learned early in life. Belief systems of the personality disordered person are seen as illogical.
- Biological relatives of people with personality disorders are more likely to develop similar disorders, supporting a genetic basis for such disorders.
- Biological explanations look at the lower-than-normal stress hormones in antisocial personality disordered persons as responsible for their low responsiveness to threatening stimuli.
- Other possible causes of personality disorders may include disturbances in family communications and relationships, childhood abuse, neglect, overly strict parenting, overprotective parenting, and parental rejection.

Applying Psychology to Everyday Life: Canadian Law and Mental Illness

13.23 *What happens to a person who is accused of a crime in Canada and is found not criminally responsible on account of a medical disorder?*

- In Canada, "not guilty by reason of insanity" was changed in 1991 to "not criminally responsible on account of a mental disorder."

- Persons who are found unfit to stand trial or not criminally responsible on account of a mental disorder will be placed in a psychiatric institution until they are deemed fit to stand trial or have significantly improved from their condition. The period of stay in the psychiatric institution, at least initially, cannot exceed the maximum sentence that would have been applied if the person had been found guilty of the crime.

13

KEY TERMS

acrophobia 531
affect 545
agoraphobia 531
all-or-nothing thinking 534
antisocial personality disorder 554
anxiety disorders 530
biological model 525
biopsychosocial model 526
bipolar disorder 547
borderline personality disorder 555
catatonic 551
claustrophobia 531
cognitive psychologists 525
conversion disorder 536
cultural relativity 526
culture-bound syndromes 526
cyclothymia 546
delusional disorder 550
delusions 549
depersonalization disorder 540
disorganized 551
dissociative disorders 538

dissociative identity disorder 538
dysthymia 546
flat affect 550
free-floating anxiety 530
gender identity disorder 541
generalized anxiety disorder 533
hallucinations 550
magnification 534
major depression 546
maladaptive 524
manic 547
minimization 534
mood disorders 545
negative symptoms 551
obsessive-compulsive disorder 532
organic or stress-induced dysfunction 542
overgeneralization 534
panic attack 532
panic disorder 533
panic disorder with agoraphobia 533
paranoid 551
paraphilia 543

pedophile 544
pedophilia 544
personality disorders 553
phobia 530
positive symptoms 551
psychological disorders 524
psychopathology 522
psychophysiological disorder 536
psychosomatic disorder 536
psychotic 549
residual 551
schizophrenia 549
sexual dysfunction 541
situational context 523
social phobia 531
somatoform disorders 536
specific phobia 531
stress-vulnerability model 553
subjective discomfort 524
transvestism 545
undifferentiated 551

TEST YOURSELF

Pick the best answer.

1. Tony periodically hears voices telling him that certain entities are evil and he must "silence" them to protect himself. Tony is likely suffering from
   a. paranoid schizophrenia.
   b. catatonic schizophrenia.
   c. antisocial personality.
   d. multiple personality or dissociative identity disorder.

2. What was the most likely reason that ancient peoples performed trepanning on others?
   a. to relieve fluid pressure on the brain
   b. to look into the brain to see what was wrong
   c. to release evil spirits that were in the person's head
   d. to restore balance to the body's humours

3. Michael decided to give up his job teaching at a small community college in Ontario and become a monk. He moved to a nearby town with a monastery, took his vows, and is now living quite happily as a member of that religious order. By what definition might Michael's behaviour be considered abnormal?
   a. statistical
   b. subjective discomfort
   c. maladaptive
   d. harmful to self

4. Which disorder is thought to be influenced by vitamin A and is seen in the Canadian Inuit?
   a. susto
   b. pibloktoq
   c. amok
   d. kora

5. Which axis of the *DSM-IV-TR* would a therapist use to classify the loss of a person's job?
   a. I
   b. II
   c. III
   d. IV

6. Elaine has been diagnosed with depression and obsessive compulsive disorder. Having two conditions at the same time is referred to as
   a. epidemiology.
   b. pyromania.
   c. morbidity.
   d. comorbidity.

7. Alex hates to go over bridges. This is a mild form of
   a. social phobia.   c. agoraphobia.
   b. specific phobia.   d. claustrophobia.

8. Which is the most common social phobia in Canada?
   a. shy bladder
   b. talking with an authority
   c. making eye contact
   d. giving a speech in front of figure others

9. Professor Cantrell always checked the door to his office before leaving for class, lunch, or home. He would pull it closed and then rattle the doorknob three times to make sure that it was locked. He does this because he keeps thinking that he hasn't locked the door well. His thoughts about this are a form of
   a. obsession.   c. anxiety attack.
   b. compulsion.   d. door phobia.

10. When a person experiences sudden attacks of intense fear, racing heart, dizziness, and other physical signs of stress, and refuses to go away from home for fear one of these attacks will happen again, it is most properly called
    a. an anxiety attack.
    b. a panic attack.
    c. panic disorder.
    d. panic disorder with agoraphobia.

11. People with this anxiety disorder often use alcohol to self-medicate.
    a. panic disorder   c. phobia
    b. obsessive-compulsive disorder   d. generalized anxiety disorder

12. Daria went to great lengths to plan her mother's seventieth surprise birthday party. "Oh, if she finds out about this, the whole thing will be ruined; it'll be a disaster!" Her sister tried to tell her that even if the party ended up not being a surprise, their mother would be happy and have fun, but Daria was convinced that it would be horrible. According to a cognitive theorist, Daria is engaging in
    a. minimization.   c. overgeneralization.
    b. all-or-nothing thinking.   d. magnification.

13. Repeated checking has been shown to
    a. increase certainty of memory recall.
    b. decrease certainty of memory recall.
    c. have no effect on memory recall.
    d. increase the accuracy of memory.

14. Henri was a soldier during World War I. He and his best friend were scouting ahead when a mine blew up nearby, killing his friend and wounding Henri in the leg. When Henri woke up after the surgeons repaired his leg, he found that he could not see. The doctors told him that there should be nothing wrong with his eyes, but Henri still could not see, though he tried. This was most likely a
    a. somatization disorder.   c. conversion disorder.
    b. hypochondriac disorder.   d. psychosomatic disorder.

15. Dissociative amnesia is different from retrograde amnesia because
    a. only memories of the past are lost in retrograde amnesia.
    b. the ability to form new memories is lost in retrograde amnesia.

   c. dissociative amnesia is caused by a physical blow to the head.
   d. dissociative amnesia is caused by psychological trauma.

16. The fact that people with dissociative identity disorder have different PET scan readouts when in their different "personalities" is evidence for the _____ explanation of dissociative disorders.
    a. biological   b. psychoanalytic
    c. behavioural   d. cognitive

17. Which mood disorder consists of mostly manic episodes with only a few episodes of depression?
    a. bipolar   c. dysthymia
    b. unipolar   d. major depression

18. Which mood disorder is a consistently sad mood?
    a. bipolar   c. mania
    b. cyclothymia   d. major depression

19. A character in an old movie was a street person who wore aluminum foil on his head to protect his brain from the thought-controlling rays of the government. This is an example of a _____ delusion.
    a. persecution   c. influence
    b. reference   d. grandeur

20. Which of the following is not a typical symptom of schizophrenia?
    a. overly rational thinking   c. delusions
    b. inappropriate emotions   d. hallucinations

21. David Koresh, leader of the ill-fated Branch Davidians in Waco, Texas, believed that he was "God's Anointed One," who would bring about the end of the world. This is a _____ delusion.
    a. jealous   c. persecutory
    b. grandiose   d. somatic

22. Jane has been diagnosed with antisocial personality disorder. Which symptom does not belong?
    a. superficial charm   c. moodiness
    b. lack of remorse   d. manipulative

23. Relatives of people who have schizotypal personality disorder have an increased risk of developing _____ when compared to unrelated persons.
    a. major depression   c. antisocial personality disorder
    b. affective psychosis   d. schizophrenia

24. In 1991, the Canadian Parliament change "not guilty by reason of insanity" to
    a. not criminally responsible on account of a mental disorder.
    b. not criminally responsible on account of insanity.
    c. not guilty or criminally responsible due to insanity.
    d. not guilty on account of insanity.

25. Which of the following disorders is the most common of the psychological problems?
    a. obsessive-compulsive disorder   c. schizophrenia
    b. conversion disorder   d. major depression

Answers: 1-a, 2-c, 3-a, 4-b, 5-d, 6-d, 7-c, 8-d, 9-a, 10-d, 11-a, 12-b, 13-b, 14-c, 15-d, 16-a, 17-a, 18-d, 19-c, 20-a, 21-b, 22-c, 23-d, 24-a, 25-d.

ScanLife™ Barcode

To access more tests and your own personalized study plan that will help you focus on the areas you need to master before your next class test, be sure to go to **www.MyPsychLab.com**, Pearson Education Canada's online psychology website, available with the access code packaged with your book.

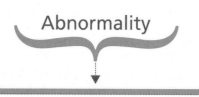

Abnormality

Psychopathology: The study of abnormal behaviour

Definitions of Abnormal Behaviour

▸ Behaviour that is statistically rare
▸ Deviates from social norms
▸ Causes subjective discomfort
▸ Does not allow normal day-to-day functioning
▸ Causes person to be dangerous to self or others

13.2

MODELS OF ABNORMALITY

Biological Models of Abnormality

Mental illness is caused by chemical or structural malfunctions in nervous system.

13.3

Psychological Viewpoints of the Causes of Abnormal Behaviour

Psychoanalytic models: repressed conflicts and urges trying to surface to consciousness

Behaviourists: learned responses

Cognitive theorists: irrational beliefs and illogical thought patterns

13.4

Psychological Disorders

Professional Descriptions of Abnormal Behaviour

Diagnostic and Statistical Manual, Version IV, Text Revision: manual of psychological disorders and symptoms

13.6

Different Psychological Disorders and Their Frequency of Occurrence

Five axes in the *DSM-IV-TR*:

1. Clinical disorders
2. Personality disorders
3. General medical conditions
4. Psychosocial and environmental problems
5. Global assessment of functioning

1 out of 5 people above 18 years old suffers from a mental disorder in a given year.

Major depression is the most common psychological disorder.

13.7

ANXIETY DISORDERS

Anxiety Disorders and Symptoms

Anxiety disorders: excessive/unrealistic anxiety

Phobias: irrational, persistent fears; three types of phobias: social, specific, and agoraphobia

Obsessive-compulsive disorder: obsessive thoughts and compulsive behaviour

Panic disorder: intense panic, physical symptoms from sympathetic nervous system

Generalized anxiety disorder: intense and unrealistic anxiety lasting at least six months

13.8

SOMATOFORM DISORDERS

Somatoform disorders: belief that one is physically ill with no corresponding physical ailment

Types: hypochondriasis, somatization disorder, and conversion disorder

13.10

Causes of Anxiety Disorders

Psychoanalytic explanations: repressed urges and desires trying to come into consciousness, creating anxiety that is controlled by abnormal behaviour

Behavioural explanations: Disordered behaviour is learned through reinforcement.

Cognitive explanations: excessive anxiety from illogical, irrational thought processes

Biological explanations:

▸ Chemical imbalances in nervous system, in particular serotonin and GABA systems
▸ Genetics may be responsible for anxiety disorders among related persons.

13.9

Causes of Somatoform Disorders

Psychoanalytic explanations: Anxiety is turned into a physical symptom.

Behavioural explanations: negative reinforcement experienced when the "ill" person escapes unpleasant situations

Cognitive explanations: People magnify physical symptoms and normal bodily changes out of irrational fear.

13.11

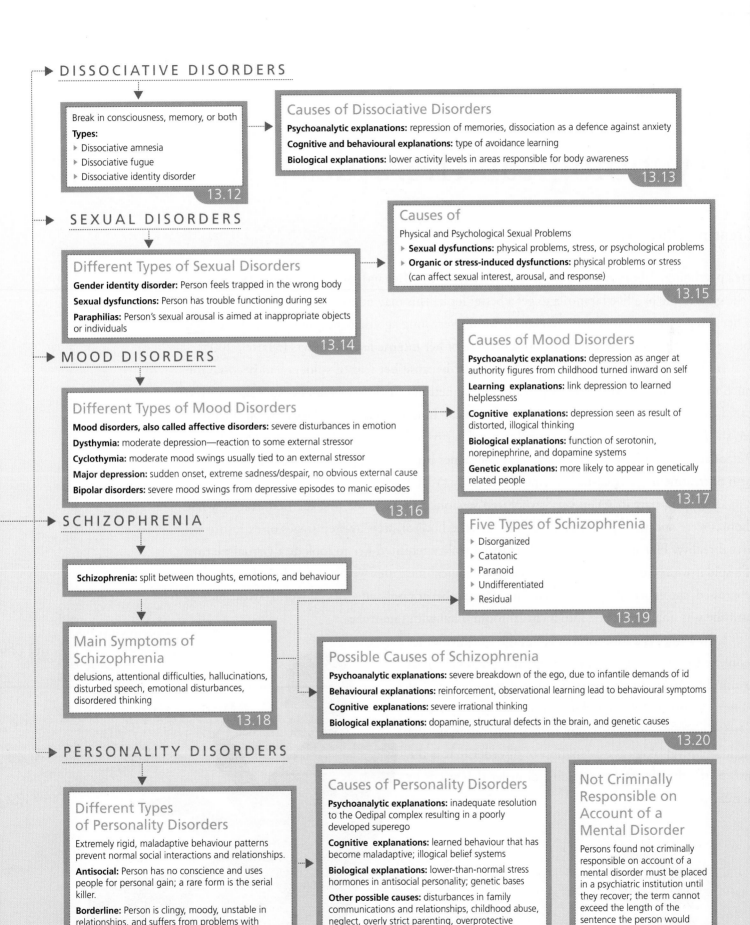

DISSOCIATIVE DISORDERS

Break in consciousness, memory, or both
Types:
▸ Dissociative amnesia
▸ Dissociative fugue
▸ Dissociative identity disorder

13.12

Causes of Dissociative Disorders

Psychoanalytic explanations: repression of memories, dissociation as a defence against anxiety

Cognitive and behavioural explanations: type of avoidance learning

Biological explanations: lower activity levels in areas responsible for body awareness

13.13

SEXUAL DISORDERS

Different Types of Sexual Disorders

Gender identity disorder: Person feels trapped in the wrong body

Sexual dysfunctions: Person has trouble functioning during sex

Paraphilias: Person's sexual arousal is aimed at inappropriate objects or individuals

13.14

Causes of

Physical and Psychological Sexual Problems
▸ **Sexual dysfunctions:** physical problems, stress, or psychological problems
▸ **Organic or stress-induced dysfunctions:** physical problems or stress (can affect sexual interest, arousal, and response)

13.15

MOOD DISORDERS

Different Types of Mood Disorders

Mood disorders, also called affective disorders: severe disturbances in emotion

Dysthymia: moderate depression—reaction to some external stressor

Cyclothymia: moderate mood swings usually tied to an external stressor

Major depression: sudden onset, extreme sadness/despair, no obvious external cause

Bipolar disorders: severe mood swings from depressive episodes to manic episodes

13.16

Causes of Mood Disorders

Psychoanalytic explanations: depression as anger at authority figures from childhood turned inward on self

Learning explanations: link depression to learned helplessness

Cognitive explanations: depression seen as result of distorted, illogical thinking

Biological explanations: function of serotonin, norepinephrine, and dopamine systems

Genetic explanations: more likely to appear in genetically related people

13.17

SCHIZOPHRENIA

Schizophrenia: split between thoughts, emotions, and behaviour

Five Types of Schizophrenia
▸ Disorganized
▸ Catatonic
▸ Paranoid
▸ Undifferentiated
▸ Residual

13.19

Main Symptoms of Schizophrenia

delusions, attentional difficulties, hallucinations, disturbed speech, emotional disturbances, disordered thinking

13.18

Possible Causes of Schizophrenia

Psychoanalytic explanations: severe breakdown of the ego, due to infantile demands of id

Behavioural explanations: reinforcement, observational learning lead to behavioural symptoms

Cognitive explanations: severe irrational thinking

Biological explanations: dopamine, structural defects in the brain, and genetic causes

13.20

PERSONALITY DISORDERS

Different Types of Personality Disorders

Extremely rigid, maladaptive behaviour patterns prevent normal social interactions and relationships.

Antisocial: Person has no conscience and uses people for personal gain; a rare form is the serial killer.

Borderline: Person is clingy, moody, unstable in relationships, and suffers from problems with identity.

13.21

Causes of Personality Disorders

Psychoanalytic explanations: inadequate resolution to the Oedipal complex resulting in a poorly developed superego

Cognitive explanations: learned behaviour that has become maladaptive; illogical belief systems

Biological explanations: lower-than-normal stress hormones in antisocial personality; genetic bases

Other possible causes: disturbances in family communications and relationships, childhood abuse, neglect, overly strict parenting, overprotective parenting, and parental rejection

13.22

Not Criminally Responsible on Account of a Mental Disorder

Persons found not criminally responsible on account of a mental disorder must be placed in a psychiatric institution until they recover; the term cannot exceed the length of the sentence the person would have received if found guilty.

13.23

14

Psychological Therapies

Treating Phobias

In a psychology laboratory of a Quebec university, Lyne Michaud calmly places her face against the glass home of a live tarantula to get a better look. This may not seem significant to you, but to her it represents a major achievement. It wasn't very long ago that she would never have been able to imagine doing something like this because of her intense fear of spiders (Martel, 2005).

In 2004, Lyne decided to contact a therapist because her fear of spiders had become too much to bear. She could no longer go camping, something she loved to do, because she was too scared that she would encounter a spider. After researching various types of therapy on the internet, she finally turned to Dr. Stéphane Bouchard, a psychologist at the Université du Québec en Outaouais, for help. Dr. Bouchard and his colleagues began treating Lyne with a relatively new form of treatment—virtual-reality exposure therapy (VRET).

Lyne took part in seven very structured sessions in which she first learned exactly what phobias were and then progressed through very methodical, step-by-step stages of exposure via virtual reality. Her first experience with virtual reality required her to look at a virtual picture of a spider while her heart rate and other physiological measures were recorded. As her sessions progressed, she experienced closer "contact" (remember it's only an artificial world) with spiders, until she was finally coached into a virtual room filled with tarantulas.

Lyne's story is a successful one, but the stories of other people with psychological disorders are not always resolved so simply. Different disorders require different kinds of therapies, and not all disorders can be completely eliminated. Therapies can take many forms, depending on the particular psychological explanation of disorder that is the basis of the therapy and the specific disorder that needs to be treated.

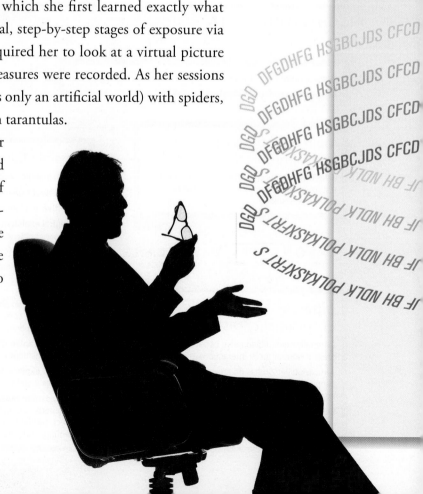

Why is it important to study therapies for psychological disorders?
There are almost as many therapy methods as there are disorders. Correctly matching the type of therapy to the disorder can mean the difference between a cure and a crisis. It is important to know the choices available for treatment and how they relate to the different kinds of disorders so that an informed decision can be made and the best possible outcome can be achieved for mental health and wellness.

TWO KINDS OF THERAPY

When talking about treating psychological disorders, there are two main types of **therapy** (treatment methods aimed at making people feel better and function more effectively). In the type of therapy that is usually more effective, people tell the therapist about their problems, and the therapist listens and tries to help them understand those problems or change the behaviour that causes them. The second type of therapy uses biological methods to bring the symptoms under control. Although the two types of treatment can be separated into two larger categories, many effective treatments combine facets of both. Just as there is no one single "cause" of a disorder (Maxmen et al., 2009), different psychological treatments are often used in tandem or combined with biomedical interventions.

14.1 *What are the two ways in which psychological disorders can be treated, and how were they treated in the past?*

The kind of therapy that involves talking things out with a professional is called **psychotherapy**, whereas the kind of therapy that uses biological methods is called **biomedical therapy**.

PSYCHOTHERAPY

The goal of almost all psychotherapy is to help both mentally healthy and psychologically disordered persons understand themselves better (Goin, 2005; Wolberg, 1977). Because understanding of one's motives and actions is called *insight*, therapies aimed mainly at this goal are called **insight therapies**. A therapy that is directed more at changing behaviour than providing insights into the reasons for that behaviour (as used in Lyne's therapy in the opening of this chapter) is called **action therapy**. Most psychological professionals use a combination of insight and action therapeutic methods.

BIOMEDICAL THERAPY

The other main type of therapy uses some biological treatment in the form of a medical procedure to bring about changes in the person's disordered behaviour. Biomedical therapies include the use of drugs, surgical methods, and electrical shock

◄─●─ Simulate on **mypsychlab**
Major Schools of Therapy

therapy
treatment methods aimed at making people feel better and function more effectively.

psychotherapy
therapy for mental disorders in which a person with a problem talks with a psychological professional.

biomedical therapy
therapy for mental disorders that directly affect the biological functioning of the body and brain to relieve symptoms.

insight therapies
therapies in which the main goal is helping people to gain insight with respect to their behaviour, thoughts, and feelings.

action therapy
therapy in which the main goal is to change disordered or inappropriate behaviour directly.

treatments. It is important to understand that biomedical therapy alone does nothing but alleviate the symptoms of the disorder, while psychotherapy addresses issues associated with the disorder, and when used together, these two types of therapy facilitate each other (Maxmen et al., 2009). For example, when medications are needed, individuals taking the proper medications are going to benefit more from psychotherapy as their symptoms will be better controlled. Furthermore, psychotherapy, not medication, is going to help them better understand what the symptoms of their disorder are and facilitate adjustment, other coping strategies, and proactive ways of addressing the disorder or its related outcomes (Maxmen et al., 2009).

THE EARLY DAYS OF THERAPY: ICE-WATER BATHS AND ELECTRIC SHOCKS

Life for the mentally ill was not pleasant in most parts of the world for many years. As discussed in Chapter Thirteen, people with severe mental illnesses were often thought to be possessed by demons or evil spirits, and the "treatments" to rid the person of these spirits were severe and deadly. Even in the supposedly more enlightened times of the past 200 years or so, the mentally ill did not always receive humane treatment.

EARLY TREATMENT OF THE MENTALLY ILL

I've seen movies about mental hospitals and they don't look like great places to be in even now—how bad was it back then? What did people do with relatives who were ill that way? The first truly organized effort to do something with mentally ill persons began in England in the middle of the sixteenth century. Bethlehem Hospital in London (later known as "Bedlam") was converted into an asylum (a word meaning "place of safety") for the mentally ill. In reality, the first asylums were little more than prisons where the mentally ill were chained to their beds. "Treatments" consisted of bloodletting (which more often than not led to death or the need for lifelong care for the patient), beatings, ice baths in which the persons were submerged until they passed out or suffered a seizure, and inducing vomiting in a kind of spiritual cleansing (Hunt, 1993). This cleansing or purging was meant to rid the body of physical impurities so that the person's mind and soul could function more effectively.

PINEL'S REFORMS

It was not until 1793 that efforts were made to treat the mentally ill with kindness and guidance—known as *moral treatment*—rather than beating them or subjecting them to the harsh physical purging that had been commonplace. In the 1780s, Philippe Pinel became very interested in mental illness after one of his friends committed suicide. He began working with the mentally ill and came to the conclusion that mental illness was not due to demonic possession but instead was an organic disorder like any other physical illness (van Walsum, 2004). Unlike others at the time, Pinel believed that mental illness was often curable, and to arrive at a diagnosis, the doctor had to observe the patient's behaviour, interview and listen carefully to the patient, and take notes (Weiner, 1992). In his late 40s, Pinel was hired as a physician at Bicêtre Hospital in Paris, France. It was here that he began working with Jean-Baptiste Pussin, who was formerly a tuberculosis patient at Bicêtre. Pussin had been successfully treated and as it was common for former (successfully treated) patients to work at the hospital, he began working at Bicêtre (Weiner, 1979). Pinel became interested in the mentally ill men who were housed in the hospital and was appalled at the conditions they

◀ I've seen movies about mental hospitals and they don't look like great places to be in even now—how bad was it back then? What did people do with relatives who were ill that way?

In this famous painting by French artist Robert Fleury, French psychiatrist Dr. Philippe Pinel orders the chains removed from patients at a Paris asylum for insane women. Pinel was one of the first psychiatrists to recommend humane treatment of the mentally ill.

were forced to live in. It was during this time that inmates at the Bicêtre were finally unchained, beginning the movement supporting the humane treatment of the mentally ill (Brigham, 1844; Curtis, 1993; Murray, 1988). There exists a controversy as to whether it was actually Pussin or Pinel who first implemented the unchaining process, but, regardless of who the initiator was, it is obvious that both men worked together to substantially improve the lives and the treatment of the mentally ill (van Walsum, 2004).

Another central figure in the humane treatment of the mentally ill was Dorothea Dix (1802–1887), a schoolteacher from Boston who implemented reforms in both the United States and Canada. Through Dix's efforts, thousands of people afflicted with mental illness were released from prisons and almshouses* and more than 30 mental hospitals were founded or enlarged in the United States, Canada, and Britain.

Although Dix's founding and enlargement of mental hospitals was the result of humane intentions and constituted a positive change in the 1800s, many started disagreeing with the idea of "warehousing" the mentally ill in the mid-1900s. Because of this opposition and advances in psychological treatment, the process of **deinstitutionalization** began. Deinstitutionalization has been occurring continuously in Canada for the past 40 years (Sealy & Whitehead, 2004). The idea behind deinstitutionalization is that some people with mental illnesses are able to leave the psychiatric hospital and receive mental health care in another setting while, at the same time, being active participants in their communities. This process has met with great criticism because it is evident that people with mental illnesses who have left psychiatric hospitals often do not receive the care that they require. As a result, many people with mental illnesses face homelessness or a life of poverty and social isolation (Sussman, 1998).

IN THE BEGINNING: PSYCHOANALYSIS

So what exactly ▶ happens in psychoanalysis? I've heard lots of stories about it, but what's it really like?

So what exactly happens in psychoanalysis? I've heard lots of stories about it, but what's it really like? In a sense, Freud took the old method of physical cleansing to a different level. Instead of a physical purge, cleansing for Freud meant removing all the "impurities" of the unconscious mind that he believed were responsible for his patients' psychological and nervous disorders. The impurities of the unconscious mind were considered to be disturbing thoughts, socially unacceptable desires, and immoral urges that originated in the id, the part of the personality that is itself unconscious and driven by basic needs for survival and pleasure. ⓁⒾⓃⓀ to *Chapter Eleven: Theories of Personality, p. 438.*

Because these unconscious thoughts were used by the person to prevent anxiety and would not be easily brought into conscious awareness, Freud designed a technique to help his patients feel more relaxed, open, and able to explore their innermost feelings without fear of embarrassment or rejection. As discussed in Chapter Eleven, this method was called **psychoanalysis**, an insight therapy that emphasizes revealing the unconscious conflicts, urges, and desires that are assumed to cause disordered emotions and behaviour (Freud, 1904; Mitchell & Black, 1996). This is the original reason for the couch in Freud's version of psychoanalysis; people lying on the couch were more relaxed and would, Freud thought, feel more dependent and childlike,

deinstitutionalization
the process of removing people with mental disorders from hospitals and placing them in the community.

psychoanalysis
an insight therapy based on the theory of Freud, emphasizing the revealing of unconscious conflicts.

---

*Almshouses: charitable housing for people who could not provide themselves with a place to live

making it easier for them to get at those early childhood memories. An additional plus was that he could sit behind the patients at the end of the couch and take notes. Because his patients were unable to see him, they remained unaffected by his reactions to what they said.

14.2   *What were the basic elements of Freud's psychoanalysis, and how is psychoanalysis conducted and viewed today?*

Freud made use of two particular techniques to try to get at the repressed information in his patients' unconscious minds. These techniques were the interpretation of dreams and free association (i.e., allowing patients to talk freely about anything that came to mind). Resistance and transference were also key elements of Freud's ideas.

DREAM INTERPRETATION

Dream interpretation, or the analysis of the elements within a patient's reported dream, formed a large part of Freud's psychoanalytic method. Ⓛ Ⓘ Ⓝ Ⓚ *to Chapter Four: Consciousness, p. 134.* Freud believed that repressed material often surfaced in dreams, although in symbolic form. The **manifest content** of the dream was the actual dream and its events, but the **latent content** was the hidden, symbolic meaning of those events that would, if correctly interpreted, reveal the unconscious conflicts that were creating the nervous disorder (Freud, 1900).

FREE ASSOCIATION

The other technique for revealing the unconscious mind was a method originally devised by Freud's co-worker, Josef Breuer (Breuer & Freud, 1895). Breuer encouraged his patients to freely say whatever came into their minds without fear of being negatively evaluated or condemned. As the patients talked, they began to reveal things that were loosely associated with their flow of ideas, often revealing what Breuer felt were hidden, unconscious concerns. Freud adopted this method, believing that repressed impulses and other material were trying to "break free" into consciousness and would eventually surface in his patients' **free associations**.

RESISTANCE

A key element in psychoanalysis was the analysis of **resistance**, the point at which the patient becomes unwilling to talk about certain topics. Freud believed that resistance from the patient meant that the conversation was coming uncomfortably close to repressed material.

TRANSFERENCE

In revealing more and more of their innermost feelings to the doctor, patients would begin to trust the therapist, who accepted anything they said and did not criticize or punish them for saying it, as they once trusted their parents. Freud believed that the therapist would then become a symbol of a parental authority figure from the past in a process he called **transference**. In transference, the patient would at first transfer positive feelings for some authority figure from the past such as a mother or father. When the therapist remained neutral and seemingly unresponsive, the patient would transfer negative feelings. Freud also believed that the transference could happen in the opposite direction—from therapist to patient. Just as patients would transfer feelings to their therapist, the therapists were also at risk of transferring their un-conscious, unresolved feelings onto the patient, in a process known as **countertransference**.

Psychotherapy often takes place one-on-one, with a client and therapist exploring various issues together to achieve deeper insights or to change undesirable behaviour.

✳ Explore on **mypsychlab**
Are Dreams Meaningful?

manifest content
the actual content of one's dream.

latent content
the symbolic or hidden meaning of dreams.

free association
Freudian technique in which a patient was encouraged to talk about anything that came to mind without fear of negative evaluations.

resistance
occurring when a patient becomes reluctant to talk about a certain topic, either changing the subject or becoming silent.

transference
in psychoanalysis, the tendency for a patient or client to project positive or negative feelings for important people from the past onto the therapist.

countertransference
in psychoanalysis, the tendency for a therapist to transfer unconscious, unresolved feelings onto the patient or client.

directive
therapy in which the therapist actively gives interpretations of a client's statements and may suggest certain behaviour or actions.

psychodynamic therapy
a newer and more general term for therapies based on psychoanalysis, with an emphasis on transference, shorter treatment times, and a more direct therapeutic approach.

"Why do you think you cross the road?"

© The New Yorker Collection 1992. Arnie Levin from cartoonbank.com. All Rights Reserved.

EVALUATION OF PSYCHOANALYSIS

Freud's original theory, on which he based his interpretations of his patients' revelations, has been criticized for several flaws, as discussed in Chapter Eleven. These included the lack of scientific research to support his claims, his unwillingness to believe some of the things revealed by his patients when those revelations did not fit into his view of the world, and his almost obsessive need to assume that problems with sex and sexuality were at the heart of nearly every nervous disorder.

Although some psychoanalysts today still use Freud's original methods, which could take years to produce results, modern psychoanalysts have greatly modified the way a psychoanalytic session is conducted. The couch is gone, and the *client* (a term used to put the therapist and the person seeking help on a more equal basis, instead of the doctor–patient concept) may sit across a desk from the therapist or in chairs. The client may stand or walk about. Rather than remaining quiet until the client says something revealing, the modern psychoanalyst is far more **directive**, asking questions, suggesting helpful behaviour, and giving opinions and interpretations earlier in the relationship, which helps speed up the therapeutic process. Today's psychoanalysts also focus less on the id as the motivator of behaviour, instead looking more at the ego or sense of self as the motivating force behind all actions (Prochaska & Norcross, 2003). Some psychoanalysts also focus on the process of transference more than on other typical aspects of traditional psychoanalysis, leading to the more general method called **psychodynamic therapy**.

The psychodynamic technique requires the client to be fairly intelligent and verbally able to express his or her ideas, feeling, and thoughts effectively. People who are extremely withdrawn or who suffer from the more severe psychotic disorders are not good candidates for this form of psychotherapy. People who have non-psychotic adjustment disorders, such as anxiety, somatoform, or dissociative disorders, are more likely to benefit from psychodynamic therapy.

PRACTICE QUIZ: HOW MUCH DO YOU REMEMBER?

Pick the best answer.

1. Psychotherapies that attempt to change disordered behaviour directly are known as _____ therapies.
   - **a.** insight
   - **b.** action
   - **c.** biomedical
   - **d.** psychoanalytic

2. In the sixteenth century, purging or _____ was sometimes used as a means to rid the body of physical impurities so that the person's mind and soul could improve.
   - **a.** ice bathing
   - **b.** bloodletting
   - **c.** beating
   - **d.** spiritual cleansing

3. In _____, a psychoanalyst encouraged the patient to talk about whatever came to mind.
   - **a.** free association
   - **b.** dream interpretation
   - **c.** resistance
   - **d.** transference

4. The psychoanalyst knows that repressed information is just "below the surface" of the conversation when the patient begins to experience
   - **a.** free association.
   - **b.** dream interpretation.
   - **c.** resistance.
   - **d.** transference.

5. Compared to traditional psychoanalysis, modern psychodynamic therapy is
   - **a.** more directive.
   - **b.** less directive.
   - **c.** more action oriented.
   - **d.** more focused on the id.

Answers: 1-b, 2-d, 3-a, 4-c, 5-a.

How common is psychodynamic therapy in Canada? Exact numbers are not available; but, according to the Canadian Association for Psychodynamic Therapy (CAPT) website, as of June 19, 2011, there were 11 institutional members (i.e., entire institutions belonging to the CAPT), 3 organizational members (i.e., entire organizations belonging to the CAPT), and 300 individual members of the CAPT.

HUMANISTIC THERAPY: TO ERR IS HUMAN

Unlike psychodynamic therapists, humanistic theorists do not focus on unconscious, hidden conflicts. Instead, humanists focus on conscious, subjective experiences of emotion and people's sense of self, as well as more immediate experiences in their daily lives rather than early childhood experiences of the distant past (Cain & Seeman, 2001; Rowan, 2001; Schneider et al., 2001). Humanistic therapy emphasizes the importance of the choices made by individuals and the potential to change one's behaviour. The two most common therapy styles based on humanistic theory are Carl Rogers's person-centred therapy and Fritz Perls's Gestalt therapy, both primarily insight therapies.

14.3 *What are the basic elements of the humanistic therapies known as person-centred therapy and Gestalt Therapy, and how are humanistic therapies viewed today?*

TELL ME MORE: ROGERS'S PERSON-CENTRED THERAPY

Chapter Eleven discussed the basic elements of Rogers's theory of personality, which emphasizes the sense of self (Rogers, 1961). To sum it up quickly, Rogers proposed that everyone has a *real self* (how people see their actual traits and abilities) and an *ideal self* (how people think they should be). The closer the real and ideal selves are to matching up, the happier and more well adjusted the person. To have these two self-concepts match, people need to receive *unconditional positive regard*, which is love, warmth, respect, and affection without any conditions attached. If people think that conditions are put on the love and affection they receive, their ideal selves will be determined by those conditions and become more difficult to achieve, resulting in a mismatch of selves and unhappiness.

So the key to getting over unhappiness would be to get the real and ideal selves closer together? How does a therapist do that? Rogers believed that the goal of the therapist should be to provide the unconditional positive regard that has been absent from the troubled person's life. He also believed that the person would actually have to do most of the work, talking out problems and concerns in an atmosphere of warmth and acceptance from the therapist, so he originally called the people in this therapy relationship *clients* instead of *patients*, to put the therapeutic relationship on a more equal footing. As a result, Rogers's therapy is mostly **non-directive** because the person actually does all the real work, with the therapist merely acting as a sounding board. Later, the term *client* was changed to the even more neutral term *person*. His therapy is now called **person-centred therapy** because the person is truly the centre of the process.

FOUR BASIC ELEMENTS Rogers saw four key elements as being necessary in any successful person–therapist relationship.

Reflection **Reflection** refers to the technique the therapist must use to allow clients to continue to talk and have insights without the interference of the therapist's interpretations and possible biases. The only way to ensure that a therapist will not control the stream of ideas coming from clients is for the therapist to simply restate what people have already said in slightly different words but with the same exact meaning. Reflection is literally a kind of mirroring of clients' statements.

Unconditional Positive Regard Another key element of person-centred therapy is the warm, accepting, completely uncritical atmosphere that the therapist must create for clients. Having respect for clients and their feelings, values, and goals, even if they are different from those of the therapist is called **unconditional positive regard**.

A Rogerian person-centred therapist listens with calm acceptance to anything the client says. A sense of empathy with the client's feelings is also important.

So the key to getting over unhappiness would be to get the real and ideal selves closer together? How does a therapist do that?

non-directive
therapy style in which the therapist remains relatively neutral and does not interpret or take direct actions with regard to the client, instead remaining a calm, non-judgmental listener while the client talks.

person-centred therapy
a less-directive insight therapy based on the work of Carl Rogers in which the client does all the talking and the therapist listens.

reflection
therapy technique in which the therapist restates what the client says rather than interpreting those statements.

unconditional positive regard
the warmth, respect, and accepting atmosphere created by the therapist for the client in person-centred therapy.

empathy
the ability of the therapist to understand the feelings of the client.

authenticity
the genuine, open, and honest response of the therapist to the client.

Gestalt therapy
form of directive insight therapy in which the therapist helps clients accept all parts of their feelings and subjective experiences, using leading questions and planned experiences such as role-playing.

👁 Watch on **mypsychlab**
Carl Rogers: Role of a Therapist

That sounds pretty much like the same thing, only with slightly different words. How is Gestalt therapy ▶ different from person-centred therapy?

In Gestalt therapy, the therapist looks at the whole person—career, family, relationships, and body language. What do the people sitting on the couch seem to be saying with their body language?

But now Gestalt ▶ therapy is beginning to sound almost like psychoanalysis with its focus on the past. How are they different?

Empathy   The therapist also has to be able to acknowledge what clients are feeling and experiencing by using a kind of understanding called **empathy**. This involves listening carefully and closely to what clients are saying and trying to feel what they feel. Therapists must avoid getting their own feelings mixed up with clients' feelings.

Authenticity   Finally, the therapist must show **authenticity** in a genuine, open, and honest response to the client. It is easier for some professionals to "hide" behind the role of the therapist, as was often the case in psychoanalysis. In person-centred therapy, the therapist has to be able to tolerate a client's differences without being judgmental.

GESTALT THERAPY

Another humanistic therapy based on Gestalt ideas is called **Gestalt therapy**. The founder of this therapeutic method is Fritz Perls, who believed that people's problems often stemmed from hiding important parts of their feelings from themselves. If some part of a person's personality, for example, is in conflict with what society says is acceptable, the person might hide that aspect behind a false "mask" of socially acceptable behaviour. As happens in Rogers's theory when the real and ideal selves do not match, in Gestalt theory the person experiences unhappiness and maladjustment when the inner self does not match the mask (Perls, 1951, 1969).

That sounds pretty much like the same thing, only with slightly different words. How is Gestalt therapy different from person-centred therapy? The two therapy types are similar because they are both based in humanism. But whereas person-centred therapy is mostly non-directive, allowing the client to talk out concerns and eventually come to insights with only minimal guidance from the therapist, Gestalt therapists are very directive. This means that a Gestalt therapist does more than simply reflect back clients' statements; instead, a Gestalt therapist actually leads clients through a number of planned experiences, with the goal of helping clients to become more aware of their own feelings and take responsibility for their own choices in life, both now and in the past. These experiences might include a dialogue that clients have with their own conflicting feelings in which clients actually argue both sides of those feelings. Clients may talk with an empty chair to reveal their true feelings toward the person represented by the chair or take on the role of a parent or other person with whom they have a conflict so that the clients can see things from the other person's point of view.

The Gestalt therapist actually confronts the client's own statements. For example, if a client complains of tenseness in his hands, the therapist would direct him to talk about how *he* feels, not how his hands feel. Once the client realizes, through active prompting from the therapist, that the tenseness is of his own creation, he can begin to control it and choose not to be tense (Perls, 1969).

But now Gestalt therapy is beginning to sound almost like psychoanalysis with its focus on the past. How are they different? Unlike psychoanalysis, which focuses on the *hidden past*, Gestalt therapy focuses on the *denied past*. Gestalt therapists do not talk about the unconscious mind. They believe everything is conscious but that it is possible for some people to simply refuse to "own up" to having certain feelings or to deal with past issues. The Gestalt therapist is more concerned about the client's "here and now" than some murky early childhood experiences. Part of that "here and now" includes attention to the body language of the client during therapy sessions. Body language, feelings both stated and unstated, and the events going on in the client's life at the time of therapy are the *gestalt* (the "whole picture") that gives this technique its name.

PRACTICE QUIZ: HOW MUCH DO YOU REMEMBER?

Pick the best answer.

1. Humanistic therapies are different from psychoanalysis because the humanistic therapies are
   a. more directive.
   b. action oriented.
   c. focused only on conscious thoughts and behaviour.
   d. insight therapies.

2. Which of the following is not one of the four basic elements of Rogers's person-centred therapy?
   a. conditional positive regard
   b. empathy
   c. reflection
   d. authenticity

3. Which of the following types of therapy makes the greatest use of body language?
   a. psychoanalysis
   b. person-centred therapy
   c. Gestalt therapy
   d. Rogerian therapy

4. Franklin's therapist has him talk to an empty chair and pretend that he is talking to his father. Franklin's therapist is most likely a _____ therapist.
   a. psychodynamic
   b. person-centred
   c. Gestalt
   d. Freudian

Answers: 1-c, 2-a, 3-c, 4-c.

EVALUATION OF THE HUMANISTIC THERAPIES

Humanistic therapies have been used not only to treat mental disorders but also to help people make career choices, deal with workplace problems, and serve as a form of marriage counselling. Some people see person-centred therapy in particular as being superior to other forms of therapy because it is so non-directive: There's nothing that the therapist says that the client has not already said, so the therapist runs no risk of misinterpretation. In addition, a lot of people do better after experiencing humanistic therapy because it provides a very warm and supportive environment in which to discuss their problems.

Unfortunately, humanistic therapies have several of the same drawbacks as psychoanalysis. There is little experimental research to support the basic ideas on which this type of therapy is founded, but humanists have always preferred to use case studies to build their theories. People must be intelligent, verbal, and able to express their thoughts, feelings, and experiences in a logical manner, which makes humanistic therapies a somewhat less practical choice for treating the more serious mental disorders such as schizophrenia.

BEHAVIOUR THERAPIES: LEARNING ONE'S WAY TO BETTER BEHAVIOUR

The last chapter talked about how behaviourists have a very different way of looking at abnormality—it's all learned. So do behaviourists do any kind of therapy? That's right—the basic concept behind behaviourism is that all behaviour, whether "normal" or "abnormal," is learned through the same processes of classical and operant conditioning. Unlike the psychodynamic and humanistic therapies, **behaviour therapies** are action-based rather than insight-based. Their aim is to change behaviour through the use of the same kinds of learning techniques that people (and animals) use to learn any new responses. The abnormal or undesirable behaviour is not seen as a symptom of anything else but rather is the problem itself. Learning created the problem, and new learning can correct it (Onken et al., 1997; Skinner, 1974; Sloan & Mizes, 1999).

behaviour therapies
action therapies based on the principles of classical and operant conditioning and aimed at changing disordered behaviour without concern for the original causes of such behaviour.

> The last chapter talked about how behaviourists have a very different way of looking at abnormality—it's all learned. So do behaviourists do any kind of therapy?

Sidney Harris

This device allows the delivery of high levels of nicotine to the smoker in a process known as *rapid smoking*. Rapid smoking is an aversive technique for helping people to quit smoking and is based on the classical conditioning principle of counterconditioning.

behaviour modification or **applied behaviour analysis**
the use of learning techniques to modify or change undesirable behaviour and increase desirable behaviour.

systematic desensitization
behaviour technique used to treat phobias, in which a client is asked to make a list of ordered fears and taught to relax while concentrating on those fears.

aversion therapy
form of behavioural therapy in which an undesirable behaviour is paired with an aversive stimulus to reduce the frequency of the behaviour.

counterconditioning
replacing an old conditioned response with a new one by changing the unconditioned stimulus.

14.4   *How do behaviour therapists use classical and operant conditioning to treat disordered behaviour?*

THERAPIES BASED ON CLASSICAL CONDITIONING

Classical conditioning is the learning of involuntary responses by pairing a stimulus that normally causes a particular response with a new, neutral stimulus. After enough pairings, the new stimulus will also cause the response to occur. **LINK** *to Chapter Five: Learning, p. 176.* Through classical conditioning, old and undesirable reflex responses can be replaced by desirable ones. Several techniques have been developed that use this type of learning to treat disorders such as phobias, obsessive-compulsive disorder (OCD), and similar anxiety disorders.

Using learning techniques to change undesirable behaviour and increase desirable behaviour has a long history (Hughes, 1993; Lovaas, 1987; Lovaas et al., 1966). Originally called **behaviour modification**, the more recent version of these techniques is **applied behaviour analysis**. Both terms refer to the use of conditioning techniques to modify behaviour.

SYSTEMATIC DESENSITIZATION   **Systematic desensitization**, in which a therapist guides the client through a series of steps meant to reduce fear and anxiety, is normally used to treat phobic disorders and consists of a three-step process.

First, the client must learn to relax through deep muscle relaxation training. Next, the client and the therapist construct a list, beginning with the object or situation that causes the least fear to the client and working up to the object or situation that produces the greatest degree of fear. Finally, under the guidance of the therapist, the client begins at the first item on the list that causes minimal fear and looks at it, thinks about it, or actually confronts it, all while remaining in a relaxed state. The idea is that the phobic object or situation is a conditioned stimulus that the client has learned to fear because it was originally paired with a real fearful stimulus—just as "Little Albert" learned to fear the rat because of the noise. By pairing the old conditioned stimulus (the fear object) with a new relaxation response that is incompatible with the emotions and physical arousal associated with fear, the person's fear is reduced and relieved. The person then proceeds to the next item on the list of fears (called a *hierarchy of fears*) until the phobia is gone.

AVERSION THERAPY   Another way to use classical conditioning is to reduce the frequency of undesirable behaviours, such as smoking or overeating, by teaching the client to pair an aversive (unpleasant) stimulus with the stimulus that results in the undesirable response in a process called **aversion therapy**. For example, someone who wants to stop smoking might go to a therapist who uses a *rapid-smoking* technique, in which the client is allowed to smoke but must take a puff on the cigarette every five or six seconds. As nicotine is a poison, such rapid smoking produces nausea and dizziness, both unpleasant effects.

Rapid smoking is a version of **counterconditioning**. In the terms of classical conditioning, discussed in Chapter Five, the old conditioned stimulus (CS) is the cigarette, including the act of putting it in one's mouth, lighting up, and so on. These things were originally paired with the nicotine, which was the unconditioned stimulus (US) that produced a pleasurable stimulation response (UR). Taking out a cigarette becomes pleasurable before the nicotine even has a chance to have its effect (CR), through the association of the two stimuli.

Rapid smoking becomes a new unconditioned stimulus (US) that produces *new* and very unpleasant responses, such as nausea and dizziness (URs), rather than pleasurable ones. When paired with the act of putting a cigarette in the mouth (CS), lighting up (CS), and so on, those old conditioned stimuli now become associated with the new unpleasant responses. Putting a cigarette in one's mouth after this conditioning triggers a new conditioned response of nausea. In fact, for some people even the thought of "lighting up" becomes nauseating (Smith, 1988). Studies have shown that people using this method have managed to remain smoke-free for relatively long periods of time (Chapelon-Clavel et al., 1997; Hajek & Stead, 2000), although some health professionals consider the quality of these studies to be poor (Joanna Briggs Institute, 2001).

Could you use aversion therapy to help someone with a phobia? Because phobias are already very unpleasant, aversive conditioning is not the most useful method of therapy. But although desensitization remains one of the more common therapies for phobias, it does not always bring quick results.

EXPOSURE THERAPIES   Behavioural techniques that introduce the client to situations, under carefully controlled conditions, which are related to their anxieties or fears are called **exposure therapies**. Exposure can be accomplished through a variety of routes and is intended to promote new learning. It can be *in vivo* ("in life"), in which the client is exposed to the actual anxiety-related stimulus; *imaginal*, in which the client visualizes or imagines the stimulus; and even *virtual*, in which virtual reality (VR) technology is used (Najavits, 2007). (For more information on VR in psychology, see the Psychology in the News section that follows).

For example, if Chang-sun has social phobia, then, for in vivo exposure, he might have to attend a social event; for imaginal exposure, he might be asked to visualize himself attending a social event; and for virtual exposure, he might experience a social event, such as attending a dinner party, through VR technology.

Exposure methods can introduce the feared stimulus gradually or quite suddenly. A gradual, or *graded,* exposure involves the client and therapist developing a fear hierarchy as in systematic desensitization: Exposure begins at the least feared event and progresses through to the most feared, similar to desensitization. If the exposure is rapid and intense, it begins with the most feared event and is called **flooding** (Gelder, 1976; Olsen, 1975). Flooding is used under very controlled conditions and, like graded exposure, produces extinction of the conditioned fear response by preventing an escape or avoidance response (e.g., Chang-sun would not be allowed to leave the party). Exposure therapy is sometimes called "exposure and response prevention" for that reason.

Eye-movement desensitization processing, or EMDR, is a type of exposure therapy used in the treatment of post-traumatic stress disorder (PTSD). It involves imaginal flooding, cognitive reprocessing and desensitization of the fearful event, and rapid eye movements or other bilateral stimulation (Shapiro, 2001). It is also used with phobias, and other anxiety-related disorders, although PTSD remains a primary disorder for which this therapy is most commonly used. Essentially, the client is instructed to think of a negative memory and an image that represents that memory (Shapiro, 1989, 1995). At this point, the client focuses on the memory while visually following the therapist's rapidly moving fingers back and forth, until the anxiety or fear has been eliminated. This is the "eye-movement desensitization" part of the process. The client is also asked to focus on some negative self-statement ("I am unlovable") during the EMDR session, and when the fear and anxiety have been removed, the client focuses on a positive thought ("I am lovable") while looking for signs of stress or tension. If such signs exist, the client will be treated with more sessions of EMDR. This is the "reprocessing" part of EMDR, in which the negative cognitions are reprocessed into positive, helpful ones.

There currently exists a controversy as to whether this type of exposure therapy is actually effective. In 2001, in an attempt to find an answer to this question, Paul Davidson and Kevin Parker of Queen's University in Kingston, Ontario, examined 34 studies investigating the impact of EMDR on different populations. They found

Could you use aversion therapy to help someone with a phobia?

◄●─⌐Simulate on **mypsychlab**
Be a Behaviour Therapist

exposure therapies
behavioural techniques that expose individuals to anxiety- or fear-related stimuli, under carefully controlled conditions, to promote new learning

flooding
technique for treating phobias and other stress disorders in which the person is rapidly and intensely exposed to the fear-provoking situation or object and prevented from making the usual avoidance or escape response.

that EMDR treatment was more effective than no treatment at all and that clients given EMDR treatment were significantly better off than they had been before the treatment was given. However, Davidson and Parker (2001) also found that EMDR treatment was no more effective than other types of exposure-based therapy and that the eye-movement component of EMDR is actually unnecessary. They concluded that much more research needs to be done in this area.

PSYCHOLOGY IN THE NEWS

Virtual Reality as a Treatment

The history of virtual reality (VR) is both interesting and complex. VR is a computer simulation of an artificial world in which the user can interact with various computer-generated stimuli. It has been in existence for decades and has been used for various purposes, including combat training for soldiers, flight simulation, and entertainment. In the past decade, VR has become increasingly popular in the treatment of various psychological disorders such as phobias and other anxiety disorders. The chapter-opening story of Lyne Michaud, who previously had a phobia of spiders (i.e., arachnophobia), is one example of how effective virtual reality exposure therapy (VRET) can be. It is becoming so popular that both the Canadian and U.S. military have invested heavily in VR research for training officers and treating PTSD symptoms, with the U.S. military spending about $4 million annually on such programs (Canadian expenditures are unknown; Carey, 2010).

Dr. Stéphane Bouchard, founder and co-director of the Cyberpsychology Laboratory at the Université du Québec en Outaouais, has been investigating the effectiveness of VRET for anxiety disorders and phobias for almost 10 years. As mentioned, it was in Bouchard's laboratory that Lyne Michaud was cured of her fear of spiders. Bouchard and colleagues have also successfully worked with clients suffering from social anxiety, such as a fear of speaking in public (Carey, 2010). Clients wear visors complete with three-dimensional video monitors and stereo headphones so that they feel as though they are actually part of the artificial world that has been created for them. They attend multiple sessions in which they are taught about the nature of phobias and are gradually exposed to fear-provoking stimuli as physiological measures such as their heart rate, breathing, and skin temperature are taken. They are taught to control their breathing in a supportive environment as they experience the therapy. In this way, Lyne Michaud was exposed to spiders in a very gradual manner. For example, in Lyne's first VR session, she was shown only a picture of a spider and was then asked to stare at it and rate how scared she felt on a scale of 1 to 10. Her exposure to spiders grew more and more significant with each session. By the end of the therapy, she was able to calmly look at the live tarantula kept in the laboratory.

Although it is still relatively new, VRET has shown great promise in the treatment of various psychological disorders. According to Bouchard, after 12 sessions of VRET, 80 percent of arachnophobics were able to stand next to an open terrarium. Because of these positive findings, VRET is starting to be used in many different parts of the world. Bouchard and his colleagues now collaborate with researchers in various places around the world—Ottawa, Montreal, San Diego, and Italy, to name just a few.

Other work conducted by Bouchard and his colleagues is discussed in the section on cybertherapy toward the end of the chapter.

Photo Dominic Boulanger, Laboratoire de cyberpsychologie, U.Q.O.

Dr. Stéphane Bouchard, founder and co-director of the Cyberpsychology Laboratory, works with a woman who has a fear of flying.

Questions for Further Discussion

1. Are there any possible drawbacks to using VR in therapy? What would these drawbacks be? What are some of the benefits (other than representing a possible cure for phobias)?

2. Use your imagination—what other types of treatment may accompany our furthering technological advancement?

3. How might VR be used to treat other problems, such as gambling or smoking?

THERAPIES BASED ON OPERANT CONDITIONING

Operant conditioning techniques include reinforcement, extinction, shaping, and modelling to change the frequency of voluntary behaviour. LINK *to Chapter Five: Learning, p. 176.* In the treatment of psychological disorders, the goal is to reduce the frequency of undesirable behaviour and increase the frequency of desirable responses.

One of the advantages of using operant conditioning to treat a problem behaviour is that results are usually quickly obtained rather than having to wait through years of more insight-oriented forms of therapy. When bringing the behaviour under control (rather than finding out why it occurs in the first place) is the goal, operant and other behavioural techniques are very practical. There's an old joke about a man whose fear of things hiding under his bed is cured by a behavioural therapist in one night. The therapist simply cut the legs off the bed.

MODELLING **Modelling**, or learning through the observation and imitation of a model, is discussed in Chapter Five. The use of modelling as a therapy is based on the work of Albert Bandura, which states that a person with specific fears or someone who needs to develop social skills can learn to do so by watching someone else (the model) confront those fears or demonstrate the needed social skills (Bandura et al., 1969). In **participant modelling**, a model demonstrates the desired behaviour in a step-by-step, gradual process. The client is encouraged by the therapist to imitate the model in the same gradual, step-by-step manner (Bandura, 1986; Bandura et al., 1974). The model can be a person actually present in the same room with the client or someone seen on videotape. For example, a model might first approach a dog, then touch the dog, then pet the dog, and finally hug the dog. A child (or adult) who fears dogs would watch this process and then be encouraged to repeat the steps that the model demonstrated.

Behavioural therapists can give parents or others advice and demonstrations on how to carry out behavioural techniques. Once a person knows what to do, modelling is a fairly easy technique. Modelling has been effective in helping children with dental fears (Klorman et al., 1980; Ollendick & King, 1998), social withdrawal (O'Connor, 1972), OCD (Roper et al., 1975), and phobias (Hintze, 2002).

USING REINFORCEMENT *Reinforcement* is the strengthening of a response by following it with some pleasurable consequence (positive reinforcement) or the removal of an unpleasant stimulus (negative reinforcement). LINK *to Chapter Five: Learning, p. 176.* Reinforcement of both types can form the basis for treatment of people with behavioural problems.

Token Economies In a **token economy**, objects that can be traded for food, candy, treats, or special privileges are called *tokens*. Clients earn tokens for behaving correctly or accomplishing behavioural goals and can later exchange those tokens for things that they want. They may also lose tokens for inappropriate behaviour. This trading system is a token economy. Token economies have also been used successfully in modifying the behaviour

modelling
learning through the observation and imitation of others.

participant modelling
technique in which a model demonstrates the desired behaviour in a step-by-step, gradual process while the client is encouraged to imitate the model.

token economy
the use of objects called *tokens* to reinforce behaviour in which the tokens can be accumulated and exchanged for desired items or privileges.

This boy is sitting in the "time-out" corner at his school. By removing the attention that he found rewarding, the teacher is attempting to extinguish the behaviour that earned the boy a time out. Do you see anything in this time-out corner that might make it less effective?

of relatively disturbed persons in mental institutions, such as people suffering from schizophrenia or depression (Dickerson et al., 1994; Glynn, 1990; McMonagle & Sultana, 2002).

Contingency Contracting   Another method based on the use of reinforcement involves making a **contingency contract** with the client (Salend, 1987). This contract is a formal agreement between therapist and client (or teacher and student, or parent and child) in which both parties' responsibilities and goals are clearly stated. Such contracts are useful in treating specific problems such as drug addiction (Talbott & Crosby, 2001), educational problems (Evans & Meyer, 1985; Evans et al., 1989), and eating disorders (Brubaker & Leddy, 2003).

For example, a contingency contract between a teenager and a parent might have one section that states the purpose of the contract (e.g., "harmony in the home") and then a specific list of behaviours that the teenager agrees to complete, such as "completing homework," "cleaning up after myself," and "using a respectful tone when speaking to Mom or Dad." There will also be a list of penalties associated with failing to perform each of these tasks (e.g., not being able to borrow the car). This written statement of the rules and penalties makes it clear to the teenager that if she fails to perform a task, she is choosing the punishment. The contract will also have a section stating the privileges that the teenager will earn when performing the tasks as agreed, such as being able to have friends over. The teenager and the parents sign the agreement.

Why does it work? The contingency contract puts everything down "in black and white." The stated tasks, stated penalties, and stated rewards are consistent, making discipline easier on both the teenager and the parents. There is no "wiggle room" for either teenager or parents to reinterpret the rules or back down on a promised privilege. Consistency is one of the most effective tools in using both rewards and punishments to mould behaviour. Ⓛ Ⓘ Ⓝ Ⓚ *to Chapter Five: Learning, p. 176.*

USING EXTINCTION   **Extinction** involves the removal of a reinforcer to reduce the frequency of a particular response. Ⓛ Ⓘ Ⓝ Ⓚ *to Chapter Five: Learning, p. 176.* In modifying behaviour, operant extinction often involves removing one's attention from the person when that person is engaging in an inappropriate or undesirable behaviour. With children, this removal of attention may be a form of **time out**, in which the child is removed from the situation that provides reinforcement (Kazdin, 1980). In adults, a simple refusal by the other persons in the room to acknowledge the behaviour is often successful in reducing the frequency of that behaviour. For example, recall Joanne from the previous chapter, the spider-phobic woman. Ⓛ Ⓘ Ⓝ Ⓚ *to Chapter Thirteen: Psychological Disorders, p. 520.* Her friends subjected Joanne to a kind of extinction process by refusing to fuss over her reactions, resulting in a reduction in both severity and frequency of her phobic reactions.

EVALUATION OF BEHAVIOUR THERAPIES

14.5 *How successful are behaviour therapies?*

Behaviour therapies may be more effective than other forms of therapy in treating specific behavioural problems, such as bedwetting, overeating, drug addictions, and phobic reactions (Burgio, 1998; Wetherell, 2002). More serious psychological disorders, such as severe depression, schizophrenia, or personality disorders, do not respond as well overall to behavioural treatments, although improvement of specific symptoms can be achieved (Glynn, 1990; McMonagle & Sultana, 2002). Bringing

contingency contract
a formal, written agreement between the therapist and client (or teacher and student) in which goals for behavioural change, reinforcements, and penalties are clearly stated.

time out
an extinction process in which a person is removed from the situation that provides reinforcement for undesirable behaviour, usually by being placed in a quiet corner or room away from possible attention and reinforcement opportunities.

symptoms under control is an important step in allowing a person to function normally in the social world, and behaviour therapies are a relatively quick and efficient way to eliminate or greatly reduce such symptoms.

COGNITIVE THERAPIES: THINKING IS BELIEVING

14.6 *What are the goals and basic elements of cognitive therapies such as cognitive-behavioural therapy and rational-emotive behaviour therapy?*

Cognitive therapy (Beck, 1979; Freeman et al., 1989) focuses on helping people change their ways of thinking. Rather than concentrating on the behaviour itself, the cognitive therapist focuses on the distorted thinking and unrealistic beliefs that lead to maladaptive behaviour (Hollon & Beck, 1994), especially those distortions relating to depression (Abela & D'Allesandro, 2002; McGinn, 2000). The goal is to help clients test, in a more objective, scientific way, the truth of their beliefs and assumptions. Then they can recognize thoughts that are distorted and negative and replace them with more positive, helpful thoughts. Because the focus is on changing thoughts rather than gaining deep insights into their causes, this kind of therapy is primarily an action therapy.

BECK'S COGNITIVE THERAPY

What are these unrealistic beliefs? Cognitive therapy focuses on the distortions of thinking. ⓁⒾⓃⓀ *to Chapter Eleven: Theories of Personality, p. 438.* Here are some of the more common distortions in thought that can create negative feelings and unrealistic beliefs in people:

- **Arbitrary inference:** This refers to "jumping to conclusions" without any evidence. Example: "Suzy cancelled our lunch date—I'll bet she's seeing someone else!"

- **Selective thinking:** In selective thinking, the person focuses only on one aspect of a situation, leaving out other relevant facts that might make things seem less negative. Example: Peter's English professor praised his paper but made one comment about needing to check his punctuation. Peter assumes that his paper is lousy and that the English professor really didn't like it, ignoring the other praise and positive comments.

- **Overgeneralization:** Here a person draws a sweeping conclusion from one incident and then assumes that the conclusion applies to areas of life that have nothing to do with the original event. Example: "I insulted my psychology professor. Now I'll flunk out of school and I'll never be able to get a decent job. I'll end up on welfare."

- **Magnification and minimization:** Here a person blows bad things out of proportion while not emphasizing the good things. Example: A student who has received good grades on every other exam believes that the C she got on the last quiz means she's not going to succeed in university.

- **Personalization:** In personalization, an individual takes responsibility or blame for events that are not really connected to the individual. Example: When Sandy's boyfriend is in a bad mood because of something that happened at work, she immediately assumes that he is angry with her.

A cognitive therapist tries to get clients to look at their beliefs and test them to see how accurate they really are. The first step is to identify an illogical or unrealistic belief, which the therapist and client do in their initial talks. Then the client is guided by the therapist through a process of asking questions about that belief, such as "When did this belief of mine begin?" or "What is the evidence for this belief?"

cognitive therapy
therapy in which the focus is on helping clients recognize distortions in their thinking and replace distorted, unrealistic beliefs with more realistic, helpful thoughts.

arbitrary inference
distortion of thinking in which a person draws a conclusion that is not based on any evidence.

selective thinking
distortion of thinking in which a person focuses on only one aspect of a situation while ignoring all other relevant aspects.

overgeneralization
distortion of thinking in which a person draws sweeping conclusions based on only one incident or event and applies those conclusions to events that are unrelated to the original.

personalization
distortion of thinking in which a person takes responsibility or blame for events that are unconnected to the person.

Don't those questions ▶ sound like critical thinking, which was discussed in Chapter One?

Don't those questions sound like critical thinking, which was discussed in Chapter One? Cognitive therapy really is a kind of critical thinking, but it is thinking specifically about one's own thoughts and beliefs rather than outside events and experiences. Just as cognitive psychology grew out of behaviourism, (L)(I)(N)(K) *to Chapter One: The Science of Psychology, p. 2*, therapies using cognitive methods have behavioural elements within them as well, leading to the term **cognitive-behavioural therapy (CBT)**.

CBT focuses on the present rather than the past (like behaviourism) but also assumes that people interact with the world with more than simple, automatic reactions to external stimuli. People observe the world and the people in the world around them, make assumptions and inferences based on those observations or cognitions, and then decide how to respond (Rachman & Hodgson, 1980). As a form of cognitive therapy, CBT also assumes that disorders come from illogical, irrational cognitions and that changing the thinking patterns to more rational, logical ones will relieve the symptoms of the disorder, making it an action therapy. Cognitive-behavioural therapists may also use any of the tools that behavioural therapists use as well to help clients alter their actions. The three basic goals of any cognitive-behavioural therapy follow.

1. Relieve the symptoms and help clients resolve the problems.
2. Help clients develop strategies that can be used to cope with future problems.
3. Help clients change the way they think from irrational, self-defeating thoughts to more rational, self-helping, positive thoughts.

ELLIS AND RATIONAL-EMOTIVE BEHAVIOUR THERAPY

Albert Ellis proposed a version of CBT called **rational-emotive behavioural therapy (REBT)**, in which clients are taught a way to challenge their own irrational beliefs with more rational, helpful statements (Ellis, 1997, 1998). Here are some examples of irrational beliefs:

* Everyone should love and approve of me (if they don't, I am awful and unlovable).
* When things do not go the way I wanted and planned, it is terrible, and I am, of course, going to get very disturbed. I can't stand it!

But I've felt that way at times. Why are these statements ▶ so irrational?

But I've felt that way at times. Why are these statements so irrational? Notice that these statements have one thing in common: It's either all or nothing. Can a person really expect the love and affection of every single person? Is it realistic to expect things to work as planned every time? REBT is about challenging these types of "my way or nothing" statements, helping people to realize that life can be good without being "perfect." In REBT, therapists take a very directive role, challenging the client when the client makes statements like those listed earlier, assigning homework, using behavioural techniques to modify behaviour, and arguing with clients about the rationality of their statements.

EVALUATION OF COGNITIVE AND COGNITIVE-BEHAVIOURAL THERAPIES

14.7 *How successful are cognitive and cognitive-behavioural therapies?*

Cognitive and cognitive-behavioural therapies are less expensive than the typical insight therapy because they are comparatively short-term therapies. As in behaviour therapy, clients do not have to dig too deep for the hidden sources of their problems. Instead, cognitive-based therapies get right

cognitive-behavioural therapy (CBT)
action therapy in which the goal is to help clients overcome problems by learning to think more rationally and logically.

rational-emotive behavioural therapy (REBT)
cognitive-behavioural therapy in which clients are directly challenged in their irrational beliefs and helped to restructure their thinking into more rational belief statements.

TABLE 14.1 CHARACTERISTICS OF PSYCHOTHERAPIES		
TYPE OF THERAPY	GOAL	KEY PEOPLE
Psychodynamic therapy	Insight	Freud
Person-centred therapy	Insight	Rogers
Gestalt therapy	Insight	Perls
Behaviour therapy	Action	Watson, Jones, Skinner, Bandura
Cognitive therapy	Action	Beck
CBT	Action	Various professionals
REBT	Action	Ellis

to the problems themselves, helping clients deal with their symptoms more directly. In fact, one of the criticisms of these therapies, as well as behaviour therapies, is that they treat the symptom, not the cause. However, it should be noted that in the cognitive viewpoint, the maladaptive thoughts are seen as the cause of the problems, not merely the symptoms. There is also an element of potential bias because of the therapist's opinions as to which thoughts are rational and which are not (Westen, 2005).

Nevertheless, cognitive and cognitive-behavioural therapies have considerable success in treating many types of disorders, including depression, stress disorders, anxiety disorders, and even some types of schizophrenia (Clark et al., 1989; DeRubeis et al., 1999; Holcomb, 1986; Jay & Elliot, 1990; Kendall, 1983; McGinn, 2000; Meichenbaum, 1996). As an offshoot of behaviourism, the learning principles that are the basis of cognitive-behavioural therapies are considered empirically sound (Masters et al., 1987).

For a summary of the various types of psychotherapies discussed up to this point, see Table 14.1.

In group therapy, several people who share similar problems gather with a therapist to discuss their feelings and concerns. The presence of others who are going through the same kind of emotional difficulties can be comforting and can provide the opportunity for insights into one's own problems by hearing about the problems of others.

GROUP THERAPIES: NOT FOR THE SHY

An alternative to individual therapy, in which the client and the therapist have a private, one-on-one session, is to gather a group of clients with similar problems together and have the group discuss problems under the guidance of a single therapist (Yalom, 1995).

14.8   *What are the various types of group therapies and the advantages and disadvantages of group therapy?*

TYPES OF GROUP THERAPIES

There are also several ways in which group therapy can be accomplished. The therapist may use either an insight or cognitive-behavioural style, although person-centred, Gestalt, and behaviour therapies seem to work better in group settings than psychoanalysis and cognitive-behavioural therapies (Andrews, 1989).

In family therapy, all family members participate in therapy sessions with the therapist guiding them through open communication. Although it appears that the young boy in the corner is the focus of this session, all family members are encouraged to see how their own behaviour may contribute to the problem behaviour.

In self-help groups, the person or persons leading a group are not specialists or therapists but just members of the group. They often have the same problem as all of the other people in the room, which is the strength of this type of program—people may be more likely to trust and open up to someone who has struggled as they have.

family counselling (family therapy) a form of group therapy in which family members meet together with a counsellor or therapist to resolve problems that affect the entire family.

self-help groups (support groups) a group composed of people who have similar problems and who meet together without a therapist or counsellor for the purpose of discussion, problem solving, and social and emotional support.

In addition to the variations in the style of therapy, the group structure can also vary. There may be small groups formed of related persons or other groups of unrelated persons that meet without the benefit of a therapist. Their goal is to share their problems and provide social and emotional support for one another.

FAMILY COUNSELLING   One form of group therapy is **family counselling** or **family therapy**, in which all of the members of a family that is experiencing some type of problem—marital problems, problems in child discipline, or sibling rivalry, for example—are seen by the therapist as a group. The therapist may also meet with one or more family members individually at times, but the real work in opening the lines of communication among family members is accomplished in the group setting (Frankel & Piercy, 1990; Pinsoff & Wynne, 1995). The family members may include grandparents, aunts and uncles, and in-laws as well as the core family. This is because family therapy focuses on the family as a whole unit or system of interacting "parts." No one person is seen as "the problem" because all members of the family system are part of the problem: They are experiencing it, rewarding it, or by their actions or inactions causing it to occur in the first place. For example, if a teenager has an addiction to online gambling and some of her family members ignore it while others lend her money, it is not just the teenager who needs help. Her family members need to realize that by ignoring the problem and lending the teenager money, they are contributing to her addiction.

The goal in family therapy, then, is to discover the unhealthy ways in which family members interact and communicate with one another and change those ways to healthier, more productive means of interaction. Family therapists work not only with families but also with couples who are in a committed relationship with the goal of improving communication, helping the couple to learn better ways of solving their problems and disagreements, and increasing feelings of intimacy and emotional closeness (Christensen et al., 1995; Heavey et al., 1993).

SELF-HELP GROUPS   Sometimes people cannot afford to attend group therapy sessions. In addition, many people may also feel that a therapist who has, for example, never had a drug problem cannot truly understand their problem and may feel that someone who has experienced addiction and beaten it is more capable of providing real help. This, rather than just concerns about money, is the main reason some people choose to meet with others who have problems similar to their own on a voluntary basis, with no therapist in charge. Called **self-help groups** or **support groups**, these groups are usually formed around the particular problem. Some examples of self-help groups are Alcoholics Anonymous, Overeaters Anonymous, and Narcotics Anonymous, all of which have groups meeting all over the country at almost any time of the day or night. There are countless smaller support groups for nearly every condition imaginable, including anxiety, phobias, having a parent with a dementia, having difficult children, depression, and stress—to name just a few. The advantages of self-help groups are that they are free and provide the social and emotional support that any group session can provide (Bussa & Kaufman, 2000). Self-help groups do not have leaders but instead have people who volunteer monthly or weekly to lead individual meetings. So the person who is in charge of organizing the meetings is also a member of the group with the same problem as all the other members.

ADVANTAGES OF GROUP THERAPY

Group therapy has several advantages:

- Lower cost. Because the therapist can see several clients at one time, this type of therapy is usually less expensive than individual therapy.

- Exposure to the ways in which other people view and handle the same kinds of problems.

- The opportunity for both the therapist and the person to see how that person interacts with others.

- Social and emotional support from people who have problems that are similar or nearly identical to one's own. This advantage is an important one; studies have shown that breast cancer patients who were part of a group therapy process had much higher survival and recovery rates than those who received only individual therapy or no psychotherapy (Fawzy et al., 1993; Spiegel et al., 1989). Another study found that adolescent girls in Africa, suffering from depression because of the stresses of the war in Uganda, experienced significant reduction in depression when treated with group therapy (Bolton et al., 2007).

DISADVANTAGES OF GROUP THERAPY

Group therapy is not appropriate for all situations, and there can be disadvantages:

- The therapist is no longer the only person to whom secrets and fears are revealed, which may make some people reluctant to speak freely.

- The client must share the therapist's time during the session.

- An extremely shy person may have great difficulty speaking up in a group setting.

- People with severe psychiatric disorders involving paranoia, such as schizophrenia, may not be able to tolerate group therapy settings.

EVALUATION OF GROUP THERAPY

Group therapy can provide help to people who might be unable to afford individual psychotherapy. It can also provide social and emotional support to people who may improve significantly from simply knowing that they are not the only people to suffer from whatever their particular problem may be. People who are not comfortable in social situations or who have trouble speaking in front of others may not find group therapy as helpful as those who are more verbal and social by nature.

William Piper and colleagues from various institutions in Quebec compared four forms of psychotherapy: short-term individual therapy, long-term individual therapy, short-term group therapy, and long-term group therapy. The results showed that long-term group therapy and short-term individual therapy produced better outcomes (and outcomes that were not significantly different from one another) than long-term individual therapy and short-term group therapy (Piper, Debbane, Bienvenu, & Garant, 1984). More recently, a survey and comparison of the effectiveness of both individual and group therapy found that group therapy is effective only if it is long-term and that it is more effective when used to promote skilled social interactions rather than attempting to decrease the more bizarre symptoms of delusions and hallucinations (Evans et al., 2000).

It is also important to note that group therapy can be used in combination with individual and biomedical therapies.

PRACTICE QUIZ: HOW MUCH DO YOU REMEMBER?

Pick the best answer.

1. Jeremy is trying to stop biting his fingernails. He wears a rubber band around each of his wrists, and whenever he finds himself biting his nails he snaps the band. Jeremy is using a form of _____ to modify his nail-biting behaviour.
- **a.** systematic desensitization
- **b.** aversion therapy
- **c.** flooding
- **d.** extinction

2. The reality television shows that deliberately force people to face their "worst fears" are most similar to which therapy technique?
- **a.** systematic desensitization
- **b.** aversion therapy
- **c.** flooding
- **d.** extinction

3. At Skinner Elementary School, teachers pass out "skinner bucks" to students who turn in papers on time, obey the teacher, and finish their homework. The paper "bucks" can be used at the end of the week to trade for special treats or game-playing time on the classroom computer. This system most resembles a
- **a.** participant modelling technique.
- **b.** contingency contract.
- **c.** group extinction procedure.
- **d.** token economy.

4. Which of the following would be an *unlikely* strategy for a rational-emotive behaviour therapist to use in treating a client?
- **a.** arguing with the client's statements
- **b.** repeating what the client, has just said without interpreting it
- **c.** giving the client homework
- **d.** pointing out irrational beliefs to the client

5. Maya is upset because her supervisor teased her about turning in her report several hours late. Although her supervisor was quite pleased with the report itself and told Maya that her work was excellent, Maya remains unhappy. Beck would say that Maya is guilty of
- **a.** arbitrary inference.
- **b.** selective thinking.
- **c.** personalization.
- **d.** defective thinking.

6. Which person might benefit the least from a group therapy environment?
- **a.** Suzanne, who has a phobia of cats
- **b.** Richard, who has a drinking problem
- **c.** Jasmine, who is painfully shy
- **d.** Elena, who suffers from depression

7. Six members of Ron's statistics class would meet every Saturday to go over their notes and try to figure out what the teacher had told them during his rambling lectures. If part of every Saturday's session is spent sharing feelings about the teacher and venting their anger and resentment, Ron's study group could be said to serve as
- **a.** a support group.
- **b.** family therapy.
- **c.** an awareness training group.
- **d.** a guided discovery group.

Answers: 1-b, 2-c, 3-d, 4-b, 5-b, 6-c, 7-a.

DOES PSYCHOTHERAPY REALLY WORK?

14.9 *How effective is psychotherapy, and how is the effectiveness of psychotherapy influenced by cultural, ethnic, and gender differences?*

> There sure are a lot of ▶ psychotherapies, but do any of them really work?

There sure are a lot of psychotherapies, but do any of them really work? In the 1950s, Hans Eysenck conducted one of the earliest investigations into the effectiveness of therapy. His conclusion was that the people receiving psychotherapy did not recover at any higher rate than those who had no psychotherapy and that the passage of time alone could account for all recovery. For more on Eysenck's study, see the Classic Studies in Psychology section later in the chapter.

Eysenck's classic survey created a major controversy within the world of clinical and counselling psychology. Other researchers began their own studies to find evidence that would contradict Eysenck's findings. One such effort reviewed studies that the researchers considered to be well controlled and concluded that the psychotherapies did not differ from one another in effectiveness (Luborsky et al., 1975). Of course, that can mean either that the psychotherapies were all equally effective or that they were all equally ineffective.

There are numerous problems with studying the effectiveness of psychotherapy. Controlled studies can be done using an experimental group of people who receive a particular psychotherapy and a control group of people who are put on a waiting list, but this is less than ideal. The control group is not getting the attention from the therapist, for one thing, and so there would be no placebo-effect expectations about getting better because of therapy (Shapiro & Shapiro, 1997). Also, not all therapies take the same amount of time to be effective. For example, psychoanalysis, even in its short form, takes longer than a behavioural therapy. In a short-term study, behavioural therapy would obviously look more effective. Action therapies such as behavioural therapies measure the success of the therapy differently than do insight therapies; in a behavioural therapy the reduction of the undesired behaviour is easy to objectively measure, but gaining insights and feelings of control, self-worth, self-esteem, and so on are not as easily evaluated (Shadish et al., 2002).

Studies that do not use empirical* procedures but instead try to determine whether the clients have been helped by the therapy in general are plagued by problems such as experimenter bias (the therapist expects the therapy to work and is also the one assessing the progress of the client), the inaccuracies of self-report information, and the same placebo effect cited by Shapiro and Shapiro (Seligman, 1995; Wampold, 1997).

Nevertheless, more recent surveys have shown that people who have received psychotherapy believe that they have been helped more often than not (*Consumer Reports*, 1995; Kotkin et al., 1996). The *Consumer Reports* research was a survey of the magazine's readers in which those who had been or were currently clients in psychotherapy rated the effectiveness of the therapy they received. Here are the findings from a summary of this and several other similar surveys (Lambert & Ogles, 2003; Seligman, 1995; Thase, 1999):

- An estimated 75 to 90 percent of people feel that psychotherapy has helped them.
- The longer a person stays in therapy, the greater the improvement.

Other studies have found that some psychotherapies are more effective for certain types of disorders (Clarkin et al., 2007; Hollon et al., 2002) but that no one psychotherapy is the most effective or works for every type of problem. Remember, all of the survey information is subject to the same flaws as any other survey information: errors in memory, inaccurate self-reporting, deliberate mistruths, and in this case even the placebo effect brought on by cognitive dissonance. L I N K *to Chapter Twelve: Social Psychology, p. 476.* People who pay for therapy more than likely expect to feel better (whether or not the therapy works).

THE SEVEN DWARFS AFTER THERAPY

©The New Yorker Collection 1991 Mike Twohy from cartoonbank.com. All Rights Reserved.

CLASSIC STUDIES IN PSYCHOLOGY

Psychotherapy: An Evaluation by Hans Eysenck

One of the earliest studies to look at the effectiveness of psychotherapy was Hans Eysenck's survey of 19 different studies reporting on the improvement or lack of improvement of clients' conditions while using psychoanalysis and **eclectic therapies**, in which the therapist used not one but several different techniques of psychotherapy (Eysenck, 1957). Eysenck compared the results of these studies with studies of people who were institutionalized for mental disorders but given no psychotherapy. Instead, these people received food, shelter, and care for their basic needs and formed the control group. (The studies in question were done in the 1930s, a time period when such custodial care was unfortunately common.)

eclectic therapies
therapy style that combines elements of several different therapy techniques.

*Empirical: capable of being verified or disproved by observation or experiment

"I like to think that each generation will need a little less therapy than the generation before."

©The New Yorker Collection 1999 Barbara Smaller from cartoonbank.com. All Rights Reserved.

After his survey of the various studies, Eysenck concluded that the data failed to prove that psychotherapy had a beneficial impact on neurotic patients' recovery. Instead, he argued that the data showed that approximately two-thirds of neurotic patients will recover or improve within about two years, regardless of whether or not they receive psychotherapy. In Eysenck's words, "From the point of view of the neurotic, these figures are encouraging; from the point of view of the psychotherapist, they can hardly be called very favourable to his claims" (Eysenck, 1957, p. 322).

However, it must be noted that Eysenck did point out that the data he collected did not necessarily disprove the possibility of psychotherapy's effectiveness and that definite proof would require a "special investigation, carefully planned and methodologically more adequate than these *ad hoc* comparisons" (Eysenck, 1957, p. 322).

Questions for Further Discussion

1. What is your opinion about Eysenck's conclusions?

2. How do you think psychotherapists reacted to his conclusions?

So how does a person ▶ with a problem know what kind of therapist to go to? How do you pick a good one?

◀◉─Simulate on **mypsychlab**

Is this Therapy Effective?

therapeutic alliance
the relationship between therapist and client that develops as a warm, caring, accepting relationship characterized by empathy, mutual respect, and understanding.

CHARACTERISTICS OF EFFECTIVE THERAPY

So how does a person with a problem know what kind of therapist to go to? How do you pick a good one? Most psychological professionals today take an eclectic view of psychotherapy, using a combination of methods or switching methods to fit the particular client's needs or specific problems. A client with a phobia may benefit from both behavioural therapy and cognitive therapy, for example. Clients who have more long-term goals of understanding themselves better might be more comfortable with psychoanalysis or one of the humanistic therapies. Finding an effective therapy (or therapist) is not so much finding one therapy that works overall but finding a specific therapy that works for a specific problem.

Several factors are important in any successful, effective therapy (Hubble et al., 1999; Seligman, 1998; Stiles et al., 1998). The most important aspect of a successful psychotherapy is the relationship between the client and the therapist, known as the **therapeutic alliance**. This relationship should be caring, warm, and accepting, and be characterized by empathy, mutual respect, and understanding. Therapy should also offer clients a protected setting in which to release emotions and reveal private thoughts and concerns and should help clients understand why they feel the way they do and provide them with ways to feel better.

An ongoing area of research in psychology is related to identifying those treatments and other aspects of treatment that work best for specific disorders. Especially in today's modern age of managed health care and tight budgets, clients benefit through evidence-based practice, or empirically validated treatment. Evidence-based practice includes systematic reviews of relevant and valid information that ranges from assessment to intervention (American Psychological Association, 2005; Hunsley & Mash, 2008; Nathan & Gorman, 2007). Some examples of evidence-based, or empirically validated, treatments are exposure therapies, cognitive-behavioural therapies, and cognitive processing for PTSD (Ehlers et al., 2010; Najavits, 2007; Resick et al., 2008), cognitive-behavioural treatment for panic disorder with agoraphobia (Barlow et al., 2007; Craske & Barlow, 2008), cognitive-behavioural group therapy for social anxiety disorder (Turk et al., 2008), cognitive therapy for depression (Young et al., 2008), and antipsychotic drugs for schizophrenia (Sharif et al., 2007).

CULTURAL, ETHNIC, AND GENDER CONCERNS IN PSYCHOTHERAPY

Consider the following situation (adapted from Wedding, 2004).

Reprinted with special permission of King Features Syndicate.

K. is a 24-year-old Korean Canadian. She lived with her parents, who were both born and reared in Korea before moving to Canada as adults. She came to a therapist because she was depressed and unhappy with her lack of independence. Her father was angry about her plans to marry a non-Korean. Her therapist immediately began assertiveness training and role-playing to prepare K. to deal with her father. The therapist was disappointed when K. failed to keep her second appointment.

This example of an actual case demonstrates a problem that exists in the therapist–client relationship for many clients when the ethnicity or culture of the client is different from that of the therapist. This cultural difference makes it difficult for therapists to understand the exact nature of their clients' problems and for clients to benefit from therapies that do not match their needs (Matsumoto, 1994; Moffic, 2003; Wedding, 2004). The values of different cultures and ethnic groups are not universally the same.

In the case of K., for example, the therapist mistakenly assumed that the key to improving K.'s situation was to make her more assertive and independent from her family, particularly her father. This Western idea runs counter to Korean cultural values. Korean culture stresses interdependence, not independence. The family comes first, obedience to one's elders is highly valued, and "doing one's own thing" is not acceptable. K.'s real problem may have been her feelings of guilt about her situation and her father's anger. She may have wanted help in dealing with her family situation and her feelings about that situation, not help in becoming more independent.

For therapy to be effective, the client must continue in treatment until a successful outcome is reached. K. never came back after the first session. One of the problems that can occur when the culture or ethnic backgrounds of the client and therapist are mismatched, as in K.'s case, is that the therapist may project his or her values onto the client, failing to achieve true empathy with the client's feelings or even to realize what the client's true feelings are and causing the client to drop out of therapy. Studies of such situations have found that members of minority racial or ethnic groups drop out of therapy at a significantly higher rate than the majority group clients (Brown et al., 2003; Cooper et al., 2003; Flaherty & Adams, 1998; Sue, 1977, 1992; Sue et al., 1994; Vail, 1976; Vernon & Roberts, 1982).

Traditional forms of psychotherapy, developed mainly in Western, individualistic cultures may need to be modified to fit the more collectivistic, interdependent cultures. For example, Japanese psychologist Dr. Shigeru Iwakabe (2008) has pointed out that, for Japanese clients, the typical "talking cure" practiced by many psychotherapists—including psychodynamic and humanistic therapists—may have to be altered to a non-talking cure that uses non-verbal tasks (such as drawing) because of the reluctance of many traditional Japanese people to talk openly about private concerns.

Are differences in gender important? For example, do women prefer female therapists, while men would rather talk to other men? Research on gender and therapist–client relationships varies. When talking about white middle-class clients, it seems that both men and women prefer a female therapist (Jones et al., 1987). But Black clients were more likely to drop out of therapy if the therapist was the *same* sex as the client (Vail, 1976), male Asian clients seemed to prefer a male therapist, and female Asian clients stayed in therapy equally long with either male or female therapists (Flaherty & Adams, 1998; Flaskerud, 1991).

Are differences in gender important? For example, do women prefer female therapists, while men would rather talk to other men?

Four barriers to effective psychotherapy exist when the culture or ethnic backgrounds of client and therapist are different (Sue & Sue, 2008):

1. *Language:* Speaking different languages becomes a problem in understanding what both client and therapist are saying and in psychological testing (Betancourt & Jacobs, 2000; Lewis, 1996).

2. *Cultural values:* Differing cultural values can cause therapists to fail at forming an empathetic relationship (Sattler, 1977; Wedding, 2004).

3. *Social class:* Clients from impoverished backgrounds may have values and experiences that the therapist cannot understand (Wedding, 2004).

4. *Non-verbal communication:* Body language, or non-verbal communication, can also differ between cultures and ethnicities. The physical distance between the client and therapist, the use of gestures, and eye contact, for example, can cause misunderstandings during the session and in interpretation of the client's moods and intentions (Galanti, 1997; Like et al., 1996). People in some cultures are content with long periods of silence while others are not; direct eye contact is desirable in some cultures and offensive in others; and even facial expressions of emotion vary from very expressive (as with Hispanic people) to non-expressive (as with many Asian people).

The American Psychiatric Association (2000a) has included a guide for therapists concerning cultural issues and culture-bound syndromes (such as *koro*). Ⓛ Ⓘ Ⓝ Ⓚ *to Chapter Thirteen: Psychological Disorders, p. 520.* All therapists need to make an effort to become aware of cultural differences, culture-bound syndromes, and possible gender issues.

CYBERTHERAPY: THERAPY IN THE COMPUTER AGE

Although psychotherapy is usually accomplished by the client or clients speaking face to face with the therapist, a new type of therapy is now available to people in need who own a computer. **Cybertherapy** refers to psychotherapy that is offered on the internet, and the people who practice it are called *cybertherapists.* Although this method of delivery may have the advantages of lower or no cost, availability of therapy opportunities for those unable to get to a therapist easily (such as people living in a remote or rural area), access to support groups online, and relative anonymity, there are dangers. There is no guarantee that the cybertherapist has any credentials or training in psychotherapy, and because there is no face-to-face or even voice-to-voice contact in most forms of cybertherapy, the therapist has no access to body language or vocal tones in trying to assess a client's emotional and psychological state. For further information on this subject, an excellent list of the various forms that cybertherapy can take and the strengths and weaknesses of each has been developed by Dr. Azy Barak, a psychologist at the University of Haifa in Israel and an expert in internet psychotherapy (Barak, 1999; Barak & Hen, 2008; Barak & Suler, 2008).

How has cybertherapy fared? Researchers in Germany found that people who were treated as in-patients and then allowed to "meet" with a group therapist in an internet chat room showed a significantly lower risk of negative changes in their mental status than a control group (Golkaramnay et al., 2007). The dropout rate from the internet group was very low, and most patients "attended" the chat-room sessions, which suggests that the ease of using a computer to connect to a group therapy session may be a viable option for some people needing continued therapy

cybertherapy
psychotherapy that is offered on the internet. Also called *online, internet,* or *web therapy* or *counselling.*

opportunities. In addition, Dr. Stéphane Bouchard and his colleagues at the Cyber-psychology Laboratory at the Université du Québec en Outaouais (whose work was discussed earlier in the Psychology in the News section) compared the effectiveness of cognitive-behavioural therapy delivered via videoconferencing to that delivered face to face and found that therapy delivered by videoconferencing was just as effective as therapy delivered face to face (Bouchard et al., 2004).

As was discussed in the Psychology in the News section, Bouchard and colleagues have used VR as an exposure therapy to treat phobias and other forms of anxiety disorders. However, according to Bouchard, VR therapy also has other uses; he and his colleagues have created a virtual therapist that they have affectionately named Mini-Me (as it looks quite a bit like Bouchard) that clients can interact with by putting on a VR headset. Bouchard and colleagues are not alone when it comes to creating virtual therapists. Researchers at the University of Southern California, for example, created a virtual woman named Angelina, whose eyes and expressions stay in sync with the person talking to "her," just as an empathetic therapist's would (Carey, 2010). Using Angelina, the researchers found that socially anxious people revealed not only more information but also more intimate information (e.g., their personal flaws and fears) about themselves when they interacted with a virtual human than they did when inter-acting with a real human in a video interview (Kang & Gratch, 2010).

Despite all the promising findings regarding cybertherapy, it is not without its critics. For example, Jaron Lanier, a computer scientist, has been very vocal about his objections and claims that even if the cybertherapy approach does work, there will be side effects that no one will be able to anticipate (Carey, 2010). Obviously, much more research needs to be conducted, but Bouchard and colleagues believe that the research thus far is very encouraging and point out that it is important to remember that virtual therapy should only ever be one of the many tools that therapists use (Carey, 2010).

BIOMEDICAL THERAPIES

Just as a therapist trained in psychoanalysis is more likely to use that technique, a ther-apist whose perspective on personality and behaviour is biological will most likely turn to medical techniques to manage disordered behaviour. Even psychotherapists who are not primarily biological in orientation may combine psychotherapy with medical treatments that are supervised by a medical doctor working with the psychologist. As medical doctors, psychiatrists are almost inevitably biological in perspective and, thus, use biomedical therapies (directly affecting the biological functioning of the body and brain) in addition to any psychotherapy technique they may favour.

The biomedical therapies fall into three categories: drug therapy, shock therapy, and surgical treatments.

PSYCHOPHARMACOLOGY

14.10   *What are the various types of drugs used to treat psychological disorders?*

The use of drugs to control or relieve the symptoms of a psychological disorder is called **psychopharmacology**. Although these drugs are sometimes used alone, they are more often combined with some form of psychotherapy and are more effective as a result (Kearney & Silverman, 1998; Keller et al., 2000). There are four basic categories of drugs used to treat psychotic disorders, anxiety disorders, the manic phase of mood disorders, and depression.

psychopharmacology
the use of drugs to control or relieve the symptoms of psychological disorders.

TABLE 14.2 TYPES OF DRUGS USED IN PSYCHOPHARMACOLOGY

CLASSIFICATION	TREATMENT AREAS	SIDE EFFECTS	EXAMPLES
Antipsychotic: Typical Neuroleptic	Positive (excessive) symptoms such as delusions or hallucinations	Motor problems, tardive dyskinesia	Chlorpromazine Droperidol Haliperodol
Antipsychotic: Atypical Neuroleptic	Positive and some negative symptoms of psychoses	Fewer than typical neuroleptics; clozapine may cause serious blood disorder	Risperidone Clozapine Aripirazole
Antianxiety: Minor Tranquilizers	Symptoms of anxiety and phobic reactions	Slight sedative effect; potential for physical dependence	Xanax Ativan Valium
Antimanic	Manic behaviour	Potential for toxic buildup	Lithium Anticonvulsant drugs
Antidepressants: MAOIs	Depression	Weight gain, constipation, dry mouth, dizziness, headache, drowsiness, insomnia, some sexual arousal disorders	Iproniazid Isocarboxazid Phenelzine sulphate Tranylcypromine sulphate
Antidepressants: Tricyclics	Depression	Skin rashes, blurred vision, lowered blood pressure, weight loss	Imipramine Desipramine Amitriptyline Doxepin
Antidepressants: SSRIs	Depression	Nausea, nervousness, insomnia, diarrhea, rash, agitation, some sexual arousal problems	Fluoxetine Hydrochloride sertraline Hydrochloride Paroxetine hydrochloride

ANTIPSYCHOTIC DRUGS   Drugs used to treat psychotic symptoms, such as hallucinations, delusions, and bizarre behaviour, are called **antipsychotic drugs**. The three categories of antipsychotic drugs are *typical neuroleptics*, *atypical neuroleptics*, and *partial dopamine agonists*. The first of the typical neuroleptics to be developed was *chlorpromazine* (Jones & Pilowsky, 2002). The term *neuroleptic* comes from the French word *neuroleptique*, which means "to have an effect on neurons."

Table 14.2 lists several of these antipsychotic drugs and their side effects.

These drugs work by blocking certain dopamine receptors in the brain, thereby reducing the effect of dopamine in synaptic transmission (Csernansky et al., 2002). However, because they block more pathways in the dopamine system than are involved in psychosis, they tend to cause problems such as *tardive dyskinesia*, a syndrome causing the person to make repetitive, involuntary jerks and movements of the face, lips, legs, and body (Jones & Pilowsky, 2002).

The atypical neuroleptics also suppress dopamine but to a much greater degree in the one dopamine pathway that seems to cause psychotic problems. These drugs also block or partially block certain serotonin receptors, resulting in fewer negative side effects and sometimes even improvement in the more negative symptoms of schizophrenia such as withdrawal, apathy, and reduced communication (Jones & Pilowsky, 2002). Scot Purdon of the University of Alberta has been investigating the effect of different neuroleptics on schizophrenia for many years. Recently, Purdon and colleagues from Nashville, Tennessee, decided to investigate the effects of four atypical neuroleptics (clozapine, olanzapine, quetiapine, and risperidone) on the neuropsychological functioning of schizophrenics. By analyzing many different studies

◄─◉─[Simulate on mypsychlab
Biomedical Therapies

antipsychotic drugs
drugs used to treat psychotic symptoms such as delusions, hallucinations, and other bizarre behaviour.

that had been conducted previously (this procedure is known as a *meta-analysis*), they found atypical neuroleptics to be superior to typical neuroleptics in improving the overall cognitive functioning of schizophrenics (Woodward, Purdon, Meltzer, & Zald, 2005).

How long do people generally have to take these antipsychotic medications? In some cases, a person might have a psychotic episode that lasts only a few months or a few years and may need drug treatment only for that time. But in most cases, especially in schizophrenia that starts in adolescence or young adulthood, the medication must be taken for the rest of the person's life.

Long-term use of neuroleptics, particularly the older typical drugs, has been associated with a decrease in cognitive functioning (Terry et al., 2002, 2003). A newer class of atypical neuroleptics, called *partial dopamine agonists*, affect the release of dopamine rather than blocking its receptors in the brain (Tamminga, 2002). (An *agonist* is any chemical substance that can stimulate a reaction within the synapse. LINK to Chapter Two: The Biological Perspective, p. 42.) Aripiprazole (which goes by the brand name Abilify) is an example of a partial dopamine agonist. It was approved by Health Canada in 2009. The hope is that these newer drugs will not only produce fewer negative side effects but also have less impact on the thought processes of those persons taking these drugs. In one recent study, the atypical neuroleptics were also found to lower the risk of violent behaviour in schizophrenic patients who are receiving their medication through community-based treatment centres (Swanson et al., 2004).

ANTIANXIETY DRUGS There are currently two kinds of drugs used to treat anxiety disorders from mild anxiety to the more serious anxiety of social phobias, simple phobias, and panic disorder. The traditional **antianxiety drugs** are the minor tranquilizers or *benzodiazepines* such as Xanax, Ativan, and Valium. All of these drugs have a sedative effect and in the right dose can relieve symptoms of anxiety within half an hour of taking the drug (Uretsky, 2002). Although many side effects are possible, the main concern in using these drugs is their potential for addiction as well as abuse in the form of taking larger doses to "escape" (CAMH, 2007; NIDA, 2002).

In the last several years, the use of the benzodiazepines to treat anxiety has declined, and physicians and therapists have begun to prescribe **antidepressant drugs** to treat anxiety disorders such as panic disorder, OCD, and PTSD. Although the antidepressants take from three to five weeks to show any effect, they are not as subject to abuse as the minor tranquilizers and have fewer of the same side effects.

ANTIMANIC DRUGS For many years, the treatment of choice for bipolar disorder and episodes of mania has been *lithium*, a metallic chemical element that in its salt form (lithium carbonate) evens out both the highs and the lows of bipolar disorder. It is generally recommended that treatment with lithium continue at maintenance levels in people with recurring bipolar disorder. Lithium affects the way sodium ions in neuron and muscle cells are transported, although it is not clear exactly how this affects mood. Side effects typically disappear quickly, although the use of lithium has been associated with weight gain. Diet needs to be controlled when taking lithium because lowered levels of sodium in the diet can cause lithium to build up to toxic levels, as can any substance that removes water from the body such as the caffeine in soft drinks, tea, and coffee.

Anticonvulsant drugs, normally used to treat seizure disorders, have also been used to treat mania. Examples are carbamazepine, valproic acid (Depakote), and lamotrigine. These drugs can be as effective in controlling mood swings as lithium and can also be used in combination with lithium treatments (Bowden et al., 2000;

◀ How long do people generally have to take these antipsychotic medications?

antianxiety drugs
drugs used to treat and calm anxiety reactions, typically minor tranquilizers.

antidepressant drugs
drugs used to treat depression and anxiety.

Thase & Sachs, 2000). When bouts of mania include psychotic symptoms (as in affective psychosis), patients are often treated with antipsychotic drugs in addition to a combination of anticonvulsants or antidepressants (Tohen et al., 2003).

ANTIDEPRESSANT DRUGS   As is so often the case in scientific discoveries, the first types of drugs used in the treatment of depression were originally developed to treat other disorders. Iproniazid, for example, was used to treat tuberculosis symptoms in the early 1950s and was found to have a positive effect on mood, becoming the first modern *antidepressant* (Trujillo & Chinn, 1996). This drug became the first of the *monoamine oxidase inhibitors (MAOIs)*, a class of antidepressants that blocks the activity of an enzyme called *monoamine oxidase*. Monoamine oxidase is the brain's "cleanup worker" because its primary function is to break down the neurotransmitters norepinephrine, serotonin, and dopamine—the three neurotransmitters most involved in control of mood. Under normal circumstances, the excess neurotransmitters are broken down *after* they have done their "job" in mood control. In depression, these neurotransmitters need more time to do their job, and the MAOIs allow them that time by inhibiting the enzyme's action.

Some common MAOIs in use today are isocarboxazid (Marplan), phenelzine sulphate (Nardil), and tranylcypromine sulphate (Parnate). These drugs can produce the following unwanted side effects, although in most cases the side effects decrease or disappear with continued treatment: weight gain, constipation, dry mouth, dizziness, headache, drowsiness or insomnia, and sexual arousal disorders. People taking MAOIs should also be careful about eating certain smoked, fermented, or pickled foods, drinking certain beverages, or taking some other medications because of a risk of severe high blood pressure in combination with these substances (Geddes & Butler, 2002).

The second category of antidepressant drug to be developed is called the *tricyclic antidepressants*. These drugs were discovered in the course of developing treatments for schizophrenia (Trujillo & Chinn, 1996). Tricyclics, so called because of their molecular structure consisting of three rings (cycles), increase the activity of serotonin and norepinephrine in the nervous system by inhibiting their reuptake into the synaptic vesicles of the neurons. **LINK** to Chapter Two: The Biological Perspective, p. 42. Some common tricyclics are imipramine (Tofranil), desipramine (Norpramin, Pertofrane), amitriptyline (Elavil), and doxepin (Sinequan, Adapin). Side effects of these drugs, which may also decrease over the course of treatment, are very similar to those of the MAOIs but can also include skin rashes, blurred vision, lowered blood pressure, and weight loss (APA, 2000b; Geddes & Butler, 2002).

The effect of the MAOIs and the tricyclics on the action of the three critical neurotransmitters led researchers to try to develop drugs that would more specifically target the critical neural activity involved in depression with fewer negative side effects. This led to the development of the *selective serotonin reuptake inhibitors (SSRIs)*, drugs that inhibit the reuptake process of only serotonin. This causes fewer side effects while still providing effective antidepressant action, making these drugs relatively safe when compared to the older antidepressants. But like the other two classes of antidepressants, the SSRIs may take from two to six weeks to produce effects. Some of the better-known SSRIs are fluoxetine hydrochloride (Prozac), sertraline hydrochloride (Zoloft), and paroxetine hydrochloride (Paxil). Side effects, although fewer in number and less intense than the other drugs, can include nausea, nervousness, insomnia, diarrhea, rash, agitation, and some sexual arousal problems (APA, 2000b; Geddes & Butler, 2002). Table 14.2 on p. 590 summarizes the various types of drugs used to treat psychological disorders.

✸—[Explore on **mypsychlab**
Drugs Commonly Used to Treat
Psychiatric Disorders

For a look at a current controversy concerning antidepressants, see the Applying Psychology to Everyday Life section at the end of this chapter.

ELECTROCONVULSIVE THERAPY

14.11   *How are electroconvulsive therapy and psychosurgery used to treat severe psychological disorders, and what are some emerging techniques?*

Many people are surprised to discover that **electroconvulsive therapy (ECT)** is still in use to treat cases of severe depression. ECT involves the delivery of an electric shock to either one side or both sides of a person's head, resulting in a seizure or convulsion of the body and the release of a flood of neurotransmitters in the brain (APA, 2001). The result is an almost immediate improvement in mood. In Canada, ECT is usually used only in very severe cases of depression or schizophrenia in which medication has not worked and patients represent a danger to themselves or to other people (Public Health Agency of Canada, 2002).

In the 1930s, doctors actually were researching the possible uses of inducing seizures in treating schizophrenia, although the seizures were induced through means of a drug (camphor) in those early experiments. It was Italian researchers Cerletti and Bini who first used electricity to induce a seizure in a schizophrenic man, who fully recovered after only 11 such treatments (Endler, 1988; Fink, 1984; Shorter, 1997). Soon doctors were using ECT on every kind of severe mental disorder. In those early days, no anaesthesia was used because the shock was severe enough to result in a loss of consciousness (most of the time). Broken bones, bitten tongues, and fractured teeth were not unusual "side effects."

ECT received more negative attention as it was portrayed in the classic 1975 film *One Flew Over the Cuckoo's Nest*, in which the little understood treatment was applied as a punishment and made to look like one. In reality, today's ECT is far more controlled and humane. It can be used only to treat severe disorders, not to control unruly behaviour. ECT has been found to be most useful for severe depression that has not responded to medications or psychotherapy and in cases in which suicide is a real possibility or has already been attempted. ECT works more quickly than antidepressant medications, so it can play an important role in helping to prevent suicide attempts (APA, 2001). However, ECT should not be considered a cure. It is a way to get a person suffering from severe depression into a state of mind that is more receptive to other forms of therapy or psychotherapy.

What are some of the side effects? Wasn't there something from an earlier chapter about this therapy affecting memory? ECT does have several negative side effects, some of which last longer than others. Memory is definitely affected, as ECT disrupts the consolidation process and prevents the formation of long-term memories. Ⓛ Ⓘ Ⓝ Ⓚ *to Chapter Six: Memory, p. 218.* This causes both retrograde amnesia, the loss of memories for events that happen close to the time of the treatment, and anterograde amnesia, the rapid forgetting of new material (APA, 2001; Lisanby et al., 2000; Weiner, 2000). The retrograde effects can extend to several months before and a few weeks after treatment and the older memories may return with time, whereas the anterograde amnesia is more temporary, clearing up in a few weeks after treatment. Only a very few patients suffer more severe and long-lasting cognitive difficulties, and it is not easy to determine whether these difficulties originate with the treatment or the disorder the person exhibits (Smith, 2001).

Physicians using ECT today try to reduce as many side effects as possible. The modern patient is given muscle relaxants to reduce the effects of the convulsion as well as a very short-term anaesthetic. In some cases, the electrodes used to induce the

electroconvulsive therapy (ECT) form of biomedical therapy to treat severe depression in which electrodes are placed on either one or both sides of a person's head and an electric current is passed through the electrodes that is strong enough to cause a seizure or convulsion.

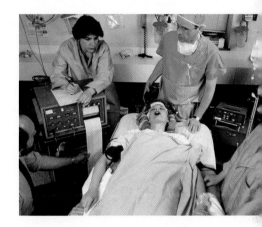

Electroconvulsive therapy consists of applying an electric shock to one or both sides of the head. The result is rapid improvement in mood. It has been shown to be most effective in treating severe depression that has not responded to medication.

◄ What are some of the side effects? Wasn't there something from an earlier chapter about this therapy affecting memory?

bilateral ECT
electroconvulsive therapy in which the electrodes are placed on both sides of the head.

unilateral ECT
electroconvulsive therapy in which the electrodes are placed on only one side of the head and the forehead.

psychosurgery
surgery performed on brain tissue to relieve or control severe psychological disorders.

prefrontal lobotomy
psychosurgery in which the connections of the prefrontal lobes of the brain to the rear portions are severed.

But I thought lobotomies left most people worse off than before—didn't it take away their emotions or something? ▶

shock are placed on both sides of the head (**bilateral ECT**) and in others only on one side and the forehead (**unilateral ECT**). Unilateral ECT causes less severe muscular convulsions and less severe memory and cognitive problems, and has been shown to be just as effective as bilateral ECT (Enns, Reiss, & Chan, 2010; Sackeim et al., 2000).

Norman Endler (1931–2003) was a very well-known Canadian psychologist. When York University was founded in Toronto in 1960, he was one of the first faculty members hired. When he passed away in 2003, he was still affiliated with York University as a distinguished research professor (emeritus). Endler's research was focused in the areas of stress, anxiety, and coping, to which he made many significant contributions. Although Endler's research was influential in the field, it is not the only thing that made him stand out. In 1977, after realizing that he was not in good psychological health, he sought psychiatric help. He was told that he was suffering from depression and was prescribed antidepressant medication. The drugs did not deliver the desired effect (and he also experienced serious side effects), so after some time, he was given a choice between two equally undesirable options: ECT or hospitalization. He chose ECT, a treatment to which he responded well.

Like many other people suffering from depression, he experienced a second episode of depression. He was prescribed more medication and then more ECT. Ultimately, after a change in diagnosis to bipolar disorder and experiencing another depressive episode and other health conditions (he had two heart attacks), Endler finally escaped from the grips of his mood disorder. He reached out to the public by discussing his personal struggles with depression and shock therapy in his book *Holiday of Darkness: A Psychologist's Personal Journey Out of His Depression*.

In 2010, the Canadian Psychological Association (CPA) issued a position paper on the use of ECT. The paper was written by Murray Enns of the University of Manitoba, Jeffrey Reiss of the University of Western Ontario, and Peter Chan, of the University of British Columbia. The paper states that although the way in which ECT works remains incompletely understood, substantial research and 70 years of clinical experience with ECT indicate that it should remain as a treatment option for major depression, bipolar disorder, and schizophrenia in Canada (Enns et al., 2010).

Research findings by Dr. Biju Mathew, a psychiatrist at the Ridge Meadows Hospital in British Columbia, and colleagues support this position. They investigated the effectiveness of ECT for patients with mood disorders. The results showed that the use of ECT resulted in substantial improvement and that this improvement lasted over a two-year follow-up period (Mathew et al., 2007).

PSYCHOSURGERY

Just as surgery involves cutting into the body, **psychosurgery** involves cutting into the brain to remove or destroy brain tissue for the purpose of relieving symptoms of mental disorders. One of the earliest and best-known psychosurgical techniques is the **prefrontal lobotomy**, in which the connections of the prefrontal lobes of the brain to the rear portions of the brain are severed. The lobotomy was developed in 1935 by Portuguese neurologist Dr. Antonio Egas Moniz, who was awarded the Nobel Prize in medicine for his contribution to psychosurgery (Cosgrove & Rauch, 1995; Freeman & Watts, 1937).

But I thought lobotomies left most people worse off than before—didn't it take away their emotions or something? Although it is true that some of the early lobotomy patients did seem less agitated, anxious, and delusional, it is also true that some early patients did not survive the surgery (about 6 percent died, in fact) and others were left with negative changes in personality: apathy, lack of emotional response, intellectual dullness, and childishness, to name a few. Fortunately, the development of antipsychotic drugs, beginning with chlorpromazine, together with the results of long-term studies that highlighted serious side effects of lobotomies, led to the discontinuation of lobotomies as a psychosurgical technique (Cosgrove & Rauch, 1995; Swayze, 1995). Some famous recipients of the last decades of lobotomies (and the disorders for which the procedure was performed) were 1940s French Canadian singer Alys Robi (violence and other disturbances), actress Francis Farmer (alcoholism), Rosemary Kennedy, sister of John F. Kennedy (mild intellectual disability), and Rose Williams, sister of playwright Tennessee Williams (schizophrenia).

There are still psychosurgical techniques in use today. The lobotomy is gone, but there is a modern replacement called the **bilateral anterior cingulotomy**, in which magnetic resonance imaging is used to guide an electrode to a specific area of the brain called the *cingulate gyrus*. This area connects the frontal lobes to the limbic system, which controls emotional reactions. By running a current through the electrode, a very small and specific area of brain cells can be destroyed. This process is called *deep lesioning*. LINK *to Chapter Two: The Biological Perspective, p. 42.* Cingulotomies have been shown to be effective in about one-third to one-half of cases of major depression, bipolar disorder, and certain forms of OCD that have not responded to any other therapy techniques (Dougherty et al., 2002; Kuhn et al., 2010; Spangler et al., 1996). Because this is deliberate brain damage and quite permanent, all other possible treatments must be exhausted before a bilateral anterior cingulotomy will be performed and, unlike the early days of lobotomies, it can be performed only with the patient's full and informed consent (Rodgers, 1992; Spangler et al., 1996). In fact, because of the ethical, social, and legal implications of psychosurgery in general, today only a very small number of such surgeries are carried out in a few medical centres around the world, such as Toronto Western Hospital (Cosgrove & Rauch, 1995).

EMERGING TECHNIQUES

As previously mentioned, depression is often treated effectively by either psychotherapy or medication or a combination of both. However, according to Burrows and Norman (1999), for up to 15 percent of people with depression, multiple pharmacological and psychotherapeutic interventions are unsuccessful. It is obvious that new treatment strategies are necessary. One such treatment that has been receiving a great deal of attention recently is **deep brain stimulation (DBS)**, which has been used effectively in helping block the tremors associated with Parkinson's disease and other related disorders. In DBS, a device known as a *brain pacemaker*, which sends electrical impulses to specific parts of the brain, is surgically implanted in the patient. This procedure is used only in severe cases of treatment-resistant depression because of its cost (roughly $40 000) and its invasiveness. A hole is bored through the skull and electrodes are implanted in the brain. These electrodes are connected to a wire that runs from the brain, behind the ear, and down the neck to a device implanted in the patient's chest. The device is not on at all times—the patient can switch it on whenever he or she feels it is necessary. When turned on, the pacemaker generates low-voltage electrical impulses that are delivered to the brain, temporarily changing the patient's neural circuitry.

Although still in its infancy, research on DBS as a treatment for depression has met with promising results. Two neuroscientists who have found that DBS helps relieve patients with treatment-resistant depression of their symptoms are Dr. Andres Lozano of Toronto Western Hospital and Dr. Helen Mayberg of Emory University in Atlanta. In fact, Lozano and Mayberg were issued a patent for the treatment in March 2008. Although very few patients have been empirically studied thus far, their clinical study at the University of Toronto found that of six participants who failed to respond to other forms of treatment, four experienced sustained remission of depressive symptoms after six months (Mayberg et al., 2005).

The woman on the left is Rosemary Kennedy, sister of former president John F. Kennedy. The man on the right is her father, U.S. Ambassador to Great Britain Joseph Kennedy. About six years after this photograph was taken, Rosemary, who had a mild intellectual disability and whose behaviour had become difficult to control, was subjected to a prefrontal lobotomy. The results were disastrous, and she remained institutionalized until her death on January 7, 2005.

bilateral anterior cingulotomy psychosurgical technique in which an electrode wire is inserted into the cingulate gyrus area of the brain with the guidance of a magnetic resonance imaging machine for the purpose of destroying that area of brain tissue with an electric current.

deep brain stimulation (DBS) delivery of low-voltage electrical impulses to the brain to temporarily change the patient's neural circuitry.

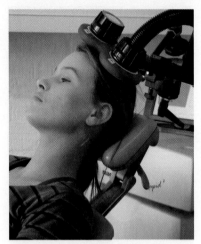

Repetitive transcranial magnetic stimulation (rTMS) uses a pulsating magnetic field.

Other new and more non-invasive techniques for effecting changes in the brain include *repetitive transcranial magnetic stimulation (rTMS)*, in which magnetic pulses are applied to the cortex, and *transcranial direct current stimulation (tDCS)*, which uses scalp electrodes to pass very low amplitude direct currents to the brain. These new and exciting strategies are being evaluated as possible treatment options for a variety of psychological disorders, including PTSD and depression (Boggio et al., 2009; Nitsche et al., 2009).

Many psychological professionals today believe that combining psychotherapy with medical therapies—particularly drug therapy—is a more effective approach to treating many disorders. A person dealing with depression may be given an antidepressant drug to alleviate symptoms but may also still need to talk about what it's like to deal with depression and with needing the medication. Cognitive-behavioural therapy in combination with drug therapy has been shown to be particularly effective in treating depression (Dew et al., 2007; Frank et al., 2007; Rohde et al., 2008). Another study has found that women with recurrent depression benefit from a combination of treatment with antidepressants and monthly maintenance psychotherapy (Frank et al., 2007).

PRACTICE QUIZ: HOW MUCH DO YOU REMEMBER?

Pick the best answer.

1. Which of the following statements about the effectiveness of psychotherapy is FALSE?
   a. In surveys, 75 to 90 percent of people reported that therapy has helped them.
   b. The longer a person stays in therapy, the less effective it is.
   c. Psychotherapy without drugs seems to work as well as psychotherapy with drugs.
   d. No one psychotherapy is effective for all disorders.

2. For psychotherapy to be effective,
   a. the therapist must provide a protected setting for clients to reveal their feelings.
   b. the therapist should maintain emotional distance from the client.
   c. clients and therapists should avoid warmth in their relationship.
   d. therapists should choose one style of therapy for all of their clients.

3. Of the following, all are potential barriers to effective therapy listed by Sue and Sue (2003) when culture or ethnic backgrounds of therapist and client are different EXCEPT
   a. language.   c. social class.
   b. cultural values.   d. gender.

4. The newest drugs being developed to treat psychotic symptoms are the
   a. typical neuroleptics.   c. anticonvulsants.
   b. atypical neuroleptics.   d. partial dopamine agonists.

5. For which disorder have antidepressants NOT been used?
   a. panic disorder
   b. dissociative amnesia
   c. obsessive-compulsive disorder
   d. post-traumatic stress disorder

6. Electroconvulsive shock therapy is useful in preventing suicide attempts because it
   a. is more effective than drug therapies.
   b. has few negative side effects.
   c. works more quickly than antidepressants.
   d. makes people happy.

7. The risk of permanent brain damage is greatest with
   a. cybertherapy.   c. psychosurgery.
   b. ECT.   d. bilateral ECT.

Answers: 1-b, 2-a, 3-d, 4-d, 5-b, 6-c, 7-c.

APPLYING PSYCHOLOGY TO EVERYDAY LIFE: SHOULD ANTIDEPRESSANTS BE PRESCRIBED FOR CHILDREN AND ADOLESCENTS?

14.12 *What are the dangers of treating children and adolescents with antidepressant drugs?*

In recent years, there has been a growing controversy over the use of antidepressant drugs for treatment of depression and anxiety-related disorders in adolescents (Breggin, 2003, 2004; Breggin & Breggin, 1994). Although such drugs are approved for use by Health Canada in adults, product warnings started to accompany the drugs in late 2004. In Canada, drug companies were required to amend their product monographs and they had to include an information sheet with drugs for consumers. In addition, doctors were sent letters explaining the risks that prescribing such medication could have on patients. These warnings, provided by Health Canada, describe that the drugs are associated with an increased risk of suicide in both children and adolescents and suggest that doctors closely monitor children and adolescents taking these drugs. Although these new warnings in Canada do not forbid the use of these drugs by children and teens (as the United Kingdom decided to do when it banned children from using six different antidepressants), it does strongly urge professionals to weigh the possible benefits of the drug against the possible negative effects.

Wait a minute. How can a drug that's meant to help depression increase the risk of suicide? Children and adolescents are often affected differently by drugs used to treat various disorders in adults. The hormonal and neurological systems—including the serotonin systems—of younger people are not yet fully functional, and drugs that would be harmless in an older person may have harmful side effects in young people. The effects of antidepressants on children and adolescents, however, are not clearly understood.

In one major study published in 2001, researchers conducted what was at that time the largest clinical trial of antidepressant use in cases of adolescent depression (Keller et al., 2001). The researchers concluded that using antidepressants in adolescents was both safe and effective. But in April 2004, researchers published the results of a meta-analysis (a comprehensive scientific review) of both the published and unpublished studies conducted by drug companies that produce antidepressants (Whittington et al., 2004). It was found that although the published research supported the safety of these drugs for use with children and adolescents, the unpublished research indicated that four out of the five drugs tested could lead to increased risk of suicide in children from ages 5 to 18. Prozac was the only antidepressant that did not have an increased risk of suicide for this age group.

Does this mean that children and adolescents should not be given these drugs to treat other conditions? At least one of the drugs in the 2004 study is approved for use in treating OCD in children. When this drug (and possibly others like it) is used to treat anxiety-related disorders rather than depression, there is no apparent increase in risk of suicide.

Obviously, the use of these drugs to treat depression is risky, especially when the research shows that there are safer drugs and alternative treatments. One study found that treating adolescents with a major depression disorder was more successful when the use of the approved antidepressant was combined with psychotherapy (March et al., 2004). Doctors and psychiatrists should exercise caution in prescribing powerful psychoactive drugs meant for adult bodies and nervous systems to younger persons.

In a surprising turn of events, researchers in Manitoba have found that in the two years following Health Canada's warnings about antidepressant use in children and adolescents, the rate of completed suicides in children and adolescents increased by 25 percent (Katz et al., 2008). After the warnings, Katz and colleagues (2008) found that children and adolescents made fewer visits to physicians. In addition, the prescription rate of antidepressants among children and adolescents decreased by 14 percent. The autopsy reports of the children and adolescents who committed suicide showed that the vast majority of them had not taken an antidepressant prior to their death. Katz and colleagues (2008) point out that although they cannot make any direct connections between the warnings issued by Health Canada and the increase in completed suicides in children and adolescents, there are concerns that the warnings could lead to untreated depression and other problems.

◀

Wait a minute. How can a drug that's meant to help depression increase the risk of suicide?

Depression is not only an adult disorder; children and adolescents such as this sad young boy also suffer from depression. Using antidepressant drugs to treat depression in children and adolescents is controversial. What other methods could be used to treat depression in this age group?

Questions for Further Discussion

1. Of the measures taken by Canada and the United Kingdom, which measure do you think is the most effective and the safest in terms of protecting the public?

2. How much input should a child be permitted to have in his or her treatment process?

3. Why would the combination of psychotherapy and drug therapy be more effective in treating depression in adolescents?

14

CHAPTER SUMMARY

Two Kinds of Therapy

14.1 *What are the two modern ways in which psychological disorders can be treated, and how were they treated in the past?*

- Psychotherapy involves a person talking to a psychological professional about the person's problems.

- Psychotherapy for the purpose of gaining understanding into one's motives and actions is called *insight therapy*, whereas psychotherapy aimed at changing disordered behaviour directly is called *action therapy*.

- Biomedical therapy uses a medical procedure to bring about changes in behaviour.

The Early Days of Therapy: Ice-Water Baths and Electric Shocks

- Mentally ill people began to be confined to institutions called *asylums* in the mid 1500s. Treatments were harsh and often damaging.

- Philippe Pinel became famous for demanding that the mentally ill be treated with kindness, personally unlocking the chains of inmates at Bicêtre Asylum in Paris, France.

In the Beginning: Psychoanalysis

- Sigmund Freud developed a treatment called *psychoanalysis* that focused on releasing a person's hidden, repressed urges and concerns from the unconscious mind.

14.2 *What were the basic elements of Freud's psychoanalysis, and how is psychoanalysis conducted and viewed today?*

- Psychoanalysis uses interpretation of dreams, free association, resistance, and positive and negative transference to help patients reveal their unconscious concerns.

- Freud's original therapy technique is criticized for its lack of scientific research and his own personal biases that caused him to misinterpret much of what his patients revealed.

- Modern psychodynamic therapists have modified the technique so that it takes less time and is much more direct, and they do not focus on the id and sexuality as Freud did.

Humanistic Therapy: To Err Is Human

14.3 *What are the basic elements of the humanistic therapies known as person-centred therapy and Gestalt therapy, and how are humanistic therapies viewed today?*

- Humanistic therapies focus on the conscious mind and subjective experiences to help clients gain insights.

- Person-centred therapy is very non-directive, allowing the client to talk through problems and concerns while the therapist provides a supportive background.

- The four basic elements of person-centred therapy are reflection of the client's statements by the therapist, unconditional positive regard given to the client by the therapist, the empathy of the therapist for the client, and the authenticity of the therapist in the client's perception.

- Gestalt therapy is more directive, helping clients to become aware of their feelings and to take responsibility for their choices in life.

- Gestalt therapists try to help clients deal with things in their past that they have denied and will use body language and other non-verbal cues to understand what clients are really saying.

- Humanistic therapies are also not based in experimental research and work best with intelligent, highly verbal persons.

Behaviour Therapies: Learning One's Way to Better Behaviour

- Behaviour therapies are action therapies that do not look at thought processes but instead focus on changing the abnormal or disordered behaviour itself through classical or operant conditioning.

14.4 *How do behaviour therapists use classical and operant conditioning to treat disordered behaviour?*

- Classical conditioning techniques for changing behaviour include systematic desensitization, aversion therapy, and exposure therapies such as flooding.

Psychology in the News: Virtual Reality as a Treatment

- Virtual reality is a computer simulation of a world, either imaginary or real, in which the user can interact with various computer-generated stimuli.

- Virtual reality has become increasingly popular in the treatment of various psychological disorders such as phobias.

- Clients attend multiple sessions of virtual reality exposure treatment (VRET) in which they are taught about the nature of phobias and are gradually exposed to fear-provoking stimuli as physiological measures are taken.

- Virtual reality shows great promise in the treatment of various psychological disorders.

- Therapies based on operant conditioning include modelling, reinforcement (with the use of token economies or contingency contracting), and extinction.

14.5 *How successful are behaviour therapies?*

- Behaviour therapies can be effective in treating specific problems, such as bedwetting, drug addictions, and phobias, and can help improve some of the more troubling behavioural symptoms associated with more severe disorders.

Cognitive Therapies: Thinking Is Believing

14.6 *What are the goals and basic elements of cognitive therapies such as cognitive-behavioural therapy and rational emotive therapy?*

- Cognitive therapy is oriented toward teaching clients how their thinking may be distorted and helping clients to see how inaccurate some of their beliefs may be.
- Some of the cognitive distortions in thinking include arbitrary inference, selective thinking, overgeneralization, magnification and minimization, and personalization.
- Cognitive-behavioural therapies are action therapies that work at changing a person's illogical or distorted thinking.
- The three goals of cognitive-behavioural therapies are to relieve the symptoms and solve the problems, to develop strategies for solving future problems, and to help change irrational, distorted thinking.
- Rational-emotive behaviour therapy is a directive therapy in which the therapist challenges clients' irrational beliefs, often arguing with clients and even assigning them homework.

14.7 *How successful are cognitive and cognitive-behavioural therapies?*

- Although cognitive-behavioural therapy has seemed successful in treating depression, stress disorders, and anxiety, it is criticized for focusing on the symptoms and not the causes of disordered behaviour.

Group Therapies: Not for the Shy

14.8 *What are the various types of group therapies and the advantages and disadvantages of group therapy?*

- Group therapy can be accomplished using many styles of psychotherapy and may involve treating people who are all part of the same family, as in family counselling.
- Group therapy can also be accomplished without the aid of a trained therapist in the form of self-help or support groups composed of other people who have the same or similar problems.
- Group therapy has the advantages of low cost, exposure to other people with similar problems, social interaction with others, and social and emotional support from people with similar disorders or problems.
- Disadvantages of group therapy can include the need to share the therapist's time with others in the group, the lack of a private setting in which to reveal concerns, the possibility that shy people will not speak up within a group setting, and the inability of people with severe disorders to tolerate being in a group.
- Group therapy is most useful to persons who cannot afford individual therapy and who may obtain a great deal of social and emotional support from other group members.

Does Psychotherapy Really Work?

14.9 *How effective is psychotherapy, and how is the effectiveness of psychotherapy influenced by cultural, ethnic, and gender differences?*

- Surveys of people who have received therapy suggest that psychotherapy is more effective than no treatment at all.
- Surveys reveal that from 75 to 90 percent of people who receive therapy improve, the longer a person stays in therapy the better the improvement, and psychotherapy works as well alone as with drugs.

- Some types of psychotherapy are more effective for certain types of problems, and no one psychotherapy method is effective for all problems.

Classic Studies in Psychology: **Psychotherapy: An Evaluation by Hans Eysenck**

- Eysenck's early survey of client improvement seemed to suggest that clients would improve as time passed, with or without therapy.
- Effective therapy should be matched to the particular client and the particular problem, there should exist a therapeutic alliance between therapist and client, and a protected setting in which clients can release emotions and reveal private thoughts is essential.
- When the culture, ethnic group, or gender of the therapist and the client differs, misunderstandings and misinterpretations can occur because of differences in cultural/ethnic values, socioeconomic differences, gender roles, and beliefs.
- The four barriers to effective psychotherapy that exist when the backgrounds of client and therapist differ are language, cultural values, social class, and non-verbal communication.
- Cybertherapy is therapy that is offered on the internet. Cybertherapists may or may not be trained in psychotherapy, but cybertherapy offers the advantages of anonymity and therapy for people who cannot otherwise get to a therapist.

Biomedical Therapies

- Biomedical therapies include the use of drugs, induced convulsions, and surgery to relieve or control the symptoms of mental disorders.

14.10 *What are the various types of drugs used to treat psychological disorders?*

- Antipsychotic drugs are used to control delusions, hallucinations, and bizarre behaviour and include the typical neuroleptics, atypical neuroleptics, and partial dopamine agonists.
- Antianxiety drugs are used to treat anxiety disorders and include the benzodiazepines and certain antidepressant drugs.
- Antimanic drugs are used to treat bipolar disorder and include lithium and certain anticonvulsant drugs.
- Antidepressant drugs are used in the treatment of depression and include monoamine oxidase inhibitors (MOAIs), tricyclic antidepressants, and selective serotonin reuptake inhibitors (SSRIs).

14.11 *How are electroconvulsive therapy and psychosurgery used to treat severe psychological disorders, and what are some emerging techniques?*

- Electroconvulsive therapy is used to treat severe depression, bipolar disorder, and schizophrenia and involves the use of a muscle relaxant, a short-term anaesthetic, and relatively mild muscular contractions.
- One of the earliest psychosurgeries was the prefrontal lobotomy, in which the front part of the frontal lobe was cut away from the back part of the brain, producing effects ranging from a disappearance of symptoms to a lack of emotional response and intellectual disability.
- Modern psychosurgery includes bilateral anterior cingulotomy, which is used to treat major depression, bipolar disorders, and certain forms of obsessive-compulsive disorder that have not responded to other forms of treatment.
- In deep brain stimulation (DBS), a brain pacemaker sends electrical impulses to specific parts of the brain after being surgically implanted in the patient.
- Although much more research needs to be conducted, research on DBS as a treatment for depression has met with promising results.

Applying Psychology to Everyday Life: Should Antidepressants Be Prescribed for Children and Adolescents?

14.12 *What are the dangers of treating children and adolescents with antidepressant drugs?*

• When both published and unpublished studies are taken into account, research shows that all but one antidepressant drug has been associated with an increased risk of suicide when used to treat depression in children and adolescents.

• Prozac, the one safe antidepressant for children and adolescents, has been found to be more effective when combined with psychotherapy.

• After Health Canada instituted regulations requiring that warnings be given to consumers and doctors who could prescribe antidepressant drugs to minors, suicide rates among children and adolescents actually increased. It is thought that the drug warnings may have scared parents away from seeking medical and/or pharmaceutical help for their children, resulting in an increase of suicidally depressed children.

14 KEY TERMS

action therapy   566
antianxiety drugs   591
antidepressant drugs   591
antipsychotic drugs   590
arbitrary inference   579
authenticity   572
aversion therapy   574
behaviour modification or applied behaviour analysis   574
behaviour therapies   573
bilateral anterior cingulotomy   595
bilateral ECT   594
biomedical therapy   566
cognitive therapy   579
cognitive-behavioural therapy (CBT)   580
contingency contract   578
counterconditioning   574
countertransference   569
cybertherapy   588
deep brain stimulation (DBS)   595

deinstitutionalization   568
directive   570
eclectic therapies   585
electroconvulsive therapy (ECT)   593
empathy   572
exposure therapies   575
family counselling (family therapy)   582
flooding   575
free association   569
Gestalt therapy   572
insight therapies   566
latent content   569
magnification and minimization   579
manifest content   569
modelling   577
non-directive   571
overgeneralization   579
participant modelling   577
personalization   579
person-centred therapy   571

prefrontal lobotomy   594
psychoanalysis   568
psychodynamic therapy   570
psychopharmacology   589
psychosurgery   594
psychotherapy   566
rational-emotive behaviour therapy (REBT)   580
reflection   571
resistance   569
selective thinking   579
self-help groups (support groups)   582
systematic desensitization   574
therapeutic alliance   586
therapy   566
time out   578
token economy   577
transference   569
unconditional positive regard   571
unilateral ECT   594

TEST YOURSELF

Pick the best answer.

1. Larisa is going to a therapist to gain a better understanding of what makes her do the things she does. This type of therapy is known as _____ therapy.
   a. insight
   b. action
   c. behavioural
   d. biomedical
2. _____ is most credited with the "moral treatment" movement for using kindness and guidance with the mentally ill.
   a. Sigmund Freud
   b. Josef Breuer
   c. Jean Martin Charcot
   d. Philippe Pinel
3. The actual content of a dream is the _____ content, according to Freud.
   a. repressed
   b. latent
   c. manifest
   d. sexual
4. The psychoanalyst does not start interpreting what the patient has said until _____ has occurred.
   a. positive transference
   b. negative transference
   c. free association
   d. dream analysis

5. In _____, a person-centred therapist must show an honest and open response to the client and not hide behind the professional role of therapist.
   a. reflection
   b. unconditional positive regard
   c. empathy
   d. authenticity
6. Gestalt therapy differs from person-centred therapy because
   a. it is based in humanistic theory.
   b. it focuses on the unconscious mind.
   c. it is directive rather than non-directive.
   d. it is an insight therapy.
7. What kind of person would probably get the least benefit from a humanistic therapy?
   a. one who is bright but confused about self-image
   b. one who is very talkative and open in discussing feelings
   c. one who enjoys exploring the inner workings of the mind
   d. one who has a hard time putting things into words in a logical manner

8. Lashonna is afraid of dogs. She wants to get over this fear, so she begins her treatment by thinking about seeing a dog while staying calm. Then she walks past her neighbour's dog in its fenced yard until she no longer feels afraid. Next, she visits a pet store and pets a dog while the sales clerk holds it. Finally, she buys herself a puppy and is no longer afraid. Lashonna's method is most like
   a. systematic desensitization.
   b. aversion therapy.
   c. flooding.
   d. extinction.

9. Virtual-reality exposure treatment is considered to be a _____ therapy.
   a. cognitive
   b. behavioural
   c. humanistic
   d. psychoanalytic

10. When the exposure to a feared object is rapid and intense rather than slow and gradual, it is called
    a. systematic desensitization.
    b. aversion therapy.
    c. flooding.
    d. extinction.

11. Carra sat down with her daughter, Morgan, and together they wrote out a list of things that Morgan was expected to do each day and the rewards she would get if she accomplished them, as well as the penalties she would face if she did not do them. This is most like which technique?
    a. token economy
    b. time out
    c. extinction
    d. contingency contracting

12. Which therapy style can be compared to a drill sergeant–private style of therapeutic relationship?
    a. person-centred
    b. Gestalt
    c. rational-emotive behavioural
    d. cognitive

13. Which of the following is NOT one of the three goals of cognitive-behavioural therapy?
    a. helping the client gain insight
    b. relieving the symptoms and resolving the problems
    c. helping the client develop strategies for future problem solving.
    d. helping the client to think in a more rational, self-helping way.

14. Stephan finds a piece of paper with a phone number he does not recognize on his wife's dresser. He immediately assumes that his wife is seeing someone else and that the phone number belongs to that man. Beck would say that Stephan has engaged in what type of distorted thinking?
    a. arbitrary inference
    b. selective thinking
    c. overgeneralization
    d. personalization

15. Which of the following is a disadvantage of group therapy?
    a. Clients share the therapist's time.
    b. Clients see how other people have handled the problem.
    c. Clients get social support from others.
    d. Clients interact with others socially.

16. When Carson began acting out, her parents took her to a therapist who suggested that her parents may have caused the problem by using the wrong kind of discipline. The kind of therapy that might best help Carson would probably be
    a. a support group of other disturbed children.
    b. an insight therapy.

    c. a cognitive therapy.
    d. family therapy.

17. Which of the following is NOT one of the problems in studying the effectiveness of psychotherapy?
    a. All therapies take the same amount of time to be effective.
    b. Control groups have no expectations about getting better.
    c. Some therapies measure success differently and are not easily evaluated.
    d. There may be experimenter bias.

18. Cindy is a white, upper-middle-class graduate student in clinical psychology doing her first internship in juvenile court. Her first client is an angry 15-year-old Black boy. Which of the following might be barriers to effective therapy in this situation?
    a. social class
    b. gender
    c. cultural values
    d. All of these might be barriers.

19. Which of the following is not one of the advantages of cybertherapy (therapy over the internet)?
    a. It is cheaper.
    b. The therapist does not have access to body language or vocal tones of the client.
    c. It offers relative anonymity.
    d. There is increased availability of therapy opportunities.

20. When a person on an antipsychotic drug develops repetitive, involuntary jerks and movements of the face, lips, legs, and body, this is called
    a. the Thorazine shuffle.
    b. neuroleptic syndrome.
    c. tardive dyskinesia.
    d. psychotic syndrome.

21. The use of antianxiety drugs to treat anxiety disorders is gradually being phased out in favour of treatment with _____ drugs.
    a. antidepressant
    b. antimanic
    c. antipsychotic
    d. sedative

22. Which neurotransmitter is not one of the three that seem to be involved in depression and the drugs that treat depression?
    a. norepinephrine
    b. serotonin
    c. dopamine
    d. epinephrine

23. Before the use of electricity, seizures were induced in psychotic patients by means of
    a. ice-cold water.
    b. bloodletting.
    c. camphor.
    d. opium.

24. In bilateral anterior cingulotomy, the
    a. front of the brain is cut away from the back.
    b. a thin wire electrode is used to destroy a small area of brain tissue.
    c. an electric shock is used to stimulate certain areas of the brain.
    d. a drug is injected into the brain to destroy a small area of brain tissue.

25. One antidepressant drug was found to be safe and most effective in treating adolescent depression when combined with
    a. other antidepressant drugs.
    b. psychotherapy.
    c. eye-movement desensitization processing.
    d. psychosurgery.

Answers: 1-a, 2-d, 3-c, 4-b, 5-d, 6-c, 7-d, 8-a, 9-b, 10-c, 11-d, 12-c, 13-a, 14-a, 15-a, 16-d, 17-a, 18-d, 19-b, 20-c, 21-a, 22-d, 23-c, 24-b, 25-b.

ScanLife™ Barcode

To access more tests and your own personalized study plan that will help you focus on the areas you need to master before your next class test, be sure to go to **www.MyPsychLab.com**, Pearson Education Canada's online psychology website, available with the access code packaged with your book.

Two Ways of Treating Psychological Disorders

1. **Psychotherapy:**
   - **Insight therapy:** understanding one's motives
   - **Action therapy:** changing disordered behaviour
2. **Biomedical therapy:** medical procedures for changes in behaviour

14.1

Treatment of Psychological Disorders in the Past

Mid 1500s: mentally ill people confined in harsh and often damaging asylums

Philippe Pinel: demanded that the mentally ill be treated with kindness

14.1

Psychotherapy

PSYCHOANALYSIS

Psychoanalysis: Freud developed psychoanalysis: focused on hidden, repressed urges and concerns from unconscious

Basic Elements of Freud's Psychoanalysis: Used to Reveal the Unconscious

- Dream interpretation
- Free association
- Resistance
- Positive and negative transference

Today's View of Psychoanalysis

Freud's theory criticized for
- Lack of scientific research
- Personal biases causing misinterpretations of patients

Modern modifications:
- Takes less time
- More direct
- Does not focus on id, sexuality

14.2

HUMANISTIC THERAPIES

Focus on conscious mind and subjective experience

Rogers's Person-Centred Therapy

- Non-directive
- Client talks through problems
- Therapist provides supportive background

Four Basic Elements
- Reflection of client's statements by therapist
- Unconditional positive regard given to the client by the therapist
- Empathy of therapist for the client
- Authenticity of therapist in client's perception

Fritz Perl's Gestalt Therapy

- More directive than person-centred therapy
- Focuses on the here and now
- Uses body language and non-verbal cues

Today's Views of Humanistic Therapies

- Not based in experimental research
- Work best with intelligent, highly verbal persons

14.3

Does Psychotherapy Really Work?

Eysenck's early survey: suggested clients improve with time, with or without therapy

Effectiveness of Psychotherapy

- Surveys suggest psychotherapy is more effective than no treatment.
- 75 to 90 percent of people who receive therapy improve.
- Longer therapy is better.
- Some psychotherapies are more effective for certain problems.
- Therapy should be matched to client and problem.

14.9

Psychotherapy's Effectiveness and Cultural, Ethnic, or Gender Differences

- Misunderstandings and misinterpretations can occur.
- Barriers to effective psychotherapy: language, cultural values, social class, non-verbal communication
- Cybertherapists (who offer therapy over the internet) may or may not be trained; cybertherapy offers anonymity and can be used by people who cannot otherwise get to a therapist

14.9

BEHAVIOUR THERAPIES

▸ Do not look at thought processes   ▸ Use conditioning to alter behaviour

Classical Conditioning and Operant Conditioning

Uses of classical conditioning: systematic desensitization, aversion therapy, exposure therapies, such as flooding, and virtual reality exposure treatment

Uses of classical conditioning: modelling, reinforcement (token economies and contingency contracting), and extinction

14.4

Effectiveness of Behaviour Therapy

Effective in treating bedwetting, drug addictions, phobias, and behavioural symptoms associated with severe disorders

14.5

COGNITIVE THERAPIES

Teaches clients that their thinking may be distorted

Goals of Cognitive-Behavioural Therapy

▸ Relieve symptoms/problems
▸ Develop strategies to solve future problems
▸ Change irrational, distorted thinking, such as arbitrary inference, selective thinking, overgeneralization, magnification and minimization, and personalization

Goals of Rational-Emotive Behaviour Therapy

Directive therapy—therapist challenges client's irrational beliefs, often arguing with clients, assigning homework.

14.6

Effectiveness of Cognitive Therapies

▸ Successful in treating depression, stress disorders, anxiety
▸ Criticized for focusing on symptoms and not causes

14.7

GROUP THERAPY

Types of Group Therapy

Can be accomplished using many styles of psychotherapy and may involve family counselling, self-help, or support groups

Advantages: Low cost, exposure to others, social interaction, and social/emotional support from others

Disadvantages: Lack of privacy to reveal concerns, shy people won't speak up, people may not tolerate groups

14.8

Biomedical Therapies

Use drugs, induced convulsions, and surgery to relieve symptoms of mental disorders

Drug Treatments

Antipsychotic drugs: control delusions, hallucinations, and bizarre behaviour, include neuroleptics, atypical neuroleptics, and partial dopamine agonists

Antianxiety drugs: treat anxiety disorders, include benzodiazepines and antidepressant drugs

Antimanic drugs: treat bipolar disorder, include lithium and anticonvulsant drugs

Antidepressant drugs: treat depression; include monoamine oxidase inhibitors (MOAIs), tricyclic antidepressants, and selective serotonin reuptake inhibitors (SSRIs)

14.10

Other Biomedical Therapies

Electroconvulsive therapy

▸ Treats severe depression, bipolar disorder, and schizophrenia—uses muscle relaxant, short-term anaesthetic, mild muscular contractions

Psychosurgery

▸ **Earliest form:** Prefrontal lobotomy can produce symptom disappearance, lack of emotional response, or mental retardation.
▸ **Modern forms:** bilateral anterior cingulotomy, used to treat major depression, bipolar disorders, and certain forms of obsessive-compulsive disorder

Deep brain stimulation

▸ A brain pacemaker is surgically implanted and sends electrical impulses to specific parts of the brain.
▸ shows great promise in treating depression

14.11

Dangers of Treating Children and Adolescents with Antidepressant Drugs

▸ All but one antidepressant drug are associated with increased suicide risk when used to treat depression in children and adolescents.
▸ Prozac more effective when combined with psychotherapy

14.12

Glossary

absolute threshold the smallest amount of energy needed for a person to consciously detect a stimulus 50 percent of the time it is present.   90

accommodation as a monocular clue, the brain's use of information about the changing thickness of the lens of the eye in response to looking at objects that are close or far away.   120

acculturative stress stress resulting from the need to change and adapt a person's ways to the majority culture.   422

acquired (secondary) drives those drives that are learned through experience or conditioning, such as the need for money or social approval.   354

acrophobia fear of heights.   531

action potential the release of the neural impulse consisting of a reversal of the electrical charge within the axon.   48

action therapy therapy in which the main goal is to change disordered or inappropriate behaviour directly.   566

activation-information-mode model (AIM) revised version of the activation-synthesis explanation of dreams in which information that is accessed during waking hours can have an influence on the synthesis of dreams.   151

activation-synthesis hypothesis theory that the higher cortical centres of the brain create dreams in response to the random activation of brain stem cells that occurs during REM sleep periods.   150

activity theory theory of adjustment to aging that assumes older people are happier if they remain active in some way, such as volunteering or developing a hobby.   341

acute stress disorder (ASD) a disorder resulting from exposure to a major stressor, with symptoms of anxiety, recurring nightmares, sleep disturbances, problems in concentration, and moments in which people seem to relive the event in dreams and flashbacks for as long as one month following the event.   400

adaptive theory theory of sleep proposing that animals and humans evolved sleep patterns to avoid predators by sleeping when predators are most active.   140

adolescence the period of life from about age 13 to the early 20s, during which a young person is no longer physically a child but is not yet an independent, self-supporting adult.   331

adrenal glands endocrine glands located on top of each kidney that secrete more than 30 different hormones to deal with stress, regulate salt intake, and provide a secondary source of sex hormones affecting the sexual changes that occur during adolescence.   78

aerial perspective the haziness that surrounds objects that are farther away from the viewer, causing the distance to be perceived as greater.   120

affect in psychology, an emotional reaction.   545

afterimage image that occurs when a visual sensation persists for a brief time even after the original stimulus is removed.   99

ageism discrimination against individuals because of their age.   336

aggression actions meant to harm or destroy.   407

aggression behaviour intended to hurt or destroy another person.   504

agonists chemical substances that mimic or enhance the effects of neurotransmitters on the receptor sites of the next cell, increasing or decreasing the activity of that cell.   51

agoraphobia fear of being in a place or situation from which escape is difficult or impossible.   531

agreeableness one of the five factors; the emotional style of a person that may range from easygoing, friendly, and likeable to grumpy, crabby, and unpleasant.   457

alcohol the chemical resulting from fermentation or distillation of various kinds of vegetable matter.   162

algorithms very specific, step-by-step procedures for solving certain types of problems that guarantee a solution to a problem providing they are used correctly.   266

all-or-none referring to the fact that a neuron either fires completely or does not fire at all.   49

all-or-nothing thinking the tendency to believe that one's performance must be perfect or the result will be a total failure.   534

alpha waves brain waves that indicate a state of relaxation or light sleep.   142

altered state of consciousness state in which there is a shift in the quality or pattern of mental activity as compared to waking consciousness.   137

altruism prosocial behaviour that is done with no expectation of reward and may involve the risk of harm to oneself.   508

amphetamines stimulants that are synthesized (made) in laboratories rather than being found in nature.   157

amygdala brain structure located near the hippocampus, responsible for fear responses and memory of fear.   68

anal expulsive personality a person fixated in the anal stage who is messy, destructive, and hostile.   445

anal retentive personality a person fixated in the anal stage who is neat, fussy, stingy, and stubborn.   445

anal stage second stage, occurring from about 1 or 1½ to 3 years of age, in which the anus is the erogenous zone and toilet training is the source of conflict.   445

analytical intelligence the ability to break down problems into component parts, or analysis, for problem solving.   273

androgens male sex hormones.   373

andropause gradual changes in the sexual hormones and reproductive system of males.   337

anorexia nervosa a condition in which a person reduces eating to the point that a weight loss of 15 percent below the ideal body weight or more occurs.   368

antagonists chemical substances that block or reduce a cell's response to the action of other chemicals or neurotransmitters.   51

anterograde amnesia loss of memory from the point of injury or trauma forward, or the inability to form new long-term memories. 230

antianxiety drugs drugs used to treat and calm anxiety reactions, typically minor tranquilizers. 591

antidepressant drugs drugs used to treat depression and anxiety. 591

antipsychotic drugs drugs used to treat psychotic symptoms such as delusions, hallucinations, and other bizarre behaviour. 590

antisocial personality disorder disorder in which a person has no morals or conscience and often behaves in an impulsive manner without regard for the consequences of that behaviour. 554

anxiety disorders disorders in which the main symptom is excessive or unrealistic anxiety and fearfulness. 530

applied behaviour analysis (ABA) modern term for a form of behaviour modification that uses shaping techniques to mould a desired behaviour or response. 202

approach–approach conflict conflict occurring when a person must choose between two desirable goals. 409

approach–avoidance conflict conflict occurring when a person must choose or not choose a goal that has both positive and negative aspects. 409

arbitrary inference distortion of thinking in which a person draws a conclusion that is not based on any evidence. 579

archetypes Jung's collective, universal human memories. 447

arousal theory theory of motivation in which people are said to have an optimal (best or ideal) level of tension that they seek to maintain by increasing or decreasing stimulation. 355

artificial intelligence (AI) the creation of a machine that can think like a human. 290

association areas areas within each lobe of the cortex responsible for the coordination and interpretation of information, as well as higher mental processing. 72

attachment the emotional bond between an infant and the primary caregiver. 323

attitude a tendency to respond positively or negatively toward a certain person, object, idea, or situation. 486

attribution theory the theory of how people explain the causes behind behaviour. 493

attribution the process of explaining one's own behaviour and the behaviour of others. 493

auditory canal short tunnel that runs from the pinna to the eardrum. 104

auditory nerve bundle of axons from the hair cells in the inner ear. 104

authenticity the genuine, open, and honest response of the therapist to the client. 572

authoritarian parenting style of parenting in which parent is rigid and overly strict, showing little warmth to the child. 339

authoritative parenting style of parenting in which parents combine warmth and affection with firm limits on a child's behaviour. 340

autobiographical memory the memory for events and facts related to one's personal life story. 251

automatic encoding tendency of certain kinds of information to enter long-term memory with little or no effortful encoding. 241

autonomic nervous system (ANS) division of the PNS consisting of nerves that control all the involuntary muscles, organs, and glands. 58

aversion therapy form of behavioural therapy in which an undesirable behaviour is paired with an aversive stimulus to reduce the frequency of the behaviour. 574

avoidance–avoidance conflict conflict occurring when a person must choose between two undesirable goals. 409

axon terminals branches at the end of the axon. 50

axon tubelike structure that carries the neural message to other cells. 45

barbiturates depressant drugs that have a sedative effect. 162

basal metabolic rate (BMR) the rate at which the body burns energy when the organism is resting. 366

basic anxiety anxiety created when a child is born into the bigger and more powerful world of older children and adults. 449

behavioural genetics field of study devoted to discovering the genetic bases for personality characteristics. 459

behaviourism the science of behaviour that focuses on observable behaviour only. 10

behaviour modification or applied behaviour analysis the use of learning techniques to modify or change undesirable behaviour and increase desirable behaviour. 574

behaviour modification the use of operant conditioning techniques to bring about desired changes in behaviour. 201

behaviour therapies action therapies based on the principles of classical and operant conditioning and aimed at changing disordered behaviour without concern for the original causes of such behaviour. 573

benzodiazepines drugs that lower anxiety and reduce stress. 162

bilateral anterior cingulotomy psychosurgical technique in which an electrode wire is inserted into the cingulate gyrus area of the brain with the guidance of a magnetic resonance imaging machine for the purpose of destroying that area of brain tissue with an electric current. 595

bilateral ECT electroconvulsive therapy in which the electrodes are placed on both sides of the head. 594

binocular cues cues for perceiving depth based on both eyes. 120

binocular disparity the difference in images between the two eyes, which is greater for objects that are close and smaller for distant objects. 121

biological model model of explaining behaviour as caused by biological changes in the chemical, structural, or genetic systems of the body. 525

biological preparedness the tendency of animals to learn certain associations, such as taste and nausea, with only one or a few pairings because of the survival value of the learning. 186

biomedical therapy therapy for mental disorders that directly affect the biological functioning of the body and brain to relieve symptoms. 566

biopsychological perspective perspective that attributes human and animal behaviour to biological events occurring in the body, such as genetic influences, hormones, and the activity of the nervous system. 12

biopsychosocial model perspective in which abnormal behaviour is seen as the result of the combined and interacting forces of biology, psychology, culture, and our social environments. 526

bipolar disorder severe mood swings between major depressive episodes and manic episodes. 547

bisexual person attracted to both men and women. 376

blind spot area in the retina where the axons of the three layers of retinal cells exit the eye to form the optic nerve, insensitive to light. 96

borderline personality disorder maladaptive personality pattern in which the person is moody, unstable, lacks a clear sense of identity, and often clings to others. 555

bottom-up processing the analysis of the smaller features to build up to a complete perception. 124

brightness constancy the tendency to perceive the apparent brightness of an object as the same even when the light conditions change. 116

Broca's aphasia condition resulting from damage to Broca's area, causing the affected person to be unable to speak fluently, to mispronounce words, and to speak haltingly. 72

bulimia a condition in which a person develops a cycle of "bingeing," or overeating enormous amounts of food at one sitting, and "purging" or using inappropriate compensatory behaviour in an attempt to get rid of the food after eating. 369

burnout negative changes in thoughts, emotions, and behaviour as a result of prolonged stress or frustration. 422

bystander effect the effect that the presence of other people has on the decision to help or not help, with help becoming less likely as the number of bystanders increases. 509

caffeine a mild stimulant found in coffee, tea, and several other plant-based substances. 159

Cannon-Bard theory of emotion theory in which the physiological reaction and the emotion are assumed to occur at the same time. 384

case study study of one individual in great detail. 20

catastrophe an unpredictable, large-scale event that creates a tremendous need to adapt and adjust as well as overwhelming feelings of threat. 399

catatonic type of schizophrenia in which the person experiences periods of statuelike immobility mixed with occasional bursts of energetic, frantic movement and talking. 551

central nervous system (CNS) part of the nervous system consisting of the brain and spinal cord. 55

central-route processing (systematic processing) type of information processing that involves attending to the content of the message itself. 490

centration in Piaget's theory, the tendency of a young child to focus only on one feature of an object while ignoring other relevant features. 318

cerebellum part of the lower brain located behind the pons that controls and coordinates involuntary, rapid, fine motor movement. 66

cerebral hemispheres the two sections of the cortex on the left and right sides of the brain. 69

cerebrum the upper part of the brain consisting of the two hemispheres and the structures that connect them. 74

character value judgments of a person's moral and ethical behaviour. 440

chromosome tightly wound strand of genetic material or DNA. 307

circadian rhythm a cycle of bodily rhythm that occurs over a 24-hour period. 137

classical conditioning learning to make a reflex response to a stimulus other than the original, natural stimulus that normally produces the reflex. 179

claustrophobia fear of being in a small, enclosed space. 531

closure the tendency to complete figures that are incomplete. 117

cocaine a natural drug derived from the leaves of the coca plant. 157

cochlea snail-shaped structure of the inner ear that is filled with fluid. 104

cognitive arousal theory theory of emotion in which both the physical arousal and the labelling of that arousal based on cues from the environment must occur before the emotion is experienced. 384

cognitive-behavioural therapy (CBT) action therapy in which the goal is to help clients overcome problems by learning to think more rationally and logically. 580

cognitive development the development of thinking, problem solving, and memory. 316

cognitive dissonance sense of discomfort or distress that occurs when a person's behaviour does not correspond to that person's attitudes. 491

cognitive map a mental representation of the environment. 205

cognitive-mediational theory theory of emotion in which a stimulus must be interpreted (appraised) by a person in order to result in a physical response and an emotional reaction. 387

cognitive perspective modern theory in which classical conditioning is seen to occur because the conditioned stimulus provides information or an expectancy about the coming of the unconditioned stimulus. 187

cognitive perspective perspective that focuses on memory, intelligence, perception, problem solving, and learning. 13

cognitive psychologists psychologists who study the way people think, remember, and mentally organize information. 525

cognitive therapy therapy in which the focus is on helping clients recognize distortions in their thinking and replace distorted, unrealistic beliefs with more realistic, helpful thoughts. 579

cognitive universalism theory that concepts are universal and influence the development of language. 293

cohort effect when participants who are born around the same time are more likely to share various characteristics with one another than with those who were born during a different time period. 305

collective unconscious Jung's name for the memories shared by all members of the human species. 447

College Undergraduate Stress Scale (CUSS) assessment that measures the amount of stress in a college or university student's life over a one-year period resulting from major life events. 402

companionate love type of love consisting of intimacy and commitment. 502

compensation (substitution) defence mechanism in which a person makes up for inferiorities in one area by becoming superior in another area. 426

compliance changing one's behaviour as a result of other people directing or asking for the change. 481

computed tomography (CT) scan brain-imaging method using computer-controlled X-rays of the brain. 63

concentrative meditation form of meditation in which a person focuses the mind on some repetitive or unchanging stimulus so that the mind can be cleared of disturbing thoughts and the body can experience relaxation. 427

conception the moment at which a female becomes pregnant. 309

concepts ideas that represent a class or category of objects, events, or activities. 264

concrete operations stage Piaget's third stage of cognitive development in which the school-age child becomes capable of logical thought processes but is not yet capable of abstract thinking. 319

conditional positive regard positive regard that is given only when the person is doing what the providers of positive regard wish. 455

conditioned emotionalresponse (CER) emotional response that has become classically conditioned to occur to learned stimuli, such as a fear of dogs or the emotional reaction that occurs when seeing an attractive person. 185

conditioned response (CR) learned reflex response to a conditioned stimulus. 180

conditioned stimulus (CS) stimulus that becomes able to produce a learned reflex response by being paired with the original unconditioned stimulus. 180

conditioned taste aversion development of a nausea or aversive response to a particular taste because that taste was followed by a nausea reaction, occurring after only one association. 186

cones visual sensory receptors found at the back of the retina, responsible for colour vision and sharpness of vision. 96

confirmation bias the tendency to search for evidence that fits one's beliefs while ignoring any evidence that does not fit those beliefs. 269

conflict psychological experience of being pulled toward or drawn to two or more desires or goals, only one of which may be attained. 409

conformity changing one's own behaviour to match that of other people. 479

conscience part of the superego that produces pride or guilt, depending on how well behaviour matches or does not match the ego ideal. 443

conscientiousness one of the five factors; the care a person gives to organization and thoughtfulness of others; dependability. 457

conscious mind level of the mind that is aware of immediate surroundings and perceptions. 441

consciousness a person's awareness of everything that is going on around him or her at any given moment. 136

conservation in Piaget's theory, the ability to understand that simply changing the appearance of an object does not change the object's nature. 318

consolidation the changes that take place in the structure and functioning of neurons when an engram is formed. 250

constructive processing referring to the retrieval of memories in which those memories are altered, revised, or influenced by newer information. 243

contact hypothesis Gordon Allport's (1954) hypothesis that intergroup contact will reduce prejudice under four conditions: those coming into contact with each other must have equal status, common goals, no competition, and an authority overseeing the contact. 499

contiguity the tendency to perceive two things that happen close together in time as being related. 118

contingency contract a formal, written agreement between the therapist and client (or teacher and student) in which goals for behavioural change, reinforcements, and penalties are clearly stated. 578

continuity the tendency to perceive things as simply as possible with a continuous pattern rather than with a complex, broken-up pattern. 118

continuous reinforcement the reinforcement of each and every correct response. 198

control group participants in an experiment who are exposed to the level of the independent variable that should not influence the dependent variable. They may receive a placebo treatment. 26

conventional morality second level of Kohlberg's stages of moral development in which the person's behaviour is governed by conforming to the society's norms of behaviour. 334

convergence the rotation of the two eyes in their sockets to focus on a single object, resulting in greater convergence for closer objects and lesser convergence if objects are distant. 121

convergent thinking type of thinking in which a problem is seen as having only one answer, and all lines of thinking will eventually lead to that single answer if the problem solver uses previous knowledge and logic. 269

conversion disorder somatoform disorder in which the person experiences a specific symptom in the somatic nervous system's functioning, such as paralysis, numbness, or blindness, for which there is no physical cause. 536

coping strategies actions that people can take to master, tolerate, reduce, or minimize the effects of stressors. 424

corpus callosum thick band of neurons that connects the right and left cerebral hemispheres. 69

correlation a measure of the relationship between two variables. 23

cortex outermost covering of the brain consisting of densely packed neurons, responsible for higher thought processes and interpretation of sensory input. 69

counterconditioning replacing an old conditioned response with a new one by changing the unconditioned stimulus. 574

countertransference in psychoanalysis, the tendency for a therapist to transfer unconscious, unresolved feelings onto the patient or client. 569

creative intelligence the ability to deal with new and different concepts and to come up with new ways of solving problems. 274

creativity the process of solving problems by combining ideas or behaviour in new ways. 269

critical periods times during which certain environmental influences can have an impact on the development of the infant. 311

critical thinking making reasoned judgments about claims. 33

cross-sectional design research design in which several different age groups of participants are studied at one particular point in time. 304

cross-sequential design research design in which participants are first studied by means of a cross-sectional design but also followed and assessed for a period of no more than six years. 304

cult any group of people with a particular religious or philosophical set of beliefs and identity. 512

cultural relativity the need to consider the unique characteristics of the culture in which behaviour takes place. 526

culture-bound syndromes disorders found only in particular cultures. 526

curve of forgetting a graph showing a distinct pattern in which forgetting is very fast within the first hour after learning a list and then tapers off gradually. 246

cybertherapy psychotherapy that is offered on the internet. Also called online, internet, or web therapy or counselling. 588

cyclothymia disorder that consists of mood swings from moderate depression to hypomania and lasts two years or more. 546

dark adaptation the recovery of the eye's sensitivity to visual stimuli in darkness after exposure to bright lights. 98

decay loss of memory because of the passage of time, during which the memory trace is not used. 247

declarative memory type of long-term memory containing information that is conscious and known. 231

deep brain stimulation (DBS) delivery of low-voltage electrical impulses to the brain to temporarily change the patient's neural circuitry. 595

deep lesioning insertion of a thin, insulated wire into the brain through which an electrical current is sent that destroys the brain cells at the tip of the wire. 62

deinstitutionalization the process of removing people with mental disorders from hospitals and placing them in the community. 568

delta waves long, slow waves that indicate the deepest stage of sleep. 143

delusional disorder a psychotic disorder in which the primary symptom is one or more delusions. 550

delusions false beliefs held by a person who refuses to accept evidence of their falseness. 549

dendrites branchlike structures that receive messages from other neurons. 45

denial psychological defence mechanism in which the person refuses to acknowledge or recognize a threatening situation. 426

dependent variable variable in an experiment that represents the measurable response or behaviour of the participants in the experiment. 25

depersonalization disorder dissociative disorder in which persons feel detached and disconnected from themselves, their bodies, and their surroundings. 540

depressants drugs that decrease the functioning of the nervous system. 157

depth perception the ability to perceive the world in three dimensions. 118

deviation IQ scores a type of intelligence measure that assumes that IQ is normally distributed around a mean of 100 with a standard deviation of about 15. 277

diffusion of responsibility occurring when a person fails to take responsibility for actions or for inaction because of the presence of other people who are seen to share the responsibility. 510

directive therapy in which the therapist actively gives interpretations of a client's statements and may suggest certain behaviour or actions. 570

direct observation assessment in which the professional observes the client engaged in ordinary, day-to-day behaviour in either a clinical or natural setting. 466

discrimination behaving differently toward people based solely or primarily on their membership within a social group. 496

discriminative stimulus any stimulus, such as a stop sign or a doorknob, that provides the organism with a cue for making a certain response in order to obtain reinforcement. 197

disorganized type of schizophrenia in which behaviour is bizarre and childish and thinking, speech, and motor actions are very disordered. 551

displaced aggression taking out one's frustrations on some less threatening or more available target; a form of displacement. 407

displacement psychological defence mechanism in which emotional reactions and behavioural responses are shifted to targets that are more available or less threatening than the original target. 407

display rules learned ways of controlling displays of emotion in social settings. 381

dispositional cause cause of behaviour attributed to internal factors such as personality or character. 493

dissociative disorders disorders in which there is a break in conscious awareness, memory, the sense of identity, or some combination. 538

dissociative identity disorder disorder occurring when a person seems to have two or more distinct personalities within one body. 538

distress the effect of unpleasant and undesirable stressors. 399

disuse another name for decay, assuming that memories that are not used will eventually decay and disappear. 247

divergent thinking type of thinking in which a person starts from one point and comes up with many different ideas or possibilities based on that point. 270

dizygotic twins often called fraternal twins, occurring when two eggs each get fertilized by two different sperm, resulting in two zygotes in the uterus at the same time. 309

DNA (deoxyribonucleic acid) special molecule that contains the genetic material of the organism. 306

dominant a gene that actively controls the expression of a trait. 307

door-in-the-face technique asking for a large commitment and being refused, and then asking for a smaller commitment. 481

double-blind study study in which neither the participants nor the experimenter knows if the participants are in the experimental or control group. 29

drive a psychological tension and physical arousal arising when there is a need that motivates the organism to act in order to fulfill the need and reduce the tension. 353

drive-reduction theory approach to motivation that assumes behaviour arises from physiological needs that cause internal drives to push the organism to satisfy the need and reduce tension and arousal. 353

dysthymia a moderate depression that lasts for two years or more and is typically a reaction to some external stressor. 546

echoic memory the brief memory of something a person has just heard. 223

eclectic therapies therapy style that combines elements of several different therapy techniques. 585

egocentrism the inability to see the world through anyone else's eyes. 318

ego ideal part of the superego that contains the standards for moral behaviour. 443

ego part of the personality that develops out of a need to deal with reality; mostly conscious, rational, and logical. 443

eidetic imagery the ability to access a visual memory for 30 seconds or more. 223

elaboration likelihood model model of persuasion stating that people will either elaborate on the persuasive message or fail to elaborate on it, and that the future actions of those who do elaborate are more predictable than those who do not. 489

elaborative rehearsal a method of transferring information from STM into LTM by making that information meaningful in some way. 229

electroconvulsive therapy (ECT) form of biomedical therapy to treat severe depression in which electrodes are placed on either one or both sides of a person's head and an electric current is passed through the electrodes that is strong enough to cause a seizure or convulsion. 593

electroencephalograph (EEG) machine designed to record the brain wave patterns produced by electrical activity of the surface of the brain. 62

embryo name for the developing organism from two weeks to eight weeks after fertilization. 311

embryonic period the period from two to eight weeks after fertilization, during which the major organs and structures of the organism develop. 311

emotional intelligence the awareness of and ability to manage one's own emotions as well as the ability to be self-motivated, able to feel what others feel, and socially skilled. 285

emotion-focused coping coping strategies that change the impact of a stressor by changing the emotional reaction to the stressor. 425

emotion the "feeling" aspect of consciousness, characterized by a certain physical arousal, a certain behaviour that reveals the emotion to the outside world, and an inner awareness of feelings. 379

empathy the ability of the therapist to understand the feelings of the client. 572

encoding failure the failure to process information into memory. 247

encoding specificity the tendency for memory of any kind of information to be improved if the physical surroundings available when the memory is first formed are also available when the memory is being retrieved. 236

encoding the set of mental operations that people perform on sensory information to convert that information into a form that is usable in the brain's storage systems. 220

endocrine glands glands that secrete chemicals called hormones directly into the bloodstream. 77

episodic memory type of declarative memory containing personal information not readily available to others, such as daily activities and events. 231

equal status contact contact between groups in which the groups have equal status, with neither group having power over the other. 500

escape or withdrawal leaving the presence of a stressor, either literally or by a psychological withdrawal into fantasy, drug abuse, or apathy. 407

estrogens female sex hormones. 373

eustress the effect of positive events, or the optimal amount of stress that people need to promote health and well-being. 399

evolutionary perspective perspective that focuses on the biological bases of universal mental characteristics that all humans share. 14

excitatory synapse the effect of the neurotransmitter in the synapse causes the receiving cell to fire. 51

expectancy-value theories incentive theories that assume the actions of humans cannot be predicted or fully understood without understanding the beliefs, values, and the importance that a person attaches to those beliefs and values at any given moment in time. 357

experiment a deliberate manipulation of a variable to see if corresponding changes in behaviour result, allowing the determination of cause-and-effect relationships. 24

experimental group participants in an experiment who are exposed to the level of the independent variable that should influence the dependent variable. 26

experimenter effect tendency of the experimenter's expectations for a study to unintentionally influence the results of the study. 29

explicit memory memory that is easily made conscious and brought from long-term storage into short-term memory, such as declarative memory. 231

exposure therapies behavioural techniques that expose individuals to anxiety- or fear-related stimuli, under carefully controlled conditions, to promote new learning 575

external validity the ability to generalize the results of an experiment to real-world situations. 29

extinction the disappearance or weakening of a learned response following the removal or absence of the unconditioned stimulus (in classical conditioning) or the removal of a reinforcer (in operant conditioning). 182

extracellular thirst thirst triggered by a loss of fluid between bodily cells. 371

extraversion one of the five factors; dimension of personality referring to one's need to be with other people. 457

extraverts people who are outgoing and sociable. 457

extrinsic motivation type of motivation in which a person performs an action because of the potential external rewards that may be obtained as a result. 352

facial feedback hypothesis theory of emotion that assumes that facial expressions provide feedback to the brain concerning the emotion being expressed, which in turn causes and intensifies the emotion. 385

false positive error of recognition in which people think that they recognize some stimulus that is not actually in memory. 240

family counselling (family therapy) a form of group therapy in which family members meet together with a counsellor or therapist to resolve problems that affect the entire family. 582

fertilization the union of the ovum and sperm. 309

fetal period the time from about eight weeks after conception until the birth of the child. 313

fetus name for the developing organism from eight weeks after fertilization to the birth of the baby. 313

figure–ground the tendency to perceive objects, or figures, as existing on a background. 117

five-factor model (Big Five) model of personality traits that describes five basic trait dimensions. 457

fixation disorder in which the person does not fully resolve the conflict in a particular psychosexual stage, resulting in personality traits and behaviour associated with that earlier stage. 444

fixed interval schedule of reinforcement schedule of reinforcement in which the interval of time that must pass before reinforcement becomes possible is always the same. 199

fixed ratio schedule of reinforcement schedule of reinforcement in which the number of responses required for reinforcement is always the same. 198

flashbulb memories type of automatic encoding that occurs because an unexpected event has strong emotional associations for the person remembering it. 241

flat affect a lack of emotional responsiveness. 550

flooding technique for treating phobias and other stress disorders in which the person is rapidly and intensely exposed to the fear-provoking situation or object and prevented from making the usual avoidance or escape response. 575

foot-in-the-door technique asking for a small commitment and, after gaining compliance, asking for a bigger commitment. 481

formal concepts concepts that are defined by specific rules or features. 264

formal operations Piaget's last stage of cognitive development in which the adolescent becomes capable of abstract thinking. 319

free association Freudian technique in which a patient was encouraged to talk about anything that came to mind without fear of negative evaluations. 569

free-floating anxiety anxiety that is unrelated to any realistic, known source. 530

frequency count assessment in which the frequency of a particular behaviour is counted. 466

frequency theory theory of pitch that states that pitch is related to the speed of vibrations in the basilar membrane. 104

frontal lobes areas of the cortex located in the front and top of the brain, responsible for higher mental processes and decision making as well as the production of fluent speech. 71

frustration the psychological experience produced by the blocking of a desired goal or the fulfillment of a perceived need. 406

fully functioning person persons who are able to accept reality, live in the present, trust their judgment, acknowledge their freedom and take responsibility for their actions, and finally, make creative contributions to the world. 455

functional fixedness a block to problem solving that comes from thinking about objects in terms of only their typical functions. 268

functionalism early perspective in psychology associated with William James, in which the focus of study is how the mind allows people to adapt, live, work, and play. 8

fundamental attribution error the tendency to overestimate the influence of internal factors in determining behaviour while underestimating situational factors. 494

gender identity disorder disorder in which a person feels psychologically dissatisfied with his or her biological sex. 541

gender identity one's perception of being male or female and the behaviour that is associated with that gender. 328

gender roles the culture's expectations for masculine or feminine behaviour, including attitudes, actions, and personality traits associated with being male or female in that culture. 328

gender schema theory theory of gender identity acquisition in which a child develops a mental pattern, or schema, for being male or female and then organizes observed and learned behaviour around that schema. 331

gender the behaviour associated with being male or female. 328

gender typing the process of acquiring gender role characteristics. 328

general adaptation syndrome (GAS) the three stages of the body's physiological reaction to stress, including alarm, resistance, and exhaustion. 410

general aggression model modern theory of aggression that states that aggression stems from a wide range of variables that influence an individual's arousal, affect, and cognitions. 508

generalized anxiety disorder disorder in which a person has feelings of dread and impending doom along with physical symptoms of stress, which lasts six months or more. 533

generativity providing guidance to one's children or the next generation, or contributing to the well-being of the next generation through career or volunteer work. 339

generativity versus stagnation seventh stage of personality development in which those in middle adulthood strive to be creative, productive, and nurturant of the next generation. 339

gene section of DNA having the same arrangement of chemical elements. 306

genetics the science of inherited traits. 306

genital stage fifth and final stage, beginning in puberty and lasting into adulthood, in which the adolescent enters into adult social and sexual behaviour. 446

germinal period first two weeks after fertilization, during which the zygote moves down to the uterus and begins to implant in the lining. 311

Gestalt psychology early perspective in psychology that focuses on perception and sensation, particularly the perception of patterns and whole figures. 9

Gestalt therapy form of directive insight therapy in which the therapist helps clients accept all parts of their feelings and subjective experiences, using leading questions and planned experiences such as role-playing. 572

g factor the ability to reason and solve problems, or general intelligence. 272

gifted the 2 percent of the population falling on the upper end of the normal curve and typically possessing an IQ of 130 or above. 282

glial cells grey fatty cells that provide support for the neurons to grow on and around, deliver nutrients to neurons, produce myelin to coat axons, and clean up waste products and dead neurons. 46

glucagons hormones that are secreted by the pancreas to control the levels of fats, proteins, and carbohydrates in the body by increasing the level of glucose in the bloodstream. 365

gonads the sex glands that secrete hormones that regulate sexual development and behaviour as well as reproduction. 78

grammar the system of rules governing the structure and use of a language. 291

groupthink kind of thinking that occurs when people place more importance on maintaining group cohesiveness than on assessing the facts of the problem with which the group is concerned. 480

gustation the sensation of a taste. 106

habits in behaviourism, sets of well-learned responses that have become automatic. 451

habituation tendency of the brain to stop attending to constant, unchanging information. 92

hallucinations false sensory perceptions, such as hearing voices that do not really exist. 550

hallucinogens drugs that cause false sensory messages, altering the perception of reality. 165

halo effect tendency of an interviewer to allow positive characteristics of a client to influence the assessments of the client's behaviour and statements. 464

hardy personality a person who seems to thrive on stress but lacks the anger and hostility of the Type A personality. 418

hassles the daily annoyances of everyday life. 403

heroin narcotic drug derived from opium that is extremely addictive. 164

hertz (Hz) cycles or waves per second, a -measurement of frequency. 103

heterosexual person attracted to the opposite sex. 376

heuristic an educated guess based on prior experiences that helps narrow down the possible solutions for a problem. Also known as arule of thumb. 266

higher-order conditioning occurs when a strong conditioned stimulus is paired with a neutral stimulus, causing the neutral stimulus to become a second conditioned stimulus. 183

hippocampus curved structure located within each temporal lobe, responsible for the formation of long-term memories and the storage of memory for location of objects. 68

homeostasis the tendency of the body to maintain a steady state. 354

homosexual person attracted to the same sex. 376

hormones chemicals released into the bloodstream by endocrine glands. 77

human development the changes that occur in people as they age from conception until death. 304

humanistic perspective the "third force" in psychology that focuses on those aspects of personality that make people uniquely human, such as subjective feelings and freedom of choice. 453

hypnosis state of consciousness in which the person is especially susceptible to suggestion. 152

hypothalamus small structure in the brain located below the thalamus and directly above the pituitary gland, responsible for motivational behaviour such as sleep, hunger, thirst, and sex. 67

hypothesis tentative explanation of a phenomenon based on observations. 17

iconic memory visual sensory memory, lasting only a fraction of a second. 222

ideal self one's perception of who one should be or would like to be. 454

identification defence mechanism in which a person tries to become like someone else to deal with anxiety. 426

identity versus role confusion fifth stage of personality development in which the adolescent must find a consistent sense of self. 334

id part of the personality present at birth and completely unconscious. 442

imaginary audience type of thought common to adolescents in which young people believe that other people are just as concerned about the adolescent's thoughts and characteristics as they themselves are. 333

immune system the system of cells, organs, and chemicals in the body that responds to attacks from diseases, infections, and injuries. 412

implicit memory memory that is not easily retrieved into conscious awareness, such as procedural memory. 230

implicit personality theory sets of assumptions about how different types of people, personality traits, and actions are related to one another. 493

incentive approaches theories of motivation in which behaviour is explained as a response to the external stimulus and its rewarding properties. 357

incentives things that attract or lure people into action. 357

independent variable variable in an experiment that is manipulated by the experimenter. 25

infantile amnesia the inability to retrieve memories from much before age 3. 251

information-processing model model of memory that assumes the processing of information for memory storage is similar to the way a computer processes memory in a series of three stages. 221

in-groups social groups with whom a person identifies; "us." 496

inhibitory synapse the effect of the neurotransmitter in the synapse causes the receiving cell to stop firing. 51

insight therapies therapies in which the main goal is helping people to gain insight with respect to their behaviour, thoughts, and feelings. 566

insight the sudden perception of relationships among various parts of a problem, allowing the solution to the problem to come quickly. 207

insomnia the inability to get to sleep, stay asleep, or get a good quality of sleep. 147

instinct approach approach to motivation that assumes people are governed by instincts similar to those of other animals. 353

instincts the biologically determined and innate patterns of behaviour that exist in both people and animals. 353

insufficient justification effect when external justification is not sufficient, dissonance is reduced by internally justifying one's behaviour. 491

insulin a hormone secreted by the pancreas to control the levels of fats, proteins, and carbohydrates in the body by reducing the level of glucose in the bloodstream. 365

integrity sense of wholeness that comes from having lived a full life and the ability to let go of regrets; the final completion of the ego. 340

integrity versus despair eighth and final stage of personality development in which those in late adulthood strive to reach wisdom, spiritual tranquility, a sense of wholeness, and acceptance of his or her life. 340

intellectual disability characterized by significant limitations both in intellectual functioning and in adaptive behaviour as expressed in conceptual, social, and practical adaptive skills. 280

intelligence quotient (IQ) a number representing a measure of intelligence, resulting from the division of one's mental age by one's chronological age and then multiplying that quotient by 100. 275

intelligence the ability to learn from one's experiences, acquire knowledge, and use resources effectively in adapting to new situations or solving problems. 272

interneuron a neuron found in the centre of the spinal cord that receives information from the sensory neurons and sends commands to the muscles through the motor neurons. Interneurons also make up the bulk of the neurons in the brain. 55

interpersonal attraction liking or having the desire for a relationship with another person. 501

interposition (overlap) the assumption that an object that appears to be blocking part of another object is in front of the second object and closer to the viewer. 120

intersex congenital anomaly of the reproductive and sexual system that makes it difficult to determine an infant's sex at birth. Intersex people are born with external genitalia, an endocrine system, and/or internal reproductive organs that are different from those of most other people. 374

intersex people/people with intersex conditions/experiences people who possess ambiguous sexual organs, making it difficult to determine actual sex from a visual inspection at birth. 373

interview method of personality assessment in which the professional asks questions of the client and allows the client to answer, either in a structured or unstructured fashion. 464

intimacy an emotional and psychological closeness that is based on the ability to trust, share, and care, while still maintaining a sense of self. 338

intimacy versus isolation sixth stage of personality development in which in which those in early adulthood strive to share who they are with another person in a close, committed relationship. 339

intracellular thirst thirst triggered by a loss of fluid within bodily cells. 371

intrinsic motivation type of motivation in which a person performs an action because the act itself is rewarding or satisfying in some internal manner. 352

introversion dimension of personality in which people tend to withdraw from excessive stimulation. 456

introverts people who prefer solitude and dislike being the centre of attention. 457

irreversibility in Piaget's theory, the inability of the young child to mentally reverse an action. 318

James–Lange theory of emotion theory in which a physiological reaction leads to the labelling of an emotion. 383

"jigsaw classroom" educational technique in which each individual is given only part of the information needed to solve a problem, causing the separate individuals to be forced to work together to find the solution. 500

just noticeable difference (jnd, or the difference threshold) the smallest difference between two stimuli that is detectable 50 percent of the time. 91

kinesthetic sense sense of the location of body parts in relation to the ground and each other. 111

language a system for combining symbols (such as words) so that an unlimited number of meaningful statements can be made for the purpose of communicating with others. 291

latency fourth stage, occurring during the school years, in which the sexual feelings of the child are repressed while the child develops in other ways. 446

latent content the symbolic or hidden meaning of dreams. 569

latent learning learning that remains hidden until its application becomes useful. 205

Law of Effect law stating that if a response is followed by a pleasurable consequence, it will tend to be repeated, and if followed by an unpleasant consequence, it will tend not to be repeated. 189

learned helplessness the tendency to fail to act to escape from a situation because of a history of repeated failures in the past. 207

learning/performance distinction referring to the observation that learning can take place without actual performance of the learned behaviour. 208

leptin a hormone that, when released into the bloodstream, signals the hypothalamus that the body has had enough food and reduces the appetite while increasing the feeling of being full. 366

levels-of-processing model model of memory that assumes information that is more "deeply processed," or proc-essed according to its meaning rather than just the sound or physical characteristics of the word or words, will be remembered more efficiently and for a longer period of time. 234

libido the instinctual energy that may come into conflict with the demands of a society's standards for behaviour. 442

light adaptation the recovery of the eye's sensitivity to visual stimuli in light after exposure to darkness. 98

limbic system a group of several brain structures located under the cortex and involved in learning, emotion, memory, and motivation. 66

linear perspective the tendency for parallel lines to appear to converge on each other. 120

linguistic relativity hypothesis the theory that thought processes and concepts are controlled by language. 293

longitudinal design research design in which one participant or group of participants is studied over a long period of time. 304

long-term memory (LTM) the system of memory into which all the information is placed to be kept more or less permanently. 227

lowball technique getting a commitment from a person and then raising the cost of that commitment. 481

LSD (lysergic acid diethylamide) powerful synthetic hallucinogen. 165

magnetic resonance imaging (MRI) brain-imaging method using radio waves and magnetic fields of the body to produce detailed images of the brain. 64

magnification the tendency to interpret situations as far more dangerous, harmful, or important than they actually are. 534

mainstreaming process of educating students with intellectual disabilities in regular schools, often in classes with students without intellectual disabilities. 281

maintenance rehearsal practice of saying some information to be remembered over and over in one's head to maintain it in short-term memory. 227

major depression severe depression that comes on suddenly and seems to have no external cause. 546

maladaptive anything that does not allow a person to function within or adapt to the stresses and everyday demands of life. 524

mammary glands glands within the breast tissue that produce milk when a woman gives birth to an infant. 373

manic having the quality of excessive excitement, energy, and elation or irritability. 547

manifest content the actual content of one's dream. 569

marijuana (pot or weed) mild hallucinogen derived from the leaves and flowers of a particular type of hemp plant. 167

MDMA (Ecstasy or X) designer drug that can have both stimulant and hallucinatory effects. 166

means–end analysis heuristic in which the difference between the starting situation and the goal is determined and then steps are taken to reduce that difference. 267

meditation mental series of exercises meant to refocus attention and achieve a trancelike state of consciousness. 427

medulla the first large swelling at the top of the spinal cord, forming the lowest part of the brain, which is responsible for life-sustaining functions such as breathing, swallowing, and heart rate. 64

memory as an active system that receives information from the senses, organizes and alters the information as it stores it away, and then retrieves the information from storage. 220

memory trace physical change in the brain that occurs when a memory is formed. 247

menopause the cessation of ovulation and menstrual cycles and the end of a woman's reproductive capability. 337

menstrual cycle monthly shedding of the blood and tissue that line the uterus (in preparation for pregnancy) when conception does not occur. 372

mental images mental representations that stand for objects or events and have a picture-like quality. 262

mental set the tendency for people to persist in using problem-solving patterns that have worked for them in the past. 269

mescaline natural hallucinogen derived from peyote cactus buttons. 166

microsleeps brief sidesteps into sleep lasting only a few seconds. 139

minimization the tendency to give little or no importance to one's successes or positive events and traits. 534

mirror neurons neurons that fire when an animal or person performs an action and also when an animal or person observes that same action being performed by another. 79

misinformation effect the tendency of misleading information presented after an event to alter the memories of the event itself. 243

modelling learning through the observation and imitation of others. 577

monocular cues (pictorial depth cues) cues for perceiving depth based on one eye only. 120

monozygotic twins identical twins formed when one zygote splits into two separate masses of cells, each of which develops into a separate embryo. 309

mood disorders a disturbance in emotion; also referred to as affective disorders. 545

morphemes the smallest units of meaning within a language. 291

morphine narcotic drug derived from opium, used to treat severe pain. 164

motion parallax the perception of motion of objects in which close objects appear to move more quickly than objects that are farther away. 120

motivation the process by which activities are started, directed, and continued so that physical or psychological needs or wants are met. 352

motor cortex section of the frontal lobe located at the back, responsible for sending motor commands to the muscles of the somatic nervous system. 71

motor neuron a neuron that carries messages from the central nervous system to the muscles and the glands of the body. Also called an efferent neuron. 55

Müller-Lyer illusion illusion of line length that is distorted by inward-turning or outward-turning corners on the ends of the lines, causing lines of equal length to appear to be different. 122

myelin fatty substances produced by certain glial cells that coat the axons of neurons to insulate, protect, and speed up the neural impulse. 46

narcolepsy sleep disorder in which a person falls immediately into REM sleep during the day without warning. 148

narcotics a class of opium-related drugs that suppress the sensation of pain by binding to and stimulating the nervous system's natural receptor sites for endorphins. 157

natural concepts concepts people form as a result of their experiences in the world. 264

natural killer cell immune system cell responsible for suppressing viruses and destroying tumour cells. 414

nature the influence of our inherited characteristics on our personality, physical growth, intellectual growth, and social interactions. 305

need a requirement of some material (such as food or water) that is essential for survival of the organism. 353

need for achievement (nAch) a need that involves a strong desire to succeed in attaining goals, not only realistic ones but also challenging ones. 354

need for affiliation (nAff) the need for friendly social interactions and relationships with others. 355

need for autonomy the psychological need that involves knowing that one's actions are self-determined rather than controlled by others. 360

need for competence the psychological need that humans have to succeed at challenging tasks and to receive positive feedback from others. 361

need for power (nPow) the need to have control or influence over others. 355

need for relatedness the psychological needs that humans have to form emotional bonds with those around them. 362

negative reinforcement the reinforcement of a response by the removal, escape from, or avoidance of an unpleasant stimulus. 192

negative symptoms symptoms of schizophrenia that are less than normal behaviour or an absence of normal behaviour; poor attention, flat affect, and poor speech production. 551

neo-Freudians followers of Freud who developed their own competing theories of psychoanalysis. 447

nerves bundles of axons coated in myelin that travel together through the body. 46

nervous system an extensive network of specialized cells that carries information to and from all parts of the body. 44

neurofeedback form of biofeedback using brain-scanning devices to provide feedback about brain activity in an effort to modify behaviour. 202

neuron the basic cell that makes up the nervous system and that receives and sends messages within that system. 45

neuroscience a branch of the life sciences that deals with the structure and function of neurons, nerves, and nervous tissue, especially focusing on their relationship to behaviour and learning. 45

neuroticism one of the five factors; degree of emotional instability or stability. 457

neurotic personalities maladaptive ways of dealing with relationships in Horney's theory. 449

neurotransmitter chemical found in the synaptic vesicles that, when released, has an effect on the next cell. 50

neutral stimulus (NS) stimulus that has no effect on the desired response. 180

nicotine the active ingredient in tobacco. 159

nightmares bad dreams occurring during REM sleep. 145

night terrors relatively rare disorder in which the person experiences extreme fear and screams or runs around during deep sleep without waking fully. 145

non-directive therapy style in which the therapist remains relatively neutral and does not interpret or take direct actions with regard to the client, instead remaining a calm, non-judgmental listener while the client talks. 571

non-REM (NREM) sleep any of the stages of sleep that do not include REM. 142

norm of reciprocity assumption that if someone does something for a person, that person should do something for the other in return. 481

nurture the influence of the environment on personality, physical growth, intellectual growth, and social interactions. 305

obedience changing one's behaviour at the command of an authority figure. 482

objective introspection the process of examining and measuring one's own thoughts and mental activities. 7

object permanence the knowledge that an object exists even when it is not in sight. 317

observational learning learning new behaviour by watching a model perform that behaviour. 208

observer bias tendency of observers to see what they expect to see. 20

observer effect tendency of people or animals to behave differently from normal when they know they are being observed. 20

obsessive-compulsive disorder disorder in which intruding, recurring thoughts or obsessions create anxiety that is relieved by performing a repetitive, ritualistic behaviour (compulsion). 532

occipital lobe section of the brain located at the rear and bottom of each cerebral hemisphere containing the visual centres of the brain. 69

Oedipus complex situation, occurring in the phallic stage, in which a child develops a sexual attraction to the opposite-sex parent and jealousy of the same-sex parent. 445

olfaction (olfactory sense) the sensation of smell. 108

olfactory bulbs areas of the brain located just above the sinus cavity and just below the frontal lobes that receive information from the olfactory receptor cells. 109

openness to experience one of the five factors; willingness to try new things and be open to new experiences. 457

operant any behaviour that is voluntary. 190

operant conditioning the learning of voluntary behaviour through the effects of pleasant and unpleasant consequences to responses. 189

operational definition a researcher's definition of a variable of interest that precisely describes the variable and how it is to be measured. 25

opium substance derived from the opium poppy, from which all narcotic drugs are derived. 164

opponent-process theory theory of colour vision that proposes four primary colours with cones arranged in pairs: red and green, and blue and yellow. 99

optimists people who expect positive outcomes. 418

oral stage first stage, occurring in the first year of life, in which the mouth is the erogenous zone and weaning is the primary conflict. 445

organic or stress-induced dysfunction sexual problem caused by physical disorder or psychological stress. 542

out-groups social groups with whom a person does not identify; "them." 496

ovaries the female gonads. 78

ovaries the female sexual glands. 372

overgeneralization distortion of thinking in which a person draws sweeping conclusions based on only one incident or event and applies those conclusions to events that are unrelated to the original. 579

overgeneralization the tendency to interpret a single negative event as a never-ending pattern of defeat and failure. 534

ovum the female sex cell, or egg. 309

pancreas endocrine gland that controls the levels of sugar in the blood. 78

panic attack sudden onset of intense panic in which multiple physical symptoms of stress occur, often with feelings that one is dying. 532

panic disorder disorder in which panic attacks occur frequently enough to cause the person difficulty in adjusting to daily life. 533

panic disorder with agoraphobia fear of leaving one's familiar surroundings because one might have a panic attack in public. 533

parallel distributed processing (PDP) model a model of memory in which memory processes are proposed to take place at the same time over a large network of neural connections. 235

paranoid type of schizophrenia in which the person suffers from delusions of persecution, grandeur, and jealousy, together with hallucinations. 551

parapsychology the study of ESP, ghosts, and other subjects that do not normally fall into the realm of ordinary psychology. 125

parasympathetic division part of the ANS that restores the body to normal functioning after arousal and is responsible for the day-to-day functioning of the organs and glands. 61

parietal lobes sections of the brain located at the top and back of each cerebral hemisphere containing the centres for touch, taste, and temperature sensations. 70

partial reinforcement effect the tendency for a response that is reinforced after some, but not all, correct responses to be very resistant to extinction. 198

participant modelling technique in which a model demonstrates the desired behaviour in a step-by-step, gradual process while the client is encouraged to imitate the model. 577

participant observation a naturalistic observation in which the observer becomes a participant in the group being observed. 20

PCP synthesized drug now used as an animal tranquilizer that can cause stimulant, depressant, narcotic, or hallucinogenic effects. 165

peak experiences according to Maslow, times in a person's life during which self-actualization is temporarily achieved. 358

pedophile a person who has recurring sexual thoughts, fantasies, or engages in sexual actions toward prepubescent (non-sexually mature) children. 544

pedophilia deriving sexual arousal and pleasure from touching or having sexual relations with prepubescent (non-sexually mature) children or fantasizing about such contact. 544

penis male reproductive organ that contains the urethra, which releases both urine and sperm. 372

perception the method by which the sensations experienced at any given moment are interpreted and organized in some meaningful fashion. 115

perceptual set (perceptual expectancy) the tendency to perceive things a certain way because previous experiences or expectations influence those perceptions. 124

peripheral nervous system (PNS) all nerves and neurons that are not contained in the brain and spinal cord but that run through the body itself. 58

peripheral-route processing (heuristic processing) type of information processing that involves attending to factors not involved in the message, such as the appearance of the source of the message, the length of the message, and other non-content factors. 491

permissive indulgent parenting style of permissive parenting in which parents are so involved that children are allowed to behave without set limits. 339

permissive neglectful parenting style of permissive parenting in which parents are uninvolved with child or child's behaviour. 339

permissive parenting style of parenting in which parent makes few, if any, demands on a child's behaviour. 339

personal fable type of thought common to adolescents in which young people believe themselves to be unique and protected from harm. 333

personality disorders disorders in which a person adopts a persistent, rigid, and maladaptive pattern of behaviour that interferes with normal social interactions. 553

personality inventory paper and pencil or computerized test that consists of statements that require a specific, standardized response from the person taking the test. 466

personality the unique and relatively stable ways in which people think, feel, and behave. 440

personalization distortion of thinking in which a person takes responsibility or blame for events that are unconnected to the person. 579

personal unconscious Jung's name for the unconscious mind as described by Freud. 447

person-centred therapy a less-directive insight therapy based on the work of Carl Rogers in which the client does all the talking and the therapist listens. 571

persuasion the process by which one person tries to change the belief, opinion, position, or course of action of another person through argument, pleading, or explanation. 488

pessimists people who expect negative outcomes. 418

phallic stage third stage, occurring from about 3 to 6 years of age, in which the child discovers sexual feelings. 445

phobia an irrational, persistent fear of an object, situation, or social activity. 530

phonemes the basic units of sound in language. 291

pineal gland endocrine gland located near the base of the cerebrum that secretes melatonin. 78

pitch psychological experience of sound that corresponds to the frequency of the sound waves; higher frequencies are perceived as higher pitches. 104

pituitary gland gland located in the brain that secretes human growth hormone and influences all other hormone-secreting glands (also known as the master gland). 77

placebo effect the phenomenon in which the expectations of the participants in a study can influence their behaviour. 28

place theory theory of pitch that states that different pitches are experienced by the stimulation of hair cells in different locations on the organ of Corti. 104

pleasure principle principle by which the id functions; the immediate satisfaction of needs without regard for the consequences. 442

pons the larger swelling above the medulla that connects the top of the brain to the bottom and plays a part in sleep, dreaming, left–right body coordination, and arousal. 65

population the entire group of people or animals in which the researcher is interested. 21

positive regard warmth, affection, love, and respect that come from the significant others in one's life. 454

positive reinforcement the reinforcement of a response by the addition or experiencing of a pleasurable stimulus. 192

positive symptoms symptoms of schizophrenia that are excesses of behaviour or occur in addition to normal behaviour; hallucinations, delusions, and distorted thinking. 551

positron emission tomography (PET) brain-imaging method in which a radioactive sugar is injected into the subject and a computer compiles a colour-coded image of the activity of the brain, with lighter colours indicating more activity. 64

postconventional morality third level of Kohlberg's stages of moral development in which the person's behaviour is governed by moral principles that have been decided on by the individual and which may be in disagreement with accepted social norms. 334

post-traumatic stress disorder (PTSD) a disorder resulting from exposure to a major stressor, with symptoms of anxiety, nightmares, poor sleep, reliving the event, and concentration problems, lasting for more than one month. 400

practical intelligence the ability to use information to get along in life and become successful. 274

pragmatics aspects of language involving the practical ways of communicating with others, or the social "niceties" of language. 292

preconscious mind level of the mind in which information is available but not currently conscious. 441

preconventional morality first level of Kohlberg's stages of moral development in which the child's behaviour is governed by the consequences of the behaviour. 334

prefrontal lobotomy psychosurgery in which the connections of the prefrontal lobes of the brain to the rear portions are severed. 594

prejudice an unsupported and often negative attitude about the members of a particular social group. 496

preoperational stage Piaget's second stage of cognitive development in which the preschool child learns to use language as a means of exploring the world. 317

pressure the psychological experience produced by urgent demands or expectations for a person's behaviour that come from an outside source. 405

primacy effect tendency to remember information at the beginning of a body of information better than the information that follows. 238

primary appraisal the first step in assessing stress, which involves estimating the severity of the stressor and classifying it as either a threat or a challenge. 414

primary drives those drives that involve biological needs of the body such as hunger and thirst. 353

primary reinforcer any reinforcer that is naturally reinforcing by meeting a basic biological need, such as hunger, thirst, or touch. 191

primary sex characteristics sexual organs present at birth and directly involved in human reproduction. 372

proactive interference memory retrieval problem that occurs when older information prevents or interferes with the retrieval of newer information. 248

problem-focused coping coping strategies that try to eliminate the source of a stress or reduce its impact through direct actions. 424

problem solving process of cognition that occurs when a goal must be reached by thinking and behaving in certain ways. 265

procedural (non-declarative) memory type of long-term memory that includes memory for skills, emotional responses, habits, and simple conditioned reflexes. These memories are not conscious but are implied to exist because they affect conscious behaviour. 230

projection defence mechanism involving placing, or "projecting," one's own unacceptable thoughts onto others, as if the thoughts actually belonged to those others and not to oneself. 464

projection psychological defence mechanism in which unacceptable or threatening impulses or feelings are seen as originating with someone else, usually the target of the impulses or feelings. 426

projective tests personality assessments that present ambiguous visual stimuli to the client and ask the client to respond with whatever comes to mind. 464

prosocial behaviour socially desirable behaviour that benefits others. 508

prostate gland gland that secretes most of the fluid that carries the male sex cells, or sperm. 372

prototype an example of a concept that closely matches the defining characteristics of a concept. 264

proximity physical or geographical nearness. 501

proximity the tendency to perceive objects that are close to each other as part of the same grouping. 117

pseudo-psychologies systems of explaining human behaviour that are not based on or consistent with scientific evidence. 34

psilocybin natural hallucinogen found in certain mushrooms. 166

psychiatric social worker a social worker with some training in therapy methods who focuses on the environmental conditions that can have an impact on mental disorders, such as poverty, overcrowding, stress, and drug abuse. 16

psychiatrist a medical doctor who has specialized in the diagnosis and treatment of psychological disorders. 15

psychoactive drugs drugs that alter thinking, perception, and memory. 156

psychoanalysis an insight therapy based on the theory of Freud, emphasizing the revealing of unconscious conflicts. 568

psychoanalysis Freud's term for both the theory of personality and the therapy based on it. 447

psychoanalysis the theory and therapy based on the work of Sigmund Freud. 9

psychoanalyst either a psychiatrist or a psychologist who has special training in the theories of Sigmund Freud and his method of psychoanalysis. 15

psychodynamic perspective modern version of psychoanalysis that is more focused on the development of a sense of self and the discovery of other motivations behind a person's behaviour than sexual motivations. 11

psychodynamic therapy a newer and more general term for therapies based on psychoanalysis, with an emphasis on transference, shorter treatment times, and a more direct therapeutic approach. 570

psychogenic drugs drugs including hallucinogens and marijuana that produce hallucinations or increased feelings of relaxation and intoxication. 157

psychological defence mechanisms unconscious distortions of a person's perception of reality that reduce stress and anxiety. 426

psychological dependence the feeling that a drug is needed to continue a feeling of emotional or psychological well-being. 156

psychological disorders any pattern of behaviour that causes people significant distress, causes them to harm others, or harms their ability to function in daily life. 524

psychologist a professional with an academic degree and specialized training in one or more areas of psychology. 16

psychology the scientific study of behaviour and mental processes. 4

psychoneuroimmunology the study of the effects of psychological factors such as stress, emotions, thoughts, and behaviour on the immune system. 412

psychopathology the study of abnormal behaviour. 522

psychopharmacology the use of drugs to control or relieve the symptoms of psychological disorders. 589

psychophysiological disorder modern term for psychosomatic disorder. 536

psychosexual stages five stages of personality development proposed by Freud and tied to the sexual development of the child. 444

psychosomatic disorder disorder in which psychological stress causes a real physical disorder or illness. 536

psychosurgery surgery performed on brain tissue to relieve or control severe psychological disorders. 594

psychotherapy therapy for mental disorders in which a person with a problem talks with a psychological professional. 566

psychotic the break away from an ability to perceive what is real and what is fantasy. 549

puberty the physical changes that occur in the body as sexual development reaches its peak. 332

punishment any event or object that, when following a response, makes that response less likely to happen again. 193

punishment by application the punishment of a response by the addition or experiencing of an unpleasant stimulus. 193

punishment by removal the punishment of a response by the removal of a pleasurable stimulus. 193

random assignment process of assigning subjects or participants to the experimental or control groups randomly, so that each subject or participant has an equal chance of being in either group. 27

rapid eye movement (REM) stage of sleep in which the eyes move rapidly under the eyelids and the person is typically experiencing a dream. 142

rating scale assessment in which a numerical value is assigned to specific behaviour that is listed in the scale. 466

rational-emotive behaviour therapy (REBT) cognitive-behavioural therapy in which clients are directly challenged in their irrational beliefs and helped to restructure their thinking into more rational belief statements. 580

rationalization psychological defence mechanism in which a person invents acceptable excuses for unacceptable behaviour. 426

reaction formation psychological defence mechanism in which a person forms an opposite emotional or behavioural reaction to the way he or she really feels to keep those true feelings hidden from the self and others. 426

realistic conflict theory theory stating that prejudice and discrimination will be increased between groups that are in conflict (e.g., competing for limited resources). 500

reality principle principle by which the ego functions; the satisfaction of the demands of the id only when negative consequences will not result. 443

real self one's perception of actual characteristics, traits, and abilities. 454

recall type of memory retrieval in which the information to be retrieved must be "pulled" from memory with very few external cues. 238

recency effect tendency to remember information at the end of a body of information better than the information ahead of it. 239

receptive meditation form of meditation in which a person attempts to become aware of everything in immediate conscious experience, or an expansion of consciousness. 428

receptor sites holes in the surface of the dendrites or certain cells of the muscles and glands, which are shaped to fit only certain neurotransmitters. 51

recessive a gene that influences the expression of a trait only when paired with an identical gene. 307

reciprocal determinism Bandura's explanation of how the factors of environment, personal characteristics, and behaviour can interact to determine future behaviour. 452

reciprocity of liking tendency of people to like other people who like them in return. 502

recognition the ability to match a piece of in-formation or a stimulus to a stored image or fact. 238

reflection therapy technique in which the therapist restates what the client says rather than interpreting those statements. 571

reflex arc the connection of the sensory neurons to the interneurons to the motor neurons, resulting in a reflex action. 55

regression psychological defence mechanism in which a person falls back on childlike patterns of responding in reaction to stressful situations. 426

reinforcement any event or stimulus that, when following a response, increases the probability that the response will occur again. 190

reinforcer any event or object that, when following a response, increases the likelihood of that response occurring again. 182

relative size perception that occurs when objects that a person expects to be of a certain size appear to be small and are therefore assumed to be much farther away. 120

reliability the tendency of a test to produce the same scores again and again each time it is given to the same person. 276

REM behaviour disorder a rare disorder in which the mechanism that blocks the movement of the voluntary muscles fails, allowing the person to thrash around and even get up and act out nightmares. 146

REM rebound increased amounts of REM sleep after being deprived of REM sleep on earlier nights. 146

replicate in research, repeating a study or experiment to see if the same results will be obtained, in an effort to demonstrate reliability of results. 19

representative sample randomly selected sample of subjects or participants from a larger population of subjects or participants. 21

repression psychological defence mechanism in which the person refuses to consciously remember a threatening or unacceptable event, instead "pushing" those events into the unconscious mind. 426

residual type of schizophrenia in which there are no delusions and hallucinations, but the person still experiences negative thoughts, poor language skills, and odd behaviour. 551

resistance occurring when a patient becomes reluctant to talk about a certain topic, either changing the subject or becoming silent.   569

resting membrane potential the state of the neuron when not firing a neural impulse.   47

restorative theory theory of sleep proposing that sleep is necessary to the physical health of the body and serves to replenish chemicals and repair cellular damage.   140

reticular formation (RF) an area of neurons running through the middle of the medulla and the pons and slightly beyond that is responsible for selective attention.   65

retrieval cue a stimulus for remembering.   236

retrieval getting information that is in storage into a form that can be used.   221

retroactive interference memory retrieval problem that occurs when newer information prevents or interferes with the retrieval of older information.   248

retrograde amnesia loss of memory from the point of some injury or trauma backward, or loss of memory for the past.   250

reuptake process by which neurotransmitters are taken back into the synaptic vesicles.   54

reversible figures visual illusions in which the figure and ground can be reversed.   117

rods visual sensory receptors found at the back of the retina, responsible for non-colour sensitivity to low levels of light.   96

romantic love type of love consisting of intimacy and passion.   502

Rorschach inkblot test projective test that uses 10 inkblots as the ambiguous stimuli.   465

scaffolding process in which a more skilled learner gives help to a less skilled learner, reducing the amount of help as the less skilled learner becomes more capable.   320

schema a mental concept formed through experiences with objects and events.   316

schizophrenia severe disorder in which the person suffers from disordered thinking, bizarre behaviour, hallucinations, and is unable to distinguish between fantasy and reality.   549

scientific method system of gathering data so that bias and error in measurement are reduced.   17

scrotum external sack that holds the testes.   372

seasonal affective disorder (SAD) a mood disorder caused by the body's reaction to low levels of sunlight in the winter months.   138

secondary appraisal the second step in assessing a threat, which involves estimating the resources available to the person for coping with the stressor.   415

secondary reinforcer any reinforcer that becomes reinforcing after being paired with a primary reinforcer, such as praise, tokens, or gold stars.   191

secondary sex characteristics sexual organs and traits that develop at puberty and are indirectly involved in human reproduction.   372

seduction hypothesis Freud's original belief that sexual abuse was responsible for causing hysteria in his patients.   450

selective attention the ability to focus on only one stimulus from among all sensory input.   224

selective thinking distortion of thinking in which a person focuses on only one aspect of a situation while ignoring all other relevant aspects.   579

self-actualization according to Maslow, the point, which is seldom reached, at which people have sufficiently satisfied the lower needs and achieved their full human potential.   357

self-actualizing tendency the striving to fulfill one's innate capacities and capabilities.   454

self-concept the image of oneself that develops from interactions with important, significant people in one's life.   454

self-determination theory (SDT) theory of human motivation in which the social context of an action has an effect on the type of motivation existing for the action.   360

self-efficacy individual's perception of how effective a behaviour will be in any particular circumstance.   452

self-fulfilling prophecy the tendency of one's expectations to affect one's behaviour in such a way as to make the expectation more likely to occur.   499

self-help groups (support groups) a group composed of people who have similar problems and who meet together without a therapist or counsellor for the purpose of discussion, problem solving, and social and emotional support.   582

self-serving bias the tendency to see and represent oneself in the most positive way possible.   495

semantic memory type of declarative memory containing general knowledge, such as knowledge of language and information learned in formal education.   231

semantic network model model of memory organization that as-sumes information is stored in the brain in a connected fashion, with concepts that are related stored physically closer to each other than concepts that are not highly related.   232

semantics the rules for determining the meaning of words and sentences.   291

sensation seeker someone who needs more arousal than the average person.   356

sensation the activation of receptors in the various sense organs.   90

sensorimotor stage Piaget's first stage of cognitive development in which the infant uses its senses and motor abilities to interact with objects in the environment.   317

sensory adaptation tendency of sensory receptor cells to become less responsive to a stimulus that is unchanging.   93

sensory conflict theory an explanation of motion sickness in which the information from the eyes conflicts with the information from the vestibular senses, resulting in dizziness, nausea, and other physical discomforts.   114

sensory memory the first stage of memory, the point at which information enters the nervous system through the sensory systems.   222

sensory neuron a neuron that carries information from the senses to the central nervous system. Also called an afferent neuron.   55

serial position effect tendency of information at the beginning and the end of a body of information to be remembered more easily and accurately than information in the middle of the body of information.   238

sexsomnia a rare Stage Four sleep disorder in which persons may groan loudly, masturbate, or even sexually assault a partner without waking and with no memory of their behaviour.   144

sexual deviance sexual behaviour that is unacceptable according to societal norms and expectations.   376

sexual dysfunction a problem in sexual functioning.   541

sexual orientation a person's sexual attraction preference for members of a particular sex. 376

s factor the ability to excel in certain areas, or specific intelligence. 272

shape constancy the tendency to interpret the shape of an object as being constant, even when its shape changes on the retina. 116

shaping the reinforcement of simple steps in behaviour that lead to a desired, more complex behaviour. 196

short-term memory (STM) the memory system in which information is held for brief periods of time while being used. 224

similarity the tendency to perceive things that look similar to each other as being part of the same group. 117

single-blind study study in which the participants do not know if they are in the experimental or the control group. 29

situational cause cause of behaviour attributed to external factors, such as delays, the action of others, or some other aspect of the situation. 493

situational context the social or environmental setting of a person's behaviour. 523

size constancy the tendency to interpret an object as always being the same actual size, regardless of its distance from the viewer. 115

skin senses the sensations of touch, pressure, temperature, and pain. 110

sleep apnea disorder in which the person stops breathing for nearly half a minute or more. 148

sleep deprivation any significant loss of sleep, resulting in problems in concentration and irritability. 140

sleepwalking (somnambulism) occurring during deep sleep, an episode of moving around or walking around in one's sleep. 144

social categorization the assignment of a person one has just met to a category based on characteristics the new person has in common with other people with whom one has had experience in the past. 493

social cognition the mental processes that people use to make sense of the social world around them. 486

social cognitive learning theorists theorists who emphasize the importance of both the influences of other people's behaviour and of a person's own expectancies on learning. 451

social-cognitive theory of hypnosis theory that people who are hypnotized are not in an altered state but are merely playing the role expected of them in the situation. 155

social cognitive theory theory in which cognitive processes are used in relation to understanding the social world. 498

social cognitive view learning theory that includes cognitive processes such as anticipating, judging, memory, and imitation of models. 451

social comparison the comparison of oneself to others to judge how well one is doing at something and how accurate one's attitudes and perceptions are, often in ways that raise one's self-esteem. 498

social facilitation the tendency for the presence of other people to have a positive impact on the performance of an easy task. 484

social identity theory theory in which the formation of a person's identity within a particular social group is explained by social categorization, social identity, and social comparison. 498

social identity the part of the self-concept that includes one's view of self as a member of a particular social category. 498

social impairment the tendency for the presence of other people to have a negative impact on the performance of a challenging task. 484

social influence the process through which the real or implied presence of others can directly or indirectly influence the thoughts, feelings, and behaviour of an individual. 478

social loafing the tendency for people to put less effort into a simple task when working with others on that task. 485

social phobia fear of interacting with others or being in social situations that might lead to a negative evaluation. 531

social psychology the scientific study of how a person's thoughts, feelings, and behaviour are influenced by the real, imagined, or implied presence of others. 478

Social Readjustment Rating Scale (SRRS) assessment that measures the amount of stress in a person's life over a one-year period resulting from major life events. 401

social-responsibility norm social expectation that people will help those who are dependent on them for help. 509

social role the pattern of behaviour that is expected of a person who is in a particular social position. 506

social support system the network of family, friends, neighbours, co-workers, and others who can offer support, comfort, or aid to a person in need. 423

sociocultural perspective perspective that focuses on the relationship between social behaviour and culture. 14

soma the cell body of the neuron responsible for maintaining the life of the cell. 45

somatic nervous system division of the PNS consisting of nerves that carry information from the senses to the CNS and from the CNS to the voluntary muscles of the body. 58

somatoform disorders disorders that take the form of bodily illnesses and symptoms but for which there are no real physical disorders. 536

somatosensory cortex area of neurons running down the front of the parietal lobes responsible for processing information from the skin and internal body receptors for touch, temperature, body position, and possibly taste. 70

somesthetic senses the body senses, consisting of the skin senses, the kinesthetic sense, and the vestibular senses. 110

source traits the more basic traits that underlie the surface traits, forming the core of personality. 456

spatial neglect condition produced by damage to the association areas of the right hemisphere resulting in an inability to recognize objects or body parts in the left visual field. 74

specific phobia fear of objects or specific situations or events. 531

spinal cord a long bundle of neurons that carries messages to and from the body and to and from the brain. Is responsible for a variety of life-saving reflexes. 55

spontaneous recovery the reappearance of a learned response after extinction has occurred. 182

stem cells special cells found in all the tissues of the body that are capable of manufacturing other cell types when those cells need to be replaced because of damage or wear and tear. 57

stereotype a set of characteristics that people believe is shared by all members of a particular social category. 493

stereotype vulnerability the effect that people's awareness of the stereotypes associated with their social group has on their behaviour. 499

stimulants drugs that increase the functioning of the nervous system. 157

stimulatory hallucinogenics drugs that produce a mixture of psychomotor stimulant and hallucinogenic effects. 166

stimulus discrimination the tendency to stop making a generalized response to a stimulus that is similar to the original conditioned stimulus because the similar stimulus is never paired with the unconditioned stimulus. 182

stimulus generalization the tendency to respond to a stimulus that is similar only to the original conditioned stimulus with the conditioned response. 182

stimulus motive a motive that appears to be unlearned but causes an increase in stimulation, such as curiosity. 355

stimulus substitution original theory in which Pavlov stated that classical conditioning occurred because the conditioned stimulus became a substitute for the unconditioned stimulus by being paired closely together. 187

storage holding on to information for some period of time. 220

stress-inoculation training (SIT) a problem-focused coping method that helps people identify their particular stressors and develop skills that will reduce the negative impact of those stressors. 428

stressors events that cause a stress reaction. 398

stress the physical, emotional, cognitive, and behavioural responses to events that are appraised as threatening or challenging. 398

stress-vulnerability model explanation of disorder that assumes a biological sensitivity, or vulnerability, to a certain disorder will develop under the right conditions of environmental or emotional stress. 553

structuralism early perspective in psychology associated with Wilhelm Wundt and Edward Titchener, in which the focus of study is the structure or basic elements of the mind. 7

subjective discomfort emotional distress or emotional pain. 524

subjective referring to concepts and impressions that are valid only within a particular person's perception and that may be influenced by biases, prejudice, and personal experiences. 465

sublimation channelling socially unacceptable impulses and urges into socially acceptable behaviour. 426

successive approximations small steps in behaviour, one after the other, that lead to a particular goal behaviour. 196

superego part of the personality that acts as a moral centre. 443

superordinate goals shared goals that can be achieved only through cooperation and that can override people's differences from one another. 500

surface traits aspects of personality that can easily be seen by other people in the outward actions of a person. 456

sympathetic division (fight-or-flight system) part of the ANS that is responsible for reacting to stressful events and bodily arousal. 59

synapse (synaptic gap) microscopic fluid-filled space between the synaptic knob of one cell and the dendrites or surface of the next cell. 50

synaptic knob rounded areas on the end of the axon terminals. 50

synaptic vesicles saclike structures found inside the synaptic knob containing chemicals. 50

synesthesia a rare condition in which some of the signals from the various sensory organs are processed in the wrong cortical areas, resulting in the sense information being interpreted as more than one sensation. 92

syntax the system of rules for combining words and phrases to form grammatically correct sentences. 291

systematic desensitization behaviour technique used to treat phobias, in which a client is asked to make a list of ordered fears and taught to relax while concentrating on those fears. 574

temperament the behavioural characteristics that are fairly well established at birth, such as easy, difficult, and slow to warm up. 323

temperament the enduring characteristics with which each person is born. 440

temporal lobes areas of the cortex located just behind the temples containing the neurons responsible for the sense of hearing and meaningful speech. 70

teratogen any factor that can cause a birth defect. 313

testes (testicles) the male sex glands. 372

testes the male gonads. 78

texture gradient the tendency for textured surfaces to appear to become smaller and finer as distance from the viewer increases. 120

thalamus part of the limbic system located in the centre of the brain, this structure relays sensory information from the lower part of the brain to the proper areas of the cortex and processes some sensory information before sending it to its proper area. 67

that's-not-all technique a sales technique in which the persuader makes an offer and then adds something extra to make the offer look better before the target person can make a decision. 481

Thematic Apperception Test (TAT) projective test that uses 20 pictures of people in ambiguous situations as the visual stimuli. 465

therapeutic alliance the relationship between therapist and client that develops as a warm, caring, accepting relationship characterized by empathy, mutual respect, and understanding. 586

therapy treatment methods aimed at making people feel better and function more effectively. 566

theta waves brain waves indicating the early stages of sleep. 142

thinking (cognition) mental activity that goes on in the brain when a person is organizing and attempting to understand information and communicating information to others. 262

thyroid gland endocrine gland found in the neck that regulates metabolism. 78

time out an extinction process in which a person is removed from the situation that provides reinforcement for undesirable behaviour, usually by being placed in a quiet corner or room away from possible attention and reinforcement opportunities. 578

token economy the use of objects called tokens to reinforce behaviour in which the tokens can be accumulated and exchanged for desired items or privileges. 577

top-down processing the use of pre-existing knowledge to organize individual features into a unified whole. 124

trait a consistent, enduring way of thinking, feeling, or behaving. 456

trait–situation interaction the assumption that the particular circumstances of any given situation will influence the way in which a trait is expressed. 458

trait theories theories that endeavour to describe the characteristics that make up human personality in an effort to predict future behaviour. 456

transduction the process of converting outside stimuli, such as light, into neural activity. 90

transference in psychoanalysis, the tendency for a patient or client to project positive or negative feelings for important people from the past onto the therapist. 569

transvestism deriving sexual arousal and pleasure from dressing in the clothing of the opposite sex. 545

trial and error (mechanical solution) problem-solving method in which one possible solution after another is tried until a successful one is found. 266

triarchic theory of intelligence Sternberg's theory that there are three kinds of intelligences: analytical, creative, and practical. 273

trichromatic theory theory of colour vision that proposes three types of cones: red, blue, and green. 99

Type A personality person who is ambitious, time conscious, extremely hard-working, and tends to have high levels of hostility and anger as well as being easily annoyed. 416

Type B personality person who is relaxed and laid-back, less driven and competitive than Type A, and slow to anger. 417

Type C personality pleasant but repressed person, who tends to internalize his or her anger and anxiety and who finds expressing emotions difficult. 417

unconditional positive regard positive regard that is given without conditions or strings attached. 454

unconditional positive regard the warmth, respect, and accepting atmosphere created by the therapist for the client in person-centred therapy. 571

unconditioned response (UCR) an involuntary response to a naturally occurring or unconditioned stimulus. 179

unconditioned stimulus (UCS) a naturally occurring stimulus that leads to an involuntary response. 179

unconscious mind level of the mind in which thoughts, feelings, memories, and other information are kept that are not easily or voluntarily brought into consciousness. 441

undifferentiated type of schizophrenia in which the person shows no particular pattern, shifting from one pattern to another, and cannot be neatly classified as disorganized, paranoid, or catatonic. 551

unilateral ECT electroconvulsive therapy in which the electrodes are placed on only one side of the head and the forehead. 594

uterus the womb in which a fetus grows during pregnancy. 372

vagina the tube that leads from the outside of a female's body to the opening of the womb. 372

validity the degree to which a test actually measures what it's supposed to measure. 276

variable interval schedule of reinforcement schedule of reinforcement in which the interval of time that must pass before reinforcement becomes possible is different for each trial or event. 200

variable ratio schedule of reinforcement schedule of reinforcement in which the number of responses required for reinforcement is different for each trial or event 198

vestibular senses the sensations of movement, balance, and body position. 111

vicarious conditioning classical conditioning of a reflex response or emotion by watching the reaction of another person. 185

visual accommodation the change in the thickness of the lens as the eye focuses on objects that are far away or close. 95

volley principle theory of pitch that states that frequencies above 100 hertz cause the hair cells (auditory neurons) to fire in a volley pattern, or take turns in firing. 105

waking consciousness state in which thoughts, feelings, and sensations are clear and organized, and the person feels alert. 136

weight set point the particular level of weight that the body tries to maintain. 365

Wernicke's aphasia condition resulting from damage to Wernicke's area, causing the affected person to be unable to understand or produce meaningful language. 74

withdrawal physical symptoms that can include nausea, pain, tremors, crankiness, and high blood pressure, resulting from a lack of an addictive drug in the body systems. 156

working memory an active system that processes the information present in short-term memory. 225

Yerkes-Dodson law law stating that performance is related to arousal; moderate levels of arousal lead to better performance than do levels of arousal that are too low or too high. This effect varies with the difficulty of the task: easy tasks require a high-moderate level while more difficult tasks require a low-moderate level. 355

zone of proximal development (ZPD) Vygotsky's concept of the difference between what a child can do alone and what that child can do with the help of a teacher. 320

zygote cell resulting from the uniting of the ovum and sperm. 309

References

AAA Foundation for Traffic Safety. (1997). *Aggressive driving: Three studies*. Washington, DC.

Abadinsky, H. (1989). *Drug abuse: An introduction*. Chicago: Nelson-Hall Series in Law, Crime, and Justice.

Abbott, K. R., & Dukas, R. (2009). Honeybees consider flower danger in their waggle dance. *Animal Behaviour, 78,* 633–635.

Abe, K., Amatomi, M., & Oda, N. (1984). Sleepwalking and recurrent sleep talking in children of childhood sleepwalkers. *American Journal of Psychiatry, 141,* 800–801.

Abdulrehman, R. Y., & De Luca, R. V. (2001). The implications of childhood sexual abuse on adult social behaviour. *Journal of Family Violence, 16,* 193–203.

Abela, J. R. Z., & D'Allesandro, D. U. (2002). Beck's cognitive theory of depression: The diathesis-stress and causal mediation components. *British Journal of Clinical Psychology, 41,* 111–128.

Aboud, F. E., & Mendelson, M. J. (1998). Determinants of friendship selection and quality: Developmental perspectives. In W. M. Bukowski, A. F. Newcomb, & W. W. Hartup (Eds.), *The company they keep: Friendship in childhood and adolescence. Cambridge studies in social and emotional development* (pp. 87–112). New York, NY: Cambridge University Press.

Abraham, S., & Llewellyn-Jones, D. (2001). *Eating disorders, the facts* (5th ed.). London, England: Oxford University Press.

Abraham, W. C., & Williams, J. M. (2003). Properties and mechanisms of LTP maintenance. *The Neuroscientist, 9*(6), 463–474.

Abramson, L. Y., Garber, J., & Seligman, M. E. P. (1980). Learned helplessness in humans: An attributional analysis. In J. Garber & M. E. P. Seligman (Eds.), *Human helplessness* (pp. 3–34). New York, NY: Academic Press.

Abramson, L. Y., Seligman, M. E. P., & Teasdale, J. D. (1978). Learned helplessness in humans: Critique and reformulation.*Journal of Abnormal Psychology, 87,* 49–74.

Acar, N., Chardigny, J. M., Darbois, M., Pasquis, B., & Sebedio, J. L. (2003). Modification of the dopaminergic neurotransmitters in striatum, frontal cortex and hippocampus of rats fed for 21 months with trans isomers of alpha-linolenic acid. *Neuroscience Research, 45,* 375–382.

Adam, K. (1980). Sleep as a restorative process and a theory to explain why. *Progressive Brain Research, 53,* 289–305.

Adams, D. B. (1968). The activity of single cells in the midbrain and hypothalamus of the cat during affective defense behavior. *Archives Italiennes de Biologie, 106,* 243–269.

Adams, R. J. (1987). An evaluation of colour preferences in early infancy. *Infant Behaviour and Development, 10,* 143–150.

Adler, A. (1954). *Understanding human nature*. New York, NY: Greenburg Publisher.

Adolphs, R., & Tranel, D. (2003). Amygdala damage impairs emotion recognition from scenes only when they contain facial expressions. *Neuropsychologia, 41,* 1281–1289.

Afifi, T. O., Cox, B. J., & Enns, M. W. (2006). Mental health profiles among married, never-married, and separated/divorced mothers in a nationally representative sample. *Social Psychiatry and Psychiatric Epidemiology, 41,* 122–129.

Aghajanian, G. K., & Marek, G. J. (1999). Serotonin and hallucinogens. *Neuropsychopharmacology, 21,* 16S–23S.

Agnati, L. F., Bjelke, B., & Fuxe, K. (1992). Volume transmission in the brain. *American Scientist, 80,* 362–373.

Agresti, A., & Finlay, B. (1997). *Statistical methods for the social sciences* (3rd ed.). Upper Saddle River, NJ: Prentice Hall.

Aguiar, A., & Baillargeon, R. (2003). Perseverative responding in a violation-ofexpectation task in 6.5-month-old infants. *Cognition, 88*(3), 277–316.

Ahern, G. L., & Schwartz, G. E. (1985). Differential lateralization for positive and negative emotion in the human brain: EEG spectral analysis. *Neuropsychologia, 23,* 745–755.

Ahlskog, J. E. (2003). Slowing Parkinson's disease progression: Recent dopamine agonist trials. *Neurology, 60,* 381–389.

Ahn, W. (1998). Why are different features central for natural kinds and artifacts? The role of causal status in determining feature centrality. *Cognition, 69,* 135–178.

Ahokas, A., Aito, M., & Rimon, R. (2000). Positive treatment effect of estradiol in postpartum psychosis: A pilot study. *Journal of Clinical Psychiatry, 61*(3), 166–169.

Aiello, J. R., & Douthitt, E. A. (2001). Social facilitation from Triplett to electronic performance monitoring. *Group Dynamics: Theory, Research, and Practice, 5*(3), 163–180.

Ainsworth, M. D. S. (1985). Attachments across the life span. *Bulletin of the New York Academy of Medicine, 61,* 792–812.

Ainsworth, M. D. S., Blehar, M. C., Waters, E., & Wall, S. (1978). *Patterns of attachment: A study of the strange situation*. Hillsdale, NJ: Erlbaum.

Aitchison, J. (1992). Good birds, better birds, & amazing birds: The development of prototypes. In P. J. Arnaud & H. Béjoint (Eds.), *Vocabulary and applied linguistics* (pp. 71–84). London: Macmillan.

Ajzen, I. (2001). Nature and operation of attitudes. *Annual Review of Psychology, 52,* 27–58.

Ajzen, I., & Fishbein, M. (2000). Attitudes and the attitude–behavior relation: Reasoned and automatic processes. In W. Stroebe & M. Hewstone (Eds.), *European review of Social Psychology* (pp. 1–33). New York, NY: Wiley.

Akil, M., Kolachana, B. S., Rothmond, D. A., Hyde, T. M., Weinberger, D. R., & Kleinman, J. E. (2003). Catechol-o-methyltransferase genotype and dopamine regulation in the human brain. *Journal of Neuroscience, 23,* 2008–2013.

Albert, D. J., & Richmond, S. E. (1977). Reactivity and aggression in the rat: Induction by alpha–adrenergic blocking agents injected ventral to anterior septum but not into lateral septum. *Journal of Comparative and Physiological Psychology, 91,* 886–896.

Alderfer, C. P. (1972). *Existence, relatedness and growth: Human needs in organisational settings.* New York, NY: Free Press.

Aldridge-Morris, R. (1989). *Multiple personality: An exercise in deception.* Hillsdale, NJ: Erlbaum.

Alexander, G., DeLong, M. R., & Strick, P. L. (1986). Parallel organization of functionally segregated circuits linking basal ganglia and cortex. *Annual Review of Neuroscience, 9,* 357–381.

Aligne, C. A., Auinger, P., Byrd, R. S., & Weitzman, M. (2000). Risk factors for pediatric asthma contributions of poverty, race, and urban residence. *American Journal of Respiratory Critical Care Medicine, 162,* 873–877.

Alkon, D. (1989). Memory storage and neural systems. *Scientific American, 261*(1), 42–50.

Allen, F. (1994). *Secret formula.* New York, NY: HarperCollins.

Allen, G., & Parisi, P. (1990). Trends in monozygotic and dizygotic twinning rates by maternal age and parity. Further analysis of Italian data, 1949–1985, and rediscussion of US data, 1964–1985. *Acta Genetic Medicine & Gemellology, 39,* 317–328.

Allen, I. V. (1991). Pathology of multiple sclerosis. In W. B. Matthews (Ed.), *McAlpine's multiple sclerosis* (pp. 341–378). Edinburgh, Scotland: Churchill Livingstone.

Allen, J. J., & Iacono, W. G. (1997). A comparison of methods for the analysis of event-related potentials in deception detection. *Psychophysiology, 34,* 234–240.

Allen, L. S., & Gorski, R. A. (1991). Sexual dimorphism of the anterior commissure and massa intermedia of the human brain. *Journal of Comparative Neurology, 312,* 97–104.

Allen, L. S., Hines, M., Shryne, J. E., & Gorski, R. A. (1989). Two sexually dimorphic cell groups in the human brain. *Journal of Neuroscience, 9,* 496–506.

Alloy, L. B., & Clements, C. M. (1998). Hopelessness theory of depression: Tests of the symptom component. *Cognitive Therapy and Research, 22,* 303–335.

Allport, G. W. (1954). *The nature of prejudice.* Cambridge, MA: Addison-Wesley.

Allport, G. W., & Odbert, H. S. (1936). Trait names: A psycho-lexical study. *Psychological Monographs, 47*(211).

Allyn, J., & Festinger, L. (1961). The effectiveness of unanticipated persuasive communications. *Journal of Abnormal and Social Psychology, 62,* 35–40.

Alperstein, L. (2001, May). *For two: Some basic perspectives and skills for couples therapy.* Paper presented at the XXXIII Annual Conference of the American Association of Sex Educators, Counselors, and Therapists. San Francisco, CA.

Alzheimer Society. (2009). *Rising tide: The impact of dementia on Canadian society.* Retrieved from http://www.alzheimer.ca/docs/RisingTide/Rising Tide_Full Report_Eng_FINAL_Secured version.pdf

Alzheimer Society Toronto. (2007). *Drug treatments.* Retrieved from http://www.alzheimertoronto.org/ad_med_aricept.htm

Alzheimer Society of Canada. (2005). *Alzheimer's disease: Statistics.* Retrieved from http://www.alzheimer.ca/english/disease/stats-intro.htm

Amabile, T., Hadley, C. N., & Kramer, S. J. (2002). Creativity under the gun. *Harvard Business Review, 80*(8), 52–60.

American Association on Intellectual and Developmental Disabilities. (2011). *FAQ on intellectual disability.* Retrieved from http://www.aaidd.org/content_104.cfm

American Association of University Women. (1992). *How schools shortchange girls.* Washington, DC: Author.

American Association of University Women. (1998). *Separated by sex: A critical look at single-sex education for girls.* Washington, DC: Author.

American Psychiatric Association. (2000a). *DSM-IV-TR: Diagnostic and statistical manual of mental disorders* (4th ed., Text Revision). Washington, DC: Author.

American Psychiatric Association. (2000b). Practice guidelines for the treatment of patients with major depressive disorder (revision). *American Journal of Psychiatry, 157*(4, Supplement): 1–45.

American Psychiatric Association Committee on Electroconvulsive Therapy. (2001). *The practice of electroconvulsive therapy: Recommendations for treatment, training, and privileging* (2nd ed.). Washington, DC: American Psychiatric Association.

American Psychological Association. (1992). Ethical principles of psychologists and code of conduct. *American Psychologist, 47,* 1597–1611.

American Psychological Association. (2005). Policy statement on evidence-based practice in psychology. Retrieved from http://www.apa.org/practice/guidelines/evidence-based.pdf

Analekta. (2011). *André Mathieu.* Retrieved from https://www.analekta.com/en/artists/Andre-Mathieu.493.html

Anand, B. K., & Brobeck, J. R. (1951.) Hypothalamic control of food intake in rats and cats. *Yale Journal of Biological Medicine, 24,* 123–146.

Anastasi, A., & Urbina, S. (1997). *Psychological testing* (7th ed.). Upper Saddle River, NJ: Prentice-Hall.

Anderson, C. A. (1987). Temperature and aggression: Effects on quarterly, yearly, and city rates of violent and nonviolent crime. *Journal of Personality and Social Psychology, 52,* 1161–1173.

Anderson, C. A. (1997). Effects of violent movies and trait hostility on hostile feelings and aggressive thoughts. *Aggressive Behavior, 23,* 161–178.

Anderson, C. A. (2003). Video games and aggressive behavior. In D. Ravitch & J. P. Viteritti (Eds.), *Kid stuff: Marketing sex and violence to America's children.* Baltimore and London: Johns Hopkins University Press.

Anderson, C. A., Berkowitz, L., Donnerstein, E., Huesmann, R. L., Johnson, J., Linz, D., . . . Wartella, E. (2003). The influence of media violence on youth. *Psychological Science in the Public Interest, 4,* 81–110.

Anderson, C. A., & Bushman, B. J. (2001). Effects of violent video games on aggressive behavior, aggressive cognition, aggressive affect, physiological arousal, and prosocial behavior: A meta–analytic review of the scientific literature. *Psych Science, 12*(5), 353–359.

Anderson, C. A., & Bushman, B. J. (2002). Media violence and the American public revisited. *American Psychologist, 57,* 448–450.

Anderson, M. C., & Neely, J. H. (1995). Interference and inhibition in memory retrieval. In E. L. Bjork & R. A. Bjork (Eds.), *Handbook of perception and cognition, Vol. 10, Memory.* San Diego, CA: Academic Press.

Andrews, J. D. W. (1989). Integrating visions of reality: Interpersonal diagnosis and the existential vision. *American Psychologist, 44,* 803–817.

Anschuetz, B. L. (1999). The high cost of caring: Coping with workplace stress. *The Journal* (the Newsletter of the Ontario Association of Children's Aid Societies), *43*(3).

Antony, M. M., Rowa, K., Liss, A., Swallow, S. R., & Swinson, R. (2005). Social comparison processes in social phobia. *Behavior Therapy, 36,* 65–75.

Antony, M. M., & Swinson, R. P. (1998). *When perfect isn't good enough: Strategies for coping with perfectionism.* Oakland, CA: New Harbinger.

Apicella, C. L., Feinberg, D. R., & Marlowe, F. W. (2007). Voice pitch predicts reproductive success in male hunter-gatherers. *Biology Letters, 3,* 682–684.

Arbuthnott, K., & Campbell, J. I. D. (2000). Cognitive inhibition in selection and sequential retrieval. *Memory and Cognition, 28,* 331–340.

Archer, J. (1991). The influence of testosterone on human aggression. *British Journal of Psychology, 82,* 1–28.

Argamon, S., Koppel, M., Fine, J., & Shimoni, A. (2003 August). Gender, genre, and writing style in formal written texts, *Text, 23*(3).

Argyle, M. (1986). Rules for social relationships in four cultures. *Australian Journal of Psychology, 38,* 309–318.

Armfield, F. (1994). Preventing post-traumatic stress disorder resulting from military operations. *Military Medicine, 159,* 739–746.

Armstrong, R. (1997). When drugs are used for rape. *Journal of Emergency Nursing, 23*(4), 378–381.

Arnett, P. A., Smith, S. S., & Newman, J. P. (1997). Approach and avoidance motivation in psychopathic criminal offenders during passive avoidance. *Journal of Personality and Social Psychology, 72,* 1413–1428.

Aron, A., Aron, E. N., & Coups, E. (2005). *Statistics for the behavioral and social sciences: A brief course* (3rd ed.). Upper Saddle River, NJ: Prentice Hall.

Aronson, E. (1997). Back to the future. Retrospective review of Leon Festinger's— A theory of cognitive dissonance. *American Journal of Psychology, 110,* 127–137.

Aronson, E., Blaney, N., Stephan, C., Sikes, J., & Snapp, M. (1978). *The jigsaw classroom.* Beverly Hills, CA: Sage.

Arrigo, J. M., & Pezdek, K. (1998). Textbook models of multiple personality: Source, bias, and social consequences. In S. Lynn (Ed.), *Truth in memory* (pp. 372–393). New York: Guilford Press.

Asarnow, R. F., Granholm, E., & Sherman, T. (1991). Span of apprehension in schizophrenia. In S. R. Steinhauer, J. H. Gruzelie, & J. Zubin (Eds.), *Handbook of schizophrenia: Vol. 5. Neuropsychology, psychophysiology and information processing* (pp. 335–370). Amsterdam, the Netherlands: Elsevier.

Asch, S. E. (1951). Effects of group pressure upon the modification and distortion of judgement. In H. Guetzkow (Ed.), *Groups, leadership and men.* Pittsburgh, PA: Carnegie Press.

Asch, S. E. (1956). Studies of independence and conformity: A minority of one against a unanimous majority. *Psychological Monographs, 70* (Whole No. 416).

Aserinsky, E., & Kleitman, N. (1953). Regularly occurring periods of eye motility, and concomitant phenomena, during sleep. *Science, 118,* 273–274.

Ash, M. G. (1998). *Gestalt psychology in German culture, 1890–1967: Holism and the quest for objectivity.* Cambridge, England: Cambridge University Press.

Atkinson, R. C., & Shiffrin, R. M. (1968). Human memory: A proposed system and its control processes. In K. W. Spence & J. T. Spence (Eds.), *The psychology of learning and motivation* (Vol. 2, pp. 89–105). New York, NY: Academic Press.

Auld, R. B., & Brock, G. (2002). Sexuality and erectile dysfunction: Results of a national survey. *Journal of Sexual and Reproductive Medicine, 2,* 50–54.

Aylward, E. H., Richards, T. L., Berninger, V. W., Nagy, W. E., Field, K. M., Grimme, A. C., . . . Cramer, S. C. (2003). Instructional treatment associated with changes in brain activation in children with dyslexia. *Neurology, 61,* 212–219.

Backer, B., Hannon, R., & Russell, N. (1994). *Death and dying: Understanding and care* (2nd ed.). Albany, NY: Delmar.

Baddeley, A. (1988). Cognitive psychology and human memory. *Trends in Neurosciences, 11,* 176–181.

Baddeley, A. D. (1986). *Working memory.* London and New York: Oxford University Press.

Baddeley, A. D. (1996). Exploring the central executive. *Quarterly Journal of Experimental Psychology, 49A,* 5–28.

Baddeley, A. D. (2003). Working memory: Looking back and looking forward. *Nature Reviews Neuroscience, 4,* 829–839.

Baddeley, A. D., & Hitch, G. (1974). Working memory. In G. A. Bower (Ed.), *The psychology of learning and motivation* (pp. 47–89). New York, NY: Academic Press.

Baehr, E. K., Revelle, W., & Eastman, C. I. (2000). Individual difference in the phase amplitude of the human circadian temperature rhythm: With an emphasis on morningness-eveningness. *Journal of Sleep Research, 9,* 117–127.

Baer, D. M., Wolf, M. M., & Risley, T. R. (1968). Some current dimensions of applied behavior analysis. *Journal of Applied Behavior Analysis, 1,* 91–97.

Bahrick, H. (1984). Fifty years of second language attrition: Implications for programmatic research. *Modern Language Journal, 68,* 105–118.

Bahrick, H. P., Hall, L. K., & Berger, S. A. (1996, September). Accuracy and distortion in memory for high school grades. *Psychological Science, 7,* 265–271.

Bailey, J., Dunne, M. P., & Martin, N. G. (2000). Genetic and environmental influences on sexual orientation and its correlates in an Australian twin sample. *Journal of Personality and Social Psychology, 78,* 524–536.

Bailey, J. M., & Pillard, R. C. (1991). A genetic study of male sexual orientation. *Archives of General Psychiatry, 48,* 1089–1096.

Bailey, J. M., Pillard, R. C., Neale, M. C., & Agyei, Y. (1993). Heritable factors influence sexual orientation in women. *Archives of General Psychiatry, 50,* 217–223.

Bailey, J. M., & Zucker, K. J. (1995). Childhood sex-typed behavior and sexual orientation: A conceptual analysis and quantitative review. *Developmental Psychology, 31,* 43–55.

Baillergeon, R. (1986). Representing the existence and location of hidden objects: Object permanence in 6- and 8-month-old infants. *Cognition, 23,* 21–24.

Baillargeon, R., & DeVos, J (1991). Object permanence in young infants: Further evidence. *Child Development, 62,* 1227–1246.

Bains, J. S., & Oliet, S. H. R. (2007). Glia: They make your memories stick. *Trends in Neuroscience, 30,* 417–424.

Baker, E. T. (1994). *Meta-analytic evidence for non-inclusive educational practices: Does educational research support current practice for special needs students?* Unpublished doctoral dissertation, Temple University.

Ball, K., Berch, D. B., Helmers, K. F., Jobe, J. B., Leveck, M. D., Marsiske, M., . . . Willis, S. J. (2002). Advanced cognitive training for independent and vital elderly study group: Effects of cognitive training interventions with older adults: A randomized controlled trial. *Journal of the American Medical Association, 288,* 2271–2281.

Baltes, P. B., Reese, H. W., & Nesselroade, J. R. (1988). *Introduction to research methods, life-span developmental psychology*. Hillsdale, NJ: Lawrence Erlbaum Associates.

Bandura, A. (1965). Influence of models' reinforcement contingencies on the acquisition of imitative responses. *Journal of Social Psychology, 1,* 589–595.

Bandura, A. (1980). The social learning theory of aggression. In R. A. Falk & S. S. Kim (Eds.), *The war system: An interdisciplinary approach* (p. 146). Boulder, CO: Westview Press.

Bandura, A. (1986). *Social foundations of thought and action: A social cognitive theory*. Englewood Cliffs, NJ: Prentice Hall.

Bandura, A. (1989). Human agency in social cognitive theory. *American Psychologist, 44,* 1175–1184.

Bandura, A. (1998). Exploration of fortuitous determinants of life paths. *Psychological Inquiry, 9,* 95–99.

Bandura, A., Blanchard, E. B., & Ritter, B. (1969). Relative efficacy of desensitization and modeling approaches for inducing behavioral, affective, and attitudinal changes. *Journal of Personality and Social Psychology, 13,* 173–199.

Bandura, A., Jeffrey, R. W., & Wright, C. L. (1974). Efficacy of participant modeling as a function of response induction aids. *Journal of Abnormal Psychology, 83,* 56–64.

Bandura, A., & Rosenthal, T. L. (1966). Vicarious classical conditioning as a functioning of arousal level. *Journal of Personality and Social Psychology, 3,* 54–62.

Bandura, A., Ross, D., & Ross, S. A. (1961). Transmission of aggression through imitation of aggressive models. *Journal of Abnormal and Social Psychology, 63,* 575–582.

Barak, A. (1999). Psychological applications on the Internet: A discipline on the threshold of a new millennium. *Applied and Preventive Psychology, 8,* 231–246.

Barak, A., & Hen, L. (2008). Exposure in cyberspace as means of enhancing psychological assessment. In A. Barak (Ed.), *Psychological aspects of cyberspace: Theory, research, applications* (pp. 129–162). Cambridge, England: Cambridge University Press.

Barak, A., & Suler, J. (2008). Reflections on the psychology and social science of cyberspace. In A. Barak (Ed.), *Psychological aspects of cyberspace: Theory, research, applications* (pp. 1–12). Cambridge, England: Cambridge University Press.

Bard, P. (1934). On emotional expression after decortication with some remark on certain theoretical views. *Psychological Review, 41,* 309–329, 424–449.

Bargh, J. A., Chen, M., & Burrows, C. (1996). Automaticity of social behavior: Direct effects of trait construct and stereotype activation on action. *Journal of Personality & Social Psychology, 71,* 230–244.

Barker, E. (1983). The ones who got away: People who attend Unification Church workshops and do not become Moonies. In E. Barker (Ed.,), *Of gods and men: New religious movements in the West*. Macon, GA: Mercer University Press.

Barlow, D. H., Allen, L. B., & Basden, S. L. (2007). Psychological treatments for panic disorders, phobias, and generalized anxiety disorder. In P. E. Nathan & J. M. Gorman (Eds.), *A guide to treatments that work* (3rd ed., pp. 351–394). New York, NY: Oxford University Press.

Barnes, A. M., & Carey, J. C. (2002, January 11). Common problems of babies with trisomy 18 or 13. *Support Organization for Trisomy 18, 13, and Related Disorders*. Rochester, NY.

Barnes, V., Schneider, R., Alexander, C., & Staggers, F. (1997). Stress, stress reduction, and hypertension in African Americans: An updated review. *Journal of the National Medical Association, 89,* 464–476.

Barnyard, P., & Grayson, A. (1996). *Introducing psychological research*. London, England: MacMillan Press.

Baron, J. N., & Reiss, P. C. (1985). Same time, next year: Aggregate analyses of the mass media and violent behavior. *American Sociological Review, 50,* 347–363.

Bar-On, R. (1997). *The Emotional Quotient Inventory (EQ-i): A test of emotional intelligence*. Toronto, ON: Multi-Health Systems.

Bar-On, R. (2006). The Bar-On model of emotional-social intelligence (ESI). *Psicothema, 18*(Suppl.), 13–25.

Baron-Cohen, S., Burt, L., Smith-Laittan, F., Harrsion, J., & Bolton, P. (1996). Synaesthesia: Prevalence and familiarity. *Perception, 25,* 1073–1080.

Barondes, S. H. (1998). *Mood genes: Hunting for origins of mania and depression*. New York, NY: Freeman.

Barone, J. J., & Roberts, H. R. (1996). Caffeine consumption. *Food Chemistry and Toxicology, 34,* 119–129.

Barsalou, L. W. (1992). *Cognitive psychology: An overview for cognitive scientists*. Hillsdale, NJ: Lawrence Erlbaum Associates.

Barsh, G. S., Farooqi, I. S., & O'Rahilly, S. (2000). Genetics of body-weight regulation. *Nature, 404,* 644–651.

Bartels, A., & Zeki, S. (2000). The neural basis of romantic love. *NeuroReport, 11,* 3829–3834.

Barth, J. M., & Boles, D. B. (1999). *Positive relations between emotion recognition skills and right hemisphere processing*. Paper presented to the 11th Annual onvention of the American Psychological Society, Denver, CO.

Bartholomew, K. (1990). Avoidance of intimacy: An attachment perspective. *Journal of Social and Personal Relationships, 7,* 147–178.

Bartlett, F. C. (1932). *Remembering: A study in experimental ad social psychology*. Cambridge, England: Cambridge University Press.

Bartlett, N. R. (1965). Dark and light adaptation. In C. H. Graham, (Ed.), *Vision and visual perception* (Chapter 8). New York, NY: Wiley.

Barton, M. E., & Komatsu, L. K. (1989). Defining features of natural kinds and artifacts. *Journal of Psycholinguistic Research, 18,* 433–447.

Bartoshuk, L. M. (1993). The biological basis for food perception and acceptance. *Food Quality and Preference, 4*(1/2), 21–32.

Basadur, M., Pringle, P., & Kirkland, D. (2002). Crossing cultures: Training effects on the divergent thinking attitudes of Spanish-speaking South American managers. *Creativity Research Journal, 14,* 395–408.

Bates, J. E. (1989). Applications of temperament concepts. In G. A. Kohnstamm, J. E. Bates, & M. K Rothbart (Eds.), *Temperament in childhood* (pp. 323–355). New York, NY: Wiley.

Battaglia, M., Bernardeschi, L., Franchini, L., Bellodi, L., & Smeraldi, E. (1995). A family study of schizotypal disorder. *Schizophrenia Bulletin, 21*(1), 33–45.

Battan, J. (1999). The "rights" of husbands and the "duties" of wives: Power and desire in the American bedroom, 1850–1910. *Journal of Family History, 24*(2), 165–186.

Baumrind, D. (1964). Some thoughts on ethics of research: After reading Milgram's "Behavioral Study of Obedience." *American Psychologist, 19,* 421–423.

Baumrind, D. (1986). Sex differences in moral reasoning: Response to Walker's (1984) conclusion that there are none. *Child Development, 57,* 511–521.

Baumrind, D. (1997). Necessary distinctions. *Psychological Inquiry, 8,* 176–182.

Bear, G. G., & Proctor, W. A. (1990). Impact of a full-time integrated program on the achievement of nonhandicapped and mildly handicapped children. *Journal of Exceptionality, 1,* 227–238.

Beardsley, T. (1995, January). For whom the bell curve really tolls. *Scientific American,* 14–17.

Beaudoin, C. M., & Cox, B. J. (1999). Characteristics of problem gambling in a Canadian context: A preliminary study using a DSM-IV based questionnaire. *Canadian Journal of Psychiatry, 44,* 483–487.

Beaujot, R., & Andersen, R. (2007). Time-crunch: Impact of time spent in paid and unpaid work, and its division in families. *Canadian Journal of Sociology, 32,* 295–315.

Beaupre, M. G., & Hess, U. (2005). Cross-cultural emotion recognition among Canadian ethnic groups. *Journal of Cross-Cultural Psychology, 36,* 355–370.

Beck, A. T. (1976). *Cognitive therapy and the emotional disorders.* New York, NY: International Universities Press.

Beck, A. T. (1979). *Cognitive therapy and the emotional disorders.* New York, NY: Penguin Books.

Beck, A. T. (1984). Cognitive approaches to stress. In C. Lehrer & R. L. Woolfolk (Eds.), *Clinical guide to stress management.* New York, NY: Guilford Press.

Beck, C. A., Metz, L. M., Svenson, L. W., & Patten, S. B. (2005). Regional variation of multiple sclerosis in Canada. *Multiple Sclerosis, 5,* 516–519.

Beck, H. P., Levinson, S., & Irons, G. (2009). Finding Little Albert: A journey to John B. Watson's infant laboratory. *American Psychologist, 64,* 605–614.

Beckman, M., & Pierrehumbert, J. (1986). Intonational structure in English and Japanese. *Phonology Year Book III,* 15–70.

Beehr, T. A., Jex, S. M., Stacy, B. A., & Murray, M. A. (2000). Work stressors and coworker support as predictors of individual strain and job performance. *Journal of Organizational Behavior, 21,* 391–405.

Beer, J. M., & Horn, J. M. (2000). The influence of rearing order on personality development within two adoption cohorts. *Journal of Personality, 68,* 789–819.

Bem, D. J., & Honorton, C. (1994). Does psi exist? *Psychological Bulletin, 115*(1), 4–18.

Bem, S. L. (1975). Sex role adaptability: The consequence of psychological androgyny. *Journal of Personality and Social Psychology, 31,* 634–643.

Bem, S. L. (1987). Gender schema theory and the romantic tradition. In P. Shaver & C. Hendrick (Eds.), *Review of personality and social psychology* (Vol. 7). Newbury Park, CA: Sage.

Bem, S. L. (1993), Is there a place in psychology for a feminist analysis of the social context? *Feminism & Psychology, 3,* 247–251.

Bemporad, J. R. (1997). Cultural and historical aspects of eating disorders. *Theoretical Medicine & Bioethics, 18*(4), 401–420.

Benasich, A. A., & Tallal, P. (1996). Auditory temporal processing thresholds, habituation, and recognition memory over the 1st year. *Infant Behavior & Development, 19,* 339–357.

Benjafield, J. J. G. (1996). *A history of psychology.* Boston, MA: Allyn and Bacon.

Benjamin, S. L. (1996). An interpersonal theory of personality disorders. In J. F. Clarkin & M. F. Lenzenweger (Eds.), *Major theories of personality disorder.* New York, NY: Guilford Press.

Benowitz, N. L. (1996). Pharmacology of nicotine: Addiction and therapeutics. *Annual Review of Pharmacology and Toxicology, 36,* 597–613.

Ben-Shakhar, G., Bar-Hillel, M., Bliu, Y., Ben-Abba, E., & Flug, A. (1986). Can graphology predict occupational success? Two empirical studies and some methodological ruminations. *Journal of Applied Psychology, 71,* 645–653.

Benson, H. (1975). *The relaxation response.* New York, NY: Morrow.

Benson, H., Beary, J., & Carol, M. (1974a). The relaxation response. *Psychiatry, 37,* 37–46.

Benson, H., Rosner, B. A., Marzetta, B. R., & Klemchuk, H. M. (1974b). Decreased blood pressure in pharmacologically treated hypertensive patients who regularly elicited the relaxation response. *Lancet, 1*(7852), 289–291.

Berenbaum, S. A., & Snyder, E. (1995). Early hormonal influences on childhood sex-typed activity and playmate preferences: Implications for the development of sexual orientation. *Developmental Psychology, 31,* 31–42.

Berent, S. (1977). Functional asymmetry of the human brain in the recognition of faces. *Neuropsychologia, 15,* 829–831.

Berg, F. (1999). Health risks associated with weight loss and obesity treatment programs. *Journal of Social Issues, 55,* 277–297.

Berk, L. S., Felten, D. L., Tan, S. A., Bittman, B. B., & Westengard, J. (2001, March). Modulation of neuroimmune parameters during the eustress of humor-associated mirthful laughter. *Alternative Therapy Health Medicines, 7*(2), 62–72, 74–76.

Berkowitz, L. (1972). *Advances in experimental social psychology* (Vol. 6). New York, NY: Academic Press.

Berkowitz, L. (1993). *Aggression: Its causes, consequences and control.* New York, NY: McGraw-Hill.

Bermond, B., Nieuwenhuyse, B., Fasotti, L., & Schuerman, J. (1991). Spinal cord lesions, peripheral feedback, and intensities of emotional feelings. *Cognition and Emotion, 5,* 201–220.

Berry, J. W., & Kim, U. (1998). Acculturation and mental health. In P. R. Dasen, J. W. Berry, & N. Sartorius (Eds.), *Health and cross-cultural psychology: Toward applications* (pp. 207–236). Newbury Park, CA: Sage.

Berry, J. W., & Sam, D. L. (1997). Acculturation and adaptation. In J. W. Berry, M. H. Segall, & C. Kagitcibasi (Eds.), *Handbook of cross-cultural psychology: Vol. 3. Social behaviour and applications* (2nd ed., pp. 291–326). Boston, MA: Allyn & Bacon.

Berscheid, E., & Reis, H. T. (1998). Attraction and close relationships. In D. T. Gilbert, S. T. Fiske, & G. Lindzey (Eds.), *The handbook of social psychology* (4th ed., Vol. 2, pp. 193–281). New York, NY: McGraw-Hill.

Best, D. L., & Williams, J. E. (2001). Gender and culture. In D. Matsumoto (Ed.), *The handbook of culture and psychology* (pp. 195–212). New York, NY: Oxford University Press.

Betancourt, J. R., & Jacobs, E. A. (2000). Language barriers to informed consent and confidentiality: The impact on women's health. *Journal of American Medical Women's Association, 55,* 294–295.

Beyer, B. K. (1995). *Critical thinking.* Bloomington, IN: Phi Delta Kappa Educational Foundation.

Bialystok, E., Craik, F. I. M., & Ryan, J. (2006). Executive control in a modified antisaccade task: Effects of aging and bilingualism. *Journal of Experimental Psychology: Learning Memory and Cognition, 32,* 1341–1354.

Bialystok, E., & Shapero, D. (2005). Ambiguous benefits: The effect of bilingualism on reversing ambiguous figures. *Developmental Science, 8,* 595–604.

Bigler, E. D., Johnson, S. C., Anderson, C. V., Blatter, D. D., Gale, S. D., Russo, A. A., . . . Abildskov, T. J. (1996). Traumatic brain injury and memory: The role of hippocampal atrophy. *Neuropsychology, 10,* 333–342.

Binet, A., & Simon, T. (1916). *The development of intelligence in children.* Baltimore, MD: Williams & Wilkins.

Bishop, G. D. (1994). *Health psychology: Integrating mind and body.* Boston, MA: Allyn and Bacon.

Bishop, K. M., & Wahlsten, D. (1997). Sex differences in the human corpus callosum: Myth or reality? *Neurosience and Biobehavioral Review, 21,* 581–601.

Bjork, R. A., & Bjork, E. L. (1992). A new theory of disuse and an old theory of stimulus fluctuation. In A. Healy, S. Kosslyn, & R. Shiffrin (Eds.), *From learning processes to cognitive processes: Essays in honor of William K. Estes* (Vol. 2, pp. 35–67). Hillsdale, NJ: Erlbaum.

Bjork, R. A., & Whitten, W. B. (1974). Recency-sensitive retrieval processes in longterm free recall. *Cognitive Psychology, 6,* 173–189.

Black, D. W., & Andreasen, N. C. (1999). Schizophrenia, schizophreniform disorder, and delusional (paranoid) disorders. In R. E. Hales et al., (Eds.), *Textbook of psychiatry* (3rd ed., pp. 425–477). Washington, D.C.: American Psychiatric Press.

Blackmore, S. (1994). Alien abduction: the inside story. *New Scientist, 144,* 29–31.

Blair, R. J. R., Sellars, C., Strickland, I., Clark, F., Williams, A. O., Smith, M., & Jones, L. (1995). Emotion attributions in the psychopath. *Personality and Individual Differences, 19,* 431–437.

Blakeslee, S. (2002, September 12). Actor regains some movement, doctor says. *New York Times.*

Blanchard, M., & Main, M. (1979). Avoidance of the attachment figure and socialemotional adjustment in day-care infants. *Developmental Psychology, 15,* 445–446.

Blanchard, R. (1989). The classification and labeling of nonhomosexual gender dysphorias. *Archives of Sexual Behaviour, 18,* 315–334.

Blanchard-Fields, F., & Horhota, M. (2005). Age differences in the correspondence bias: When a plausible explanation matters. *Journals of Gerontology: Psychological Sciences, 60B,* 259–267.

Blass, T. (1991). Understanding behavior in the Milgram obedience experiment: The role of personality, situations, and their interactions. *Journal of Personality and Social Psychology, 60,* 398–413.

Blass, T. (1999). The Milgram paradigm after 35 years: Some things we now know about obedience to authority. *Journal of Applied Social Psychology, 25,* 955–978.

Blatt, S. D., Meguid, V., & Church, C. C. (2000). Prenatal cocaine: What's known about outcomes? *Contemporary Ob/Gyn, 9,* 67–83.

Blazer, D. G., Kessler, R. C., McGonagle, K. A., & Swartz, M. S. (1994). The prevalence and distribution of major depression in a national community sample: The National Comorbidity Survey. *American Journal of Psychiatry, 151,* 979–986.

Bledsoe, C. H., & Cohen, B. (1993). *Social dynamics of adolescent fertility in Sub-Saharan Africa.* Washington DC: National Academy Press.

Blehar, M. C., & Oren, D. A. (1997). Gender differences in depression. *Medscape General Medicine, 1*(2). Retrieved www.medscape.com/viewarticle/408844

Bleuler, E. (1911, reissued 1950). *Dementia praecox or the group of schizophrenias.* New York, NY: International Universities Press.

Block, N. (2005). Two neural correlates of consciousness. *Trends in Cognitive Sciences, 9,* 41–89.

Bloom, L. (1974). Talking, understanding and thinking. In R. Schiefelbusch & L. L. Lloyd (Eds.), *Language perspectives: Acquisition, retardation and intervention.* New York, NY: Macmillan.

Bloom, P. (2000). *How children learn the meaning of words.* Cambridge, MA: MIT Press.

Blumer, D. (2002). The illness of Vincent van Gogh. *American Journal of Psychiatry, 159*(4), 519–526.

Bock, R. (1993, August). *Understanding Klinefelter Syndrome: A guide for XXY males and their families.* National Institutes of Health, Office of Research Reporting. Publication No. 93-3202.

Bodrova, E., & Leong, D. J. (1996). *Tools of the mind: The Vygotskian approach to early childhood education.* Englewood Cliffs, NJ: Prentice Hall.

Bogle, K. D. (2000). Effect of perspective, type of student, and gender on the attribution of cheating. *Proceedings of the Oklahoma Academy of Science, 80,* 91–97.

Bolton, P., Bass, J., Betancourt, T., Speelman, L., Onyango, G., Clougherty, K. F., . . . Verdeli, H. (2007). Interventions for depression symptoms among adolescent survivors of war and displacement in northern Uganda. *Journal of Medical Association, 298,* 519–527.

Bond, R. A., & Smith, P. B. (1996). Culture and conformity: A meta–analysis of studies using Asch's (1952, 1956) line judgment task. *Psychological Bulletin, 119,* 111–137.

Bondarenko, L. A. (2004). Role of methionine in nocturnal melatonin peak in the pineal gland. *Bulletin of Experimental Biological Medicine, 137,* 431–432.

Bonnelykke, B. (1990). Maternal age and parity as predictors of human twinning. *Acta Genetic Medicine & Gemellology, 39,* 329–334.

Bonnet, M., & Arand, D. (1995). We are chronically sleep deprived. *Sleep, 18,* 908–911.

Boor, M. (1982). The multiple personality epidemic: Additional cases and inferences regarding diagnosis, etiology, dynamics, and treatment. *Journal of Nervous and Mental Disease, 170,* 302–304.

Booth-Butterfield, S. (1996). Message characteristics. *Steve's primer of practical persuasion and influence.* Retrieved from http://www.as.wvu.edu/ ~sbb/comm221/chapters/message.htm

Borgeat, F., & Goulet, J. (1983, June). Psychophysiological changes following auditory subliminal suggestions for activation and deactivation. *Perceptual & Motor Skills, 56,* 759–766.

Borges, M. A., Stepnowsky, M. A., & Holt, L. H. (1977). Recall and recognition of words and pictures by adults and children. *Bulletin of the Psychonomic Society, 9,* 113–114.

Bornstein, M. H. (1985). Habituation of attention as a measure of visual information processing in human infants: Summary, systematization, and synthesis. In G. Gottleib & N. A. Krasnegor (Eds.), *Measurement of audition and vision in the first year of postnatal life: A methodological overview* (pp. 253–300). Norwood, NJ: Ablex.

Bornstein, M. H., & Benasich, A. A. (1986). Infant habituation: Assessments of individual differences and short-term reliability at 5 months. *Child Development, 57,* 87–99.

Bors, D. A. (1994). Is the nature-nurture debate on the verge of extinction? *Canadian Psychology, 35,* 231–243.

Boswell, S. (2002). Former Miss America receives cochlear implant. *The ASHA Leader Online.* AGS Publishing. Retrieved from www.asha.org/ about/publications/leader-online/archives/2002/q4/021109a.htm

Bosworth, H. B., & Schaie, K. W. (1997). The relationship of social environment, social networks, and health outcomes in the Seattle Longitudinal Study: Two analytical approaches. *Journals of Gerontology Series B: Psychological Sciences and Social Sciences, 52*(5), 197–205.

Bottos, S., & Dewey, D. (2004). Perfectionists' appraisals of daily hassles and chronic pain. *Headache: The Journal of Head and Face Pain, 44,* 772–779.

Botwin, M. D., & Buss, D. M. (1989). The structure of act data: Is the five-factor model of personality recaptured? *Journal of Personality and Social Psychology, 56,* 988–1001.

Bouchard, C. (1997). Genetic determinants of regional fat distribution. *Human Reproduction, 12*(Suppl 1), 1–5.

Bouchard, C., Tremblay, A., Nadeau, A., Dussault, J., Despres, J. P., Theriault, G., et al. (1990). Long-term exercise training with constant energy intake. 1: Effect on body composition and selected metabolic variables. *International Journal on Obesity, 14*(1), 57–73.

Bouchard, S., Paquin, B., Payeur, R., Allard, M., Rivard, V., Fournier, T., . . . Lapierre, J. (2004). Delivering cognitive-behavior therapy for panic disorder with agoraphobia in videoconference. *Telemedicine Journal and e-Health, 10* (1), 13–24.

Bouchard, T. (1994). Genes, environment, and personality. *Science, 264,* 1700–1701.

Bouchard, T. J., Jr. (1997). Whenever the twain shall meet. *The Science, 37* (5), 52–57.

Bouchard, T. J., & Segal, N. L. (1985). Environment and IQ. In B. B. Wolman (Ed.), *Handbook of intelligence: Theories, measurements, and applications* (pp. 391–464). New York, NY: Wiley.

Bouchard, T. J., Lykken, D. T., McGue, M., Segal, N. L., & Tellegen, A. (1990). Sources of human psychological differences: The Minnesota study of twins reared apart. *Science, 250*(4978), 223.

Bowden, C. L., Calabrese, J. R., McElroy, S. L., Gyulai, L., Wassef, A., Petty, F., et al. (2000). For the Divalproex Maintenance Study Group. A randomized, placebo-controlled 12-month trial of divalproex and lithium in treatment of outpatients with bipolar I disorder. *Archives of General Psychiatry, 57,* 481–489.

Bower, G. H., Thompson, S. S., & Tulving, E. (1994). Reducing retroactive interference: An interference analysis. *Journal of Experimental Psychology: Learning, Memory, and Cognition, 20,* 51–66.

Bowers, K. S., & Woody, E. Z. (1996). Hypnotic amnesia and the paradox of intentional forgetting. *Journal of Abnormal Psychology, 105,* 381–390.

Bowman, E. S. (1996). Delayed memories of child abuse: Part II: An overview of research findings relevant to understanding their reliability and suggestibility. *Dissociation: Progress in the Dissociative Disorders, 9,* 232–243.

Boyd, L. A., & Winstein, C. J. (2004). Cerebellar stroke impairs temporal but not spatial accuracy during implicit motor learning. *Neurorehabilitation and Neural Repair, 18*(3), 134–143.

Boyson-Bardies, B., deHalle, P., Sagart, L., & Durand, C. (1989). A cross-linguistic investigation of vowel formats in babbling. *Journal of Child Language, 16,* 1–17.

Bracey, G. (1997). A few facts about poverty. *Phi Delta Kappan, 79,* 163–164.

Bradshaw, W. (1997). Evaluating cognitive-behavioral treatment of schizophrenia: Four single-case studies. *Research in Social Work Practice, 7,* 419–445.

Bradshaw, W. (1998). Cognitive-behavioral treatment of schizophrenia: A case study. *Journal of Cognitive Psychotherapy: An International Journal, 12*(1), 13–25.

Braun, B. G. (Ed.) (1986). *Treatment of multiple personality disorder.* Washington, DC: American Psychiatric Press.

Braun, S. (1996). *Buzz: The science and lore of alcohol and caffeine* (pp. 107–192). New York, NY: Oxford University Press.

Brawman-Mintzer, O., & Lydiard, R. B. (1997). Biological basis of generalized anxiety disorder. *Journal of Clinical Psychiatry, 58*(3), 16–25.

Brazelton, T. B. (1992). *Touchpoints: Your child's emotional and behavioral development.* Reading, MA: Addison-Wesley.

Brecher, M., Wang, B. W., Wong, H., & Morgan, J. P. (1988). Phencyclidine and violence: Clinical and legal issues. *Journal of Clinical Psychopharmacology, 8,* 397–401.

Breggin, P. R. (2003/2004). Suicidality, violence and mania caused by selective serotonin reuptake inhibitors (SSRIs): A review and analysis. *International Journal of Risk & Safety in Medicine, 16,* 31–49.

Breggin, P. R., & Breggin, G. R. (1994). *Talking back to Prozac.* New York, NY: St. Martin's Press.

Bregman, A., & Campbell, J. (1971) Primary auditory stream segregation and perception of order in rapid sequence of tones. *Journal of Experimental Psychology, 89,* 244–249.

Breier A., Albus M., Pickar D., Zahn, T. P., Wolkowitz, O. M., & Paul, S. M. (1987). Controllable and uncontrollable stress in humans: Alterations in mood, neuroendocrine and psychophysiological function. *American Journal of Psychiatry, 144,* 1419–1425.

Brennan, J. F. (2002). *History and systems of psychology* (6th ed.). Upper Saddle River, NJ: Prentice Hall.

Brennan, P. A., Raine, A., Schulsinger, F., Kirkegaard-Sorensen, L., Knop, J., Hutchings, B., . . . Mednick, S. A. (1997). Psychophysiological protective factors for male subjects at high risk for criminal behavior. *American Journal of Psychiatry, 154,* 853–855.

Breslau, N., Chilcoat, H. D., Kessler, R. C., Peterson, E. L., & Lucia, V. C. (1999). Vulnerability to assaultive violence: Further specification of the sex difference in posttraumatic stress disorder. *Psychological Medicine, 29,* 813–821.

Breslau, N., Davis, G. C., Andreski, P., & Peterson, E. L. (1997). Sex differences in posttraumatic stress disorder. *Archives of General Psychiatry, 54,* 1044–1048.

Breuer, J., & Freud, S. (1895). *Studies on hysteria (cathartic method).* [Special edition]. *2,* 1–309.

Brewer, M. B. (2001). Ingroup identification and intergroup conflict: When does ingroup love become outgroup hate? In R. D. Ashmore, L. Jussim, & D. Wilder (Eds.), *Social identity, intergroup conflict, and conflict reduction.* New York, NY: Oxford University Press.

Brick, J. (2003). The characteristics of alcohol: Chemistry, use and abuse. In J. Brick (Ed.), *Handbook of the medical consequences of alcohol and drug abuse* (pp. 1–11). New York, NY: Haworth Medical Press.

Briggs, K. C., & Myers, I. B. (1998). *The Myers-Briggs Type Indicator-Form M.* Palo Alto, CA: Consulting Psychologists Press.

Brigham, A. (1844). Asylums exclusively for the incurably insane. Classic article in *The American Journal of Psychiatry, 151,* 50–70.

Broadbent, D. (1958). *Perception and communication.* Elmsford, NY: Pergamon.

Brockington, I. F., Winokur, G., & Dean, C. (1982). Puerperal psychosis. In I. F. Brockington & R. Kumar (Eds.), *Motherhood and mental illness* (pp. 37–69). London, England: Academic Press.

Brockner, J., Greenberg, J., Brockner, A., Bortz, J., Davy, J., & Carter, C. (1986). Layoffs, equity theory, and work performance: Further evidence of the impact of survivor guilt. *Academy of Management Journal, 29*, 373–384.

Brondolo, E., Rieppi, R., Erickson, S. A., Bagiella, E., Shapiro, P. A., McKinley, P., & Sloan, R. P. (2003). Hostility, interpersonal interactions, and ambulatory blood pressure. *Psychosomatic Medicine, 65*, 1003–1011.

Brooks, J. G., & Brooks, M. G. (1993). *In search of understanding: The case for constructivist classrooms.* Alexandria, VA: The Association for Supervision and Curriculum Development.

Brotman, E. (2001). *How to toilet train your cat: The education of Mango.* Sherman Oaks, CA: Bird Brain Press.

Brown, C., Taylor, J., Green, A., Lee, B. E., Thomas, S. B., & Ford, A. (2003). *Managing depression in African Americans: Consumer and provider perspectives.* (Final Report to Funders). Pittsburgh, PA: Mental Health Association of Allegheny County.

Brown, G. L., & Linnoila, M. I. (1990). CSF serotonin metabolite (5–HIAA) studies in depression, impulsivity, and violence. *Journal of Clinical Psychiatry, 51*(4, suppl.), 31–43.

Brown, J. (1958). Some tests of the decay theory of immediate memory. *Quarterly Journal of Experimental Psychology, 10*, 12–21.

Brown, P. K., & Wald, G. (1964). Visual pigments in single rods and cones of the human retina. *Science, 144*, 45.

Brown, R., & McNeill, D. (1966). The "tip of the tongue" phenomenon. *Journal of Verbal Learning & Verbal Behavior, 5*, 325–337.

Brown, R. W. A. (1973). *First language: The early stages.* London, England: George Allen and Unwin.

Brown, Y. A., Barlow, D. H., & Liebowitz, M. R. (1994). The empirical basis of generalized anxiety disorder. *American Journal of Psychiatry, 151*, 1272–1280.

Browne, D. (2004). Do dolphins know their own mind? *Biology & Philosophy, 19*, 633–653.

Brubaker, D. A., & Leddy, J. J. (2003). Behavioral contracting in the treatment of eating disorders. *The Physician and Sportsmedicine, 31*(9).

Bruck, M., Ceci, S. J., Francoeur, E., and Barr, R. (1995). "I hardly cried when I got my shot." Influencing children's reports about a visit to their pediatrician. *Child Development, 66*, 193–208.

Brunet, A., Orr, S. P., Tremblay, J., Robertson, K., Nader, K., & Pitman, R. K. (2008). Effect of post-retrieval propranolol on psychophysiologic responding during subsequent script-driven traumatic imagery in post-traumatic stress disorder. *Journal of Psychiatric Research, 42*(6), 503–506.

Brunner, E. J., Hemingway, H., Walker, B., Page, M., Clarke, P., Juneja, M., . . . Marmot M. G. (2002). Adrenocortical, autonomic and inflammatory causes of the metabolic syndrome: Nested case-control study. *Circulation, 106*, 2659–2665.

Brunner, L., Nick, H. P., Cumin, F., Chiesi, M., Baum, H. P., Whitebread, S., . . . Levens, N. (1997). Leptin is a physiologically important regulator of food intake. *International Journal of Obesity Related Metabolic Disorders, 21*, 1152–1160.

Bryan, E. B., & Hallett, F. (2001). *Guidelines for professionals. Twins and triplets: The first five years and beyond.* London, England: Multiple Births Foundation.

Bryan, J., & Freed, F. (1982). Corporal punishment: Normative data and sociological and psychological correlates in a community college population. *Journal of Youth and Adolescence, 11*(2), 77–87.

Bryant, R. A., & McConkey, K. M. (1989). Hypnotic blindness: A behavioral and experimental analysis. *Journal of Abnormal Psychology, 98*, 71–77.

Brym, R. J., & Lenton, R. L. (2001). *Love online: Digital dating in Canada.* Retrieved from www.nelson.com/nelson/harcourt/sociology/newsociety3e/ loveonline.pdf

Brzustowicz, L. M., Simone, J., Mohseni, P., Hayter, J. E., Hodgkinson, K. A., Chow, E. W., & Bassett, A. S. (2004). Linkage disequilibrium mapping of schizophrenia susceptibility to the CAPON region of chromosome 1q22. *American Journal of Human Genetics, 74*, 1057–1063.

Bubenik, G. A., & Bubenik, P. G. (2008). Palmated antlers of moose may serve as a parabolic reflector of sounds. *European Journal of Wildlife Research, 54*(3), 533–535.

Bucher, B. D., & Lovaas, O. I. (1967). Use of aversive stimulation in behavior modification. In M. R. Jones (Ed.), *Miami Symposium on the Prediction of Behavior 1967: Aversive Stimulation,* 77–145.

Buck, R. (1980). Nonverbal behavior and the theory of emotion: The facial feedback hypothesis. *Journal of Personality and Social Psychology, 38*, 811–824.

Budney, A. J., Hughes, J. R., Moore, B. A., & Novy, P. L. (2001). Marijuana abstinence effects in marijuana smokers maintained in their environment. *Archives of General Psychiatry, 58*, 917–924.

Bunge, M. (1984). What is pseudoscience? *The Skeptical Inquirer, 9*(1), 36–46.

Bunge, M. B., & Pearse, D. D. (2003). Transplantation strategies to promote repair of the injured spinal cord. *Journal of Rehabilitative Research & Development, 40*(4), 55–62.

Burger, J. J. M. (1997). The psychoanalytic approach: Neo-Freudian theory, application, and assessment. *Personality* (4th ed.). Pacific Grove, CA: Brooks/Cole.

Burger, J. M., (1986). Increasing compliance by improving the deal: The that's not all technique. *Journal of Personality and Social Psychology, 51*, 277–283.

Burger, J. M., & Petty, R. E. (1981). The low-ball compliance technique: Task or person commitment? *Journal of Personality and Social Psychology, 40*, 492–500.

Burgio, K. L. (1998). Behavioral vs. drug treatment for urge urinary incontinence in older women: A randomized controlled trail. *Journal of the American Medical Association, 280*, 1995–2000.

Burke, D. M., MacKay, D. G., Worthley, J. S., & Wade, E. (1991). On the tip of the tongue: What causes word finding failures in young and older adults. *Journal of Memory and Language, 30*, 542–579.

Burks, N., & Martin, B. (1985). Everyday problems and life change events: Ongoing versus acute sources of stress. *Journal of Human Stress, 11*, 27–35.

Burrows, G. D., & Norman, T. R. (1999). Treatment-resistant unipolar depression. In M. Lader & D. Naber (Eds.), *Difficult clinical problems in psychiatry* (pp. 57–73). London, England: Martin Dunitz.

Bushman, B. J., & Huesmann, L. R. (2000). Effects of televised violence on aggression. In D. G. Singer & J. L. Singer (Eds.), *Handbook of children and the media* (pp. 223–254). Thousand Oaks, CA: Sage.

Buss, D. M., Larsen, R. J., Westen, D., & Semmelroth, J. (1992). Sex differences in jealousy: Evolution, physiology, and psychology. *Psychological Science, 3*, 251–255.

Bussa, B., & Kaufman, C. (2000). What can self-help do? *Journal of the California Alliance of the Mentally Ill, 2*(2).

Butcher, J. N., Graham, J. R., Ben-Poarth, Y. S., Tellegen, A., Dahlstrom, W. G., & Kaemmer, B. (2001). *Minnesota Multiphasic Personality Inventory-2. Manual for administration, scoring, and interpretation* (rev. ed.). Minneapolis, MN: University of Minnesota Press.

Butcher, J. N., & Rouse, S. V. (1996). Personality: Individual differences and clinical assessment. *Annual Review of Psychology, 47*, 87–111.

Butcher, J. N., Rouse, S. V., & Perry, J. N. (2000). Empirical description of psychopathology in therapy clients: Correlates of MMPI-2 scales. In J. N. Butcher (Ed.), *Basic sources on the MMPI-2* (pp. 487–500). Minneapolis, MN: University of Minnesota Press.

Butler, K. (1993). Too good to be true? *Networker, 6,* 19–31.

Byne, W. (1995). Science and belief: Psychobiological research on sexual orientation. *Journal of Homosexuality, 28*, 303–344.

Cabeza, R., Anderson, N. D., Locantore, J. K., & McIntosh, A. R. (2002). Aging gracefully: Compensatory brain activity in high-performing older adults. *NeuroImage, 17*, 1394–1402.

Cabeza, R., & Nyberg, L. (2000). Imaging cognition II: An empirical review of 275 PET and fMRI studies. *Journal of Cognitive Neuroscience, 12*, 1–47.

Cain, D., & Seeman, J. (Eds.). (2001). *Humanistic psychotherapies: Handbook of research and practice.* Washington, DC: APA.

Califia, P. (1997). *Sex changes: The politics of transgenderism.* San Francisco, CA: Cleis Press.

Calvert, D. R. (1992). *Descriptive phonetics.* New York, NY: Stuttgart, Germany: Thieme.

Camara, W. J., Nathan, J. S., & Puente, A. E. (2000). Psychological test usage: Implications in professional psychology. *Professional Psychology: Research and Practice, 31*(2), 141–154.

Cambridge Dictionaries Online (2011). *Child prodigy.* Retrieved from http://dictionary.cambridge.org/dictionary/british/child-prodigy

Cameron, J., Banko, K. M., & Pierce, W. D. (2001). Pervasive negative effects of rewards on intrinsic motivation: The myth continues. *The Behavior Analyst, 24,* 1–44.

Cameron, J. A., Alvarez, J. M., Ruble, D. N., & Fuligni, A. J. (2001). Children's lay theories about ingroups and outgroups: Reconceptualizing research on prejudice. *Personality and Social Psychology Review, 5,* 118–128.

Cameron, J. R., Hansen, R., & Rosen, D. (1989). Preventing behavioral problems in infancy through temperament assessment and parental support programs. In W. B. Carey & S. C. McDevitt (Eds.), *Clinical and educational applications of temperament research* (pp. 155–165). Amsterdam, the Netherlands: Swets & Zeitlinger.

Cameron, L., & Bartel, L. (2008, February 9). Homework a homewrecker: Report. *Toronto Star.*

Cami, J., Farre, M., Mas, M., Roset, P. N., Poudevida, S., Mas, A., . . . de la Torre, R. (2000). Human pharmacology of 3,4-methylenedioxymethamphetamine ("ecstasy"): Psychomotor performance and subjective effects. *Journal of Clinical Psychopharmacology, 20,* 455–466.

Campbell, J. C., & Wolf, A. D. (2003). Risk factors for femicide in abusive relationships: Results from a multisite case control study. *American Journal of Public Health, 93*(7), 1089–1097.

Campos, J. J., Langer, A., & Krowitz, A. (1970). Cardiac responses on the visual cliff. *Science, 170,* 196–197.

Canadian Centre for Justice Statistics. (1999). Crime statistics in Canada. *Juristat, 20*(5).

Canadian Council on Learning. (2007). *Equality in the classroom: The educational placement of children with disabilities.* Retrieved from http://www.ccl-cca.ca/CCL/Templates/LessonsInLearning.aspx?N RMODE=Published&NRORIGINALURL=%2fCCL%2fReports %2fLessonsInLearning%2fLinL20070502_Disability_Provincial_ differences%2ehtm&NRNODEGUID=%7bA85EEB82-B368-48BF-ADB0-02B9E8E3F891%7d&NRCACHEHINT=NoModifyGu est#_edn2

Canadian Down Syndrome Society. (2011). *New parents.* Retrieved from http://www.cdss.ca/blog/information/new-parent-information/

Canadian Encyclopedia, The (2011). *André Mathieu.* Retrieved from http://www.thecanadianencyclopedia.com/index.cfm?PgNm=TCE &Params=U1ARTU0003903

Cannon, W. B. (1927). The James-Lange theory of emotion: A critical examination and an alternative theory. *American Journal of Psychology, 39,* 10–124.

Cannon, W. B., & Washburn, A. L. (1912). An explanation of hunger. *American Journal of Physiology, 29,* 444–454.

Capek, J., & Capek, K. (1923). *"R.U.R." (Rossum's Universal Robots).* London, England: Oxford University Press.

Carducci, B. (1998). *The psychology of personality.* Pacific Grove, CA: Brooks/Cole Publishing Co.

Carey, B. (2010, November 22). In cybertherapy, avatars assist with healing. *New York Times.* Retrieved from www.nytimes.com

Carlberg, C., & Kavale, K. (1980). The efficacy of special versus regular class placement for exceptional children: A meta-analysis. *Journal of Special Education, 14,* 295–309.

Carlson, G. A., Jensen, P. S., & Nottelmann, E. D. (Eds.). (1998). Current issues in childhood bipolarity [special issue]. *Journal of Affective Disorders, 51.*

Carpenter, P. A., Just, M. A., & Shell, P. (1990). What one intelligence test measures: A theoretical account of the processing in the Raven Progressive Matrices test. *Psychological Review, 97*(3), 404–431.

Carr, E. G., & Lovaas, O. I. (1983). Contingent electric shock as a treatment for severe behavior problems. In S. Axelrod & J. Apsche (Eds.), *The effects of punishment on human behavior* (pp. 221–245). New York, NY: Academic Press.

Carrion, V. G., Weems, C. F., & Reiss, A. L. (2007). Stress predicts brain changes in children. A pilot longitudinal study on youth stress, posttraumatic stress disorder, and the hippocampus. *Pediatrics, 119*(3), 509–516.

Carroll, R. T. (2000). Eye movement desensitization and reprocessing (EMDR). *The Skeptic's Dictionary.* Retrieved from http://www. skepdic.com/ pseudosc.html

Carroll, R. T. (2002). ESP: Extrasensory perception. *Skeptic's Dictionary.* Retrieved from http://skepdic.com/esp.html

Carruthers, M. (2001). A multifactorial approach to understanding andropause. *Journal of Sexual and Reproductive Medicine, 1,* 69–74.

Carskadon, M. A., & Dement, W. C. (2005). Normal human sleep overview. In M. H. Kryger, T. Roth, & W. C. Dement (Eds.), *Principles and practice of sleep medicine* (4th ed., pp. 13–23). Philadelphia, PA: Elsevier/Saunders.

Carson, R. C. (1969). *Interaction concepts of personality.* Chicago, IL: Aldine.

Carver, C. S., & Antoni, M. H. (2004). Finding benefit in breast cancer during the year after diagnosis predicts better adjustment 5 to 8 years after diagnosis. *Health Psychology, 26,* 595–598.

Carver, L. J., & Bauer, P. J. (2001). The dawning of a past: The emergence of longterm explicit memory in infancy. *Journal of Experimental Psychology: General, 130,* 726–745.

Carveth, D. L. (2006, October 22). *Sigmund Freud today: What are his enduring contributions?* Lecture presented to the Oraynu Congregation for Humanistic Judaism, Toronto, ON.

Cassiday, K. L., & Lyons, J. A. (1992). Recall of traumatic memories following cerebral vascular accident. *Journal of Traumatic Stress, 5,* 627–631.

Cassidy, A., Bingham, S., & Setchell, K. D. R. (1994). Biological effects of a diet of soy protein rich in isoflavones on the menstrual cycle of premenopausal women. *American Journal of Clinical Nutrition, 60,* 333–340.

Castillo, R. J. (1997). Eating disorders. In R. J. Castillo (Ed.), *Culture and mental illness: A client-centered approach* (p. 152). Pacific Grove, CA: Brooks/Cole.

Cattell, R. B. (1950). *Personality: A systematic, theoretical, and factual study.* New York, NY: McGraw-Hill.

Cattell, R. B. (Ed.). (1966). *Handbook of multivariate experimental psychology.* Chicago, IL: Rand McNally.

Cattell, R. B. (1990). Advances in Cattellian personality theory. In L. A. Pervin (Ed.), *Handbook of personality: Theory and research* (pp. 101–110). New York, NY: Guilford.

Cattell, R. B. (1994). *Sixteen Personality Factor Questionnaire* (5th ed.). Champaign, IL: Institute for Personality and Ability Testing.

Cattell, R. B. (1995). Personality structure and the new fifth edition of the 16PF. *Educational & Psychological Measurement, 55,* 926–937.

Cattell, R. B., & Kline, P. (1977). *The scientific analysis of personality and motivation.* New York, NY: Academic Press.

Cave, K. R., & Kim, M. (1999). Top-down and bottom-up attentional control: On the nature of interference from a salient distractor. *Perception & Psychophysics, 61,* 1009–1023.

CBC News (2008, July 7). Steven Truscott: The search for justice. Retrieved from http://www.cbc.ca/news/background/truscott/

CBC News (2010, August 5). Deep brain stimulation tested for Alzheimer's. Retrieved from http://www.cbc.ca/health/story/2010/08/05/alzheimer-deep-brain-stimulation-toronto.html

Centers for Disease Control and Prevention (CDC). (2004). *Parents' guide to childhood immunization.* Atlanta, GA: U.S. Department of Health and Human Services, Public Health Service.

Centerwall, B. S. (1989). Exposure to television as a risk factor for violence. *American Journal of Epidemiology, 129,* 643–652.

Centre for Addiction and Mental Health (CAMH). (2008). *Treatment for Anxiety Disorders.* Retrieved from http://www.camh.net/About_Addiction_Mental_Health/Mental_Health_Information/Anxiety_Disorders/ treatment_anxiety.html

Cermak, L., & Craik, F. (1979). *Levels of processing in human memory.* Hillsdale, NJ: Erlbaum.

Cha, J. H., & Nam, K. D. (1985). A test of Kelley's cube theory of attribution: A cross-cultural replication of McArthur's study. *Korean Social Science Journal, 12,* 151–180.

Chadda, R. K., & Ahuja, N. (1990). Dhat syndrome: A sex neurosis of the Indian subcontinent. *British Journal of Psychiatry, 156,* 577–579.

Chaiken, S., & Eagly, A. H. (1978). Communication modality as a determinant of message persuasiveness and message comprehensibility. *Journal of Personality and Social Psychology, 34,* 605–614.

Chang, P. P., Ford, D. E., Meoni, L. A., Wang, N., & Klag, M. J. (2002). Anger in young men and subsequent premature cardiovascular disease: The precursors study. *Archives of Internal Medicine, 162,* 901–906.

Chapelon-Clavel, F., Paoletti, C., & Benhamou, S. (1997). Smoking cessation rates 4 years after treatment by nicotine gum and acupuncture. *Preventive Medicine 26,* 25–28.

Charlesworth, W. R., & Kreutzer, M. A. (1973). Facial expression of infants and children. In P. Ekman (Ed.), *Darwin and facial expression: A century of research in review.* New York, NY: Academic.

Chen, R., & Ende, N. (2000). The potential for the use of mononuclear cells from human umbilical cord blood in the treatment of amyotrophic lateral sclerosis in SOD1 mice. *Journal of Medicine, 31,* 21–31.

Cheng, H., Cao, Y., & Olson, L. (1996). Spinal cord repair in adult paraplegic rats: Partial restoration of hind limb function. *Science, 273,* 510–513.

Cherry, E. C. (1953). Some experiments on the recognition of speech, with one and with two ears. *Journal of the Acoustical Society of America, 25,* 975–979.

Chess, S., & Thomas, A. (1986). *Temperament in clinical practice.* New York, NY: Guilford.

Chesterton, L. S., Barlas, P., Foster, N. E., Baxter, G. D., & Wright, C. C. (2003). Gender differences in pressure pain threshold in healthy humans. *Pain, 101,* 259–266.

Chiu, C., Hong, Y., & Dweck, C. S. (1997). Lay dispositionism and implicit theories of personality. *Journal of Personality and Social Psychology, 73,* 19–30.

Choi, I., & Nisbett, R. E. (1998). Situational salience and cultural differences in the correspondence bias and in the actor–observer bias. *Personality and Social Psychology Bulletin, 24,* 949–960.

Choi, I., Nisbett, R. E., & Norenzayan, A. (1999). Causal attribution across cultures: Variation and universality. *Psychological Bulletin, 125,* 47–63.

Chomsky, N. (1957). *Syntactic structures.* The Hague: Mouton.

Chomsky, N. (1964). *Current issues in linguistic theory.* The Hague: Mouton.

Chomsky, N. (1981). Principles and parameters in syntactic theory. In N. Hornstein & D. Lightfoot (Eds.), *Explanation in linguistics: The logical problem of language acquisition.* London, England: Longman.

Chomsky, N. (1986). *Knowledge of language: Its nature, origin and use.* New York, NY: Praeger.

Chou, S. Y., Grossman, M., & Saffer, H. (2004). An economic analysis of adult obesity: Results from the behavioral risk factor surveillance system. *Journal of Health Economics, 23,* 565–587.

Christensen, A., Jacobson, N. S., & Babcock, J. C. (1995). Integrative behavioral couple therapy. In N. S. Jacobson & A. S. Gurman (Eds.), *Clinical handbook of couple therapy* (pp. 31–64). New York, NY: Norton.

Chu, J. A., Frey, L. M., Ganzel, B. L., & Matthews, J. A. (1999). Memories of childhood abuse: Dissociation, amnesia, and corroboration. *American Journal of Psychiatry, 156,* 749–755.

Chwalisz, K., Diener, E., & Gallagher, D. (1988). Autonomic arousal feedback and emotional experience: Evidence from the spinal cord injured. *Journal of Personality and Social Psychology, 54,* 820–828.

Cialdini, R., Vincent, J., Lewis, S., Catalan, J., Wheeler, D., & Darby, B. (1975). Reciprocal concessions procedure for inducing compliance: The door–in–the–face technique. *Journal of Personality and Social Psychology, 31,* 206–215.

Cialdini, R., Wosinska, W., Barrett, D., Butner, J., & Gornik–Durose, M. (1999). Compliance with a request in two cultures: The differential influence of social proof and commitment/consistency on collectivists and individualists. *Personality and Social Psychology Bulletin, 25,* 1242–1253.

Cialdini, R. B., Trost, M. R., & Newsom, J. T. (1995). Preference for consistency: The development of a valid measure and the discovery of surprising behavioral implications. *Journal of Personality and Social Psychology, 69,* 318–328.

Ciardiello, A. (1998). Did you ask a good question today? Alternative cognitive and metacognitive strategies. *Journal of Adolescent & Adult Literacy, 42,* 210–219.

Cincirpini, P. M., Lapitsky, L., Seay, S., Wallfisch, A., & Kitchens, K. V. V. H. (1995). The effects of smoking schedules on cessation outcome: Can we improve on common methods of gradual and abrupt nicotine withdrawal? *Journal of Consulting and Clinical Psychology, 63,* 388–399.

Cinnirella, M., & Green, B. (2007). Does cyber-conformity vary cross-culturally? Exploring cultural effects on conformity using a computer-mediated Asch paradigm. *Computers in Human Behavior, 23,* 2011–2025.

Cioffi, F. (1998). *Freud and the question of pseudoscience* (pp. 210–239). Chicago, IL: Open Court.

CityNews.ca Staff (2008, July 7). Steven Truscott receives $6.5M in compensation for wrongful murder conviction. Retrieved from http://www.citytv.com/toronto/citynews/news/local/article/3158-steven-truscott-receives-6-5m-in-compensation-for-wrongful-murder-conviction

Clark, D. A. (2004). *Cognitive-behavior therapy for OCD.* New York, NY: Guilford.

Clark, D. A., Beck, A. T., & Brown, G. (1989). Cognitive mediation in general psychiatric outpatients: A test of the content-specificity hypothesis. *Journal of Personality and Social Psychology, 56,* 958–964.

Clarke, J. (1994). Pieces of the puzzle: The jigsaw method. In S. Sharan (Ed.), *Handbook of cooperative learning methods* (pp. 34–50). Westport, CT: Greenwood Press.

Clarkin, J. F., Levy, K. N., Lenzenweger, M. F., & Kernberg, O. F. (2007). Evaluating three treatments for borderline personality disorder: A multiwave study. *American Journal of Psychiatry, 164*(6), 922–928.

Coates, J. (1986). *Women, men, and language.* New York, NY: Longman.

Coccaro, E. F., & Kavoussi, R. J. (1996). Neurotransmitter correlates of impulsive aggression. In D. M. Stoff & R. B. Cairns (Eds.), *Aggression and violence* (pp. 67–86). Mahwah, NJ: Erlbaum.

Cohen, E. (2007). Chris Benoit. Retrieved from http:// prowrestling.about.com/od/thewrestlers/p/chrisbenoit.htm

Cohen, L., Berzoff, J., & Elin, M. (1995). *Dissociative identity disorder: Theoretical and treatment controversies.* New York, NY: Human Sciences Library.

Cohen, L. J. (1997). Rational drug use in the treatment of depression. *Pharmacotherapy, 17,* 45–61.

Cohen, N. J., Eichenbaum, R., Decedo, J. C., & Corkin, S. (1985). Preserved learning capacity in amnesia: Evidence for multiple memory systems. In L. S. Squire & N. Butters (Eds.), *Neuropsychology of memory.* New York, NY: Gilford Press.

Cohen, S., & Herbert, T. B. (1996). Health psychology: Psychological factors and physical disease from the perspective of human psychoneuroimmunology. *Annual Review of Psychology, 47,* 113–142.

Colapinto, J. (2000). *As nature made him: The boy who was raised as a girl.* New York, NY: HarperCollins.

Colcombe, S. J., Erickson, K. I., Raz, N., Webb, A. G., Cohen, N. J., McAuley, E., & Kramer A. F. (2003). Aerobic fitness reduces brain tissue loss in aging humans. *Journal of Gerontology Series A: Biological Sciences and Medical Sciences, 58,* 176–180.

Colligan, J. (1983). Musical creativity and social rules in four cultures. *Creative Child and Adult Quarterly, 8,* 39–44.

Collins, A. M., & Loftus, E. F. (1975). A spreading activation theory of semantic processing. *Psychological Review, 82,* 407–428.

Collins, A. M., & Quillian, M. R. (1969). Retrieval time from semantic memory. *Journal of Verbal Learning and Verbal Behaviour, 8,* 240–247.

Collins, C. J., Hanges, P. J., & Locke, E. A. (2004). The relationship of achievement motivation to entrepreneurial behavior: A meta-analysis. *Human Performance, 17*(1), 95–117.

Committee on Animal Research and Ethics. (2004). *Research with animals in psychology.* APAOnline. Retrieved from http://www.apa.org/science/animal2.html

Conrad, R., & Hull, A. J. (1964). Information, acoustic confusion, and memory span. *British Journal of Psychology, 55,* 429–432.

Consumer Reports. (1995, November). Mental health: Does psychotherapy help? 734–739.

Conway, M. A., Cohen, G., & Stanhope, N. (1992). Very long-term memory for knowledge acquired at school and university. *Applied Cognitive Psychology, 6,* 467–482.

Coolidge, F. L. (2006). *Dream interpretation as a psychotherapeutic technique.* London, England: Radcliffe.

Cooper, L. A., Gonzales, J. J., Gallo, J. J., Rost, K. M., Meredith, L. S., Rubenstein, L. V., . . . Ford D. E. (2003). The acceptability of treatment for depression among African-American, Hispanic, and white primary care patients. *Medical Care, 41,* 479–489.

Corkin, S. (1984). Lasting consequences of bilateral medial temporal lobe lobectomy: Clinical course and experimental findings in H.M. *Seminars in Neurology, 4,* 249–259.

Cormier, J. F., & Thelen, M. H. (1998). Professional skepticism of multiple personality disorder. *Professional Psychology: Research and Practice, 29,* 163–167.

Cornell, E. H., & Heth, C. D. (2006). Home range and the development of children's wayfinding. In R. Kail (Ed.), *Advances in Child Development and Behavior, 34* (pp. 173–206). New York, NY: Elsevier.

Cosgrove, G. R., & Rauch, S. L. (1995). Psychsurgery. *Neurosurgery Clinics of North America, 6,* 167–176.

Costa P. T., Jr., & McCrae. R. R. (1989). Personality continuity and the changes of adult life. In M. Storandt & G. R. VandenBos (Eds.), *The adult years: Continuity and change* (pp. 45–77). Washington, DC: American Psychological Association.

Costa, P. T., Jr., & McCrae, R. R. (2000). The Revised NEO Personality Inventory (NEO PI-R). In J. Cheek & E. M. Donahue (Eds.), *Handbook of personality inventories.* New York, NY: Plenum.

Courage, M. L., & Howe, M. L. (2002). From infant to child: The dynamics of cognitive change in the second year of life. *Psychological Bulletin, 128,* 250–277.

Cowan, N. (1988). Evolving conceptions of memory storage, selective attention, and their mutual constraints within the human information processing system. *Psychological Bulletin, 104,* 163–191.

Cox, B. J., & Stevens, S. (1999). Anxiety disorders: Panic and phobias. In T. Millon, P. Blaney, & R. Davis, (Eds.), *Oxford textbook of psychopathology* (pp. 81–113). Oxford, England: Oxford University Press.

Cox, B. J., Yu, N., Afifi, T. O., & Ladouceur, R. (2005). A national survey of gambling problems in Canada. *Canadian Journal of Psychiatry, 50,* 213–217.

Crago, M. B., Shisslak, C. M., & Estes, L. S. (1996). Eating disturbances among American minority groups: A review. *International Journal of Eating Disorders, 19,* 239–248.

Craik, F. I. M. (1970). The fate of primary memory items in free recall. *Journal of Verbal Learning and Verbal Behavior, 9,* 143–148.

Craik, F. I. M. (1994). Memory changes in normal aging. *Current Directions in Psychological Science, 3*(5), 155–158.

Craik, F. I. M. (2002). Levels of processing: Past, present. . . and future? *Memory, 10,* 305–318.

Craik, F. I. M., & Lockhart, R. S. (1972). Levels of processing. A framework for memory research. *Journal of Verbal Learning and Verbal Behaviour, 11,* 671–684.

Craik, F. I. M., & Tulving, E. (1975). Depth of processing and the retention of words in episodic memory. *Journal of Experimental Psychology: General, 104,* 268–294.

Cramer, P. (2000). Defense mechanisms in psychology today: Further processes for adaptation. *American Psychologist, 55,* 637–646.

Craske, M. G., & Barlow, D. H. (2008). Panic disorder and agoraphobia. In D. H. Barlow (Ed.), *Clinical handbook of psychological disorders* (pp. 1–64). New York, NY: Guilford Press.

Crawford, M., & Unger, R. (2004). *Women and gender: A feminist psychology* (4th ed.). Boston, MA: McGraw-Hill.

Crowley, A. E., & Hoyer, W. D. (1994). "An integrative framework for understanding two–sided persuasion," *Journal of Consumer Research, 20,* 561–574.

Crozier, W. R., & Alden, L. E. (2001). *International handbook of social anxiety: Concepts, research and interventions relating to the self and shyness.* New York, NY: Wiley.

Csernansky, J. G., Mahmoud, R., & Brenner, R. (2002). A comparison of reperidone and hloperidol for the prevention of relapse in patients with schizophrenia. *New England Journal of Medicine, 346,* 16–22.

Csikszentmihalyi, M. (1996). *Creativity: Flow and the psychology of discovery and invention.* New York, NY: Harper Perennial.

Csikszentmihalyi, M. (1997). *Finding flow: The psychology of engagement with everyday life.* New York, NY: Basic Books.

CTV.ca News. (2003). Broken soldiers: Combating military stress. Retrieved from http://www.ctv.ca/servlet/ArticleNews/story/CTVNews/1047060032429_37///?hub=Specials

CTV.ca News. (2006). Canadians are a stressed-out bunch, poll finds. Retrieved from http://www.ctv.ca/servlet/ArticleNews/story/CTVNews/20061220/canada_stress_061220?s_name=&no_ads=

CTV.ca News. (2007). Foul play suspected in wrestler family's death. Retrieved from http://www.ctv.ca/servlet/ArticleNews/story/CTVNews/20070625/chris_benoit_070625?s_name=&no_ads

Cua, A. B., Wilhelm, K. P., & Maibach, H. I. (1990). Elastic properties of human skin: Relation to age, sex and anatomical region. *Archives of Dermatology Research, 282,* 283–288.

Culbertson, F. (2003). *The phobia list.* Retrieved from http://www.phobialist.com

Cummings, J. L., & Coffey C. E. (1994). Neurobiological basis of behavior. In C. E. Coffey, & J. L. Cummings (Eds.), *Textbook of geriatric neuropsychiatry* (pp. 72–96). Washington, DC: American Psychiatric Press.

Cummings, S. R., & Melton, L. J., III. (2002). Epidemiology and outcomes of osteoporotic fractures. *Lancet, 359,* 1761–1767.

Curtis, R. C., & Miller, K. (1986). Believing another likes or dislikes you: Behaviors making the beliefs come true. *Journal of Personality and Social Psychology, 51,* 284–290.

Curtis, R. H. (1993). *Great lives: Medicine.* New York, NY: Scribner's.

Cytowic, R. E. (1989). Synesthesia and mapping of subjective sensory dimensions. *Neurology, 39,* 849–850.

Czeisler, C. A. (1995). The effect of light on the human circadian pacemaker. In D. J. Chadwick & K. Ackrill (Eds.), *Circadian clocks and their adjustment* (pp. 254–302). West Sussex, England: Wiley.

Czeisler, C. A., Weitzman, E. D., Moore-Ede, M. C., Zimmerman, J. C., & Knauer, R. S. (1980). Human sleep: Its duration and organization depend on its circadian phase. *Science, 210,* 1264–1267.

Dabbs, Jr, J. M., Riad, J. K., & Chance, S. E. (2001).Testosterone and ruthless homicide. *Personality and Individual Differences, 31*(4), 599–603.

Dalenberg, C. J. (1996). Accuracy, timing and circumstances of disclosure in therapy of recovered and continuous memories of abuse. *The Journal of Psychiatry and Law, 24,* 229–275.

Dallman, M., Pecoraro, N., Akana, S., la Fleur, S. E., Gomez, F., Houshyar, H., . . . Manalo, S. (2003). Chronic stress and obesity: A new view of "comfort food." *Proceedings of the National Academy of Sciences, 100,* 11696–11701.

Daly, M., Wilson, M., & Weghorst, S. J. (1982). Male sexual jealousy. *Ethology and Sociobiology, 3,* 11–27.

Damasio, H., Grabowski, T., Frank, R., Galaburda, A. M., & Damasion, A. R. (1994). The return of Phineas Gage: Clues about the brain from the skull of a famous patient. *Science, 264,* 1102–1105.

Darley, J. M., & Latané, B. (1968). Bystander intervention in emergencies: Diffusion of responsibility. *Journal of Personality and Social Psychology, 8,* 377–383.

Darwin, C. (1859). The origin of species by means of natural selection. London, England: John Murray.

Darwin, C. (1898). The expression of the emotions in man and animals. New York, NY: D. Appleton & Co.

Daum, I., & Schugens, M. M. (1996). On the cerebellum and classical conditioning. *Current Directions in Psychological Science, 5,* 58–61.

David, D. H., & Lyons, R. K. (2005). Differential attachment responses of male and female infants to frightening maternal behavior: Tend or befriend versus fight or flight. *Infant Mental Health Journal, 26,* 1–18.

Davidson, P. R., & Parker, K. C. H. (2001). Eye movement desensitization and reprocessing (EMDR): A meta-analysis. *Journal of Consulting and Clinical Psychology, 69,* 305–316.

Davidson, R. J., Ekman, P., Saron, C. D., Senulis, J. A., & Friesen, W. V. (1990). Approach-withdrawal and cerebral asymmetry: Emotional expression and brain physiology I. *Journal of Personality and Social Psychology, 58*(2), 330–341.

Davidson, R. J., Putman, K. M., & Larson, C. L. (2000). Dysfunction in the neural circuitry of emotion regulation—A possible prelude to violence. *Science, 289,* 591–594.

Davies, I. R. L, Laws, G., Corbett, G. G., & Jerrett, D. J. (1998a). Crosscultural differences in colour vision: Acquired "colour blindness" in Africa. *Personality and Individual Differences, 25,* 1153–1162.

Davies, I. R. L., Sowden, P., Jerrett, D. T., Jerrett, T., & Corbett, G. G. (1998b). A cross-cultural study of English and Setswana speakers on a colour triads task: A test of the Sapir-Whorf hypothesis. *British Journal of Psychology, 89,* 1–15.

Davis, C., & MacDonald, S. (2004). Threat appraisals, distress, and the development of positive life changes after September 11th in a Canadian sample. *Cognitive Behavioral Therapy, 33*(2), 67–78.

Davis, J. O., & Bracha, H. S. (1996). Prenatal growth markers in schizophrenia: A monozygotic co-twin control study. *American Journal of Psychiatry, 153,* 1166–1172.

Davis, K. F., Parker, K. P., & Montgomery, G. (2004). Sleep in infants and young children: Part 1, Normal sleep. *Journal of Pediatric Healthcare, 18*(2), 65–71.

Davis, K. L., Kahn, R. S., Ko, G., & Davidson, M. (1991). Dopamine in schizophrenia: A review and reconceptualization. *American Journal of Psychiatry, 148,* 1474–1486.

Davis, M., & Whalen, P. J. (2001). The amygdala: Vigilance and emotion. *Molecular Psychiatry 6,* 13–34.

Dawood, K., Pillard, R. C., Horvath, C., Revelle, W., & Bailey, J. M. (2000). Familial aspects of male homosexuality. *Archives of Sexual Behavior, 29*(2).

Day, R. H., & McKenzie, B. E. (1981). Infant perception of the invariant size of approaching and receding objects. *Developmental Psychology, 17,* 670–677.

Dean, G., & Kelly, I. W. (2000). Does astrology work? Astrology and skepticism 1975–2000. In P. Kurtz (Ed.), *Skepticism: A 25 year retrospective* (pp. 191–207) Amherst NY: Prometheus Books.

Dean, G., Kelly, I. W., Sakolfske, D. H., & Furnham, A. (1992). Graphology and human judgment. In B. L. Beyerstein & D. F. Beyerstein (Eds.), *The write stuff: Evaluations of graphology— the study of handwriting analysis* (pp. 342–396). Amherst NY: Prometheus Books.

DeAngelis, T. (2002). Promising treatments for anorexia and bulimia: Research boosts support for tough-to-treat eating disorders. *APA Monitor on Psychology, 33*(3), 38–43.

DeCasper, A. J., & Fifer, W. P. (1980). Of human bonding: Newborns prefer their mothers' voices. *Science, 208,* 1174–1176.

DeCasper, A. J., & Spence, M. J. (1986). Prenatal maternal speech influence on newborns' perception of sounds. *Infant Behaviour and Development, 9,* 133–150.

deCharms, R. (1968). *Personal causation.* New York, NY: Academic Press.

Deci, E. L., Eghrari, H., Patrick, B. C., & Leone, D. R. (1994). Facilitating internalization: The self-determination theory perspective. *Journal of Personality, 62,* 119–142.

Deci, E. L., Koestner, R., & Ryan, R. M. (1999). A meta-analytic review of experiments examining the effects of extrinsic rewards on intrinsic motivation. *Psychological Bulletin, 125,* 627–668.

Deci, E. L., & Ryan, R. M. (1985). *Intrinsic motivation and self–determination in human behavior.* New York, NY: Plenum.

DeCoster, J., & Claypool, H. M. (2004). A meta-analysis of priming effects on impression formation supporting a general model of informational biases. *Personality and Social Psychology Review, 8*(1), 2–27.

DeGrandpre, R. J. (2000). A science of meaning: Can behaviorism bring meaning to psychological science? *American Psychologist, 55,* 721–739.

Dehaene, S., Naccache, L., Cohen, L., Le Bihan, D., Mangin, J. F., Poline, J. B., & Rivière, D. (2001). Cerebral mechanisms of word masking and unconscious repetition priming. *Nature Neuroscience, 4,* 752–758.

Deinzer, R., Kleineidam, C. H., Winkler, R., Idel, H., & Bachg, D. (2000). Prolonged reduction of salivary immunoglobulin A (sIgA) after a major academic exam. *International Journal of Psychophysiology, 37,* 219–232.

Delagrange, P., & Guardiola-Lemaitre, B. (1997). Melatonin, its receptors, and relationships with biological rhythm disorders. *Clincal Neuropharmacology, 20,* 482–510.

DeLongis, A., Lazarus, R. S., & Folkman, S. (1988). The impact of daily stress on health and mood: Psychological and social resources as mediators. *Journal of Personality and Social Psychology, 54,* 486–495.

De Luca, R. V., Boyes, D. A., Grayston, A. D., & Romano, E. (1995). Sexual abuse: Effects of group therapy on preadolescent girls. *Child Abuse Review, 4,* 263–277.

Dement, W. (1974). *Some must watch while some must sleep.* San Francisco, CA: W.H. Freeman.

Dement, W. (1997). *Sleepless at Stanford: What all undergraduates should know about how their sleeping lives affect their waking lives.* Retrieved from http://www.stanford.edu/~dement/sleepless.html

Dement, W. C. (1960). The effect of dream deprivation. *Science, 131,* 1705–1707.

Dement, W. C., Henry, P., Cohen, H., & Ferguson, J. (1969). Studies on the effect of REM deprivation in humans and animals. In K. H. Pribram (Ed.), *Mood, states, and mind.* Baltimore, MD: Penguin.

Demers, R. A. (1988). Linguistics and animal communication. In Newmeyer (Ed.), *Language form and language function* (pp. 314–335). Cambridge, MA: MIT Press.

Dennett, D. C. (1991). *Consciousness explained.* New York, NY: Little, Brown, & Company.

Denno, D. W. (2002). Crime and consciousness: Science and involuntary acts. *Minnesota Law Review, 87,* 269–399.

Deregowski, J. B. (1969). Perception of the two-pronged trident by two- and threedimensional perceivers. *Journal of Experimental Psychology, 82,* 9–13.

Derfel, A. (2007, November 28). Catching a whiff of danger: Our noses can tell friend from stranger. *The Gazette.* Retrieved from http://www.canada.com/ottawacitizen/features/bestofcanwest/story.html?id= da9f4948-cde0-439d-8a62-9777e1475a29

DeRubeis, R. J., Gelfand, L. A., Tang, T. Z., & Simons, A. D. (1999). Medications versus cognitive behavior therapy for severely depressed outpatients: Megaanalysis of four randomized comparisons. *American Journal of Psychiatry, 156,* 1007–1013.

De Valois R. L., & Jacobs G. H. (1968). Primate color vision, *Science, 162,* 533–540.

Dew, M. A., Whyte, E. M., Lenze, E. J., Houck, P. R., Mulsant, B. H., Pollock, B. G., . . . Reynolds, C. F. (2007). Recovery from major depression in older adults receiving augmentation of antidepressant pharmacotherapy. *American Journal of Psychiatry, 164*(6), 892–899.

Diamond, L. M. (2003). What does sexual orientation orient? A biobehavioral model distinguishing romantic love and sexual desire. *Psychological Review, 110,* 173–192.

Diamond, M. (1995). Biological aspects of sexual orientation and identity. In L. Diamant & R. McAnulty (Eds.), *The psychology of sexual orientation, behavior and identity: A handbook* (pp. 45–80). Westport, CT: Greenwood Press.

Diamond, M., & Sigmundson, H. K. (1997). Sex reassignment at birth. Long-term review and clinical implications. *Archives of Pediatric Adolescent Medicine, 151*(3), 298–304.

Diamond, M. C. (1991). Hormonal effects on the development of cerebral lateralization. *Psychoneuroendocrinology, 16,* 121–129.

Dickens, W. T., & Flynn, J. R. (2001 April). Heritability estimates vs. large environmental effects: The IQ paradox resolved. *Psychological Review, 108,* 346–369.

Dickerson, F., Ringel, N., Parente, F., & Boronow, J. (1994). Seclusion and restraint, assaultiveness, and patient performance in a token economy. *Hospital and Community Psychiatry, 45,* 168–170.

Digman, J. M. (1990). Personality structure: Emergence of the five-factor model. *Annual Review of Psychology, 41,* 417–440.

Dillard, J. (1990). Self-inference and the foot–in–the–door technique: Quantity of behavior and attitudinal mediation. *Human Communication Research, 16,* 422–447.

Dillard, J. (1991). The current status of research on sequential–request compliance techniques. *Personality and Social Psychology Bulletin, 17,* 282–288.

Dimberg, U., Thunberg, M., & Elmehed, K. (2000). Unconscious facial reactions to emotional facial expressions. *Psychological Science, 11,* 86–89.

Dinges, D. F. (1995). An overview of sleepiness and accidents. *Journal of Sleep Research, 4*(2), 4–14.

Dion, K. K., & Dion, K. L. (1993). Individualistic and collectivistic perspectives on gender and the cultural context of love and intimacy. *Journal of Social Issues, 49*(3), 53–69

Dodge, K. A., Bates, J. E., & Pettit, G. S. (1990). Mechanisms in the cycle of violence. *Science, 250,* 1678–1683.

Doidge, N. (2006, May). Sigmund Freud: The doctor is back in. *Maclean's.*

Dollard, J., Doob, L. W., Milller, N. E., Mowrer, O. H., & Sears, R. R. (1939). *Frustration and aggression.* New Haven, CT: Yale University Press.

Dollard, J., & Miller, N. (1950). *Personality and psychotherapy: An analysis in terms of learning, thinking and culture.* New York, NY: McGraw-Hill.

Domhoff, G. W. (1996). *Finding meaning in dreams: A quantitative approach.* New York, NY: Plenum Publishing Co.

Domjan, M., Cusato, B., & Villarreal, R. (2000), Pavlovian feed-forward mechanisms in the control of social behavior. *Behavioral and Brain Sciences, 23,* 235–282.

Dorahy, M. J. (2001). Dissociative identity disorder and memory dysfunction: The current state of experimental research and its future directions. *Clinical Psychology Review, 21*(5), 771–795.

Dornin, R., & Reiss, A. (2007). "Roid rage" questions surround Benoit murdersuicide. CNN. Retrieved from http://www.cnn.com/2007/US/06/27/wrestler/index.html

Dougherty, D. D., Baer, L., Cosgrove, G. R., Cassem, E. H., Price, B. H., Nierenberg, A. A., . . . Rauch, S. L. (2002). Prospective long-term follow-up of 44 patients who received cingulotomy for treatment-refractory obsessive-compulsive disorder. *American Journal of Psychiatry, 159,* 269–275.

Dove, A. (1971). The "Chitling" Test. In Lewis R. Aiken, Jr. (Ed.), *Psychological and educational testings.* Boston, MA: Allyn and Bacon.

Dreger, A. D. (1998). "Ambiguous sex"—or ambivalent medicine? Ethical issues in the treatment of intersexuality. *Hastings Center Report, 28*(3), 24–35.

Dreger, A. D. (1999). *Intersex in the age of ethics.* Hagerstown, MD: University Publishing Groups.

Drenth, P. J., Thierry, H., Willems, P. J., & de Wolff, C. J. (1984) *Handbook of work and organizational psychology.* Chichester, England: Wiley.

Druckman, D., & Bjork, R. A. (Eds.). (1994). *Learning, remembering, believing: Enhancing human performance.* (Study conducted by the National Research Council). Washington, DC: National Academy Press.

Drummond, K. D., Bradley, S. J., Peterson-Badali, M., & Zucker, K. J. (2008). A follow-up study of girls with gender identity disorder. *Developmental Psychology, 44*(1), 34–45.

Duben, A., & Behar, C. (1991). *Istanbul households: Marriage, family and fertility 1880–1940.* Cambridge, England: Cambridge University Press.

Dubowitzm, H., & Bennett, S. (2007). Physical abuse and neglect of children. *Lancet, 369*(9576), 1891–1899.

Dufresne, T. (2000). *Tales from the Freudian crypt: The death drive in text and context.* Stanford, CA: Stanford University Press.

Dufresne, T. (2007). *Against Freud: Critics talk back.* Stanford, CA: Stanford University Press.

Duker, P. C., & Seys, D. M. (1995). *Long-term use of electrical aversion treatment with self-injurious behavior.* Paper presented at BILD Conference.

Dulcan, M. K. (2010). *Dulcan's textbook of child and adolescent psychiatry.* Arlington, VA: American Psychiatric Publishing.

Duncan, R. M. (1995). Piaget and Vygotsky revisited: Dialogue or assimilation? *Developmental Review, 15,* 458–472.

Durrant, M. (Ed.). (1993). *Aristotle's De anima in focus.* London, England: Routledge.

Durso, F., Rea, C., & Dayton, T. (1994). Graph-theoretic confirmation of restructuring during insight. *Psychological Science, 5,* 94–98.

Durston, S. (2003). A review of the biological bases of ADHD: What have we learned from imaging studies? *Mental Retardation and Developmental Disabilities Research Reviews, 9,* 184–195.

Dutton, D. G., & Aron, A. P. (1974) Some evidence for heightened sexual attraction under conditions of high anxiety. *Journal of Personality and Social Psychology, 30,* 510–517

Dutton, D. G., & Aron, A. P. (1989). Romantic attraction and generalized liking for others who are sources of conflict-based arousal. *Canadian Journal of Behavioural Science, 21,* 246–257.

Dweck, C. (1986). Motivational processes affecting learning. *American Psychologist, 41,* 1040–1048.

Dweck, C., & Elliott, E. (1983). Achievement motivation. In P. Mussen (Ed.), *Handbook of child psychology: Vol. 4. Socialization, personality, and social development* (pp. 643–691). New York, NY: Wiley.

Dweck, C. S. (1999). *Self-theories: Their role in motivation, personality and development.* Philadelphia, PA: Psychology Press.

Dweck, C. S., Chiu, C., & Hong, Y. (1995). Implicit theories and their role in judgments and reactions: A world from two perspectives. *Psychological Inquiry, 6,* 267–285.

Dweck, C. S., & Leggett, E. L. (1988). A social-cognitive approach to motivation and personality. *Psychological Review, 95,* 256–273.

Dworet, D., & Bennett, S. (2002). A view from the north—Special education in Canada. *Teaching Exceptional Children, 34*(5), 22–27.

Dykens, E. M., Hodapp, R. M., & Leckman, J. F. (1994). *Behavior and development in Fragile X syndrome.* Thousand Oaks, CA: Sage.

Eagly, A., & Chaiken, S. (1975). An attribution analysis of the effect of communicator characteristics on opinion change: The case of communicator attractiveness. *Journal of Personality and Social Psychology, 37,* 136–144.

Eagly, A. H. (1987). *Sex difference in social behavior: A social-role interpretation.* Hillsdale, NJ: Erlbaum.

Eagly, A. H., Ashmore, R. D., Makhijani, M. G., & Longo, L. C. (1991). What is beautiful is good, but . . . : A meta-analytic review of the physical attractiveness stereotype. *Psychological Bulletin, 110,* 109–128.

Eagly, A. H., & Chaiken, S. (1993). *The psychology of attitudes.* Fort Worth, TX: Harcourt Brace.

Eagly, A. H., & Chaiken, S. (1998). Attitude structure and function. In D. T. Gilbert, S. T. Fiske, & G. Lindzey (Eds.), *The handbook of social psychology* (4th ed., pp. 269–322). New York, NY: McGraw-Hill.

Eagly, A. H., Wood, W., & Diekman, A. B. (2000). Social role theory of sex differences and similarities: A current appraisal. In T. Eckes & H. M. Trautner (Eds.), *The developmental social psychology of gender* (pp. 123–174). Mahwah, NJ: Erlbaum.

Eaker, E. D., & Castelli, W. P. (1988). Type A behavior and mortality from coronary disease in the Framingham Study. *New England Journal of Medicine, 319,* 1480–1481.

Ebbinghaus, H. (1913). *Memory: A contribution to experimental psychology.* New York, NY: Teachers College Press. (Translated from the 1885 German original.)

Eddy, J., Fitzhugh, E., & Wang, M. (2000). Smoking acquisition: Peer influence and self-selection. *Psychological Reports, 86,* 1241–1246.

Edelmann, R. J., & Iwawaki, S. (1987). Self-reported expression of embarrassment in five European cultures. *Psychologia: An International Journal of Psychology, 30,* 205–216.

Ehlers, A., Bisson, J., Clark, D. M., Creamer, M., Pilling, S., Richards, D., . . . Yule, W. (2010). Do all psychological treatments really work the same in posttraumatic stress disorder? *Clinical Psychology Review, 30*(2), 269–276.

Eich, E., & Metcalfe, J. (1989). Mood dependent memory for internal versus external events. *Journal of Experimental Psychology: Learning, Memory, and Cognition, 15,* 443–455.

Eich, J. E. (1980). The cue dependent nature of state-dependent retrieval. *Memory and Cognition, 8*(2), 157–173.

E I Skills Group (2011). *About the MSCEIT.* Retrieved from http://www.emotionaliq.com/MSCEIT.html

Ekman, P. (1973). Darwin and cross-cultural studies of facial expression. In P. Ekman (Ed.), *Darwin and facial expression: A century of research in review.* New York, NY: Academic Press.

Ekman, P. (1980). Asymmetry in facial expression. *Science, 209,* 833–834.

Ekman, P., & Friesen, W. (1969). The repertoire of nonverbal behavior: Categories, origins, usage, and coding. *Semiotica, 1,* 49–98.

Ekman, P., & Friesen, W. (1971). Constants across cultures in the face and emotion. *Journal of Personality and Social Psychology, 17*(2), 124–129.

Ekman, P., & Friesen, W. V. (1978). *The facial action coding system.* Palo Alto, CA: Consulting Psychologists Press.

Ekman, P., Sorensen, E. R., & Friesen, W. V. (1969). Pan-cultural elements in facial displays of emotion. *Science, 164,* 86–88.

Elias, L. J., Saucier, D. M., Hardie, C., & Sarty, G. E. (2003). Dissociating semantic and perceptual components of synaesthesia: Behavioural and functional neuroanatomical investigations. *Cognitive Brain Research, 16,* 232–237.

Elkind, D. (1985). Egocentrism redux. *Developmental Review, 5,* 218–226.

Elliott, E., & Dweck, C. (1988). Goals: An approach to motivation and achievement. *Journal of Personality and Social Psychology, 54,* 5–12.

Elliott, L., & Brantley, C. (1997). *Sex on campus: The naked truth about the real sex lives of college students.* New York, NY: Random House.

Ellis, A. (1997). *The practice of rational emotive behavior therapy.* New York, NY: Springer.

Ellis, A. (1998). *The Albert Ellis reader: A guide to well-being using rational emotive behavior therapy.* Secaucus, NJ: Carol.

Ellis, A., & Knaus, W. J. (1977). *Overcoming procrastination.* New York, NY: Signet Books.

Ellis, B. J., McFayden-Ketchum, S. A., Dodge, K. A., Pettit, G. S., & Bates, J. E. (1999). Quality of early family relationships and individual differences in the timing of pubertal maturation in girls: A longitudinal test on an evolutionary model. *Journal of Personality and Social Psychology, 77,* 387–401.

Ellis, H. D. (1983). The role of the right hemisphere in face perception. In A. W. Young (Ed.), *Functions of the right cerebral hemisphere.* London, England: Academic Press.

Ellis, L., Ames, M. A., Peckham, W., & Burke, D. (1988). Sexual orientation of human offspring may be altered by severe maternal stress during pregnancy. *Journal of Sex Research, 25,* 152–157.

Ellis, L. K., Gay, P. E., & Paige, E. (2001). *Daily pleasures and hassles across the lifespan.* Poster presented at the annual meeting of the American Psychological Association, San Francisco, CA.

EMDR. (2004). *Eye movement desensitization and reprocessing.* Retrieved from http:// www.emdr.com

Endler, N. S. (1988). The origins of electroconvulsive therapy (ECT). *Convulsive Therapy, 4,* 5–23.

Endler, N. S., Macrodimitris, S. D., & Kocovski, N. L. (2000). Controllability in cognitive and interpersonal tasks: Is control good for you? *Personality and Individual Differences, 29,* 951–962.

Engelhardt, C. R., Bartholow, B. D., Kerr, G. T., & Bushman, B. J. (in press). This is your brain on violent video games: Neural desensitization to violence predicts increased aggression following violent video game exposure. *Journal of Experimental Social Psychology.*

Engle, R. W., & Kane, M. J. (2004). Executive attention, working memory capacity, and a two-factor theory of cognitive control. *The Psychology of Learning and Motivation, 44,* 145–199.

Enns, J. T., & Coren, S. (1995). The box alignment illusion: An orientation illusion induced by pictorial depth. *Perception & Psychophysics, 57,* 1163–1174.

Enns, M. W., Reiss, J. P., & Chan, P. (2010). Electroconvulsive therapy. *Canadian Journal of Psychiatry, 55*(6), 1–11.

Epping-Jordan, M., Waltkins, S. S., Koob, G. F., & Markou, A. (1998). Dramatic decreases in brain reward function during nicotine withdrawal. *Nature, 393,* 76–79.

Erdley, C. A., & Dweck, C. S. (1993). Children's implicit personality theories as predictors of their social judgments. *Child Development, 64,* 863–878.

Erikson, E. (1980). Elements of a psychoanalytic theory of psychosocial development. In S. Greenspan & G. Pollock (Eds.), *The course of life* (Vol. 1, pp. 11–61). Washington, DC: U.S. Dept. of Health and Human Services.

Erikson, E. H. (1950). *Childhood and society.* New York, NY: Norton.

Erikson, E. H. (1959). Growth and crises of the healthy personality. *Psychological Issues, 1,* 50–100.

Erikson, E. H. (1982). *The life cycle completed.* New York, NY: Norton.

Erikson, E. H., & Erikson, J. M. (1997). *The life cycle completed.* New York, NY: Norton.

Eriksson, P., Jakobsson, E., & Fredriksson, A. (2001). Brominated flame retardants: A novel class of developmental neurotoxicants in our environment? *Environmental Health Perspectives, 109,* 903–908.

Eskenazi, B., Bradman, A., & Castorina, R. (1999). Exposures of children to organophosphate pesticides and their potential adverse health effects. *Environmental Health Perspectives, 107*(Suppl. 3), 409–419.

Evans, D., Hodgkinson, B., O'Donnell, A., Nicholson, J., & Walsh, K. (2000). The effectiveness of individual therapy and group therapy in the treatment of schizophrenia. In *Best Practice, 5*(3), 1–54. Australia: Joanna Briggs Institute for Evidence Based Nursing and Midwifery.

Evans, I. M., & Meyer, L. H. (1985). *An educative approach to behavior problems: A practical decision model for interventions with severely handicapped learners.*Baltimore, MD: Brookes.

Evans, W. H., Evans, S. S., & Schmid, R. E. (1989). *Behavior and instructional management: An ecological approach.* Boston, MA: Allyn and Bacon.

Everson, S. (1995). Psychology. In J. Barnes (Ed.), *The Cambridge companion to Aristotle* (pp. 168–194). Cambridge, England: Cambridge University Press.

Exner, J. E. (1980). But it's only an inkblot. *Journal of Personality Assessment, 44,* 562–577.

Eysenck, H. (1994). *Test your IQ.* Toronto, ON: Penguin Books.

Eysenck, H. J. (1957). The effects of psychotherapy: An evaluation. *Journal of Consulting Psychology, 16,* 319–324.

Eysenck, H. J. (1994). Synergistic interaction between psychosocial and physical factors in the causation of lung cancer. In C. Lewis, C. O'Sullivan, & J. Barraclough (Eds.), *The psychoimmunology of human cancer* (pp. 163–178). London, England: Oxford University Press.

Eysenck, H. J., & Eysenck, S. B. G. (1993). *Eysenck Personality Questionnaire [Revised].* London, England: Hodder & Stoughton Educational.

Fagot, B. I., & Hagan, R. (1991). Observations of parent reactions to sexstereotyped behaviours: Age and sex effects. *Child Development, 62,* 617–628.

Fahey, V. (1993). How sleep deprived are you? *Health, 7*(5), 3–4.

Fanselow, M. S., & Gale, G. D. (2003). The amygdala, fear, and memory. *Annals of the New York Academy of Sciences, 985,* 125–134.

Fantz, R. L. (1961). The origin of form perception. *Scientific American, 204,* 66–72.

Fantz, R. L. (1964). Visual experience in infants: Decreased attention to familiar patterns relative to novel ones. *Science, 146,* 668–670.

Faraone, S. V., Tsuang, M. T., & Tsuang, D. W. (1999). *Genetics of mental disorders: A guide for students, clinicians, and researchers.* New York, NY: Guilford Press.

Farmer, A. E. (1996). The genetics of depressive disorders. *International Review of Psychiatry, 8*(4).

Farthing, W. (1992). *The psychology of consciousness.* Upper Saddle River, NJ: Prentice-Hall.

Faucett, J., Gordon, N., & Levine, J. (1994). Differences in postoperative pain severity among four ethnic groups. *Journal of Pain Symptom Management, 9,* 383–389.

Fawzy, F. I., Fawzy, N. W., Hyun, C. S., Elashoff, R., Guthrie, D., Fahey, J. L., & Morton, D. L. (1993). Malignant melanoma effects of an early structured psychiatric intervention, coping, and affective state on recurrence and survival 6 years later. *Archives of General Psychiatry, 50,* 681–689.

FDA MedWatch Safety Alert. (2004, October 15). Public health advisory: Suicidality in children and adolescents being treated with antidepressant medications. Retrieved from http://www.fda.gov/ medwatch/ SAFETY/2004/safety04.htm#ssri

Fechner, G. T. (1860). *Elemente der Psykophysik.* Leipzig, Germany: Breitkopf und Härtel.

Fedoroff, I. C., & McFarlane, T. (1998). Cultural aspects of eating disorders. In S. S. Kazarian & D. R. Evans (Eds.), *Cultural clinicalm psychology: Theory, research and practice* (pp. 152–176). New York, NY: Oxford University Press.

Feinberg, D. R., Jones, B. C., Smith, M. J. L., Moore, F. R., DeBruine, L. M., Cornwell, S. G., . . . Perrett, D. I. (2006). Menstrual cycle, trait estrogen, and masculinity preferences in the human voice. *Hormones and Behaviour, 49,* 215–222.

Feingold, A. (1992). Good-looking people are not what we think. *Psychological Bulletin, 111,* 304–341.

Feldman, D. H. (2003). Cognitive development in childhood. In R. M. Lerner, M. A. Easterbrooks, J. Mistry, & I. B. Weiner (Eds.), *Handbook of psychology: Developmental psychology* (Vol. 6, pp. 195–201). New York, NY: Wiley.

Ferber, S. G., & Makhoul, I. R. (2004). The effect of skin-to-skin contact (kangaroo care) shortly after birth on the neurobehavioral responses of the term newborn: A randomized, controlled trial. *Pediatrics, 857*(4), 857–866.

Ferguson, G. A. (1982). Psychology at McGill. In M. J. Wright & C. R. Myers (Eds.), *History of academic psychology in Canada* (pp. 33–67). Toronto, ON: Hogrefe.

Ferguson, N. B., & Keesey, R. E. (1975). Effect of a quinine-adulterated diet upon body weight maintenance in male rats with ventromedial hypothalamic lesions. *Journal of Comparative Physiological Psychology, 89,* 478–488.

Fernandez, E., & Sheffield, J. (1996). Relative contributions of life events versus daily hassles to the frequency and intensity of headaches. *Headache, 36*(10), 595–602.

Feroah, T. R., Sleeper, T., Brozoski, D., Forder, J., Rice, T. B., & Forster, H. V. (2004). *Circadian slow wave sleep and movement behavior are under genetic control in inbred strains of rat.* Paper presented at the American Physiological Society Annual Conference, April 17–21, 2004, at the Washington, DC, Convention Center.

Ferron, F., Considine, R. V., Peino, R., Lado, I. G., Dieguez, C., & Casanueva, F. F. (1997). Serum leptin concentrations in patients with anorexia nervosa, bulimia nervosa and non-specific eating disorders correlate with the body mass index but are independent of the respective disease. *Clinical Endocrinology (Oxford), 46,* 289–293.

Festinger, L. (1954). A theory of social comparison processes. *Human Relations, 7,* 117–140.

Festinger, L. (1957). *A theory of cognitive dissonance.* Stanford, CA: Stanford University Press.

Festinger, L., & Carlsmith, J. (1959). $1/$20 Experiment: Cognitive consequences of forced compliance. *Journal of Abnormal and Social Psychology, 58.*

Fiatarone, M. (1996). Physical activity and functional independence in aging. *Research Quarterly for Exercise & Sport, 67,* 70–75.

Fiatarone, M. A., O'Neill, E. F., Doyle, N., Clements, K. M., Roberts, S. B., Kehayias, J. J., . . . Evans, W. J. (1993). The Boston FICSIT study: The effects of resistance training and nutritional supplementation on physical frailty in the oldest old. *Journal of American Geriatrics, 41,* 333–337.

Fink, M. (1984). Meduna and the origins of convulsive therapy. *American Journal of Psychiatry, 141,* 1034–1041.

Finke, R. (1995). Creative realism. In S. Smith, T. Ward, & R. Finke (Eds.), *The creative cognition approach* (pp. 301–326). Cambridge, England: Cambridge University Press.

Finkel, D., & McGue, M. (1997). Sex differences and nonadditivity in heritability of the Multidimensional Personality Questionnaire scales. *Journal of Personality and Social Psychology, 72,* 929–938.

Finlay, B., & Love, G. D. (1998). Gender differences in reasoning about military intervention. *Psychology of Women Quarterly, 22,* 481–485.

Fischer, A. (1993). Sex differences in emotionality: Fact or stereotype? *Feminism & Psychology, 3,* 303–318.

Fischl, B., Liu, A., & Dale, A. M. (2001). Automated manifold surgery: Constructing geometrically accurate and topologically correct models of the human cerebral cortex. *IEEE Transactions on Medical Imaging, 20,* 70–80.

Fisher, W., Boroditsky, R., & Morris, B. (2004). The 2002 Canadian contraceptive survey: Part 2. *Journal of Obstetrics and Gynaecology Canada, 26,* 646–656.

Fiske, S. T. (1998). Stereotyping, prejudice, and discrimination. In D. T. Gilbert & S. T. Fiske (Eds.), *The handbook of social psychology* (4th ed., Vol. 2, pp. 357–411). New York, NY: McGraw-Hill.

Fitzgerald, J. (2004, October 11). "Superman" star Christopher Reeve, an advocate for spinal cord research, dies at age 52. *Associated Press.*

Fivush, R., Haden, C., & Reese, E. (1996). Remembering, recounting, and reminiscing: The development of autobiographical memory in social context. In D. C. Rubin (Ed.), *Remembering our past: Studies in autobiographical memory* (pp. 341–359). New York, NY: Cambridge University Press.

Fivush, R., & Nelson, K. (2004). Culture and language in the emergence of autobiographical memory. *Psychological Science, 15,* 573.

Flaherty, J. A., & Adams, S. A. (1998). Therapist–patient race and sex matching: Predictors of treatment duration. *Psychiatric Times, 15*(1).

Flaskerud, J. H. (1991). Effects of an Asian client–therapist language, ethnicity and gender match on utilization and outcome of therapy. *Community Mental Health Journal, 27,* 31–42.

Flavell, J. H. (1999). Cognitive development: Children's knowledge about the mind. *Annual Review of Psychology, 50,* 21–45.

Fleming, M. F., & Barry, K. L. (1992). Clinical overview of alcohol and drug disorders. In M. F. Fleming & K. L. Barry (Eds.), *Addictive disorders.* St. Louis, MO: Mosby Year Book.

Flemons, W. W. (2002). Obstructive sleep apnea. *New England Journal of Medicine, 347,* 498–504.

Flett, G. L., Blankstein, K. R., Hicken, D. J., & Watson, M. S. (1995). Social support and help-seeking in daily hassles versus major life events stress. *Journal of Applied Social Psychology, 25,* 49–58.

Fogel, S., & Smith, C. (2006). Procedural-learning-dependent changes in stage 2 sleep and sleep spindle density. *Journal of Sleep Research, 15,* 250–255.

Folkman, S. (1997). Positive psychological states and coping with severe stress. *Social Science & Medicine, 45,* 1207–1221.

Folkman, S., & Chesney, M. A. (1995). Coping with HIV infection. In M. Stein and A. Baum (Eds.), *Perspectives in behavioral medicine* (pp. 115–133). Hillsdale, NJ: Erlbaum.

Folkman, S., & Lazarus, R. S. (1980). An analysis of coping in a middle-aged community sample. *Journal of Health and Social Behavior, 21*(3), 219–239.

Follett, K. J., & Hess, T. M. (2002). Aging, cognitive complexity, and the fundamental attribution error. *Journal of Gerontology: Psychological Sciences, 57B,* 312–323.

Foulkes, D. (1982). *Children's dreams.* New York, NY: Wiley.

Foulkes, D., & Schmidt, M. (1983). Temporal sequence and unit comparison composition in dream reports from different stages of sleep. *Sleep, 6,* 265–280.

Frank, D. A., Augustyn, M., Knight, W. G., Pell, T., & Zuckerman, B. (2001). Growth, development, and behavior in early childhood following prenatal cocaine exposure. *Journal of the American Medical Association, 285,* 1613–1625.

Frank, E., Kupfer, D. J., Buysse, D. J., Swartz, H. A., Pilkonis, P. A., Houck, P. R., . . . Stapf, D. M. (2007). Randomized trial of weekly, twice-monthly, and monthly interpersonal psychotherapy as maintenance treatment for women with recurrent depression. *American Journal of Psychiatry, 164*(5), 761–767.

Frankel, B. R., & Piercy, F. P. (1990). The relationship among selected supervisor, therapist, and client behaviors. *Journal of Marital and Family Therapy, 16,* 407–421.

Frea, W. D., & Vittimberga, G. L. (2000). Behaviour interventions for children with autism. In J. Austin & J. E. Carr (Eds.), *Handbook of applied behaviour analysis* (pp. 247–274). Reno, NV: Context Press.

Fredrickson, B. L., Maynard, K. E., Helms, M. J., Haney, T. L., Siegler, I. C., & Barefoot, J. C. (1999). Hostility predicts magnitude and duration of blood pressure response to anger. *Journal of Behavioral Medicine, 23,* 229–243.

Freedman, J., & Fraser, S. (1966). Compliance without pressure: The foot-in-thedoor technique. *Journal of Personality and Social Psychology, 4,* 195–202.

Freeman, A., Simon, K. M., Beutler, L. E., & Arkowitz, H. (Eds.) (1989). *Comprehensive handbook of cognitive therapy.* New York, NY: Plenum Press.

Freeman, J. (2001). *Gifted children grown up.* London, England: Fulton.

Freeman, W., & Watts, J. W. (1937). Prefrontal lobotomy in the treatment of mental disorders. *Southern Medical Journal, 30,* 23–31.

Freese, J., Powell, B., & Steelman, L. C. (1999). Rebel without a cause or effect: Birth order and social attitudes. *American Sociological Review, 64,* 207–231.

Frensch, P. A., & Runger, D. (2003). Implicit learning. *Current Directions in Psychological Science, 12,* 13–18.

Freud, A. (1946). *The ego and the mechanisms of defense* (American ed.). New York, NY: I.U.P.

Freud, S. (1900). *The interpretation of dreams. The Standard Edition of the Complete Psychological Works of Sigmund Freud [S.E.], 4–5.* (cf. Joyce Crick, Trans., 1999). London, England: Oxford University Press.

Freud, S. (1901). *The psychopathology of everyday life. S.E., 6,* 1–290.

Freud, S. (1904). *Freud's psycho-analytic procedure, S.E., 7,* 249–254.

Freud, S. (1915). *Repression. S.E., 14,* 146–158.

Freud, S. (1923). *The ego and the id, S.E., 19,* 12–66.

Freud, S. (1930). *Civilization and its discontents.* New York, NY: Jonathon Cape.

Freud, S. (1931). Female sexuality. *Pelican Freud Library, 7,* 367.

Freud, S. (1933). *New introductory lectures on psycho-analysis.* London, England: Hogarth.

Freud, S. (1940). Splitting of the ego in the process of defence. *International Journal of Psychoanalysis, S.E., 22,* 65 [1938], *23,* 275–278.

Freud, S., & Gay, P. (1977). *Inhibitions, symptoms and anxiety. Standard edition of the complete works of Sigmund Freud.* New York, NY: Norton.

Freud, S., Strachey, J., & Riviere, J. (1990). *The ego and the id (The Standard Edition of the Complete Psychological Works of Sigmund Freud).* New York, NY: Norton.

Friedlander, L. J., Reid, G. J., Shupak, N., & Cribbie, R. (2007). Social support, self-esteem, and stress as predictors of adjustment to university among firstyear undergraduates. *Journal of College Student Development, 48,* 259–274.

Friedman, J. M. (2000). Obesity in the new millennium. *Nature, 404,* 632–634.

Friedman, J. M. (2003). A war on obesity, not the obese. *Science, 299,* 856–858.

Friedman, J. M., & Halaas, J. L. (1998). Leptin and the regulation of body weight in mammals. *Nature, 395,* 763.

Friedman, M., & Kasanin, J. D. (1943). Hypertension in only one of identical twins. *Archives of Internal Medicine, 72,* 767–774.

Friedman, M., & Rosenman, R. H. (1959). Association of specific behavior pattern with blood and cardiovascular findings. *Journal of the American Medical Association, 169,* 1286–1296.

Frontera, W. R., Hughes, V. A., Lutz, K. J., & Evans, W. J. (1991). A cross-sectional study of muscle strength and mass in 45- to 78-year-old men and women. *Journal of Applied Physiology, 71,* 644–650.

Fujii, Y., Suzuki, K., Sato, T., Murakami, Y., & Takahashi, T. (1998). Multiple personality disorder in Japan. *Psychiatry and Clinical Neurosciences, 52,* 299.

Fulcher, J. S. (1942). "Voluntary" facial expression in blind and seeing children. *Archives of Psychology, 38,* 1–49.

Fumeron, F., Betoulle, D., Aubert, R., Herbeth, B., Siest, G., & Rigaud, D. (2001). Association of a functional 5–HT transporter gene polymorphism with anorexia nervosa and food intake. *Molecular Psychiatry, 6,* 9–10.

Gackenbach, J., Kuruville, B., & Dopko, R. (2009). Video game play and dream bizarreness. *Dreaming, 19*(4), 218–231.

Galanter, M. (1983). Unification Church ("Moonie") dropouts: Psychological readjustment after leaving a charismatic religious group. *American Journal of Psychaiatry, 140,* 984–989.

Galanti, G. A. (1997). *Caring for patients from different cultures* (2nd ed.). Philadelphia, PA: University of Pennsylvania Press.

Galea, S., Resnick, H., Kilpatrick, D., Bucuvalas, M., Gold, J., & Vlahov, D. (2002, March 28). Psychological sequelae of the September 11 terrorist attacks in New York City. *New England Journal of Medicine, 346,* 982–987.

Galef, B. G., & Whiskin, E. E. (1995). Learning socially to eat more of one food than of another. *Journal of Comparative Psychology, 109,* 99–101.

Gamwell, L., & Tomes, N. (1995). *Madness in America: Cultural and medical perspectives of mental illness before 1914.* Ithaca, NY: Cornell University Press.

Ganchrow, J. R., Steiner, J. E., & Munif, D. (1983). Neonatal facial expressions in response to different qualities and intensities of gustatory stimuli. *Infant Behavior Development, 6,* 473–478.

Ganellen, R. J. (1996). *Integrating the Rorschach and the MMPI-2 in personality assessment.* Mahwah, NJ: Erlbaum.

Garb, H. N., Florio, C. M., & Grove, W. M. (1998). The validity of the Rorschach and the Minnesota Multiphasic Personality Inventory: Results from metaanalyses. *Psychological Science, 9,* 402–404.

Garcia, J., & Koelling, R. A. (1966). Relation of cue to consequence in avoidance learning. *Psychonomic Science, 4,* 123.

Garcia, J., Brett, L. P., & Rusiniak, K. W. (1989). Limits of Darwinian conditioning. In S. B. Klein & R. R. Mowrer (Eds.), *Contemporary learning theories: Instrumental conditioning theory and the impact of biological constraints on learning* (pp. 237–275). Hillsdale, NJ: Erlbaum.

Gardner, H. (1993a). *Creating minds: An anatomy of creativity seen through the lives of Freud, Einstein, Picasso, Stravinsky, Eliot, Graham, and Ghandi.* New York, NY: Basic Books.

Gardner, H. (1993b). *Multiple intelligences: The theory in practice.* New York, NY: Basic Books.

Gardner, H. (1998). Are there additional intelligences? The case for naturalist, spiritual, and existential intelligences. In J. Kane (Ed.), *Education, information, and transformation* (pp. 111–131). Upper Saddle River, NJ: Merrill-Prentice Hall.

Gardner, H. (1999a). *Intelligence reframed: Multiple intelligences for the 21st century.* New York, NY: Basic Books.

Gardner, H. (1999b, February). Who owns intelligence? *Atlantic Monthly,* 67–76.

Gardner, H., Kornhaber, M. L., & Wake, W. K. (1996). *Intelligence: Multiple perspectives.* Orlando, FL: Harcourt Brace.

Gardner, J., & Oswald, A. J. (2004). How is mortality affected by money, marriage, and stress? *Journal of Health Economics, 23,* 1181–1207.

Gardner, R. J. M., & Sutherland, G. R. (1996). Chromosome abnormalities and genetic counseling. *Oxford Monographics on Medical Genetics No. 29.* New York, NY: Oxford University Press.

Garland, E. J., & Smith, D. H. (1991). Simultaneous prepubertal onset of panic disorder, night terrors, and somnambulism. *Journal of American Academic Child and Adolescent Psychiatry, 30,* 553–555.

Garner, D. M., & Garfinkel, P. E. (1980). Socio-cultural factors in the development of anorexia nervosa. *Psychological Medicine, 10,* 647–656.

Garver-Apgar, C. E., Gangestad, S. W., Thornhill, R., Miller, R. D., & Olp, J. J. (2006). Major histocompatibility complex alleles, sexual responsivity, and unfaithfulness in romantic couples. *Psychological Science, 17,* 830–835.

Gathercole, S. E., & Hitch, G. J. (1993). Developmental changes in short-term memory: A revised working memory perspective. In A. F. Collins, S. E. Gathercole, M. A. Conway, & P. E. Morris (Eds.), *Theories of memory* (pp. 189–209). Hove, United Kingdom: Erlbaum.

Geary, D. C. (2000). Evolution and proximate expression of human paternal investment. *Psychological Bulletin, 126,* 55–77.

Gebhard, P. H., & Johnson, A. B. (1979/1998). *The Kinsey data: Marginal tabulations of 1938–1963 interviews conducted by the Institute for Sex Research.* Philadelphia, PA: Saunders.

Geddes, D. P. (Ed.). (1954). *An analysis of the Kinsey reports.* New York, NY: New American Library.

Geddes, J., & Butler, R. (2002). Depressive disorders. *Clinical Evidence, 7,* 867–882.

Geddes, J. R., Carney, S. M., Davies, C., Furukawa, T. A., Kupfer, D. J., Frank, E., & Goodwin, G. M. (2003). Relapse prevention with antidepressant drug treatment in depressive disorders: A systematic review. *Lancet, 361,* 653–661.

Geen, R. G., & Thomas, S. L. (1986). The immediate effects of media violence on behavior. *Journal of Social Issues, 42,* 7–27.

Gelder, M. (1976). Flooding. In T. Thompson & W. Dockens (Eds.), *Applications of behavior modification.* New York, NY: Academic Press.

Geliebter, A. (1988). Gastric distension and gastric capacity in relation to food intake in humans. *Physiological Behavior, 44,* 665–668.

Geller, B., Williams, M., Zimerman, B., Frazier, J., Beringer, L., & Warner, K. L. (1998). Prepubertal and early adolescent bipolarity differentiate from ADHD by manic symptoms, grandiose delusions, ultra-rapid or ultradian cycling. *Journal of Affective Disorders, 51*(2), 81–91.

Gelman, S. A. (1988). The development of induction within natural kind and artifact categories. *Cognitive Psychology, 20,* 65–95.

Gelman, S. A., & Markman, E. M. (1986). Categories and induction in young children. *Cognition, 23,* 183–209.

Gerdes, H. and Mallinckrodt, B. (1994). Emotional, social and academic adjustment of college students: A longitudinal study of retention. *Journal of Counseling and Development, 72,* 281–288.

Gershoff, E. (2000). The short- and long-term effects of corporal punishment on children: A meta-analytical review. In D. Elliman

& M. A. Lynch (Eds.), *The physical punishment of children, 83,* 196–198.

Gershoff, E. T. (2002). Parental corporal punishment and associated child behaviors and experiences: A meta-analytic and theoretical review. *Psychological Bulletin, 128,* 539–579.

Gevensleben, H., Holl, B., Albrecht, B., Vogel, C., Schlamp, D., Kratz, O., . . . Heinrich H. (2009). Is neurofeedback an efficacious treatment for ADHD? A randomized controlled clinical trial. *Journal of Child Psychology and Psychiatry, 50*(7), 780–789.

Gibbons, J. L., Stiles, D. A., & Shkodriani, G. M. (1991). Adolescents' attitudes toward family and gender roles: An international comparison. *Sex Roles, 25,* 625–643.

Gibson, E. J., & Walk, R. D. (1960). The "visual cliff." *Scientific American, 202,* 67–71.

Giedd, J. N., Blumenthal, J., Jeffries, N. O., Castellanos, F. X., Liui, H., Zijdenbos, A., . . . Rapoport, J. L. (1999). Brain development during childhood and adolescence: A longitudinal MRI study. *Nature Neuroscience, 2,* 861–863.

Gilberg, C., & Coleman, M. (2000). *The biology of the autistic syndromes* (3rd ed.). London, England: MacKeith Press.

Gilbert, P. B., Peterson, M. L., Follmann, D., Hudgens, M. G., Francis, D. P., Gurwith, M., . . . Berman, P. W. (2005). Correlation between immunologic responses to a recombinant glycoprotein 120 vaccine and incidence of HIV-1 infection in a phase 3 HIV-1 preventive vaccine trial. *Journal of Infectious Diseases, 191,* 666–677.

Gilbert, S. J. (1981). Another look at the Milgram obedience studies: The role of the graduated series of shocks. *Personality and Social Psychology Bulletin, 7,* 690–695.

Gill, S. T. (1991). Carrying the war into the never-never land of psi. *Skeptical Inquirer, 15*(1), 269–273.

Gillespie, M. A., Kim, B. H., Manheim, L. J., Yoo, T., Oswald, F. L., & Schmitt, N. (2002). The development and validation of biographical data and situational judgment tests in the prediction of college student success. In A. M. Ryan (Chair), *Beyond g: Expanding thinking on predictors of college success.* Symposium conducted at the 14th Annual Convention of the American Psychological Society, New Orleans, LA.

Gillham, B., Tanner, G., Cheyne, B., Freeman, I., Rooney, M., & Lambie, A. (1998). Unemployment rates, single parent density, and indices of child poverty: Their relationship to different categories of child abuse and neglect. *Child Abuse and Neglect, 22*(2), 79–90.

Gilligan, C. (1982). I*n a different voice: Psychological theory and women's development.* Cambridge, MA: Harvard University Press.

Gillund, G., & Shiffrin, R. M. (1984). A retrieval model for both recognition and recall. *Psychological Review, 91,* 1–67.

Gilmour, J., & Skuse, D. (1999). A case-comparison study of the characteristics of children with a short stature syndrome induced by stress (hyperphagic short stature) and a consecutive series of unaffected "stressed" children. *Journal of Child Psychology and Psychiatry and Allied Disciplines, 40*(6), 969–978.

Ginzburg, K., Solomon, Z., Koifman, B., Keren, G., Roth, A., Kriwisky, M., . . . Bleich, A. (2003). Trajectories of post-traumatic stress disorder following myocardial infarction: A prospective study. *Journal of Clinical Psychiatry, 64,* 1217–1223.

Gittelman-Klein, R. (1978). Validity in projective tests for psychodiagnosis in children. In R. L. Spitzer & D. F. Klein (Eds.), *Critical issues in psychiatric diagnosis* (pp. 141–166). New York, NY: Raven Press.

Gleaves, D. H. (1996). The socio-cognitive model of dissociative identity disorder: A reexamination of the evidence. *Psychological Bulletin, 20,* 42–59.

Glick, P., & Fiske, S. (2001). An ambivalent alliance: Hostile and benevolent sexism as complementary justifications for gender inequality. *American Psychologist, 56,* 109–118.

Glynn, S. M. (1990). Token economy approaches for psychiatric patients: Progress and pitfalls over 25 years. *Behavior Modification, 14,* 383–407.

Goel, V., & Grafman, J. (1995). Are the frontal lobes implicated in "planning" functions? Interpreting data from the Tower of Hanoi. *Neuropsychologia, 33,* 623–642.

Goin, M. K. (2005). Practical psychotherapy: A current perspective on the psychotherapies. *Psychiatric Services, 56*(3), 255–257.

Goldman-Rakic, P. S. (1998) The prefrontal landscape: Implications of functional architecture for understanding human mentation and the central executive. In A. C. Roberts, T. W. Robbins, & L. Weiskrantz (Eds.), *The prefrontal cortex: Executive and cognitive functions* (pp. 87–102). Oxford, England: Oxford University Press.

Goldsmith, H. H., & Campos, J. (1982). Toward a theory of infant temperament. In R. Emde & R. Harmon (Eds.), *The development of attachment and affiliative systems: Psychobiological aspects* (pp. 161–193). New York, NY: Plenum Press.

Goleman, D. (1982). Staying up: The rebellion against sleep's gentle tyranny. *Psychology Today, 3,* 24–35.

Goleman, D. (1995). *Emotional intelligence: Why it can matter more than IQ.* New York, NY: Bantam Books.

Golkaramnay, V., Bauer, S., Haug, S., Wolf, M., & Kordy, H. (2007). The exploration of the effectiveness of group therapy through an Internet chat as aftercare: A controlled naturalistic study. *Pychotherapy and Psychosomatics, 76,* 219–225.

Gonsalves, B., Reber, P. J., Gitelman, D. R., Parrish, T. B., Mesulam, M. M., & Paller, K. A. (2004). Neural evidence that vivid imagining can lead to false remembering. *Psychological Science, 15,* 655–660.

Gonzalez, J. S., Penedo, F. J., Antoni, M. H., Durán, R. E., Fernandez, M. I., McPherson-Baker, S., . . . Schneiderman, N. (2004). Social support, positive states of mind, and HIV treatment adherence in men and women living with HIV/AIDS. *Health Psychology, 23,* 413–418.

Goodglass, H., Kaplan, E., & Barresi, B., (2001). *The assessment of aphasia and related disorders* (3rd ed.). Baltimore, MD: Lippincott, Williams and Wilkins.

Gordon, T., (1989). *Discipline that works.* New York, NY: Plume Books.

Gorn, G. J. (1982). The effects of music in advertising on choice behaviour: A classical conditioning approach. *Journal of Marketing, 46*(1), 94–101.

Gosselin, R. E., Smith, R. P., Hodge, H. C., & Braddock, J. E. (1984). *Clinical toxicology of commercial products* (5th ed.). Sydney, Australia: Williams & Wilkins.

Gotlib, I. H., Sivers, H., Canli, T., Kasch, K. L., & Gabrieli, J. D. E. (2001). Neural activation in depression in response to emotional stimuli. In I. H. Gotlib (Chair), *New directions in the neurobiology of affective disorders.* Symposium presented at the Annual Meeting of the Society for Research in Psychopathology, Madison, WI.

Gottesman, I. I. (1991). *Schizophrenia.* New York, NY: Freeman.

Gottesman, I. I., & Shields, J. (1976). A critical review of recent adoption, twin and family studies of schizophrenia: Behavioural genetics perspectives. *Schizophrenia Bulletin, 2,* 360–401.

Gottesman, I. I., & Shields, J. (1982). *Schizophrenia, the epigenetic puzzle.* New York, NY: Cambridge University Press.

Gottman, J. M., & Krokoff, L. J. (1989). Marital interaction and satisfaction: A longitudinal view. *Journal of Consulting and Clinical Psychology, 57,* 47–52.

Gough, H. G. (1995). *California Psychological Inventory* (3rd ed.). Palo Alto, CA: Consulting Psychologist-Press.

Gould, J. L., & Gould, C. G. (1994). *The animal mind.* New York, NY: Scientific American Library.

Gould, S. J. (1981). *The mismeasure of man.* New York, NY: Norton.

Gould, S. J. (1996). *The mismeasure of man.* New York, NY: Norton.

Gouldner, A. W. (1960). The norm of reciprocity: A preliminary statement. *American Sociological Review, 25,* 161–178.

Graber, J. A., Brooks-Gunn, J., & Warren, M. P. (1995). The antecedents of menarcheal age: Heredity, family environment, and stressful life events. *Child Development, 66,* 346–359.

Grammer, K., & Thornhill, R. (1994). Human (homo sapiens) facial attractiveness and sexual selection: The role of symmetry and averageness. *Journal of Comparative Psychology, 108,* 233–242.

Grandjean, P., Weihe, P., White, R. F., Debes, F., Araki, S., Yokoyama, K., . . . Jørgensen, P. J. (1997). Cognitive deficit in 7-year-old children with prenatal exposure to methylmercury. *Neurotoxicology and Teratology, 19*(6), 417–428.

Granqvist, P., Fredrikson, M., Unge, P., Hagenfeldt, A., Valind, S. Larhammar, D., & Larsson, M. (2005). Sensed presence and mystical experiences are predicted by suggestibility, not by the application of transcranial weak complex magnetic fields. *Neuroscience Letters, 379,* 1–6.

Grant, J., Courtemanche, J., Duerden, E. G., Duncan, G. H., & Rainville, P. (2010). Cortical thickness and pain sensitivity in Zen meditators. *Emotion, 10*(1), 43–53.

Greenwald, A. G., Draine, S. C., & Abrams, R. L. (1996). Three cognitive markers of unconscious semantic activation. *Science, 273,* 1699–1702.

Gregory, R. L. (1990). *Eye and brain, the psychology of seeing.* Princeton, NJ: Princeton University Press.

Gresham, L. G., & Shimp, T. A. (1985). Attitude toward the advertisement and brand attitudes: A classical conditioning prospective. *Journal of Advertising, 14*(1), 10–17, 49.

Gribbons, B., & Herman, J. (1997). True and quasi-experimental designs. *Practical Assessment, Research & Evaluation, 5*(14).

Grigorenko, E. L., Jarvin, L., & Sternberg, R. J. (2002). School-based tests of the triarchic theory of intelligence: Three settings, three samples, three syllabi. *Contemporary Educational Psychology, 27,* 167–208

Grimshaw, G. M., Adelstein, A., Bryden, M. P., & MacKinnon, G. E. (1998). First-language acquisition in adolescence: Evidence for a critical period for verbal language development. *Brain and Language, 63,* 237–255.

Grön, G., Schul, D., Bretschneider, V., Wunderlich, A. P., & Riepe, M. W. (2003). Alike performance during nonverbal episodic learning from diversely imprinted neural networks. *European Journal of Neuroscience, 18,* 3112–3120.

Gross, C. G. (1999). A hole in the head. *The Neuroscientist, 5,* 263–269.

Grumbach, M. M., & Kaplan, S. L. (1990). The neuroendocrinology of human puberty: An ontogenetic perspective. In M. M. Grumbach, P. C. Sizonenko, & M. L. Aubert (Eds.), *Control of the Onset of Puberty* (pp. 1–6). Baltimore, MD: Williams & Wilkins.

Grumbach, M. M., & Styne, D. M. (1998). Puberty: Ontogeny, neuroendocrinology, physiology, and disorders. In J. D. Wilson, D. W. Foster, H. M. Kronenberg, & P. R. Larsen (Eds.), *Williams Textbook of Endocrinology* (9th ed., pp. 1509–1625). Philadelphia, PA: Saunders.

Grünbaum, A. (1984). *The foundations of psychoanalysis: A philosophical critique.* Berkeley, CA: University of California Press.

Guilford, J. P. (1967). *The nature of human intelligence.* New York, NY: McGraw-Hill.

Gupta, M. (1994). Sexuality in the Indian sub-continent. *Sex and Marital Therapy, 9,* 57–69.

Gustavson, C. R., Kelly, D. J., Seeney, M., & Garcia, J. (1976). Prey lithium aversions I: Coyotes and wolves. *Behavioral Biology, 17,* 61–72.

Haber, R. N. (1979). Twenty years of haunting eidetic imagery: Where's the ghost? *The Behavioral and Brain Sciences, 2,* 583–619.

Hack, T. F., Osachuk, T. A., & De Luca, R. V. (1994). Group treatment for sexually abused preadolescent boys. *Families in Society, 75,* 217–228.

Hajek, P., & Belcher, M. (1991). Dream of absent-minded transgression: An empirical study of a cognitive withdrawal symptom. *Journal of Abnormal Psychology, 100,* 487–491.

Hajek, P., & Stead, L. F. (2000). *Aversive smoking for smoking cessation.* Oxford, England: The Cochrane Library.

Hall, C. (1966). Studies of dreams collected in the laboratory and at home. *Institute of Dream Research Monograph Series* (No. 1). Santa Cruz, CA: Privately printed.

Hall, N. C., Perry, R. P., Chipperfield, J. G., Clifton, R. A., & Haynes, T. L. (2006). Enhancing primary and secondary control in achievement settings through writing-based attributional retraining. *Journal of Social and Clinical Psychology, 25,* 361–391.

Hamani, C., McAndrews, M. P., Cohn, M., Oh, M., Zumstey, D., Shapiro, C. M., . . . Lozano, A. M. (2008). Memory enhancement induced by hypothalamic/fornix deep brain stimulation. *Annals of Neurology, 63,* 119–123.

Hamann, S., Herman, R. A., Nolan, C. L., & Wallen, K. (2004). Men and women differ in amygdale response to visual sexual stimuli. *Nature Neuroscience, 7,* 411–419.

Hamer, D. H., Hu, S., Magnuson, V. L., Hu, N., & Pattatucci, A. M. L. (1993). A linkage between DNA markers on the X chromosome and male sexual orientation. *Science, 261,* 321–327.

Hamilton, D. L., & Gifford, R. K. (1976). Illusory correlation in interpersonal perception: A cognitive basis of stereotypic judgments. *Journal of Experimental Social Psychology, 12,* 392–407.

Hamilton, J. A. (1982). The identity of postpartum psychosis. In I. F. Brockington & R. Kumar (Eds.), *Motherhood and mental illness* (pp. 1–17). London, England: Academic Press.

Hammen, C. (2005). Stress and depression. *Annual Review of Clinical Psychology, 1,* 293–319.

Hammond, D., Fong, G., Borland, R., Cummings, K., McNeill, A., & Driezen, P. (2007). Text and graphic warnings on cigarette packages: Findings from the international tobacco control four country study. *American Journal of Preventive Medicine, 32,* 202–209.

Hammond, D., Fong, G., McDonald, P., Brown, K., & Cameron, R. (2004). Graphic Canadian warning labels and adverse outcome: Evidence from Canadian smokers. *American Journal of Public Health, 94,* 1442–1445.

Hampton, J. A. (1998). Similarity-based categorization and fuzziness of natural categories. *Cognition, 65,* 137–165.

Handel, S. (1989). Listening: An introduction to the perception of auditory events. Cambridge, MA: MIT Press.

Hansemark, O. C. (2003). Need for achievement, locus of control and the prediction of business start-ups: A longitudinal study. *Journal of Economic Psychology, 24,* 301–319.

Hansen, C. P. (1988). Personality characteristics of the accident involved employee. *Journal of Business and Psychology, 2,* 346–365.

Hare, R. D. (1996). Psychopathy: A clinical construct whose time has come. *Criminal Justice and Behavior, 23,* 25–54.

Harkness, K. L., Bruce, A. E., & Lumley, M. N. (2006). The role of childhood abuse and neglect in the sensitization to stressful life events in adolescent depression. *Journal of Abnormal Psychology, 115,* 730–741.

Harlow, H. F. (1958). The nature of love. *American Psychologist, 13,* 573–685.

Harlow, H. F. (1959). Love in infant monkeys. *Scientific American, 200,* 68, 70, 72–73.

Harman, G. (1999). Moral philosophy meets social psychology: Virtue ethics and the fundamental attribution error. *Proceedings of the Aristotelian Society, 1998–99, Vol. 99,* 315–331.

Harris, G. T., Rice, M. E., & Cormier, C. A. (1991). Length of detention in matched groups of insanity acquittees and convicted offenders. *International Journal of Law and Psychiatry, 14,* 223–236.

Harrison, P. J. (1999). The neuropathology of schizophrenia: A critical review of the data and their interpretation. *Brain, 122,* 593–624.

Hart, P. (1998). Preventing groupthink revisited: Evaluating and reforming groups in government. *Organizational Behavior & Human Decision Processes, 73,* 306–326.

Hart, S. D., & Roesch, R. (2007). Mental disorder and the law. In P. Firestone & D. J. A. Dozois (Eds.), *Abnormal Psychology* (3rd ed., pp. 453–472). Toronto, ON: Pearson.

Hartfield, E. (1987). Passionate and companionate love. In R. J. Sternberg & M. L. Barnes (Eds.), *The psychology of love* (pp. 191–217). New Haven, CT: Yale University Press.

Hartfield, E., & Rapson, R. L. (1992). Similarity and attraction in intimate relationships. *Communication Monographs, 59,* 209–212.

Hauck, S. J., & Bartke, A. (2001). Free radical defenses in the liver and kidney of human growth hormone transgenic mice. *Journal of Gerontology and Biological Science, 56,* 153–162.

Havighurst R. J., Neugarten B. L., & Tobin S. N. S. (1968). Disengagement and patterns of aging. In B. L. Neugarten (Ed.), *Middle age and aging: A reader in social psychology* (pp. 161–172). Chicago, IL: University of Chicago Press.

Hay, P., & Bacaltchuk, J. (2002). Bulimia nervosa. *Clinical Evidence, 8,* 914–926.

Hayflick, L. (1977). The cellular basis for biological aging. In C. E. Finch & L. Hayflick (Eds.), *Handbook of biology of aging* (p. 159). New York, NY: Van Nostrand Reinhold.

Hazan, C., & Shaver, P. (1987). Romantic love conceptualized as an attachment process. *Journal of Personality and Social Psychology, 52,* 511–524.

Health Canada. (2002a). *Healthy Canadians: A federal report on comparable health indicators.* Retrieved from http://www.hc-sc.gc.ca/iacb-dgiac/arad-draa/ english/accountability/indicators.html

Health Canada. (2002b). *A report on mental illnesses in Canada.* Catalogue No. 0-662-32817-5. Retrieved from http://www.phac-aspc.gc.ca/publicat/miic-mmac/pdf/men_ill_e.pdf

Health Canada. (2005). Canadian tobacco use monitoring survey (CTUMS) 2005. Retrieved from http://www.hc-sc.gc.ca/hl-vs/pubs/tobactabac/ctums-esutc-2005/wave-phase-1_summary-sommaire_e.html

Heavey, C. L., Layne, C., & Christensen, A. (1993). Gender and conflict structure in marital interaction: A replication and extension. *Journal of Consulting and Clinical Psychology, 61,* 16–27.

Hebb, D. O. (1949). *The organization of behavior.* New York, NY: Wiley.

Hebb, D. O. (1955). Drives and the C.N.S. (Conceptual Nervous System). *Psychological Review, 62,* 243–254.

Heider, F. (1958). *The psychology of interpersonal relations.* New York, NY: John Wiley & Sons.

Heilman, K., Watson, R., & Valenstein, E. (1993). Neglect and related disorders. In K. Heilman & E. Valenstein (Eds.), *Clinical neuropsychology.* New York, NY: Oxford University Press.

Heine, S. J., & Hamamura, T. (2007). In search of East Asian self-enhancement. *Personality and Social Psychology Review, 11,* 1–24.

Heine, S. J., & Lehman, D. R. (1997). Culture, dissonance, and self-affirmation. *Personality and Social Psychology Bulletin, 23,* 389–400.

Heinicke, C. M., Goorsky, M., Moscov, S., Dudley, K., Gordon, J., Schneider, C., & Guthrie, D. (2000). Relationship-based intervention with at-risk mothers: Factors affecting variations in outcome. *Infant Mental Health Journal, 21,* 133–155.

Heinrich, B. (2000). Testing insight in ravens. In C. Heyes & L. Huber (Eds.), *The evolution of cognition.* Cambridge, MA: MIT Press.

Helms, J. E. (1992). Why is there no study of cultural equivalence in standardized cognitive ability testing? *American Psychologist, 47*(9), 1083–1101.

Helmstetter, E., Peck, C. A., & Giangreco, M. F. (1994). Outcomes of interactions with peers with moderate or severe disabilities: A statewide survey of high school students. *Journal of the Association for Persons with Severe Handicaps, 13,* 20–27.

Henningfield. J. E. (1995). Nicotine medications for smoking cessation. *New England Journal of Medicine, 333,* 1196–1203.

Henningfield. J. E. Clayton, R., & Pollin, W. (1990). Involvement of tobacco in alcoholism and illicit drug use. *British Journal of Addition, 85,* 279–292.

Herberman, R. B., & Ortaldo, J. R. (1981). Natural killer cells: Their role in defenses against disease. *Science, 214,* 24–30.

Herman, C. P., Roth, D. A., & Polivy, J. (2003). Effects of the presence of others on food intake: A normative interpretation. *Psychological Bulletin, 129,* 873–886.

Herman, L. M., Pack, A. A., & Morrell-Samuels, P. (1993). Representational and conceptual skills of dolphins. In H. L., Roitblatt, L. M. Herman, & P. E. Nachtigall (Eds.), *Language and communcation: Comparative perspectives.* Hillsdale, NJ: Erlbaum.

Hernandez, D., & Fisher, E. M. (1996). Down syndrome genetics: Unravelling a multifactorial disorder. *Human Molecular Genetics, 5,* 1411–1416.

Herrnstein, R. J., & Murray, C. (1994). *The bell curve: The reshaping of American life by differences in intelligence.* New York, NY: Free Press.

Hersh, S. M. (2004, May 10). Annals of national security: Torture at Abu Ghraib. *The New Yorker.*

Hershberger, S. L., Plomin, R., & Pedersen, N. L. (1995, October). Traits and metatraits: Their reliability, stability, and shared genetic influence. *Journal of Personality and Social Psychology, 69,* 673–685.

Hershcovis, S. M., & Barling, J. (2007). Towards a relational model of workplace aggression. In J. Langan-Fox, C. L. Copper, & R. J. Klimoski (Eds.), *Research companion to the dysfunctional workplace: Management challenges and symptoms* (pp. 268–284). Northhampton, MA: Edward Elgar.

Heslegrave, R. J., & Rhodes, W. (1997). Impact of varying shift schedules on the performance and sleep in air traffic controllers. *Sleep Research, 26,* 198–208.

Hetherington, A. W., & Ranson, S. W. (1940). Hypothalamic legions and adiposity in rats. *Anatomical Records, 78,* 149–172.

Hewstone, M., Rubin, M., & Willis, H. (2002). Intergroup bias. *Annual Review of Psychology, 53,* 575–604.

Heyes, C. M. (1998). Theory of mind in nonhuman primates. *Behavior and Brain Science, 21,* 101–148.

Hicklin, J., & Widiger, T. A. (2000). Convergent validity of alternative MMPI-2 personality disorder scales. *Journal of Personality Assessment, 75,* 502–518.

Hilgard, E. R. (1991). A neodissociation interpretation of hypnosis. In S. Lynn & J. Rhue (Eds.), *Theories of hypnosis* (pp. 83–104). New York, NY: Guilford Press.

Hilgard, E. R., & Hilgard, J. R. (1994). *Hypnosis in the relief of pain* (Rev. ed.). New York, NY: Brunner/Mazel.

Hill, D. (1990, April). Causes of smoking in children. In B. Durston & K. Jamrozik (Eds.), *Smoking and health 1990—The global war. Proceedings of the Seventh World Conference on Smoking and Health* (205–209). Perth: Health Department of Western Australia.

Hill, D. R., & Persinger, M. A. (2003). Application of transcerebral, weak (1 microT) complex magnetic fields and mystical experiences: Are they generated by field-induced dimethyltryptamine released from the pineal gland. *Perceptual Motor Skills, 97,* 1049–1050.

Hill, P. C., & Butter E. M. (1995). The role of religion in promoting physical health. *Journal of Psychology and Christianity, 14*(2), 141–155.

Hilton, J. L., & von Hipple, W. (1996). Stereotypes. *Annual Review of Psychology, 47,* 237–271.

Hinton, G. E., McClelland, J. L., & Rumelhart, D. E. (1986). Distributed representations. In D. E. Rumelhart, J. L. McClelland, & the PDP Research Group (Eds.), *Parallel distributed processing: Explorations in the microstructure of cognition, Vol. 1, Foundations* (pp. 77–109). Cambridge, MA: MIT Press.

Hintze, J. M. (2002). Interventions for fears and anxiety problems. In M. R. Shinn, H. R. Walker, & G. Stoner (Eds.), *Interventions for academic and behavior problems II: Preventive and remedial approaches* (pp. 939–954). Bethesda, MD: National Association of School Psychologists.

Hobson, J. (1988). *The dreaming brain.* New York, NY: Basic Books.

Hobson, J., Pace-Schott, E., & Stickgold, R. (2000). Dreaming and the brain: Towards a cognitive neuroscience of conscious states. *Behavioral and Brain Sciences, 23,* 793–1121.

Hobson, J. A., & McCarley, R. (1977). The brain as a dream state generator: An activation-synthesis hypothesis of the dream process. *American Journal of Psychiatry, 134,* 1335–1348.

Hochman, J. (1994). Buried memories challenge the law. *National Law Journal, 1,* 17–18.

Hodges, J. R. (1994). Retrograde amnesia. In A. Baddeley, B. A. Wilson, & F. Watts (Eds.), *Handbook of memory disorders* (pp. 81–107). New York, NY: Wiley.

Hodgson, B. (2001). *In the arms of Morpheus: The tragic history of laudanum, morphine, and patent medicines.* New York, NY: Firefly Books.

Hodson, D. S., & Skeen, P. (1994). Sexuality and aging: The hammerlock of myths. *Journal of Applied Gerontology, 13,* 219–235.

Hoebel, B. G., & Teitelbaum, P. (1966). Weight regulation in normal and hypothalamic hyperphagic rats. *Journal of Comparative Physiological Psychology, 61,* 189–193.

Hoff, E. (2005). *Language development.* Belmont, CA: Thomson Wadsworth.

Hoff, T. L. (1992). Psychology in Canada one hundred years ago: James Mark Baldwin at the University of Toronto. *Canadian Psychology, 33,* 683–694.

Hoffer, T. B., Hess, M., Welch, V., Jr., & Williams, K. (2007). *Doctorate Recipients from United States Universities: Summary Report 2006.* Chicago, IL: National Opinion Research Center.

Hoffmann, A. (1998). *Paradigms of artificial intelligence: A methodological and computational analysis.* London, England: Springer-Verlag.

Hoffrage, U., Hertwig, R., & Gigerenzer, G. (2000). Hindsight bias: A by-product of knowledge updating? *Journal of Experimental Psychology: Learning, Memory, and Cognition, 26,* 566–581.

Hofstede, G. H. (1980). *Culture's consequences, international differences in workrelated values.* Beverly Hills, CA: Sage.

Hofstede, G. J., Pedersen, P. B., & Hofstede, G. H. (2002). *Exploring culture: Exercises, stories, and synthetic cultures.* Yarmouth, ME: Intercultural Press.

Hogg M. A., & Hains S. C. (1998). Friendship and group identification: A new look at the role of cohesiveness in groupthink. *European Journal of Social Psychology, 28*(1), 323–341.

Holahan, C. K., & Sears, R. R. (1996). *The gifted group at later maturity.* Stanford, CA: Stanford University Press.

Holcomb, W. R. (1986). Stress inoculation therapy with anxiety and stress disorders of acute psychiatric patients. *Journal of Clinical Psychology, 42,* 864–872.

Holden, C., & Vogel, G. (2002). Plasticity: Time for a reappraisal? *Science, 296,* 2126–2129.

Hollon, S., These, M., & Markowitz, J. (2002). Treatment and prevention of depression. *Psychological Science in the Public Interest, 3,* 39–77.

Hollon, S. D., & Beck, A. T. (1994). Cognitive and cognitive-behavioral therapies. In A. E. Bergin & S. L. Garfield (Eds.), *Handbook of psychotherapy and behavior change* (4th ed., p. 428). Chichester, England: Wiley.

Holmes, T. H., & Masuda, M. (1973). Psychosomatic syndrome: When mothersin- law or other disasters visit, a person can develop a bad, bad cold. *Psychology Today, 5*(11), 71–72, 106.

Holmes, T. H., & Rahe, R. H. (1967). The Social Readjustment Rating Scale. *Journal of Psychosomatic Research II,* 213–218.

Holroyd, J. (1996). Hypnosis treatment of clinical pain: Understanding why hypnosis is useful. *International Journal of Clinical and Experimental Hypnosis, 44,* 33–51.

Holt-Lunstad, J., Uchino, B. N., Smith, T. W., Cerny, C. B., & Nealey-Moore, J. B. (2003). Social relationships and ambulatory blood pressure: Structural and qualitative predictors of cardiovascular function during everyday social interactions. *Health Psychology, 22,* 388–397.

Hood, D. C. (1998). Lower-level visual processing and models of light adaptation. *Annual Review of Psychology, 49,* 503–535.

Hopfinger, J. B., Buonocore, M. H., & Mangun, G. R. (2000). The neural mechanisms of top-down attentional control. *Nature Neuroscience, 3,* 284–291.

Horley, J. (2001). Frotteurism: A term in search of an underlying disorder? *Journal of Sexual Aggression, 7*(1), 51–55.

Horne, J. A., & Staff, C. H. (1983). Exercise and sleep: Body heating effects. *Sleep, 6,* 36–46.

Horney, K. (1939). *New ways in Psychoanalysis,* New York, NY: Norton.

Horney, K. (1967/1973). *Feminine psychology.* New York, NY: Norton.

Horowitz, D. L. (1985). *Ethnic groups in conflict*. Berkeley, CA: University of California Press.

Hortaçsu, N. (1999). The first year of family and couple initiated marriages of a Turkish sample: A longitudinal investigation. *International Journal of Psychology, 34*(1), 29–41.

Hoshino-Browne, E., Zanna, A. S., Spencer, S. J., Zanna, M. P., Kitayama, S., & Lackenbauer, S. (2005). On the cultural guises of cognitive dissonance: The case of Easterners and Westerners. *Journal of Personality and Social Psychology, 89*(3), 294–310.

Hovdestad, W. E., & Kristiansen, C. M. (1996). A field study of "false memory syndrome": Construct validity and incidence. *Journal of Psychiatry and Law, 24*, 299–338.

Hovland, C. I. (1937). The generalization of the conditioned responses. I. The sensory generalization of conditioned responses with varying intensities of tone. *Journal of General Psychology, 17*, 125–148.

Howe, M. L., & O'Sullivan, J. T. (1990). The development of strategic memory: Coordinating knowledge, metamemory, and resources. In D. F. Bjorklund (Ed.), *Children's strategies: Contemporary views of cognitive development* (pp. 129–155). Hillsdale, NJ: Erlbaum.

Hu, P., & Meng, Z. (1996). *An examination of infant–mother attachment in China*. Poster presented at the meeting of the International Society for the Study of Behavioral Development, Quebec City, Quebec, Canada.

Hu, S., Pattatucci, A. M. L., Patterson, C., Li, L., Fulker, D. W., Cherny, S. S., . . . Hamer, D. H. (1994). Linkage between sexual orientation and chromosome Xq28 in males but not in females. *Nature Genetics, 11*, 248–256.

Hubble, M. A., Duncan, B. L., & Miller, S. D. (1999). Directing attention to what works. In M. A. Hubble, B. L. Duncan, & S. D. Miller (Eds.), *The heart and soul of change: What works in therapy* (pp. 407–447). Washington, DC: American Psychological Association.

Huesmann, L. R., & Miller, L. S. (1994). Long-term effects of repeated exposure to media violence in childhood. In L. R. Huesmann (Ed.), *Aggressive behavior: Current perspectives* (pp. 153–183). New York, NY: Plenum Press.

Huesmann, L. R., Moise, J. F., & Podolski, C. L. (1997). The effects of media violence on the development of antisocial behavior. In D. M. Stoff, J. Breiling, & J. D. Maser (Eds.), *Handbook of antisocial behavior* (pp. 181–193). New York, NY: Wiley.

Huesmann, L. R., Moise-Titus, J., Podolski, C. L., & Eron, L. D. (2003). Longitudinal relations between children's exposure to TV violence and their aggressive and violent behavior in young adulthood: 1977–1992. *Developmental Psychology, 39*(2), 201–221.

Hugenberg, K., & Bodenhausen, G. V. (2003). Facing prejudice: Implicit prejudice and the perception of facial threat. *Psychological Science, 14*, 640–643.

Hughes, J. (1993). Behavior therapy. In T. R. Kratochwill & R. J. Morris (Eds.), *Handbook of psychotherapy with children and adolescents* (pp. 185–220). Boston, MA: Allyn and Bacon.

Hull, C. L. (1943). *Principles of behavior*. New York, NY: Appleton-Century.

Hummer, R. A., Rogers, R. G., Nam, C. B., & Ellison, C. G. (1999). Religious involvement and U.S. adult mortality. *Demography, 36*(2), 273–285.

Hunsley, J., & Mash, E. J. (2008). Developing criteria for evidence-based assessment: An introduction to assessments that work. In J. Hunsley & E. J. Mash (Eds.), *A guide to assessments that work* (3rd ed.). New York, NY: Guilford Press.

Hunt, E. (2001). Multiple views of multiple intelligence. [Review of the book *Intelligence reframed: Multiple intelligence in the 21st century*, by H. Gardner] *Contemporary Psychology, 46*, 5–7.

Hunt, M. (1993). *The story of psychology*. New York, NY: Doubleday.

Hurley, D. (1989). The search for cocaine's methadone. *Psychology Today, 23*(7/8), 54.

Hurley, S., & Nudds, M. (Eds.) (2006). *Rational animals?* Oxford, England: Oxford University Press.

Hurst, S., & Milkewicz, N. (2000). Eye movement desensitization and reprocessing: A controversial treatment technique. Retrieved from www.netpsych.com/health/emd.htm

Hurvich, L. M. (1969). Hering and the scientific establishment. *American Psychologist, 24*, 497–514.

Hurwitz, T. A. (1989). Approach to the patient with psychogenic neurological disturbance. In W. N. Kelley (Ed.), *Textbook of internal medicine* (Vol. 2, pp. 2518–2521). Philadelphia, PA: Lippincott.

Hutcheson, J., & Snyder, H. M. (2004). Ambiguous genitalia and intersexuality. *eMedicine Journal, 5*(5). Retrieved from http://author.emedicine.com/PED/topic1492.htm

Hyde, J. S., & Kling, K. C. (2001). Women, motivation, and achievement. *Psychology of Women Quarterly, 25*, 264–378.

Hyde, J. S., & Plant, E. A. (1995). Magnitude of psychological gender differences. *American Psychologist, 50*, 159–161.

Hyman, I. E., Gilstrap, L. L., Decker, K., & Wilkinson, C. (1998). Manipulating remember and know judgements of autobiographical memories. *Applied Cognitive Psychology, 12*, 371–386

Hyman, I. E., Jr., & Loftus, E. F. (1998). Errors in autobiographical memories. *Clinical Psychology Review, 18*, 933–947.

Hyman, I. E., Jr., & Loftus, E. F. (2002). False childhood memories and eyewitness memory errors. In M. L. Eisen, J. A. Quas, & G. S. Goodman (Eds.), *Memory and suggestibility in the forensic interview* (pp. 63–84). Mahwah, NJ: Erlbaum.

Imaizumi, Y. (1998). A comparative study of twinning and triplet rates in 17 countries, 1972–1996. *Acta Genetic Medicine & Gemellology, 47*, 101–114.

Internet World Stats. (2008.) World internet users and population stats. *Internet usage: The internet big picture*. Retrieved from http://www.internetworldstats.com/stats.htm

Intersex Initiative (2008). *Intersex FAQ (frequently asked questions)*. Retrieved from http://www.intersexinitiative.org/articles/intersex-faq.html

Ioannidis, J. P. A. (1998, January 28). Effect of the statistical significance of results on the time to completion and publication of randomized efficacy trials. *Journal of the American Medical Association, 279*, 281–286.

Irwin, M., Mascovich A., Gillin, J. C., Willoughby, R., Pike, J., & Smith, T. L. (1994). Partial sleep deprivation reduces natural killer cell activity in humans. *Psychosomatic Medicine, 56*, 493–498.

Irwin, M., McClintick, J., Costlow, C., Fortner, M., White, J., & Gillin, J. C. (1996). Partial night sleep deprivation reduces natural killer and cellular immune responses in humans. *The Federation of American Societies for Experimental Biology Journal, 10*, 643–653.

Isabel, J. (2003). *Genetics: An introduction for dog breeders*. Loveland, CO: Alpine Publications.

Iwakabe, S. (2008). Psychotherapy integration in Japan. *Journal of Psychotherapy Integration, 18*(1), 103–125.

Iwamoto, E. T., & Martin, W. (1988). A critique of drug self-administration as a method for predicting abuse potential of drugs. *National Institute on Drug Abuse Research Monograph, 1046*, 81457–81465.

Iyengar, S. S., & Brockner, J. (in press). Cultural differences in self and social influence. In B. Cialdini (Ed.), *The practice of social influence in multiple cultures*. Mahweh, NJ: Lawrence Erlbaum Associates.

Izard, C. (1988). Emotion-cognition relationships and human development. In C. Izard, J. Kagan, & R. Zajonc (Eds.), *Emotions, cognition, and behavior* (Chapter 1). New York, NY: Cambridge University Press.

Izard, C. E. (1968). Cross-cultural research findings on development in recognition of facial behavior. *Proceedings of the 76th Annual Convention of the American Psychological Association, 3*, 727.

Izard, C. E. (1969). The emotions and emotion constructs in personality and culture research. In R. B. Cattell (Ed.), *Handbook of modern personality theory*. Chicago, IL: Aldine Press, 1969.

Jackson, D. N. (1984). *Personality Research Form manual*. Port Huron, MI: Research Psychologists Press.

Jackson, R. (2001). *Plato: A beginner's guide*. London, England: Hoder & Stroughton.

Jackson, T., Iezzi, T., Gunderson, J., Fritch, A., & Nagasaka, T. (2002). Gender differences in pain perception: The mediating role of self-efficacy beliefs. *Sex Roles, 47*, 561–568.

Jacobson, S. G., Cideciyan A. V., Regunath, G, *Rodriguez, F. J., Vandenburgh, K., Sheffield, V. C., & Stone, E. M.* (1995). Night blindness in Sorsby's fundus dystrophy reversed by vitamin A. *Nature Genetics, 11*, 27–32.

Jaeger, J. J., Lockwood, A. H., Van Valin, R. D., Kemmerer, D. L., Murphy, B. W., & Wack, D. S. (1998). Sex differences in brain regions activated by grammatical and reading tasks. *Neuroreport, 9*, 2803–2807.

James, W. (1884). What is an emotion? *Mind, 9*, 188–205.

James, W. (1890). *Principles of psychology*. New York, NY: Holt.

James, W. (1890, 2002). *The principles of psychology* (Vols. 1 and 2). Cambridge, MA: Harvard University Press.

James, W. (1894). The physical basis of emotion. *Psychological Review, 1*, 516–529.

Janeck, A. S., Calamari, J. E., Riemann, B. R., & Heffelfinger, S. K. (2003). Too much thinking about thinking? Meta-cognitive differences in obsessivecompulsive disorder. *Journal of Anxiety Disorders, 17*, 181–195.

Jang, K. L., Livesley, W. J., & Vernon, P. A. (1996). Heritability of the Big Five personality dimensions and their facets: A twin study. *Journal of Personality, 64*, 577–591.

Jang, K. L., McCrae, R. R., Angleitner, A., Riemann, R., & Livesley, W. J. (1998). Heritability of facet-level traits in a cross-cultural twin sample: Support for a hierarchical model of personality. *Journal of Personality and Social Psychology, 74*, 1556–1565.

Janicki, M. P., Heller, T., Seltzer, G., & Hogg, J. (1995). *Practice guidelines for the clinical assessment and care management of Alzheimer and other dementias among adults with mental retardation*. Washington, DC: American Association on Mental Retardation.

Janis, I. (1972). *Victims of groupthink*. Boston, MA: Houghton-Mifflin.

Janis, I. (1982). *Groupthink* (2nd ed.) Boston, MA: Houghton-Mifflin.

Janos, P. M. (1987). A fifty-year follow-up of Terman's youngest college students and IQ-matched agemates. *Gifted Child Quarterly, 31*, 55–58.

Janowitz, H. D. (1967). Role of gastrointestinal tract in the regulation of food intake. In C. F. Code (Ed.), *Handbook of physiology: Alimentary canal 1*. Washington, DC: American Physiological Society.

Janus, S. S., & Janus, C. L. (1993). *The Janus report on sexual behavior*. New York, NY: Wiley.

Jarmul, D. (2002, March.) Canada's quieter stem cell debate: A conversation with Janet Rossant. *HHMI Bulletin, 15*(1). Retrieved from www.hhmi.org/bulletin/pdf/mar2002/Canada.pdf

Jay, S. M., & Elliot, C. H. (1990). A stress inoculation program for parents whose children are undergoing medical procedures. *Journal of Consulting and Clinical Psychology, 58*, 799–804.

Jensen, A. R. (1969). How much can we boost IQ and scholastic achievement? *Harvard Educational Review, 39*, 1–123.

Jimerson, D. C., Wolfe, B. E., Metzger, E. D., Finkelstein, D. M., Cooper, T. B., & Levine, J. M. (1997). Decreased serotonin function in bulimia nervosa. *Archives of General Psychiatry, 54*, 529–534.

Joanna Briggs Institute. (2001). Smoking cessation interventions and strategies. In *Best Practice, 5*(3), 1329–1874. Australia: Joanna Briggs Institute for Evidence Based Nursing and Midwifery.

John, O. P., Angleitner, A., & Ostendorf, F. (1988). The lexical approach to personality: A historical review of trait taxonomic research. *European Journal of Personality, 2*, 171–203.

Johnson, D., Johnson, R., & Smith, K. (1991). *Active learning: Cooperation in the college classroom*. Edna, MN: Interaction Book Company.

Johnson, G. (1995, June 6). Chimp talk debate: Is it really language? *New York Times*.

Johnson, G. B. (1966). Penis-envy? Or pencil-needing? *Psychological Reports, 19*, 758.

Johnson, J., Cohen, P., Pine, D. S., Klein, D. F., Kasen, S., & Brook, J. S. (2000). Association between cigarette smoking and anxiety disorders during adolescence and early adulthood. *Journal of the American Medical Association, 284*, 2348–2351.

Johnson-Down, L., O'Loughlin, J., Koski, K. G., & Gray-Donald, K. (1997). High prevalence of obesity in low income and multiethnic school-children: A diet and physical activity assessment. *Journal of Nutrition, 127*, 2310–2315.

Jones, E. E., & Harris, V. A. (1967). The attribution of attitudes. *Journal of Experimental Social Psychology, 3*, 1–24.

Jones, E. J., Krupnick, J. L., & Kerig, P. K. (1987). Some gender effects in a brief psychotherapy. *Psychotherapy, 24*, 336–352.

Jones, G. W. (1997). Modernization and divorce: Contrasting trends in Islamic Southeast Asia and the West. *Population and Development Review, 23*(1), 95–113.

Jones, H. M., & Pilowsky, L. S. (2002). Dopamine and antipsychotic drug action revisited. *British Journal of Psychiatry, 181*, 271–275.

Juffer, F., & Rosenboom, L. G. (1997). Infant–mother attachment of internationally adopted children in the Netherlands. *International Journal of Behavioral Development, 20*(1), 93–107.

Jung, C. (1933). *Modern man in search of a soul*. New York, NY: Harcourt Brace.

Kabat-Zinn, J., Lipworth, L., & Burney, R. (1985). The clinical use of mindfulness meditation for the self-regulation of chronic pain. *Journal of Behavioral Medicine, 8*, 163–190.

Kabat-Zinn, J., Lipworth, L., Burney, R., & Sellers, W. (1986). Four year follow-up of a meditation-based program for the self regulation of chronic pain: Treatment outcomes and compliance. *Clinical Journal of Pain, 2*, 159–173.

Kachgal, M. M., Hansen, L. S., & Nutter, K. T. (2001). Academic procrastination prevention/intervention: Strategies and recommendations. *Journal of Developmental Education, 25*(1), 2–12.

Kahan, M., & Sutton, N. (1998). Overview: Methadone treatment for the opioiddependent patient. In B. Brands & J. Brands (Eds.), *Methadone maintenance: A physician's guide to treatment* (pp. 1–15). Toronto, ON: Addiction Research Foundation.

Kales, A., Soldatos, C., Bixler, E., Ladda, R. L., Charney, D. S., Weber, G., & Schweitzer, P. K. (1980). Hereditary factors in sleepwalking and night terrors. *British Journal of Psychiatry, 137,* 111–118.

Kamin, L. J. (1995, February). Behind the curve. *Scientific American,* 99–103.

Kamphaus, R. W. (1993). *Clinical assessment of children's intelligence.* Boston, MA: Allyn & Bacon.

Kandel, E. R., & Schwartz, J. H. (1982). Molecular biology of learning: Modulation of transmitter release. *Science, 218,* 433–443.

Kanne, S. M., Balota, D. A., Storandt, M., McKeel, D. W., Jr., & Morris, J. C. (1998). Relating anatomy to function in Alzheimer's disease: Neuropsychological profiles predict regional neuropathology 5 years later. *Neurology, 50,* 979–985.

Kantrowitz, B., & Springen, K. (1987). For the parents, a delicate balance. *Newsweek, (110)*21, 64.

Karau, S. J., & Williams, K. D. (1993). Social loafing: A meta-analytic review and theoretical integration. *Journal of Personality and Social Psychology, 65,* 681–706.

Karau, S. J., & Williams, K. D. (1997). The effects of group cohesiveness on social loafing and social compensation. *Group Dynamics: Theory, Research and Practice, 1,* 156–168.

Karayiorgou, M., Altemus, M., Galke, B., Goldman, D., Murphy, D., Ott, J., & Gogos, J. A. (1997). Genotype determining low catechol-O-methyltransferase activity as a risk factor for obsessive-compulsive disorder. *Proceeds of the National Academy of Science, 94,* 4572–4575.

Kastenbaum, R., & Costa, P. T., Jr. (1977). Psychological perspective on death. *Annual Review of Psychology, 28,* 225–249.

Katada, E. K., Sato, K., Sawaki, A., Dohi, Y., Ueda, R., & Ojika, K. (2003). Long-term effects of donepezil on P300 auditory event-related potentials in patients with Alzheimer's disease. *Journal of Geriatric Psychiatry and Neurology, 16*(1), 39–43.

Katz, L. Y., Kozyrskvi, A. L., Prior, H. J., Enns, M. W., Cox, B. J., & Sareen, J. (2008). Effect of regulatory warnings on antidepressant prescription rates, use of health services and outcomes among children, adolescents and young adults. *Canadian Medical Association Journal, 178,* 1005–1011.

Kaufman, J., & Zigler, E. (1993). The intergenerational transmission of abuse is overstated. In R. J. Gelles & D. R. Loseke (Eds.), *Current controversies on family violence.* Newbury Park, CA: Sage.

Kaufmann, G. R., Bloch, M., Zaunders, J. J., Smith, D., & Cooper, D. A. (2000). Long-term immunological response in HIV-1 infected subjects receiving potent antiretroviral therapy. *AIDS, 14,* 959–969.

Kazdin, A. E. (1980). Acceptability of time out from reinforcement procedures for disruptive behavior. *Behavior Therapy, 11*(3), 329–344.

Kearney, C. A., & Silverman, W. K. (1998). A critical review of pharmacotherapy for youth with anxiety disorders: Things are not as they seem. *Journal of Anxiety Disorders, 12,* 83–102.

Keillor, J., Barrett, A., Crucian, G., Kortenkamp, S., & Heilman, K. (2002). Emotional experience and perception in the absence of facial feedback. *Journal of the International Neuropsychological Society, 8*(1), 130–135.

Keirsey, D. (1998). *Please understand me II: Temperament, character, intelligence.* Del Mar, CA: Prometheus Nemesis.

Keller, M. B., McCullough, J. P., Klein, D. N., Arnow, B., Dunner, D., Gelenberg, A., . . . Zajecka, J. (2000). A comparison of nefazodone, the cognitive behavioralanalysis system of psychotherapy, and their combination for the treatment of chronic depression. *New England Journal of Medicine, 342,* 1462–1470.

Keller, M. B., Ryan, N. D., Strober, M., Klein, R. G., Kutcher, S. P., Birmaher, B., . . . McCafferty, J. P. (2001). Efficacy of paroxetine in the treatment of adolescent major depression: A randomized, controlled trial. *Journal of the Academy of Child and Adolescent Psychiatry, 40*(7), 762–772.

Kellner, R. (1986). *Somatization and hypochondriasis.* New York, NY: Praeger- Greenwood.

Kelly, I. (1980). The scientific case against astrology. *Mercury, 10,* 13.

Kendall, P. (1983). Stressful medical procedures: Cognitive-behavioral strategies for stress management and prevention. In D. Meichenbaum & M. Jaremko (Eds.), *Stress reduction and prevention.* New York, NY: Plenum Press.

Kendler, K. S. (1985). Diagnostic approaches to schizotypal personality disorders: A historical perspective. *Schizophrenia Bulletin, 11,* 538–553.

Kendler, K. S., & Prescott, C. A. (1999). A population-based twin study of lifetime major depression in men and women. *Archives of General Psychiatry, 56*(1), 39–44.

Kendler, K. S., & Walsh, D. (1995). Schizotypal personality disorder in parents and the risk for schizophrenia in siblings. *Schizophrenia Bulletin, 21*(2), 47–52.

Kenny, A. (1968). Mind and body. In *Descartes: A study of his philosophy* (p. 279). New York, NY: Random House.

Kenny, A. (1994). Descartes to Kant. In A. Kenny (Ed.), *The Oxford history of western philosophy* (pp. 107–192). Oxford, England: Oxford University Press.

Kenrick, D. T., Griskevicius, V., Neuberg, S. L., & Schaller, M. (2010). Renovating the pyramid of needs: Contemporary extensions built upon ancient foundations. *Perspectives on Psychological Science, 5,* 292–314.

Keromoian, R., & Leiderman, P. H. (1986). Infant attachment to mother and child caretaker in an East African community. *International Journal of Behavioral Development, 9,* 455–469.

Kessler, S. (1998). *Lessons from the intersexed.* Piscataway, NJ: Rutgers University Press.

Kety, S. S., Wender, P. H., Jacobsen, B., Ingaham, L. J., Jansson, L., Faber, B., & Kinney, D. K. (1994). Mental illness in the biological and adoptive relatives of schizophrenic adoptees. *Archives of General Psychiatry, 51,* 442–455.

Kiecolt-Glaser, J. K., Fisher, L. D., Ogrocki, P., Stout, J. C., Speicher, C. E., & Glaser, R. (1987). Marital quality, marital disruption, and immune function. *Psychosomatic Medicine, 49,* 13–34.

Kiecolt-Glaser, J. K., Glaser, R., Gravenstein, S., Malarkey, W. B., & Sheridan, J. (1996). Chronic stress alters the immune response to influenza virus vaccine in older adults. *Processes of the National Academy of Science, 93*(7), 3043–3047.

Kiecolt-Glaser, J. K., Marucha, P. T., Malarkey, W. B., & Marcado, A. M. (1995). Slowing of wound healing by psychological stress. *Lancet, 346,* 1194–1196.

Kiecolt-Glaser, J. K., McGuire, L., Robles, T., & Glaser, R. (2002). Psychoneuroimmunology: Psychological influences on immune function and health. *Journal of Consulting and Clinical Psychology, 70,* 537–547.

Kihlstrom, J., Mulvaney, S., Tobias, B., & Tobis, I. (2000). The emotional unconscious. In E. Eich, J. Kihlstrom, G. Bower, J. Forgas, & P. Niedenthal (Eds.), *Cognition and emotion* (pp. 30–86). New York, NY: Oxford University Press.

Kihlstrom, J. F. (1985). Hypnosis. *Annual Review of Psychology, 36,* 385–418.

Kihlstrom, J. F. (1987). The cognitive unconscious. *Science, 237,* 1445–1452.

Kihlstrom, J. F. (1999). Conscious and unconscious cognition. In R. J. Sternberg (Ed.), *The nature of cognition* (pp. 173–203). Cambridge, MA: MIT Press.

Kihlstrom, J. F. (2001). Hypnosis and the psychological unconscious. In Howard S. Friedman (Ed.), *Assessment and therapy: Specialty articles from the Encyclopedia of Mental Health.* San Diego, CA: Academic Press.

Kihlstrom, J. F. (2002). Memory, autobiography, history. *Proteus: A Journal of Ideas, 19*(2), 1–6.

Kihlstrom, J. F., Couture, L. J., Schacter, D. L., & Cork, R. L. (1998). Anesthesia, effects on cognitive functions. In G. Adelman (Ed.), *The encyclopedia of neuroscience* (2nd ed.). Amsterdam, the Netherlands: Elsevier.

Kim, H., & Markus, H. R. (1999). Deviance or uniqueness, harmony or conformity? A cultural analysis. *Journal of Personality and Social Psychology, 77,* 785–800.

Kimura, D. (1994). Body asymmetry and intellectual pattern. *Personality and Individual Differences, 17,* 53–60.

Kimura, D. (1999). *Sex and cognition.* Cambridge, MA: MIT Press.

Kimura, D. (2002, May 13). Sex differences in the brain. *Scientific American.*

Kinsey, A. C., Pomeroy, W. B., & Martin, C. E. (1948). *Sexual behavior in the human male.* Philadelphia, PA: Saunders.

Kinsey, A. C., Pomeroy, W. B., Martin, C. E., & Gebhard, P. H. (1953). *Sexual behavior in the human female.* New York, NY: Saunders.

Kirby, J. S., Chu, J. A., & Dill, D. L. (1993). Correlates of dissociative symptomatology in patients with physical and sexual abuse histories. *Comprehensive Psychiatry 34,* 250–263.

Kirmayer, L. J. (1991). The place of culture in psychiatric nosology: Taijinkyofusho and the DSM-III-R. *Journal of Nervous and Mental Disease, 179,* 19–28.

Kirouac, G., & Hess, U. (1999). Group membership and the decoding of nonverbal behavior. In P. Philippot, R. Feldman, & E. Coats (Eds.), *The social context of nonverbal behavior* (pp. 182–210). New York, NY: Cambridge University Press.

Kirsch, I. (2000). The response set theory of hypnosis. *American Journal of Clinical Hypnosis, 42*(3/42, 4), 274–292.

Kirsch, I., & Lynn, S. J. (1995). The altered state of hypnosis: Changes in the theoretical landscape. *American Psychologist, 50,* 846–858.

Kitayama, S., Snibbe, A. C., Markus, H. R., & Suzuki, T. (2004). Is there any free choice? Self and dissonance in two cultures. *Psychological Science, 15,* 527–533.

Klaver, C. C., Wolfs, R. C., Vingerling, J. R., Hofman, A., & de Jong, P. T. (1998). Age-specific prevalence and causes of blindness and visual impairment in an older population: The Rotterdam Study. *Arch Ophthalmol, 116,* 653–658.

Klehe, U. -C., & Anderson, N. (2007). The moderating influence of personality and culture on motivation in typical versus maximal performance situations. *International Journal of Selection and Assessment, 15,* 250–262.

Klein, D., Schwartz, J., Rose, S., & Leader, J. (2000). Five-year course and outcome of dysthymic disorder: A prospective, naturalistic follow-up study. *American Journal of Psychiatry, 157*(6), 931–939.

Klein, R. M. (1999). The Hebb legacy. *Canadian Journal of Psychology, 53,* 1–3.

Klein, S. B., & Mowrer, R. R. (1989). Contemporary learning theories: Pavlovian conditioning and the status of traditional learning theory. Hillsdale, NJ: Erlbaum.

Kleinot, M. C., & Rogers, R. W. (1982). Identifying effective components of alcohol misuse prevention programs. *Journal of Studies on Alcohol, 43,* 802–811.

Kligman, A. M., & Balin, A. K. (1989). Aging of human skin. In A. K. Balin & A. M. Kligman (Eds.), *Aging and the skin* (pp. 1–42). New York, NY: Raven Press.

Klorman, R., Hilpert, P. L., Michael, R., LaGana, C., & Sveen, O. B. (1980). Effects of coping and mastery modeling on experienced and inexperienced pedodontic patients' disruptiveness. *Behavior Therapy, 11,* 156–168.

Kluft, R. P. (1984). Introduction to multiple personality disorder. *Psychiatric Annals, 14,* 19–24.

Kluft, R. P. (1988). The phenomenology and treatment of extremely complex multiple personality disorder. *Dissociation, I,* 47–58.

Klüver, H., & Bucy, P. C. (1939). Preliminary analysis of functions of the temporal lobes in monkeys. *Archives of Neurological Psychiatry, 42,* 979–1000.

Knauth, P. (1993). The design of shift systems. *Ergonomics, 36*(1–3), 15–28.

Knight, A. (1996). The life of the law: *The people and cases that have shaped our society, from King Alfred to Rodney King.* New York, NY: Crown.

Knight, J. A. (1998). Free radicals: Their history and current status in aging and disease. *Annals of Clinical and Laboratory Science, 28,* 331–346.

Knight, W. (2003). Man vs. machine chess match ends in stalemate. *NewScientist.com News Service, February.* Retrieved from http://www .newscientist.com/news/news.jsp?id=ns99993370

Kobasa, S. (1979). Stressful life events, personality, and health: An inquiry into hardiness. *Journal of Personality and Social Psychology, 37*(1), 1–11.

Koenig, H. G., Hays, J. C., Larson, D. B., George, L. K., Cohen, H. J., McCullough, M. E., . . . Blazer, D. G. (1999). Does religious attendance prolong survival? A six-year follow-up study of 3,968 older adults. *Journal of Gerontology, 54A,* M370–M377.

Koenig, H. G., McCullough, M. E., & Larson, D. B. (2001). *Handbook of religion and health.* Oxford, England: Oxford University Press.

Koh, J. K. (1996). A guide to common Singapore spiders. *BP Guide to Nature* series. Singapore: Singapore Science Center.

Kohlberg, L. (1969). Stage and sequence: The cognitive-developmental approach to socialization. In D. A. Goslin (Ed.), *Handbook of socialization: Theory in research* (pp. 347–480). Boston, MA: Houghton-Mifflin.

Kohlberg, L. (1973). Continuities in childhood and adult moral development revisited. In P. Baltes & K. W. Schaie (Eds.), *Lifespan development psychology: Personality and socialization.* San Diego, CA: Academic Press.

Köhler, W. (1925). *Mentality of apes* (E. Winter, Trans.). London, England: Routledge & Kegan Paul.

Kohler, W. (1992). Gestalt psychology: An introduction to new concepts in modern psychology (reissue). New York, NY: Liveright.

Kolb, B., Cioe, J., & Whishaw, I. Q. (2000). Is there an optimal age for recovery from motor cortex lesions? II. Behavioral and anatomical consequences of unilateral motor cortex lesions in perinatal, infant, and adult rats. *Restorative Neurology and Neuroscience, 17*(2–3), 61–71.

Kolers, P. A. (1975). Specificity of operations in sentence recognition. *Cognitive Psychology, 7,* 289–306.

Kolodny, R. C. (2001, August). In memory of William H. Masters. *Journal of Sex Research,* 274–276.

Konowal, N. M., Van Dongen, H. P. A., Powell, J. W., Mallis, M. M., & Dinges, D. F. (1999). Determinants of microsleeps during experimental sleep deprivation. *Sleep, 22*(1 Suppl.), 328.

Korn, S. (1984). Continuities and discontinuities in difficult/easy temperament: Infancy to young adulthood. *Merrill Palmer Quarterly, 30,* 189–199.

Kosslyn, S. M. (1983). Mental imagery. In Z. Rubin (Ed.), *The psychology of being human.* New York, NY: Harper and Row.

Kosslyn, S. M., Alpert, N. M., Thompson, W. L., Maljkovic, V., Weise, S. B., Chabris, C. F., . . . Buonanno, F. S. (1993). Visual mental imagery activates topographically organized visual cortex: PET investigations. *Journal of Cognitive Neuroscience 5,* 263–287.

Kosslyn, S. M., Ball, T. M., & Reiser, B. J. (1978). Visual images preserve metric spatial information: Evidence from studies of image scanning. *Journal of Experimental Psychology: Human Perception and Performance, 4,* 47–60.

Kosslyn, S. M., Ganis, G., & Thompson, W. L., (2001). Neural foundations of imagery. *Nature Reviews Neuroscience 2,* 635–642.

Kosslyn, S. M., Pascual-Leone, A., Felician, O., Camposano, S., Keenan, J. P., Thompson, W. L., . . . Alpert, N. M. (1999). The role of area 17 in visual imagery: Convergent evidence from PET and rTMS. *Science 284,* 167–170.

Kosslyn, S. M., Thompson, W. L., Wraga, M. J., & Alpert, N. M. (2001). Imagining rotation by endogenous and exogenous forces: Distinct neural mechanisms for different strategies. *Neuroreport,* 12, 2519–2525.

Kotkin, M., Daviet, C., & Gurin, J. (1996). The *Consumer Reports* mental health survey. *American Psychologist, 51,* 1080–1082.

Kouri, E. M., Pope, H. G., & Lukas, S. E. (1999). Changes in aggressive behavior during withdrawal from long-term marijuana use. *Psychopharmacology, 143,* 302–308.

Kourtis, A. P., Bulterys, M., Nesheim, S. R., & Lee, F. K. (2001). Understanding the timing of HIV transmission from mother to infant. *Journal of the American Medical Association, 285,* 709–712.

Kratofil, P. H., Baberg, H. T., & Dimsdale, J. E. (1996). Self-mutilation and severe self-injurious behavior associated with amphetamine psychosis. *General Hospital Psychiatry, 18,* 117–120.

Kreipe, R. E. (1992). Normal somatic adolescent growth and development. In E. McAnarney, R. E., Kreipe, D. Orr, & G. Comerci (Eds.), *Textbook of adolescent medicine* (pp. 44–68). Philadelphia, PA: Saunders.

Krosnick, J. A., Betz, A. L., Jussim, L. J., & Lynn, A. R. (1992). Subliminal conditioning of attitudes. *Personality and Social Psychology Bulletin, 18,* 152–162.

Kryger, M., Lavie, P., & Rosen, R. (1999). Recognition and diagnosis of insomnia. *Sleep, 22,* S421–S426.

Kübler-Ross, E. (1997). *The wheel of life: A memoir of living and dying.* New York, NY: Touchstone.

Kuhn, H. W., & Nasar, S. (Eds.) (2001). *The essential John Nash.* Princeton, NJ: Princeton University Press.

Kuhn, J., Gründler, T. O. J., Lenartz, D., Sturm, V., Klosterkötter, J., & Huff, W. (2010). Deep brain stimulation for psychiatric disorders. *Deutsches Ärzteblatt International, 107*(7), 105–113.

Kuiper, N. A., Grimshaw, M., Leite, C., & Kirsh, G. (2004). Humor is not always the best medicine: Specific components of sense of humor and psychological well-being. *Humor: International Journal of Humor Research, 17,* 135–168.

Kuiper, N. A., & Martin, R. A. (1998). Is sense of humor a positive personality characteristic? In W. Ruch (Ed.), *The sense of humor: Explorations of personality characteristics* (pp. 159–178). New York, NY: Mouton de Gruyter.

Kulik, J. A., & Mahler, H. I. M. (1989). Social support and recovery from surgery. *Health Psychology, 8,* 221–238.

Kulik, J. A., & Mahler, H. I. M. (1993). Emotional support as a moderator of adjustment and compliance after coronary bypass surgery: A longitudinal study. *Journal of Behavioral Medicine, 16,* 45–63.

Kumar, R. (1994). Postnatal mental illness: A transcultural perspective. *Social Psychiatry and Psychiatric Epidemiology, 29*(6), 250–264.

Kumar, S., & Oakley-Browne, M. (2002). Panic disorder. *Clinical Evidence, 7,* 906–912.

Kunkel, P., & Mead, K. P. (1991). *How to toilet train your cat: 21 days to a litter-free home.* New York, NY: Workman.

Kupfer, D. J., & Reynolds, C. F. III. (1997). Management of insomnia. *New England Journal of Medicine, 336*(5), 341–346.

LaBar, K. S., LeDoux, J. E., Spencer, D. D., & Phelps, E. A. (1995). Impaired fear conditioning following unilateral temporal lobectomy to humans. *Journal of Neuroscience, 15,* 6846–6855.

LaBerge, D. (1980). Unitization and automaticity in perception. In J. H. Flowers (Ed.), *Nebraska symposium on motivation* (pp. 53–71). Lincoln, NB: University of Nebraska Press.

Lacayo, A. (1995). Neurologic and psychiatric complications of cocaine abuse. *Neuropsychiatry, Neuropsychology, and Behavioral Neurology, 8*(1), 53–60.

Ladouceur, R. (1996). The prevalence of pathological gambling in Canada. *Journal of Gambling Studies, 12,* 129–142.

LaFromboise, T., Coleman, H. L. K., & Gerton J. (1993). Psychological impact of biculturalism: Evidence and theory. *Psychological Bulletin, 114,* 395–412.

Laguna, F., Adrados, M., Alvar, J., Soriano, V., Valencia, M. E., Moreno, V., et al. (1997). Visceral leishmaniasis in patients infected with the human immunodeficiency virus. *European Journal of Clinical Microbiology and Infectious Diseases, 16,* 898–903.

Lalancette, M-F, & Standing, L. G. (1990). Asch fails again. *Social Behavior and Personality, 18*(1), 7–12.

Lam, R. W., & Levitt, A. J. (1999). *Canadian consensus guidelines for the treatment of seasonal affective disorder.* Vancouver, BC: Clinical and Academic Publishing.

Lam, R. W., Levitt, A. J., Levitan, R. D., Enns, M. W., Morehouse, R., Michalak, E. E., & Tam, E. M. (2006). The CANSAD study: Randomized controlled trial of the effectiveness of light therapy and fluoxetine in patients with winter seasonal affective disorder. *American Journal of Psychiatry, 163,* 805–812.

Lambert, M. J., & Ogles, B. M. (2003). The efficacy and effectiveness of psychotherapy. In M. J. Lambert (Ed.), *Handbook of psychotherapy and behavior change* (5th ed.). New York, NY: Wiley.

Lamerson, C. D., & Kelloway, E. K. (1996). Towards a model of peacekeeping stress: Traumatic and contextual influences. *Canadian Psychology, 37,* 195–204.

Lance, C. E., LaPointe, J. A., & Fisicaro, S. A. (1994). Tests of three causal models of halo rater error. *Organizational Behavior and Human Decision Performance, 57,* 83–96.

Landy, D. (1985). Pibloktoq (hysteria) and input nutrition. Possible implication of hypervitaminosis A. *Social Science & Medicine, 21,* 173–185.

Lane, R. D., Kivley, L. S., DuBois, M. A. Shamasundara, P., & Schwartz, G. E. (1995). Levels of emotional awareness and the degree of right hemisphere dominance in the perception of facial emotion. *Neuropsychologia, 33,* 525–538.

Lang, S. L. (2001). American and Chinese recall memories differently. *Human Ecology, 29,* 23.

Lange, C. (1967). The emotions. Reprinted in Lange and James (Eds.), *The emotions.* New York, NY: Harner. (Original work published 1885)

Langer, E. J., & Rodin, J. (1976). The effects of enhanced personal responsibility for the aged: A field experiment in an institutional setting. *Journal of Personality and Social Psychology, 34,* 191–198.

Langford, C. (2002). *Sexually transmitted diseases: Frequently asked questions.* National Women's Health Information Center, U.S. Department of Health and Human Services.

Langone, M. C. (1996). Clinical update on cults. *Psychiatric Times, 13*(7).

Lapsley, D. K., Milstead, M., Quintana, S. M., Flannery, D., & Buss, R. R. (1986). Adolescent egocentrism and formal operations: Tests of a theoretical assumption. *Developmental Psychology, 22,* 800–807.

Larzelere, R. (1986). Moderate spanking: Model or deterrent of children's aggression in the family? *Journal of Family Violence, 1*(1), 27–36.

Lashley, K. S. (1938). The thalamus and emotion. *The Psychological Review, 45,* 21–61.

Lasnik, H. (1990). Metrics and morphophonemics in early English verse. *University of Connecticut Working Papers in Linguistics* (Vol. 3, pp. 29–40).

Latané, B., & Darley, J. M. (1968). Group inhibition of bystander intervention in emergencies. *Journal of Personality and Social Psychology, 10,* 215–221.

Latané, B., & Darley, J. M. (1969). Bystander "apathy." *American Scientist, 57,* 244–268.

Latané, B., Williams, K., & Harkins, S. (1979). Many hands make light the work: The causes and consequences of social loafing. *Journal of Personality & Social Psychology, 37,* 822–832.

Lauer, J., Black, D. W., & Keen, P. (1993). Multiple personality disorder and borderline personality disorder: Distinct entities or variations on a common theme? *Annals of Clinical Psychiatry, 5,* 129–134.

Laumann, E. O., Paik, A., & Rosen, R. C. (1999). Sexual dysfunction in the United States: Prevalence and predictors. *Journal of the American Medical Association, 281,* 537–544.

Launer, L., Masaki, K., Petrovitch, H., Foley, D., & Havlik, R. (1995). The association between midlife blood pressure levels and late-life cognitive function. *Journal of the American Medical Association, 272,* 1846–1851.

Lavergne, G. M. (1997). *A sniper in the tower: The true story of the Texas Tower massacre.* New York, NY: Bantam.

Lavoie, J. A. A., & Pychyl, T. A. (2001). Cyberslacking and the procrastination superhighway: A web-based survey of online procrastination, attitudes and emotion. *Social Science Computer Review, 19,* 431–444.

Laws, G., Davies, I., & Andrews, C. (1995). Linguistic structure and nonlinguistic cognition: English and Russian blues compared. *Language and Cognitive Processes, 10,* 59–94.

Lay, C., & Nguyen, T. T. I. (1998). The role of acculturation-related and acculturation non-specific daily hassles: Vietnamese-Canadian students and psychological distress. *Canadian Journal of Behavioural Science, 30*(3), 172–181.

Lazarus, R. S. (1991). *Emotion and adaptation.* New York, NY: Oxford University Press.

Lazarus, R. S. (1993). From psychological stress to the emotions: A history of changing outlooks. *Annual Review of Psychology, 44.*

Lazarus, R. S. (1999). *Stress and emotion: A new synthesis.* New York, NY: Springer.

Lazarus, R. S., & Folkman, S. (1984). *Stress, appraisal and coping.* New York, NY: Springer.

Leary, M. R., & Forsyth, D. R. (1987). Attributions of responsibility for collective endeavors. *Review of Personality and Social Psychology, 8,* 167–188.

Leask, J., Haber, R. N., & Haber, R. B. (1969). Eidetic imagery in children: II. Longitudinal and experimental results. *Psychonomic Monograph Supplements, 3,* 25–48.

Leccese, A. P., Pennings, E. J. M., & De Wolff, F. A. (2000). Combined use of alcohol and psychotropic drugs. A review of the literature. *Academisch Ziekenhuis Leiden (AZL),* Leiden.

Leclerc, C. M., & Hess, T. M. (2007). Age differences in the bases for social judgments: Tests of a social expertise perspective. *Experimental Aging Research, 33,* 95–120.

LeDoux, I. (1994). Emotion, memory and the brain. *Scientific American, 270,* 32–39.

Lee, F., Hallahan, M., & Herzog, T. (1996). Explaining real life events: How culture and domain shape attributions. *Personality and Social Psychology Bulletin, 22,* 732–741.

Lee, M., & Shlain, B. (1986). *Acid dreams: The complete social history of LSD: The CIA, the sixties, and beyond.* New York, NY: Grove Press.

Lee, P. A. (1995). Physiology of puberty. In K. L. Becker (Ed.), *Principles and practice of endocrinology and metabolism* (pp. 822–830). Philadelphia, PA: Lippincott.

Lehr, U., & Thomae, H. (Hrsg.) (1987). Patterns of psychological aging. *Results from the Bonne Aging Longitudinal Study (BOLSA).* Stuttgart, Germany: Enke.

Leibel, R. L., Rosenbaum, M., & Hirsch, J. (1995). Changes in energy expenditure resulting from altered body weight. *The New England Journal of Medicine, 332,* 621–628.

Leonard, L. (1997). *Children with specific language impairment.* Cambridge, MA: MIT Press, pp. 89–117.

Leong, F. T. L., Hartung, P. J., Goh, D., & Gaylor, M. (2001). Appraising birth order in career assessment: Linkages to Holland's and Super's models. *Journal of Career Assessment, 9,* 25–39.

LePoncin, M. (1990). *Brain fitness.* New York, NY: Ballantine Books.

Leroy, C., & Symes, B. (2001). Teachers' perspectives on the family backgrounds of children at risk. *McGill Journal of Education, 36*(1), 45–60.

Lesch, K. P., Bengel, D., Heils, A., Sabol, S. Z., Greenberg, B. D., Petri, S., . . . Murphy, D. L. (1996). Association of anxiety-related traits with a polymorphism in the serotonin transporter gene regulatory region. *Science, 274,* 1527–1531.

Leslie, M. (2000, July/August). The vexing legacy of Louis Terman. *Stanford Magazine.*

LeVay, S. (1991). A difference in hypothalamic structure between heterosexual and homosexual men. *Science, 253,* 1034–1037.

LeVay, S., & Hamer, D. (1994). Evidence for a biological influence in male homosexuality, *Scientific American, 270,* 44–49.

Levenson, R. W. (1992). Autonomic nervous system differences among emotions. *Psychological Sciences, 3,* 23–27.

Levenson, R. W., Ekman, P., Heider, K., & Friesen, W. V. (1992). Emotion and autonomic nervous system activity in the Minangkabau of West Sumatra. *Journal of Personality and Social Psychology, 62,* 972–988.

Levy, B. R., Slade, M. D., Kunkel, S. R., & Kasl, S. V. (2002). Longevity increased by positive self-perceptions of aging. *Journal of Personality and Social Psychology, 83,* 261–269.

Levy, S. R., Stroessner, S. J., & Dweck, C. S. (1998). Stereotype formation and endorsement: The role of implicit theories. *Journal of Personality and Social Psychology, 74,* 1421–1436.

Lewin, K. (1935). *A dynamic theory of personality.* New York, NY: McGraw-Hill.

Lewin, K. (1936). *Principles of topological psychology.* New York, NY: McGraw-Hill.

Lewis, D. K. (1996, June). A cross-cultural model for psychotherapy: Working with the African-American client. *Perspectives on Multiculturalism and Cultural Diversity, 6*(2).

Like, R., Steiner, P., & Rubel, A. (1996). Recommended core curriculum guidelines on culturally sensitive and competent care. *Family Medicine, 27,* 291–297.

Lilienfeld, S. O. (1999). Projective measures of personality and psychopathology: How well do they work? *Skeptical Inquirer, 23*(5), 32–39.

Lin, P. J., & Schwanenflugel, P. J. (1995). Cultural familiarity and language factors in the structure of category knowledge. *Journal of Cross-Cultural Psychology, 26,* 153–168.

Lin, P. J., Schwanenflugel, P. J., & Wisenbaker, J. M. (1990). Category typicality, cultural familiarity, and the development of category knowledge. *Developmental Psychology, 26,* 805–813.

Lindemann, B. (1996) Taste reception. *Physiological Review, 76,* 719–766.

Links, P. S., Heslegrave, R., & van Reekum, R. (1998). Prospective follow-up study of borderline personality disorder: Prognosis, prediction of outcome, and Axis II comorbidity. *Canadian Journal of Psychiatry, 43,* 251–259.

Lipsitt, L. P., Kaye, H., & Bosack, T. N. (1966). Enhancement of neonatal sucking through reinforcement. *Journal of Experimental Child Psychology, 4,* 163–168.

Lisanby, S. H., Maddox, J. H., Prudic, J., Devanand, D. P., & Sackeim, H. A. (2000). The effects of electroconvulsive therapy on memory of autobiographical and public events. *Archives of General Psychiatry, 57,* 581–590.

Livesley, J. W., (Ed.). (1995). *The DSM-IV Personality disorders.* New York, NY: Guilford Press.

Lock, M. (1994). Menopause in cultural context. *Experimental Gerontology, 29*(3–4), 307–317.

Loehlin, J. C. (1992). *Genes and environment in personality development.* Newbury Park, CA: Sage.

Loehlin, J. C., McCrae, R. R., Costa, P. T., Jr., & John, O. P. (1998). Heritabilities of common and measure-specific components of the Big Five personality factors. *Journal of Research in Personality, 32,* 431–453.

Loehlin, J. C., Willerman, L., & Horn, J. M. (1985). Personality resemblances in adoptive families when the children are late-adolescent or adult. *Journal of Personality and Social Psychology, 48,* 376–392.

Loftus, E. (1975). Leading questions and the eyewitness report. *Cognitive Psychology, 7,* 560–572.

Loftus, E. (1987, June 29). Trials of an expert witness. *Newsweek.*

Loftus, E. F., Miller, D. G., & Burns H. J. (1978). Semantic integration of verbal information into a visual memory. *Journal of Experimental Psychology: Human Learning, 4,* 19–31.

Loftus, E. F., & Pickrell, J. E. (1995). The formation of false memories. *Psychiatric Annals, 25,* 720–725.

Logue, M. W., Vieland, V. J., Goedken, R. J., & Crowe, R. R. (2003). Bayesian analysis of a previously published genome screen for panic disorder reveals new and compelling evidence for linkage to chromosome 7. *American Journal of Medical Genetics, 121B,* 95–99.

Lohr, J. M., Kleinknecht, R. A., Tolin, D. F., & Barrett, R. H. (1995). The empirical status of the clinical application of eye movement desensitization and reprocessing. *Journal of Behavior Therapy and Experimental Psychiatry, 26,* 285–302.

Lohr, J. M., Tolin, D. F., & Lilienfield, S. O. (1998). Efficacy of eye movement desensitization and reprocessing: Implications for behavior therapy. *Behavior Therapy, 29,* 123–156.

Lord, T. R. (2001). 101 reasons for using cooperative learning in biology teaching. *The American Biology Teacher, 63*(1), 30–38.

Lovaas, O. I. (1964). Cue properties of words: The control of operant responding by rate and content of verbal operants. *Child Development, 35,* 245–256.

Lovaas, O. I. (1987). Behavioral treatment and normal educational and intellectual functioning in young autistic children. *Journal of Consulting and Clinical Psychology, 55,* 3–9.

Lovaas, O. I. Berberich, J. P., Perloff, B. F., & Schaffer, B. (1966). Acquisition of imitative speech by schizophrenic children. *Science, 151,* 705–707.

Lu, S., & Ende, N. (1997). Potential for clinical use of viable pluripotent progenitor cells in blood bank stored human umbilical cord blood. *Life Sciences, 61,* 1113–1123.

Lubinski, D. (2000). Scientific and social significance of assessing individual differences: "Sinking shafts at a few critical points." *Annual Review of Psychology, 51,* 405–444.

Luborsky, L., Singer, B., & Luborsky, L. (1975). Comparative studies of psychotherapies: Is it true that "everyone has won and all must have prizes"? *Archives of General Psychiatry, 32,* 995–1008.

Luchins, A. S. (1957). Primacy-recency in impression formation. In C. Hovland (Ed.), *The order of presentation in persuasion* (pp. 33–40, 55–61). New Haven, CT: Yale University Press.

Lucy, J. A., & Shweder, R. A. (1979). Whorf and his critics: Linguistic and nonlinguistic influences on color memory. *American Anthropologist, 81,* 581–615.

Lundstrom, J. N., Boyle, J. A., Zatorre, R. J., & Jones-Gotman, M. (2008). Functional neuronal processing of body odors differs from that of similar common odors. *Cerebral Cortex, 18,* 1466–1474.

Luria, A. R. (1968). *The mind of a mnemonist.* (pp. 24, 25). New York, NY: Basic Books.

Lurito, J. T., Dzemidzic, M., Mathews, V. P., Lowe, M. J., Kareken, D. A., Phillips, M. D., & Wang, Y. (2000). Comparison of hemispheric lateralization using four language tasks. *Neuroimage, 11,* S358.

Lutkenhaus, P., Grossmann, K. E., & Grossman, K. (1985). Infant–mother attachment at twelve months and style of interaction with a stranger at the age of three years. *Child Development, 56,* 1538–1542.

Lykken, D. T. (1995). *The antisocial personalities.* Hillsdale, NJ: Erlbaum.

Lykken, D. T., & Tellegen, A. (1996). Happiness is a stochastic phenomenon. *Psychological Science, 7,* 186–189.

Lynch, E. B., Coley, J. D., & Medin, D. L. (2000). Tall is typical: Central tendency, ideal dimensions, and graded category structure among tree experts and novices. *Memory & Cognition, 28*(1), 41–50.

Lytton, H., & Romney, D. M. (1991). Parents' sex-differentiated socialization of boys and girls: A meta-analysis. *Psychological Bulletin, 109,* 267–296.

Lyvers, M. (2003). The neurochemistry of psychedelic experiences. *Science & Consciousness Review, 1,* 1–5.

Lyznicki, J. M., Doege, T. C., Davis, R. M., & Williams, M. A. (1998). Sleepiness, driving, and motor-vehicle crashes. Council on Scientific Affairs, American Medical Association. *Journal of the American Medical Association, 279*(23), 1908–1913.

Maccoby, E. E. (1998). *The two sexes: Growing up apart: Coming together.* Cambridge, MA: Belknap Press of Harvard University Press.

MacDonald, A. P. (1970). Internal-external locus of control and the practice of birth control. *Psychological Reports, 27,* 206.

MacDonald, D., Kabani, N., Avis, D., & Evens, A. C. (2000). Automated 3D extraction of inner and outer surfaces of cerebral cortex from MRI. *Neuro- Image, 12,* 340–356.

MacDonald, S., Uesiliana, K., & Hayne, H. (2000). Cross-cultural and gender differences in childhood amnesia. *Memory, 8,* 365–376.

MacDonald, S. E., Spetch, M. L., Kelly, D. M., & Cheng, K. (2004). Strategies in landmark use by children, adults, and marmoset monkeys. *Learning and Motivation, 35,* 322–347.

Mack, J. E. (1994). *Abduction.* New York, NY: Scribner.

MacKenzie, S. B., Lutz, R. J., & Belch, G. E. (1986, May). The role of attitude toward the ad as a mediator of advertising effectiveness: A test of competing explanations. *Journal of Marketing Research, 23,* 130–143.

MacMillan, H. L., Fleming, J. E., Streiner, D. L., Lin, E., Boyle, M. H., Jamieson, E., . . . Beardslee, W. R. (2001). Childhood abuse and lifetime psychopathology in a community sample. *American Journal of Psychiatry, 158,* 1878–1883.

Macquet, P., & Franck, G. (1996). Functional neuroanatomy of human rapid eye movement sleep and dreaming. *Nature, 383,* 163–166.

Macrae, C. N., & Bodenhausen, G. V. (2000). Social cognition: Thinking categorically about others. *Annual Review of Psychology, 51,* 93–120.

Madsen, K. M., Hviid, A., Vestergaard, M., Schendel, D., Wohlfahrt, J., Thorsen, P., . . . Melbye, M. (2002). A population-based study of measles, mumps, rubella vaccine and autism. *New England Journal of Medicine, 347,* 1477–1482.

Magarinos, M., Zafar, U., Nissenson, K., & Blanco, C. (2002). Epidemiology and treatment of hypochondriasis. *CNS Drugs, 16*(1), 9–22.

Maguire, E. A., Burgess, N., Donnett, J. G., O'Keefe, J., & Frith, C. D. (1998). Knowing where things are: Parahippocampal involvement in encoding object locations in virtual large-scale space. *Journal of Cognitive Neuroscience, 10*(1), 61–76.

Mahe, V., & Dumaine, A. (2001). Oestrogen withdrawal associated psychoses. *Acta Psychiatrica Scandinavica, 104*(5), 323–331.

Mahowald, M. W., & Schenck, C. H. (1996). NREM sleep parasomnias. *Neurologic Clinics, 14,* 675–696.

Mai, J. K., Triepel, J., & Metz, J. (1987). Neurotensin in the human brain. *Neuroscience, 22,* 499–524.

Maier, S. F., & Watkins, L. R. (1998). Cytokines for psychologists: Implications of bidirectional immune-to-brain communication for understanding behavior, mood, and cognition. *Psychological Review, 105,* 83–107.

Main, M., & Cassidy, J. (1988). Categories of response to reunion with the parent at age 6: Predictable from infant attachment classifications and stable over a 1-month period. *Developmental Psychology, 24,* 415–426.

Main, M., & Hesse, E. (1990). Parents' unresolved traumatic experiences are related to infant disorganized attachment status: Is frightened and/or frightening parental behaviour the linking mechanism? In M. T. Greenberg, D. Cicchetti, & E. M. Cummings (Eds.), *Attachment in the preschool years: Theory, research and intervention* (pp. 161–182). Chicago, IL: University of Chicago Press.

Main, M., & Solomon, J. (1990). Procedures for identifying infants as disorganized/ disoriented during the Ainsworth Strange Situation. In M. T. Greenberg, D. Cicchetti, & E. M. Cummings (Eds.), *Attachment in the preschool years: Theory, research and intervention* (pp. 121–160). Chicago, IL: University of Chicago Press.

Makeig, S., Delorme, A., Westerfield, M., Jung, T., Townsend, J., Courchesne, E., & Sejnowski, T. J. (2004). Electronic brain dynamics following manually responded visual targets. *Public Library of Science: Biology, 2*(6), e176.

Malan, J. R., Norton, G. R., & Cox, B. J. (1993). Panic attacks and alcoholism: Primacy and frequency of attacks. *Alcoholism Treatment Quarterly, 10,* 95–105.

Mandler, G. (1967). Organization and memory. In K. W. Spence & J. T. Spence (Eds.), *The psychology of learning and motivation* (Vol. 1, pp. 327–372). New York, NY: Academic Press.

Mandler, J. M. (2000). Perceptual and conceptual processes. *Journal of Cognition and Development, 1,* 3–36.

Mandler, J. M. (2003). Conceptual categorization. In D. H. Rakison & L. M. Oakes (Eds.), *Early category and concept development: Making sense of the blooming, buzzing confusion* (pp. 103–131). Oxford, England: Oxford University Press.

Manson, J., Greenland, P., LaCroix, A. Z., Stefanick, M. L., Mouton, C. P., Oberman, A., . . . Siscovick, D. S. (2002). Walking compared with vigorous exercise for the prevention of cardiovascular events in women. *New England Journal of Medicine, 347*(10), 716–725.

March, J., Silva, S., Petrycki, S., Curry, J., Wells, K., Fairbank, J., ... Severe, J. [Treatment for Adolescents with Depression Study (TADS) Team]. (2004). Fluoxetine, cognitive-behavioral therapy, and their combination for adolescents with depression: Treatment for Adolescents with Depression Study (TADS) randomized controlled trial. *Journal of the American Medical Association, 292,* 807–820.

Marcus, D. K., Gurley, J. R., Marchi, M. M., & Bauer, C. (2007). Cognitive and perceptual variables in hypochondriasis and health anxiety: A systematic review. *Clinical Psychology Review, 27,* 127–139.

Maren, S., & Fanselow, M. S. (1996). The amygdala and fear conditioning: Has the nut been cracked? *Neuron, 16,* 237–240.

Marik, P. E. (2000). Leptin, obesity, and obstructive sleep apnea. *Chest, 118,* 569–571.

Markland, D. (2011). *Exercise motivation management.* Retrieved from http://pages.bangor.ac.uk/~pes004/exercise_motivation/breq/theory.htm

Markovitz, J. H., Lewis, C. E., Sanders, P. W., Tucker, D., & Warnock, D. G. (1997). Relationship of diastolic blood pressure with cyclic GMP excretion among young adults (the CARDIA study): Influence of a family history of hypertension. *Journal of Hypertension, 15*(9), 955–962.

Mars, A. E., Mauk, J. E., & Dowrick, P. (1998). Symptoms of pervasive developmental disorders as observed in prediagnostic home videos of infants and toddlers. *Journal of Pediatrics, 132,* 500–504.

Martel, R. (2005). Real fears, virtual therapy. University Affairs website. Retrieved from http://www.universityaffairs.ca/2005/06/06/real-fears-virtual-therapy.aspx

Martin, C. L. (2000). Cognitive theories of gender development. In T. Eckes & H. M. Trautner (Eds.), *The developmental social psychology of gender* (pp. 91–121). Mahwah, NJ: Erlbaum.

Martin, J. A., & Buckwalter, J. J. (2001). Telomere erosion and senescence in human articular cartilage chondrocytes. *Journal of Gerontology and Biological Science, 56*(4), 172–179.

Martin, L. (2004). Can sleepwalking be a murder defense? Retrieved from http://www.mtsinai.org/pulmonary/Sleep/sleep-murder.htm

Martin, R. A. (2007). *The psychology of humour: An integrative approach.* Burlington MA: Elsevier.

Martin, R. A., & Lefcourt, H. M. (1983). Sense of humor as a moderator of the relation between stressors and moods. *Journal of Personality and Social Psychology, 45,* 1313–1324.

Maruta, T., Colligan, R. C., Malinchoc, M., & Offord, K. P. (2002, August). Optimism- pessimism assessed in the 1960s and self-reported health status 30 years later. *Mayo Clinic Proceedings, 77,* 748–753.

Maslow, A. (1971). *The farther reaches of human nature.* New York, NY: Viking Press.

Maslow, A. (1987). *Motivation and personality* (3rd ed.). New York, NY: Harper & Row.

Maslow, A., & Lowery, R. (Ed.). (1998). *Toward a psychology of being* (3rd ed.). New York, NY: Wiley.

Maslow, A. H. (1943). A theory of human motivation. *Psychological Review 50,* 370–396.

Maslow, A. H. (1968). *Toward a psychology of being.* Princeton, NJ: Van Nostrand Reinhold.

Massaro, D. W., & Cowan, N. (1993). Information processing models: Microscopes of the mind. *Annual Review of Psychology, 44,* 383–426.

Master, Z., McLeod, M., & Mendez, I. (2007). Benefits, risks, and ethical considerations in translation of stem cell research to clinical applications in Parkinson's Disease. *Journal of Medical Ethics, 33*(3), 169–173.

Masters, J. C., Burish, T. G., Holton, S. D., & Rimm, D. C. (1987). *Behavior therapy: Techniques and empirical finding.* San Diego, CA: Harcourt Brace Jovanovich.

Masters, W., & Johnson, V. (1966). *Human sexual response.* Boston, MA: Little, Brown.

Masters, W., Johnson, V., & Kolodny, R. (1995). *Human sexuality* (5th ed.). New York, NY: Harpers-Collins.

Masters, W. H., & Johnson, V. E. (1970). *Human sexual inadequacy* (pp. 316–351). Boston, MA: Little, Brown.

Masuda, T., Ellsworth, P., Mesquita, B., Leu, J., Tanida, S., & Veerdonk, E. (2008). Placing the face in context: Cultural differences in the perception of facial emotion. *Journal of Personality and Social Psychology, 94,* 365–381.

Masuda, T., & Nisbett, R. E. (2001). Attending holistically versus analytically: Comparing the context-sensitivity of Japanese and Americans. *Journal of Personality and Social Psychology, 81,* 922–934.

Masuda, T., & Nisbett, R. E. (2006). Culture and change blindness. *Cognitive Sciences, 30,* 381–399.

Mathew, B., Dawson, M. Y, B. A., Kozanitis, C., Bright, B., Gopinath, H. V., . . . Lam, R. W. (2007). Psychosocial outcomes following electroconvulsive therapy in a community setting: Retrospective chart review with 2-year follow-up. *Canadian Journal of Psychiatry, 52,* 598–604.

Matsumoto, D. (1994). *People: Psychology from a cultural perspective* (pp. 144–147). Pacific Grove, CA: Brooks-Cole.

Matthews, K. A., Gump, B. B., Harris, K. F., Haney, T. L., & Barefoot, J. C. (2004). Hostile behaviors predict cardiovascular mortality among men enrolled in the Multiple Risk Factor Intervention Trial. *Circulation, 109,* 66–70.

Maurer, D., & Young, R. (1983). Newborns' following of natural and distorted arrangements of facial features. *Infant Behaviour and Development, 6,* 127–131.

Mavromatis, A. (1987). *Hypnagogia: The unique state of consciousness between wakefulness and sleep.* London, England: Routledge & Kegan Paul.

Mavromatis, A., & Richardson, J. T. E. (1984). Hypnagogic imagery. *International Review of Mental Imagery, 1,* 159–189.

Mawhinney, T. A. (1983). A picture vocabulary test for the Eastern James Bay Cree. In S. H. Irvine & J. W. Berry (Eds.), *Human assessment and cultural factors.* New York, NY: Plenum.

Maxfield, L., & Melnyk, W. T. (2000). Single session treatment of test anxiety with eye movement desensitization and reprocessing (EMDR). *International Journal of Stress Management, 7*(2), 87–101.

Mayberg, H. S., Lozano, A. M., Voon, V., McNeely, H. E., Seminowicz, D., Hamani, C., . . . Kennedy, S. H. (2005). Deep brain stimulation for treatment-resistant depression. *Neuron, 45,* 651–660.

Mayer, J. D. (September 1999). Emotional intelligence: Popular or scientific psychology? *APA Monitor Online, 30*(8) [*Shared Perspectives* column]. Washington, DC; American Psychological Association. Retrieved from http://www.apa.org/monitor/sep99/sp.html

Mayer, J. D., & Geher, G. (1996). Emotional intelligence and the identification of emotion. *Intelligence, 22,* 89–113.

Mayer, J. D., Salovey, P., & Caruso, D. R. (2000). Models of emotional intelligence. In R. J. Sternberg (Ed.), *Handbook of human intelligence* (2nd ed., pp. 396–420). New York, NY: Cambridge.

Maziade, M., Bissonnette, L., Rouillard, E., Martinez, M., Turgeon, M., Charron, L., . . . Mérette, C. (1997). 6p24–22 region and major psychoses in the Eastern Quebec population. Le Groupe IREP. *American Journal of Medical Genetics, 74,* 311–318.

Mazzoni, G. A. L., Loftus, E. F., & Kirsch, I. (2001). Changing beliefs about implausible autobiographical events: A little plausibility goes a long way. *Journal of Experimental Psychology: Applied, 7*(1), 51–59.

McCann, S. J. H., & Stewin, L. L. (1988). Worry, anxiety, and preferred length of sleep. *Journal of Genetic Psychology, 149,* 413–418.

McCarthy, J. (1959). Programs with common sense. In *Mechanisation of thought processes, proceedings of the Symposium of the National Physics Laboratory* (pp. 77–84). London, England: Her Majesty's Stationery Office.

McCauley, C. (1998). Group dynamics in Janis's theory of groupthink: Backward and forward. *Organizational Behavior & Human Decision Processes, 73*(2–3), 142–162.

McClelland, D. C. (1961). *The achieving society.* Princeton, NJ: Van Nostrand.

McClelland, D. C. (1987). *Human motivation.* Cambridge, MA: Cambridge University Press.

McClelland, J. L., & Rumelhart, D. E. (1988). *Explorations in parallel distributed processing.* Cambridge, MA: MIT Press.

McCrae, R. R., & Costa, P. T. (1990). *Personality in adulthood.* New York, NY: Guilford Press.

McCrae, R. R., & Costa, P. T., Jr. (1996). Toward a new generation of personality theories: Theoretical contexts for the five-factor model. In J. S. Wiggins (Ed.), *The five-factor model of personality: Theoretical perspectives* (pp. 51–87). New York, NY: Guilford.

McCrae, R. R., Costa, P. T., Jr., Ostendorf, F., Angleitner, A., Hrebickova, M., Avia, M. D., . . . Smith, P. B. (2000). Nature over nurture: Temperament, personality, and life span development. *Journal of Personality and Social Psychology, 78,* 173–186.

McCrae, R. R., & Terracciano, A. (2006). National character and personality. *Current Directions in Psychological Science, 15,* 156–161.

McDermott, J. F. (2001). Emily Dickinson revisited: A study of periodicity in her work. *American Journal of Psychiatry, 158,* 686–690.

McDonald, J., Becker, D., Sadowsky, C., Jane, J., Conturo, T., & Schultz, L. (2002). Late recovery following spinal cord injury. *Journal of Neurosurgery: Spine, 97,* 252–265.

McDougall, W. (1908). *An introduction to social psychology.* London, England: Methuen.

McEwen, B. S. (2000). The neurobiology of stress: From serendipity to clinical relevance. *Brain Research, 886,* 172–189.

McGinn, L. K. (2000). Cognitive behavioral therapy of depression: Theory, treatment, and empirical status. *American Journal of Psychotherapy, 54,* 254–260.

McGinnis, J. M., & Foege, W. H. (1993). Actual causes of death in the United States. *Journal of the American Medical Association, 270,* 2207–2212.

McGrath, E., Keita, G. P., Strickland, B. R., & Russo, N. F. (1992). *Women and depression: Risk factors and treatment issues.* Washington, DC: American Psychological Association.

McHugh, P. R. (1993). Multiple personality disorder. *Harvard Mental Health Newsletter, 10*(3), 4–6.

McKenzie, B. E., Tootell, H. E., & Day, R. H. (1980). Development of visual size constancy during the 1st year of human infancy. *Developmental Psychology, 16,* 163–174.

McKenzie, I. A., Biernaskie, J., Toma, J. G., Midha, R., & Miller, F. D. (2006). Skin-derived precursors henerate myelinating Schwann cells for the injured and dysmyelinated nervous system. *Journal of Neuroscience, 26,* 6651–6660.

McLaughlin, S. K., & Margolskee, R. F. (1994). Vertebrate taste transduction. *American Scientist, 82,* 538–545.

McMillan, H. L., Boyle, M. H., Wong, M. Y., Duku, E. K., Fleming, J. E., & Walsh, C. A. (1999). Slapping and spanking in childhood and its association with lifetime prevalence of psychiatric disorders in a general population sample. *Canadian Medical Association Journal, 161,* 805–809.

McMonagle, T., & Sultana, A. (2002). Token economy for schizophrenia (Cochrane Review). In *The Cochrane Library, Issue 2.* Oxford, England: Update Software.

McPherson, M., Smith-Lovin, L., & Cook, J. M. (2001). Birds of a feather: Homophily in social networks. *Annual Review of Sociology, 27,* 415–444.

McWilliams, L. A., & Bailey, S. J., (2010). Associations between adult attachment ratings and health conditions: Evidence from the national comorbidity survey replication. *Health Psychology, 29*(4), 446–453.

Meadow, P. W., & Clevans, E. G. (1978). A new approach to psychoanalytic teaching. *Modern Psychoanalysis, 3*(1), 29–43.

Medicine, B. (2002). Directions in gender research in American Indian societies: Two spirits and other categories. In W. J. Lonner, D. L. Dinnel, S. A. Hayes, & D. N. Sattler (Eds.), *Online readings in psychology and culture* (Unit 3, Chapter 2) Bellingham, WA: Center for Cross-Cultural Research, Western Washington University.

Mehrabian, A. (2000). Beyond IQ: Broad-based measurement of individual success potential or "emotional intelligence." *Genetic, Social, and General Psychology Monographs, 126,* 133–239.

Meichenbaum, D. (1985). *Stress inoculation training.* NewYork, NY: Pergamon Press.

Meichenbaum, D. (1993). Changing conceptions of cognitive behavior modification: Retrospect and prospect. *Journal of Consulting and Clinical Psychology, 61,* 202–204.

Meichenbaum, D. (1996). Stress inoculation training for coping with stressors. *The Clinical Psychologist, 49,* 4–7.

Meissner, K. K., Kirkham, D. L., & Doering, L. C. (2005). Transplants of neurosphere cell suspensions from aged mice are functional in the mouse model of Parkinson's. *Brain Research, 1057*(1–2), 105–112.

Melzack, R., & Wall, P. D. (1965). Pain mechanisms: A new theory. *Science, 150,* 971–979.

Melzack, R., & Wall, P. D. (1996). *The challenge of pain.* London, England: Penguin Books.

Mendel, M. P. (1995). *The male survivor: The impact of sexual abuse.* London, England: Sage.

Menon, T., Morris, M., Chiu, C. Y., & Hong, Y. I. (1999). Culture and the construal of agency: Attribution to individual versus group dispositions. *Journal of Personality and Social Psychology, 76,* 701–727.

Merikle, M. P. (2000). Subliminal perception. In A. E. Kazdin (Ed.), *Encyclopedia of Psychology* (Vol. 7, pp. 497–499). New York, NY: Oxford University Press.

Merikle, P. M., & Daneman, M. (1998). Psychological investigations of unconscious perception. *Journal of Consciousness Studies, 5,* 5–18.

Merriam-Webster. (2003). *Merriam-Webster's collegiate dictionary* (11th ed.). Merriam-Webster, Publisher.

Merskey, H. (1992). The manufacture of personalities: The production of multiple personality disorder. *British Journal of Psychiatry, 160,* 327–340.

Mervis, C. B., & Rosch, E. (1981). Categorization of natural objects. *Annual Review of Psychology, 32,* 89–115.

Meyrick, J. (2001). Forget the blood and gore: An alternative message strategy to help adolescents avoid cigarette smoking. *Health Education, 101*(3), 99–107.

Mezzich, J. E., Kleinman, A., Fabrega, H., & Parron, D. L. (1996). *Culture and psychiatric diagnosis.* Washington DC: American Psychiatric Association.

Michaels, J. W., Blommel, J. M., Brocato, R. M., Linkous, R. A., & Rowe, J. S. (1982). Social facilitation and inhibition in a natural setting. *Replications in Social Psychology, 2,* 21–24.

Miles, D. R., & Carey, G. (1997). Genetic and environmental architecture of human aggression. *Journal of Personality and Social Psychology, 72,* 207–217.

Milgram, S. (1964a). Behavioral study of obedience. *Journal of Abnormal and Social Psychology, 67,* 371–378.

Milgram, S. (1964b). Issues in the study of obedience: A reply to Baumrind. *American Psychologist, 19,* 848–852.

Milgram, S. (1974). *Obedience to authority: An experimental view.* New York, NY: Harper and Row.

Miller, G. A. (1956). The magical number seven, plus or minus two: Some limits on our capacity for processing information. *Psychological Review, 63,* 81–97.

Miller, J. G. (1984). Culture and the development of everyday social explanation. *Journal of Personality and Social Psychology, 46,* 961–978.

Miller, K. E., & Graves, J. C. (2000). Update on the prevention and treatment of sexually transmitted diseases. *American Family Physician, 61,* 379–386.

Miller, L. H., & Smith, A. D. (1993). *The stress solution.* New York, NY: Pocket Books.

Miller, M., & Kantrowitz, B. (1999, January 25). Unmasking Sybil: A re-examination of the most famous psychiatric patient in history. *Newsweek.*

Miller, M., & Rahe, R. H. (1997). Life changes scaling for the 1990s. *Journal of Psychosomatic Research, 43*(3), 279–292.

Miller, M. E., & Bowers, K. S. (1993). Hypnotic analgesia: Dissociated experience or dissociated control? *Journal of Abnormal Psychology, 102,* 29–38.

Miller, M. N., & Pumariega, A. (1999). Culture and eating disorders. *Psychiatric Times, 16*(2), 1–4.

Miller, N. E., Sears, R. R., Mowrer, O. H., Doob, L. W., & Dollard, J. (1941). The frustration-aggression hypothesis. *Psychological Review, 48,* 337–342.

Miller, P. M. (1976). *Behavioral treatment of alcoholism.* Elmsford, NY: Pergamon Press.

Mills, M. A., Edmondson, D., & Park, C. L. (2007). Trauma and stress response among Hurricane Katrina evacuees. *American Journal of Public Health, 97*(1), 116–123.

Milner, B., Corkin, S., & Teuber, H. L. (1968). Further analysis of the hippocampal syndrome: 14-year follow-up study of H. M. *Neuropsychologia, 6,* 215–234.

Milner, J. (1992, January). Risk for physical child abuse: Adult factors. *Violence Update.*

Milner, J. (2007). Chris Benoit. *Slam Sports.* Retrieved from http://slam. canoe.ca/Slam/Wrestling/Bios/benoit.html

Milton, J., & Wiseman, R. (2001). Does psi exist? Reply to Storm and Ertel (2001). *Psychological Bulletin, 127,* 434–438.

Miner, M. H., & Dwyer, S. M. (1997). The psychosocial development of sex offenders: Differences between exhibitionists, child molesters, and incest offenders. *International Journal of Offender Therapy and Comparative Criminology, 41,* 36–44.

Mintz, L. B., & Betz, N. E. (1988). Prevalence and correlates of eating disordered behaviors among undergraduate women. *Journal of Counseling Psychology, 35,* 463–471.

Mischel, W. (1966). A social learning view of sex differences in behaviour. In E. E. Maccoby (Ed.), *The development of sex differences* (pp. 56–81). Stanford, CT: Stanford University Press.

Mischel, W. (1968). *Personality and assessment.* New York, NY: Wiley.

Mischel, W., & Shoda, Y. (1995). A cognitive-affective system theory of personality: Reconceptualizing situations, dispositions, dynamics, and invariances in personality structure. *Psychological Review, 102,* 246–268.

Mishell, D. R. (2001). Menopause. In M. A. Stenchever, W. Droegemueller, A. L. Herbst, & D. R. Mishell (Eds.), *Comprehensive gynecology* (4th ed., pp. 1217–1258). St. Louis, MO: Mosby.

Mitchell, J. E. (1985). *Anorexia nervosa & bulimia, diagnosis and treatment.* Minneapolis, MN: University of Minnesota Press.

Mitchell, S. A., & Black, M. J. (1996). *Freud and beyond: A history of modern psychoanalytic thought* [Reprint edition]. New York, NY: HarperCollins.

Miyatake, A., Morimoto Y., Oishi, T., Hanasaki, N., Sugita, Y., Iijima, S., . . . Yamamura, Y. (1980). Circadian rhythm of serum testosterone and its relation to sleep: Comparison with the variation in serum luteinizing hormone, prolactin, and cortisol in normal men. *Journal of Clinical Endocrinology and Metabolism, 51,* 1365–1371.

Moffic, H. S. (2003). Seven ways to improve cultural competence. *Current Psychiatry (2*), 78.

Mogil, J. S. (1999). The genetic mediation of individual differences in sensitivity to pain and its inhibition. *Proceedings of the National Academy of Sciences of the United States of America, 96*(14), 7744–7751.

Mokdad, A, H., Bowman, B. A., Ford, E. S., Dietz, W. H., Vinicor, F., Bales, V. S., & Marks, J. S. (2001). Prevalence of obesity, diabetes, and obesity related health risk factors. *Journal of the American Medical Association, 289,* 76–79.

Moldofsky, H. (1995). Sleep and the immune system. *International Journal of Immunopharmacology, 17*(8), 649–654.

Möller, A., & Hell, D. (2002). Eugen Bleuler and forensic psychiatry. *International Journal of Law and Psychiatry, 25,* 351–360.

Mondlach, C. J., Lewis, T. L., Budreau, R. D., Maurer, D., Dannemiller, J. L., Stephens, B. R., & Kleiner-Gathercoal, K. A. (1999). Face perception during early infancy. *Psychological Science, 10,* 419–422.

Money, J. (1994). *Sex errors of the body and related syndromes.* Baltimore, MD: Brookes.

Money, J., & Mathews, D. (1982). Prenatal exposure to virilizing progestins: An adult follow-up study of 12 women. *Archives of Sexual Behavior, 11*(1), 73–83.

Money, J., & Norman, B. F. (1987). Gender identity and gender transposition: Longitudinal outcome study of 24 male hermaphrodites assigned as boys. *Journal of Sex and Marriage Therapy, 13,* 75–79.

Montgomery, R. W., & Ayllon, T. (1994). Eye movement desensitization across subjects: Subjective and physiological measures of treatment efficacy. *Journal of Behavior Therapy and Experimental Psychiatry, 25,* 217–230.

Moody, R., & Perry, P. (1993). *Reunions: Visionary encounters with departed loved ones.* London, England: Little, Brown.

Moore, T. E. (1988). The case against subliminal manipulation. *Psychology and Marketing, 5,* 297–316.

Moore-Ede, M. C., Sulzman, F. M., & Fuller, C. A. (1982). *The clocks that time us.* Cambridge, MA: Harvard University Press.

Moorhead, G., Neck, C. P., & West, M. S. (1998). The tendency toward defective decision making within self-managing teams: The relevance of groupthink for the 21st century. *Organizational Behavior & Human Decision Processes, 73,* 327–351.

Mora, G. (1985). History of psychiatry. In H. I. Kaplan & B. J. Sadock (Eds.), *Comprehensive textbook of psychiatry* (pp. 2034–2054). Baltimore, MD: Williams & Wilkins.

Moreland, R. L., & Zajonc, R. B. (1982). Exposure effects in person perceptions: Familiarity, similarity, and attraction. *Journal of Experimental Social Psychology, 18*(5), 395–415.

Morgan, C. D., & Murray, H. A. (1935). A method for investigating fantasies: The Thematic Apperception Test. *Archives of Neurology and Psychiatry, 34,* 298–306.

Morris, C. (2010). *Some general occupations profiting from a multiple intelligences perspective.* Retrieved from http://www.igs. net/~cmorris/smo_comments.html

Morris, J. S., Friston, K. J., Buche, L. C., Frith, C. D., Young, A. W., Calder, A. J., & Dolan, R. J. (1998). A neuromodulatory role for the human amygdala in processing emotional facial expressions. *Brain, 121,* 47–57.

Morris, M., Nisbett, R. E., & Peng, K. (1995). Causal understanding across domains and cultures. In D. Sperber, D. Premack, & A. J. Premack (Eds.), *Causal cognition: A multidisciplinary debate.* Oxford, England: Oxford University Press.

Morris, M. W., & Peng, K. (1994). Culture and cause: American and Chinese attributions social and physical events. *Journal of Personality and Social Psychology, 67,* 949–971.

Morrison, J. (1995). *The clinician's guide to diagnosis.* New York, NY: Guilford Press.

Morrongiello, B. A., & Lasenby-Lessard, J. (2006). Finding the daredevils: Development of a sensation-seeking scale for children that is relevant to physical risk-taking. *Accident Analysis and Prevention, 38,* 1101–1106.

Morrongiello, B. A., & Matheis, S. (2007). Addressing the issue of falls off playground equipment: An empirically-based intervention to reduce fall-risk behaviors on playgrounds. *Journal of Pediatric Psychology, 32,* 819–830.

Moruzzi, G., & Magoun, H. W. (1949). Brainstem reticular formation and activation of the EEG. *Electroencephalographs in Clinical Neurophysiology, 1,* 455–473.

Mowat, F. (1988). *Woman in the mists: The story of Dian Fossey and the mountain gorillas of Africa.* New York, NY: Warner Books.

Muller-Oerlinghausen, B., Berghofer, A., & Bauer, M. (2002). Bipolar disorder. *Lancet, 359,* 241–247.

Munroe, R. (1980). Male transvestism and the couvade: A psychocultural analysis. *Ethos, 8,* 49–59.

Murdock, B. B., Jr. (1962). The serial position effect in free recall. *Journal of Experimental Psychology, 64,* 482–488.

Muris, P., Harald, M., Irit, H., & Sijsenaar, M. (1998). Treating phobic children: Effects of EMDR versus exposure. *Journal of Consulting and Clinical Psychology, 66,* 193–198.

Murphy, C. C., Boyle, C., Schendel, D., Decouflé, P., & Yeargin-Allsopp, M. (1998). Epidemiology of mental retardation in children. *Mental Retardation and Developmental Disabilities Research Reviews, 4,* 6–13.

Murphy, L. R. (1995). Managing job stress: An employee assistance/human resource management partnership. *Personnel Review, 24*(1), 41–50.

Murphy, M., & Donavan, S. (1997). *The physical and psychological effects of meditation: A review of contemporary research with a comprehensive bibliography.* Petaluma, CA: Institute of Noetic Sciences.

Murray, D. J. (1983). *A history of western psychology.* Englewood Cliffs, NJ: Prentice-Hall.

Murray, D. J. (1988). *A history of western psychology* (2nd ed.). Englewood Cliffs, NJ: Prentice-Hall.

Murray, D. J., & Hitchcock, C. H. (1969). Attention and storage in dichotic listening. *Journal of Experimental Psychology, 81,* 164–169.

Muter, P. (1978). Recognition failure of recallable words in semantic memory. *Memory & Cognition, 6*(1), 9–12.

Mysterud, I. (2003). Long live nature via nurture! [Review of the book *Nature via Nurture: Genes, Experience and What Makes us Human,* by M. Ridley]. *Evolutionary Psychology, 1,* 188–191.

Nadeau, K. G., Quinn, P., & Littman, E. (2001). *AD/HD Self-Rating Scale for Girls.* Springfield, MD: Advantage Books.

Naitoh, P., Kelly, T. L., & Englund, C. E. (1989). *Health effects of sleep deprivation.* Naval Health Research Centre, Report No. 89–46.

Najavits, L. M. (2007). Psychosocial treatments for posttraumatic stress disorder. In P. E. Nathan & J. M. Gorman (Eds.), *A guide to treatments that work* (3rd ed., pp. 513–530). New York, NY: Oxford University Press.

Nasar, S. (1998). A beautiful mind: A biography of John Forbes Nash, Jr., winner of the Nobel Prize in economics 1994. New York, NY: Simon & Schuster.

Nash, A. (2004, October). Christopher Reeve: A hero onscreen and off. *Reader's Digest,* 23–25.

Nathan, P. E., & Gorman, J. M. (2007). *Psychosocial treatments for postraumatic stress disorder* (3rd ed.). New York, NY: Oxford University Press.

National Commission on Sleep Disorders. (1997). Lack of sleep America's top health problem, doctors say. CNN Interactive: Health Story Page. Retrieved from http://www.cnn.com/HEALTH/9703/17/nfm/ sleep .deprivation/index.html

National Institutes of Health. (1998). *Understanding vaccines.* NIH Publication #98–4219.

National Institutes of Health. (2000). *NIH publishes final guidelines for stem cell research.* Retrieved from http://www.nih.gov/news/pr/aug2000/od-23.htm

National Sleep Foundation. (2008). *How sleep works. Myths and facts about sleep.* Retrieved from http://www.sleepfoundation.org/site/ c.huIXKjM0IxF/b.2417141/k.2E30/The_National_Sleep_Foundation.htm

Neale, M. C., Rushton, J. P., & Fulker, D. W. (1986). The heritability of items from the Eysenck Personality Questionnaire. *Personality and Individual Differences, 7,* 771–779.

Neary, N. M., Goldstone, A. P., & Bloom, S. R. (2004). Appetite regulations: From the gut to the hypothalamus. *Clinical Endocrinology, 60*(2), 153–160.

Neimeyer, R. A., & Mitchell, K. A. (1998). Similarity and attraction: A longitudinal study. *Journal of Social and Personality Relationships, 5,* 131–148.

Neisser, U. (1982). Snapshots or benchmarks? In U. Neisser (Ed.), *Memory observed: Remembering in natural contexts* (pp. 43–48). San Francisco, CA: Freeman.

Neisser, U., Boodoo, G., Bouchard, T. J., Boykin, A. W., Brody, N., Ceci, S. J., . . . Urbina, S. (1996). Intelligence: Knowns and unknowns. *American Psychologist, 51,* 77–101.

Neisser, U., & Harsch, N. (1992). Phantom flashbulbs: False recollections of hearing the news about *Challenger.* In E. Winograd & U. Neisser (Eds.), *Affect and accuracy in recall: Studies of "flashbulb memories."* New York, NY: Cambridge University Press.

Nelson, K. (1978). Semantic development and the development of semantic memory. In K. E. Nelson (Ed.), *Children's language* (Vol. 1). New York, NY: Gardner Press.

Nelson, K. (1993). The psychological and social origins of autobiographical memory. *Psychological Science, 4,* 7–14.

Neto, F. (1995). Conformity and independence revisited. *Social Behavior and Personality, 23*(3), 217–222.

Neumarker, K. (1997). Mortality and sudden death in anorexia nervosa. *International Journal of Eating Disorders, 21,* 205–212.

Neumeister, A., Bain, E., Nugent, A. C., Carson, R. E., Bonne, O., Luckenbaugh, D. A., . . . Drevets, W. C. (2004). Reduced serotonin Type 1a receptor binding in panic disorder. *Journal of Neuroscience, 24,* 589–591.

Neville, H. J., & Bavelier, D. (2000). Specificity and plasticity in neurocognitive development in humans. In M. S. Gazzaniga, (Ed). *The New Cognitive Neurosciences* (2nd ed., pp. 83–99). Cambridge, MA: MIT Press.

Newcomer, R. R., & Perna, F. M. (2003). Features of posttraumatic distress among adolescent athletes. *Journal of Athletic Training, 38,* 163–166.

Nicholson, N., Cole, S., & Rocklin, T. (1985). Conformity in the Asch situation: A comparison between contemporary British and US students. *British Journal of Social Psychology, 24,* 59–63.

Nickerson, R. S., & Adams, J. J. (1979). Long-term memory for a common object. *Cognitive Psychology, 11,* 287–307.

NIDA (National Institute on Drug Abuse). (2002). Research report series— Prescription drugs: Abuse and addiction. National Institutes of Health (NIH). Retrieved from http://drugabuse.gov/ResearchReports/Prescription/ prescription5.html

Nieto, F., Young, T. B., Lind, B. K., Shahar, E., Samet, J. M., Redline, S., . . . Pickering, T. G. (2000). Association of sleep-disordered breathing, sleep apnea, and hypertension in a large, community-based study. *Journal of the American Medical Association, 283,* 1829–1836.

Nigg, J. T., & Goldsmith, H. H. (1994). Genetics of personality disorders: Perspectives from personality and psychopathology research. *Psychological Bulletin, 115,* 346–380.

Nijenhuis, E. R. (2000). Somatoform dissociation: Major symptoms of dissociative disorders. *Journal of Trauma and Dissociation, 1*(4), 7–29.

NIMH Genetics Workgroup. (1998). *Genetics and mental disorders.* NIH Publication No. 98-4268. Rockville, MD: National Institute of Mental Health.

Nisbett, R. E. (1972). Hunger, obesity, and the ventromedial hypothalamus. *Psychological Review, 79,* 433–453.

Nisbett, R. E., & Masuda, T. (2003). Culture and point of view. *Proceedings of the National Academy of Sciences, USA, 100,* 11163–11170.

Nishino, S., Ripley, B., Overeem, S., Lammers, G. J., & Mignot, E. (2000). Hypocretin (orexin) deficiency in human narcolepsy. *Lancet, 355,* 39–40.

Nolen-Hoeksema, S. (1990). *Sex differences in depression.* Palo Alto, CA: Stanford University Press.

Norenzayan, A., Choi, I., & Nisbett, R. E. (1999). Eastern and Western perceptions of causality for social behavior: Lay theories about personalities and situations. In D. A. Prentice & D. T. Miller (Eds.), *Cultural divides* (pp. 239–272). New York, NY: Russell Sage Foundation.

Norrbrink Budh, C., Lund, I., Hultling, C., Levi, R., Werhagen, L., Ertzgaard, P., & Lundeberg, T. (2003). Gender-related differences in pain in spinal cord injured individuals. *Spinal Cord, 41,* 122–128.

Noseworthy, J. H. (1999). Progress in determining the causes and treatment of multiple sclerosis. *Nature, 399,* 40–47.

Nyberg, L., & Tulving, E. (1996). Classifying human long-term memory: Evidence from converging dissociations. *European Journal of Cognitive Psychology, 8*(2), 163–183.

O'Brien, W. K. (2002). *Applying the transtheoretical model to academic procrastination.* Unpublished doctoral dissertation, University of Houston.

Ocholla-Ayayo, A. B. C., Wekesa, J. M., & Ottieno, J. A. M. (1993). *Adolescent pregnancy and its implications among ethnic groups in Kenya.* International Population Conference of the International Union for the Scientific Study of Population, Montreal, QC.

Ochsner, K., & Kosslyn, S. M. (1994). Mental imagery. In V. S. Ramaschandran (Ed.), *Encyclopedia of human behavior.* New York, NY: Academic Press.

O'Connor, L. E. (1994). Empirical studies of shame and guilt: Development of a new measure, the Interpersonal Guilt Questionnaire. *Process Notes, 1*(1), 12–15.

O'Connor, L. E., Berry, J. W, Weiss, J., Bush, M., & Sampson, H. (1997). The Interpersonal Guilt Questionnaire: Development of a new measure. *Journal of Clinical Psychology, 53*(1), 74–89.

O'Connor, R. D. (1972). Relative efficacy of modeling, shaping, and the combined procedures for modification of social withdrawal. *Journal of Abnormal Psychology, 79,* 327–334.

Offit, P. A., & Bell, L. M. (1998). *What every parent should know about vaccines.* New York, NY: Macmillan.

Offord, D. R., Boyle, M. H., Campbell, D., Goering, P., Lin, E., Wong, M., & Racine, Y. A. (1996). One-year prevalence of psychiatric disorders in Ontarians 15 to 64 years of age. *Canadian Journal of Psychiatry, 41,* 559–563.

Ofshe, R., & Watters, E. (1994). *Making monsters: False memories, psychotherapy and sexual hysteria.* New York, NY: Scribners.

Oinonen, K. A., & Mazmanian, D. (2007). Facial symmetry detection ability changes across the menstrual cycle. *Biological Psychology, 75,* 136–145.

Olin, B. R., (Ed.). (1993). Central nervous system drugs, sedatives and hypnotics, barbiturates. In *Facts and comparisons drug information* (pp. 1398–1413). St. Louis, MO: Facts and Comparisons.

Oliver, J. E. (1993). Intergenerational transmission of child abuse: Rates, research, and clinical interpretations. *American Journal of Psychiatry, 150,* 1315–1324.

Ollendick, T. H., & King, N. J. (1998). Empirically supported treatments for children with phobic and anxiety disorders: Current status. *Journal of Clinical Child Psychology, 27*(2), 156–167.

Olsen, P. (1975). *Emotional flooding.* Baltimore, MD: Penguin Books.

Olson, H. C., & Burgess, D. M. (1997). Early intervention for children prenatally exposed to alcohol and other drugs. In M. J. Guralnick (Ed.), *The effectiveness of early intervention.* Baltimore, MD: Brookes.

Olson, J. M., Vernon, P. A., Harris, J. A., & Jang, K. L. (2001). The heritability of attitudes: A study of twins. *Journal of Personality and Social Psychology, 80,* 845–860.

Olson, J. M., & Zanna, M. P. (1993). Attitudes and attitude change. *Annual Review of Psychology, 44,* 117–154.

Oman, C. M. (1990). Motion sickness: A synthesis and evaluation of the sensory conflict theory. *Canadian Journal of Physiological Pharmacology, 68,* 294–303.

Onken, L. S., Blaine, J. D., & Battjes, R. J. (1997). Behavioral therapy research: A conceptualization of a process. In S. W. Henggeler & A. B. Santos (Eds.), *Innovative approaches for difficult-to-treat populations* (pp. 477–485). Washington, DC: American Psychiatric Press.

Oster, G. D., & Crone, P. G. (2004). *Using drawings in assessment and therapy*: A guide for mental health professionals. New York, NY: Brunner-Routledge.

Oswald, I. (1959). Sudden bodily jerks on falling asleep. *Brain, 82,* 92–103.

Oswalt, R., Anderson, M., Hagstrom, K., & Berkowitz, B. (1993). Evaluation of the one-session eye-movement desensitization reprocessing procedure for eliminating traumatic memories. *Psychological Reports, 73,* 99–104.

Otis, N., & Pelletier, L. G. (2005). A motivational model of daily hassles, physical symptoms, and future work intentions among police officers. *Journal of Applied Social Psychology, 35,* 2193–2214.

Overeem, S., Mignot, E., Gert van Dijk, J., & Lammers, G. J. (2001). Narcolepsy: Clinical features, new pathophysiological insights, and future perspectives. *Journal of Clinical Neurophysiology, 18*(2), 78–105.

Overmier, J. B., & Seligman, M. E. P. (1967). Effects of inescapable shock on subsequent escape and avoidance behavior. *Journal of Comparative Physiology and Psychology, 63,* 23–33.

Owen, M. T., Easterbrooks, M. A., Chase-Lansdale, L., & Goldberg, W. A. (1984). The relation between maternal employment status and the stability of attachments to mother and to father. *Child Development, 55,* 1894–1901.

Padayatty, S. J., & Levine, M. (2001). New insights into the physiology and pharmacology of vitamin C [editorial]. *Canadian Medical Association Journal, 164*(3), 353–355.

Padian, N. S., Shiboski, S. C., & Jewell, N. P. (1991). Female-to-male transmission of human immunodeficiency virus. *Journal of the American Medical Association, 266*(12), 1664–1667.

Paivio, A. (1971). *Imagery and verbal processes.* New York, NY: Holt, Rinehart & Winston.

Paivio, A. (1986). *Mental representations: A dual coding approach.* New York, NY: Oxford University Press.

Palmer, S. E. (1992). Common region: A new principle of perceptual grouping. *Cognitive Psychology, 24*(3), 436–447.

Pan, A. S. (2000). Body image, eating attitudes, and eating behaviors among Chinese, Chinese-American and non-Hispanic White women. *Dissertation Abstracts International, Section B: The Sciences and Engineering, 61*(1-B), 544.

Papousek, I., & Schulter, G. (2002). Covariations of EEG asymmetries and emotional states indicate that activity at frontopolar locations is particularly affected by state factors. *Psychophysiology 39,* 350–360.

Pargament, K. I. (1997). The psychology of religion and coping: Theory, research, and practice. New York, NY: Guilford.

Paris, J. (2004). Gender differences in personality traits and disorders. *Current Psychiatry Reports, 6,* 71–74.

Park, J., Turnbull A. P., & Turnbull H. R. (2002). Impacts of poverty on quality of life in families of children with disabilities. *Exceptional Children, 68,* 151–170.

Parker, J. D. A., Hogan, M. J., Eastabrook, J. M., Oke, A., & Wood, L. M. (2006). Emotional intelligence and student retention: Predicting the successful transition from high school to university. *Personality and Individual Differences, 41,* 1329–1336.

Parkinson, W. L., & Weingarten, H. P. (1990). Dissociative analysis of ventromedial hypothalamic obesity syndrome. *American Journal of Physiology: Regulatory, Integrative, and Comparative Physiology, 259,* R829–R835.

Parobek, V. M. (1997). Distinguishing conversion disorder from neurologic impairment. *Journal of Neuroscience Nursing, 29*(2), 128.

Patten, S. B. (2006). A major depression prognosis calculator. *Clinical Practice and Epidemiology in Mental Health 2006, 2,* 13.

Patten, S. B., Wang, J. L., Williams, J. V. A., Currie, S., Beck, C. A., Maxwell, C. J., & el-Guebaly, N. (2006). Descriptive epidemiology of major depression in Canada. *Canadian Journal of Psychiatry, 51,* 84–90.

Paunonen, S. V., Ashton, M. C., & Jackson, D. N. (2001). Nonverbal assessment of the Big Five personality factors. *European Journal of Personality, 15,* 3–18.

Paunonen, S. V., Jackson, D. N., & Keinonen, M. (1990). The structured nonverbal assessment of personality. *Journal of Personality, 58,* 481–502.

Paunonen, S. V., Keinonen, M., Trzbinski, J., Forsterling, F., Grishenko-Roze, N., Kouznetsova, L., & Chan, D. W. (1996). The structure of personality in six cultures. *Journal of Cross Cultural Psychology, 27,* 339–353.

Pavlov, I. (1926). *Conditioned reflexes.* London, England: Oxford University Press.

Penfield, W., & Boldrey, E. (1937). Somatic motor and sensory representation in the cerebral cortex of man as studied by electrical stimulation. *Brain, 60,* 389–443.

Penfield, W., & Rasmusson, T. (1950). *The cerebral cortex of man: A clinical study of localization of function.* New York, NY: MacMillan.

Peng, K., Ames, D. R., & Knowles, E. D. (2000). Culture and human inference: Perspectives from three traditions. In D. Matsumoto (Ed.), *The handbook of culture and psychology* (pp. 245–264). New York, NY: Oxford University Press.

Peng, Y., Zebrowitz, L. A., & Lee, H. K. (1993). The impact of cultural background and cross-cultural experience on impressions of American and Korean male speakers. *Journal of Cross Cultural Psychology, 24,* 203–220.

Penn, D. L. (1998). Assessment and treatment of social dysfunction in schizophrenia [Supplemental bulletin]. *Clinicians Research Digest, 18,* 1–2.

Peplau, L. A., & Taylor, S. E. (1997). *Sociocultural perspectives in social psychology: Current readings.* Upper Saddle River, NJ: Prentice-Hall.

Pepperberg, I. M. (1998). Talking with Alex: Logic and speech in parrots. *Scientific American Presents: Exploring Intelligence, 9*(4), 60–65.

Pereira, M. A., Kartashov, A. I., Van Horn, L., Slattery, M., Jacobs, D. R., Jr., & Ludwig, D. S. (2003, March). *Eating breakfast may reduce risk of obesity, diabetes, heart disease.* Paper presented at the American Heart Association's 2003 Annual Conference on Cardiovascular Disease Epidemiology and Prevention, Miami, FL.

Perls, F. (1951). *Gestalt therapy.* New York, NY: Julian Press.

Perls, F. (1969). *Gestalt therapy verbatim.* Moab, UT: Real People Press.

Perlstein, W. M., Carter, C. S., Noll, D. C., & Cohen, J. D. (2001). Relation of prefrontal cortex dysfunction to working memory and symptoms in schizophrenia. *American Journal of Psychiatry, 156,* 1105–1113.

Perrin, S., & Spencer, C. (1980). The Asch effect—a child of its time. *Bulletin of the British Psychological Society, 33,* 405–406.

Perry, R. P. (2003). Perceived (academic) control and causal thinking in achievement settings. *Psychology, 44,* 312–331.

Perry, R. P., Hladkyj, S., Pekrun, R. H., & Pelletier, S. T. (2001). Academic control and action control in the achievement of college students: A longitudinal field study. *Journal of Educational Psychology, 93,* 776–789.

Persaud, R. (2001). *Staying sane: How to make your mind work for you.* New York, NY: Bantam.

Peters, K. R., Smith, V., & Smith, C. T. (2007). Changes in sleep architecture following motor learning depend on initial skill level. *Journal of Cognitive Neuroscience, 19,* 817–829.

Peters, W. A. (1971). *A class divided.* Garden City, NY: Doubleday.

Peterson, L. R., & Peterson, M. J. (1959). Short-term retention of individual items. *Journal of Experimental Psychology, 58,* 193–198.

Petrakis, I. L, Gonzalez, G., Rosenheck, R., & Krystal, J. H. (2002). Comorbidity of alcoholism and psychiatric disorders. *Alcohol Research and Health, 26*(2), 81–89.

Petri, H. (1996). *Motivation: Theory, research and application* (4th ed.). Belmont, CA: Wadsworth.

Petrova, P. K., Cialdini, R. B., & Sills S., J. (2003). Compliance, consistency, and culture: Personal consistency and compliance across cultures. *Journal of Experimental Social Psychology* [Submitted]. Retrieved from http:// www.public.asu.edu/~liulang/Compliance.pdf

Pettigrew, T. F., & Tropp, L. R. (2000). Does intergroup contact reduce prejudice? Recent meta-analytic findings. In S. Oskamp (Ed.), *Reducing prejudice and discrimination: Social psychological perspectives* (pp. 93–114). Mahwah, NJ: Erlbaum.

Petitto, L. A., Holowka, S., Sergio, L. E., & Ostry, D. (2001). Language rhythms in baby hand movement. *Nature, 413,* 35.

Petty, R., & Cacioppo, J. (1986). *Communication and persuasion: Central and peripheral routes to attitude change.* New York, NY: Springer-Verlag.

Petty, R., & Cacioppo, J. (1996). *Attitudes and persuasion: Classic and contemporary approaches,* reprint. Boulder, CO: Westview Press.

Petty, R. E. (1995). Attitude change. In A. Tesser (Ed.), *Advances in social psychology* (pp. 194–255). New York, NY: McGraw-Hill.

Petty, R. E., Wheeler, S. C., & Tormala, Z. L. (2003). Persuasion and attitude change. In T. Millon & M. J. Lerner (Eds.), *Handbook of psychology, Vol. 5, Personality and social psychology* (pp. 353–382). Hoboken, NJ: Wiley.

Pezdek, K., & Hodge, D. (1999). Planting false childhood memories in children: The role of event plausibility. *Child Development, 70,* 887–895.

Pezdek, K., Finger, K., & Hodge, D. (1997). Planting false childhood memories: The role of event plausibility. *Psychological Science, 8,* 437–441

Pfeiffer, W. M. (1982). Culture-bound syndromes. In I. Al-Issa (Ed.), *Culture and psychopathology* (pp. 201–218). Baltimore, MD: University Park Press.

Phan, T., & Silove, D. (1999). An overview of indigenous descriptions of mental phenomena and the range of traditional healing practices amongst the Vietnamese. *Transcultural Psychiatry, 36,* 79–94.

Phillips, K. A. (2001). Somatoform and factitious disorders. *Review of Psychiatry, 20*(3), 27–65.

Piaget, J. (1926). *The language and thought of the child.* New York, NY: Harcourt Brace.

Piaget, J. (1952). *The origins of intelligence in children.* New York, NY: W. W. Norton.

Piaget, J. (1954) *The construction of reality in the child.* New York, NY: Basic Books.

Piaget, J. (1962). *Play, dreams and imitation in childhood.* New York, NY: W. W. Norton.

Piaget, J. (1983). Piaget's theory. In W. Kessen (Ed.), *Handbook of child psychology* (Vol. 1, pp. 103–128). New York, NY: Wiley.

Pierce, S. H., & Lange, G. (2000). Relationships among metamemory, motivation, and memory performance in young school age children. *British Journal of Developmental Psychology, 18,* 121–135.

Pierce, D. W., Heth, D. C., Owczarczyk, J. C., Russell, J. C., & Proctor, S. D. (2007). Overeating by young obesity-prone and lean rats caused by tastes associated with low energy foods. *Obesity, 15,* 1969–1979.

Pihl, R. O., & Peterson, J. B. (1993). Alcohol, serotonin and aggression. *Alcohol Health and Research World, 17,* 113–116.

Pilkington, J. (1998). "Don't try and make out that I'm nice": The different strategies women and men use when gossiping. In J. Coates (Ed.), *Language and gender: A reader.* Oxford: Blackwell.

Pilson, T. (2000). Jericho, Benoit mastered craft in Hart dungeon. *Slam Sports.* Retrieved from http://slam.canoe.ca/SlamWrestlingJericho/jericho_00may28.html

Pinker, S. (1995). Language acquisition. In L. R. Gleitman & M. Liberman (Eds.), *An invitation to cognitive science* (2nd ed.). Cambridge, MA: MIT Press.

Pinker, S., & Bloom, P. (1990). Natural language and natural selection. *Behavioral and Brain Sciences, 13,* 707–784.

Pinsof, W. M., & Wynne, L. C. (1995). The efficacy of marital and family therapy: An empirical overview, conclusions, and recommendations. *Journal of Marital and Family Therapy, 21,* 585–613.

Piper, W. E., Debbane, E. G., Bienvenu, J. P., & Garant, J. (1984). A comparative study of four forms of psychotherapy. *Journal of Consulting and Clinical Psychology, 52,* 268–279.

Pittam, J., Gallois, C., Iwawaki, S., & Kroonenberg, P. (1995). Australian and Japanese concepts of expressive behavior. *Journal of Cross-Cultural Psychology, 26*(5), 451–473.

Plomin, R. (1994). The nature of nurture: The environment beyond the family. In R. Plomin (Ed.), *Genetics and experience: The interplay between nature and nurture* (pp. 82–107). Thousand Oaks, CA: Sage.

Plomin, R. N. L., Pederson, G. E., McClearn, J. R., Nesselroade, C. S., & Bergman, H. F. (1988). EAS temperaments during the last half year of the life span: Twins reared apart and twins raised together. *Psychology of Aging, 4,* 43–50.

Plomin, R., & DeFries, J. C. (1998, May). Genetics of cognitive abilities and disabilities. *Scientific American,* 62–69.

Plug, C., & Ross, H. E. (1994). The natural moon illusion: A multi-factor angular account. *Perception, 23,* 321–333.

Plum, F., & Posner, J. B. (1985). *The diagnosis of stupor and coma.* Philadelphia, PA: Davis.

Polivy, J., & Herman, C. P. (2002). Causes of eating disorders. *Annual Review of Psychology, 53,* 187–213.

Pomerleau, A., Bolduc, D., Malcuit, G., & Cossette, L. (1990). Pink or blue: Environmental gender stereotypes in the first two years of life. *Sex Roles, 22,* 359–367.

Pornpitakpan, C., & Francis, J. N. P. (2001). The effect of cultural differences, source expertise, and argument strength on persuasion: An experiment with Canadians and Thais. *Journal of International Consumer Marketing, 13,* 77–101.

Porter, S., & Peace, K. (2007). The scars of memory: A prospective, longitudinal investigation of the consistency of traumatic and positive emotional memories in adulthood. *Psychological Science, 18,* 435–441.

Pormerleau, C. S., & Pormerleau, O. F. (1994). Euphoriant effects of nicotine. *Tobacco Control, 3,* 374.

Postman, L. (1975). Tests of the generality of the principle of encoding specificity. *Memory & Cognition, 3,* 663–672.

Potts, T. J. (1987). Predicting procrastination on academic tasks with self-report personality measures. *Dissertation Abstracts International, 48,* 1543.

Powers, M. H. (1984). A computer assisted problem solving method for beginning chemistry students. *The Journal of Computers in Mathematics and Science Teaching, 4*(1), 13–19.

Pratkanis, A. R. (1992). The cargo-cult science of subliminal persuasion. *Skeptical Inquirer, 16,* 260–272.

Pratkanis, A. R., & Greenwald A. G., (1988). Recent perspectives on unconscious processing: Still no marketing applications. *Psychology and Marketing, 5,* 337–353.

Pratt, J. A. (1991). Psychotropic drug tolerance and dependence: Common underlying mechanisms? In E. Pratt (Ed.), *The biological bases of drug tolerance and dependence.* London, England: Academic Press, Harcourt Brace Jovanovich.

Priester, J. M., & Petty, R. E. (1995). Source attributions and persuasion: Perceived honesty as a determinant of message scrutiny. *Personality and Social Psychology Bulletin, 21,* 637–654.

Prigerson, H. G., Bierhals, A. J., Kasi, S. V., Reynolds, C. F., Shear, M. K., Day, N., . . . Jacobs, S. (1997). Traumatic grief as a risk factor for mental and physical morbidity. *American Journal of Psychiatry, 154I,* 616–623.

Pritchard, R. M. (1961). Stabilized images on the retina. *Scientific American, 204,* 72–78.

Prochaska, J. O., & Norcross, J. C. (2003). *Systems of psychotherapy* (5th ed.). Belmont, CA: Wadsworth.

ProSpeakers Bureau (2011). *Dave Farrow.* Retrieved from http://www. prospeakersbureau.com/davefarrow/

Public Health Agency of Canada. (1998). Hospitalizations for pelvic inflammatory disease in Canada, 1983/84–1993/94. *Canadian Communicable Disease Report, 24*(01). Retrieved from www.phac-aspc.gc.ca/publicat/ ccdr-rmtc/98vol24/dr2401ea.html

Public Health Agency of Canada. (2002). *Schizophrenia: A handbook for families.* Retrieved from http://www.phac-aspc.gc.ca/mh-sm/pubs/ schizophrenia-schizophrenie/chpt08-eng.php

Public Health Agency of Canada. (2002a). Chapter 1: An overview. *A report on mental illness in Canada.* Retrieved from http://www. phac-aspc.gc .ca/publicat/miic-mmac/chap_1_e.html

Public Health Agency of Canada. (2002b). Chapter 4: Anxiety disorders. *A report on mental illness in Canada.* Retrieved from http://www. phac-aspc .gc.ca/publicat/miic-mmac/chap_4_e.html

Public Health Agency of Canada. (2002c). Chapter 2: Mood disorders. *A report on mental illness in Canada.* Retrieved from http://www. phac-aspc .gc.ca/publicat/miic-mmac/chap_2_e.html

Public Health Agency of Canada. (2002d). Chapter 3: Schizophrenia. *A report on mental illness in Canada.* Retrieved from http://www. phacaspc. gc.ca/publicat/miic-mmac/chap_3_e.html

Public Health Agency of Canada. (2002e). Chapter 7: Suicidal Behaviour. *A report on mental illness in Canada.* Retrieved from http://www .phac-aspc.gc.ca/publicat/miic-mmac/chap_7_e.html

Public Health Agency of Canada. (2003). *Down syndrome: Background information.* Retrieved from http://www.phac-aspc.gc.ca/ccasn-rcsac/ct2003/ bgds_e.html

Public Health Agency of Canada. (2005). *Mumps.* Retrieved from http://www.phacaspc. gc.ca/tmp-pmv/info/mumps_e. html#symptoms

Public Health Agency of Canada. (2006). *Canadian immunization guide, seventh edition—2006.* Retrieved from http://www.phac-aspc. gc.ca/publicat/cig-gci/ p04-mump-orei-eng.php

Public Health Agency of Canada. (2007). *National HIV prevalence and incidence estimates for 2005.* Retrieved from http://www.phac-aspc. gc .ca/aids-sida/publication/epi/pdf/epi2007_e.pdf

Pullum, G. K. (1991). *The great Eskimo vocabulary hoax: And other irreverent essays on the study of language.* Chicago, IL: University of Chicago Press.

Pumariega, A. J., & Gustavson, C. R. (1994). Eating attitudes in African-American women: The essence. *Eating Disorders: Journal of Treatment and Prevention, 2,* 5–16.

Purcell, S. (1985, August). *Relation between religious orthodoxy and marital sexual functioning.* Paper presented at a meeting of the American Psychological Association, Los Angeles, CA.

Purdon, C., & Clark, D. A. (1993). Obsessive intrusive thoughts in nonclinical subjects: Part1, Content and relation with depressive, anxious, and obsessional symptoms. *Behaviour Research and Therapy, 31,* 713–720.

Quintero, J. E., Kuhlman, S. J., & McMahon, D. G. (2003). The biological clock nucleus: A multiphasic oscillator network regulated by light. *Journal of Neuroscience, 23,* 8070–8076.

Raaijmakers, J. G. W., & Shiffrin, R. M. (1992). Models for recall and recognition. *Annual Review of Psychology, 43,* 205–234.

Rachman, S. (1990). The determinants and treatments of simple phobias. *Advances in Behavioral Research and Therapy, 12*(1), 1–30.

Rachman, S. J., & Hodgson, R. J. (1980). *Obsessions and compulsions.* Englewood Cliffs, NJ: Prentice Hall.

Radomsky, A. S., Gilchrist, P. T., & Dussault, D. (2006). Repeated checking really does cause memory distrust. *Behaviour Research and Therapy, 44,* 305–316.

Raikkonen, K., Matthews, K. A., & Salomon, K. (2003). Hostility predicts metabolic syndrome risk factors in children and adolescents. *Health Psychology, 22,* 279–286.

Ramón y Cajal, S. (1995.) *Histology of the nervous system of man and vertebrates* (N. Swanson & L. M. Swanson, Trans.). New York, NY: Oxford University Press.

Randi, J. (1980). *Flim-flam!* New York, NY: Lippincott/Crowell.

Randi, J. (1982). *Flim-flam! Psychics, ESP, unicorns and other delusions.* Buffalo, NY: Prometheus.

Ranke, M. B., & Saenger, P. (2001, July 28). Turner's syndrome. *Lancet, 358,* 309–314.

Rao, S. C., Rainer, G., & Miller, E. K. (1997) Integration of what and where in the primate prefrontal cortex. *Science, 276,* 821–824.

Raynor, H. A., & Epstein, L. H. (2001). Dietary variety, energy regulation and obesity. *Psychological Bulletin, 127*(3), 325–341.

Reder, L. M., Anderson, J. R., & Bjork, R. A. (1974). A semantic interpretation of encoding specificity. *Journal of Experimental Psychology, 102,* 648–656.

Reinders, A., Quak, J., Nijenhuis, E. R., Korf, J., Paans, A. M., Willemsen, A. T., & den Boer, J. A. (2001). Identity state-dependent processing of neutral and traumatic scripts in Dissociative Identity Disorder as assessed by PET. Oral Presentation: 7th Annual Meeting of the Organisation for Human Brain Mapping, June 10–14, Brighton, England. *NeuroImage 13* (supplement), S1093.

Reiner, W. G. (1999). Assignment of sex in neonates with ambiguous genitalia. *Current Opinions in Pediatrics, 11*(4), 363–365.

Reiner, W. G. (2000). *The genesis of gender identity in the male: Prenatal androgen effects on gender identity and gender role.* Talk given at New York University Child Study Center, Grand Rounds Summary.

Reisenzein, R. (1983). The Schachter theory of emotion: Two decades later. *Psychological Bulletin, 94,* 239–264.

Reisenzein, R. (1994). Pleasure-arousal theory and the intensity of emotions. *Journal of Personality and Social Psychology, 7*(6), 1313–1329.

Reiter, R., & Milburn, A. (1994). Exploring effective treatment for chronic pelvic pain. *Comtemporary Ob/Gyn, 3,* 84–103.

Renchler, R. (1993). Poverty and learning. *ERIC Digests,* ERIC Clearinghouse on Educational Management, Eugene, OR. Retrieved from http:// www.ed.gov/databases/ERIC_Digests/ ed357433.html

Renfrey, G., & Spates, R. C. (1994). Eye movement desensitization: A partial dismantling study. *Journal of Behavior Therapy and Experimental Psychiatry, 25,* 231–239.

Renner, M. J., & Mackin, R. S. (1998). A life stress instrument for classroom use. *Teaching of Psychology, 25,* 47.

Rescorla, R. (1988). Pavlovian conditioning—It's not what you think. *American Psychologist, 43,* 151–160.

Rescorla, R. A. (1968). Probability of shock in the presence and absence of CS in fear conditioning. *Journal of Comparative and Physiological Psychology, 66,* 1–5.

Resick, P. A., Monson, C. M., & Rizvi, S. (2008). Posttraumatic stress disorder. In D. H. Barlow (Ed.), *Clinical handbook of psychological disorders* (pp. 65–122). New York, NY: Guilford Press.

Reuters. (2006). Canada troops battle 10-foot Afghan marijuana plants. Retrieved January 13, 2008, from http://news.bbc.co.uk/2/hi/south_asia/6052270.stm

Rezvani, A. H., & Levin, E. D. (2001). Cognitive effects of nicotine. *Biological Psychiatry, 49,* 258–267.

Rhine, J. B. (1935). *Extrasensory perception.* Boston, MA: Bruce Humphries.

Richards, C. F., & Lowe, R. A. (2003). Researching racial and ethnic disparities in emergency medicine. *Academic Emergency Medicine, 10,* 1169–1175.

Rideout, T. M. (2005). *Eating disorders: Anorexia and bulimia.* Holistic-online.com: Eating Disorders Infocenter. Retrieved from http://www. holistic-online.com/Remedies/EatingD/EatD_anorxia-bulemia.htm

Ridgeway, D. (2006). Strategic grouping in the spatial span memory task. *Memory, 14,* 990–1000.

Ridley, M. (1999). *Genome: The autobiography of a species in 23 chapters.* London, England: Fourth Estate.

Rieber, R. W., & Robinson, D. K. (2001). *Wilhelm Wundt in history: The making of a scientific psychology.* New York, NY: Kluwer.

Rieger, E., Touyz, S. W., Swain, T., & Beumont, P. J. (2001). Cross-cultural research on anorexia nervosa: Assumptions regarding the role of body weight. *International Journal of Eating Disorders, 29,* 205–215.

Ritenbaugh, C., Shisslak, C., & Prince, R. (1992). Eating disorders: A cross-cultural review in regard to DSM-IV. In J. E. Mezzich, A. Kleinman, & H. Farega et al., (Eds.), *Cultural Proposals for DSM-IV.* Submitted to the DSM-IV Task Force by the NIMH Group on Culture and Diagnosis. Pittsburgh, PA: University of Pittsburgh.

Ritts, V. (1999). *Infusing culture into psychopathology: A supplement for psychology instructors.* Retrieved from http://www.stlcc.cc.mo.us/mc/ users/vritts/psypath.htm

Roberts, S. C., Gosling, L. M., Carter, V., & Petrie (2008). MHC-correlated odour preferences in humans and the use of oral contraceptives. *Proceedings of the Royal Society B: Biological Sciences, 275*(1652), 2715–2722.

Robins, L. N. (1996). *Deviant children grown up.* Baltimore, MD: Williams & Wilkins.

Robins, S. L. (2008). *In the matter of Steven Truscott: Advisory opinion on the issue of compensation.* Retrieved from http://www. attorneygeneral.jus.gov.on.ca/english/about/pubs/truscott/robins_report.pdf

Robinson, J. W., & Preston, J. D. (1976). Equal status contact and modification of racial prejudice: A reexamination of the contact hypothesis. *Social Forces, 54,* 911–924.

Robinson, P. (1993). *Freud and his critics.* Berkeley, CA: University of California Press.

Rockwood, K., & Middleton, L. (2007). Physical activity and the maintenance of cognitive function. *Alzheimer's & Dementia, 3*(2), S38–S44.

Rodgers, J. E. (1992). *Psychosurgery: Damaging the brain to save the mind.* New York, NY: HarperCollins.

Rodin, J. (1981). Current status of the internal-external hypothesis for obesity. *American Psychologist, 36,* 361–372.

Rodin, J. (1985). Insulin levels, hunger, and food intake: An example of feedback loops in body weight regulation. *Health Psychology, 4,* 1–24.

Rodin, J., & Langer, E. J. (1977). Long-term effects of a control-relevant intervention among the institutionalized aged. *Journal of Personality and Social Psychology, 35,* 275–282.

Roediger, H. L. (1990). Implicit memory: Retention without remembering. *American Psychologist, 45,* 1043–1056.

Roediger, H. L., III (2000). Why retrieval is the key process to understanding human memory. In E. Tulving (Ed.), *Memory, consciousness and the brain: The Tallinn Conference* (pp. 52–75). Philadelphia, PA: Psychology Press.

Roediger, H. L., III, & Crowder, R. G. (1976). A serial position effect in recall of United States presidents. *Bulletin of the Psychonomic Society, 8,* 275–278.

Roediger, H. L., III, & Guynn, M. J. (1996). Retrieval processes. In E. L. Bjork & R. A. Bjork (Eds.), *Memory* (pp. 197–236). New York, NY: Academic Press.

Roffman, R. A., Stephens, R. S., Simpson, E. E., & Whitaker, D. L. (1988). Treatment of marijuana dependence: Preliminary results. *Journal of Psychoactive Drugs, 20*(1), 129–137.

Roffwarg, H. P., Muzio, J. N., & Dement, W. C. (1966). Ontogenetic development of the human sleep-dream cycle. *Science, 152,* 604–619.

Rogers, C. (1961). *On becoming a person: A therapist's view of psychotherapy.* Boston, MA: Houghton Mifflin.

Rogers, R. W., & Mewborn, C. R. (1976). Fear appeals and attitude change: Effects of a threat's noxiousness, probability of occurrence, and the efficacy of the coping responses. *Journal of Personality and Social Psychology, 34,* 54–61.

Rogoff, B. (1994). Developing understanding of the idea of communities of learners. *Mind, Culture, and Activity, 1*(4), 209–229.

Rohde, A., & Marneros, A. (1993). Postpartum psychoses: Onset and long-term course. *Psychopathology, 26,* 203–209.

Rohde, P., Silva, S. G., Tonev, S. T., Kennard, B. D., Vitiello, B., Kratochvil, C. J., . . . March, J. S. (2008). Achievement and maintenance of sustained improvement during TADS continuation and maintenance therapy. *Archives of General Psychiatry, 65*(4), 447–455.

Roid, G. H. (2003). *Stanford-Binet intelligence scales* (5th ed.). Ithaca, IL: Riverside Publishing.

Roos, P. E., & Cohen, L. H. (1987). Sex roles and social support as moderators of life stress adjustment. *Journal of Personality and Social Psychology, 3,* 576–585.

Roper, G., Rachman, S., & Marks, I. (1975). Passive and participant modeling in exposure treatment of obsessive-compulsive neurotics. *Behaviour Research and Therapy, 13,* 271–279.

Rorschach, H. (1921). *Psychodiagnostik.* Bern, Switzerland: Bircher.

Rosch, E. (1973). On the internal structure of perceptual and semantic categories. In T. E. Moore (Ed.), *Cognitive development and the acquisition of language.* New York, NY: Academic Press.

Rosch, E. (1977). Human categorization. In N. Warren (Ed.), *Advances in crosscultural psychology, 1.* London, England: Academic Press.

Rosch, E., & Mervis, C. (1975). Family resemblances: Studies in the internal structures of categories. *Cognitive Psychology, 7,* 573–605.

Rosch, E., Mervis, C. B., Gray, W. D., Johnson, D. M., & Boyes-Braem, P. (1976). Basic objects in natural categories. *Cognitive Psychology, 8,* 382–439.

Rosch-Heider, E. (1972). Universals in color naming and memory. *Journal of Experimental Psychology, 93,* 10–20.

Rosch-Heider, E., & Olivier, D. C. (1972). The structure of the color space in naming and memory for two languages. *Cognitive Psychology, 3,* 337–354.

Rose, S., Kamin, L. J., & Lewontin, R. C. (1984). *Not in our genes: Biology, ideology and human nature.* Harmondsworth, England: Penguin.

Roselli, C. E., Larkin, K., Resko, J. A., Stellflug, J. N., & Stormshak, F. (2004). The volume of a sexually dimorphic nucleus in the ovine medial preoptic area/anterior hypothalamus varies with sexual partner preference. *Endocrinology, 145,* 478–483.

Rosenbaum, R. S., Kohler, S., Schacter, D. L., Moscovitch, M., Westmacott, R., Black, S. E., . . . Tulving, E. (2005). The case of K. C.: Contributions of a memoryimpaired person to memory theory. *Neuropsychologia, 43,* 989–1021.

Rosenman, R. H., Brand, R. I., Jenkins, C. D., Friedman, M., Straus, R., & Wurm, M. (1975). Coronary heart disease in the Western Collaborative Group Study, final follow-up experience of 8½ years. *Journal of the American Medical Association, 233,* 812–817.

Rosenthal, N. E., Sack, D. A., Gillin, J. C., Lewy, A. J., Goodwin, F. K., Davenport, Y., & Wehr, T. A. (1984). Seasonal affective disorder: A description of the syndrome and preliminary findings with light therapy. *Archives of General Psychiatry, 41,* 72–80.

Rosenthal, R., & Jacobson, L. (1968). *Pygmalion in the classroom.* New York, NY: Holt, Rinehart and Winston.

Rosenzweig, M. R., Leiman, A. L., & Breedlove, A. M. (1996). *Biological psychology.* Sunderland, MA: Sinaur.

Ross, S. E., Niebling, B. C., & Heckert, T. M. (1999). Sources of stress among college students. *College Student Journal, 33,* 312–318.

Rossiter, T. R., & La Vaque, T. J. (1995). A comparison of EEG biofeedback and psychostimulants in treating attention deficit hyperactivity disorders. *Journal of Neurotherapy,* 48–59.

Rothenberg, A. (2001). Bipolar illness, creativity, and treatment. *Psychiatric Quarterly, 72*(2), 131–147.

Rotter, J. B. (1954). *Social learning and clinical psychology.* New York, NY: Prentice Hall.

Rotter, J. B. (1966). Generalized expectancies for internal versus external control of reinforcements. *Psychological Monographs, 80,* Whole No. 609.

Rotton, J., & Frey, J. (1985). Air pollution, weather, and violent crime: Concomitant time-series analysis of archival data. *Journal of Personality and Social Psychology, 49,* 1207–1220.

Rotton, J., Frey, J., Barry, T., Milligan, M., & Fitzpatrick, M. (1979). The air pollution experience and physical aggression. *Journal of Applied Social Psychology, 9,* 397–412.

Rouse, B. A. (1998). *Substance and mental health statistics source book.* Rockville, MD: Department of Health and Human Services, Substance Abuse and Mental Health Services Administration (SAMHSA).

Rovet, J. (1993). The psychoeducational characteristics of children with Turner's syndrome. *Journal of Learning Disabilities, 26,* 333–341.

Rowan, J. (2001). *Ordinary ecstasy.* Hove, England: Brunner-Routledge.

Rowe, D. C., Almeida, D. A., & Jacobson, K. C. (1999). School context and genetic influences on aggression in adolescence. *Psychological Science, 10,* 277–280.

Roysircai-Sodowsky, G. R., & Maestas, M. V. (2000). Acculturation, ethnic identity, and acculturative stress: Evidence and measurement. In R. H. Dana (Ed.), *Handbook of cross-cultural and multicultural assessment* (pp. 131–172). Mahwah, NJ: Erlbaum.

Ruble, D., Alvarez, J., Bachman, M., Cameron, J., Fuligni, A., Garcia Coll, C., . . . Rhee, E (2004). The development of a sense of "we": The emergence and implications of children's collective identity. In M. Bennett & F. Sani (Eds.), *The development of the social self.* New York, NY: Psychology Press.

Rudd, P., & Osterberg, L. G. (2002). Hypertension: Context, pathophysiology, and management. In E. J. Topol (Ed.), *Textbook of cardiovascular medicine* (pp. 91–122). Philadelphia, PA: Lippincott Williams and Wilkins.

Rumelhart, D. E., Hinton, G. E., & McClelland, J. L. (1986). A general framework for parallel distributed processing. In D. E. Rumelhart, J. L. McClelland, & the PDP Research Group (Eds.), *Parallel distributed processing: Explorations in the microstructure of cognition: Vol. 1. Foundations.* Cambridge, MA: MIT Press.

Rundus, D. (1971). An analysis of rehearsal processes in free recall. *Journal of Experimental Psychology, 89,* 63–77.

Ruscio, A. M., Borkovec, T. D., & Ruscio, J. (2001). A taxometric investigation of the latent structure of worry. *Journal of Abnormal Psychology, 110,* 413–422.

Rushton, P. J. (1991). Mongoloid-caucasoid differences in brain size from military samples. *Intelligence, 15,* 351–359.

Rushton, P. J. (1992). Contributions to the history of psychology: XC evolutionary biology and heritable traits (with reference to oriental-white-black differences). *Psychological Reports, 71,* 811–821.

Russell, D. E. (1986). *The secret trauma: Incest in the lives of girls and women.* New York, NY: Basic Books.

Rutherford, E. (1886). A new theory of hearing. *Journal of Anatomy and Physiology, 21,* 166–168.

Rutherford, M. D. (2008). *The development of a fast and objective tool for identifying early autism.* Poster presented at the International Meeting for Autism Research, London, England.

Ryan, R. M., & Deci, E. L. (2000). Intrinsic and extrinsic motivations: Classic definitions and new directions. *Contemporary Educational Psychology, 25,* 54–67.

Rynn, M., Scherrer, J., & True, W. R. (2000, November). Generalized anxiety disorder. *Best Practice of Medicine.*

Sackeim, H. A., Prudic, J., Devanand, D. P., Nobler, M. S., Lisanby, S. H., Peyser, S., . . . Clark, J. (2000). A prospective, randomized, double-blind comparison of bilateral and right unilateral electroconvulsive therapy at different stimulus intensities. *Archives of General Psychiatry, 57,* 425–434.

Sacks, O. (1990). *The man who mistook his wife for a hat and other clinical tales.* New York, NY: HarperPerennial.

Sacks, O. (1995). *An anthropologist on Mars.* London, England: Picador.

Sadker, M., & Sadker, D. (1994). *Failing at fairness: How America's schools cheat girls.* New York, NY: Scribner.

Sagan, C. (1977). *The dragon of Eden: Speculations on the evolution of human intelligence.* New York, NY: Random House.

Salend, S. J. (1987). Contingency management systems. *Academic Therapy, 22,* 245–253.

Salovey, P., & Mayer, J. D. (1990). Emotional intelligence. *Imagination, Cognition, and Personality, 9,* 185–211.

Salthouse, T. A. (1984). The skill of typing. *Scientific American, 250*(2), 128–135.

Sands, L. P., & Meredith, W. (1992). Intellectual functioning in late midlife. *Journal of Gerontological and Psychological Science, 47,* 81–84.

Sapir, E. S. (1921). *Language: An introduction to the study of speech.* New York, NY: Harcourt, Brace.

Sapolsky, R. M. (2004). *Why zebras don't get ulcers* (3rd ed., pp. 1, 144–145). New York, NY: Owl Books.

Sarbin, T. R., & Coe, W. C. (1972). *Hypnosis: A social psychological analysis of influence communication.* New York, NY: Holt, Rinehart, & Winston.

Sareen, J., Cox, B. J., Stein, M. B., Afifi, T. O., Fleet, C., & Asmundson, G. J. G. (2007). Physical and mental comorbidity, disability, and suicide behavior associated with posttraumatic stress disorder in a large community sample. *Psychosomatic Medicine, 69,* 242–248.

Sartori, G., & Umilta, C. (2000). How to avoid the fallacies of cognitive subtraction in brain imaging. *Brain and Language, 74,* 191–212.

Sastry, K. S., Karpova, Y., Prokopovich, S., Smith, A. J., Essau, B., Gersappe, A. . . . Kulik, G. (2007). Epinephrine protects cancer cells from apoptosis via activation of cAMP-dependent protein kinase and BAD phosphorylation. *Journal of Biological Chemistry, 282*(19), 14094–14100.

Satcher, D. (2001). *The surgeon general's national strategy to prevent suicide.* Washington, DC: Office of the Surgeon General of the United States.

Satterly, D. (1987). Piaget and education. In R. L. Gregory (Ed.), *The Oxford companion to the mind.* Oxford, England: Oxford University Press.

Sattler, J. M. (1977). The effects of therapist–client racial similarity. In A. S. Gurman & A. M. Razin. (Eds.), *Effective psychotherapy: A handbook of research* (pp. 252–290). Elmsford, NY: Pergamon.

Saunders, B., & Goddard, C. R. (1998). Why do we condone the "physical punishment" of children? *Children Australia, 23,* 23–28.

Savage-Rumbaugh, S., & Lewin, R. (1994). *Kanzi.* New York, NY: Wiley.

Savage-Rumbaugh, S., Shanker, S., & Taylor, T. J. (1998). *Apes, language and the human mind.* Oxford: Oxford University Press.

Schachter, S., & Singer, J. E. (1962) Cognitive, social and physiological determinants of emotional states. *Psychological Review, 69,* 379–399.

Schafer, M., & Crichlow S. (1996). Antecedents of groupthink: A quantitative study. *Journal of Conflict Resolution, 40,* 415–435.

Schaller, M., Miller, G. E., Gervais, W. M., Yager, S., & Chen, E. (2010). Mere visual perception of other people's disease symptoms facilitates a more aggressive immune response. *Psychological Science, 21,* 649–652.

Schlenger, W. E., Caddell, J. M., Ebert, L., Jordan, B. K., Rourke, K. M., Wilson, D., . . . Kulka, R. A. (2002). Psychological reactions to terrorists attacks: Findings from the National Study of Americans' reactions to September 11. *JAMA, 288,* 581–588.

Schmitt, D. P. (2002). Personality, attachment and sexuality related to dating relationship outcomes: Contrasting three perspectives on personal attribute interaction. *British Journal of Social Psychology, 41*(4), 589–610.

Schmitz, C., Wagner, J., & Menke, E. (2001). The interconnection of childhood poverty and homelessness: Negative impact/points of access. *Families in Society, 82*(1), 69–77.

Schneider, K. J., Bugental, J. F. T., & Fraser, J. F. (Eds.). (2001). *Handbook of humanistic psychology.* Thousand Oaks, CA: Sage.

Schneider, R. H., Staggers, F., Alexander, C. N., Sheppard, W., Rainforth, M., Kondwani, K., . . . Gaylord King, C. (1995). A randomized controlled trial of stress reduction for hypertension in older African Americans. *Hypertension, 26*(5), 820–827.

Schneider, W., Dumais, S., & Shriffrin, R. (1984). *Automatic and control processing and attention.* London, England: Academic Press.

Schneidman, E. (1983). *Death of man.* New York, NY: Jason Aronson.

Schneidman, E. (1994). *Death: Current perspectives.* New York, NY: McGraw-Hill.

Schöls L., Haan J., Riess O., Amoiridis G., & Przuntek H. (1998). Sleep disturbance in spinocerebellar ataxias: Is the SCA3 mutation a cause of restless legs syndrome? *Neurology, 51,* 1603–1607.

Schreiber, F. R. (1973, reissued 1995). *Sybil.* New York, NY: Warner.

Schroeder, S. R. (2000). Mental retardation and developmental disabilities influenced by environmental neurotoxic insults. *Environmental Health Perspectives 108* (Suppl. 3), 395–399.

Schroth, M. L., & McCormack, W. A. (2000). Sensation seeking and need for achievement among study-abroad students. *Journal of Social Psychology, 140,* 533–535.

Schwanenflugel, P., & Rey, M. (1986). Interlingual semantic facilitation: Evidence from common representational system in the bilingual lexicon. *Journal of Memory and Language, 25,* 605–618.

Schwartz, S. H. (1975). The justice of need and the activation of humanitarian norms. *Journal of Social Issues, 31*(3), 111–136.

Schweickert, R. (1993). A multinomial processing tree model for degradation and redintegration in immediate recall. *Memory and Cognition, 21,* 168–175.

Schwitzgebel, E. (1999). Representation and desire: A philosophical error with consequences for theory-of-mind research. *Philosophical Psychology, 12,* 157–180.

Scoboria, A., Mazzoni, G., & Kirsch, I. (2006). Effect of misleading questions and hypnotic memory suggestion on memory reports: A signal-detection analysis. *International Journal of Clinical and Experimental Hypnosis, 54,* 340–359.

Scoboria, A., Mazzoni, G., Kirsch, I., & Milling, L. S. (2002). Immediate and persisting effects of misleading questions and hypnosis on memory reports. *Journal of Experimental Psychology: Applied, 8*(1), 26–32.

Scott, S. K., Young, A. W., Calder, A. J., Hellawell, D. J., Aggleton, J. P., & Johnson, M. (1997). Impaired auditory recognition of fear and anger following bilateral amygdala lesions. *Nature, 385*(6613), 254–257.

Sealy, P., & Whitehead, P. C. (2004). The impact of deinstitutionalization of psychiatric hospitals on psychological distress of the community in Canada. *Journal of Health and Social Policy, 21*(4), 73–94.

Segall, M. H., Campbell, D. T., & Herskovits, M. J. (1966). *The influence of culture on perception.* Indianapolis, IN: Bobbs-Merrill.

Segerstrom, S. C., Taylor, S. E., Kemeny, M. E., & Fahey, J. L. (1998). Optimism is associated with mood, coping, and immune change in response to stress. *Journal of Personality and Social Psychology, 74,* 1646–1655.

Seligman, L. (1998). Selecting effective treatments: A comprehensive guide to treating mental disorders. San Francisco, CA: Jossey-Bass.

Seligman, M. (1989). *Helplessness.* New York, NY: Freeman.

Seligman, M. E. P. (1970). On the generality of the laws of learning. *Psychological Review, 77,* 406–418.

Seligman, M. E. P. (1975). *Helplessness—On depression, development, and death.* San Francisco, CA: Freeman.

Seligman, M. E. P. (1995). The effectiveness of psychotherapy: The *Consumer Reports* study. *American Psychologist, 50,* 965–975.

Seligman, M. E. P. (1998). *Learned optimism: How to change your mind and your life* (2nd ed.). New York, NY: Pocket Books.

Seligman, M. E. P. (2002). *Authentic happiness*. New York, NY: Free Press.

Seligman, M. E. P., & Maier, S. F. (1967). Failure to escape traumatic shock. *Journal of Experimental Psychology, 74,* 1–9.

Selye, H. (1956). *The stress of life*. New York, NY: McGraw-Hill.

Selye, H. (1976). *The stress of life* (rev. ed.). New York, NY: McGraw-Hill.

Selye, H. A. (1936). Syndrome produced by diverse nocuous agents. *Nature, 138,* 32.

Separate lives. (2005). *WFive*. Retrieved from http://www.ctv.ca/ servlet/ ArticleNews/story/CTVNews/20050507/WFIVE_separate_lives_ 050506/20050507

Sestir, M. A., & Bartholow, B. D. (2010). Violent and nonviolent video games produce opposing effects on aggressive and prosocial outcomes. *Journal of Experimental Social Psychology, 46,* 934–942.

Shackelford, T. K., Buss, D. M., & Bennett, K. (2002). Forgiveness or breakup: Sex differences in responses to a partner's infidelity. *Cognition and Emotion, 16,* 299–307.

Shadish, R., Cook, T. D., & Campbell, D. T. (2002). *Experimental and quasiexperimental designs for generalized causal inferences*. New York, NY: Houghton Mifflin.

Shafto, P., & Coley, J. D. (2003). Development of categorization and reasoning in the natural world: Novices to experts, naïve similarity to ecological knowledge. *Journal of Experimental Psychology: Learning, Memory & Cognition, 29,* 641–649.

Shafton, A. (1995). Dream reader: Contemporary approaches to the understanding of dreams (SUNY series in dream studies) (pp. 40–46). New York, NY: State University of New York Press.

Shapiro, A. K., & Shapiro, E. (1997). *The powerful placebo*. Baltimore, MD: Johns Hopkins University Press.

Shapiro, C. M., Trajanovic, N. N., & Fedoroff, J. P. (2003). Sexsomnia: A new parasomnia. *Canadian Journal of Psychiatry, 48,* 311–317.

Shapiro, F. (1989). Eye movement desensitization: A new treatment for posttraumatic stress disorder. *Journal of Behavior Therapy and Experimental Psychiatry, 20,* 211–217.

Shapiro, F. (1995). *Eye movement desensitization and reprocessing: Basic principles, protocols, and procedure*. New York, NY: Guilford.

Shapiro, K. L., Jacobs, W. J., & LoLordo, V. M. (1980). Stimulus relevance in Pavlovian conditioning in pigeons. *Animal Learning and Behavior, 8,* 586–594.

Sharif, Z., Bradford, D., Stroup, S., & Lieberman, J. (2007). Pharmacological treatment of schizophrenia. In P. E. Nathan & J. M. Gorman (Eds.), *A guide to treatments that work* (3rd ed., pp. 203–241). New York, NY: Oxford University Press.

Shaywitz, S. E. (1996). Dyslexia. *Scientific American, 275*(5), 98–104.

Shean, R. E., de Klerk, N. H., Armstrong, B. K., & Walker, N. R. (1994). Sevenyear follow-up of a smoking-prevention program for children. *Australian Journal of Public Health, 18,* 205–208.

Sheeber, L. B., & Johnson, J. H. (1992). Child temperament, maternal adjustment, and changes in family life style. *American Journal of Orthopsychiatry, 62*(2), 178–185.

Sheehy, R., & Horan, J. J. (2004). Effects of stress inoculation training for 1st-year law students. *International Journal of Stress Management, 11,* 41–55.

Shekelle, P. G., Hardy, M. L., Morton, S. C., Maglione, M., Mojica, W. A., Suttorp, M. J., & Gagné, J. (2003). Efficacy and safety of ephedra and ephedrine for weight loss and athletic performance: A meta-analysis. *Journal of the American Medical Association, 289,* 1537–1545.

Shelley, M. (1969). *Frankenstein* (12th ed.). Oxford, England: Oxford University Press. (Original work published 1818)

Shepard, R. N., & Metzler, J. (1971). Mental rotation of three-dimensional objects. *Science, 171,* 701–703.

Shepard, T. H. (2001). *Catalog of teratogenic agents* (10th ed.). Baltimore, MD: Johns Hopkins University Press.

Sherif, M. (1936). *The psychology of social norms*. New York, NY: Harper & Row.

Sherif, M., Harvey, O. J., White, B. J., Hood, W. R., & Sherif, C. W. (1961). *Intergroup conflict and cooperation: The Robber's Cave experiment*. Norman, OK: University of Oklahoma Book Exchange.

Sherry, P. (1991). Person environment fit and accident prediction. *Journal of Business and Psychology, 5,* 411–416.

Sherry, P., Gaa, A., Thurlow-Harrison, S., Graber, K., Clemmons, J., & Bobulinski, M. (2003). *Traffic accidents, job stress, and supervisor support in the trucking industry*. Paper presented at the International Institute for Intermodal Transportation at the University of Denver, Denver, CO.

Shneidman, E. S. (1994). Clues to suicide reconsidered. *Suicide and Life-Threatening Behavior, 24,* 395–397.

Shore, L. A. (1990). Skepticism in light of scientific literacy. *Skeptical Inquirer, 15*(1), 3–4.

Shorey, G. (2001). Bystander non-intervention and the Somalia incident. *Canadian Military Journal,* 19–27.

Shorter E. (1997). *A history of psychiatry: From the era of the asylum to the age of Prozac*. New York, NY: Wiley.

Showalter, E. (1997). *Hystories: Hysterical epidemics and modern culture*. New York, NY: Columbia University Press.

Shuglin, A. (1986). The background chemistry of MDMA. *Journal of Psychoactive Drugs, 18*(4), 291–304.

Shurkin, J. N. (1992). *Terman's kids; The groundbreaking study of how the gifted grow up*. Boston, MA: Little, Brown.

Siegal, A., Roeling, T. A. P., Gregg, T. R., & Kruk, M. R. (1999). Neuropharmacology of brain-stimulation-evoked aggression. *Neuroscience and Biobehavioral Reviews, 23,* 359–389.

Siegel, S. (1969). Effects of CS habituation on eyelid conditioning. *Journal of Comparative and Physiological Psychology, 68*(2), 245–248.

Siegler, I. C., Costa, P. T., Brummett, B. H., Helms, M. J., Barefoot, J. C., Williams, R. B., . . . Rimer, B. K. (2003). Patterns of change in hostility from college to midlife in the UNC alumni heart study predict high-risk status. *Psychosomatic Medicine, 65,* 738–745.

Siegler, R. S. (1989). Mechanisms of cognitive development. *Annual Review of Psychology, 40,* 353–379.

Siegler, R. S. (1996). *Emerging minds: The process of change in children's thinking*. New York, NY: Oxford University Press.

Silva, C. E., & Kirsch, I. (1992). Interpretive sets, expectancy, fantasy proneness, and dissociation as predictors of hypnotic response. *Journal of Personality & Social Psychology, 63,* 847–856.

Silver, F. W. (1996). Management of conversion disorder. *American Journal of Physical Medicine and Rehabilitation, 75,* 134–140.

Silver, S. M., Brooks, A., & Obenchain, J. (1995). Eye movement desensitization and reprocessing treatment of Vietnam war veterans with PTSD: Comparative effects with biofeedback and relaxation training. *Journal of Traumatic Stress, 8,* 337–342.

Silverman, I., Choi, J., Mackewn, A., Fisher, M., Moro, J., & Olshansky, E. (2000). Evolved mechanisms underlying wayfinding: Further studies on the huntergatherer theory of spatial sex differences. *Evolution and Human Behavior, 21,* 201–213.

Simeon, D., Guralnik, O., Hazlett, E. A., Spiegel-Cohen, J., Hollander, E., & Buchsbaum, M. S. (2000). Feeling unreal: A PET study of depersonalization disorder. *American Journal of Psychiatry, 157,* 1782–1788.

Simon, E. (2007, October 11). The phantom cellphone. *Globe and Mail.* Retrieved from http://www.theglobeandmail.com/servlet/story/RTGAM.20071010.wgtphantom101007/BNStory/Technology/?cid=al_gam_nletter_newsUp

Singer, M. T., & Lalich, J. (1995). *Cults in our midst.* San Francisco, CA: Jossey-Bass.

Singh-Manoux, A., Richards, M., & Marmot, M. (2003). Leisure activities and cognitive function in middle age: Evidence from the Whitehall II study. *Journal of Epidemiology and Community Health, 57,* 907–913.

Siqueland, E. R., & Lipsitt, L. P. (1966). Conditioned head-turning in human newborns. *Journal of Experimental Child Psychology, 3,* 356–376.

Skinner, B. F. (1938). *The behavior of organisms: An experimental analysis.* New York, NY: Appleton-Century-Crofts.

Skinner, B. F. (1953). *Science and human behavior.* New York, NY: MacMillan.

Skinner, B. F. (1954). The science of learning and the art of teaching. *Harvard Educational Review, 24*(2), 86–97.

Skinner, B. F. (1956). A case history in scientific method. *American Psychologist, 11,* 221–233.

Skinner, B. F. (1961). *Cumulative record: Definitive edition.* New York, NY: Appelton- Century-Crofts.

Skinner, B. F. (1971). *Beyond freedom and dignity.* New York, NY: Knopf.

Skinner, B. F. (1974). *About behaviorism.* New York, NY: Knopf.

Skinner, B. F. (1989). The origins of cognitive thought. *American Psychologist, 44,* 13–18.

Skinner, N. F. (1997). Failure to support a test for penis envy. *Psychological Reports, 80,* 754.

Skolnick, A. (1986). Early attachment and personal relationships across the life course. In P. B. Baltes, D. L. Featherman, & R. M. Lerner (Eds.), *Life-span development and behavior* (Vol. 7). Hillsdale, NJ: Erlbaum.

Skrandies, W., Reik, P., & Kunze, C. (1999). Topography of evoked brain activity during mental arithmetic and language tasks: Sex differences. *Neuropsychologia, 37,* 421–430.

Slater, A. (2000). Visual perception in the young infant: Early organisation and rapid learning. In D. Muir and A. Slater (Eds.), *Infant development: The essential readings.* Oxford, England: Blackwells.

Slater, A., Mattock, A., & Brown, E. (1990). Size constancy at birth: Newborn infants' responses to retinal and real size. *Journal of Experimental Child Psychology, 49,* 314–322.

Slater, A., Murison, V., & Rose, D. (1984). Habituation in the newborn. *Infant Behavior Development, 7,* 183–200.

Slipp, S. (1993). *The Freudian mystique: Freud, women and feminism.* New York, NY: New York University Press.

Sloan, D. M., & Mizes, J. S. (1999). Foundations of behavior therapy in the contemporary healthcare context. *Clinical Psychology Review, 19,* 255–274.

Smith, C. (2001). Sleep states and memory processes in humans: Procedural versus declarative memory systems. *Sleep Medicine Reviews, 5,* 491–506.

Smith, C. (2003). The REM sleep window and memory processing. In P. Maquet, C. Smith, & R. Stickgold (Eds.), *Sleep and brain plasticity* (pp. 117–133). Oxford, England: Oxford University Press.

Smith, C. T., Nixon, M. R., & Nader, R. S. (2004). Posttraining increases in REM sleep intensity implicate REM sleep in memory processing and provide a biological marker of learning potential. *Learning & Memory, 11,* 714–719.

Smith, D. (2001). Shock and disbelief. *Atlantic Monthly, 2,* 79–90.

Smith, D. G., Standing, L., & de Man, A. (1992). Verbal memory elicited by ambient odor. *Perceptual and Motor Skills, 74,* 339–343.

Smith, G. N., Flynn, S. W., McCarthy, N., Meistrich, B., Ehmann, T. S., MacEwan, W. G., . . . Honer, W. G. (2001). Low birth-weight in schizophrenia: Prematurity or poor fetal growth? *Schizophrenia Research, 47,* 177–184.

Smith, J. D., & Mitchell, A. (2001). "Me? I'm not a drooler. I'm the assistant": Is it time to abandon mental retardation as a classification. *Mental Retardation, 39*(2), 144–146.

Smith, J. W. (1988). Long term outcome of clients treated in a commercial stop smoking program. *Journal of Substance Abuse Treatment, 5*(1), 33–36.

Smith, M. C., Bibi, U., & Sheard, D. E. (2003). Evidence for the differential impact of time and emotion on personal and event memories for September 11, 2001. *Applied Cognitive Psychology, 17,* 1047–1055.

Smith, M. C., & Phillips, M. R., Jr. (2001). Age differences in memory for radio advertisements: The role of mnemonics. *Journal of Business Research, 53,* 103–109.

Smith, M. K. (2002) Howard Gardner and multiple intelligences. *The encyclopedia of informal education.* Retrieved from http://www.infed.org/thinkers/gardner. htm

Snyder, M., Tanke, E. D., & Berscheid, E. (1977). Social perception and interpersonal behavior: On the self-fulfilling nature of social stereotypes. *Journal of Personality and Social Psychology, 35,* 656–666.

Sodowsky, G. R., Lai, E. W., & Plake, B. S. (1991). Moderating effects of sociocultural variables on acculturation attitudes of Hispanics and Asian Americans. *Journal and Counseling and Development, 70,* 194–204.

Soomro, G. M. (2001). Obsessive-compulsive disorder. *Clinical Evidence, 6,* 754–762.

Sowell, E. R., Thompson, P. M., Holmes, C. J., Jernigan, T. L., & Toga, A. W. (1999). In vivo evidence for post-adolescent brain maturation in frontal and striatal regions. *Nature Neuroscience, 2,* 859–861.

Spangler, W. D. (1992). Validity of questionnaire and TAT measures of need for achievement: Two meta-analyses. *Psychological Bulletin, 112,* 140–154.

Spangler, W. J., Cosgrove, G. R., Ballantine, H. T., Jr., Cassem, E. H., Rauch, S. L., Nierenberg, A., & Price, G. H. (1996). Magnetic resonance image-guided stereotactic cingulotomy for intractable psychiatric disease. *Neurosurgery, 38,* 1071–1076.

Spanos, N. P. (1994). Multiple identity enactments and multiple personality disorder: A socio-cognitive perspective. *Psychological Bulletin, 116,* 143–165.

Spanos, N. P. (1996). *Multiple identities and false memories: A socio-cognitive perspective.* Washington, DC: American Psychological Association.

Spanos, N. P., Flynn, D. M., & Gabora, N. J. (1989). Suggested negative visual hallucinations in hypnotic subjects: When no means yes. *British Journal of Experimental and Clinical Hypnosis, 6*(2), 63–67.

Spanos, N. P., Menary, E., Gabora, N. J., DuBreuil, S. C., & Dewhirst, B. (1991). Secondary identity enactments during hypnotic past-life regression. A sociocognitive perspective. *Journal of Personality and Social Psychology, 61,* 308–320.

Spanos, N. P., Weekes, J. R., & Bertrand, L. D. (1985). Multiple personality: A social psychological perspective. *Journal of Abnormal Psychology, 94,* 362–376.

Sparing, R., Mottaghy, F., Ganis, G., Thompson, W. L., Toepper, R., Kosslyn, S. M., & Pascual-Leone, A. (2002).Visual cortex excitability increases during visual mental imagery—A TMS study in healthy human subjects. *Brain Research, 938,* 92–97.

Spearman, C. (1904). "General intelligence" objectively determined and measured. *American Journal of Psychology, 15,* 201–293.

Speca, M., Carlson, L. E, Goodey, E., & Angen, E. (2000). A randomized wait-list controlled clinical trial: The effects of a mindfulness meditation-based stress reduction program on mood and symptoms of stress in cancer outpatients. *Psychosomatic Medicine, 6,* 2613–2622.

Sperling, G. (1960). The information available in brief visual presentations. *Psychological Monographs,* 74(11), 1–29.

Speroff, L., Glass, R. H., & Kase, N. G. (1999). Recurrent early pregnancy loss. In *Clinical Gynecologic Endocrinology and Infertility* (pp. 1042–1055). Philadelphia, PA: Lippincott Williams and Wilkins.

Sperry, R. W. (1968). Mental unity following surgical disconnection of the cerebral hemispheres. *The Harvey Lectures* (Series 62), 293–323. New York, NY: Academic Press.

Spetch, M. L., Cheng, K., & MacDonald, S. E. (1996). Learning the configuration of a landmark array: I. Touch-screen studies with pigeons and humans. *Journal of Comparative Psychology, 110,* 55–68.

Spiegel, D., Bloom, J. R., & Gottheil, E. (1989). Effects of psychosocial treatment on survival of patients with metastatic breast cancer. *Lancet, 2,* 888–891.

Spiegel, H., & Borch-Jacobsen, M. (1997). Sybil—The making of a disease. *New York Review of Books,* 44(7).

Sports Legacy Institute. (2007). *Sports Legacy Institute announces findings of forensic examinations on wrestler Chris Benoit's brain.* Retrieved from http://www.bio-medicine.org/medicine-technology-1/Sports-Legacy-Institute-Announces-Findings-of-Forensic-Examinations-on-Wrestler-Chris-Benoits-Brain-198-3

Springer, S. P., & Deutsch, G. (1998). *Left brain, right brain: Perspectives from cognitive neuroscience* (5th ed.). New York, NY: Freeman.

Squire, L., & Kandel, E. (1999). *Memory: From mind to molecule.* New York, NY: Scientific American Library.

Squire, L. R., Knowlton, B., & Musen, G. (1993). The structure and organization of memory. *Annual Review of Psychology, 44,* 453–495.

Squire, L. R., & Slater, P. C. (1978). Anterograde and retrograde memory impairment in chronic amnesia. *Neuropsychologia, 16,* 313–322.

Squire, L. R., Slater, P. C., & Chace, P. M. (1975). Retrograde amnesia: Temporal gradient in very long-term memory following electroconvulsive therapy. *Science, 187,* 77–79.

Stancl, C. (2006). Chance at life. *WFive.* Retrieved from http://www.ctv.ca/servlet/ArticleNews/story/CTVNews/20060421/WFIVE_chance_life_060421/20060422

Standing, L., Conezio, J., & Haber, R. N. (1970). Perception and memory for pictures: Single-trial learning of 2500 visual stimuli. *Psychonomic Science, 19,* 73–74.

Stapleton, J. A., Taylor, S., & Asmundson, G. J. G. (2007). Efficacy of various treatments for PTSD in battered women: Case studies. *Journal of Cognitive Psychotherapy,* 21(1), 91–102.

Statistics Canada. (2003, September 3). Canadian community health survey: Mental health and well-being. *The Daily.* Retrieved from http:// www.statcan.ca/Daily/English/030903/d030903a.htm

Statistics Canada. (2004, December 9). Alcohol and illicit drug dependence. *The Daily.* Retrieved from http://www.statscan.ca/Daily/ English/041209/d041209b.htm

Statistics Canada. (2004). Supplement to health report, Vol. 15. Statistics Canada Catalogue 82-003. Retrieved from http://www.statcan.ca/english/freepub/82-003-SIE/82-003-SIE2004000.htm

Statistics Canada. (2007a, May 3). The income of Canadians. *The Daily.* Retrieved from http://www.statcan.ca/Daily/English/070503/d070503a.htm

Statistics Canada. (2007b). Pregnancy outcomes by province or territory of residence: Fetal loss, 2004. Retrieved from http://www40.statcan.ca/l01/cst01/hlth64d.htm

Staub, D., & Peck, C. A. (1995). What are the outcomes for nondisabled students? *Educational Leadership, 6,* 36–40.

Steel, P. (2007). The nature of procrastination: A meta-analytic and theoretical review of quintessential self-regulatory failure. *Psychological Bulletin, 133,* 65–94.

Steele, C. M. (1992). Race and the schooling of black Americans. *The Atlantic Monthly,* 269(4), 68–78.

Steele, C. M. (1997). A threat in the air: How stereotypes shape intellectual identity and performance. *American Psychologist, 52,* 613–629.

Steele, C. M. (1999, August). Thin ice: "Stereotype threat" and Black college students. *The Atlantic Monthly, 284,* 44–54.

Steele, C. M., & Aronson J. (1995). Stereotype threat and the intellectual test performance of African Americans. *Journal of Personality and Social Psychology, 69,* 797–811.

Stein, H. T. (2001). Adlerian overview of birth order characteristics. Alfred Adler Institute of San Francisco. Retrieved from http://ourworld. compuserve.com/homepages/hstein/birthord.htm

Stein, M. B., Torgrud, L. J., & Walker, J. R. (2000). Social phobia symptoms, subtypes, and severity: Findings from a community survey. *Archives of General Psychology, 57,* 1046–1052.

Stein, S. (1984). *Girls and boys: The limits of non-sexist rearing* (pp. 12–14). London, England: Chatto and Windus.

Stein-Behrens, B., Mattson, M. P., Chang, I., Yeh, M., & Sapolsky, R. (1994). Stress exacerbates neuron loss and cytoskeletal pathology in the hippocampus. *Journal of Neuroscience, 14,* 5373–5380.

Steinberg, L., & Silverberg, S. B. (1987). Influences on marital satisfaction during the middle stages of the family life cycle. *Journal of Marriage and the Family, 49,* 751–760.

Steriade, M., & McCarley, R. W. (1990). *Brainstem control of wakefulness and sleep.* New York, NY: Plenum.

Stern, W. (1912). The psychological methods of testing intelligence. (G. M. Whipple, Trans.). *Educational Psychology Monographs,* no. 13.

Sternberg, R. J. (1986). A triangular theory of love. *Psychological Review, 93,* 119–135.

Sternberg, R. J. (1988a). The triarchic mind: A new theory of human intelligence. New York, NY: Viking-Penguin.

Sternberg, R. J. (1988b). Triangulating love. In R. Sternberg & M. Barnes (Eds.), *The psychology of love* (pp. 119–138). New Haven, CT: Yale University Press.

Sternberg, R. J. (1996). *Successful intelligence: How practical and creative intelligence determine success in life.* New York, NY: Simon & Schuster.

Sternberg, R. J. (1997a). Construct validation of a triangular love scale. *European Journal of Social Psychology, 27,* 313–335.

Sternberg, R. J. (1997b). The triarchic theory of intelligence. In P. Flannagan, J. L. Genshaft, & P. L. Harrison (Eds.), *Contemporary intellectual assessment: Theories, tests, and issues* (pp. 92–104). New York, NY: Guilford Press.

Sternberg, R. J. (2006). *Cognitive psychology* (4th ed.). Belmont, CA: Thomson.

Sternberg, R. J., & Kaufman, J. C. (1998). Human abilities. *Annual Review of Psychology, 49,* 479–502.

Stevens, J. R. (1988). Schizophrenia and multiple sclerosis. *Schizophrenia Bulletin, 14,* 231–241.

Stiff, J. B., & Mongeau, P. A. (2002). *Persuasive communication* (2nd ed.). New York, NY: Guilford.

Stiles, W. B., Agnew-Davies, R., Hardy, G. E., Barkham, M., & Shapiro, D. A. (1998). Relations of the alliance with psychotherapy outcome: Findings in the second Sheffield Psychotherapy Project. *Journal of Consulting and Clinical Psychology, 66,* 791–802.

Stitzer, M. L., & De Wit, H. (1998). Abuse liability of nicotine. In N. L. Benowitz (Ed.), *Nicotine safety and toxicity* (pp. 119–131). New York, NY: Oxford University Press.

Stockhorst, U., Gritzmann, E., Klopp, K., Schottenfeld-Naor, Y., Hübinger, A., Berresheim, H., . . . Arnold Gries, F. (1999). Classical conditioning of insulin effects in healthy humans. *Psychosomatic Medicine, 61,* 424–435.

Storch, A. (2004, April). *Conversion of adult bone marrow cells into stem cells for transplantation.* Paper presented at the American Academy of Neurology 56th Annual Meeting in San Francisco, CA.

Stowell, J. R., Kiecolt-Glaser, J. K., & Glaser, R. (2001). Perceived stress and cellular immunity: When coping counts. *Journal of Behavioral Medicine, 24,* 323–339.

Stratton, K., Gable, A., & McCormick, M. C. (Eds.) (2001a). *Immunization safety review: Thimerosal-containing vaccines and neurodevelopmental disorders.* Washington, DC: National Academies Press.

Stratton, K., Wilson, C. B., & McCormick, M. C. (Eds.). (2001b). *Immunization safety review: Measles-mumps-rubella vaccine and autism.* Washington, DC: National Academies Press.

Straus, M. A. (2000). Corporal punishment of children and adult depression and suicidal ideation. *Beating the devil out of them: Corporal punishment in American families and its effects on children* (pp. 60–77). New York, NY: Lexington Books.

Straus, M. A., & Stewart, J. H. (1999). Corporal punishment by American parents: National data on prevalence, chronicity, severity, and duration, in relation to child, and family characteristics. *Clinical Child and Family Psychology Review, 2,* 55–70.

Straus, M. A., & Yodanis, C. L. (1994). Physical abuse. In M. A. Straus (Ed.), *Beating the devil out of them: Corporal punishment in American families* (pp. 81–98). San Francisco, CA: New Lexington Press.

Strawbridge, W. J., Cohen, R. D., Shema, S. J., & Kaplan, G. A. (1997). Frequent attendance at religious services and mortality over 28 years. *American Journal of Public Health, 87,* 957–961.

Strober, M., Freeman, R., Lampert, C., Diamond, J., & Kaye, W. (2000). Controlled family study of anorexia nervosa and bulimia nervosa: Evidence of shared liability and transmission of partial syndromes. *American Journal of Psychiatry, 157,* 393–401.

Stromeyer, C. F., III, & Psotka, J. (1971). The detailed texture of eidetic images. *Nature, 237,* 109–112.

Stuss, D. T., Binns, M. A., Murphy, K. J., & Alexander, M. P. (2002). Dissociations within the anterior attentional system: Effects of task complexity and irrelevant information on reaction-time speed and accuracy. *Neuropsychology, 16*(4), 500–513.

Sue, D. W., & Sue, D. (2003). *Counseling the culturally different: Theory and practice* (4th ed.). New York, NY: Wiley.

Sue, S. (1977). Community mental health services to minority groups: Some optimism, some pessimism. *American Psychologist, 32,* 616–624.

Sue, S. (1992). Ethnicity and mental health: Research and policy issues. *Journal of Social Issues, 48*(2), 187–205.

Sue, S., Zane, N., & Young, K. (1994). Research on psychotherapy in culturally diverse populations. In A. Bergin & S. Garfield (Eds.), *Handbook of psychotherapy and behavior change* (pp. 783–817). New York, NY: Wiley.

Sullivan, M. J. L., Bishop, S. R., & Pivik, J. (1995). The pain catastrophizing scale. Development and validation. *Psychological Assessment, 7,* 524–532.

Sulloway, F. J. (1996). Born to rebel: Birth order, family dynamics, and creative lives. New York, NY: Pantheon.

Suryani, L., & Jensen, S. (1993). Trance and possession in Bali: A window on western multiple personality, possession disorder, and suicide. New York, NY: Oxford University Press.

Sussman, S. (1998). The first asylums in Canada: A response to neglectful community care and current trends. *Canadian Journal of Psychiatry, 43,* 260–264.

Sutcliffe, N., Clarke, A. E., Levinton, C., Frost, C., Gordon, C., & Isenberg, D. A. (1999). Associates of health status in patients with systemic lupus erythematosus. *Journal of Rheumatology, 26,* 2352–2356.

Sutherland, P. (1992). Cognitive development today: Piaget and his critics. London, England: Paul Chapman.

Swann, J. (1998). Talk control: An illustration from the classroom of problems in analyzing male dominance of conversation. In J. Coates (Ed.), *Language and gender: A reader.* Oxford, England: Blackwell.

Swanson, H. (1994). Index of suspicion. Case 3. Diagnosis: Failure to thrive due to psychosocial dwarfism. *Pediatric Review, 15*(1), 39, 41.

Swanson, J. W., Swartz, M. S., & Elbogen, E. B. (2004). Effectiveness of atypical antipsychotic medications in reducing violent behavior among persons with schizophrenia in community-based treatment. *Schizophrenia Bulletin, 30*(1), 3–20.

Swartz, M. (1990). Somatization disorder. In L. N. Robins (Ed.), *Psychiatric disorder in America* (pp. 220–257). New York, NY: Free Press.

Swartz, M., Blazer, D., George, L., & Winfield, I. (1990). Estimating the prevalence of borderline personality disorder in the community. *Journal of Personality Disorders, 4,* 257–272.

Swayze V. W., II, (1995). Frontal leukotomy and related psychosurgical procedures in the era before antipsychotics (1935–1954): A historical overview. *American Journal of Psychiatry, 152*(4), 505–515.

Szabo, E., Rampalli, S., Risueño, R. M., Schnerch, A., Mitchell, R., Fiebig-Comyn, A., . . . Bhatia, M. (2010). Direct conversion of human fibroblasts to multilineage blood progenitors. *Nature, 468,* 521–526.

Taglialatela, J. P., Savage-Rumbaugh, E. S., & Baker, L. A. (2003). Vocal production by a language-competent bonobo (Pan Paniscus). *International Journal of Comparative Psychology, 24,* 1–17.

Tajfel, H., & Turner, J. C. (1986). The social identity theory of intergroup behaviour. In S. Worchel & W. G. Austin (Eds.), *The psychology of intergroup relations* (Vol. 2). New York, NY: Nelson Hall.

Takeuchi, T., Ogilvie, R. D., Murphy, T. I., & Ferrelli, A. V. (2003). EEG activities during elicited sleep onset. REM and NREM periods reflect difference mechanisms of dream generation. *Clinical Neurophysiology, 114*(2), 210–220.

Talbott, G. D., & Crosby, L. R. (2001). Recovery contracts: Seven key elements. In R. H. Coombs (Ed.), *Addiction recovery tools* (pp. 127–144). Thousand Oaks, CA: Sage.

Tamminga, C. A. (2002). Partial dopamine agonists in the treatment of psychosis. *Journal of Neural Transmission, 109,* 411–420.

Tart, C. (1986). *Waking up: Overcoming the obstacles to human potential.* Boston, MA: New Science Library.

Tart, C. T. (1970). Marijuana intoxication: Common experiences. *Nature, 226,* 701.

Taylor, B., Miller, E., Farrington, C. P., Petropoulos, M. C., Favot-Mayaud, I., Li, J., & Waight, P. A. (1999). Autism and measles, mumps, and rubella vaccine: No epidemiological evidence for a causal association. *Lancet, 353,* 2026–2029.

Taylor, C. T., & Alden, L. E. (2005). Social interpretation bias and generalized social phobia: The influence of developmental experiences. *Behaviour Research and Therapy, 43,* 759–777.

Taylor, D. M., & Moghaddam, F. M. (1994). *Theories of intergroup relations: International social psychological perspectives* (2nd ed.). Westport, CT: Praeger.

Taylor, F. W. (1985). *Principles of scientific management* (pp. 5–29). New York, NY: Harper. (Original work published 1911)

Taylor, M. J., Carney, S., Geddes, J., & Goodwin, G. (2004). Folate for depressive disorders (Cochrane Review). In *The Cochrane Library* (Issue 2). Chichester, England: Wiley.

Taylor, S., & Asmundson, G. J. G (2004). *Treating health anxiety.* New York, NY: Guilford.

Taylor, S., Thordarson, D. S., Jang, K. L., & Asmundson, G. J. G. (2006). Genetic and environmental origins of health anxiety: A twin study. *World Psychiatry, 5,* 47–50.

Taylor, S. E., Klein, L. C., Lewis, B. P., Gruenewald, T. L., Gurung, R. A. R., & Updegraff, J. A. (2000). Biobehavioral responses to stress in females; tend-andbefriend, not fight-or-flight. *Psychological Bulletin, 107,* 411–429.

Taylor, S. E., Repetti, R., & Seeman, T. (1997). Health psychology: What is an unhealthy environment and how does it get under the skin? *Annual Review of Psychology, 48,* 411–447.

Teigen, K. (1994). Yerkes–Dodson: A law for all seasons. *Theory & Psychology, 4,* 525–547.

Temoshok, L., & Dreher, H. (1997). *The Type C connection: The behavioral links to cancer and your health.* New York, NY: Random House.

Terman, L. M. (1916). *The measurement of intelligence.* Boston, MA: Houghton Mifflin.

Terman, L. M. (1925). *Mental and physical traits of a thousand gifted children (I).* Stanford, CA: Stanford University Press.

Terman, L. M., & Oden, M. H. (1947). *The gifted child grows up: 25 years' followup of a superior group: Genetic studies of genius* (Vol. 4). Stanford, CA: Stanford University Press.

Terman, L. M., & Oden, M. H. (1959). *The gifted group at mid-life, thirty-five years follow-up of the superior child: Genetic studies of genius* (Vol. 3). Stanford, CA: Stanford University Press.

Terracciano, A., Abdel-Khalek, A. M., Adam, N., Adamovová, L., Ahn, C. -K., Ahn, H. -N., . . . McCrae, R. R. (2006). National character does not reflect mean personality trait levels in 49 cultures. *Science, 310,* 96–100.

Terry, A. V., Jr., Hill, W. D., Parikh, V., Evans, D. R., Waller, J. L., & Mahadik, S. P. (2002). Differential effects of chronic haloperidol and olanzapine exposure on brain cholinergic markers and spatial learning in rats. *Psychopharmacology, 164*(4), 360–368.

Terry, A. V., Jr., Hill, W. D., Parikh, V., Waller, J. L., Evans, D. R., & Mahadik, S. P. (2003). Differential effects of haloperidol, risperidone, and clozapine exposure on cholinergic markers and spatial learning performance in rats. *Neuropsychopharmacology, 28*(2), 300–309.

Tesser, A. (1993). On the importance of heritability in psychological research: The case of attitudes. *Psychological Review, 100,* 129–142.

Thase, M. E. (1999). When are psychotherapy and pharmacotherapy combinations the treatment of choice for major depressive disorders? *Psychiatric Quarterly, 70*(4), 333–346.

Thase, M. E., & Sachs, G. S. (2000). Bipolar depression: Pharmacotherapy and related therapeutic strategies. *Biological Psychiatry, 48*(6), 558–572.

Thiedke, C. C. (2001). Sleep disorders and sleep problems in childhood. *American Family Physician, 63,* 277–284.

Thigpen, C. H., & Cleckley, H. M. (1992, revised). *The three faces of Eve.* London, England: Secker & Warburg.

Thomas, A., & Chess, S. (1977). *Temperament and development.* New York, NY: Brunner/Mazel.

Thomas, M., Thorne, D., Sing, H., Redmond, D., Balkin, T., Wesensten, N., et al. (1998). The relationship between driving accidents and microsleep during cumulative partial sleep deprivation. *Journal of Sleep Research, 7*(2), 275.

Thomas, N. J. T. (2001). Mental imagery. In E. N. Zalta, (Ed.), *The stanford encyclopedia of philosophy* (Winter 2001 Edition).

Thoresen, C. E., & Harris, H. S. (2002). Spirituality and health: What's the evidence and what's needed? *Annals of Behavioral Medicine, 24,* 3–13.

Thorndike, E. L. (1911). *Animal intelligence: Experimental studies.* New York, NY: MacMillan.

Thorndike, E. L. (1920). A constant error on psychological rating. *Journal of Applied Psychology* (Vol. IV), 25–29.

Thornton, A., & Hui-Sheng, L. (1994). Continuity and change. In A. Thornton & L. Hui-Sheng (Eds.), *Social change and the family in Taiwan.* Chicago, IL: University of Chicago Press.

Thurstone, L. L. (1938). *Primary mental abilities.* Chicago, IL: University of Chicago Press.

Tiwari, S. K., & Wang, J. (2006). The epidemiology of mental and substance userelated disorders among White, Chinese, and other Asian populations in Canada. *Canadian Journal of Psychiatry, 51,* 904–912.

Tjepkema, M. (2004). Adult obesity in Canada: Measured height and weight. *Nutrition: Findings from the Canadian Community Health Survey.* Retrieved from http://www.statcan.ca/english/research/82-620-MIE/2005001/articles/ adults/aobesity.htm#5

Tobach, E. (2001). Development of sex and gender. In J. Worell (Ed.), *Encyclopedia of women and gender* (pp. 315–332). San Diego, CA: Academic Press.

Todd, D. (2010). Mates and kids more important than self-realization: Study. *The Vancouver Sun.* Retrieved from http://communities.canada.com/vancouversun/blogs/thesearch/archive/2010/08/27/mates-and-kids-more-important-than-self-realization-study.aspx

Toga, A. W., & Thompson, P. M. (2003). Mapping brain asymmetry. *Natural Neuroscience, 4,* 37–48.

Tohen, M., Vieta, E., Calabrese, J., Ketter, T. A., Sachs, G., Bowden, C., . . . Breier, A. (2003). Efficacy of olanzapine and olanzapine-fluoxetine combination in the treatment of bipolar I depression. *Archives of General Psychiatry, 60*(11), 1079–1088.

Tolman, E. C. (1932). *Purposive behavior in animals and man.* New York, NY: Century.

Tolman, E. C., & Honzik, C. H. (1930). Introduction and removal of reward and maze learning in rats. *University of California Publications in Psychology, 4,* 257–275.

Tombs, S., & Silverman, I. (2004). Pupillometry. A sexual selection approach. *Evolution and Human Behaviour, 25,* 221–228.

Torgersen, S. (2000). Genetics of patients with borderline personality disorder. *Psychiatric Clinics of North America, 23,* 1–9.

Torrance, E. P. (1962). Non-test ways of identifying the creatively gifted. *Gifted Child Quarterly, 6*(3), 71–75.

Torrance, E. P. (1993). The Beyonders in a thirty-year longitudinal study of creative achievement. *Roeper Review, 15*(3), 131–135.

Torrey, E. F. (1986). Witchdoctors and psychiatrists. The common roots of psychotherapy and its future. New York, NY: Harper & Raw.

Torrey, E. F. (1987). Prevalence studies in schizophrenia. *British Journal of Psychiatry, 150,* 598–608.

Trappey, C. (1996). A meta-analysis of consumer choice and subliminal advertising. *Psychology and Marketing, 13,* 517–530.

Tremblay, A., Doucet, E., & Imbeault, P. (1999). Physical activity and weight maintenance. *International Journal of Obesity, 23*(3), S50–S54.

Tremblay, M. S., & Willms, J. D. (2003). Is the Canadian childhood obesity epidemic related to physical inactivity? *International Journal of Obesity, 27,* 1100–1105.

Tresniowski, A. (1999, July 12). Troubled sleep. *People Weekly,* 56–59.

Triandis, H. (1971). *Attitude and attitude change.* New York, NY: Wiley.

Trocmé, N., MacLaurin, B., Fallon, B., Daciuk, J., Billingsley, D., Tourigny, M., . . . McKenzie, B. (2001). *Canadian incidence study of reported child abuse and neglect: Final report* (pp. 30–31). Ottawa, ON: Minister of Public Works and Government Services Canada.

Troisi, A., & McGuire, M. (2002). Darwinian psychiatry and the concept of mental disorder. *Human Ethology & Evolutionary Psychology, 23*(4), 31–38.

Tropepe, V., Coles, B. L., Chiasson, B. J., Horsford, D. J., Elia, A. J., McInnes, R. R., & van der Kooy, D. (2000). Retinal stem cells in the adult mammalian eye. *Science, 287,* 2032–2036.

Trujillo, K. A., & Chinn, A. B. (1996). Antidepressants. Drugs and the Brain. California State University. Retrieved from http://www.csusm.edu/ DandB/AD.html#history

Trut, L. M. (1999). Early canid domestication: The Farm-Fox Experiment. *Science, 283.*

Tsai, J. L., Simeonova, D. I., & Watanabe, J. T. (2004). Somatic and social: Chinese Americans talk about emotion. *Personality and Social Psychology Bulletin, 30,* 1226–1238.

Tsapogas, J. (2006). *Characteristics of doctoral scientists and engineers in the United States: 2003,* NSF, 06–320. Arlington, VA: National Science Foundation, Division of Science Resources Statistics.

Tugade, M. M., & Fredrickson, B. L. (2004). Resilient individuals use positive emotions to bounce back from negative emotional experiences. *Journal of Personality and Social Psychology, 86,* 320–333.

Tukuitonga, C. F., & Bindman, A. B. (2002). Ethnic and gender differences in the use of coronary artery revascularisation procedures in New Zealand. *New Zealand Medical Journal, 115,* 179–182.

Tulving, E. (1972). Episodic and semantic memory. In E. Tulving & W. Donaldson (Eds.), *Organization of memory* (pp. 381–403). New York, NY: Academic Press.

Tulving, E., & Thomson, D. M. (1973). Encoding specificity and retrieval processes in episodic memory. *Psychological Review, 80,* 352–373.

Turner, W. J. (1995). Homosexuality, Type 1: An Xq28 phenomenon. *Archives of Sexual Behavior, 24*(2), 109–134.

Turner's Syndrome Society of Canada. (n.d.) *About Turner's Syndrome.* Retrieved from http://www.turnersyndrome.ca

Turton, S., & Campbell, C. (2005). Tend-and-befriend versus fight-or-fight: Gender differences in behavioral responses to stress among university students. *Journal of Applied Biobehavioral Research, 10,* 209–232.

Tusel, D. J., Piotrowski, N. A., Sees, K., Reilly, P. M., Banys, P., Meek, P., & Hall, S. M. (1994). Contingency contracting for illicit drug use with opioid addicts in methadone treatment. In L. S. Harris (Ed.), *Problems of drug dependence: Proceedings of the 56th Annual Scientific Meeting. National Institute on Drug Abuse research monograph 153* (pp. 155–160). Washington, DC: U.S. Goverment Printing Office.

Turk, C. L., Heimberg, R. G., & Magee, L. (2008). Social anxiety disorder. In D. H. Barlow (Ed.), *Clinical handbook of psychological disorders* (pp. 123–163). New York, NY: Guilford Press.

Tversky, A., & Kahneman, D. (1974). Judgment under uncertainty: Heuristics and biases. *Science, 185,* 1124–1130.

Tversky, A., & Shafir, E. (1992). The disjunction effect in choice under uncertainty. *Psychological Science, 3*(5), 305–309.

Tweed, R. G., & Lehman, D. R. (2002). Learning considered within a cultural context: Confucian and Socratic approaches. *American Psychologist, 57,* 89–99.

UBC Public Affairs. (2007, September 17). *New way to diagnose Alzheimer's disease promises earlier treatment.* Retrieved from www.publicaffairs.ubc.ca/media/releases/2007/mr-07-084.html

Unger, R. (1979). Toward a redefinition of sex and gender. *American Psychologist, 34,* 1085–1094.

University of Rochester (2008). *Self-determination theory.* Retrieved from http://www.psych.rochester.edu/SDT/theory.php

University of Windsor. (n.d.). Altruistic motivation for psychology prof. *Daily News: Public Affairs and Communications.* Retrieved from http://www.uwindsor.ca/ units/pac/nvdailynews/nvdn.nsf/264f80f204e5088a85256a7a004a4bfb/ fabbda924fc55fdd852573fa004d4786!OpenDocument&Click=

Uretsky, S. D. (2002). Antianxiety drugs. *Gale Encyclopedia of Medicine.* The Gale Group. Retrieved from http://www.healthatoz.com/ healthatoz/Atoz/ency/antianxiety_drugs.html#

Vail, A. (1976). Factors influencing lower class, black patients' remaining in treatment. *Clinical Psychology, 29,* 12–14.

Vaillant, G. E. (2002). Adaptive mental mechanisms: Their role in a positive psychology. *American Psychologist, 55,* 89–98.

Van de Castle, R. (1994). *Our dreaming mind.* New York, NY: Ballantine Books.

van der Merwe, A., & Garuccio, A. (Eds.). (1994). *Waves and particles in light and matter.* New York, NY: Plenum Press.

Van Dongen, H. P. A., Maislin, G., Mullington, J. M., & Dinges, D. F. (2003). The cumulative cost of additional wakefulness: Dose-response effects on neurobehavioral functions and sleep physiology from chronic sleep restriction and total sleep deprivation. *Sleep, 26,* 117–126.

Van Til, R. (1997). *Lost daughters: Recovered memory therapy and the people it hurts.* Grand Rapids, MI: Eerdmand.

van Walsum, K. L. (2004). Nos malades: Three examples of Christian influences in care for the insane in pre-revolutionary France and Belgium. *Journal of Psychology and Christianity, 23,* 219–233.

Vartanian, L. R. (2000). Revisiting the imaginary audience and personal fable constructs of adolescent egocentricism: A conceptual review. *Adolescence, 35,* 639–661.

Vaughan, K., Armstrong, M. S., Gold, R., O'Connor N., Jenneke, W., & Tarrier, N. (1994). A trial of eye movement desensitization compared to image habituation training and applied muscle relaxation in post-traumatic stress disorder. *Journal of Behavior—Therapy and Experimental Psychology, 25,* 283–291.

Vaughan, S. (2000). *Half empty, half full: The psychological roots of optimism.* New York, NY: Harcourt.

Veasey, S. C. (2003). Serotonin agonists and antagonists in obstructive sleep apnea: Therapeutic potential. *American Journal of Respiratory Medicine, 2*(1), 21–29.

Vernon, S. W., & Roberts, R. E. (1982). Use of RDC in a tri-ethnic community survey. *Archives of General Psychiatry, 39,* 47.

Veteran Affairs Canada. (2008). Minister's message. *2006–2007 performance report.* Retrieved from http://www.tbs-sct.gc.ca/dpr-rmr/2006- 2007/inst/dva/dva01-eng.asp

Villani, S. (2001). Impact of media on children and adolescents: A 10-year review of the research. *Journal of the American Academy on Child and Adolescent Psychiatry, 40*(4), 392–401.

Vine, C., & Challen, P. (2002). *Gardens of shame: The tragedy of Martin Kruze and the sexual abuse at Maple Leaf Gardens.* Vancouver, BC: Greystone Books.

Vink, T., Hinney, A., Van Elburg, A. A., Van Goozen, S. H., Sandkuijl, L. A., Sinke, R. J., . . . Adan, R. A. (2001). Association between an agouti-related protein gene polymorphism and anorexia nervosa. *Molecular Psychiatry, 6,* 325–328.

Visser, P. S., & Krosnick, J. A. (1998). Development of attitude strength over the life cycle: Surge and decline. *Journal of Personality and Social Psychology, 75,* 1389–1410.

Vogel, G. W. (1975). A review of REM sleep deprivation. *Archives of General Psychiatry, 32,* 749–761.

Vogel, G. W. (1993). Selective deprivation, REM sleep. In M. A. Carskadon (Ed.), *The encyclopedia of sleep and dreaming.* New York, NY: Macmillan Publishing Company.

Vokey, J. R., & Read J. D., (1985). Subliminal messages: Between the devil and the media. *American Psychologist, 40,* 1231–1239.

von Helmholtz, H. (1852). On the theory of compound colours. *Philosophical Magazine, 4,* 519–535.

von Helmholtz, H. L. F. (1863). Die Lehre von den Tonempfindungen als physiologische Grundlage fur die Theorie der Musik published in translation (1954). On the sensations of tone as a physiological basis for the theory of music. New York, NY: Dover.

Voyer, D., & Rodgers, M. (2002). Reliability of laterality effects in a dichotic listening task with nonverbal material. *Brain & Cognition, 48,* 602–606.

Voyer, D., Voyer, S., & Bryden, M. (1995). Magnitude of sex differences in spatial abilities: A meta-analysis and consideration of critical variables. *Psychological Bulletin, 117,* 250–270.

Vygotsky, L. S. (1934/1962). *Thought and language.* Cambridge, MA: MIT Press.

Vygotsky, L. S. (1978). *Mind in society: The development of higher psychological processes.* Cambridge, MA: Harvard University Press.

Vygotsky, L. S. (1987). Thought and word. In R. W. Riebe & A. S. Carton (Eds.), *The collected works of L. S. Vygotsky: Vol. 1. Problems of general psychology* (pp. 243–288). New York, NY: Plenum.

Wagar, B. M., & Cohen, D. (2003). Culture, memory, and the self: An analysis of the personal and collective self in long-term memory. *Journal of Experimental Social Psychology, 39,* 468–475.

Wahlsten, D. (1997). The malleability of intelligence is not constrained by heritability. In B. Devlin, S. E. Fienberg, & K. Roeder (Eds.), *Intelligence, genes, and success: Scientists respond to the bell curve* (pp. 71–87). New York, NY: Springer.

Walker, J. (2004). The death of David Reimer: A tale of sex, science, and abuse. *Reason Online.* Retrieved from http://reason.com/links/links052404.shtml

Walker, L. J. (1984). Sex differences in the development of moral reasoning: A critical review. *Child Development, 55,* 677–691.

Walker, L. J. (1986). Sex differences in the development of moral reasoning: A rejoinder to Baumrind. *Child Development, 57,* 522–526.

Walker, L. J. (1989). A longitudinal study of moral reasoning. *Child Development, 60,* 157–166.

Walker, L. J. (1991). Sex differences in moral reasoning. In W. M. Kurtines & J. L. Gewirtz (Eds.), *Handbook of moral behavior and development: Vol. 2. Research* (pp. 333–364). Hillsdale, NJ: Lawrence Erlbaum.

Walsh, M., Hickey, C., & Duffy, J. (1999). Influence of item content and stereotype situation on gender differences in mathematical problem solving. *Sex Roles, 41,* 219–240.

Wampold, B. E. (1997). Methodological problems in identifying efficacious psychotherapies. *Psychotherapy Research, 7,* 21–43.

Wang, M. C., & Baker, E. T. (1985-86). Mainstreaming programs: Design features and effects. *Journal of Special Education, 19,* 503–521.

Ward, A. S., Li, D. H., Luedtke, R. R., & Emmett-Oglesby, M. W. (1996). Variations in cocaine self-administration by inbred rat strains under a progressiveratio schedule. *Psychopharmacology, 127*(3), 204–212.

Ward, C., & Rana-Deuba, A. (1999). Acculturation and adaptation revisited. *Journal of Cross-Cultural Psychology, 30,* 422–442.

Ward, I. L. (1992). Sexual behavior: The product of parinatal hormonal and prepubertal social factors. In A. A. Gerall, H. Moltz, & I. L. Ward. (Eds.), *Handbook of behavioral neurobiology, Vol. 11, Sexual differentiation.* New York, NY: Plenum Press.

Ward, J., Mattic, K. R. P., & Hall, W. (1999). *Methadone maintenance treatment and other opioid replacement therapies.* Sydney, Australia: Harwood Academic Publishers.

Ward, M. M., Lotstein, D. S., Bush, T. M., Lambert, R. E., van Vollenhoven, R., & Neuwelt, C. M. (1999). Psychosocial correlates of morbidity in women with systemic lupus erythematosus. *Journal of Rheumatology, 26,* 2153–2158.

Wartner, U. G., Grossmann, K., Fremmer-Bombik, E., & Suess, G. (1994). Attachment patterns at age six in south Germany: Predictability from infancy and implications for preschool behavior. *Child Development, 65,* 1014–1027.

Washington University in St. Louis, School of Medicine (2002, September). Questions and answers about Christopher Reeve's recovery of movement and the Washington University spinal cord injury program.

Wasserman, E. A., & Miller, R. R. (1997). What's elementary about associative learning? *Annual Review of Psychology, 48,* 573–607.

Watkins, C. E., Campbell, V. L., Nieberding, R., & Hallmark, R. (1995). Contemporary practice of psychological assessment by clinical psychologists. *Professional Psychology: Research and Practice, 26,* 54–60.

Watkins, C. E., Jr., & Savickas, M. L. (1990). Psychodynamic career counseling. In W. B. Walsh & S. H. Osipow (Eds.), *Career counseling: Contemporary topics in vocational psychology* (pp. 79–116). Hillsdale, NJ: Lawrence Erlbaum.

Watson, D. L., Hagihara, D. K., & Tenney, A. L. (1999). Skill-building exercises and generalizing psychological concepts to daily life. *Teaching of Psychology, 26,* 193–195.

Watson, J. B. (1913). Psychology as the behaviorist views it. *Psychological Review, 20,* 158–177.

Watson, J. B. (1924). *Behaviorism.* New York, NY: Norton.

Watson, J. B., & Rayner, R. (1920). Conditioned emotional responses. *Journal of Experimental Psychology, 3,* 1–14.

Watt, H. M. G. (2000). Measuring attitudinal change in mathematics and English over the 1st year of junior high school: A multi-dimensional analysis. *Journal of Experimental Education, 68,* 331–361.

Webb, C. T., & Levinson, D. F. (1993). Schizotypal and paranoid personality disorder in the relatives of patients with schizophrenia and affective disorders: A review. *Schizophrenic Research, 11*(1), 81–92.

Webb, W. B. (1992). *Sleep: The gentle tyrant* (2nd ed.). Bolton, MA: Ander.

Wechsler, D. (1975). *The collected papers of David Wechsler.* New York, NY: Academic Press.

Wechsler, D. (1981). *Weschler Adult Intelligence Scale—Revised.* San Antonio, TX: The Psychological Corporation.

Wechsler, D. (1990). *Wechsler Preschool and Primary Scale of Intelligence—Revised.* Sidcup, Kent: Psychological Corporation.

Wechsler, D. (1991). *Wechsler Intelligence Scale for Children-Third Edition.* New York, NY: Psychological Corporation.

Weckwerth, A. C., & Flynn, D. M. (2006). Effect of sex on perceived support and burnout in university students. *College Student Journal, 40, 237–249.*

Wedding, D. (2004). Cross-cultural counseling and psychotherapy. In R. J. Corsini & D. Wedding (Eds.), *Current Psychotherapies* (7th ed., p. 485). Itasca, IL: Peacock.

Wedekind, C., Seebeck, T., Bettens, F., & Paepke, A. J. (1995). MHC-dependent mate preferences in humans. *Proceedings of the Royal Society B: Biological Sciences, 260,* 245–249.

Weinberger, D. R. (1987). Implications of normal brain development for the pathogenesis of schizophrenia. *Archives of General Psychiatry, 44,* 660–668.

Weiner, B. (1985). An attributional theory of achievement motivation. *Psychological Review, 92,* 548–573.

Weiner, D. (1979). The apprenticeship of Philippe Pinel: A new document, "Observations of Citizen Pussin on the Insane." *American Journal of Psychiatry, 136,* 1128–1134.

Weiner, I. B. (1997). Current status of the Rorschach Inkblot Method. *Journal of Personality Assessment, 68,* 5–19.

Weiner, R. D. (2000). Retrograde amnesia with electroconvulsive therapy: Characteristics and implications. *Archives of General Psychiatry, 57,* 591–592.

Weis, S., Klaver, P., Reul, J., Elger, C. E., & Fernandez, G. (2004). Temporal and cerebellar brain regions that support both declarative memory formation and retrieval. *Cerebral Cortex, 14,* 256–267.

Weisman, A. (1972). *On dying and denying.* New York, NY: Behavioral Publications.

Weiss, J. M. (1972). Psychological factors in stress and disease. *Scientific American, 26,* 104–113.

Weisse, C. S. (1992). Depression and immunocompetence: A review of the literature. *Psychological Bulletin, 111,* 475–489.

Weissman, M. M., Bland, R., Joyce, P. R., Newman, S., Wells, J. E., & Wittchen, H. U. (1993). Sex differences in rates of depression: Cross-national perspectives. *Journal of Affective Disorders, 29,* 77–84.

Weissman, M. M., Bland, R. C., Canino, G. J., Faravelli, C., Greenwald, S., Hwu, H. G., . . . Yeh, E. K. (1997). The cross-national epidemiology of panic disorder. *Archives of General Psychiatry, 54,* 305–309.

Weissman, M. M., & Klerman, G. L. (1977). Sex differences and the epidemiology of depression. *Archives of General Psychiatry, 34,* 98–111.

Weizenbaum, J. (1976). *Computer power and human reason.* San Francisco, CA: Freeman.

Wenneberg, S. R., Schneider, R. H., Walton, K. G., Maclean, C. R., Levitsky, D. K., Mandarino, J. V., . . . Wallace, R. K. (1997). Anger expression correlates with platelet aggregation. *Behavioral Medicine, 22*(4), 174–177.

Wen-Shing, T., & Strelzer, J. (Eds.). (1997). *Culture and psychopathology: A guide to clinical assessment.* Bristol, PA: Brunner/Mazel.

Werker, J. F., & Lalonde, C. E. (1988). Cross-language speech perceptions: Initial capabilities and developmental change. *Developmental Psychology, 24,* 672–683.

Wertheimer, M. (1982). *Productive thinking.* Chicago, IL: University of Chicago Press.

Westen, D. (2005). Cognitive neuroscience and psychotherapy: Implications for psychotherapy's second century. In G. Gabbard, J. Beck, & J. Holmes (Eds.), *Oxford textbook of psychotherapy.* Oxford, England: Oxford University Press.

Wetherell, J. L. (2002). Behavior therapy for anxious older adults. *Behavior Therapist, 25,* 16–17.

Whiskin, E. E., & Bielavska, E. (1997). Interaction with demonstrator rats changes observer rats' affective responses to flavors. *Journal of Comparative Psychology, 111,* 393–398.

White, G. L. (1980). Physical attractiveness and courtship progress. *Journal of Personality and Social Psychology, 39,* 660–668.

White, M. (2010, April 26). Why did nobody help, asks mugged man, 79. *Toronto Star.* Retrieved from www.thestar.com

White, S. (2000). The transgender debate (the crisis surrounding gender identity). Reading, England: Garnet Publishing.

Whitley, B. E., Jr. & Kite, M. E. (2006). Prejudice based on gender, sexual orientation, and age. In B. E. Whitley, Jr., & M. E. Kite (Eds.), *The psychology of prejudice and discrimination* (pp. 344–394). Toronto, ON: Thomson-Wadsworth.

Whittington, C. J., Kendall, T., Fonagy, P., Cottrell, D., Cotgrove, A., & Boddington, E. (2004). Selective serotonin reuptake inhibitors in childhood depression: Systematic review of published versus unpublished data. *Lancet, 363,* 1341–1345.

WHO International Consortium in Psychiatric Epidemiology. (2000). Crossnational comparisons of the prevalences and correlates of mental disorders. *Bulletin of the World Health Organization, 78,* 413–426.

Whorf, B. L. (1956). *Language, thought and reality.* New York, NY: Wiley.

Wicker, A. W. (1971). An examination of the "other variables" explanation of attitude– behavior inconsistency. *Journal of Personality and Social Psychology, 19,* 18–30.

Widiger, T. A., & Weissman, M. M. (1991). Epidemiology of borderline personality disorder. *Hospital and Community Psychiatry, 42,* 1015–1021.

Wiesenthal, D. L., & Wiener, N. I. (1996). Privacy and the human genome project. *Ethics and Behavior, 6*(3), 189–201.

Williams, M. E. (1995). The American Geriatrics Society's complete guide to aging and mental health. New York, NY: Random House.

Williams, R. B. (1999). A 69-year-old man with anger and angina. *Journal of the American Medical Association, 282,* 763–770.

Williams, R. B., Haney, T. L., Lee, K. L., Kong, Y. H., Blumenthal, J. A., & Whalen, R. E. (1980). Type A behavior, hostility, and coronary atherosclerosis. *Psychosomatic Medicine, 42*(6), 539–549.

Williamson, A. M., & Feyer, A. M. (2000). Moderate sleep deprivation produces impairments in cognitive and motor performance equivalent to legally prescribed levels of alcohol intoxication. *Journal of Occupational and Environmental Medicine, 57,* 649–655.

Williamson, D. L., & Fast, J. E. (1998). Poverty and medical treatment: When public policy compromises accessibility. *Canadian Journal of Public Health, 89*(2), 120–124.

Wilson, R. S., Mendes de Leon, C. F., Barnes, L. L., Schneider, J. A., Bienias, J. L., Evans, D. A., & Bennett, D. A. (2002). Participation in cognitively stimulating activities and risk of incident Alzheimer disease. *Journal of the American Medical Association, 287,* 742–748.

Wilson, S., Becker, L., & Tinker, R. (1995). Eye movement desensitization and reprocessing (EMDR) treatment for psychologically traumatized individuals. *Journal of Consulting and Clinical Psychology, 63,* 928–937.

Winningham, R. G., Hyman, I. E., Jr., & Dinnel, D. L. (2000). Flashbulb memories? The effects of when the initial memory report was obtained. *Memory, 8,* 209–216.

Witelson, S. F. (1991). Neural sexual mosaicism: Sexual differentiation of the human temporo-pariatal region for functional asymmetry. *Psychoneuroendocrinology, 16,* 131–153.

Wolberg, L. R. (1977). *The technique of psychotherapy.* New York, NY: Grune & Stratton.

Wood, J. M., Nezworski, M. T., & Stejskal, W. J. (1996). The comprehensive system for the Rorschach: A critical examination. *Psychological Science, 7*(1), 3–10, 14–17.

Woodward, N. D., Purdon, S. E., Meltzer, H. Y., & Zald, D. H. (2005). A metaanalysis of neuropsychological change to clozapine, olanzapine, quetiapine, and risperidone in schizophrenia. *International Journal of Neuropsychopharmacology, 8,* 457–472.

WordIQ.com. (2002). Cults. Retrieved from http://www.wordiq .com/ definition/Cult

World Health Organization, Joint Commission on International Aspects of Mental Retardation. (1985). *Mental retardation: Meeting the challenge* (WHO offset publication, no. 86). Geneva, Switzerland: Author.

Wright, M. J., & Myers, C. R. (Eds.). (1982). History of academic psychology in Canada. Toronto, ON: Hogrefe.

Wu, C., Tashkin, D., Djahed, B., & Rose, J. E. (1988). Pulmonary hazards of smoking marijuana as compared with tobacco. *New England Journal of Medicine, 318,* 347–351.

Wynne, C. (1999). Do animals think? The case against the animal mind. *Psychology Today, 32*(6), 50–53.

Yalom, I. (1995). *The theory and practice of group psychotherapy* (4th ed.). New York, NY: Basic Books.

Yamagata, S., Suzuki, A., Ando, J., Ono, Y., Kijima, N., Yoshimura, K., . . . Jang, K. L. (2006). Is the genetic structure of human personality universal? A cross-cultural twin study from North America, Europe, and Asia. *Journal of Personality and Social Psychology, 90,* 987–998

Yamaguchi, S., Isejima, H., Matsuo, T., Okura, R., Yagita, K., Kobayashi, M., & Okamura, H. (2003). Synchronization of cellular clocks in the suprachiasmatic nucleus. *Science, 302,* 1408–1412.

Yang, L., Krampe, R. T., Baltes, P. B. (2006). Basic forms of cognitive plasticity extended into the oldest-old: retest learning, age, and cognitive functioning. *Psychology and Aging, 21,* 372–378.

Yarmey, A. D., & Bull, M. P. (1978). Where were you when President Kennedy was assassinated? *Bulletin of the Psychonomic Society, 11,* 133–135.

Yarmey, A. D., Yarmey, A. L., Yarmey, M. J., & Parliament, L. (2001). Commonsense beliefs and identification of familiar voices. *Applied Cognitive Psychology, 15,* 283–299.

Yerkes, R. M., & Dodson, J. D. (1908). The relation of strength of stimulus to rapidity of habit formation. *Journal of Comparative Neurology and Psychology, 18,* 459–482.

Ying, Y. W. (1990). Explanatory models of major depression and implications for help-seeking among immigrant Chinese-American women. *Culture, Medicine, and Psychiatry, 14,* 393–408.

Young, J. E., Rygh, J. L.,Weinberger, A. D., & Beck, A. T. (2008). Cognitive therapy for depression. In D. H. Barlow (Ed.), *Clinical handbook of psychological disorders* (pp. 250–305). New York, NY: Guilford Press.

Yule, G. (1996). *Pragmatics.* Oxford, England: Oxford University Press.

Zajonc, R. B. (1965). Social facilitation. *Science, 149,* 269–274.

Zajonc, R. B. (1968) Attitudinal effects of mere exposure. *Journal of Personality and Social Psychology, 9*(2), 1–27.

Zajonc, R. B. (1980). Feeling and thinking: Preferences need no inferences. *American Psychologist, 35,* 151–175.

Zajonc, R. B. (1984). On the primacy of affect. *American Psychologist, 39,* 117–123.

Zajonc, R. B. (1998). Emotions. In D. T. Gilbert & S. T. Fiske (Eds.), *Handbook of social psychology* (4th ed., Vol. 1, pp. 591–632). New York, NY: McGraw-Hill.

Zajonc, R. B., Heingartner, A., & Herman, E. M. (1970). Social enhancement and impairment of performance in the cockroach. *Journal of Social Psychology, 13*(2), 83–92.

Zamboni, P., Galeotti, R., Menegatti, E., Malagoni, A. M., Mascoli, F., Dall-Ara, S. . . . Salvi, F. (2009). A prospective open-label study of endovascular treatment of chronic cerebrospinal venous insufficiency. *Journal of Vascular Surgery, 50,* 1348–1358.

Zanarini, M. C. (2000). Childhood experiences associated with the development of borderline personality disorder. *Psychiatric Clinics of North America, 23*(1), 89–101.

Zeki, S. (2001). Localization and globalization in conscious vision. *Annual Review of Neuroscience, 24,* 57–86.

Zendel, B. R., & Alain, C. (2010, November 16). Musicians less likely to experience age-related changes in the auditory cortex. *ScienceDaily.* Retrieved from http://cms.sfn.org/am2010/press/OmniPress/data/ press/008.pdf

Zentall, T. R. (2000). Animal intelligence. In R. J. Sternberg (Ed.), *Handbook of intelligence.* Cambridge, MA: Cambridge University Press.

Zhou, J. N., Hofman, M. A., Gooren, L. J. G., & Swaab, D. F. (1995). A sex difference in the human brain and its relation to transsexuality. *Nature, 378,* 68–70.

Zilles, K. (1990). Cortex. In G. Paxinos (Ed.), *The human nervous system* (pp. 757–802). San Diego, CA: Academic.

Zillmann, D., Baron, R., & Tamborini, R. (1981). Social costs of smoking: Effects of tobacco smoke on hostile behavior. *Psychology Journal of Applied Social, 11,* 548–561.

Zimbardo, P. (1971). The pathology of imprisonment. *Society, 9*(4–8), 4.

Zimbardo, P., Maslach, C., & Haney, C. (2000). Reflections on the Stanford Prison Experiment: Genesis, transformations, consequences. In T. Blass (Ed.), *Obedience to authority: Current perspectives on the Milgram paradigm.* London, England: Lawrence Erlbaum.

Zimbardo, P. G. (1970). The human choice: Individuation, reason, and order versus deindividuation, impulse, and chaos. In N. J. Arnold & D. Levine (Eds.), *Nebraska Symposium on Motivation, 1969.* Lincoln, NE: University of Nebraska Press.

Zimbardo, P. G., & Hartley, C. F. (1985). Cults go to high school: A theoretical and empirical analysis of the initial stage in the recruitment process. *Cultic Studies Journal, 2,* 91–148.

Zimmer, L., & Morgan, J. P. (1997). *Marijuana myths, marijuana facts: A review of the scientific evidence.* New York, NY: Lindesmith Center.

Zisapel, N. (2001). Circadian rhythm sleep disorders: pathophysiology and potential approaches to management. *CNS Drugs, 15*(4), 311–328.

Zorilla, E. P., Luborsky, L., McKay, J. R., Rosenthal, R., Houldin, A., Tax, A., . . . Schmidt, K. (2001). The relationship of depression and stressors to immunological assays: A meta-analytic review. *Brain, Behavior, and Immunity, 15,* 199–226.

Zucker, K. J., & Blanchard, R. (1997). Transvestic fetishism: psychopathology and theory. In D. R. Laws and W. T. O'Donohue (Eds.), *Handbook of sexual deviance: theory and application.* New York, NY: Guilford.

Zuckerman, M. (1979). *Sensation seeking: Beyond the optimal level of arousal.* Hillsdale, NJ: Lawrence Erlbaum.

Zuckerman, M. (1994). Behavioral expression and biosocial bases of sensation seeking. New York, NY: Cambridge University Press.

Zuckerman, M. (2002). Zuckerman-Kuhlman Personality Questionnaire (ZKPQ): An alternative five-factorial model. In B. De Raad & M. Perugini (Eds.), *Big five assessment* (pp. 377–396). Seattle, WA: Hogrefe & Huber Publishers.

Zuo, L., & Cramond, B. (2001). An examination of Terman's gifted children from the theory of identity. *Gifted Child Quarterly, 45*(4), 251–259.

Zvolensky, M. J., Schmidt, M. B., & Stewart, S. H. (2003). Panic disorder and smoking. *Clinical Psychology: Science and Practice, 10,* 29–51.

Credits

Front Matter

Page i M. Dykstra/Shutterstock; Page xxi © mauritius images GmbH / Alamy;

Chapter 1

Page 2–3 (water surface) © David Joyner/iStock; Page 2 (fish) Yuri Arcurs /Shutterstock; Page 2–3 (bubbles) Valentina R. /Shutterstock; Page 2 (hummingbird) Al Mueller /Shutterstock; Page 2 (rectangular object) 3d4medical.com; Page 2 (elephant) Photodisc/Getty Images; Page 2 (bow) © ushama/iStock; Page 2 (key) Thomas Northcut /Photodisc/Getty Images; Page 3 (flower) © Dorling Kindersley; Page 3 (spider) James L. Davidson / Shutterstock; Page 3 (sheep) GK Hart/Vikki Hart/Photodisc/Getty Images; Page 3 (man) DEX IMAGE/Getty Images; Page 3 (house) © Margojh/ Dreamstime.com; Page 5 Jeff Greenberg/The Image Works; Page 7 (Top) Hulton Archives/Getty Images; Page 7 (Bottom) Darrin Henry /Shutterstock; Page 8 Courtesy of the University of Toronto Archives; Page 9 © INTERFOTO/Alamy; Page 10 (Top) © Bettmann/CORBIS; Page 10 (Bottom) © Underwood & Underwood/CORBIS; Page 12 (Top) Time & Life Pictures/Getty Images; Page 12 (Bottom) Courtesy of Arthur W. Toga and Dr. aul M. Thompson of the Laboratory of Neuro Imaging, UCLA; Page 13 (Right) Montreal Neurological Institute, McGill University; Page 14 © Getty Images/Thinkstock; Page 16 Stock Boston- Mike Grecco; Page 17 ©Bob Daemmrich / The Image Works; Page 19 Michael K. Nichols/National Geographic Stock; Page 20 PhotoEdit/ Jonathan Nourok; Page 21 University of Iowa Department of Neurology and Image Analysis Facility Source: Hanna Damasio, M.D.; From H. Damasio, T. Grabowski, R. Frank, A.M. Galaburda, A.R. Damasio, The Return of Phineas Gage: Clues about the brain from the skull of a famous patient. Science 264:1102-1105, 1994.; Page 22 © George Price /The New Yorker Collection/www.cartoonbank.com; Page 23 (Bottom) © Leo Cullum /The New Yorker Collection/www.cartoonbank.com; Page 25 Bill Aron / PhotoEdit; Page 26 (Bottom) © Peter Mueller /The New Yorker Collection/ www.cartoonbank.com; Page 28 (Top) Mendil / Photo Researchers, Inc.; Page 31 © Tom Chalkkey /The New Yorker Collection/www.cartoonbank. com; Page 33 (Top) Hulton Archives/Getty Images; Page 34 (Top) © Roger Ressmeyer/CORBIS; Page 34 AridOcean /Shutterstock;

Chapter 2

Page 42 (rectangular object) 3d4medical.com; Page 42–43 (nervous system) 3d4medical.com; Page 43 (man) Ryan McVay /Getty Images; Page 45 (Left) Jurgen Berger/Max-Planck Institute Photo Researchers Inc.; Page 45 (Right) © Dorling Kindersley; Page 50 (Left) © Illustration Dorling Kindersley; Page 50 (Right) E.R. Lewis, T.E. Everhart, Y.Y. Zeevi; Visuals Unlimited; Page 52 (Top) James L. Davidson /Shutterstock; Page 52 (Bottom) Olivier Douliery/ABACAUSA.COM /The Canadian Press; Page 53 (Top) © Image Source / Alamy; Page 55 Andrew Paul Leonard Photo Researchers Inc.; Page 59 Amy Myers /Shutterstock; Page 60 Jean Levac / Canwest News

Service). CNS-OLY-MHKY The Canadian Press Images/Ottawa Citizen; Page 61 Johnny Crawford/The Atlanta-Journal Constitution; Page 63 (Top Left) SPL / Photo Researchers Inc; Page 63 (Top Right) Alfred Pasieka / Photo Researchers Inc.; Page 63 (Bottom Left) © Pete Saloutos/CORBIS; Page 63 (Bottom Right) Tim Beddow / Photo Researchers Inc. Page 66 Copyright: JustASC /Shutterstock; Page 68 shock/Shutterstock; Page 70 (top) © Bettmann/CORBIS; Page 70 (Bottom) Robert Kneschke /Shutterstock; Page 73 (Top) S.Miller /Custom Medical Stock; Page 73 (Bottom) Courtesy Mike Benoit; Page 80 Stockbyte/Thinkstock;

Chapter 3

Page 88–89 (music notes) Kirsty Pargeter /Shutterstock; Page 88–89 (flower) © Dorling Kindersley; Page 89 PM Images/Getty Images; Page 93 © Tim Pelling/firstlight.ca; Page 97 Ralph C. Eagle, Jr. / Photo Researchers, Inc.; Page 98 © Bryan Allen/CORBIS; Page 99 Time & Life Pictures/ Getty Images; Page 100 (Bottom) Lowell Handler; Page 103 (Top) © Charles Barsotti /The New Yorker Collection/www.cartoonbank.com; Page 103 (Bottom) The Plain Dealer; Page 106 (Top) JOHN BAVOSI/ SCIENCE PHOTO LIBRARY; Page 103 (Bottom) © Daniel Giry/ Sygma/CORBIS; Page 107 (Bottom Right) Omikron / Photo Researchers Inc.; Page 110 Superstock; Page 111 Robin Sachs / PhotoEdit; Page 112 AP Images/STEPHEN MORTON; Page 114 © Munson, John/Star Ledger/CORBIS; Page 118 © John O'brien/The New Yorker Collection/www. cartoonbank.com; Page 119 Mark Richards / PhotoEdit; Page 121 (Top Left) Surkov Vladimir /Shutterstock; Page 121 (Top Right) © Dorling Kindersley; Page 121 (Bottom Left) iStockphoto/Thinkstock; Page 121 (Bottom Right) Linhsiaowei /Shutterstock; Page 123 Larry Landolfi / Photo Researchers Inc.; Page 127 Paul M. Valliant, Professor, Department of Psychology, Laurentian University;

Chapter 4

Page 134 (sheep) GK Hart/Vikki Hart/Photodisc/Getty Images; Page 134–135 (clock) Dmitry Fisher /Shutterstock; Page 135 (woman) Jean Luc Morales/Image Bank/Getty Images; Page 137 flashgun /Shutterstock; Page 137 (Top) PhotoEdit/ Michael Newman; Page 139 (Top) PhotoEdit/ Michael Newman; Page 139 (Bottom) Michael Newman / PhotoEdit; Page 140 Mihail Zhelezniak /Shutterstock; Page 141 (Top) Comstock/Thinkstock; Page 141 (Bottom Left) Photos.com/Thinstock; Page 141 (Bottom Right) Ryhor M Zasinets /Shutterstock; Page 142 Chuck Nacke, Woodfin Camp and Associates; Page 144 © Joe Dator/The New Yorker Collection/ www.cartoonbank.com; Page 146 Globe & Mail - Erik Christensen/The Canadian Press; Page 146 Globe & Mail - Erik Christensen/The Canadian Press; Page 147 © Envision/CORBIS; Page 148 (Top) David Weinstein & Associates/Custom Medical Stock; Page 148 (Bottom) www.cartoonstock. com; Page 149 © Dana Fradon /The New Yorker Collection/www.cartoonbank.com; Page 151 (Middle) © Sven Hagolani/CORBIS; Page 154 © Bettmann/CORBIS; Page 154 © Firefly Productions/CORBIS; Page 158 (Top) The Granger Collection, NYC — All rights reserved.; Page 158

Name Index

Subject Index

Note: '*f*' indicates a figure; '*t*' indicates a table.